A Biographical Dictionary
of
ARTISTS

Waterfall by Arshile Gorky; oil on canvas; 155×114cm (61×45in); 1943. Tate Gallery, London (see page 271)

A BIOGRAPHICAL DICTIONARY

OF

ARTISTS

—— GENERAL EDITOR ——

SIR LAWRENCE GOWING

Facts On File®

AN INFOBASE HOLDINGS COMPANY

Project Editor Valerie Mendes
Picture Research Diana Morris, Jo Rapley
Additional Research Mel Cooper
Production Clive Sparling
Design Trevor Vincent
Art Editor Jerry Burman
Text Editors Janet Graham, Robert Peberdy,
 Chris Murray
Index Sandra Raphael

AN ANDROMEDA BOOK

Planned and produced by
Andromeda Oxford Limited
9–15 The Vineyard, Abingdon
Oxfordshire, England OX14 3PX

Facts On File, Inc.
460 Park Avenue South
New York NY 10016–7382

Library of Congress Cataloguing-in-
Publication Data

Biographical dictionary of artists / Sir Lawrence Gowing [editor]. --
Rev. ed.
    p.   cm.
    Includes bibliographical references and index.
    ISBN 0-8160-3252-1
    1. Artists--Biography--Dictionaries.   I. Gowing, Lawrence.
N40.B53 1995
709'.2'2--dc20
[B]   94-38801
                                                          CIP

This edition first published in the United
States by Facts On File.

Facts On File books are available at
special discounts when purchased in bulk
quantities for businesses, associations,
institutions or sales promotions. Please
call our Special Sales Department in New
York at 212/683-2244 or 800/322-8755

Printed in Spain by Fournier
Artes Gráficas, S.A., Vitoria

10 9 8 7 6 5 4 3 2 1

Note

The chronological tables on pages x–xv show the life-spans (or, in the case of most medieval artists, the active periods) of a selection of major figures.

Technical matter in the contributions and captions has been edited according to the following conventions. Titles of works are given in English, except where a title in another language is more familiar. Wherever possible the locations of works are provided, by reference to the full name of an institution and to the town or city in which it stands. Names of institutions in English, French, German, and Italian are normally given in their original forms. Others have been translated except where an original name is familiar or because an idiomatic translation is not possible. The names of some major institutions have been abbreviated. A statement of location does not necessarily imply a statement about ownership.

The suggestions for "Further reading" usually specify the latest editions. Where possible, details of publication in both England and the United States are given.

In the captions dimensions are given in the order height × width (× depth in the case of sculpture). Measurements for most works are given to the nearest centimeter with, in parentheses, an imperial equivalent to the nearest inch. Where possible, the media of works are also given, but for many works, especially those from the period of European painting when tempera and oils were both in common use, media have not been specified because the binders and pigments of such works have not been analyzed.

Andromeda wishes to thank the following individuals and institutions for their help in the preparation of this work:

INDIVIDUALS: Margaret Amosu, Professor Manolis Andronikos, Janet Backhouse, Claudia Bismarck, John Boardman, His Grace the Duke of Buccleugh, Richard Calvocoressi, Lord Clark, Curt and Maria Clay, James Collins, Bryan Cranstone, Mrs E.A. Cubitt, Mary Doherty, Judith Dronkhurst, Rosemary Eakins, Mark Evans, Claude Fessaguet, Joel Fisher, Jean-Jacques Gabas, Dr Oscar Ghez, Paul Goldman, G. St G.M. Gompertz, Zoë Goodwin, Toni Greatrex, A.V. Griffiths, Victor Harris, Barbara Harvey, Maurice Howard, A.D. Hyder, Jane Jakeman, Peg Katritzky, Moira Klingman, Andrew Lawson, Betty Yao Lin, Christopher Lloyd, Jean Lodge, Richard Long, Lorna McEchern, Eunice Martin, Shameem Melluish, Jennifer Montagu, Sir Henry Moore, Richard Morphet, Elspeth O'Neill, Alan Peebles, Professor Dr Chr. Pescheck, Pam Porter, Professor P.H. Pott, Alison Renney, Steve Richard, Andrew Sherratt, Richard Shone, Lawrence Smith, Don Sparling, Graham and Jennifer Speake, Annamaria Petrioli Tofani, Mary Tregear, the late Jim Tudge, Betty Tyers, Ivan Vomáčka, Tom Wesselmann.

INSTITUTIONS: Ashmolean Museum, Oxford; Bibliothèque Nationale, Paris; Bodleian Library, Oxford; British Library, London; British Museum, London; Courtauld Institute of Art, London; Gulbenkian Foundation, Lisbon; Louvre, Paris; Merseyside County Museums, Liverpool; Metropolitan Museum, New York; Museum of Modern Art, New York; Museum of Modern Art, Oxford; Oriental Institute, Oxford; Oxford City Library; Petit Palais, Geneva; Phaidon Press, Oxford; Pitt Rivers Museum, Oxford; Sainsbury Centre for the Visual Arts, Norwich; Sotheby Parke Bernet & Co., London; Tate Gallery, London; Victoria and Albert Museum, London; Warburg Institute, London.

Andromeda wishes to thank the numerous individuals, agencies, museums, galleries, and other institutions who kindly supplied the illustrations for this book.

Andromeda also wishes to acknowledge the important contributions of Judith Brundin, Ann Currah, Bernard Dod, Herman and Polly Friedhoff, the late Juliet Grindle, Jonathan Lamède, Giles Lewis, Andrew McNeillie, Penelope Marcus and Louise Pengelley.

CONTENTS

PREFACE

It was a bold man who first guessed that a collection of artists' biographies would be one of the most delightful books in the world. Not just incidentally interesting or entertaining, but germane to the essence of art, relevant to all its pleasures and meanings.

The fact is that the Western conception of art, which has flourished since Giorgio Vasari published his *Lives* four centuries ago, is a conception of artistic identity and personality. A meaningful work is the production of a more or less identifiable artist. His achievement is relative to an outlook which is in the strict sense no one's but his, the communicator of an individual purpose which could not have been expressed in any other way. The more works we know by an artist, the more each of them will signify.

The dictionary of artists is one of the prime imaginative achievements of our culture and it is my pleasure to introduce as distinguished and useful an example of its kind as I know. The range is wide. This *Dictionary* deals with more than three times the number of artists who figure in the only previous volumes of equal readability and convenience. No major Western artist is missing and the relatively minor names, which we might be in doubt whether to seek here, are listed in summary form in the Index. The artists of other cultures of whom we have an impression personal enough to compare with those of our own are included too.

I dare promise that whenever you open this book you will both profit and gain enjoyment.

LAWRENCE GOWING
(1918–91)

DAVID FREKE
Director, Rescue Archaeology Unit, University of Liverpool

RICHARD FREMANTLE
Author of *Florentine Gothic Painters from Giotto to Masaccio*

JOHN FREW
Lecturer, Department of Fine Art, University of St Andrews

MARTIN GAUGHAN
Senior Lecturer in the History and Theory of Art, South Glamorgan Institute of Higher Education, Cardiff

JOHN GLAVES-SMITH
Lecturer in the History of Art, North Staffordshire Polytechnic, Stoke-on-Trent

BASIL GRAY
Former Keeper of Oriental Antiquities (Retired), British Museum, London

MICHAEL GREENHALGH
Senior Lecturer, History of Art, University of Leicester

ALASTAIR GRIEVE
Senior Lecturer, School of Fine Arts and Music, University of East Anglia

KEITH HARTLEY
Assistant Keeper, Scottish National Gallery of Modern Art, Edinburgh

ADELHEID HEIMANN
Former Assistant Curator of the Photographic Collection, Warburg Institute, London

JAMES HOLLOWAY
Assistant Keeper of Art, National Museum of Wales, Cardiff

CHARLES HOPE
Lecturer in Renaissance Studies, Warburg Institute, London

JOHN HOUSE
Lecturer in the History of Art, Courtauld Institute of Art, London

MAURICE HOWARD
Lecturer in the History of Art, University of Sussex

PETER HUMPHREY
Lecturer in the History of Art, University of St Andrews

OLIVER IMPEY
Assistant Keeper of Eastern Art, Ashmolean Museum, Oxford

CHRISTOPHER JOHNSTONE
Curator of Education and Information, National Gallery of Scotland, Edinburgh

MARTIN KEMP
Professor and Chairman of the Department of Fine Art, University of St Andrews

PETER KIDSON
Reader in the History of Art, Courtauld Institute of Art, London

HELEN LANGDON
Author of *The Mitchell Beazley Pocket Art Gallery Guide*, and *Everyday Life Painting*

PETER LASKO
Director, Courtauld Institute of Art, London

CHRISTINA LODDER
Lecturer, Department of Fine Arts, University of St Andrews

SHEILA MADDISON
Tutor, Open University, West Yorkshire Region

JODY MAXMIN
Associate Professor, Department of Art, Stanford University

HUGH MELLER
Historic Buildings Representative, The National Trust, Devon

HAMISH MILES
Director, Barber Institute of Fine Arts, Birmingham

JOHN MILNER
Senior Lecturer, Department of Fine Art, University of Newcastle-upon-Tyne

PARTHA MITTER
Lecturer in South Asian History, University of Sussex

JENNIFER MONTAGU
Curator of the Photographic Collection, Warburg Institute, London

KATHLEEN MORAND
Professor and Head of Department of Art, Queen's University, Kingston, Ont.

JOHN M. NASH
Senior Lecturer, Department of Art, University of Essex

PATRICK NOON
Assistant Curator, Yale Center for British Art, New Haven, Conn.

OLGA PALAGIA
Lecturer in Archaeology, University of Athens

RONALD PARKINSON
Head of the Department of Education, Victoria and Albert Museum, London

RONALD PICKVANCE
Richmond Professor of History of Fine Arts, University of Glasgow

GRISELDA POLLOCK
Lecturer in the History of Art, University of Leeds

ANTHONY RADCLIFFE
Keeper of Sculpture, Victoria and Albert Museum, London

BENEDICT READ
Deputy Witt Librarian, Courtauld Institute of Art, London

HON. JANE ROBERTS
Curator of the Print Room, Royal Library, Windsor Castle

†KEITH ROBERTS
Former Associate Editor, *Burlington Magazine*, and sometime Commissioning Editor for Phaidon Press, Oxford

GILES ROBERTSON
Professor Emeritus, Department of Fine Art, University of Edinburgh

RUTH RUBINSTEIN
Warburg Institute, London

ROBIN SIMON
Director, Institute of European Studies, London

LAWRENCE R.H. SMITH
Keeper of Oriental Antiquities, British Museum, London

ROBIN SPENCER
Lecturer, Department of Fine Arts, University of St Andrews

PAUL SPENCER-LONGHURST
Assistant to the Director, Barber Institute of Fine Arts, Birmingham

GERETH SPRIGGS
Freelance writer and authority on English medieval manuscript illumination

JOHN STEER
Head of Department of History of Art, Birkbeck College, London

MARY-ANNE STEVENS
Lecturer, History and Theory of Art, University of Kent at Canterbury

NEIL STRATFORD
Keeper of Medieval and Later Antiquities, British Museum, London

SARAH SYMMONS
Lecturer, Department of Art, University of Essex

ALAN TAIT
Reader in the History of Art, University of Glasgow

MARY TREGEAR
Keeper of Eastern Art, Ashmolean Museum, Oxford

NICHOLAS TURNER
Assistant Keeper, Department of Prints and Drawings, British Museum, London

WILLIAM VAUGHAN
Reader in the History of Art, University College, London

NICHOLAS WADLEY
Head of Department of Art History, Chelsea School of Art, London

CHRISTOPHER WAKELING
Lecturer in Fine Art, University of Keele

ERNST WANGERMANN
Reader in Modern History, University of Leeds

MALCOLM WARNER
Freelance writer; coauthor of *The Phaidon Companion to Art and Artists in the British Isles*

ANTHONY WHITE
Managing Director, Frederick Muller Ltd, London

ALAN G. WILKINSON
Curator of the Henry Moore Sculpture Centre, Art Gallery of Ontario, Toronto

D.J.R. WILLIAMS
Research Assistant, Department of Greek and Roman Antiquities, British Museum, London

CHRISTOPHER WRIGHT
Freelance writer; publications include *Rembrandt and His Art*, *Paintings in Dutch Museums*

ERIC YOUNG
Distinguished authority on Spanish painting; publications include *Francisco Goya*

GEORGE ZARNECKI
Professor of the History of Art, Courtauld Institute of Art, London

CHRONOLOGY OF ARTISTS: ROMANESQUE TO BAROQUE

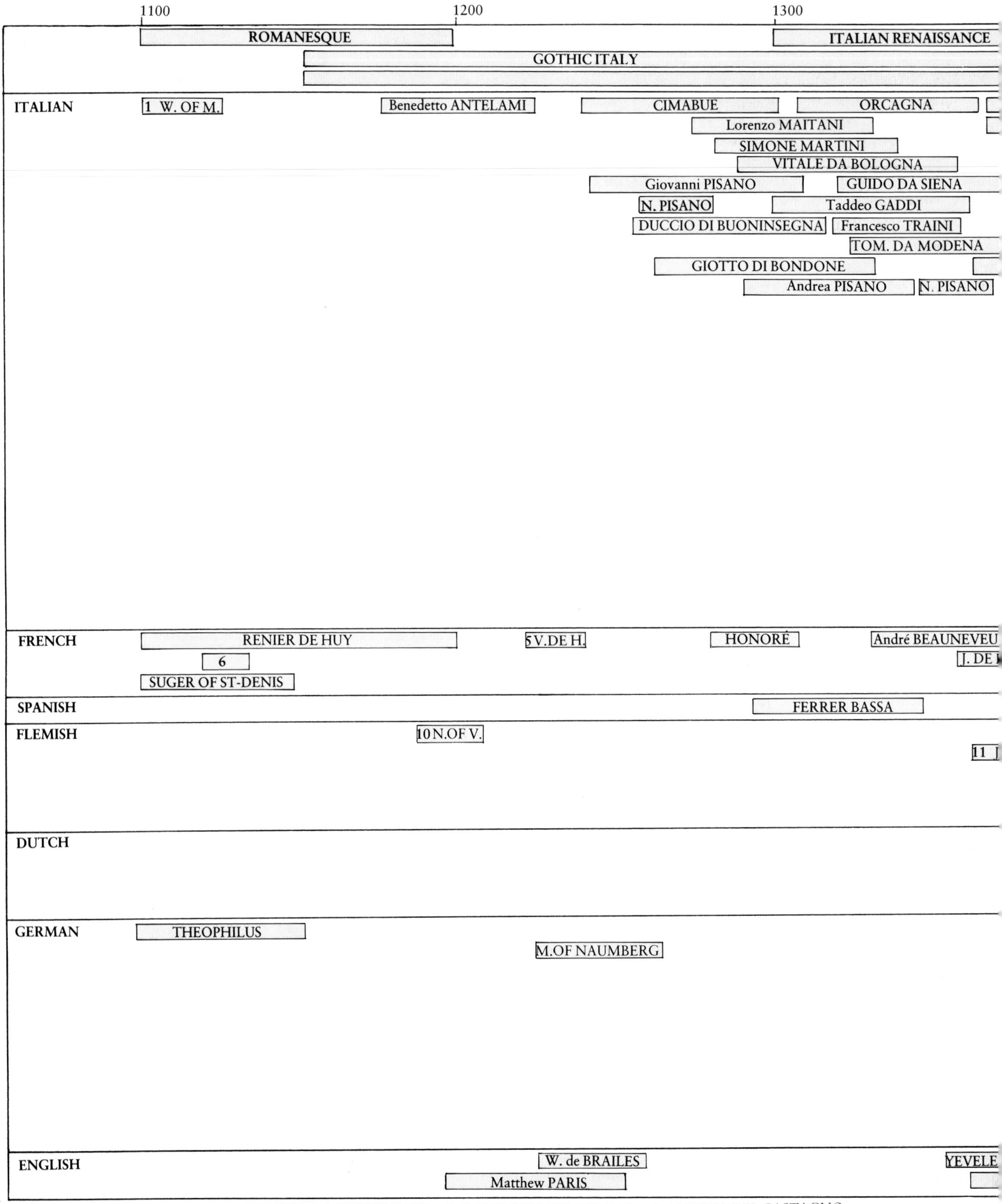

	1100	1200	1300
	ROMANESQUE		ITALIAN RENAISSANCE
		GOTHIC ITALY	

ITALIAN

1 W. OF M.
Benedetto ANTELAMI
CIMABUE
ORCAGNA
Lorenzo MAITANI
SIMONE MARTINI
VITALE DA BOLOGNA
Giovanni PISANO
GUIDO DA SIENA
N. PISANO
Taddeo GADDI
DUCCIO DI BUONINSEGNA
Francesco TRAINI
TOM. DA MODENA
GIOTTO DI BONDONE
Andrea PISANO
N. PISANO

FRENCH

RENIER DE HUY
5 V.DE H.
HONORÉ
André BEAUNEVEU
6
J. DE
SUGER OF ST-DENIS

SPANISH

FERRER BASSA

FLEMISH

10 N.OF V.
11 J

DUTCH

GERMAN

THEOPHILUS
M.OF NAUMBERG

ENGLISH

W. de BRAILES
YEVELE
Matthew PARIS

1 WILIGELMO OF MODENA   2 DESIDERIO DA SETTIGNANO   3 DOMENICO VENEZIANO   4 ANDREA DEL CASTAGNO
5 VILLARD DE HONNECOURT   6 GILABERTUS OF TOULOUSE   7 Jean de BEAUMETZ   8 BOUCICAUT MASTER   9 NUNO GONÇALVES
10 NICHOLAS OF VERDUN   11 Jean BONDOL   12 Melchior BROEDERLAM 13 Nikolaus GERHAERT VAN LEYDEN
14 GEERTGEN TOT SINT JANS   15 MASTER FRANCKE   16 Herman SCHEERRE

1400 1500

MANNERISM

NORTHERN RENAISSANCE

BAROQUE

GOTHIC OUTSIDE ITALY

Cennino CENNINI
Donato BRAMANTE
Il TINTORETTO

ENT. DA FABRIANO
Giovanni BELLINI
Giovanni BOLOGNA

SASSETTA
LEONARDO DA VINCI
Paolo VERONESE

GIOVANNI DE PAOLO
Andrea PALLADIO

UCCELLO
SEBASTIANO DEL PIOMBO

PISANELLO
Filippino LIPPI
Francesco PRIMATICCIO

DONATELLO
Il SANSOVINO

Lorenzo GHIBERTI
Fra BARTOLOMMEO
Lodovico CARRACCI

copo della QUERCIA
Antonio CORREGGIO
Agostino CARRACCI

Filippo BRUNELLESCHI
PERUGINO
Ludovico CIGOLI

Fra ANGELICO
PIERO DI COSIMO
Annibale CARRACCI

MASACCIO
Dom. GHIRLANDAIO
Jacopo PONTORMO
CARAVAGGIO

Leon Battista ALBERTI
MICHELANGELO
PIETRO DA CORTONA

Fra Filippo LIPPI
Vittore CARPACCIO
Alessandro ALGARDI

PIERO DELLA FRANCESCA
ROSSO FIORENTINO
Francesco BORROMINI

Agostino di DUCCIO
Lorenzo LOTTO

2 D. DA S.
GIORGIONE

Gentile BELLINI

NICCOLO ALUNO
Agnolo BRONZINO

Cosmè TURA
GIULIO ROMANO

ANT. DA MESSINA
PALMA VECCHIO

Andrea MANTEGNA
Giorgio VASARI

VERROCCHIO
TITIAN

3 D.V.
RAPHAEL

4 A. DEL C.
Benvenuto CELLINI

Alessandro BOTTICELLI

Jean FOUQUET
Philibert DELORME

7
Simon MARMION

8 B.M.

9 N.G.
Gil de SILOE

LIMBURG
Hugo van der GOES
Pieter BRUEGEL E.

12 M.B.
Gerard DAVID
Jan BRUEGEL

Jan van EYCK
Quentin MASSYS
Anthony van DYCK

Rogier van der WEYDEN
Jan GOSSAERT

Joachim PATENIER

MALOUEL
13 N.G. VAN L.
LUCAS VAN LEYDEN
Hendrick GOLTZIUS

Dieric BOUTS

Hieronymus BOSCH

14 G.T.S.J.

Stefan LOCHNER
H. HOLBEIN THE ELDER
A. ELSHEIMER

Hans MULTSCHER
Matthias GRÜNEWALD

15 M.F.
Michael PACHER

MASTER OF LIESBORN

Martin SCHONGAUER
Hans HOLBEIN Y.

Michael WOLGEMUT

Bernt NÖTKE

Veit STOSS

Albrecht DÜRER

Lucas CRANACH THE ELDER

Albrecht ALTDORFER

16 H.S.
Nicholas HILLIARD

ohn SIFERWAS
Inigo JONES

CHRONOLOGY OF ARTISTS: BAROQUE TO REALISM

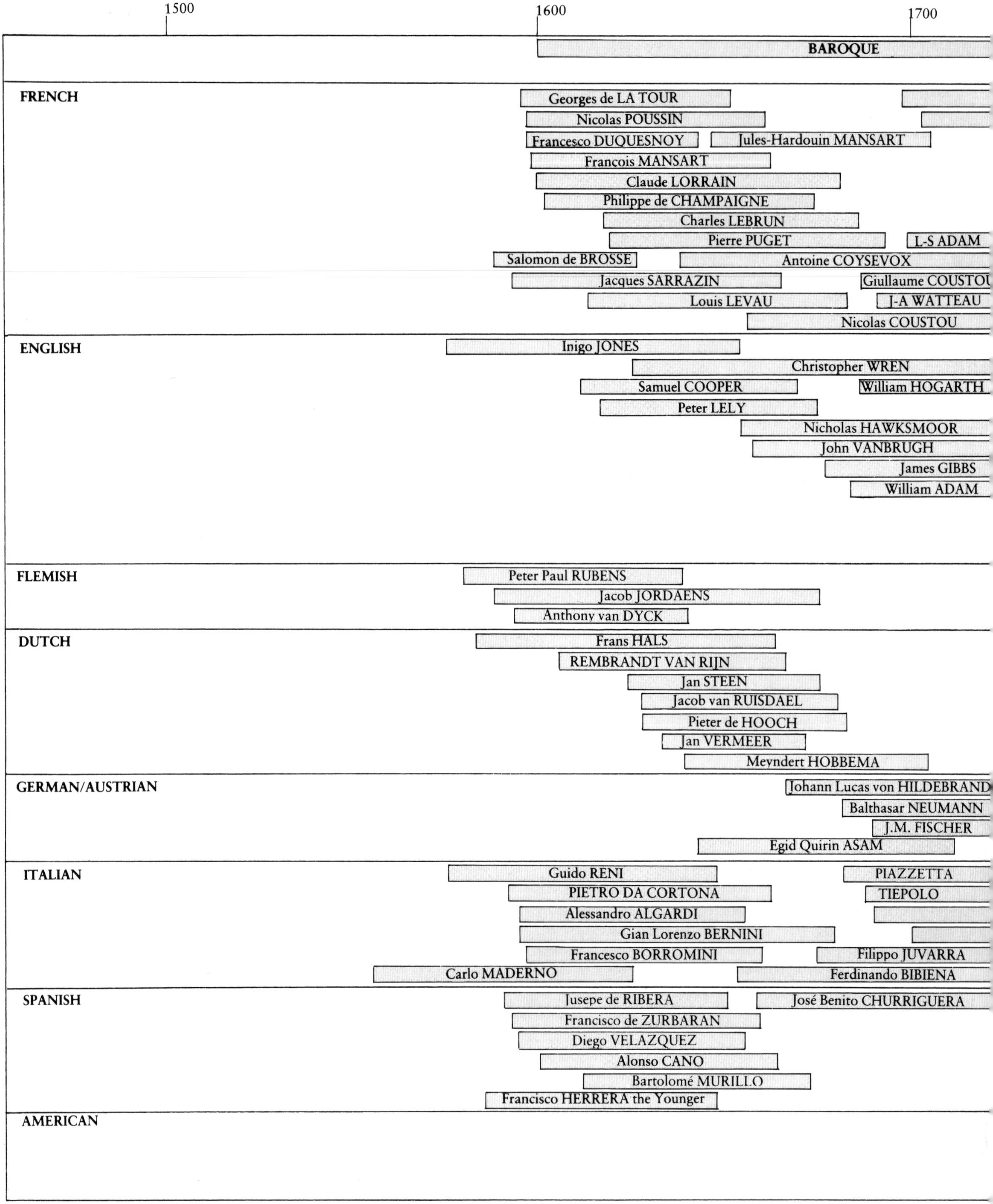

1500	1600	1700

BAROQUE

FRENCH

- Georges de LA TOUR
- Nicolas POUSSIN
- Francesco DUQUESNOY
- Jules-Hardouin MANSART
- François MANSART
- Claude LORRAIN
- Philippe de CHAMPAIGNE
- Charles LEBRUN
- Pierre PUGET
- L-S ADAM
- Salomon de BROSSE
- Antoine COYSEVOX
- Jacques SARRAZIN
- Giullaume COUSTOU
- Louis LEVAU
- J-A WATTEAU
- Nicolas COUSTOU

ENGLISH

- Inigo JONES
- Christopher WREN
- Samuel COOPER
- William HOGARTH
- Peter LELY
- Nicholas HAWKSMOOR
- John VANBRUGH
- James GIBBS
- William ADAM

FLEMISH

- Peter Paul RUBENS
- Jacob JORDAENS
- Anthony van DYCK

DUTCH

- Frans HALS
- REMBRANDT VAN RIJN
- Jan STEEN
- Jacob van RUISDAEL
- Pieter de HOOCH
- Jan VERMEER
- Meyndert HOBBEMA

GERMAN/AUSTRIAN

- Johann Lucas von HILDEBRAND
- Balthasar NEUMANN
- J.M. FISCHER
- Egid Quirin ASAM

ITALIAN

- Guido RENI
- PIAZZETTA
- PIETRO DA CORTONA
- TIEPOLO
- Alessandro ALGARDI
- Gian Lorenzo BERNINI
- Francesco BORROMINI
- Filippo JUVARRA
- Carlo MADERNO
- Ferdinando BIBIENA

SPANISH

- Jusepe de RIBERA
- José Benito CHURRIGUERA
- Francisco de ZURBARAN
- Diego VELAZQUEZ
- Alonso CANO
- Bartolomé MURILLO
- Francisco HERRERA the Younger

AMERICAN

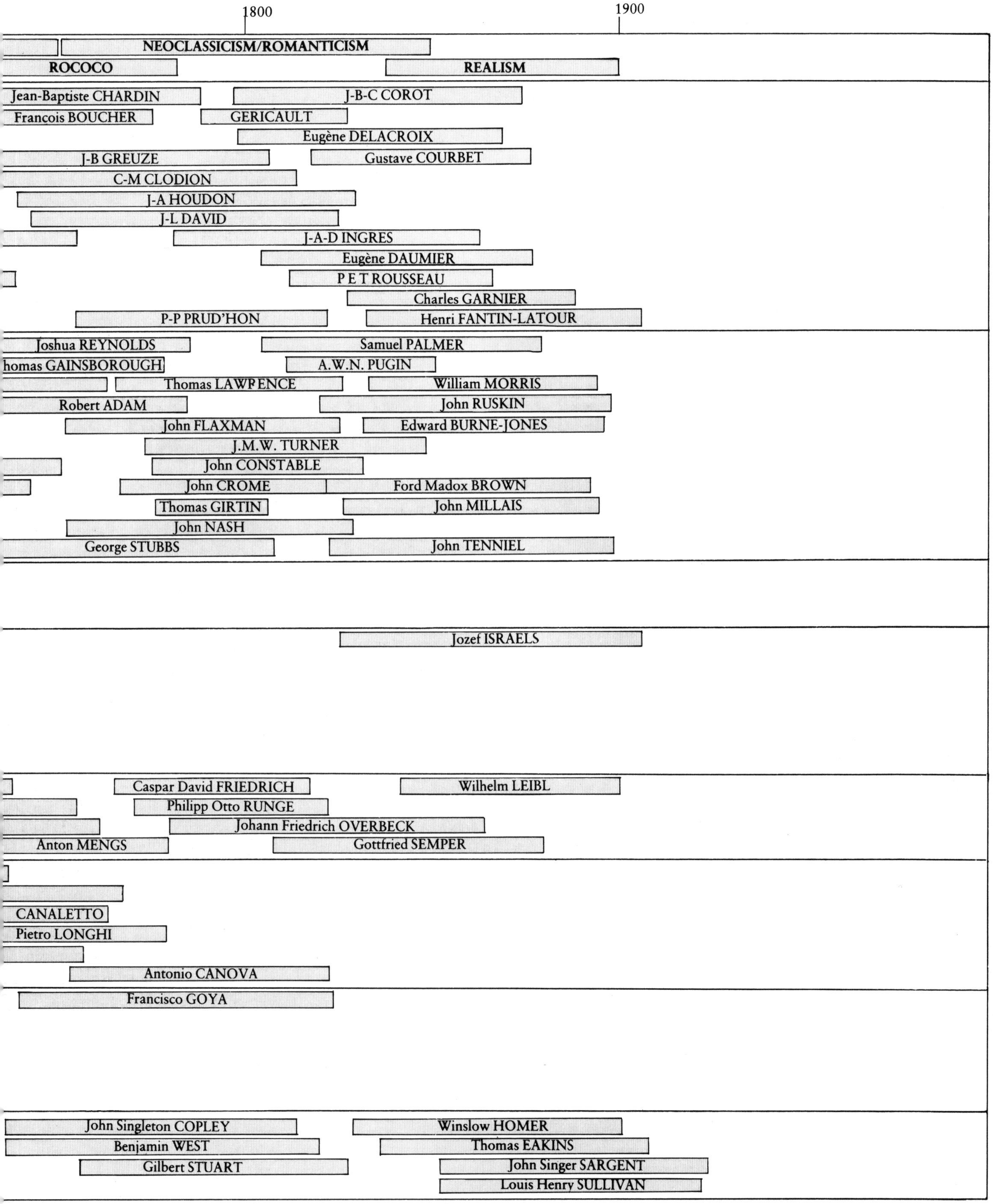

1800   1900

NEOCLASSICISM/ROMANTICISM

ROCOCO   REALISM

Jean-Baptiste CHARDIN

J-B-C COROT

Francois BOUCHER

GERICAULT

Eugène DELACROIX

J-B GREUZE

Gustave COURBET

C-M CLODION

J-A HOUDON

J-L DAVID

J-A-D INGRES

Eugène DAUMIER

P E T ROUSSEAU

Charles GARNIER

P-P PRUD'HON

Henri FANTIN-LATOUR

Joshua REYNOLDS

Samuel PALMER

Thomas GAINSBOROUGH

A.W.N. PUGIN

Thomas LAWRENCE

William MORRIS

Robert ADAM

John RUSKIN

John FLAXMAN

Edward BURNE-JONES

J.M.W. TURNER

John CONSTABLE

John CROME

Ford Madox BROWN

Thomas GIRTIN

John MILLAIS

John NASH

George STUBBS

John TENNIEL

Jozef ISRAELS

Caspar David FRIEDRICH

Wilhelm LEIBL

Philipp Otto RUNGE

Johann Friedrich OVERBECK

Anton MENGS

Gottfried SEMPER

CANALETTO

Pietro LONGHI

Antonio CANOVA

Francisco GOYA

John Singleton COPLEY

Winslow HOMER

Benjamin WEST

Thomas EAKINS

Gilbert STUART

John Singer SARGENT

Louis Henry SULLIVAN

CHRONOLOGY OF ARTISTS: SINCE IMPRESSIONISM

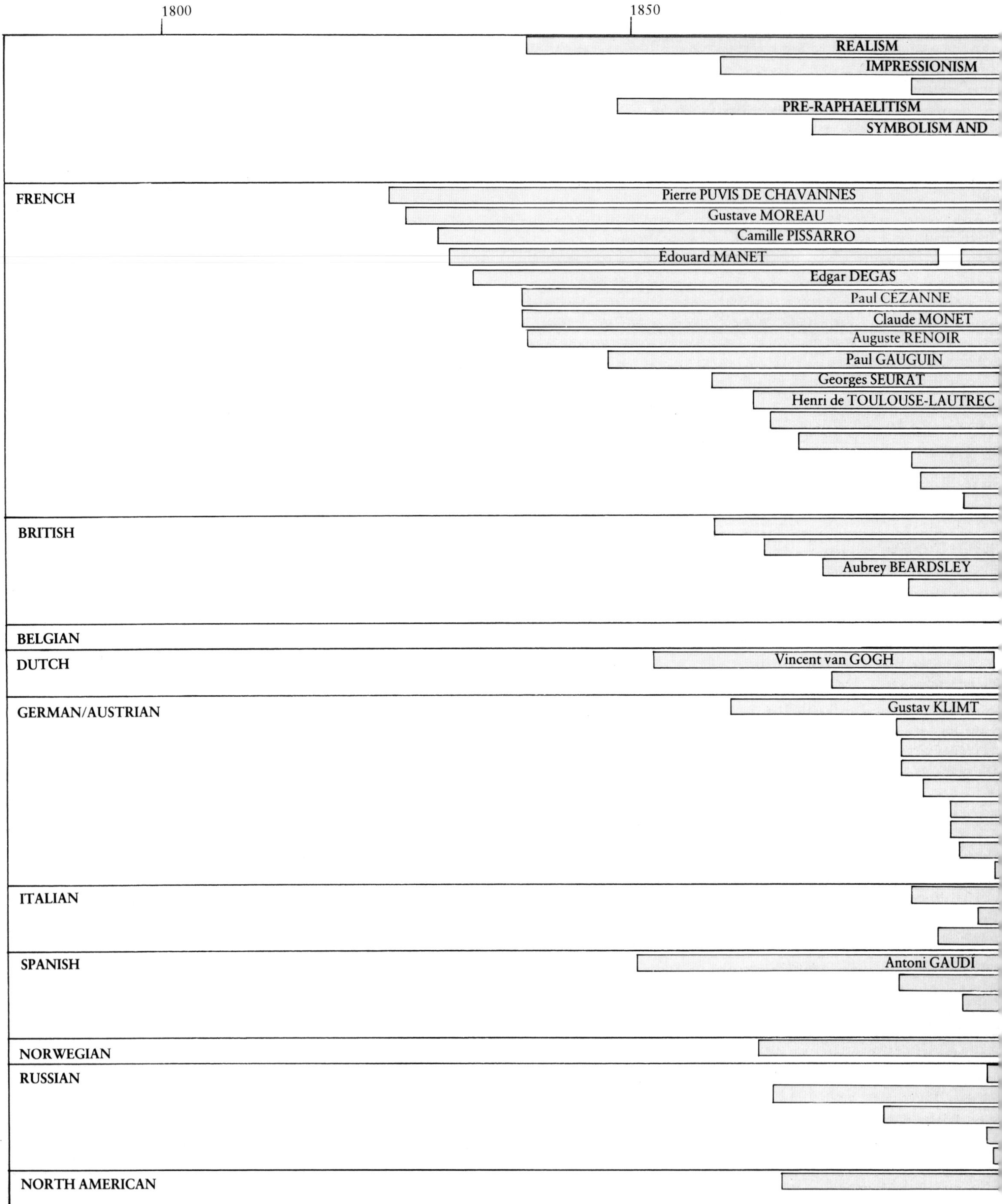

	1800		1850	

REALISM

IMPRESSIONISM

PRE-RAPHAELITISM

SYMBOLISM AND

FRENCH

Pierre PUVIS DE CHAVANNES

Gustave MOREAU

Camille PISSARRO

Édouard MANET

Edgar DEGAS

Paul CEZANNE

Claude MONET

Auguste RENOIR

Paul GAUGUIN

Georges SEURAT

Henri de TOULOUSE-LAUTREC

BRITISH

Aubrey BEARDSLEY

BELGIAN

DUTCH

Vincent van GOGH

GERMAN/AUSTRIAN

Gustav KLIMT

ITALIAN

SPANISH

Antoni GAUDÍ

NORWEGIAN

RUSSIAN

NORTH AMERICAN

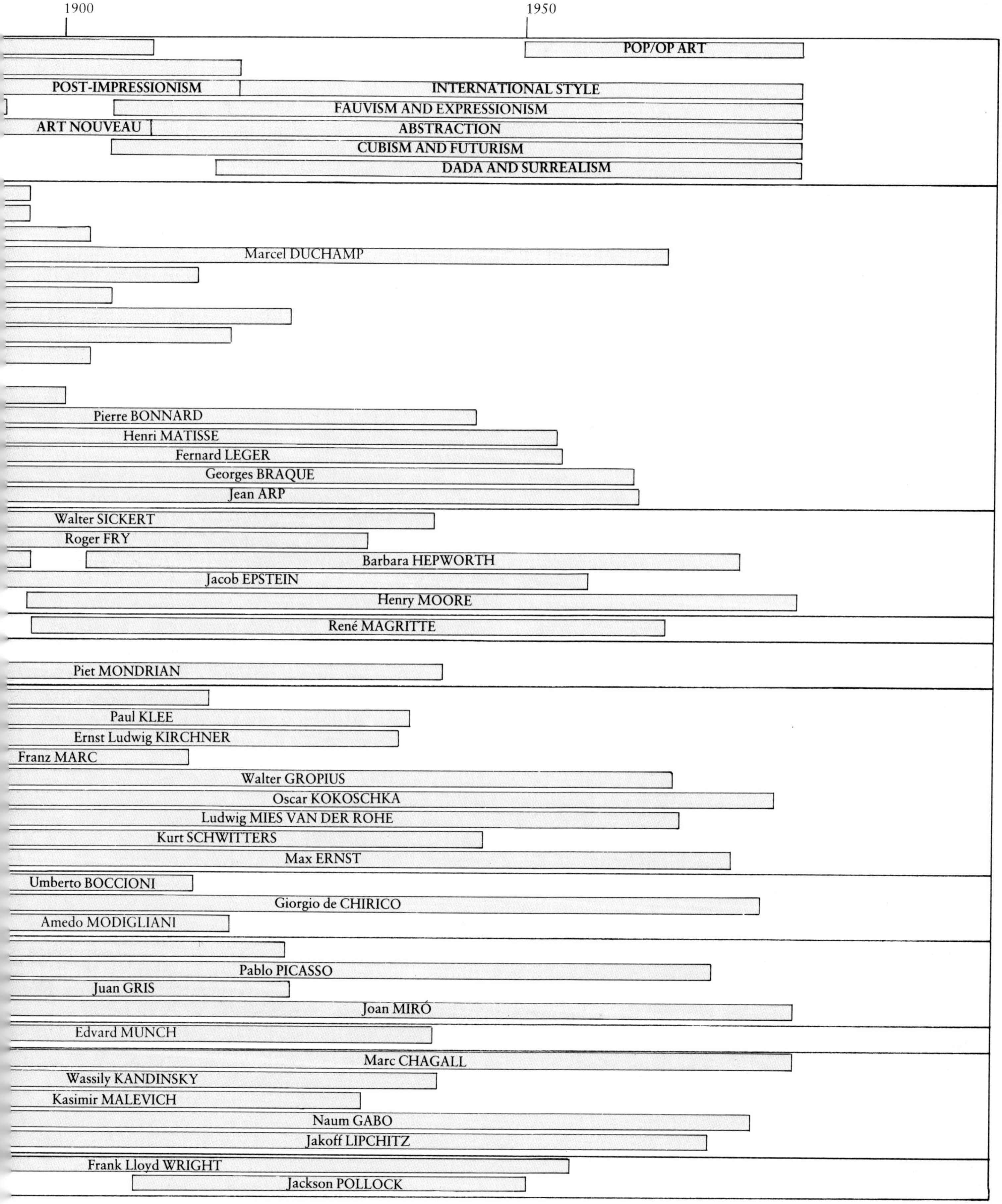

1900		1950	

POP/OP ART

POST-IMPRESSIONISM   INTERNATIONAL STYLE

FAUVISM AND EXPRESSIONISM

ART NOUVEAU   ABSTRACTION

CUBISM AND FUTURISM

DADA AND SURREALISM

Marcel DUCHAMP

Pierre BONNARD

Henri MATISSE

Fernard LEGER

Georges BRAQUE

Jean ARP

Walter SICKERT

Roger FRY

Barbara HEPWORTH

Jacob EPSTEIN

Henry MOORE

René MAGRITTE

Piet MONDRIAN

Paul KLEE

Ernst Ludwig KIRCHNER

Franz MARC

Walter GROPIUS

Oscar KOKOSCHKA

Ludwig MIES VAN DER ROHE

Kurt SCHWITTERS

Max ERNST

Umberto BOCCIONI

Giorgio de CHIRICO

Amedo MODIGLIANI

Pablo PICASSO

Juan GRIS

Joan MIRÓ

Edvard MUNCH

Marc CHAGALL

Wassily KANDINSKY

Kasimir MALEVICH

Naum GABO

Jakoff LIPCHITZ

Frank Lloyd WRIGHT

Jackson POLLOCK

PICTURE ACKNOWLEDGMENTS

Aberdeen Art Gallery: 197, 203. Albright-Knox Art Gallery, Buffalo: 23. Alinari, Florence: 7, 31, 91, 140, 157, 181, 225, 240, 366, 380, 391, 408, 414, 445, 450 (photo: Anderson), 485, 504, 527, 541, 547, 552,(photo: Anderson), 589, 592, 612 (photo: Anderson), 614, 615, 616bl and tr, 650, 660, 677, 679, 681. Alte Pinakothek, Munich: 212, 289, 502. Andromeda Picture Archive, Oxford: 6b, 10, 11, 12, 13, 16, 19, 24t, 24b (c DACS 1995), 27b, 29, 30, 31r, 32t and b, 35, 42, 44, 50t and b, 51, 52br, 53 (c DACS 1995), 59, 60, 64b, 66t (c ADAGP/SPADEM Paris and DACS London 1995), 66b, 69, 72, 77, 81 (c ADAGP Paris and DACS London 1995), 82 (c ADAGP Paris and DACS London 1995), 88, 89, 94, 99, 101t, 103, 105, 106, 107 (c DACS 1995), 112, 114, 116, 120, 121b, 123t, 124, 125t, 129, 133tl and br, 136, 139, 141, 142, 144, 145b, 147t, 148bl, 150t and b, 151, 154, 155t, 158 (c Demart Pro Arte BV/DACS London 1995), 159r, 163, 165, 167, 174t, 175 (c ADAGP Paris and DACS London 1995), 178, 180t, 182, 188, 202b, 205t (c Richard Estes/DACS London/VAGA New York 1995), 207, 211, 212, 213, 215, 216, 222, 227, 228, 231br, 232, 237, 239t and b, 243, 247, 248, 249b, 253t and b, 254, 256, 261b, 263, 267, 269, 274, 275, 278, 281, 285, 286, 289, 294, 299, 301t, 301b (c Richard Hamilton 1995 All rights reserved DACS), 305, 310, 311br, 312, 315t and b, 317, 332, 334 (c DACS 1995), 347, 360t, 361t and b, 362, 363, 364, 365, 369, 376t and b, 377, 383l and r, 384t, 384b (c Roy Lichtenstein/DACS 1995), 386, 387t (c ADAGP Paris and DACS London 1995), 390, 391l, 393, 394t and b, 396, 397b, 399, 403l, 405t and b, 407 (c DACS 1995), 412, 414b, 417t and b, 418, 422, 423, 431, 432t and b, 434, 435tr and br, 437 (c Succession H Matisse/DACS 1995), 442, 448, 449, 451, 452, 454, 457, 460, 468, 469b, 473tr, 478, 484l and r, 491 (c Angela Verren-Taunt 1995 All rights reserved DACS), 498, 507br, 515, 521l (c ADAGP/SPADEM Paris and DACS London 1995), 521r, 528, 530tl, 543br (c ARS New York and DACS London 1995), 548l and r, 549, 551, 553t, 555, 556, 557, 558, 561t, 562, 565b, 567, 568, 569, 571, 572, 573, 575, 576r, 577bl and tr, 579br, 582, 586, 588l and r, 593, 595, 597 (c ADAGP Paris and DACS London 1995), 599, 600b, 601, 602, 604, 605, 607, 608, 610, 613tr, 619bl and tr, 620b, 621, 622tl, 623, 625 (c DACS London 1995), 626, 627, 629, 630, 631 (c ADAGP Paris and DACS London 1995), 632, 635b, 637 (c DACS 1995), 638, 641, 642, 644, 645, 649 (c ADAGP Paris and DACS London 1995), 651 (c ADAGP Paris and DACS London 1995), 667b, 669, 672, 673t, 676 (c DACS 1995), 677tl, 680, 685tr, 689, 690, 692, 694 (c ADAGP Paris and DACS London 1995), 695l and r, 701, 702, 705 t and b, 706, 709, 710r, 713t (c ADAGP Paris and DACS London 1995), 713b, 715 (c DACS 1995), 716, 721t and b, 724, 726, 730, 731t, 732bl (c ADAGP Paris and DACS London 1995), 735, 737, 740. Archivio Fotografico d'Arte A Villani a Figli, Bologna: 710l. Art Gallery of New South Wales: 373. Art Institute of Chicago: 354 (c DACS 1995), 411b, 732tr. Arxiu MAS, Barcelona: 127. Ashmolean Museum, Oxford: 14. Bergen Art Gallery: 480 (c The Munch Museum/The Munch-Ellingsen Group/DACS 1995). Bibliotheque Nationale, Paris: 242. Bildarchiv Foto Marburg: 353b, 433, 499, 622br. O Bohm, Venice: 711b. Boymans van Beunigen Museum, Rotterdam: 339b. J Brennan, Oxford: 370. Bridgeman Art Library, London: 40, 45, 76, 95cr, 238b, 307, 358, 402, 438 (c Succession H Matisse/DACS 1995), 473bl, 477. British Library, London: 429. British Museum, London: 36, 58, 100, 318, 531. Brooks Memorial Art Gallery, Memphis, Tenn.: 74. Bulloz, Paris: 37, 38, 161, 261, 340, 443, 501. Busch-Reisinger Museum, Cambridge, Mass.: 349, 458 (c DACS 1995). Butler Institute of American Art, Youngstown, Ohio: 321b. Caisse Nationale des Monuments Historiques et des Sites, Paris: 533, 643. Central Museum of Art, Utrecht: 62. Chester Beatty Library, Dublin: 503 (photo: Pieterse Davison International). City of Birmingham Museums and Art Gallery: 105t, 111b, 293, 327, 539. Cleveland Museum of Art, Ohio: 241l. Corpus Christi College, Cambridge: 509r. Dallas Museum of Fine Art: 462. (Munger Fund). Detroit Institute of Arts: 186 (c ADAGP Paris and DACS London 1995), 223b, 579tl, 727. Collection of H M Queen Elizabeth II: 598, 739. Equinox Archive: 731b. William Hayes Fogg Art Museum, Cambridge, Mass.: 214t (Gift of Dr G Stevens Jones, c DACS 1995), 633 (Louise E Betters Fund) Freer Gallery of Art, Washington DC: 121t, 581br. Frick Collection, New York: 712. Gabinetto Fotografico Nazionale, Rome: 9, 459. Gemaldegalerie Alte Meister, Dresden: 673b. Giraudon, Paris: 3b, 26, 39, 41, 48, 75l and r, 85, 87, 97, 110, 122, 147, 148t, 149, 159l, 160, 169, 212, 219, 241, 252, 260, 272, 404, 410, 481, 530. Solomon R Guggenheim Museum, New York: 353t (c Estate of Franz Kline/DACS London/VAGA New York 1995). Frans Hals Museum, Haarlem: 52tl. Robert Harding Associates, London: 231tl, 436. Joseph Hirschhorn Museum, Washington DC: 488. Michael Holford, Essex: 250, 338, 517b, 733. Holle Verlag, Baden: 135. Imperial War Museum, London: 382t. Sidney Janis Gallery, New York: 476 (c Estate of Robert Motherwell/DACS London/VAGA New York 1995), 497t (Carroll Janis Collection). Kenwood House, London: 658. A F Kersting, London: 2, 4, 33, 119, 156l, 176, 177t, 303, 738. Kress Foundation, New York: 515. Kunsthistorisches Museum, Vienna: 23, 264. Andrew Lawson, Oxford: 348. Lefevre Gallery, London: 95tl. Los Angeles County Museum of Art: 401t, 708 (c ADAGP Paris and DACS London 1995). Marlborough Gallery of Fine Art, London: 350. Mansell Collection, London: 427t (photo: Anderson). Pierre Matisse Gallery, New York: 172 (c ADAGP Paris and DACS London 1995). Metropolitan Museum, New York: 27t, 70 (Brisbane Dick Fund), 126, 199, 259, 392, 496 (Steiglitz Collection c ARS New York and DACS London 1995), 508, 581tl, 592, 609t, 707, 741. Ministry of Public Buildings and Works, London: 667t. Minneapolis Institute of Arts: 554. Modern Museum, Stockholm: 367 (c ADAGP Paris and DACS London 1995). Montreal Museum of Fine Arts: 214b (c DACS 1995). Musee d'Art Moderne, Geneva: 666. Museo Nazionale, Florence: 15. Museum Ludwig, Cologne: 341. Museum of Fine Arts, Antwerp: 202t (c DACS 1995). Museum of Fine Arts, Boston: 47, 238t, 283, 657. Museum of Fine Art, Houston: 190. Museum of Modern Art, New York: 63 (Lillie P Bliss Bequest), 118t (Goodyear Fund), 118b (c ADAGP Paris and DACS London 1995), 164 (c Estate of Stuart Davis/DACS London/VAGA New York 1995), 204b (c SPADEM/ADAGP Paris and DACS London 1995), 219b (c ARS New York and DACS London 1995), 288 (c DACS 1995), 330, 344 (c ADAGP Paris and DACS London 1995), 350t (c DACS 1995), 360b (Inter American Fund c DACS 1995), 382b (c ARS New York and DACS London 1995), 420 (c Escobar Marisol/DACS London/VAGA New York 1995), 427 (c ADAGP Paris and DACS London 1995), 439 (c ADAGP Paris and DACS London 1995), 509l (Blanchette Rockefeller Fund), 670 (c ADAGP Paris and DACS London 1995), 736. National Gallery, London: 21, 73, 86, 108, 117, 131, 179, 201, 221, 234b, 308, 313, 322, 355, 416, 419t, 425, 430,440, 446, 470, 473, 487, 500, 510, 513t, 516, 518, 526, 533t, 542, 543tl, 545, 576l, 591t, 611, 618, 620t, 647, 652, 665, 671br, 684, 696, 698, 699, 725, 730, 733. National Gallery of Art, Washington DC: 49, 110t (Chester Dale Collection), 209 (Mellon Collection), 226, 388, 389 (Kress Collection), 395 (Widener Collection), 444 (Kress Collection), 455l, 471, 513br (Kress Collection), 584 (Kress Collection), 646 (Kress Collection). National Gallery of Ireland, Dublin: 276, 682. National Gallery of Scotland, Edinburgh: 17br, 85, 321t, 323, 540tl, 560, 561b, 570, 600t, 719. National Gallery of Victoria, Melbourne: 333b, 512. National Maritime Museum, Greenwich: 199r, 700. National Museum of Stockholm: 125b (c DACS 1995). National Museum of Wales, Cardiff: 249t (c ADAGP Paris and DACS London 1995). National Palace Museum, Taipei: 326, 441r, 717, 736b. National Portrait Gallery, London: 245, 300, 337t. William Rockhill Nelson Gallery, Kansas City, Mo: 634, 722. The National Trust, London: 205b. Offentliche Kunstsammlung, Kunstmuseum Basel: 178r (c DACS 1995), 315b. Osterreiche Galerie, Vienna: 441l. Pennsylvania Academy of the Fine Arts, Philadelphia: 723. Maria Perotti, Milan: 457t. Philadelphia Museum of Art: 189 (c ADAGP Paris and DACS London 1995), 233t, 309t, 333t, 371 (c DACS 1995), 421, 507tl, 514. Pollok House, Glasgow: 282. A Raichele, Ulm: 54. Rijksmuseum, Amsterdam: 25, 339t. Rijksmuseum Vincent Van Gogh, Amsterdam: 411tr. Robert Harding Picture Library, London: 436. Royal Academy of Art, London: 138. Royal Albert Memorial Museum, Exeter: 304. Royal Library, Windsor: 320. Saint Louis Art Museum, Missouri: 609b. San Diego Museum of Art: 613bl. Scala, Florence: 5, 17t, 20, 53l, 57, 68, 79, 92, 98b, 101b, 109, 113, 130, 152, 153, 187, 192, 233b, 235tl, 246, 258, 262, 280, 292, 342, 343, 401b, 403r, 426, 443br, 490, 502, 505, 517t, 532, 535, 536, 537, 544, 546, 553b, 559, 674, 704. R V Schoder, Chicago: 482. Anton Schroll and Co, Vienna: 441. Scottish National Portrait Gallery, Edinburgh: 483. Seattle First National Bank: 497b (c Jules Olitski/DACS London/VAGA New York 1995). Service de Documentation Photographique de la Reunion des Musees Nationaux, Paris: 34b, 319, 428, 538. Olive Smith (photo Edwin Smith), Saffron Walden: 75b. Staatliche Antikensammlungen, Munich: 206 (photo Moessener), 208. Staatliche Museen zu Berlin, Germany: 446t. Stadtische Kunsthalle, Mannheim: 46tl (c DACS 1995), 479 (c DACS 1995). State Art Museum, Copenhagen: 3t. Stedelijk Museum, Amsterdam: 409. Tate Gallery, London: 6t (c DACS 1995), 34t, 46br, 61, 64t, 95bl, 135, 137, 157l, 170 (c Paul Delvaux Foundation/St Idesbald Belgium/DACS London 1995), 225b (c ARS New York and DACS London 1995), 230, 252t, 268, 270 (c ADAGP Paris and DACS London 1995), 271 (c ADAGP Paris and DACS London 1995), 279, 296, 306, 309b, 314, 316, 325b, 335, 336 (c Jasper Johns/DACS London/VAGA New York 1995), 337b, 352 (c ADAGP Paris and DACS London 1995), 362b, 374, 397t, 419b (c DACS 1995), 455r (c ADAGP Paris and DACS London 1995), 467, 475, 492, 493b, 494 (c Kenneth Noland/DACS London/VAGA New York 1995), 520 (c Tom Phillips 1995 All rights reserved DACS), 523 (c DACS 1995), 524bl (c DACS 1995), 564 (c Robert Rauschenberg/DACS London/VAGA New York 1995), 565t (c Man Ray Trust/ADAGP Paris and DACS London 1995), 578, 580, 585, 590 (c James Rosenquist/DACS London/VAGA New York 1995), 591b, 594, 596 (c ARS New York and DACS London 1995), 617, 635t, 636, 650t, 653, 655, 659 (c DACS London 1995), 660, 661 (c DACS 1995), 662 (c ADAGP Paris and DACS London 1995), 664, 686, 687, 718, 728. E Teitelman, Camden, NJ: 96, 191t. Thorvaldsen Museum, Copenhagen: 668. Toledo Museum of Art, Ohio: 540br. UNESCO, Paris: 98t (c ADAGP Paris and DACS London 1995), 493t. Vautier Phototheque, Paris: 8. Victoria and Albert Museum, London: 43, 691. Virginia Museum of Fine Arts, Richmond Va: 583. Wadsworth Atheneum, Hartford, Conn.: 328. Walker Art Center, Minneapolis: 235br. Walker Art Gallery, Liverpool: 729. Wallace Collection, London: 65, 220, 223, 290, 325t, 375, 398b. Wallraf-Richartz Museum, Cologne: 489. Walters Art Gallery, Baltimore: 161b, 711t. Whitney Museum of American Art, New York: 347b, 356. Wilhelm-Lehmbruck Museum, Duisburg: 387b (c Estate of Jacques Lipchitz/DACS London/VAGA New York 1995). Yale University Art Gallery, New Haven: 683. York City Art Gallery: 180b. Zefa Picture Library, London: 145t, 173, 184, 200, 218, 234t, 251, 295.

Private Collections: 71 (c Fernando Botero/DACS London/VAGA New York 1995), 83 (c ADAGP Paris and DACS London 1995), 168 (c ADAGP Paris and DACS London 1995), 171 (c DACS 1995), 191b (c DACS 1995), 204t (c SPADEM/ADAGP Paris and DACS London 1995), 311br (c Estate of Roger Hilton 1995 All Rights reserved DACS 1995), 363t (ADAGP Paris and DACS London 1995), 406 (c ADAGP Paris and DACS London 1995), 411tl (c ADAGP Paris and DACS London 1995), 469t (c DACS 1995), 622b (c DACS 1995), 654 (c ARS New York and DACS London 1995), 678 (c ADAGP Paris and DACS London 1995), 706 (c ADAGP Paris and DACS London 1995)

Works by the following artists are still in copyright: Joseph Albers, Alexander Archipenko, Arman, Kenneth Armitage, Keith Arnatt, Conrad Atkinson, Frank Auerbach, Francis Bacon, Giacomo Balla, Ernst Barlach, George Bellows, Charles Biederman, Peter Blake, David Bomberg, Fernando Botero, Edward Burra, Alberto Burri, Reg Butler, Anthony Caro, Lynn Chadwick, Christo, Bernard Cohen, James Collins, Stuart Davis, Charles Demuth, Robyn Denny, Jim Dine, Otto Dix, Jacob Epstein, Richard Estes, Alexander Exter, Michael ffolkes, Dan Flavin, Sam Francis, Helen Frankenthaler, Roger Fry, Naum Gabo, Eric Gill, Fritz Glarner, Arshile Gorky, Adolf Gottlieb, Duncan Grant, Gropius, Philip Guston, Richard Hamilton, Duane Hanson, Barbara Hepworth, Patrick Heron, Roger Hilton, Ivon Hitchens, David Hockney, Hans Hofmann, Edward Hopper, John Hoyland, Robert Indiana, Augustus John, Jasper Johns, Allen Jones, Donald Judd, Ellsworth Kelly, Philip King, Ernst Ludwig Kirchner, R B Kitaj, Franz Kline, Willem de Kooning, Gaston Lachaise, Peter Lanyon, John Latham, Wilhelm Lehmbruck, Wyndham Lewis, Sol Le Witt, Max Liebermann, Richard Lindner, Jakoff Lipchitz, El Lissitzky, Richard Long, Morris Louis, L S Lowry, Stanton Macdonald-Wright, F E McWilliam, Kasimir Malevich, Marino Marini, Kenneth Martin, Laszlo Moholy-Nagy, Henry Moore, Giorgio Morandi, Robert Motherwell, Edvard Munch, Elie Nadelman, Louise Nevelson, Barnett Newman, Ben Nicholson, Isamu Noguchi, Sidney Nolan, Georgia O'Keeffe, Claes Oldenburg, Orozco, Eduardo Paolozzi, Victor Pasmore, Tom Phillips, Jackson Pollock, Jose Posada, Maurice Prendergast, Ceri Richards, Bridget Riley, Diego Rivera, Alexander Rodchenko, Mies van der Rohe, Mark Rothko, Oskar Schlemmer, Charles Sheeler, Walter Sickert, Matthew Smith, Richard Smith, Tony Smith, Robert Smithson, Stanley Spencer, Philip Wilson Steer, Saul Steinberg, Frank Stella, Clyfford Still, Vladimir Tatlin, Pavel Tchelitchew, Jean Tinguely, Carl Tubby, William Turnbull, Frank Lloyd Wright, Andrew Wyeth, Jack Yeats

BIOGRAPHICAL DICTIONARY
OF ARTISTS

Edvard Munch: Self-portrait in Blue Suit; cil on canvas; 100×110cm (39×43in); 1909
Bergen Art Gallery (see page 480)

A

Aalto Alvar 1898–1976

Alvar Aalto was one of the most original and inventive architects of this century. Born at Kuortane in Finland, son of a forester, he studied architecture at the Helsinki Polytechnic, and in 1927 won a competition for a library at Viipuri. His second major work of the early "white" period was the Paimio Sanatorium (1929–33), a reinforced concrete building in the International style, for which he also designed the equipment (bent plywood furniture, used here for the first time).

Aalto's work was distinguished by a remarkable sensitivity to natural materials, especially to timber which featured prominently in his Finnish Pavilions at the Paris Exhibition (1937) and the New York World Fair (1939). He showed an almost instinctive approach to the creation of forms, which prevented his work from lapsing into any of the architectural clichés of his day. And he was able to integrate his architecture with landscape and with local building tradition.

After the Second World War, Aalto began building in red brick and timber. A fine example from this so-called "red" period is the Civic Center at Säynätsalo (1950–2). In the early 1950s, his work upon the redesigning of Helsinki began in earnest. Projects included the Otaniemi Polytechnic (begun 1955), and the Cultural Center (1955–8). The main building of the Institute of Technology in Otaniemi (executed 1961–4) and Finlandia house in Helsinki are among of his last major works.

Further reading. Quantrill, M. *Alvar Aalto: A Critical Study*, New York (1983).

Abbate Niccolò dell' 1509?–71

Born at Modena, west of Bologna, Niccolò dell'Abbate was a fresco painter, mainly of secular subjects. The details of his early career at Modena are obscure. He was probably familiar with Raphael's *bella maniera*, with the work of Pordenone and Correggio, and with that of Parmigianino with whose work some of his own has been confused. His affinity with the Dossi brothers is even stronger. His earliest decoration, on the facade of the Beccherie (1537; fragments are now in the Galleria Estense, Modena), introduced a characteristically piquant theme of Venetian origin, that of amorous genre, with the actors in romantic costumes. The theme reached the height of elegance in his work in the Palazzo Poggi (now the University) at Bologna, c1550–2. His second decorative commission, for the Rocco di Scandiano (c1540; now in the Galleria Estense, Modena), introduced delicately observed landscape which is developed into a sophisticated contrivance for delight. During his residence in Bologna from c1548 his already synthetic style was influenced by the refinements of contemporary Florentine figurative painting.

Niccolò's work in the Palazzo Poggi, which was to affect Bolognese painting later in the century, was left unfinished. In 1552, perhaps on the recommendation of Primaticcio, Niccolò was called to the court of Henry II of France. He was the last important Italian painter to establish himself at Fontainebleau, but most of his work there has perished.

Niccolò's activity as a decorator was directed by Primaticcio. His own style, while sympathetic to Primaticcio's, was not altogether subservient to it. He embroidered it with engaging superfluities, anticipating in spirit some of the qualities of the French Rococo. The finest surviving works from the last decade of his life are two large panoramic landscapes on canvas, filled with topographical fantasies and magical artifices of light (Louvre, Paris, and National Gallery, London).

Abd Allah 16th century

Abd Allah was court painter in Bukhara (now in Uzbekistan) under Abd al-Aziz (1540–9) and Yar Muhammad (1550–7) and may have been active until c1575. Said to have been a pupil of Mahmud, Abd Allah developed the tendency towards flat, decorative painting, increasing the emphasis on the silhouette, first seen in a *Bustan* of Sa'di of 1542 on which he collaborated with Mahmud (Gulbenkian Foundation, Lisbon) and in the *Gulistan* of Sa'di dated 1543 (Bibliothèque Nationale, Paris). His separate figure drawings show the development even more clearly.

Alvar Aalto: a lecture theater at the Institute of Technology, Otaniemi, Finland; built 1964

Nicolai Abildgaard: The wounded Philoctetes; oil on canvas; 123×174cm (48×69in); 1774–5. State Art Museum, Copenhagen

Abildgaard Nicolai 1743–1809

The Danish history painter and decorative artist Nicolai Abraham Abildgaard studied at the Royal Academy, Copenhagen (1764–7) and then in Italy (1772–7). Through meeting the Swedish sculptor Johan Sergel in Rome, he was influenced by Henry Fuseli's subject matter. In the 1780s, he carried out the decorations of the Palace of Charlottenburg in Denmark, where he is best known for his Neoclassical figures and his contribution to the applied arts, including furniture, medals, and sculpture. Abildgaard's later paintings were often based on the writings of Apuleius and Terence, and, in their relaxed elegance, they contrast with the darker, more dramatic compositions of his earlier years.

Abul Hasan 1589–1616

Born 1589 in the Mughal Imperial household, India, Abul Hasan was the son of the Persian painter Aqa Riza. He started work in the Akbar period, but attained eminence in Jahangir's reign (1605–27). Jahangir gave him the title Nadir-al-Zaman ("Wonder of the Age") and wrote in his autobiography that his work was "perfect, and his picture is one of the *chefs d'oeuvre* of the age. At the present time he has no rival". Specializing in allegorical portraits, he copied and in turn was influenced by European art, particularly in the treatment of light and color. Natural history was another subject area in which he excelled; his painting *Squirrels in a Chennar Tree* (India Office Library, London) is a marvel of observation and sensitivity, and surpasses even the best works of Mansur. Among his known works are *Portrait of Jahangir Holding Picture of Akbar* (Musée Guimet, Paris), *Jahangir Standing on a Globe* (Chester Beatty Library, Dublin), *Durbar of Jahangir* (c1620; Boston Museum of Fine Arts), and several in the St Petersburg Album (Hermitage, St Petersburg).

Adam Lambert Sigisbert 1700–59

Lambert Sigisbert Adam was both a sculptor and the business head of a large family workshop in Paris, together with his brothers Nicolas Sébastien (1705–78) and François Gérard (1710–61). Their father was the provincial Nancy sculptor, Jacob Sigisbert Adam (1670–1747). Lambert Sigisbert provided the principal competition for J.B. Lemoyne the younger and Edmé Bouchardon during the second quarter of the 18th century.

After working under his father, and at Metz, Adam arrived in Paris in 1719. He won the *premier prix* at the Académie in 1723, then left for Rome with Bouchardon. Patronized there by Cardinal de Polignac and Pope Clement XII, he was joined by Nicolas Sébastien in 1726 and later by François Gérard. Adam won the competition for designing the Fontana di Trevi, but failed to gain the commission.

In 1733, Adam returned to Paris where his *Neptune Calming the Waves* (Louvre, Paris) was completed in 1737. The statue's debt to Bernini was self-evident, but its dramatic flamboyance and vitality compensate for its lack of originality. This immensely decorative treatment also proved ideal for the central group of *Neptune and Amphitrite*, executed in lead by the family workshop for the Basin de Neptune at Versailles. Completed in 1740, this exuberant group was a great success, but the same principles as applied to the bust of *Louis XV as Apollo* (before 1741; terracotta; Victoria and Albert Museum, London) result in empty grandiloquence. Nicolas Sébastien's *Monument to Queen Catharina Opalinska* (set up 1749, Notre-Dame de Bon Secours, Nancy) is a finer, less ostentatious work.

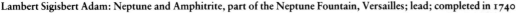

Lambert Sigisbert Adam: Neptune and Amphitrite, part of the Neptune Fountain, Versailles; lead; completed in 1740

Robert Adam: the Tapestry Room at Nostell Priory, West Yorkshire; 1767. Tapestries were added in the early 19th century

Adam family 18th century

The Adam family were Scottish architects. William Adam (1689–1748), Master Mason to the Ordnance in North Britain, was the leading architect of his generation in Scotland. His robust style resembles that of Vanbrugh (1664–1726), and is well represented at Hopetoun House, Midlothian (1723–48). Of his four sons, Robert (1728–92) and James (1730–94) were architects; and it is with the former that the family name is chiefly associated.

Robert Adam was born in Kirkcaldy. He matriculated at Edinburgh University in 1743, and was already established as an independent architect before he set off on

The Grand Tour in 1754. Arriving in Rome he befriended Piranesi, made an exhaustive study of antique, Renaissance, and post-Renaissance architecture, and undertook an archaeological expedition to Spalato (now Split, in Croatia), the fruits of which were published in 1764 as *The Ruins of the Palace of the Emperor Diocletian at Spalato in Dalmatia*.

He returned to Britain in 1758, established himself in London in partnership with his brother James, and immediately began to promote a self-acclaimed "revolution" in British domestic architecture.

The new style was characterized by an intricate, linear style of interior decoration, Pompeian in origin, but also inspired by

the "antique" wall frescoes of Raphael and Peruzzi. The brothers achieved a free but elegant interpretation of the Classical orders, defended as being in "the spirit" rather than in "servile imitation" of Antiquity. Most important of all, the Adam style contributed "movement", defined by the brothers as "the rise and fall, the advance and recess with other diversity of form, in the different parts of a building, so as to add greatly to the picturesque of the composition". The principle had important implications for the exterior as well as the interior of the country house; it expressed itself most fully in an imaginative use of screen columns, and a preference for spatially contrasting apartments, frequently arranged in imitation of Roman Imperial baths.

Much of the "revolution" had been anticipated by Vanbrugh and Kent, but it proved sufficiently innovatory to excite a public bored by the repetitive formalism of late Palladianism. For almost 15 years (c1760–75) Robert Adam was the most fashionable architect in Britain. Of the many buildings with which he was associated during this period, those that best represent the Adam style include Kedleston Hall in Derbyshire (c1761), Osterley Park (1763–80) and Syon House (1762–9) in Middlesex, and Luton Hoo in Bedfordshire (1766–70).

But as early as 1772, the style had produced at least one serious imitator, James Wyatt, and when, in 1774, a speculative venture decimated the family fortune, Adam's attention returned again to Scotland where the expansion of Edinburgh provided him with an opportunity to display his talents in the sphere of civic architecture. Register House (1774–92), Edinburgh University (c1789–92), and Charlotte Square (designed 1791) introduce a monumentality almost entirely lacking in the elegant sophistication of his earlier work. His new style culminated in the romantic massing of his Scottish castles, of which Culzean, Ayrshire (1777–90) is the largest and most impressive.

Further reading. Beard, G. *The Work of Robert Adam*, London (1978). Bolton, A.T. *The Architecture of Robert and James Adam* (2 vols.), London (1922). Fleming, J. *Robert Adam and his Circle in Edinburgh and Rome*, London (1978). Oresko, R. (ed.) *The Works in Architecture of Robert and James Adam*, London (1975).

Adams Robert 1917–

An English sculptor born in Northampton, Robert Adams studied at the Northampton School of Art in evening classes from 1933 to 1942. Between 1949 and 1960 he taught industrial design at London's Central School of Art and Design.

Adam's first mature sculptures were carvings in wood and stone based on the figure, influenced by reproductions of the works of Henry Moore and Barbara Hepworth. In 1949 he began welding vertical, open, linear constructions in various metals inspired by the Spanish sculptor Julio Gonzalez (1876–1942), and continued in this manner until 1965. Contrasts of transparency and solidity are apparent in his wood carvings and bronzes of the early 1950s, which consist of rectilinear forms and planes. His *Large Screen Form No.2* (1962) is in the Tate Gallery, London. From 1963, his major output has been uncompromisingly Abstract, juxtaposing simple planes of bronzed steel which retain openings or perforations. Since 1970, his sculptures in marble and polished bronze have introduced curved surfaces.

Aertsen Pieter 1508–75

The Flemish painter Pieter Aertsen was probably born in Amsterdam, where he originally trained. In 1535 he was registered as a master in the Antwerp guild, though he returned to Amsterdam in his later years. Aertsen was famous in his day as a painter of altarpieces, but many of these were destroyed in the widespread image-breaking in Amsterdam during the 1560s. Among the few that survive are some panels in the Royal Museum of Fine Arts at Antwerp and an *Adoration of the Magi* of 1555–60 (Rijksmuseum, Amsterdam).

Aertsen's chief historical significance lies in his contribution to the development of small Netherlandish genre subjects, (popularized by the Bruegel workshop) into life-size, monumental paintings. His scenes of peasants in everyday domestic settings give weight to foreground detail, which is usually tilted toward the spectator. The figures are also close to the picture plane in half- or three-quarter-length, as in the *Pancake Bakery* of 1560 (Boymans-van Beuningen Museum, Rotterdam). In his rather humorless treatment of the figures, Aertsen rejects the moralizing or ironic comment found in Bruegel. His style is more sculptural, and closer to the Romanist school of Flemish painting. Sometimes an ostensibly genre subject provides the foreground for a religious scene, and takes visual precedence over it. For example, in the *Butcher's Shop* (Royal Collection of Uppsala University) the carefully arranged meat and cooking utensils of the foreground frame a scene of the Flight into Egypt seen through an opening on to the landscape.

Aertsen's genre subjects anticipate similar works by several late-16th-century Italian artists, notably Annibale Carracci. Technically, his vigorous, broad brushwork places him in the Flemish tradition that was to produce such artists as Rubens and Jordaens in the 17th century.

Agam Yaacov 1928–

An Israeli painter and sculptor, Yaacov Agam was born in Rishon-le-Zion. He studied at Bezalel School of Art, Jerusalem, and from 1949 to 1951 at the School of Arts and Crafts, Zurich. He then settled in Paris, but went to teach at Harvard University during 1968–9. Entirely Abstract, Agam's paintings depend either on spectator movement or manual manipulation, devices developed in Paris during the early 1950s. His highly-structured painted reliefs—"polymorphic paintings"—in bright colors change as the spectator moves past, often from isolated color areas to grids, fusing independent themes into new relationships. Agam's "transformables" consist of linear elements in wood and metal, pivoted against plain grounds. From 1969 he has made stainless steel sculptures of repeated elements. His artistic career has included work with sound, tactile sculpture, and both interior and exterior architectural projects.

Agoracritus 5th century BC

The work of the Greek High Classical sculptor Agoracritus represents the Rich style. He emigrated from his native Paros to Athens, presumably to collaborate on the Parthenon sculptures, and became the favorite pupil of Pheidias. His style was a direct development of his master's: it shows a special interest in the sensuous renderings of richly contrasted draperies that seem almost independent of the human body. To Agoracritus and his workshop have been attributed the reliefs on the marble parapet around the temple of Athena Nike on the Acropolis (Acropolis Museum, Athens) and the sculptural decoration of the temple of Nemesis at Rhamnus.

An apocryphal tradition had it that Pheidias was the lover of Agoracritus, and had even made his pupil's two most renowned works: the colossal marble cult-statues of *Nemesis* at Rhamnus and of the *Mother of Gods* in Athens. Nemesis was the Greek goddess of retribution; appropriately, the statue was thought to have been carved in a piece of Parian marble abandoned by the Persians after their invasion of Attica. Agoracritus is reputed to have been defeated by his rival Alcamenes in a competition for a statue of Aphrodite in Athens, and subsequently to have sold his version to Rhamnus as *Nemesis*. Fragments of the statue and its elaborate base survive in the National Museum, Athens,

Agoracritus: statue of Hera; marble; a Roman copy of a late Hellenistic version possibly of the original of c430 BC. Vatican Museums, Rome

and in the British Museum, London, and there are many copies. The goddess was represented standing with a libation bowl in her right hand and an apple bough in her left. She was crowned with a wreath of deer and little victories. The signature of Agoracritus was inscribed on a small tablet attached to the bough. The *Mother of Gods* was described as seated on a throne holding a tambourine and flanked by lions. Another famous work of his was the bronze group of *Athena and Hades*, in Coronea, now lost.

Albani Francesco 1578–1660

Born in Bologna, Francesco Albani studied with Denys Calvaert (1540–1619), and then at the Carracci Academy, before joining Annibale Carracci's Roman studio *c*1602. He implemented Annibale's designs for frescoes in the S. Diego chapel in S. Giacomo degli Spagnuoli (1604–7). Between 1609 and 1615 he executed important fresco cycles, including painted ceil-

ings in the Palazzo Giustiniani, Bassano di Sutri (1609), and in the Palazzo Verospi (*post* 1609). Although he adhered to Domenichino's classicism and was influenced by Raphael, his style is gentler and sweeter. He returned to Bologna in 1616, visiting Rome briefly in the 1620s. His most successful late works are small, idyllic paintings of mythological and allegorical subjects in landscape settings.

Albers Josef 1888–1976

The American painter and designer Josef Albers was born in Bottrop, Germany. He first worked in the Expressionist tradition of Erich Heckel and Karl Schmidt-Rottluff. In 1920 he entered the Bauhaus school at Weimar, where he became a teacher. After the school's closure by the Nazis in 1933, he emigrated to America. He taught first at the Black Mountain College in North Carolina (1933–49) and then at Yale, where he was Chairman of the Department of Architecture and Design

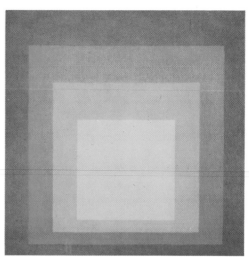

Josef Albers: Study for Series Homage to the Square: Departing in Yellow; oil on board; 76×76cm (30×30in); 1964. Tate Gallery, London

(1950–8). Albers is best known for his famous series of paintings and lithographs based on the square which exploit very subtle chromatic harmonies. *Homage to the Square*, as the series is generally known (Tate Gallery, London, and many other galleries), was a development of an interest in abstraction which went back to the 1920s. Albers' work included furniture design: he designed a pioneering bent laminated chair, intended for mass production.

Further reading. Albers, J. *Interaction of Colour*, London and New Haven (1971). Spies, W. *Josef Albers*, London (1971).

Alberti Leon Battista 1404–72

The Italian art theorist, architect, author, and diplomat Leon Battista Alberti was probably born at Genoa. He was the illegitimate son of the Florentine Lorenzo Alberti, who had been exiled in 1401. After a humanist education under Gasparino da Barzizza (1359–1431) at Padua, he studied law at the University of Bologna, entered minor orders, and became a papal civil servant. He remained in papal service for most of his life; although he lived principally in Rome, his duties took him to a number of Italian cities and possibly as far afield as the Netherlands.

Throughout his life, Alberti wrote constantly, composing plays, philosophical works, treatises, and letters on a wide variety of subjects. Between 1434 and 1436 he was in Florence (which he seems to have regarded as his home, despite his cosmopolitan life) and it is during this

Francesco Albani: The Earth, from The Four Elements; oil on canvas; diameter 180cm (71in); c1626–8. Galleria Sabauda, Turin

period that his interest in the visual arts first becomes apparent. The undated treatise *Della Statua (On Sculpture)* was probably his first essay in this field. In it, Alberti recommends the sculptor to be guided both by an observation of nature and by academic study, entailing a knowledge of proportional theory. It also contains the first known definition of sculpture as an additive process, as in clay modeling, or a subtractive one, as in carving.

His better-known and more ambitious *Della Pittura (On Painting)* was written in Latin in 1435 and translated into Italian the following year. Divided into three books, it deals with the technicalities of "one-point" perspective, the theory of human proportions, composition, and the use of color, and considers the nature of beauty and the behavior appropriate to an artist. When compared with earlier treatises, *Della Pittura* emerges as a fundamentally new departure: the first Rennaissance treatise on art. Although partly a humanist utopia, replete with numerous Classical references, the treatise was also a working handbook. As Alberti's dedication to Brunelleschi and his references to Masaccio, Donatello, Luca della Robbia, and Ghiberti imply, the book was a codification of current Florentine artistic practice. In certain respects, particularly in his observations on aerial perspective, Alberti's theory went further and was actually in advance of contemporary practice. His request, at the beginning of Book One, that he be judged as a painter rather than as a mathematician, is the only surviving evidence that Alberti himself painted. Although no surviving works by his hand have been identified, there seems to be little reason to doubt this claim.

Alberti seems to have turned to architecture in the 1440s. His treatise *De Re Aedificatoria (On Architecture)* was substantially complete in 1452. Drawing upon a critical reading of Vitruvius and a firsthand antiquarian knowledge of Classical remains, he put forward the first coherent theory of the use of the five orders since Antiquity, relating their use to different classes of building. He also expounded a lucid theory of architectural beauty, dependent upon the harmonic relationship between certain fixed proportions, mitigated by ornamental forms. As the first comprehensive treatise on Renaissance architecture, this book is in many respects comparable with the earlier *Della Pittura*, although it was more a work of original

Leon Battista Alberti: the exterior of the Tempio Malatestiano (church of S. Francesco), Rimini; conversion begun c1450 but never completed

research, and was more influential.

By this time Alberti appears to have been employed as a papal consultant on town planning and the conservation of Classical remains. His first known architectural commission was undertaken c1450 for Sigismondo Malatesta of Rimini. This prince, who was as steeped in Classical culture as Alberti himself, wished to convert the Gothic church of S. Francesco in Rimini into a splendid mausoleum for himself and his court. Faced with this unprepossessing task, Alberti's solution was both ingenious and simple. Retaining the interior with minor decorative modifications, he enclosed the old fabric within an architectural shell. The facade was recast as a temple front incorporating a triumphal facade motif, and the sides were masked with a massive series of piers, framing deep, round-head niches. The walls were taken up to a sufficient height to conceal the church within. It seems that the crossing was to have been crowned with a huge semicircular dome, though this was never built. Despite its incomplete state, the church stands as an austere evocation of Roman Antiquity, such as had never before been seen in the Quattrocento.

Shortly afterwards, Alberti was called upon to complete the facade of the church of S. Maria Novella in Florence. Incor-

porating the extant Gothic arcading of the lower story, Alberti monumentalized the facade with the addition of a great arched central doorway, and unified it with side pilasters and a high attic zone. As at Rimini, the end result is a triumphal arch motif. In the upper story, he retained the old circular window and surrounded it with a visually dominating square element. Decorated with pilasters and surmounted by a pediment, this formed an applied temple front. The difference in height between this story and the aisles was effectively masked by a pair of great volutes. At S. Maria Novella, Alberti had formulated a lucidly structured Classical facade, working within the traditional Tuscan formal repertoire dictated by the existing building. The true genius of his design is that it appears as a convincing aesthetic whole and in no way as a compromise.

Alberti's last two church designs were for new buildings, commissioned by Ludovico Gonzaga of Mantua. The first, S. Sebastiano, was begun in 1460 but never properly completed. It was conceived as a central cube spanned by an enormous domical vault, contained within a Greek cross. Three arms ended in apses, the fourth led out to a pedimented facade with a broken entablature. The main story was elevated upon a crypt, giving a strange emphasis to the facade. This would probably have been masked by a mighty stairway, firmly anchoring the facade to street level, but it was never built. The second church S. Andrea, was begun in 1470 and completed according to Alberti's plans after his death. On a Latin cross plan, the church was enclosed with a great coffered barrel vault. This coffering was echoed in the chapels that lined the nave, in the entrance porch that serves as a centerpiece to the facade, and in the remarkable window niche that stands high above the majestic main pediment and its giant order. Both churches were of an extremely unconventional design, although they reveal a deliberate application of proportional theory, and the use of a wide range of antique sources, closely related to the theories in *De Re Aedificatiora*.

In addition to these works, Alberti designed the Palazzo Rucellai and the tiny shrine of the Holy Sepulcher (Rucellai Chapel) in the adjoining church of S. Pancrazio. His total oeuvre is small, but highly significant. With his unparalleled knowledge of antique architecture, Alberti set out to transcend his models. In so doing, and in providing a literary explanation of his aims and ideas, he provided a secure basis for the subsequent development of the classical style in European architecture. When his other literary works, in particular his treatises on sculpture and painting, are added to this achievement, his contribution to Renaissance culture justly appears immense. Alberti is often regarded as the embodiment of the *Uomo Universale,* but the range and quality of his activities are not typical of his own or any other age.

Further reading. Alberti, L.B. (trans. and ed. Orlandesi, G. and Portoghesi, P.) *L'Architettura di Leon Battista Alberti* (2 vols), Milan (1966). Alberti, L.B. (trans. and ed. Grayson, C.) *On Painting and On Sculpture,* London (1972). Borsi, F. *Leon Battista Alberti,* Oxford (1977). Heydenreich, L. and Lotz, W. *Architecture in Italy: 1400–1600,* Harmondsworth (1974). Wittkower, R. *Architectural Principles in the Age of Humanism,* London (1949).

Albright Ivan 1897–1983

The American painter Ivan Le Lorraine Albright was born in Harvey, Illinois. He studied architecture at the University of Illinois and later studied art both in Europe (the École des Beaux-Arts, Nantes) and America (the Art Institute of Chicago). The

dominant influence on his style, though, was his father, a painter who had studied under Thomas Eakins. Albright's works show an obsession with the relentless decay wrought by time, their mood one of the poignancy of unfulfilled ambitions and missed opportunities—the work which established his career, *That Which I Should Have Done I Did Not Do* (1931–41; Art Institute of Chicago), shows a withered hand reaching for a funeral wreath hanging on a weathered door. His painstaking attention to minute details of fabrics and wrinkled skin, finely etched against a dark background, creates images of hallucinatory intensity, as in one of his best-known portraits, *Fleeting Time Thou Hast Left Me Old* (1929–30; Metropolitan Museum of Art, New York).

Alcamenes 5th Century BC

The Greek High Classical sculptor Alcamenes came from Athens or Lemnos, and was a member of the Attic School. He is said to have won a competition against Agoracritus for a statue of Aphrodite commissioned by Athens. Medieval tradition believed he had been a rival of Pheidias for the bronze *Athena Promachos.* He was one of the strongest artistic personalities of his time; the Greeks attributed to him works ranging in date from 480 BC to the end of the 5th century BC. It is possible that he worked on the pediments of the temple of Zeus at Olympia (468–456 BC) as a young man, and later collaborated in the Parthenon.

Alcamenes executed a number of cult-statues for the temples of Athens, notably an ivory and gold *Dionysos* and a bronze group of *Athena and Hephaestus* (Hephaestus' club foot disguised by falling drapery). He also carved an *Ares,* now tentatively identified as the prototype of the *Ares Borghese* (Louvre, Paris). His statue of Aphrodite, which used to stand in the "Gardens" (a suburb of Athens), was much praised for its lovely hands, while the finishing touches were ascribed to Pheidias.

Some of Alcamenes' sculptures seem to have embodied archaistic features along with innovations, following a trend of the period. He created the much imitated type of *Hecate,* with three bodies in archaistic dress set around a pillar, which stood on the bastion of the Athena Nike temple on the Acropolis. Inscribed copies of a herm by Alcamenes have been found in Ephesus and Pergamon.

Aleijadinho: the Prophet Hosea, a detail of one of the 12 prophets carved for the church of Bom Jesus de Matozinhos, Congonhas do Campo, Brazil; stone; 1800–5

Aleijadinho 1738–1814

The great Brazilian sculptor and architect António Francisco Lisboa is best known by his nickname, "O Aleijadinho" or "the little cripple". He was a mulatto, son of the Portuguese architect Manuel Francisco Lisboa.

Aleijadinho was the most original exponent of the Rococo in the Americas; he worked in the province of Minas Gerais, which in the 18th century was booming with the gold and diamond rush. He designed, built, and decorated the church of São Francisco, Ouro Preto (1766–94), a rare example of a building in a completely unified style. His sculptural work includes processional images of the Passion (1797–99) and 12 remarkable, dynamic, open-air statues of the prophets (1800–5) at Bom Jesus de Matozinhos, Congonhas do Campo. His simple and dignified Rococo interiors use straight columns and refined ornament.

Algardi Alessandro 1598–1654

The Italian sculptor Alessandro Algardi was born in Bologna. For one brought up in a city without a local stone an inclination towards modeling seems natural and was to prove as fundamental to his art as was the support of Bolognese patrons to his career.

Algardi studied with the painter Lodovico Carracci as well as with the sculptor Giulio Cesare Conventi, with whom he collaborated on the stucco statues of the four patron saints of Bologna in the Oratory of S. Maria della Vita. At the age of 19 he went to Mantua, where he worked for the Duke and became familiar with antique works of art placed in his care as well as with the paintings of Giulio Romano (c1499–1546).

In 1625, after a brief visit to Venice, he arrived in Rome where artistic life was dominated by Bernini. For many years Algardi earned his living by restoring antiques and making small models which were cast either in bronze or in precious metals. His first major commission was for the tomb of Pope Leo XI in St Peter's (1634–44), followed by that for the marble *St Philip Neri* in the sacristy of the Vallicella (1635?–46). Some of his rivals in Rome doubted his ability to work in marble. To silence them he carved *Sleep* (1635–6) in the harder medium of black marble (Museo e Galleria Borghese, Rome). Meanwhile, for the high altar of the Spada church of S. Paolo in Bologna, he produced the two-figure marble group of the *Beheading of St Paul*.

With the election of Innocent X in 1644 and the disgrace of Bernini, Algardi had a chance to exercise his talents more extensively. He carved the high-relief altarpiece of *Leo and Attila* in St Peter's (1646–53), the altar group of *St Nicholas of Tolentino* (begun 1651; S. Nicola da Tolentino, Rome); and made the full-scale model for the unexecuted altar relief of the *Miracle of St Agnes* (Vallicella, Rome). He also designed the delicate stucco reliefs of the Villa Pamphili which were to prove so influential for the Neoclassicists of Robert Adam's generation.

Throughout his life, Algardi produced numerous portrait busts, many of them for tombs. They are marked by a feeling for solidity and a sensitivity to surface texture and detail, and are imbued with a straightforward naturalism and life-like veracity.

As the principal rival to Bernini, Algardi is often regarded as a classicist, and indeed his major sculptures in white marble are comparatively detached and undramatic, avoiding the more spectacular effects of the Baroque. But he displays an inventive talent in his decorative ornamentation.

Further reading. Pope-Hennessy, J. *Italian High Renaissance and Baroque Sculpture*, London (1963). Wittkower, R. *Art and Architecture in Italy, 1600–1750*, London (1958).

Alessandro Algardi: Leo and Attila; marble relief; model 1646, relief executed 1646–53. St Peter's, Vatican, Rome

Allston Washington 1779–1843

Washington Allston was the first major American Romantic landscape painter. Born near Charleston, Virginia, he went to London in 1801 to study with Benjamin West. From 1803 to 1808 he traveled in Europe with a fellow American, John Vanderlyn, studying particularly in the Louvre, then filled with spoils from Napoleon's wars. His taste ranged from Claude Lorrain to Salvator Rosa to Fuseli to Turner; the work of the latter may have influenced Allston's *Rising of a Thunderstorm at Sea* (1804; Museum of Fine Arts, Boston). Allston returned to America in 1818, tried and failed to become a history painter, and instead became one of the precursors of the Hudson River School.

Lawrence Alma-Tadema: The Tepidarium; oil on panel; 24×33cm (9×13in); 1881. Lady Lever Art Gallery, Port Sunlight

Alma-Tadema Lawrence
1836–1912

The painter Sir Lawrence Alma-Tadema was born in Holland, but became a naturalized Englishman. Trained in Antwerp, he began by painting imitation Dutch 17th-century works, then turned to subjects from Merovingian history such as *Venantius Fortunatus* (1862; Dordrecht Museum). Later he made increasing use of subjects from Antiquity (occasionally Egyptian but predominantly Classical) for scenes of historical and domestic genre. Technically brilliant, they depicted modern sentiment in both generalized and historical settings. An example of the first is *There He Is* painted in 1875 (Walker Art Gallery, Liverpool), and of the second, *The Roman Flower Market* of 1868 (City of Manchester Art Gallery). Some works like *A Favourite Custom* (1909; Tate Gallery,

London) were mildly pornographic, but all were very popular, and their allure should not obscure the artist's thoughtful skill.

Almonacid Sebastián de
c1460–1526

Sebastián de Almonacid was born in Torrijos, near Toledo, and became a significant figure in the transition to the Renaissance in Spanish sculpture. His four major works are the cloister door of Segovia Cathedral (completed by 1487), the tomb of the Condestable Álvaro de Luna and his wife, the high altar in Toledo Cathedral (by 1505), and a monument to Cardinal Alonso Carrillo de Acuña (*ob.* 1482) in Alcalá de Henares. It is probably wrong to attribute to him the famous *Doncel de Sigüenza* in Sigüenza Cathedral. His style is of Flemish derivation, possibly acquired from Flemish-trained craftsmen in Toledo.

Altdorfer Albrecht c1480–1538

A German painter born at Regensburg, Albrecht Altdorfer was the son of a painter of illuminated manuscripts. Among his earliest surviving dated works are drawings of 1506, one of which copies the dancing muses in the Italian print after the *Parnassus* of Mantegna. Other Italian influences on his style included engravings after the architecture of Bramante. His painting of architectural space remained empirical, however: the *Nativity of the Virgin* (1520–5; Alte Pinakothek, Munich) takes place in a church setting, but only the ring of joyful angels gives credence to an otherwise fanciful grouping of piers and side-chapels.

Altdorfer's major contribution to the history of European painting is his powerful imaginative vision of landscape. Two journeys along the Danube, c1503–5 and

1511, had a decisive impact on his style and brought him into contact with the Danube school of landscape art. Early works such as the *St John the Evangelist and St John the Baptist* (c1510; Alte Pinakothek, Munich) show a dense, untamed landscape which dominates the figures. Perhaps in response to the influence of Cranach, Altdorfer increased the size and scope of his work by c1515. His figures become more slender. In 1518 he completed a major altarpiece for St Florian, near Linz. In the *Resurrection of Christ* panel (still at St Florian) the cavernous setting and brightly colored figures, illuminated by Christ's presence, are set before a landscape with a stormy sky. Here he seems to have captured the vigorous and highly charged emotional style of Cranach's early religious paintings.

The dominance of nature over man is a permanent feature of the artist's work. In the early *Nativity of Christ* (c1515; Staatliche Museen, Berlin) vegetation invades the cracks of a rambling, decaying brick and wood structure where the Holy Family kneel cowed in a corner. The sharp contrast of light and dark is accentuated by the stippled effect of highlights on the brickwork and foliage. In the masterpiece of his later years, the *Battle of Alexander* (1529; Alte Pinakothek, Munich), the field of battle is seen from a great height with the landscape stretching away to an infinite blue distance where sky and mountainous horizon meet. The artist avoids confusion in the multitude of figures by showing the clear direction the battle is taking. The outcome is shown by the cord hanging from the inscription above the scene, which points to Alexander, and by the sun setting on the side of the eventual victors. In less ambitious paintings, Altdorfer created some of the first pure landscapes in Northern art, including the small *Landscape with a Footbridge* (c1518–20; National Gallery, London), where only a distant church suggests the presence of man.

Altdorfer's output was small and he painted little in his last years when his duties as a city councillor of Regensburg took precedence. In 1535 he traveled to Vienna to explain the city's religious views to the authorities. He died at Regensburg.

Further reading. Benesch, O. *Der Maler Albrecht Altdorfer*, Vienna (1940). Ruhmer, E. *Albrecht Altdorfer*, Munich (1965). Winzinger, F. (ed.) *Albrecht Altdorfer: Graphik*, Munich (1963).

Albrecht Altdorfer: Nativity of Christ; limewood panel; 36×25cm (14×10in); c1515. Staatliche Museen, Berlin

Altichiero *fl.* 1369–c1390

Altichiero and Avanzo are the two names associated with the fresco decoration of the chapel of St James in the Santo, Padua, and the Oratory of St George nearby. Recently discovered documents show, however, that only Altichiero should be credited with the work. Altichiero is a distinct artistic personality about whom much is known. Avanzo, on the other hand, could be one of several painters of that name, and remains a shadowy figure.

He should now be excluded from Altichiero's work.

Altichiero, a Veronese painter probably trained in Tuscany, was one of the most gifted and interesting north-Italian painters of his time. He is documented in Verona in 1369, but his major surviving Veronese fresco, in the Cavalli Chapel, S. Anastasia, should probably be dated to the late 1380s. Between these dates he was probably working in Padua. He was paid for painting the Chapel of St James in 1379 and the Oratory of St George in 1384.

Altichiero: The Presentation in the Temple; fresco; c1384. Oratory of St George, Padua

Every possible surface of the Chapel of St James is painted, creating a rich decorative impression when combined with the white and red marble paterns of the floor and facade, and the sculptures of Andriolo dei Santi. The *Crucifixions* here and in the Oratory are powerfully naturalistic and full of realistic detail. Altichiero was profoundly influenced by Giotto, but his scenes are characterized by their diffuse, anecdotal realism, and bewilderingly sophisticated architecture, rather than by Giottesque dramatic power.

Altichiero was remarkable for his scholarly interest in Classical Antiquity, and it is easy to see in his work interests similar to those of the artists of the early Renaissance, including Donatello and Mantegna, who were active in Padua barely a generation or so after his death.

Amaral Tarsila do 1896–1973

The Brazilian painter and sculptor Tarsila do Amaral was born in Sao Paulo. She studied there with Pedro Alexandrino in 1917, and at the Académie Julian in Paris from 1920. She later met Léger, Lhôte, and Gleizes, who oriented her towards a classical Cubism. On returning to Brazil in 1924 she was active not only as a painter but in promoting modern art. She exhibited in Paris and Sao Paulo. A fine colorist, she adapted Cubism to create bold, simple forms, using local Brazilian subject matter. Increasingly modernist from the 1940s, she sent works to the First and Second Sao Paulo Biennales, and at the Seventh Biennale in 1963 she exhibited 51 works in a special room. Her famous painting *EFBG* (1924) is in the Museum of Modern Art, Sao Paulo.

Amasis Painter c560–525 BC

Amasis was an Athenian-trained potter of black-figure vases, and was probably the father of the potter Kleophrades. He signs eight complete vases "made by Amasis". These, and more than 90 other pieces, were painted by one man, probably by Amasis himself, but in the absence of a painter's signature, we must call him the Amasis Painter. "Amasis" is a Hellenization of the common Egyptian name "Ahmosis" and there are additional reasons for believing that he was born in Egypt: he introduced to Athens the so-called alabastron—a clay equivalent of an Egyptian shape made of alabaster; and his rival Exekias named two black men on his *amphorae* "Amasis" and "Amasos".

He enjoyed a long career and had at every stage of his work a favorite shape. His earliest vases are panel *amphorae* decorated with centripetally arranged figures. A fine *amphora* in New York (Metropolitan Museum) shows a warrior putting on his greaves, and facing him, a robust lady holding his spear and *aryballos*. Surrounding the group, like parentheses within parentheses, are a pair of perky youths, reminiscent of contemporary *kouroi*. The lustrous black figures are pleasantly taut, their incised features precise and elegant.

A slightly later *amphora* in Berlin, (Antikenabteilung) showing the *Introduction of Herakles to Olympus*, illustrates the painter's early development. The composition has fewer figures than before and the center of attention (Zeus) is moved to the edge of the panel. The picture has a warm, friendly atmosphere: Zeus, sporting informal dress, chats with Hermes; next come Athena and a nude youth with an impatient Herakles between them. For Amasis, the august introduction becomes a casual family get-together, complete with two restless dogs.

His small vases, later than early *amphorae*, are of the same high quality and reveal the work of a gifted miniaturist with an engaging flair for decoration. The shapes are exquisitely fine and painted with neat, elastic figures, nude or dressed in robes with delicate fringes and colorful embroidery. Some unusual scenes occur on his small vases—a wedding procession by torchlight (Metropolitan Museum, New York), women preparing and weaving wool (Metropolitan Museum, New York)—as well as some quite ordinary scenes: winged youths and horsemen (National Museum, Athens), heated combat (Museum Haaretz, Tel Aviv), and Dionysos with his entourage (Cabinet des Médailles, Paris).

Amasis loved to paint satyrs and maenads and in contrast to the sober Exekias, Dionysos was his favorite god. A later *amphora* in the Antikenmuseum, Basel, shows Amasis in his element: great bearded satyrs vintaging, with Dionysos as supervisor. A very hairy and bottom-heavy satyr stands in a large bowl, trampling the slippery grapes and holding on to a loop above for balance. The new wine rushes out of the bowl and into a pot sunk in the ground. Facing him, a satyr pours water into the bowl and helps himself to some wine from a mug. Dionysos holds out his *kantharos* for a fill while the satyr behind him pipes a tune in his ear. To the right, a spirited couple rush forward in strangling embrace. The face, arms, and feet of the maenad are outlined in black paint (as are a number of his other late females): an indication of his acknowledged role in the formation of the red-figure technique.

His latest pots are neck-*amphorae*, decorated with two or three large figures and spirals winding under the handles. The neck-*amphora* with Achilles receiving armor from Thetis (Museum of Fine Arts, Boston) typifies his late career: the old jollity has almost vanished, yielding to a lofty atmosphere of heroic figures full of grandeur and even a hint of gravity. But these late, serious pictures seem more a matter of inspiration from his colleague Exekias than a natural expression of Amasis' own personality. Exekias and his figures seem touched by something deep within, perhaps the thought of death; while Amasis and his figures seem touched by nothing deeper than the joy of being alive.

Amberger Christoph c1505–62

The German painter Christoph Amberger was born in Augsburg where he may have trained under his father-in-law, Leonhard Beck, and where he was registered Master in 1530. He was a successful portraitist, first in the Augsburg style established by Hans Burgkmair the Elder, as in the *Portrait of Charles V* (1532; Staatliche Museen, Berlin) and later in a style influenced by Venetian painting. The visits of Titian and Paris Bordone to Augsburg in the 1540s probably influenced such works as the *Portrait of Christoph Fugger* (Alte Pinakothek, Munich) where the sitter is shown three-quarter length before a niche and curtain in contemporary Venetian style.

Amigoni Jacopo 1682–1752

Jacopo Amigoni was born in Naples, but when very young moved to Venice. There, influenced by Giordano, Ricci, and Tiepolo, he developed a charming Rococo style and became internationally successful. He spent about 12 years in the service of the Bavarian court and painted frescoes in Nymphenburg, Ottobeuren, and Schlessheim. From 1729 to 1739 he lived in England, where he painted portraits and executed decorative commissions. He returned to Venice in 1739, and from 1747 spent his final years as court painter in Madrid where he worked at the palaces of Aranjuez and Buen Retiro.

Amman Jost 1539–91

The Swiss draftsman Jost Amman was born in Zurich. In 1560 he settled at Nuremberg where he took citizenship in 1577. His large output of more than 540 graphic works remains a valuable record of contemporary German life and customs, as in *Fireworks at Nuremburg*, a print of 1570. His book illustrations are especially important. These include works on heraldry, costume, animals, and Roman history, and also the Frankfurt Bible of 1564 which was to be a major influence on the young Rubens. His illustrations served as designs for a wide range of applied arts, including jewelry. (*See* overleaf.)

Ammanati Bartolomeo 1511–92

Born near Florence, the sculptor Bartolomeo Ammanati trained in the workshop of Pisa Cathedral, where his first independent work is found (1536). Next he worked with Giovanni Angelo Montorsoli (1507?–63), a follower of

Jacopo Amigoni: Juno receives the Head of Argus; oil on canvas; 1730–2. Moor Park, Hertfordshire

Jost Amman: detail of The Arrival of the Turkish Ambassadors in Frankfurt; woodcut; 1562.
Ashmolean Museum, Oxford

chio (components now in the Museo Nazionale, Florence). Ammanati's best-known sculpture is the *Fountain of Neptune* in the Piazza della Signoria, Florence (*c*1560–75): the central figure was carved out of a colossal block of marble (height approximately 30 ft, 9 m.), already begun by Bandinelli, which inhibited Ammanati's treatment. More successful are the surrounding bronze figures of marine deities, fauns, and satyrs, modeled and cast under his supervision. These figures and his *Ops*, a female nude statuette, which Ammanati contributed to the *Studiolo* of Francesco de' Medici (1572–3), epitomize his style, which is distantly derived from Michelangelo, but concentrates on grace of form at the expense of emotion. Ammanati also rivaled Vasari as a Mannerist architect, with his amazingly bold but capricious rustication in the courtyard of the Pitti Palace (1558–70) and his graceful bridge of S. Trinità (1567–70). By 1582 the sculptor was so strongly influenced by the Counter-Reformation as to denounce on moral grounds the public display of nude sculpture.

Andokides Painter *fl. c*530–510 BC

The unknown artist who painted four of the vases signed by the potter Andokides is referred to simply as "the Andokides Painter". He worked in Athens and may well have been the first to use the red-figure technique regularly. He decorated mainly large *amphorae*. On several of these and on a cup in the Museo Archeologico Nazionale, Palermo (Inv. V. 650), one side was painted in the black-figure technique. There is considerable doubt as to whether the same artist painted both sides, and it is generally held that the black-figure side was painted by the Lysippides Painter and that both were pupils of the vase-painter Exekias. These "bilingual" vases seem to be the Andokides Painter's earlier works. On them he struggled with the new technique, still using large splashes of added red and elaborately patterned drapery in the black-figure manner. He was hesitant in overlapping his figures and for the internal markings used the solid relief line, where black-figure artists had used incision and later red-figure artists were to use the diluted glaze line.

On his later works he no longer collaborated with the Lysippides Painter. His subjects are taken from myth and the realm of Dionysos, but he also loved scenes

Michelangelo, on a tomb for Naples. Later he went to Urbino. In 1540 he tried to make his mark in Florence with a private commission for a tomb, but it was sabotaged by the jealous Baccio Bandinelli, leaving only the effigy and the good allegorical group *Victory* (both Museo Nazionale, Florence), closely based on Michelangelo's projected groups for his tomb of Pope Julius II. Ammanati retreated to Venice where he was helped and influenced by his fellow-countryman Jacopo Sansovino, who was already established there. His principal sculptures in north Italy were Michelangelesque al-

legories for the palace and tomb of the humanist M.M. Benavides in Padua.

On the election of Pope Julius III (1550) Ammanati moved to Rome and executed, in a chapel designed by Vasari under the supervision of Michelangelo, the sculpture on the paired monuments to members of the Papal family (Del Monte) in S. Pietro in Montorio: these effigies and allegories are among Ammanati's masterpieces. Moving with Vasari to Florence, he entered the service of the Medici Dukes, producing a spectacular *Fountain of Juno* with six over-life-size marble figures mounted on a rainbow for the Hall of the Palazzo Vec-

of daily life, in which he reflected the refinement of Pisistratid Athens. An *amphora* in the Antikenabteilung, Berlin (Inv. 2159), shows on one side Herakles struggling with Apollo for the Delphic tripod, while Athena and Artemis watch from the wings—a scene which no doubt symbolized some historical attempt to take over control of Apollo's oracle at Delphi. The other side shows two pairs of wrestlers and a trainer. The style is now much more mannered, faces are rather too pretty, gestures too refined, and drapery rich but lifeless. In the wrestlers, however, we can perhaps see the beginnings of an interest in new poses and actions which were to grip the "Pioneers" of the next generation—Euphronios, Euthymides, and Phintias.

André Carl 1935–

The American Minimalist sculptor and poet Carl André was born in Quincy, Massachusetts. He studied with Patrick Morgan at Phillips Academy, Andover from 1951 to 1953. During the years 1955–6 he served as an intelligence analyst in the U.S. army and worked for the Pennsylvania Railroad from 1960 to 1964.

Influenced by Brancusi, André's first major sculptures in carved wood date from 1958–9, when he was working in Frank Stella's New York studio. A series of stacked sculptures in modular units of wood, styrofoam, and concrete followed, until 1966 when he deployed eight groups of 120 bricks directly on a gallery floor in rectangular formats: *Equivalents VIII* (Tate Gallery, London). He has since emphasized the horizontal ground plane in sculptures made from square metal plates, timber and other materials.

Further reading. Waldman, D. *Carl André*, New York (1970).

Andrea da Firenze *fl.* 1343–77

The work of Andrea da Firenze (Andrea Bonaiuti) is typical of much contemporaneous Florentine painting which was influenced by Sienese art. As a result, Andrea's work is full of elegant decorative qualities of line and color, and the space in

Bartolomeo Ammanati: Victory; marble; height 262cm (103in); 1540. **Museo Nazionale, Florence** his pictures is often imaginatively unrealistic.

His major surviving works are two fresco decorations: the frescoes in the Spanish Chapel in the Dominican church of S. Maria Novella, Florence, and three scenes from *The Life of S. Ranieri* in the Camposanto, Pisa. In 1365 he was given two years to finish the Spanish Chapel frescoes, which may have been started in the previous decade. The subject matter owes much to *The Mirror of True Penitence*, a devotional work by the painter Passavanti who was a friend of the merchant who paid for the building and its frescoes, Buonamico di Lapo Guidalotti. On the Chapel's left-hand wall is the *Apotheosis*

of *St Thomas Aquinas*, on the right, an allegory of the *Road to Salvation*, on the altar wall the *Road to Calvary, Crucifixion*, and *Descent into Limbo*. The vault contains the *Navicella*, *Resurrection*, *Pentecost*, and *Ascension*; while on the entrance wall are scenes from the *Life of St Peter Martyr*. Perhaps the most famous of these is the *Road to Salvation*, with intriguing details including a view of the Cathedral at Florence (Andrea was on its building advisory committee in 1366), a group of delightful dancing girls, and Christian sheep protected by black and white dogs representing Dominicans (a pun on the Latin *domini canes*, "the dogs of the Lord".)

Andrea da Firenze: detail of the Church Militant and Triumphant; fresco; c1365. Spanish Chapel, S. Maria Novella, Florence

Andrea was paid in 1377 for the S. Ranieri frescoes in Pisa. Although little else can be connected with him, in his surviving frescoes Andrea shows himself to be more strongly influenced than any of his Florentine contemporaries by Sienese artists, especially by Simone Martini and the Lorenzetti brothers.

Andrea del Castagno *fl.* 1440–57

The Italian painter Andrea del Castagno was one of the most capable Florentine artists of the generation following Masaccio.

The identity of Castagno's master is not known, but his association with Uccello is an important factor the results of which are seen throughout his career. His first recorded works were the portraits of the rebels hanged after the Battle of Anghiari (the *Impiccati*) painted c1440 on the exterior of the Bargello, now the Museo Nazionale, Florence, which gave Castagno a reputation for the vivid portrayal of the

Andrea del Castagno: The Last Supper; detached fresco; 470×975cm (185×384in); 1447. Refectory of Sant'Apollonia, Florence

human figure. Following a visit to Venice *c*1442, where he signed frescoes in the church of S. Zaccaria, Andrea embarked upon a prolific series of works for buildings in and around Florence, which ended with his death from the plague in 1457.

An important group of Passion scenes in the monastery of S. Apollonia (Florence) now forms the core of a museum of Castagno's works (the Cenacolo di Sant'-Apollonia). These paintings reveal his ability to portray movement and drama in the scientific depiction of space. The emotional atmosphere depends to a great extent on his use of vivid color contrasts.

His later works, such as the frescoes of *Famous Men and Women*, formerly in the Villa Carducci, Legnaia (*c*1450; now in the Uffizi, Florence) show an emotion and linear quality akin to Donatello's works of the 1440s. These features are also seen in the equestrian portrait of Niccolò da Tolentino (1455–6, Florence Cathedral) painted as a pendant to Uccello's Hawkwood fresco of 1436

Andrea del Sarto 1486–1530

Andrea del Sarto was born Andrea d'Agnolo in Florence where he trained first with Piero di Cosimo and then Raffaellino del Garbo. This experience left its mark on the figures and the setting of the *c*1509 *Pietà* (Museo e Galleria Borghese, Rome). It also influenced both the style of the landscapes and the small scale of the actors in the series of frescoes of 1509–10 in SS. Annunziata, Florence, *Scenes from the Life of S. Filippo Benizzi*.

The painter's early work reveals his study of early-16th-century Florentine painting by Leonardo, Fra Bartolommeo, and Raphael. The work of these three painters probably suggested the psychological energy of the Christ Child in the small *Madonna* of 1509 (Galleria Nazionale d'Arte Antica, Rome). A similar energy is found in Andrea's *Marriage of St Catherine* (Gemäldegalerie Alte Meister, Dresden) of *c*1512. There the excitement pervades both the angels who hold back

Andrea del Sarto: Self-portrait (?); panel; 86×67cm (34×26in). National Gallery of Scotland, Edinburgh

the Baldacchino and the saints who are more involved in the action than are those of Fra Bartolommeo. The figure of St John the Baptist at the bottom of the panel has been positioned to create not just the usual pyramidal grouping but a diamond that echoes the form of Andrea's signature. Other altars of this decade continue the inventive approach to the compositional principles introduced by Leonardo. The *Madonna of the Harpies* (Uffizi, Florence) of 1517 retains the symmetrical balance achieved by Fra Bartolommeo, but the twisting poses of the saints are contrasted and their balletic movement looks forward to Mannerism. The sculptural quality that Andrea achieves is the result of his collaboration with Jacopo Sansovino, who prepared wax *modelli* for him.

Andrea's development as a frescoist was slower. Although the Benizzi frescoes show his appreciation of Leonardo's *Adoration of the Magi* (1481; Uffizi, Florence), in their spacing of the figures they also look back to the Quattrocento. He only fully breaks with this heritage in the *Birth of the Virgin* of 1514 (SS. Annunziata, Florence) whose bulky figures are comparable to those of Leonardo's London cartoon (*c*1494–5; National Gallery). In the following year he returned to the cloister of the Scalzo, where he had already painted a *Baptism* some five years earlier, to continue the grisaille frescoes of scenes from the life of St John the Baptist. The pyramidal *Preaching* of 1515 draws upon Dürer's *Passion* cycle, including many bizarre details among the spectators, and later frescoes also draw upon Roman sources. The *Capture* of 1517 probably reflects Michelangelo's near-contemporary design of the *Flagellation* in S. Pietro in Montorio for Sebastiano del Piombo. The final frescoes in the series (the *Feast of Herod* and the *Visitation*) show Andrea's new feeling for the space within which the figures move, which may have been suggested by Raphael's Stanza d'Eliodoro in the Vatican.

This development is matched in the late altars from the 1520s, where his interest in both Raphael and Michelangelo leads to a new elegance. Elegance never became an end in itself, as in the work of Pontormo (1494–1557); the energy with which the saints react and are composed into schemes that derive from Leonardo and Fra Bartolommeo mark Andrea del Sarto as the last representative (in painting) of the High Renaissance.

Further reading. Comandé, G.B. *L'Opera di Andrea del Sarto*, Palermo (1952). Freedberg, S.J. *Andrea del Sarto* (2 vols.), Cambridge, Mass. (1963). Shearman, J. *Andrea del Sarto* (2 vols.), Oxford (1965).

Angelico Fra *c*1400–55

Fra Angelico was the popular name given to the major painter of the Florentine Renaissance, Fra Giovanni da Fiesole. His real name was Guido di Pietro, and he was born in the Mugello a decade later than has been traditionally thought. Still a layman in 1417, he is not mentioned as Fra Giovanni until 1423.

The young Angelico was proposed to a Florentine church guild in 1417 by Battista di Biagio Sanguigni, an illuminator of antiphonaries. His familiarity with a miniature-painting milieu probably included Lorenzo Monaco's school in the Camaldolese convent of S. Maria degli Angeli. This would explain the peculiar translucence and brilliance of his tempera style. That Angelico himself worked as a miniaturist is testified by Vasari; his hand has now been detected in at least one missal at S. Marco (no. 558; *c*1428–30) and in a single leaf of the *Crucifixion* at S. Trinità (*c*1435–40).

By 1418 he was already known as a panel painter. His early repertoire—conventional Gothic triptychs with *predelle* below—represents a synthesis of Sienese-influenced tradition (Lorenzo Monaco), International Gothic intrusion (Gentile da Fabriano), and Florentine innovation (Masaccio). A comparison between his first major surviving altarpiece (*c*1424–5; S. Domenico, Fiesole) with the later *San Pietro Martire* triptych (1429; Museo di San Marco, Florence) shows that Masaccio's influence was decisive.

By the 1430s Angelico had arrived at his own indubitable style. We recognize it in the *Annunciation* in the Museo Diocesano, Cortona (*c*1432). Here, volume reminiscent of Masaccio has been chastened into something more slender, but no less spacious, as in the proportions of the arcaded loggia which accommodates the Virgin and the vermilion-clad angel before her.

To the same period belongs the Tabernacle commissioned by the Arte dei Linaiuoli, the guild of flax workers (1432–3; Museo di San Marco). Derived from the Madonna of Humility as evolved by Lorenzo Monaco and Gentile da Fabriano, the type of the Linaiuoli Madonna was to appear in

a whole series of devotional Madonnas of the utmost gentleness which Angelico and his workshop produced during the 1430s. Variants occur in the two polyptychs painted for Cortona (1435–6) and Perugia (1437), and in the central panel of a dismantled polyptych now in the Uffizi, Florence (*c*1440).

Aided by an increasingly productive workshop, Angelico, during these years, was working in the secluded Dominican Observant house at S. Domenico in Fiesole. He was, despite growing fame in the outside world, preeminently a conventual painter—"most gentle and temperate, living chastely, removed from the cares of the world", said Vasari—and it is this "medieval" reclusion which has led to him being considered as somehow reactionary. On the contrary: the works Angelico produced during the later 1430s were fundamentally innovative in composition, color harmony, perspective, portraiture, and landscape. Progress in all these directions gained momentum in the decade following the removal of the Dominican Observants from Fiesole to the former Silvestrine convent of S. Marco in Florence (1436). Cosimo de' Medici, who instigated its reconstruction, commissioned Angelico to paint a major new altarpiece for the church's high altar (1438). The central panel (Museo di San Marco, Florence)—an enthroned Madonna, encircled by a meditative entourage of angels and saints—is full of novel features: the prototype of the typically Renaissance *sacra conversazione*.

The panel is much damaged, and to form an impression of Angelico's tempera style at its most brilliant we must consider the *Deposition* he painted for the Strozzi Chapel in S. Trinità (*c*1442–5; Museo di San Marco, Florence). Originally commissioned from Lorenzo Monaco (who completed the three pinnacles on top), the limitations of the panel's tripartite shape have been resolved by Angelico's unified figural composition. Unlike Rogier van der Weyden's almost contemporary *Deposition* in the Prado, Madrid, Angelico's version has been given a spatial setting of unparalleled depth. It is as if a door has been flung open on the confined schemata of Florentine panel-painting and we have emerged into the real world. Its flowers are before us. And as we advance into the picture space, a majestic panorama unfolds before us: Jerusalem on one side, dominated by its ziggurat-like Temple of Solomon, and on the other, the hills of Tuscany receding, with the most fastidious gradations of light, into haziness. Angelico shows equal lucidity in his variation of color: delicate mutations preponderantly of pink, vermilion, lilac, and blue reinforce the spatial construction.

It is above all for his frescoes in S. Marco (the majority c1440–5) that Angelico is remembered. They fall into two groups: those for communal contemplation (of which the *Annunciation*, at the top of the stairs leading to the upper corridor, is again set in an arcaded loggia), and those for private meditation in the individual cells (among these the *Noli Me Tangere*, the *Coronation of the Virgin*, and the *Transfiguration* are especially beautiful).

At the call of Pope Eugenius IV, Angelico left Florence for Rome (c1445), where, in the Vatican Palace, he decorated the Cappella del Sacramento with scenes from the Life of Christ. These were destroyed by Paul III in the following century.

On Eugenius IV's death, Pope Nicholas V commissioned Angelico to decorate his own small private chapel in the Vatican. It survives intact (1447–8). Angelico's frescoes—richer in style than those in S. Marco—form an ensemble. Narrative scenes in magnificent architectural settings, from the lives of St Stephen (upper lunettes) and St Lawrence (lower rectangles), are flanked by eight full-length Doctors of the Church (on the lateral pilasters). On the ceiling are the Four Evangelists; the embrasures of the two windows are decorated with alternating prophet heads and rosettes; the lower wall surfaces are painted with a green textile design. Documents show that Angelico did not produce this alone: in May 1447 his workshop included Benozzo Gozzoli and four other assistants. But the speed at which he

worked, despite studio assistance, is remarkable. In the summer of 1447 he painted frescoes on part of the ceiling of the Capella di S. Brizio in Orvieto Cathedral. In 1449 he began, and apparently completed, the decoration of the study of Pope Nicholas V (lost).

Angelico probably left Rome at the end of 1449. In the following year he succeeded his brother as Prior of S. Domenico in Fiesole. After serving his term, he returned to Rome, where he died in February 1455. He is buried in the Dominican Church of S. Maria sopra Minerva.

Further reading. Baldini, U. *L'opera Completa dell'Angelico*, Milan (1970). Berti, L. *Angelico*, Florence (1967). Cohn, W. "Il Beato Angelico e Battista di Biagio Sanguigni", *Rivista d'Arte* vol. 30, Rome (1955). Pope-Hennessy, J. *Fra Angelico*, London (1974).

Fra Angelico: The Annunciation; fresco; 230×321cm (91×126in); c1440 or c1449. Upper corridor of S. Marco, Florence

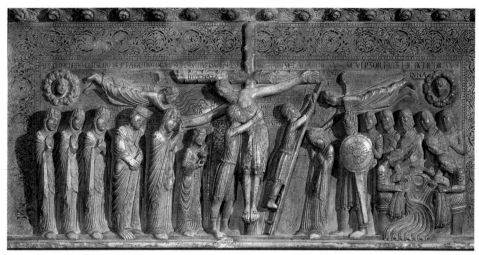

Benedetto Antelami: Deposition from the Cross; marble relief; 1178. Parma Cathedral

Antelami Benedetto *fl. c1175–1225*

Benedetto Antelami was an Italian architect and sculptor during the period of transition from Romanesque to Gothic. His first known work is the relief, probably an altar frontal or part of a screen, showing the *Deposition from the Cross*, in Parma Cathedral, signed and dated 1178. It is a worthy descendant of the art of Wiligelmo of Modena; austere in form and expression but also indebted to French art emanating from Chartres.

Antelami and his assistants worked at Borgo S. Donnino (richly decorated facade, c1185) and at the Abbey of S. Andrea at Vercelli (1219–24), but it is the baptistery of Parma Cathedral that is considered his masterpiece. This massive, octagonal structure was started in 1196 in an essentially Romanesque style, with some Gothic features such as ribbed vaulting. Of the three deeply recessed portals, one is devoted to the Virgin and another to the Last Judgment, the iconography derived from France. Surprisingly, there are no column-figures here, as could be expected in works whose inconography and style both show links with French art. The portals are flanked by niches with large statues; there is a decorative frieze encircling the building and numerous reliefs.

It is often said that the style of Antelami's sculptural works originated in Provence (St-Gilles, Arles), but the Provençal art of the second half of the 12th century is in itself very Italianate. It is far more likely that Antelami grew up in the traditions of Italian art, itself so strongly rooted in the art of the Roman past; he may have made one or even two journeys to France, and seen there the early Gothic churches, and also absorbed some ideas from the emerging proto-Gothic style in sculpture.

Anthemius and Isidore
6th century AD

Anthemius and Isidore were Byzantine *mechanikoi*—architects with a grounding in mathematics. They designed and built S. Sophia in Constantinople (532–7) for the Emperor Justinian, apparently producing plans for this extraordinary structure in only 39 days, after the destruction of its predecessor during the Nika Riot (532). Procopius of Gaza in *The Buildings* (c560) mentions them again only in connection with a dam at Dara in Mesopotamia. The 6th-century historian Agathias, however, implies that Anthemius was responsible for other buildings; later Byzantine tradition associated the church of the Holy Apostles in Constantinople with him. Anthemius, from Tralles, wrote a treatise on reflectors. Isidore, from Miletus, published works of the mathematician Archimedes (*ob.* 212 BC) and wrote a commentary on a 3rd-century AD work on vaulting. His nephew Isidore the Younger rebuilt the dome of S. Sophia after it collapsed in 558.

Antonello da Messina *c1430–79*

Antonello da Messina was the only major painter of the 15th century who originated in the south of Italy. Today he is considered important mainly for his brief stay in Venice (1475–6), and also as the most direct link in Italy with the art of Jan van Eyck (c1390–1441).

According to Summonte, writing in 1524,

Antonello was the pupil of Colantonio in Naples, but by 1456 he had settled in Messina. His earliest dated work, the *Salvator Mundi* (1465; National Gallery, London) shows a strong Flemish influence both in format and in the oil technique employed: it is clear that by this date he had been in contact with Flemish art. This could have occurred either through direct contact with Flemish artists (we know that Antonello returned home from a "long journey" in 1460) or through his familiarity with the Flemish paintings recorded at an early date in Neapolitan collections.

The group of early works still in museums in southern Italy consists chiefly of altarpieces of the old-fashioned polyptych type. He made a great advance in the altarpiece for S. Cassiano, Venice, *The Madonna and Saints*, the most important work of his Venetian stay. Only three fragments survived its partial destruction in the 17th century (Kunsthistorisches Museum, Vienna); but Johannes Wilde's scholarly reconstruction of its original appearance shows that here, probably for the first time in Venice, the architecture of the single arched frame was extended into the picture to act as the setting for the figures surrounding the Virgin's throne. The brilliant clarity of the lighting seen in the fragments from this painting is also found in Antonello's portraits, many of which were executed during the Venetian stay (for example *Il Condottiere*, 1475; Louvre, Paris; and the *Portrait of a Man*, 1476; Museo Civico, Turin).

Apelles   4th century BC

The Greek painter Apelles was trained in Sicyon and Ephesus, and worked mainly in the east Greek area during the second half of the 4th century BC. He was best known for his portraits of Alexander the Great, and it was said that Alexander was a regular visitor to his studio and would allow no other artist to paint him. No works survive, but Pliny describes his style and career in some detail, attributing to him grace and subtlety. These qualities can be detected in certain Roman wall-paintings which may copy or derive from his work (panels by him were known to have been brought to Rome).

Antonello da Messina: Portrait of a Man; oil on poplar panel; 36×25cm (14×10in); c1475. National Gallery, London

His most famous works were an *Aphrodite* rising from the sea, wringing out her hair, on the island of Cos; *Alexander* with a thunderbolt, in the Temple of Artemis at Ephesus; and a number of personifications, for example, *War*. By this period extreme realism in painting was readily achieved: Apelles was said to have painted a horse so realistically that live horses neighed at it. A famous anecdote tells how Apelles visited the rival painter Protogenes; finding he was away, Apelles left as identification a very fine line drawn across a panel. Protogenes on his return drew an even finer one over it; at which Apelles, with ultimate finesse, split the two. He was also alleged to have fallen in love with and been awarded Alexander's favorite, Pankaspe, after painting her in the nude. Apelles was charged with political conspiracy against Ptolemy. He celebrated his eventual acquittal by creating a famous painting of Calumny with other allegorical figures. The story inspired Botticelli's *Calumny of Apelles* (*c*1495; Uffizi, Florence).

Apollinaire Guillaume 1880–1918

The French poet, author, and art critic Guillaume Apollinaire was the originator of the terms "Orphism" and "Surrealism". Born in Rome, he first came to Paris in 1898; between 1912 and his death he was one of the most influential creative figures among Parisian painters and poets. A friend of Matisse, Picasso, Delaunay, and Duchamp, Apollinaire was one of the first to acclaim these artists. His seminal influence was later acknowledged by the Dadaists and the Surrealists. His most important critical writing was probably the collected essays *Les Peintres Cubistes* (1913). Among Apollinaire's own works, the lyrics *Bestiaire ou Cortège d'Orphée* (1911), *Alcools* (1913), and *Calligrammes* (1918) typify his originality.

Apollodorus 5th century BC

An Athenian painter of the later 5th century BC, little is known of Apollodorus and no original work by him survives, but it is clear that he was an artist of influence and importance. He was said to have first developed *skiagraphia* or shading. There had earlier been an unsystematic use of shading in painting (on vases and no doubt also on panels), but the essentially linear effect of Greek painting and drawing allowed little realistic rendering of figures or limbs in the round until the principles of shading were observed and understood. This was an important step in the progress to the *trompe-l'oeil* painting of the 4th century BC.

Appel Karel 1921–

The Dutch expressionist Karel Appel studied at the Royal Academy of Fine Arts, Amsterdam (1940–3). In 1948 he helped to create the Experimental Group in Amsterdam, which later formed the basis of CoBrA. He moved to Paris in 1950 and has lived in France ever since.

During the late 1940s and early 1950s, Appel captured the postwar mood of reconstruction and fresh beginnings by trying to see things with the eyes of a child. Like Jean Dubuffet (1901–85), Appel painted monumental graffiti-like images of people, animals, and primitive carvings, in which influences of late works by Klee, Miró, and Nolde can be detected. About 1953 Appel's style became more painterly; the figures formed part of a violently swirling mass of bright paint, like mythical creatures welling up from the unconscious. This surrealist-automatic approach gave way in the 1970s to a more decorative style.

Aqa Riza fl. 1585–1625

The Persian painter Aqa Riza was the father of the famous Abul Hasan. He trained under Muhammadi of Herat, then served the Mughal Emperor Jahangir (1605–27) from *c*1589, when the latter was still Prince Selim. Jahangir did not regard him as highly as Abul Hasan or Mansur. Riza introduced the new Persian style which prevailed during the first part of the reign of Shah Abbas (1587–1629). He was liked for his charming drawings and colors rather than for original works. His paintings and drawings are to be found in the British Museum *Anwar-i-Suhayli*, in the Museum of Fine Arts, Boston, and on borders of the Jahangir Album (Gulistan Palace Library, Teheran).

Archermus 6th century BC

A Greek sculptor of the Archaic period, from Chios, Archermus was the father of the artists Bupalus and Athenis, famous for their caricature of the satiric poet Hipponax. Archermus was reputedly the first to represent Victory with wings. The base of a votive sculpture from Delos signed by Archermus as sculptor and Micciades as dedicant is associated with a marble flying Victory found near it (mid 6th century BC; National Museum, Athens). Archermus' signature also survives on a fluted column base of the dedication (now lost) of Iphidice on the Acropolis of Athens.

Archipenko Alexander 1887–1964

The Russian-born sculptor Alexander Archipenko worked in Paris from 1908 to 1921. He emigrated to America in 1923, and lived there until his death.

Archipenko was one of the leading sculptors mixing in Cubist circles from *c*1912. In his sculpture he explored some of Cubism's ideas: the interaction of space and form, the separation of colors from forms, and the use of new materials.

Walking Woman (1912; Denver Art Museum) was one of the first pierced-form sculptures, and turned conventional form: space ratios upside down—the densest solids of torso and head are voids, penetrated by space and light. In *Médrano* (1915; Solomon R. Guggenheim Museum, New York) he improvised elements of tin, glass, wood and oil-cloth—some painted, some transparent—into a circus figure standing on a colored base, against a colored screen. It is a whimsical puppet-like image: an inventive, shifting dialogue of flat and curved planes and lines.

In his later works, the *Archipentura* (1924) and "light modulators" (1946 onwards; internally lit Plexiglass constructions) he continued to explore color, light, movement, and space. Archipenko was influential as a teacher in various American universities and at his sculpture school in New York from 1937 to 1964.

Arcimboldo Giuseppe *c*1530–93

Born in Milan, Giuseppe Arcimboldo was court painter in Prague from 1562 to 1587 when he returned to his birthplace. He worked in Milan Cathedral (1549–58), designed tapestries for Como (1558), and was a successful portrait painter. He is best known for his Mannerist fantasies of monstrous human faces of figures made from fish, flowers, fruit, and commonplace objects. Some are allegorical representations, containing subtle moral allusions, of *The Four Seasons* or *The Four Elements*. Others are personifications; *The Librarian* (Collection of Baron von Essen, Skoklos-

Kenneth Armitage: Family Going for a Walk; bronze; 20×27×14cm (8×11×6in); c1951. Albright-Knox Art Gallery, Buffalo

Giuseppe Arcimboldo: Winter; limewood panel; 67×51cm (26×20in); 1563. Kunsthistorisches Museum, Vienna

ter, Sweden) is constructed entirely of books. Several pictures he painted for Rudolf II are now in Vienna (Kunsthistorisches Museum) and a complete *Seasons* series, 1573, at the Louvre, Paris.

Arman Augustin 1928–

The French/American Artist Augustin Fernandez Arman studied in Nice and at the École du Louvre in Paris. In 1946 he met Yves Klein. In 1960 the group *Nouveaux-Réalistes* formally came into being. Arman was a co-founder and signatory of their manifesto, along with Yves Klein, Claude Pascal, and Pierre Restany. Their aim was to develop "new perceptive approaches of the real". In Arman's work this took the shape of accumulations of everyday objects (for example toy automobiles or the

contents of a friend's wastebasket), packed into a box or block of transparent plastic (*Garbage I*, 1960; assemblage; Kaiser Wilhelm Museum, Krefeld). He moved to the U.S.A. in 1963 and became a citizen of the United States.

Armitage Kenneth 1916–

An English sculptor born in Leeds, Kenneth Armitage studied at Leeds College of Art (1934–7) and the Slade School of Fine Art, London (1937–9). He taught at the Bath Academy of Art (1946–56), and was Gregory Fellow at Leeds University from 1953 to 1955. The stone carvings of his earlier years led in 1946 to flat groups of small limbed figures in plaster with metal armatures, cast in bronze. In the mid 1950s the groups became more massive

and less frontal and he began single figures which during the period 1960–3 were extremely abstract; later figures had flanges and funnels for limbs. In 1965, his series based on the legend of the Yugoslavian town Skadar introduced a flat frontal plane with protruding limbs and breasts. During the late 1960s he used fiberglass and aluminum plate for casting smooth, doll-like figures, either in silhouette or rounded joined to tables, plinths, and screens, with drawn or silkscreened details.

Further reading. Lynton, N. *Art in Progress: Kenneth Armitage*, London (1962). Spencer, C. *Kenneth Armitage*, London (1973).

Arnolfo di Cambio *fl.* 1264–?1302

The Italian sculptor and architect Arnolfo di Cambio was a pupil of Nicola Pisano. He almost certainly worked with Pisano on the shrine of St Dominic in the church of S. Domenico at Bologna (1264–7) and definitely assisted him in the construction of the Siena Cathedral pulpit (1265–8). Arnolfo's next works were in Rome: the tomb of Cardinal Annibaldi della Molara in S. Giovanni in Laterano (1276), which has been ascribed to him on stylistic grounds, and the seated statue of Charles of Anjou (Palazzo dei Conservatori, Rome) probably completed by 1277.

His tomb of Cardinal de Braye (*ob.* 1282) in S. Domenico at Orvieto is a key work in the history of sepulchral monuments. It has been reconstructed and is no longer

Arnolfo di Cambio: Madonna of the Nativity; marble; length 174cm (69in); c1296–1302. Museo dell'Opera del Duomo, Florence

crowned by its original Gothic canopy which showed the body of the dead man on a bier and the Madonna and Child above—a pattern followed and developed by Giovanni Pisano, Tino di Camaino, and others during the next century.

Arnolfo designed altar canopies (*ciboria*) for two Roman churches: S. Paolo fuori le Mura (1285) and S. Cecilia in Trastevere (1293). On the evidence of a lost inscription, the tomb of Boniface VIII (Grotte Vaticane, Rome) has been ascribed to him. Documented as master mason of Florence Cathedral in 1300, he was probably responsible for the design of the western bays of the nave and the lower part of the facade, for which he made a number of sculptures. Also attributed to him, on stylistic grounds, are S. Croce and the church of the Badia, both in Florence.

The fragmentary nature of his surviving work and the lack of documentary evidence make it difficult to draw conclusions about his artistic personality. However, works that are definitely attributable to Arnolfo show a highly original mind. Restrained in organization, he was receptive to and skillful in the manipulation of antique, Romanesque, and Gothic styles.

Arp Jean 1887–1966

The Alsatian sculptor, painter, and poet Jean (or Hans) Arp was a leading member of the Dada movement and was later associated with the Surrealists. He was born in Strasbourg, and between 1904 and 1907 studied in art schools there and in Weimar and Paris. In 1908 he returned to his family in Weggis in Switzerland, and devoted himself to studying literature, philosophy, and modern art. By 1910 he had painted his first abstract pictures. He visited Kandinsky in Munich in 1911, and was briefly associated with the *Blaue Reiter* group. On the eve of the First World War, he traveled to Paris, where he remained for several months, associating with Apollinaire, Modigliani, Picasso, and Delaunay. He was deeply impressed by Delaunay's "Orphic" paintings and by recent developments in Cubist painting and collage. Regarded in Paris as an enemy alien, Arp decided to return to neutral Switzerland, and settled in Zurich in 1915.

In Zurich, Arp met his future wife, the dancer and painter Sophie Taeuber (1889–1943). From this time on, they often collaborated on projects and were influenced by each other's work; in general, however, Taeuber's work was more geometrical and abstract than Arp's. Together they joined the group in Hugo Ball's *Cabaret Voltaire* in 1916, helped to engineer the transformation into Dada, and figured prominently in all the Dada activities in Zurich. In 1919 they joined Max Ernst in Cologne and Arp collaborated with him on Dada events there.

In 1914 Arp had made his first reliefs, creating them from superimposed layers of wood. In some, like *Stag* (1914; private collection), his mature style, which he later described as "concretion", is already present in its essentials. Its characteristics are simplified, asymmetrical, organic forms that are abstracted, but still suggestive of natural forms, spontaneous, flowing, unbroken

contours, clarity and economy of execution, freedom of composition, a sense of movement, and lightness of mood.

Sharing the Dadas' disrespect for the European artistic heritage, Arp experimented with diverse materials and techniques, employing automatic procedures in his poems and allowing chance to intervene in the creation of some of his collages. Stressing the importance of the life of the unconscious, he believed that a new and pure kind of beauty was released when the artist relaxed his conscious control. He felt that an abstract art employing the vocabulary of primitive, organic forms could have a regenerative function and was, indeed, equivalent to nature itself. Works such as *Forest* (1916; private collection) realize this ideal.

In 1925, Arp settled in Meudon, outside Paris, and, except for the war years, lived there for the rest of his life. He became involved with the Surrealists, without sacrificing his independence. He later joined two abstract-oriented groups—*Cercle et Carré* ("Circle and Square") in 1930, *Abstraction-Création* in 1932—while maintaining contact with Surrealism. The most important development in his art at this time was his decision, in 1930, to translate his ideas into three-dimensional, freestand-

Jean Arp: Portrait of Tristan Tzara; relief of painted wood; 51×50×2cm (20×20×1in); 1916. On loan to the Musée d'Art et d'Histoire, Geneva

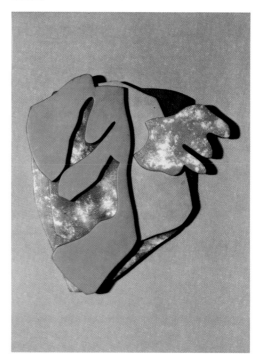

ing sculptures; these were even richer than his reliefs in the multiplicity of suggestions of plant, animal, and human life.

Like Brancusi, whose work has much in common with his, Arp has had a profound and widespread influence, particularly in the 1920s on such Surrealist painters as Miró, Tanguy, and Dali, and on the later generation of Moore and Hepworth.

Further reading. Arp, H. (ed. Jean, M.; trans, Neugroschel, J.) *Collected French Writings*, London (1973). Read, H. *Arp*, London (1968). Seuphor, M. *Arp*, Paris (1964).

Asam family 17th and 18th centuries

The Asams were the dominant artistic personalities in the creation of the Bavarian Baroque style. The family included Hans Georg Asam (1649–1711) and his sons Cosmas Damian (1686–1739) and Egid Quirin (1692–1750). Hans Georg's importance lies principally in the two extensive cycles of frescoes he painted in the abbey churches of Benediktbeuern (1683–1686) and Tegernsee (1688–94). Trained in Munich, Hans Georg had later traveled to northern Italy and on his return became Bavaria's first significant fresco-painter.

In the execution of his last frescoes, decorating the pilgrimage church at Freystadt in the Upper Palatinate (1708), Hans Georg was assisted by the young Cosmas Damian. After Georg's death the brothers were sent by their patron, Abbot Quirin Millon of Tegernsee, to study in Rome. Cosmas Damian studied under the painter Pierleone Ghezzi and in 1713 won a prize at the Accademia di San Luca; the nature of Egid Quirin's activities is not known. Cosmas Damian's earliest known frescoes in Germany, in the abbey church of Ensdorf, are signed and dated 1714; Egid Quirin presumably continued his training, now with Andreas Faistenberger in Munich, until 1716.

In 1714 Cosmas Damian received his first architectural commission, for the rebuilding of the abbey church of Weltenburg (consecrated 1716, major decorations completed by 1740). From the middle of the 1720s Cosmas Damian was mainly active as a fresco-painter, with Egid Quirin working as a sculptor and *stuccatore*, but both occasionally worked as architects. The huge frescoes executed by Cosmas Damian in the abbey church of Weingarten (1718–20) are a landmark in the development of fresco painting in southern Ger-

Jan Asselijn: The Threatened Swan; oil on canvas; 144×171cm (57×67in). Rijksmuseum, Amsterdam

many. The strongly Berninesque high altars at Weltenburg and the nearby abbey church of Rohr (both 1721–3) reveal the full maturity of the Bavarian Baroque.

The Asam brothers worked as a team for the decoration of the abbey church of Aldersbach (1720), St Jakobi in Innsbruck (1722–3), Freising Cathedral (1724), and above all the great abbey church of Einsiedeln in Switzerland (1724–6). Cosmas Damian also undertook independent fresco commissions further afield, including Kladruby and Břevnov in Bohemia (mid 1720s). Attempts have been made to identify a development towards the Rococo in the work of the Asams. Rococo forms are undoubtedly included in their decorative repertoire, for example in Freising Cathedral, but the spirit remains firmly Baroque. Vast illusionistic frescoes by Cosmas Damian in the abbey church of Legnickie Pole in Silesia (1733) and in S. Maria de Victoria at Ingolstadt (1734) recall the late Baroque vault decorations of Rome. The Asams collaborated earlier on the immensely rich interior of the abbey church of Osterhoven (1728–32), but their interpretation of the Baroque *Gesamtkunstwerk* reaches its climax in the Nepomukkirche which the brothers designed and built for their own use in Munich (1733–46).

Asselijn Jan 1610–52

Jan Asselijn was a Dutch painter whose career was dominated by the experience of Italian landscape, and especially its interpretation in the Arcadian paintings of Claude Lorrain (1600–82). Asselijn, like Claude, rearranged natural forms on his canvas to achieve pictorial balance or effects of distance. In this and the suffusion of his scenes with golden light he is distinct from the naturalistic painters of his native landscape. His paintings frequently depict the Campagna di Roma and its ancient ruins, and they often include beggars, peasants, and other genre motifs. He also produced more exotic, semi-imaginary pictures of ports and harbors on the Mediterranean littoral. His most famous animal painting, *The Threatened Swan*, his *Italian Landscape*, and *View in an Italian Port* are in the Rijksmuseum, Amsterdam.

Attavante degli Attavanti
1452–c1525

Attavante degli Attavanti was one of the major Florentine miniaturists of the Renaissance. The undeserved obscurity into which he soon sank—the fate of nearly all artists whose works are consigned to manuscript—is exemplified in the garbled

Attavante degli Attavanti: Crucifixion, a leaf from the missal illuminated for Thomas James, Bishop of Dol; 1483. Nouveau Musée des Beaux-Arts, Le Havre

account of him which Vasari anachronistically appended to his "Life of Fra Angelico". Attavante's mature style, based on a study of antique ornament and on contemporary Florentine art, belongs essentially to the latter part of the 15th century and the first years of the 16th century.

Born into a Florentine noble family, Attavante was trained during 1471–2 in the workshop of Francesco d'Antonio del Cherico, the most distinguished Florentine miniaturist during the third quarter of the 15th century. Later he seems to have collaborated with his master on the illumination of the Bible for Federico da Montefeltro (1476; Vatican Library, Rome; Urb. lat. 1 and 2).

Established as an independent miniaturist by the 1480s, Attavante's first signed and dated work is the sumptuous missal for Thomas James, Bishop of Dol in Brittany (1483; Lyons Cathedral). A loose leaf from the missal (Nouveau Musée des Beaux-Arts, Le Havre) depicts the Crucifixion, with a superb background panorama of Rome, where the Bishop had been Castellan of the Castel S. Angelo.

Two years after its completion, Attavante began working for Matthias Corvinus, King of Hungary, a lover of humanism whose library of lavishly illuminated Italian manuscripts in Budapest was dispersed soon after his death. The first of the many manuscripts illuminated for him by Attavante (over 30 have been identified) is the signed and dated missal in Brussels

(1485; Bibliothèqe Royale Albert I; Cod. 9008). The classical style of its ornate title page is especially indebted to Domenico Ghirlandaio (1449–94), who led the archaeological study of the Antique in late 15th century Florence. Like many of the miniatures Attavante and his workshop produced for Corvinus, it shows sarcophagus reliefs, candelabra panels, acanthus scrolls, imitation cameos, medallions, and similar motifs.

Not all the codices commissioned by Corvinus had been completed on his death in 1490 (for example the beautiful *breviarium* in the Vatican Library: Urb. lat. 112). Some were bought by Lorenzo de' Medici, who shared a taste for Attavante's work, as several manuscripts preserved in the Biblioteca Laurenziana, Florence, testify. An important documented work of Attavante's subsequent career is the monumental Bible donated by Pope Julius II to King Emanuel of Portugal (1494; Archivo Nacional da Torre do Tombo, Lisbon): Attavante's hand is discernible in six of its seven volumes.

We have meager but conflicting reports of Attavante's later career. He was distinguished enough in 1503 to sit on the committee chosen to recommend a location for Michelangelo's *David,* but was also so impoverished that he borrowed money from Leonardo da Vinci—perhaps the flow of secular commissions was drying up. At all events he seems, in old age, to have concentrated on ecclesiastical work, including a series of antiphonaries for Florence Cathedral (c1510).

Audubon John 1785–1851

John James Audubon was an American artist and naturalist. He was born in Haiti, the son of a French sea captain and his creole mistress. He may have studied in Paris with Jacques-Louis David, but at 18 was sent to the United States to enter business. Most of his life was devoted to the recording of animal and bird life in America, resulting in his *magnum opus* illustrating at life size *The Birds of America, from Original Drawings with 435 Plates Showing 1,065 Figures.* Because of lack of interest in America, this was first published in England, between 1827 and 1838. Audubon's two sons, John and Victor, worked with him both on this project and on his later study of American quadrupeds. Audubon was one of the greatest artist-naturalists of all time.

Auerbach Frank 1931–

The British painter Frank Auerbach was born in Berlin. He came to Britain in 1939 and trained at the St Martin's School of Art (1948–52) and at the Royal College of Art (1952–5). He also attended evening classes given by David Bomberg, by whom he was considerably influenced, particularly through the thick textures of Bomberg's mature style. Auerbach has developed this feature to the point where the pigment can be as much as an inch (2.5 cm) thick, giving his imagery a tactile as well as a painterly character. The imagery itself is often rather conventional, in a Euston Road School manner.

Avercamp Hendrick 1585–1634

The Dutch painter Hendrick Avercamp was known to his contemporaries as "Die Stomme van Campen" ("the Mute of Kampen", the town where he spent most of his life). Certain features of his style, such as the high horizon line of his landscapes and his thinly painted figures, suggest a training with an artist of the Bruegel school, possibly David Vinckeboons. There is little stylistic development through surviving paintings, dated from 1608 to 1632, probably because he specialized almost exclusively in winter landscapes. The circular *Winter Scene* (c1609; National Gallery, London) is a skillful blend of contemporary figures and idealized setting in which the colors become transparent so as to suggest distance.

Avery Milton 1893–1965

Although he studied briefly at the Connecticut League of Art at Hartford, the American painter Milton Avery was largely self-taught. At a time when many progressive American artists were responding to Cubism and Futurism (Charles Demuth, Max Weber and Joseph Stella, for example) and others were developing various home-grown forms of realism (Edward Hopper and Thomas Benton, among them), Avery was one of the few to be inspired by Matisse. Avery's style, consequently, is characterized by flat areas of luminous, finely harmonized colors, the simplified forms enclosed by flowing outlines. His many portraits of friends and family include *Seated Blond* (1946; Walker Art Center, Minneapolis). In his seascapes—he lived at Cape Cod for many

Frank Auerbach: Mornington Crescent; oil on board; 122×147cm (48×58in); 1967. Metropolitan Museum, New York

years—he often employed elements of childlike naivety (such as schematic birds) and a simplicity of form that is close to total abstraction, for example *Green Sea* (1954; Metropolitan Museum, New York). His many etchings are more Expressionist in character. Through his in-creasingly free use of broad areas of flat color, Avery strongly influenced Abstract artists such as Adolph Gottlieb and Mark Rothko.

Further reading. Haskell, B. *Milton Avery*, New York (1982).

Hendrick Avercamp: detail of A Winter Landscape; panel; full size 25×34cm (10×13in). Wallraf-Richartz Museum, Cologne

B

Bacon Francis 1909-92

The British painter Francis Bacon was born in Dublin. In 1928 or 1929 he went to London where he worked as an interior decorator. He was self-taught as a painter; the small number of his surviving works from before 1944 show the influence of Picasso in their distorted, attenuated figures. This influence is also apparent in his earliest important painting, *Three*

Studies for Figures at the Base of a Crucifixion (1944; Tate Gallery, London), a triptych depicting sinister, stunted creatures, both threatening and agonized, starkly modeled in gray against a piercing orange background. The impact this made when first exhibited in London in April 1945 should be understood not only in the light of contemporary events, but also in contrast to the apparent trend in British painting towards mellow romanticism, or a new humanism.

His later paintings are similarly horrific. They include a series of *Popes* with mouths wide open in a scream or a yawn based on

Veláquez, a motif he began to use in 1949 which reappears throughout his work. The juxtaposition of living flesh alongside hunks of meat in these pictures and elsewhere acts as a *memento mori*. Their similarity is emphasized by Bacon's handling of paint, heavily worked in smears to suggest the vulnerability and flexibility of flesh and blood. His technical procedures result in a blurring of the image reminiscent of photography, a constant source for Bacon. He was fascinated by the way in which a figure caught in violent action loses its human identity, a theme he explored in paintings based on Eadweard Muybridge's studies of the body in motion.

Bacon's art is dominated by a sense of risk, an element he believed vital to life; it is expressed both in his intense, unpremeditated manner of working, which necessitated the destruction of many spoiled paintings, and in the mood of the finished canvas. Even portraits of friends are precariously poised in the briefest indication of support and space.

Further reading. Hobhouse, J. "Francis Bacon: Retrospective at the Grand Palais", *Arts* vol. XLVI, New York (1972). Russell, J. *Francis Bacon*, London (1971). Sinclair, A. *Francis Bacon: His Life and Violent Times*, London (1993).

Bacon John, the Elder 1740-99

The self-taught English sculptor John Bacon the Elder worked in a picturesque style, and his statues and decorative sculpture were much in demand. He was the designer for Eleanor Coade's artificial-stone factory, and for the Wedgwood and Derby porcelain factories. His largest work is the Chatham monument in Westminster Abbey (1779-83). Although his work could be monumental, his technique indicates a preference for modeling rather than carving. Bacon was considered the most fashionable sculptor of his day, and his prolific output was aided by his invention of an efficient pointing machine, by means of which a mason could hew marble in half the time previously taken.

Baiitsu Yamamoto 1783-1856

A Japanese painter, Yamamoto Baiitsu was one of the last masters of the *Bunjinga* (scholar-painting) style. Born in Nagoya, he moved to Kyoto as a young man and studied Chinese styles. With access to

Francis Bacon: After Muybridge—Woman Emptying a Bowl of Water and Paralytic Child on all Fours; canvas; 197×147cm (78×58in); 1965. Private collection

Léon Bakst: part of the design for Diaghilev's ballet based on Scheherazade by Rimsky-Khorsakov; 1910. Musée des Art Décoratifs, Paris

original works not available to earlier *Bunjinga* artists, he developed a style as close to the Chinese as possible, without losing Japanese feeling. Equally talented in ink monochrome landscape or colored bird-and-flower compositions, he shows a beauty and facility of brushwork unequaled in the school, but he lacks the originality of some of his predecessors. His masterpiece is the pair of sixfold screens depicting scholars in a lakeside landscape (Freer Gallery of Art, Washington, D.C.).

Bakst Léon 1866–1924

Léon Bakst was a Russian painter and stage designer. Born in St Petersburg and called Lev Samilovich Rosenberg, he studied in Moscow and Paris. He became involved with Sergei Diaghilev and Alexandre Benois in the attempt to reinvigorate Russian art, both by establishing closer contacts with the West through exhibitions, and by the publication from 1898 of a review, *Mir Iskusstva* ("World of Art"). The three friends then became interested in ballet as a total expression of their modernist theories. Bakst designed his first stage sets and costumes in 1902.

Among his outstanding designs are those for *Scheherazade* (1908) and *L'Après-midi d'un Faune* (1912) for Diaghilev's Russian Ballet. The latter was first produced in Paris in 1912.

Further reading. Pruzhan, I. *Bakst*, Harmondsworth (1987).

Balchand c1570–1650

The Hindu painter Balchand was the brother of the painter Payag at the Mughal court; his work spanned the reigns of Akbar (1556–1605), Jahangir (1605–27) and Shah Jahan (1627–56). He was one of the most versatile painters, particularly of the last monarch, showing great skill both in penetrating portraiture and in historical subjects. He contributed to the manuscript history of Shah Jahan's reign, the *Shah Jahan-nama* (Royal Library, Windsor). A famous work is the equestrian portrait of Shah Jahan with three sons (Victoria and Albert Museum, London). His *Royal Lovers at Twilight* (private collection), dated c1645, with its hazy background landscape, is typical of the romantic phase of Mughal art. The figures, Shah Shuja and

his mistress, are not idealized but treated with sympathy, and details like the eyelashes are meticulously rendered.

Baldovinetti Alesso c1425–99

The Florentine painter Alesso Baldovinetti also worked extensively in glass and mosaic. His early work was influenced by Domenico Veneziano. The major works of his maturity include frescoes and panel paintings for the Cardinal of Portugal's chapel in S. Miniato (1466–73) and, also in Florence, frescoes (mostly destroyed) at S. Trinità (1471–97?). Their poor condition is evidence of unsuccessful technical experiments. He was curator of the Baptistery mosaics in the 1480s. Baldovinetti's works are lovingly executed; with their purity of line, the freshness and charm of their figures, and their exquisite landscape backgrounds, they are the quintessence of later Quattrocento painting in Florence.

Balduccio Giovanni fl. 1315–49

The sculptor Giovanni Balduccio was born in Pisa, and worked in several places in the first half of the 14th century. He carved the tomb of St Peter Martyr (1339; S. Eustorgio, Milan), and the reliquary of St Augustine (S. Pietro in Ciel d'Oro, Pavia) which derives from it. His was the main workshop in the Po Valley. The tomb in S. Eustorgio is his masterpiece and was clearly influenced by the *arca* of Nicola Pisano in S. Domenico, Bologna. The tabernacle that tops the work can be connected with Tino da Camaino's tomb of Cardinal Petroni (*c*1318; Siena Cathedral). Giovanni's style hovers between that of Nicola and that of Giovanni Pisano: sometimes austere and consciously monumental in the manner of Nicola, sometimes sinuous and intricate like that of Giovanni.

Baldung (Grien) Hans
1484/5–1545

Hans Baldung (Grien) was a German painter and engraver. He was born at Swäbisch-Gmünd but settled in Strasbourg where he became a member of the city council in his later years. He is said to have worked with Albrecht Dürer *c*1503, but this assertion rests on stylistic evidence alone since documentary links are tentative. His first dated work, the St Sebastian altar (1507) for the Stadtkirche, Halle (now in the Germanisches Nationalmuseum, Nuremberg) shows a painterliness uncharacteristic of Dürer. Baldung is at his most original in works where a visionary theme allows freedom of action for painterly effects; in *The Trinity and Mystic Pietà* (1512; National Gallery, London) a tiny frieze of donor figures witnesses an explosion of vivid yellow and red surrounding the devotional image of Christ in the tomb.

Baldung remained constantly inventive as a painter and engraver of religious subjects, rarely repeating compositional ideas. Perhaps his most important commission was to paint the high altar for Freiburg Minster in 1516. Generally, however, his later work is dominated by secular subjects, where he indulges his fascination for the elemental and supernatural.

The painter's friendship with the literary circles of Strasbourg may explain the origin and meaning of the often obscure allegorical references found in his nonreligious work. *Death and the Woman* (1517; Öffentliche Kunstsammlung, Kunstmuseum Basel) comments on the transience of life. The *Two Witches* (1523; Städelsches Kunstinstitut, Frankfurt am Main) are portrayed naked against a livid

sky of contrasting colors. Woodcuts explore similar themes, such as the power of animal instinct in the series of *Horses* of the 1530s, and *The Spellbound Stable Boy* of 1544 which has been most convincingly explained as an allegory of lust.

Balla Giacomo 1871–1958

An Italian painter, born in Turin, Giacomo Balla's early style, seen, for example, in *Bankrupt* (1902; Giuseppe Cosmelli Collection, Rome) evoked personal drama through an acute observation of the environment. By 1910, when he signed the *Manifesto of Futurist Painters,* he had become an established artist, his work of that time seeking to capture the abstract values of velocity and light. It then evolved from the charming *Dynamism of a Dog on a Leash* (1912; Conger Goodyear Collection, New York), through the study of organic and mechanical motion, to the cosmic motion implied in *Mercury Passing the Sun* (1914; Gianni Matteoli Collection, Milan). After 1918 his painting was Abstract and colorful, but static.

Further reading. Balla, G. (et al.) *Manifesto dei Pittori Futuristi,* Milan (1910). Dortch-Dorazio, V. *Giacomo Balla: an Album of his Life and Works,* New York (1970). Martin, M.W. *Futurist Art and Theory,* Oxford (1968).

Balthus 1908–

The French painter Balthus (Balthasar Klossowski de Rola), whose Polish father was a painter and art critic, was born in Paris but spent most of his childhood in Switzerland with his mother. Encouraged from an early age by the poet Rainer Maria Rilke and later the artists Derain and Bonnard, he was largely self-taught. By the 1930s he had developed a distinctive style; the almost doll-like, self-absorbed figures and blending of the everyday and the mysterious create a Surrealistic mood of stillness and brooding intensity, as in his *Street* (1933; Museum of Modern Art, New York). He painted a few landscapes and several striking portraits (*André Derain,* 1936; Museum of Modern Art, New York), but his most characteristic works depict adolescent girls asleep or daydreaming in quiet, middle-class interiors, their poses languidly erotic. This eroticism creates an ambiguous relationship between the frank and nostalgic depiction of awakening sexuality, and

Giacomo Balla: Speed of an Automobile and Lights; oil and paper on cardboard; 50×70cm (20×28in); 1913. Collection of M.G. Neumann, Chicago

thinly disguised voyeurism. He also designed stage sets, notably for Antonin Artaud.

Further reading. Carandente, G. *Balthus,* New York (1983).

Bambocciati *fl.* 1630–60

The Bambocciati were a group of artists, predominantly Dutch and Flemish, who worked in Rome from *c*1630 to 1660 painting small-scale genre scenes of everyday life set in Rome and the nearby Campagna. They were so-called, in scorn, after the nickname of their hunchbacked leader Pieter van Laer, *il Bamboccio* ("big baby, fool"). The group's concentration on the antics of the poorest classes, which were recorded with great realism, was felt by many native Italian artists and their patrons to be foreign to the idealizing function of high art. The diversions of the vulgar could not be admired by the learned, whose interests the Bambocciati appeared to flout.

In their depiction of the real, often enlivened with dramatic effects of light, the Bambocciati appeared to contemporary critics to be the heirs of Caravaggio and his followers, and so they inherited the derisory criticisms to which this earlier group of painters had been subjected. Despite this welter of opposition, their paintings were occasionally bought by such well-known collectors as Vincenzo Giustiniani and Niccolò Simonelli; but their clientele came largely from the middle classes.

Pieter van Laer (1592/5–1642), leader of the Bambocciati, was a Dutch painter, born in Haarlem. By 1625 he had moved to Rome where he joined the *Schildersbent,* an association of northern artists.

Already a fully trained painter, he sold his works through dealers and rapidly established a successful practice in small genre scenes. Shortly before his death he returned to Haarlem.

Bandinelli Baccio 1488–1560

The Italian sculptor Baccio Bandinelli first trained in Florence under his father, a Medicean goldsmith, and later under Giovanni Francesco Rustici (1474–1555), the sculptor associated with Leonardo da Vinci. He was also influenced by the work of Michelangelo and dedicated his career to emulating it. His family's old allegiances brought Bandinelli commissions from Cardinals, Popes, and Dukes of the Medici, his earliest being a *St Peter* in Florence Cathedral (1515). He excelled when carving variations of Classical themes (for example *Orpheus and Cerberus*, 1519, Palazzo Medici, Florence) and when working in low relief (*Triumphal Scene*, under the statue of *Giovanni delle Bande Nere*, Piazza S. Lorenzo, Florence). Bandinelli's attempts to rival Michelangelo, or predecessors such as Donatello, were recognized as failures in his own day, for instance his *Hercules and Cacus* (Piazza delle Signoria, Florence), unveiled in 1534 and intended as a pendant to the *David*. Even so, Bandinelli was unchallenged as court sculptor to Duke Cosimo I until the return of Benvenuto Cellini from France in 1545: then they became fierce rivals, as we know from their respective autobiographies. Bandinelli produced drawings, paintings, and engravings, as well as bronze statuettes and busts.

Banks Thomas 1735–1805

The Neoclassical sculptor Thomas Banks worked mostly on a small scale. He produced reliefs of Classical subjects, and from 1772 worked in Italy where he was influenced by Henry Fuseli (1741–1825), and by the theories of Johann Winckelmann (1717–68). For a year he worked in St Petersburg where he was patronized by Catherine the Great. His "poetic statue", *The Falling Titan* (1784; Royal Academy of Arts, London), is typical of his lofty approach to sculpture.

Barbari Jacopo de' c1445?–1516

The painter and engraver Jacopo de' Barbari is called "Venetian" in some documentary sources, but he is also referred to as "Jacob Walch", suggesting German origins. He certainly worked in Venice, where he produced a celebrated and highly accurate woodcut map of the city in 1500. In the same year he was appointed court painter to the Emperor Maximilian at Nuremberg, and his life thereafter was spent at the courts of Germany and the Netherlands. His engraved work includes Classical subjects influenced by Italian art, by Mantegna in particular. Among his few surviving pictures is one of the earliest "still-life" subjects (1504; Alte Pinakothek, Munich).

Baccio Bandinelli: The Dead Christ supported by Nicodemus; marble; c1554–60. SS. Annunziata, Florence

Jacopo de' Barbari: SS. Giovanni e Paolo with the old Scuola di Sant'Orsola, a detail of his woodcut map of Venice; 1500

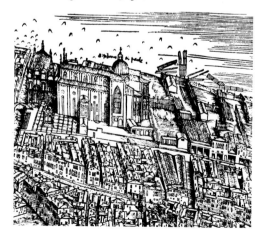

Barlach Ernst 1870–1938

The Expressionist sculptor and writer Ernst Barlach was born in Wedel, near Hamburg, in 1870. He studied at the Hamburg Technical School (1888–91), at the Dresden Academy (1891–5), and settled in Gustrow, Mecklenburg in 1910. Following a visit to Russia in 1906 he abandoned Art Nouveau and quickly developed his characteristic style. In Barlach's work draped figures and groups, carved in wood and stone, or cast in bronze, express single emotions through gestures. *Frenzy* (1910; Ernst Barlach Haus, Hamburg) and *Avenger* (1914; Herman D. Shickman Collection, New York), are typical figures, imbued with spiritual power and humanity, derived from Gothic sculpture and German mysticism. Though he was awarded national honors, his work was later classed as "degenerate" by the Nazis and many works were destroyed.

Barna da Siena *fl.* mid 14th century

Nothing is known about the life of the 14th-century Sienese painter Barna da Siena, but he was the most important follower of Simone Martini and was surely a pupil of his, if not related to him. He was active in the middle of the century and his major work is *The Life of Christ* fresco cycle in the Collegiata church at S. Gimignano. These scenes were probably painted *c*1350 and cover the right-hand aisle wall

Ernst Barlach: Have Pity; bronze; height 37cm (15in); 1919. Ernst Barlach Haus, Hamburg

Barna da Siena: Crucifixion and (above) Massacre of the Innocents; fresco; c1350–5. Collegiata, San Gimignano

of the nave. Arranged in three tiers, there are 26 scenes including a large *Crucifixion*. The series displays great skill in narrative composition, dramatic power, and characterization, for example, in *The Pact of Judas*.

Barragán Luis 1902–88

On leaving Mexico University, the Mexican architect Luis Barragán traveled widely in Europe, where he was strongly influenced by Corbusier and by the traditional architecture of the Mediterranean, particularly the Moorish architecture of Spain. His first works on his return to Mexico were in the International Style,

though by the mid 1940s he had evolved a personal idiom that combined a spare Minimalism with traditional Mexican influences (including rich textures and vibrant colors, such as pink and yellow). He argued for what he called an "emotional architecture", one that concerned itself not only with function, but also with developing a sense of beauty, serenity and "other spiritual values". His designs strive to achieve an intimate relationship with the natural environment.

Further reading. Ambasz, E. *The Architecture of Luis Barragán*, New York (1976). Portugal, A.S. *Barragán*, New York (1992).

Barry Charles 1795–1860

A prolific early Victorian English architect, Charles Barry made a Grand Tour of Europe and the Near East when a young man. He built in the Greek, Gothic, and Renaissance styles. In the latter, his best-known works are the Travellers' Club (1830–2) and the neighboring Reform Club (1838–40) in London.

Barry's grandest achievement was the Houses of Parliament (1840–65), a masterly fusion of balanced and irregular features, of the Classical and the Picturesque, with late Gothic detail and interior work by the Catholic and remarkable neo-Gothic architect A.W.N. Pugin (1812–52).

Barry James 1741–1806

The Irish history painter James Barry was probably self-taught. In 1766, after spending a year in London, he traveled to Italy where he developed a heroic, linear style based on painstaking analysis of Renaissance masters. His major work, the series of paintings comprising *The Progress of Human Culture* (1777–83; Royal Society of Arts, London), was enthusiastically received and established his reputation as the period's leading history painter. Thereafter his career declined, largely as a result of his independent but quarrelsome temperament which exasperated his patrons and alienated his fellow artists. He died in extreme poverty in 1806.

Charles Barry: Bridgewater House, London; begun in 1848

Bartolo di Fredi c1330–c1410

The Sienese painter Bartolo di Fredi was a
follower of Simone Martini. We know he
was active from 1353 to 1397. His most
important paintings are his frescoes in the
Collegiata church at S. Gimignano (1367)
and *The Adoration of the Magi* in Siena
(1390?; Pinacoteca Nazionale, Siena). His
style is similar to that of the brothers
Lorenzetti and of Barna da Siena. Barna
also worked in the Collegiata at S. Gimignano, painting *The Life of Christ* fresco
cycle during the 1350s. Bartolo's compositions are crowded and vital, and sometimes, as in *The Crossing of the Red Sea* at
S. Gimignano, show a propensity for
horror and violence. Their main effect
comes from anecdote and the accumulation of detail. The decorative nature of the
drawing accentuates the flatness of the
space within the picture, thereby increasing its teeming life.

Bartolommeo Fra 1472–1517

Fra Bartolommeo was born Baccio della
Porta in Florence where he trained in the
workshop of Cosimo Roselli. His first
work, the *Annunciation*, dated 1497 (Volterra Cathedral) shows his assimilation of
the complex overweighted draperies of his
contemporary Lorenzo di Credi.

  In 1499 he began the upper part of *The
Last Judgment* for S. Maria Nuova (now in
the Museo di San Marco, Florence), which
was left unfinished when, under the belated influence of Savonarola, he retired in
1500 to the Dominican monastery of S.
Marco. It was completed by Albertinelli
(1474–1515) and shows in embryo the
principles of High Renaissance art. Fra
Bartolommeo was influenced by Leonardo,
after the latter's return to Florence in
1500. His *Vision of St Bernard* (Galleria
dell' Academia, Florence), begun in 1504,
still shows the heavy drapery folds of his
Quattrocento training, but has already
been influenced by Leonardo's *sfumato*
and softer handling of color. Fra Bartolommeo was not, however, affected by
the more somber chiaroscuro of Leonardo's later work; a visit to Venice in 1508,

**Above: James Barry: King Lear Weeping over
the Dead Cordelia; oil on canvas; 269×367cm
(106×144in); 1786–8. Tate Gallery, London**

**Left: Bartolo di Fredi: The Presentation of
Christ in the Temple; panel; 180×125cm
(71×49in); c1390. Louvre, Paris**

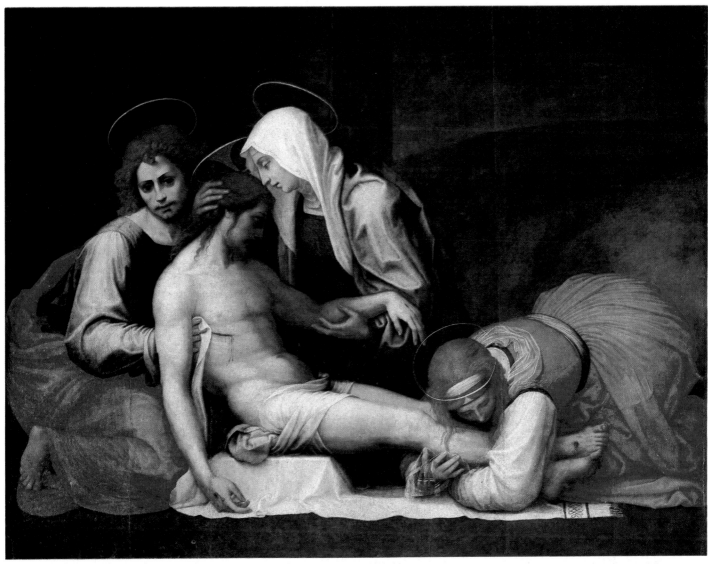

Fra Bartolommeo: Pietà; panel; 158×199cm (62×78in); c1516–17. Palazzo Pitti, Florence

when he came into contact with the stronger, brighter colors of Venetian art, had a marked effect on his development. Venetian influence can be seen, for example, in *The Marriage of St Catherine* (1511; Louvre, Paris) which shows a knowledge of Bellini's altarpiece *Virgin and Child for Saints* painted in 1505 for the church of S. Zaccaria, Venice, although Bartolommeo's figures have a breadth and assurance which is central Italian and can only have come from Leonardo.

By this time Fra Bartolommeo was a High Renaissance artist, and the balanced scheme of *The Marriage of St Catherine*, which also reflects Raphael's *Madonna del Baldacchino* (1507–8; Galleria Palatina di Palazzo Pitti, Florence), is extended in a number of other large commissions, in which the holy figures are set on flights of steps in grand architectural settings. In these the interplay of balancing and contrasting shapes becomes increasingly complex; but, for all the rhetoric of the figures, their movements remain comparatively soft and gentle, and the overall mood is sweet.

Around 1514 Fra Bartolommeo visited Rome and the movement and contrapposto of his later paintings show the influence of Raphael's Roman works. This can be seen in the heroic figures of *St Paul* and *St Peter* (unfinished) which he painted for S. Silvestro while in Rome (now in the Vatican Museums) and in large altarpieces like the *Madonna della Misericordia* of 1515 (Pinacoteca Nazionale di Palazzo Ducale, Lucca) and the *Salvator Mundi* of 1516 (Palazzo Pitti, Florence) commissioned after his return. In these there is an energy not found in his earlier paintings. The figures are in vigorous contrapposto, and the architecture—for example the background of the *Salvator Mundi*—shows knowledge of Bramante's Roman work. Tenderness remains, however, the hallmark of Fra Bartolommeo's most personal and successful work and this can be seen in the touching humanity of his late *Presentation of Christ in the Temple* (c1516; Kunsthistorisches Museum, Vienna).

Further reading. *Catalogue of the Drawings of Landscapes and Trees by Fra Bartolommeo*, London (1957). Patch, T. *The Life of Fra Bartolommeo*, Florence (1972).

Bartolozzi Francesco 1727–1815

Francesco Bartolozzi trained in Florence, and there became an accomplished engraver. His importance rests with his popularizing of the stipple process of color engraving which, by using a "dotted" technique, avoids the harsh contours of line engraving. This was particularly suitable for the soft interpretation of the Old Masters favored by 18th-century engravers. His most celebrated Old Master engravings are after Guercino (1591–1666), whose drawings in Windsor (Royal Art Collection) he engraved in 1772. He lived in London from 1772, and reproduced the work of many of his European contemporaries, including Cipriani, Copley, and Angelica Kaufmann.

Barye Antoine-Louis 1796–1875

The French Romantic sculptor Antoine-Louis Barye was noted for his spirited portrayal of wild animals. He studied painting under Jean-Antoine Gros, and was influenced by Géricault and Delacroix. His works, based on drawings made in the Jardin des Plantes zoo in Paris (for example *Lion Crushing a Serpent*; bronze; 1832; Louvre, Paris) were admired by the Romantics. He sculpted decorative groups in stone for the Louvre (1854–60) and made an equestrian statue (*Napoleon I as a Roman Emperor*; bronze; 1860; Place de Gaulle, Ajaccio). His works, showing realism and fine craftsmanship, often depict scenes of natural savagery as in *Jaguar Devouring a Hare* (bronze; 1852; Louvre, Paris).

Basawan 1556–1605

A Hindu of the Ahir caste from Uttar Pradesh, Basawan was the major Mughal painter of the Akbar period (1556–1605); he ceased work c1600. The chronicler Abul Fazl writes: "In designing, portrait-painting, coloring ... and painting illusionistically ... he became unrivaled in the world and many connoisseurs prefer him to Daswanth". His apprenticeship involved work on the first great project of Akbar's studio, the *Hamza-nama* produced in the 1580s (collections of miniatures from this are in the Österreichisches

Francesco Bartolozzi: Lady Smythe and Children; stipple engraving after a painting by Joshua Reynolds; 30×23cm (12×9in); 1789. British Museum, London

Museum für Angewandte Kunst, Vienna, and the Victoria and Albert Museum, London). His mature style can be found in the *Akbar-nama* (Victoria and Albert Museum, London), the *Babur-nama* (British Library, London), the *Razm-nama* (Maharaja Sawai Man Singh II Museum, Jaipur), and in the *Murakka-i-Gulshan* (the *Gulshan* Album; Gulistan Palace Library, Teheran). Although all these albums were painted in collaboration with other artists, Basawan's style remains perceptible. Works entirely by his own hand include the *Darab-nama* (British Library, London), the *Tuti-nama* (Cleveland Museum of Art), the *Baharistan* of Jami (Bodleian Library, Oxford), and the *Anwar-i-Suhayli* (Bharat Kala Bhavan, Varanasi).

The strong features of his art are dramatic composition, the depiction of diverse human types, and the experimental use of perspective and foreshortening. He learned a great deal from European paintings.

Baselitz Georg 1938–

The German painter and sculptor Georg Baselitz came to prominence as one of the leading figures of the Neo-Expressionist movement of the 1970s and '80s. His style

Antoine-Louis Barye: Lion Crushing a Serpent; bronze; height 135cm (53in); modeled 1832, cast 1835. Louvre, Paris

(reminiscent of early Expressionists such as Christian Rohlfs and Emil Nolde) is characterized by vivid colors, vigorous, gestural brushwork, and distorted forms. He has denied that art has any social or political meaning, art being totally autonomous, though his disturbing images have been interpreted as vivid expressions of contemporary (often specifically German) anxiety and insecurity. Typically, his figures are painted upside down, as in *The Girls of Olmo* (1981; National Museum of Modern Art, Paris). During the 1980s he worked increasingly as a sculptor (usually of roughly hewn wood carvings) and as a photographer. He remains a controversial figure: some see his work as bold and relevant, others as facile and inflated.

Bassano family 15th–17th centuries

A family of provincial Venetian painters who took the name from their native city of Bassano, this group of artists were otherwise known by the name of "da Ponte" apparently from the fact that their

Jacopo Bassano: Susannah and the Elders; oil on canvas; 85×125cm (33×49in); 1571. Musée des Beaux-Arts, Nimes

house in Bassano lay near the bridge.

Francesco da Ponte [1] (1470/80–c1540) was a painter of purely local interest, but his son Jacopo (1510/19–92) was an important painter of the generation of Tintoretto. He presumably received his first teaching from his father in Bassano but we know that he was in Venice in 1535 and he may have been there earlier. He was strongly influenced by the expatriate Veronese painter Bonifazio di Pitati (1487–1553) in whose studio he probably worked. It is unlikely that he worked in Titian's studio but like all painters of his generation he was influenced by his works, and also by those of Pordenone (c1484–1539). He seems to have soon returned to Bassano where he then lived permanently although he probably visited Venice on later occasions. In his earlier work we can also trace the influence of Central Italian and German engravings.

Jacopo's earliest datable works are three canvases painted for the Palazzo Pubblico in Bassano, *Nebuchadnezzar and The Three Children*, *Christ and the Adulteress*, and *Susannah and the Elders* (1534–6; Museo Civico, Bassano del Grappa) in which the influence of Bonifazio is plainly seen. *The Way to Calvary* (c1540; Fitzwilliam Museum, Cambridge) borrows its composition *via* an engraving from Raphael, and the *Adoration of the Magi* (c1540; National Gallery of Scotland, Edinburgh) shows the influence of Albrecht Dürer in its background architecture. In *The Rest on the Flight into Egypt* (1550; Pinacoteca Ambrosiana, Milan) we can see the influence Parmigianino (1503–40) probably exercised through the medium of engravings. This is an important factor in Jacopo's development.

The great *Crucifixion* (1562; Museo Civico Luigi Bailo, Treviso) is a highly original and striking work. The main image probably derives from Titian, but with the sharp contrast between the horizontal streaks of cloud and the vertical accents of the cross, the Virgin, and St John, the composition becomes almost abstract. It seems a transcendental evocation of the gospel narrative on which St Jerome—portrayed more naturalistically in the foreground with stone and open book—is meditating. This type of kneeling St Jerome exists in several versions as a separate composition. He is accompanied by a donkey rendered naturalistically (for example, *St Jerome in his Cave*; Alte Pinakothek, Munich); this type of treatment leads on to genre compositions of peasants and domestic animals, often with biblical subject matter. Such scenes, which are particularly characteristic of the productions of the Bassano family as a whole, make their first fully-fledged appearance in *The Departure of Jacob for Canaan* (c1565; Hampton Court Palace, London). The way in which these subjects are treated seems to reflect contemporary developments in Northern painting, but their great popularity among Venetian patrons may also be linked to the extensive development of land-reclamation and farming on the *terra firma* at this period.

The votive lunette of *The Rectors Moro and Capello before the Virgin* (1572; Museo Civico, Vicenza) is painted in a rather different, more monumental style and, in addition to its obvious dependence on Titian's *Madonna of the Pesaro Family* altarpiece (1519–26; S. Maria dei Frari, Venice), shows the influence of Tintoretto. This is also to be seen in his portraits, one of the finest of which is the *Portrait of a Man* (c1570; National Gallery of Scotland, Edinburgh). In his later work Jacopo seems to have received considerable help from his sons and probably painted little during the last decade of his life.

Four of Jacopo's sons were painters. Francesco da Ponte [II] (1549–92) assisted his father in some of his later work and produced a number of peasant and animal pictures in his father's manner such as the *Spring* and *Autumn* (c1575?; Kunsthistorisches Museum, Vienna). In 1579 he left Bassano and established himself in Venice, participating, unlike his father, in the great scheme for the redecoration of the Doge's Palace after the disastrous fire of 1577. Here he executed the central oval in the ceiling of the Sala del Scrutinoio and four historical scenes in the Sala del Maggior Consiglio. He was to have assisted Paolo Veronese (1528–88) in the execution of the *Paradise* on the end wall of this room, but this was prevented by Veronese's death; the commission passed to Tintoretto.

Another son, Giambattista (1553–1613), was also active as a painter as was the youngest son Gerolamo (1566–1613), but neither of them was an independent artist of great significance. Leandro (1557–1622) was a more considerable figure. He completed some of the works in the Doge's Palace undertaken by his brother Francesco but left unfinished at his death, and executed other works there on his own. He was best known as a portrait painter, and it was for his eminence in this field that he was knighted by Doge Marin Grimani c1596.

Further reading. Berenson, B. *Italian Painters of the Renaissance*, London (1898). Freeberg, S. *Painting in Italy, 1500–1600*, London (1970). Hale, J. *Italian Renaiss-*

Leandro Bassano: Penelope; oil on canvas; 92×85cm (36×33in); c1575–85. Musée des Beaux-Arts et d'Archéologie, Rennes

ance Painting, Oxford (1977). Marano, M. "The Jacopo Bassano Exhibition", *Burlington Magazine* vol. XCIX, London (1957). Tietze, H. and Tietze-Conrat, E. *The Drawings of the Venetian Painters*, New York (1944).

Batoni Pompeo 1708–87

The Italian painter Pompeo Batoni was born in Lucca. In 1727 he came to Rome where he was to remain all his life. He studied briefly with Sebastiano Conca and Agostino Masucci, but was largely self-educated. By 1740 he had established a reputation rivaling that of Mengs, but he was not prolific and his fame was not based on any extensive decorative schemes. He painted the altarpiece, *The Fall of Simon Magus* (1746–55) for St Peter's. From 1754 he specialized in portraits, his clientele including Englishmen on the Grand Tour. Batoni was influenced by Raphael and the Antique.

Baudelaire Charles 1821–67

The French poet and critic Charles Baudelaire was most famous for his controversial poems *Les Fleurs du Mal*, but he was also a perceptive and original commentator on the art of his day. He evolved a critical method which rejected a cold, neutral approach in favor of one "partial, impassioned, and political", as well as being amusing and poetic.

Baudelaire's first Salon review of 1845 was unremarkable and primarily factual, and although it showed the influence of Diderot and Stendhal its most important feature was the first of many homages to Delacroix, who was to constitute Baudelaire's artistic yardstick—the painter by whom all others were judged. The Salon

of 1846 showed a transition from factual to philosophical preoccupations, and encapsulated his critical theories, including his definition of Romanticism as being expressed by "intimacy, spirituality, color, and aspiration towards the infinite". This latter point was the basis of an argument against the clichés and restrictions of the ideal beauty of the classicists, in favor of the variable beauty reflected in contemporary taste. A lengthy appraisal of Delacroix also appeared, as did a section entitled "The Heroism of Modern Life", in which Baudelaire urged painters to look to the present for subjects rather than choosing retrospective themes. This idea was expanded in relation to Constantin Guys, an illustrator of military subjects and Parisian life, in the essay "The Painter of Modern Life" (1863).

Baudelaire was commissioned to write a series of articles on the *Exposition Universelle* of 1855 for *Le Pays*. He concentrated on Delacroix, whom he praised as usual, and on Ingres, condemned for lacking the essential quality of imagination. In the Salon of 1859 he critized what he saw as the prevailing artistic mediocrity and again turned to Delacroix as the paragon of the modern artists.

While recognizing the practical applications of photography, Baudelaire condemned artists who adopted a "photographic" approach to painting, attempting to copy nature in every detail. He believed with Delacroix that "Nature is but a dictionary" from which the artist must select the elements of his painting, combining them under the transforming power of imagination which he called "the Queen of Faculties". This aesthetic opposed him to the Realist school, though he was for a period in close association with Courbet and other Realists.

Baudelaire was a close friend of Manet from 1858 onwards; yet although the latter was the victim of much adverse criticism, Baudelaire never wrote in his defence. While recognizing Manet's talent and praising his quality of modernity, Baudelaire found that Manet's forthright, visual approach did not agree with some of his own most cherished principles formulated from the art of Delacroix.

Baudelaire wrote an extended critical

Lubin Baugin: Dessert with Wafers; panel; 52×40cm (20×16in). Louvre, Paris

essay on Delacroix on the occasion of the painter's death in 1863, and also essays on Poe (1856–7) and Wagner (1861), whom he saw as representing Romanticism in literature and music. His essays on caricature, which appeared in 1857, assert its validity as a form of fine art, and defends the talent of Honoré Daumier.

Baugin Lubin c1610–63

Born in Pithiviers (Loiret) the painter Lubin Baugin is occasionally called "le petit Guide", because he introduces a sentiment reminiscent of Guido Reni (1575–1642) into his compositions. Some of his paintings also derive from Parmigianino (1503–40), probably through the latter's fine etchings. Baugin is notable, in the art politics of 17th-century France, for being forced by the new Academy of Painting and Sculpture to close his public drawing school. He had joined the old Corporation of Painters in 1645 and, when this was amalgamated with the new Academy in 1651, apparently went his own way. Indeed, legal action was required to make a success of the new body, and in 1663 it was declared what we would call a "closed shop": those within got work, those without did not. Baugin died in Paris the same year.

Bazille Frédéric 1841–70

The French painter Frédéric Bazille was born in Montpellier. In 1862 he entered Charles Gleyre's studio in Paris, where he met Monet, Renoir, and Sisley; Monet and Renoir became his close friends. Some of his paintings were accepted at the Salon in the late 1860s, for instance his *Family Reunion*, an open-air group portrait, shown in 1868 (Musée du Jeu de Paume, Paris); however, in 1870 the Salon jury rejected his more conventional *La Toilette* (Musée Fabre, Montpellier). He favored a broad handling of paint and a bold modeling of figures, in the tradition of Manet; less devoted to open-air painting than his friends, he treated both monumental modern subjects and more traditional themes. He was killed in the Franco-Prussian War in November 1870.

Baziotes William 1912–63

William Baziotes was one of the original members of the New York School. Like Robert Motherwell, he was closer than most American painters to the European Surrealist exiles in New York during the Second World War. By 1939 Baziotes was painting strangely juxtaposed marine forms in a boxed framework; by 1946 he

was using automatism to produce floating biomorphic figures against a lyrical Abtract ground. He continued to develop this formula in works such as *Congo*, painted in oils in 1954 (Los Angeles County Museum of Art, Los Angeles). In 1948 he was co-founder, with Robert Motherwell, Barnett Newman, and Mark Rothko of "The Subject of the Artist", an informal teaching group central to the New York School in the late 1940s.

Beardsley Aubrey 1872–98

The English illustrator Aubrey Vincent Beardsley was born in Brighton. He began his professional life in 1888 as a clerk in a surveyor's office in London, transferring shortly afterwards to the Guardian Life Insurance Company—cruel irony, since he was already suffering from the tuberculosis that was to claim his life. To counteract the boredom of his routine office job, he resorted during his free time to music, literature, and, especially, drawing. By 1890 he was determined to put his talents as a draftsman to more appropriate use. In 1891 he met Edward Burne-Jones, who encouraged him to study art seriously and to pursue it as a profession. He attended classes at the Westminster School of Art under Fred Brown and, although his initial enthusiasm for instruction soon waned, it was revived within the same year when Beardsley saw Whistler's *Harmony in Blue and Gold: the Peacock Room* (1876–7; Freer Gallery of Art, Washington, D.C.). Whistler's adaptation and transformation of Japanese motifs fascinated Beardsley and encouraged him to collect original Japanese prints. He also became interested in the work of Mantegna, Pollaiuolo, and Botticelli, which he saw in the National Gallery, and in the work of Albrecht Dürer, studied in reproductions.

Beardsley discovered additional sources of inspiration when he went to Paris in 1892. Armed with a letter of introduction from Burne-Jones, he went to see Puvis de Chavannes who repaid Beardsley's compliment of a visit by praising the young artist's work.

Public recognition first came to Beardsley when the owner of a bookshop, Frederick Evans, recommended him to the publisher John Dent as the most suitable illustrator

Frédéric Bazille: View of the Village; canvas; 130×89cm (52×35in); 1868. Musée Fabre, Montpellier

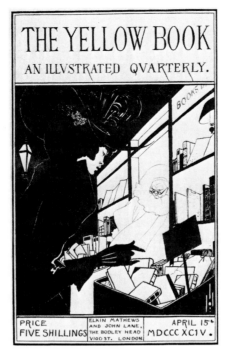

Aubrey Beardsley: prospectus cover for The Yellow Book; drawing; 20×18cm (8×7in); 1894. Victoria and Albert Museum, London

for Dent's republication of Malory's *Morte d'Arthur*. Dent granted Beardsley the commission, which occupied him for the next 18 months. One of these illustrations, *Merlin and Nimüe* (in *Morte d'Arthur*, vol. I, London, 1893) serves to demonstrate his early style. Beardsley's treatment of this subject, depicted earlier by Burne-Jones, retains some of the details of the older master's style. Merlin is still the robe-swathed magus outwitted and undone by his powerful pupil, the beautiful Nimüe. The setting remains naturalistic—the action takes place in an appropriate forest glade. Yet there is a languid, morbid mood to the scene, underlined by the facial expressions, which is altogether absent from the work of Burne-Jones. This departure from his master's style is taken even further in the border: a riot of vegetable forms swirls around the central illustration while a snake emerges from the foliage to support the *banderole* of the title. Some of these elements may derive from Japanese decoration, but the composition as a whole defies the identification of specific prototypes.

Beardsley's next noteworthy commission involved the illustration of Oscar Wilde's *Salome*. Here Whistler's influence becomes overt, as witnessed in *The Peacock Skirt* (1894; William Hayes Fogg Art Museum, Cambridge, Mass.). The principal motif comes directly from Whistler's decorative scheme which Beardsley had seen three years earlier. But again, he forsakes the application of the original for a flight of fancy peculiar to himself. The peacock

does not simply adorn the skirt, it appears in a cloud-like vision at the upper left. Peacock feathers form a crown from the left-hand figure, and dart from this point to the corners of the drawing. The curving, sinuous line, the fantastic exaggeration of natural forms, and the emphasis on the dramatic potential of black and white were later to become incorporated into the language of the international Art Nouveau style.

Contemporary with the *Salome* illustrations was Beardsley's appointment as art editor of the *Yellow Book*. His contributions to this periodical brought his work before a wider, and generally hostile audience. The critics objected to the grotesque misrepresentation of famous figures and recoiled from the macabre and perverse imagination responsible for their distortion.

This adverse reaction to his work, together with his tenuous links with Wilde, led to Beardsley's dismissal from the *Yellow Book* following the Wilde scandal of 1895. Shortly afterwards, he joined the staff of the recently founded *Savoy Magazine*, in which some of his best designs were published. *The Rape of the Lock* drawings display a knowledge of 18th-century French art, well-illustrated in *The Battle of the Beaux and the Belles* (1896; Barber Institute of Fine Arts, Birmingham, England), which uses intermediate tones reminiscent of stipple engraving. This conveys a warmer, more sympathetic atmosphere than the stark juxtaposition of black and white values found in his earlier work. However, in keeping with his graphic style as a whole, certain aspects of the drawing remain highly stylized and are intended for strictly decorative effects.

At the end of his life, Beardsley regretted some of his transgressions against conventional taste and morals. He wrote to his publisher and patron, Leonard Smithers, requesting that his morally questionable drawings be destroyed. Despite this plea, Smithers preserved all his drawings and saved a representative selection of the grotesque creations of a brilliant draftsman.

Further reading. Gallatin, A.E. and Wainwright, A.D. *The Gallatin Beardsley Collection in the Princeton University Library,* Princeton (1952). Reade, B. and Dickinson, F. *Aubrey Beardsley Exhibition Catalogue,* London (1966). Walker, R.A. *The Best of Beardsley,* London (1947).

Beaumetz Jean de *fl. 1361–96*

The 14th-century Franco-Flemish painter Beaumetz was active in Artois, Paris, and Burgundy. He owned property in Arras, and by 1361 is recorded in Valenciennes with the title "bourgeois". In 1375 he was in Paris, where he was engaged as court painter to Philip the Bold. With a large atelier, he designed altarpieces and adorned the vault of the Chartreuse de Champmol in Dijon. He also painted murals for the castle chapel of Argilly from 1388 to 1391 and several rooms for the Duchess in the castle at Germolles. In 1393 Philip the Bold sent Beaumetz with Claus Sluter to see the new works André Beauneveu had executed for Duke John of Berry at Mehun-sur-Yèvres. Beaumetz also went on a mission to Bruges.

Though his career is richly documented, his surviving works are a matter of controversy. Attributed to Beaumetz and a collaborator are a *Crucifixion* in the Cleveland Museum of Art depicting an emaciated, blood-spattered figure of Christ and a bulky Carthusian monk at the foot of the cross; so is a *Crucifixion* in the Louvre, with somewhat different proportions. Both show a mixture of Netherlandish and Sienese stylistic traits, a common feature in painting assigned to the Dijon School.

Beauneveu André *c1330–c1400*

The French sculptor, painter, and illuminator André Beauneveu was born in Valenciennes in the county of Hainaut. The 14th-century chronicler Froissart (himself a native of Hainaut) regarded him as the supreme sculptor and painter of his time, but the destruction of work known to have been commissioned from him has been heavy, and his career is now traceable only in documents and in two extant groups of works: a series of tomb effigies executed for Charles V of France between 1364 and 1366, and 24 illuminated pages showing prophets and apostles in a Psalter made for the Duke of Berry *c1386*.

Nothing survives of Beauneveu's early activity as painter and sculptor in Valenciennes, but he entered the service of Charles V in 1364 as an esteemed and highly paid artist with workshop assistants. Of the four royal tombs commissioned from him for the abbey of St-Denis only three effigies survive; only that of Charles V, distinguished by its sensitive portrayal of the King's features, is considered to be entirely by Beauneveu.

André Beauneveu: St Philip, from the Berry Psalter; *c1386*. Bibliothèque Nationale, Paris

Between the completion of the tombs and 1372 Beauneveu's whereabouts are unknown, though he may have visited England. Froissart, who implies this, was at the English court of Philippa of Hainaut until her death in 1369—and the Queen is known to have been hospitable to her countrymen.

The remainder of Beauneveu's career falls into two main phases: between 1372 and 1384, when his activity was concentrated in Flanders and northeast France, and a final phase from 1386 until his death *c1400* when he was in the service of the Duke of Berry, primarily in Bourges.

From the documents he emerges as a somewhat restless artist. The Flemish phase, when his leading patron was Louis de Mâle, Count of Flanders, was dominated by the construction of a tomb, commissioned in 1374, but still incomplete in 1384 when the count died after a period of political turmoil. A figure of St Catherine in the church of Notre-Dame at Courtrai is probably the only survival of what was once intended to be a sumptuous funerary chapel. Beauneveu was also active in Valenciennes (1374), Malines (1374–5 and 1383–4), Ypres (1377), Cambrai (1377–8), and Ghent (1384). No works are known to survive.

By 1386 at the latest, Beauneveu was employed at Bourges as the Duke of Berry's leading sculptor; he also seems to have acted as director of works in the extravagant decoration of the Duke's château at Mehun-sur-Yèvre and in the Ste-Chapelle of the palace at Bourges. Various fragments of sculpture and stained glass survive from these now-destroyed buildings. Beauneveu's participation in their design or execution has to be gauged by comparison with the authenticated but more unusual commission for 24 miniatures in the Berry Psalter (Bibliothèque Nationale, Paris; Ms. fr. 13091). They reveal him as a sculptor rather than a painter, and are stylistically connected with some half-life-size prophets from the Ste-Chapelle at Bourges (Hôtel Jacques Coeur, Bourges) and stained glass now in Bourges Cathedral.

Beccafumi Domenico *c*1486–1551

The highly individual style of the Sienese painter Domenico Beccafumi is sometimes associated with early Mannerism. Very little is known of his training and early career, and a period in Rome (1510–12), coinciding with Raphael's earlier work in the Vatican Stanze, seems to have made little permanent impact on his art. Beccafumi's mature works are characterized by an illogical treatment of spatial recession and human proportion, showing a greater concern for emotional expressiveness than for classical beauty, and by a very personal use of eerie lighting and glowing color, with which the early works of Rosso Fiorentino (1494–1540) provide the only contemporary parallel.

Further reading. Ciaranfi, A. *Domenico Beccafumi*, Florence (1966).

Beckmann Max 1884–1950

Trained at the Weimar Academy of Art, Max Beckmann worked at first in a conser-

Domenico Beccafumi: Tanaquil; panel; 91×53cm (36×21in). National Gallery, London

Max Beckmann: Pierette and Clown; oil on canvas; 160×100cm (63×39in); 1925. Städtische Kunsthalle Mannheim

vative style. Later his experiences in the First World War led him to paint brutally expressive images of physical and psychological mutilation, emphasized by tension between forms and space (for example, *The Night*, 1918–19; Kunstsammlung Nordrhein-Westfalen, Düsseldorf). During the 1920s his work was influenced by medieval art. His less morbid compositions, in black and a few strong colors, are concerned with general humanitarian themes rather than with specific postwar conditions. His work was included in *Die Neue Sachlichkeit* exhibition in Mannheim in 1925. He moved to Amsterdam in 1937 and then to America in 1947. His most important works were allegorical triptychs such as *The Departure* (1932–5; Museum of Modern Art, New York).

Behrens Peter 1868–1940

Initially a painter, the German artist Peter Behrens moved into architecture *via* design and the Arts and Crafts movement. He was a co-founder of the *Vereinigte Werkstätten* ("United Workshops") in Munich for which he designed glassware. His first building, in 1901, was a house in Darm-

stadt; this displayed rationalist tendencies as well as the influence of Henri van de Velde and Charles Rennie Mackintosh. In 1907 he was appointed designer and architect to AEG (the Allgemeine Elektricitäts-Gesellschaft, German power company). His responsibilities included both small-scale and large-scale design problems, ranging from factories to electrical products, including lamps and cookers. His functionally designed AEG turbine factory (in Berlin; built 1908–9) advanced the use of glass and steel to span a wide space, and the serious design of factory buildings by architects without resorting to decorative styles from the past.

After 1914 Behrens designed in an Expressionist idiom, using steel-framed construction faced with brick for the dye-works at Höchst am Main (1920–5). For prestigious offices Behrens used a style he called "Scraped Classicism" (for example, the administrative buildings of the Mannesmann Corporation in Düsseldorf; 1913–23). Later he worked in the International style, as in his design for the State Tobacco Administration (Linz, Austria; 1930). Although he was a pioneer in the use of glass and steel, Behrens' work showed an essentially classical feeling for proportion. This can be seen in the solid structural walls of a country house at

Vanessa Bell: Portrait of Mrs Hutchinson; oil on board; 74×58cm (29×23in); 1915. Tate Gallery, London

Schlachtensee (Berlin; 1920) and in a luxury house in the Taunus Mountains (near Frankfurt am Main; 1932).

Bell Vanessa 1879–1961

The British painter and designer Vanessa Bell was born in London, the daughter of Sir Leslie Stephen and sister of Virginia Woolf. She studied under Sir Arthur Cope (c1899–1900) and then at the Royal Academy of Arts (1901–4). In 1907 she married the writer and critic Clive Bell, and must always be considered a key member of the so-called Bloomsbury Group. Between 1913 and 1920 she worked as a designer for the Omega Workshops, founded by Roger Fry. Her early paintings are in the New English Art Club tradition but she soon came under the spell of the Fauves (with side-glances at Lautrec and Van Gogh), partly as a result of the two Post-Impressionist exhibitions mounted by Fry in London in 1910–11 and 1912. She showed four pictures at the second of these. After c1920, however, she reverted to a conventional form of Impressionism, retaining from her best and most interesting "Fauve period" only the liking for strong colors. She painted still life (for example, *Still Life on Corner of a Mantelpiece*, 1914; Tate Gallery, London), landscape, domestic interiors, and portraits of E.M. Forster, Virginia Woolf, Aldous Huxley, and Roger Fry among others. Examples of her work can be seen in the Courtauld Institute Galleries, London.

Further reading. Spalding, F. *Vanessa Bell*, London (1983).

Bellange Jacques 1594–1638

Jacques Bellange was a French painter and etcher. He is documented in Nancy between 1600 and 1617 as a portrait-painter, and also as the executor of large-scale murals and designs for theatrical performances and pageants for the Duke of Lorraine. Nothing survives of all this, and Bellange's authenticated output consists entirely of prints and drawings, mostly religious in subject matter, but partly also genre. The elegant attenuation of his figures, and the disturbing ambiguity of his treatment of space, derive principally from the School of Fontainebleau; but at the same time, his art expresses a religious intensity characteristic of the Counter-Reformation.

Jacques Bellange: The Three Maries at the Tomb; etching touched with burin; 43×28cm (17×11in). Museum of Fine Arts, Boston

Bellechose Henri *fl.* 1415–40

The Franco-Flemish painter Henri Bellechose was born in Brabant. Court painter to the Dukes of Burgundy, he succeeded Jean Malouel in 1415 as *valet de chambre* to John the Fearless. In 1416 Bellechose received colors to complete an altarpiece of the life of St Denis, begun by Malouel for the Chartreuse de Champmol in Dijon. *The Martyrdom of St Denis*, a panel usually credited to Bellechose, has episodes from the life of the saint flanking Christ on the cross; the lavishly embroidered pluvials (cloaks) and sinuous figure of the executioner of St Denis show affinities with Sienese painting. From 1416 to 1425 Bellechose adorned the ducal palace in Dijon and the castles at Talant and Saulx. At Saulx he painted an altarpiece of the Virgin and Child, with John the Fearless, Philip the Good, and their patron saints.

Bellini family 15th and 16th centuries

The Bellini were a family of Italian painters active in the second half of the 15th century and in the early 16th, during which time they dominated artistic life in Venice.

Henri Bellechose: The Holy Communion and Martyrdom of St Denis; panel; 161×210cm (63×83in); 1416. Louvre, Paris

Very few authenticated works by Jacopo (c1400–70/1) survive, though many are known from records. According to a lost inscription he was apprenticed to Gentile da Fabriano after whom he named his eldest son; he may be identifiable with one Jacopo, a pupil of Gentile da Fabriano who was charged with assault in Florence in 1423. These Tuscan connections must be responsible for his highly decorative International Gothic style, enriched with Renaissance detail and with at least some interest in the spatial experiments then occupying the foremost Florentine artists (seen in, for example, *Madonna and Child*; Uffizi, Florence). Jacopo is documented in Padua and Verona in the 1430s and in 1441 was chosen, in preference to Pisanello, to execute Leonello d'Este's portrait: his activity as portraitist is well recorded in literature but no certain portraits survive from his hand. In Venice, where he died, Jacopo executed large-scale paintings (now lost) for the Doge's Palace and for the major *scuole*.

Jacopo was the master of both his sons Gentile and Giovanni, and with them he signed a now-lost altarpiece in Padua in 1460. What are probably his most important surviving works, two sketchbooks (Louvre, Paris, and British Museum,

London), contain studies, which were used as models by Gentile and Giovanni and also by Andrea Mantegna who in 1454 married their sister Nicolosia. These books contain more than 230 studies and provide precious evidence of artistic practice in Renaissance Italy: several sheets are devoted to studies of antique fragments, some of which certainly formed part of Jacopo's collection of antiquities, later to be inherited by Giovanni.

Gentile (c1429–1507), as the eldest son, appears to have taken over the management of his father's studio and replaced him in his position as the foremost painter of the Venetian Republic. In 1469 he was ennobled by the Emperor Frederick III, and ten years later visited Constantinople to paint portraits of Sultan Mahomet II. During the 1470s he was occupied in the execution of a cycle of paintings of historical subjects for the Sala del Maggior Consiglio in the Doge's Palace in Venice, a task that involved the replacement of some paintings dating from his father's time. These paintings by Gentile were destroyed in the great fire of 1577. As is the case with his father, therefore, Gentile's most important work is now lost and we must judge him from his lesser (but nonetheless impressive) works such as the cycle of paint-

ings for the Scuola di S. Giovanni Evangelista in Venice and the canvases he contributed to the series for the Scuola Grande di S. Marco (Pinacoteca di Brera, Milan, and Gallerie dell'Accademia, Venice). In these we can appreciate his skill in depicting large crowd scenes and panoramas: together with similar paintings by Carpaccio, who owed much to Gentile, they are superb records of the ceremony and pomp that filled the lives of Venetians c1500.

From the point of view of art history, Giovanni (c1430–1516) was the most important member of the Bellini family. More than any other Venetian artist he paved the way for the innovations to be found in the art of Giorgione and Titian, and was therefore responsible for the conversion of Venice from an artistic backwater into one of the most important centers of the Italian High Renaissance. From 1479 Giovanni collaborated with Gentile in the important (but now lost) series of paintings for the Doge's Palace and he received important State commissions thereafter. In 1506 Albrecht Dürer, during his second visit to Venice, wrote that Giovanni "though he is old, is still the best in painting" in the city.

Giovanni's art progressed from a style clearly learned in the studio of Jacopo, but enriched by the influence of his brother-in-law Mantegna—as in Giovanni's *Transfiguration* of the 1450s (Museo Correr, Venice)—to one relying heavily on a thorough study of light and color. Antonello da Messina's visit to Venice in 1475/6 was crucial in the development of Giovanni's style both for the introduction of the technique of oil painting (first seen in the Pesaro Altarpiece, c1475) and in introducing Giovanni to the unified altarpiece in which the painted space is an extension of that occupied by the beholder (for example the S. Giobbe Altarpiece, c1480; Gallerie dell'Accademia, Venice).

In his later work other spatial devices are used as subjects are more and more often set outdoors. In the S. Corona Altarpiece (1500s; S. Corona, Vicenza) the figures are clearly related to the landscape background by means of both light and color; in addition the drapery becomes increasingly important. Another crucial late work is *The Feast of the Gods* (National Gallery of Art, Washington, D.C.) completed by Giovanni in 1514 for Alfonso d'Este but subsequently worked on by Titian. Here figures and objects in the painting are treated as in a still life, a quality more easily studied in small-scale devotional paintings and portraits (for example, *The Doge Leonardo Loredan*, *c*1501–5; National Gallery, London). During the later years of his long life Giovanni saw his pupils—particularly Titian and Giorgione—rise in popularity and importance. Giorgione's short life was contained within Giovanni's own, and the changes that artist brought about, both in painterly style and in subject matter, must have impressed the older artist. A painting such as *The Drunk-*

enness of Noah (Musée des Beaux-Arts, Besançon) which dates from Bellini's last years, shows how he adapted his style to suit the new post-Giorgione era.

Further reading. Goloubew, V. *Les Dessins de Jacopo Bellini au Louvre et au British Museum* (2 vols), Brussels (1912). Heinemann, F. *Giovanni Bellini e i Belliniani*, Venice (1962). Robertson, G. *Giovanni Bellini*, Oxford (1968). Walker, J. *Bellini and Titian at Ferrara*, London (1956).

Bellotto Bernardo 1720–80

Bernardo Bellotto, an Italian painter of townscapes and topographical views, was taught by his uncle Canaletto, whose name he later adopted. His earliest paintings of Venice imitate Canaletto's style. He visited Rome *c*1742, and Florence, Turin, and Verona in 1744, painting views in each town. He left Venice in search of employment, settling in Dresden where, from 1747 to 1757, he painted views of the city. He lived in Vienna from 1757 to 1761, moving finally to Warsaw in 1763. His

Giovanni Bellini: The Feast of the Gods; oil on canvas; 170×188cm (67×74in); 1514. National Gallery of Art, Washington, D.C.

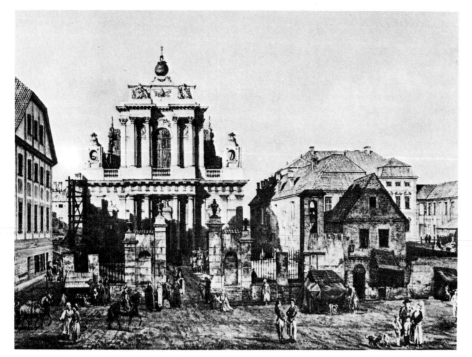

Bernardo Bellotto: The Carmelite Church on Krakowskie Pzedmiescie, Warsaw; oil on canvas; 113×170cm (44×67in); 1780. National Museum, Warsaw

colors, darker than those of Canaletto, accurately record the light of central and northern Europe.

Bellows George 1882–1925

The American realist George Wesley Bellows studied under Robert Henri and was closely associated with The Eight. Like them, he painted urban scenes, delighting in the teeming life of New York's poorer districts. He also excelled at sporting subjects—he had trained as a football player—among his best-known works being *The Stag at Sharkey's* (1907; Museum of Art, Cleveland). His early work was characterized by vigorous brushwork and somber tones, his later works, often landscapes and portraits, by a more colorful palette and a more studied approach to composition and style. This increased concern with formal qualities marked a decline in his spontaneity and vigor, though some of his late portraits are among the finest of the period. An outstanding graphic artist, he was one of the major figures in the revival of lithography in the United States.

Further reading. Mason, L. and Ludman, J. *The Lithographs of George Bellows*, New York (1977). Morgan, C. H. *George Bellows: Painter of America*, New York (1965).

Benedetto da Maiano: Madonna and Child; terracotta; Staatliche Museen, Berlin

Benedetto da Maiano 1442–97

The Italian sculptor Benedetto da Maiano matriculated in the sculptor's guild at Florence in 1473, after training as a wood carver; he was associated with Antonio Rossellino. His portrait busts of Pietro Mellini and Filippo Strozzi (Museo Nazionale, Florence) are almost photographic likenesses, and may be compared with paintings by Domenico Ghirlandaio. Benedetto's strength was in narrative reliefs, for example the Franciscan scenes on the pulpit in S. Croce, Florence (terracotta models in the Victoria and Albert Museum London), and *The Annunciation* in S. Anna dei Lombardi, Naples, as well as many versions of the Virgin and Child. Benedetto's style influenced sculptors of the High Renaissance such as Andrea Sansovino and Michelangelo.

Bening family
15th and 16th centuries

The Benings were a family of Flemish book illuminators. Alexander (Sanders) Bening joined the guild of painters in Ghent in 1469 and was sponsored by Hugo van der Goes and Justus van Ghent. He also joined the Bruges guild for a year in 1486 and at various later dates. He died in Ghent in 1519. No documented work by him has come to light.

Alexander married Catherine van der Goes, who was perhaps a niece of Hugo, and had two sons, Paul and Simon. No works by Paul are known, but Simon, born in Ghent in 1483, joined the Bruges guild in 1508 and became the leading illuminator of his time. Among the major works attributable to him are a Missal at Dixmude (payments made to him in 1530), *The Genealogy of the House of Portugal* (British Library, London; Add. MS. 12531; documented as begun in 1530), the Hours of Cardinal Albrecht of Brandenburg (Bodleian Library, Oxford; Astor Deposit, c1521–3).

Simon's daughter, Levina, who married George Teerlinc, also had a considerable reputation and was called to England by Henry VIII in 1545. She painted a portrait of Queen Elizabeth as princess in 1551, the whereabouts of which is not known, and she died in 1576.

Benozzo c1420–97

Benozzo di Lese Gozzoli, called Benozzo, was a Florentine painter. He was a pupil of

Ghiberti and an assistant of Fra Angelico. Fra Angelico had achieved a particularly happy union between International Gothic and the style of Masaccio. Benozzo substituted a highly decorative anecdotal style more simply related to International Gothic. This is typified in his most famous work, the *Journey of the Magi*, commissioned in 1459 for the Medici Palace (Palazzo Medici-Riccardi, Florence). The frescoes cover all four walls of the tiny chapel and overwhelm the spectator by sheer richness and detail of decoration. It seems clear that Benozzo was influenced by such works as Gentile da Fabriano's *Adoration of the Magi* (Uffizi, Florence) painted about 40 years earlier. Benozzo's other important work is a fresco cycle of Old Testament scenes in the Camposanto at Pisa (1468–84).

Benozzo: detail of Journey of the Magi; fresco; c1459. Palazzo Medici-Riccardi, Florence

Benton Thomas 1889–1975

The American painter and muralist Thomas Hart Benton founded the so-called Regionalist School. Born in Neosho, Missouri, he studied briefly in Chicago, visited Paris, and, under the influence of Stanton Macdonald-Wright, became an Abstract artist. Benton rapidly abandoned modernism for a highly stylized, rather frenetic and folksy realism. In works such as *Boom Town* (1928; Memorial Art Gallery of the University of Rochester, N.Y.) Benton records pioneer small-town life in the Midwest. He worked widely as a muralist, especially in the New York School for Social Research, New York, and in the Missouri State Capitol. Always a contentious figure, Benton aimed to produce a native American art free of the supposed decadence of Europe.

Berchem Nicolaes 1620–83

The Dutch landscape painter Nicolaes Pietersz. Berchem was born at Haarlem, the son of Pieter Claesz, a painter of still life. He is reputed to have studied with Jan van Goyen before entering the Haarlem guild in 1642. He then paid an extended visit to Italy, making sketches of landscapes and figures which furnished ideas for paintings on his return. His first works, for example *The Education of Bacchus* (1648; Royal Museum of Art, Mauritshuis, The Hague) attempted to emulate the large-scale Flemish decorative tradition then popular at court; but he soon specialized in small landscape subjects.

Following the return from Italy of Jan Both in 1641 the fashion for Italianate landscape painting grew rapidly in Holland. Berchem's output extends to about 800 landscapes, of largely small-scale pastoral subjects with figures painted in bright local colors against softly lit skies of pink and gray. Works such as *The Round Tower* (1656; Rijksmuseum, Amsterdam) show the dominantly picturesque qualities of his art. There is generally a carefree attitude about his figures, even when they are set against grandiose ruins as in the painting of *Ruins* (c1650; Alte Pinakothek, Munich). Berchem's proficiency led to his employment as a figure-painter in the landscapes of Jacob van Ruisdael and Meyndert Hobbema.

His extensive workshop produced artists following his own style, such as Karel Dujardin, and others with quite different specialities such as Pieter de Hooch. Ber-

Nicolaes Berchem: Ramparts at Winter Time; panel; 40×50cm (16×20in); 1647. Frans Hals Museum, Haarlem

chem's work was both highly praised and highly priced during the 18th century. It prefigures the *capriccio* landscape of the Rococo style, and it was at that period that a great many overtly picturesque engravings after his work were produced.

Berg Claus (c1485–c1535)

The German wood sculptor Claus Berg was born in Lübeck. He spent most of his working life in Denmark where he kept a workshop at Odense. His work there includes the complex carved altarpiece of 1517–22 whose delicate, rather brittle, late Gothic scrollwork forms a frame for scenes from the Passion of Christ. At the center is a combined representation of *The Crucifixion*, *The Coronation of the Virgin*, and *The Tree of Jesse*. The vigorous and rather mannered 11 Apostles in Gustrow Cathedral from the 1530s are probably his last known work. He appears to have left Denmark at the onset of the Reformation, and little is known of him thereafter.

Berlinghieri Berlinghiero 1200–43

Milanese by birth, Berlinghiero Berlinghieri was a painter active in Lucca in the second quarter of the 13th century, and is best thought of as a Tuscan artist. He is the earliest Italian panel-painter known by name and is mentioned in a document of 1228 together with his painter sons, Barone, Marco, and Bonaventura. The basis for identifying his work is a splendid signed *Crucifixion* for the Church of S. Maria degli Angeli, Lucca. Christ is shown still alive (typical of Tuscan painting of this period) with the figures of the Virgin and St John on the apron of the cross.

Bonaventura Berlinghieri (*ob.* 1274?), his son, signed and dated the altarpiece of *St Francis and Scenes from his Life* (S. Francesco, Pescia). This was painted in 1235, only nine years after the death of St Francis.

Berlin Painter *fl. c505–460 BC*

The Berlin Painter is the conventional name for the painter of the splendid tall *amphora* F. 2160 of *c*490 BC in the Staatliche Museen, Berlin; one side shows Hermes and the satyr Oreimachos, the other features the satyr Orochares. The Berlin Painter was one of the greatest painters of large vases of his generation in Athens, second only to the Kleophrades Painter. His earliest work may be the fine cup from the Agora at Athens, which owes much to Phintias. Two very early *pelikai*, however, show clearly his greater debt to Euthymides (no. 11200 in the Archaeological Museum, Madrid, and no. 50755 in the Villa Giulia, Rome).

His career can be divided into three main phases. After the initial works, mentioned above, comes his long early period to which his best pieces belong. One of these is an *amphora* of rather rare shape in New York (Metropolitan Museum; 56.171.38). On one side a youth, richly clad, plays a

Berlinghiero Berlinghieri: St Francis and scenes from his life; panel; 1235. S. Francesco, Pescia

Berlin Painter: a red-figure hydria showing the god Apollo; height 52cm (20in); early 5th century BC. Vatican Museums, Rome

kithara with great passion, his head held back, mouth open, and body gently swaying. The bearded trainer on the other side is a sharp contrast: he is tense, intent only on the purity of the youth's notes. Both figures are isolated in a sea of black glaze, unsupported by a groundline. This system, which can be seen first among the works of Euphronios and his followers, was particularly loved by the Berlin Painter. He also reveals a surprisingly constant scheme for delineating the details of the anatomy of the body. His tense, long-limbed figures seem always about to move.

His middle period is shorter. The figures are slightly more massive, less nimble, and more rigidly conventional. In his last period all is mechanical. Here belong his prize Panathenaic *amphorae* (for example, the one in the Vatican Museums, Rome), which demonstrate that he, like the Kleophrades Painter, was also adept at black-figure. The Berlin Painter can be seen to have had several pupils: first the Providence Painter, then Hermonax, and finally the Achilles Painter (*fl. c*460–430 BC), who was one of the greatest masters of the pure Classical style in vase-painting.

Bernard Émile 1868–1941

Émile Bernard was a French artist, poet, book-illustrator, critic, and editor. His paintings, executed during the second half of the 1880s, were among the first to reject the traditional photographic representation of nature.

Born in Lille, Bernard moved to Paris in 1878 and joined the Atelier Cormon in 1884. Here he met Toulouse-Lautrec and Vincent van Gogh, formed a friendship with Louis Anquetin (1861–1932), and, through the latter, was introduced to the literary Symbolist circles of Paris. In the spring of 1886 he was dismissed from the Atelier for insubordinate behavior.

Dissatisfied with all other styles of art, Bernard sought to create a new sort of painting based upon the Old Masters' respect for form and the Impressonists' adherence to brilliant, pure color. He passed rapidly through Impressionism and Neo-Impressionism, then turned his attention to the early work of Cézanne, the pastels of Degas, Japanese prints, stained-glass windows, and paintings and drawings from Van Gogh's Dutch period. By the summer of 1887, these studies provided the basis for a new style of painting, "Cloisonnisme", evolved with the help of Anquetin and well illustrated in Bernard's *Portrait of the Artist's Grandmother* (1887; Rijksmuseum Vincent van Gogh, Amsterdam). The bold outline and areas of flat color provide an evocation rather than a photographic representation of the old lady. A year after this "decorative" deformation of nature there emerged Synthetism, or Pictorial Symbolism.

In mid August 1888 at Pont-Aven, Brittany, Bernard introduced Gauguin to Pictorial Symbolism in the form of his *Breton Women in the Meadow* (1888; Collection of D. Denis, St-Germain-en-Laye). This painting provided Gauguin with the solution to his long search for a visual vocabulary capable of creating symbolic rather than representational painting. Gauguin then applied these new principles to his *Vision after the Sermon* (1888; National Gallery of Scotland, Edinburgh). Bernard's painting also established a fruitful, but ultimately ill-fated collaboration between the two artists. They became the leaders of the School of Pont-Aven. Together with Émile Schuffenecker, they mounted their influential "manifesto" exhibition at the Café Volpini on the edge of the Paris *Exposition Universelle* of 1889.

The relationship broke up in 1891. The critic Albert Aurier wrote an article published in February of that year in which he heralded Gauguin as the initiator of Pictorial Symbolism, a position seconded by Gauguin himself at his atelier sale of 24 February. In addition, Bernard had passed through a religious crisis during the winter of 1890–1 and this directed his artistic interests away from Gauguin's experiments and towards the schools of Byzantine and Northern primitive painting. After brief flirtations with the Nabis and with Sar Peladan's Salon de la Rose et Croix, Bernard left for Egypt in 1893.

Émile Bernard: Madonna and Child supported by two Music-making Angels; pen on paper; including frame 34×27cm (13×11in); 1894. Collection Flamand-Charbonnier, Paris

Bernard returned to France in 1904, having traveled in Spain and Italy as well, and he founded (and edited) the review *La Rénovation Esthétique*. Apart from articles on Cézanne, Baudelaire, and Pictorial Symbolism, the paintings and writings he completed between 1904 and his death in 1941 reflect a complete rejection of contemporary art and society. He called for a return to the aesthetic ideals of the Old Masters, which he practiced in his own paintings such as *Après le Bain: Nymphes* (1906; Musée d'Art Moderne de la Ville de Paris). He also published correspondence with Van Gogh, Gauguin, Redon and Cézanne.

Bernini 1598–1680

Gian Lorenzo Bernini, the Italian sculptor, architect, and occasional painter, was a brilliant exponent of the Italian Baroque. His career was spent almost exclusively in Rome. His contemporaries rated his genius as highly as Michelangelo's, but in his affable and worldly manner he possessed a temperament utterly different. Whereas Michelangelo was a solitary artist who rarely communicated the essence of his art to others, Bernini was a great teacher capable of delegating many tasks to his flourishing school. He could thereby undertake the vast building projects for which he was employed by the papacy, ambitious for the material aggrandizement of Rome.

Bernini was born in Naples. His father, Pietro Bernini (1562–1629), was a Florentine sculptor who worked in a late Mannerist style. By about 1584 Pietro had moved to Naples where he had executed, among other works, the *Madonna* in the Certosa di S. Martino. In 1604/5 Pietro Bernini was called to Rome by Camillo Borghese (created Pope Paul V in 1605), to assist in the sculptural decoration of the Cappella Paolina, S. Maria Maggiore; his work in this chapel includes the relief, *The Assumption of the Virgin*. Gian Lorenzo, who had moved to Rome with his family in 1604/5, and who was by all accounts a prodigy, was trained by his father. He was thus able to master quickly the techniques of marble carving. In Rome he studied antique sculpture as well as the works of Raphael and Michelangelo. The influence of Hellenistic marbles is visible in the realistic rendering of one of his first surviving works, *The Goat Amalthea* (c1615; Museo e Galleria Borghese, Rome) which was itself long thought to be an antique marble.

With his father's employment by Paul V, Bernini gained access to Borghese patronage, particularly that of the Pope's nephew Scipione Borghese for whom his first large sculpture, the *Aeneas, Anchises, and Ascanius* (Museo e Galleria, Borghese, Rome) was executed c1619. Here the delicate Mannerist style of his father can be seen in the richness of detail, but the spiraling movement of the intertwined figures recalls the sculpture of the Florentine, Giovanni da Bologna (1524–1608). There then followed a brilliant series of large, freestanding marble sculptures, commissioned by the same patron and still in the Museo e Galleria Borghese, Rome. Here Bernini tried in sculpture to equal the naturalism attained by the paintings of the Carracci School in Rome. Works in this series include *Pluto and Persephone* (1621–2), *Apollo and Daphne* (1622–5), and *David* (1623–4). In each one Bernini created a painterly effect: texture is subtly varied and marble achieves plastic effects never before obtained. In the *David*, the last of the series, the closed form of High Renaissance sculpture is denied by the figure's vigorous centrifugal motion. The representation of instantaneous movement had become the property of sculpture as well as painting.

With the election of a Barberini to the papacy as Urban VIII (1623–44) Bernini found another devoted patron. It was for Urban that Bernini undertook his first architectural commission, the building of the entrance facade and portico of the church of S. Bibiana, Rome. For the high altar of the same church he carved his first major religious sculpture, *S. Bibiana at her Martyrdom*. Here Bernini's new sculptural techniques, developed in the Borghese statues, were put to the services of the religious zeal of the Counter-Reformation.

Urban wished to embellish the completed Basilica of St Peter's. He called upon Bernini, who was made architect of St Peter's in 1629, to erect a monumental canopy or *baldacchino* over the site of the tomb of St Peter. The Baldacchino (built 1624–33), which was made of bronze, was composed of four giant twisted columns surmounted by four volutes terminated by an orb and a cross. It successfully created a point of emphasis at the center of the building. To decorate further the zone of the crossing, Bernini was directed to supervise the placing of four monumental statues in niches of his design in the four giant piers. Only one of the statues, the *Longinus*, 1629–38, is his. It was designed to be seen at a distance and in the context of the immense space of the crossing. Its open form of white marble was intended as a striking contrast to the colored background of the niche. Its surface was therefore not worked with intricate detail but left rough so that its broad masses could be readily comprehended.

In 1632 Bernini interrupted his work for Urban in St Peter's to make a portrait bust of Scipione Borghese (Museo e Galleria Borghese, Rome). In this sculpture he developed his skill in capturing the momentary. He showed the Cardinal turning briefly to the spectator as if in conversation. His employment by Scipione Borghese was only an interlude in his work for Urban. Besides the projects already mentioned, this included the completion of the Palazzo Barberini (1629–33), the tomb of Countess Matilda, St Peter's (1633–7, in which a moderate classical phase in the sculptor's development is best seen), the tomb of Urban VIII, St Peter's (1628–47, which was to be a prototype for later Baroque papal tombs), the project to construct lateral towers for the facade of St Peter's (1637–41), and the Triton fountain, Piazza Barberini (1642–3).

With Urban's death in 1644 and upon the election to the papacy of Innocent X, Pamphili (1644–55), Bernini fell out of favor. Innocent, who was opposed to Urban's extravagance, at first no longer required Bernini's services. Unfettered by official commissions, Bernini was able to undertake work for private patrons. His chief commission of this period, executed for Cardinal Federigo Cornaro, was the decoration of the Cornaro Chapel, S. Maria della Vittoria, Rome, 1647–c55. The marble group on the high altar, the *Ecstasy of St Theresa*, is perhaps Bernini's greatest masterpiece in sculpture and shows the moment in one of the Saint's ecstatic visions when she believed an angel was stabbing at her heart. The group receives dramatic illumination from a hidden window at the rear of the altar niche. Reliefs representing members of the Cornaro family, who appear to witness this event, are placed in shallow panels in the two side-walls of the Chapel. This combination of architecture, painting, and sculpture brought together into one unified whole gives an impression of theater.

However, it was not long before Innocent was to employ Bernini. In 1648 he commissioned the sculptor to erect a large fountain representing the Four Rivers in the middle of the Piazza Navona, Rome. The fountain symbolizes the center of the world and has the form of a rock on which personifications of four major rivers are seated: the Danube, the Nile, the Plate, and the Ganges. On top of the rock an obelisk rises, surmounted by a dove.

With the pontificate of Alexander VII, Chigi (1655–67), Bernini was again restored to favor. Turning his attention increasingly towards architecture, Bernini now built his two most famous churches,

S. Andrea al Quirinale, Rome, and S. Maria dell'Assunzione, Ariccia. Cardinal Camillo Pamphili commissioned him to build S. Andrea. He tried to create in the space of this oval church a fitting environment for the representation of a religious event—the ascension into heaven of the Apostle. By so doing he extended the theatrical conception of the Cornaro Chapel to a far larger field. To narrate this event he populated the lower dome with sculpted figures, headed by St Andrew who floats above the pediment of the high altar. Bernini invigorated the space of his churches with sculptural decorations; but this drama is not integral to the architecture itself as it is in the churches of Borromini.

Like Urban before him, Alexander was anxious to embellish St Peter's. The piazza in front of the Basilica, in which pilgrims frequently congregated for papal benediction, required definition. Bernini worked on the project from 1656–67. To enclose the space he constructed two massive colonnades which form an oval piazza symbolizing the world gathered together before the Pope, and which correspond to the arms of the church open in greeting. Inside the Basilica he placed a monumental reredos at the high altar. Contained in this construction (known as the *Cathedra Petri*) is the throne of St Peter, a symbol of the Apostle's power as Christ's vicar and a witness to papal legitimacy. The *Cathedra* uses several different media: bronze in the throne and in the four "Fathers" of the church that support it, stucco and wood in the glory of angels above. Illumination through a window with orange lights tints the whole structure. Bernini intended that from the nave, the *Cathedra* should be seen framed by the columns of the *baldacchino*. Also for St Peter's, 1663–6, he constructed the Scala Regia, a stairway leading from the Vatican Palace to St Peter's. It occupies a narrow site between the Basilica and the Sistine Chapel. By constructing an illusionistic colonnade on the main flight of stairs, and by cleverly creating light-filled caesuras on the landings, he turned what was formerly a dark passage into a gracious stairway.

In 1665 Bernini went to Paris, ostensibly to supervise the erection of a new facade on the east front of the Louvre, the plans for which he had already submitted to Louis XIV's first minister, Colbert. The visit was a diplomatic slight to Alexander VII whom Louis XIV desired to humiliate for political reasons. Bernini had to relinquish his work on St Peter's to undertake the journey. His visit is vividly described in a diary written by Sieur de Chanteloup who was directed to accompany the sculptor throughout his stay. In Paris Bernini made a portrait bust of the King, now in the Louvre. In his final plan for the east facade, Bernini used a design that abandons the curves present in the first two projects. It resembles the facade he had already designed for the Palazzo Chigi-Odescalchi, under construction when he left Rome. Although foundations for the facade were laid while Bernini was in Paris, building was abandoned in 1666—the year after he had left the city.

Bernini's late works executed in Rome after 1665 have a strong spiritual and subjective quality. The origins for this style are already present in *Truth Revealed by Time* (1646; Museo e Galleria Borghese, Rome), a statue that shows an unclassical distortion of the figure through an emphasis on feeling and expression. The development is continued in four other statues: *Habakkuk* and *Daniel* (1655–61; S. Maria del Popolo, Rome); *St Mary Magdalen* and *St Jerome* (1661–3; Siena Cathedral). But the best examples of his mystical late style are the over-life-size *Angel with the Crown of Thorns* and *Angel with the Superscription* (1668–9; S. Andrea delle Fratte, Rome). These two statues were commissioned by Clement IX for the decoration of the Ponte S. Angelo, Rome, but were never erected there because they were considered too precious for exposure in the open air. Bernini's spirituality is further shown in other late works: the altar and *ciborium* (1673–4; Cappella del SS. Sacramento, St Peter's Rome), the tomb of Alexander VII (1671–1678; St Peter's Rome), and the *Death of the Blessed Ludovica Albertoni* (1674; S. Francesco a Ripa, Rome). He was not so extensively employed at the end of his life, partly through old age and partly because of the increasing poverty of the papacy which could no longer finance large-scale commissions.

Bernini possessed great personal charm and was much admired by his contemporaries. His brilliant universal achievements were well summed up by the English diarist John Evelyn who attended an opera given by Bernini "wherein he painted the scenes, cut the statues, invented the engines, composed the music, writ the comedy and built the theatre".

Further reading. Baldinucci, F. (ed.; trans. Enggass, C.) *The Life of Bernini*, University Park, Pa. (1966). Hibbard, H. *Bernini*, Harmondsworth (1965). Wittkower, R. *Bernini*, Oxford (1981).

Berruguete family (15th and 16th centuries)

The painter Pedro Berruguete (1450–1504) was born in Paredes de Nava. He began his career in Spain, but by 1480 was painting at the court of Duke Federico da Montefeltro in Urbino, where he worked with Justus van Ghent, Piero della Francesca, Luca Signorelli, and Melozzo da Forli. He collaborated in the decoration of the ducal library and Studiolo and in 1480–1 finished a portrait of *Duke Federico da Montefeltro and his Son* (Galleria Nazionale delle Marche, Urbino). On the death of Federico in 1482 he returned to Spain, working first on the murals of Seville Cathedral (now lost) and later on the frescoes of Toledo Cathedral. After 1490 he obtained, through a family connection with Torquemada, the contract to decorate the Dominican house of St Thomas in Avila. Although he is essentially a painter of the Renaissance, Berruguete's style maintains some traces of Hispano-Flemish tradition.

Pedro's son Alonso Berruguete (1488–1561) was also born at Paredes de Nava. He studied painting with his father, but studied also in Rome and Florence—especially with Michelangelo—and turned his interest to sculpture. On his return to Spain (c1517–19) he established himself in Valladolid, although he also worked in Salamanca, Medina del Campo, and Toledo. His early project for the Royal Chapel of Granada (1523) was rejected, but from 1527 to 1532 he worked on his masterpiece, the complex altarpiece of S. Benito in Valladolid, which involves both independent figures and figures in relief.

In 1529 he carved the altarpiece of the Irish College in Salamanca. From 1539 to 1543 he executed the Epistle-side choir-stalls and the bishop's throne in Toledo Cathedral at the invitation of Cardinal Taverao. He also did the alabaster *Transfiguration* (1543–8). His style displays little concern for naturalism, or for precise representation of the human figure; but his deliberately dramatic distortions are effective in suggesting emotional and spiritual tensions.

Pedro Berruguete: Duke Federico da Montefeltro and his Son; oil on panel; 134×77cm (53×30in); 1480–1. Galleria Nazionale delle Marche, Urbino

Bertoldo di Giovanni *c*1420–91

The origins of the Italian bronze sculptor Bertoldo di Giovanni are obscure. He made his name as one of the assistants who helped the elderly Donatello to work up narrative reliefs for the bronze pulpits of S. Lorenzo, *c*1460–70. He was an associate of the Medici, producing small bronze statuettes, reliefs, plaquettes, and medals, mostly for their circle. His most famous works are *Battle of the Horsemen*, originally set over a mantelpiece in the Medici Palace (now in the Museo Nazionale, Florence) and a medal recording the assassination of Giuliano de' Medici in the Pazzi Conspiracy (1478). At the end of his career he was made curator of the Medici collections of sculpture, and played a role in the training of talented young artists handpicked by Lorenzo the Magnificent. In this capacity he formed a living link between his master Donatello and Michelangelo, who may have learned the techniques of modeling from Bertoldo *c*1490.

Beuys Joseph 1921–86

The German sculptor Joseph Beuys was born in Cleves. Following war service as a pilot in the German Air Force, he studied under Ewald Mataré at the Düsseldorf Academy of Art from 1947 to 1952. Throughout the 1950s he created a succession of highly original sculptures, assemblages in a variety of materials, and cast bronzes such as *SaFG-SaUG* (1953–8; Hessisches Landesmuseum, Darmstadt), their imagery drawn from his personal experiences, natural science, and mythology. He also created a group of intensely personal drawings (exhibited in 1974 as *The Secret Block for a Secret Person in Ireland*), whose imagery he would use consistently during the 1960s and 1970s.

In 1961 Beuys was appointed Professor of Sculpture at the Düsseldorf Academy, a post he held until 1972 when he was dismissed for his political activity. In the early 1960s his work and reputation were linked to the Fluxus group. But a succession of "actions" (performances) *Siberian Symphony, Section 1* (1963; Düsseldorf), *The Chief* (1964; Berlin), and *How to Explain Pictures to a Dead Hare* (1965; at the opening of his first solo exhibition, Düsseldorf) took him away from Fluxus concerns into his own highly personal forms of creativity. These first performances contained the essential elements of his actions for the next decade: fat, felt, batteries, dead hare, and blackboards. Most of his sculptures were created during or resulted from actions, such as *Eurasia* (1966; Galerie René Block, West Berlin), *Three Pots Action Object* (1974; Scottish National Gallery of Modern Art, Edinburgh), *Directional Forces* (1974; Nationalgalerie, West Berlin), and *Tallow* (1979; Art Institute of Chicago). In Edinburgh in 1970 he combined action with lecture for the first time in *Celtic (Kinloch Rannoch) Scottish Symphony*. Of the many actions, *Coyote* (1974; Ronald Feldman Gallery, New York) in which he spent a week in a gallery with a wild coyote, is

Thomas Bewick: The Wild Bull in the Park at Chillingham Castle, Northumberland; wood engraving; including border 26×18cm (10×7in); 1789. British Museum, London

probably the most memorable.

In the late 1960s Beuys' art and political ideas came together in a unified aesthetic in which art is inseparable from social organization. He was instrumental in setting up several political groups; most significantly he founded the Free International University, whose manifesto he and the novelist Heinrich Böll wrote in 1972. In 1976 Beuys represented West Germany in the Venice Biennale with one work *Tram Stop* (1976; Kröller-Müller Museum, Otterlo). He was given a major retrospective exhibition at the Solomon R. Guggenheim Museum, New York, in 1979.

Further reading. Beuys, J. "Joseph Beuys: Public Dialogue", *Avalanche*, New York (May/June 1974). Jappe, G. "A Joseph Beuys Primer", *Studio International*, London (September 1971). Mauer, O. *Beuys*, Eindhoven (1968). Tisdall, C. *Joseph Beuys*, London (1979).

Bewick Thomas 1753–1828

The animal artist and draftsman Thomas Bewick is usually considered to be the father of 19th-century wood engraving and among the most outstanding of English graphic artists. He was born in Newcastle upon Tyne where he established a school of engravers. His most famous illustrations are those of birds and animal life in *Select Fables* (1784) and *A History of British Birds* (1797 and 1804). Bewick's vignettes and tailpieces of natural life and landscape show acute observation. By using the end grain rather than the plank, and cutting it with a burin, Bewick achieved a wide range of middle tones for foliage and textures. This method of engraving did much to arrest the decline of engraving into a primarily reproductive technique.

Bibiena family
17th and 18th centuries

The Bibieni were a family of theatrical designers who worked in many European countries. The name "da Bibiena" derives from the birthplace of the father of the family, Giovanni Maria Galli (1625–65). Moving from his home town to Bologna, he studied under Francesco Albani with whom he remained as an assistant. His more famous son Ferdinando (1657–1743) founded the family's fortunes. After studying painting under Carlo Cignani, and architecture under several masters, he designed theater sets, decorations, and several buildings for the Farnese of Parma. Subsequently, he worked for the Hapsburgs, first in Barcelona, later in Vienna.

His son Giuseppe (1696–1756) decorated the new theaters at Dresden and Bayreuth, and designed the sets for operas at Vienna, Linz, Venice, and Berlin. He also designed catafalques, triumphal arches, and similar ephemeral decorations. His career included work in Prague, Munich, Augsburg, Stuttgart, Frankfurt, and Paris. (Eight of his designs survive in the Department of Prints and Drawings, British Museum, London.) Like his father, Giuseppe's son Carlo (1728–*c*78) was employed by the Imperial aristocracy—at Bayreuth, Württemberg, Brunswick, and Berlin. Carlo worked at Naples and Padua and visited France, the Netherlands, Britain, and Russia.

Other artist members of the Bibiena family include the children of Giovanni Maria—Maria Oriana (1656–1749) and Francesco (1659–1739), the three sons of Ferdinando—Alessandro (1687–*ante* 1769), Antonio (1700–74), and Giovanni Maria the Younger (*c*1739–69), and Francesco's son Giovanni Carlo (?–1760).

Because their chosen medium was so inherently perishable, the Bibieni are often forgotten. However, in their day, the family enjoyed European renown for their illusionistic stage sets and must be counted among the creators of the Baroque opera. Some of their drawings survive, notably in collections at Vienna, Dresden, and Munich. Two hundred of their designs were reproduced in contemporary prints.

Bichitr *c*1550–*c*1650

Bichitr was one of the most polished Mughal portraitists of the Shah Jahan period (1628–58), though the active life of this Hindu painter spans the reigns of the previous two emperors—Akbar and Jahangir—as well. His refined draftsmanship shows evidence of European influence. The painting of a saint in the Chester Beatty Library, Dublin, shows a mastery of facial expression. His paintings, consisting of enamel-like surfaces, express majestic solidity. He often used a low horizon to underline the importance of the central figure, as in the portrait of Asaf Khan. He employed bluish tones to convey atmospheric perspective, and reduced distant architectural background to abstract shapes. The *Shah Jahan-nama* (Royal Art Collection, Windsor) contains his work.

Biederman Charles 1906–

Charles Biederman, the most important American Constructivist artist and theorist, was born of Czech parents in Cleveland, Ohio, and lived in Red Wing, Min-

Charles Biederman: No. 23, Red Wing; painted aluminum; 98×79×14cm (38×31×6in); 1968–9. Collection of Mr and Mrs Carl R. Erickson, Minnesota

nesota after 1942. A major retrospective was held at the Minneapolis Institute of Arts in 1976. Following the publication of his magisterial study *Art as the Evolution of Visual Knowledge* (Red Wing, Minn., 1948), Biederman's influence as a theorist has been profound. Later books include *The New Cézanne* (Red Wing, 1958) and *Towards a New Architecture* (Red Wing, 1979).

Biederman studied at the Art Institute of Chicago School (1926–9). He moved to New York in 1934 and lived in Paris from 1936 to 1937. There he met Mondrian, Léger, and other mainstream artists, coming under the influence of Mondrian, *De Stijl*, and Constructivism. During these years his obviously derivative paintings ranged from Cézannesque landscapes and still lifes to geometric and biomorphic abstraction. He gradually revealed a concern for three-dimensional sculptural forms in space, such as *Paris, March 7,*

1937 (artist's collection). From 1937 he has worked exclusively in the relief format, designating his style as "Structurist" in 1952 to disassociate his works and himself from all previous Constructivist and *De Stijl* theory and practice.

Since 1949 his aluminium, spray-painted reliefs have taken on their distinctive and unique appearance. At first he relied on vertical elements alone, perpendicular to the background plane, as in *No. 36, Red Wing* (1950; artist's collection). He later added horizontal and slanting elements (*No. 39, Red Wing*, 1961–71; artist's collection). He uses no more than ten colors for each relief; their essential quality is the balance of color, space, and light, creating structural unity. According to Biederman, the reliefs emulate the structure and building methods of nature, and depend upon varying natural light and the changing viewpoint of the spectator to create an infinite number of readings.

Bihzad Kamal al-Din *c*1450–1536

The Persian miniature painter Kamal al-Din Bihzad worked in Herat where he was a pupil of Miraq. He was patronized by the minister and poet Mir Ali Shir Nawa'i and by his master Sultan Husayn Bayqara, the Timurid ruler of Khurasan (1469–1506). During his lifetime he achieved an unrivaled reputation which has persisted in Iran and Mughal India; his work has therefore been much copied and imitated, often with the addition of forged signatures. His genuine surviving work is hard to identify with certainty. The best attested are three miniatures in a *Gulistan* of Sa'di (private collection) dated 1486, four miniatures and a double-page frontispiece showing Sultan Husayn at a picnic in a garden courtyard in a *Bustan* of Sa'di dated 1488 (Egyptian National Library, Cairo), a double-page album picture of the same Sultan in a garden enclosure in his harem, *c*1485 (Gulistan Library, Teheran), five miniatures added to a *Khamsa* of Nizami (originally copied in 1442) in 1486, 1490, or 1493, according to different readings of a date on one of them (British Library, London; Add. MS. 25900), and the frontispiece and five miniatures, one dated 1494, in a second Nizami manuscript (British Library, London; Or. 6810).

In a manuscript of the *Concert of the Birds* by Attar dated 1483 (Metropolitan Museum, New York) a Bihzadian miniature of a *Beggar at Court* is dated 1487/8, while at least one more—a funeral procession—is worthy of his hand. Probably also by Bihzad are six double-page scenes illustrating the *Zafar-nama* (the history of the conquests of Timur) copied in Herat in 1467. They have suffered much overpainting in India and the date of their production is controversial; they are either early work of *c*1480, or later work from the 1490s. They stand apart from the other works in subject, but are masterly in dynamic composition and include single figures within the repertory of Bihzad (The Walters Art Gallery, Baltimore).

Bihzad was a Timurid and Herati painter, excelling in that tradition. He was no innovator, but an artist of great sensibility and color sense, an expressive draftsman and brilliant at composition. Light is shed on the working of his studio by the identification of tightly knit groups of figures transferred from one composition to another, sometimes in reverse.

Bill Max 1908-

The Swiss painter, sculptor, designer, theorist, and teacher Max Bill was born in Winterthur. He trained as a silversmith at the Kunstgewerbeschule, Zurich (1924–7) and at the Dessau Bauhaus (1927–9). He was a member of *Abstraction-Création* from 1932 to 1936. Bill was both co-founder and Rector of the Hochschule für Gestaltung, Ulm, heading the architecture and product-design departments from 1951 to 1956.

Bauhaus ideals and the works of Mondrian (1872–1944) and Georges Vantongerloo (1886–1965) all contributed to Max Bill's constructivism and the formulation of the principles of Concrete art in 1936. He first attempted to interpret the Möbius strip in 1935, achieving success in 1953. Thereafter, his sculptures in carved stone, polished bronze, and stainless steel explore the properties of continuous surfaces in space. His paintings are strictly logical and geometric structures of color, exploiting optical properties combined with rhythmical sequences of forms.

Bishndas c1550–c1650

Bishndas was a Hindu portraitist at the Mughal court, the nephew of the painter Nanha. He collaborated with Nanha on *Babur-nama* (British Museum, London) and with the painter Inayat on a *Shah-nama*, during the Akbar period (1556–1605). A portrait by Daulat in the *Gulshan* Album (Gulistan Palace Library, Teheran) shows him as a young man. Bishndas rose to prominence during the reign of Jahangir (1605–27) who considered him "unequalled in his age for taking likenesses". He was sent to Persia to paint the portraits of the Shah and his courtiers (1613–20), and on his return was awarded an elephant. *The Sultan of Baghdad and Chinese Princess* (1599–1600) in the British Museum *Anwar-i-Suhayli* (a book of fables) is one of his finest works, showing movement, agility, and restrained emotions. Among his portraits are one of Shaikh Phul (Chester Beatty Library, Dublin), a simple but perceptive painting of Suraj Singh of Jodhpur, and two paintings of Shah Abbas in the Hermitage, St Petersburg.

Blake Peter 1932-

The British painter Peter Blake was born at Dartford in Kent, and studied at the Gravesend School of Art from 1946 to

Peter Blake: Tattoed Woman; pen and ink with collage on paper; 79×41cm (31×16in); 1961. Collection of Mr and Mrs Gordon House, London

1951. After National Service in the Royal Air Force he studied at the Royal College of Art from 1953 to 1956. In 1956 he won a Leverhulme Research Award to study popular art and traveled in Holland, Belgium, France, Italy, and Spain. He was influenced by American realist painters and was a pioneer in the development of Pop art in Britain. *On the Balcony* (1955–7; Tate Gallery, London) is characteristic of his sharp, precise, almost *trompe-l'oeil* style, and reveals his fondness for the details of life: old magazines, snapshots, badges, and buttons.

Blake William 1757–1827

William Blake, born in London where he spent all but three years of his life, was both poet and visionary artist. Despite having a number of artist friends, he was one of the first unrecognized geniuses of the Romantic age. Partly inspired by Henry Fuseli, James Barry, and John Hamilton Mortimer, he evolved a completely personal style, closely linked in imagery and symbolism to the mythology and to the personal form of Christian philosophy found in his writings. He saw both poetry and the visual arts as aspects of a single poetic or prophetic genius

which expressed eternal truths, the only justification for true art.

In 1767 Blake entered Henry Pars' drawing school and from 1772 to 1779 was apprenticed to the engraver James Basire (1730–1802) for whom he made copies of Gothic tombs in Westminster Abbey. He continued engraving for the rest of his life, both in an individual manner for his own designs and in a more conventional style for the commercial world by which he hoped to earn his living. In 1779 he entered the Royal Academy Schools, but was dissatisfied with the emphasis placed on richness of chiaroscuro and drawing from life.

Blake first exhibited at the Royal Academy in 1780 and then at infrequent intervals until 1808, arousing neither public nor critical interest. His early works show a development from the rather flaccid Neoclassicism of his watercolor illustrations of English history (for example, *The Death of Earl Godwin*, c1779; British Museum, London), to the more powerful and accomplished Neoclassicism of the three watercolors illustrating the story of Joseph in Egypt exhibited in 1785 (Fitzwilliam Museum, Cambridge). The first appearance of one of Blake's most personal images, *Glad Day* or *The Dance of Albion*, is thought to date from this period, though the engravings bearing the date 1780 were probably executed considerably later. "Ideal" dates, relating to the date of a work's first conception rather than its actual execution, occur more than once in Blake's work. At this time he was associated with such political radicals as Joseph Johnson, Thomas Paine, Joseph Priestley, Mary Wollstonecraft, and William Godwin.

From 1788 until 1795 Blake developed his own unique combination of text and illustration in a series of "illuminated books" in which he simultaneously printed both his verses and his designs, coloring the latter at a second stage; examples are *Songs of Innocence* (1789) and *Songs of Experience* (1794), *The Marriage of Heaven and Hell* (1790–3), *America* (1793), and *Europe* (1794), copies of which are in the British Museum, London, Fitzwilliam Museum, Cambridge, and elsewhere. At first the coloring was done in watercolor, but in *Urizen* (1794) Blake started printing the colors in his own form of tempera (based on glue rather than the egg-yolk of the Renaissance masters). This technique produced a rich, heavy texture suited to the imagery of the book, and was soon used by Blake in separate color-prints of designs taken from the books. In 1795 he used the same technique for the splendid set of 12 large color prints of subjects taken from such diverse sources as the Bible, Shakespeare, Milton, and history. These illustrate Blake's views of the predicament of mankind following a fall from grace—the division of the unified man into his diverse, conflicting elements. (The best selection from the series, ten in all, is in the Tate Gallery, London.) *Elohim Creating Adam* shows the Creation as a completely negative act; *Nebuchadnezzar* is man in his purely bestial aspect, and *Newton* in his purely rational, for instance.

In 1799 Blake found his most important patron, the minor government official Thomas Butts, and began painting small

pictures of Biblical subjects, at first in tempera and then, from 1800 to *c*1805, in watercolor (examples in the Tate Gallery, London, and elsewhere). Although more direct illustrations of their subjects than the large color prints, they also contain many examples of Blake's personal imagery. These works were followed by Blake's first series of watercolor illustrations to the Book of Job (*c*1805–6; Pierpont Morgan Library, New York), and by a number of sets of illustrations to Milton's poems. Some of these, including those to *Paradise Lost*, 1808 (mainly in the Boston Museum of Fine Arts), duplicate with variations sets already done for another patron, the Revd Joseph Thomas (Huntington Library and Art Gallery, San Marino).

Meanwhile Blake had suffered three setbacks. The first was the three years he

spent living at Felpham near Chichester (1800–3). There he worked for the well meaning but unimaginative poet and man of letters, William Hayley, who employed him on such uncongenial tasks as decorating his library, illustrating his books, and painting miniature portraits. The second was over his illustrations to Robert Blair's poem *The Grave*, which were published in 1806, engraved by the fashionable Luigi Schiavonetti instead of by Blake himself, as had been promised. The third was Blake's exhibition of his own works at his brother's house (1809–10), which aroused hardly any comment and that mostly hostile. It included the subsequently engraved painting of *The Canterbury Pilgrims* (Pollok House, Glasgow), *The Spiritual Form of Nelson*, and *The Spiritual Form of Pitt* (both Tate Gallery, London).

William Blake: The Good and Evil Angels; color-printed monotype, finished with pen and watercolor; 45×59cm (18×23in); 1795. Tate Gallery, London

These and other failures to achieve commercial success led to a period of neglect, occupied largely by further illustrations to Milton and the completion of the poems *Milton* (c1804–15) and *Jerusalem* (c1804–1820; the only complete fully colored copy is in the Paul Mellon Collection, U.S.A.). However, from 1818 onwards Blake became friendly with a group of young artists: John Linnell, Samuel Palmer, George Richmond, and Samuel Calvert. For Linnell's teacher, John Varley, Blake drew, mainly in 1819, his notorious *Visionary Heads:* heads or complete figures of personages reputedly seen in visions (though it is at least possible that he was partly teasing his credulous friend). These include Biblical and historical personages and the *Ghost of a Flea* (both a drawing of the head and a full-length painting are in the Tate Gallery, London).

For Linnell, Blake painted a second series of Job watercolors (1821; mainly in the William Hayes Fogg Art Museum, Cambridge, Mass.) which were subsequently engraved. He also painted over 100 illustrations to Dante's *Divine Comedy* (1824–7; dispersed, between the Tate Gallery, London, the William Hayes Fogg Museum, Cambridge, Mass., the National Gallery of Victoria, Melbourne, etc). Again Blake's illustrations embodied his own ideas and criticisms of the texts.

Also from these last years are the tiny woodcut illustrations for Dr Thornton's schoolboys' edition of Virgil. Relatively untypical in their stress on landscape, these proved to have the greatest influence of all Blake's works on subsequent British artists—not only on Palmer, Richmond, and Calvert but also well into the 20th century in the early work of Paul Nash (1889–1946) and Graham Sutherland (1903–80). The years following Blake's death saw him almost forgotten, but the publication of Alexander Gilchrist's *Life of William Blake* in 1863 and the enthusiasm of D.G. Rossetti (1828–82) and his circle started a cult of Blake as poet-painter-philosopher that has grown to this day.

Further reading. Bentley, G.E. Jr *Blake Records,* Oxford (1969). Bentley, G.E. Jr and Nurmi, M. *A Blake Bibliography,* Minneapolis (1964). Bindman, D. *Blake as an Artist,* London (1977). Blunt, A. *The Art of William Blake,* London and New York (1959). Butlin, M. *The Paintings and Drawings of William Blake,* London (1981). Erdman, D.V. *Blake, Prophet against Empire,* Princeton (1969). Erdman, D.V. *The Illuminated Blake,* London (1975) and New York (1976). Gilchrist, A. *Life of William Blake,* London (1863, revised 1945). Keynes, G. *The Complete Writings of William Blake,* London (1957).

Blakelock Ralph Albert
1847–1919

The American landscape painter Ralph Albert Blakelock was born in New York. He first worked in the Romantic style of the Hudson River school, and after several years traveling in Western states (1869–72) he introduced motifs such as the campfire at evening. His work was not, however, a celebration of the grandeur of the American landscape (in the manner of Bierstadt [1830–1902], for example), but an evocation of its poetic moods; typically, trees are silhouetted against evening or night skies, the mood one of melancholy reverie, as in *Moonlight Sonata* (c1888; Museum of Fine Arts, Boston). Endless financial difficulties, coupled with critical neglect and then hostility, took their toll and in 1899 he was committed to an insane asylum. He was released shortly before he died, largely unable to appreciate his growing critical acclaim.

Further reading. Gebhard, D. *Ralph A. Blakelock,* New York (1969).

Bloemaert Abraham 1564–1651

The principal importance of the Dutch painter Abraham Bloemaert lies in his influence as the teacher of such artists as Jan Both and several members of the Utrecht School (notably Terbrugghen and Gerrit van Honthorst). His paintings include brightly colored Biblical and mythological works, such as *The Marriage of Peleus and Thetis* (1638; Royal Museum of Art, Mauritshuis, The Hague): pictures in which his early Mannerist figure-style was gradually replaced by a more classical idiom. Figures are subordinated to landscape in many of his historical and mythological paintings, and it is for landscapes that Bloemaert is principally remembered. These are rather schematic in character when compared with the drawings of natural details on which they were based, and especially when compared with realistic Dutch landscapes of the later 17th century. Their depth is somewhat shallow and they are usually composed of carefully arranged motifs of a rustic or picturesque kind: tumbledown farmhouses, groups of peasants or shepherds, farm animals and implements, and clumps of gnarled trees. The "Drawing Book" Bloemaert compiled from his pen and chalk studies influenced the many pupils who trained under him.

Boccioni Umberto 1882–1916

Umberto Boccioni was an Italian Futurist painter and sculptor. Works like the Romantic *Paola and Francesco* (1908; Palazzoli Collection, Milan) reflect the feeling for Symbolism and Impressionism outside France. Other works are neo-Impressionist evocations of the new industrial city on the outskirts of Milan.

Boccioni was fired by the poet Filippo Marinetti's *Manifesto of Futurism* (1909), which called for a violent rejection of the cultural past and glorified the machines of the new technological age in a style reminiscent of political manifestos: "a roaring motor car, which looks as though it runs on shrapnel, is more beautiful than the *Victory* of Samothrace". He adapted Marinetti's ideas in his *Technical Manifesto of the Futurist Painters* (1910), in which the goal of dynamism in painting is first stated. At first Boccioni could find no suitable technical means to express it. Although he chose aggressive, modern subject matter, as in *The City Rises* (1911; Museum of Modern Art, New York), dynamism is conveyed by the pattern of rapid brush strokes delineating strenuous, heroic men and horses, and not through the use of the mechanical images of the *Manifesto*.

The stylistic liberation of Boccioni and the Futurists came through exposure to Cubism in Paris in 1911. The effect can be traced in his sketches for the *States of Mind* project, pictures with the contemporary theme of leave-taking at a railway station. The earliest sketches of limp linear waves gives way to Cubist angularity, with numbers and fragments of machinery.

The Futurists' concern for "states of mind" is a version of the then fashionable idea of "simultaneity". This was elaborated by the French philosopher Henri Louis Bergson (1859–1941), who argued that life is experienced as a series of fleeting, intuitively grasped impressions. Boccioni and the Futurists interpreted this both in a simple way, by superimposing transient visual data, and also in a more sophisticated manner, by attempts to

Umberto Boccioni: Unique Forms of Continuity in Space; cast bronze; 112×89×41cm (44×35×16in); 1913. Museum of Modern Art, New York

depict the response of the mind to all sorts of stimuli.

Boccioni also tried to convey the essence of movement, although his images of horses, cyclists, and figures tended to be organic rather than mechanical. The most striking of these attempts is the polished bronze *Unique Forms of Continuity in Space* (1913; Museum of Modern Art, New York), an analysis of a man walking.

The choice of subject was never a matter of indifference to Boccioni: one that involved him intensely was his mother. She appears throughout his work as an hierarchic, monolithic image, emanating "lines of force". Her presence is maintained even in the extraordinary series of sculptures we know only from photographs. These were assembled from incongruous, but logical, materials—a fragment of a window frame,

plaster, wire, and cardboard.

Boccioni was called up in 1914 to fight in the war the Futurists had glorified. He was killed in a fall from his horse, while on maneuvers.

Further reading. Balla, G. *Boccioni*, Milan (1964). Tisdall, C. and Bozzola, A. *Futurism*, London (1977). Zeno, B. (ed.) *Umberto Boccioni: Gli Scritti Editi e Inediti*, Milan (1971).

Böcklin Arnold 1827–1901

Born in Basel, the Swiss painter Arnold Böcklin studied painting at the Düsseldorf Academy under Johann Schirmer. His early work embodied ideas based on German Romanticism. During a visit to Paris in 1848 he studied the work of Corot

and Thomas Couture. The paintings he did in Rome between 1850 and 1857 interpret Classical landscapes through mythical figures from Antiquity (for example, *Pan Among the Rushes*, 1857; Neue Pinakothek, Munich). He worked in Munich and in Basel, where he was a successful portrait painter (for example, *The Actress Jenny Janauschek*, 1861; Städelsches Kunstinstitut, Frankfurt am Main) and muralist (for example, the staircase of the Kunstmuseum Basel, 1868–70). But he drew his inspiration from Italian art, particularly from Raphael, whose Vatican frescoes he first admired in 1862. In 1874 he met the German painter Hans von Marées in Florence, and with him shared an interest in depicting pseudo-Classical figures in mysterious landscape settings.

His mature work is reminiscent of French Symbolist paintings such as those of Gustave Moreau (for example, *Couple in the Tuscan Landscape*, 1878; Nationalgalerie, Berlin). It also shows the influence of the Old Masters, including Northern painters of the 16th and 17th centuries such as Grünewald, Dürer, and Ruysdael; but Böcklin's landscapes were more intense both in mood and atmosphere. These somber characteristics are evident in his best-known work, *The Island of the Dead* (1880; five versions from the first, in tempera, which is in the Öffertliches kunstsammlung, Kunstmuseum Basel; one is in the Metropolitan Museum, New York). The title was invented by a dealer, not by the artist: Böcklin described the painting simply as "a picture for dreaming about". His reputation in Europe was eclipsed during the 19th century by developments in France; but Böcklin's art came into its own in the 20th century when it was reassessed by the Expressionists and Surrealists, particulary by de Chirico and Salvador Dali.

Boffrand Gabriel-Germain
1667–1754

The French architect Gabriel-Germain Boffrand was a pupil of J.H. Mansart. His eminence lies in his exportation of the French ideal of royal architecture. He was employed at Luneville (1702–6) by the Duke of Lorraine, whose Premier Architect he became, at Bouchefort by the Elector of Bavaria (1705), and he designed both the Residenz at Würzburg (1723) and Schloss Favorite at Mainz (1724). All these works were on a regal scale and in a style derived from the Baroque of Louis Levau (1612–1670). But he was eclectic and his domed centralized schemes such as those for Bouchefort or his second project for Malgrange (1712) demonstrated his versatility and imaginative range. His stylistic vocabulary ran from echoes of Vaux-le-Vicomte at Malgrange to Palladio's Villa Capra at Bouchefort. For this reason he marks a turning point between the Baroque and the advent of Neoclassicism; he had some influence in the latter movement through the publication of his *Livre d'Architecture* in 1745.

Bol Ferdinand 1616–80

The Dutch painter Ferdinand Bol was born at Dordrecht but spent most of his working life in Amsterdam. In the 1630s he became one of Rembrandt's closest and most esteemed pupils and he adopted his master's portrait style of that period, often placing his sitters at an open window. The *Portrait of Elizabeth Jacobsdr. Bas* (c1635–45; Rijksmuseum, Amsterdam), once attributed to Rembrandt, is now recognized as a work of Bol. In succeeding years his style lightened in tone as that of Rembrandt darkened, and though he remains close to his master in religious works (for example, *Jacob's Dream*, c1635–45; Gemäldegalerie Alte Meister, Dresden), his portraits are more obviously fashionable. His last dated work is of 1669.

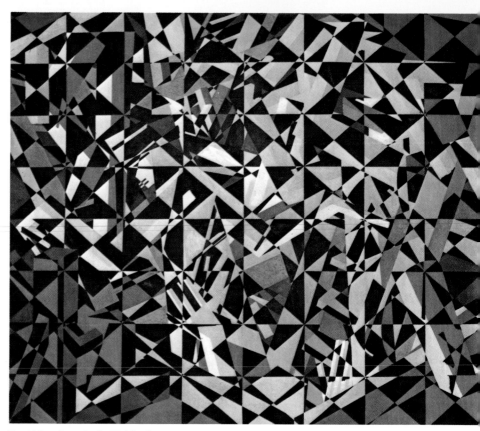

David Bomberg: In the Hold; oil on canvas; 196×231cm (77×91in); 1913–14. Tate Gallery, London

Ferdinand Bol: Ferdinand Bol and his wife Elisabeth Dell; oil on canvas; 205×180cm (81×71in); 1654. Louvre, Paris

Bomberg David 1890–1957

The British painter David Bomberg was born in Birmingham, the fifth son of a Polish immigrant leather-worker. Apprenticed to a lithographer (1906–7), but more interested in becoming a painter, he studied at the Slade School of Fine Art (1911–13) and in 1914 was a founder member of the London Group. Bomberg's historical significance lies in his four major early works (for example *The Mud Bath*, 1913–14; Tate Gallery, London), in which he applies Cubist-inspired forms to relatively traditional subjects. They should also be seen in the context of Vorticism. In the mid 1920s, Bomberg moved away from abstraction to a heavily worked, representational style somewhat Expressionist in character. He gained recognition near the end of his life. In 1953 his pupils formed a School around him, the Borough Bottega, which lasted until his death.

Further reading. Cork, R. *David Bomberg*, New Haven (1987).

Bondol Jean fl. 1368–81

The Flemish-born artist Jean Bondol became "Painter and Valet de Chambre" to Charles V of France in 1368. His only known works were created within the milieu of the French court, where he was known as "Jean" or "Hennequin de Bruges". He was granted a pension for life in 1380 and is last recorded in March 1381.

Bondol is best known as the designer of the cartoons for the Angers *Apocalypse* (Musée des Tapisseries, Angers), one of the longest series of tapestries in the world and a rare survival from the 14th century of a complex subject portrayed in this medium. The series was commissioned by the King's brother, Louis, Duke of Anjou, who borrowed both the King's painter and an illustrated text of the Apocalypse from the royal collection to help with the designs. Cartoons and weaving progressed simultaneously, and the task, begun after 1373, was probably completed by 1380. The most famous weaver in Paris, Nicolas Bataille, translated Bondol's full-scale cartoons into tapestry. The tapestry, renowned throughout the Middle Ages, suffered some mutilation during and after the French Revolution. The disposition of scenes in two registers and in seven sections, each associated with the figure of a reader under a tall architectural setting, is original. Bondol clearly drew for inspiration on more than one illustrated text of the Apocalypse. He evokes the vision of St John and the events recorded in the Book of Revelation in a highly dramatic way; his figures show great individuality both in character and in their reaction to events.

Although Jean Bondol is invariably described in documents as a painter and not as an illuminator, the only other work undoubtedly by his hand is a dedication miniature in a Bible given to Charles V by his counsellor Jean de Vaudetar in March 1372 (Rijksmuseum Meermanno-Westreenianum, The Hague; MS. 10 B 23). A Latin inscription facing the miniature tells us it was painted by order of King Charles, and also that John of Bruges, painter to the King, made it with his own hand. The painting shows the counsellor kneeling and presenting a Bible to the seated King, who is dressed in the gown and close-fitting cap of a Master of the University of Paris. Grisaille painting gives a sculptural effect to the figures, and the setting is presented in a sophisticated way by the perspectival treatment of the floor pattern and the implication that space continues behind the arch of the frame. The rest of the Hague Bible is lavishly illustrated in styles associated with the workshop of the Maître aux Boqueteaux, so-called because of the clumps of little umbrella-like trees (or *boqueteaux*) featured in his landscapes. Juxtaposition of this Master's work with the authenticated work of Bondol has led some authorities to identify him with this illuminator. The evidence is inconclusive. Tendencies towards an earthy realism, often regarded as characteristically Flemish, may well have been intensified by the influence of Bondol on other Flemish artists working in Paris from the 1350s onward and employed by Charles V as illuminators.

Bonington Richard Parkes
1801–28

Richard Parkes Bonington was born in Arnold near Nottingham, where his father was a drawing master. In 1817 the family moved to Calais, France, where Richard's father set up a lace factory. Here Richard received tuition from François Louis Francia, who was familiar with the Girtin school of English watercolor painting. Thus Bonington's initial teaching was within the English tradition. About 1818, while studying Flemish artists in the Louvre, Bonington met Eugène Delacroix. Afterwards he entered the École des Beaux-Arts and became a pupil of Baron Gros.

Before his debut at the 1822 Salon, where he exhibited watercolors of Normandy, Bonington toured northern France. In

Richard Parkes Bonington: The Doge's Palace, Venice; watercolor; 20×27cm (8×11in); c1827. Wallace Collection, London

1823 he made a tour of medieval towns, the probable basis of his lithographs for Baron Taylor's *Voyage Pittoresque dans l'Ancienne France*. Bonington's prowess in landscape is again evident in five contributions to the "English" Salon of 1824. In 1825 he visited England with Delacroix and was impressed by the work of Turner. After this, Bonington and Delacroix shared a studio in Paris and their close friendship influenced the development of both artists. Bonington began to paint "costume pieces" with themes drawn from medieval history. In 1826 he traveled in Italy, studying the Venetian school, and in 1827 exhibited views of Venice as well as history pieces in the Salon: a mastery of rich color and atmosphere replaced an earlier affiliation to cool grays and greens.

Ill with consumption, Bonington returned in 1828 to England where he exhibited at the British Institution and at the Royal Academy of Arts. He died in London—his funeral cortege was led by Sir Thomas Lawrence and representatives of the Academy.

Bonington worked in both watercolor and oil, rapidly developing a luminosity and breadth of style which were later to engage the attention of Corot. His costume pieces and picturesque landscapes place him firmly within the Romantic tradition.

Bonnanus of Pisa   12th century

Bonnanus of Pisa (also known as Bonnano or Bonnano da Pisa) was a bronze-founder who, in the 1180s, cast two doors for Pisa Cathedral, only one of which survives. These were followed in 1186 by a bronze door for Monreale Cathedral in Sicily. Unlike the Carolingian bronze doors at Aachen, the Ottonian at Hildesheim, and the Romanesque at Gniezno (Poland), which are cast as two complete halves, the Italian bronze doors consist of small panels, which are then nailed on to a wooden core. Bonnanus, like most Pisan artists of the Romanesque period, was profoundly influenced by Byzantine art: some of his reliefs are copies of Greek ivories. Andrea Pisano (c1290–1348/9) must have known Bonnanus' work when he revived the art of casting doors in Florence in 1330.

Bonnard Pierre   1867–1947

The French painter, book-illustrator, and graphic artist Pierre Bonnard was born near Paris. He studied law from 1885 to 1888, but after failing his examination he attended classes at the École des Beaux-Arts and then at the Académie Julian, where he met Maurice Denis, Paul Sérusier, and Jean Édouard Vuillard. In 1889, he produced his first poster, *France-*

Pierre Bonnard: Standing Nude; oil on canvas; 125×109cm (49×43in); c1908. Musées Royaux d'Art et d'Histoire, Brussels

Post-Impressionist palette (and he absorbed the lessons of Monet and Renoir, especially in their late styles). He also produced more landscapes. Yet he always remained a devotee of the human figure, expressed above all in an extensive series of nudes. A "dry" middle period produced its reaction. Color and light flooded back into his pictures, and pattern and texture were now combined with a taut, simple composition.

Further reading. Fermigier, A. *Pierre Bonnard*, New York (1987).

Bordone Paris 1500–71

The Trevisan painter Paris Paschalinus Bordone worked principally in Venice and was trained there by Titian. The starting point for his many paintings of the Madonna and Child with saints seated in a landscape is Titian's early work; but his style, both in figures and landscape, gradually becomes more Mannerist, with oddly tilted figures, sharply silhouetted planes, and artificial foliage.

His *Bathsheba* (Wallraf-Richartz-Museum, Cologne), typical of a number of quasi-erotic paintings with nudes, shows these qualities. It displays, too, a charac-

Champagne. After military service (1889–1890) he took a studio in Paris with Vuillard. From 1891, he exhibited regularly at the Salon des Indépendants. He became friendly with the Natanson brothers and hence produced illustrations for *La Revue Blanche*; he produced theater designs for several avant-garde theaters and worked with Alfred Jarry.

A meeting with Ambroise Vollard in 1894 led to the publication of Bonnard's lithographs, *Quelques Aspects de la Vie de Paris* (1895), *Parallèlement* (1900), and *Daphnis and Chloë* (1902). In 1904, he illustrated Jules Renard's *Histoires Naturelles*. He met Maria Boursin in 1895. She became his mistress, his model, and in 1925 his wife. She died in 1940.

In 1896 Bonnard held his first one-man show at Durand-Ruel's gallery, but he subsequently signed an exclusive contract with Bernheim-Jeune. From 1900 he began to concentrate on painting. He knew both Renoir and Monet, and was a pall-bearer at Monet's funeral in 1926. He spent some of his time in the Seine Valley, where he

had a house, and some in the South, where in 1925 he bought a small villa at Le Cannet. He died there in 1947.

In the 1890s, Bonnard was a member of the group known as Les Nabis: they were influenced by Post-Impressionism, especially by Gauguin. They were also greatly attracted to Japanese prints, and none more so than Bonnard who was known as "Le Nabi Japonard". The Nabis wished to move away from what they considered the tyranny of the easel-picture: hence their contributions to poster and theatrical designs, to screens, tapestries, and book illustrations. Bonnard became a master of lithography, using shapes, color, and line with decorative wit and subtle changes of texture. His brilliancy as a designer in the 1890s matched that of Toulouse-Lautrec. His paintings of the same decade share similar features of flattened shapes and witty arabesques, but their *intimisme* is conveyed in dark, even somber colors, as though Impressionism and Gauguin had never existed.

After 1900, Bonnard began to use a more

Paris Bordone: Nude Woman; black pencil and white chalk on blue card; 32×20cm (12½×8in). Uffizi, Florence

teristic contrast between a decorative front plane and an architectural perspective background, which creates a typically Mannerist dislocation of space. This artificial perspective vista is likely to have been suggested by the Renaissance theater; after Bordone, it finds its way into the early works of Tintoretto and El Greco.

Bordone visited Lombardy in the late 1520s and was influenced by Moretto and by Brescian painting. He also seems to have visited France.

Borrassá Lluís c1390–1424

The Spanish painter Lluís Borrassá was born in Gerona. He was the leading Catalan exponent of the International Gothic style which, at the end of the 14th century, succeeded the Italo-Catalan tradition founded by Ferrer Bassa (c1290–1348). He painted the altarpiece of the archangel Gabriel in Barcelona Cathedral by 1390; his later works include the altarpieces of Vich, Tarrasa, and Cruilles. His sense of color is characterized by powerful reds and greens, and careful use of light and shade. His works convey a striking impression of violent movement, for example, the Retable of Peter (1411–13; Museum of S. Maria, Tarrassa); and the Retable of S. Clara (1414–15; Episcopal Museum of Archaeology and Art, Vich): this manner is foreign to the essentially static traditions of earlier Spanish painting.

Borromini Francesco 1599–1667

The Italian architect Francesco Borromini was born at Bissone on Lake Lugano, the son of the architect Giovanni Domenico Castelli. After a stay in Milan, he arrived at Rome c1620. At this time, his relation Maderno was the architect in charge of St Peter's. After Borromini had worked for a while as a stone-carver on decorative features of the new Basilica, Maderno employed him as an architectural draftsman. In this capacity, he worked not only on St Peter's, but also on the Palazzo Barberini and on the church and dome of S. Andrea della Valle. After his kinsman's death in 1629, Borromini worked under Bernini, who was appointed architect to the first two of these projects. From the appearance of certain architectural details executed during this period, it would appear that Bernini allowed his assistant a certain freedom of action in matters of design. With the completion of the major part of

the Palazzo Barberini in 1633, the two architects parted company.

In the following year Borromini received his first independent commission, the design for the monastery of S. Carlo alle Quattro Fontane. Building began in 1638 and was completed by 1641, with the exception of the facade. Working on a small, irregular site, Borromini designed not only a masterpiece of compression, but also a highly innovatory work of art—a most important milestone in the history of High Baroque. Rejecting the modular system of proportion usual in Renaissance architecture, he constructed the church on a diamond configuration of two equilateral triangles laid base to base. The severe geometry upon which this design rests is mitigated by capacious niches that break through the angles of the diamond. The resultant effect is of a sinuous oval space. This is taken up by the true oval of the honeycombed dome, the whole being held in play by an attached colonnade and a powerful entablature. The basic forms of the church interior find some reflection in that of the monastery cloister—an essentially oblong space softened by convex curvatures at the corners and enlivened by the elongated octagonal disposition of the colonnade.

As early as 1632 Bernini had recommended Borromini to the authorities of the Roman Archiginnasio as the architect to complete their scheme for the Archiginnasio (later Rome University). In 1642 Borromini began their church, S. Ivo, at the east end of the cortile built by Giacomo della Porta in the previous century. By 1650 work was substantially complete. Once again, Borromini turned to the geometry of the equilateral triangle—this time interpenetrated to form a hexagon. He tamed the angles of this underlying construction by manipulating the wall space into three semicircular bays interposed with three straight-sided ones culminating in convex curvatures. This sophisticated spatial configuration is varied still further by the use of three different types of wall niche—major ones of alternating type forming a central element to each bay, framed by pairs of a smaller uniform type. Borromini kept this highly pitched composition in order with stringcourses, a giant order of pilasters, and a heavy entablature. The entablature emphasizes the hexagonal form upon which the whole ensemble is based, and serves as a secure foundation for the extreme verticality of

the dome which maintains this star shape up to the circular terminating point of the lantern. The exterior of S. Ivo was as innovatory as its interior. On the outside the fundamentally hexagonal drum appears as a lobed circle. In place of an orthodox dome, this is surmounted by a stepped pyramid, itself vertically divided by concave ribs which spring outwards from the center to be let down by pedestals on to the perimeter of the drum. The lantern is also six-sided, consisting of paired columns framing concave faces which contrast with the convex forms of the dome and drum. Above this the building terminates in a remarkable ziggurat-like spiral.

With its complex and unorthodox orchestration of form, its rhythmical sense of movement and its dramatic intensity, S. Ivo was Borromini's masterpiece. Although he never surpassed this work as an artistic statement, he received many other important commissions. In 1646 he was faced with the difficult task of restoring the decayed interior of the Lateran basilica while preserving the old fabric. The architect resolved these contradictory requirements by encasing consecutive columns of the nave within a series of broad pillars, each framed by a pair of giant pilasters echoing the original disposition of the interior. In 1653 he was asked to complete the church of S. Agnese in Agone (Piazza Navona), which Rainaldi had begun the previous year. Borromini was only in charge of the work for two years before work was suspended, to be resumed two years later by the original architect. By careful alterations to the plan, Borromini succeeded in leaving his characteristic stamp of monumentality and spatial variety upon the ultimate design. The interior was recast as an octagon, enlivened by wall openings of varying size, and ennobled by a lofty drum; the facade was redesigned as a concave form with a slight central projection, the whole framed by two lofty towers.

Between 1653 and 1665, Borromini turned to S. Andrea delle Frate, adding a massive dome with a contrasting tower of intriguing complexity. During the 1650s, he began S. Maria dei Sette Dolori which remained unfinished on his death. In 1662 he began the church of the Propaganda Fide—to a daring design in which the verticals of the wall pilasters are continued by strips across the ceiling, forming a net vault. Between 1665 and 1667 he returned

Francesco Borromini: the facade of the Oratory of St Philip, Rome; begun in 1637

Further reading. Blunt, A. *Borromini*, Harmondsworth (1979). Portoghesi, P. "Borromini, Francesco", *Encyclopedia of World Art* vol. II, London (1960). Portoghesi, P. *Borromini nella Cultura Europea*, Rome (1964). Wittkower, R. *Art and Architecture in Italy: 1600–1750*, Harmondsworth (1973). Wittkower, R. "Francesco Borromini, his Character and Life" in Wittkower, R. *Studies in the Italian Baroque*, London (1975).

Bosch Hieronymus c1450–1516

Hieronymus Bosch spent his working life in 's-Hertogenbosch, a peaceful Dutch city. References to his life and to professional transactions occur in the municipal archives from 1474, and in those of the Brotherhood of our Lady, of which Bosch was a member from 1486 to 1516. Apart from these few documented facts, information is sparse. Nothing is known of Bosch's training or journeys, there are no dated or datable paintings, and his iconography is unusual and often baffling. Both his subject matter and his free and painterly brushwork, which contrasts sharply with the jewel-like brilliance of the Eyckian tradition, set him apart from the mainstream of Flemish art.

Bosch's outlook was deeply pessimistic and his art gave vivid expression to the profound anxieties that troubled the human mind as the Gothic world drew to its close. He was obsessed by sin and depravity, by the snares laid by the devil for the unwary human soul on its perilous journey through this life, and by the torments of hellfire. Bosch's powerful imagination created a haunted world where good and evil wage perpetual war. It is filled with strange monsters and hideous plants bearing evil fruits; fantastic structures and strange mineral forms are scattered through fiery landscapes. Yet, despite its difficulties, Bosch's art must be examined in the context of the orthodox religious beliefs of his time. Many of the sources of his iconography may be found in contemporary language, proverbs, and folklore, and in late medieval sermons and visionary poetry.

Bosch's chronology is highly controversial. A small group of biblical scenes and didactic genre paintings, characterized by

Hieronymus Bosch: detail of the Garden of Earthly Delights; panel; c1500–5. Prado, Madrid

to his first church, S. Carlo alle Quattro Fontane, to execute the facade. This consists of three two-story bays—a convex center, framed by concave elements. The horizontal "ripple" this imparts is matched by a vertical movement as the central bay abruptly switches from convex to concave at mid-upper story height before terminating in an oval medallion, which projects diagonally forwards and upwards. Although Borromini's fame rests primarily upon his church designs, he also executed a number of domestic buildings. The most important of these are the Oratory of St Philip Neri (1637–50), the Collegio di Propaganda Fide (1646–67), and the remodeling of the Palazzo Falconieri (c1640).

Borromini is a fascinating contrast to his great contemporary Bernini. The latter was an outgoing man of the world, the former a brooding melancholic who ultimately committed suicide. Bernini was an all-rounder, as much a sculptor as an architect; Borromini was an architectural specialist of great technical expertise. Like the rest of his contemporaries, Bernini sought to enhance the Renaissance tradition, which he could not seriously call into question. Borromini, on the other hand, broke with the past by a combination of fearless invention and respect for geometrical form and structural principles: it is precisely these characteristics that his work shares with the Gothic buildings it sometimes seems to imitate. And it was these same qualities that made Borromini the most revolutionary architect of his day.

stiff, awkwardly placed figures and hard, sharp brushwork, are generally accepted as early works. The themes of the genre paintings—*The Ship of Fools*, (Louvre, Paris), *The Stone Operation* (Prado, Madrid), and the *Seven Deadly Sins* (Prado, Madrid)—are those of contemporary satirical writing. Bosch castigates the vices of charlatans and quacks, of rich men, and of lecherous monks and nuns.

Two important triptychs, *The Last Judgment* (Alte Pinakothek, Munich) and *The Haywain* (Prado, Madrid), stand at the center of Bosch's middle period (c1485–1500). In the central panel of *The Last Judgment* Bosch created a highly original hellish landscape, infested by a swarm of devils and covered by burning pits and furnaces, bizarre constructions, and instruments of torture. Many of the monsters are half animal, half human. Others combine animal forms with inanimate ones, and startling juxtapositions of scale increase the horror of the effect—as in the egg, pierced by an arrow, that scuttles about on booted legs. Some of Bosch's imagery is developed from traditional medieval symbols and he was further inspired by the grotesques that appear on medieval manuscripts; yet there is no precedent for the extraordinary fertility of his invention.

The subject of *The Haywain* was new in Netherlandish art. The inner and outer wings show the Creation and Fall of Man (inner) and Hell (outer). On the central panel a crowd of demons pulls a vast haycart, with a pair of lovers on top, towards hell. Behind ride dignitaries of Church and State, while beside it an unruly mob fight over handfuls of hay. Their greed and depravity is the subject of the painting. Bosch's source was a contemporary ballad or proverb; the hay also symbolizes the worthlessness of all material gain.

The Deadly Sin of Lust is almost certainly the subject of Bosch's most difficult triptych, *The Garden of Earthly Delights* (Prado, Madrid), probably painted after 1500. The central panel, again set between the Creation of Man and Hell, shows a garden landscape of enchanting and fragile beauty, painted in pearly pinks and blues. Here, groups of small nude figures, spread out decoratively as though on a tapestry, indulge in every kind of sexual activity. They ride on beasts, cavort in ponds and streams, nibble at luscious fruits, and entwine themselves with giant birds. Almost all the details are erotic symbols drawn

Abraham Bosse: Hearing, from the series The Five Senses; etching. Metropolitan Museum, New York

from contemporary folklore. Bosch certainly intended to represent not innocence but depravity; the surface beauty of the painting underlines the alluring and deceptive pleasures of sin, and the soft fruits symbolize the transience of carnal pleasure.

Especially in his later years, Bosch was fascinated by the temptations and torments that beset those hermits and holy men who sought to achieve union with God by a life spent in contemplation and mortification of the flesh. A series of paintings on this theme culminates in the brilliantly colored, signed triptych of *The Temptation of St Anthony* (c1500; National Museum of Art, Lisbon). Bosch drew the details of the story from the *Lives of the Fathers* and *The Golden Legend*. The left and right wings show traditional scenes—the saint attacked by demons and rescued, unconscious, by his friends, and his temptation by a naked devil-queen. The central scene, however, is far more complex and its details have been interpreted in many different ways. St Anthony, his hand raised in blessing, kneels before a ruined tomb. He is surrounded by a throng of devils who symbolize the temptations that had beset him in the desert. They cluster and press around him with a terrifying intensity, and many of their bodies are fearsome mixtures of human, animal, and inanimate forms.

Bosch painted many other traditional Christian subjects from the life of Christ, especially scenes from the Passion. The

triptych of the *Adoration of the Magi* (Prado, Madrid) is one of his most baffling works. The scene takes place before a dilapidated hut, in which lurks a crowd of men with menacing faces and bizarre clothing. Their presence has never been satisfactorily explained, but they suggest the universal conflict of good and evil: reminders of the all-pervading presence of evil recur throughout the splendid panoramic landscape which links the three panels. A series of half-length paintings of the Passion of Christ, which may date from late in Bosch's life, are more straightforward. These exploit to the full the contrast between Christ's humility and the bestiality of his persecutors. In Bosch's last Passion scene, *Christ carrying the Cross* (Museum of Fine Arts, Ghent), the deformed and leering faces of the mob are grotesquely ugly. Yet Christ remains aloof and serene; his carrying of the cross promises a victory over evil which was Bosch's final message.

Further reading. Galdass, L. von *Hieronymous Bosch*, London (1960). Gibson, W. *Hieronymous Bosch*, London (1973). Whinney, M. *Early Flemish Painting* London (1968).

Bosse Abraham 1602–76

The French print-maker and book-illustrator Abraham Bosse wrote one of the first treatises on engraving. His early work consists of illustrations to novels and religious books. During the 1630s he produced prints illustrating contemporary life, including the *Mariage à la Ville* and *Mariage à la Campagne* series, 1633. He also produced biblical prints, notably the *Wise and Foolish Virgins* series (c1635) in which the figures are depicted in contemporary bourgeois costume.

Botero Fernando 1932–

Botero was born in the remote provincial capital of Medellín, Colombia. By the age of 16 he was contributing illustrations to the local newspaper, *El Colombiano*, and in 1951 was given his first one-man show in Bogotá. His early watercolors were influenced by Orozco (1883–1949) and Picasso (1881–1973). From 1952 to 1955 he lived in Europe, studying at the Academy of Fine Arts of San Fernando in Madrid and subsequently in Florence, spending vacations in Paris. Although he was interested in modern art, he concentrated on the Old Masters in the Prado, the Louvre, and in Italy. By the late 1950s he was elaborating his idiosyncratic mature style. He has described a crucial discovery made when seeing how a small mark placed on the drawing of a mandoline emphasized its plasticity and monumentality. He began to treat all his subject matter in this way, rendering figures, fruits, still lives, and landscapes in huge, visually powerful forms. Images that he plundered from such European painters as Mantegna, Velazquez, Rubens, Ingres, Manet, and Bonnard he dealt with in the same way, sometimes subtly altering the original. When asked why he painted fat figures, he replied, "I don't. They all look rather slim to me." His figures are not so much fat as rendered formally massive through carefully adjusted changes of scale.

The world Botero creates is imaginary, a poetic distortion of the ordinary world, but rooted in Latin America. "Latin America is one of the few places left in the world which can be transformed into myths", he said. "People have a cloudy idea about Latin America and that is a good thing for an artist. Places which have been overexplained and overexposed offer little possibility for poetic transformation..." Botero finds this transformation easier at a distance, and having lived in Mexico City and in the U.S.A. now lives in Paris. He draws his subject matter from the provincial towns of his youth: parents and children, priests, nuns (as in *The Nun*,

1979; private collection), bishops, cardinals, soldiers gaze impersonally out of the canvas as in anonymous *ex-votos* (see, for example, his *New-born Nun*, 1975, and *Mother Superior Levitating*; both in private collections). He has made sculptures based on the figures in his oil paintings, and he also draws abundantly. The sensual brilliance of his color, particularly in his studies of tropical fruit (for example, *Still Life with Water Melon*, 1974; Collection of Mrs Frances K. Lloyd, Paris), is sometimes unjustly overlooked.

Both Jan c1618–52

Jan Both was a Dutch landscape painter and etcher. After training under Bloemaert in Utrecht he traveled to Rome, where between 1638 and 1641 he developed a style of painting which was to make him, along with Asselijn, Dujardin, and Nicolaes Berchem, one of the principal Dutch "Italianizing" landscapists of the mid 17th century. Claude's ideal landscapes of the Roman Campagna, with their warm, golden light and Arcadian settings, were a decisive influence, although Both's own paintings reveal a rather more objective, precise approach to naturalistic detail and light effects. His views are less often imaginary than Claude's, and he tended to replace figures from myth or legend with peasants, travelers, or such motifs as artists sketching. These figures and the grazing animals in Both's scenes may sometimes have been the result of collaboration with other painters. Both was instrumental in popularizing Italianate landscapes in Holland, and his serene views with their

Fernando Botero: The Nun; oil on canvas; 150×170cm (59×67in); 1979. Private collection

mellow light effects were also influential on those artists such as Aelbert Cuyp (1620–91) who remained faithful to their native scenery. He painted a few pictures of the Dutch countryside himself, but it was his Italianate landscapes that collectors admired, and which gave him an international reputation until the mid 19th century.

Botticelli Sandro 1444–1510

The nickname "Botticelli", meaning "little barrels", was given to Alessandro dei Filipepi, one of the leading Italian painters of the Florentine school. Vasari describes him as the pupil of Filippo Lippi, and he was probably among that master's assistants during the painting of the frescoes at Prato and Spoleto in the 1460s. He is also mentioned as being a member of the Compagnia di San Luca in Florence "with" Filippino Lippi in 1472. His first datable work is *Fortitude* (Uffizi, Florence) for which he was paid in 1470. This panel was intended for the Council Room of the Mercatanzia in Florence, together with six other personifications of Virtues by Piero del Pollaiuolo. It is therefore not surprising that the work of that artist proved an important influence on Botticelli. The linearity of contour this new contact brought about can be seen particularly clearly in *St Sebastian* (Staatliche Museen, Berlin) which was apparently dated January 1473 on its original frame.

From 1474 Botticelli's name appears regularly in the account books of members of the Medici family, for whom he painted banners, portraits, and altarpieces as well as paintings with allegorical or mythological subject matter. The *Adoration of the Magi* (c1477; Uffizi, Florence) which originally hung in the church of S. Maria Novella, contains portraits of several members of the Medici family and other prominent Florentine citizens. The composition, with its strong pyramidal structure and partly architectural background, acts as an important predecessor to Leonardo's unfinished *Adoration* of 1481–1482. A similar solidarity and mastery of spatial contruction is seen in the frescoed figure of *St Augustine* painted by Botticelli at the same time as Ghirlandaio's compan-

Jan Both: A View on the Tiber near the Ripa Grande, Rome (?); oak panel; 43×56cm (17×22in). National Gallery, London

ion fresco of *St Jerome*, which is dated 1480.

In the following year Botticelli, with Ghirlandaio, Perugino, and Cosimo Rosselli, was called to Rome by Pope Sixtus IV to decorate the walls of the Sistine Chapel with scenes from the Old and New Testaments. Botticelli was in control of the scheme and executed three of the frescoes: *The Story of Moses, The Punishment of Korah*, and *The Temptation of Christ*. The large scale of these works and the attempt to include several stages of narrative in one composition were not fully mastered by the artist: they remain confused and disorganized.

Botticelli's allegorical paintings, his most successful and best-known works, are largely undocumented but should be dated in the late 1470s. Their precise meaning, as well as the circumstances surrounding their commissioning, is still uncertain. The *Primavera* (Uffizi, Florence) was probably painted for Lorenzo di Pierfrancesco de' Medici (a member of a cadet branch of the family) to hang in the Villa di Castello which Lorenzo bought in 1477. The theme was almost certainly provided by the Humanist Poliziano, and concerns Mercury with the three Graces, Spring, Flora, and a nymph being pursued by Zephyr or

the North Wind. Precise identification of the figures is frustrated by the fact that Botticelli's female types rarely change, whether he is depicting the Virgin Mary, Pallas, or Venus. This observation has led Sir Ernst Gombrich, among others, to believe that the allegories were partially intended as exemplars, with Venus and Pallas representing Beauty and Reason. The *Primavera* is clearly related to *The Birth of Venus* (Uffizi, Florence), in which the precise event depicted is clearer. Complex political undertones have been read into *Pallas and the Centaur* (Uffizi, Florence), in which the Medicean connection is stressed by the family emblems adorning Pallas's gown. To these allegories must be added Botticelli's exquisite illustrations to Dante's *Inferno*, drawn for Lorenzo di Pierfrancesco de' Medici (now divided between the Staatliche Museen in West and East Berlin and the Vatican Library, Rome). Apart from his works for members of the Medici family, Botticelli received many commissions from other prominent members of Florentine society. Among his allegorical paintings these included an important (but now fragmentary) series of frescoes at the Villa Lemmi, which probably commemorated the marriage of Lorenzo Tornabuoni to Giovanna degli

Albizzi in 1486 (Louvre, Paris). *Mars and Venus* (National Gallery, London) was probably painted for a member of the Vespucci family. Although we know nothing about the commissioning of the *Calumny of Apelles* (c1495; Uffizi, Florence), Vasari reports having seen it in the house of Fabio Segni.

Both the *Calumny* and the Dante illustrations can be dated on stylistic and historical evidence to the last decades of the 15th century. In them we see a heightening of emotion, an elongation of human proportions, and the development of a swirling and swaying movement which is more characteristic of late Gothic than of Renaissance art. These antinaturalistic tendencies of Botticelli's late works are seen at their most extreme in religious works: the *Allegory of the Cross* (William Hayes Fogg Art Museum, Cambridge, Mass.), the Munich *Pietà* (Alte Pinakothek, Munich), and the *Mystic Nativity* (1500; National Gallery, London). All of these are datable to the last decade of the artist's life, and are related to the preaching activity of Savonarola in the 1490s. In the *Mystic Nativity*, Botticelli's only signed work, the scale of the figures is decided by their relative importance rather than their distance from the viewer: the dramatic intensity resembles the work of contemporary artists of northern Europe (particularly Grünewald) rather than that of any Italian of the period.

The *Mystic Nativity* is Botticelli's last major work, although he did not die until 1510, nine years after it was completed. His previous standing among the leading artists of his day ensured that even though the new generation of artists, such as Leonardo, Raphael, and Michelangelo, received the most important commissions, Botticelli's opinion was still valued. In 1502 Francesco Malatesta suggested to Isabella d'Este that Botticelli should be invited to complement Mantegna's contribution to her Studiolo, and two years later he was among those who were called upon to decide on the placing of Michelangelo's *David* in Florence.

Further reading. Ettlinger, L.D. and H.S. *Botticelli*, London (1976). Gombrich, E. "Botticelli's Mythologies", *Journal of the Warburg and Courtauld Institutes* vol. VIII, London (1945). Salvini, R. *Tutta la Pittura di Botticelli*, Milan (1958). Santi, B. *Botticelli*, New York (1986). Venturi, L. *Botticelli*, London (1961).

Botticini Francesco 1446–97

The Florentine painter Francesco Botticini trained under Neri di Bicci. His only documented work is the *Tabernacle of the Holy Sacrament* (Galleria della Collegiata, Empoli), commissioned in 1484, delivered in 1491, then finished by his son Raffaello in 1504. All other works are attributions. Their variety of styles betrays a variety of influence—Verrochio, Antonio Pollaiuolo, and Botticelli among others. This may indicate a rather unimaginative eclecticism or possibly the inclusion in his oeuvre of works not actually his. The *Assumption of the Virgin* (c1474–6; National Gallery, London) is a rare instance in the Quattrocento of the depiction of a heresy.

Bouchardon Edmé 1698–1762

Born at Chaumont, the son of a provincial sculptor, Edmé Bouchardon was a pupil first of his father and later, in Paris, of Guillaume I Coustou. In 1722 he won the first prize for sculpture at the Académie in Paris, and the following year left for Rome. He was to remain there for nine years, gaining considerable fame. His bust of Philipp Stosch (1727; Staatliche Museen, Berlin) in strict classical Roman form is representative of this period. Bouchardon was the champion of the return to classical values in French sculpture; his style is a complete antithesis of that of Jean-Baptiste Lemoyne, who represents the Rococo current. He was an artist of reason and

Francesco Botticini (attrib.): Madonna and Child; panel; 81×66cm (32×26in). Brooks Memorial Art Gallery, Memphis, Tenn.

Edmé Bouchardon: Christ at the Column;
stone; height 240cm (94in); c 1735.
St-Sulpice, Paris

François Boucher: Diana Resting after her Bath; oil on canvas; 57×73cm (22×29in); 1742. Louvre,
Paris

intellect, rather than of passion and
expression; his work appealed to the intel-
ligentsia of the time rather than to the
King, who preferred Lemoyne.

In his day Bouchardon was thought to be
the greatest sculptor alive—a reputation
not wholly deserved. His art has proved a
little too frigid and cerebral for the taste of
later generations. Bouchardon was one of
the finest draftsmen of his time, and his
monumental sculpture, such as the fountain of the Rue de Grenelle, Paris (commissioned in 1739), is superbly designed. In
his last years he was occupied with the
colossal equestrian statue of Louis XV for
the Place de la Concorde. The work was

designed as a reevocation of a Roman
Imperial monument; it was completed
after Bouchardon's death by Jean-Baptiste
Pigalle, and was destroyed during the
Revolution.

Boucher François 1703–70

The French artist François Boucher was
born in Paris. The son of a minor painter,
he spent some months as a pupil of François Lemoyne. However, his talents as a
draftsman attracted him to book illustration, and he worked for the prolific engraver J.F. Cars. This in turn led him in the
early 1720s to work on the *Oeuvre Gravée*
of Watteau, sponsored by Jean de Julli-
enne. His intense study of Watteau's works
confirmed his spirited and graceful draftsmanship, his sense of fantasy, and his fine
observation. The results of this influence
are to be seen in his elegant and celebrated
illustrations to an edition of Molière's
works (1734). Meanwhile, he had won the
Prix de Rome in 1723, and traveled to
Italy in 1728. He spent three years in
Rome and almost certainly north Italy and
Venice. He took note of the lighter aspects
of late Baroque and Rococo art in Rome,
where Franco-Italian artistic relations were
close.

His reception piece for the Académie,
Rinaldo and Armida (1734; Louvre, Paris)
already displays the amorous subject
matter, graceful style, and artificial color
of his maturity. In the same year, Oudry
employed him as a designer at the tapestry

works in Beauvais. Among his most delightful and amusing designs for Beauvais
are those with fanciful Chinese subjects
(oil sketches c1742; Musée des Beaux-
Arts, Besançon) for the *Chinese Tapestries*
given by Louis XV to Emperor Ch'ien
Lung of China, which reveal Boucher's
brilliance and facility. In 1755, he was
made Inspector of the Gobelins tapestry
works. Working on tapestry design encouraged the decorative qualities of
Boucher's art, and many of his paintings
were made for a specific decorative context. Thus, together with other artists, he
executed paintings for the new Rococo
rooms at the Hotel de Soubise by Boffrand,
and for the *Petits Appartements* at Versailles in the mid–late 1730s. His work perfectly suited the smaller and more intimate
scale of 18th-century Parisian interiors.
His subjects are mainly shepherds and
shepherdesses, or minor gods and goddesses, sporting in impossibly pastel Arcadian landscapes.

With the ascendancy of Madame de Pompadour in the favor of Louis XV, during
the 1740s, Boucher found a ready patroness: their names will always be linked,
Boucher expressing her fashionable and
influential Rococo taste. He also made
some sensitive and cultivated portraits of
her. The most important pictures that
Boucher painted for her are the *Rising*- and
the *Setting of the Sun* (1753; Wallace
Collection, London); these were originally
designed as tapestry cartoons, but were
completed and acquired for Madame de

Eugène Boudin: Entering the Port of Le Havre; oil on canvas; 42×55cm (17×22in); 1864. Private collection

Pompadour's Château de Bellevue. They represent Boucher's grand manner, and mark the high point of his career. In 1765, he was made First Painter to the King, and Director of the Académie.

By the 1760s Boucher's pictures had become rather cluttered and his style more mannered. His work failed to appeal to that rising taste for a more "serious" art which culminated in Neoclassicism, and he was increasingly attacked by critics such as Denis Diderot.

Boucicaut Master *fl. c1400–c20*

The Boucicaut Master is the name by which the anonymous artist of a Book of Hours made for the Maréchal de Boucicaut c1405–8 (Musée Jacquemart-André, Paris, MS. 2) is known. The 42 full-page miniatures in this work supply the basis for further attributions to the artist or his workshop, and show that he was extremely active in Paris during the first two decades of the 15th century.

The Boucicaut Master ranks as one of the important forerunners of 15th-century Flemish realism. His outstanding innovations were in landscape painting, where he was a pioneer of aerial perspective (for example the *Visitation* in the Boucicaut Hours), and also in the development of architectural interiors conceived as realistic settings for figure compositions. In religious manuscripts, church interiors are often associated with the scene of the Annunciation or with the celebration of the Mass for the Dead (for example the Book of Hours MS. 16997 in the British Library, London). Domestic settings that encourge the depiction of naturalistic detail are also explored. The most sumptu-

ous is in the *Dialogues de Pierre Salmon* (Bibliothèque Publique et Universitaire, Geneva); it shows Charles VI receiving Salmon in the presence of princes. The consistency with which he pursues the investigation of these specific artistic problems distinguishes his entire career.

In Paris the Boucicaut Master clearly associated with the most distinguished artists and patrons of his time. His "international style" developed there, but it also owes much to Italy and Flanders. Numerous surviving works, now scattered throughout the world, include a Book of Hours bearing the arms of the Visconti family of Milan (Biblioteca Reale, Turin).

The identification of the Boucicaut Master with Jacques Coene, a member of a family of painters in Bruges, has been suggested. Coene was living in Paris in 1398, when he dictated notes for a treatise on painting (published in Merrifield, M. *Original Treatises dating from the 12th–18th centuries on the Arts of Painting . . .*, London, 1849). In 1399 he was sent to Milan to design the Cathedral; but he returned to Paris before 1404, when he was one of three artists illustrating a Bible commissioned by Philip the Bold, Duke of Burgundy. No authenticated works by him are known to survive, but his identification with the Boucicaut Master would be compatible with the origins of the latter's style.

Boudin Eugène 1824–98

The French painter Eugène Boudin was born in Honfleur. In 1844 he opened a stationery shop in Le Havre, the town in which he met Constant Troyon, Eugène Isabey, Thomas Couture, and Millet. He became a painter in the late 1840s, studying in Paris and the Low Countries, and began to paint coastal scenes in the 1850s. He met the young Monet c1856, and introduced him to landscape painting. Boudin is best known for his paintings of Trouville beach, from 1862 onwards (of which there are many examples in the Nouveau Musée des Beaux-Arts, Le Havre), which show the resort's fashionable holidaymakers. He also traveled widely to paint—to the Low Countries, to Venice, and all over France. He greatly valued the spontaneity of his first impressions of nature, but seems to have worked up his paintings in the studio.

Bourdon Sébastien 1616–71

The French painter Sébastien Bourdon was born in Montpellier. After living for some time in Paris, he spent the years 1634–7 in Rome. Here he imitated the styles of the Bambocciati and Castiglione, as well as those of Poussin and Claude. He visited Venice, then returned to Paris. He was appointed Court Painter to the Queen of Sweden in 1652. Returning to Paris in 1654 he then spent the years 1659–63 in Montpellier. Bourdon is the perfect mirror to the development of French 17th-century painting (and its fashionable expansion through Europe) because of his imitative abilities. He moved from genre scenes, which always sold well, to imitations of Claude that verged on fraud (hence Claude's *Liber Veritatis*—to protect him against copyists). He found success in Paris with a loose, Venetian-based Baroque style, and also as a portrait-painter. But in the mid 1650s he adopted the very severe manner of Poussin, as in his *Martyrdom of St Andrew* (Musée Fabre, Montpellier).

Bourgeois Louise 1911–

The French-born American artist Louise Bourgeois studied mathematics at the Sorbonne, Paris, then art at the École de Louvre, the Académie des Beaux-Arts and in the studio of Ferdinand Léger. She emigrated to America in 1938 and in the 1940s produced totem-like sculptures consisting of slender wooden forms (often painted black or white) loosely suggesting groups of human figures. Sensitive to the work of sculptors such as Isamu Noguchi, she had by the 1960s evolved her mature style. Using latex and plaster, she created a variety of semi-Abstract forms which, with breast-like domes, phallic columns, fleshy openings and deep hollows, are strongly if obscurely reminiscent of the body, with a sometimes disturbingly visceral, fetishistic quality, as in *The Quartered One* (1964–65; Museum of Modern Art, New York).

Further reading. Wye, D. *Louise Bourgeois*, New York (1982).

Bouts Dieric c1415–75

The painter Dieric Bouts, born in Haarlem, had settled in Louvain by 1457; he had married there c1448. His solemn works

Dieric Bouts: The Last Supper; oil on panel; 180×150cm (71×59in); c1464–7. St Pierre, Louvain

are full of religious feeling; they are deliberately restrained in gesture and expression, and occasionally border on a naive stiffness. He was a gifted colorist and exceptionally sensitive to the effects of light.

He was early influenced by Albert van Ouwater, but in Flanders came into contact, perhaps as a pupil, with Rogier van der Weyden. The attitude of the latter is strong in a group of early works, among them a *Deposition* in the Louvre, Paris, and a triptych of the *Deposition* (Royal Chapel Museum, Granada). Bouts' figures are calmer than van der Weyden's and his compositions less powerfully rhythmical.

Two fully documented works date from late in his life. In the triptych of *The Last Supper* (1464–7; St Pierre, Louvain) Christ's dramatic words are greeted by the Apostles with deep reverence. The scene, set in a realistic Flemish interior, is hushed and still. In the four wing panels Bouts excels as a landscapist; the terrain is rocky and open, and his treatment of the effects of shimmering light on distant hills shows a remarkable understanding of atmospheric perspective.

Two large panels, *The Judgment of the Emperor Otto* (Musées Royaux des Beaux-Arts de Belgique, Brussels) belong to an uncompleted commission for four paintings about the administration of justice, ordered by the town council of Louvain in 1468. In the right panel a hideous injustice is revealed and the austere control of the tall, dignified figures underlines the pathos of the situation. His one dated work is the *Portrait of a Man* (1462; National Gallery, London). He also did a series of tender paintings of the Virgin and Child.

Brailes W. de *fl.* 1230–60

The English medieval illuminator W. de Brailes can almost certainly be identified with a resident of Oxford called William de Brailes. De Brailes appears to have been an ecclesiastic head of a professional workshop that produced liturgical books illustrated in a distinctive style. His signed portrait is to be found in two of these. One of them consists of picture leaves from a Psalter (*c*1240–50; Fitzwilliam Museum, Cambridge) where his soul is shown being received by St Michael in a Last Judgment.

De Brailes was often dependent upon earlier native traditions of imagery; for example the beasts beneath the feet of

Christ and the type of mouth of hell shown in the Last Judgment can be found in Anglo-Saxon and later English art. In many of his illustrations an unusual aspect of a subject is given prominence, or a particular figure in the action vividly characterized, thus revealing the artist's considerable originality. Among the scenes in a Book of Hours (*c*1250; British Library, London) are some episodes from Christ's Passion. By juxtaposing these with the three denials of St Peter, as well as adding the weeping saint outside the frame, de Brailes interprets a standard biblical subject as a human story seen from an individual point of view. A similar lively and idiosyncratic approach to narrative illustration is found in the scene from a Psalter (*c*1250–60; New College, Oxford) of Jonah being thrust vigorously into the mouth of a whale. This is probably the latest manuscript known from the workshop because it is the most advanced in style.

Particularly characteristic of de Brailes' personal style are the tightly drawn, openeyed faces of his neat, active figures. However, the arrangement of the compositions in medallions, the delicate foliate ornament, and the elegant proportions of the figures are more generally typical of mid-13th-century English Gothic painting.

Bramante Donato *c*1444–1514

Donato Bramante, considered by his contemporaries to have restored the true principles of ancient architecture, is acknowledged today as the founder of the High Renaissance architectural style. Under the patronage of Julius II (1503–13), Bramante, Michelangelo, and Raphael renewed the artistic greatness appropriate to Rome as heir to the Roman Empire and as the center of Christendom. The city's heritage was symbolized by Bramante redesigning St Peter's as "the dome of the Pantheon over the vaults of the Temple of Peace".

Although we know nothing of his early life, Bramante was probably trained as a painter in Urbino, near his birthplace. At the court of Federico da Montefeltro he could have met Alberti, Piero della Francesca, and, most important as an architectural influence, Francesco di Giorgio. His first certain work, the facade painting of the Palazzo del Podestà, Bergamo (1477), already demonstrates an interest in architecture, as well as in perspective illusion. A

signed engraving of 1481 contains many elements which were to appear in his buildings in Milan, where he was by then living, attracted, like Leonardo, to the court of Lodovico il Moro. Leonardo's architectural drawings, the early Christian churches of Milan, and the logical harmonies of the buildings in Urbino, were the formative influences on Bramante's architecture. Alberti's Mantuan churches are also reflected in Bramante's first church, S. Maria presso S. Satiro (1482–6). During his work on this building it developed from a simple rectangular oratory to a Latin Cross basilica with nave and aisles. Site restrictions forced him to truncate the choir into a *trompe-l'oeil* backcloth, using the perspectival skills of his painter's training. The somber monumentality of the nave, with its massive arch and pier system and illusionistically coffered barrel vault, owes something to Alberti's S. Andrea.

The tribune of S. Maria delle Grazie (1493) was commissioned by Lodovico Sforza as a vast family mausoleum. The plan is like a gigantic version of Brunelleschi's Old Sacristy, with semicircular apses added on three sides. The uncluttered articulation of huge spaces foreshadows Bramante's mature Roman works. His other Milanese work was at S. Ambrogio: it includes the elegant Corinthian loggia of the Canonica (1492), with its bizarre tree-trunk columns at the corners, and the Doric cloister (1497–8), whose upper story suggests a first-hand knowledge of ancient Roman examples. From 1488 he was consulted, as were Leonardo and Francesco di Giorgio, about the rebuilding of the Duomo at Pavia. At Vigevano (1492) he designed the town's central piazza, whose arcaded sides were painted with illusionistic frescoes.

By 1499 the French occupation of Milan had forced Bramante to Rome. Taken up by the entourage of Alexander VI, he first designed the cloister of S. Maria della Pace. More consistently antique than his S. Ambrogio cloisters, it retains the graceful linearity characteristic of Urbino. The commission for the *tempietto* at S. Pietro in Montorio followed. Despite the inscription dated 1502, the masterly design of this tiny round church has often earned it a later dating. The first Renaissance building to employ correctly the full Doric order, it was inspired both by the column-encircled temples of Antiquity and by Francesco di Giorgio's architectural drawings. Bramante's "House of Raphael" (Palazzo

Donato Bramante: the cloister of S. Maria della Pace, Rome; designed in 1499, built 1500-4

Caprini, now destroyed) probably also dates from before 1505. Built in the new street leading to the Vatican, it provided a perfect model for the small palaces needed by the expanding papal bureaucracy. Its sequence of rusticated ground floor with shops and applied Classical orders on the first floor influenced domestic architecture up to the 20th century, as did its innovatory use of stucco-covered brick.

Bramante was to be the architect of Julius II's plan for the renewal of Rome. It began at the Vatican, where he connected the palace and the Villa Belvedere with an ascending series of courtyards flanked by arcaded corridors. From the papal apartments a perspectival vista (now interrupted by a library wing) ran through ramps and fountains to an *exedra* at the uppermost level. While its axiality recalled the ancient temple complex at Palestrina, the symbolism of the Cortile del Belvedere (1507-7) combined overtones of Roman villa and theater. Julius II's most optimistic project was to replace Old St Peter's with a great

new basilica. The foundation medal and Bramante's "parchment plan" give some idea of the unexecuted first project: a vast Greek Cross with four subsidiary crosses and corner towers, it recalled Leonardo's centralized church plans. The single-shelled Pantheon-type dome was to be supported on four great isolated piers of original and influential design. Work began on these piers; by Bramante's death in 1514 they had been vaulted with crossing arches, and a choir had been built, using the 15th-century foundations built for Nicholas V. A giant pilaster order— Doric on the exterior, Corinthian on the inside—gave vertical unity.

The plan for the new Rome extended beyond the Vatican. Across the river in the old city Bramante built a new street, the Via Giulia, to be dominated by a colossal Palace of Justice, of which only the rusticated base was executed. The church of S. Celso (now destroyed), a small scale version of the first St Peter's plan, was begun (in 1509) on another new street, the Via

de' Banchi. The tribune of S. Maria del Popolo (c1507-9) remains relatively unchanged. Here Bramante added a funerary chapel and choir to an existing church. The coffered barrel vault and simplified shell-niche apse are a stripped version of the destroyed St Peter's choir, and the square tomb chapel is lit by the so-called "Serliana" windows invented by Bramante.

As Vasari realized, the ambition of Julius II was necessary for the fulfillment of Bramante's architectural genius. Their joint enthusiasm for destruction and renewal earned the architect the nickname "Bramante ruinante", and in a contemporary satirical dialogue the dead Bramante is heard outlining to St Peter his plan for the redevelopment of heaven.

Further reading. Bruschi, A. *Bramante*, London (1977). Heydenreich, L. and Lotz, W. *Architecture in Italy: 1400–1600*, Harmondsworth (1974). Murray, P. *The Architecture of the Italian Renaissance*, London (1969).

Bramantino c1460–1536

The Lombard painter Bartolommeo Suardi known as Bramantino was, as his name suggests, trained by Bramante. His style remained relatively free from the influence of Leonardo, and his works, for instance the *Adoration of the Magi* (1501–3; National Gallery, London) and *Crucifixion*, (1510–11; Pinacoteca di Brera, Milan) show a severe, static, and monumental vision of Antiquity. He was inspired partly by Milanese masters like Vincenzo Foppa, but also by Mantegna and the still, mathematical tradition of Piero della Francesca, which he must have learned from his master. All his figures are like statues, and his backgrounds, often very abstracted, are rocky and of a steely hardness. In 1508 Bramantino was sufficiently successful to be summoned to Rome to paint in the Stanze of the Vatican, but he was soon replaced by Raphael and returned to Milan. Alongside Leonardo he had a considerable influence on the next generation of Lombard painters, notably on Bernardino Luini and Gaudenzio Ferrari, though his later works were increasingly dry and abstracted.

Brancusi Constantin 1876–1957

Constantin Brancusi left his peasant family in the village of Hobitza in Rumania when he was 11 years old. He lived and worked in Paris for over 50 years, becoming the great innovator in early modern sculpture. But he never broke his ties with his homeland, and in his old age his peasant roots became a significant part of his legend.

After leaving home, Brancusi supported himself by menial work, first at Tirgu Jiu, later at Craiova where, in 1895, he entered the School of Arts and Crafts and specialized in sculpture. After graduating with honors in 1898, he went on to the School of Fine Arts in Bucharest for a further three years' study. During this period he won several prizes and modeled a number of portraits of flawless academic competence. An outstanding work was his lifesize *écorché* anatomical figure (without the skin, displaying the muscles) which he made under the guidance of his anatomy instructor. A cast of this *écorché* is now in the Medical Institute, Jassy.

Leaving Bucharest in 1903, Brancusi traveled slowly across Europe. He arrived in Paris in 1904 and in 1905 enrolled at the École des Beaux-Arts. Few works from these years have survived, though the re-cords taken by Brancusi himself—he was an enthusiastic photographer—show that by 1906, when he was 30, he was a sculptor of ability and refinement. Yet he remained a student, perhaps because he received a small grant from Rumania, perhaps because he had yet to discover his own vision. Two works that do survive, *Portrait of Nicolae Darascu* (1906; bronze; Museum of Art, Bucharest) and *Torment* (also called *Pain*; bronze; David Thompson Collection, Pittsburgh, Pa.), the bust of a small boy, are works of real power, strongly influenced by Rodin. Indeed, Brancusi worked briefly in Rodin's studio. But he quickly left, saying: "nothing can grow in the shadow of great trees".

Nineteen hundred and seven was the turning point for Brancusi, as for other artists of his generation. Because of his age, he had to leave the École des Beaux-Arts. Also, he received a commission to make a memorial (now in Dumbrava Cemetery, Buzau, Rumania) to Petre Stanescu (completed in 1910). The bronze figures—a bust of Stanescu and a symbolic naked female mourner—are modeled in bold, simple forms. It was a determined rejection of Rodin and the tradition Brancusi later called "beefsteak" sculpture. He emphasized this rejection most significantly when he chose Rodin's most famous motif for his own major work of 1907. Brancusi's *The Kiss* is the antithesis of Rodin's; it is directly carved, not modeled in clay, its forms are simple and block-like, and, above all, it is spiritual not sensual. This *Kiss*, the first of six versions, marked Brancusi's conversion: he called it his "road to Damascus". (*The Kiss*, 1908, limestone, is in the Musée National d'Art Moderne, Paris, as are three versions from 1910).

In the following three years he experimented with styles of simplification and primitivism, like his contemporaries Picasso, Derain, and Epstein. Throughout his career, Brancusi was to invent a handful of basic motifs and make numerous variations on them. By 1910, he had established the most important of these motifs, a female head and neck often called *The Muse* (marble; Solomon R. Guggenheim Museum, New York). The strange variant of this—the head on its side, like an egg—was later developed as *The Sleeping Muse* (two versions from 1908: plaster in Musée d'Art Moderne de la Ville de Paris, bronze example in the Art Institute of Chicago), *Prometheus* (1911; marble; Philadelphia Museum of Art), *The New Born* (1915; marble; Philadelphia Museum of Art), *Sculpture for the Blind* (1924; Philadelphia Museum of Art), and the fragmentary *Female Torso* (1909; marble; Craiova Museum of Art). In 1912 he created the first *Maiastra* (white marble; Museum of Modern Art, New York)—the golden bird of Slav folklore—which led to numerous birds throughout his career, including at least 16 versions of *Bird in Space*: an image like a frozen flame. (The first version, from 1919, in polished bronze, is in the Museum of Modern Art, New York.)

By 1910, Brancusi was one of the circle of the avant-garde in Paris. His friends included Picasso, Matisse, and Apollinaire. He taught Modigliani to carve: his own *Head of a Girl* of 1907 (now lost) anticipates Modigliani's style. In 1913, he had five pieces in the famous Armory Show in New York. The following year he had his first one-man exhibition in New York, at Alfred Stieglitz's Gallery of the Photo-Secession. It was also in New York, in the same year, that he found his most important patron, the lawyer John Quinn. By the time Quinn died, in 1924, he had bought 27 pieces by Brancusi for almost 21,000 dollars.

Because of his nationality, Brancusi was exempt from French military service during the First World War and worked steadily throughout it. He emerged to become one of the most famous sculptors of the day, celebrated by the international smart set of the 1920s. In 1921 *The Little Review* devoted an entire issue to him.

By this time Brancusi had developed two distinctive kinds of image. There were the images he would develop in several or many versions, in marble or bronze, or in both. These images appear at first sight to quite abstract and very simple, geometrical and symmetrical. But in fact they are always representational and their forms are elusive and subtle. As Brancusi said: "they are imbeciles who call my work Abstract; that which they call Abstract is the most realist, because what is real is not the exterior form but the idea, the essence of things."

These extremes of simplification lead to ambiguities. *Princess X* was removed from the Salon des Indépendants of 1920 because her bosom, neck, and head had been reduced to bulbous curves that looked undeniably phallic. And in 1926, U.S.

Constantin Brancusi: The Prodigal Son; oak on stone base; height 45cm (18in); c1915. Philadelphia Museum of Art

Georges Braque: The Guéridon; oil on canvas; 117×81cm (46×32in); 1912. Musée National d'Art Moderne, Paris

Customs officials declared that a *Bird in Space* (the one now in the Museum of Modern Art, New York) in polished bronze was a object of manufacture, not a work of art. Only after a court case, which lasted throughout 1927–8, was judgment given in the artist's favor.

When he turned to wood carving, Brancusi's imagery was utterly different. He had studied the craft as a student at Craiova and returned to it for many works after 1913. His wood carvings are essentially rough and primitive, echoing peasant craftsmanship and tribal art. He seldom created variants on these images in wood. Yet the polish of the marbles and bronzes and the crudity of the wood carvings are aspects of the same imagination; they are sometimes combined in one piece, such as the two versions of *Fish* (1928–30) each with a fetish-like wooden pedestal. On rare occasions, Brancusi did carve in wood the smooth forms of his marble and bronze images: these pieces include *Torso of a Young Man* (versions of 1922 in Philadelphia Museum of Art and Musée d'Art Moderne de la Ville de Paris), *Cock* (1924; Museum of Modern Art, New York), and two portraits, of *Nancy Cunard* (1928; Collection of Mrs Marcel Duchamp, New York) and *Mrs Eugene Meyer Jr* (*Undisdainful Queen*, 1910; Musée National d'Art Moderne, Paris).

In 1926 Brancusi was 50; in the following years, although he produced new variations of earlier motifs, he conceived only three new images: *Nocturnal Animal* (1930?), *The Seal* (first version 1936), and *Turtle* (1941 in wood, Musée National d'Art Moderne, Paris; and 1943, marble, Solomon R. Guggenheim Museum, New York). This was because his creative imagination had taken a new direction in the 1930s. He had become interested in mysticism and in particular the writings of the Tibetan, Milarepa. Then, in 1933, he met the Maharajah of Indore, who bought three versions of *Bird of Space* and proposed that Brancusi should design a Temple of Meditation. Despite a visit to India in 1937, the project fell through. However, another commission, of greater importance, was executed. In 1934, he was asked to design a memorial to the heroes of the First World War for Tirgu Jiu, the town where Brancusi himself had spent his adolescence. By 1937, he had created three monuments that are as much architectural as sculptural, designed for spiritual as well as aesthetic contemplation. The *Endless*

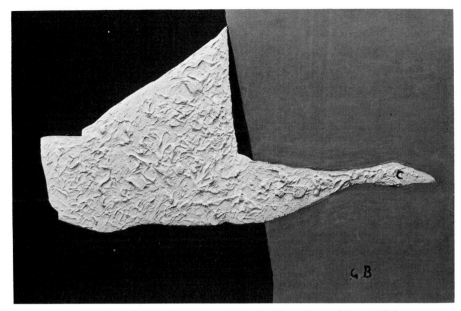

Georges Braque: Le Canard; oil and gouache on paper; 60×84cm (24×33in); 1956. Private collection

Column, based on a peasant decorative motif that Brancusi had used for several earlier versions, is a rigid rosary of rhomboidal beads reaching over 96 ft (32 m) into the sky. In the public park a *Table of Silence* set on the grass is like a giant millstone set round with 12 stone stools. The *Gate of the Kiss* (also in the park) is his crowning achievement, completing the development that began in 1907. Its pair of massive rectangular columns and lintel are developed from his own *Kiss*, now refined to a hieroglyph, a symbol of the fusion of opposites: it is a union transcending sexuality, with male and female as equal halves of the whole, the ultimate antithesis of Rodin's *Gates of Hell*.

Brancusi lived to be 81, producing little in his last 20 years. He survived as a legendary figure. At the last, he became a French citizen and left his studio and its contents to the French nation.

Further reading. Geist, S. *Brancusi, a Study of the Sculpture*, London (1968). Miller, S. *A Survey of Constantin Brancusi's Work*, Oxford (1994). Varia, R. *Brancusi*, New York (1987).

Braque Georges 1882–1963

The French painter Georges Braque was one of the major artists of the 20th century, whose partnership with Picasso from 1908 to 1914 generated Cubism.

The son of a house painting contractor, Braque decided at 15 to become a painter, but his characteristic caution prompted him at first to follow his family's trade in Le Havre. He enrolled as a part-time student at the local art school in 1897 and was apprenticed to a painter-decorator in 1899. He went to Paris in 1900, continuing his trade apprenticeship until his military service in 1901. He then studied mainly at the Académie Humbert and briefly at the École des Beaux-Arts.

His boyhood friends Raoul Dufy and Orthon Friez probably introduced him to the Fauve group, with whom he exhibited in 1906. His Fauvism was not of the muscular variety of Derain and Vlaminck, but was more meditative and lyrical, with luminous bright colors and a strong constructive element (for example, *Landscape of l'Estaque*, 1906; Galerie Beyeler, Basel).

In 1907 he subdued his colors and strengthened the underlying constructive qualities reminiscent of Cézanne, but was then galvanized by Picasso's newly painted *Les Demoiselles d'Avignon* (1907; Museum of Modern Art, New York). Braque's *Grand Nu* (1908; Collection of Mme Marie Cuttoli, Paris) was the earliest coherent response to Picasso's startling initiative; it was the start of their association which produced Cubism and lasted until 1914. The critic Louis Vauxcelles inadvertently christened the movement in a review of Braque's first one-man show at Kahnweiler's in 1908 when he referred to the reduction of forms to "little cubes".

Braque's contribution to Cubism was considerable: he was responsible for the development of the overlapping planes that created the new Cubist space; he first used letters as part of composition (*Le Portugais*, 1911; Öffentliches Kunstsammlung, Kunstmuseum Basel); and soon after Picasso had created the first *collage*, Braque made the first *papier collé* (*Fruit Dish and Glass*, September 1912; Douglas Cooper Collection, France), which was of great importance to his philosophy of art.

Braque enlisted in 1914, breaking the already weakening partnership. He was wounded in 1915 at Artois, and when he returned to painting in 1917 he found he was unable to concur with the paths Picasso and other artists had taken. He continued working the themes of his prewar works but the forms became bolder and more recognizable and the colors tended towards dark grays, browns, and greens with creams and whites vigorously scrubbed over them. His personal Cubist vision is continued in works like *The Marble Table* (1925; Musée d'Art Moderne de la Ville de Paris), in which simplified Cubist forms create volume rather than space, and house painter's imitation marbling becomes the occasion for a virtuoso display. While retreating from actual *collage* or *papier collé* he went on using the formal possibilities revealed by them.

He continued to respond to some of Picasso's thematic innovations; for instance he painted a series of Classically inspired figures called *Canephorae* from 1922 (examples in Musée d'Art Moderne de la Ville de Paris). Their characteristics are frontality, massiveness, a peculiar treatment of the drapery, and an obsessive pattern of lines describing the stomach. His reaction to Picasso's beach scenes of the late 1920s was to produce a series of *Bathers* in 1931 (an example in the Collection of M. and Mme Claude Laurens, Paris), which lack Picasso's sharpness but have a strong arabesque linear quality.

Braque painted several series of works on similar themes, which enabled him to build up slowly to complex pictures. The "studio" series, for instance, begins in the mid 1930s and reaches its first climax in 1939 in *The Painter and his Model* (Collection of Walter P. Chrysler Jr, New York). This brings together the Classical figure, the image of the Artist (bearded, so not a self-portrait), imitation wood graining, the picture within a picture, and collage-like panels. The human relationship implied is immediately taken over by the demands of art: the focus is on the brightly colored picture on the easel, and the two figures minister to it.

The awareness of Art as the subject of art is increasingly apparent throughout the 1940s; palettes, easels, and pictures within pictures appear regularly, culminating in a series of five paintings each called *The Studio* in 1949. In numbers I, II, III, and IV of these the bird motif, which had occurred earlier in his work, takes on its metaphys-

ical function as the symbol of aspiration. In his later paintings the symbolism of the bird takes over from the hitherto basic earthiness of his vision.

Braque worked in many graphic media: book illustrations which include drawings for Paul Reverdy's *The Roof Slates* (1918), etchings for Hesiod's *Theogony* published by Ambrose Vollard (1931), lithographs for Reverdy's *Liberty of Seas* (1959), and engravings for *The Order of Birds* with poems by Saint-John Perse (1962). He also designed sets for Diaghilev's ballets *The Bores* (1923) and *Zephyrus and Flora* (1925), as well as sets and costumes for the ballet *Salade* with music by Milhaud (1924) and the sets for Molière's *Tartuffe* (1949). In 1952–3 he decorated the ceiling of the Etruscan room in the Louvre, and in 1954 he produced mural decorations for the Mas Bernard at St-Paul-de-Vence and stained-glass windows for the small church at Varengeville.

Braque's achievement was recognized during his career by ever-widening circles of acclaim. He won the Carnegie Prize in 1937, was given a special exhibit at the Salon d'Automne in 1943, and won the Grand Prize at the Venice Biennale of 1948. In 1961 the Louvre honored him with a reconstruction of his studio, exhibiting the work of a living artist for the first time in the museum's history.

Further reading. Cogniat, R. *Georges Braque*, New York (1980). Zurcher, B. *Georges Braque Life and Work*, New York (1988).

Breton André 1896–1966

The French poet and writer André Breton was dominant in Parisian Dadaism and was the co-founder and the leader, and principal theorist of the Surrealist movement. Author of the Surrealist manifestos of 1924 and 1929, and of such important Surrealist texts as *Les Champs Magnétiques* (with Philippe Soupault; 1920) *Nadja* (1928), and *L'Amour Fou* (1937), Breton was also the chief apologist of Surrealist painting: he published his pioneering essay *Le Surréalisme et la Peinture* in 1928. A refugee in America from 1941 to 1946, he came into fruitful contact with young artists there, including Arshile Gorky; he was sympathetic to Abstract Expressionism and Tachism, and continued to support new Surrealist artists.

Breuer Marcel 1902–81

Born in Hungary, Marcel Lajos Breuer was a student at the Bauhaus and became head of its furniture workshop in 1925. His major contribution to design was in furniture. In 1925–6 he furnished the Dessau Bauhaus and produced his first chair from tubular steel, simplifying this in the S-shaped cantilever chair of 1928. He worked in Berlin as an architect and designer from 1928, moving to London in 1935. Two years later he joined Walter Gropius at Harvard, and from 1946 had an architectural practice in New York. His later architecture, such as the Unesco building, Paris (with Zehrfuss and Nervi, 1953), appears less functionally determined than his prewar work.

Bril Paul 1554–1626

Paul Bril was a Flemish landscape painter who worked in Rome. He was born at Antwerp though his family came originally from Breda. He is mentioned in the workshop of Daniel Wortelmans in 1568. In 1574 he left Antwerp and, after a stay at Lyons, settled in Rome, where his brother Matthew (1550–83) was already working as a landscape painter. Both brothers obtained commissions for extensive fresco work. Paul Bril painted six frescoes in the Lateran Palace (1589), others for S. Cecilia in Trastevere, and the *Seascape with St Clement* for the Sala Clementina in the Vatican (1602).

His fame now rests mainly on the smaller landscapes he painted for private patrons; these ensure his place in the development of the classical landscape at Rome in the 17th century. The earliest of them are small, often on copper; they follow the style of late-16th-century Mannerist painters, with emphatic diagonals into depth and sharply divided planes of light and dark accented by bright color contrasts. The influence of the German artist Adam Elsheimer (1578–1610), also resident at Rome, helped Bril to a new style based on closer observation of nature. *The Roman Forum with the Temple of Castor and Pollux and the Basilica of Hadrian* (1600; Gemäldegalerie Alte Meister, Dresden, and several early copies, including one in the Fitzwilliam Museum, Cambridge) shows a more gentle recession of space. The highly idealized setting of the Forum is used as a stage for a blend of the everyday and the picturesque: a scene of a cattle market. By the time he painted *Fishermen* (1624;

Paul Bril: Pan and Syrinx; 38×60cm (24×15in); c1620. Louvre, Paris

Louvre, Paris) he had anticipated, on a small scale, the coloring and quiet, poetical mood of later classical landscapes. In this respect it is significant that one of Bril's Roman pupils was Agostino Tassi, the teacher of Claude Lorrain.

Broederlam Melchior

fl. 1381–1409

Melchior Broederlam was a Flemish painter from Ypres, first documented in 1381 as court painter to the Count of Flanders, Louis of Male. With the Count's death in 1384 Flanders passed to his son-in-law Philip the Bold, Duke of Burgundy. Broederlam joined the Burgundian court, and was granted a salary. Occasional documentary evidence shows him to have been in the Duke's employment throughout the next two decades, though from 1392 he seems also to have run his own workshop at Ypres. His major commission from the Duke was the decoration of an altarpiece for the Chartreuse (Carthusian monastery) at Champmol near Dijon, the burial place of the ducal family. The work, paid for in 1394 but probably not installed till 1399, involved painting the exterior of the wings of the large wooden altarpiece carved by Jacques de Baerze. Broederlam is last mentioned in 1409.

References to him convey some idea of the duties of a late medieval court painter. During the years 1386 to 1392 he undertook the decoration of the Duke's castle at Hesdin in the county of Artois. He made tournament equipment, including pavilions, repaired machinery for springing practical jokes on the Duke's guests, painted flags and banners, and designed tiled floors. In 1386 he directed the decoration of ships being prepared for an expedition against England. At his workshop in Ypres he carried out commissions for glass windows, worked as a goldsmith, and fitted out civic dignitaries with uniforms. In this variety of undertakings Broederlam is typical of Franco-Flemish artists of his time; also typical is that almost all his work has been lost or destroyed (much of it was of a temporary nature).

His only surviving work, the Dijon altarpiece (Musée des Beaux-Arts, Dijon) consists of two panels, each containing a pair of New Testament scenes. The left-hand panel shows *The Annunciation and the Visitation*, the right-hand *The Presentation and the Flight into Egypt*. The figures, with their soft flowing draperies, are French in style, but the architecture and landscape background contain strong echoes from Italian painting, particularly from the work of the early-14th-century Sienese artists Simone Martini and the Lorenzetti brothers. Many of the details are symbolic. Mary in *The Annunciation* holds a skein of purple wool, a reference to the account in the Apocrypha in which she is interrupted by the angel while working the wool for a new veil for the Temple. The three windows in the same scene, representing the light of the Trinity, are an example of architecture being used for symbolic pur-

poses. This sort of imagery was expanded and used extensively by later Flemish painters like the Master of Flémalle (c1375–1444) and Jan van Eyck (c1390–1441). With its figure-style, gold background, rich coloring, delicate, exquisite detail, and its realism (particularly the much-imitated rustic figure of Joseph drinking from his water flask), the Dijon altarpiece is a major example of the International Gothic style current in Europe c1400.

Bronzino 1503–72

Born Angelo or Agnolo di Cosimo near Florence, Bronzino studied under Raffaellino del Garbo before joining Jacopo da Pontormo's workshop in 1519. This relationship was important throughout Bronzino's career, for he helped with Pontormo's decoration of the Medicean villas at Careggi and Castello in the 1530s and completed the frescoes in the choir of S. Lorenzo, Florence (now destroyed) after Pontormo's death in 1557. Bronzino was slow to develop; the early *Temptation of St Benedict* (1526–8; Badia, Florence) sets stiff, awkward figures (at best a crude approximation to those of Pontormo) in a simplified landscape that has its origin in the Quattrocento.

The *Pietà* that Bronzino painted for SS. Trinità (Uffizi, Florence) at the end of the 1520s draws away from Pontormo both in its somber tonality and its composition, reminiscent of Andrea del Sarto. His first portrait, that of Guidobaldo delle Rovere (Uffizi, Florence) was painted while he was working at the Villa Imperiale near Pesaro from 1530 to 1532. It depends on the influence of Titian for the introduction of the dog on which the Duke rests his hand; the pose, although stiffer than in Titian, has not yet achieved the artificiality of Bronzino's mature portraits. This is reached in the portrait of Duke Cosimo I (Uffizi, Florence). The twist of the shoulders is set against the head and this, with the expressionless gaze, freezes the figure and gives it the unnatural elegance of art. His portraits show a considerable range: some of those from the 1530s in which the buildings in the background are used as attributes rather than as settings look back to Pontormo, while in others the sitters hold a book or a statue. The *Eleonora of Toledo with her Son* (Uffizi, Florence) of the 1540s shows no emotion, but every detail of the brocade of her dress is accurately recorded.

Further reading. Baccheschi, E. *L'Opera Completa del Bronzino*, Milan (1973). Freedberg, S.J. *Painting in Italy: 1500–1600*, Harmondsworth (1979). McCorquodale, C. *Bronzino*, London (1981). Smyth, C.H. *Bronzino as a Draughtsman, an Introduction*, Locust Valley (1971).

Bronzino: Venus, Cupid, Folly, and Time; panel; 147×117cm (58×46in); c1540–5. National Gallery, London

Brosse Salomon de 1571–1626

Salomon de Brosse stands in French architectural history between Philibert Delorme (c1510–70) and François Mansart (1598–1666), though he was a less sensitive and inventive designer than either of them. Like Mansart, whom he influenced, he worked essentially in the provinces around Paris, but few of his buildings have survived. His grandest and most intriguing work is the Luxembourg Palace, begun in 1615 for Marie de Medici; fortunately this building remains largely intact. In it de Brosse showed a much more unified composition than in his earlier châteaux of Blerancourt (1612) and Verneuil (c1608), both now ruined. The Luxembourg Palace, was followed by the equally monumental Palais du Parlement at Rennes (1618) and later by the more ponderous exercise in Vitruvian principles, the Protestant Temple of Charenton (1623) which set the form for much 17th-century Protestant architecture.

Brown Ford Madox 1821–93

The English painter Ford Madox Brown was associated with the Pre-Raphaelite movement though he never actually became a member of the Brotherhood. He was born in Calais where his father, a ship's purser of English birth, had chosen to retire. In 1833 the family moved to Belgium to allow their talented son to study art. Brown attended various studios culminating in that of Baron Gustaf Wappers in Antwerp. Between 1840 and 1844 he lived in Paris. Brown then entered the important cartoon competitions for the decoration of the new Houses of Parliament at Westminster in 1844 and 1845. After passing the winter of 1845–6 in Rome, Brown, encouraged by the state of English history painting, settled permanently in London.

His early works reflect his mixed training, carrying a flavor of French Romanticism, but also strongly biased towards the archaicism of the Nazarene School of painters whom he admired and visited in

From 1540 Bronzino began the decoration of Eleonora's chapel in the Palazzo Vecchio, Florence. Scenes from the life of Moses appear on the walls and four saints on clouds decorate the ceiling, which is divided by a framework of swags and putti. The style of the frescoes is Roman, although Bronzino had not at this date visited Rome, and comparable to that of his near-contemporary Francesco Salviati in his 1538 *Visitation* (S. Giovanni Decollato, Rome). The style that Bronzino achieves in these frescoes was repeated in his later altars in S. Croce and SS. Annunziata, and also in *Venus, Cupid, Folly, and Time* (c1540–5; National Gallery, London). In the later 1540s he designed tapestries for the Medici and while the first of them share the complexity of this style the later, most notably the suite of scenes from the life of Joseph (Palazzo del Quirinale, Rome), achieve a new clarity in their handling of narrative. His last major work, the *Martyrdom of St Lawrence* in S. Lorenzo, Florence (c1565–9) shows a belated reaction to Michelangelo's *Last Judgment*. He has modified the bulk of the figures in his search for greater complexity of movement; the result, however, is unpleasant.

Salomon de Brosse: the Luxembourg Palace, Paris; begun in 1615

Rome. In 1848 Rossetti made himself Brown's pupil, and promoted his works among the gathering Pre-Raphaelite circle, but Brown refused to become a full member. In 1851 he turned to Realism, taking his whole canvas out of doors. In 1852 he began his greatest pictures, *The Last of England* (City of Birmingham Museums and Art Gallery) and *Work* (City of Manchester Art Gallery).

The Last of England shows an emigrant family setting out from Dover. Inspired by the experiences of the Pre-Raphaelite sculptor Thomas Woolner, it combines close character study with a wider sense of the picture as a social document. *Work*, a much larger painting, was not completed until 1865. Then, in a retrospective exhibition, Brown wrote long catalog notes to prove that the picture could be approached as a sociological tract akin to the writings of Ruskin and Carlyle. *Work* is one of the great achievements of the English Realist school. The scene, centered upon navvies laying drains in Hampstead, contains all levels of society including the unemployed poor and the idle rich, and all is, as the artist himself claimed, "rendered exactly as it would appear".

After 1860, Brown's work became more decorative, reflecting his involvement with the firm Morris, Marshall, Faulkner and Company, of which he was a founder member. The most significant of his late works are the murals in the Town Hall, Manchester, a series of symbolic and historical scenes which occupied him from 1878 until his death. Brown was an individualist, and his idiosyncratic outlook is reflected in his art. During the 1850s he lived in penury, but after receiving some recognition he moved from Hampstead to Bloomsbury where, during the 1860s and 1870s, his house was a center of intellectual and artistic life. (*See* overleaf.)

Ford Madox Brown: Work; oil on canvas; 135×196cm (53×77in); 1852–65. City of Manchester Art Gallery

Bruegel family

16th and 17th centuries

Pieter Bruegel the Elder (1525–69), Pieter Bruegel the Younger (c1564–1637/8), and Jan Bruegel (1568–1625) were a family of Flemish painters. Pieter the Elder, the greatest moralist in the Netherlands since Bosch (c1450–1516), and a major landscape artist, was born at Breda. His origins are uncertain; the claim made by van Mander in 1604 that he was of peasant stock may be only an attempt to explain the original subject matter of his pictures and to excuse a number of picturesque stories. There is little documentary evidence either for the assertion that he trained in the workshop of Pieter Coecke van Aelst (1502–50), though he did eventually marry his daughter, Mayken. In 1551 he was registered as Master in the Antwerp guild but left for a journey through France and Italy shortly afterwards. He reached Reggio Calabria and Sicily and is recorded at Rome in 1553.

The journey south did not have the predictable impact on a Northern artist. His interest was more in landscape and particularly the mountainous scenery so foreign to his homeland, than in contemporary art or the Antique. His landscape drawings seek to convey the expanse and atmosphere of his surroundings rather than exact geographical detail; they are the first step toward an imaginative use of his experience of landscape in his paintings.

On his return to the Netherlands (by 1555) Bruegel's first success came through drawings for engravings published by Hieronymous Cock in Antwerp. They are the first indication of a strong moralizing tendency in his work and a talent for illustrating proverb and parable. It is significant that Cock issued Bruegel's *Big Fish eat Little Fish* of 1556 as a work of Hieronymus Bosch. Many contemporaries, and especially Italian critics like Vasari, saw Bruegel's panoramic settings and half-man, half-animal forms as successors to the paintings of Bosch. He comes closest to Bosch in works of 1562 such as *The Triumph of Death* (Prado, Madrid) and *The Fall of the Rebel Angels* (Musées Royaux des Beaux-Arts de Belgique, Brussels). In other works such as *Netherlandish Proverbs* (Staatliche Museen, Berlin), he replaces Bosch's blend of the playful and the demonic by a ruthless observation of everyday action as the basis for moral comment. The *Battle between Carnival and Lent* (1559; Kunsthistorisches Museum, Vienna) is perhaps the most vivid of these early works which juxtapose the lighthearted and the darker sides of man's existence, here enacted as a play of Netherlandish Shrovetide customs. The market square, seen from the high viewpoint common to his early works, has become a stage for the contest between greed and self-denial.

Bruegel's work appealed chiefly to private patrons and connoisseurs. For the Antwerp art collector Nicholas Jonghelinck he painted a series of pictures (1565–6) representing the months. Only five of these survive from a possible original 12. Their panoramic landscapes mark the high point of Bruegel's use of observed reality for imaginative purpose. The *Hunters in the Snow* (Kunsthistorisches Museum, Vienna) probably depicts January. The viewpoint is slightly lowered from earlier works and transition from foreground to background is effected by sharply plunging diagonals. Throughout the series the artist's message seems to be that the changing face of season and landscape dominates and determines human activity.

The relative insignificance of man in Bruegel's world picture is manifest even in some of his religious works; *The Conversion of St Paul* (1567; Kunsthistorisches Museum, Vienna) is a tiny detail in a vast mountain-top landscape. Other religious works, however, show a marked increase of figure-scale to picture-field. The *Adoration of the Kings* (1564; National Gallery, London) dispenses with landscape; and a grisaille painting of 1565, *Christ and the Woman Taken in Adultery* (Home House Collection, Courtauld Institute of Art, London) shows an expansive space dominated by monumental figure forms and a lack of any setting at all.

A lower viewpoint and much larger figure forms are used in his last scenes of peasant life, such as the *Peasant Wedding* (Kunsthistorisches Museum, Vienna) and his late allegories. In the *Blind leading the Blind* (1568; Museo e Gallerie Nazionali di Capodimonte, Naples) the figures move as in a frieze across the canvas towards the man falling into the ditch at the right. Bruegel has moved away from the bright juxtapositions of color in his early works to a muted and delicate palette of browns, greens, and shades of gray. His technique of painting had always been to apply his colors thinly, edging the contours with soft, black lines; in the Naples picture the landscape is hardly more than a thin wash of transparent colors.

The Magpie on the Gallows (1568; Hessisches Landesmuseum, Darmstadt) is probably his last work. It seems to mark a new departure in the reconciliation of a high viewpoint with the soft light and color of other late works. In this respect it is close to the style of the landscape drawings, where light and atmosphere are rendered by short, meticulous pen strokes, echoed here in the dappled treatment of the foliage. Numerous studies of the peasant figures that populate his paintings also survive, many of them annotated with color and descriptive notes. Direct preparatory studies are rare, however; Bruegel's artistic process was one of assimilation of observed detail rather than direct transcription.

Bruegel's impact on Flemish painting in the century after his death was due partly to engravings after his work and partly to the family workshop which continued his style. Pieter the Younger, his elder son, became Master at Antwerp in 1585 and efficiently produced copies and derivations

Pieter Bruegel the Elder: detail of Hunters in the Snow; oil on canvas; full size 117×162cm (46×64in); c1565. Kunsthistorisches Museum, Vienna

of his father's work for much of his long career; he often changed landscape settings or extracted groups of figures for variant compositions. He was called "Hell Bruegel" because he exploited the growing market for pictures of hell-fire and demons, the origins of which are found in his father's work. He was father of Pieter III, born in 1589, Master in Antwerp in 1608.

Jan, the younger son, was more talented than Pieter II. In his early twenties he traveled in Italy and became a member of the Guild of St Luke at Rome. In 1604 he is recorded at Prague. His ability to paint on a small scale led to his fame as a painter of cabinet pictures and he painted some of the finest early flower pieces. He collaborated with a number of artists, including the young Rubens (for example, *Virgin with a Garland*; Prado, Madrid). His sons Ambrosius (1617–75) and Jan II (1601–78) were also artists, as was Jan II's son, Abraham (1631–90).

Further reading. Gerson, H. *Art and Architecture in Belgium: 1600–1800*, Harmondsworth (1960). Gibson, W. *Bruegel*, London (1977). Grossman, F. *Bruegel, the Paintings*, London (1973). Klein, H.A. *Graphic Works of Pieter Bruegel the Elder*, New York (1963). Munz, L. *Bruegel, the Drawings*, London (1961). Tolnay, C. de *Pierre Bruegel l'Ancien*, Brussels (1935).

Brunelleschi Filippo 1377–1446

The Florentine artist Filippo Brunelleschi was architect, engineer, and sculptor. He was the son of Ser Brunellesco Lippi, a Florentine notary who held important offices in the Republic and was sometimes entrusted with diplomatic missions. Filippo was enrolled as a master of the goldsmiths' guild in 1398; in the following year he was active in the shop of Lunardo di Matteo Ducci da Pistoia, for whom he made some silver figures for the altar of S. Jacopo in Pistoia Cathedral. The significance of a document mentioning a second matriculation by Brunelleschi in the goldsmiths' guild in 1404 has not been explained.

Brunelleschi first came to prominence as a result of the competition for the second bronze door of the Florence Baptistery, held in 1401, in which he participated alongside Ghiberti and five other sculptors. This contest has been described as the first art competition since Antiquity. In fact, it seems to have been common late medieval practice for a patron to invite several artists to submit designs before concluding a contract. Ghiberti and the anonymous biographer of Brunelleschi, believed to be Antonio di Tuccio Manetti, differ in their accounts of the result of this contest. While Ghiberti states that he won outright, the biographer claims that Brunelleschi and Ghiberti were invited to share the commission and that Brunelleschi subsequently withdrew.

Although Brunelleschi is known to have been involved in sculptural commissions c1409 and in 1415, he seems to have turned away from sculpture during the decade following the competition. Between 1404 and 1406 he served as a consultant on the fabric of Florence Cathedral, and it was probably around this time that he first visited Rome. It is not known precisely when Brunelleschi formulated the principles of "one-point" perspective which were subsequently employed by Masaccio and codified by Alberti, although his discovery could hardly have been made later than the second decade of the 15th century. There is little evidence that Brunelleschi was interested in painting; the two small perspectival views with which he is said to have demonstrated his ideas imply that his studies of this subject were primarily directed towards the requirements of architecture.

Little is known of Brunelleschi's work as an architect before 1417, when he was called upon to give his opinion on the dome of Florence Cathedral. Although the approximate design of the dome had been established as early as 1367, its actual execution remained a supremely difficult engineering problem. Originally working alongside Ghiberti, Brunelleschi soon acquired control over the supervision of the work. The completion of this enterprise spanned the rest of his life and it remains his most famous achievement. He overcame the main task of enclosing the enormous drum (which was already standing) by introducing a double-shell dome. This required a series of ingenious technical innovations to reduce weight and ensure maximum strength. The scaffolding and the weight-lifting devices needed to erect the massive superstructure of the dome posed serious difficulties in themselves. Brunelleschi surmounted every problem as it arose, with a brilliant display of engineering skill and meticulous attention to each detail of the construction.

Brunelleschi's earliest surviving public building is the Ospedale degli Innocenti, Florence, begun in 1419. Its long semicircular arcade reveals a clear debt to the Tuscan Romanesque, but the precision with which these medieval forms are applied, and the modular system of proportion with which the disposition of the whole design is governed, are entirely Classical. In 1421, Brunelleschi began the church of S. Lorenzo. Here he brought the traditional basilican plan up to date with a rigid application of modular theory, embracing the arcade bays, the span of the nave, and the equally-sized transepts, choir, and crossing, each of which stands in a precise proportional ratio to the others. The clarity of Brunelleschi's thought is well exemplified by the Old Sacristy of the church, adjoining the main building. A simple cube, rationally linked by pendentives to its dome above, it stands as virtually the first of a succession of centrally planned Renaissance structures.

With S. Spirito, begun in 1436 but completed after his death, Brunelleschi continued to develop his ideas upon the basilican church without being hampered, as he had been at S. Lorenzo, by an existing ground plan. The design was tightened up by continuing the aisle in an unbroken band around the transepts, choir, and west front, and by simplifying the ratio of arcade to clerestory from 5:3 to 1:1. Brunelleschi's original design incorporated a ring of semicircular chapel niches, visible from the outside, which established a formal congruity between the exterior wall and the interior configuration of the building.

Although Brunelleschi was commissioned to design the Pazzi Chapel in the cloister of S. Croce in 1429, the building seems to have progressed slowly and was not completed until many years after the architect's death. It consists of a domed central square, extended to an oblong by barrel-vaulted side bays, and further elaborated by a square, domed choir and a barrel-vaulted portico. This runs longitudinally across the facade of the building, firmly knitting the new structure into the cloister within which it stands. The exquisitely balanced proportions of the design are underscored by the subtle polychromy of the gray moldings set against the paler walls, and enlivened by the glazed majolica roundels on the walls and in the spandrels of the dome. It was partly because of this innovatory system of interior decoration that the Pazzi Chapel proved so influential upon subsequent generations of architects.

Unfortunately, Brunelleschi's design for S. Maria degli Angeli (1434–7) was never completed. Consisting of a domed octagonal lantern surrounded by a ring of eight chapels, it would have been the first true centrally planned building of the Renaissance—it marks a high point in Brunelleschi's development as an architect. In 1436 he designed a last centrally planned structure: the lantern of Florence Cathedral. An octagonal *tempietto*, braced against the ribs of the dome by flying buttresses, this design aptly demonstrates the structural purpose of the lantern and at the same time provides a superb conclusion to Brunelleschi's great composition.

In addition to these works, Brunelleschi's name has been associated with other important Florentine buildings, including the Palazzo della Parte Guelfa and even the Palazzo Pitti which was not begun until long after his death. Uniting his vast store of traditional engineering expertise with a new awareness of Classical models, and a personal genius for coherent and rational design, Brunelleschi transformed the outlook of the Florentine architectural world. More than any other individual, he established the forms and demonstrated the preoccupations of Italian Renaissance architecture.

Filippo Brunelleschi: the cupola and lantern of Florence Cathedral; built 1425–67

Bartolomeo Buon: the facade of the Ca' d'Oro, Venice; 1421–34

Further reading. Heydenreich, L. and Lotz, W. *Architecture in Italy: 1400–1600*, Harmondsworth (1974). Klotz, H. *Die Frühwerke Brunelleschis und der Mittelalterliche Tradition*, Berlin (1970). Manetti, A. (trs. and ed. Saalman, H.) *The Life of Brunelleschi by Antonio di Tuccio Manetti*, Pennsylvania and London (1970). Prager, F.D. and Scaglia, G. *Brunelleschi, Studies of His Technology and Inventions*, Cambridge, Mass. (1970). Sanpaolesi, P. *Brunelleschi*, Milan (1962).

Bruyn Nicholaes de 1571–1656

The Flemish engraver Nicholaes de Bruyn was born in Antwerp, the son of the engraver Abraham de Bruyn. He entered the printmakers' guild of his home town in 1601. Around 1617 he moved to Rotterdam, where he died. Nicholaes completed over 200 engravings. A large proportion of these are reproductions of the designs of other artists, primarily near-contemporary figures such as Gills van Coninxloo, David Vinckboons, and Jacob Savery, but occasionally earlier artists including Lucas van Leyden and Albrecht Dürer. He also prepared original compositions, some of which he entrusted to other engravers, including Aswerus van Londerseel and Claes Jans Visscher. The majority of his works, both his copies and his own designs, are religious in subject matter, although he also undertook profane themes and ornamental compositions.

Bryaxis *fl.* 355–300 BC

Bryaxis was a Greek sculptor of the late Classical or early Hellenistic period. A signed early base of a votive tripod in the National Museum, Athens, indicates that he was probably an Athenian, although his name also occurs in Caria. He collaborated with Scopas and Leochares in the Mausoleum of Halicarnassus and later worked mostly in eastern Greece. His fame rested mainly on two cult-statues: the *Apollo Pythius* at Daphne near Antioch in Syria, made of gilded wood with the nude parts in marble (known to us from coins); and the Hellenic-Egyptian god *Serapis* in Alexandria, an original, dark blue creation of rare metals and precious stones.

Brygos Painter *fl. c495–470 BC*

The Brygos Painter is the conventional name for a prolific Greek vase-painter in Athens who painted five of the finest cups signed by the potter Brygos. He painted mainly cups, on one of which he experimented with painting on a white ground (Staatliche Antikensammlungen, Munich; Inv. 2645). Onesimos was his teacher. His early work runs parallel to the later work of Onesimos, when that artist's figures were beginning to become rather delicate: the Brygos Painter gave them back their vigor. He was a master of movement, but was also capable of quiet grandeur; his faces are passionate, his subjects lively. He loved myth and abandoned carousals. A large school of artists who painted in a similar manner gathered around him. In his later works his style becomes weaker, his figures more attenuated, and his subjects repetitive.

Buncho Tani *1763–1840*

The Japanese painter Tani Buncho was the first great master to be born and to work mainly in Edo (Tokyo). He was basically a *Bunjinga* (Chinese-style scholar-artist), but he could and did paint in every current style. He lived in the metropolis, where he moved in high circles and became a popular hero, but throughout his life he traveled widely in Japan, sketching from nature; so his landscapes are native in flavor in spite of their Chinese models. His most original landscape style is a fusion of chunky construction and bold outline filled with delicate atmospheric washes. As a virtuoso in pure ink he is in the first rank. He illustrated many books, and was a major influence on Japanese painting.

Buon Bartolomeo *fl. 1421–64*

Bartolomeo Buon was a Venetian stonemason and sculptor, and from *c*1440 until his death he was the principal sculptor in Venice. He undertook all types of work in stone and marble: stone decoration of brick buildings (windows, ornamental moldings, statues), elaborate doorways, and tombs. His was an elaborate late Gothic style with classical elements, but his incomplete facade for the Ca' del Duca Palace (*c*1460) is classical, entirely in stone, and innovatory for Venice. His most important documented statue, *Justice*, on the Porta della Carta, Doge's Palace (*c*1440) is in a style developed from that of

the works of Jacobello and Pierpaolo dalle Masegne (*fl.* 1383–1403) but the figure has more solidity, the draperies are ampler, and the face fleshier and more placid.

Buontalenti *1536–1608*

The architect and stage designer Buontalenti (Bernardo dalle Guandole) worked mainly for the Medici court in and around Florence. He completed the Uffizi, begun by Vasari, and designed the Chapel of the Princes at S. Lorenzo. He also built a canal between Pisa and Leghorn, contrived some trick fountains at the Villa Pratolino, and designed other works requiring a high degree of technical skill. He showed a talent for decorative invention in architectural detail which links him closely to Mannerism. Examples include the Porta delle Suppliche (Uffizi, Florence), where the two halves of a broken pediment are reversed, and the altar steps for S. Trinità (now at S. Stefano), which cannot in fact be climbed. He was one of the major innovators of Baroque stage design.

Burchfield Charles *1893–1967*

Born and raised in Ohio, the American landscape artist Charles Burchfield spent most of his adult life in Buffalo. Usually painting in watercolors, he was one of the first American Scene painters, his earliest works being based on memories of his childhood in Ohio. Created in response to fits of deep depression and anxiety, they show buildings and nature animated by strong and sometimes sinister forces. They are characterized by distortions, strong and often agitated rhythms, and childlike fantasy—in one of his best-known works, *Church Bells Ringing, Rainy Winter Night* (1917; Cleveland Museum, Ohio) a church spire has become a birdlike head, and the windows are faces. In the 1920s and 1930s he concentrated on depicting the drabness of small, Midwestern towns, the buildings derelict and ghostly, his style more restrained, though by the 1940s he had returned to the visionary landscapes of his early period.

Further reading. Baur, J. *Charles Burchfield, 1893–1967*, New York (1982).

Burgkmair Hans, the Elder *1473–1531*

The German painter and draftsman Hans Burgkmair the Elder was born in Augsburg

where he was registered Master in 1498. He trained first under his father Thoman. On stylistic grounds it seems likely that he then studied in Martin Schongauer's workshop on the upper Rhine in the late 1480s.

Burgkmair's style, like that of his contemporary Albrecht Dürer, was decisively influenced by travel in Italy. About 1505 he was in Lombardy and Venice, and thereafter Italian Renaissance forms become assimilated into his work.

His portraits similarly show a grafting of Italian ideas on to the realistic traditions of Northern Europe. The *Portrait of Hans Schellenberger* (1505; Wallraf-Richartz-Museum, Cologne) has an elegance reminiscent of the highly self-conscious, gentlemanly self-portraits of Dürer. His woodcut portraits include a medallion study of *Pope Julius II* (1511). Other woodcuts show imaginative range and a command of ornamental design.

Burne-Jones Edward *1833–98*

The English painter and designer Sir Edward Coley Burne-Jones was a leading figure in the second wave of the Pre-Raphaelite movement. Born in Birmingham, he was originally destined for a career in the Church. With this intention he went up to Exeter College, Oxford, in 1853, but soon became disillusioned by the apathetic atmosphere. However, he did meet William Morris, a kindred spirit who shared his enthusiasm for medieval legend and poetry and who later guided him toward the artistic path. Inspired by the writings of Ruskin, the Pre-Raphaelite periodical *The Germ*, a summer visit to northern France, and a meeting with D.G. Rossetti, Burne-Jones left the University in 1856 and went to London to become a painter.

He was admitted to Rossetti's studio as a pupil and remained under his tutelage for several years; together with Morris he helped Rossetti to paint the wall decorations of the Oxford Union Debating Chamber in 1857. Through Rossetti, Burne-Jones met various members of the Pre-Raphaelite circle, including Arthur Hughes, Thomas Woolner, and Ford Madox Brown. Morris, who had joined Burne-Jones in London in 1856, pursued his own artistic studies. In 1861 he founded the firm of Morris, Marshall, Faulkner and Company for which Burne-Jones made tapestry and stained glass designs, as well as cartoons for furniture decorations.

Edward Burne-Jones: The Arming of Perseus; gouache; 152×127cm (60×50in); 1877.
Southampton Art Gallery

until the opening of the Grosvenor Gallery in 1877. With this event, Burne-Jones was finally hailed as England's most influential painter. The delay in public acclaim had been caused by a disturbed exhibition history. He had exhibited with the Old Watercolour Society in the 1860s, but resigned from the Society in 1870 following a dispute, and did not exhibit again in public until the first Grosvenor Gallery exhibition. He also refrained from exhibiting at the Royal Academy Summer Exhibition. Consequently his fame only became established in the late 1870s and 1880s. One of his most celebrated paintings, *King Cophetua and the Beggar Maid* (1880–4; Tate Gallery, London) was shown at the Grosvenor in 1884 and won a First Class medal at the Paris International Exhibition of 1889.

Burne-Jones was elected an Associate of the Royal Academy in 1885 and, as a concession to this unsought honor, he exhibited one painting, *The Depths of the Sea* (1885–6; private collection) at the annual Summer Exhibition of 1886. In 1893 he resigned from the Royal Academy without becoming a full Academician. He received a baronetcy in 1894.

Though his style changed during his career, his vision of painting as an amalgamation of the poetic and the aesthetic never wavered, as can be seen in his illustrations to William Morris' Kelmscott Press edition of *The Works of Geoffrey Chaucer* (printed 1896). Burne-Jones' conception of a picture as "a beautiful romantic dream of something that never was, never will be" resulted in the creation of a dreamworld haunted by wistful figures set within landscapes whose space was deliberately indeterminate.

Further reading. Spalding, F. *Magnificent Dreams: Burne-Jones and the Late Victorians*, London (1978).

Burra Edward 1905–76

The British painter Edward Burra was born in London. He studied at Chelsea Polytechnic (1921–3) and at the Royal College of Art (1923–4). His early work shows some affinity with that of George Grosz but Burra soon moved closer to Surrealism. He joined Paul Nash's short-lived group Unit One in 1933 (as did Ben Nicholson, Henry Moore, and Barbara Hepworth) and exhibited with the English Surrealists in 1936 and 1938. His mature

His best-known contributions in stained glass are those with large, single-figure compositions representing saints or virtues. Thus Morris and Burne-Jones gave practical expression to their shared desire to elevate the handicrafts to the level of Art.

Burne-Jones' first visit to Italy in 1859 revealed to him the glories of true "pre-Raphael" painting in the works of Orcagna, Signorelli, Mantegna, Botticelli, and Michelangelo. Three years later, in the company of Ruskin, he discovered the splendor of the Venetians. From this time on, his work moved away from the luxuriant, decorative treatment of Rossetti to the sparser forms and muted tones of the Italian primitives. His great love of literary

themes remained with him, and he drew upon many such sources for his subject matter. A favorite subject, *The Beguiling of Merlin* (1874; Lady Lever Art Gallery, Port Sunlight) taken from Mallory's *Morte d'Arthur*, demonstrates his adherence to poetic imagery and displays many of the peculiar characteristics of his art. The clear muscular delineation of Merlin and Nimuë, (seen for example in *Merlin and Nimuë* in the Victoria and Albert Museum, London), the languid poses, the androgynous quality of the faces and figures, the muted yet rich coloring, the suspension of movement, the creation of an ethereal, otherworldly mood—all these elements distinguish the Burne-Jones style.

This style was not, however, recognized

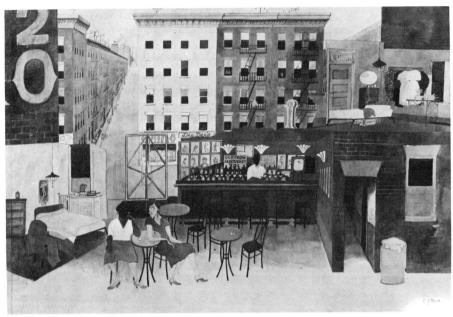

Edward Burra: Scene in Harlem (Simply Heavenly); watercolor; 72×112cm (28×44in); 1952. Lefevre Gallery, London

style, already developed by the mid 1930s and little changed since, is characterized by a strong visual rhythm, simplified forms, grotesque figures, and a mood that is invariably sinister and sometimes menacing. He always worked in watercolor and his later work shows a marked preference for landscape.

Burri Alberto 1915–

The Italian painter and collage artist Alberto Burri was born in Città di Castello. He took a medical degree in 1940 and practiced in the Italian Army. Captured in North Africa in 1943, he spent 18 months in a Prisoner of War camp in Hereford, Texas, where he began to paint in 1944. Returning to Rome in 1945 Burri gave up

Alberto Burri: Sacking and Red; sacking, glue, and plastic paint on canvas; 86×100cm (34×39in); 1954. Tate Gallery, London

his medical practice to become an artist; his first exhibition was held in 1947. His second important exhibition was the *Origine* group show in 1951 where he exhibited with Ballocco, Capogrossi, and Colla. Burri's earliest paintings were worked in thick opaque materials. These were followed by the collages in burlap, wood, iron, and plastic on hardboard for which he is now best known, for example *Sackcloth 1953* (1953; burlap, sewn, patched, and glued over canvas; Museum of Modern Art, New York).

Busch Wilhelm 1832–1908

The German illustrator and painter Wilhelm Busch studied at the Düsseldorf and Munich Academies (1851–2, 1854–5). He visited Antwerp in 1852, and the impact of Dutch and Flemish art turned his interest towards realism and comic genre painting. His contact with the bohemian circle of "Young-Munich" led to commissions for the humorous newspaper *Fliegende Blätter* (1858–71). Busch progressed from illustrating stories to providing his own verse-captions to picture-cycles. These *Bildergeschichten* are full of Schopenhauerian pessimism and *Schadenfreude* ("Max and Moritz", 1865), relying on a mixture of realism and the grotesque. Busch never exhibited his paintings, which seem to foreshadow Expressionism in the violence of their technique.

Bushnell John c1630–1701

The English sculptor John Bushnell trained under the London mason Thomas Burman. He gained firsthand knowledge of Baroque sculpture by working in Italy, France, and Flanders. He settled in Venice where he executed a large tomb with complex battle reliefs for the Mocenigo family in S. Lazzaro dei Mendicanti, Venice, in 1663–4. After returning to England, probably c1669, he received commissions for a number of royal portraits, as well as for tombs in Westminster Abbey. Bushnell's style is characterized by a Baroque bravura, and a knowledge of Bernini's sculpture; but his unstable temperament is reflected in the uneven quality of much of his work.

Yosa Buson: Landscape; 1771. Museum für Ostasiatische Kunst, Cologne

Buson Yosa 1716–83

The Japanese painter and poet Yosa Buson (born Taniguchi Buson) is considered, with Taiga (1723–76), one of the greatest masters of the *Bunjinga* (scholar-painters). Born near Osaka to a wealthy family, he moved to Tokyo as a young man; he became a *haiku* poet, with a reputation second only to that of the 17th-century master Basho. As a result he became adept at the abbreviated line-and-wash style of painting called *Haiga*, used to illustrate the poems. This humorous style is seen in his screens of parts of Basho's *Narrow Road to the Deep North* (Yamagata Art Gallery), where three-quarters of the paper is filled with text. Its racy vigor was handed on to his pupil in poetry and painting, Goshun, and thence to the *Shijo* School.

Buson left Tokyo in 1742, and until c1760 traveled and studied painting, especially the Chinese school of Nagasaki. A late developer, he did not achieve a mature *Bunjinga* style until middle age; but by 1768 he was better known in his adopted town of Kyoto as a painter than as a poet. His best work of this period is the *Ten Conveniences and Ten Pleasures* album, done with Taiga, a small-scale masterpiece of the pure Chinese scholar spirit. Always learning, Buson was influenced later in life by the new naturalism of Okyo; in his last years he produced the soft, rhapsodic, leafy, usually springtime landscapes which are so in accord with Japanese sentiment. They include the famous *Cuckoo over Springtime Forest* (Hiraki Collection, Tokyo) and the screens *Bridle Path Through a Willow Grove* (Yabumoto Collection, Tokyo).

Bustelli Francesco 1723–63

The eminent porcelain modeler Francesco Antonio Bustelli (also known as Franz Anton) was born in Locarno. Nothing is known of his training or early activity before 1754, when he is documented at Neudeck in Bavaria as a modeler of figures. He remained there until 1761 when the porcelain factory was transferred to Nymphenburg, near Munich. In 1759 he had been appointed "Arcanista", indicating other forms of technical expertise. The elegant figures made by Bustelli during his nine years in Bavaria are closely related in style to the sculpture of Ignaz Günther; his sophisticated bust of *Count Sigismund Haimhausen* (1761) is one of the finest examples of Bavarian Rococo court portraiture.

Butler Reg 1913–81

The English sculptor Reg Cottrell Butler was born at Buntingford, Hertfordshire. He trained as an architect from 1933 to 1937, practicing until 1950 under the name of Cottrell Butler. He was Gregory Fellow at Leeds University 1950–3. In 1953 he was Grand Prizewinner in "The Unknown Political Prisoner" International Sculpture Competition, and was a visiting lecturer at the Slade School of Fine Art, London.

Reg Butler sculpted figures as a child. His early wood carvings and bronzes, influenced by Henry Moore, were succeeded in 1948 by open, linear forged iron figures and groups; from 1951 he also worked in cast iron. He introduced closed forms within a linear, skeletal structure. During

William Butterfield: the pulpit of All Saints church, Margaret Street, London; designed 1849

1953 he concentrated on single gesturing figures in bronze, supported by architectural constructions which become cages to suspend them in space. Between 1960 and 1963 he experimented with rectilinear maquettes for tower sculptures and from 1967 to 1972 he developed a series of larger-than-life female nudes in bronze, naturalistically painted with false eyes and hair, in exaggerated and provocative poses.

Butterfield William 1814–1900

The English architect William Butterfield was born in London. During his early

training with a builder he developed an interest in the practical aspects of building. He combined this with a commitment to the revival of medieval architecture and ritual, as advocated by the magazine *The Ecclesiologist*, to which he contributed. Most of his large practice was devoted to church-building and restoration. His assertive use of colored brickwork and his bold pattern-making at All Saints, Margaret Street, London (1849–59), introduced into the Gothic Revival a new vigor and richness which was displayed on a fuller scale in his masterpiece, Keble College, Oxford (1867–75).

C

Caffiéri family
17th and 18th centuries

The distinguished Caffiéri family of sculptors and bronze founders were descended from Daniel Caffiéri (1603–39), a papal engineer who worked in Rome. His son Philippe (1634–1729) was summoned to France by Mazarin in 1660 and worked under Charles Lebrun. Philippe's elder son, François-Charles (1667–1729), like his descendants Charles-Philippe (1695–1755) and Charles-Marie (1736–*post* 1744), specialized in decorative marine sculpture. Philippe's other son, Jacques (1678–1755), was the outstanding bronze founder and chiseler at the French court, where he was followed by his eldest son Philippe (1714–74). His younger son, Jean-Jacques (1725–92), studied under J.B. Lemoyne and became an outstanding sculptor of portrait busts.

Calamis 5th century BC

The Greek sculptor Calamis may have come from Athens. He worked in bronze, in marble, and in ivory and gold. It is uncertain whether he belonged to the early Classical or the Classical period, or both. He was commissioned to make a statue of *Zeus Ammon* by Pindar in Thebes, and for an *Aphrodite* by Callias, brother-in-law of the Athenian general Cimon. (The signed base of this work was found on the Acropolis.) Calamis collaborated with Onatas in the bronze group of a chariot and horses erected at Olympia by Dinomenes, King of Syracuse (467–466 BC). He also made an *Apollo, Averter of Evil*, possibly dedicated by the Athenians after the plague of 430 BC.

Calder Alexander 1898–1976

The American sculptor Alexander Calder was born in Philadelphia; his father was a sculptor, his mother a painter. He was at first interested in engineering, and in 1919 graduated from the Stevens Institute of Technology as a mechanical engineer. It was not until 1922 that he became seriously interested in art; he attended the Art Students' League in New York from 1923 until 1926, when his first paintings were exhibited. That same year, after a visit to England, he went on to Paris. He stayed

Jean-Jacques Caffiéri: bust of Jean-Philippe Rameau; terracotta; height 75cm (30in); 1760. Musée des Beaux-Arts, Dijon

there for a time, making a series of animated toys and also his first wire sculpture, inspired by the circus. For some years he continued to make wire sculpture, light in form and witty in tone, at times even reminiscent of drawings by Paul Klee (for example, *Romulus and Remus*, 1928; Solomon R. Guggenheim Museum, New York).

In 1930 Calder was attracted by the more austere work of Piet Mondrian and the Constructivists (notably Naum Gabo). He

also met Joan Miró and Jean Arp, who influenced his style. He began to produce very light, Abstract sculptures in wire and wood (Arp called them "stabiles", a word always associated with Calder's work). He also experimented with manual and motorized mobiles, which went through prescribed programs of movements (for example, *The White Frame*, 1934; Modern Museum, Stockholm).

From these experiments it was but a short step to the type of mobile Calder was to

Alexander Calder: The Spiral; metal mobile; height 500cm (197in); 1958. Unesco Complex, Paris

make his own: the series of flat, often brightly painted disks and metal shapes, suspended either from a ceiling or from an arm linked to a base on the floor. These works were held in balance, yet needed only the slightest draft of air to set them moving in ever-changing patterns (examples, *Lobster Trap and Fish Tail*, 1939; Museum of Modern Art, New York—a suspended mobile; *The Spiral*, 1958; Unesco Complex, Paris—an outdoor standing mobile). During the 1950s and 1960s, Calder received many commissions for large-scale outdoor sculpture: the Unesco mobile is 30 ft (10 m) high, while *Man*, the stabile he created for Montreal's EXPO 67, is 94 ft (31 m) high. Among the most inventive of 20th-century sculptors, Calder also worked as a book-illustrator and painter. In 1971 he was awarded the Gold Medal for Sculpture by America's National Institute of Arts and Letters.

Further reading. Calder, A. *An Autobiography with Pictures*, New York (1966). Cate, C. "Calder Made Easy", *Horizon*, New York (Winter 1972). Davidson, J. *Calder at the Zoo*, Washington, D.C. (1974).

Callot Jacques 1592–1635

The French engraver Jacques Callot was born at Nancy in Lorraine where his father was King-at-Arms to Duke Charles III. After being apprenticed to a local goldsmith, Callot left for Rome *c*1610 where he learned the art of line engraving. Late in 1611 he moved to Florence where his greatest success was in recording the festivals staged by the Grand Duke Cosimo II. Such plates as the *Florentine Fete* (1619) depict hundreds of people skillfully controlled in a coherent pattern within the panorama. His ability to build up large numbers of small figures into a unified composition was probably influenced by engravings after the works of Bosch and Bruegel. He also showed an interest in the grotesque, producing small plates of *Gobbi* (hunchbacks) and beggars, or, as in *Pantaloons*, borrowing characters from the *Commedia dell'Arte*. Here, characteristically, he juxtaposes these bizarre figures with the affectedly elegant courtiers who promenade in the background.

In 1621 the Grand Duke died, and Callot lost his pension. He returned to Lorraine and became a leading figure among the late Mannerists working in Nancy. He continued to produce his series of *Fetes* and engraved the finest of his studies in the grotesque, *Gypsies* (1622). He also produced a number of religious etchings in which the witty artificiality of court Mannerism gives way to a poignant and more dramatic feeling. In 1625 he was called upon to depict *The Siege of Breda*, and in 1629 *The Capture of La Rochelle*. In Paris he produced some of his most notable topographical works.

Returning to Nancy, Callot produced in 1633 his last great series, the *Grandes Misères de la Guerre* (British Museum, London). Though partly influenced by the Thirty Years War (marked in 1633 by Richelieu's invasion of Lorraine) the scenes also draw on past experience, such as *The Siege of Breda*.

Calvaert Denys 1540–1619

Denys Calvaert (also called Dionisio Fiammingo) was a Flemish painter from Antwerp. He emigrated to Italy *c*1560–2 and there became an important member of the Bolognese school. In 1570 he went to Rome, where he helped Lorenzo Sabbatini with decorative work at the Vatican. He later founded a teaching academy in Bologna, which provided a model for the more famous academy created by the Carracci *c*1585–6. Calvaert taught over 130 artists, notably the Bolognese painters Guido Reni and Domenichino.

Canaletto 1697–1768

Antonio Canale, nicknamed Canaletto, was born in Venice; he was the son of a scene painter and started his career in his father's workshop. About 1720 he turned to the painting of views and concentrated on this for the rest of his life, raising the genre to a new artistic level. His progenitors as *veduta* painters were Luca Antonio Carlevaris and the Dutch-born Jaspar van Wittel or Vanvitelli, but Canaletto's superiority to them was early recognized by his contemporaries.

His views of his native city were intended for export. Through the Irish impresario Owen MacSwiny and through Joseph Smith, a merchant resident in Venice who became British Consul in 1744, he acquired a large clientele in England. Smith's own collection of 54 paintings and over 140 drawings was sold to George III and many are still in the Royal Art Collection at Windsor.

In 1745, partly as a result of the War of the Austrian Succession, which made travel difficult for his patrons, Canaletto went to England. He lived mainly there until 1755, painting many views of the Thames and its bridges, of Whitehall, and

Denys Calvaert: The Presentation of Mary; oil on canvas; 93×78cm (37×31in). Pinacoteca Nazionale, Bologna

Canaletto: Venice, The Rialto Bridge from the South; oil on copper; 46×63cm (18×25in); c1729. Collection of the Earl of Leicester, Holkham Hall, Norfolk

of a number of country houses including Warwick Castle and Badminton.

In these, as in all his works, the topography is extraordinarily accurate. He made detailed pen and ink drawings, which are often annotated, and seems to have used a *camera obscura* in order to notate with detailed precision the minutiae of a scene before him. All his works employ linear perspective, which is used not only as an illusionistic device but as a means to aesthetic order. He often employs wide-angle or birds-eye views with several vanishing points; the perspective is handled so as to control the way the painting is seen, leading the eye on a structured voyage of exploration through its complex spaces.

His Venetian views are very varied, moving from the enclosed irregular spaces of the smaller Venetian *campi* to wide panoramas of the Grand Canal and the Bacino di San Marco. In the careful distribution of accents across the surface they show a sense of interval which is classical and deeply satisfying: but this is combined with a feeling for extended effects of air and atmosphere which is essentially Rococo and comparable with Tiepolo.

Canaletto's early works, such as the so-called *Stonemason's Yard* in the National Gallery, London, favor picturesque effects of surface and texture. Some of his greatest paintings of this period, for example, the *View of S. Cristoforo* (Royal Art Collection, Windsor) have open, Corotesque brushwork, evoking effects of light comparable to early Impressionism. Later, however, the need for elaborate detail and spatial precision led to a harder, more schematic notation, with many twirls and twiddles of the brush: in his very late work, the style became somewhat mannered and dry.

This mature style was well suited to engravings, and Visentini's several engraved series of Canaletto's Venetian views (1732; 1745) are important extensions of the painter's art and influence.

Further reading. Barker, C. *Canaletto*, London (1994). Brandi, C. *Canaletto*, Milan (1960). Bromberg, R. *Canaletto's Etchings*, London (1974). Constable, W.G. *Canaletto, Giovanni Antonio Canal*, Oxford (1976). Links, J.G. *Canaletto and his Patrons*, London (1977).

Cano Alonso 1601–67

The Spanish painter, sculptor, and architect Alonso Cano was born in Granada. He went early to Seville, and was apprenticed in 1616 to the painter Francisco Pacheco, becoming the fellow pupil of Diego Velázquez. Though painting was his major activity, Cano was early attracted to the polychromed wood sculpture that was popular in Seville; he may have received some training as a sculptor from Juan Martínez Montañés (1568–1648).

His large sculpture of the *Virgin and Child* in the retable in the church of Santa Maria at Lebrija (Seville; 1621–31), shows striking originality in a Baroque idiom —the sweeping folds of the Virgin's draperies from head to feet give her an unprecedented air of majestic dignity. In the design of the architectural framework of that retable, Cano displayed even greater originality, abandoning the normal balanced proportions to make the lower story twice the height of the upper one and framing it in a giant order of Palladian inspiration.

Cano's early paintings in Seville were tenebrist, but he soon adopted a more colorful style. Among his works for religious orders, *St John the Evangelist's Vision of Jerusalem* (1635–7; Wallace Collection, London), for the nuns of Santa Paula, was an outstanding achievement. The painting displays a sculptural modeling and foreshortening prominent in a vigorous Baroque diagonal composition. The signed *St Agnes*, probably from the same period, was destroyed in Berlin in 1945. It made skillful use of shadows to add suppleness to a sculpturesque figure in a more static composition.

In Madrid (1638–52) Cano was mostly active as a painter and his work reflected renewed contact with Velázquez. He received royal commissions and frequently worked for religious bodies. Among many representations of the Virgin is *The Immaculate Conception* (c1650–2), in the Provincial Museum at Vitoria, in which the contrapposto attitude of the body gives a spiral movement to the wind-blown mantle. The beautifully modeled figure of Eve, a rare example of a female nude in this period, is notable in the *Christ in Limbo* (c1646–52; Los Angeles County Museum of Art, Los Angeles) though this composition is uneven in quality. In spite of increasing success, Cano returned to Granada embittered by false accusations that he had murdered his second wife.

Becoming a prebendary of Granada Cathedral, Cano again turned his attention to sculpture. Still in the cathedral are large busts of *Adam* and *Eve* (c1666–7), and a small *Immaculate Conception* (1656), originally decorating the lectern he designed. Notable among late paintings in Granada are seven enormous canvases of *The Life of the Virgin*, placed high in the cathedral sanctuary with simple compositions, most effective in the *Annunciation* and *Visitation* (1652–6). He also provided the design for the main facade of the cathedral, which was not completed until after his death.

Cano was the most versatile artist of his period in Spain. His reputation has suffered from the legends arising from his volatile temperament, together with the unevenness of his production and the disappearance of many important recorded works. But at its best his achievement as a painter and sculptor was of a high level, and he was a superb draftsman.

Canova Antonio 1757–1822

The Italian Neoclassical artist Canova became, internationally, the most famous sculptor of the 18th century. He began his career as a stonemason in northern Italy, but moved to Venice in 1768 and was apprenticed to a minor sculptor. In 1780 he arrived in Rome where almost immediately he discarded the skillful naturalistic style of his early work. He began to study Greco-Roman art and was influenced by the theories of Neoclassical collectors, archaeologists, and theorists, like Gavin Hamilton. In a short time Canova created the style that became the most expressive sculptural statement of the whole Neoclassical movement. His new inspiration depended on antique subject matter, but Canova also imbued his work with a personal concept of the ideal. His first major Neoclassical work, *Theseus and the Minotaur* (1781–3; Victoria and Albert Museum, London), is a figure that emulates the style of a Classical statue without being a slavish copy. Canova made constant use of the most diverse artistic precedents. His first important monument, *Pope Clement XIV* (1783–7; SS. Apostoli, Rome), was another personal adaptation from Bernini's Baroque tomb convention which Canova freely adapted into a Neoclassical idiom.

Canova was a prolific workman who ran a large studio in Rome. He usually finished the marble himself but he also employed a great many assistants. These worked on the marble and enlarged Canova's models (*bozzetti*) and preliminary designs with the aid of machinery. The sculptor could thus produce replicas of his work for an international market. Canova was always aware of the dangers of mechanical reproduction in sculpture and used numerous techniques for avoiding them. He made terracotta models, sometimes to scale, on which the details might be emphasized. When the assistants copied these models in marble they were less likely to lose surface animation and could preserve the dy-

namics of Canova's original image.

While Canova's style seems rooted in J.J. Winckelmann's Neoclassical creed (which demanded a smooth, calm sculpture with closed, compact outlines), the surfaces of Canova's figures are never monotonous like those of his contemporaries and imitators. This was perhaps due to the artist's early training. Canova's quest for truth to the Classical ideal was tempered by his insight into the possibilities of sculpture itself. His freestanding figures have an all-round viewpoint which maintains their antique derivation. Canova also systematically refined his work, bringing the details and textures to a highly polished state. This deliberate over-refinement often makes Canova's sculpture appear simultaneously frigid and sensual. It expresses the restraint and harmony that Winckelmann regarded as the essence of the best Greek sculpture; it also invests Canova's work with immense originality. Part of this originality came from the artist's fascination with different materials. Whether he worked in stone, marble, or clay Canova always displayed an understanding of the demands of each medium in relation to the shape he was trying to evolve. Many of his figures assume static, compact poses which allow little movement to disturb their integral form. Nevertheless, they are works of art that glory in physical beauty; they are never purely intellectual abstractions of a remote ideal. Canova himself cautioned admiring spectators never to forget the sculptor's struggle with the material: "I do not aim in my works at deceiving the beholder," he said. "We know that they are marble, mute, and immobile."

This overwhelming interest in techniques also influenced Canova's approach to the Antique. *Hebe* (c1808–14; Duke of Devonshire Collection, Chatsworth, Derbyshire), for example, was originally colored in order to make it correspond more closely to antique precedents, and Canova added a gilt ewer and cup. He was criticized for this scholarly departure from the Neoclassical rule of consistency and restraint in sculpture, but the figure became one of his most popular images.

The unorthodox nature of his Neoclassical sculpture made his work highly prized in the early 19th century. The sensuality of Canova's marble figures invited spectators to touch—or even kiss—the marble. When Canova saw the Elgin marbles during his visit to London at the end of 1815, he recognized the animation and passion of genuine Classical carving. It was this sense of passion and movement that gave a Romantic character to Canova's work.

Canova's work spanned many regimes and nations. He worked for the Emperor Francis II of Austria, Catherine the Great of Russia, the Duke of Wellington, and Napoleon. He made many memorable portraits, the most bizarre of which was a nude statue of Napoleon in marble, 10 ft (3 m) high, which now stands in the Wellington Museum at Apsley House in London. An equally famous (or notorious) nude portrait was that of Napoleon's sister Pauline Borghese reclining as a *Venus Vincitrice* (1805–7; Museo e Galleria Borghese, Rome). Napoleon invited Canova to live and work in Paris but the sculptor declined; he remained in Rome, working for the Papal court.

In 1815 Canova became the Pope's representative in restoring to Italian collections works of art that had been looted by Napoleon during the Italian campaign. He traveled to Paris and London, where he was received as a major celebrity. The Pope made him Marchese d'Ischia in 1816, and Canova retired to his home village of Possagno near Treviso. Here he built a studio which now houses the most important collection of his works, particularly his models and his collection of antiquities. During the 19th century Canova's popu-

Jan van de Capelle: State Barge saluted by the Home Fleet; oil on panel; 64×93cm (25×37in); 1650. Rijksmuseum, Amsterdam

larity as a sculptor declined, but his style remained influential for serious historical sculpture, particularly in England. His work was celebrated by major poets such as Keats, Shelley, and Heinrich Heine.

Further reading. Honour, H. *Neoclassicism*, London (1968). Missirini, M. *Della Vita di Antonio Canova*, Milan (1824).

Antonio Canova: Pauline Borghese as Venus; marble; 87×185×65cm (34×73×26in); 1805–7. Museo e Galleria Borghese, Rome

Capelle Jan van de 1626–79

Jan van de Capelle was a wealthy Amsterdam dyer and self-taught painter who became one of Holland's greatest marine artists. His pictures are less often seascapes than views of estuaries and harbors (for example, *The Calm*, 1651; Art Institute of Chicago). In these, Dutch merchant or naval ships lie quietly at anchor, the pattern of verticals created by their masts outlined against the large, fleecy clouds which fill three quarters or more of his canvases. The artist probably painted some of these views from his own pleasure yacht. His early works are silver-gray in tonality; later pictures have warmer colors, and convey a sense of moist but luminous atmosphere. Sunlight picks out detail at great distances in his translucent paintings; the effect is one of spaciousness and serenity. He also painted subtly composed and colored winter scenes, for example *Bridge Across a Frozen Canal* (1653; Royal Museum of Art, Mauritshuis, The Hague).

Capogrossi Giuseppe 1900–72

The Italian painter Guarna Giuseppe Capogrossi began his career in law but turned to painting between 1927 and 1933 while in Paris. Here his art gradually evolved from realism to abstraction under the influence of such artists as Joan Miró.

From 1933 he lived in Rome, and in 1949 he founded the "Origine" group with Burri, Colla, and Ballocco. Capogrossi's nonfigurative ideograms also appeared in 1949 and remained central to his work. These signs often take the form of hand-like graffiti ranged in opposing pairs over the whole canvas (for example, *Section 4*, 1953; oil on canvas; Museum of Modern Art, New York).

Caravaggio 1573–1609/10

Michelangelo Merisi, called Caravaggio, was born in Caravaggio near Bergamo, Lombardy. From 1584–8 he was apprenticed to Simone Peterzano, a Bergamesque late-Mannerist artist, and as a young man he absorbed the traditions of Savoldo, Moretto, and Lotto. Some time c1592–3 Caravaggio moved to Rome.

His temperament was violent and anarchic; throughout his life he was involved in brawls, continually skirmishing with the authorities, and sometimes in prison. His powerfully original art was also violent and showed no respect for authority. In Rome he quickly gained a reputation as an uncompromising realist who painted only what he saw. He worked straight on to the canvas without the use of preliminary drawings; he used strong, bright local colors, very different from the subtleties of Mannerist hues.

Caravaggio believed it required as much skill to paint a good picture of flowers as one of figures; it seems likely that he began his career as a still-life painter. His *Basket of Fruit* (Pinacoteca Ambrosiana, Milan) was probaby painted for Cardinal del Monte. From 1596 Caravaggio was attached to his household and painted for him and his circle a series of half-length figures of boys playing lutes, with carafes holding wine or flowers, or offering baskets of fruit. Among these works are *Self-Portrait as Young Bacchus (Bacchino Malato)* and the *Boy with a Basket of Fruit* (both Museo e Galleria Borghese, Rome), *A Musical Scene* (Metropolitan Museum, New York), and *Bacchus* (Uffizi, Florence). The figures are shown against plain but warm backgrounds. The paint is smooth, and the superbly accomplished still-life elements are painted in bright colors with precise, fresh details of surface and texture. There is, however, a hint of uncertainty in the placing of the figures in space. Though genre paintings, these are not realistic works. The boys have a lan-

guid elegance, and the clear beauty of their youth is mingled with their obvious knowledge of less innocent pleasures. The erotic appeal is made shamelessly explicit in *Victorious Love* (Staatliche Museen, Berlin), probably painted c1602.

From 1598 Caravaggio began to paint altarpieces. His most important commissions for the remainder of his stay in Rome were scenes from *The Life of St Matthew*, (Contarelli Chapel, S. Luigi dei Francesi) painted between 1599 and 1602, *The Conversion of St Paul* and *The Crucifixion of St Peter*, 1601 (Cerasi Chapel, S. Maria del Popolo), *The Entombment of Christ* (Vatican Museums, Rome) painted in 1602 for S. Maria in Vallicella, and the *Death of the Virgin* (Louvre, Paris) painted 1602–4 for S. Maria della Scala in Trastevere.

In these works Caravaggio created a deeply original religious style. They are distinguished by a startlingly direct dramatic appeal to the spectator, and a sense of profound compassion for the sufferings and complexities of humanity, both new in painting. The Contarelli Chapel paintings, in oil on canvas, consist of an altarpiece, *St Matthew and the Angel*, and two side paintings, *The Calling of Matthew* and *The Martyrdom of St Matthew*. These works mark a turning point in 17th-century art. Caravaggio's approach was realistic and he painted from humble models. A first version of the altarpiece, *St Matthew and the Angel* (formerly Kaiser-Friedrich Museum, Berlin; destroyed) was rejected by the clergy as improper. The saint was shown as a burly peasant whose dirty feet seemed to jut out of the painting towards the spectator. A graceful angel, erotically close to him, guided his hand. The final version was more conventional. *The Calling of St Matthew* shows a squalid setting and unheroic figures; the saint and his flashy gambling companions sit at a table in the courtyard of a Roman Palace. Their complex psychological reactions to the appearance of Christ are shown with a new and vivid narrative realism. To a public accustomed to Raphael's idealization, these were startling works.

Caravaggio abandoned the even lighting of his early work and began to place the figures in semi-darkness lit by a harsh beam of light. The lighting was contrived in the studio and is irrational: the dramatic and poetic contrasts of light and dark create a deeply spiritual atmosphere. In *The Calling of St Matthew* there is a

large dark area above the figures and the symbolic light falls from the right, accompanying the gesture of Christ, to penetrate the darkness of the unconverted. The composition is relatively simple; the figures are located in the foreground and the space behind closed.

The plebeian characters, stark settings and confined space occur in other works. In the *Death of the Virgin* Caravaggio shows the Virgin as a bloated corpse. The painting was rejected by the Carmelites as indecorous, yet it is a work of moving gravity.

Dramatic crises were heightened by the use of great gestures which seem to burst out of the picture-plane and fuse the world of the picture with the world of the spectator. In *The Conversion of St Paul* the saint lies at the foot of his horse; his dramatically foreshortened body and outflung arms are intended to draw the worshiper into the drama. Paul's eyes are closed and the conversion is within him; there is no excited recognition of supernatural powers.

At this period the figures themselves are solidly modeled and elaborately posed and the compositions clear and compact. *The Entombment of Christ* is Caravaggio's most severely constructed work; the figures have a grandiose, almost sculptural solidity. The corner of the stone slab on which the bearers of Christ's body are standing juts out towards us, and the whole composition seems to expand into our space. The emotions of the figures are expressed in expansive gestures.

In 1606 Caravaggio killed a man in a fight and had to flee Rome. In 1607 he was in Naples; his most important works there are *The Seven Works of Mercy* (church of the Pio Monte della Misericordia, Naples) of 1607 and *The Flagellation* (S. Domenico Maggiore, Naples), possibly 1610. The former is distinguished by its human warmth of feeling and astonishing freedom of composition, the latter by its somber brutality.

Caravaggio was in Malta in 1607–8. He was commissioned by the Grand Master of the Knights of Jerusalem to paint *The Execution of John the Baptist* for the cathedral of St John in Valletta. This huge canvas (12 by 17 ft; 4 by 5.6 m.) is remarkable for its austerely symmetrical

Caravaggio: The Entombment of Christ; oil on canvas; 300×203cm (118×80in); 1602–4. Vatican Museums, Rome

composition and for its unusual technical spontaneity. The executioner is about to lift the saint's head into a bowl held out by Salome, and the frozen stillness of the participants underlines the horror of the scene. In his detailed rendering of extreme violence Caravaggio typifies one important aspect of 17th-century emotional response.

After trouble with the authorities in Malta, Caravaggio fled to Sicily and then returned to Naples; he died of a fever on his way to Rome in 1610. In Sicily Caravaggio had painted *The Burial of St Lucy* (Church of S. Lucia, Syracuse), *The Raising of Lazarus* (Museo Nazionale, Messina), and *The Nativity with St Francis and St Lawrence* (S. Lorenzo, Palermo). In these works both composition and gesture are even less traditional than before. The dark areas are often larger than in his earlier works and darkness seems to engulf the figures, who are themselves less solidly modeled. In *The Raising of Lazarus* emotions are rendered with a new expressionist urgency. In *The Burial of St Lucy* Caravaggio makes a painful contrast between the scale of the grave diggers—massive and unmoved in the foreground—and the small pathetic body of the saint stretched out beside the grave.

Although realism and lighting are the aspects of his style most often discussed, it should be stressed that Caravaggio did not paint scenes from everyday life but chose the traditional subjects of Italian figure-painters. Nor was his humble approach appreciated by the people or the lower clergy; he was patronized by cardinals and by the most cultivated members of the aristocracy.

Caravaggio did not have pupils nor did his imitators form a school or a homogenous group. Artists would adapt certain aspects of his style, or else, after undergoing a Caravaggesque phase, would turn to other styles. Nonetheless his influence spread rapidly and dramatically throughout Europe. In Rome it was most important between 1610 and 1620. His most significant Italian followers were Orazio Gentileschi, Orazio Borgiani, Carlo Saraceni, and Bartolomeo Manfredi. A group of Northern artists working in Rome, including the French Valentin de Boulogne, popularized the coarser versions of Caravaggio's early genre scenes throughout western Europe.

By 1620 the movement had finished in Rome, but Northern artists who had visited Rome had established a center in Utrecht. The most important of these were Dirck van Baburen, Gerrit van Honthorst (a specialist in candle-light scenes), and Hendrick Terbrugghen. Caravaggio's influence was most profound and lasting in the Spanish colony of Naples and in Spain itself; the Neapolitan Caracciolo and the Spaniard Jose de Ribera were both attracted by his chiaroscuro and by his violent subject matter. His influence also spread to north Italy, Sicily, and France. Many of the greatest artists of the period—Rubens, Rembrandt, Velazquez, Georges de la Tour, and Vermeer—were deeply affected by his art.

Further reading. Friedländer, W. *Caravaggio Studies*, Princeton (1955). Hinks, R. *Michelangelo Merisi da Caravaggio*, London (1953). Kitson, M. *The Complete Painting of Caravaggio*, New York (1967). Mori, A. *Caravaggio and his Copyists*, New York (1976). Mori, A. *The Italian Followers of Caravaggio*, Cambridge, Mass. (1967). Nicolson, B. *The International Caravaggesque Movement*, Oxford (1979).

Carducho Vicente 1578–1638

The Spanish painter and theorist Vicente Carducho was born in Florence. In 1585 he went to Spain with his brother Bartolomé (1560–1608). He became Bartolomé's pupil and eventually succeeded him as King's Painter in 1609, becoming virtual dictator in artistic matters at Madrid.

Outstanding among his enormous production as a painter in a naturalistic style are the 56 large canvases for the Charterhouse of El Paular near Madrid (1626–31), now distributed among various collections in Spain.

His theories were expounded in his *Diálogos de la Pintura* (1633), which indirectly reveal envy of the success of the young Velázquez at Court.

Carlevaris Luca 1665–1731

Mathematician as well as artist, the Venetian view painter Luca Carlevaris is best remembered for his series of large reception pieces. *The Procession of the Earl of Manchester* (City of Birmingham Museums and Art Gallery) of 1707 is typical: it is composed like a school photograph with many small figures competing for attention. This vast work was not painted

from life but was built up from fluent oil sketches (now in the Victoria and Albert Museum, London) whose bravura appealed to Canaletto (1697–1768).

More influential in his own time was the series of 103 etchings (1703) which expanded the small number of stock Venetian views. These stimulated an interest in less familiar views of the city: a demand that was later met by Canaletto and Francesco Guardi.

Caro Anthony 1924–

The English sculptor Anthony Alfred Caro was born in London. He took his Master's degree in engineering at Cambridge University in 1944. He then studied at the Royal Academy Schools under Charles Wheeler, 1947–52. During 1951–3 he worked as a part-time assistant to Henry

Luca Carlevaris: The Arrival of the Fourth Earl of Manchester in Venice; oil on canvas; 132×264cm (52×104in); 1707. City of Birmingham Museums and Art Gallery

Moore. He taught at St Martin's School of Art from 1953 to 1956, and again from 1968 to 1973. He spent the years 1963 to 1965 teaching at Bennington College, Vermont, U.S.A.

From 1954 to 1959 Caro modeled expressionist figures in clay, cast in bronze. After visiting the United States in 1959, influenced by the sculptor David Smith and the critic Clement Greenberg, he began making large, painted nonfigurative sculptures. These were welded and bolted from steel scrap, and placed directly on the ground. In 1962 he ceased painting his work, but from 1971 allowed them to rust and then varnished them. His working procedures are entirely distinctive. Since

Anthony Caro: Prospect II; painted steel; 260×215×31cm (102×85×12in); 1964. Museum Ludwig, Cologne

1966 he has made smaller pieces, especially for plinths, at the same time as full-scale works. Caro's work has had tremendous influence on other artists, both in Britain and the United States, where he had a retrospective exhibition at New York's Museum of Modern Art in 1975.

Further reading. Fried, M. "Caro's Abstractness", *Art Forum*, New York (April 1972). Whelan, R. *Anthony Caro*, Harmondsworth (1974).

Carpaccio Vittore 1472–1526

The Italian painter Carpaccio worked almost exclusively in Venice where he specialized in the production of huge panoramic paintings, depicting a large number of figures. In these he followed in the steps of Gentile (and Jacopo) Bellini, in whose workshop he probably received his training; in 1507 he was named among Giovanni Bellini's assistants.

Carpaccio's first dated work is the canvas depicting *The Arrival of St Ursula in Cologne* (1490). This is one of a series of nine paintings dated 1490–5 portraying scenes from the saint's life, which originally hung in the Scuola di S. Orsola and are now in the Gallerie dell'Accademia, Venice. In common with Carpaccio's other narrative works, the action of these paintings takes place in settings that provide detailed evidence for contemporary architecture, fashion, and many other aspects of Venetian life. In the later paintings of the cycle, for instance *The Reception of the English Ambassadors*, his mastery of per-

spective, color, and the depiction of a large number of figures in space is far advanced: thereafter his style changes very little. *The Miracle of the True Cross* (c1495; Gallerie dell'Accademia, Venice) was commissioned by the Scuola di San Giovanni Evangelista as part of a series of canvases by different artists; it is particularly rich in authentic contemporary detail.

On a smaller scale are Carpaccio's paintings representing scenes from the lives of Saints George and Jerome; these are still preserved in the Scuola di San Giorgio degli Schiavoni, Venice, for which they were painted in the first decade of the 16th century. Carpaccio painted other cycles for the Scuola degli Albanesi and the Scuola di San Stefano; he also contributed paintings

to the series of historical subjects in the Sala del Gran' Consiglio of the Ducal Palace (destroyed in the fire of 1577).

There are in addition a handful of religious and secular works, with several others recorded in drawings. Among Carpaccio's earliest works is the panel depicting *Christ and the Four Apostles* (Contini Bonaccossi Collection, Florence), showing elements derived from Antonello da Messina. His altarpieces generally have an exterior setting and do not usually employ the semi-illusory framework evolved by Antonello and by Giovanni Bellini. Carpaccio's historical importance lies almost entirely in his panoramic views; apart from his two sons, who were both painters of minor importance, he had no true artistic heirs.

Vittore Carpaccio: detail of The Disputation of St Stephen; oil on canvas; full size 147×172cm (58×68in); 1514. Pinacoteca di Brera, Milan

Carpeaux Jean-Baptiste 1827–75

Carpeaux was the major French sculptor of his day. His works have qualities of movement and rhythm that contrast with contemporary academic sculpture, and make him the precursor of Rodin. He also produced a number of oil paintings.

He studied at the École des Beaux-Arts under François Rude, won the Prix de Rome in 1854, and spent the years 1856–62 in Italy. He neglected his studies of the Antique to observe the daily life of the people, which furnished the basis for his *Fisherboy with a Seashell* (plaster; 1855–9; Louvre, Paris). In Rome he began *Ugolino* (bronze; 1861–3; Louvre, Paris), a dramatic work using a pyramidal composition of five figures in tortuous poses, influenced by Michelangelo.

On his return to France he was introduced into the circle of Princesse Mathilde, cousin of Napoleon III, and this led to commissions for a number of portrait busts of the ruling classes of the Second Empire. These combine the elegance of the work of Houdon (1741–1828) with a new frankness and liveliness: for example his bust of the Empress Eugénie (plaster; 1866; Musée du Petit Palais, Paris). He received a commission for the decoration of the Pavillon de Flore of the Louvre (stone; 1866), in which he used fuller forms based on Flemish painting. He sculpted a group for the front of the Paris Opéra, *The Dance* (stone; 1869; Louvre, Paris). This joyous, rhythmical work was considered immoral.

Carpeaux's last major monumental work was his fountain for the Paris Observatory (bronze; 1874); it includes four figures symbolizing the points of the compass, represented as ethnic types, and supporting the celestial sphere.

Carrà Carlo 1881–1966

The Italian painter Carlo Carrà was born in Piedmont. A self-taught artist, he worked first as a decorator. In 1910 he signed the *Manifesto of Futurist Painters*. He adopted the Cubist technique of breaking up a subject into facets in order to create repetitive rhythms that expressed Futurist dynamism. In 1914 he also used collage, incorporating printed letters implying noise—another Futurist fetish. He eventually became dissatisfied with the Futurist style, which lacked the solidity of form he admired in the work of Giotto (1266–1337). His paintings of 1916 depict

Carlo Carrà: Woman at a Window (Simultaneity); oil on canvas; 147×133cm (58×52in); 1912. Collection of Dr Riccardo Jucker, Milan

doll-like but fully rounded figures; these were to develop into the dummies in eerie deserted settings that characterize his metaphysical period (a response to the influence of de Chirico). This phase lasted from 1917 to 1921. Afterwards the fantastical element in Carrà's work became subdued in favor of muted classical treatment of landscape and the figure.

Carracci family
16th and 17th centuries

The Carracci—the brothers Agostino (1557–1602) and Annibale (1560–1609), and their cousin Lodovico (1555–1619)—were a family of Italian painters active in Bologna and Rome. It was above all Annibale, the most talented of the three, who, by reviving a classical and naturalistic style, broke away from the late Mannerist painting predominant in Italy from 1620. The Carracci worked closely together in Bologna in the 1580s; their studio, known as the Carracci Academy, in which life-drawing was regularly taught, attracted many younger artists to train there. In his Roman work, particularly in the ceiling of the Farnese Gallery (Palazzo Farnese, Rome) Annibale effectively restored the artistic language of Antiquity and of Raphael (1483–1520) and Michelangelo (1475–1564). This he combined with Venetian colorism to produce a style of painting rich in naturalistic form which was to remain influential throughout the 17th century.

Agostino, who trained with his cousin Lodovico, was principally an engraver. He made prints after the work of, among others, Barocci and Tintoretto (he met the latter in Venice in 1582). He was a gifted teacher, and among the first to systematize the teaching of life-drawing. Under his direction it was a step-by-step procedure: the student first learned to draw the different parts of the human anatomy, such as the eyes, the nose, and the mouth, before combining them together into a whole head. His anatomical drawings were engraved and the prints were widely used in later artist academies. Agostino was only periodically occupied as a painter; his work was inspired more by Annibale than by Lodovico. The paintings he executed in Bologna in the 1580s and 1590s before his visit to Rome include *Adoration of the Shepherds* (c1584; Madonna della Pioggia, Bologna), and *The Last Communion of St Jerome* (c1593; Pinacoteca Nazionale, Bologna). The composition of the latter work was developed by Domenichino in a famous painting of the same subject now in the Vatican Museums. In 1597 Agostino was in Rome where he helped Annibale with the decoration of the Farnese Gallery ceiling; his work there can be seen in the stories *Peleus and Thetis* and *Cephalus and Aurora*. After quarreling with Annibale he went to Parma where he worked for Duke Ranuccio Farnese in the Palazzo del Giardino. The frescoes he painted there are rather dry variations of Annibale's Roman work.

Annibale was born in Bologna where he trained under Lodovico. He soon gained experience of frescoe painting in decorating the Palazzi Fava and Magnani, in which all three Carracci collaborated. To begin with, his paintings showed elements of Mannerism; this can best be seen in the early *Crucifixion* (1583; S. Niccolò, Bologna). Soon there was a change: the results of a visit to Parma, where he studied the works of Correggio, became visible in his paintings. In 1585, still under the influence of Correggio, he painted *The Baptism of Christ* (S. Gregorio, Bologna) where his forms began to soften and became more naturalistic. By 1587, in *Assumption of the Virgin* (Gemäldegalerie Alte Meister, Dresden), his dependence on Correggio was even more complete. But after a stay in Venice his experience of Venetian painting, particularly of the work of Titian and Veronese, began to reveal itself, above all in another *Assumption of the Virgin*

(1592; Pinacoteca Nazionale, Bologna). The result was that he started using blocks of bright color together with the muted tones derived from Correggio: the combination is one of two essential ingredients of Annibale's later pre-Roman work. The other ingredient is a tendency towards classical solidity of form where figures are conceived monumentally. This became apparent even before his visit to Rome and before his close familiarity with the works of the High Renaissance masters and the Antique. The development is best seen in *The Almsgiving of St Roch* (Gemäldegalerie Alte Meister, Dresden), painted from *c*1590.

Annibale visited Rome in 1595; he stayed in the city, apart from making a few unimportant excursions, for the rest of his life. It was here that Annibale's art reached the high point of its development, and his classical and naturalistic style came to maturity. He had been called to the city by Cardinal Odoardo Farnese to paint the Camerino and the Gallery of the Palazzo Farnese. It was also intended that Annibale should decorate the Gran' Salone, in the same palace, with frescoes illustrating the deeds of Prince Alessandro Farnese. He was prevented from doing this by his early death. The decoration of the Camerino, a small room which was used as the Cardinal's study, was Annibale's first undertaking: it occupied him from 1595 to 1597. The stories of Hercules and Ulysses he painted there illustrate the triumph of virtue; their complicated allegorical theme was devised by the Cardinal's tutor and adviser, Fulvio Orsini. In the central painting, *The Choice of Hercules* (now Museo e Gallerie Nazionali di Capodimonte, Naples) Annibale showed himself capable of interpreting pictorially a subtle narrative theme.

The style employed by Annibale in the Camerino was successfully developed and extended to a larger scale in the ceiling of the Gallery, painted immediately afterwards (1557–1600). Here the frescoes illustrate love scenes of the gods taken from Ovid's *Metamorphoses*; the whole was conceived as an epithalamium, probably to celebrate the marriage of the Cardinal's brother, Duke Ranuccio Farnese. The program was frankly pagan in character, in contrast with the vast religious decorations of the preceding century, particularly Michelangelo's Sistine Chapel ceiling. Intended to show how love dominates action, the mood of the ceiling is light-

Annibale Carracci: Christ Appears to St Peter (Domine Quo Vadis?); oil on canvas; 77×56cm (30×22in); c1602. National Gallery, London

hearted and mischievous, the colors bright and joyous. In the structure of the ceiling Annibale used a design which—with its lateral divisions and its use of *ignudi* framing medallions—resembles that of Michelangelo's Sistine Chapel ceiling. This he combined with the type of simple frieze decoration employed earlier in the Palazzi Fava and Magnani. The scenes themselves are separate from the framework and are attached to it like transferred easel pictures (*quadri riportati*). Annibale borrowed this device from the ceiling frescoes of Raphael's Loggie in the Vatican, as well as from Tibaldi's ceiling decorations in the Palazzo Poggi, Bologna. The ceiling was not fully illusionistic; but the later Baroque ceilings it influenced, such as Pietro da Cortona's ceiling in the Palazzo Barberini, Rome, were to be so. Together with Michelangelo's Sistine Chapel ceiling, and Raphael's frescoes in the Vatican, Annibale's Farnese ceiling was rated as one of the masterpieces of Roman painting.

Towards the end of his life illness forced Annibale to be less active. But a number of history paintings from his later years were to influence artists like Domenichino and Poussin by their classical purity. They include *Christ Appears to St Peter (Domine Quo Vadis?)* (*c*1602; National Gallery, London) and the *Pietà* (*c*1602–7; Louvre, Paris). In both, Annibale restricted the number of figures within the composition and concentrated on the communicative force of gesture and facial expression.

Annibale was also a landscape-painter of great originality. His early experiments depended on Venetian landscapes but he later evolved a classical type in which the

different scenic elements are logically arranged. *The Flight into Egypt* (Galleria Doria Pamphili, Rome) is a fine example of Annibale's late landscape-painting. Also, particularly at the beginning of his career, Annibale experimented with informal genre painting of which *The Butcher's Shop* (Christ Church Picture Gallery, Oxford) is an example.

Lodovico was the eldest of the Carracci. He was the dominant figure in the studio at the beginning of the 1580s and it was he who first indicated the path away from contemporary Mannerism. He spent his career almost entirely in Bologna, and for this reason his development was quite different from that of Agostino and Annibale, both of whom were to respond to the art of Rome. The paintings of Lodovico therefore show different preoccupations: far from exploring natural form in terms of classical structure, he aimed at transient effects achieved by means of light and shade. Anatomical accuracy was secondary to compositional unity. This can be seen in his painting, *The Holy Family with SS. Joseph and Francis* (1591; Pinacoteca Civica, Cento) where the figures, which are placed in darkened surroundings, are picked out by highlights. Their interrelationship in space is not clear, and the composition is held together by the gestures and glances of the figures. Lodovico's work, inspired by Tintoretto and Correggio, has more affinities with the developing Baroque style, (particularly the work of Lanfranco and Guercino), than with Annibale's classicism. After 1597, with Agostino's departure from Bologna, Lodovico was left in charge of the Carracci studio. As a result it was his work rather than Annibale's that inspired a new generation of younger Bolognese artists, among them Tiarini and Cavedone. But with the absence of his cousins, Lodovico's work became by degrees increasingly old-fashioned.

Further reading. Boschloo, A. *Annibale Carracci in Bologna*, The Hague (1974). Posner, D. *Annibale Carracci: A Study in the Reform of Italian Painting around 1590*, London (1971). Wittkower, R. *The Drawings of the Carracci*, London (1952).

Right: Lodovico Carracci: The Bargellini Madonna; oil on canvas; 282×188cm (111×74in); 1588. Pinacoteca Nazionale, Bologna

Carriera Rosalba 1675–1757

Lightness of palette and charm secured the Venetian painter Rosalba Carriera her immense success. She was honored and feted in many European capitals as well as in her native Venice. Although other pastelists were later to equal and to surpass her, she can lay claim to have been the inventor of Rococo portraiture. Rosalba started her career by decorating the ivory lids of snuff boxes. From this she turned to miniature painting—her pastel portraits always retained the feeling of enlarged miniatures. At her best, as in her self-portrait (Royal Art Collection, Windsor), she was capable of a penetrating psychological insight.

Carrière Eugène 1849–1906

Eugène Carrière was a French painter of portraits and religious pictures. The work he did during the last 20 years of his life made him popular with Symbolist artists and writers alike. Brought up in Strasbourg and trained as a lithographer, he came to Paris in 1869 to study under Alexandre Cabanel. Although his early work was naturalistic in style, both its subject matter and its low-toned palette point forward to the change in his style at the end of the 1880s. His work is characterized by absence of color and vagueness of form enveloped in mists; this transformed specific studies of his wife or of the

Eugène Carrière: Portrait of Verlaine; oil on canvas; 31×22.5cm (12×9in); 1891. Musée Tavet-Delacour, Pontoise

Mary Cassatt: The Boating Party; oil on canvas; 90×117cm (35×46in); 1893–4. National Gallery of Art, Washington, D.C.

sculptor Rodin into generalized statements about human states (for example *Maternité*, c1890–5; National Museum of Wales, Cardiff) and human activities, such as creativity. Carrière was a close friend of Verlaine, Daudet, Gauguin, Anatole France, and Rodin; it was the latter who arranged an honorary banquet for Carrière two years before the painter's death from throat cancer.

Carstens A.J. 1754–98

In 1776 the Danish history painter and portraitist Asmus Jakob Carstens studied at the Royal Academy, Copenhagen, under Nicolai Abildgaard. He made several visits to Italy, the first in 1783, and he lived in Rome from 1794 until his death. His idealized subject matter, executed in the Neoclassical manner, was derived from ancient and mythical sources. While living in Rome he was on close terms with Alberto Thorvaldsen, and others, and was an important influence on the Nazarene group of artists.

Cassatt Mary 1845–1926

Mary Cassatt was an American painter and printmaker. After a period of study in Italy, Spain, and Holland, she settled in Paris in the mid 1870s and remained in France until her death. She was a close friend of Degas and exhibited with the Impressionists. Her work in oil and pastel is characterized by firm drawing and unusual compositions; her subject matter consists predominantly of figures (she painted virtually no landscapes or still life) culminating in a long series of *Maternités*. She produced a significant number of prints, especially a group of colored aquatints during the early 1890s which demonstrated her mature assimilation of Japanese prints, for example, *Woman Bathing*. She also encouraged American collectors, especially the Havemeyers, to buy a great many French Realist and Impressionist paintings.

Castiglione Giovanni 1616–70

Giovanni Benedetto Castiglione was born in Genoa where he studied under two local painters and also worked in van Dyck's Genoese studio. He was a many-sided and versatile artist, technically both original and supremely skillful. He invented the monotype, and probably the soft ground etching, and he created a highly original series of brush "drawings" in oil on paper. He was most famous for his processions of animals in landscapes which often illustrate the journeys of the patriarchs; these were influenced by Flemish artists working in Genoa and by works of the Bassano family.

During the early 1630s Castiglione was in Rome and briefly in Naples (1635). In Rome he was attracted by Poussin's early romantic style, and by the copying of fragments of Classical sculpture, an activity that absorbed artists associated with the learned antiquarian Cassiano dal Pozzo. By the end of the 1630s his etchings show a knowledge of Rembrandt unique in Italy at that date.

Back in Genoa, from 1640 to 1647 he produced large, religious paintings, including the Rubensian *St James Driving the Moors from Spain* (S. Giacomo della Marina). His subject matter widened and he began to paint and etch romantic, mysterious allegories; he was obsessed by the theme of the devouring power of time, and created an atmosphere of ruined splendor by the use of picturesque Classical motifs.

Vincenzo Catena: The Adoration of the Shepherds; oil on canvas; 122×207cm (48×81in); c1510. Private collection

From 1647 to 1651 he was again in Rome. In 1651 he entered the service of the Duke of Mantua; between 1659 and 1663 he was in Venice and Genoa. He died in Mantua. His late style has an ecstatic spirituality reminiscent of Bernini.

Catena Vincenzo c1470–1531

The early works of this Venetian painter are crude variants after Giovanni Bellini's paintings of the 1490s. He seems, however, to have quickly evolved his mature style. This reflects the values of Venetian humanism, can be seen in two minor masterpieces: *The Martyrdom of St*

Giovanni Castiglione: The Angel Appearing to the Shepherds; oil on canvas; 107×161cm (42×63in); c1640. City of Birmingham Art Gallery

Christina (1520) in S. Maria Corpus Domini, Venice, and the *Warrior Adoring the Virgin and the Infant Christ* in the National Gallery, London. In these the influence of Giorgione is clear (he is described in an inscription of 1506 as a "colleague" of Giorgione), as is the influence of Giovanni Bellini's later work. In Catena's soft planes of warm, singing color and gently rounded forms, all the tension of Giorgione's art has been ironed out to create a mood of idyllic calm. A portrait of the humanist *Giangiorgio Trissino* (Louvre, Paris) further reveals his links with Venetian humanism.

Cavalcanti Emiliano di 1897–1976

The Brazilian painter Emiliano di Cavalcanti was born in Rio de Janeiro, where he abandoned his law studies to become an artist. He first exhibited caricatures in 1916, and in 1922 helped to organize the "Week of Modern Art" in Sao Paulo. From 1923 to 1925 he studied in Paris, where he met Picasso, Braque, and Matisse, and discovered the works of Cézanne, Gauguin, and Toulouse-Lautrec. He returned several times to Europe but never settled there. Although his work shows the influence of contemporary European painting, it is essentially figurative; his favorite subjects were landscape, still life, and local Brazilian motifs, especially mulatto girls. At the 2nd Sao Paulo Biennal (1953) he shared the prize for the "best national painter" and at the 7th Biennale was honored with a retrospective exhibition.

Cavallini Pietro c1250–1330

Pietro Cavallini was a Roman painter; his name is associated with those of Cimabue and Giotto in the movement towards greatly increased naturalism in painting which took place in the latter part of the 13th and the first part of the 14th centuries. It is significant that most of Cavallini's activity was in Rome, for during the last quarter of the 13th century a program of restoration and redecoration of Early Christian monuments was commissioned there by the Papal court.

One of the works that Pope Nicholas III (1277–80) was involved in was the restoration of a cycle of Early Christian frescoes in the huge basilica of S. Paolo Fuori le Mura: these were scenes from the *Lives of SS. Peter and Paul* dateable to 1277–9. On

Pietro Cavallini: detail of the Last Judgment fragment; fresco; c1293. S. Cecilia in Trastevere, Rome

the opposite, right, wall of the nave, Cavallini painted scenes from the Old Testament. All these frescoes were destroyed in a fire in 1823, but records of them survive in 17th-century manuscript copies. The scenes were divided in the Roman manner by twisted columns (a similar arrangement to that of *The Legend of St Francis* at Assisi). It is clear that in these scenes Cavallini was tackling the problem of creating a realistic sense of space by the use of architecture painted in perspective, and by the disposition of his figures. The surviving ciborium over the high altar of S. Paolo by Arnolfo di Cambio was completed in 1285, and this is the likely period of Cavallini's work in the church.

The influence of Gothic sculpture, and particularly of Arnolfo di Cambio, plays a considerable part in Cavallini's pioneering achievement; we find the two working at the same time in S. Cecilia in Trastevere. The church was frescoed by Cavallini and contains a ciborium by Arnolfo with the date 1293. The surviving fragment of Cavallini's *Last Judgment* displays rich, sculptural folds in the drapery, a new naturalism in the modeling of faces and hands, and the creation of a general sense of solid volume and weight in the figures. Although there are iconographical precedents for the form of this *Last Judgment*, it is transformed by Cavallini's revolutionary style.

It is perhaps more difficult to recognize a similar originality in his mosaics in S. Maria in Trastevere because he was using a

far less flexible medium. The mosaics are in the apse: there are six scenes from *The Life of the Virgin*, and a votive group. Even allowing for the difference in medium it seems clear that these lovely mosaics represent a slightly earlier stage than the S. Cecilia frescoes. Cavallini's latest work is to be found in S. Maria Donna Regina, Naples (being built 1307–c20) where the paintings appear to be the products of a large workshop. The frescoes include a few outstanding figures of commanding naturalism, such as that of *David*, which must be the last known works of the master himself.

Cellini Benvenuto 1500–71

The Italian goldsmith and sculptor Benvenuto Cellini trained in Florence. He worked in Rome from 1519 until 1540, with occasional visits to Florence and Venice. He traveled to France in 1537. Seals, medals, and cope-fastenings for noblemen and prelates were among his works: like most of his generation, he was influenced by Michelangelo and tended towards Mannerist elaboration of detail.

From 1540 to 1545 he was employed by King Francis I of France and extended his range into sculpture on a large scale, for example *The Nymph of Fontainebleau* (Louvre, Paris), a bronze lunette designed for the entrance of the palace. His most ambitious project, for 12 silver statues of gods and goddesses, never reached completion, though a *Jupiter* was ready by 1544. Cellini's masterpiece as a goldsmith was his Saltcellar (Kunsthistorisches Museum, Vienna) begun in Italy and finished for Francis I. It is the epitome of a Mannerist work of art: intricate in design, complex in theme, and technically brilliant. Its style betrays the influence of Primaticcio and Rosso, the Italians who worked at Fontainebleau.

Under suspicion of embezzlement, Cellini returned to Florence and persuaded Cosimo I de' Medici to commission a bronze statue of *Perseus and Medusa* for the Piazza della Signoria, to rival Donatello's earlier *Judith and Holofernes*. It is the most obviously Mannerist sculpture in Florence, with its decorative marble base including four large statuettes (unveiled in 1554). Meanwhile, Cellini produced a col-

Benvenuto Cellini: Ganymede on the Eagle; bronze; height 62cm (24in); 1545–7. Museo Nazionale, Florence

ossal bust in bronze of Cosimo, originally parcel-gilt and enameled (Museo Nazionale, Florence)—one of the most dynamic portraits of the century. To meet a challenge from Bandinelli he turned to marble carving: several statues are in the Museo Nazionale, Florence, but the best is his *Crucifix* (now in the Escorial, near Madrid). By 1560, Cellini's popularity was waning and he turned to writing, completing his *Autobiography* in 1562 and his *Treatises on Goldsmithing and Sculpture* in 1565. Because of these works, we are better informed about Cellini and his art than about almost any other Renaissance artist.

Cennini Cennino c1370–c1440

The Italian artist and writer Cennino d'Andrea Cennini was born in Colle di Val d'Elsa. He studied under Agnolo Gaddi and was presumably active in Florence. Although no surviving works by his hand have been identified, he is remembered because of his treatise, *Il Libro dell'Arte* ("The Book of Art").

Cennini's book was not printed until 1821, but several manuscript copies exist and it is generally supposed that it was written during the 1390s. It consists of over 100 short sections, the vast majority of which cover the different aspects of the painter's craft from drawing to making glue, from how to paint a face to the best manner of gilding. As a contemporary guide to the techniques used by Italian artists of the day, the historical importance of *Il Libro dell'Arte* is unequaled. It has often been unfavorably and unfairly compared with Alberti's *Della Pittura*. The former is a basic textbook written by a practicing craftsman, while the latter is a theoretical treatise composed by a humanist intellectual.

Cennini's observation that painting "justly deserves to be enthroned next to theory, and to be crowned with poetry" has a surprisingly modern ring. His attitude on such issues as fidelity to nature implies that Cennini should be placed among the more conservative painters of his generation. He considered himself an heir to the tradition of Giotto, which had been transmitted *via* Taddeo and Agnolo Gaddi. This outlook may indicate dissatisfaction with the general rejection of the precepts of Giotto, characteristic of Tuscan art of the second half of the Trecento.

Cephisodotus 4th century BC

The Athenian sculptor Cephisodotus was an elder relation of Praxiteles, and may have been his father. Praxiteles' son, also a sculptor, was allegedly named after Cephisodotus. His sister was the first wife of the Athenian general Phocion. He is best known to us from copies of his allegorical bronze group of *Peace holding the Infant Wealth*, erected in Athens shortly after the establishment of a public cult of Peace in 374 BC. (The best copy is in the Glyptothek, Munich.)

This work inspired a series of similar groups, including *Hermes holding the Infant Dionysos* at Olympia. It embodies the spirit of the beginning of late Classicism and heralds the art of Praxiteles. A new sensibility pervades the grouping of the woman and child, represented standing as never before in Classical art. The traditional High Classical drapery of *Peace* is balanced by her relaxed stance, the protruding hip which supports the infant, her smiling face with the soft features, the triangular forehead, and, above all, the new intimacy between the two figures. The representation of grandeur is tempered with softness and grace, and with sentimentality.

Cephisodotus is also recorded as having made a bronze *Athena* with a spear for the sanctuary of Zeus Savior in Piraeus, and to have collaborated in a group of Muses on Mount Helicon.

César 1921–

The French sculptor César (César Baldiccini) was born at Marseille and studied there under Cornu in 1935. From 1943 he studied with Gâumont and Saupique at the École des Beaux-Arts, Paris. The plaster and iron figures he made in 1947 represented an attempt to break away from his classical training. In 1950 he began to weld metal industrial waste into seated figures, and between 1954 and 1958 into fantastic creatures. His casts in bronze of 1957–8 show greater solidity than his earlier work. Until 1965 he continued to create figurative works. Meanwhile, in 1960, he produced his first "Compressions": cubic sculptures made from mechanically crushed car bodies. Their random juxtaposition of diverse elements creates rhythmic abstract surfaces. In the mid 1960s he experimented with plastics for casting, evolving in 1967 his "Expansions". These are bright monochromatic

Giuseppe Cesari: Moses; detail of the frescoes in S. Prassede, Rome; c1593–5

forms in expanded polyurethane. He demonstrated his technique in public in many countries from 1967 to 1969. Later he made smaller expansions, cast in stainless steel. In 1967 César refused a prize at the Sao Paulo Bienal.

Cesari Giuseppe 1568–1640

Giuseppe Cesari, known as "Il Cavaliere d'Arpino", was the most favored of the decorative painters in Rome under Pope Clement VIII. His drawing was dexterous and artificial, his figures elegantly bloodless, and his color ingratiatingly Sienese.

Yet he disciplined his Mannerist inheritance at an early date through reference to the balanced compositions of High Renaissance classicism—so that a contemporary coupled his name with Domenichino's. He was the head of an efficient workshop. His principal frescoes are in S. Martino at Naples (1589), and at Rome in S. Prassede (c1593–5), the Palazzo dei Conservatori, and S. Giovanni in Laterano. He designed the mosaics in the cupola of St Peter's in 1603, but by this time his style had become dully anachronistic. Certain works by Fréminet, van Dyck, Reni, and G.B. Crespi reflect his influence.

Cézanne Paul 1839–1906

Born on 19 January 1839, at Aix-en-Provence, the son of a French banker and a former hat manufacturer, Paul Cézanne persevered throughout a career of failure and neglect to become recognized as one of the most profoundly original painters of the modern period.

His youthful letters to his boyhood friend Émile Zola reveal a schoolboy romantic, exuberantly scribbling verses and sketches without obvious talent for either. In 1858, when he was already thinking of becoming an artist, his father made him study law. He abandoned those studies in 1861 and went to Paris to join Zola and become an artist. He drew at the Académie Suisse and there met Camille Pissarro. But that September, apparently disillusioned, he returned to Aix, to work as a clerk in his father's bank. Months of scribbling in the ledgers convinced him and even his father of his vocation. In November 1862, he went back to Paris and painting.

From that time he was committed to art, though years of discouragement lay ahead. He had his friends. He knew the circle of the Café Guerbois, who, in addition to Zola and Pissarro, included Manet, Degas, Renoir, and Monet. Pissarro certainly respected his determination and his artistic promise. But Cézanne was not easy to know and like. He was uncouth in appearance, shy and sardonic. Though he admired Manet, who had praised his still lifes, he said to him at the Café Guerbois "I am not offering my hand to you, Monsieur Manet, I haven't washed for eight days."

His career failed to develop. He was not admitted to the École des Beaux-Arts and, from 1863, his works were regularly rejected by the Salon. He became notorious, even caricatured in the press, for his stubborn refusal to admit his own incompetence. Once, in 1882, his friend Antoine Guillemet used his privilege as a member of the Salon jury to exhibit a single canvas by his "pupil" Cézanne. The "pupil" was then 43, three years older than his "master". The picture went unnoticed.

For over a quarter of a century Cézanne depended on an allowance from his father. After 1869, when Hortense Fiquet became his mistress, part of that allowance went to keep her and their son in secrecy, while Cézanne lived in terror of discovery. The people of Aix regarded him and his works with derision. When they asked to see his paintings, he snarled at them "be damned to you!"

But his painting had its admirers. Dr Gachet, a friend of the Impressionists (and later of Van Gogh) and himself an amateur artist, bought several canvases. Cézanne's most important patron after 1875 was a customs officer, Victor Choquet, who not only had his portrait painted several times and acquired more than 35 works by Cézanne, but also became a good friend of the artist. At the first Impressionist exhibition of 1874, although his three canvases attracted ridicule from the critics, Count Doria bought his *Maison du Pendu* (1873–4; Louvre, Paris) for 300 francs.

Cézanne only exhibited once more with the Impressionists, at their third exhibition in 1877. But there he showed 16 works, which were given a place of honor, and hung together in the main room.

It would not have been surprising if Cézanne had become a recluse. Yet, despite his temperament and the considerable distance between Aix and Paris, for two decades there was hardly a year he did not travel north. There was a period of isolation between 1882 and 1888, when he made only one visit north (in 1885) to visit Zola at Medan, following a mysterious love affair. But even during this period, he met both Monet and Renoir on their visits to the south. It was his work as a portrayer of Provence, as much as his solitary temperament, that kept him in the south.

On 28 April 1886, he married Hortense Fiquet; six months later his father died, leaving him a considerable fortune. The most significant event of that year, however, was the end of his friendship with Zola. Since boyhood, his friendship with Zola had been assured. During the novelist's years of success he had provided Cézanne with money as well as encouragement. But in 1886, Zola sent Cézanne his new novel *L'Oeuvre*. In the central character, Claude Lantier—a talentless artist who eventually commits suicide—Cézanne saw a grotesquely misconceived caricature of himself. On 4 April 1886, he sent Zola an impersonal note thanking him, and never saw him or wrote to him again.

Although he had not exhibited in Paris for over ten years, by the time he was 50 Cézanne was becoming known. In 1890 he was invited to exhibit with Les Vingt, the avant-garde group in Brussels, and in 1895 Pissarro persuaded Vollard to organize a large exhibition of Cézanne's work at his gallery in the Rue Lafitte in Paris.

In his last years, after 1900, Cézanne became more solitary. His wife and son lived mostly in Paris while he, as his letters reveal, could think only of his work and of the failing health that interfered with it. Critics were becoming interested in his art and younger artists would make a pilgrimage to meet him; in 1904 the Salon d'Automne devoted a room to his works; Cézanne was unimpressed, for recognition had come too late. By then he was certain of his own worth. As he wrote in his last letter to his son: "compared to me all my compatriots are hogs". In October 1906 he was caught in a storm while out painting; after several hours in the rain he was brought home in a laundry cart, The next morning, after working on a portrait of his gardener Vallier in the garden, he came into the house desperately ill. He died on 22 October 1906.

Cézanne had virtually no public career. Even the annual rejections by the Salon were hardly more than an extension of his private anxieties. His serious attention was devoted solely to the development of his art.

His early works were crude, and at first he was often in despair over his lack of ability. He never developed skill in academic draftsmanship; his figures were curiously proportioned, their features clumsily drawn. He laid on the paint with an inept vigor, often using a palette knife. He chose subjects that were violent or erotic or both, including *The Temptations of St Anthony* (1869; Stiftung Sammlung E.G. Bührle, Zurich) *The Abduction* (1867; J.M. Keynes Collection) and *The Rape* (c1870, E. Roche Collection, Paris). Yet even these works were not merely uncontrolled youthful fantasies.

Cézanne studied profoundly the art of the past, visiting and copying in the Louvre when he was in Paris. He based his painting on the study of Poussin, Rubens, and, above all, the 16th-century Venetian masters. It was in their art that he found precedents for his erotic imagery. And it was in their art, particularly in that of Tintoretto, that he discovered the powerful pictorial rhythms his own work always possessed. He dismayed his academic contemporaries by ignoring superficial refinement and finish, and leaving bare the constructional skeleton on which his painting was built. His early works were vigorous caricatures of earlier pictorial forms.

Among the artists of his own century, he imitated Delacroix, Daumier, and Courbet. Some of his most powerful early works were studies, portraits, landscapes,

Paul Cézanne: The Black Marble Clock; oil on canvas; 55×74cm (22×29in); c1869–70. Collection of Stavros S. Niarchos, Paris

and still lifes influenced by Courbet. Like Courbet, Cézanne laid on his pigment with a palette knife, but with exaggerated breadth. It was this broad handling that gave studies of his *Uncle Dominique* (c1866; Museum of Modern Art, New York), his *Father Reading* (1866; Lecomte Collection, Paris) and two portraits of his friend *Valabrègue* (1870; private collection) a massive dignity. The masterpiece of these years is *The Black Clock* (1869–70; Stavros Niarchos Collection, Paris). Some of the forms, notably the cup, seem clumsily drawn, but the composition has an architectural solidity, and the vertical folds of the white napkin have the massive dignity that he later depicted on a grander scale in his painting of the quarry called Bibémus.

Cézanne had met Pissarro in 1861, and in 1866 had written to Zola that "all pictures painted inside, in the studio, will never be as good as the things done outside"; but it was not until 1872 that he visited Pissarro at Pontoise and worked alongside him. Under Pissarro's discreet guidance, Cézanne made the discoveries that were to be the foundation of his mature art. He learned to see forms as patterns of colored light and shade and to represent them as small patches of color. At first, he continued to compose in the manner of Courbet but

with a new luminosity. Later, he adopted a much smaller brush stroke. But he never became a true Impressionist: he was not interested in the transient effects of light, in qualities of weather or of the time of day or year. Rather, he transposed the crude, broad rhythms of his early compositions to the small scale of the Impressionist brush stroke, and created a complex mosaic of delicately balanced touches of color. Most important of all, he learned that this pictorial structure must be discovered through long contemplation of the motif. In this way, Cézanne at the age of 33 found himself beginning what he came to call his "researches".

The way in which Cézanne's vision differed from that of the Impressionists may be seen in the magnificent landscape he painted at Auvers, *La Maison du Pendu* (1873–4; Louvre, Paris). Though a country scene, it is not a true landscape, despite a glimpse of trees on the horizon. The greater area of the canvas is packed with solid surfaces: walls, thatched roofs, tree trunks, and slabs of earth, all painted in encrusted pigment. The picture is itself a feat of architecture, its surface like plastered masonry.

At the first Impressionist exhibition of 1874, Cézanne showed, together with *La Maison du Pendu*, a strange small canvas:

The New Olympia (1872–3; Louvre, Paris). Like many of his earlier canvases, it was an erotic subject, but with a fresh irony. As its title suggests, it is a parody of Manet's famous painting. It shows the black servant stripping away the sheet to expose the naked Olympia cowering before the passive gaze of a clothed male spectator—an ambiguous connoisseur who is included within the picture. It is also a satire of Cézanne's own early ambitions. The composition still recalls Delacroix and the Venetians, but the brilliant color is applied with a new flowing deftness of touch appropriate to this small, light, witty sketch.

The New Olympia was one of a number of small studies of voyeurist themes. In the most striking, *The Eternal Feminine* (private collection), an artist's model is unveiled to a fanfare before an audience of men, including a bishop. After 1875, Cézanne abandoned overtly sexual motifs and began instead a series of landscapes with bathers (male and female, but never both together) which he continued until the year before his death.

After his visit to Pissarro, the major part of Cézanne's work was painted from a motif: portrait, still life, and, above all, landscape. The countryside of his native Provence was decisive in the development of his mature vision. In 1876 he wrote to Pissarro: "The sun is so terrific here that it seems to me as if the objects were silhouetted not only in black and white, but in blue, red, brown, and violet ... this seems to me to be the opposite of modeling." The southern light and the evergreen foliage led Cézanne away from Impressionism to a slower contemplation of his subject. And the land itself, the scene of his childhood, had a significance far more important to him than the mere effects of light. Montagne Sainte-Victoire became the most important character he portrayed.

From 1875, Cézanne's art developed with rigorous logic. He worked slowly and with intense concentration, creating his pictorial forms out of an unprecedented scrutiny of his motifs. The subject matter, whether landscape, still life, portrait, or composition, was not an assembly of items but a harmonious relationship of forms. Each work was a search for a new resolution between the three-dimensional relationships perceived in nature and the two-dimensional relationships possible in painting, and between the colors of nature and the scale of the Impressionist palette.

He had learned the analysis of appearances from Pissarro. Now Cézanne sought to discover in nature equivalences to the synthetic pictorial patterns he had learned from the Venetians in his youth.

His later letters to such young admirers as Joachim Gasquet and Émile Bernard show that Cézanne was well aware of the paradoxical nature of his art. He believed that art grew out of the perception of nature, but also out of prolonged reflection which little by little modifies the artist's vision until "at last comprehension comes to us". He wrote to Émile Bernard on 26 May 1904: "One is neither too scrupulous nor too sincere nor too submissive to nature: but one is more or less master of one's model, and, above all, of the means of expression."

In the great works of his last years, it seems to matter very little whether—like the late landscapes of *Mount Sainte-Vic-toire*, the *Château Noir* (one example in the Sammlung Oskar Reinhart "Am Römerholz", Winterthur), or *Bibémus* (one example in the Museum Folkwang, Essen), or the still lifes with their amazing baroque rhythms—they are painted from the motif; or whether like the last heroic compositions of *Bathers*, they are invented or reconstructed from life-drawings of his youth. In all these works there is a symphonic resonance: a resolution of the perceived and the abstract, the sensuous and the intellectual, that transcends analysis. As Cézanne wrote in his last letter to his son (15 October 1906) "As with me sensations are at the root of all things, I am, I believe, impenetrable."

Further reading. Anderson, W. *Cézanne's Portrait Drawings*, Cambridge, Mass. (1970). *Cézanne, Les Dernières Années: 1895–1906*, Paris (1978). Cézanne, P. (ed. Rewald, J.) *Letters*, Oxford (1977). Chappuis, A. *The Drawings of Paul Cézanne*, London (1973). Dunlop, I. and Orienti, S. *The Complete Paintings of Cézanne*, London (1972). Fry, R. *Cézanne, a Study of his Development*, London (1927). Reff, T. (ed. Rubin, W.) *Cézanne, the Late Works*, London (1978). Schapiro, M. *Cézanne*, New York (1965). Venturi, L. *Cézanne: Son Art, Son Oeuvre*, Paris (1936).

Chadwick Lynn 1914–

The English sculptor Lynn Chadwick was born in London, and trained as an architect. After serving as a pilot in the Second World War he started making sculptures; he concentrated on mobiles, influenced by Calder, and on constructions mainly in welded iron. In 1954 he developed his mature style: armatures of mild steel filled with composition, which from 1956 were

Paul Cézanne: Bathing Women; oil on canvas; 130×195cm (51×77in); c1900–5. National Gallery, London

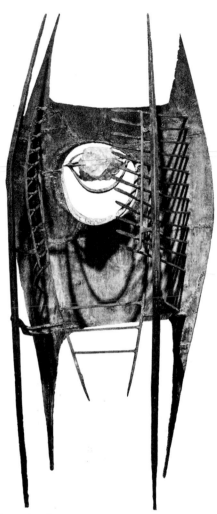

Lynn Chadwick: Inner Eye; wrought iron and molten glass; height 230cm (91in); 1952. Museum of Modern Art, New York

cast in bronze; these resembled birds, animals, and figures. In the mid 1960s he began to reduce his figures to pyramidal shapes, sometimes in laminated wood, but he later returned to winged and seated figures in which he combined realistic modeling and flat planes, with both polished and dull surfaces. Chadwick was awarded the International Sculpture Prize at the Venice Biennale in 1956.

Chagall Marc 1889–1985

The Russian painter Marc Chagall was born in Vitebsk, Belorussia, of a Jewish family. In 1907 he went to St Petersburg to study art, spending some time at the school of Leon Bakst who introduced him to advanced French art. He returned to Vitebsk in 1909, having already painted a number of scenes from Jewish life; these were done in a strident, primitive manner which reflected his period of apprenticeship to a sign-painter. In 1910 he traveled to Paris where he discovered Cubism, the methods of which he adapted to a highly personal fantasy rooted in the village life of his boyhood. *To Russia, to Asses, and to Others* (1911; Musée National d'Art Moderne, Paris) has a faceted treatment of the sky reminiscent of Picasso's 1908 landscapes; but when in Chagall's picture the milkmaid loses her head, this is not a Picasso-like pictorial fragmentation but a physical decapitation.

His greatest admirers were not other painters but the poets Blaise Cendrars, Max Jacob, and Guillaume Apollinaire. Because of its nostalgic subject matter, his work had a distinct literary appeal compared with most other avant-garde painting in Paris at the time. For Chagall, Cubism was not a rigid dogma; it was the gateway to an art that could ignore the law of gravity, naturalistic color, and the traditional treatment of space, to express a poetic vision. *I and the Village* (1911; Museum of Modern Art, New York) brings together diverse images within a single plane by means of arbitrary disparities of scale.

When war broke out in 1914 Chagall returned to Russia, and after the Revolution was appointed Commissar of Fine Arts in Vitebsk; he left the post after disagreements with Malevich about the conduct of art education. In 1919 he became designer for the State Jewish Theater in Moscow. He left Russia for Paris in 1923 and was commissioned by Vollard to make a series of etchings illustrating Gogol's *Dead Souls*. During the 1920s and 1930s his art became more lyrical, the aggressive sharp edges of his earlier work giving way to a flowing treatment. This development coincided with more sentimental subject matter. Lovers lie in a bouquet of flowers or float blissfully through the sky. While less ingenious in form than his earlier works, these paintings are more inventive in their imagery. Animals and musicians

Marc Chagall: I and the Village; oil on canvas; 162×151cm (64×59in); 1911. Museum of Modern Art, New York

become musical instruments, and flying fishes play violins.

For all its element of escapist fantasy, Chagall's art was nonetheless affected by the Second World War which drove him to the U.S.A. in 1941. His palette acquired a sombre tone, and his flying figures became an expression of panic rather than ecstasy. He returned to France in 1947. After the War he continued to paint and also produced ceramics and stone sculptures. In the latter medium he produced a series based on Old Testament themes. His gift for intense decorative color led to several commissions for stained glass, notably those he made for the United Nations building, New York, in 1964. His airborne figures made him the natural choice to paint a new ceiling for the Paris Opéra, also installed in 1964.

Because of his penchant for visual metaphor, critics have related Chagall to the Surrealists. He never in fact had any formal contact with the group. The religious basis of many of his images, as well as the uncomplicated affirmative content of his art, with its romantic and tender vision of eroticism, is far from their subversive spirit.

Further reading. Carson, J. *Chagall*, New York (1965). *Chagall*, Zurich (1967). Chagall, M. *My Life*, London (1965). Erben, W. *Marc Chagall*, London (1966). Haftmann, W. *Marc Chagall*, New York (1972). Malraux, A. *The Ceramics and Sculptures of Chagall*, Monaco (1972). McMullen, R. *The World of Marc Chagall*, London (1968).

Chamberlain John 1927–

The American sculptor and painter John Chamberlain was born in Rochester, Indiana. He studied at the Art Institute of Chicago (1951–2), taught sculpture at Black Mountain College (1955–6), and then moved to New York. He began carving and modeling in 1951, turning to metal and welding the following year. Influenced by David Smith, his early sculpture was linear and open, constructed largely from iron piping. In 1957 he began to use scrap from wrecked cars, found at the home of the painter Larry Rivers, but continued his previous formal concerns. A year later he welded pieces of crushed and crumpled car bodies, retaining their original metallic colors. The energetic volumes and surfaces of these works allied him to

the Abstract Expressionists, especially to Willem de Kooning (1904–). During the mid 1960s he made sculptures from simply tied urethane foam and painted paper; in 1970 he worked in mineral-coated plexiglass. Chamberlain made his first experimental film in 1967.

Chambers Sir William 1723–96

The architect Sir William Chambers was the first Treasurer of the Royal Academy. He was born in Sweden, educated in England, and had already visited India and China before entering the studio of the French academician J.F. Blondel in 1749. From France he traveled to Italy where he remained for five years, returning to England in 1755. He developed an eclectic but conservative style, drawn almost exclusively from Renaissance sources, exemplified by his masterpiece, Somerset House, London (1776–96). His *Treatise on Civil Architecture* (1759) was very influential and provided an important counterweight to the innovations of his contemporary and arch-rival Robert Adam, with whom he temporarily shared the post of Architect of the King's Works.

Champaigne Philippe de 1602–74

Philippe de Champaigne trained in Brussels as a landscape painter and moved to Paris in 1621. He developed the classical qualities of economy and restraint admired in France, yet these remain tempered by an enduring debt to his Northern heritage. His works display a feeling for the beauty of domestic interiors, for the individuality of his sitters, and for realistic detail and effects of light in his landscapes.

Before 1643 he worked almost exclusively for Marie de Medici, Richelieu, and Louis XIII. He did many mural decorations, including frescoes in the dome of the Sorbonne, and undertook some important large commissions, among them *The Vow of Louis XIII* (1638; Musée des Beaux-Arts, Caen) and the *Échevins of the City of Paris* (1648; Louvre, Paris). His style from c1629–30 is a modified version of the Baroque. His religious works are indebted to the glowing color and billowing draperies of Rubens, and his official portraits tone down the Baroque magnificence

Sir William Chambers: Chinese Pagoda; 1757–63. Kew Gardens, London

of van Dyck's Genoese portraits. A *Triple Portrait of the Head of Richlieu* (National Gallery, London) was intended as a working model for the sculptor Francesco Mochi.

About 1643 Champaigne became interested in the doctrines of the Jansenists of Port Royal, an austere Catholic sect. At the same time he began to move towards a more classical style. In *The Marriage of the Virgin* (1644; Wallace Collection, London) the composition is arranged as a frieze, the drapery has the sharp lines of antique sculpture, and the gesture and expression of each figure plays a distinct part. Champaigne was basing his art on Poussin, Raphael, and the Antique; like Poussin, he was deeply concerned with questions of historical and archaeological accuracy.

Between 1643 and 1661 de Champaigne began working for a wider public and it was then that he was most active as a portraitist; he painted sovereigns, ecclesiastics, merchants, lawyers, ministers, writers, and magistrates. His portraits are sober and restrained, the colors limited; his sitters rarely smile and the compositions are of the utmost simplicity. *Charles Coiffier* (private collection) rests his hands on a window sill, a portrait type perhaps developed from 15th-century Flemish precedents; the latent vitality of hands and features contrasts sharply with the stone-colored parapet and the severity of geometric shapes.

His most famous late work is the votive picture made after the miraculous recovery from paralysis of his daughter, a nun at Port Royal (*Mère Agnès and Soeur Catherine de Ste-Suzanne Praying*, 1662; Louvre, Paris). He avoids drama; in a very simple composition the prioress kneels beside the sick girl. There is the same feeling of stillness in his painting of the vision of *St Julienne* (Barber Institute of Fine Arts, Birmingham) where again the true subject is the communion of the soul with God. This quality of calm immobility links Champaigne more closely to Georges de la Tour (1593–1652) and Louis Lenain (c1593–1648) than to the visions and ecstasies of his Baroque contemporaries.

Philippe de Champaigne: Self-portrait (a copy by his nephew Jean-Baptiste de Champaigne); oil on canvas; 120×91cm (47×36in); 1668. Louvre, Paris

Chao Meng-fu 1254–1322

Chao Meng-fu was a traditionally educated Confucian scholar and the pupil of the eminent figure painter Ch'ien Hsuan. From his teacher he had learned the styles of T'ang dynasty figure-painting, and the Northern Sung academic styles of landscape and bird-and-flower painting. Since he left Wu Hsing in 1286 to take up official posts in Peking, he has been traditionally referred to as "a traitor" for he had been a servant of the Mongol Yuan court. However, he was outstanding in his period as a painter and calligrapher and was much admired as an exponent of the classical styles; he was also revered as a great poet and scholar. Unfortunately only fragments of his studies remain. These show he was a sincere, straightforward, and elegant draftsman with a strong instinct for the old masters. He seems to have deserved his imposing reputation as a scholar painter of taste and erudition and a stylist of the highest order.

Chao Meng-fu was a leader, with his teacher, of the movement that purposely turned its face towards the Old Masters and away from the sophisticated romanticism of the Hsia-Ma and Ch'an Schools. This was a period of reunification of China, though under foreign rule, and there was an acute awareness of former artistic standards. This led to a rejection of the Southern Sung courtly styles, and an attempt to reassess the old ideals. Chao Meng-fu as a traditional scholar official

Chao Meng-fu (attributed): detail of Horses Crossing a River; ink and color on paper; full size 17×87cm (7×34in); Freer Gallery of Art, Washington, D.C.

was ideal for the role; with his fellow official, Kao K'o-kung, who painted in the Mi Fei idiom, he overshadowed the very early Yuan period and was the epitome of the scholar-painter. The connotation of this term has varied through the ages. At that period it meant the well-educated man who painted for his own enjoyment and that of his friends, and who aimed at a directness of expression through the methods of the old masters, rejecting all technical "cleverness" but handling his brush with the skill of a well-trained calligrapher. To judge by the small sketch of the Ch'iao and Hua Mountains in the National Palace Museum, Taipei, Chao Meng-fu was the sort of painter who "wrote out" his ideas and his work seems close in spirit to that of Huang Kung-wang (1269–1354).

Chardin Jean-Baptiste 1699–1779

Jean-Baptiste-Siméon Chardin was a French painter of still-life and genre subjects. Born in Paris, the son of a carpenter, he entered the studio of P.-J. Cazes in 1718 and two years later worked as an assistant to N.N. Coypel. In 1728, he was received at the Académie with the still-life picture of a fish *The Skate* (*La Raise*; Louvre, Paris). This picture had caught the attention of some academicians at an exhibition, and it was at their suggestion that Chardin joined their ranks. The essential elements of his later still lifes are present in this painting, though the later works are less dramatic.

Simplicity, sobriety, and naturalness are the hallmarks of his still-life paintings, which vary little in style and content over 40 years. On a wooden or stone ledge will be arranged fruits, such as apples, grapes, peaches, and pears; a glass or bottle of wine or water; vegetables with copper or earthenware pots; a knife, a pipe, occasionally a piece of fine porcelain—the objects one would expect to find in any stable bourgeois household. Indeed, Chardin elevates that sober and unpretentious world to the status of an ideal.

This applies also to his figure-subjects, which he painted from the early 1730s to the mid 1750s. These show servants at work in austere, uncluttered kitchens—extensions of some of the still lifes, as it were; or they depict mothers and governesses instructing children in reading or in the domestic arts. Such paintings to some extent reflect progressive ideals of the period. They seem to recommend a return to what is natural and simple in life, as opposed to the glitter and formality of the court. They advocate education and a reasoned approach to the upbringing of children. Through such subject matter, Chardin expressed the bourgeois standards of his time. His technique was one of carefully modulated light and shade. He used muted earthy colors, with some powdery blues, grays, and pinks, an impastoed, deliberate brushwork, and a solid and powerful sense of structure and design.

Many of the great French private collectors of the age bought his work, as did foreigners such as the King of Sweden and the Empress of Russia. He also painted three overdoors for the Château de Choisy. Some academically minded critics thought his art low and vulgar, because he did not aspire to the great tradition of history painting—indeed, engravings of his art were popular with a wide general public. In his figure-pieces he retains something of the delicacy of Watteau, while never descending to the boorishness of certain Dutch 17th-century genre paintings. The latter were widely collected in 18th-century France, and influenced Chardin's interior scenes in a general way. He ceased inventing figure-subjects in the mid 1750s, probably capitulating before the rising star of the more sentimental art of J.-B. Greuze. He made a number of portraits in pastel during the 1770s.

Jean-Baptiste Chardin: The Attributes of Music; oil on canvas; 91×145cm (36×57in); 1765. Louvre, Paris

Charonton Enguerrand *c1410–61*

The French painter Enguerrand Charonton was born in Laon. In spite of his obscure northern origins, and the fact that only two paintings can be attributed to him with certainty, he is considered one of the masters of medieval painting in Provence. He worked in Aix, Arles, and Avignon for at least 22 years. His *Vièrge de la Miséricorde* and the great *Coronation of the Virgin* from the Hospice of Villeneuve-lès-Avignon present a decorative, highly tactile style suggestive of sculptural origins. His paintings also display the brilliance of light and harshness of line characteristic of the school of Avignon.

Chassériau Théodore *1819–56*

The French painter Théodore Chassériau was born in the Antilles. His work shows affinities with the supposedly antithetical styles of both Ingres and Delacroix. He painted portraits showing the influence of his teacher Ingres (for example, *The Two Sisters*, 1840; Louvre, Paris) but *c*1845 he became disenchanted with pure "Ingrisme". He adopted the atmospheric color and chiaroscuro of Delacroix; while retaining Ingres' preoccupation with contour (for example, *The Tepidarium*, 1853; Louvre, Paris). His subject matter reflects the Romantics' interest in Shakespeare (*Desdemona*, 1849; Louvre, Paris) and in the East (*Moorish Dancers*, 1849; Louvre, Paris), which was reinforced by his visit to Algeria in 1846.

Chicago Judy *1939–*

The American multimedia artist Judy Chicago (pseudonym of Judy Cohen) studied art at Los Angeles and helped to establish the first feminist art courses in America, first at Fresno State College and the California Institute of Arts. She became the focus of feminist art debate with *The Dinner Party* (1974–79; a traveling exhibit), a triangular table with place settings for 39 women, real and mythical, who have contributed to Western cultural history, but have been "ignored, maligned, or obscured by that history". A collective work, it is executed in crafts traditionally associated with women, such as needlework and painted china. She continued her

Enguerrand Charonton: Coronation of the Virgin; panel; 183×220cm (72×87in); 1454. Hospice, Villeneuve-lès-Avignon

Théodore Chassériau: The Two Sisters; oil on canvas; 180×135cm (71×53in); 1843; Louvre, Paris

frank exploration of "women's achievement and struggle" in subsequent works. She also began exploring her own Jewish heritage, and in the mid 1980s, together with her husband, the photographer Donald Woodman, began *Holocaust Project*, a collection of paintings, photographs, tapestries and texts relating to the Holocaust and to the need for "what are sometimes called the 'feminine values' of compassion and nurturance".

Further reading. Chicago, J. *Through the Flower*, New York (1975).

Chikuden Tanomura *1777–1835*

Tanomura Chikuden was a Japanese painter of the *Bunjinga* (scholar-painters) School, born in Takeda in Kyushu. He became head of the Confucian school of his local lord, and head of his family, but decided to devote his life to painting. He traveled a great deal in Japan, but of all the *Bunjinga* he comes closest to the true Chinese spirit. He must have seen good original works imported through Nagasaki. He favored landscapes and bird-and-flower albums; these are painted with a dry, apparently hesitant brush which conceals great strength of purpose. His landscapes are often many-layered.

Chillida Eduardo 1924–

The Spanish Basque sculptor Eduardo Chillida was born in San Sebastian. He studied architecture at Madrid University from 1943 to 1947. He lived in Paris from 1948 to 1950, in Villenes 1950–1, returned to Hernani until 1957, and then moved back to San Sebastian.

His figure-carvings of 1948–9 led to Abstract sculptures in 1950 and to work in forged iron from 1951. Small in scale, and concerned with enclosed space within forms, these were jagged iron pieces owing something to Julio Gonzalez (1876–1942) and to local traditional techniques. They were followed in the mid 1950s by sculptures made from cut and twisted iron bars. He began wood carvings in 1959 and from 1964 also worked in alabaster. These media introduced a new emphasis on solidity and mass. As well as reliefs he has done many *papiers collés*, drawings, and graphics.

Ch'i Pai-shih 1851–1957

The Chinese painter Ch'i Pai-shih was born of humble parentage in Hsiang-tan, Hunan. He had a few years of schooling and then earned his keep on the family land as a woodcutter. He took up wood carving and learned to paint, doing mostly portraits and decoration for the villagers. He was helped by local writers, who introduced him to classical literature and poetry. During his twenties he gradually progressed to seal cutting, poetry, and painting, seeing for the first time works by Shih T'ao and Chu Ta. After a few years in which he traveled widely through his own country, Ch'i returned home and began seriously to write poetry and to paint.

He had by this time come under the influence of the painting of Wu Ch'ang-shih (1844–1927). Ch'i followed his master closely, especially in his flower painting; but the younger man used a wider range of subject matter and a different style of painting, which he would often combine with Wu's. Ch'i was a most acute observer of birds and flowers, but he seems to have had a special affection for insects and painted them with great sensitivity. From the age of 60 Ch'i Pai-shih lived in Peking; his paintings became popular and he himself became a cult figure. This very popularity perhaps led to a certain slackening of style and even a triteness which is never present in the painting of his master Wu Ch'ang-shih. There are many copies of

Ch'i Pai-shih: A Faded Lotus; ink and color on paper; 35×34cm (14×13½in); 1953. National Gallery, Prague

Ch'i's paintings which makes it difficult to identify with certainty the work of this forthright and, at his best, fine, poetic, and decorative painter.

Chirico Giorgio de 1888–1978

The Italian painter Giorgio de Chirico founded the Metaphysical School and had a vital influence on the development of Surrealist art. Born in Volo, Greece, he began studying art in Athens in 1900. In 1906 his parents moved to Munich, where de Chirico enrolled in the Academy of Fine Arts and came under the influence of late-19th-century German painters and philosophers, especially Böcklin and Nietzsche. Their joint example encouraged him to reject naturalism and to concentrate instead on poetic, imaginary, and visionary subjects. In 1909 the family moved to Milan where de Chirico painted mythological scenes closely based on Böcklin.

Traveling by way of Florence and Turin, where the arcaded buildings, statues, and desolate squares deeply affected him, he

settled in Paris in 1911. His first characteristic works date from 1910–11. Subject to illness and depression, haunted by the writings of Nietzsche and by nostalgic recollections of Greece and Italy, a prey to hallucinations, de Chirico depicted a mysterious and troubling world which was for him as real as the banal world of everyday life.

In such works as *The Rose Tower* (1913; Peggy Guggenheim Collection, Venice), he created a sense of enigma in images of trance-like stillness and silence. The period of time is ambiguous, the space impossibly deep, and the perspective inconsistent, and objects are irrationally juxtaposed. The strangeness is heightened by the almost naive lucidity of his style. Sometimes spatially agoraphobic, sometimes claustrophobic, these paintings, with their looming statues and shadows, are full of tension and menace. They suggest, through an apparently unconscious symbolism of towers, arcades, and trains, feelings of panic and sexual frustration.

In 1915 de Chirico was drafted into the

army in Ferrara, but continued to paint. His work by now showed a debt to Cubism in the shallowness of the pictorial space, the use of collage-like effects, and its imagery of abstracted mathematical instruments. In January 1917 he was joined by Carlo Carrà and together they founded the Metaphysical School, whose tenets were a rationalization of the artistic aims de Chirico had held since 1910–11. Although short-lived, the association helped to draw attention to de Chirico's concept of poetic painting, which was to have a profound effect on such Surrealist painters as Dali, Ernst, Magritte, and Tanguy.

Daniel Chodowiecki: The Artist Having a Horse Shod; pen and ink; 11×19cm (4×7in); 1773

Giorgio de Chirico: The Child's Brain; oil on canvas; 1914. National Museum, Stockholm

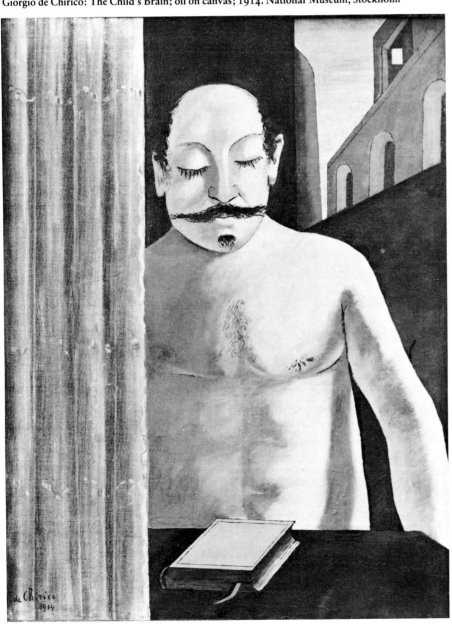

After 1917, when he painted masterpieces like *The Disquieting Muses*, (Gianni Mattioli Collection, Milan), de Chirico's work declined, although he created a series of remarkable still lifes and portraits in 1919. At the end of the war, he moved to Rome and turned his back on Metaphysical imagery; he became increasingly concerned with questions of pictorial technique and produced works imitative of the Old Masters. From this time onwards, when he did return to his early manner it was to make copies or pastiches. Nevertheless, the visionary intensity of his metaphysical work was recaptured briefly in his extraordinary novel *Hebdomeros* (1929).

Further reading. Brunio, C. *Catalogo Generale: Giorgio de Chirico* (3 vols.) Milan (1971). Chirico, G. de *De Chirico by De Chirico*, New York (1971). Gaffé, R. *Giorgio de Chirico, Le Voyant*, Brussels (1946). Rubin, W. (ed.) *De Chirico*, New York (1982). Sloane, J.C. "Giorgio de Chirico and Italy", *Art Quarterly*, Detroit (Spring 1958). Soby, J.T. *Giorgio de Chirico*, New York (1966).

Chodowiecki Daniel 1726–1801

Born in Danzig, the painter Daniel Nikolaus Chodowiecki went to Berlin in 1743 to work as a shop assistant. He soon turned to painting and established a reputation as a miniature painter. In 1757 he started engraving and painting in oils. The 12 paintings illustrating scenes from Lessing's *Minna von Barnhelm*, for the Berlin Calendar in 1768, proved to be a watershed in his career. In these he imbued the Rococo with a new realism. His later work, painted for the middle class of

Berlin, is remarkable for the directness and sensitivity of his response to unpretentious indoor scenes. These are comparable to the work of Chardin (1699–1779) in their approach.

Chokuan Soga *fl.* 1596–1610

The Japanese painter Soga Chokuan was the founder of the later Soga School. Little is known of his life, and his connections with the Muromachi Soga painters are obscure. He lived and worked in the prosperous part of Sakai, near Osaka, and his patrons were probably rich merchants and samurai. Chokuan specialized in ink monochrome painting of aggressive birds, especially hawks, often in a landscape dominated by foreground rocks, trees, and foliage. The brush work of his stabbing, horizontally jutting tree boughs recalls that of Yusho (1533–1615), but his composition is more dynamic and less elevated. Many hawk paintings are attributed to him; the authentic ones have a splendid, controlled ferocity.

Choshun Miyagawa 1683–1753

Miyagawa Choshun was a Japanese artist of the *Ukiyoe* School, born in Owari Province. He worked in Edo (Tokyo), but was never tempted into the woodblock medium. As the most sensitive colorist among *Ukiyoe* painters he probably found the print techniques of his day inadequate. He is said to have helped redecorate the Tokugawa mausoleum at Nikko; this would seem to indicate a rise in status of the *Ukiyoe* School, which had once been considered frivolous. Choshun's paintings nearly all depict women in softly sensuous, pleasurable situations, such as *Girl Enjoying Scent* (Tokyo National Museum), and more than any other artist he seems to give substance to the erotic dreams of the Edo world.

Christo 1935–

The Bulgarian sculptor Christo Javacheff, known simply as Christo, was born in Gabravo. He studied at the Fine Arts Academy, Sofia (1952–6), and moved to Paris in 1958. Since 1964 he has lived in New York. Christo's early association with the Paris Nouveaux Réalistes allied him with a movement critical of modern consumerism and waste. He is best known for his wrapped objects begun in 1958–9.

Petrus Christus: Portrait of a Carthusian; tempera and oil on wood; 29×20cm (11½×8in); 1446. Metropolitan Museum, New York

At first he wrapped bottles and cans, but later wrapped famous monuments and buildings, adding a significant political dimension. In 1969 he wrapped part of the Australian coast. Since 1961 he has used stacked empty oil drums as a parallel theme. His major projects, achieved at great cost and through technological innovation, include *Valley Curtain* (1971–2; Rifle, Colorado) and *Running Fence* (1976; California).

Christus Petrus *fl.* 1444–72/3

Petrus Christus was the major painter in Bruges in the mid 15th century, and the principal follower of Jan van Eyck, who may have been his teacher. It has been suggested that Christus completed some of van Eyck's unfinished works and, less convincingly, that he introduced Eyckian techniques to Italian artists, notably Antonello da Messina (c1430–79). While his work seems to have been popular in Italy, there is no evidence that he ever went there; he may have traveled to Germany, but he worked mainly in Bruges.

The chronology of his paintings is uncertain, despite an unusually large number of dated works from 1446–57. The earliest of these are two portraits, one of Edward Grymestone (Collection of the Earl of Verulam, St Albans), the other of a Carthusian (Metropolitan Museum, New York). The former is innovatory in placing the sitter in a domestic interior, as though the setting of the van Eyck's *Arnolfini Marriage* (National Gallery, London) had been combined with an Eyckian portrait bust. *The Exeter Madonna* (Staatliche Museen, Berlin) may belong to the same period: it is clearly indebted to Jan van Eyck's *The Madonna of Chancellor Rolin* (Louvre, Paris) for its architectural setting and competent perspective, though the figures are anatomically less convincing. The more complex *St Eligius* (1449; Metropolitan Museum, New York) combines half-length figures with a meticulously detailed interior (a goldsmith's shop; Eligius is the patron saint of metalworkers). The precise rendering of individual objects reveals Christus as a master of still life.

A pair of altar wings showing the *Annunciation*, *Nativity*, and *Last Judgment* (1452; Staatliche Museen, Berlin) combine motifs from the work of Jan van Eyck and Rogier van der Weyden. That Christus was influenced by the emotional intensity of van der Weyden is demonstrated by the large *Lamentation* (Musées Royaux des Beaux-Arts de Belgique, Brussels) a work variously dated to the very beginning and the end of Christus' career. But it is as a truthful recorder of the physical world that Christus is chiefly remarkable. He was a master of linear perspective and modeled surfaces, an underrated artist whose work represents, in pictorial terms, a development from the achievement of van Eyck.

Chu Jan *fl. 960–80*

A younger contemporary of Tung Yuan, the Chinese painter Chu Jan is known by his monastic name. Like Tung Yuan he came from Chiangnan and worked at first for the Southern T'ang court. However, when this State capitulated to the Sung rulers he retired to a monastery. Specializing in landscape painting, Chu Jan was a master of composition, building up imposing "master mountain" landscapes in which he expressed the piles of rocks by his own distinctive "hemp fiber" *ts'un*. This is the earliest example of a brush stroke associated with a particular artist; although we must regard attributions of such a remote date with circumspection, it is possible to glimpse a most original painter at work. The smooth, repetitive curves and carefully accented dots create not only a sense of great volume and grandeur, but also a mild atmosphere characteristic of the southern area in which he worked. His landscapes are clearly related to those of the later 13th–14th-century group of southern painters of the Chiangnan district in the Yuan dynasty.

Alberto Churriguera: the Ayuntamiento in the Plaza Mayor, Salamanca; 1728

Churriguera family
17th and 18th centuries

The Churriguera family were Spanish architects. Arriving in Madrid in the 1670s, they brought from Barcelona an ornate style of Catalan Baroque decoration which they applied first to altarpieces and later to whole buildings.

José Benito de Churriguera (1665–1725), the leading member of the family, was the son of José Simón de Churriguera (José the Elder) a sculptor (*fl.* 1670–9). José Benito began with conventional designs like that of the main altarpiece of San Esteban, Salamanca (1693). This uses six large twisted columns in the lower story, with the center pair continued above by pilasters in the upper story. (These serve to frame a great canvas by Claudio Coello.) José's architectural activity began in 1709 with the planning of the new town of Nuevo Baztán. The tall, narrow church and adjoining horizontal palace are in a severe style. In spite of their asymmetrical contrasting masses, they distantly recall Juan de Herrera's work at the Escorial. But José's achievement was neither extensive nor markedly original.

His brother Joaquín (1674–1724) was even less venturesome, reverting to an elaborately ornamented Plateresque style in the dome of Salamanca Cathedral (1714; later destroyed) and elsewhere in that city.

The youngest brother, Alberto (1676–c1747), constructed the Plaza Mayor, Salamanca (1728). The most successful town-planning scheme of the period, it was executed in a restrained Baroque style still reminiscent of Plateresque in its ornament.

The principal followers of the Churriguera family were Pedro de Ribera, Narciso Tomé, and Andrés García Quiñones who worked at Salamanca, Valladolid, and Toledo. It was the work of these later architects that gave the term "Churrigueresque" a note of opprobrium for its lavish, riotous ornament. This was sometimes inspired (as in the case of Ribera) by the French Rococo; but it lacked the elegance of that style. Tomé's *Transparente* (1721–32), a theatrical blending of painting, sculpture, and architecture in the ambulatory of Toledo Cathedral, is the most striking achievement of this extreme phase.

Chu Ta 1626–1705

The Chinese painter Chu Ta, who often signed himself by his monastic name Pa Ta Shan Jen, was a descendant of the Ming royal house; he retired to become a monk at the fall of the dynasty. He had a reputation for eccentricity which perhaps indicates some form of mental instability. He was subject to periods of depression and elation and drank wine to sustain himself. He eventually gave up speaking altogether, putting a notice "dumb" on his door. His painting is strong and entirely personal; he painted birds and flowers in the Ch'an School, using a deft skill in composition and a marvelously controlled ink tone. He did not use color. His birds and fish have a baleful, humorous quality,

and critics have perceived social comment in his animal painting.

The bird and flower paintings, scrolls or album leaves and fans, are done on paper; but when, more rarely, Chu Ta painted landscape he seems to have favored white satin as a base on which to paint in ink. The weave of the satin, encouraging a spiky spread of the ink, gives Chu Ta's wet ink style a brittle quality. His landscape composition is conventional, unlike the experimentalism of Tung Ch'i-ch'ang (1555–1636); the "bones" of the landscape are the subject, and little weight is given to considerations of atmosphere or light, or even to the natural world. These ascetic landscapes are a considerable contrast to those of his contemporary, Shih T'ao (1630–1707).

Cigoli 1559–1613

Lodovico Cardi da Cigoli, often known as "Il Cigoli", was a Florentine painter of the transition from late Mannerism to early Baroque. He was named after his birthplace near Empoli. He was also an architect and a poet, and a friend of Galileo. A close contemporary of the Carracci, Cigoli shared their desire to create a new pictorial language based on warm color and intense emotion. This was probably a reaction to the highly artificial and mannered style of his master, Alessandro Allori. Almost from the beginning, his works show the influences of Correggio, Barocci, and the Venetians. He also admired the work of Florentine painters such as Santi di Tito, who similarly rejected the more extreme forms of Mannerism in the interest of a greater simplicity and clarity.

Fundamental to Cigoli's artistic purpose was the effective expression of his religious subject matter, in accordance with the spirit of the Counter-Reformation. This may be seen in a mature work such as *The Martyrdom of St Stephen* of c1597 (Galleria Palatina di Palazzo Pitti, Florence), which in many ways anticipates the high Baroque of Pietro da Cortona, and even of Rubens. At the same time, Cigoli's formulation of the new style was much less radical than that of the Carracci; he remained to a much greater extent tied to Florentine traditions of incisive draftsmanship and hardness of color. Although his art had a pervasive influence on 17th-century painting in Florence, it had far less effect in Rome, where he settled after 1604.

Cimabue c1240–c1301

The Florentine painter Cimabue was also known as Cenni di Pepo (from Bencivieni di Pepo). He was long considered to have been Giotto's master. Whether or not this was true, Cimabue confronted many of the same artistic problems as Giotto. His work displays a similar, essentially Florentine, concern with a realistic sense of space and volume and the desire to create a human, dramatic interpretation of divine subjects.

The first mention we have of Cimabue records his presence in Rome in 1272, just a year before we hear of Pietro Cavallini there; this is significant in view of the importance of Rome for the development of painting at that time. Among Cimabue's surviving works only one is documented: the figure of *St John* in the apse mosaic in the Duomo at Pisa (1302). There is thus some controversy about attributions, but there is a small core of universally accepted works. Of these, the earliest seem to be his frescoes in the upper church of St Francis at Assisi. The frescoes cover the vaults of the crossing (*Four Evangelists*), the walls of the apse (*Life of the Virgin*), the left transept (*Apocalyptic Scenes* and *Crucifixion*) and the lower part of the right transept (*Lives of SS. Peter and Paul* and *Crucifixion*.) The *Evangelists* in the vault contain a possible heraldic clue to the date of the decoration, which seems to have been c1277–9. The frescoes are poorly preserved, but enough remains to show that the *Crucifixion* in the left transept, for example, is a work of enormous dramatic power. The same vastness of conception applies to the organization of the whole scheme, which combines the actual architectural space and the painted pictorial space into a satisfying unity. This approach is partly developed by succeeding painters in *The Legend of St Francis* in the nave of the same church, and more fully by Giotto in his Capella dell'Arena, Padua.

There is another fresco by Cimabue at Assisi, down in the lower church: the *Madonna and Child with Angels and St Francis*. This fresco, and a later Cimabue workshop *Madonna and Child* (Louvre, Paris) may both reflect the influence of Duccio's *Rucellai Madonna* (1285; Uffizi, Florence). Cimabue's major surviving altarpiece, however, the S. Trinità *Madonna* (Uffizi, Florence) is likely to date from shortly before 1285. Like the *Rucellai Madonna* it is one of the grandest of the series of huge gabled panel paintings of the Madonna and Child which culminates in

Giotto's *Ognissanti Madonna* (*c*1307; Uffizi, Florence). The throne is presented in convincing perspective, suggesting a central vanishing point. The accompanying

Cimabue (follower of?): Madonna and Child; panel; 424×276cm (167×109in); c1290–5. Louvre, Paris

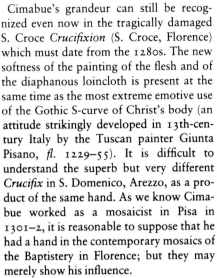

angels are securely situated on its steps, and altogether the painting marks a major advance in the Florentine development of realistic space.

Cimabue's grandeur can still be recognized even now in the tragically damaged S. Croce *Crucifixion* (S. Croce, Florence) which must date from the 1280s. The new softness of the painting of the flesh and of the diaphanous loincloth is present at the same time as the most extreme emotive use of the Gothic S-curve of Christ's body (an attitude strikingly developed in 13th-century Italy by the Tuscan painter Giunta Pisano, *fl.* 1229–55). It is difficult to understand the superb but very different *Crucifix* in S. Domenico, Arezzo, as a product of the same hand. As we know Cimabue worked as a mosaicist in Pisa in 1301–2, it is reasonable to suppose that he had a hand in the contemporary mosaics of the Baptistery in Florence; but they may merely show his influence.

Despite the fragmentary nature of his surviving work, it is still possible to recognize Cimabue as a major innovator.

Further reading. Battisti, E. *Cimabue*, Milan (1963). Bologna, F. *Cimabue*, Milan (1963). Salvini, R. *Cimabue*, Rome (1946). Sindona, E. *L'Opera Completa de Cimabue*, Milan (1975).

Cima da Conegliano

*c*1459–1517/18

Giovanni Battista Cima was an Italian painter known as Cima da Conegliano after his birthplace near Treviso. His first dated work is an altarpiece in Vicenza (painted for the church of S. Bartolomeo, now in the Museo Civico) of 1489 whose style, in common with all the artist's later works, suggests an early association with Giovanni Bellini (*c*1430–1516). From 1492 until 1516/18 he worked chiefly in Venice, before returning to Conegliano where he died. Cima's style developed little, and without the dates inscribed on many of his works it would be impossible to place them in any logical sequence. The altarpieces are in general derived from a Bellinesque type: for example the 1492 Conegliano altarpiece (Conegliano Cathedral) and the St Peter Martyr altarpiece, commissioned approximately 14 years later (Pinacoteca di Brera, Milan). He also painted many devotional panels showing the Madonna and Child seated in front of an open landscape. Two small roundels representing mythological subjects (Galleria Nazionale, Parma) are exceptions in an *oeuvre* chiefly concerned with religious subjects. (*See* overleaf.)

Cima da Conegliano: Madonna and Child with St Jerome and St Louis of Toulouse; canvas; 212×139cm (83×55in); c1495. Gallerie dell'Accademia, Venice

Ciurlionis 1875–1911

The Lithuanian painter Mikolojus Konstantinas Ciurlionis originally trained as a musician. He took up painting in 1904, working in a Symbolist manner reminiscent of Odilon Redon. He used a technique of tempera on paper to gain subtle translucent effects which accorded well with his cosmic subject matter. Claims have been made for him as the first Abstract painter, a misunderstanding arising out of his attempts to find visual equivalents for musical forms. *Fugue* (M.K. Ciurlionis State Art Museum, Kaunas) is basically a landscape in which the outlines of the hills and forest undulate in an analogy with musical counterpoint. Ciurlionis also painted in series, each painting representing one of the movements of a sonata.

Claude Lorrain 1600–82

Born Claude Gellée in the village of Chamagne in Lorraine, the French painter known as Claude Lorrain can be considered as the greatest landscapist of the 17th century. Apart from a short visit to Germany and France from 1625 to 1627, he spent his whole working life in Italy, and his art should be examined in the context of the Roman school of the period. His paintings of landscape relate to major concerns of 17th-century Italian art—the study of nature and the exploration of light. His achievements in these fields rank him with the greatest of his contemporaries. He restricted his investigation of those themes to landscape painting, unlike other pioneers such as Rubens, Rembrandt, and Poussin for whom this was only one aspect of their approach. Claude radically extended the concept of landscape, giving it historical significance without sacrificing his sensibility to effects of nature. In doing so, he further developed the classical tradition of landscape painting which had evolved in Italy since the Renaissance.

There are two sources for the life of Claude: biographies by Joachim von Sandrart and by Filippo Baldinucci. Sandrart (1606–88) was a contemporary of Claude during his early years in Italy. He was one of the many Northern artists who flocked to Rome in the early 17th century and with whom Claude was initially associated. Sandrart accompanied Claude on many of those expeditions in the countryside around Rome that remained his greatest inspiration. His biography is particularly valuable for its firsthand account of Claude's working method—especially of the studies from Nature which form the basis of Claude's landscape art. Baldinucci (1624–96), of a generation later than Claude's, obtained most of his information from the artist's nephew. His is a more professional type of biography, detailed and objective, but less circumstantial. Both tended to stress the supposed naivety of the painter, but the modern view more justly appreciates the intellectual content of his art and the seriousness of purpose of this careful and conscientious artist.

Two traditions exist about Claude's early training (he was the third of five sons). Sandrart claimed that he was originally apprenticed to a pastry cook; Baldinucci claimed that he began in the studio of his elder brother, a wood engraver in Strasbourg. However, his significant training

Claude Lorrain: The Embarkation of St Ursula; detail; oil on canvas; full size 113×149cm (44×59in); 1641. National Gallery, London

began in Italy where he had arrived by 1615. He may have worked for the German painter Gottfried Wals in Naples for the first two years. The first certain evidence is his apprenticeship to Agostino Tassi in Rome in 1618. He stayed with this artist until 1625. Tassi was a major influence on the formation of Claude's style. As a decorative landscapist working predominantly in fresco, his art was firmly based on the classical traditions of land-

scape. It used the elements of landscape, and coast scenes, with pastoral, Biblical, or mythological figures, architecture, and shipping. All these themes are to be found later in the work of Claude. After his return to Italy in 1627, Claude received commissions for frescoes in the palaces of certain high churchmen in Rome. However, he quickly abandoned this medium in favor of easel painting. His patrons remained drawn from aristocratic circles—

the Medici, Pope Urban VIII, Philip IV of Spain. In this he differed from his contemporary, Poussin, whose paintings were generally commissioned by the intellectual bourgeoisie.

In his first period, up to the 1640s, Claude produced many seascapes and landscapes which greatly developed the rather schematic compositions of the landscapes of Tassi and Bril. He succeeded in connecting the planes of his compositions by subtle aerial gradations which achieved real unity of atmosphere. His landscapes are suffused with light—a result of his observations of nature, also evidenced in the many studies he made in the open air. He was the first to attempt to depict the sun on canvas and to explore its effects as accurately as possible.

In his second period, from the 1640s to his death, Claude's naturalism is increasingly affected by a classical humanist feeling. This derives from his study of the art of Domenichino (1581–1641) and of Annibale Carracci (1560–1609), especially as seen in the latter's contributions to frescoes in the Palazzo Aldobrandini, Rome (c1604). His artistic purpose became more ambitious with the inclusion of specific subjects drawn from Classical mythology or the Bible. His compositions were more posed and complicated than the earlier pastorals, and can be considered as fully historical: the form of the landscape depends directly on the significance of the subject matter, and the figures play an integral part in the composition. This mature style is brilliantly represented by pictures such as Landscape with Dancers (1669; Hermitage Museum, Leningrad) and View of Carthage (1676; Hamburger Kunsthalle, Hamburg) in which Claude has manipulated the figures and the scenery with great dramatic effect.

In search of a more severe, epic style, Claude turned for inspiration to Virgil's Aeneid which increasingly suited his mood towards the end of his life. The last paintings achieve a supreme blend of poetic feeling and decorative skill equal in sublimity to that of the Classical poet. There is no perceptible falling off in technical ability. The acceptance of the qualities of Mannerism now allow his very personal handling of his figures to be recognized as an essential ingredient of his art, and not as the failing they had for long been considered. This is quite evident in his last painting, Ascanius Shooting the Stag of Silva (Ashmolean Museum, Oxford), painted in his 82nd year.

Throughout his career, Claude kept a careful record of his compositions and his patrons in the so-called Liber Veritatis. This is a chronological series of copies in pen and ink of his major commissions: the 195 drawings serve as an indication of his style and its development.

Claude's vision of the Classical world was quite different in conception to that of Poussin, the artist who worked most closely to him during his life. The latter's landscapes are intellectual constructs that depend directly on the imagination of the artist. The landscapes of Claude, while no less ideal, are rooted in his observation of the natural world. It was this quality that made his art of such consistent appeal to later generations, especially to those who fell under the spell of the Classical terrain of Italy. In 18th-century England this admiration was translated by the aristocracy and landed gentry into real terms in the Classical arrangement of their parks. It is Claude's ability to observe that makes his interpretation of nature of interest today, as much on the intellectual as on the sensuous level.

Further reading. Cecchi, D. L'Opera Completa di Claude Lorrain, Milan (1975). Friedländer, W. Claude Lorrain, Berlin (1921). Hind, A.M. Claude Lorrain and Modern Art, Cambridge (1926). Kitson, M. Claude Lorrain: Liber Veritatis, London (1978). Kitson, M. The Art of Claude Lorrain, London (1969). Röthlisberger, M. Claude Lorrain: the Drawings (2 vols.), Berkeley (1968). Röthlisberger, M. Claude Lorrain: the Paintings (2 vols.), New Haven (1961).

Cleve Joos van c1490–1540/1

Originally from Cleves, the Flemish painter Joos van Cleve trained at Antwerp. His earliest works were in the style of late-15th-century painters such as Gerard David (c1460–1523). The ambitious Death of the Virgin (1515; Wallraf-Richartz-Museum, Cologne) shows an unexpected mastery of interior space. He may have traveled in Italy; his later works were infused with a soft Italianate chiaroscuro technique grafted on to the traditional Flemish format. An example is his Virgin and Child (c1520–30; Fitzwilliam Museum, Cambridge). He became a successful court portraitist, since he avoided any penetrating analysis of character and achieved an immaculate smooth finish of skin and costume textures, as in the Portrait of Henry VIII (c1536; Hampton Court Palace, London).

Clodion 1738–1814

Born at Nancy, Claude Michel, known as Clodion, was the tenth child of Thomas Michel who was First Sculptor to the King of Prussia. On his mother's side Clodion was related to the Adam family of sculptors. Such connections were quite common among French master-craftsmen, with whom sculptors were numbered. In 1781 he married the daughter of the sculptor Augustin Pajou.

Clodion and three of his brothers came to Paris in 1755 and worked under their uncle, Lambert-Sigisbert Adam, moving on his death in 1759 to the studio of Jean-Baptiste Pigalle. Almost immediately, however, Clodion won the Academy Prize. Following the usual custom, he then left for a period of State-financed study at Rome, where he remained from 1762 to 1771. After 1767 he worked there privately for Catherine II of Russia who was a Francophile and an international patron of the arts.

By the time of his return to Paris he was producing many small-scale works, inspired by the more irreverent subjects of antique sculpture. He quickly established a workshop, assisted by his brother and a few craftsmen, in the Place Louis XV (now the Place de la Concorde). They created a succession of statuettes, groups, reliefs, and vases depicting nymphs, fauns, satyrs, and bacchantes in playful and bucolic settings. These were gay, charming figurines, delicately modeled, and evocative of childhood or rejuvenation.

The majority were executed in the supremely pliable medium of terracotta, the potential of which had been revealed by Robert Le Lorrain (1666–1743), and later extolled by the collector, Lalive de Jully. Clodion was the first sculptor to concentrate on terracotta; by doing so he freed himself from the lengthy struggles inevitably connected with work on and payment for large-scale monuments. Nevertheless he did receive some official commissions, and the most obvious proof of his abilities as a sculptor in marble on a large scale is his Montesquieu (final version 1783; Institut, Paris) commissioned by the Crown.

He was elected to the Académie Royale in 1773; but he failed to submit the statutory reception piece and was hence never a full Academician, though he became an Associate in 1793. So popular was his style that after 1783 he could afford not to exhibit at the Salon (where there was pressure to submit less frivolous pieces), and none of his more brilliant terracotta groups was shown there.

Clodion's output before the Revolution was vast, and works were often duplicated in porcelain and bronze for incorporation

Clodion: Cupid and Psyche; terracotta; height 59cm (23in); c1798–1804. Victoria and Albert Museum, London

of detail. All are small, and they include *A Man with a Book* (Royal Art Collection, Windsor) and *Guillaume Budé* (Metropolitan Museum, New York). He has generally been credited with the famous state portrait of Francis I (c1520; Louvre, Paris).

Clouet was almost certainly the author of portrait miniatures that anticipate the work of Hans Holbein the Younger and Nicholas Hilliard; he also anticipates Holbein as a portrait draftsman. About 120 drawings of the heads of royal and courtly persons, mostly done in black and red chalks, can be attributed to him (most are in the Musée Condé, Chantilly). Remarkable alike for their draftsmanship and their psychological acumen, they brought an essentially Florentine, even Leonardesque technical authority to the earlier forms of French portrait drawing.

François (c1510–72), the son of Jean Clouet, was perhaps born at Tours; he died in Paris. He succeeded his father as painter to the King, and was then described as having "already imitated him very well". This, and the fact that both painters were nicknamed Janet, has led to confusion. François continued to make portrait drawings in the manner of his father (major collections in the Musée

Jean Clouet: portrait of Antoine de la Barre, Archbishop of Tours; black and red chalk drawing; 28×20cm (11×8in); c1520–5. Musée Condé, Chantilly

into objects like candelabra and clocks. But since much is undated, it is often difficult to distinguish his own work from that of his many assistants.

During the Revolution, he retreated to Nancy. Afterwards he staged a Parisian comeback with his austere, sensational work for the Salon of 1800, *Déluge* (since destroyed) which was in tune with contemporary heroic preoccupations. He was subsequently given work on Napoleonic monuments, such as the Colonne Vendôme (or Column of the Grande Armée, Place Vendôme, Paris) of 1806–10, the Arc de Triomphe (1806), and the Carrousel monument.

Clouet family 16th century

The father and son Jean and François Clouet were French painters. Jean (1485/90–1541), possibly born in the Netherlands, is named in the accounts of Francis I for 1516. His first known residence was at Tours, and his wife was French. After 1525 he moved to Paris and probably died there. All the surviving paintings that can be associated with his name are portraits. Only about eight of them have serious claims to authenticity. They are characterized by strong, luminous areas of smoothly applied color, restrained in chromatic range, yet sharpened by a vivid sense

François Clouet: Portrait of Francis I of France; gouache on vellum mounted on wood; 27×22cm (11×9in); c1540. Louvre, Paris

Cochin the Younger (1715–90) executed freer compositions from his own drawings. His brilliant career was crowned by his appointment as keeper of the Cabinet du Roi. Even in his own day it was observed that Cochin's work was pretty and elegant rather than monumental. He was a master of the vignette, whose style was ideally suited to the fanciful taste of the court of Louis XV.

Cohen Bernard 1933–

The English painter Bernard Cohen is the younger brother of the painter Harold Cohen. Born in London, he studied at St Martin's School of Art (1950–1) and at the Slade School of Fine Art (1951–4). He taught at Ealing College of Art (1961–4), at the Slade from 1967, and at the University of New Mexico, Albuquerque (1969–70). From 1957 Cohen reacted against English semiabstraction with rigorously Abstract paintings emphasizing process, time, subconcious fantasy and light. The structured paintings of 1959–61 were followed by works displaying loosely sprayed and painted linear, organic imagery. Later he began to blend ground and image by using tape, stripped off after he had sprayed or painted over the top. During 1965 he created dense, luminous paintings, and soon afterwards abandoned the use of line. The paintings that followed, until 1972, were made by covering small disks of color with expansive layers of white. In 1973 he began to use tilted canvases and reintroduced judiciously placed disparate colored marks. These gradually came to fill the entire canvas.

Cohen Harold 1928–

The English painter Harold Cohen is the elder brother of Bernard Cohen. He was born in London, studied at the Slade School of Fine Art (1948–52) and then lectured on art history at Camberwell School of Art (1952–4). He taught painting at the Slade from 1962 until he moved in 1969 to the University of California, San Diego, where from 1974 onwards directed the project for Art Science Studies.

Cohen abandoned Abstract Expressionism after visiting the U.S.A. from 1959 to 1961. His work retained a neutral ground for stripes and colored structures, gradually making use of disparate marks or complexes emphasizing drawing. In the mid 1960s color took on a new import-

Condé, Chantilly, and Bibliothèque Nationale, Paris), though they sacrifice incisiveness to charm. He also painted portraits, for example *Pierre Quthe* (1562; Louvre, Paris), *A Lady in her Bath* (c1570; National Gallery of Art, Washington, D.C.); mythology (*Diana Bathing*, 1550s; Musée des Beaux-Arts et de la Ceramique, Rouen); and genre works. These make clear his knowledge of the school of Fontainebleau, and of painting at Antwerp. In all his works there are strong naturalistic tendencies.

Clovio Giulio 1498–1578

The miniature painter Giulio Clovio was of Croatian origin, but worked mainly in Rome. According to tradition, he learned his art from the Veronese Girolamo dai Libri (1474–1555) in the late 1520s, and his subsequent production in Rome included not only illuminated manuscripts, but also pictures on a minute scale. His most famous work is the Book of Hours decorated for Cardinal Alessandro Farnese (Pierpont Morgan Library, New York). This shows the overwhelming influence of Michelangelo in its figure types. However, in keeping with a typically Mannerist eclecticism, it draws freely on a wide range of sources that also includes Raphael, Dürer, and the 15th-century Netherlandish Grimani Breviary (Biblioteca Marciana, Venice).

Cochin family 18th century

The Cochins were Parisian engravers from an old family of printmakers originally based in Troyes. Charles Nicolas Cochin the Elder (1688–1754) produced engravings after Watteau, François Lemoyne, and other contemporary French painters.

Instead of painstakingly reproducing the work of other artists, Charles Nicolas

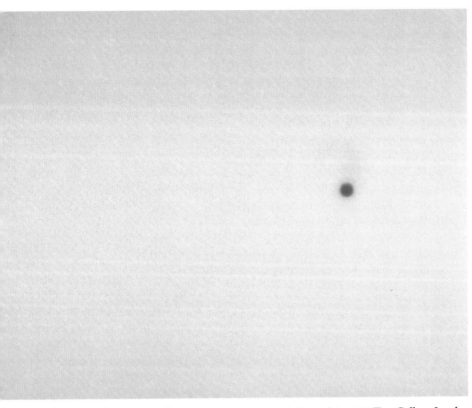

Bernard Cohen: Blue Spot; acrylic on canvas; 244×335cm (96×132in); 1966. Tate Gallery, London

ance, as Cohen used unified fields of dots against ambiguous backgrounds. While in the U.S.A. Cohen has worked with computers to solve problems of color relationships and to create drawings and paintings.

Coldstream Sir William 1908–87

Sir William Coldstream was one of the most distinguished of post-1945 British portrait-painters. Born in Northumberland and trained at the Slade School of Fine Art in London, he exhibited with the New English Art Club and the London Group. In 1934 he turned his attention to the cinema, taking a post with the film unit of the General Post Office. Coldstream started painting again in 1936 and in 1938 founded the Euston Road School with Claude Rogers and Victor Pasmore. In 1943 he was made an Official War Artist, and posted to Cairo; in 1949 he was appointed Slade Professor at University College, London. Coldstream's style is representational and subdued in mood. The earlier landscapes and portraits are often suffused with atmosphere. His later work is more cerebral and suggests the underlying influence of Cézanne.

Cole Thomas 1801–48

The American landscape painter Thomas Cole was the founder of the Hudson River School and an early member of the National Academy. Born in Lancashire, England, he was brought to America in 1820, where he worked as an apprentice engraver in Ohio. Cole was deeply influenced by the mezzotints of the English painter John Martin and traveled a good deal in Europe and England, but his major works are distinctly American in outlook. The best of them are grouped in series, such as *The Voyage of Life* (1894; Munson-Williams-Proctor Institute, Utica, N.Y.). These huge landscapes are approached in a poetical and philosophical spirit; in them Cole shows an appreciation of man's responsibilities in the face of the potential wealth and strength of the New World.

Colombe Jean 1430/5–1529

Jean Colombe was a French illuminator, the brother of the sculptor, Michel Colombe. His property transactions in Bourges are recorded in the 1460s. Jean's atelier became one of the most productive in the second half of the 15th century.

Probably during the 1470s he illuminated a massive Book of Hours for Louis Laval (Bibliothèque Nationale, Paris; MS. Lat. 920). Through the patronage of Charlotte of Savoy in the 1480s he received important commissions, including one for illustrations in the *Livre des Douze Périls d'Enfer* (Bibliothèque nationale, Paris; MS. Fr. 449) and the *Roméléon* (Bibliothèque Nationale, Paris; MS. Fr. 364), a book which contains the artist's anagram "Molbeco". Colombe completed works that had been left unfinished earlier in the 15th century, including an Apocalypse now in the Escorial near Madrid, begun by Jean Bapteur and Perronet Lamy. He also finished parts of the *Très Riches Heures* (Musée Condé, Chantilly; MS. 65), begun by the Limburg brothers, for the Duke of Berry. He added ornate gilt framework and some rather powerful and diverse figures, and he preferred tricky perspective views to the delicate atmospheric rendering of his predecessors.

Colombe Michel 1430/5–1512

The French sculptor Michel Colombe was the brother of the miniaturist Jean Colombe. Not much is known of Michel's work before 1500 when he was almost 70 years old and working in Tours. There he is known to have designed works, including a medal in 1500, for the triumphal entry of Louis XI into Tours upon his return from Italy. Under the patronage of Anne of Brittany, Colombe's major work was a tomb for her parents, François II, Duke of Brittany, and his Duchess, Marguerite de Foix. Designed by Jean Perréal, the sarcophagus was executed by Michel with several Italian assistants, and was installed in 1507 in the Carmelite church in Nantes (now in Nantes Cathedral).

Colombe was one of the first 15th-century French sculptors to adopt Italianate ornament. He incorporated into the sarcophagus a round arcade with grotesques and pilasters in the antique manner; but his large corner-figures of the Virtues retained a Burgundian richness of material and naturalism of facial expression. About 1508–9, Colombe sculpted an altarpiece for the castle chapel at Gaillon; his relief of *St George and the Dragon*, now in the Louvre, Paris, shows evidence of Italian collaboration in its framework. The relief itself is the least Italianate of his works. A valiant St George pinions a giant scaly dragon. The diminutive princess is overwhelmed by a mountainous space that shows none of the experimental features to be found in the works of Donatello or Uccello. The designer, Perréal, wanted Colombe to collaborate with him again on a ducal tomb in Brou, but that project was not realized.

Colonia Juan de c1415–81

The mason Juan de Colonia probably came from Cologne. Invited to Spain by the Bishop of Cartagena, he was one of several Northern architects to go there in the 15th century. From c1442–c58 he worked on Burgos Cathedral (begun c1220), particularly on the octagonal west spires which have openwork tracery in the German late Gothic manner. His magnificent *Cimborio* unfortunately collapsed, to be replaced by an equally elaborate 16th-century example designed by his grandson Francisco. Juan's other great work, begun in 1461, is the Miraflores Charterhouse Chapel near Burgos, which houses the monuments of King Juan II and Queen Isabella. A large church without aisles, it was completed by his son Simon.

Colvin Marta 1917–

The Chilean-born sculptor Marta Colvin studied sculpture under Julio Antonio Vasquez at the Santiago Academy. She visited Europe in 1948, working in wood and metal in the international sculptural idiom of the 1950s. In Paris she studied sculpture under Ossip Zadkine (1890–1967); her organic curvilinear sculpture—part abstract, part figurative—reflected an interest in the work of Laurens and Brancusi, whom she met. In the 1950s she lived in Paris and London and became acquainted with Henry Moore. Later she taught sculpture at the Santiago Academy, and in her carving was influenced by Pre-Columbian and primitive American sculpture.

Conrad von Einbeck fl. 1383–1416

Conrad von Einbeck was a German architect and sculptor. In 1383 he began the choir of St Moritz at Halle an der Saale, a design that shows the influence of the Parler workshops in Prague, particularly in its window tracery. Inside are several stone sculptures signed by Conrad, all of which combine emotional intensity with careful naturalism. The *Mourning Virgin*, for instance, expresses grief both in her face and through her gestures; but, as though for additional emphasis, her eyes are shown rimmed with meticulously carved tears. The style is basically the so-called "Soft style" of the contemporary "Beautiful Madonnas", but without their courtliness. The bracket carved as a bust in the north aisle was inspired by the portrait busts in Prague Cathedral. Usually regarded as Conrad's self-portrait, it shows a youngish man with heavy features, deep-set eyes, and a brooding expression.

Conrad von Scheyern

early 13th century

Conrad von Scheyern was a German illuminator. Five manuscripts from Scheyern Abbey in Bavaria contain references to a man, "Cuonradus", who has often been regarded as their scribe and illuminator; in fact the works vary too much in script and decoration to be the work of one hand. A *Glossarium Salomonis* (Staatsbibliothek, Munich; Clm. 17403) dated 1241 is copied from a manuscript of 1158–65 from Prüfening near Regensburg; but the hard lines of the original are replaced by a gentler, rounded style with only a hint of the current "Jagged style" (*Zackenstil*) in the draperies. The splendid full-page illustrations to the *Liber Matutinalis* (Staatsbibliothek, Munich; Clm. 17401) made between 1206 and 1225 are nearer the Byzantine style of the late-12th-century *Hortus Deliciarum* which was formerly at Strasbourg.

Conrad von Soest fl. c1390–c1425

Conrad von Soest was an important German painter, working in Westphalia during the first quarter of the 15th century. His artistic personality can be surmised from the magnificent high altar of the church of St Nicholas at Bad Wildungen which is signed and dated 1404. It is painted in the so-called "Soft style", closely related to the International Gothic, and indebted to Franco-Burgundian painting. The lyrical elegance of many of the figures is contrasted with an everyday realism in the details. Subsequently he painted the high altar of the church of the Virgin at Dortmund (c1420) of which substantial fragments survive.

Constable John 1776–1837

Constable is considered one of the two greatest masters of landscape painting in Britain, the other being J.M.W. Turner (1775–1851). Born on 11 June 1776 at East Bergholt, Suffolk, the son of a prosperous mill-owner, Constable was from an early age responsive to the natural beauties of his birthplace. "I associate my 'careless boyhood'", he wrote later, "with all that lies on the banks of the Stour. Those scenes made me a painter, and I am grateful."

He showed an early interest in painting and drawing, and was encouraged by John Dunthorne, a local plumber and glazier and amateur artist. He was also introduced to the famous patron and amateur painter Sir George Beaumont, and to the professional engraver J.T. Smith. After working for a time in his father's mill, he went to London and in 1799, with the encour-

John Constable: The Valley of the Stour; oil on paper laid on canvas; 50×60cm (20×24in); c1805. Victoria and Albert Museum, London

John Constable: A Country Lane; oil on paper; 20×30cm (8×12in); c1810. Tate Gallery, London

agement of the landscape painter Joseph Farington, he began training at the Royal Academy Schools. Through Beaumont, Smith, and Farington, he became familiar with the European landscape tradition, particularly the works of Claude Lorrain (1600–82) and the Dutch painters of the 17th century. But Constable was already dedicated to depicting the countryside around his native Stour Valley in his own more direct and informal way. As early as 1802, the year he exhibited his first landscape at the Academy exhibition, he wrote to Dunthorne: "For these past two years I have been running after pictures and seeking the truth at second hand ... I shall make some laborious studies from nature ... There is room enough for a natural painter." Although he was to paint several portraits—sometimes with success when he was intimately concerned with the sitter, as is shown by the portrait of his fiancée Maria Bicknell (1816; Tate Gallery, London)—his main concern for the whole of his career was with the painting of the English landscape.

Constable's early development as an artist was slow; drawings made during sketching tours of the Peak District in 1801 and of the Lake District in 1806 show the diverse influences of Beaumont, Gainsborough, the Cozens, and Girtin. But he found that picturesque sights and mountain scenery did not greatly appeal to him, and he did not undertake such tours again. He wanted to depict nature directly and accurately, as is shown by the notes he made on drawings recording the time of day, the climatic conditions, and so on; but some of his paintings, such as Dedham

Vale (1802; Victoria and Albert Museum, London), are composed in the formal manner of Claude, an artist Constable always admired.

From about this time he began to explore more intensely the pictorial possibilities of the countryside around his Suffolk home, making small oil sketches in the open air and experimenting with brighter, more varied colors to convey the effects of light and atmosphere. He also made small pencil studies, notably those in the sketchbooks of 1813 and 1814 (Victoria and Albert Museum, London). With immediacy and brilliance, he recorded his observations, not only of details of foliage, of agricultural equipment, of men at work and at rest, but also of any scene that might be used later as the basis for a composition. These outdoor sketches in oil and pencil were intended as preparatory work for the highly finished oils he painted in his studio and exhibited annually at the Royal Academy. On one apparently unique occasion, however, when he was working on Boatbuilding near Flatford Mill (1815; Victoria and Albert Museum, London), Constable painted wholly in the open air.

In 1816, after a long and difficult courtship, Constable married Maria Bicknell, and by 1820 had settled in Hampstead, London. It was in 1819, the year he was elected an Associate of the Royal Academy, that he revealed the full results of his studies and the extent of his talent in his painting of The White Horse (Frick Collection, New York). This was the first in a series of six large canvases (approximately 4 by 6 ft, 1.3 by 2 m) depicting everyday

life and work on the River Stour. Like his earlier painting Flatford Mill on the Stour (1817; Tate Gallery, London) these works were intended to raise the status of his landscape painting at the Academy. The most famous of the series is The Hay Wain (1821; National Gallery, London) which was exhibited at the Royal Academy as simply Landscape: Noon. This picture not only exemplifies the verdant, sunny qualities of the English countryside in summer, but also creates a quiet mood of utter contentment. Man is seen here as completely at one with his environment: an image that perfectly illustrates one aspect of the Romantic attitude towards the relationship between man and nature.

For The Hay Wain, and for some other larger works, Constable made a full-size preliminary sketch in oils. This practice doubtless inspired the greater freedom of handling evident in his exhibited works of the 1820s, for example his use of the palette knife as well as the brush to apply paint, and his extensive use of touches of white to give a glittering surface texture. By 1825, when he painted the last in the great series, The Leaping Horse (Royal Academy of Arts, London), he was undecided whether to send the finished oil to the Academy exhibition, or the preparatory sketch (1825; Victoria and Albert Museum, London). The two works were almost identical in their degree of finish and their loose, rapid brush strokes.

There is always evident in Constable's mature works an impressive confidence in the beauties of nature itself; he once claimed that his "limited and abstract art is to be found under every hedge and in every lane." He wrote to his friend John Fisher in 1821: "old rotten planks, slimy posts, and brickwork, I love such things ... as long as I do paint, I shall never cease to paint such places." It is one indication of his originality that he expressed this view when the formality of the classical and picturesque styles of landscape painting was still universally expected and admired.

Although Constable traveled very little in England, places outside Suffolk became familiar and important to him as subjects for painting during these years. There was Salisbury, which he first visited in 1811. There he met John Fisher who was to be a life-long friend and whose uncle, the Bishop of Salisbury, commissioned the famous view of the Cathedral (1823; Victoria and Albert Museum, London). There was Brighton, where he first took his

John Constable: Cloud Study—Horizon and Trees; 25×29cm (10×11in); 1821. Royal Academy of Arts, London

family in 1824 because of his wife's poor health, and where he painted some remarkably fresh and vivid beach scenes. The periods he spent at his home in Hampstead encouraged his interests in climatic change, particularly in the formation of clouds.

Despite his belated election to full membership of the Royal Academy in 1829, his later years were unhappy. In 1828 Maria died, leaving him with seven children, and his friend Fisher died four years later. Constable never fully recovered from these bereavements. His sporadic black moods seem to be expressed in the stormy atmosphere and restless brushwork of his paintings during these years, for example *Hadleigh Castle* (1829; Paul Mellon Center for British Art, New Haven) and the dramatic preparatory oil sketch for that picture (c1829; The Tate Gallery, London). Also c1829 Constable began work on designs to

be engraved in mezzotint by David Lucas and published as a series entitled *English Landscape Scenery*, a project presumably undertaken in emulation of Claude and Turner, and intended as a summary of the artist's ideas and achievements. Some of Constable's opinions on landscape were expressed in the accompanying text, and were expanded and extended in lectures he gave in Hampstead in 1833 and 1835. He died on 30 March 1837.

In the 1830s Constable achieved more expressiveness in his work; he aimed less at the careful naturalistic depiction of a scene and more at an immediate record of the light and atmosphere of the moment and their fleeting effect on the sky, foliage, and water. This expressiveness is seen at its most intense in the later outdoor sketches in watercolors, a medium he used more frequently in these years, and in the elaborate finished oils such as *The Valley Farm*

(1835; Tate Gallery, London), the last great Suffolk picture. The most turbulently Romantic of all the later works is perhaps the remarkable watercolor *Stonehenge* (1835; Victoria and Albert Museum, London), in which the mystery of the subject is enhanced by the disturbing presence of the double rainbow and the dramatically ominous sky.

The naturalism of Constable's work was recognized in his own day; Henry Fuseli remarked to Callcott in 1823 that Constable "makes me call for my greatcoat and umbrella". He achieved this naturalism largely by close observation, at times of a scientific intensity. He not only consulted scientific treatises, concerning meteorology for example, but also believed, as he stated in a lecture given in 1836, that his profession was "*scientific* as well as *poetic*". He was particularly interested in the effects of light and shadow, with which he attempted to suggest the transient qualities of the scene before him, to depict what he called the "chiaroscuro of nature". The advice he received from the President of the Royal Academy, Benjamin West, in 1802, that "light and shadow never stand still" was described by Constable as the best lecture on chiaroscuro he had ever heard.

Constable's place in early-19th-century Romantic art is assured partly by this interest in the transience of nature, but mainly by his belief that "painting is with me but another word for feeling". For Constable, a landscape could express a poetic mood, as in *The Cornfield* (1826; National Gallery, London), which gives a visual interpretation of the lines from James Thomson's poem *Summer* which accompanied the picture when it was exhibited at the British Institution in 1827:

> ... A fresher gale
> Begins to wave the woods and stir the
> streams
> Sweeping with shadowy gusts the fields of
> corn.

The boy drinking from the stream in the foreground of the picture also calls to mind certain passages from Wordsworth's *The Prelude*. Constable also possessed a grand, cosmic vision, different from that of Turner but no less intense. Both artists were able to convey their own feelings for the basic forces of nature, for the powerful vibrancy of the living landscape.

Constable's achievement, like Turner's, was so original and individual that he had few followers among English artists; his closest imitator was Frederick William Watts (1800–62). However, his paintings were much copied and forged. Although he never traveled abroad, his work was known in France; several works were exhibited and sold in Paris, notably *The Hay Wain* which won a Gold Medal at the 1824 Salon. Delacroix, among others, especially admired Constable's work, calling him "one of the glories of England" and adopting to some extent his loose, broken handling of paint. Constable's principal influence in France was more far-reaching; his work was admired by the Barbizon group of landscape painters, whose consequent interest in naturalism and outdoor painting was to provide a suitable background for the Impressionists later in the century.

There are works by Constable in London at the National and Tate Galleries, and at the Royal Academy of Arts; he is also represented in galleries elsewhere in Britain and abroad. The main collection of sketches in oils, watercolors, and pencil is at the Victoria and Albert Museum, London, mainly because of the bequest in 1888 by the artist's daughter Isabel.

Further reading. Beckett, R. B. (ed.) *John Constable's Correspondence*, vol. 1, Woodbridge (1976); vols. 2–6, Ipswich (1962–9). Leslie, C.R. (ed.) *Memoirs of the Life of John Constable*, Oxford (1951). Reynolds, G. *Catalogue of the Constable Collection in the Victoria and Albert Museum*, London (1973). Reynolds, G. *Constable, the Natural Painter*, London (1965).

Cooper Samuel 1609–72

The work of the English miniaturist Samuel Cooper marked a break with the tradition of Nicholas Hilliard and Isaac Oliver, and introduced the Baroque into English miniature painting. Cooper was first apprenticed to his uncle John Hoskins, but was working on his own by 1642. He soon learned to absorb the influence of van Dyck, and echoes of Lely's compositions are also discernible in his work. His most characteristic effect is a soft pearly-grayish tone. Cooper's work was highly prized during his lifetime, and his services were much in demand both by Cromwell and by Charles II after the Restoration.

Samuel Cooper: Portrait of an Unknown Man; watercolor on vellum; 7.3×5.7cm (2⅞×2¼in); 1645. Collection of H.M. Queen Elizabeth II

Copley John 1738–1815

The American painter John Singleton Copley had two separate careers: one as America's first great portrait-painter and one, from 1774, as a history painter and precursor of Romantic painting in London.

Copley was born in Boston. Although he was the stepson of Peter Pelham, a London-trained engraver of mezzotints, he was largely self-taught; yet he produced a personal portrait style far superior to any he had ever seen. In *Henry Pelham (Boy with a Squirrel)* of 1765 (Boston Museum of Fine Arts) Copley painted with an objective clarity, acuteness of characterization, and sheer professionalism unknown previously in the American colonies. From the 1760s he produced a magnificent record of his native New England clientele such as *Mrs John Winthrop* (1773; Metropolitan Museum, New York) and of heroes of the revolutionary period such as *Paul Revere* (1765–70; Boston Museum of Fine Arts).

However, Copley felt cut off from artistic developments in Europe; the political situation made his economic survival as a portraitist in America doubtful, and as the son-in-law of a prominent tea-merchant his family position was precarious. All these factors conspired to make him leave permanently for England in 1774. In London the influence of Sir Joshua Reynolds and Benjamin West made Copley's portrait style lose its vivacity and his interest changed to large-scale history paintings. His best historical works were of modern subjects, and, like those of West, in contemporary dress.

In *Brook Watson and the Shark* (1778; Boston Museum of Fine Arts) Copley's interest was in man's exposure to natural hazard rather than in historical significance; his success was greater here with an essentially Romantic theme than in set pieces such as *The Collapse of the Earl of Chatham in the House of Lords* (1779–80; Tate Gallery, London). Despite outstanding success with the latter and with *The Death of Major Pierson* (1783; Tate Gallery, London) Copley's later life was darkened by an ever-growing melancholy, exacerbated by his permanent exile.

Coppo di Marcovaldo c1225–74

Coppo di Marcovaldo was a Florentine painter who worked between 1250 and 1270. In 1261 he signed the *Madonna del*

Bordone (S. Maria dei Servi, Siena), a work monumental both in design and size (7 ft 3 in by 4 ft; 2.2 by 1.3 m). A similar work, in the same rich yet somber coloring, is the *Madonna and Child* in Orvieto (S. Maria dei Servi). Within a framework of Byzantine style, Coppo's work displays a new sense of physical and moral weight. He tries, both by means of the still linear "creases" which serve for folds of drapery, and by setting the body and legs of the Virgin at an angle to the picture-plane, to indicate that they occupy a position in space. Other works attributed to him are disputed; his known work in fresco—Pistoia Cathedral, *c*1265—is now lost.

Cornelius Peter 1783–1867

Peter Cornelius was a German draftsman and painter. Despite a thoroughly classical training (Düsseldorf Academy, 1795–1800), Cornelius shared his generation's enthusiasm for the Middle Ages. His illustrations to Goethe's *Faust* (1808–16) and to the *Niebelungenlied* (1812–17) show the influence of Dürer's line drawings and a search for specifically German subject matter.

In 1811 he went to Rome to study early Italian painting and became a member of the group of artists known as the Nazarenes. Cornelius' contribution to the frescoes they painted in a room of the house of the Prussian Consul in Rome (the *Story of Joseph* in the Casa Bartholdi, now in the Nationalgalerie, East Berlin; 1815–16) bears the fruit of these studies; the human warmth they express shows the influence of Johann Friedrich Overbeck (1789–1869). The designs Cornelius painted for the ceiling of the Dante room in the Casino Massimo, Rome, show his ability to summarize symbolically a subject's spiritual content. His stay in Rome and his work on the frescoes helped to revive German art and in 1819 he eagerly accepted the offer to decorate the Glyptothek in Munich.

In keeping with his Nazarene principles, he treated the Classical myths required by the commission as symbolically foreshadowing Christian ideas. The result was intellectual and cold. The frescoes are more mannerist than his Roman works,

Coppo di Marcovaldo: Madonna del Bordone; panel; 220×130cm (87×52in); 1261. S. Maria dei Servi, Siena

Corot: View of Florence from the Boboli Gardens; oil on canvas; 51×74cm (20×29in); c1836. Louvre, Paris

color is neglected for the sake of line, and there is frequent overcrowding; but Cornelius has successfully integrated his pictures into their architectural setting.

The driving force behind Cornelius' subsequent work was the belief that underlying Christianity there were basic truths all sects should embrace. Unfortunately his intellectual treatment of Christian iconography and his lack of sensuous appeal (for example, his frescoes in the Ludwigskirche, Munich; 1830–40) prevented him from making the spiritual impact he sought.

Cornell Joseph 1903–72

Joseph Cornell was an untaught, highly original American artist. His works consist of collections of objects and fragments in small-scale box-like constructions such as *Box with a Perched Bird* (1945), *Dovecote* (c1950), both at Xavier Fourcade Inc., New York. His juxtaposition of unlikely objects in poetic disarray owes much to Dada, and especially to Kurt Schwitters. But whereas Schwitters constructed out of *Merz* (his coinage for rubbish or garbage),

Cornell builds up a gem-like quality. A man of great breadth of knowledge, he learned about Surrealism—particularly the work of Max Ernst—from the Julian Levy Gallery in the 1930s. During the 1940s he was close to the European Surrealists in exile in New York. He wrote several books and also made films.

Corot 1796–1875

The French landscape and figure-painter Jean-Baptiste-Camille Corot played an important part in the development of plein-air painting. He began working within the framework of the classical French Italianate landscape tradition as seen in the work of Claude (1600–82) and Poussin (1615–75), but revitalized the style by the freshness of his observation. Though he was never to forsake his classical principles completely, he made important technical advances. He particularly emphasized the quality of the sketch as an artistic production equal to, or even greater in value than the finished studio composition.

Born in Paris in 1796 into a prosperous commercial family, he was educated at

Rouen and then worked as an assistant in a draper's shop. Only in 1822, at the age of 26, was he able to persuade his parents to let him turn to painting full time. He studied with the painters Achille Michallon (1796–1822) and Jean-Victor Bertin (1775–1842), and at the Académie Suisse, and made the first of three trips to Italy in 1825. His first Salon painting was shown in 1827, and though he was only slowly accepted as a talented artist, his work was never as controversial as that of Rousseau. He visited England and Holland, and spent an itinerant life painting in many parts of the French provinces.

Corot began painting out of doors in 1822 on the advice of his first teacher, Michallon. His trip to Italy from 1825 to 1828 confirmed his dedication to the classical principles of landscape, which he was to adapt but never forsake. Here, through painting on the site, he developed his technique of treating distance in terms of tonal values rather than drawing. As he was working primarily on plein-air studies during his first Italian trip, there are many sketches but few finished works from this period. One of the most famous studio compositions is *Le Pont de Narni* (National Gallery of Canada, Ottawa), which he sent to the Salon of 1827. When this is compared with sketches of the same site, it becomes clear that he made several alterations to the landscape in the studio painting, changing the disposition of the ground and trees for compositional reasons. This classical practice became less and less frequent in Corot's landscape work over the years.

The artist made two trips to Italy in 1834 and 1843. The intense sunlight, which tended to bleach color, led him to develop his characteristic technique of mixing white with all his colors: this gives an effect of opacity, and unites the painting through chromatic harmony. In 1834 he painted a view of Volterra (Louvre, Paris) which he sent to the Salon of that year: this was the first Salon entry he had painted in front of the motif.

In France, Corot painted on numerous sites, one of his favorite subjects being views of his parents' home at Ville d'Avray, near Paris. He preferred to paint calm rather than turbulent scenes, and rarely depicted violent effects of weather, or objects in motion. In the late 1840s he developed a more misty style, with feathery treatment of trees; this is characteristic of his later landscapes, such as *The Church of Marissel, near Beauvais* (1866; Louvre, Paris). He also painted several "topographical" landscapes, which give clear records of the views depicted, for example *The Cathedral of Chartres* (c1830; Louvre, Paris).

Corot's historical landscapes, which place figures of religious or Classical history in backgrounds of scenery, were painted for exhibition at the Salons. They were assembled from various sketches done in the open air, and are now perhaps the least admired of his works, as their distance from original inspiration results in a lack of spontaneity. One of his best paintings of this type is *Homer among the Shepherds* (1845; Musée de St-Lô).

The lyrical or fantastic landscapes Corot painted later in his career (c1850 onwards) use an atmospheric, Claudesque style, and show the influence of the Rococo and the French 18th century. The forms are softened and the colors reduced to a very narrow range, carefully graded and silvery in hue. Peopled with nymphs and bathers, set at dawn or dusk in a misty atmosphere, these charming works were much admired by Corot's contemporaries (for example,

Souvenir de Mortefontaine, 1864; Louvre, Paris).

From the start of his career Corot painted portraits of his family and close friends. They depict the prosperous commercial bourgeoisie from which he sprang (for example, *Portrait of Claire Sennegon*, 1837; Louvre, Paris). He occasionally included a figure-subject in his Salon entries, for example in 1859 in *La Toilette* (private collection). Most of his figure-subjects are late works, however. Mainly pictures of women, either against neutral backgrounds or in Corot's studio, they are posed and motionless, silent and melancholy (for example, *Woman with a Pearl*, 1869; Louvre, Paris; *Lady in Blue*, 1874; Louvre, Paris).

Corot was in touch with the artists of the Barbizon School, and was particularly close to Daubigny; they often painted together in the Forest of Fontainebleau and elsewhere. Open-hearted in character, he showed great generosity to his friends, notably to Daumier, and to Millet's widow. He had great personal prestige among younger artists, and by 1850 had a number of disciples, including Antoine Chintreuil and François-Louis Français. During the mid 1860s he was in occasional contact with the young Impressionists.

Though admired by many critics, and named by Baudelaire in 1845 as the head of the modern French landscape school, he never enjoyed official patronage to any great extent and was forced to rely on the considerable enthusiasm of private collectors. By the 1860s they were collecting his sketches as well as finished works.

A single-minded artist with few interests outside his work, Corot was a "pure" painter and had little concern with depicting his own period. While his subject matter remained very conventional—particularly in his liking for the Italian scenes renounced by many avant-garde artists—he made innovations in plein-air painting and in techniques, which prepared the way for the Impressionists.

Further reading. Arts Council *Corot*, London (1965). Herbert, R. *Barbizon Revisited*, Boston (1962). Roberts, K. *Corot*, London (1965).

Correggio c1490–1534

Correggio, whose real name was Antonio Allegri, was a north Italian painter, and a master of illusion and sentiment, whose

Correggio: Jupiter and Io; oil on canvas; 163×74cm (64×29in); 1531. Kunsthistorisches Museum, Vienna

dome decorations and altarpieces exercised a profound influence upon Baroque and Rococo art.

His reputation has never regained the peak of esteem it deservedly achieved during the 17th and 18th centuries. No contemporary artist rivaled his ability to set huge spaces in motion with form and color, or equaled the fluid design, soft forms, and engaging emotion of his easel paintings.

His father acted as guarantor in the contract for his first recorded commission in 1514, *The Madonna of St Francis* (Gemäldegalerie Alte Meister, Dresden) which he painted for the church of S. Francesco in Correggio, his home town. A local law required such a guarantor for an artist under the age of 25. The altarpiece, finished in 1515, containing echoes of the work of Lorenzo Costa (c1460–1535) and and perhaps also of Leonardo and

Raphael, but the main influence is that of Mantegna's *Madonna della Vittoria* of *c*1494–6 in Mantua (now Louvre, Paris). Correggio had almost certainly visited the city and may have been responsible for the *Four Evangelists* in Mantegna's funerary chapel, and for two fresco roundels (S. Andrea, Mantua).

The influence of Albrecht Dürer's prints is apparent in two of his earliest paintings, *The Mystic Marriage of St Catherine* (*c*1513; Detroit Institute of Arts) and *Christ Taking Leave of His Mother* (*c*1512; National Gallery, London).

The Albinea Madonna (now lost) and the *Four Saints* (Metropolitan Museum, New York), both works probably begun in 1517, give little indication that Correggio was to develop into anything more than a provincial painter. The relatively sudden sophistication and amplitude of his figure-style after 1518 may result from at least one visit to Rome and direct experience of the works of Michelangelo and Raphael.

His first fully mature paintings are the Raphaelesque *Diana* and cherubs in the Camera di San Paolo in the Benedictine convent at Parma. The suite of rooms of Gioanna da Piacenza, the Abbess, possessed little of the enclosed atmosphere of an ordinary convent, but served as a center for humanist intellectual activity. Correggio's vault decorations accordingly contain learned images illustrating Classical themes and based substantially upon Roman coins. Above these images, painted to look like sculpture, playful cherubs are visible through holes in a painted trellis of fruit and vegetation.

His success with this vault may have led to his being asked to paint the dome, apse, and friezes of S. Giovanni Evangelista, Parma. Payments made between 1520 and 1525 record the steady progress and completion of the frescoes. His entirely original conception transforms the whole dome into the vision of St John the Evangelist on Mount Patmos, who crouches in awe on the section of cornice nearest the nave. Above him, Michelangelesque Apostles are seated in a ring, while the upper region dissolves into a radiant vision of sky teeming with nebulous angels. The foreshortened figure of Christ miraculously floats in an indefinable space above the spectator. His apse decoration for the same church, the *Coronation of the Virgin*, survives only in fragments (Galleria Nazionale, Parma, and National Gallery, London).

In 1526 he received the first payment for the even grander project for the huge dome of Parma Cathedral (commissioned 1522). Work was to continue until 1530. The dome arises from an octagonal base, punctuated by round windows between which stand excited Apostles. To enhance the illusion, Correggio has carried some sections of the plaster upon which the draperies are painted across the edges of the window frames. In the dome itself, the Virgin ascends towards a luminous heaven through a vast, floating, celestial funnel composed of biblical characters and flying angels. She is greeted by a heavenly messenger (the adolescent Christ?) flying free on the opposite side. The spectator's viewpoint is placed off-center towards the nave, so that the inner surface of the divine cylinder is more visible on the Virgin's side.

During the painting of the domes, he also completed a series of major altarpieces, whose overlapping chronology is difficult to disentangle. *The Madonna of St Sebastian* (Gemäldegalerie Alte Meister, Dresden) finished *c*1526 and the *Madonna of St Jerome* (Galleria Nazionale, Parma) possibly commissioned in 1523 but painted later, show the development of fluid, flickering compositions based upon complex patterns of light and color, often with daring asymmetry.

In the justly famous *Nativity* (*La Notte*; Gemäldegalerie Alte Meister, Dresden) commissioned in 1522 and finished *c*1528–30, asymmetry is combined with a brilliant exposition of divine light radiating from the child. Correggio increasingly highlights sentiment, expressing sweetness and reverent delight. In what may be one of his later works, *The Martyrdom of Saints Placidus, Flavia, Eutichius, and Victorinus* (*c*1528–30, but often dated earlier; Galleria Nazionale, Parma, formerly in the Del Bono Chapel, S. Giovanni Evangelista) the saints welcome their deaths with a swooning ecstasy which is repeated in countless Baroque altarpieces.

Also during the 1520s he was patronized by Isabella d'Este Federico Gonzaga, producing a series of mythologies and allegories for the ducal palaces in Mantua. These began with *The Education of Cupid Anteros* (*c*1524; National Gallery, London), reminiscent of Leonardo's *Leda*, continued with the disconcertingly seductive *Virtues* (*c*1529; Louvre, Paris), and reached great heights of sensual appeal in the luscious *Io* (*c*1530; Kunsthistorisches Museum, Vienna). The scale of his artistic activity appears to have diminished greatly in the last four years of his life.

After his death, Correggio was followed in Parma by a school of imitators and by the young Parmigianino; but his major impact was to be felt in the late 16th and early 17th centuries, when Federico Barrocci, the Carracci, and Lanfranco translated his style into the language of Baroque art.

Further reading. Gould, C. *The Paintings of Correggio*, London (1976). Panofsky, E. *The Iconography of Correggio's Camera di San Paolo*, London (1961). Popham, A.E. *Correggio's Drawings*, London (1957). Ricci, C. *Correggio*, London (1930).

Cossa Francesco del *c*1435–*c*77

The Italian painter Francesco del Cossa came from Ferrara. He was first recorded in 1456; his earliest authenticated works, some frescoes in the Palazzo Schifanoia, Ferrara, date from 1469–70. They illustrate the months and include much astrological subject matter. The remainder of his working life he spent at Bologna painting religious pictures, notably the dismembered Griffoni Chapel triptych (*c*1473; center panel in the National Gallery, London) and an altarpiece dated 1474 (Pinacoteca Nazionale, Bologna). Cossa's style draws its grace and clarity from Florentine draftsmanship, its hardness and tautness from the works of Mantegna and Cosmé Tura. Its characteristics include contrived rocky landscapes and, in the Ferrara frescoes, engaging details of human activities.

Costa Lorenzo *c*1460–1535

Lorenzo Costa, known as Costa the Elder, was a Ferrarese painter who worked in Bologna and Mantua. He was in Bologna by 1483 where he undertook several commissions for the ruling Bentivoglio family, notably frescoes in their chapel in S. Giacomo Maggiore (1488–90). Costa's partnership there with Francesco Francia ended when he succeeded Mantegna as court painter at Mantua in 1506. His Mantuan works included two allegories for Isabella d'Este's Studiolo (both in the Louvre, Paris). He was superseded by Giulio Romano *c*1524. Costa's earlier paintings show the influence of Cosmé

Lorenzo Costa: Isabella d'Este Crowned by Love; oil on canvas; 158×193cm (62×76in); c1504–6. Louvre, Paris

Tura (c1430–95) and particularly Ercole de' Roberti (1456?–96). His later style was softened by the elegance of Francia's works, which introduced Costa to Umbrian styles.

Cotman John Sell 1782–1842

The landscape artist John Sell Cotman was one of the most important figures in the development of English watercolor painting. Born in Norwich, he moved to London in 1798, though by 1806 he was back in his home town, where he was to become one of the leaders of the Norwich School, a group of landscape painters who painted the English countryside in a style strongly influenced by 17th-century Dutch painting. His own style, however, was highly original: flat, crisply defined areas of clear color created landscapes structured by abstract shapes and patterns. Among his finest works are those he made on his trips to Yorkshire between 1803 and 1805, such as *Greta Bridge* (1805; British Museum).

Cotte Robert de 1656–1735

Robert de Cotte was a French architect of the early Rococo period. His early years were spent assisting his brother-in-law J. Hardouin Mansart, whom he succeeded as *Premier Architecte* to Louis XIV in 1709, in which capacity he completed Mansart's unfinished chapel at Versailles. His independent work consists mainly of town houses in Paris and the provinces. The gallery of his Hotel de la Vrillière, Paris (1719), is a gem of Rococo decoration. The Palais Rohan, Strasbourg, is one of his principal works outside Paris. Cotte is important for the role he played in disseminating French architectural ideas abroad during the early 18th century.

Gustave Courbet: Portrait of P.J. Proudhon; oil on canvas; 147×198cm (58×78in); 1853. Musée du Petit Palais, Paris.

Robert de Cotte: Schloss Schleissheim in Schleissheim, Munich

Courbet Gustave 1819–77

The French painter Gustave Courbet, born at Ornans (Doubs) on 10 June 1819, was a self-confessed Realist, painting only what he could see and hostile to every kind of idealist art. After the Revolution of 1848, he was identified as an artist of the Left; later generations have seen him as one of the originators of the modern movement.

Intended for the law by his father, a rich farmer of peasant stock, Courbet left home for Paris in 1840. For a decade he struggled to establish himself as an artist. He was virtually self-taught, drawing at the Atelier Suisse and studying composition and technique at the Louvre. His early works were mediocre, aping the worst excesses of contemporary Romanticism. They were also narcissistic: he was his own model for such works as *Self-portrait with a Black Dog* (1844; Musée du Petit Palais, Paris), *The Sculptor* (1845; private collection), and the famous *Man with a Leather*

Belt (?1845; Louvre, Paris). But gradually he discovered the true sources for his art: works by the Italian painters Caravaggio (1573–1609/10), and Guercino (1591–1666), by the Spaniard Zurbaran (1598–1664), and, after a visit to Holland in 1847, by Hals (c1580–1666) and Rembrandt (1606–1669).

It was in 1847 that Courbet painted his only commissioned altarpiece, *St Nicholas Resurrecting the Children*, for the church of the local parish of Saules. But success in Paris eluded him. To four successive Salons after 1844 he submitted a total of 18 works, but only three were accepted. The 1848 Revolution and the brief Second Republic eventually established Courbet as a Revolutionary artist, but this did not happen immediately. It is true he designed a crude masthead for his friend Baudelaire's revolutionary paper *Le Salut Public* in 1848. But otherwise he simply took advantage of the jury-less Salon that year to show ten of his early works. These attracted little attention, but he returned to Ornans to paint the canvas that in 1849 did establish his reputation.

Even this work, *After Dinner at Ornans* (Musée des Beaux-Arts, Lille), was not strikingly revolutionary in either an aesthetic or a political sense. It was described in Courbet's own subtitle: "It was in November, we were at our friend Cuénot's house, Marlet had just returned from the hunt, and we had persuaded Promayet to play his violin for my father". But this autobiographical incident, a trivial pastoral occasion, was painted on a heroic scale (over 6 by 8 ft; 2 by 2.6 m) with a mastery that demanded comparison with Caravaggio or Rembrandt. It was bought by the State and presented to Lille's museum. More important, it won Courbet a second-class medal and the right to exhibit what he chose at future Salons.

Again returning to Ornans, Courbet began the three works that made him notorious when they were exhibited in the Salon of 1850–1. The most scandalous was the enormous *A Burial at Ornans* (1849; Louvre, Paris), 10 ft high and 7 yds long (3.3 by 7 m). Flattered by Courbet's second-class medal, more than 45 citizens of Ornans, including the artist's relatives and friends, posed for this frieze of life-sized mourners. But when the painting was seen in Paris alongside the degraded proletariat in *The Stonebreakers* (1849; formerly in Dresden; destroyed in 1945) and *The Peasants of Flagey Returning from the Fair* (1850; Musée des Beaux-Arts, Besançon) the public believed that Courbet was satirizing contemporary social values, and the bourgeois *Burial* was thought a caricature. Courbet, supported by his friend the Socialist Pierre-Joseph Proudhon, acknowledged his own socialist political ideals. But aesthetically his ideal was Realism. He thought the word Realism was a misnomer, but in 1861 he defined his art as independent of teachers or traditions, concerned only to represent "*real and existing things ... Imagination in art consists in knowing how to find the most complete expression of an existing thing*". In practice, Courbet painted the surfaces of things vividly and vigorously with his unique palette-knife technique. This gives *The Stonebreakers* a poignant immediacy, without revealing the subjects' faces or using heroic poses, as Millet would have done.

After the *coup d'état* of 1851 and the coming of the Second Empire, Courbet's paintings became less obviously political. *Young Ladies of the Village Giving Alms* (1851; Metropolitan Museum, New York) shows his sisters giving alms to a cowgirl, an inoffensive enough image of charity. The broad, naked buttocks of *The Bather* (1853; Musée Fabre, Montpellier) offended by their realistic vulgarity: the Emperor likened the model to a draft horse. The painting was, however, bought by a rich eccentric, Alfred Bruyas, who became Courbet's patron and friend.

In turning away from political commitment, Courbet's art became increasingly egotistical. Of the many works he painted for Bruyas, the most revealing is *The Meeting* (1854; Musée Fabre, Montpellier) in which the artist arrogantly confronts his patron and manservant who deferentially doff their hats to him.

In the autumn of 1854, to prove that he was "not dead yet, or realism either" Courbet undertook a second immense painting, 12 ft high by 20 ft long (4 by 6.6 m), *The Artist's Studio: a real allegory defining a seven year period of my life* (Louvre, Paris). Painted at Ornans, it shows his Paris studio, with Courbet himself at work on a landscape, but he is surrounded by 27 other figures, including a life model. On the right are his friends, including Baudelaire, Bruyas, Proudhon, and Champfleury. On the left are "the others, the world of trivialities: the common people ... those who thrive on death". This immense fantasy, painted in little over two months, seems far from socialist in spirit.

Courbet had expected that both *A Burial at Ornans* and *The Artist's Studio* would be accepted for the Paris International Exhibition of 1855. When they were rejected, he angrily opened his own pavilion. This was a novel enterprise, later emulated by Manet, but it attracted little attention.

Courbet's *The Return from the Conference* depicts drunken clergy and was refused even for the Salon des Refusés of 1863: it was bought and destroyed by a strict Catholic. Apart from this painting and *Young Ladies on the Banks of the Seine*, 1857; Musée du Petit Palais, Paris). Courbet produced few works in later years with overt social messages. He painted what he liked and what he was commissioned to paint: splendid landscapes of his native Franche-Comté, hunting scenes, deer in woodland, and female nudes, sensual and even deliberately indecent. In 1861, he opened a studio for a few months, but then declared he was not and could not be a teacher. In the Commune of 1871 he was made President of the Art Commission and was implicated in the destruction to the Vendôme Column. This was his last political act. When the Commune fell in May 1871, Courbet was arrested and imprisoned.

While in prison he painted a number of exquisite still lifes. Released in 1872, he fled to Switzerland where he spent the rest of his life. In those years of exile, he drank heavily and employed assistants to paint salable Swiss landscapes in his broad palette-knife style. He died at Le Tour de Peilz, near Vevey, on 31 December 1877.

Further reading. Aragon, L. *L'Exemple de Courbet*, Paris (1952). Arts Council of Great Britain *Gustave Courbet 1819–1877*, London (1978). Boas, G. *Courbet and the Naturalistic Movement*, Baltimore (1938). Bowness, A. "Courbet and Baudelaire", *Gazette des Beaux-Arts*, Paris (December 1977). Clark, T.J. "A Bourgeois Dance of Death", *The Burlington Magazine*, London (April, May 1969). Clark, T.J. *Image of the People: Gustave Courbet and the 1848 Revolution*, London (1973). Fernier, R. *La Vie et L'Oeuvre de Gustave Courbet*, Lausanne (1978). Leger, C. *Courbet et Son Temps*, Paris (1948). Mack, G. *Gustave Courbet*, New York (1951). Nicolson, B. *Courbet: The Studio of the Painter*, London (1973). Riat, G. *Gustave Courbet, Peintre*, Paris (1906).

Courtois brothers 17th century

The French painter Jacques Courtois (1621–75) was born at St-Hippolyte, Doubs. After a period serving in the Spanish army in Milan he had arrived in Rome by 1640 and spent the rest of his life there. He worked in the manner of Salvator Rosa (1615–73) and Michelangelo Cerquozzi (1602–60), and is best known as a painter of battles; these are full of verve, light, and smoke, thanks to his loose, glittering technique. His works are extremely popular with collectors. His name is sometimes italianized to "Il Borgognone".

Guillaume Courtois (1628–79), his younger brother, was also born at St-Hippolyte. A pupil of Pietro da Cortona, he was primarily a religious painter, working in Rome. He was known in Italy as "Guglielmo Cortese". Among his many works are the high altar of S. Andrea al Quirinale, Rome (c1670) and *The Battle of Joshua* (1657; Palazzo del Quirinale, Rome). He also engraved religious subjects.

Coustou family
17th and 18th centuries

Nicolas Coustou (1658–1733) and his brother Guillaume (1677–1746) were French sculptors. They were born at Lyons, sons of the wood sculptor François Coustou and his wife Claudine who was the sister of the sculptor Antoine Coysevox. They thus began their careers as nephews of the leading court sculptor of the day. Louis XIV said of Nicolas that he was "born a great sculptor". The brothers were pupils first of their father, and later of their uncle in Paris. Both in turn won first prize for sculpture at the Academy, Nicolas in 1682 and Guillaume in 1697, and each made the journey to Rome, where they were influenced by Baroque sculpture. After his return to Paris in 1687 Nicolas pursued an active career as a court sculptor, working (later in conjunction with his brother) at the Royal Châteaux of Versailles, the Trianon, and Marly.

Nicolas was perhaps the finer artist of the two although less versatile and imaginative than his brother. Guillaume is the more

Above: Guillaume Coustou: one of the Chevaux de Marly; marble; erected in 1745. Place de la Concorde, Paris

Below: Nicolas Coustou: Pietà; marble; 230×280cm (91×110in); 1712–28. Notre Dame de Paris

celebrated. His great marbles of horse tamers, the *Chevaux de Marly*, erected at Marly in 1745 and now in the Place de la Concorde, Paris, are the most famous French sculptures of their time.

Guillaume had a son, Guillaume II Coustou (1716–77). A less distinguished artist than his father, he nevertheless enjoyed a long, prosperous career as a court sculptor, his style gradually moving away from the Baroque. His highly original monument to the Dauphin at Sens (1766–77) is one of the earliest great Neoclassical sculptures.

Cox David 1783–1859

David Cox was an English watercolorist whose anecdotal genre subjects enjoyed considerable popularity in the 19th century. He studied under John Varley and first exhibited at the Royal Academy in 1805. After living in London from 1829 to 1841 he retired to Harborne near Birmingham, and made annual sketching tours to the Welsh mountains. His watercolors are painted in a broad, free style, and after 1836 he began to paint on a coarse Scottish paper which was commercially marketed as "Cox Paper". Cox published several works on landscape painting of which *Treatise on Landscape Painting and Effect in Water-colour* (1841) is the best known.

David Cox: The Brocas, Eton; watercolor; 21×33cm (8×13in); c1812. British Museum, London

Coypel family
17th and 18th centuries

The Coypels were a family of French painters. Noël (1628–1707) worked in the general manner of Poussin; he was a leading light of the French Academy of Painting and Sculpture from 1663, and became a Professor in 1664. He went to Italy as Director of the French Academy in Rome in 1672, returning two years later. His main work was the decoration of the Invalides (Paris, 1700–7).

Antoine Coypel (1661–1722) was the son of Noël, and went with his father to Rome. He became Director of the Academy of Painting and Sculpture in 1714. His chief work was the ceiling of the chapel at Versailles (1708), which was an important assertion of the continuing values of the Roman Baroque in court circles.

Noël Nicolas (1690–1734) was half-

Antoine Coypel: Chaste Susanna being Denounced; 48×70cm (19×28in); c1700. Musée des Beaux-Arts, Angers

Antoine Coysevox: Louis XIV; marble; 89×80cm (35×31in); 1686. Musée des Beaux-Arts, Dijon

brother to Antoine. His career was less successful than that of his son Charles-Antoine (1694–1752), who was made *Premier Peintre du Roi* (1743) and Director of the Academy (1747). He is significant for his part in the formation of an *École des Élèves Protégés*, who were fed on a wholesome diet of Classical learning and historical texts. The institution became the foundation stone of a strong French school of Neoclassicism.

Coysevox Antoine 1640–1720

The French sculptor Antoine Coysevox was born at Lyons. In 1657 he went to Paris, where he studied under Louis Lerambert and at the Académie. In 1666 he gained the title of *Sculpteur du Roi*.

Between 1667 and 1671 he worked at Saverne in Alsace for Cardinal Egon, Bishop of Strasbourg. After a brief return to Lyons, where he seems to have thought of establishing himself, he settled in Paris from 1667, and embarked on a busy career as a Royal Sculptor, producing works for Versailles, the Trianon, Marly, Saint-Cloud, and the Invalides. A brilliant portraitist, he made busts of most of the leading public figures of the time, and was the first French sculptor to portray fellow artists and friends, establishing a tradition that was to remain a special feature of French sculpture. Working in both bronze and marble, he produced several major sepulchral monuments, sometimes in collaboration with other Royal Sculptors.

Coysevox epitomizes the restrained Baro-

que style favored by Louis XIV, and was the dominant figure in French sculpture in the latter part of the reign. He exercised a powerful influence on the development of French sculpture in the first half of the 18th century. The foremost sculptors of the succeeding generation, Nicolas and Guillaume I Coustou, were his nephews and pupils. Coysevox's output was very large, but many of his important works have not survived; several of those that have have been moved from their original locations. His best-known statues, *Mercury* and *Fame*, originally carved in 1702 for Marly, have since 1719 stood at the entrance to the Jardins des Tuileries in Paris. There is an extensive and varied collection of his work in the Louvre, Paris.

Alexander Cozens: Sun Breaking through Clouds; pen and wash; 21×28cm (8×11in); 1746. British Museum, London

John Robert Cozens: The Oak; etching tinted with Indian ink; 24×32cm (9×12½in); 1789. British Museum, London

Cozens family 18th century

The English landscape painter and drawing master Alexander Cozens (c1717–86) was born in St Petersburg, but by 1742 he had settled in London. His dated sketchbooks (British Museum, London) confirm that he visited Rome in 1746. In England he painted and exhibited landscapes in oil, but he is best known for his monochrome landscape drawings and his teachings on art. His landscape compositions are almost always imaginary and reflect his deep respect for the classical tradition of Claude (1600–82). In 1771 he published an artist's manual on 32 varieties of trees. In his last publication, *A New Method of Assisting the Invention in Drawing Original Compositions of Landscape* (1785), he advocated his method of composing landscapes by applying ink to a sheet of paper at random, and then working the abstract markings into a finished representation. His emphasis on invention was not new; but his wash technique, which allowed extreme simplification of forms and a patterned massing of areas of light and shade, departed radically from the methods then in use.

John Robert Cozens (1752–97) was the only son of Alexander, from whom he received his early training as a landscape painter. In 1776 he exhibited a historical landscape in oils at the Royal Academy and then departed for Italy, via Switzerland. He was accompanied by Richard Payne Knight who was later to become an important theorist of the Picturesque. Cozens returned to England in 1779 but within three years set off again for Rome, on this occasion as draftsman to William Beckford. From 1783 Cozens lived in London and produced, on commission, a steady stream of watercolors based on sketches culled from his two Italian trips. In 1792 he suffered a nervous breakdown from which he never fully recovered.

Cozens' works are almost exclusively watercolor paintings of Italian and Swiss scenes, in which he reveals a heightened sensitivity to the most poetic and contemplative states of nature. His range of colors was limited, but he used them to create the most varied atmospheric effects. His technical innovations with watercolor and his moving response to nature were formative influences on Turner and Girtin, both of whom acknowledged their debt to his achievement.

Cranach Lucas, the Elder
1472–1553

Lucas Cranach the Elder was one of the most influential and prolific German artists of the 16th century. He was born at Kronach in northern Franconia, and received his early training in the workshop of his father, Hans Maler, who taught him the art of engraving. It was a journey along the Danube to Vienna that inspired the first and perhaps the most inventive phase of his career. On either the outward or the return journey he may have passed through Nuremburg and gained knowledge of Albrecht Dürer's woodcut style and technique. His own *St George* woodcut of 1507 is possibly the first true chiaroscuro print in Germany.

The influence of the Danube school of painting, with its distinctive landscape style and dramatic contrasts of color and lighting, is seen in Cranach's paintings, such as the *Crucifixion* of 1503 (Alte Pinakothek, Munich). This work is also highly original for its ingenious composi-

tion. The cross is placed at an angle to the picture-plane, so that the spectator's vision of the crucified Christ and his relationship to the other mourning figures are given a new psychological impact. In the same year Cranach painted what are probably his most successful and sympathetic portraits, those of the historian Johannes Cuspinian and of his wife Anna (both in the Sammlung Oskar Reinhart "Am Römerholz", Winterthur).

By 1505 Cranach had been appointed court painter to Frederick the Wise, Elector of Saxony, at Wittenberg. There he set up a large workshop to carry out variations and copies of his major compositions, where his sons, Hans (*ob.* 1537) and Lucas the Younger (1515–86) were trained. The characteristic features of a recognizable workshop style became quickly established and underwent little development after *c*1520.

Lucas Cranach the Elder: The Ill-matched Couple; originally wood panel, now canvas; 79×57cm (31×22in); c1532. Musée des Beaux-Arts, Besançon

The portraits of Duke Henry the Pious and his wife (1514; Gemäldegalerie Alte Meister, Dresden) are early examples of his most familiar style. The figures are flattened and their contours outlined against a dark background. The tall format makes them dominate the picture-field and removes the need for any spatial setting. The elaborate surface patterning of their costumes is accentuated at the expense of anatomical accuracy. The *Three Graces* (1535; William Rockhill Nelson Gallery, Kansas City) shows this style transferred to a mythological subject. The delicate nude forms are traditionally northern in character, sinuous and rhythmical in contour with bluish, pearl-like flesh tones. Hair and drapery (in other nude subjects jewelry as well) lend an erotic quality to these works.

Many of Cranach's later works are difficult to distinguish from the best of the workshop's productions. Originals such as the *Nymph of the Fountain* (1518; Museum der Bildenden Künste, Leipzig), *Adam and Eve*, and *The Ill-matched Couple* are repeated in many copies (one example of the latter is in the Musée des Beaux-Arts, Besançon).

Apart from his reputation as a court artist, Cranach holds an important place as a portrait painter of the German Reformation. His friendship with Martin Luther was very close and several portraits by Cranach of the Reformer and his wife survive. Cranach's last years were shaped by the wars resulting from the religious conflicts of his time. In 1550 he followed his patron, the exiled Elector John Frederick I, first to Augsburg and then to Weimar, where the artist died in 1553.

Further reading. Dornik-Eger, H. *Die Druckgraphik Lucas Cranachs und Seiner Zeit*, Vienna (1972). Friedländer, M.H. and Rosenberg, J. (eds.) *The Paintings of Lucas Cranach*, London (1978). Ruhmer, E. *Cranach*, London (1963). Schade, W. *Die Malerfamilie Cranach*, Dresden (1974).

Cresilas *fl.* 450–425 BC

Cresilas was a Greek sculptor from Crete; he was influenced by Pheidias in Athens where he probably collaborated on the Parthenon marbles. In his day he was famous for his noble portrait of Pericles; this stood on the Acropolis, and seems to have been an ideal characterization of a

Cresilas: Pericles; marble; height 50cm (20in); Roman copy derived from original of mid 5th century BC. Vatican Museums, Rome

general and statesman, perhaps portrayed in heroic nudity. Only copies of the head survive, as in the herm in the British Museum, London, and a Roman copy in the Vatican Museums, Rome. His bronze *Amazon* from Ephesus (Roman copy in the Capitoline Museum, Rome) is probably represented in copies showing her wounded under the right armpit, her right hand resting on her head, her left elbow on a pillar. The pathetic gesture, drooping head, and archaistic drapery were combined in an elegant style. The new, bold device of the supporting pillar was exploited later by Praxiteles (*fl. c*370–330 BC).

Crespi Daniele *c*1590–1630

Daniele Crespi was an Italian painter who worked in Milan. With Guglielmo Moncalvo he painted the dome of S. Vittore al Corpo in 1619. He later enrolled in Cerano's painting class in the Ambrosiana, Milan. His masterpiece is *The Fast of S. Carlo Borromeo* (S. Maria della Passione, Milan). In his last years he painted frescoes in the nave of the Certosa di Garegnano and in the choir of the Certosa di Pavia (both Carthusian monasteries). He died of the plague. His paintings are realistic, with strong effects of light and color developing later into cool silvery tonality.

Crespi Giuseppe Maria
1665–1747

Giuseppe Maria Crespi was an Italian painter, also known as "Lo Spagnuolo". He was born in Bologna. A specialist in genre painting, he portrayed the idiosyncrasies of man's everyday behavior with both sympathy and irony. He drew inspiration from the work of Bolognese painters as diverse as Lodovico Carracci (1555–1619), Domenico Maria Canuti (1620–1684), Guercino (1591–1666), and Lorenzo Pasinelli (1629–1700), as well as from the Umbrian painter Federico Barocci (1526–1612). From all these influences he developed an entirely individual style. In 1708 he was working in Florence where he was employed by the Grand Duke. On his return to Bologna soon afterwards he painted the famous cycle of *The Seven Sacraments* (Gemäldegalerie Alte Meister, Dresden).

Critius 5th century BC

Critius was a sculptor of the early Classical period; he worked with Nesiotes in Athens, specializing in bronze. Their greatest creation was *The Tyrannicides Harmodius and Aristogeiton*, heroes of the Athenian democracy; the statue was set up in Athens in 477 BC. Copies in Naples (Museo Archeologico Nazionale) and elsewhere present them in the act of killing Hipparchus, brother of the tyrant Hippias. The marble *Boy* attributed to Critius (Acropolis Museum, Athens) is one of the finest examples of the early Classical style in which Archaic frontality is abandoned and the weight rests on one leg.

Crivelli family
15th and 16th centuries

The Crivelli were a family of Italian painters, of Venetian origin. The first reference to Carlo Crivelli (1430/5–*c*1495) occurs in 1457 when he was sentenced to imprisonment in Venice for adultery. He seems to have left Venice soon after this date and in 1465 is recorded as living in Zara, Dalmatia. Thereafter he appears to have settled in the Marches of central Italy. His surviving works consist entirely of religious paintings, which retain the same highly

Daniele Crespi: The Last Supper; oil on canvas; 210×230cm (83×91in); *c*1624–5. Pinacoteca di Brera, Milan

decorated, hard edged, and rather provincial character throughout his life. Richly patterned fabrics and gold, embossed with elaborate patterns, form an essential part of his art.

We know nothing of Carlo Crivelli's early training, but his style, as seen for instance in the Demidoff Altar of 1476 (National Gallery, London), appears to derive from the Vivarini school: the elaborate frames surrounding his paintings would also confirm such a connection. Other paintings, such as the *Annunciation* of 1486 (National Gallery, London) contain reminiscences of works by Mantegna and Antonello. The Brera *Coronation of the Virgin* of 1493 (Pinacoteca di Brera, Milan) includes female types and ecstatic sentiment closer to works by Botticelli than to those of any other painter of this date. Carlo Crivelli's paintings are full of natural phenomena, especially fruit and vegetables, depicted with a very high degree of accuracy; these objects are often used as part of the elaborate structure of symbolism employed in his works.

Vittorio Crivelli (*fl.* 1481–1501/2) was probably Carlo's younger brother and is first recorded in 1481 when he signed and dated the now dismembered Vinci polyptych (Philadelphia Museum of Art). He worked in a style close to Carlo's, and like him found his chief patrons among the religious houses of the Italian Marches.

Crome John 1768–1821

The English landscape painter John Crome spent most of his life in Norwich. He trained as a coach painter until 1790. His ambition to become a landscape painter was encouraged by Thomas Harvey of Catton who made available a large collection of Dutch and English pictures for Crome to study. He rapidly assimilated the achievements of Hobbema (1638–1709), Jan Wynants (c1625–84), Richard Wilson (1714–82), and Thomas Gainsborough (1727–88). By the early 1800s he had developed his own version of the picturesque landscape, infused with sensitively observed details, always based on his rustic East Anglian terrain. In 1803 he helped to found the Norwich Society of Artists, a group of gifted painters to whom he was

Carlo Crivelli: St George and the Dragon; tempera on canvas; 90×46cm (35×18in); c1476. Isabella Stewart Gardner Museum, Boston

John Crome: Houses and Wherries on the Wensum; pencil and watercolor on paper; 30×40cm (12×16in); c1809–10. Whitworth Art Gallery, Manchester

the senior adviser. He exhibited landscape paintings annually with the Society from their first exhibition in 1805 to his death.

George Cruikshank: Monstrosities of 1825 and 1826; etching; 22×36cm (8½×14in); 1826. British Museum, London

Cruikshank George 1792–1878

The painter, illustrator, and cartoonist George Cruikshank was born in Bloomsbury, London; coming from a family of cartoonists and engravers, he learned the trade from his father Isaac (c1756–c1811) who had been a book illustrator and caricaturist of some popularity. When the caricaturist James Gillray died in 1815, Cruikshank took over his last plates. He was associated with Dickens, for whom he illustrated *Sketches by Boz* (1836) and *Oliver Twist* (1838). He worked with equal success for Harrison Ainsworth on his magazines (*Bentley's Miscellany, Ainsworth's Magazine*, etc) on *Jack Sheppard* (1839) and *The Tower of London* (1840), as well as illustrating numerous other books and pamphlets. From 1847 he was actively involved in the Temperance Movement, for which he produced a great deal of propaganda.

Cuvilliés Jean-François de 1695–1768

The French architect and decorator Jean-François de Cuvilliés was of Flemish origin. Tiny in stature, he was appointed as court dwarf by Max Emanuel of Bavaria in 1708 while Max Emanuel was living in exile in France. In 1715 Cuvilliés returned

Jean-François de Cuvilliés: detail of the main saloon of the Amalienburg hunting lodge, Schloss Nymphenburg; 1734–9

The decoration of Falkenlust is in the same style, which reaches its climax in the interiors of the Amalienburg in the park of Schloss Nymphenburg (1734–9).

In the facades of his palaces in Munich (now mostly destroyed or damaged) Cuvilliés blended French discipline with the Bavarian love of surface decoration. The masterpiece of his later years is the interior of the Residenz Theater in Munich (1751–3) in which classical columns are replaced by naturalistic palm trees.

Cuyp Aelbert 1620–91

The Dutch landscape painter Aelbert Cuyp (or Cuijp) was born and died in Dordrecht. He was the son of the painter Jacob Gerritsz. Cuyp, and early works such as his *Landscape with Cattle* (1639; Musée des Beaux-Arts, Besancon) may reflect his father's style. For a time he painted landscapes in the tonal manner of Jan van Goyen (1596–1656); but by the early 1640s Cuyp's style began to reflect the influence of those artists, such as Jan Both (*c*1618?–52), whose vision of landscape had been formed by travel in Italy.

Cuyp is best known for his river scenes and seascapes in which the moist atmosphere bathed in soft golden light lends an Arcadian quality to his work. The mood of his pictures is generally calm and silent and there is a degree of generalization in his rendering of specific localities; the *View of Nijmegen* (Indianapolis Museum of Art) is an example of this. Sometimes he takes a close and very low viewpoint as in the *Herdsman and Five Cows by a River* (National Gallery, London). Cuyp seems to have avoided narrative pictures wherever possible; his scenes of action are his least successful works. (An example is *Christ Entering Jerusalem*; Glasgow Art Gallery and Museum.)

The Maas at Dordrecht (Kenwood, The Iveagh Bequest, London) is one of several representations of the mouth of the river in his native town. Though there is no documentary evidence that he ever left Dordrecht, paintings and drawings suggest that he traveled to Utrecht and along the Rhine. Through his marriage in 1658 he belonged to the wealthy merchant class of Dordrecht, and he later purchased a country estate. The chronology of his work is difficult to establish since he dated so few of his pictures; but it does appear that his financial security enabled him to give up painting in the last years of his life.

Cuyp had little influence on painters outside Dordrecht, but he became a favorite of collectors, especially in England, where some of his finest works remain.

Aelbert Cuyp: River Landscape (detail); oil on canvas; full size 123×241cm (48×95in); c1655–60. Private collection

to Munich with the Elector. After five years' work as a draftsman for the Generalbaudirektor in Munich, Cuvilliés was sent to Paris for further training under François Blondel the Younger. In 1726, after Max Emanuel's death, the Elector Karl Albrecht appointed him Hofbaumeister, thus supplanting Joseph Effner. From 1728, Cuvilliés was also in the service of Karl Albrecht's brother, Clemens August, the Archbishop Elector of Cologne.

Apart from work on the Schloss Brühl near Bonn, Cuvilliés was responsible between 1729 and 1740 for the elegant hunting lodge Falkenlust, which is in the park there. In 1729 there was a disastrous fire in the Munich Residenz which destroyed most of the rooms newly completed by Effner. Cuvilliés redecorated the Reiche Zimmer (1730–7), with elaborate naturalistic *rocaille* work executed by the *stuccatore* J.B. Zimmermann and the woodcarvers J. Dietrich and W. Mirofsky. This introduced the fully developed Rococo into Germany for the first time.

D

Dadd Richard 1819–87

Richard Dadd was an English faery painter and illustrator. Born in Chatham, Kent, Dadd began drawing at the age of 14 and entered the Royal Academy Schools in 1837. His promising career was interrupted by a sudden mental breakdown during a trip to the Holy Land (1842–3). Dadd returned to London and murdered his father. Committed as insane in 1844, Dadd spent the rest of his life in care. In London's Bethlem Hospital he painted his meticulously worked oils *Oberon and Titania* (1854–8; private collection) and *The Faery Feller's Master Stroke* (1855–1864; Tate Gallery, London). In 1864 he was moved to Broadmoor; he continued to paint well on into the 1880s.

Bernardo Daddi: The Meeting of St Joachim and St Anne at the Golden Gate; tempera on panel; c1340. Uffizi, Florence

Richard Dadd: The Faery Feller's Master Stroke; oil on canvas; 54×39cm (21×15in); 1855–64. Tate Gallery, London

Daddi Bernardo c1280–1348

The Florentine painter Bernardo Daddi worked in the manner of Giotto between c1312 and 1345. In 1328 he signed a triptych (now in the Uffizi, Florence) of *The Madonna with SS. Matthew and Nicolas*. Other important works are his frescoes in the Pulci Beraldi Chapel in S. Croce, Florence (1324). His acquaintance with the manner of the Lorenzetti meant that those frescoes, while recognizably Giottesque in their massive bodies and characteristic drapery and shadings, contain elements of Sienese style as well—a higher color tone and much richer detail. These make his work less austere and more decorative than anything by Giotto himself. They seem to point to a certain dilution of the Giotto manner in the years after the painter's death.

Daedalus 7th century BC

Daedalus was originally a Greek mythological figure personifying the qualities of craftsman and engineer implicit in his name (Daedalic means "skillful"). His legendary career was set in the Bronze Age and he was credited with a number of inventions and engineering works such as the Cretan Labyrinth and the wax wings that flew him from Crete to Sicily. Another

Daedalus, who may or may not have been a historical figure, lived in the early Archaic period (7th century BC) and was said to have introduced monumental sculpture in Greece. The first generations of Archaic sculptors claimed him as their teacher.

"Daedalic" is a conventional term for a Greek artistic style of the 7th century BC. It is characterized by the flat, angular appearance of the human form, notably the head, which has wig-like hair fashioned in horizontal layers, a triangular face, pointed nose, and large eyes. It was formed under Near Eastern influence and is commonly found on the Aegean islands, Crete, and in the Peloponnese, on mold-made clay figurines, small bronzes, ivories, gold jewelry, and statuettes of limestone or wood.

The first large marble sculptures in Greece were also conceived in this style, the technique of stone carving having been borrowed from Egypt. They are draped women of a columnar appearance, free-standing or in relief, used for architectural decoration or votive offerings. The modeling is shallow. The shoulders and back of each figure are covered by a shawl, the waist accentuated by a large girdle of metallic form; drapery patterns are picked out in color, and are sometimes also incised. The statue dedicated by Nikandre to Artemis on Delos is one of the earliest and finest (National Museum, Athens). The Daedalic conventions for the head were used in the early male standing nudes (*Kouroi*) *c*600 BC, some of which also retained the large belt.

Dahl Michael 1656–1743

The Swedish-born painter Michael Dahl rivaled Sir Godfrey Kneller in maintaining a flourishing portrait practice in England. After studying in Stockholm he came to England in 1682 and was patronized by Prince George of Denmark and Queen Anne. However, unlike Kneller, Dahl was content with commissions from less illustrious subjects, and his observation and understanding were reserved for sitters such as merchants and naval officers (a series of portraits is in the National Maritime Museum, London). Dahl's technique was light and feathery; his portraits have an unmistakable resemblance to the European Rococo style, which may be due to his knowledge of contemporary French painting.

Dali Salvador 1904–89

The Spanish painter and writer Salvador Dali was at one time a member of the Surrealist movement. Born in Figueras, he studied at the Madrid School of Fine Art. His paintings of the mid 1920s show the influence of Carrà and de Chirico and of Surrealism. In Spain in 1928, he and his contemporary Luis Bunuel made the film *An Andalusian Dog*, which was received rapturously in Paris by the Surrealists. From this point onwards, Dali divided his time between Spain and France.

In such works as *Illumined Pleasures* (1929; Museum of Modern Art, New York), Dali employed a meticulously smooth, *trompe-l'oeil* style; he evolved a system of shading that resulted in a hallucinatory luminosity and dramatically receding perspectives. This contributed to the resurgence of illusionism in Surrealist painting in the late 1920s. In these paintings Dali's exposure of his neurotic sexual fantasies and fears (often by means of Freudian symbols) asserted the Surrealists' belief that art should be unflinchingly self-revelatory.

During the years 1929 and 1930, Dali developed his "paranoiac-critical method", which he used in both his paintings and his art criticism. It involved the ability to perceive unexpected analogies between forms and objects: thus Mae West's face is also a furnished room (*Mae West*, *c*1936; Art Institute of Chicago).

In 1930 Dali and Bunuel made the classic Surrealist film, *The Golden Age*. During this decade Dali was a leader in the Surrealist cult of the object. But his self-promotional stunts and his flirtation with Fascism eventually led to his exclusion from the movement. After the Second World War he worked in a style imitative of Vermeer and J.-L.-E. Meissonnier; his paintings express his erotic and religious fantasies, and his obsession with the Catalonian landscape, his wife Gala, and himself.

Salvador Dali: Autumnal Cannibalism; oil on canvas; 65×65cm (26×26in); 1936. Tate Gallery, London

Further reading. Dali, S. *Dali by Dali*, New York (1970). Dali, S. *Diary of a Genius*, London (1974). Gerard, M. (ed.) *Dali*, New York (1968). Morse, A.R. *Dali, a Guide to his Works in Public Museums*, Cleveland (1974). Tapie, M. *Dali*, Paris (1957).

Daliwes Jaques *fl.* early 15th century

The superb draftsman who signed his name Jaques Daliwes on the first of a series of drawings on 12 boxwood panels now in Berlin (Öffentliche Wissenschaftliche Bibliothek; Lib. pict. A. 74) is otherwise unknown. He was clearly a major artist, probably Franco-Flemish in origin but aware of Italian trends. A profile female portrait in The National Gallery of Art, Washington D.C., formerly attributed to Pisanello, closely resembles one of the Daliwes Berlin drawings and may be by the same hand. The panels include religious and animal subjects as well as heads; they are iconographically adventurous, and were probably intended as a model-book.

Dalmau Luís *fl.* 1428–61

The Spanish artist Luís (or Lluís) Dalmau was born in Valencia. By 1428 he was official painter to the city and to Alfonso V of Aragon. From 1431 to 1436 he studied with Jan van Eyck in Bruges; his surviving work, the Altarpiece of the Councillors, suggests a synthesis of Flemish experience with the International Gothic of Catalonia. The five Councillors of Barcelona are disposed with the Virgin, St Andrew, and St Eulalia, and angels, in a manner reminiscent of van Eyck's altarpiece at St-Bavon. In this work, landscape, buildings, and the treatment of detail and dimension all testify to Flemish origins. Dalmau's style had some influence in Castille and León, as well as throughout Catalonia.

Dalou Aime-Jules 1838–1902

The French sculptor Aime-Jules Dalou was born in Paris. He fled to London after the Paris Commune in 1871. In the following decade he worked in England on terracotta sculptures, naturalistically depicting scenes of family life; this class of subject, which appealed greatly to the Victorian love of domesticity, had previously been confined to painting. His ambition was to become a monumental sculptor, and on his return to Paris in 1880 he had already secured the

Aime-Jules Dalou: The Triumph of the Republic; bronze; completed in 1899. Place de la Nation, Paris

commission for *The Triumph of the Republic* (completed 1899, Place de la Nation, Paris), the largest of the many monuments sponsored under the Third Republic. He worked in secret on a *Monument to Labour* (sketches in Musée de l'École Supérieure des Beaux-Arts, Paris) intended as a socialist complement to the *Triumph*. This was never completed, but a large number of his small realist figures of workers survive.

Danti Vincenzo 1530–76

The Italian goldsmith and sculptor Vincenzo Danti was born in Perugia, where he matriculated as a goldsmith in 1548. His earliest sculpture is a monumental bronze figure of *Pope Julius III Enthroned*, erected outside Perugia Cathedral (1553–1556). From 1557 until 1573 Danti worked as a sculptor at the court of Cosimo I, Grand Duke of Florence. His masterpiece there was a bronze group on the Baptistery, depicting *The Beheading of St John the Baptist* (1571). In this and all his other works, the figures are gracefully elongated and set in balletic poses characteristic of sculpture in the age of Mannerism. For the Medici he cast a bronze statuette of *Venus Anadyomene* for the

Vincenzo Danti: Honor Triumphant over Falsehood; marble; c1561. Museo Nazionale, Florence

Studiolo in the Palazzo Vecchio, Florence (c1573) and a large narrative relief of *Moses and the Brazen Serpent* (now Museo Nazionale, Florence) for the altar-frontal of the Medici private chapel. Danti also carved in marble during the 1560s (for example, *Honor Triumphant over Falsehood* and *Duke Cosimo I*; both Museo Nazionale, Florence). In 1567 he published a treatise on proportion. He retired after 1573 to Perugia, where he was honored as an Academician. Danti's sculpture has a delicacy of detail and an elegance of line reminiscent of many another goldsmith turned sculptor, for example Ghiberti and Cellini.

Jacques Daret: The Circumcision, a panel from the St Vaast Altarpiece; oil on panel; c1434. Musée du Petit Palais, Paris

Daret Jacques c1404–70

Jacques Daret was a Flemish painter from Tournai. During the years 1427–32 he was apprenticed to Robert Campin, an artist who is identified by some scholars with the Master of Flémalle. Rogier van der Weyden was one of Daret's fellow students. In 1434 Daret was commissioned to paint an altarpiece for St Vaast, Arras. Four panels are regarded as belonging to his work; they are divided between the Staatliche Museen, Berlin, Paris (Musée du Petit Palais), and New York (Pierpont Morgan Library). These are his only documented extant paintings, though an *Annunciation* (Musée d'Art Ancien, Brussels) copied from the Master of Flémalle's Mérode Altarpiece has been attributed to him. He also produced designs for tapestries, festivals (including the wedding of Charles the Bold, 1468), and he also probably illuminated manuscripts.

The St Vaast panels, with their steep perspectives and ornamental naturalistic details, recall the conventions used in Tournai and Arras tapestries. Both documentary evidence and the surviving works suggest that Daret's talent was primarily that of a decorative artist.

Daswanth c1550–84

The Mughal painter Daswanth's remarkable talent and tragic life made him a legendary figure in his own time. The son of a palanquin bearer, his compulsive interest in drawing even on walls attracted the attention of the Mughal Emperor Akbar (1556–1605). Akbar arranged for the young man to study art under Abd al-Samad. Daswanth soon reached the height of his profession and was widely regarded as the greatest painter of his time. A melancholic figure who suffered from fits of depression, he took his own life at an early age. Despite his artistic reputation he remains a shadowy figure. The only surviving picture done entirely by his hand is in the *Tuti-nama* (Cleveland Museum of Art). Other works of his were the product of artistic collaboration. However, some 30 turbulent works in the *Razm-nama* (Maharaja Sawai Man Singh II Museum, Jaipur) bear the unmistakable imprint of his passionate, expressionist style.

Daubigny Charles-François
1817–78

Charles-François Daubigny was a French landscape painter and engraver. He studied under his father, a minor landscapist, and went to Italy in 1836. He concentrated on graphic work early in his career, turning to systematic plein-air painting in the 1850s. His *Villerville-sur-Mer* (1864–72; Hendrik Willem Mesdag Museum, The Hague) was painted completely from the motif, breaking the traditional practice of finishing works in the studio. His favorite subjects were tranquil water scenes painted from his studio boat on the major French rivers (for example, *Women Washing Along the Oise*, 1859; Louvre, Paris). Like the Impressionists, of whom he was a major precursor, he was criticized for rendering only an "impression" of nature.

Daucher family
15th and 16th centuries

The sculptors Adolf Daucher (1460–1523/4) and his son Hans (c1485–1538) worked at Augsburg. The altarpiece of the Fugger Chapel there (finished by 1518) is usually attributed to Hans, but it may reveal a collaboration between father and son. The stone figure-group of *Christ supported by the Virgin, St John, and an Angel* on top of the altar is one of the first freestanding groups in Northern altarpiece design. The scenes of the Passion below it show Hans' talent for relief sculpture. This was also evident in later work he carried out for the Hapsburg family, such as *The Meeting of Charles V and his brother Ferdinand* (post 1518; Pierpont Morgan Library, New York).

Daulat 16th century

A Muslim artist at the Mughal Court, Daulat was one of the ablest illustrators in the reign of the Emperor Akbar (1556–1605). He achieved prominence in Jahangir's reign (1605–27) but continued even in the Shah Jahan period (1628–58). Jahangir held a high opinion of him and ordered a portrait of the artist to be painted for inclusion in the *Khamsa* (Dyson Perrins Collection). Daulat in his turn did thumbnail sketches of five contemporary painters in the *Gulshan* Album (Gulistan Palace Library, Teheran). His works are in the *Akbar-nama* (Victoria and Albert Museum, London), *Babur-nama* (Indian Museum, Delhi), *Iyar-i-Danish*,

Charles-François Daubigny: Sunset on the Banks of the Oise; oil on canvas; 39×67cm (15×26in); 1865. Louvre, Paris

Shah Jahan-nama (Royal Art Collection, Windsor), and in the Rothschild Collection, Paris.

Daumier Honoré 1808–79

Honoré Daumier was an important French lithographer and painter. His lithographs are valuable documents for the political and social history of his period, and his paintings, largely unappreciated during his lifetime, are now held in high esteem.

He studied briefly in an academic studio before learning lithography. The Revolutions of 1830 and 1848 gave him the opportunity to express his republican sentiments in his caricatures. At other times, censorship confined him to social satire (he was even imprisoned in 1833 for criticizing the government). In the mid 1840s he became increasingly interested in painting, while still producing lithographs for his livelihood. Contemporaries knew him mainly as a graphic artist: in his lifetime he showed only six paintings in official exhibitions.

During the 1830s Daumier's political cartoons—published in the newspapers *La Caricature* and *Le Charivari*—included *Gargantua* (1831), an earthy caricature of Louis-Philippe's corrupt government, and the famous *Rue Transnonain 14 April*

1834 (1834), in which he abandons the satirical manner to show the pathetic aftermath of a military slaughter of civilians.

In 1836 Daumier began a series on the invented character Robert Macaire, personifying the chicanery of commercial society. He produced several great series of

lithographs in the 1840s, for example *Ancient History* (1842), a lampoon of Neoclassicism. His targets were often pomposity and pretentiousness, as in the series *Men of Justice* (1845–8): here the flowing robes and black–white contrast of the legal costume allowed impressive pic-

Honoré Daumier: The First-Class Carriage; crayon and watercolor on paper; 21×30cm (8×12in); c1858–60. Walters Art Gallery, Baltimore

torial effects. He invented the character of Ratapoil, of which he also made a sculpture in bronze (1850; Louvre, Paris) to satirize the unscrupulous brigands of Napoleon III.

Daumier entered the competition for an allegorical figure of the Republic in 1848: he was placed eleventh, but never completed the painting, the sketch for which is now in the Louvre, Paris. Works he did at this period owe some debt to Rubens, for example, *The Miller, his Son, and the Ass* (c1848–9; Burrell Collection, Glasgow). A number of Daumier's paintings were inspired by contemporary events, for example *The Uprising* (c1848; The Phillips Collection, Washington, D.C.). Others are everyday scenes, such as *Third Class Carriage* (1863–5; National Gallery of Canada, Ottawa). The sculptural nature of his drawing is seen in *The Washerwoman* (1863–4; Louvre, Paris).

Daumier often depicted clowns and acrobats (for example, *Saltimbanque*, c1855–60; Louvre, Paris) and theater scenes (for example, *Crispin and Scapin*, 1858–60; Louvre, Paris). *Don Quixote and Sancho Panza* (c1870; Courtauld Institute Galleries, London) is one of a group of paintings on this subject, showing the loose handling and calligraphic brushwork of his late years. His paintings were not given the degree of finish expected by his contemporaries, but they have an evocative quality resulting from this sketchiness which gives them a particular appeal today. Daumier uses a tentative and broken line, so that the contours are made indefinite by the surrounding light, in an Impressionistic manner.

Further reading. Escholier, R. *Daumier et Son Monde*, Paris (1965). Kist, J.R. *Daumier, Eyewitness of an Epoch*, London (1976). Larkin, O.W. *Daumier, Man of his Time*, London (1967). Maison, K.E. *Honoré Daumier, Catalogue Raisonné of the Paintings, Watercolours, and Drawings* (2 vols.), London (1968). Passeron, R. *Daumier*, Oxford (1981).

David Gerard c1460–1523

The Flemish painter Gerard David was born in Oudewater, near Gouda. He may have trained under his father, Jan, or possibly under Geertgen tot Sint Jans. In 1484 he entered the Bruges painters' guild, of which he became Dean in 1501. He married Cornelia Cnoop, herself a

miniaturist and the daughter of the Dean of the goldsmiths' guild, in 1496. David was admitted to the Antwerp guild in 1515, but by 1519 he was back in Bruges where he subsequently died.

After the death of Memling (1494), David's position as the leading artist in Bruges was unassailable. Although very few of his works are identifiable by documentation, a large group of paintings has been associated with his name. A high percentage of these were clearly produced by his workshop, but enough autograph pictures survive to reconstruct his artistic development in some detail. David's early style as illustrated by *Christ Nailed to the Cross* (c1480–5; National Gallery, London) reveals a brutal realism that relates to the work of Hugo van der Goes (c1436–82) and, more generally, to the Dutch tradition. By the time of the *Justice of Cambyses* (State Museum, Bruges) diptych of 1498, the tense drama of his earlier manner had been substantially toned down—although the flaying alive of the unjust judge Sisames in the left-hand panel is depicted with an excruciating objectivity. Owing to this work's double function as a narrative theme and a disguised group portrait, the two compositions are inevitably crowded and somewhat lacking in visual coherence.

The slightly later altar shutter of *Canon Bernardinus de Salviatis and Three Saints* (c1501; National Gallery, London) is a great deal more monumental in conception. The weighty poise of the four main figures implies a perceptive study of the work of Jan van Eyck (c1390–1441). This impression deepens as David's style progresses. His *Mystic Marriage of St Catherine* (c1505; National Gallery, London) is a centralized composition of five massive figures, tightly focused upon the simply articulated form of the Virgin and Child. By comparison, the Rouen *Virgin and Child with Saints* (Musée des Beaux-Arts) of 1509 is no less symmetrical, but much less static. A high point in David's art is reached with the approximately contemporary Bruges triptych of *The Baptism of Christ* (State Museum). In this painting, exquisite variety of detail and sensitivity of handling is combined with a striking monumentality of design, in a fashion closely reminiscent of the founding generation of Early Netherlandish painting.

A distinct duality is apparent in David's late productions. The many variants of his *Virgin and Child with a Milk Bowl* (ex-

amples in the Musée Royaux des Beaux-Arts de Belgique, Brussels; Galleria di Palazzo Bianco, Genoa) are pervaded by a gentle domesticity. On the other hand, a painting such as the Genoa *Crucifixion* (Galleria di Palazzo Bianco) indicates that he could also produce dramatic compositions of stark simplicity. While David was undoubtedly the last great master of the 15th-century Netherlandish style, it would be wrong to classify him as an old-fashioned artist. His students, particularly Ambrosius Benson and Adriaen Isenbrandt, prolonged his style of painting until almost the middle of the 16th century. David's return to the origins of the tradition within which he worked was fundamentally creative, as it allowed a rediscovery of the monumental values that had eluded many of his contemporaries. A later generation of artists, including Quentin Massys (1465/6–1530) and Jan Gossaert (c1478–1532), began by following his precepts before discovering a new formal vocabulary in Italian art.

David Jacques-Louis 1748-1825

The early career of the French painter Jacques-Louis David (often known as Louis David) followed a well established pattern. Born in Paris, he trained initially in the studio of a successful painter, finishing his education at the French Academy in Rome. On his return to France, he emerged as a leading exponent of Neoclassicism. He held official positions during both the Revolutionary period and the Empire, and was particularly active in the former. Throughout his life he was also much in demand as a portrait-painter. Exiled at the Restoration of 1815 for his continued support of Napoleon, he passed the remaining ten years of his life in Brussels, painting some outstanding works.

The France in which David grew up was ripe for both political and artistic revolution. The Rococo style of the previous generation—best exemplified by the decorative, sentimental, and sometimes overtly erotic work of François Boucher (1703–70) and Fragonard (1732–1806)—was fading. A reaction was taking place in the paintings of such artists as David's teacher Joseph-Marie Vien, who favored a return to the more classical tendencies of French art, particularly those portrayed in the 17th century by Poussin. In addition, theorists such as J.J. Winckelmann were becoming fashionable by stressing the

Jacques-Louis David: The Intervention of the Sabine Women; oil on canvas; 386×520cm (152×205in); 1799. Louvre, Paris

beauty, and above all the correctness, of antique Greek and Roman art. At the same time, archaeologists were bringing to light antiquities which profoundly affected artists' conceptions of bygone days.

David progressed slowly towards the style that was to make him the most influential French painter of his time. His *Antiochus and Stratonice* (1774; Musée de l'École Supérieure des Beaux-Arts, Paris), won him the Prix de Rome, entitling him to spend four years in Italy at the French government's expense. The picture does not break radically with the taste of the day. The classicizing style that was to dominate French art under David's leadership is evident in its subject matter, but the Rococo is still strongly suggested in the crowded composition and consciously pretty colors. David's five years in Rome, from 1775 to 1780, which he spent studying ancient monuments and sculptures as well as works of the Renaissance and the Baroque, convinced him of the need to

adopt a more rigorously classical approach.

Back in France, David finally drew together all the elements associated with Neoclassicism in his *Oath of the Horatii* (1785; Louvre, Paris), called by one contemporary critic "the most beautiful painting of the century". The background is as sparse and rigid as a Greek theater; the figures of the warriors, as unbending in their bearing as in their intent, are placed in parallel rather than receding planes. The painting echoes perfectly the "noble simplicity and calm grandeur" so favored by Winckelmann. This work has often been cited as heralding the Revolution. Although this seems far-fetched, David himself quickly became involved when hostilities began in 1789. He voted for the death of the King in 1793, as a member of the National Assembly, and allied himself with the extreme faction headed by Maximilien Robespierre. His support of the group led to his imprisonment in 1795, but fortunately he was not long incarcerated. All his

work of this period demonstrates his involvement, be it his organization of festivals celebrating Revolutionary events, or such a drawing as the *Oath of the Tennis Court* (1791; William Hayes Fogg Museum of Art, Cambridge, Mass.). Echoing in its gestures the *Oath of the Horatii*, the work breaks new ground in showing a large number of identifiable figures engaged in an important contemporary event.

Another side of David's work is shown by his portraits—often intimate, even when executed on a large scale as in *Lavoisier and his Wife* (1791; Metropolitan Museum, New York). The superb *Death of Marat* (1793; Musées Royaux des Beaux-Arts de Belgique, Brussels) is much more than the mere representation of a man known and admired by David: it is conceived almost in the manner of an icon, glorifying the Revolutionary who has been assassinated in his bath for his beliefs. Portraiture remained an important element in David's art throughout his life, and it assumes a new importance in his relations with Napoleon Bonaparte, who, David declared, was "his hero". Napoleon knew nothing about art, but, recognizing David's fame, he wished to have him at his service in order to fulfil his aim of propagating his image throughout Europe. David's first Napoleonic commission was *Bonaparte Crossing the Saint Bernard Pass* (1800; Versailles), very different in conception from the somber *Death of Marat*. This latter, painted in quiet shades of green and brown, has none of the splendor in the portrait of the ambitious and victorious Consul and General. Under the Napoleonic regime, when David became *Premier Peintre* to the Emperor, he did not entirely neglect his first love, classical painting. However, as can be seen from *Leonidas at Thermopylae* (Louvre, Paris), worked and reworked from 1800 to 1814, this style could not compete with the brilliance of contemporary reality. Depicting as it does a group of warriors condemned in advance to defeat, the work was totally out of key with the times. As Napoleon himself told David, "You are wasting your time painting losers".

The two vast works David executed to commemorate Napoleon's coronation, *The Coronation of Josephine* or *Le Sacre* (1808; Louvre, Paris), and the *Distribution of the Eagles* (1810; Versailles), are much more successful. Here David draws his inspiration from the Flemish school, especially Rubens, rather than from the Antique; he even visited Belgium to study Flemish works *in situ* before embarking on his own paintings. Both of these immense canvases caused David considerable trouble, as he had to fit his conception to the vacillating demands of the self-conscious Emperor, over-anxious to ensure a flattering likeness to himself and his retinue. Despite the difficulties, however, these works are unrivaled in showing, if not the truth of life under Napoleon, then the glory he wished to evoke.

At the Restoration David was in an untenable position. True to Napoleon, he refused to sign an oath of loyalty to the new monarch, Louis XVIII, and was forced into exile, living in Brussels until his death. There he continued to paint, and kept in touch with his former pupils: many of them, for example Gros, Gérard, and Ingres, had now become famous. David's own art had suffered, however. He was still convinced that the Antique was the only serious subject for a painter, but was unable to forget the influence of contemporary events; the work of his last years lacks the tautness and vitality that had made him preeminent.

Further reading. Brookner, A. *Jacques-Louis David*, London (1980). Friedländer, W. *David to Delacroix*, Cambridge, Mass. (1966). Hautecoeur, L. *Louis David*, Paris (1954). Herbert, R.L. *David's "Brutus"*, London (1972). Rosenblum, R. *Transformations in late 18th Century Art*, Princeton (1970).

Davie Alan 1920–

The Scottish painter, jeweler, and jazz musician Alan Davie was born in Grangemouth. He studied at Edinburgh College of Art in 1937, was Gregory Fellow at Leeds University from 1956 to 1959, and taught at the Central School of Art and Design, London, from 1954 to 1957 and again in 1960.

Davie's paintings are never entirely Abstract. Those dating from the late 1940s depend upon an imaginative vocabulary of

Stuart Davis: Lucky Strike; oil on canvas; 84×46cm (33×18in); 1921. Museum of Modern Art, New York

symbols relating to primitive magic, mysticism, and Zen. A strong autobiographical and unconscious content, often erotic, runs through his work. The painter's thick, gestural brushstrokes in somber, earthy colors and bright, jewel-like flashes became more controlled in the late 1950s. He began to develop detail-encrusted images, using lighter colors and smoother paint. His earlier spontaneity was gradually replaced by a reworking of themes. In the late 1960s the figuration in his paintings became less ambiguous and he introduced interior settings for his imagery.

Davis Stuart 1894–1964

Stuart Davis was one of the most consistent, adventurous, and relatively unrecognized of American modern painters. He was a radical illustrator before the First World War, and by the 1920s was creating Abstract paintings composed of shapes and mass-produced objects, such as *Lucky Strike* (1921; Museum of Modern Art, New York). A visit to Paris from 1928 to 1929 did not have a profound effect on his style, but did much to enhance his self-confidence. Davis painted murals such as *Swing Landscape* (1938; Indiana University) in the 1930s. His enthusiasm for jazz syncopation and for the internal visual development of his work provided a more genuine structure than slavish adaptation of contemporary European models.

Degas 1834–1917

Hilaire-Germain-Edgar de Gas (who signed his works "degas" or "Degas" after 1870) was the great draftsman of his age. He rivaled the virtuosity of his hero Ingres, and developed boldly original pictorial forms in his scenes of contemporary life.

Degas was born on 19 July 1834, in Paris. Both his parents were descendants of French *emigrés*—his father came from Naples and his mother from New Orleans. But despite several journeys to Italy during his youth, and a visit to an uncle in New Orleans in 1873, Degas remained essentially a Parisian. All his major themes were taken from Parisian life. He did paint one masterpiece in the United States, *The Cotton Exchange at New Orleans* (1873; Musée des Beaux-Arts, Pau). But he felt uneasy there, saying: "one makes an art out of what one knows well."

Degas' father was a banker, director of the Paris branch of the family business;

Degas: Ballet Rehearsal; oil on canvas; 85×75cm (33×30in); 1875. Musée du Jeu de Paume, Paris.

when Edgar preferred painting to the law, he received an income that made him independent of academic recognition and patronage. It was only after 1875—when he sacrificed most of his inheritance to save his brother Achille from bankruptcy—that he had to earn his living as a professional artist.

His financial independence reinforced his solitary and aristocratic temperament. He never submitted works to the Salon after 1870. Although he was a close friend of Manet, and a founder member of the *Société Anonyme des Artistes, Peintures, Sculpteurs, Graveurs*, later known as the Impressionists, he was never himself a true Impressionist. His fascination with indoor figure-groups places him apart from the Impressionists, though his increasingly brilliant palette and interest in the fleeting makes him akin to them.

Degas' art was rooted in tradition. When he was 21 he entered the École des Beaux-Arts; there he was taken under the wing of Louis Lamothe, who had been a pupil of Ingres. At the Beaux-Arts, and on his first visit to Italy, Degas studied and copied the works of Old Masters. As he said: "No art was ever less spontaneous than mine. What I do is the result of reflection and the study of the great masters." He also believed that "the study of nature is of no significance, for painting is a conventional art."

Although he met Manet in 1862, Degas was slow to treat contemporary subjects. His early compositions were taken from history, and included such works as *Semiramis Founding a City* (Louvre, Paris), *Young Spartans Exercising* (National Gallery, London), and *Jephthah's Daughter* (c1861–4; Smith College Museum of Art, Northampton, Mass.). Each of these works was constructed from careful preliminary studies in the academic tradition. The only history painting he exhibited at that time was *Scenes of War in the Middle Ages* (1865; Louvre, Paris) at the Salon of 1865. Degas' disquieting image of mounted archers discharging their shafts at naked women was admired by Puvis de Chavannes, but was generally unnoticed.

The one modern subject he exhibited at the Salon also went unregarded. This was the *Fallen Jockey* (1866; private collection) which, although prepared from careful drawings in the traditional way, was a large, unconventional composition. Apart from a few, usually small, racecourse subjects, Degas approached modern subject matter obliquely during the 1860s. Beginning with an enormous canvas, *The Bellilli Family* (1858; Louvre, Paris) showing his aunt's family in Florence, he painted a brilliant series of portraits that showed his sitters in elaborate interiors, and so combined subtle and polished characterizations with original, even bizarre, compositions. One of the earliest is *Woman with Chrysanthemums* (1865; Metropolitan Museum, New York). *Mme Camus* (1870; National Gallery, Washington, D.C.) is silhouetted against a golden wall that dominates the composition, creating an abstract arabesque that suggests Japanese woodcuts.

But by that time, Degas was beginning to look out for modern subjects: he listed potential motifs in notebooks. Among the earliest of these studies was *The Orchestra of the Paris Opera* (1868–9; Louvre, Paris). This was developed from portrait studies—including one of the composer Chabrier. The heads of the players were related in a complex wedge of forms, while the ostensible spectacle (the dancers) was reduced to a fringe of legs and tulle along the top of the canvas.

The dancers were given their due importance in the series of ballet dancers at rehearsal, painted in the 1870s, such as the *Dancing Class at the Ballet School of the Opera* (1872; Louvre, Paris). These are the most remarkable works of Degas' career, yet none is large; several in fact are remarkably small (for example, *The Foyer*, 1872, Metropolitan Museum, New York, is 7½ by 10½ in, 19 by 27 cm) and are all muted in color. In many ways they are traditional, with precursors among the works of Watteau (1684–1721) and Hogarth (1697–1764), yet at the same time are completely original. In ballet rehearsals, Degas found a curious blend of charm and tedium, grace and ungainliness, with figures grouped not dramatically, but accidentally, according to ritual and repetition. In the bleak rehearsal rooms, with large mirrors and long windows, he discovered uncanny perspectives: a world that mixed dream and drab reality.

Ever since the Franco-Prussian war of 1870 Degas had suffered from failing eyesight, and in the 1880s he abandoned the small scale of his first ballet scenes. Instead, he began experimenting in a range of media, pastel in particular. His motifs included racecourses, theaters, laundresses, milliners, and cafés and cabarets. But the two themes he made his own were the ballet and a woman at her toilette. On these subjects he made pastels of almost abstract brilliance, showing powerfully the influence of Japanese art. His series of a woman taking a bath has images at once intimate and anonymous, close-up, yet abstract and detached. In this way they differ completely from the many monotypes he made of brothel scenes: these are filled with a bawdy wit and a light line that is a brilliant complement to the economy of Japanese draftsmanship.

During his lifetime, Degas exhibited only a single piece of sculpture, a wax of *The Little Dancer of 14 Years* dressed in specially made muslin tutu, linen bodice, and satin shoes, which he showed at the sixth Impressionist exhibition of 1881. (Bronzes can be seen at the Tate Gallery, London, and elsewhere.) But after his death, 74 smaller pieces, mainly in wax, were found in his studio, including dancers, bathers, and horses. Modeled broadly yet precisely, they established Degas as one of the great sculptors of the 19th century.

Despite a prickly temperament, Degas supported younger artists he admired. At his death, his collection included works by Cézanne, Gauguin, Pissarro, Sisley, Morisot, and Van Gogh. Although attracted to women, Degas appears to have been both timid and proud; he never married. In his last years he went almost completely blind, and in 1912, when he had to leave the studio he had used for many years, he stacked up his canvases and never worked again. He was often to be seen stalking through the Paris streets until his death in 1917 at the age of 83.

Further reading. Degas, E. (ed. Guerin, M.) *Letters*, Oxford (1947). Degas, E. (ed. Reff. T.) *The Notebooks of Edgar Degas*, Oxford (1976). Millard, C.W. *The Sculpture of Edgar Degas*, Princeton (1976). Minervino, F. *L'Opera Completa di Degas*, Milan (1970). Reff, T. *Degas: the Artist's Mind*, New York (1976). Reff, T. "The Pictures within Degas' Pictures", *Metropolitan Museum Journal*, New York (1968). Rivière, G. *Degas, Bourgeois de Paris*, Paris (1935).

Delacroix Eugène 1798–1863

The greatest French painter of the first half of the 19th century, Eugène Delacroix is generally considered to have been the leader of the Romantic school—opposed to the Neoclassicism of Ingres. Delacroix's emotive use of color, relative subordination of line, and dramatic composition contrast with Ingres' insistence on draftsmanship and carefully balanced static composition.

The public and many critics saw Delacroix as an indiscriminate iconoclast: he was elected to the Institut only in 1857, at his seventh attempt, and suffered much adverse criticism. In personality, however, he was very different from the turbulent young Romantics who gathered round Victor Hugo. His aloof and aristocratic nature emerges from his *Self-portrait* (1835–7; Louvre, Paris).

He was born in 1798 into a family of the *haute bourgeoisie* (although evidence suggests that he may have been the natural son of Talleyrand), and received a thorough classical education. In 1816 he entered the studio of Pierre-Narcisse Guérin, a distinguished Neoclassicist; there he met Géricault, who influenced him profoundly. He visited England in 1825 and Morocco in 1832. After his return he received a number of important decorative commissions through friendship in official circles. In 1855 he was made a Commander of the

Legion of Honor, and also had 35 works shown in the *Exposition Universelle*. He died in 1863: Baudelaire, his greatest and most discerning champion, wrote an obituary *L'Oeuvre de Delacroix*.

Géricault's *The Raft of the Medusa* (1819; Louvre, Paris) was the inspiration of Delacroix's *Dante and Virgil Crossing the Styx* (1822; Louvre, Paris), his first Salon painting, which was generally admired. His color here is still close to Géricault's, showing a predominantly earthy palette and marked chiaroscuro; but the painting also shows the expressive use of color that he was to develop later in his career.

A decisive innovation in Delacroix's style took place under the influence of Constable, whose paintings he saw in Paris in 1823. In the Salon of 1824, Delacroix exhibited the *Massacre at Chios* (Louvre, Paris). He is thought to have retouched the painting using Constable's procedure of adding flecks of paint of various colors to the foreground to animate the surface, and to bind the composition together through chromatic harmony.

The *Massacre at Chios* and *Greece Expiring on the Ruins of Missolonghi* (1827; Musée des Beaux-Arts de Bordeaux) illustrate subjects inspired by the Greek War of Independence, interest in which was stimulated by Byron. *The Death of Sardanapalus* (1827; Louvre, Paris) depicts a subject drawn from Byron, and, like *Massacre at Chios*, typifies Romantic interest in exoticism and suffering. The composition of *Sardanapalus* is highly animated, showing baroque, diagonal lines of force; vibrant reds and golds are used to underline the violent nature of the scene.

In the four years that followed his visit to England, Delacroix's major works used subjects from English literature: *The Murder of the Bishop of Liège* (1829; Louvre, Paris) was based on Sir Walter Scott, and *The Execution of the Doge Marino Faliero* (1827; Wallace Collection, London) on Byron. The treatment of the latter relies heavily on the influence of Bonington (1801–28), while the *Portrait*

Eugène Delacroix: Lion Hunt; oil on canvas; 76×98cm (30×39in); 1861. Art Institute of Chicago

of *Baron Schwitter* (1827; National Gallery, London) shows the influence of Sir Thomas Lawrence (1769–1830), whom Delacroix met on his trip to London. The Revolution of 1830 inspired Delacroix to paint *Liberty Leading the People* (1831; Louvre, Paris), which combines idealism with vivid, realistic description.

On his visit to Morocco in 1832 Delacroix found that the Arabs, in their bearing, dress, and way of life, represented a living link with the ancient world. Their natural dignity contrasted with the cold formality of Neoclassical depictions of the Greeks and Romans. For his Moroccan sketches he reverted to the English watercolor techniques of his friends Bonington and Thales Fielding, in an attempt to render the freshness of his impressions. The intensity of the north African light sharpened his observation of the interaction of light and color in nature. He applied these discoveries in *Women of Algiers* (1834; Louvre, Paris), modifying the local colors according to the intensity of the light falling on them, and using contrasts of complementary colors. A series of paintings grew out of this journey, including *Jewish Wedding in Morocco* (1841; Louvre, Paris), and *The Sultan of Morocco Surrounded by his Court* (1845; Musée des Augustins, Toulouse).

Delacroix's major decorative commissions in Paris under Louis Philippe were the Salon du Roi (1833–7) and the Library (1838–47) of the Palais Bourbon, the Library of the Luxembourg Palace (1841–6), a *Pietà* at St Denis du Saint Sacrement (1843), a ceiling in the Galerie d'Apollon of the Louvre (1849–51), the Salon de la Paix of the Hôtel de Ville (1851–3; destroyed), and the Chapelle des Anges in St-Sulpice (c1856–61). The works are conceived in the tradition of Baroque mural painting, but within this framework Delacroix made considerable advances in his use of color. He was preoccupied with luminosity; he decreased the quantity of black in his work, and began using white underpainting, a technique later adopted by the Impressionists.

Delacroix's color theories were derived from two sources: close observation of nature and scientific theories of the interactions of color, such as those of Eugène Chevreul. In Delacroix's *Entry of the Crusaders into Constantinople* (1841; Louvre, Paris), there is a systematic use of contrasts of complementary colors, which can be seen in the standards carried by the Crusaders. In contrast to Ingres, who concealed his brush strokes, Delacroix made his quite obvious. In his mature work, for example *The Justice of Trajan* (1840; Musée des Beaux-Arts de Bordeaux), he developed this technique, using a broken style of brush work to animate the surface of the painting.

Throughout his career, Delacroix produced a number of colorful, lively easel paintings. These include many animal paintings (for example, *Lion Hunt*, 1855; Musée des Beaux-Arts de Bordeaux), scenes of Arab life (for example, *Fanatics of Tangier*, 1831; Jerome Hill Collection; New York), and subjects from medieval history and from literature (for example, *Hamlet and the Gravedigger*, 1839; Louvre, Paris). He painted many successful portraits, for example those of *Chopin* (1836; Louvre, Paris), *Paganini* (1831; The Phillips Collection, Washington, D.C.), and *Jenny Leguillou* (1840; Louvre, Paris).

Delacroix was deeply concerned with the theory of art: he began, but never completed, a dictionary of the fine arts. His journal, kept from 1822 to 1824 and again from 1847 to 1863, is a particularly valuable source of information about his personal and professional life, and about his aesthetic theories.

Further reading. Baudelaire, C. (trans. Mayne, J.) *The Painter of Modern Life and Other Essays*, London (1964). Baudelaire, C. (trans. Mayne, J.) *Art in Paris 1845–1862*, London (1965). Delacroix, E. (ed. Wellington, H., trans. Horton, L.) *The Journal of Eugène Delacroix*, Oxford (1980). Huyghe, R. (trans. Griffin, J.) *Delacroix*, London (1963).

Delaunay Robert 1885–1941

The French painter Robert Delaunay was apprenticed to a stage designer in 1902. He took up a painting career in 1904, but his work always continued to show his concern for the qualities of design.

He rapidly moved away from traditional practices. By 1905 he was painting in large patches of bright color in the manner of the Fauves. In 1908, under the influence of Cubism, his color was temporarily subdued, but he soon reintroduced it in a fractured, prismatic form.

A major work, *La Ville de Paris* (1912; Musée d'Art Moderne de la Ville de Paris) demonstrates the then-popular idea of "simultaneity", as elaborated by the French philosopher Henri Louis Bergson. Both Delaunay and the Italian Futurists

Robert Delaunay: Rhythm 579; oil on canvas; 113×145cm (44×57in); 1934. Private collection

explored this idea, which contends that the world impresses itself upon the consciousness as fleeting, intuitively understood sensations. In *La Ville de Paris*, Delaunay was not concerned to depict how Paris looked, but how it felt from minute to minute; he indicated the speed and pressure of life in a big city with overlapping and fragmented forms including an iron bridge and the Eiffel Tower. "Simultaneity" was seen as a particularly appropriate description of modern life, and Delaunay painted a series of views of contemporary Paris which conveyed a sense of urgency and movement, as in *The Cardiff Team* (1912–13; Van Abbe Museum, Eindhoven).

After 1912 this dynamism changes to more regular rhythmic form: rectangular shapes in the *Fenêtres* series, and circular shapes in the *Disks*. Some of these paintings could be considered Abstract, but they contain an insistent strain of cosmic symbolism. Brilliant light and color are enhanced by "simultaneous contrast", an effect of spatio-temporal juxtapositions—attempted by Michel Eugène Chevreul, Toulouse-Lautrec, and Seurat in the 19th century—in which color is a primary element. Delaunay and the Duchamp brothers combined Fauve color with Cubist forms in penetrating simultaneous views of the same object either at the same time or at successive moments. In 1912, Apollinaire gave a lecture at an exhibition of Delaunay's work in Berlin; he labeled the artist's style "Orphism". It had a great effect on the German *Blaue Reiter* group—Franz Marc, Auguste Macke, and Wassily Kandinsky—as well as on Paul Klee, Fernand Léger, and Marc Chagall.

In 1910 Delaunay married the Russian artist Sonia Terk; she used Orphism as the basis of a style of decoration. Delaunay spent the years 1914 to 1921 in Spain and Portugal. After his return to Paris, his work became stiff and lacking in spontaneity. He painted large mural decorations such as the *Ville de Paris* (1925; Exhibition of Decorative Arts, Paris), and a gigantic *Rhythm* in the Hall of Air for the 1937 Paris International Exhibition.

Further reading. Cohen, A. (ed.) *The New Art of Color: the Writings of Robert and Sonia Delaunay*, New York (1978). Dorival, B. *Robert Delaunay et le Cubisme*, Saint-Étienne (1973). Pernes, R. *Robert et Sonia Delaunay à Portugal*, Lisbon (1972). Schmidt, G. *Robert Delaunay*, Paris (1957).

Philibert Delorme: The chapel of the château at Anet; 1549–52

Delorme Philibert c1510–70

The French architect Philibert Delorme (or De L'Orme) came from Lyons. He lived in Rome from c1533 to 1536, but returned to Lyons to begin his career as an architect. On the accession of Henri II in 1547 he was appointed superintendent of buildings. In this capacity and in that year, he took over the newly begun château at Anet; on commission from Diane de Poitiers, he built the side-wings between 1549 and 1551, the chapel between 1549 and 1552, and the entrance pavilion in 1552. The rather old-fashioned courtyard plan was not impressive, but Delorme's centralized chapel anticipated that of Palladio at Maser. The ingenious mixture of medieval and classical in the entrance pavilion was a vital step forward in French architecture. His later work at Chenonceaux and the Tuileries show a refinement of these bold innovations. As a canon of Notre Dame of Paris he oversaw work on the cathedral. In 1567, he published his popular *Le Premier Tome de l'Architecture*, which included French versions of the Classical orders; the book helped to establish the respectability of his own works, and of French architecture in general.

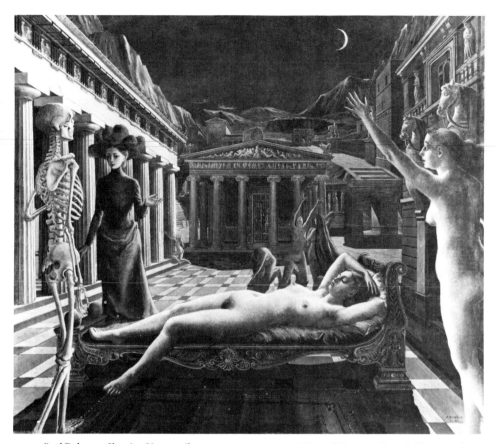

Paul Delvaux: Sleeping Venus; oil on canvas; 173×199cm (68×78in); 1944. Tate Gallery, London

Delvaux Paul 1897–1994

The Belgian painter Paul Delvaux was associated with the Surrealists, although he was never actually a member of the movement. After studying architecture in Brussels he took up painting, at first working in a style derived from the Impressionists. In 1936 he came under the transforming influence of Chirico and Magritte, and after that his work altered little. His characteristic paintings are illusionistic in style and dream-like in imagery: naked or partially clothed women, sometimes observed by respectably dressed men, move silently and expressionlessly within improbable architectural settings. These superficially tranquil scenes are invested with an atmosphere of muffled sexual tension.

Further reading. Butor, M. and Clair, J. *Paul Delvaux: Catalogue Raisonné*, Brussels (1974). Terrasse, A. *Paul Delvaux*, Paris (1972).

Demuth Charles 1883–1935

The American painter Charles Henry Demuth was born at Lancaster in Pennsylvania. Lame from childhood, he was always frail. He studied at the Pennsylvania Academy of Fine Arts (1905–10), and made two visits to Europe (1907–8; 1912–14), where he met Gertrude Stein and her circle. He had an opportunity to see the art of Cézanne and the Fauves which influenced his style. His preferred medium was watercolor. He was eclectic, borrowing from both Cubism and Expressionism; his finest watercolors combine a simplified sense of space with a delicate command of color.

Demuth was fond of circus themes, and still life; but he also became an illustrator, for example for the two Henry James' stories, *The Turn of the Screw* (1918–19) and *The Beast in the Jungle* (1919–20). Alongside his more naturalistic work he also developed a Cubist-based style that he applied to urban subject matter such as streets and factories. His most famous work, the oil painting of 1928 known as *I Saw the Figure Five in Gold* (Metropolitan Museum, New York) belongs to this more abstract idiom.

Further reading. Eiseman, A. *Charles Demuth*, New York (1982).

Denis Maurice 1870–1943

The French artist and art theorist Maurice Denis was a founder member of the group of painters known as the Nabis. He was the most prominent spokesman of the generation that followed in the footsteps of Gauguin, Émile Bernard, and Cézanne.

Born at Granville, he spent almost all his life at St Germain-en-Laye outside Paris. After attending the Lycée Condorçet, where he met the future artists Vuillard and K.-X. Roussel, Denis joined the Académie Julian in 1888. It was here that he met Paul Sérusier, Pierre Bonnard, and Paul Ranson and in the autumn of 1888 saw the result of Sérusier's lesson in Pictorial Symbolism, *The Talisman* (1888; Collection of J.E. Denis, St Germain-en-Laye). This painting acted as a catalyst for the young art students. Denis and his friends formed themselves into a revolutionary group and christened themselves the "Nabis", or "prophets". They dedicated themselves to the rejection of three things: the photographic representation of Nature in painting, the use of trivial anecdotal subject matter, and belief in the superiority of the easel painting. Furthermore, they believed in the unity of the arts and the serious and revelatory mission of the arts in proclaiming the existence of the idea.

Denis, with the help of Sérusier, published this program of artistic reform in two articles entitled "Définition du Néo-Traditionnisme" in the periodical *Art et Critique* (August, 1890). This was the first of a series of theoretical writings on art, the most important being his *Théories* published in 1912. The pictorial equivalent to this program can be seen in Denis' *Taches de Soleil sur la Terrasse* (1890; Collection of D. Denis, St Germain-en-Laye). Influenced by Gauguin, Bernard, Puvis de Chavannes, and Japanese prints, the work's title alone helps the spectator to discern the line of trees receding on the right-hand side of the panel with their red shadows cast across the orange path.

Gauguin's departure to Tahiti in 1891 caused a vacuum in the Nabis' artistic leadership which, as Denis later recalled, they filled by turning to literature. In response to this change, Denis produced between 1891 and 1898 a number of "synthesist" stage, costume, and program designs for the Symbolist *Théâtre de l'Oeuvre* founded by his friend, the actor and impresario Lugné-Poë. He also turned his attention to book illustration,

During the decade of the 1890s, Denis visited Italy three times. Confronted with the Classical traditions of Ancient Rome and the Renaissance, he gradually modified his two-dimensional, non-naturalistic Nabis style and adopted the more vigorously classical vocabulary seen in his painting *Jeux Aquatiques* (1908; private collection).

Denis' output covered both easel painting and decorative cycles. For subject matter he relied heavily upon representations of his family as participators or actors in scenes from the Bible (for example *Sinite Paevulos*, 1900; private collection). Denis was a deeply committed Roman Catholic. He believed that his gift as an artist should be placed at the service of the Church. He undertook a number of large decorative cycles for churches (for instance *La Glori-fication de la Croix*, 1898–9; Collège de la Sainte-Croix, Le Vésinet) and in response to the parlous state of contemporary church art he founded the Atelier d'Art Sacré in 1918, together with the artist Georges Desvallières. This Atelier undertook the complete decoration of church interiors, including frescoes, altarpieces, and stained glass windows—such as are found in Perret's church, Notre-Dame de Raincey, Paris (1922–3).

Further reading. Brilliant, M. *Maurice Denis*, Paris (1930). Denis, M. *Du Symbolisme au Classicisme: Théories*, Paris (1964). Denis, M. *Journal: 1884–1943*, Paris (1959). *Exposition Maurice Denis*, Albi (1963).

Denny Robyn 1930–

The British painter Robyn Denny was born in Abinger, Surrey, in 1931. He studied at St Martin's School of Art (1951–3) and at the Royal College of Art (1953–7). In 1966 he represented Britain at the Venice Biennale and in 1973 became the youngest living artist ever to have a retrospective exhibition at the Tate Gallery, London. His large-scale paintings of the late 1950s were influenced by Abstract Expressionism and he was included in the "Situation" exhibition (1960). But at the same time he was developing a hard edged rectilinear style. This led to symmetrical compositions in which a centralized "image", comprising bands and later blocks of color, was disposed against a color ground. In the late 1970s the paintings became asymmetrical with fewer colors.

Maurice Denis: Three Portraits of Yvonne Lerolle; oil on canvas; 170×110cm (67×43in); 1897.
Private collection

producing work just as radical as his painting and stage designs. He believed that an illustration "must find that form of decoration without servitude to the text", and he sought in the designs such as those executed for André Gide's *Voyage d'Urien* (1893; Librairie de l'Art Indépendant, Paris) to create "an embroidery of arabesque on the page, an accompaniment of expressive lines".

Derain André 1880–1954

The French painter André Derain was born at Chatou. He rapidly gained prominence in Paris after studying at the Académie Carrière (1898–9) and the Académie Julian (1904), and was given a contract by the art dealer Ambrose Vollard in 1905. He was one of the boldest of the Fauve group, which included Matisse, Vlaminck, Braque, and Marquet.

Derain's series of landscapes from 1905 to 1907 are vigorously painted with dabs of intense color, rapidly applied and held together by spontaneous and powerful compositions which combine to give dramatic expression to the picture space (for example, *Westminster Bridge*, 1906; private collection).

He was soon open to new possibilities and was the first of the Fauve group to consider seriously using ethnographic art as a source, although Vlaminck is credited with starting the vogue for collecting it. Later, Derain's impressionable nature brought him under the influence of Picasso, Braque, and Cézanne, whose posthumous exhibition in 1907 led him to a reappraisal of his treatment of structure and space (for example, *Old Bridge at Cagnes*, 1910; National Gallery of Art, Washington D.C.).

After 1912 his paintings exhibited a fusion of Cubist and Neoclassical styles. After his first one-man show in 1918 at the Galerie Paul Guillaume in Paris, neoclassicism predominated, entailing a corresponding loss of verve. Derain received First Prize in the Carnegie International in Pittsburgh in 1928 for *La Chasse*.

He was also active as an illustrator and made drawings for Apollinaire's *L'Enchanteur Pourrissant* of 1909, as well as illustrating the works of many other writers.

Further reading. Diehl, G. (trans. Hamilton) *Derain*, New York (1964). Sutton, D. *André Derain*, London (1959).

André Derain: The Artist and his Family in the Artist's Studio; oil on canvas; 116×89cm (46×35in); 1920–1. Pierre Matisse Gallery, New York

Deschamps Jean 13th century

Jean Deschamps was a 13th-century French architect. In 1248 he began work on Clermont-Ferrand Cathedral. Like its exact contemporary at Cologne, it is a monumental example of northern French Gothic imported into a region that had no earlier experience of the style. Certain features of the design, notably the deep side-chapels surrounding the choir and the restricted size of the clerestory windows, suggest a deliberate rejection of the "glass cage" effect favored in the North. The increased emphasis on plane surfaces and spatial effects was to become characteristic of southern French and Catalan Gothic in the following century. In 1286 Deschamps was appointed architect to Narbonne Cathedral, but its design is quite different in style to Clermont-Ferrand and had probably already been settled when work started in 1272. He may have been the father of Pierre Deschamps, an architect of the same area of France who died in the early 14th century.

Desiderio da Settignano c1428–64

The Italian sculptor Desiderio was born in the quarry-town of Settignano near Florence. Like the Rossellino brothers, Desiderio came of a family of stonemasons from whom he learned his craft. He matriculated into the Sculptors' Guild of Florence in 1453 and was associated in that year with Antonio Rossellino. Desiderio was a brilliant carver both of marble and of the gray sandstone known as *pietra serena*. His style shows the strong

Jean Deschamps: Narbonne Cathedral

influence of Donatello, particularly in his reliefs, but lacks Donatello's drama and emotional intensity. Only two works from his brief career can be approximately dated: the monument to Chancellor Carlo Marsuppini (*ob.* 1453) at S. Croce, Florence, and the Altar of the Sacrament in S. Lorenzo, Florence, in 1461. A number of reliefs showing the Virgin and Child, as well as busts of boys and young women, may be reliably attributed to him.

Desportes Alexandre-François
1661–1743

The French painter Alexandre-François Desportes moved to Paris from Champagne at the age of 12. He studied under a pupil of the Flemish painter Frans Snyders, learning to specialize in still life and hunting scenes. After a brief period in Poland as Court Painter to King John Sobieski, Desportes returned to Paris and was appointed painter to the Royal Hunt. He decorated a number of palaces including Anet and Chantilly, and designed a series of eight large hunting scenes for Gobelins

Alexandre-François Desportes: A Tiger Walking; chalks. Louvre, Paris

tapestry factory. The Flemish style of both Chardin (1699–1779) and Oudry (1686–1755) is due more to the influence of Desportes than to Flemish painting itself.

Devis family 18th century

The British brothers Arthur and Anthony Devis specialized in painting conversation pieces and portraits. Their clientele was drawn mainly from the merchant classes whom they depicted as living in a secure world of middle-class values. The elder brother Arthur (1711–87) is supposed to have studied under the landscape painter Peter Tillemans (1684–1734); his work was regarded as cliché-ridden, even during his own lifetime. His brother Anthony (1729–1816) worked in London as a painter of conversation pieces from 1742. His work presents a meticulous inventory of a family's estate and possessions, with formally posed figures which have a certain naive charm.

Dexamenos 5th century BC

Dexamenos was a Greek gem-engraver, native of the island of Chios, who worked in the third quarter of the 5th century BC. He is the foremost exponent of the Classical style in gem-engraving, working on scarab-shaped gems of chalcedony, about ¾ in (2 cm) long. His style is characterized by originality of subject matter and extreme precision of technique, including the hand-cutting of fine linear detail where usually wheel-cut work was considered adequate. Four signed gems survive. One in the Museum of Fine Arts, Boston, from Attica, shows a bearded male head which has been regarded by many scholars as one of the earliest examples of a portrait in Greek art. It is likely, however, to be a

Arthur Devis: The Rookes-Leeds Family; oil on canvas; 91×124cm (36×49in); c1763. Private collection

characterization of a male type such as is seen elsewhere in Greek art, contrasting with the idealizing features of Athenian art. On two other stones (British Museum, London, with a boxer; Staatliche Museen, Berlin, with a beardless head) that can be attributed to Dexamenos, the same features and wild hair appear.

A gem in the Fitzwilliam Museum, Cambridge, shows a seated woman and her maid, the maid holding a mirror and a wreath. Two gems in the Hermitage Museum, Leningrad, found on Greek sites in south Russia, have studies of herons—one flying, the other preening itself, with a locust beside it. These are prime animal studies in an art that lent itself especially to this genre at this period. A few other stones can be attributed to Dexamenos, including one with a riderless horse in the Museum of Fine Arts, Boston, and another in the Hermitage Museum, Leningrad, with a still-life study of a wine jar of the type made on his native island of Chios. The quality of his work is unrivaled in this period and it is likely that he also worked in other materials but his name is not mentioned by any ancient author.

Dharamdas c1556–c1605

Dharamdas was an artist of Hindu origin, an excellent painter of animals and historical scenes, who worked during the period of the Mughal Emperor Akbar (1556–1605). His early work can be seen in the *Darab-nama* in the British Library, London. He also contributed to the *Akbarnama* in the Chester Beatty Library in Dublin, the scenes *Akbar Receiving Congratulations on Murad's Birth*, *Shahbaz Khan Taking the Fort of Dunara*, and *Shahbaz Khan Marching against Kumbhalmer*. Other works he helped to illustrate include the *Timur-nama*, *Iyar-i-Danish*, *Babur-nama*, and the *Khamsa* (British Library, London) and the *Jami-al-Tawarikh* of Rashid al-Din (Gulistan Palace Library, Teheran).

Diaghilev 1872–1929

The Russian impresario Sergei Pavlovich Diaghilev was born in the city of Perm. He went to St Petersburg in 1890 to study law. In 1898 he published the first issue of *The World of Art*, in collaboration with a group of artists including Alexandre Benois and Leon Bakst; it ran until 1904. Reacting against the literary tendencies of

Diaghilev: scenery for the ballet Le Coq d'Or designed by Natalia Gontcharova; 1913–14. Musée de l'Opéra, Paris

contemporary Russian painting these young men promulgated an "art for art's sake" doctrine. Through this journal and through exhibitions, Diaghilev introduced foreign painting—including works by the French Post-Impressionists and the Nabis—to the Russian art-world. In 1906 he presented an exhibit of Russian painting at the Paris Salon d'Automne; he followed this with concerts of Russian music in 1907 and a production of Mussorgsky's opera *Boris Godunov* in 1908.

These activities introduced to Paris existing aspects of Russian culture. His creation of the *Ballets Russes*, which first appeared in Paris in 1909, was genuinely innovatory: it rejected classical tradition in order to treat music, dance, and design as equal components in an artistic entity. He employed painters for costumes and settings, to escape from the time-honored conventions of specialist designers—a practice that gave scope for the sumptuous exoticism of Bakst, and the 18th-century revivalism of Benois. Natalia Goncharova's designs for *Le Coq d'Or* (1914) introduced her version of Cubism to Paris.

After the outbreak of war, Diaghilev's company left these headquarters and became Paris-based. He continued to employ outstanding painters, often assiduously courting the avant-garde. *Parade* (1917) used noise music by Erik Satie and unwieldy costumes by Picasso reminiscent of his Cubist works. *La Chatte* (1927) had Constructivist settings by Antoine Pevsner and Naum Gabo. It is largely due to Diaghilev that designing for opera and ballet is today considered a worthy activity for a serious artist. Diaghilev's influence on 20th-century ballet cannot be exaggerated.

Diaz de la Pena 1808–76

Virgilio-Narcisse Diaz de la Pena was a French painter of landscapes and genre subjects. He had a brief academic training, and in his early works combined a rococo manner derived from the 18th century with the vivid color of Delacroix. These light-hearted and charming paintings depict nymphs, gypsies, and bathers (for example, *Descent of the Bohemians*; Museum of Fine Arts, Boston). Under the influence of Rousseau, he painted an increasing number of pure landscapes during the 1840s. These works, often painted at Barbizon, used dappled colors on a darker background; they were heavily glazed to give a lustrous, shimmering finish, as in the *Forest Interior* (c1867; Washington University Gallery of Art, Steinberg Hall, St Louis, Mo.).

Dibbets Jan 1941–

The Dutch artist Jan Dibbets was born in Weert, the Netherlands. He attended art school in Tilburg (1959–63) and studied at St Martin's School of Art, London, in 1967. There he abandoned Abstract painting and turned to still photography (later adding film and video). His *Perspective Corrections* (1968–9) rely on the monocular viewpoint of the static camera for their effect. His later works, *Panoramas* and *Dutch Mountains*, for example, comprise sequences of images recorded by the camera as it turns on its axis according to predetermined procedures. The mounted photographs give paradoxical, abstract, poetic, and anti-Euclidean images of the world. His 24-minute television film of

T.V. as a Fireplace was transmitted on Westdeutsches Fernsehen on 31 December 1969. Dibbets represented the Netherlands at the 1972 Venice Biennale. He lives and works in Amsterdam.

Diebenkorn Richard 1922–93

Richard Diebenkorn was one of a group of American West Coast artists based on the San Francisco Bay area who abandoned abstraction and reverted to figurative art. Diebenkorn, Elmer Bischoff (1916–) and David Park (1911–60) all taught at the California School of the Arts, San Francisco, and developed figurative styles that showed some debt to their earlier Abstract Expressionism. Diebenkorn began his figurative work in 1955, using broad areas of color in carefully structured wedge shapes. He achieved a sense of thoughtful quiet and isolation in his figure studies, as in *Man and Woman in Large Room* (1957; Joseph Hirshhorn Museum, Washington, D.C.), and a pleasing sense of cool space in his landscapes.

Dientzenhofer family
17th and 18th centuries

The Dientzenhofers were a remarkably talented family of architects whose activities extended over almost a century in central Germany and Bohemia. Georg Dientzenhofer (1614–89) assisted Abraham Leutner on the abbey church of Waldassen (from 1681) and at the end of his career designed Kappel nearby (1685–1689). His son Christoph (1655–1722) was almost certainly responsible for a series of major churches in Bohemia employing Guarinesque vault designs, including Obořistě (c1699–1712), Smiřice (c1700–13), sv. Mikulaš, Malà Strana, in Prague (1703–11) and St Margaret's (1719–21) attached to the Benedictine monastery of Brevnov (Breunau).

Another of Georg's sons, Johann Leonhard (1660–1707), was most important as a designer of monasteries (Ebrach, 1687–98; St Michael at Bamberg, 1696–1702; and Schöntal, 1700–17). A third son, Johann (1663–1726), studied in Rome, as is revealed by his cathedral at Fulda (1704–12). Johann's brilliant de-

signs for the abbey church of Banz (1710–1718) reflect the vaulting patterns employed by his brother Christoph in nearby Bohemia; his secular masterpiece is Schloss Pommersfelden (1711–18). A fourth brother, Wolfgang (1648–1706) was also active as an architect.

The major figure of the third generation was Christoph's son Kilian Ignaz (1689–1751). He was the principal church architect active in Bohemia during the second quarter of the 18th century, and was responsible for the dome and tower of St Niklas, Mala Strana (1737–52).

Above: Georg Dientzenhofer: the pilgrimage church at Kappel; 1685–9

Below: Johann Dientzenhofer: Schloss Pommersfelden; 1711–18

Left: Johann Leonhard Dientzenhofer: detail of the interior of the abbey church at Ebrach; designed 1687–98, built in the early 18th century

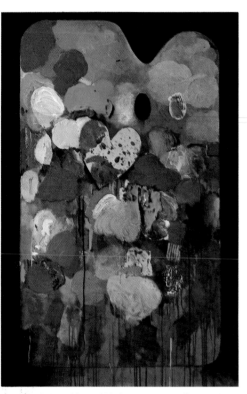

Jim Dine: Pleasure Palette; paper and canvas; 152×102cm (60×40in); 1969. Museum Ludwig, Cologne

Dine Jim 1935–

Jim Dine is, with Robert Rauschenberg and Jasper Johns, one of the American Pop artists closest in technique to Abstract Expressionism. His approach is the juxtaposition of fluent Abstract brush work with man-made objects: ties, tuxedos, toothbrushes, tumblers, washbasins, shower baths, and a wealth of modern products are all physically incorporated into his works. The tradition is one culled from Dada and the works of Marcel Duchamp. It was developed in New York in the late 1950s and 1960s by Allan Kaprow in his Happenings at the Reuben Gallery. In 1960 Dine created an Environment exhibition called *The House* in conjunction with Claes Oldenburg's *The Street*. Dine has remained one of the most versatile of the American Pop painters.

Dionysios of Fourna
18th century AD

Dionysios of Fourna was a Greek painter and author. As a Byzantine monk who spent much of his life on Mount Athos, he wrote the *Exposition of the Art of Painting*, the only surviving manual of Byzantine iconography. This work, first made known to the West in a French translation in 1845, consists of technical and iconographic instructions. It is based on a series of earlier texts dating from about the 16th century and also upon the author's personal observations. It deals in particular with the works of the painters Panselinos and Theophanes of Crete. Some of the iconographic instructions are based on Western models, such as that of the *Apocalypse* which was derived from Dürer's etchings. Several icons and wall paintings by Dionysios are preserved at Fourna and Mount Athos. They are mediocre imitations of earlier models.

Dioskourides late 1st century BC

The Greek gem-engraver Dioskourides worked principally in Italy and especially for the family of Caesar. He is mentioned by Pliny as making a famous gem portrait of Augustus Caesar which the Emperor used as his seal. Three of his sons are also mentioned as distinguished engravers—Eutyches, Herophilos, and Hyllos—all known from extant signed stones. Of their father's work about a dozen signed pieces are preserved, but his name was often forged on the skillful classicizing stones of the 18th and 19th centuries AD or was added to less distinguished ancient gems. His portraits may have included a study of Julius Caesar, known to us today only from later copies.

Original signed works by Dioskourides include a carnelian intaglio in the Duke of Devonshire's Collection (Chatsworth, Derbyshire) showing Diomedes escaping from Troy, an amethyst with the head of Demosthenes (private collection), studies of Hermes, a bust of Io (in the Uffizi, Florence), the figure of *Alexander the Great posing as Achilles* (Museo e Gallerie Nazionali di Capodimonte, Naples), and a cameo with *Herakles Capturing Cerberus* (Antikenabteilung, Berlin).

He was the foremost Greek engraver serving the Roman nobility and the new Imperial family, in common with other Greek artists who had been brought by the Romans. Their style, like their names and signatures, is wholly Greek, and the sub-

Otto Dix: The Artist's Parents; oil on canvas; 101×115cm (40×45in); 1921. Öffentliche Kunstsammlung, Kunstmuseum Basel

jects they cut are also Greek except where portraiture was required. The work of Dioskourides in particular characterizes the classicizing style of the early Empire, apparent in many sculptural and decorative works of the day.

Dix Otto 1891–1969

The German painter Otto Dix was born in Untermhausen in Thuringia. He studied at the Dresden and Düsseldorf Academies. He was professor at the Kunstakademie Dresden from 1927 to 1933, when he was dismissed by the National Socialists. In 1937 he was included in the Nazi "Degenerate Art" exhibition. After the Second World War he lived in seclusion until his death in 1969. Although he painted until he died, Dix's most important work dates from the 1920s. He illustrated postwar German society, both through figure-subjects—cripples, prostitutes, and war profiteers—and through pitilessly realistic portraits which border on caricature. He was included in the 1925 "Neue Sachlichkeit" exhibition in Mannheim.

Further reading. Dube, W.-D. *The Expressionists*, London (1972). Löffler, F. *Otto Dix: Life and Work*, New York (1982).

Dobson William 1610–46

William Dobson was probably the most accomplished native portrait-painter working in England before the advent of William Hogarth (1697–1764). His short career was mainly confined to the period after 1642, during the time the English royal court was in Oxford, when he painted a number of portraits of King Charles I and his officers. His portraits have a distinctly blunt and realistic feel about them, quite unlike the dash and glamor found in the work of van Dyck, by whom Dobson appears to have remained uninfluenced. A love of accessories and detail, rich coloring, and unusual three-quarter compositions are typical of his original style.

Doesburg Theo van 1883–1931

Theo van Doesburg, whose real name was Christian Emil Marie Küpper, was a Dutch polemicist, painter, and architect. His early paintings were Fauvist and Expressionist in style. He first painted in an Abstract manner under the influence of Kandinsky,

whose *Concerning the Spiritual in Art* he read during his war service. By 1917, aware of the painting of Bart Anthony van der Leck and Mondrian, his work became simplified and geometric.

In August of that year Doesburg founded *De Stijl*, the magazine of the Dutch contribution to the modern movement. He collaborated on interiors with two architect members of the group, Jan Wils and J.J.P. Oud. In the early 1920s Doesburg undertook lecture tours, notably in Germany; with some success he attacked the teaching methods of the Bauhaus at Weimar, particularly its emphasis on individual expression. In the same period Doesburg worked as a Dadaist, writing

Theo van Doesburg: Composition VI; 1917. Private collection

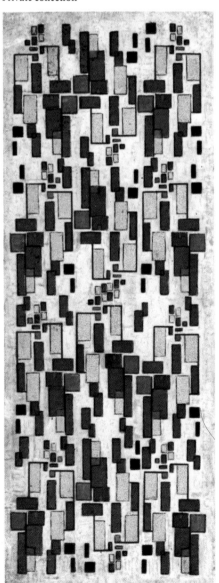

Dada poetry, editing the Dada magazine *Mecano*, and both organizing and performing in Dada "Evenings" in 1923 on a tour of Holland, with Schwitters.

Increasingly concerned with architecture, Doesburg joined two new members of *De Stijl*, van Eestern and Rietveld, in exhibiting architectural projects at the Galerie de l'Effort Moderne, Paris, in 1923. In the following year he moved away from the strict horizontal-vertical aesthetic of *De Stijl*, feeling that it limited expression. He introduced the diagonal, calling the new style "counter-composition".

In 1926 Doesburg published the *Elementarist Manifesto*. Elementarism opposed the balanced relationship of Neo-Plasticism with non-balanced counter-composition based on the diagonal and on color-dissonance. A commission with Jean Arp for the design of the Aubette restaurant in Strasbourg, 1927 (completed 1928), gave him the opportunity to put his Elementarist ideas into practice. His last important work was the design for his own house at Meudon, outside Paris. He became editor of *Art Concret* in Paris in 1929, and was involved in the formation of a broadly based group of Abstract artists.

Further reading. Doig, A. *Theo van Doesburg*, Cambridge (1986).

Dolci Carlo 1616–86

The Italian painter Carlo Dolci spent almost his entire career in his native Florence, where he was taught by Jacopo Vignali. Of a profoundly religious temperament, he specialized in the painting of sacred subjects. These devotional works, for example *The Martyrdom of St Andrew* (1646; Galleria Palatina di Palazzo Pitti, Florence), were small in size and intended for private chapels and apartments; their execution was deliberately laborious and highly wrought. From this approach to painting, Dolci earned himself the reputation of being a slow worker. Displaying a great sensitivity to color and light, his paintings also express a sentimental poignancy. (*See* overleaf.)

Domenichino 1581–1641

Domenico Zampieri, called Domenichino, was born in Bologna and later entered the Carraccis' Academy. In 1602 he went to Rome, where he helped Annibale Carracci decorate the Gallery ceiling of the Palazzo

Carlo Dolci: The Young St John Asleep; oil on canvas; 45×58cm (18×23in); 1670. Galleria Palatina di Palazzo Pitti, Florence

Farnese. He lived in Rome from 1602 to 1617 and again from 1621 to 1631. By 1617 he had become the leading artist in Rome, admired as the defender of classical *disegno*, and a friend of the influential

Domenichino: Portrait of Monsignor Agucchi; oil on canvas; 61×46cm (24×18in); c1621–3. York City Art Gallery

theorist Monsignor Agucchi.

Domenichino owed his severe style and use of careful preparatory drawings to Annibale's teaching. His most important works were a series of fresco decorations in Rome. *The Scourging of St Andrew* (1608; S. Gregorio Magno) and the *Scenes from the Life of S. Cecilia* (1611–14; S. Luigi dei Francesi, Rome) show the development of an austere classicism influenced by Raphael (1483–1520) and the Antique. Space is lucidly defined, and carefully balanced groups of elaborately studied figures are arranged parallel to the picture-plane.

Between 1616 and 1618 Domenichino executed ten scenes from the legend of Apollo for the Villa Aldobrandini at Frascati (eight are now in the National Gallery, London). His frescoes in the tribune of S. Andrea della Valle, Rome (1624–8) are freer and more Baroque in style. In 1631 he began work in Naples on frescoes in the chapel of S. Gennaro in the cathedral; these were left uncompleted at his death.

Domenichino also painted in oil: altarpieces, a few portraits, and landscapes. His famous *The Last Communion of St Jerome* (1614; Vatican Museums) is distinguished by its warmth and clarity. His grandiose ideal landscapes lead on to the mature style of Claude.

Domenico Veneziano *fl.* 1438–61

Domenico Veneziano (Domenico di Bartolomeo di Venezia) was an Italian painter of the Florentine school, although his name denotes a Venetian origin. Very few paintings survive that are definitely by his hand, but from the scattered contemporary records concerning his life we obtain some idea of his undoubted importance in the history of art. The first record of Domenico is in a letter dated Perugia, April 1438, in which he offers his services to Cosimo de' Medici and demonstrates his intimate knowledge of the artistic life of Florence, where he had presumably lived for some time.

In 1439 he began work on an important but now lost series of frescoes of the life of the Virgin in the choir of the church of S. Egidio, Florence, where he is documented until 1445. At that time Piero della Francesca "sta con lui", implying that Piero was Domenico's pupil and assistant.

His principal surviving work is the signed St Lucy Altarpiece from the church of S. Lucia dei Magnoli, Florence (Uffizi, Florence; predella panels in the Staatliche Museen, Berlin, Fitzwilliam Museum, Cambridge, and National Gallery of Art, Washington, D.C.). The Virgin is shown seated within a loggia, with the Christ child on her knee, and Saints Francis, John the Baptist, Zenobius, and Lucy standing at either side. The figures occupy a single unified space, in a *sacra conversazione*, rather than being divided into separate compartments by the frame, as would previously have been the case. The development of the *sacra conversazione* was an important step in the evolution of Renaissance art, and the St Lucy Altarpiece was among the first of the type to be painted. Each figure in this painting is lit by a single light source, and depicted in soft but richly varied colors. The painted architecture, which provides the main stresses in the picture, is composed of pink, green, and blue, as well as white and black marble. Domenico's interest in and mastery of perspective, which was inherited by his pupil Piero della Francesca, is seen in the complicated recession of the colored geometric floor design in the foreground.

The St Lucy Altarpiece is probably from the 1440s; the only other signed work by the artist, the much damaged *Carnesecchi Tabernacle* (National Gallery, London) is certainly earlier. The pose of the Madonna, her facial type, and her throne, with its

Domenico Veneziano: St Lucy, detail of the St Lucy Altarpiece; panel; full size 209×216cm (82×85in); c1445. Uffizi, Florence

filled with statues by Ghiberti, by Donatello himself, by Nanni di Banco, Verrocchio, and others. The *St Mark* stands weightily on its cushion base, one leg as straight as a column, the other trailing in true contrapposto. Equally important, the slight twist of the body, together with the powerful expression on the face and the tension in the hands, spelled a strong psychological presence; Vasari tells of Donatello cursing one of his statues for not actually speaking.

An expression of vigorous physical and mental life is evident in all Donatello's work, and is shown with greater delicacy in the half-assured, half-reticent figure of *St George* (c1416), also intended for a niche on Orsanmichele (now Museo Nazionale, Florence; replaced in Orsanmichele by a copy). The pedestal of this statue contains the famous relief of *St George and the Princess* (c1420). It is celebrated as one of the first examples of the use of linear perspective to construct a convincing representation of space and, indeed, atmosphere on a basically two-dimensional surface. We may imagine that the relief was studied with great interest by painters. Occasionally, there is a similarity between the sculptor and the painter—as in Donatello's *Christ giving the Keys to St Peter* (Victoria and Albert Museum, London) and Masaccio's *Tribute Money* in the Brancacci Chapel of S. Maria del Carmine, Florence, both works dating from c1427.

Around the time of the *St George*, Donatello began a series of *Prophets* for the Campanile of Florence Cathedral (1415 onwards), of which the last and most startling was *Habbakuk* (sometimes called *Lo Zuccone*) of 1427–36. If the *St George* was classical in its stasis and graceful monumentality, this work broke the bounds of the classical style, and created almost a new category of nervous, single-minded passion which was later to attract painters like Andrea del Castagno and the Pollaiuolo brothers.

In certain works Donatello uses antique elements in a totally new way, and thereby turns classicism on its head. This is the case in the Cavalcanti Altar (c1435; S. Croce, Florence) where the vocabulary of Classical architecture is abused and maltreated for decorative ends. It appears even more menacingly in the riotous and uncontrollable *putti* of the Cantoria for Florence Cathedral (1433–9; now Museo dell'Opera del Duomo). This work is in strong

steeply receding perspective, are reminiscent of the work of Gentile da Fabriano or even Jacopo Bellini; this would accord well with Domenico's apparently Venetian origins.

Further reading. Wohl, H. *The Paintings of Domenico Veneziano: a Study in Florentine Art of the Early Renaissance*, Oxford (1980).

Donatello *c1386–1466*

The Florentine artist Donato di Niccolò di Betto Bardi was known as Donatello. He is generally considered the most important sculptor of the Florentine Quattrocento and, indeed, one of the most influential of all Renaissance artists. There is no definite record of his activity before 1403, when he is recorded by name as an assistant to the sculptor Lorenzo Ghiberti. He would have learned bronzeworking in that busy workshop, then making the first set of doors for the Florence Baptistery. Vasari believed that Donatello visited Rome with Brunelleschi (the sculptor, goldsmith, and, later, architect) in 1402/4, but modern opinion tends to date the visit to c1410. Before that year there was no sign of the influence of Classical Antiquity in his basically Gothic style—witness the *Little Prophets* for the Porta della Mandorla of Florence Cathedral (1406–8).

The first work that pointed the direction in which his style would develop was the *St Mark* (1411) for a niche on the facade of Orsanmichele, a guildhall, which might be called the battleground or showcase of Florentine sculptural pretensions during the Quattrocento. Other niches were to be

contrast with Luca della Robbia's majestically calm choir gallery which faced it across the nave. Often an evocation of Antiquity vies with a potent expressionism, as in the bas-relief of *The Dance of Salome*, made in Florence *c*1425 for the font of the Baptistery of S. Giovanni in Siena. Here, the massiveness of the antique arches is the setting for a scene of unmitigated horror.

Donatello's relationship to Classical Antiquity is therefore more complicated than the clarity and serenity of a Luca della Robbia or a Masaccio. He sees it as a source for interesting motifs (and indeed uses Etruscan and Gothic motifs on occasion), not as a vision of restraint, logic, and order. Donatello's art can have a demonic quality akin to that in some of Michelangelo's work: in both cases, lesser artists have tended to copy the motifs without attaining the inner vision that makes such subjects live.

Such considerations do not, of course, diminish the important influence of Antiquity on his art. This is clear from a study of the bronze *David* (*c*1433; Museo Nazionale, Florence) which reflects Donatello's visit to Rome in 1432–3 and possibly conversations there with Leon Battista Alberti. He may well have seen there something in the manner of Praxiteles—but the serenity of the work is disturbed by the playful inclusion of a long feather on Goliath's helmet, which tickles the top of the young hero's leg.

The anti-Classical nature of some of his art is confirmed by his reported argument with his friend Brunelleschi about the two doors, the Door of the Apostles and the Door of the Martyrs, which Donatello made in 1440–3 for the Old Sacristy of S. Lorenzo, Florence. Brunelleschi, who had designed the plain, serene architecture of the Sacristy, did not like the doors, which show fiercely arguing pairs of figures. He probably liked the eight terracotta roundels set within his architecture even less, for four of them thrust upon the spectator Donatello's continuing interest in the intricacies and emotional potential of violent perspective.

Possibly as a result of the quarrel, Donatello went to Padua in 1443 and made a bronze crucifix for the Basilica of St Anthony. This led to the most splendid,

Donatello: Jeremiah; marble; height approximately 200cm (79in); 1423–6. Museo dell'Opera del Duomo, Florence

varied and influential of all his commissions, the high altar for the same church (c1446–50). The altar consisted of a group of seven bronze statues of the Virgin and Child and saints, four bas-reliefs of scenes of the *Miracles of St Anthony*, four reliefs of symbols of the Evangelists, one relief of a *Pietà*, 12 reliefs of singing angels, and a stone panel of *The Entombment of Christ*. The altar was dismembered in 1579/82, and the original arrangement of the various elements is now disputed. The statues stood on the altar table, sheltered by a canopy (the design of which is perhaps reflected in Mantegna's S. Zeno altarpiece), and reliefs were no doubt arranged around the skirt of the altar. Yet some of the reliefs might have decorated the architectural canopy, and some of the saints might have faced to the rear of this large pilgrimage church.

Donatello's other great Paduan work is the equestrian statue of *Gattamelata*, the condottiere (1446–53; Piazza del Santo, Padua). The warrior is represented as an antique hero, perhaps following the example of the celebrated Regisole of Pavia, now lost. However, the armor is only pseudo-Roman. The powerful impact of the group derives from the uprightness of the soldier, and the geometry that governs every detail and seems to be a metaphor for the inflexible strength of will that Donatello here exalts. The condottiere looks straight to the front, controlling both horse and invisible army by willpower, not force. This statue was to be the model for the final version of Leonardo's equestrian monument to Francesco Sforza, a piece that was, unfortunately, never cast. Both have clear links with that most famous of all antique equestrian groups, the Marcus Aurelius, now on the Capitol in Rome.

A comparison between the heroic *Gattamelata* and the Santo Altar demonstrates the great range of style and emotion of which Donatello was capable. The central focus of the Altar is the group of the Virgin and Child, surrounded by a *sacra conversazione* of saints (which may have prompted Giovanni Bellini's predilection for the form). Compared with the rigidly central, hieratic, rather Byzantine Virgin, the saints are supple, naturalistic, noble, and serene. The four plaques of *The Miracles of St Anthony* proclaim the grandeur of Roman architecture; but the figure-style, by contrast, is nervous and frenetic. The stone relief of *The Deposition* intensifies this manner, with its violent gestures and crammed, despairing bodies; it continues that cult of ugliness begun as early as 1425 in *The Dance of Salome* in Siena. The slow nobility of Classical art, breathing serenely in naturalistic space, has been discarded in favor of deliberate confusion and contortion, which together present an emotional intensity unequaled until Michelangelo.

The change from the relatively serene work of Donatello's youth can be appreciated by contrasting the *St George* with the *Mary Magdalen* (polychrome wood; 1453–5; Baptistery, Florence), which he made before his final return to Florence in 1455. This depicts spiritual yearning and repentance by bodily degradation. Even more apposite is the group of *Judith and Holofernes* (1455/60; Piazza della Signoria, Florence), which has similar heroic intentions. This was originally commissioned to decorate a fountain, but was placed on its present site in 1495 on the expulsion of the Medici, when it became a symbol of the right for freedom against tyranny. It must, indeed, have been in the forefront of Michelangelo's mind when he conceived the nature of his gigantic *David*.

The *Judith and Holofernes* is unusual in Donatello's work because it is made to be viewed from the rear and sides as well as from the front. All his other works have painterly characteristics. This group is unthinkable in two dimensions, for its full horror and deliberate awkwardness are revealed only by walking around it. The implacable and pensive Judith, standing with one foot on the twisted arm of the victim, the other pressed to his crotch, waits to strike a second blow to sever the gory head from the limp and distorted body, the legs of which flop over the sides of the triangular pedestal. Judith's extravagant drapery is Gothic in its emotional intricacy—and probably inspired Benvenuto Cellini to produce something similar in his *Perseus*, which faces Donatello's group from its position at the front of the Loggia dei Lanzi.

When Donatello died, work was well in hand on two pulpits for S. Lorenzo, Florence; certain panels were completed by assistants. The north pulpit is decorated with five bronze reliefs of *The Agony in the Garden, Christ before Caiaphas and Christ before Pilate, The Crucifixion, The Descent from the Cross*, and *The Deposition*. The south pulpit has six reliefs: *The Three Women at the Tomb, The Descent into Limbo, The Resurrection, The Ascension, Pentecost*, and *The Martyrdom of St Lawrence*. The pulpits display the tragic breadth of vision that sometimes visits artists in extreme old age: certain mature works by Michelangelo, Titian, and Rembrandt make a similarly strange, almost terrifying impact. In *The Descent from the Cross* the confusion of gesticulating bodies—against the cowled stillness of the Virgin supporting her Son—lends a tragic significance that transcends the immediate Christian reference. Raphael and Michelangelo were much in his debt.

Further reading. Janson, H.W. *The Sculpture of Donatello*, Princeton (1962). Janson, H.W. "Donatello and the Antique" in *Donatello e il Suo Tempo*, Florence (1968).

Donner Georg 1693–1741

Born near Vienna, and trained under Giovanni Giuliani at Heiligenkreuz, the Austrian sculptor Georg Raphael Donner worked briefly in Salzburg as a medalist (1726) and contributed to the staircase of Schloss Mirabell (1726–7). His figure of *Paris* (signed and dated 1726) with its relaxed pose and mellifluous outline points the way to his mature style.

Summoned to Bratislava in 1729 by the Prince-Bishop Emmerich Count Esterhazy, Donner was responsible for his funerary chapel in Bratislava Cathedral (consecrated 1732) and for the high altar (consecrated 1735). The latter consisted of *St Martin and the Beggar* within a semicircular colonnade, of which only the lead central group with two angels and the *Passion* reliefs survive. The rationalism of the 18th century is reflected in the figure of St Martin who is represented not in armor but in the dress of a Hungarian hussar.

Donner's selection of lead, with its softness and silky sheen, is an essential element in the composition and emphasizes his detachment from Baroque dynamism. Nevertheless, his personal move towards classicism was based on Mannerist principles rather than any anticipation of Neoclassicism. We can discern the influence of Giovanni Bologna (c1524–1608) in the elongation and the twisted poses of the lead figures representing the *Rivers Ybbs, Traun, March*, and *Enns*. Arranged around the central figure of *Providence*, these are the dramatic components of Donner's famous fountain for the Mehlmarkt in Vienna (1737–9; now in Österreichische Galerie, Vienna). The lead

Georg Donner: Providence, the central figure of the Mehlmarkt fountain; lead and tin alloy; 1737–9. Österreichische Galerie, Vienna

Dou Gerrit 1613–75

The Dutch genre painter Gerrit Dou, the son of a Leiden glass-maker, was Rembrandt's first pupil. The religious subjects of his early years were influenced by his teacher, and he also attempted to master the chiaroscuro effects of Rembrandt's paintings. But he never exploited contrasts of light and dark for expressive purposes; although he frequently used Rembrandt's studio props—even the same models—his work lacks the latter's sense of drama and mystery. Increasingly Dou concentrated on small domestic scenes whose detailed realism (often achieved with the aid of a magnifying glass) and enamel-like finish brought him wealth and an international reputation.

Dove Arthur 1880–1946

The American painter Arthur Garfield Dove was among the very first pioneers of Abstract art. On leaving Cornell University he moved to New York and began working as an illustrator for magazines such as *Scribners*, a job that supported him until the 1930s. He lived in Europe from 1907 to 1909, where he absorbed the influences of Cézanne and the Fauves, and on his return to the United States began experimenting with Abstraction, exhibiting at Alfred Stieglitz' 291 Gallery in New York. In 1913 he exhibited at the Armory Show. Dove developed his Abstract works, which he called "extractions", by refining and simplifying objects and scenes until color and rhythmic forms took on a life of their own. Yet despite his emphasis on non-naturalistic qualities—he saw painting in terms of music—he was concerned to remain close to nature, and the origins of his Abstract forms in landscapes and plants can often be glimpsed. *Nature Symbolized No. 2* (1914; Art Institute of Chicago) is among his best-known works. In the 1920s he experimented with collage, often with great inventiveness and wit, as in his *Portrait of Alfred Stieglitz* (1925; Museum of Modern Art, New York), in which he used springs and camera lenses (among other things) to depict the photographer.

Further reading. Morgan, A.L. *Arthur Dove: Life and Work*, New York (1984).

Right: Gerrit Dou: Interior with a Young Violinist; panel; 31×24cm (12×9in); 1637. National Gallery of Scotland, Edinburgh

Pietà for Gurk Cathedral in south Austria was completed in the year of Donner's death, and his Mannerist classicism was to dominate Viennese taste for almost half a century.

Dossi Dosso c1490–1542

The Italian artist Dosso Dossi was for nearly 30 years court painter to the Este at Ferrara. Beginning in 1514, his duties entailed designing stage sets and wedding decorations, and even varnishing carriages, besides painting mythologies, portraits, and altarpieces. His earlier works were an extension of Giorgione's pastoral fantasies, with figures set in beautiful, impressionistic landscapes. In the 1520s, while retaining the rich Venetian colors, he adopted a more monumental Roman figure-style. An example can be seen in the altarpiece in Modena Cathedral (1522).

Jean Dubuffet: Setting Snares; oil on canvas; 130×196cm (52×78in); 1963. Detroit Institute of Arts

Dubuffet Jean 1901–85

The French painter and sculptor Jean Dubuffet was born in Le Havre of middle-class parents. Although he began training as a painter in 1916, he felt that art was irrelevant to common experience; he did not work as a full-time artist until 1942. He looked for an alternative inspiration in the art of the insane. This he discovered in 1923 in H. Prinzhorn's *The Artistry of the Mentally Ill*, which claimed that such art was able to express drives usually repressed by civilization.

Dubuffet took the themes of his earliest exhibited paintings from the familiar life of the city and the countryside. These were first shown in Paris just after the liberation in 1944. He abandoned spatial illusionism for a childlike hieratic style with garish colors. In a situation where the future of painting was presumed to lie either in realism or in lyrical abstraction, Dubuffet created a scandal. Particularly controversial were the *Hautes Pâtés* ("thick impastos"), exhibited in 1946. His imagery was as startling as his style: the canvases were dominated by ungainly bodies drawn like crude graffiti. This idea was taken to extremes in the series of *Dames* of 1950–1, in which heads and limbs are mere adjuncts to uneven, flat, rectangular torsos like table-tops on which anything might be scrawled.

During the 1950s Dubuffet developed these preoccupations, devoting a series of paintings to evoking the surface of the earth in terms of collage or thick oil-paint. He also used crumpled silver paper, vinyl plastics, and polyester resins from 1959. After 1962, he confined himself to red, white, black, and blue pigment in a further attempt to resist aesthetic blandishments. His life's work was rooted in an attempt to rehabilitate values that fall outside aesthetic preconceptions.

Further reading. Damisch, H. (ed.) *Jean Dubuffet: Prospectus et Tous Écrits Suivants,* Paris (1967). Gagnon, F. *Jean Dubuffet aux Sources de la Figuration Humaine,* Montreal (1972). Loreau, M. *Jean Dubuffet: Stratégies de la Creation,* Paris (1973).

Duccio Agostino di 1418–81

Agostino di Duccio was an Italian sculptor, a native of Florence. His first dated work is an *antependium* in Modena Cathedral carved in high relief with scenes from the life of S. Gemignano (1442). The provincial style of this work suggests that he received his artistic training outside Florence.

Duccio's most important work is the carved decoration within the Tempio Malatestiano at Rimini (from 1447), where an inscription records him as the sculptor responsible for the transformation of Gothic church to Renaissance "temple". There is, however, some doubt about the exact part Duccio played in the introduction of the neo-Attic low relief style of carving so characteristic of this building: the reliefs in the Chapel of the Sibyls and the Arca degli Antenati are documented as his works, and much of the rest of the sculpture was probably his too.

From 1457 to 1462 Duccio was active in Perugia where he executed the sculptured facade of the Oratory of S. Bernardino (dated 1461), much of which is derived directly from Rimini. Thereafter he divided his time between Perugia, Bologna, and Florence where he was commissioned in 1463 to carve a *Gigante* (giant) for the Duomo. Work on another colossal figure begun the following year was abandoned after two months; the block remained with the cathedral authorities until Michelangelo used it to carve his celebrated figure of David. But Duccio is known chiefly for his work in low relief, and many reliefs of the Madonna and Child.

Duccio di Buoninsegna
c1255–1319

The Italian painter Duccio di Buoninsegna worked chiefly in Siena, whose first great artist he was. Records of Duccio's name occur in 1278 and 1279, when he was paid for decorating bookcovers for the Siena town government. His first major commission came from the Confraternity of the Virgin Mary in Florence in 1285: this was for a painting of the Madonna and Child for the church of S. Maria Novella, and is today generally identified with the so-called *Rucellai Madonna* (Uffizi, Florence), in spite of Vasari's attribution of the picture to Cimabue. Duccio is again recorded in Siena in the 1290s, and in 1295 he helped Giovanni Pisano with the preliminaries for the erection of the Fonte d'Ovile, Siena.

Seven years later, he was responsible for painting a *Maestà* (Madonna and Child enthroned in Glory, with Saints and Angels) for the Chapel of the Council of Nine in Siena town hall. That work is now lost but most of another and greater *Maestà,* commissioned in 1308 for Siena

Agostino di Duccio: Philosophy, a relief carving in the Tempio Malatestiano, Rimini

Cathedral, has survived. As the only fully documented surviving work by Duccio this must act as the key to an understanding of his style, and to the attribution of other works to his hand. The painting, which Duccio contracted to execute unaided by assistants, was probably not completed until 1311, when it was carried in solemn procession from Duccio's workshop to the Cathedral, there to take its place on the high altar.

Duccio's art, although clearly based in the Byzantine style then current in Italy, gradually enriches this tradition with a new life and humanity. The early *Rucellai Madonna* conforms to the shape and type of altarpiece of Cimabue's S. Trinità *Madonna* (which probably precedes it by a few years) to the extent of copying the frame, with roundels connected by ornamental strips. Duccio's Virgin is shown holding the Christ-child with his right arm raised in blessing, enthroned in the centre of an upright panel pointed at the top. The vast scale of the image of the Virgin is emphasized by the small scale of the three angels crouched at either side of her elaborate throne. In these figures the painter's skill is seen in the clear but delicate coloring of the drapery of each angel, complemented by the coloring of the angels on the opposite side of the throne.

Some of the panel paintings of smaller dimensions can on stylistic grounds be placed between the *Rucellai Madonna* and the *Maestà*. One of these is the *Madonna with Three Franciscan Monks* (Pinacoteca Nazionale, Siena); here the flowing "Gothic" line, already apparent in the Virgin's hemline of the Florentine painting, can be seen again. The rich golden ground behind and around the Virgin is partly obscured by a richly decorated cloth of honor, as it is in a later panel, now in the National Gallery, London. In both these panels, the Virgin and Child are seated between angels much smaller in scale; but the subsidiary figures now have a less ethereal nature and begin to stand more firmly on the ground.

That is certainly the case in the great Siena Cathedral *Maestà* of 1308–11. This work, now dismantled, was originally made up of two parts, each demanding a different talent from the artist. The front, facing the congregation, showed the Virgin and Child enthroned in the center of an oblong panel; angels and saints were ranged in three rows, two standing and one kneeling, at either side of the throne.

Duccio di Buoninsegna: The Entry into Jerusalem, a panel from the Maestà; size of panel 102×54cm (40×21in); 1308–11. Museo dell'Opera del Duomo, Siena

Crucifixion scene occupied the large upper central area (26 panels in all). The greater part of this vast altarpiece survives in the cathedral museum (Museo dell'Opera del Duomo) at Siena. However, the panels from the predella are scattered through public and private collections in Europe and America (examples in the National Gallery, London; Frick and Rockefeller Collections, New York; National Gallery of Art, Washington, D.C.).

In the small panels of the *Maestà*, Duccio reveals himself as a master of pictorial narrative. In many cases he follows a pattern of storytelling inherited from Byzantine artists. But he enriches the traditional iconography with many new incidents intended to provoke greater contemplation in the devout beholder. The individual figures have a sensitivity of characterization which reinforces Duccio's importance in the prehistory of Italian Renaissance art, and clearly distinguishes him from his Florentine contemporary Cimabue. He places these figures within a convincing spatial setting which is used, for narrative purposes, in a brilliantly inventive manner. For instance, Christ appears before Annas in the upper floor of a building, on the ground floor of which St Peter's denial is shown, with a staircase linking the two floors.

It is probably Duccio's skill as colorist that is made clearest in the *Maestà*. The figure of Christ, clad in a glowing red and blue robe which becomes striated with gold after the Crucifixion, can be traced passing from panel to panel. The jewel-like quality of color seen in Duccio's work was to remain of fundamental importance to the painters of the Sienese school throughout the next 200 years.

Further reading. Brandi, C. *Duccio*, Florence (1951). Carli, E. *Duccio di Buoninsegna*, Milan (1951). Cattaneo, G. *L'Opera Completa di Duccio*, Milan (1972). Weigelt, C.H. *Duccio di Buoninsegna*, Leipzig (1911). White, J. *Duccio: Tuscan Art and the Mediaeval Workshop*, London (1979).

Ducerceau family
16th and 17th centuries

The Ducerceau were a family of French architects and architectural theorists. The elder Ducerceau (Jacques I, *c*1515–*c*84) was probably connected with two buildings, both now destroyed: Charleval, a vast rural palace begun in 1568 for Charles IX,

Above the main figures, in separate compartments of the no-longer-extant original frame, were half-length figures of saints. Crowning it all, in separate gabled panels, were six scenes narrating the life of the Virgin, with her Death and Assumption in the center.

The reverse side of the *Maestà* was occupied by panels depicting the life of Christ. The ten predella panels narrated his early life and ministry, and the crowning gabled panels his appearances following the Resurrection. The story of Christ's Passion adorned the main area, shown in two bands, each two panels deep, progressing from bottom left to top right; while the

and Verneuil of 1570. He is mainly known for his many architectural and ornamental engravings. He illustrated the principal French châteaux in two volumes (1576; 1579).

In 1559, Jacques I wrote *Livre d'Architecture* and in 1561 a second *Livre d'Architecture*. Both books were rag-bags of ideas with little emphasis on the practical, and they may well have hindered rather than helped his career. His sons, Baptiste, (*c*1555–*c*90) and the more famous Jacques II (1556–1614) continued the architectural rather than the literary traditions of their father. Jacques II built the Petite Galerie des Tuileries in Paris, *c*1608, and at the Louvre the Pavilion de Flore, *c*1607; this followed his earlier work on the western part of the Grande Galerie of the Louvre, with its impressive use of the giant order. The architecture of the Ducerceau family strengthened and extended the naturalization of Serlio's Italian manner.

Duchamp Marcel 1887–1968

The French artist Marcel Duchamp was a leading exponent of Dada principles and was later associated with the Surrealists. He was born in Blainville, Normandy, the son of a notary. His two elder brothers, Gaston (1875-1963), known as Jacques Villon and Raymond Duchamp-Villon (1876–1918), were also artists. Duchamp began painting in 1902, and two years later joined his brothers in Paris, where he studied for a year at the Académie Julian. From 1905 to 1910 he worked

Marcel Duchamp: Portrait of Chess-Players; oil on canvas; 102×102cm (40×40in); 1911. Philadelphia Museum of Art

sporadically as a cartoonist for popular periodicals, and he also began to frequent his brothers' avant-garde poet and painter friends.

Duchamp's paintings of 1910–11 reflect the influence of Cézanne and of Fauvism, but they also have Symbolist overtones in their imagery of female nudes and lovers. An awareness of Cubism is shown in his works of 1911–12. Influenced by Futurism and Étienne-Jules Marey's Chrono-photography, Duchamp also began to depict movment by means of successive images of the body in motion. *Dulcinea* (1911; Philadelphia Museum of Art) and his most important painting up to that time, *Nude Descending a Staircase* (no. 2; 1912; Philadelphia Museum of Art), both employed this method. In neither work, however, was there any sign of the Futurists' optimistic attitude to modern life. Rejected from the Indépendants exhibition in Paris, *Nude Descending a Staircase* had a *succès de scandale* when it was shown in the Armory Show in New York in 1913.

In 1912, Duchamp was in close association with Apollinaire and Picabia; with them he evolved a critical attitude to the nature and purpose of art that prefigures the studied iconoclasm of Dada. On a visit to Munich that summer, he painted *The Passage from the Virgin to the Bride* (Museum of Modern Art, New York) and *Bride* (Philadelphia Museum of Art), in which sexual intercourse and the loss of virginity are symbolized cryptically in semiorganic, semimechanical terms. Duchamp had by now moved far from Cubism, which he had come to regard as too "retinal". As he repeatedly stated, his aim was to reintroduce the cerebral into painting at the expense of pure visual beauty.

Nineteen-thirteen was a crucial year in Duchamp's development. Apparently as a "diversion" he created his first so-called "Ready-made" (*The Bicycle Wheel*; original lost; replica, Museum of Modern Art, New York), which consisted of a bicycle wheel upended on a stool. Implicit in this gesture is a Dadaist contempt for the traditional notions of what constitutes a work of art, and the suggestion that the essential factor in the creation of art is not skill but choice. *The Chocolate Grinder* (no. 1; 1913; Philadelphia Museum of Art) was almost the last of Duchamp's oil paintings: in it he employed all the resources of academic illusionism in the portrayal of a simple implement, thus

directing his irony against both academic and avant-garde artists. At the same time, he developed a quasi-scientific system, "canned chance", to incorporate random effects into his work. Thus, in *Three Standard Stoppages* (1913–14; Museum of Modern Art, New York), the design was established by dropping three one-meter lengths of string from a height of one meter on to the floor.

Duchamp settled in New York in 1915. He spent most of the rest of his life there, becoming an American citizen in 1955. With Man Ray, Picabia, and others, he founded the New York Dada group. Periodically, he manufactured Ready-mades. One of the most notorious of these was *Fountain* (1917; original lost; replica, private collection), which was an upended urinal. Another was *L.H.O.O.Q.* (1919; private collection)—a reproduction of the *Mona Lisa* defaced by a mustache, beard, and inscription, which he made while staying in Paris.

Duchamp's most important work, *The Bride Stripped Bare by her Bachelors, Even*, or *Large Glass*, was begun in 1915 and abandoned unfinished in 1923 (Philadelphia Museum of Art). Notes and studies for it dated back to 1912. In this complex work, executed in mixed media on glass, the Bride's domain occupies the top half, and the organic vocabulary of the 1912 paintings is employed; the Bachelors, in the lower half, represented by nine "malic moulds", are controlled by an elaborate pseudo-mechanical apparatus dominated by the Chocolate Grinder. Despite the strenuous efforts of the Bachelors, aided by the Oculist Witnesses (represented by optical charts), and despite the Bride's encouraging messages (the cloud-like forms at the top), sexual union is never achieved. Through the metaphor of impotent machines and the medium of glass, Duchamp makes an ironic and pessimistic comment on human sexuality. For the Surrealists, who immediately recognized Duchamp's importance, the *Large Glass* was a key work, comparable to the great occult creations of the Middle Ages.

In the 1920s, Duchamp became increasingly interested in optics and cinematic techniques. He experimented with the visual effects created by rotating disks, and in 1926 made a short film, *Anemic Cinema*, with Man Ray. In the 1930s he spent less time on artistic activities as he became increasingly involved in chess-playing at an international level. He concentrated on the publication in 1934 of *The Green Box*, a complete facsimile of his notes and drawings for the *Large Glass*; he also designed installations for Surrealist exhibitions. The legend that he had given up art to play chess began to circulate, and had a considerable influence on avant-garde artists in the 1950s and 1960s.

In fact, however, Duchamp had been engaged secretly for some 20 years, from 1946, on making the illusionistic tableau-assemblage, *Given: 1. the waterfall, 2. the illuminating gas* (Philadelphia Museum of Art). In essence, this extraordinary construction is a further extension of the erotic theme of the *Large Glass*. Revealed only after his death in 1968, the work had been preceded by a number of erotic objects during the 1950s.

The influence of Duchamp's ideas and of his work has been vital: his Ready-mades were a major stimulus to Surrealist object-making and to Pop art. His belief that living is the true art form, and his emphasis on the cerebral content of art, have deeply affected such avant-garde developments as Conceptual art.

Further reading. Cabanne, P. *Dialogues with Marcel Duchamp*, New York (1959). Golding, J. *Duchamp: The Bride Stripped bare by her Bachelors, Even*, London (1972). Harnoncourt, A. d' and McShine, K. *Marcel Duchamp*, London (1974) and New York (1973). Lebel, R. *Marcel Duchamp*, London and New York (1959). Paz, O. (trans. Phillips, R. and Gardner, D.) *Marcel Duchamp: Appearance Stripped Bare*, New York (1979). Sanouillet, M. and Peterson, E. *The Essential Writings of Marcel Duchamp*, London (1975). Schwarz, A. *The Complete Works of Marcel Duchamp*, New York (1969). Tomkins, C. *The World of Marcel Duchamp*, New York (1966).

Duchamp-Villon Raymond 1876–1918

The French Cubist sculptor Raymond Duchamp-Villon was the brother of Marcel Duchamp and Jacques Villon. Born in Rouen, he settled in Paris 1901, having first taken up sculpture during a convalescence from 1899 to 1900. His early terracottas had an Art Nouveau stylization, and a dynamic sense of the spiral remained vital to his art.

Under the influence of Cubism he used increasingly angular forms. An example is

Raymond Duchamp-Villon: The Larger Horse; bronze; height 150cm (59in); 1914. Museum of Fine Arts, Houston

his *Baudelaire* (1911; Museum of Modern Art, New York). In other works he made reliefs analogous to Cubist painting in their compressed space and formal dislocation.

His bronze *Horse* (1914; Museum of Modern Art, New York) is one of the most famous and revered of Cubist sculptures. Close in spirit to Léger and to Futurism, it is a dynamic machine-age image, blending ideas of animal energy with mechanistic forms and using the play of light on turning surfaces.

The increasing abstraction of his last bronze, *Professor Gosset* (1917–18; Albright-Knox Art Gallery, Buffalo), has prompted much speculation about how his art might have developed. His career at the center of the Cubist movement was curtailed by his early death from typhoid, contracted during service at the Front in the First World War.

Dudok Willem 1884–1974

The Dutch architect Willem Marinus Dudok was born in Amsterdam. An admirer of the work of H.P. Berlage (1856–1934), he quickly evolved his own distinctive style. He was in contact with the *De Stijl* movement but was not a member. Most of his important works were public buildings for the town of Hilversum, where he was made municipal architect in 1915.

Dudok's work is largely in exposed brick, asymmetrically composed, often with a tower and long horizontal strips of window. The interlocking of massive rec-

tangular blocks is effective. His best building, the Hilversum Town Hall (1924–30), was admired in England where his work as a whole—less radical than that of his friend J.J.P. Oud (1890–1963)—was seen as representing the softer stream of modernism.

Dufy Raoul 1877–1953

The French painter Raoul Dufy was born at Le Havre. After studying at the École des Beaux-Arts in Le Havre (1900) he developed a brightly colored style influenced by Van Gogh and the Impressionists. Much impressed by the work of Matisse, he joined the Fauves in 1905. From printed fabric made in 1910 he evolved his familiar decorative style of luminous washes and calligraphic notations evoking scenes of elegant life. He executed one of the largest murals ever painted on the theme of Scientific Progress for the Palace of Electricity at the 1937 Paris World Fair.

Further reading. Perez-Tibi, D. *Dufy*, New York (1989).

Dujardin Karel 1622–78

The Dutch painter and etcher Karel Dujardin painted genre scenes, life-size portraits, and occasional religious pictures, but is best known for his landscapes. These are usually, like those of his teacher, Berchem, in the Italianate tradition deriving from Claude. Unlike most Italianizing painters from the north, Dujardin combined clear, warm light effects and such classical pastoral motifs as shepherds and grazing animals with a Dutch setting and a particularizing approach to natural forms. Dujardin's bucolic landscapes found a ready market in his native Amsterdam.

Duquesnoy François 1597–1643

The Flemish sculptor François Duquesnoy acquired his fame in Rome, where he became generally known as "Il Fiammingo". Born in Brussels, he was trained by his father, the sculptor Jérôme Duquesnoy the Elder. No works survive from this period and his later works do not display any marked Flemish characteristics.

He reached Rome in 1618 with a pension from Archduke Albert, for whom he had previously executed some minor works. The Archduke died in 1621, and Duques-

Willem Dudok: Hilversum Town Hall; 1924–30

Raoul Dufy: Races at Goodwood; watercolor; 50×66cm (20×26in); 1930. Private collection

noy earned his living by producing small sculptures in ivory and metal, and by restoring antiques. He was fortunate in securing powerful patrons. He received commissions from Cardinal Francesco Barberini, for whom he carved the busts of *Bernardo Guglielmi* and *John Barclay* (1627); from Cardinal Connestabile Filippo Colonna, for whom he modeled an inkwell; and from Marchese Giustiniani, for whom he designed a frontispiece and created small bronze statuettes of *Mercury* and *Apollo*.

Duquesnoy made only two over-life-size marble statues. One of these, the *St Andrew* (1633–9; in the crossing of St Peter's, Rome) was based on a model prepared by Bernini. The other, *S. Susanna* (1630–3; S. Maria di Loreto, Rome), was one of the most influential statues carved in modern times. The graceful, curving form of *S. Susanna* combined a warm classicism with gentle sentiment. It achieved that perfect statement of the ideal for which its slow-working creator was

François Duquesnoy: S. Susanna; marble; 1630–33. S. Maria di Loreto, Rome.

constantly striving, and its style impressed itself upon a host of later imitators.

Apart from the busts already mentioned, Duquesnoy carved a portrait of Cardinal Maurice of Savoy. He created a fascinating study of the dwarf who accompanied the Duc de Créqui on his embassy to Rome (1633–4), and modeled a bust of the wife of his friend Nicolas Poussin.

His most popular and influential contribution to art was his treatment of *putti* (babies), which in his hands attained a new veracity and charm. Some are to be seen in the three surviving small tombs of Adrien Vryburch (1629) and Ferdinand van den Eynde (1633–40) in S. Maria dell'Anima, and of Jacob de Hase (*post* 1634) in S. Maria in Campo Santo, Rome, and others are in reliefs such as the *Bacchanal of Putti* and *Amor Sacro and Amor Profano* in the Galleria Doria Pamphili, Rome. There are further examples in his *Musician Angels* on the Filomarino Altar in SS. Apostoli in Naples (1640–2), and there are also numerous small models, such as that of the Colonna inkwell.

Despite his small output, much of it in such "minor" genres, Duquesnoy achieved a perfection that places him among the great sculptors of the Roman Baroque. Such was his fame in his own day that he was summoned to work for the King of France; it was at Leghorn, on the journey to Paris, that he died.

Durand-Ruel Paul 1831–1922

Paul Durand-Ruel was the leading French dealer in the works of the French Impressionists. He inherited his father's Paris gallery in 1865, and initially concentrated on the work of the Barbizon School and their contemporaries, as well as some earlier French painters and Old Masters. He met Monet and Pissarro in London during the Franco-Prussian War of 1870–1, and bought much from the Impressionists and from Manet between 1871 and 1873, though he continued to buy the work of Academic artists such as Adolphe William Bouguereau. Financial difficulties prevented him from investing further in the work of the Impressionists until the 1880s, but from then onwards he was the principal agent of their increasing success, in the United States, in France, and elsewhere in Europe.

Dürer Albrecht 1471–1528

The German painter, printmaker, and theorist Albrecht Dürer is generally acknowledged to be the most significant figure in the history of European art outside Italy in the period of the Renaissance. His prints especially had an enormous influence on all forms of the pictorial and decorative arts both in northern Europe and Italy. A critical understanding of Dürer's art is facilitated by the large quantity of personal information that survives in the form of letters, theoretical writings, and carefully annotated drawings. This constant comment on his work is more sustained than that of any other north European artist of the period.

Dürer was born at Nuremberg, the son of a goldsmith of Hungarian origin in whose workshop he originally trained. At the age of 13 his precocious talents were sufficiently developed to produce the earliest of many self-portraits, the accomplished silverpoint drawing in the Graphische Sammlung Albertina, Vienna. His apprenticeship, in the strict sense, was in the workshop of the Nuremberg painter Michael Wolgemut; he gained his general artistic education through years of travel from 1490 to 1494.

It is significant, in the light of Dürer's mastery of the graphic arts, that the aim of one of his journeys was to reach the workshop of the leading German engraver of the day, Martin Schongauer of Colmar; but in this he was frustrated by Schongauer's death. Dürer was already gaining a reputation as a designer of woodcuts for printed books; while at Basel in 1492 he designed a *St Jerome in his Study* for an edition of the saint's letters. Many copies of this print were duly painted, following the contemporary tradition of treating the woodcut as a network of lines demanding filling-in of color to resemble the effect of stained glass. But Dürer's attempt to render interior space, and his careful hatching of light and shade, point the way to a freeing of the woodcut from dependence on applied color.

Dürer's earliest knowledge of Italian art was through prints; by 1494 he was copying the mythological engravings of Mantegna. His desire to travel south was not curbed by his marriage to Agnes Frey in Nuremberg in 1494. Shortly after this, he left alone for his first visit to Italy. The watercolors that survive from his journey across the Alps are some of the earliest evidence of Dürer's curiosity about the world around him. Many of them are rapid sketches of broad areas of color, conveying not only the landscape of mountains of Alpine towns new to him, but also the effects of atmosphere and light, as in *The Pond in a Wood* (British Museum, London). From comments made on a second visit to Italy ten years later, it is clear that Dürer reached Venice on this journey; but where else he may have traveled in Italy remains speculative. By the spring of 1495 he had returned to Nuremberg.

In the following years, Dürer established a workshop in his native city and received commissions from several German patrons, including Frederick the Wise, Elector of Saxony, for portraits and religious works. One of the most significant of the latter was the Paumgärtner Altar of 1503 (Alte Pinakothek, Munich), the central panel of which reflects a blend of northern and Italian ideas. The tiny donor figures with their armorial devices are placed in the foreground of a ruined courtyard, with plunging diagonals towards a background landscape. Portraits of this period include the tense characterization of *Oswolt Krell* (1499; Alte Pinakothek, Munich) and two self-portraits which show Dürer's highly self-conscious approach to his status as an artist. The 1498 *Self-portrait* (Prado, Madrid), though indebted to Flemish portrait conventions in format, is also highly Italian in its use of modish dress and in its relaxed elegance of pose. Here Dürer seems to wish to present the artist as a cultured gentleman. The 1500 *Self-portrait* (Alte Pinakothek, Munich) seeks to elevate the position of the artist, in a religious rather than social sense: the physical equation of Dürer with the image of Christ suggests the artist as creator, as a unique figure with God-given talents.

It was, however, with the production of woodcuts and engravings that Dürer was chiefly preoccupied at this time, and it is here that the lessons of Italy are most manifest. He not only designed but published his own graphic work, thus establishing a link between his artistic judgment and the market for prints. He was therefore able to risk the unusual, as when he issued the *Pig with Six Feet*, depicting a freak of nature that he himself had seen. The *Men's Bathhouse* woodcut of 1496–7 shows an effort at classicism. Half-length figures in the foreground are placed to show the back and front views of the same human form; the composition is centered

**Albrecht Dürer: Large Piece of Turf;
watercolor; 41×32cm (16×12½in); 1503.
Graphische Sammlung Albertina, Vienna**

on the figure of the flautist, who provides a point of stability. As in his religious paintings of this period, Dürer adds a northern landscape, again evoking the direct contrast between his local artistic origins and the Italian style.

The engravings of these years are increasingly refined in style and detail, achieving effects in tone and texture not possible in woodcuts. By working slowly on one small area of the copper plate at a time, Dürer transformed the engraving technique of his day. He replaced the current rigid linear style with a fine but repetitive method of hatching. Using flexible draftsmanship, he varied the length and pressure of his incision with the engraver's tool, the burin, to produce a multiplicity of curved lines and cross-hatchings. *The Fall of Man* of 1504 demonstrates this achievement in the fine detail of animals and trees which are symbolic allusions to the main figure-subject. The figure of Adam is indebted to the Classical sculpture of the *Apollo Belvedere*.

Dürer's most influential work in the period between his two visits to Italy was probably the series of woodcuts illustrating major biblical themes; at this time he began the *Great Passion* series and finished the *Apocalypse* (1497–9). The latter consists of 14 full-page woodcuts issued as a book. For the first time, the text in German and Latin is clearly aligned with the illustrations. He appears to have worked on two or more of the woodcuts simultaneously, so that there is a close interrelation between the development of subjects. Nevertheless, certain works of the 14 stand out as being

Albrecht Dürer: St Michael from the series of woodcut illustrations of the Apocalypse; 39×28cm (15×11in); 1498

Albrecht Dürer: The Painter's Father; panel; 51×40cm (20×16in); 1497? National Gallery, London

exceptionally powerful: for example, *The Four Horsemen*. Here the narrative is most forceful in the depiction of the irresistible forces of Death, War, Famine, and Pestilence. More than any other work of this period, the *Apocalypse* series spread Dürer's fame throughout Germany and Italy. As visionary subjects, they echoed the troubled mood of the close of the century. And, on an artistic level, the fact that they are related to earlier woodcuts on the same theme only underlines the superiority of Dürer's skill and narrative power.

The first published reference to Dürer is in a German chronicle of 1505 which confirms the profound impact of his prints upon Italian artists; it is interesting that he paid his second visit to Italy in this year. His stay at Venice is well documented by letters home to his friend, the humanist Willibald Pirckheimer. In these he contrasts the respected position of the Italian artist with the lower social status of the artist in Germany.

During the visit, he consciously tried to equal the painterly skill of the leading Venetian artists of the day. *The Feast of the Rose Garlands* (1506; National Gallery, Prague) was painted for the German national church in Venice. Thematically, it combines the cult of the rosary with the idea of the universal brotherhood of Christianity—showing Pope and Emperor leading the spiritual and temporal worlds in adoration of the Virgin and Child. Its centralized composition and richness of color, much subdued in its present damaged state, are reminiscent of Venetian altarpieces. A tribute to Giovanni Bellini, who befriended the artist on this visit, is found in the single music-playing angel at the base of the throne. The *Portrait of a Young Woman* (c1506; Staatliche Museen, Berlin) shows Dürer attempting to emulate contemporary Venetian portraiture; the figure is placed against a blue background and her features, though Germanic in character, are modeled in light and shade rather than in his usually incisive drawing style.

After his return to Nuremberg in 1507 Dürer appears to relinquish the freedom of brushwork and color that marked his Venetian works, perhaps under pressure from northern patrons. The altarpiece he painted for the Frankfurt merchant Jacob Hellar (1508–9; now lost; copy in the Historisches Museum, Frankfurt am Main) was executed with meticulous care

for detail, as is made clear in Dürer's letter on the subject. His *Trinity Adored by Saints* (1511; Kunsthistorisches Museum, Vienna) is also painstakingly finished. At this period Dürer's initial inspiration is reserved increasingly for the preparatory stages of the painted work, in many drawings in a variety of media, including chalk or brush on prepared ground. Throughout his life, his skill and reputation as a painter and his conscious attempt to equal his contemporaries in this field was a hard-won triumph; whereas in the graphic arts his supremacy was unchallenged.

More woodcut series, such as the *Life of the Virgin*, were completed in succeeding years. But the period 1511 to 1514 is most remarkable for Dürer's successful "Master" engravings, which exhibit his most mature graphic style. *Melencolia I* of 1514 is the representation of reason reduced to inertia by the melancholy spirit; its counterpart, the *St Jerome in his Study* of the same year, presents the security, comfort, and fulfillment of scholarship. The latter engraving especially shows the refined technique of the late works, in its depiction of surfaces, and of light passing across them through multiple variations of cross-hatching.

Dürer worked in his later years for the Emperor Maximilian and designed the enormous print of a *Triumphal Arch* (1515–17) made up of 192 blocks of woodcut and standing more than 27 ft (9 m) high (one example in the British Museum, London). Its exceedingly complex design detracts considerably from the visual impact, suggesting that here the artist was not working on his own initiative. His inventiveness was still reserved for the curious, the everyday details of life as he viewed it. From his journey to the Netherlands of 1520–1 his drawings include, alongside highly finished portraits in charcoal, a single pen sketch of the *Harbour at Antwerp* (Graphische Sammlung Albertina, Vienna) and the *Head of a Walrus* in pen and watercolor (British Museum, London) drawn from a real animal specimen washed up on the shore. His last years were troubled by the coming of the Reformation. There is considerable evidence that he turned Protestant; he certainly held great faith in the teachings of Luther. Luther's translations of writings by the apostles are found at the foot of his panels of the *Four Apostles*, presented to the town council of Nuremberg in 1526 (now Alte Pinakothek,

Munich). Significantly, the quotations refer to the dangers of excessive religious zeal, reflecting the mood of uncertainty created by extremism on both sides of the controversy. These are among Dürer's last painted works; the monumental forms of the Apostles fill the picture-space, and the bold simplicity of their drapery underlines the powerful message of the panels.

Dürer was also preoccupied at this time with preparations for his books on measurement and proportion. His treatise on measurement appeared in 1525 and his books on human proportion were published posthumously, following his death in 1528. His books are attempts to rationalize his approach to art, based on knowledge of Italian forerunners in the field of artistic theory. Yet perhaps Dürer's ultimate importance lies not so much in his theories as in the general attitudes to art he displayed in the practice of his profession. It lies, too, in his many-sided impact on the work of his contemporaries both north and south of the Alps. The degree of self-consciousness apparent in everything he undertook, from commissioned works to self-portraits to spontaneous drawings, suggests an artist convinced of his unique gifts and their value to posterity. In the Germany of his day, his belief that originality and inventiveness were worth more than simple diligence and traditional craftsmanship was revolutionary.

Further reading. Conway, M. *The Writings of Albrecht Dürer*, London (1958). Kurth, W. *The Complete Woodcuts of Albrecht Dürer*, London (1927). Levey, M. *Dürer*, London (1964). Panofsky, E. *The Life and Art of Albrecht Dürer*, Princeton (1955). Strauss, W. *Albrecht Dürer: the Complete Engravings, Etchings and Drypoints*, New York (1971). White, C. *Dürer, the Artist and his Drawings*, London (1971). Wölfflin, H. (trans. Grieve, A. and H.) *The Art of Albrecht Dürer*, London (1971).

Dyce William 1806–64

William Dyce was a Scottish painter and art educationalist. Born in Aberdeen, he trained in Edinburgh and London; he then visited Italy from 1825 to 1829, studying early Italian painting and meeting the Nazarene group of artists. On his return he produced works based on the manner of the Italian masters (for example, *Madonna and Child*, c1840; Tate Gallery, London).

William Dyce: A scene on Arran; oil on board; 35×50cm (14×20in); 1858–9. Aberdeen Art Gallery

He evolved a precise style which resembled but predated Pre-Raphaelitism, painting religious, historical, and modern subjects, often in landscape settings (for example, *Pegwell Bay*, 1859–60; Tate Gallery, London). He was involved in the attempted revival of fresco painting in the 1840s and was Director of the Government School of Design at Somerset House (1838–43).

Dyck Anthony van 1599–1641

Sir Anthony van Dyck holds a special place in 17th-century art as the creator of the Baroque court portrait. He had a highly developed sense of elegance and refinement, and made from his courtly sitters an image of ideal aristocracy that has retained a lasting hold on the European imagination.

Born in Antwerp, he was apprenticed in 1609 to Hendrik van Balen. He was a precocious artist, endowed with a remarkable fluency in the handling of paint. By c1616–18 he already had his own studio and assistants; at that date he was creating a series of paintings of Christ and the Apostles. Between 1618 and 1621 he worked as principal assistant to Rubens. Under that master's influence he modified his harsh, robust early style, and began to use smoother paint and delicate, silvery tonalities. There are sketches and copies of figure-subjects, both after Rubens and from prints by Renaissance masters, contained in van Dyck's Antwerp sketchbook; these provide evidence of the thoroughness and breadth of his education as a religious and historical painter.

The ambitious figure-compositions of his first period in Antwerp (1599–1620) already reveal a profound debt to Rubens and Titian that was to last throughout his life. Yet his *Samson and Delilah* (Dulwich College Picture Gallery, London), *The Betrayal of Christ* (c1617; Prado, Madrid), and *The Continence of Scipio* (c1620–1; Christ Church Picture Gallery, Oxford) also show a highly personal preference for shallow space and frieze-like designs, for a sophisticated grace of gesture and expressions, and for decorative surface patterns of light and shade. Van Dyck's early self-portraits are of astonishing quality; they combine informality with elegance and their rich clothing and slightly narcissistic appeal seem to demonstrate his claims to be considered a prince among painters. By c1621–2 his portrait style had moved away from the conventional designs of his earliest years towards a new naturalness and freedom of pose.

In 1621, after an abortive visit to the court of James I in London in 1620, he left for Italy; he spent longest in Genoa and Rome but also traveled to Florence, Venice, and Sicily. His Italian sketchbook (British Museum, London) shows how deeply he studied the works of Titian in these years; he responded to his glowing color, the openness of his compositions, and the lyrical poetry of his early allegories. His own most Titianesque work is the *Four Ages of Man* (c1622–7; Museo Civico, Vicenza). He was also influenced by Bolognese art, particularly by Guido Reni's expression of intense religious feeling.

In Genoa van Dyck painted a magnificent series of portraits of the aristocracy; these were often full-length, some of them equestrian. Rubens, in Genoa 15 years earlier, had already created the new *mise-en-scène* of the terrace or palace. Now van Dyck transformed Rubens' robust power into grace and elegance. In his spectacular *Marchesa Elena Grimaldi* (1625; National Gallery of Art, Washington, D.C.) the reticent majesty of the figure is enhanced by the magical beauty of the terrace setting, by the Italian light on the distant hills, and by the luxurious, almost ceremonial, dress. The painting seems to capture the essence of aristocracy.

In 1627 van Dyck returned to Antwerp; in 1630 he was made court painter at

Anthony van Dyck: Mountjoy Blount, Earl of Newport; oil on canvas; 215×130cm (85×51in); c1633. Private collection

Brussels by the Archduchess Isabella Clara Eugenia. In his second Antwerp period he painted many portraits of collectors, fellow artists, and of the Spanish court in Brussels, and he fulfilled several great commissions for churches. Van Dyck's Flemish sitters wear black, and the cool blacks and whites are relieved only by the brilliant reds of the studio properties. His portrait style became more severe and monumental. He developed superb mastery over the double portrait, creating subtle composi-

tional links that are full of psychological significance. He also began to work on the *Iconography*, a collection of engravings after portraits of celebrated persons. The religious works he painted at this period are deeply indebted to the heightened emotionalism of Guido Reni. In 1632 van Dyck moved to London where he was knighted by Charles I, named Principal Painter, and granted a house at Blackfriars. He visited Antwerp in 1634 and 1640, but died in London in 1641.

Charles I was a learned patron of the arts who shared van Dyck's love of Titian. Van Dyck's portraits of the King and courtiers show how sensitive the artist was to the ethos and aspirations of the Caroline court. He painted shimmering, silvery portraits of the Queen and the ladies of the court, and within the formal trappings of the state portrait he managed to convey the restless charm of Charles' five children. Above all, he painted Charles I in many roles which interpret with poetic beauty Charles' vision of the monarchy. In 1633 he painted him as king and warrior in the equestrian portrait (National Gallery, London) based on Titian's Charles V (Prado, Madrid); and again in the *Charles I on Horseback, with M. de St Antoine* (Collection of H.M. Queen Elizabeth II). This work, which shows the King riding through an archway, gave scope to van Dyck's thwarted ambitions as a large-scale designer; it is his most magnificent use of Baroque illusionism. *Charles I Hunting* (1635; Louvre, Paris) shows the king as the perfect cavalier. In 1636 he painted him as a robed monarch (Collection of H.M. Queen Elizabeth II). He also painted Charles' head from three different positions on one canvas (c1637; Royal Art Collection, Windsor). This triple portrait was intended as a model for the sculptor Bernini, who is said to have exclaimed over Charles' melancholy expression.

Van Dyck's portraits of the English aristocracy revolutionized English painting. He brought to the art of portraiture a wide new range of designs, a rhythmic elegance of composition, and a nervous, flickering beauty of touch. The influence of his brilliant painterly surface and his landscape settings may be seen at its best in full-length portraits by Gainsborough. Van Dyck also did some unusually spontaneous watercolors and drawings of the English countryside. One or two subject paintings from his late period survive; the delicate voluptuousness and light coloring of the *Cupid and Psyche* (c1639–40; Collection of H.M. Queen Elizabeth II) seem to anticipate the Rococo.

Further reading. Cust, L. *Anthony van Dyck*, London (1900). Gerson, H. and Kuile, E.H. ter *Art and Architecture in Belgium: 1600–1800*, Harmondsworth (1960). Glück, G. *Rubens, van Dyck, und Ihr Kreis*, Vienna (1933). Jaffé, M. *Van Dyck's Antwerp Sketchbook*, London (1966).

E

Eakins Thomas 1844–1916

Thomas Eakins was possibly the greatest of all American artists. Masterpieces such as *Max Schmitt in a Single Scull* (1871; Metropolitan Museum, New York) mark a high point of psychological realism in 19th-century art, displaying brilliant control over perspective, anatomy, mechanical drawing, and the study of the human form in motion. In all Eakins' art the human figure is central; his composition is enlivened by a use of light that derives from Rembrandt (1606–69) and Velazquez (1599–1660) and yet is wholly personal and American in execution and feeling.

Eakins worked in Philadelphia, where he

Thomas Eakins: Portrait of Louis N. Kenton (The Thinker); oil on canvas; 208×107cm (82×42in); 1900. Metropolitan Museum, New York

studied art at the Pennsylvania Academy of the Fine Arts and anatomy at Jefferson Medical College. From 1866 to 1869 he studied under Jean Léon Gérôme in Paris, and went to Spain to see the works of Velazquez and Ribera. Returning to Philadelphia in 1870, he began a series of family portraits; he also painted scenes of sporting and outdoor life such as *Max Schmitt*. Eakins' second masterpiece, *The Gross Clinic* (1875; Jefferson Medical College, Philadelphia), painted for the Philadelphia Centennial, was rejected for the art exhibition because of its depiction of blood and was shown in the medical section instead.

Eakins was also a great teacher, and the study of the nude was the pivot of his teaching method. He taught at the Pennsylvania Academy of the Fine Arts from 1876, became its head in 1879, and resigned in 1886 because of opposition to his insistence on the total nudity of the model. His students followed him, and he thus became a decisive influence on the realism of the so-called Ash Can School. Eakins' interest in motion led to his making wax and bronze figures to help in compositions such as *The Swimming Hole* (1883; Fort Worth Art Museum). His enquiries paralleled, and were aided by, the photographic studies made by Eadweard Muybridge of the human body and the horse in movement. The climax of Eakins' art was his series of late portraits of artists, musicians, and other prominent figures. The excellence of works like *Mrs Edith Mahon* (1904; Smith College Museum of Art, Northampton, Mass.) elevates Eakins above all his American contemporaries.

Further reading. Goodrich, L. *Thomas Eakins*, Washington, D.C. (1961). Porter, F. *Thomas Eakins*, New York (1959). Siege, T. *The Thomas Eakins Collections: Philadelphia Museum of Art*, Philadelphia, Pa (1978).

Eastlake Charles 1793–1865

The English painter Sir Charles Eastlake was also a scholar and administrator. Born in Plymouth, he trained in London at the Royal Academy Schools and under B.R. Haydon. In Italy from 1816 to 1830, he painted landscapes and genre scenes, and successfully continued these on returning to England. Historical (for example, *The Escape of the Carrara Family*, 1849; Tate

Charles Eastlake: Napoleon on board the "Bellerophon" in Plymouth Sound, 1815; oil on canvas; 259×184cm (102×72in); 1815. National Maritime Museum, Greenwich, London

Gallery, London) and less specific (for example, *Haidée: A Greek Girl*, 1827; Tate Gallery, London) they embody refined sentiment and warm, Venetian-inspired coloring. Eastlake's wide and discriminating knowledge of art brought many professional commitments—Presidency of the Royal Academy, first Directorship of the National Gallery—which he outstandingly fulfilled.

Egas Enrique c1455–c1534

The Spanish architect Enrique Egas was the nephew of Anequin Egas of Brussels and Toledo; he was one of the first architects to give a distinctive character to the Plateresque style. Several attributions to the early years of his career are dubious, but it is certain that between 1499 and 1515 Egas planned and directed the works of the three Royal Hospitals founded by Isabel the Catholic. These were cruciform buildings based on a central chapel, at Santiago de Compostela (1499–1511), Granada (1511), and Toledo (by 1514). He subsequently carried out extensive work in the cathedrals of Toledo and Jaen and designed the Chapel Royal of Granada, the burial place of Ferdinand and Isabella now incorporated in Granada Cathedral.

Eiffel Alexandre-Gustave
1832–1923

A French structural engineer, Alexandre-Gustave Eiffel is famous for the 984 ft (300 m) tower that bears his name. The Eiffel Tower, largely responsible for the integration of steel into the language of architecture, was built for the 1889 Paris Exhibition. It is a masterpiece of intricate rolled iron and steel construction and was greatly admired by later artists and architects for its unsurpassed variety of exciting spatial experiences. It was developed from Eiffel's bridge building in steel lattice-work (Douro Bridge 1877; Garabit viaduct 1880–4), which displays a similar talent for combining technical skill with formal daring. After 1910, Eiffel became a specialist in aerodynamics.

Eilbertus of Cologne *fl. c1220–60*

The goldsmith Eilbertus is known only from an inscription on the base of the portable altar in the Guelph Treasure, now in the Kunstgewerbemuseum, Staatliche Museen, Berlin. The altar, one of the finest examples to survive, is decorated with champlevé enamels on its top and sides. On the top the enamels show scenes from the life of Christ with gilt figures against blue and green backgrounds. Plaques with the 12 apostles surround a transparent rock crystal altar stone mounted in the center over an illumination showing Christ in Majesty, with symbols of the four Evangelists. On the sides standing figures of 18 Old Testament Prophets (one is missing) are shown on a gilt ground in imitation of Byzantine gold cloisonné enameling. The date of the altar is not recorded, but is likely to be between 1130 and 1160. The central illumination is by the same hand as a *Christ in Majesty* in a gospel book from St Vitus, Gladbach, now in the Hessisches Landesmuseum, Darmstadt (Cod. 508), which has been dated to *c*1140.

A number of other goldsmiths' works have been attributed to Eilbertus on the basis of style, including parts of the shrine of St Victor, Xanten (soon after *c*1129) and *The Cardinal Virtues*, a portable altar, also in the Guelph Treasure (Kunstgewerbemuseum, Staatliche Museen, Berlin). His lively, sketchy drawing technique and his fine sense of color were influential both in Rhenish metalwork, and in east German workshops in Hildesheim and Brunswick, throughout the second half of the 12th century.

Eitoku Kano 1543–90

The Japanese painter Kano Eitoku was the son of Kano Naonobu (Shoei) and grandson of Kano Motonobu. He was a pioneer of decorative screen painting of the Momoyama period. The sliding doors of the Jukoin of the Daitokuji Temple, Kyoto, done in 1566 with his father, show the arrival of a bold new talent. Across four doors spreads a gnarled plum tree, overhanging a stream with ducks and rocks of bold triangular shape. There is hardly any background, all attention being on the dynamic shape of the tree. There are touches of color and extensive gold washes. These are in great contrast to his father's gentle landscapes, though they are still in the ink-painting tradition.

His full-scale adoption of gold-leaf backgrounds, which led to the Momoyama style proper, probably came from the influence of the *Tosa* School. They can be seen in the 1574 screens of scenes in Kyoto, where numerous glimpses of the city and its people are seen through gaps in thick, gold-leaf clouds. The logical step from this was a combination of *Kano* brushwork with *Tosa* color and gold. We can see this in the six-fold screens of *c*1582, *Kara-shishi* (Imperial Collection, Tokyo) portraying the two lion-dogs, peace and dignity, and *Cypress Trees* (Tokyo National Museum). This is a masculine style of pure decoration, which must have been used in the Azuchi Castle (now destroyed) of the dictator Nobunaga. Eitoku was invited to decorate the Castle

Alexandre-Gustave Eiffel: The Eiffel Tower; steel; height 300m (984ft); finished in 1889; Paris

in 1576; it was the first of the huge commissions that are said to have caused his early death from overwork. His great pupil was Kano Sanraku.

Elsheimer Adam 1578–1610

Adam Elsheimer's surviving works are few, but his art opened up new possibilities to the 17th-century painter. He worked mostly for private patrons and painted on copper panels of extremely small dimensions. Minute details of plants and costumes are shown with miraculous precision, yet his works retain the power of large-scale art. He brought a fresh simplicity and truth to landscape painting, and he depicted the moods of nature, whether idyllic or dramatic, as reflecting a human emotion. Revolutionary in his use of light, he studied the natural effects of sun and moon, fires and torchlight, and the mysterious shadows cast in dark interiors by oil lamp and candle. He brought to the interpretation of biblical and mythological scenes a tenderness, intimacy, and directness that leads to Rembrandt.

Elsheimer was born in Frankfurt am Main and probably studied under the local painter Philipp Uffenbach. His roots are in German art; his treatment of landscape evolves from the work of artists of the Danube school, and his tenebrism is indebted to Altdorfer's nocturnal world. His figure-style is based on Schongauer and Dürer.

In 1599 he arrived in Venice where he worked with the group of artists influenced by the German painter Hans Rottenhammer. *The Baptism* (National Gallery, London) shows how he responded to the complex rhythms, glowing colors, and rich draperies of Bassano and Veronese. By 1600 he was in Rome, where he became famous for his rendering of night scenes and use of several sources of illumination. *The Burning of Troy* (Alte Pinakothek, Munich) and *St Paul on Malta* (National Gallery, London) explore the dramatic potential of flood and fire, while recording the events with deeply human realism. In *St Paul on Malta* shipwrecked travelers cluster naked around fires and attempt to dry their clothes; his narrative style avoids the grandiloquent and depends on vivid detail.

Elsheimer's best documented work was a seven-part house-altar of *The Story of the True Cross* (c1603–5) once owned by the Grand Duke of Tuscany (panels now in

Adam Elsheimer: St Paul on Malta; oil on copper; 17×21cm (7×8in); c1600. National Gallery, London

the Städelsches Kunstinstitut and in the Städtische Galerie Liebighaus, both in Frankfurt am Main). The scenes are presented with touching realism.

Elsheimer's late landscapes show a greater emphasis on mood; their delicate light and tender melancholy which so perfectly capture the essence of the story were later to inspire Claude. *The Flight into Egypt* (1609; Alte Pinakothek, Munich) is an astonishingly naturalistic rendering of the Milky Way and the constellations of the northern hemisphere; yet it is also an intensely poetic work in which the tiny figures are sheltered by the dark and infinite spaces of nature.

The painter was a withdrawn character, subject to melancholy. His small output became widely known throughout Europe, however, largely through the engravings of his pupil, Hendrick Goudt. He was admired by the Dutch landscape artists, by Rubens and Rembrandt; Claude understood and developed the idyllic element in Elsheimer's art.

Further reading. Andrews, K. *Adam Elsheimer: Paintings, Drawings, and Prints*, Oxford (1977).

Ensor James 1860–1949

James Ensor was a Belgian painter, printmaker, and writer. He was born in Ostend, of an English father and a Belgian mother; his parents ran a souvenir shop, selling seashells, puppets, toys, and carnival masks. His childhood was unhappy: his businesslike mother dominated his well educated and artistic father, who died of alcoholism in 1887. Ensor studied at the Brussels Academy from 1877 to 1881. His early works—landscapes and still lifes—were influenced by Courbet and Manet, but by 1882 his *Woman Eating Oysters* (Royal Museum of Fine Arts, Antwerp) showed a competent handling of Impressionist light and color.

His submissions to the Brussels Salon of 1883 were rejected: the following year he joined the avant-garde group called Les Vingt. But even there, his most important single work, *The Entry of Christ into Brussels* (Casino Communal, Knokke-le-Zoute, Belgium) was refused in 1888. Ensor imagines Christ's entry on a new Palm Sunday. It becomes an indictment of modern society: Christ, a minute figure in the center mounted on an ass, is dwarfed by a strident mob waving banners; towards the front, faces harden into masks.

Ensor's use of masks continued in a series of paintings attacking the hypocrisy of society. His attacks on the social order were even more vitriolic in a set of etchings of the seven cardinal sins (1892 and 1904). After 1900 his fury subsided; his later pictures were often bland reworkings of his earlier ones. He spent his life in Ostend: some of his seascapes are reminiscent of J.M.W. Turner's late work. An idiosyn-

James Ensor: The Fall of the Rebel Angels; oil on canvas; 108×132cm (43×52in); 1889. Museum of Fine Arts, Antwerp

cratic Expressionist and Symbolist, his work influenced the Dadas and Surrealists and, later, the work of Jean Dubuffet.

Further reading. Croquez, A. *L'Oeuvre Gravé de James Ensor*, Geneva (1947). Haesaerts, P. (trans. Guterman, N.) *James Ensor*, London and New York (1959). Tannenbaum, L. *James Ensor*, New York (1977).

Epiktetos *fl. c*520–490 BC or later

Epiktetos (or Epictetus) was a prolific cup-painter in Athens who also potted some of his own pieces. He frequently signed his name, though his late pieces are unsigned. Like those of his contemporary, Oltos, a number of his early cups are decorated in black-figure technique on the inside, but in red-figure technique on the exterior. One such early cup (British Museum, London; E.3), is signed by Epiktetos as painter, by Hischylos as potter. It has a black-figure mounted horseman on the interior, and on each side of the exterior—between evil-averting eyes—a satyr armed with a shield. Instead of spears, one satyr has a jug, the other a drinking horn. (The basic shape of the cup and the use of eyes were innovations of Exekias.) Epiktetos' drawing is clean and delicate, his figures spruce and energetic. He used only a minimum of internal markings, his drawing relying solely on the sureness of his outlines.

Epiktetos also painted a series of plates which demonstrated his unsurpassed mastery of compositions in a circular field.

Epiktetos: Archer in Scythian Costume; diameter 20cm (8in); late 6th century BC. British Museum, London

One of the most pleasing of these depicts two revelers (British Museum, London; E.137). In the foreground stands a youth playing the pipes, his pipe-case over his arm; in the background a bearded reveler stoops to set on the ground his huge *skyphos*, probably full to the brim with wine, before beginning to dance. Around these graceful figures runs the painter's signature, binding the whole composition together. On his later pieces he displays a knowledge of the new researches of Euphronios and Euthymides but he never lost himself in the exploration of anatomy as they did. It is possible that he continued to paint in his own fashion into the second decade of the 5th century BC, although he does seem to have been influenced by Douris, the most graceful cup-painter of the next generation.

Epimenes *fl. c*500 BC.

Epimenes was a Greek gem-engraver of c500 BC. There is one signed gem in Boston (Museum of Fine Arts), showing a youth restraining a restive horse. A gem in the Metropolitan Museum, New York, with a young archer testing his arrow has been attributed to him; so have another gem in Boston, with an archer crouching to draw his bow, and a gem in Lausanne (private collection) with an athlete. He belongs to a period when the best Archaic work was done on scarab-shaped gems and scaraboids of carnelian or chalcedony, most of it produced in the east Greek world or on the Greek islands. Generally this work presents conventional Archaic motifs rendered with precision and subtlety but without ambitious modeling.

Epimenes is exceptional in attempting miniature sculptural poses; he rendered figures barely $\frac{1}{2}$ in (1 cm) high in intaglio in poses that at that date were rarely attempted by sculptors of larger reliefs. His best are the first two named above, with studies of youths in a twisting three-quarter back view, and the last, where a plausible profile view of a stooping figure is achieved. In many respects these *tours de force* are inappropriate to the scale and nature of the medium, and their sculptural qualities are not seen again in Greek gem-engraving until the 4th century BC.

Epstein Jacob 1880–1959

The sculptor Sir Jacob Epstein was born in New York, the son of Russian-Polish immigrants. He studied briefly in New York at the Art Students League in the mid 1890s, and decided to become a sculptor c1900. In 1902 he moved to Paris, studying at the École des Beaux-Arts and the Académie Julian until 1904. After traveling on the Continent and visiting Florence, he moved to London in 1905. He was commissioned by the architect Charles Holden in 1907 to carve 18 figures for Holden's new British Medical Association building. They were completed in 1908, and caused much controversy in the press. This early incident gave Epstein such notoriety that none of his subsequent public sculptures escaped noisy press comment, which embittered the artist and may have had a bearing on his subsequent development.

In 1910 he received the commission for the tomb of Oscar Wilde; this was eventually erected in the Père-Lachaise cemetery in Paris in 1912, at which time Epstein met Picasso, Brancusi, and Modigliani. In 1913 he settled at Pett Level, Sussex, and during a period of intense activity executed *The Rock Drill* (Tate Gallery, London). This jagged work, which integrates a robot-like figure with a real rock drill, represents Epstein's closest identification with modernism, both in form and conception. While *The Rock Drill* is a unique achievement its origins are in Cubism and Futurism: it has affinities with works by Boccioni, and with the "Ready-mades" of Duchamp which originated in the same year. *The Rock Drill* coincided with the beginnings of Vorticism in England; Epstein contributed drawings to the periodical *Blast*, but did not otherwise align himself with the Vorticists, in spite of similarities of style and attitude. *Rock Drill* was not publicly exhibited until 1915; the following year, a truncated version—minus drill—was exhibited, signaling Epstein's abdication from a pioneering role. Other notable works of this brief phase are *Female Figure* (1913; Tate Gallery, London), *Venus* (1913/14; Yale University), and *Doves* (1915; marble version in Tate Gallery, London).

From the beginning, however, Epstein was a portraitist; throughout his career, and during his spasmodic preoccupation with carving, he sought human likeness in clay. His best portraits, such as *Head of a Baby* (1907 version, Scottish National Gallery of Modern Art, Edinburgh), *Jacob Kramer* (1921; Tate Gallery, London), *Paul Robeson* (1928; Museum of Modern

Jacob Epstein: Oriel; bronze; height 55cm (21in); 1931. Aberdeen Art Gallery

Art, New York), *Ernest Bevin* (1943; Tate Gallery, London) entrap likeness and expression in a mobile and "unfinished" surface. But there are many other commissioned busts that lack vitality.

From c1917 when he began *The Risen Christ* (1919; Scottish National Gallery of Modern Art, Edinburgh), Epstein regularly sculpted thematic works, often with a religious content, either in response to a personal compulsion or as a result of commissions. These figures and groups, particularly the carvings, are often awkward in form while possessing a strong emotional content. For example *Genesis* (1930; private collection) displays a combination of delicacy and primitivism. *Ecce Homo* (1935; Coventry Cathedral) is crude yet dignified. Other works of this kind include *Adam* (1938; Collection of the Earl of Harewood), the massive *Jacob and the Angel* (1940; private collection), and *Lazarus* (1948; New College Chapel, Oxford). Epstein died in London in 1959. To younger English artists such as Henry Moore, Epstein was both the representative of modernism, and also the man who smoothed their path by drawing the fire of the Philistines. His *Madonna and Child* (1950–2; Convent of the Holy Child Jesus, Cavendish Square, London), is one of his finest works.

Further reading. Buckle, R. *Jacob Epstein, Sculptor*, London and New York (1963). Epstein, J. *Epstein, an Autobiography*, London (1963) and New York (1975). Epstein, J. and Haskell, A.L. *Sculpture Speaks: a Series of Conversations on Art*, New York (1976).

Ernest John 1922–

John Ernest was born in Philadelphia in 1922, but since studying sculpture at St Martin's School of Art in London (1952–6) he has lived and worked in Britain, teaching at the Chelsea School of Art. A leading British Constructivist, he has worked in various media, including wood, metal, and formica, since 1956. His work is based partly on conceptual or theoretical models which are usually mathematical, but also on topological figures such as the Möbius strip. Works such as *Relief Painting: Iconic Group Table* (1977; artist's collection) illustrate his continuing interest in the structure of groups.

Ernst Max 1891–1976

The German painter and sculptor Max Ernst was the cofounder of the Cologne branch of Dada, and later became a leading Surrealist artist. He was born in Brühl, near Cologne. His father was a teacher of the deaf and dumb, but also a painter with a local reputation. In 1909, Ernst enrolled in Bonn University where he studied philosophy, psychiatry, and art history, while painting small landscapes in the manner of Van Gogh. By 1910 he had decided to devote himself to painting—though he never received any formal training.

In 1911, Ernst joined *Das Junge Rheinland*, a group of liberally minded painters and poets which included August Macke. Through Macke he became associated with the *Blaue Reiter* group in Munich; in 1913 he exhibited in the *Der Sturm* gallery in Berlin beside Kandinsky, Klee, Macke, Chagall, and Delaunay. His work both at this time and during the First World War, when he served in the artillery, shows the marked influence of these contacts and of Futurism. It is characterized by the qualities that persisted throughout his career: fantastic, dream-like imagery, whimsical humor, and an emphasis on poetic content rather than plastic form.

The war over, Ernst—who was fully informed about the Dada group in Zurich—founded a Dada group in Cologne with the left-wing activist, Johannes Baargeld (1891–1927). They were joined by Arp. In 1919, Ernst published *Fiat Modes*, eight lithographs which, with their imagery of bizarre stuffed dummies and impossible perspective systems, revealed the influence of de Chirico. Among his other Dada works were pictures of unstable semimechanical, semiarchitectural

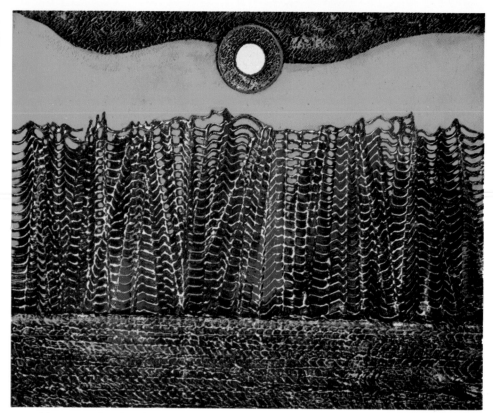

Max Ernst: The Edge of a Forest; oil on canvas; 1926. Private collection

structures, which were created from rubbings taken from large wooden printing type. In his collages, some of which were made in collaboration with Arp, Ernst combined cutouts from wallpaper, advertisements, illustrations in scientific textbooks, and photographs, evoking monstrous and fantastic landscapes, interiors, animals, and anthropomorphic beings.

Following the success among the Surrealist poets of an exhibition of his collages, Ernst moved to Paris in 1922 and immediately began collaborating with the Surrealists. He found himself naturally in sympathy with their interests in hypnotism, dreams, madness, and the subconscious, and he shared their admiration for de Chirico. His paintings of 1921 to 1924, such as *Oedipus Rex* (1922; private collection), are justly described as the first Surrealist paintings, with their irrational juxtapositions of objects, their allusions to dreams, their Freudian-inspired symbolism, and their avoidance of visual "beauty". With de Chirico's Metaphysical paintings, they also provided the basis for the resurgence of illusionism in Surrealist painting in the late 1920s and 1930s.

In 1925, Ernst developed the *frottage* (rubbing) technique. Taking rubbings from such surfaces as floorboards, leaves, and sacking, he found a pictorial equivalent for the automatic-writing procedures of the Surrealist poets, and answered Breton's call for "pure, psychic automatism". A collection of *frottages* was published in 1926 as *Histoire Naturelle*.

Ernst employed a related technique, *grattage* (scraping), in his paintings—placing objects under a canvas covered with layers of paint and scraping the paint from the raised portions. In complete contrast to the precise imagery of his earlier paintings, these are spontaneous, full of movement and flux—vague, expressionistic representations of birds, monsters, horses, forests and flowers, which frequently convey the uninhibited violence and passion that the Surrealists recognized as fundamental to human nature.

In 1929, he published the first of his collage-novels, *La Femme 100 Têtes* (the title is a pun in French: "The hundred-headed Woman" or "The Woman without a Head"). In this and subsequent "novels", such as *Une Semaine de Bonté* ("A Week of Goodness", 1934) Ernst subtly altered popular 19th-century engravings through the collage process, evoking dramas of unparalleled fantasy, and implying that the forces of desire lurk beneath even the most respectable facade. It is in these collage-novels, and in his *frottages*, that Ernst is most original and provocative.

In 1934, Ernst made his first sculptures, carving low-reliefs on large granite stones and creating his first independent sculptures from modified *objets trouvés* such as flowerpots. In the 1930s the imagery of the *grattage* paintings tended to become more clearly defined and the subject matter more menacing: savage monsters and skeletal,

Max Ernst: Stratified Rocks, Nature's Gift of Gneiss Lava, Iceland Moss, two kinds of Lungwort, two kinds of Ruptures of the Perineum, Growths of the Heart (b) the same thing in a well-polished Box somewhat more expensive; anatomical engraving altered with gouache and pencil; 15×21cm (6×8in); 1920. Museum of Modern Art, New York

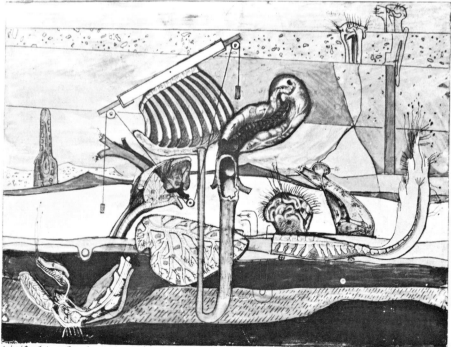

low-lying cities were among Ernst's favorite motifs. At this period he also reverted to conventional oil-painting techniques and an illusionistic manner in, for instance, the *Garden Airplane-Trap* (example in Centre Georges Pompidou, Musée National d'Art Moderne, Paris) series of 1935 and *The Angel of Hearth and Home* (private collection) series of 1937. In works like *Lust for Life* (1936; private collection), Ernst expressed his anxiety about the worsening political situation in images of a ruined Eden, overgrown with rank vegetation and inhabited by predatory creatures.

Interned by the French as an enemy alien at the outbreak of war in 1939, Ernst emigrated to New York in 1941. There, with Breton and Duchamp, he edited a new Surrealist review *VVV*. In the years of the Second World War his work became increasingly rich in color and in detailed, elaborate imagery. He now used to dazzling effect the *decalcomania* technique of the Surrealist painter Oscar Dominguez (1906–57). Ernst created impressions of coral reefs, seabeds, spongy vegetation, and rotting matter, in works like the apocalyptic *Europe after the Rain II* (1940–2; Wadsworth Atheneum, Hartford, Conn.). His most ambitious sculptural project was realized in his house in Sedona, Arizona, both in wall-decorations and in the monumental, freestanding group *Capricorn* (1948; bronze cast; Centre Georges Pompidou, Paris). In its hieratic image of a semihuman, semianimal "royal" family, *Capricorn* epitomizes Ernst's mythic concept of man.

In 1953 Ernst returned to France and in 1958 became a French citizen. His work after the War was varied in style and technique, becoming increasingly bright and lyrical in color and sanguine in mood.

Prolific and eclectic throughout his career, Ernst had the most significant impact on the painters who joined the Surrealist movement after *c*1927. His intelligence and wide culture undoubtedly also contributed to the development and the ever-broadening range of Surrealist artistic and philosophical thinking.

Further reading. Ernst, M. (ed. Motherwell, R.) *Max Ernst: Beyond Painting and Other Writings by the Artist and his Friends*, New York (1948). Russell, J. *Max Ernst: Life and Work*, London and New York (1967). Schneede, U. *The Essential Max Ernst*, London (1972). Waldberg, P. *Max Ernst*, Paris (1958).

Richard Estes: Bus Window; acrylic on canvas; 62×84cm (24×33in); 1969. Neue Galerie, Sammlung Ludwig, Aachen

Estes Richard 1936–

The American Photo-Realist painter Richard Estes was born in Evanston, Illinois. He studied at the Chicago Art Institute (1952–6) and had his first solo exhibition in 1968 in New York, when he first came to public prominence. His paintings of urban scenery are based on color photographs that he takes himself (for example, *Food Shop*, 1967; Museum Ludwig, Cologne). Ever since his most important earlier works such as *Booths* (1967; Haigh Cundey Collection, New York) he has been attracted to images that include multiple reflections in glass and metal. His pictures are usually devoid of dirt and other evidence of people's lives, rather simplified and idealized, even in drug store scenes like *Ice cream* (1976; Allan Stone Gallery, New York).

Further reading. Lucie-Smith, E. *Super Realism*, Oxford (1979). Raymond, H. "The Real Estes", *Art and Artists*, London (August 1974).

Etty William 1787–1849

The English figure-painter William Etty was a baker's son, born in York. After serving a printing apprenticeship, he moved to London in 1805, entering the Royal Academy Schools. On tours abroad he studied Rubens, Titian, and French Academic painting. He exhibited a succession of grand history pictures, such as *The Combat* (1825; National Gallery of Scot-

William Etty: Standard Bearer; oil on panel; 43×34cm (17×13in); c1843. Fairhaven Collection, Anglesey Abbey, Cambridgeshire

land, Edinburgh) and *Venus and her Satellites* (1835; private collection). A more marketable line, however, lay in nude studies, painted freely from the life. By 1847, when he finished his huge *Joan of Arc* triptych, which fetched 2,500 guineas, he had become England's most respected painter.

Euphranor 4th century BC

The Greek sculptor and painter Euphranor came from Isthmia and was a contemporary of Praxiteles. He became an eminent member of the Attic school and carried out a number of public commissions in Athens, including the pictorial decoration of the Stoa of Zeus with historical and mythical scenes, and the cult statue of Apollo Patroos, patron of the city (Agora Museum, Athens). His grandiose style was particularly suitable for the representation of gods, heroes, and battles. He also wrote treatises on colors and on proportions. Among his most famous bronze statues were a *Paris* and the portraits of Philip and Alexander (a copy of his *Alexander* is in Glyptothek, Munich). The bronze *Athena* from Piraeus (National Museum, Athens) has been attributed to him.

Euphronios *fl. c510–465 BC*

Euphronios was a Greek vase-painter whose name is known from about 20 vases. Some of these he signed as painter, the others, which are all later, as potter. His long career thus divides into two

Euphronios: Athenian Cavalryman dressed in a Thessalian Cloak on a red-figure cup; c510 BC. Staatliche Antikensammlungen, Munich

phases: until c500 BC he painted vases, thereafter he fashioned them. In this later period he was apparently the master of a flourishing workshop, able to afford a dedication to Athena, which has been found on the Acropolis.

His earliest works as a painter owe something to the Andokides Painter, but they have none of his mannered elegance. Instead, the figure of a running Amazon on his early cup in Munich (Staatliche Antikensammlungen; Inv. 8953) is so powerfully drawn that the circular frame scarcely seems able to hold her. Euphronios together with two contemporary painters, Euthymides and Phintias, looked beyond the simple silhouette technique of black-figure to a more detailed observation of the human body; they experimented with new poses and views as well as with rudimentary foreshortenings, and are considered pioneers in the development of the art of that period. Euphronios' mature works display inventive iconography and a fascination for the muscles of the body. A *kalyx-krater* in Paris (Louvre; G.103) gives us a splendid study of power and tension in the figures of Herakles and the giant Antaeus (Antaios) wrestling to the death. A fully mature work in New York (Metropolitan Museum) is a *kalyx-krater*, with the winged figures of Sleep and Death lifting the limp body of the hero Sarpedon from the battlefield. There a marvelously constructed composition is matched by remarkable observation of relaxed limbs. On his last preserved work his figures no longer interact. They are a mere lifeless procession, all tension lost.

At this point, when he was perhaps already well into his middle age and surrounded by a new generation of painters, he changed to potting. As a potter, specializing in cups, he continued to work for a further 25 years: his earliest pieces were decorated by Onesimos, and his latest by the Pistoxenos Painter, both of whom were the greatest cup-painters of their time.

Euthymides *fl. c520–500 BC*

Euthymides was a Greek vase-painter who worked in Athens. Along with the other so-called pioneers, Euphronios and Phintias, he experimented with new poses and views of the body which incorporated rudimentary foreshortenings. In an inscription he wrote beside three dancing revelers on an *amphora* in Munich (Staatliche

Antikensammlungen; Inv. 2307), Euthymides boasted that his rival Euphronios had never painted better; the inscription reads simply: "as Euphronios never". More of the lively rapport between the "Pioneers" can be seen on a *hydria* by his friend Phintias (Staatliche Antikensammlungen, Munich; Inv. 2421) who both toasts and depicts him. Euthymides' figures, with their massive chests and shoulders, are like Nestor's heroes of an earlier age. One of his pupils was the Kleophrades Painter who became the greatest painter of large vessels in the next generation. The Berlin Painter also owed much to him.

Eutychides
late 4th–early 3rd century BC

Eutychides, a Greek early Hellenistic sculptor from Sicyon, was a pupil of Lysippos. His art marks an advance in realism as he tried to capture the third dimension and imitate the texture of skin and draperies. His most influential creation was the colossal bronze group the *Tyche* of Antioch, in which Antioch is personified in the figure of Tyche, goddess of Fortune, and its river, the Orontes, is a youth emerging from the ground. The type survives in reduced copies in the Vatican Museums and in private collections: Fortune is a girl with a city-crown, heavily draped; seated on a rock, she leans above the swimming Orontes. Their poses are momentary and characterized by abrupt transitions.

Eworth Hans *fl. 1540–c74*

The portrait painter Hans Eworth was born in Antwerp. He is now identified with the artist who signed himself HE and who worked in England. He is probably the "Jan Eeuworts" listed as a freeman of Antwerp in 1540 and working in England by 1549. Eworth is known to have painted Mary I (notably a portrait in the Royal Museum of Fine Arts, Antwerp) and to have worked for Elizabeth I on court festival designs from 1572 to 1574. He was patronized by both nobility and gentry. Portraits such as that of *Lady Dacre* (National Gallery of Canada, Ottawa) show that his style was derived

Hans Eworth: Portrait of Lady Dacre; oil on panel; 74×58cm (29×23in); 1540. National Gallery of Canada, Ottawa

from the work of Holbein the Younger, his predecessor in favor at the royal court. The allegorical portrait of *Sir John Luttrell* (Courtauld Institute Galleries, London) is a unique example of contemporary French influence on his work.

Exekias *fl. c545–530 BC*

Exekias was an Athenian black-figure painter and potter. His name appears on 12 vases and fragments, usually as potter, but also on two *amphorae* as both potter and painter. He decorated a wide variety of shapes, and can probably be credited with the invention of the "eye-cup" and *kalyx-krater*.

His earliest vase is a neck-*amphora* in Berlin, signed in his meticulous handwriting as potter and painter. The *amphora* has the same compact and well-proportioned body as the powerful Herakles who wrestles with the Nemean Lion on the obverse. Herakles and his nervous nephew Iolaos are painted with steady, careful brush strokes whose sharp edges and deep sheen recall bronze statues. Equally clean and metallic are the slowly winding spirals and friezes of floral ornament above and below the main scene. The reverse shows two armed warriors standing quietly by their handsome steeds: horses and humans alike are given names. Exekias' devotion to horses was a lifelong passion, equaled only by the consummate skill with which he drew them. These early horses have all the dignity and good manners of his later thoroughbreds, and a statuesque elegance reminiscent of Archaic horses in marble and bronze.

A *kylix* in the Staatliche Antikensammlungen, Munich, signed by Exekias as potter, represents a new form of wine-cup, perhaps invented by this artist. He departs from Athenian tradition by filling the interior with a single picture, unrestricted by groundlines or borders: Dionysos reclining in his vine-laden ship sails freely across a sea alive with dolphins. The outside is decorated with scenes of combat which are forced around and under the handles by a broad, decorative scheme, new to Attic cups: graceful eyebrows, a nose and two large eyes. An apparent parody of the "eye-cup" by Exekias' rival, Amasis, suggests that the shape of the cup and the ornamental eyes were regarded as the property of Exekias. Under each handle sits a defecating hound and between them an enormous siren whose body consists of

Exekias: Dionysos on his Vine-laden Ship; black-figure painting on a kylix; c530 BC. Staatliche Antikensammlungen, Munich

the Exekian eye. Exekias lashed back at his rival on two vases: a neck-*amphora* (British Museum, London) with Memnon and his black squires, one of whom is named Amasis; and an *amphora* (Philadelphia Museum of Art) with Ajax lifting the dead Achilles, while a Greek pursues a scrawny black man who is named Amasos. Such amicably biting gestures anticipate the friendly jabs and greetings written on the vases of Euthymides, Phintias, and other red-figure "pioneers".

One of his finest works is the *amphora* in the Vatican Museums, Rome, signed as potter and painter. Achilles and Ajax sit absorbed in their board-game, in much the same composition as Cézanne's *Card Players* (c1890–2; Collection Pellerin, Paris). Their elaborately engraved hair, beards, and cloaks reveal a master in full control of his difficult technique. The heroes are thoughtful, well-bred men with the lordly bearing of Olympians. The mood of the picture exemplifies Exekias' preference for quiet, reflective figures en-

gaged in unhurried activity—a rare and unusually "classical" preference, in stark contrast to the lively action scenes beloved of Archaic painters.

The solemn mourners on his funeral plaques (Staatliche Museen, Berlin) show a rare delicacy of emotion that was seldom equaled in Greek painting. And his *Ajax* (Musée des Beaux-Arts et d'Archéologie, Boulogne)—who is depicted slowly and carefully fixing the suicidal sword in the earth—is portrayed with a grave inwardness, perhaps reflecting the painter's own personality.

Exekias represents black-figure painting at its finest hour. To a spirit of great sensitivity he joined faultless technical control, revealing to his contemporaries and all who followed that the upper limits of black-figure work were far higher than any of them had ever imagined. His latest paintings show no sign of influence from the new red-figure technique, and so his brief but brilliant career must have come to an end shortly before 530 BC.

Eyck brothers

14th and 15th centuries

The brothers Hubert (1366/70–1426) and Jan (c1390–1441) van Eyck were the founders of the Flemish school of painting. Jan van Eyck was undoubtedly the most famous painter of his age; his paintings broke completely with the art of the Middle Ages. His supreme excellence lay in his power to represent the visible world by the patient observation of an endless variety of detail. Unlike his Italian contemporaries, van Eyck had no knowledge of the laws of mathematical perspective, nor of anatomy. It is his study of the fall of light that gives reality to the objects and unifies the scene. His creation of a convincing space was achieved empirically. A feeling for the beauty of the surface and texture of things, of flowers, rocks, jewels, fabrics, and metals, remained characteristic of Flemish art. His technical mastery was outstanding and he perfected the art of oil painting: by enabling the artist to apply the paint in transparent layers, the new technique gave colors a fresh intensity and made possible sparkling highlights and subtle half-tones.

Jan's relationship to his brother, Hubert, is one of the most difficult problems in the history of art. In 1823 an inscription on the *Adoration of the Lamb* altarpiece (St-Bavon Cathedral, Ghent) was published. The altarpiece was the most renowned of all early Flemish paintings. The inscription—partly indecipherable and postdating the execution of the work—began a controversy, which still continues, about the share each of the two artists may have had in the painting of the altarpiece. It reads:

> ... ubertus eyck maior quo nemo repertus
> incepit pondusq johannes arte secundus
> ... iodici vyd prece fretus
> versu sexta mai vos collocat acta tueri

This may be translated:

> The painter Hubrecht Eyck, than whom none was greater, began this work, which his brother Jan, who was second to him in art, completed at the behest of Jodoc Vijdt, and which he invites you by this verse to contemplate on 6 May [1432].

Jan van Eyck: the Annunciation; oil on panel transferred to canvas; 93×36cm (37×14cm). National Gallery of Art, Washington, D.C.

The date is given by a chronogram in the last line.

We know almost nothing about Hubert (or Hubrecht); a 16th-century tradition suggests that both artists probably came from Maaseyck in Limborg. Their birth dates are unknown. Hubert died in 1426; no separate works can be attributed to him on external evidence. He is usually identified with a painter mentioned, in documents in Ghent, in 1425 and 1426 as "Hubrecht", "Ubrechts" etc.

By contrast Jan's career is well documented, and his artistic activity is known from a series of signed and dated works from 1432 to 1441. From 1422 to 1425 he worked at The Hague as *peintre et valet de chambre* of John Count of Holland. On John's death he entered the service of Philip, Duke of Burgundy. Philip also employed him as confidential agent and in 1426, 1428, and 1436 he was sent to Portugal to negotiate the Duke's marriage with the Infanta Isabella. He worked at Lille and Bruges and was patronized by the Burgundian court and by Italian merchants at Bruges.

The *Adoration of the Lamb* is the major achievement of 15th-century Flemish art and its new realism of figure and landscape mark the break with the art of the 14th century. This large polyptych, which consists of 20 panels, shows three rows of figures when the shutters are closed. At the top are figures of prophets and sibyls. Beneath them, spreading across four panels, is an Annunciation, set in a room with a view of a Flemish town from the window. The bottom row shows the donors, Josse or Jodocus Vijdt and his wife; and between them, in grisaille paintings that imitate stone sculpture, are the figures of St John the Baptist and St John the Evangelist. The color is a brownish monochrome though the portraits are in scarlet and green.

The brilliance of the interior is a startling contrast. The central panel of the lower row shows an Adoration of the Lamb. Processions of worshipers advance across a flowery meadow towards the altar of the Lamb. Before the Lamb is the Fountain of life, symbol of Redemption, and above is the Holy Dove. Twelve prophets gather on the left, behind them the Patriarchs. The Apostles are on the right, and behind them the martyrs. Further groups of saints gather in the distance. In the four wings on either side of the central panel the procession continues. The Just Judges and the Warriors of Christ move in from the left, the Holy Hermits and the Holy Pilgrims from the right. In this row the figures are small and the five panels unified by one continuous landscape; in the distance are the spires of the Heavenly City.

In the upper row the figures are larger. In the center is God the Father, to the left and right the Virgin and St John the Baptist. On either side of them are angels making music, and on the outermost panels Adam and Eve.

In this interior the new technique of oil painting may be seen in all its splendor. The painting is deeply religious and its beauties seem a paean of praise to the glory of God. In the Paradisal landscape of the lower row the colors are brilliant, scarlets and blues against a startlingly bright green ground; there is a rich profusion of lovingly observed plants and trees, and wonderful effects of light falling on distant meadows and Gothic towers. The plants can all be identified, and the palms, cypresses, and orange trees must postdate Jan's journey to Portugal. Several of the buildings can also be named. The Knights and the Judges are richly dressed in shining armor and with decorated bridles; in the upper row jeweled crowns, robes, and lavish brocades create a still richer effect.

The love of delicate detail and gorgeous costumes and jewelry is already present in Gothic art—we are reminded of the early-15th-century *Très Riches Heures du Duc de Berry* by the Limburg brothers (Musée Condé, Chantilly). But Jan's observation is more scientific and his study of light gives the landscape a new unity. The nude figures of Adam and Eve create a startling contrast to the more hieratic figures in the center of the upper row. The nude is represented with an entirely new and almost harsh realism. Unlike the other figures in that row they were designed to be seen from below, and Adam's foot seems to jut out of the niche in which he stands.

No opinion has been generally accepted as to how much of the altarpiece Hubert had completed on his death in 1426. There are certainly discrepancies of style within the work as a whole. The most widely held view is that Jan, between 1430 and 1432, repainted an altarpiece that had been designed and partly completed by Hubert before 1426. Most authorities assign wholly to Jan the most "advanced" parts of the altarpiece, the Adam and Eve and the beautiful rendering of atmospheric perspective in the upper part of the landscape in the lower row.

After the Ghent altarpiece we have a series of signed and dated works by Jan. His earliest portrait, dated 1432, is *A Young Man* or *Timotheos* (National Gallery, London); *The Man in a Turban* (National Gallery, London) was painted in the following year. The *Young Man* is shown against a plain background and behind a stone parapet; he holds a script in his hand. His plain features are un-idealized; his face is turned towards a gentle light that falls from the left and models the features with great subtlety. The stone parapet, which is inscribed with the words *Leal Souvenir* ("loyal remembrance") and with the signature and date, is one of the marvels of Jan's art; the surface of the stone, cracked and pitted, is faithfully recorded. These works mark the beginnings of modern portraiture. The three-quarter view is new; so is the detailed description of the face—the wrinkles of the skin, the texture of the hair, the light in the eyes. The *Man in a Turban* looks out of the painting towards the spectator, thus creating a sense of lifelike immediacy; it is possibly the first instance in the history of painting of this connective gaze, and it has been suggested that the painting may be a self-portrait.

The most famous of Jan's portraits is the *Arnolfini Wedding* (1434; National Gallery, London). This shows the marriage ceremony between Giovanni Arnolfini and his wife Giovanna Cenami; the vows are taken within their own room, surrounded by their own objects; the marriage was witnessed by van Eyck himself, whose reflection appears in a convex mirror hanging on the back wall. His presence is confirmed by the inscription on the wall over the mirror, which reads, "Johannes de eyck fuit hic" ("was here") 1434. The small scale of the painting gives it a sense of magic. The nuptial chamber is full of objects—a small dog, cast-off shoes, fruit, a chandelier, a bed, a chair-back topped by a statuette of St Margaret—several of which contain symbolic references to marriage. There are beautifully controlled effects of light on the chandelier and on the wall. The technical supremacy of the convex mirror is a *tour de force*; around it are 10 small round panels showing, in minute detail, scenes from the Passion of Christ. This detailed description of a private and domestic scene, the creation of a convincing space, and the observation of

Jan van Eyck: St Donation, a detail of the Madonna with Canon van der Paele; oil on panel; full size 122×157cm (48×62in); 1436. State Museum, Bruges

the fall of light lead on to 17th-century Dutch genre painting. Jan van Eyck's later dated portraits include the *Jan de Leeuw* (1436; Kunsthistorisches Museum, Vienna) and the *Margaretha van Eyck* (1439; State Museum, Bruges). With these may be associated the *Portrait of Cardinal Albergati* (Kunsthistorisches Museum, Vienna).

In the religious paintings of the mid 1430s, the *Madonna with Canon van der Paele* (State Museum, Bruges) and the *Dresden Triptych* (1437; Gemäldegalerie Alte Meister, Dresden), van Eyck was concerned with the problem of setting figures in space, and with the splendor of effects of light and surface texture. The former work shows the Virgin enthroned within the apse of a Romanesque church. The donor, one of van Eyck's most powerful portraits, kneels on the right with St George; on the left is St Donation. The massive figures are pushed back in space and the composition has a classical severity. There is an astonishing clarity, sharpness of detail, and contrast of textures—of carpets, tiles, brocades, armor, glass, and stone. The figures have a strange immobility; the total effect is calm and remote, and this quality is characteristic of Jan's mature work. His later religious works, *St Barbara* (1437; Royal Museum of Fine Arts, Antwerp) and *The Madonna at the Fountain* (1439; Royal Museum of Fine Arts, Antwerp), tend to be less realistic, simpler, and more restrained. The unsigned *Madonna of Chancellor Rolin* (1435; Louvre, Paris) contains one of van Eyck's most wonderful landscapes, remarkable for its unparalleled breadth of vision. A river crossed by a bridge leads the eye from a town in the foreground through an extensive sweep of rich countryside to the blue of distant hills.

The van Eycks' early style is highly controversial. The problem works consist of five or six paintings and the illuminations in the Hours of Turin. The *Three Maries at the Sepulchre* (Boymans-van Beuningen Museum, Rotterdam) is usually agreed to be an Eyckian picture, often attributed to Hubert. In 1902 a group of miniatures were discovered in the Turin library which formed part of the Hours of Turin. A further series were found in the Biblioteca Trivulziana, Milan (now in the Museo Civico, Turin). Turin library and the miniatures were destroyed by fire in 1904, but the brief reappearance of these works had started a long argument as to their authorship. The manuscripts may almost certainly be dated to 1416 and anticipate in an astonishing way later developments in 15th-century art. They have a new feeling for light and atmosphere and show an ambitious attempt to set figures in space. It is possible that they show the Eyckian style as it moves towards the Ghent altarpiece. Some authorities have attributed them to Hubert on the grounds that they show a concentration on figures in action that we do not associate with Jan. Others have suggested the possibility of collaboration; others, that they represent the early style of the young Jan.

The van Eycks will doubtless continue to be the focus of controversies. Yet their supreme position in the history of Flemish art will remain unchallenged. All later Flemish artists were affected by them and later in the 15th century their achievement began to influence artists of the Italian Renaissance.

Further reading. Baldass, L. *Jan van Eyck*, London (1952). Hughes, R. and Faggin, G. *The Complete Paintings of the van Eycks*, London (1970). Whinney, M. *Early Flemish Painting*, London (1968).

F

Fabré Jaime *fl. c1300–39*

Jaime Fabré was a Spanish architect. A native of Palma in Majorca, he was appointed in 1317 as architect to Barcelona Cathedral, where work had begun in 1296 to a plan based on the plan of the cathedral at Narbonne. By 1321 Fabré was in charge at Narbonne itself and also at Gerona Cathedral, another Narbonne-influenced design which had been started c1312. However, Barcelona differs from Narbonne in not following the usual two tier, basilican spatial arrangement. Instead the heights of chapels and aisles are staggered in a way that recalls Toledo Cathedral, which was begun before 1224. The circular clerestory windows and low triforium derive from the inner aisles at Toledo. This so-called "spatial" Gothic achieved its finest expression at S. Maria del Mar in Barcelona, a church begun in 1323 by Berenguer de Montagut and Ramón Despuig.

Fabritius Carel   1622–54

The Dutch painter Carel Fabritius was the most gifted of Rembrandt's pupils, and is historically important as a link between Rembrandt and Vermeer. After his apprenticeship in the early 1640s he followed Rembrandt in attempts at dramatic biblical narratives, also employing something of the freedom of his teacher's application of paint. Later, after settling in Delft, he turned instead to portraiture, genre, and still-life painting. His colors became paler and cooler, and he increasingly stressed purely pictorial effects rather than the projection of a particular mood. This is evident in his portraits (where personality is partially subordinated to the organization of shapes, colors, and tones). It is perhaps even more apparent in such paintings as *The Goldfinch* (1654; Royal Museum of Art, Mauritshuis, The Hague): a superb demonstration of balance in an asymmetrical composition.

Fabritius' interest in the abstract components of a design, the architectural character of some of his compositions, his study of the fall of light on objects, and of optical problems in general all reappear in the work of Vermeer—who was probably his pupil and certainly owned some of his

Carel Fabritius (attrib.): Portrait of a Young Man; oil on canvas; 63 × 51cm (25 × 20in). Alte Pinakothek, Munich

pictures. Very few of Fabritius' paintings have survived; the Delft gunpowder factory explosion that caused his early death probably also destroyed many of his pictures.

Falconet Étienne-Maurice 1716–91

The Parisian sculptor Falconet was trained first by his uncle, and then—like his later rival, Jean-Baptiste Pigalle—at the studio of Jean-Baptiste Lemoyne (1704–78). He was accepted at the Académie Royale in 1744 on the strength of his plaster model for *Milo of Crotona* (marble version, 1754; Louvre, Paris). From 1745 to 1765 he exhibited regularly at the Salon, and in 1783 became Professor at the Académie— a rare honor for a sculptor of that period.

Falconet was the favorite sculptor of Mme de Pompadour, mistress of Louis XV, and for her he created *L'Amour Menaçant* and *La Baigneuse* in 1757 (both

Étienne-Maurice Falconet: Louis XV; biscuit porcelain; height 33cm (13in). Musée Lambinet, Versailles

Henri Fantin-Latour: Roses and a Glass Jug; oil on canvas; 44×56cm (17×22in); 1889. Musée des Beaux-Arts, Lyons

now in the Louvre, Paris). The former was conceived in a Rococo spirit, while the latter had a more classical tendency. Through the influence of his patroness he was appointed that year as Director of the Sèvres Porcelain Factory, where many of his boudoir pieces, usually soft female nudes, were reproduced as statuettes in biscuit (unglazed porcelain), a recently-popularized genre.

The ambitious Falconet never actually secured a commission from Louis XV. In 1766, he was working on a large-scale marble of *St Amboise* destined for the Invalides, but since destroyed. Diderot offered him Catherine II's commission for a bronze *Equestrian Statue to Peter the Great* at St Petersburg. He finished this powerful and highly original piece in 1769, casting it himself, but he left Russia before the unveiling, dissatisfied with his fees.

He was a thinker, and unusually literate for a sculptor of the time. In 1761 he published *Réflexions sur la Sculpture*, ad-

vocating realism and modernity as against servile copying from ancient prototypes. He himself never visited Italy.

Fan K'uan *fl.* 990–1030

The Chinese painter Fan K'uan came from Hua Yuan; he lived a solitary life, roaming at first between Loyang and Yung but later living in T'ai-hua in Chung-nan. He is described as a man of stern and old-fashioned manner and appearance, a rustic and Taoist. Yet he seems to have had a warm character for which he was much respected. Fan K'uan apparently followed the Chinese artistic tradition, first studying Li Ch'eng closely and then developing his own style. The remark attributed to him, and echoed by many Chinese artists, sums up his attitude: "My predecessors have not yet tried to seize things as they really are; surely it is better to take the things themselves than men as teachers, and a still better teacher than material objects is the

heart". This order of study is recommended repeatedly, but artists are always told to follow a thorough grounding in the techniques of painting by study of the Old Masters. Most of Fan K'uan's own painting seems to have been of classical mountain landscape. He apparently mastered the structure of his subject and then painted directly without self-conscious regard for brush stroke.

Fantin-Latour Henri 1836–1904

The French painter Ignace Henri Jean Joseph Théodore Fantin-Latour was born in Grenoble and worked in Paris. His most ambitious works were allegories inspired by his love of the music of Berlioz and Wagner, with elusive figures evoked in feathery brush strokes achieving a Romantic rather than Impressionist haze. These paintings are an important link between the late Delacroix and the younger French Symbolist painters. His commercial success was gained by flower painting, a genre he found less congenial than the allegories. His flower pieces gave full scope to his skillful control of tone. Like his friend J.A.M. Whistler, he achieved this by the use of very thin paint which exposed the texture of the canvas.

Feininger Lyonel 1871–1956

The American painter Lyonel Feininger was born in New York. He studied at the Hamburg School of Applied Arts, then at the Berlin Academy, and later in Paris. He worked successfully as a cartoonist for some years, but by 1909 was concentrating on painting. In 1911, during a visit to Paris, he discovered Cubism and began to use its formal qualities for his expressive aims. He met members of *Die Brücke* Expressionist group in 1912. Feininger has sometimes been categorized as an Expressionist, but his paintings are cooler in

Robert Feke: The Family of Isaac Royall; oil on canvas; 143×197cm (56×78in); 1741. Harvard University, Cambridge, Mass.

Lyonel Feininger: Yellow Street II; oil on canvas; c1917. The Montreal Museum of Fine Arts

color than most Expressionist works; they are also more contemplative in content, dealing with subjects like churches and the sea. He was appointed to the Bauhaus staff on its establishment in 1919, and directed its print workshop until 1923. He later joined the exhibiton group "Blue Four", with Kandinsky, Klee, and Jawlensky. Feininger returned to America in 1938.

Feke Robert *fl.* 1724–c67

Robert Feke was an American portrait-painter who worked in the Colonial style. He has been described as the best American-born artist before J.S. Copley (1738–1815). Historically, Feke is a somewhat shadowy figure. The facts about his life are very sparse: he is thought to have been a mariner, and to have made several visits to England. Born between 1705 and 1710, he was, by 1741, an established portraitist based in Boston. His *Family of Isaac Royall* (1741; Harvard University, Cambridge, Mass.) is one of his earliest best-known works. He was married in 1742. In succeeding years he traveled between Newport and Philadelphia and disappeared from accounts until his death in Bermuda or the West Indies. His portraits are the first in the art history of the U.S.A. to achieve something that belongs distinctly to that nation.

Ferrari Gaudenzio *c1475–1546*

The Italian painter and sculptor Gaudenzio Ferrari was a native of Valduggia. He worked in Piedmont and Lombardy, where his major works are still to be found. Between 1523 and 1528 he worked at the Sacre Monte in Varallo (where 45 chapels are grouped on a hill) where he did frescoes and sculptures in the chapels of the Crucifixion and Adoration of the Magi. His combination of fresco and painted terracotta resembles a *tableau vivant* and is reminiscent of German Gothic sculpture. His other major works are in S. Cristoforo, Vercelli (1529–32) and in Saronno (1534–6). In his painting, Ferrari reveals the influence of both Leonardo da Vinci and Perugino.

Ferrer Bassa *c1290–1348*

Born at Sasgaioles, near Barcelona, Ferrer was the effective founder of a tradition of Catalan painting. Although it was at times subject to external pressures and international fashions, Catalan painting preserved its individuality from the early 14th century until the death of Jaime Huguet. The first phase of this tradition, represented at its best by Ferrer, was characterized by the combination of personal originality with marked Italian—particularly Sienese—influence. This had reached Spain by way of Mallorca but also through Simone Martini and the School of Avignon. By 1320 Ferrer was painting at the court of Jaime II where he also seems to have taken part in other activities. His association with the court continued for most of his working life: he subsequently worked for Alfonso IV to illuminate the *Usages of Barcelona and the Customs of Cataluña*—the so-called *Usajes*; the work has not survived.

In 1344 Ferrer was appointed painter to the court of Pedro IV, a post that carried with it the opportunity to travel in the royal service. Some time after 1335, possibly during this period of official travel, he went to Avignon, thereby fortifying the connection between Cataluña and the Sienese School. In 1344 he apparently painted the principal altarpiece of the Chapel Royal of Barcelona; this work was replaced in 1464, at the order of D. Pedro, Condestable of Portugal, by one painted by Jaime Huguet.

In 1344 Ferrer began the only work—fortunately an extensive one—that has survived to the present day: the decoration of the chapel of S. Miguel in the Convent

Gaudenzio Ferrari: The Flight into Egypt; fresco; 267×130cm (105×51in); c1511–13. S. Maria delle Grazie, Varallo

of the Nuns of St Clare at Pedralbes, near Barcelona. This is a narrative cycle of paintings with a largely didactic purpose, in accordance with the precepts of St Bernard on the education of the faithful. It shows the life of the Virgin Mary and the life and Passion of Christ. Though the effects of Florentine and Sienese painting (particularly of Giotto and Duccio) are clear, Ferrer's work is by no means without originality. The arrangement of figures

in formalized rows and the diagonal, slightly sly lines of the faces are unmistakably Sienese. In common with almost all Italo-Catalan painting, the series shows little interest in effects of depth, and the backgrounds are perfectly flat. The comfortable grace and the careful detail of the Sienese style are absent: greater simplicity is reinforced by a tension that sometimes characterizes later Spanish art almost to the point of melodrama. The faces have a harshness of expression amounting at times to distortion which suggests, if not outward beauty, a considerable inner turbulence.

As the most obvious Italian influences died away, or yielded before the pressure of new fashions, the sense of drama and spiritual tension introduced by Ferrer persisted. His immediate followers, before the weight of the International Gothic style was fully felt, were Ramón Destorrents and the Serra brothers.

Feti Domenico _c1589–1624_

The Italian painter Domenico Feti (or Fetti) was born in Rome, where he was later taught by Cigoli. He was influenced by the realism and dramatic lighting of Caravaggio and his followers, but he did not himself become a Caravaggist. The work of Elsheimer, who was a painter of tiny highly realistic landscapes, also made an impact on him. His patron was Cardinal Ferdinando Gonzaga; on becoming Duke of Mantua in 1613, Gonzaga left Rome taking Feti with him to be his court painter.

In Mantua Feti became closely acquainted with the work of Rubens, who had been court painter to Vincenzo Gonzaga from 1600 to 1608, and also with the work of the Venetians, whose paintings were well represented in the ducal collection. Feti's best known pictures date from the beginning of his stay in Mantua. The combination of influences from Elsheimer and Rubens led Feti to develop a highly individual style of genre painting which was both rich in color and subtle in tone, and in which the action often conveyed melancholy. _The Pearl of Great Price_ (William Rockhill Nelson Gallery, Kansas City) is such an example. Small in size, it is one of a set of 12 paintings of parables made for Ferdinando Gonzaga; it illustrates the parable in Matthew 13 and shows a market scene with dealers haggling over pearls. Other genre scenes are more explicitly tragic, for example, _The Blind Leading the Blind_ (Barber Institute of Fine Arts, Birmingham, England). In 1621 Feti moved to Venice, and lived there until his death.

Domenico Feti: The Flight into Egypt; oil on canvas; 73×82cm (29×32in); c1621–3. Kunsthistorisches Museum, Vienna

Feuerbach Anselm 1829–80

The German painter Anselm Feuerbach studied from 1845 to 1848 at the Academy in Düsseldorf, then the center of German Neoclassicism. A brief stay in Antwerp (1850–1) taught him the importance of realism; but it was between the years 1851 and 1854 in Paris, where he attended Thomas Couture's studio, that he achieved a balance between the intellect and the senses. This ideal, dear to his heroes Goethe and Schiller, seemed embodied in the works of the Italian Renaissance masters. When he moved to Rome in 1856 he, like other Deutsch-Römer (German-Romans), copied many of them for Count Schack. His art was profoundly influenced by this experience. He treated Classical subjects and portraits with increasing simplicity of line and color (usually subdued and chalky). His paintings often express a Roman *gravitas* through their monumental poses and frieze-like compositions (for example, *Iphigenie*, 1862; Hessisches Landesmuseum, Darmstadt).

Filarete c1400–69

The Florentine sculptor and architect Antonio di Pietro Averlino was known as Filarete. He was trained under Ghiberti, a degenerate version of whose relief-style he used in the bronze door commissioned from him by Pope Eugenius IV for St Peter's in Rome (1433–45). Accused of stealing sacred relics and expelled from Rome by the Pope, Filarete traveled to northern Italy and in 1451 became architect to his protector Francesco Sforza, for whom he designed the Ospedale Maggiore in Milan (1456). It was to Sforza that he later dedicated his *Trattato d'Architettura* (1461–4), a diverting architectural treatise cast in the form of a project for the construction of an ideal city, Sforzinda, and its port, Plusiapolis.

Finiguerra Maso 1426–64

Maso Finiguerra was a Florentine goldsmith. According to Vasari, he was the inventor of engraving, but the claim has no documentary proof. However, his fame as a craftsman in niello—a process very similar to engraving—suggests that the ascription to him of several engravings is probably correct. These, usually dated to the 1460s, are done in the so-called Fine Manner: for example, the series of *Planets* (British Museum, London). In 1463 Finiguerra was commissioned to make drawings for *intarsia* (wood inlay) panels for the north sacristy of Florence Cathedral. These drawings (now in the Museo dell'Opera del Duomo, Florence) are his only positively authenticated works.

Fischer J.M. 1691–1766

The prolific South German architect Johann Michael Fischer claimed responsibility for no less than 32 churches, 23 monasteries, and "very many" secular works, according to his tombstone. He ranks with Balthasar Neumann among the greatest of the Germanic architects of the 18th century.

Born in the Upper Palatinate, the son of a municipal master mason, Fischer worked as a foreman in Moravia (c1715–16) before moving on to Munich. There he worked for Johann Mayr, mason to the city, before becoming a master mason himself in 1722. Thus at the outset of his long career Fischer was familiar with a wide range of contemporary architecture including the Austrian Baroque and, probably, the buildings of G. Santini and C. Dientzenhofer in Bohemia and Moravia.

His first independent commission was for the reconstruction of the choir of the abbey church of Niederaltaich (begun 1724). In the church of St Anna-am-Lehel in Munich (begun 1727) Fischer clearly reveals the impact of the designs of C. Dientzenhofer (for example Obořiště and Smiřice). Unfortunately the Asams' decorations in St Anna were destroyed in 1944.

In the abbey church at Osterhoven (1727–8) the Bohemian elements are more explicit and the convex gallery fronts are contrasted with the concave faces of the piers. This creates an undulating effect inspired, no doubt, by C. Dientzenhofer's nave of sv. Mikuláš, Malá Strana, in Prague. Again the immensely rich decoration was executed by the Asams (1728–35). In the abbey church of Berg-am-Laim, on the outskirts of Munich, Fischer was able to explore the possibilities of interlinked centrally-planned spaces on a considerable scale (1738–42).

Fischer's role as architect was generally confined to the structure of the building and during the 1720s and early 1730s he usually worked with the Asams as decorators. In the mid 1730s he turned instead to the teams of Wessobrunn *stuccatori* and painters working in the Rococo style. His designs for the abbey church at Zwiefalten (1744–65) were circumscribed by the reuse of existing foundations. The length of the church is undeniably excessive, but the stuccos by J.M. Feichtmayr and the swirling frescoes of F.J. Spiegler are highly successful.

Less rigid limitations applied to the huge abbey church of Ottobeuren where Fischer, from 1748, was again able to explore the possibilities of a large central vaulted space with equal emphasis laid on the nave and choir. The team of J.M. Feichtmayr moved on from Zwiefalten to decorate Ottobeuren together with the painters F.A. and J.J. Zeiller. The centralizing tendencies in Fischer's designs reach their most extreme in the abbey church of Rott-am-Inn (1759–63), where the interior is dominated by the great central octagon with its fresco by M. Günther. The clarity of the architectural forms takes on a new strength through the reduced amount of Rococo stucco work.

Fischer von Erlach J.B. 1656–1723

The first major architect active in central Europe since the Middle Ages, Johann Bernhard Fischer von Erlach was the son of a sculptor in Graz, Austria. He left his homeland in 1674 to study for 12 years in Italy. During this period, in Rome and Naples, he continued to work as a sculptor and two medals executed by him then are known. After his return to Austria he submitted designs for the decoration of the Mausoleum in Graz (c1687). These were unsuccessful; but by 1690 he was well established in Vienna, and designed two triumphal arches for the entry of Joseph I. These introduced the ideas of the Roman High Baroque into Vienna. In 1705 he was appointed Chief Imperial Inspector of all Buildings for Court and Festivities, a post he retained until his death.

Fischer von Erlach's sculptural work on the Pest Column in Vienna was done during the years 1687 to 1689. Much of his earliest work was more sculptural than architectural, though the first project for the palace of Schönbrunn (outside Vienna) can be dated to c1690. During the mid 1690s he began two important churches in Salzburg, while working on the central section of Prince Eugene's town palace in Vienna (1695–1700). The Dreifaltigkeitskirche (1694–1702) is remarkable for its sharply concave facade flanked by low towers, and the clearly articulated longi-

J.M. Fischer: the basilica of the Benedictine abbey of Ottobeuren; mid 18th century

tudinal oval which forms the nave. He developed these ideas further in the Karlskirche. In contrast, the much larger Kollegienkirche is a modified Greek cross in plan, with a strongly convex central section to the facade, held in check by the twin towers. The vitality of the designs is enhanced by the limited decoration; in the Kollegienkirche the dazzling white plasterwork of the later high altar by Diego Carlone provides a fitting climax.

The palace of Schönbrunn was modified during construction (1696–*post* 1711), and once again for the Empress Maria Theresa, so that today it bears little resemblance to Fischer von Erlach's intentions. However, the richly articulated facades of the Bohemian Chancellery in Vienna (*post* 1708–14) and the Clam Gallas Palace in Prague (begun 1713) reveal his dynamic mature style.

In 1715 Fischer von Erlach began his work on his masterpiece, the Karlskirche in Vienna. The structure was completed by his son Joseph Emmanuel with modifica-

tions in 1725. The relatively low central portico is flanked by two enormous columns, and the facade is completed by a pair of bell towers over archways. The tension between these elements, and the dome behind, provides both the basis for the dynamic balance of the facade, and a foretaste of the vigorous treatment of the oval nave. In the Karlskirche Fischer von Erlach strove to create a specifically Imperial Baroque style; these ideas reached their climax in his Imperial Library in Vienna, begun the year before his death.

Further reading. Kunoth, G. *Die Historische Architektur Fischers von Erlach*, Düsseldorf (1956). Sedlmayr, H. *Johann Bernhard Fischer von Erlach*, Munich (1956).

Flandrin J.-H. 1809–64

The French painter Jean-Hippolyte Flandrin was born in Lyons. He moved to Paris and entered the studio of J.-A.-D. Ingres in

1829. He became one of Ingres' most zealous followers, and won the Prix de Rome in 1832. After six years in Italy he returned to France. There he developed a style that combined early Renaissance formal austerity with a characteristic mid-19th-century sentimentality. The strength of Flandrin's style appears to be particularly well-suited to portraiture, in which he was extremely gifted. He was also to become one of the most important 19th-century religious artists, as his murals in the church of St-Germain-des-Près, Paris, demonstrate.

Flavin Dan 1933–

Dan Flavin is an American sculptor in light. He uses columns of tubular light to create open-ended paintings in a darkened gallery area. Flavin's work is part of a trend towards systematic and optical art which began in the 1960s; it is related to the painting of Richard Anuszkiewicz, Frank Stella, and Kenneth Noland, and to

J.-H. Flandrin: Theseus Recognized by his Father; oil on canvas; 115×146cm (45×57in); 1832. École des Beaux-Arts, Paris

Dan Flavin: untitled, to the "innovator" of Wheeling Peachblow; pink, gold, and daylight fluorescent light; 244×244cm (96×96in); 1966–8. Museum of Modern Art, New York

the later sculptures of Richard Lippold. With its use of modern technology and lighting, Flavin's work is also a direct development of early "color-field" painting: in many ways his works are the electrified equivalent of paintings by Barnett Newman (1905–1970), such as Newman's earlier *Vir Heroicus Sublimus* (1950; Museum of Modern Art, New York).

Flaxman John 1755–1826

The English Neoclassical artist John Flaxman was probably the most internationally famous British sculptor before the 20th century. Flaxman was trained at the Royal Academy in the early 1770s and began his career designing for Josiah Wedgwood's pottery factory. Flaxman was interested in all kinds of archaic and primitive art, including Gothic and early Renaissance, as well as having a conventional admiration for Antiquity. He managed to establish a reputation as a tomb sculptor in England and visited Italy in 1787, remaining in Rome until 1794. He studied as many different styles as possible, filling small notebooks with his researches, and the result of these studies appears in the works of his Italian period.

Flaxman was friendly with the Italian sculptor Canova whose influence secured a few important patrons for the British artist. His greatest Roman statue was *The Fury of Athamas* (1790–4; Ickworth House, Suffolk), a marble group of four figures, 7 ft (2.1 m) high, which depicts a subject from Ovid's *Metamorphoses*. Although the patron, Lord Bristol, admired the carefully researched "Antique" style of the work, he was not prepared to pay the sculptor adequately. Flaxman was forced to find new commissions and, in doing so, produced a series of graphic masterpieçes—outline illustrations to Dante, Homer, and Aeschylus. These were engraved in black and white lines which recalled the flat, painted decorations on the sides of Archaic vases. The success of these outlines confirmed Flaxman's reputation abroad and they were copied by artists as diverse as Ingres, Goya, Géricault, and Seurat.

On his return to England Flaxman became a leading society sculptor, designing famous tombs which included those for Lord Mansfield (1795–1801; Westminster Abbey, London), Admiral Nelson (1808–18; St Paul's Cathedral, London), and Dr

Joseph Warton (1804; Winchester Cathedral). Flaxman's main talent appears in relief work, and his memorial plaques often convey a simple moral message. Like his outline illustrations, his achievement in relief was revolutionary in the placing of firm silhouettes or sinuous contours against a plain background. In this way his graphic work and the images he made in relief anticipate later styles, such as Art Nouveau. Flaxman also made very beautiful small models in terracotta or plaster, based on Classical designs, as in the *Sketch Model for a Monument to Barbara Lowther* (1807; University College, London). These models, however, were less successful when enlarged to the required size for a finished tomb.

Despite his eminence among foreign contemporaries, Flaxman's popularity in England declined in the two decades before his death. His market was taken by more successful artists like Chantrey, and Flaxman died bankrupt. It was not until the 1850s, when his studio models and drawings were acquired by University College in London, that his reputation in England revived. On the Continent, however, Flaxman never lost his popularity. During a visit to Paris in 1802 he was received as a celebrity by his French fellow artists. In 1865 Ingres included Flaxman's portrait among the elect in the second version of

G.T. Flinck: A Young Negro Archer; oil on panel; 68×52cm (27×20in); 1639–40. Wallace Collection, London

The Apotheosis of Homer (Louvre, Paris); Goethe and A.W. von Schlegel in Germany also admired Flaxman's work and wrote the earliest critical accounts of his outline illustrations.

In 1817 Flaxman published a final set of illustrations, to the poems of Hesiod, and these were engraved by his friend William Blake. They were less popular than the previous designs, but they were collected abroad, especially in Germany where Flaxman's reputation as one of the greatest graphic artists of the 19th century has survived.

Flinck G.T. 1615–60

Govert Teunisz. Flinck was a Dutch painter. Although he was born in Cleves, on the German side of the border, he studied at Leeuwarden and spent most of his working life in Amsterdam. His early works reveal the powerful influence of Rembrandt, with whom he studied in the 1630s. In the following decade he adopted a lighter, more Flemish style, which suggests a knowledge of works by van Dyck and van der Helst.

Although his fame has been obscured by that of his greater contemporaries, Flinck enjoyed a considerable reputation in his day. A prolific artist, he received several important state commissions. The contract for *The Conspiracy of Julius Civilis*, intended for Amsterdam town hall, was only given to Rembrandt to realize after Flinck's premature death.

Floris brothers 16th century

Frans Floris (c1518–70) and his brother Cornelis (1514–75), were Flemish artists of Antwerp. Frans was a painter who traveled extensively in Italy in the 1540s. His most important work, *The Fall of the Rebel Angels* (1554; formerly Antwerp Cathedral, now Royal Museum of Fine Arts, Antwerp) shows evidence that he had studied Italian Mannerist painting and Michelangelo's *Last Judgment* in the Sistine Chapel. He was also a successful portraitist.

Cornelis was a sculptor who absorbed a number of influences—Italian, Classical, and French—and whose work was in demand in a number of north European centers (see his tomb of Christian III of Denmark, 1568; Roskilde Cathedral). The large Floris family workshop dominated Netherlandish design in the 1560s.

Fontana Carlo c1636–1714

Carlo Stefano Fontana was an Italian architect and engineer. After leaving his native north Italy, he served as assistant to Cortona, Rainaldi, and Bernini. After Bernini's death, he emerged as the most influential architect in the Holy City.

His facade of S. Marcello al Corso, Rome (1682–3), with its comparatively static and orderly articulation, reveals a dramatic contrast with the exuberant compositions of his predecessors. Other important commissions, such as the Jesuit church and college at Loyola in Spain, have been criticized for their cold eclecticism.

Despite such failings, Fontana's numerous smaller buildings, plans, drawings, and notes reveal his immense energy. Deeply respected by the following generation, his work was an important influence upon late Baroque classicism.

Fontana Domenico 1543–1607

The architect Domenico Fontana was born in northern Italy but worked mainly in Rome and Naples. During his Roman period, his fortunes depended very much on those of his patron, Cardinal Felice Peretti, who became Pope Sixtus V in 1585, for whom he had built the Villa Montalto. After Peretti's death in 1590 Fontana found it difficult to obtain further work in Rome and went to Naples to work for the Viceroy.

Due to Peretti, Fontana was able to play a major role in no less than three papal palaces. He built a new wing at the Vatican (which houses the present papal apartments) and a new library in the Cortile del Belvedere; he worked at the Quirinale, and was responsible for the Lateran Palace (completed 1587) which was Sixtus' summer residence. In accordance with the Pope's program of urban renewal Fontana also designed new streets and waterworks.

Fontana was perhaps best known in his own day for the erection of two Egyptian obelisks, remarkable features of Rome's skyline, one in front of the choir of S. Maria Maggiore and the other in St Peter's Square. He describes this immense operation in *Della Transportatione dell'Obelisco Vaticano* (1590). In fact, he placed it a few degrees off the principal axis of Michelangelo's St Peter's. He served Sixtus literally until the end, building his mausoleum at S. Maria Maggiore.

In Naples his main work was the Palazzo Reale (1600–2), which helped to spread

Roman classicism in the city. His style is often criticized as monotonous and severe, and in the case of the Lateran palace it is plainly derivitive (from Sangallo's Palazzo Farnese).

Fontana Lucio 1899–1968

The Italian sculptor, painter, and ceramist Lucio Fontana was born in Rosario, Argentina. He spent his childhood in Milan, then in 1922 returned to Rosario where he opened a sculpture studio. From 1928 to 1930 he studied under Wildt at the Brera Academy, Milan. In 1935 he became a member of the *Abstraction-Création* group in Paris. Fontana lived in Argentina from 1939 to 1947. In 1946 he was a cofounder of the avant-garde Academia Altamira in Buenos Aires, which led to the publication of his *Manifesto Blanco*. In 1947 he returned to Milan, where he issued the *Manifesto Spaziale,* founding the "Spazialismo" movement. He died in Comabbio in 1968.

Fontana made his first Abstract sculptures in 1934. He returned to figurative art from 1939 to 1946 (and until 1960 as a subsidiary activity). From 1947 to 1949 he created ceramic sculptures. Fontana made his first pierced canvases in 1949, and in 1958 began to make cuts (*atese*). These were made either in raw canvas, on monochrome grounds, or combined with informal painting, graffiti, drawing, glass, and stone collage. From the early 1950s onwards Fontana worked in pierced sheet metal, terracotta, and bronze. Beginning in 1948, his environmental and architectural projects incorporated neon, painting, holes, and suspended sculpture.

Vincenzo Foppa: Adoration of the Magi; poplar panel; 239×211cm (94×83in). National Gallery, London

Foppa Vincenzo 1427/30–1515/16

Vincenzo Foppa was an Italian painter, from Brescia. His first signed work is a *Crucifixion* (Galleria dell'Academia Carrara, Bergamo) dated 1456. Resident in Pavia by 1458, he worked extensively there, in Milan, and in Genoa, primarily for the Sforza Dukes of Milan. He returned to Brescia *c*1489–90.

Foppa was the most important painter of the Milanese School before Leonardo da Vinci. Traces of late Gothic in his early style soon yielded to the influence of Giovanni Bellini and Mantegna. His paintings, often bathed in silvery-gray light, tend to have a rather coarse finish. An example is the *Virgin and Child with Saints* (1485; Pinacoteca di Brera, Milan).

Forain Jean-Louis 1852–1931

The French painter and illustrator Jean-Louis Forain was born at Reims. He had little formal training, but by the late 1870s he was painting in a style derived from Edouard Manet and Edgar Degas. He exhibited with the Impressionists, mostly interior scenes, for instance of backstage at the Opera. His work displayed sharp observation of modern life in Paris. He is now remembered less for his painting than for his illustrations in the weekly press, where his incipient satirical bent found freer rein. His output of caricatures was considerable; but he continued to paint, and some of his courtroom scenes recall Daumier's caustic comments on the legal profession.

Foster Norman 1935–

The British architect Norman Foster is one of the leading exponents of "hi-tech" architecture, an approach in which technology, instead of being hidden or disguised, is made explicit, often with structure and services being exposed. He studied at the universities of Manchester and Yale, and in the early 1960s formed a design partnership with Richard Rogers (and their wives) known as Team 4, which ended in 1967. One of his first outstanding buildings was the Sainsbury Centre for the Visual Arts, Norwich University (1976–78), a work uncompromising in its use of modern materials and engineering, and typical of Foster in its elegant detail and innovative use of space and light (for example, electronic shutters in the roof, subtly controlling the flow of daylight). His skillful use of technology in determining form can also be seen in his best-known building, the Hong Kong and Shanghai Bank, Hong Kong (1979–85), and in the Stansted Airport Terminal, Essex, England. Since 1988 Foster has been employed on the redevelopment of a site around Kings Cross railroad station in central London.

Fouquet Jean c1420–c80

Jean Fouquet was born in Tours. Although he is the principal French painter of the 15th century, little is known of his initiation into the craft. By 1447 he was certainly in Rome, where he painted a portrait of Pope Eugenius IV with his nephews—a privilege that would only have been bestowed on a painter of some distinction. The portrait, now lost, attracted the praise of the theorist Filarete, whose opinion remains on record. Fouquet appears to have been familiar with Rome. He also knew Paris and may have studied there though much of his working life was spent in the provinces. In his miniatures, he has depicted monuments of both these cities.

On his return to Tours in 1447 he was taken under royal patronage by Charles VII—patronage that was extended after 1461 by Louis XI. Of more immediate importance was his acquaintance with Étienne Chevalier, diplomat, treasurer of France, and friend of both kings. For Chevalier, Fouquet painted the miniatures of the magnificent *Hours of Étienne Chevalier*; 13 of these illustrations and the text have been lost, but the remaining 47 miniatures constitute Fouquet's finest work. (Forty of the miniatures are in the Musée Condé, Chantilly, two are in the Louvre, Paris, one is in the British Library, London, and the other four are in private collections.) On the death of Chevalier's wife, Cathérine Budé, in 1452, Fouquet was commissioned to paint the diptych for her tomb in Notre-Dame de Melun; Chevalier himself appears as donor, together with St Stephen. Fouquet's *Portrait of Charles VII* (Louvre, Paris) and his decoration of the church of Notre-Dame-la-Riche in Tours date from the same very productive period, as do the miniatures for Boccaccio's *Les Cas des Nobles Hommes et Femmes Malheureuses* painted for Laurens Gyrard (1458; Staatsbibliothek, Munich).

Jean Fouquet (attrib.): Portrait of a Man; panel; 47×40cm (18×16in); 1456. Liechtenstein'sche Fürstliche Sammlungen, Vienna

Until 1458 Fouquet's style is consistent, and suggests some slight debt to Fra Angelico. Single figures or groups offer a point of focus, in architectural settings of the utmost solidity, sometimes with considerable fidelity to recognizable models. In the few paintings from the *Hours of Étienne Chevalier* where crowds are portrayed, there is always a figure that provides a center of attention.

After 1458 Fouquet's work shows evidence of a greater dispersion of subject matter, concern with altogether less intimate scenes, and an increasing regard for the landscapes of France. The *Chronicles of the Kings of France* (1458; Bibliothèque Nationale, Paris) abandoned a relatively static style for the dynamic possibilities of the battlefield. This new dynamism is also seen in the illustrations to the *Jewish Antiquities* of Josephus (1470–6; Bibliothèque Nationale, Paris) painted for Jacques d'Armagnac, Duke of Nemours. Fouquet's versatility was considerable: his portraits *Charles VII* and *Guillaume Juvénal des Ursins* (Louvre, Paris), and his self-portrait, demonstrate his sensitivity to human features. His style as a miniature painter shows constant evolution, and his influence continued long after his death. The work at Notre-Dame-la-Riche and at Nouans suggests ability in a larger dimension. The overall effect of his achievement was to release French painting from the last ties of a persistent and belated Gothicism.

Fragonard Jean-Honoré
1732–1806

Jean-Honoré Fragonard was the last of the French Rococo painters. He outlived the movement, and died poor and unnoticed during the heyday of Neoclassicism. He was born at Grasse in Provence, but his family moved to Paris before Fragonard was 10 years old. He trained at first under Chardin, leaving after only 6 months to work in Boucher's studio.

In 1751, Fragonard became the pupil of François Boucher, who was at the height of his career; Fragonard must have learned his fluent handling of paint, speed of execution, and pure professionalism from the elder painter. More important, he may have learned how to draw; for under Boucher, superb academic drawings formed the backbone of studio production. Fragonard's graphic style is unlike his master's, however, being more vivacious and independent. In many of his smaller oil paintings and sketches the paint is literally drawn on with a brush.

Fragonard was something of a prodigy. He won the highly coveted Prix de Rome at his first attempt in 1752, but instead of leaving France immediately he went to the École des Élèves Protégés to study under Carle van Loo. Fragonard had won the prize for his painting *Jeroboam Sacrificing to the Idols* (1752; École des Beaux-Arts, Paris), an Old Testament subject that gave the artist scope to work in the grand style. It is a skillful painting with tension created by two groups of dramatically opposed figures. This was not the sort of work that Boucher produced. Fragonard had based his work on the style of the contemporary Venetian history painter Giovanni Battista Pittoni, simplifying the Venetian's crowded compositions and gaining an increased intensity.

Fragonard made his mark with the *Jeroboam*, and to his peers and contemporaries he seemed destined for great things. He studied under van Loo for three years, then in 1756 left Paris for the French Academy in Rome. Whatever he learned and however much he studied in Rome, Fragonard was a disappointment to his teachers. Natoire, the Director of the French Academy, accused him of not being the painter of the *Jeroboam*; he criticized his pupil's carelessness and lack of fire.

Jean-Honoré Fragonard: The Swing; oil on canvas; 81×65cm (32×26in); 1767. Wallace Collection, London

Perhaps not surprisingly, very few paintings are known from his time in Rome. In Paris his drawings were more admired than his paintings.

Although Fragonard may not have been a model pupil at the Academy, his Italian sojourn was not wasted. His very individual response to Italian art may have raised eyebrows at the French Academy; for Fragonard admired not the works of Raphael and the Antique, but the modern artists Pietro da Cortona, Solimena, and Giambattista Tiepolo. Fragonard was to become the greatest of late French Rococo painters; he was sensible to study at firsthand works by the founders of the movement. Italy to Fragonard meant Italian landscape as well as art, in particular the gardens of the Villa d'Este at Tivoli.

Although landscape was never a major part of his output in the way that it was with his English contemporary Gainsborough, his response to it was highly unusual. Trees and clouds have a pulsating life of their own, far more intensely alive then the little manikin figures that inhabit their world. Landscape, especially in Fragonard's drawing, is a natural force, never a pretty back-cloth to a *fête galante*. This was Fragonard's own discovery, which he did not share even with his close friend and colleague Hubert Robert. It is a facet of his art that seems closer to Romantic painting of the 19th century than to the Rococo. At Tivoli, Fragonard worked with Robert under their patron the Abbé de Saint-Non. It was with Saint-Non that Fragonard visited Naples and Venice, and with whom he made his long leisurely journey back to Paris, visiting and revisiting the towns and cities of northern Italy.

Fragonard returned to Paris in 1761. He may then have worked for art dealers—producing landscapes in the style of Ruisdael and Castiglione, painting a series of character heads in the manner of Rembrandt and Tiepolo, and probably even producing fakes. In 1765 he exhibited *Coresus and Callirrhoé* (Louvre, Paris) at the Salon; the picture brought his name back into the public eye and established him as the master of contemporary history painting. This was a role Fragonard was unwilling to accept, for he very soon turned his back on the Salon, exhibiting there for the last time in 1767. He became a private painter, valuing his independence from the art establishment as much as many painters do today.

A work produced *c*1768 or 1769 has the type of subject matter that Fragonard was often to choose during the years that followed his break with the Salon. The commission for *The Swing* (*L'Escarpolette*, 1767; Wallace Collection, London) was originally given by the Baron de Saint-Julien to the religious painter Doyen. The patron asked Doyen to paint his mistress on a swing with a bishop pushing her; the painter was instructed to place him, Saint-Julien, in a good position to see her pretty legs. Doyen was scandalized and rejected the commission, but suggested Fragonard's name.

The delightful painting that resulted must have pleased the Baron, for he later owned a similar erotic painting by Fragonard. The surface of *The Swing* is very carefully worked, in Fragonard's finished rather than freely sketched manner. The same is true of the canvases he painted for Madame du Barry a few years later at the beginning of the 1770s. *The Progress of Love* (1771–2; Frick Collection, New York) a set of four amorous scenes, is Fragonard's masterpiece. Indeed these are among the greatest decorations of any age. Amusing and charming, they are not frivolous—though Madame du Barry may have believed them to be so when she rejected them for her Neoclassical pavilion at Louveciennes.

In *The Progress of Love* the lovers make their advances and form their alliances against an enchanted background where statues and landscape are alive, encouraging and protecting them. Whatever the reasons for Madame du Barry's action (and it was something that Fragonard refused to discuss), her rejection of the paintings was evidence of a break with Rococo taste well over a decade before the political revolution took over.

In 1789, the Revolution brought about an abrupt change of patronage. Until that year Fragonard still had plenty of patrons, indeed he was extremely active. After 1789 his fortunes declined, and it was only through the help of Jacques-Louis David that he managed to obtain the administrative posts that provided his inadequate income. His later works may have been adapted for the change in artistic climate; erotic girls and cherubs became contented mothers and children, and the settings of his paintings were more likely to be the hearth and the classroom than the bedroom.

Outliving his era, Fragonard left no successors; it was not until with Renoir that France produced an artist of similar vitality, decorativeness, and originality.

Further reading. Goncourt, E. and J. de *French Eighteenth-Century Painters*, Oxford (1981). Nolhac, P. de *J.-H. Fragonard, 1732–1806*, Paris (1906 and 1931). Wildenstein, G. *Fragonard Aquafortiste*, Paris (1956). Wildenstein, G. (trans. Chilton, C.W. and Kitson, A.L.) *The Paintings of Fragonard*, London (1960).

Francesco di Giorgio Martini
1439–1502

Francesco di Giorgio Martini was an Italian artist of the Sienese school. He was active chiefly as an architect, although his first documented work is a carved wooden figure of *St John the Baptist* paid for in 1464 (Pinacoteca Nazionale, Siena). In the 1470s he worked for Federico da Montefeltro at Urbino, where he was responsible for the completion of work in the Ducal Palace begun by Luciano Laurana (*ob.* 1479).

The most important of Francesco's surviving architectural projects is the church of S. Maria del Calcinaio outside Cortona (1484–5) which is a model of early Renaissance purity. His treatise on architecture (*c*1500) shows an indebtedness to Alberti but is more practical in approach. Francesco executed small-scale sculptural works throughout his life, particularly in bronze. There are authenticated paintings by him in Siena, showing a tender linearity akin to Botticelli.

Francia Francesco *c*1450–1517

Francesco Francia was a Bolognese goldsmith and painter. He matriculated in the goldsmiths' guild in 1482. Save for some medals and coins nothing of this side of his activities remains. First recorded as a painter in 1486, he seems to have specialized in devotional Madonnas and altarpieces. An example is *The Adoration* (1499; Pinacoteca Nazionale, Bologna). About 30 of these altarpieces survive, many signed. Highly esteemed by his contemporaries, Francia avoided the Ferrarese style, which dominated the Bolognese art of his day, by adopting the softer, mellower forms of Perugino. Typical of his paintings are the gentle, rather wistful facial expressions of his figures, and the pleasing but simple landscape backgrounds.

Francesco di Giorgio Martini: The Nativity; detail; panel; c1486–94. S. Domenico, Siena

Francis Sam 1923–

Sam Francis is a second generation Californian Abstract Expressionist who was based in Paris from 1950 to 1961. During the 1950s his work was better known in Europe than that of American painters like Pollock and Rothko; and Francis' association with Parisian *Art Informel* led to an erroneous conclusion that New York School painting was part of an international movement. Francis' own painting moved from a dense overall Abstract Expressionist technique as in *Blue Black* (oil; 1952; Albright-Knox Art Gallery, Buffalo), to the creation of a neutral center or large areas of dusty canvas enlivened by peripheral action as in *Abstraction* (oil; 1959; Whitney Museum of American Art, New York) which presages "color-field" painting.

Francken family
16th and 17th centuries

The Francken were a family of 14 painters active mainly at Antwerp over five generations. In the second generation Hieronymus I (1540–1610), Frans I (1542–1616),

and Ambrosius I (1544–1618) accepted the Venetianizing Mannerism of Maerten de Vos, turning in middle life to a harsh, classicizing formality (examples in the Royal Museum of Fine Arts, Antwerp).

Frans II (1581–1642), in the third generation, was the most widely known of the family. He combed mythology, history, and the Bible for subjects for small genre pictures, prolifically and repetitively produced, apparently for collectors of middle rank. Frans Francken made use of opulent and exotic accessories in a manner reminiscent of Lastman and Vignon. His figures have a pert, theatrical elegance; later they became rounder, and blander in color, under the influence of Rubens. Francken is represented in many of the older collections in northern and central Europe such as the Rijksmuseum, Amsterdam.

Frankenthaler Helen 1928–

The American artist Helen Frankenthaler is one of the most original and consistent of the painters who matured in the 1950s after the main achievements of the Abstract Expressionists. Frankenthaler was

Sam Francis: Around the Blues; oil and acrylic on canvas; 43×76cm (108×192in); 1957 and 1962. Tate Gallery, London

Helen Frankenthaler: Mountains and Sea; detail; oil on canvas; full size 220×298cm (87×117in); 1952. Private collection, on loan to the National Gallery of Art, Washington, D.C.

helped by Meyer Shapiro, Clement Greenberg, and Hans Hoffman to an appreciation of recent events in American painting, in particular to the aims and techniques of Jackson Pollock and Arshile Gorky. Frankenthaler's own painting was from the outset more "open" than that of the Abstract Expressionists. As early as 1952 in *Mountains and Sea* (private collection) she developed a "soak-stain" technique, applying thin washes of paint in lyrical and carefully articulated areas on a relatively empty canvas. The technique was later used extensively by Kenneth Noland and Morris Louis.

Further reading. Baro, G. "The Achievement of Helen Frankenthaler", *Art International*, Zurich (September 1967). Rose, B. *Frankenthaler*, New York (1972).

Freud Lucian 1922–

Born in Berlin, the British artist Lucian Freud, grandson of Sigmund Freud, came to England in the early 1930s, and in the 1940s studied briefly at the East Anglian School of Drawing and Painting. Freud's early works—he has concentrated largely on portraits of friends and relatives throughout his career—are in a taut, linear style, his sitters remote and ambiguous, their eyes and lips exaggerated: see *Girl with a Kitten* (1947; British Council). By

the late 1950s, however, he had evolved a far more painterly style, his subjects, often nudes of a disturbing frankness and vulnerability, acquiring an intense physical presence that deepens their emotional remoteness. For Freud, this physicality is intimately linked with the act of painting: "As far as I am concerned the paint *is* the person. I want it to work for me just as flesh does." *Night Portrait* (1985–86; Smithsonian Institution, Washington, D.C.) is typical.

Further reading. Gowing, L. *Lucian Freud*, London (1982).

Friedrich Caspar David
1774–1840

Caspar David Friedrich was the leading landscape painter in Germany during the Romantic era. His views of the desolate coastlands of his native Pomerania and of the mountainous regions of central Europe combine a careful observation of natural features with a deep sense of the spiritual.

Friedrich's pantheistic approach to landscape, shared by so many writers and painters of his generation, seems to have derived from his home background. The son of a prosperous soap-boiler and candlemaker in the Baltic harbor town of Greifswald, he was taught from 1790 to 1794 by J.G. Quistorp, the drawing master

at the local university. Through Quistorp he came into contact with the poet and pastor L.T. Kosegarten, a writer who combined the nature sentiment of J.-J. Rousseau and such English poets as Thomson and Gray with a traditional north German pietism.

In 1794 Friedrich went to study at the leading art academy of northern Europe, the Copenhagen Academy. From such teachers as Jens Juel and Christian Lorentzen he learned the current modes of picturesque local views and sublime stormy and mountainous scenes. A series of exquisite watercolors of the parklands around Copenhagen—notably the *Landscape with a Pavilion* (1795; Hamburger Kunsthalle, Hamburg)—show how fully he mastered his teachers' use of nature to convey sentimental moods. At the same time his study in the drawing classes of the Academy developed the habit of using a fine outline for describing the forms of his pictures. This practice, which remained with him throughout his life, enabled him to achieve great precision in the balancing of his compositions.

In 1798 Friedrich moved to Dresden. The town was then a leading art center, because of both its superb gallery and the local landscape school that had grown up in emulation of the Dutch 17th-century masters. He was to remain there for the rest of his life, apart from a number of return visits to Pomerania (the longest being for 18 months in 1801–2) and frequent tours of the Harz, the Riesengebirge, and other scenic areas in central Europe.

Friedrich first built a reputation as a painter of views of his Baltic homeland. These were executed for the most part in sepia, a monochrome technique that gave full scope for the Neoclassical emphasis on form. While specializing in this method, Friedrich developed a careful control of lighting effects, most effective for misty and nocturnal scenes, as in *View of Arkona with Rising Moon* (1806; Graphische Sammlung Albertina, Vienna).

At the same time Friedrich began to invest his landscapes with the religious and national themes made topical in Dresden by such Romantic writers and critics as Ludwig Tieck and the Schlegel brothers. This can be seen in the two sepias that were awarded a prize by Goethe at the Weimar exhibition of 1805, *Summer Landscape with a Dead Oak* and *Pilgrimage at Sunrise* (Schlossmuseum, Staatliche

Caspar David Friedrich: Stages of Life; oil on canvas; 73×94cm (29×37in); c1834. Museum der Bildenden Künste, Leipzig

Kunstsammlungen, Weimar). The latter is particularly explicit in its imagery, showing a procession bearing a monstrance towards a wayside cross and passing between two trees which lean together in the form of a Gothic arch. Despite this interweaving of religion and nature, the scene was sufficiently conventional in its presentation for Goethe, who was deeply suspicious of the new movement, to concentrate on praising its naturalism and technical expertise.

It was not possible, however, to ignore the spiritual nature of the work that caused a sensation three years later, *The Cross in the Mountains* (1808; Gemäldegalerie Alte Meister, Dresden). Intended as an altarpiece for a private chapel, it took the remarkable step of presenting the Christian faith in terms of pure landscape. Even more striking were the means by which the artist conveyed his message, for he discarded the conventions of landscape composition to concentrate upon the silhouette of the triangular top of a mountain against the setting sun. Such radicalism could also

be found in the two works he exhibited in Berlin in 1810, which were bought by the Prussian Crown Prince: *Abbey in the Oakwoods* and *Monk by the Sea* (Schloss Charlottenburg, Berlin). The latter conveyed the sense of isolation with unprecedented intensity.

It is a mark of Friedrich's increasing self-confidence and reputation that these large works, like the majority of his pictures after 1807, were painted in oil. The growing nationalist movement in Germany that followed on the Napoleonic invasions of 1806 also favored his art, with its emphasis on northern spirituality. Friedrich was in fact an ardent nationalist himself, and celebrated the defeat of the French in 1814 with a number of patriotic landscapes. One of these shows a French dragoon lost in a Germanic forest of firs (private collection).

After the Napoleonic Wars Friedrich's life became more settled. In 1816 he was elected to the Dresden Academy, and in 1818 he married a local girl, Caroline Bommer. At the same time he began to

abandon his repertoire of monks, ruins, and other theatrical motifs in favor of more contemporary themes. Under the influence of the Norwegian painter Dahl, who settled in Dresden in 1819, his painting manner became more spontaneous, and he adopted the fresh greens and blues associated with naturalism. While strongly opposed to the scientific analysis of natural phenomena (he refused to assist Goethe in his study of cloud formations), Friedrich followed Dahl in making *plein air* oil sketches at this time (for example, *Evening*, 1824; Städtisches Kunsthalle, Mannheim).

Despite these changes, Friedrich did not abandon the spiritual approach to landscape. Such topical themes as the *Arctic Shipwreck* (1824; Hamburger Kunsthalle, Hamburg), in which a ship is crushed to pieces beneath an ice-floe, were every bit as symbolic as his earlier more arcane images. A recurrent motif in his pictures during the 1820s was the inclusion of figures, viewed from behind, contemplating the landscape (for example, *Moonrise over the Sea*,

1822; Nationalgalerie, Berlin). Such works emphasized the importance of the individual response to nature. It was this attitude—so evident in a series of critical aphorisms that he wrote *c*1830—that made him increasingly unpopular with the younger generation.

Friedrich was an isolated, lonely figure whose fatalism has often been seen as the outcome of a personal melancholia. However, his art has a universal dimension, which made him a source of inspiration for later Symbolist painters.

Further reading. Börsche-Supan, H. *Caspar David Friedrich*, London and Munich (1974). Sumowski, W. *Caspar David Friedrich Studien*, Wiesbaden (1970).

Froment Nicolas *c*1435–*c*86

Born in Uzès, the Provençal artist Nicolas Froment was the last great painter of the Avignon School. His work displayed a

Nicolas Froment: center panel of The Burning Bush triptych; height 410cm (161in); 1476. Cathedral of the Holy Savior, Aix-en-Provence

taste for distortion and the grotesque which was not typical of 15th-century Provençal painting. For this reason his style can be interpreted in two different ways. He may have been an eccentric individualist, but within the Provençal tradition, or he may have been a decadent artist subject to Flemish or German influence. His earliest known work, the triptych of *The Raising of Lazarus* (Uffizi, Florence), dates from 1461; his masterpiece is the highly complex and symbolic triptych of *The Burning Bush* (1476) in the Cathedral of the Holy Savior, Aix-en-Provence.

Fry Roger 1866–1934

The English painter Roger Fry was also an important art critic and theorist. He read for a science degree at Cambridge between 1885 and 1888. During these years he began to paint and to study the history of Italian painting with J.H. Middleton. In 1888 he studied painting with Francis Bate, a member of the New English Art Club, and made his first trip to Italy in 1891. In 1894 he began giving University Extension lectures on the Italian Renaissance. From 1900 onwards he wrote articles and reviewed exhibitions for *Athenaeum*, *The Monthly Review*, and *The Burlington Magazine*.

Roger Fry was Curator of Painting at the Metropolitan Museum in New York from 1905 to 1910. In December 1910 he arranged the exhibition "Manet and the Post-Impressionists" at the Grafton Galleries, London, which established his reputation as an advocate of modern painting. In 1912 he organized the "Exposition de Quelques Indépendents Anglais" in Paris and the "Second Post-Impressionist Exhibition of English, French and Russian Artists" at the Grafton Galleries.

In 1913 Fry opened the Omega Workshops Ltd; it involved such artists as Duncan Grant, Vanessa Bell, and Wyndham Lewis—until its closure in 1919. Fry was given a retrospective exhibition at the London Artist's Association in 1931 and he gave three highly successful series of lectures in 1927, 1932, and 1934, at the Queen's Hall, London. These were sponsored by the National Art Collections Fund. Fry was made Slade Professor of Fine Art at Cambridge in 1933. He published numerous articles and books of art criticism and aesthetic theory, among them *Giovanni Bellini* (1899), *Vision and*

Design (1920), *Transformations* (1926), *Cézanne: A Study of his Development* (1927), and *Henri Matisse* (1930).

Fry's own painting (for example *White Road with Farm*, *c*1912; Scottish National Gallery of Modern Art, Edinburgh) was very important to him; but it is overshadowed by his importance as an exhibition organizer, writer, and lecturer on aesthetics and the history of art. By 1904 Fry was recognized for his study of the Old Masters, particularly for his interest in the Italian Primitives. But by 1910 he had become known as an advocate of the modern movement.

Most important to Fry's theories was the role of plastic values. It was this that led him to the "discovery" of Cézanne in 1906 and the organization of the "Manet and the Post-Impressionists" exhibition in 1910. The first English critic to acknowledge Cézanne's importance, Fry was much criticized for his seeming abandonment of the Old Masters. However it was his ability to recognize the formal virtues of the new art, and to see the continuity of these same virtues down the ages, that led him to his own oversimplification, that the essence of the art lay in *disegno*, in its formal values.

After 1920 Fry was not closely concerned with avant-garde art, though he was still considered a spokesman for modern French painting. He will be best remembered for his involvement with the major artistic endeavors of the 1910s, for the critical recognition in England of the importance of French and British modern painting, and for his writings, which are rich in insight into individual works of art.

Further reading. Bell, Q. *Roger Fry*, Leeds (1964). Fry, R. *Vision and Design*, London (1957). Shone, R. *Bloomsbury Portraits*, Oxford (1975). Woolf, V. *Roger Fry*, London (1957).

Fu Pao-shih 1904–65

Fu Pao-shih was born in Kiangsi and spent much of his life in east-central China. He went to Japan for a few years from 1935 onwards, to study in the Imperial Academy. An academically trained painter, he seems to have been a follower of Shih T'ao; like that 17th-century master, he wrote a great deal about the theory and philosophy of painting. Fu became professor of painting at the National Central

Roger Fry: The Barn; oil on canvas; 25×36cm (10×14in); c1916. Private collection

and from these diverse sources forged a distinctive personal style.

In 1779 Fuseli returned to London and began exhibiting history paintings regularly at the Royal Academy. His picture *The Nightmare* (1782; Tate Gallery, London) was an immediate success, and in 1786 he was commissioned to paint nine illustrations for Boydell's Shakespeare Gallery (opened 1789). In 1800 he exhibited 47 paintings of subjects from Milton which had occupied him during the 1790s. He became a member of the Royal Academy in 1799, Professor of Painting in 1800, and Keeper in 1804. His important contributions to the literature and theory of art included his series of lectures to the students of the Royal Academy and his additions to *Pilkington's Lives of the Artists* (1805).

The characteristics of Fuseli's mature style were well defined before his departure from Italy. They included dramatic foreshortening of figures, strong light–shade contrasts, extravagant gestures and distortions of scale, and a preference for new, often obscure, literary subjects which stressed the demonic side of human nature. In his works, the aesthetic of the Sublime was given its most extreme visual articulation.

University, and at the time of his death was Principal of the Nanking Academy of Art.

Fu Pao-shih's own painting is in various styles, ranging from an archaistic figure-painting of beauties to a romantic painting of landscape. He built upon Shih T'ao's experiments with color and texture, following a Japanese interest in the actual surface of the paper. Using a coarse fiber paper, Fu used to scuff up the surface, achieving some very beautiful effects. He became one of the leading painters of the mid 20th century, and has had great influence over his contemporaries and students. He and Kuan San-yueh collaborated on some of the major paintings for the new Chinese State after Liberation (1949), notably the large wall painting in the Hall of the People, Peking, depicting the sun rising over the eastern hills.

Fuseli John Henry 1741–1825

John Henry Fuseli (Johann Heinrich Fussli) was born into a family of distinguished Zurich intellectuals and artists. In 1761 he was ordained a Zwinglian minister after studying with the influential literary critics J.J. Breitinger and J.J. Bodmer. It was Bodmer who introduced him to the writings of Milton and Shakespeare and who supported his early interest in art. In 1764 he went to London where he worked as an illustrator and published an English translation of Winckelmann's *Gedanken* (*Reflections...*; 1765). Determined to become a history painter, he was encouraged by Reynolds to study in Italy,

and to this end he departed for Rome in 1769. His years in Rome, from 1770 to 1778, influenced him profoundly. He soon found himself at the center of a talented group of like-minded English and continental artists which included Alexander Runciman, Johan Tobias Sergel, and Nicolai Abildgaard. In addition to the Antique, Fuseli studied carefully the works of Michelangelo and certain Mannerists,

John Henry Fuseli: The Nightmare; canvas; 101×127cm (40×50in); 1782. Detroit Institute of Arts

G

Gabo Naum 1890–1977

The Russian sculptor and painter Naum Gabo was born in Briansk. He spent the years 1910 to 1914 studying natural science in Munich; his only contact with the fine arts during this period came through attendance at Heinrich Wölfflin's lectures in art history. In 1913 and 1914 he made frequent trips to Paris where his brother Antoine Pevsner was working as a painter. When the First World War began he went to Scandinavia; in 1915 his brother joined him in Oslo.

There he made his first sculptures, a series of heads which rejected the use of solid volumes, building up forms instead from a series of curved planes. Archipenko's constructed figures certainly influenced him, but unlike Archipenko he did not use a painterly treatment to compensate for the lack of solid modeling. Gabo's monochrome works boldly postulated the possibility of sculpture in which space takes precedence over mass.

After the Revolution of 1917 both Gabo and Pevsner returned to Russia. In 1920 they published the *Realistic Manifesto*, actually written entirely by Gabo, to accompany an outdoor exhibition of their work in Moscow. It proclaimed the failure of Cubism and Futurism to create an art appropriate to the new civilization arising out of the Revolution. Rejecting applied color as being an "idealizing agent", it advocated "freeing the volume of mass", justifying this by reference to the principles of engineering. The works that followed this manifesto were totally Abstract and used thin planes of plastic, wood and glass to define space, while employing transparent materials to render the structure clear to the spectator.

While sharing the Constructivists' concerns, Gabo disagreed with Tatlin and Rodchenko's view that in a Socialist state pure art was a redundant luxury, and that the artist should devote himself to tasks of direct practical value. He believed that to be of the greatest value to society the artist should keep his independence. In 1922, aware that the more narrowly utilitarian view of art prevailed, he left Russia for Berlin. Moving to Paris in 1932, he joined the international *Abstraction-Création* group. In 1935 he visited England, where

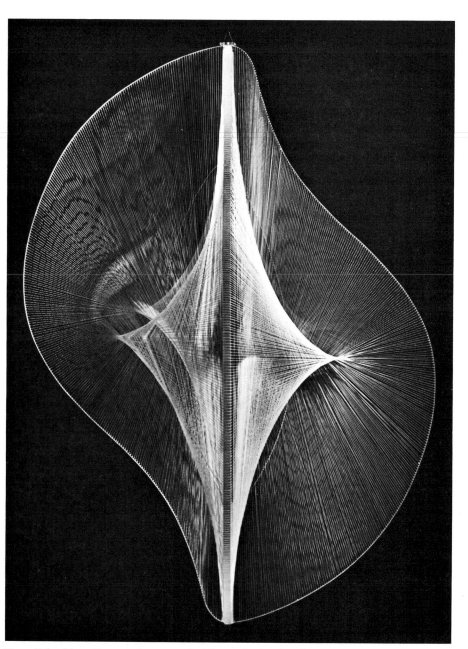

Naum Gabo: Linear Construction no. 2; plexiglass and nylon thread; 114×84×84cm (45×33×33in); 1968–9. Tate Gallery, London

his presence was to stimulate the growing interest in Abstract art whose adherents included Ben Nicholson and Barbara Hepworth. In 1937 he co-edited *Circle*, a publication in which advanced architects and Abstract artists sought to explain their ideas to a wider public.

At that time a new element entered his work, and space was defined by line as well as surface. This was achieved by incised lines across the surface of transparent perspex, and later by stretching taut steel or plastic threads across an overall framework. This defined space with the minimum of volume, and built a three-dimensional void logically from an outline in space. In 1946 Gabo moved to New York. During the 1950s he was at last able to realize his ideas on a monumental scale, through commissions such as that for the sculpture outside the Bijenkorf building in Rotterdam in 1957.

Further reading. Pevsner, A. *A Biographical Sketch of my Brothers, Naum Gabo and Antione Pevsner*, Amsterdam (1964). Read, H. and Martin, L. *Naum Gabo*, Cambridge, Mass. and London (1964).

Jacques-Ange Gabriel: the Petit Trianon, Versailles; 1763–9.

Gabriel Jacques-Ange 1698–1782

Jacques-Ange Gabriel was the greatest French architect of the 18th century and a talented decorative draftsman. He was the pupil and colleague of his father, Jacques Gabriel (1667–1742), also known as Gabriel Père, from whom he took over the reconstruction of the Royal Palace at Fontainebleau in 1742.

At the age of 30 he was made *Contrôleur-Général des Bâtiments du Roi* and a member of the Académie Royale. He trained in Paris, never went to Italy, and built almost exclusively for Louis XV and his mistress, Madame de Pompadour. At first this restricted his work to additions or alterations to Royal Palaces, but he was lucky in that the second half of the King's reign saw a great increase in public building.

From 1755 to 1775 he laid out the Place Louis XV in Paris (now the Place de la Concorde). His Hotel de Crillon (1757–75) and Gardemeuble (1758–66, now the Ministry of Marine) echo the Louvre Colonnade by Perrault (begun 1667), thus bypassing Rococo architecture in favor of the French classical tradition of François Mansart (1598–1666).

At the École Militaire (begun 1751) and the perfectly cubic Petit Trianon, Versailles (1763–9), he worked in a more mixed spirit, combining elements of Antiquity (which was increasingly popular in the 1760s) and Palladianism.

His blend of elegance and restraint determined the style of official architecture under Louis XV. The "style Gabriel" was widely imitated, influencing among others the Neoclassical architect Claude-Nicolas Ledoux (1736–1806) in his early designs.

Gaddi family 14th century

The Gaddi were a family of Florentine painters, the greatest being Taddeo Gaddi (1300–66). Taddeo's father Gaddo Gaddi (*fl. c*1308–30) was a painter and mosaicist, and traditionally the author of some of the surviving work in the Cathedral and the Baptistry in Florence. None of his work is now known with certainty.

Taddeo Gaddi was Giotto's pupil and assistant for 24 years. His first independent work dates from the mid 1320s, a *Madonna and Child* in S. Francesco, Castelfiorentino. Not surprisingly it is a highly individual version of Giotto's *Ognissanti Madonna* (Uffizi, Florence). Taddeo's

Taddeo Gaddi: the Annunciation to the Shepherds; fresco; 1332–8. Baroncelli Chapel, S. Croce, Florence

Agnolo Gaddi: The Legend of the Holy Cross; fresco series; c1380. S. Croce, Florence

fresco decoration of the Baroncelli Chapel, S. Croce, Florence, with *The Life of the Virgin*, probably dates from 1328 to 1330. As the altarpiece of the chapel is signed by Giotto (a workshop product) it seems possible that Taddeo carried out the frescoes according to ideas Giotto left behind when he went to Naples in 1329. There are several major innovations in the chapel, including some *trompe-l'oeil* still-life cupboards, and a *nocturne* scene of the Annunciation to the Shepherds. A rare survival from this period is Taddeo's drawing on paper for *The Presentation of the Virgin* (Louvre, Paris).

All his work is most distinctive, and shows a deep understanding of Giotto together with a feeling for beautiful color,

as is clearly seen in the tiny, delicate Franciscan Scenes on 29 cupboard door panels (Galleria dell'Accademia, Florence). His *Last Supper* in the Refectory of S. Croce is extraordinarily realistic and foreshadows 15th-century frescoes of the same subject.

Taddeo was an influential artist and teacher; among his pupils were his three painter sons, Giovanni, Niccolò, and Agnolo, of whom Agnolo (c1350–96) is the most important. He developed even further his father's love of color. Some idea of his contemporary standing as an artist can be gained from his commission to decorate the main chapel behind the high altar in S. Croce, with *The Legend of the Holy Cross* (c1380).

Gaibano Giovanni *fl.* 1253–93

Giovanni Gaibano was an Italian miniaturist who worked a great deal in Padua. First heard of in 1253 near Ferrara, he is known chiefly for his illuminated Epistolary in the Chapter Library of Padua Cathedral (c1260). One of the miniatures (f. 98v.) probably shows Giovanni himself at work on the book. He died in 1293.

The Padua Epistolary is illustrated with 16 full-page miniatures on a gold ground. These show scenes relating to the chief festivals of the Christian year, such as the Nativity and the Epiphany. As so often with miniatures of this date, they are surprisingly well-preserved; the bright blues, reds, and greens, with white detail, give life to a style of illumination which is of high quality, if unadventurous.

Gainsborough Thomas 1727–88

The English painter and landscape draftsman Thomas Gainsborough was born at Sudbury in Suffolk. About 1740 he went to London where he trained with Gravelot; later he assisted Francis Hayman with the painted decorations at Vauxhall Gardens. During his years in London he also studied the paintings of the 17th-century Dutch landscapists, in particular Wynants and Jacob Ruisdael. He contributed his most important early landscape, *The Charterhouse*, to the Foundling Hospital, London in 1748. He returned to Suffolk and by 1752 was settled in Ipswich, where he painted landscapes while supporting his family by portraiture. His early portraits, of which *Mr and Mrs Andrews* (1748/9; National Gallery, London) is the most remarkable example, feature small figures casually disposed in landscape settings and are close in style to the contemporary conversation pieces by Hayman. His approach to landscape during this period was an ornamental blend of French and Dutch influences enriched by sensitive observations of light effects and of naturalistic detail. This is seen in such pictures as the so-called *Gainsborough's Forest* (*Cornard Wood*; 1748; National Gallery, London) and *River Scene with Figures* (c1747; National Gallery of Scotland, Edinburgh).

Upon moving to Bath in 1759, Gainsborough rapidly established a fashionable portrait practice. He began painting on life scale, at first retaining the informal poses of his Ipswich style, but gradually introducing a more conventional elegance in emulation of van Dyck. Among the mas-

Thomas Gainsborough: River Landscape with Figures in a Boat; oil on canvas; 119×168cm (47×66in); c1768–70. Philadelphia Museum of Art

terpieces of the Bath period are *Mary, Countess Howe* (*c*1765; Kenwood, The Iveagh Bequest, London); *Jonathan Buttall* (known as *The Blue Boy*, 1770; Huntington Library and Art Gallery, San Marino); and *Elizabeth and Mary Linley* (1772; Dulwich College Picture Gallery, London). He continued to paint landscapes in the picturesque vein, peopling his woodlands with an increasingly idealized peasantry. As lyrical evocations of an idyllic world, such paintings as *Return from Market* (1767–8; Toledo Museum of Art, Toledo, Ohio) and *The Harvest Wagon* (1767; Barber Institute of Fine Arts, Birmingham) are rivaled in the 18th century only by the landscape masterpieces of Boucher.

Gainsborough was a founder member of the Royal Academy in 1768. He moved to London in 1774, and became the favorite painter of the royal family soon afterwards. He had a series of quarrels with the Academy, and after 1784 exhibited only in his own studio. From the late 1770s, "fancy pictures" of beggar children in rustic settings began to figure more prominently in his work. He experimented with techniques of transparency painting, mixed media drawing, and printmaking, as well as new subject matter, including historical scenes and seascapes. His portrait style became increasingly impressionistic, while his late landscapes reveal great stylis-

tic diversity and a new poetic force.

In the history of Western painting, Gainsborough ranks with the greatest technicians and colorists. His approach to art combined empiricism and imagination, and he generally shunned the intellectual-

ism of contemporary academic theory. His influence on English portraiture was small in comparison to that of his rival, Reynolds; but his importance to subsequent genre and landscape painting in England was considerable.

Further reading. Hayes, J. *The Drawings of Thomas Gainsborough* (2 vols.), London and New Haven (1970). Waterhouse, E. *Gainsborough*, London (1958).

Galilei Alessandro 1691–1737

Alessandro Galilei was an Italian architect. Leaving his native Florence in 1714, he spent five years in England, before returning home to become court architect to the Medici. The Florentine Pope Clement XII called Galilei to Rome in 1730.

He won the competition (1732) for the facade of S. Giovanni in Laterano, Rome (completed 1736). The acceptance of his severely classical design marks the beginning of late Baroque classicism in Rome. While it has been suggested that his design reveals a knowledge of nascent English Neo-Palladianism, it also derives from the Roman tradition of Carlo Maderno and Michelangelo. Other important Roman works of Galilei were the Corsini Chapel, also in S. Giovanni, and the facade of S. Giovanni dei Fiorentini.

Alessandro Galilei: the facade of S. Giovanni in Laterano, Rome; completed 1736

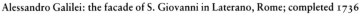

Gallegos Fernando *fl. 1467–1507*

The Spanish painter Fernando Gallegos (or Gallego) was born in Salamanca, and was foremost among the few painters known to have been working in that province in the late 15th century. His first work was the six-paneled altarpiece of San Ildefonso in Zamora Cathedral (1467), commissioned by Cardinal Juan de Mella. He later painted in Valencia Cathedral, and in the University Chapel and the old cathedral of Salamanca (*c*1507). His facial types are unmistakably Spanish, but his spatial effects, dream-like clarity of background, sculptural notions of form, and heavily decorative textiles suggest affinities with Flemish painting, especially that of Dieric Bouts.

Ganku Kishi *c1749–1838*

The Japanese painter Kishi Ganku (or Kishi Ku) was the founder of the *Kishi* School. Little is known of his life. He was evidently known in Kanazawa and achieved some sort of official rank in that part of Japan, though he worked mainly in Kyoto. He was greatly influenced by the Nagasaki Chinese-style artists, but developed his own unmistakable manner, combining powerful, chunky line with delicacy of wash and detail. He was especially renowned for his paintings of tigers—animals he had never seen, but which he reconstructed from skins. One of his best examples is in the British Museum, London. Ganku's school gradually adopted the *Shijo* style, though they retained his thick, angled outlines of rocks and trees.

Garnier Charles *1825–98*

Charles Garnier was a French architect of the Second Empire. His best-known building, the neo-Baroque Opéra in Paris, is generally thought to epitomize the Second Empire taste for splendor and almost vulgar luxury. After winning the Grand Prix of the Academy in 1848, Garnier visited Rome and Athens. In 1861 he won the competition for the new opera house, but the building was not finished until 1875. This ornate work—very elaborate both on paper and in reality—stands as a focal point at the end of one of Baron Haussman's wide new boulevards which revolutionized the look of Paris. Garnier's Casino at Monte Carlo (1878) is an equally grandiose building.

Charles Garnier: the Casino at Monte Carlo; 1878

Garnier Tony *1869–1948*

Born in Lyons, the French architect Tony Garnier won the Prix de Rome in 1899. He soon began work on the designs that have since assured him a place in the history of modern architecture: for a Cité Industrielle, Lyons (1901–4). This embodied a new conception of urban planning and was greatly admired by Le Corbusier. Garnier's chosen material, reinforced concrete, was then in its infancy, and the forms he created were ones only made possible by the new material. Consequently, many of his designs anticipate developments of 20 or more years later. In Lyons Garnier built the Abattoir (1909–13), the Olympic Stadium (1913–16), and other public works. His Town Hall of Boulogne-Billancourt (1931–4) served as a prototype for many later administrative buildings.

Garofalo: A Pagan Sacrifice; oil on canvas; 128×185cm (51×73in); 1526. National Gallery, London

Garofalo 1481–1559

Benvenuto Tisi, known as Garofalo was a worthy if not markedly individual Italian painter in the Ferrarese tradition. His illusionistic ceiling decorations in Ferrara (Palazzo del Seminario, 1517–19; Palazzo di Ludovico il Moro) show him practicing the North Italian style which had been initiated by Andrea Mantegna (1431–1506). His religious paintings range from early Holy Families reminiscent of the work of Giorgione (1477–1510), to monumental late altarpieces. These may show the influence of two visits he probably made to Rome, where he is thought to have seen works by Raphael, Michelangelo, and Sebastiano del Piombo.

Gaudí 1852–1926

The Catalan architect Antoni Gaudí y Cornet came from a family of coppersmiths and wrought-ironworkers. He studied in Barcelona, graduating in 1878, and became interested in a variety of subjects: aesthetics, philosophy, medieval art and craft, Viollet-le-Duc's interpretation of Gothic architecture, and the nostalgic and primitivist sentiments of Catalan nationalism. The latter led him to the study of nature as a source of decorative and structural forms.

Like other architects brought up in a craft tradition Gaudí possessed an innate feeling for the properties of his material, in this case metal. In his first commission, the Casa Vicens in Barcelona (1878–80), one interesting detail is the naturalistic wrought ironwork of the gates and railings. The building as a whole carries connotations of both Moorish and Gothic architecture; this was also to be a feature of Gaudí's *magnum opus*, the Sagrada Familia church in Barcelona (1884–1926). Gaudí was put in charge of this building in 1883 and continued to work on it until his death.

With the Sagrada Familia, the architect gradually transformed what had been a normal neo-Gothic design into a fantastic confection, highly idiosyncratic. "Grotesque" is perhaps the only word to describe this product of Gaudí's imagination. The transept towers, crowned by pinnacles that resemble crustacea, call to mind such bizarre phenomena as Hittite caves eroded by the wind, or stalagmites. Indeed, the whole church is a giant grotto whose skin is molded into a continuously curving, twisting construction, studded with stone

Gaudí: the Parque Güell; 1900–14

sculpture and fragments of glass, china, tile, and mosaic.

Even more sculptural are Gaudí's two major secular works, the blocks of flats in Barcelona, the Casa Batlló (1905–7), which he remodeled, and the Casa Milá (1905–10). Here Art Nouveau breaks away from surface ornament to dictate the shape of the entire building, inside and out. The result, in the case of the Casa Milá, is a rippling, bulging organism, embossed with spiky wrought iron balconies, pierced by windows that look like eyes, and topped with crazy twirls. The interior has no straight walls or level ceilings.

In the Parque Güell (1900–14; now the Municipal Park of Barcelona), glass and ceramic mosaic are again prominent means towards Gaudí's monstrous ends, along with broken plates, bottles, china dolls, and other relics. They are all part of an extremely colorful, almost Surrealist collage, which spreads itself all along the serpentine seat-parapet of this sunny Barcelona park. As an antidote to the puritanism and rationalism of the International style, the Parque Güell—or any other of Gaudí's creations—is without equal.

Further reading. Casanelles, E. *Antonio Gaudí: a Reappraisal*, Greenwich, Conn. and London (1968). Collins, G.R. *Antonio Gaudí*, London and New York (1960). Sert, J.L. and Sweeney, J.J. *Antonio Gaudí*, London and New York (1960).

Gaudier-Brzeska Henri
1891–1915

The French-born sculptor Henri Gaudier-Brzeska was born Henri Gaudier, at St-Jean-de-Braye, Loiret, France. He met the Polish Sophie Brzeska in Paris. They lived together from 1910 and he added her name to his in 1911; the couple moved to London in the same year. Powerful portraits such as *Ezra Pound* (1914; Yale University Art Gallery, New Haven, Conn.) and *Horace Brodzky* (1913; Kettle's Yard, Cambridge) celebrate the new friendships he formed at this period. He was associated with the Omega Workshops, and then with the rival Vorticists. Gaudier made many drawings of animals, and in 1914 produced such vivid sculptures as the semi-Abstract *Stags* (alabaster; 1914; Art Institute of Chicago) and the stark, stylized *Bird Swallowing a Fish*

Henri Gaudier-Brzeska: Crouching Figure; marble; 22×30×10cm (9×12×4in); c1914. Walker Art Center, Minneapolis

(1914; alabaster in Kettle's Yard, Cambridge). He joined the French army in 1914 at the outbreak of the First World War. An artist of incalculable potential, he was killed at Neuville-Saint-Vaast at the age of 24.

Further reading. Brodzky, H. *Henri Gaudier-Brzeska, 1891–1915*, London (1933). Cole, R. *Burning to Speak*, Oxford (1978). Ede, H.S. *Savage Messiah: a Life of Gaudier-Brzeska*, London (1931).

Gauguin Paul 1848–1903

The French painter Paul Gauguin was also a sculptor, ceramist, and printmaker. He was born in Paris; his mother was Aline-Marie Chagal the daughter of the political activist Flora Tristan (1803–44) and the engraver André Chagal. Gauguin's parents decided to emigrate from the France of Louis Napoleon to Peru in 1851: his father Clovis Gauguin, a liberal journalist, died on the voyage. In Peru, his mother's relatives, rich and politically powerful, provided a tropical paradise the infant Paul was to remember all his life. He was six years old when his mother returned with him to France.

Gauguin left school at 17; he was a merchant seaman from 1865 to 1867, and served in the French navy from 1868 to 1871. When his mother died (aged only 41) in 1868, a wealthy banker, Gustave Arosa, became his legal guardian. It was through his guardian that Gauguin entered a stockbroker's office in Paris in 1871. Two years later he married Mette Sophie Gad, a Danish governess whom he had met through Arosa; in 1874, the first of their five children was born. Early in his married life Gauguin became a Sunday painter, introduced to this too by Arosa, and attended evening classes. He exhibited at the Salon in 1876 and about this time met Pissarro. In 1879 he exhibited with the Impressionists and became a regular contributor to their last four group shows between 1880 and 1886.

Enjoying moderate financial success, he started collecting paintings by Manet, Monet, Renoir, and Degas, buying one or two by each of them. Above all he collected works by Cézanne and Pissarro. His own early paintings were strongly influenced by these two painters and by Degas. In 1883, he gave up his job to become a full-time painter. The following year he went to Rouen, and then to Copenhagen; but he was unable to find patrons in either place and, humiliated by his Danish relatives, he returned to Paris in 1885. Estranged from his family, beset by poverty and debt, prone to illness, longing for a tropical paradise, Gauguin existed from 1886 onwards in repeating phases of hope and despair.

His odyssey took him to Brittany, Provence, the West Indies, and, finally, Oceania. Between 1886 and 1891, he spent most of his time in Brittany at Pont Aven and Le Pouldu, broken by his visits to Panama and Martinique in 1887, his two months' stay with Van Gogh in Arles (from October to December 1888), and his sojourns in Paris. His Breton works began as continuations of the lessons he had learned from Pissarro and Cézanne. But his restless, experimental nature—not least, the excitement of producing pottery—drove him to search for a new means of pictorial expression. During these years he was sustained by the Japanese prints and Javanese and Indonesian art he saw at the Paris World Fair of 1889. He found refreshment in contact with the Symbolist poets Mallarmé, Morice, and Moréas, and he picked up religious and Symbolist impulses from two younger friends, Bernard and Aurier. Two Dutchmen gave him financial help at this time, the art dealer Theo van Gogh, and the artist Meyer de Haan.

Gauguin was never a prolific artist—his total oeuvre amounts only to some 600 paintings and pastels. Nor did his development proceed in a straightforward way: he would push far ahead into unexplored stylistic territory, and then withdraw. His landscapes, still lifes, and even portraits were produced without deliberate Symbolist overtones. His use of color was often arbitrary, his line simplified and abrupt. Words like "Synthetism" and "Cloissonism" were used to describe the characteristics of his art at that time: Post-Impressionism is the later, all-embracing term.

Gauguin once wrote of his Breton pictures: "I love Brittany. I find a wildness and a primitiveness there. When my wooden shoes ring out on its granite soil, I hear the muffled, dull, and powerful note I am looking for in my painting." Important pictures from this period include the *Vision after the Sermon* or *Jacob Wrestling with the Angel* (1888; National Gallery of Scotland, Edinburgh), the *Yellow Christ* (1889; Albright-Knox Art Gallery, Buffalo), *Christ in the Garden of Olives* (1889; Norton Gallery, West Palm Beach) and *Loss of Virginity* (1891; Collection of Walter P. Chrysler Jr, New York). Gauguin and his friend Meyer de Haan collaborated in decorating the dining-room of a Breton inn, which they carried out in a fully liberated, nonnaturalistic style. Gauguin's ceramics and his sculpture, especially the painted wood relief *Be in Love and You Will be Happy* (1889; Museum of Fine Arts, Boston) proclaim his Symbolist tendencies. He often theorized about his art, in letters to his friends, in articles, and in illustrated manuscripts.

Gauguin's yearning for a tropical paradise led him to organize a sale of his work in Paris in 1891. By June of that year he was in Tahiti, where he remained until August 1893. He did not find a primitive paradise or a primitive art, nor did he discover a primitive religion being practiced. He had therefore to create his own myths, his own series of allegorical works, which were interspersed with "straight" landscapes, still lifes, and portraits. He took with him photographs of Greek, Roman, and Egyptian art, of the works of French 19th-century painters (Delacroix, Degas, Puvis de Chavannes), and of the Buddhist reliefs at the Javanese temple of Borobudur. An account of Tahitian society published in 1837 provided the basis for his illustrated manuscript, *Ancien Culte Mahorie*. From this source he composed his semiautobiographical, semi-imaginary account of his first Tahitian visit, *Noa Noa (Fragrance)*. As illustrations, Gauguin prepared a set of colored woodcuts, which were themselves a landmark in the history of printmaking. In Paris in November 1893, a one-man show of his Tahitian paintings revealed their bright, flat colors, exotic subject matter, esoteric titles (often in misunderstood Tahitian), and their Symbolist intent.

Gauguin revisited Brittany in 1894; unhappily he broke an ankle in a brawl, and eventually—after another sale of his work in Paris—left France for good in June 1895. He returned to Tahiti. He worked at a slower rate during this second stay—producing only 100 paintings between 1895 and 1903, as against 90 between 1891 and 1893. The paintings became direct and bold in spatial organization, although often more grave and somber in both color and mood than his earlier works. Many of them suggest a mural scale and style. Privation and illness continued to haunt the artist's life. Eighteen ninety-seven was a disastrous year for him, culminating in the news of the death of his favorite daughter, Aline, and the final rupture with Mette. In utter despair, he planned his largest and most philosophically ambitious picture, *Where Do We Come From? What Are We? Where Are We Going?* (1897; Museum of Fine Arts, Boston). He wrote of it: "My dream is intangible, it implies no allegory. To quote Mallarmé: 'a musical poem, it needs no libretto'". After completing it, he made an unsuccessful suicide attempt.

Paul Gauguin: Ea Haere Ia Oe (Where are you going?); oil on canvas; 91×72cm (36×28in); 1892/3. Hermitage Museum, Leningrad

Paul Gauguin: Where Do We Come From? What Are We? Where Are We Going?; oil on canvas; 139×375cm (55×148in); 1897. Museum of Fine Arts, Boston

He painted little during his last years in Tahiti (nothing at all, for example, in 1900). But after moving to the Marquesas Islands in 1901, his enthusiasm revived and several important canvases date from

Il Gaulli: St John the Baptist; oil on canvas; 184×119cm (72×47in); c1676. City of Manchester Art Gallery

the last two years of his life. He continued to sculpt, and in January 1903 he completed a rambling piece of autobiography, *Avant et Après*. After his death a large retrospective exhibition, one of the most important of the century, at the Salon d'Automne of 1906, guaranteed his continuing influence on 20th-century art.

Further reading. Bodelsen, M. *Gauguin's Ceramics*, London (1964). Gray, C. *Sculpture and Ceramics of Paul Gauguin*, Baltimore (1963). Rewald, J. *Post-Impressionism*, New York (1956). Wildenstein, G. and Cogniat, R. *Gauguin*, Paris (1964).

Gaulli Il 1639–1709

The Italian painter Giovanni Battista Baciccia was known as Il Gaulli. Born in Genoa, he left his native city in 1657 to follow a career in Rome. There he painted large illusionistic frescoes, among which is the *Triumph of the Name of Jesus* (1676–9) in the nave vault of the Gesù. In Genoa he was influenced by the colorism of the work of van Dyck and Rubens. This, combined with the impact of the sculpture of Bernini (whose circle he joined in Rome), led to his developing one of the most exuberant painting styles of the High Baroque.

Geertgen tot Sint Jans
1455/65–1485/95

Very little is known about the career of the Netherlandish painter Geertgen. He was probably born in Leiden, but he seems to have worked mainly in Haarlem, where he apparently died at the age of only 28. His name ("Little Gerard of the Order of St John") indicates that he was a lay brother of the Confraternity of St John the Baptist, for whose church he painted his most important work. This was an altarpiece showing on one side the Passion of Christ and on the other episodes from the Life of John the Baptist. The commission may well have been connected with the gift of a relic of St John to the church in 1484. Only two fragments from the altarpiece still exist, the *Lamentation over the Body of Christ* and the *Burning of the Bones of the Baptist* (both in the Kunsthistorisches Museum, Vienna). These panels show the influence of Flemish artists such as Dieric Bouts and Rogier van der Weyden, and above all of Hugo van der Goes: one figure, in fact, is a direct quotation from the latter's Monforte Altarpiece (Staatliche Museen, Berlin).

It is possible that Geertgen learned about the work of these painters in Bruges, where he may have served an apprenticeship in the guild of goldsmiths and illuminators in 1475–6; but his use of Flemish art was wholly personal and idiosyncratic. The most characteristic feature of his style is the reduction of figures to simple geometric forms, with spherical, almost doll-like heads and very little indication of facial details. At the same time his work reveals a delight in genre elements and a humorous approach. These qualities can to a certain extent be paralleled in manuscript illumination in Holland at this period, as well as in the masterpieces of 17th-century Dutch painting. Geertgen's simple and unpretentious style seems to reflect the influence of his teacher Albert van Ouwater, who also worked in Haarlem. Ouwater's only securely identified work, *The Raising of Lazarus* (Staatliche Museen, Berlin) was certainly the major source for Geertgen's early *Holy Family in a Church* (Rijksmuseum, Amsterdam).

Geertgen's masterpiece is probably *St John the Baptist in the Wilderness* (Staatliche Museen, Berlin). The Baptist is shown in a state of bemused contemplation in a rich and poetic landscape, which is painted with a marvelous luminosity and remarkably sure sense of recession. The preoccupation with light is perhaps this painter's most outstanding quality—reflected in his extraordinary *Nativity of Christ* (National

Arent de Gelder: The Artist painting a Portrait of an Old Woman; oil on canvas; 142×169cm (56×67in); 1685. Städelsches Kunstinstitut, Frankfurt am Main

strokes and his practice of creating variously textured surfaces with palette knife, brush handle, and fingers also follow Rembrandt's practices.

Gallery, London). This is the earliest known true night scene in European painting, in that it uses nonsolar light sources within the picture itself. Together with the Berlin panel, Geertgen's *Nativity* reveals him as one of the most innovative artists of his generation.

Gelder Arent de 1645–1727

Arent de Gelder was a Dutch painter from Dordrecht who was the last important artist to study under Rembrandt. Although not himself capable of Rembrandt's expressive power or dramatic impact, he became and remained a profound admirer of his master's late paintings; he continued to work in a similar style into the 18th century. His early scenes from biblical and secular history have something of Rembrandt's strong, warm color, and also his teacher's liking for Oriental types and costumes (for example, *The Holy Family*, c1685; Staatliche Museen, Berlin). In these pictures and in several sympathetic portraits, de Gelder's thick, broken brush

Gentile da Fabriano c1370–1427

Gentile da Fabriano was an influential, itinerant painter from the Italian Marches, who disseminated the International Gothic style through northern and central Italy. The high reputation he enjoyed during his lifetime must be partially taken on trust, since many of his works have disappeared or survive only in a fragmentary state.

He was born to a prominent family in Fabriano, but little is known of his training and early career. Though influenced by the art of his fellow-townsmen Allegretto Nuzi and Francesco di Cecco Ghissi, he seems to have assimilated the International Gothic style mainly from the miniaturists and painters of Lombardy. Signs of this are evident in what is perhaps his earliest surviving panel, the signed *Madonna and Child with St Nicholas, St Catherine, and Donor* (c1395; Staatliche Museen, Berlin), painted for the church of S. Niccolò in Fabriano.

Between 1395 and 1400 Gentile painted the Coronation Altarpiece for the Franciscan convent in Fabriano (now divided between two private collections) and the more advanced Valle Romita Polyptych for the hermits' church of S. Maria di Valdisasso, near Fabriano (now in the Pinacoteca di Brera, Milan). In this signed polyptych—long dismantled, but now re-

Gentile da Fabriano: The Presentation in the Temple; tempera on panel; 26×61cm (10×24in); 1423. Louvre, Paris

assembled in a modern frame—the Lombard International style is tempered by a new softness, as in the features of the Madonna and the undulation of her silk gown.

Gentile must have traveled to Venice *c*1406 or 1407; there is a record of his presence there in 1408. A 1581 guide to Venice mentions an altarpiece by Gentile in S. Felice, and murals by him in the Grand Hall of the Ducal Palace: none of these survive—all of Gentile's Venetian works are now lost. But the fact that he—an immigrant artist—was commissioned to paint the main hall of the Ducal Palace is proof of his reputation.

From 1414 to 1419 Gentile worked at the cosmopolitan court of Brescia in Lombardy, where he painted a chapel for Pandolfo Malatesta (destroyed at the beginning of the 19th century). On its completion, he accepted an invitation to work for Pope Martin V, who was making his way south to Rome. But owing to the Pope's delay, it was another seven years before Gentile entered his service. He might have returned to a career of provincial obscurity in Fabriano, has not his arrival in Florence, in the Pope's footsteps, occurred at an opportune moment: at a time, that is, when the rich Florentine burghers were beginning to ape the tastes of the courts of northern Italy and France.

Gentile catered to this taste. His versions of *The Madonna of Humility* (examples in the Museo Nazionale, di S. Matteo, Pisa, and Fitzwilliam Museum, Cambridge; both *c*1420/22) are refined and aristocratic. Fashion predominates over saintliness, as in his Washington *Madonna* (*c*1422; National Gallery of Art, Washington D.C.), her tunic sleeve, under a mulberry-red robe, embroidered in gold with a pomegranate pattern.

The fashionable International Gothic style Gentile brought to Florence was already known there, but in a diluted, Sienese version. Gentile expressed its full force in the signed and dated altarpiece he painted for the wealthy Florentine businessman Palla Strozzi (1423; Uffizi, Florence). It consists of a single main panel of the *Adoration of the Magi*; there are lunettes above the three arches at the top of the panel, and a three-panel *predella* below. An inseparable component is the Gothic frame, of which the polygonal corner posts are painted with miniature panels of Mediterranean flowers. In the main panel, Gentile depicts the Epiphany as a courtly cavalcade. Sumptuously at-

Artemisia Lami (Gentileschi): Judith Beheading Holofernes; oil on canvas; 199×162cm (78×64in); c1620. Uffizi, Florence

tired in gold-encrusted brocades, the three Kings have dismounted before the Madonna. A veritable menagerie (which may have been painted by Gentile's friend Pisanello) accompanies the entourage that crowds the foreground. In the background, passing through cities and castles on their way, the Magi journey towards Bethlehem: a seemingly endless procession meandering flamboyantly from one side of the panel to the other. The *predella* panels show an attempt—new in Italian painting—to represent real sky instead of a gold background: the Nativity by night, the Flight into Egypt by day.

Soon after finishing the Strozzi Altarpiece, Gentile began work on another Florentine private commission: the polyptych painted for the Chapel of the Quaratesi family in S. Niccolò sopr'Arno. Vasari called this "indubitably the best of all the works of this artist which I have seen". Consisting of five gabled panels and a *predella*, the Quaratesi Polyptych was

unfortunately dismantled in the early 19th century, its frame (with the date 1425) destroyed, and the panels dispersed throughout various collections. The central panel of the *Madonna and Child with Angels* is now in London (Hampton Court Palace) and the side panels of saints are in Florence (Uffizi). Once again, the emphasis is on sumptuous accoutrements, as in the Magdalen's ermine-lined mantle and the embroidered stole of St Nicholas.

After May 1425 Gentile went to Siena, where he painted a now-lost *Madonna and Saints*. At the end of the same year, traveling south, he frescoed a *Madonna and Child* in Orvieto Cathedral; although damaged, this gives some impression of his more monumental late style.

Arriving in Rome in 1426, Gentile finally entered the service of Pope Martin V, for whom he executed frescoes of *St John the Baptist* in the Lateran Basilica (1427). These were later destroyed to make way for Borromini's Baroque interior. Gentile's last work in Rome seems to have been a *Madonna and Saints* in S. Maria Novella described by Vasari but now lost. It was in the adjoining convent that he died in the autumn of 1427. The Lateran frescoes were completed by Pisanello, who has left one or two drawings that relate to them, and who inherited Gentile's belongings. Though nothing appears to have survived of Gentile's work in Rome (apart from a ruined *Madonna and Child* in Velletri), its importance cannot be minimized. The first great Quattrocento artist to work in the city after the return of the Papacy, he laid the foundations of Renaissance painting there, as to some extent he had already done in Venice and Florence.

Further reading. Christiansen, K. *Gentile da Fabriano*, New York (1982). Colnaghi, D.E. *A Dictionary of Florentine Painters*, London (1928). Degenhart, B. and Schmitt, A. "Gentile da Fabriano in Rom und die Anfänge des Antikenstudiums", *Münchner Jahrbuch der Bildenden Kunst* vol. 11, Munich (1960). Grassi, L. *Tutta la Pittura di Gentile da Fabriano*, Milan (1953). Molajoli, B. *Gentile da Fabriano*, Fabriano (1934).

Gentileschi family
16th and 17th centuries

Born in Pisa, Orazio Lomi Gentileschi (1562–c1639) worked from 1576 until 1621 in Rome, where he was influenced by Caravaggio. Later he reverted to the elegance and light colors of Florentine art. He spent periods in Genoa, Turin, and Paris. Then in 1626 he became painter to the English monarch Charles I. He held this post till the end of his life, painting nine canvases for the hall of the Queen's House at Greenwich.

In 1638 he was visited by his painter daughter, Artemisia Lomi (1597–1651). Besides working in England, she was also active in Rome, Florence, and Naples. Artemisia's work shows the influence of the brutality of Neapolitan Caravaggism; she liked violent subject matter and dramatic contrasts of light and shade.

Orazio Gentileschi: Danaë; detail; oil on canvas; full size 162×229cm (64×90in); 1621–2. Cleveland Museum of Art

Baron Gérard: Corinne at Cape Misène; oil on canvas; 256×277cm (101×109in); c1819–22. Musée des Beaux-Arts, Lyons

Gérard Baron 1770–1837

The French painter Baron François-Pascal-Simon Gérard was born in Rome, but moved to Paris when he was 10 years old. He studied in the studios of the sculptor Augustin Pajou and the painter Brenet, before working under J.-L. David in 1786. In 1789, he won the second Prix de Rome, and spent the years 1791 and 1793 there. On his return he was allotted a studio in the Louvre. His great popularity stemmed from his *Cupid and Psyche* (Salon, 1798; now Louvre, Paris), which is similar in its slightly erotic and porcelain Neoclassicism to the contemporary sculpture of Canova (marble also in the Louvre, Paris). At the time, it was praised for its "primitive" appearance—a feature that appears again in his several versions of the popular Ossian theme.

In spite of some work as a battle painter, his main claim to fame is for his career as a portraitist which lasted through several regimes from Napoleon to Louis XVIII. He was loaded with honors, and created "Baron" in 1819. His *Mme Récamier* (1805; Musée Carnavalet, Paris), preferred by the lady to David's version, displays an atmosphere of subdued and graceful grandeur. In his basically Baroque portrait manner, and in the types of commissions he accepted, he bears comparison with Sir Thomas Lawrence in England.

Gérard Jean 1803–47

The French illustrator and caricaturist Jean-Ignace-Isidore Gérard was also known as Jean Grandville. He was born in Nancy in 1803, and was taught by his father, a miniaturist, until he left for Paris in 1820. He created two early series of lithographs, *Chaque Âge à ses Plaisirs* (1827) and *Les Dimanches d'un Bourgeois de Paris* (1828). These were followed by *Les Métamorphoses du Jour* (1829), an album of 72 colored lithographs consisting of scurrilous caricatures which ascribed appropriate animal guises to the human subjects. Analogies of facial types with animals have been commonplace since Antiquity, but Gérard developed the metamorphosis to a point at which satire took on a dream-like existence of its own.

A fierce anti-Royalist, Gérard was among the artists who collaborated on the journals published by Charles Philipon. From

Jean Gérard: Madame Moon paints a Self-portrait; 1844

LA LUNE PEINTE PAR ELLE-MÊME.

1835, after these had been suppressed, he concentrated on illustrating books, notably *Fables de La Fontaine* (1838), *Gulliver's Travels* (1839), and *Robinson Crusoe* (1840). A later series of lithographs, *Scènes de la Vie Privée et Publique des Animaux* (1842), made his direction clear; the only theme of his masterpiece, *Un Autre Monde* (1844) was his determination to follow his fantasy wherever it led. ("I myself claim to act as guide to myself." Standing on his head he added, "Vive la liberté".) Thus were Philipon's republican aspirations transposed into the realm of graphic imagination. Many of the obsessions that haunted his time appeared undisguised in this remarkable book, introduced by an invocation to Heaven to protect an innocent pencil setting out on its journey alone. Nothing protected its creator; he died insane in 1847.

Gerhaert van Leyden Nikolaus c1430–73

The Dutch sculptor Nikolaus Gerhaert van Leyden was presumably born in Leiden. He was probably trained in the Low Countries, and is first documented in 1462 as the carver of the tomb of Archbishop von Sierck in Trier (its lid and effigy survive in the Bischöfliches Museum, Trier). The walnut *Crucifixion* in the high altar of the church of St George, Nördlingen, generally attributed to him, was made the same year. It therefore seems likely that Gerhaert was based in Strasbourg for some time before 1463, when he is first recorded in the city, and that these early works were executed on excursions from there. From 1463 to 1467 he lived in Strasbourg, although he also worked in Constance. After two invitations from Emperor Frederick III, he moved to Wiener Neustadt, where he remained until his death.

The destruction of Gerhaert's early work in Holland and the loss of his most substantial wooden retable, the high altarpiece in Constance Cathedral, renders proper assessment of his stylistic development extremely difficult. His Trier tomb effigy is very deeply and vigorously carved, with a tremendous sense of volume, while the complexly undercut drapery of the Nördlingen figures imbues them with tense and dynamic movement. About 1464 Gerhaert carved a sandstone portal for the New Chancellery in Strasbourg, of which three fragments survive in Strasbourg (Musée de l'Oeuvre Notre-Dame) and Frankfurt am

Main (Städtische Galerie Liebighaus, Museum Alter Plastik). These heads have astonishing realism and it seems likely that one of them, of a man deep in thought (Musée de l'Oeuvre Notre-Dame, Strasbourg), is actually a self-portrait. The 1464 monument of Canon Conrad von Busnang in Strasbourg Cathedral depicts Gerhaert's patron bust-length before the Virgin and Child within an illusionistic niche: a novel sculptural theme which has points of contact with Netherlandish art.

Gerhaert executed his altarpiece of the Virgin and Child in Constance Cathedral during the years 1465–7. Its loss has repercussions which extend far beyond his own oeuvre, as the influence of this major work upon South German sculpture was extensive. In 1467 he carved the sandstone Crucifix which stands in the Old Cemetery at Baden-Baden. Although it may be broadly associated with Claus Sluter's Dijon *Crucifixion*, and Christ's fluttering loincloth could derive from Rogier van der Weyden's representations of the theme, the stunning naturalism of this figure remains entirely personal.

After his move to Wiener Neustadt, Gerhaert's last years were devoted to the red marble tomb effigy of Frederick III in St Stephen's Cathedral, Vienna. The Emperor's effigy, within the shadows of a cavernous Flamboyant Gothic niche, is surrounded by heraldic symbols. Gerhaert's relief is so remarkably pictorial that it quite belies its function as a horizontal effigy and would function more appropriately as a vertical composition. Other works frequently attributed to him include a walnut Virgin and Child in Berlin (Staatliche Museen) and a sandstone representation of the same subject in Hamburg.

Compared with the work of earlier sculptors, Gerhaert's figures have an entirely new dynamism and expansiveness combined with profound characterization. The widespread diffusion of his style was stimulated not only by his own travels across the breadth of the Empire, but also by the prints of the Master ES and Martin Schongauer, which incorporate many features of Gerhaert's art. More than any other individual, he prepared the way for the great period of German sculpture which spanned the late 15th and the early 16th centuries.

Géricault: study for The Wounded Cuirassier; oil on canvas; 55×46cm (22×18in); c1814. Brooklyn Museum, New York.

Géricault 1791–1824

One of France's first Romantic painters, Jean-Louis-André-Théodore Géricault lived as well as painted with all the verve of the Romantic style. Independently wealthy, he could indulge his twin passions, for painting and horses, as and when he wished. He had less formal training than most artists of his day, and only applied himself seriously to his art when inspired—as with his masterpiece, *The Raft of the Medusa* (1819; Louvre, Paris). His untimely death came after many months of suffering following a fall from a horse.

Born the son of a wealthy bourgeois in Rouen, Géricault moved to Paris as a boy. During his youth, he was fascinated by all aspects of equestrianism, such as races, circuses, and riding schools. When in 1808 he joined his first studio, it was that of Carle Vernet, who was primarily a horse painter. In 1810 he transferred to the studio of Pierre Guérin for more serious academic training; but his real artistic education was derived from the three years he spent copying in the Louvre (1811–14). His first Salon exhibit, *Officers of the Imperial Guard* (1812; Louvre, Paris) is a blaze of color and movement, quite natural in the context of Imperial France; it is strongly reminiscent of the work of A.-J. Gros, who was much admired by Géricault. Until his departure for Rome in 1816, most of Géricault's work was in this vein, and he was sufficiently inspired by the military life actually to enlist for a few months in 1814.

Géricault spent a year in Italy, where he fell under the spell of Michelangelo. The monumentality of the latter is instantly visible in the series of sketches of the famous *Race of the Riderless Horses*; the series is also strongly affected by Géricault's study of the Parthenon frieze. Some sketches are basically realistic, and concentrate on capturing the life and color of 19th-century Rome with crowds cheering these brave men who struggle to restrain the bucking, prancing horses. Perhaps the most impressive, however, is *The Riderless Horse Race in Rome* (1816–17; Louvre, Paris). It transposes the event to a timeless era, uniting the heavily muscled figures from Michelangelo (particularly those on the extreme right) with the flat relief-like depiction of the horse in the center, so like the friezes of Greek art.

On his return to Paris in the autumn of 1817, Géricault was in a quandary. His work had gained power through his study of the Renaissance, but he was dissatisfied with works like the *Race of the Riderless Horses* which did not depict specific happenings. A child of France's most heroic age, he could not ignore the dynamic representation of contemporary reality as practiced by artists like Gros, nor the influence of the increasingly popular British Romantic writers, notably Byron and Walter Scott. He wanted to paint a subject from modern life in monumental terms. Having experimented rather unsuccessfully with various themes, he came across a pamphlet describing the privations of those who had survived the raft of the "Medusa". Left to their fate on the raft by a mutinous crew, the survivors returned to France to tell a horrifying tale of exposure and near starvation, avoided only by cannibalism. Burning with enthusiasm, Géricault interviewed the authors of the pamphlet, and determined to paint a vast canvas. He toyed with sketches of many different scenes before he settled on the final version, but once decided he worked with complete dedication. To force himself to remain in his studio, he shaved his head; and to ensure the correct representation of dead bodies, he worked in the company of corpses. *The Raft of the Medusa* (1819; Louvre, Paris) is a truly innovative painting, not only in raising a subject from modern life to the proportions once reserved for paintings of the Antique, but also in its construction. Géricault was extremely daring in organizing his painting around a pyramid, which culminates in the figure of the Negro waving a rag in the direction of the rescue ship, faintly visible on the horizon. However, this composition gives such power to the expression of hope among the shipwrecked survivors that it succeeds admirably.

Despite its qualities, the *Medusa* was not well received by the critics, nor was it bought by the government as Géricault had hoped it would be. Disillusioned by his relative failure after so much intense work, he took the painting to England early in 1820; he made a considerable amount of money by showing it there in a traveling exhibition. In England, Géricault's style again underwent a radical change. He had been, in 1817, one of the first artists to take up the newly invented process of lithography; he now put this expertise to good use, producing a series of 13 plates illustrating the life of the English poor. These engravings are inspired in part by the work of English genre painters, although they have nothing of the maudlin sentimentality of the latter. The most important work he produced in England is undoubtedly *The Epsom Derby* (1821; Louvre, Paris). Returning to his first love, horses, Géricault here conceives the movement of that most gracious of animals in entirely new terms. The whole impression given is one of movement, with the horses shown galloping flat out to increase the feeling of speed. Minor English sporting painters may have suggested this style to Géricault, but it is essentially new, and no echo of it is found in French art until the advent of Degas, almost 50 years later.

Géricault's entire history is one of change and innovation, and nothing is more novel than his portraits of the insane. Painted for a Dr Georget, one of the pioneers of psychiatry, each of these paintings illustrates a different psychotic condition such as kleptomania, delusions of grandeur, and so forth. It is not certain whether these works were painted by Géricault as a favor to Dr Georget, or whether they were in fact a kind of occupational therapy prescribed by Georget for one of Géricault's frequent bouts of depression. Géricault painted ten of these canvases in all; only five are extant, a fine example being *The Mad Assassin* (1822/3; Museum of Fine Arts, Ghent). The uniqueness of the works lies in the fact that they were among the first to depict an abnormal mental state as an illness, rather than as a subject for laughter.

Between his return to France in 1822, and his death two years later, Géricault painted very little, the only really significant work being *The Lime Kiln* (1822–3; Louvre, Paris). Successive equestrian accidents weakened him, and as he was unwilling to take good care of himself, he eventually died. Near death, he exclaimed in typical Romantic but essentially untrue fashion: "If only I had painted five pictures: but I have done nothing, absolutely nothing."

Further reading. Berger, K. *Géricault and his Work*, Lawrence, Kan. (1955). Eitner, L. *Géricault's Raft of the Medusa*, London (1972). Friedländer, W. trans. Goldwater, R. *David to Delacroix*, Cambridge, Mass. (1952).

Gerthner Madern c1391–c1430

A group of works is closely connected with the name of the German sculptor and architect Madern Gerthner, who was

Gheeraerts family
16th and 17th centuries

The Gheeraerts family are held responsible for a series of full length costume-portraits which were produced in England between *c*1590 and *c*1625. The work of individual hands is difficult to disentangle, but their style originates in the Flemish studio work of the Jacobean period. Marcus Gheeraerts the Elder (1516/21–1604) came from Bruges. He worked in England between 1568 and 1577, and married a sister of John de Critz, another Anglo-Flemish painter who also came from Bruges. Marcus Gheeraerts the Younger (1561–1635) also intermarried with the de Critz family, and his daughter became the second wife of the miniature painter Isaac Oliver. The Gheeraerts' highly decorative portraits can be found in English country houses such as Woburn Abbey, Bedfordshire, Penshurst Place, Kent, and Welbeck Abbey, Nottinghamshire.

Ghiberti Lorenzo 1378–1455

Lorenzo Ghiberti was the major Florentine sculptor of the early Renaissance. His autobiography (the first to be left by a Western artist) begins with his professional debut in 1400, when he left Florence for Pesaro to paint murals for Pandolfo Malatesta. He had been trained as a goldsmith in the workshop of Bartoli di Michele, known as Bartoluccio.

Ghiberti was recalled to Florence in 1401 by news of the competition announced by the Arte di Calimala (cloth guild) for the commission of a new bronze door to the Baptistery, to match the one completed by Andrea Pisano in 1338. The competition involved casting a specimen panel in relief on the subject of the Sacrifice of Isaac. Brunelleschi, Jacopo della Quercia, and Ghiberti were among the seven finalists. Ghiberti, the youngest, won; a comparison between his competition relief and Brunelleschi's (the only two to survive: both in the Museo Nazionale, Florence) suggests he deserved to do so. Artistically more mature than his rival's and technically more advanced, it already establishes his taste for figures *all'antica* (the nude kneeling figure of Isaac derives from an antique torso). In fact, the relief combines a mixture of Classical and Gothic influence which, in varying measures, to persist in his art to the end.

When the contract for the new Baptistery door was eventually signed in 1403, a New

Marcus Gheeraerts the Younger: Portrait of Elizabeth I; oil on canvas; 241×152cm (95×60in); 1592. National Portrait Gallery, London

active in the lodge of Frankfurt am Main Cathedral. These display an extremely painterly treatment of sculptural style. Gerthner sculpted monuments to Werner Weiss von Limpurg (Karmelitenkirche, Frankfurt am Main) and Siegfried zum Paradies (Nikolaikirche, Frankfurt am Main). They point the way to the *Adoration of the Magi* on the south portal of the Liebfrauenkirche in Frankfurt (*c*1420) and the lyrical figures on the Memorienpforte of Mainz Cathedral (*c*1424–5). The climax of Gerthner's achievement is reached, however, in the effigy of Archbishop Konrad von Daun (*ob.* 1434) in Mainz Cathedral.

Testament program of 28 quatrefoil panels, arranged four in a row, was stipulated. The work, which was interrupted by other commissions, spanned two decades. Ghiberti's workshop increased in size during this period. In 1407 he was employing 11 assistants, and later he added more—Donatello, Uccello, Michelozzo, and Benozzo Gozzoli among them. It was the largest and most influential sculptor's workshop in Florence during the first half of the 15th century. By c1415 most of the quatrefoil reliefs had been cast. The frame surrounding them was cast afterwards. There were 48 heads of prophets at its corners (many derived from Roman sculpture), and the bronze jambs and lintel were foliated with wild roses, daisies, crocuses, violets, forget-me-nots, pine cones, and hazel nuts. It was not until April 1424 that the Baptistery north door was finally installed. Ghiberti, who had begun it as a young man, was now in his mid forties.

He had concurrently undertaken other commissions: designs for stained glass (for Florence Cathedral), papal miters, and jewelry. Three Florentine guilds had commissioned from him three bronze statues for the exterior niches of the guild church of Orsanmichele: *John the Baptist* (1413–14); *St Matthew* (1419–22); and *St Stephen* (1425–29). The first of these was predominantly International Gothic in style; the second was Classical (influenced by Donatello and Nanni di Banco); and the third synthesized the two. Technically, all three show Ghiberti's unrivaled mastery of large-scale casting in bronze.

Several shallow bronze reliefs belong to the same years: the two reliefs for the Baptismal Font of Siena (1420–7), the tomb plaque of Leonardo Dati (1425–7; S. Maria Novella, Florence), and the shrine of Saints Protus, Hyacinth, and Nemesius (Museo Nazionale, Florence). Their growing pictorial accomplishment culminates in the four superb reliefs of the shrine of St Zenobius (1432–42; Florence Cathedral); the Classical nature of these reflects Ghiberti's visit to Rome (c1425–30). The visit profoundly influenced the new style he developed during the 1430s, notably in the new Florence Baptistery door commissioned by the Arte di Calimala in 1425 (eight months after the north door had been installed).

Ghiberti claimed he had been given *carte blanche* over the design of the new door, but it is possible that the Old Testament program was drawn up by Florentine humanists. In any case, the new door abandons the quatrefoil pattern of its predecessor. The doors measure 8 ft 6 in by 3 ft 7 in (2.35 m by 1.1 m). They consist of ten 31 in by 31 in (79.5 cm by 79.5 cm) relief panels; each wing, consisting of five panels, is surrounded by a frame ornamented with 24 heads of prophets in roundels, alternating with 24 statuettes in niches, with four reclining figures above and below. Michelangelo is said to have dubbed the new door "The Gates of Paradise", though the story is probably apocryphal.

Apart from their size, it is their pictorial quality and narrative complexity that differentiate the new panels from those of the north door. They display both linear and aerial perspective, reinforced by a gradation from high relief in the foreground to shallow relief in the background, corresponding to the diminution in the size of the figures. Ghiberti described the perspective

Lorenzo Ghiberti: the north doors of the Baptistery, Florence; cast bronze; 457×251cm (180×99in); 1403–24

system in his autobiography. He also emphasized that his narratives were "abounding with figures"—an International Gothic preoccupation. What he omitted to say is that many of these figures, in contrast to his previous *all'antica* repertoire, were derived from Roman sarcophagus reliefs visible in Rome. Ghiberti must certainly have made drawings of them. Yet it is paradoxical that his style, in spite of prolific antique borrowings, never achieves the Classicism of Donatello, who assimilated the Antique without quoting it so directly.

The ten panels of the Gates of Paradise took a decade to cast (*c*1428–37), but work on the chasing and the frames continued into the 1440s. It was not until 1452, after the final process of gilding, that the Gates of Paradise—Ghiberti's finest achievement—were installed at the east entrance to the Baptistery. Three years later Ghiberti was dead.

On his death, he left a flourishing workshop (which Vittorio, his younger son, took over), a distinguished collection of antiquities, and, in manuscript, an incomplete vernacular history and theory of the figurative arts, his three-part *Commentarii*. The first book treats of ancient art, the second of modern, while the fragmentary third is devoted to theoretical problems. Book two represents a pioneer attempt by an artist to describe his predecessors' achievements and thus articulate the epoch we now designate as Early Renaissance.

Ghiberti's status in Quattrocento Renaissance art remains contentious: to some he is one of its fathers; to others he is a late Gothic sculptor, outstripped in his lifetime by the relentlessly progressive Donatello. Undoubtedly Donatello did eventually erode Ghiberti's early unassailable lead in Florentine sculpture. Yet Ghiberti's career exemplifies the artist's new role in postfeudal society, so that to regard him merely as a reactionary champion of International Gothic (the style which had so powerfully influenced his youth) is absurd. The *Commentarii* show to what an extent he grappled with the fundamental pictorial problems underlying a true Renaissance style, and the Gates of Paradise what pains he took to resolve them.

Further reading. Goldscheider, L. *Ghiberti*, London (1949). Krautheimer, R. *Lorenzo Ghiberti* (2 vols.), Princeton, N.J. (1970). Schlosser, J. von *Leben und Meinungen des Florentinischen Bildners Lorenzo Ghiberti*, Basel (1941).

Domenico Ghirlandaio: Head of an Old Woman; black and white chalk on paper; 37×22cm (14×9in); c1486–90. Collection of the Duke of Devonshire, Chatsworth, Derbyshire

Ghirlandaio Domenico 1449–94

The Italian painter Domenico Ghirlandaio was born in Florence in 1449. It is said that he once demanded, "Let me work ... now that I've begun to know how to do it, I only regret that I haven't been commissioned to paint narrative pictures on all the walls of Florence." Though never granted the commission in question, Ghirlandaio did receive many others for portraits, altarpieces, and frescoes. For a decade, between 1480 and 1490, he was the city's most popular and prolific artist.

Ghirlandaio's fresco cycles are evocative pageants of Florentine life. Whatever the ostensible subjects, they contain numerous portraits of his patrons, their families and friends. The tastes and values of his patrons—usually wealthy bankers—are reflected in the impeccable craftsmanship and restrained grandeur of his paintings. While responsive to his immediate surroundings, he also looked to the past for inspiration. In his last and most important works, he established an influential revival of the monumental tradition of Tuscan painting.

Little is known about Ghirlandaio's early training. According to Vasari, he began his

career as a goldsmith but learned to paint from Alesso Baldovinetti. There is no strong evidence of training with Baldovinetti in Ghirlandaio's work. He always painted rather in the manner of a goldsmith. His paintings, early and late, are richly ornamented and metallic. Ruskin cruelly but perceptively summed him up as "a goldsmith selling plated goods". Ghirlandaio was not unique, for a similar goldsmith's style of painting dominated Florence during the late Quattrocento. Two goldsmith painters, Verrocchio and Antonio Pollaiuolo, deeply influenced not only Ghirlandaio but all the important artists who came to maturity during the 1470s, including Leonardo da Vinci, Botticelli, and Perugino.

Much like those artists, during the 1470s and early 1480s Ghirlandaio turned from the static style of mid-century Florentine painting to nurture a striking if stilted vitality. In early works—such as the frescoes of the S. Fina Chapel (1475; Collegiata, San Gimignano), *The Last Supper* in the refectory of the Ognissanti (1480; Florence), and the *St Jerome in his Study* (1480; Ognissanti, Florence)—Ghirlandaio adopted a linear style in which sharp highlights and shadows fragment hard, shiny forms into small, clear facets. Such angular, gleaming forms give tense energy to his early paintings.

Ghirlandaio's most famous works are those he painted during the 1480s. They include the frescoes of the Sala dei Gigli (1482; Palazzo Vecchio, Florence), the frescoes and altarpiece of the Sassetti Chapel (1482–85; S. Trinità, Florence), *The Last Supper* in S. Marco (c1485; Florence), and *The Visitation* (1491; Louvre, Paris). During this decade he constantly augmented the monumentality of his paintings, though he never fully embraced the austere nobility of his early Renaissance models. His late paintings are grand, but they are also garrulous. He always retained something of the vivacity of his early style, partly because he enlivened all his paintings with an abundance of naturalistic or Classical details.

The symbolic isolation of naturalistic elements in Flemish painting attracted Ghirlandaio. For example, he borrowed the bundle of wheat in *The Adoration of the Shepherds* (1485; S. Trinità, Florence) from the rich array of such naturalistic symbols in Hugo van der Goes' *Adoration of the Shepherds* (c1478; Uffizi, Florence), a painting that had only recently arrived in the city.

Similarly, Ghirlandaio shared his contemporaries' enthusiasm for antique art. He amassed an influential vocabulary of antique ornament and pictorial motifs which he used to enrich his paintings. In the *Adoration of the Shepherds* of 1485, for example, he placed the Christ Child before an antique marble sarcophagus with a Latin inscription prophesying His birth. In the Sala dei Gigli Ghirlandaio depicted six Roman heroes within painted architecture reminiscent of Roman triumphal arches, but imitative of no single antique model.

The culmination of Ghirlandaio's career was his decoration of the Tornabuoni Chapel, the presbytery chapel of S. Maria Novella in Florence. The ensemble is vast; there are 19 scenes from the lives of the Virgin, the Baptist, and Dominican saints. Ghirlandaio also designed, though he did not execute, the stained glass windows of the Chapel, and the altarpiece of the *Madonna in Glory* (now in the Alte Pinakothek, Munich).

In those paintings Ghirlandaio actively pursued a sweeping grandeur which helped to shape the artistic goals of younger artists such as Raphael and Michelangelo. He spread vast landscape panoramas across the low horizons to fling open the scenes. He gave the figures an impressive dignity and monumentality. And, perhaps with the help of the Florentine architect Giuliano di San Gallo, he constructed immense Classical architectural settings which ennoble the narrative scenes.

The Tornabuoni frescoes are at once religious narratives and magnificent pageants of Renaissance life. The architectural settings are idealized but also unabashedly contemporary. For instance, Ghirlandaio depicted *The Birth of the Virgin* in the richly decorated room of an opulent Florentine palace. His figures, too, depict the personages of his own era. He portrayed Ludovica Tornabuoni, one of the daughters of the family who were donors of the chapel; she is seen at the head of a group of solemn women in 15th-century costume who visit the Virgin's mother, St Anne.

Ghirlandaio had always used an anachronistic approach, placing portraits of contemporaries alongside religious figures. His settings are pastiches of classicizing fictions

Domenico Ghirlandaio: Portrait of a Lady, called Giovanna Tornabuoni; panel; 76×50cm (30×20in); 1488. Thyssen-Bornemisza Collection, Lugano

and real places. In the Sassetti Chapel, for instance, he showed *The Granting of the Rule to St Francis* in a lofty portico located in Florence's Piazza della Signoria.

Besides being invaluable records of Florentine culture, Ghirlandaio's paintings are also significant artistic achievements. He forged a distinctive, eclectic style from widely disparate elements in Florentine, Flemish and Classical art. His style commands special attention both because of the range of his borrowings and because of his effort to weave those borrowings together. His attempt to achieve a synthesis reflects an unprecedented self-consciousness about the personal and cultural implications of artistic style. The marked range and rapidity of change in Ghirlandaio's manner of painting, and in that of his great heirs Raphael and Michelangelo, sprang partly from this new approach to artistic style.

Further reading. Davies, G.S. *Ghirlandaio*, London (1908). Lauts, J. *Domenico Ghirlandaio*, Vienna (1943). Vasari, G. *Lives of the Great Painters* (4 vols.), London (1969).

Giacometti Alberto 1901–66

The Swiss painter and sculptor, Alberto Giacometti was born in Stampa, the son of a successful post-Impressionist painter. After a year as an art student in Geneva, Giacometti traveled in Italy. He settled in Paris in 1922 and for the next three years studied under the sculptor Antoine Bourdelle.

Influenced by Cubism and by African and Cycladic art, his sculpture of the years 1925–9 became semiabstract, consisting either of simple, compact, tablet-like forms, or else of complex, openwork, cage-like structures. Between 1930 and 1935, he was active in the Surrealist group. Often his Surrealist constructions imply movement; some are actually kinetic. Some of his works, like *The Palace at 4 a.m.* (1932–3; Museum of Modern Art, New York), suggest complete environments and dramatic situations; most are nightmarish, evocative of violent torture, mutilation, and physical confinement.

In 1935, Giacometti's decision to work from nature led to his exclusion from the Surrealist group. Henceforward, his subject matter was taken only from the "real" world—the single human figure and full-length or portrait bust predominating.

Periods of working from the model or from memory alternated.

Throughout his career, Giacometti was obsessed by the desire to render exactly his sensation of the living reality of his subject. In 1940, he felt a compulsion to create miniature statuettes; but in 1945, he found that only exceptionally tall and thin figures came close to reality as he experienced it. From this time on, the surfaces of all his sculptures became deeply pitted, while, in his paintings and drawings, the forms were built up slowly by means of multiple lines and contours. Invariably the figures are frontal; occasionally they are given an environmental setting. Their gouged surfaces and attenuated silhouettes suggest physical decay; while the concentration on the single figure—even in the groups there is no communication between individuals —suggests man's tragic isolation.

Further reading. Genet, J. *L'Atelier d'Alberto Giacometti*, Paris (1958). Giacometti, A. "Ma Realité" in *XXᵉ Siecle*, new series no. nine, Paris (June 1957). Matter, H. *Alberto Giacometti*, London (1988).

Giaquinto Corrado 1699–c1765

Corrado Giaquinto, a Neapolitan Painter, was one of the most important Italian Rococo artists in the first half of the 18th century. A pupil of Francesco Solimena, he moved to Rome in 1723. He worked both

Alberto Giacometti: Seated Nude; lithograph; 57×76cm (22×30in); 1961. **National Museum of Wales, Cardiff**

in Rome, where he decorated many churches (of which the most important is S. Lorenzo in Damaso; 1734), and in Turin, where he acquired something of the extreme sophistication and light and lovely colors of the French Rococo. His most important works are six voluptuous and magical scenes from *The History of Aeneas* (Palazzo Quirinale, Rome). From 1753 to 1762 he was court painter in Madrid, where his decorations at the Royal Palace form the climax of his career; he then returned to Naples.

Gibbons Grinling 1648–1721

The fame of the Rotterdam-born sculptor Grinling Gibbons rests upon the skillful

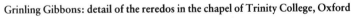

Grinling Gibbons: detail of the reredos in the chapel of Trinity College, Oxford

woodcarvings he made in England as Master Carver in Wood to the Crown. In England, where he lived from c1672, Gibbons decorated the choir stalls of St Paul's Cathedral, London, for Sir Christopher Wren. His virtuoso carvings of fruit, flowers, and animals can also be seen at Windsor Castle and Hampton Court, where he worked under the patronage of Charles II. He maintained a flourishing practice, and also worked in marble and bronze.

Gibbs James 1682–1754

The Scottish architect James Gibbs was born in Aberdeen. About 1703 he traveled to Rome where, after briefly contemplating a career as a painter, he entered the studio of Carlo Fontana. Fontana's influence is discernible in the bold, sculptural treatment of Gibbs' first London commission, the church of St Mary-le-Strand (1714–17). Thereafter the influence of Roman Baroque architecture was eliminated in favor of a more restrained, but still recognizably Baroque style. His manner was derived from Christopher Wren rather than Vanbrugh, and established him as the only mid-18th-century British architect to resist seriously the Neo-Palladianism of Campbell, Burlington, and Kent.

St Martin-in-the-Fields (1722–6), the largest of his London churches, was by far his most influential work. The interior repeated the formula of Wren's St James, Piccadilly (1682–4). But the exterior, with its steeple rising immediately behind the apex of the boldly projecting entrance portico, was entirely new; it was imitated by church builders throughout the 18th and 19th centuries. His country houses—for instance Ditchley, Oxfordshire (1720–5)—were less original. They are frequently distinguishable from their Palladian counterparts only by their elaborate, Italianate interiors, invariably ornamented by the stuccoists Artari and Bugatti.

As a Catholic and a Tory (possibly with Jacobite sympathies) Gibbs necessarily worked independently of the Whig establishment. His *Book of Architecture* (1728) exerted a considerable influence on British architecture, but he inspired no direct heir. His late masterpiece, the circular Radcliffe

James Gibbs: the Radcliffe Camera, Oxford; 1737–49

Camera, Oxford (1737–49) has strong Mannerist and Baroque features despite contemporary trends, and is considered one of the last fully Baroque buildings to be constructed in Britain.

Gilabertus of Toulouse
fl. c1120–30

Gilabertus of Toulouse was a Romanesque sculptor active between c1120 and 1130. His works are now in the Musée des Augustins, Toulouse, and include almost life-size figures of Apostles from the chapter house of the Cathedral of St Étienne, and a series of capitals from the cloister. The Apostles are carved as four pairs and four single figures. It was at one time assumed that these figures formed part of a doorway; but it has recently been claimed that they were used inside the chapter house as *atlantes*, supporting the vaulting. However, this view is not universally accepted. Not all of the figures are by Gilabertus: some are in a different angular style which is related to that of the portal of Moissac. Two of the single figures originally had the signature of Gilabertus on them, but these are now obliterated.

The style of this sculptor has no precedents in Languedoc. It is soft and flowing, with gentle facial expressions, and shows a delight in ornamental details such as the jewel-studded hems of the robes. His method of carving is also new. Previously, a figure in a niche was carved from the front surface of a block of stone into its depth. Gilabertus attacked the block from two adjoining sides, so that the figure emerged from the diagonal axis of the block and not frontally. This method was universally adopted in carving Gothic column-figures.

Gilbert Alfred 1854–1934

The British sculptor Sir Alfred Gilbert was born in London. His work reflected both the Art Nouveau style and the growing interest in mixed-media sculpture. Trained at the Royal Academy and in Paris, he then spent six years in Rome, before his debut at the Royal Academy in 1882. Lord Leighton encouraged him to return to live in England, where success came quickly. He received commissions from private bodies (for the Caldecott memorial, 1890; Westminster Abbey, London), from the State (for the memorial to Lord Shaftesbury, the Eros fountain, 1892; Piccadilly

Alfred Gilbert: Eros; aluminum; 1892. Piccadilly Circus, London

Circus, London), and from the Crown. He was elected to the Royal Academy in 1892. But success vied with overcommitment and financial mismanagement, and Gilbert was declared bankrupt in 1901. He fled to Bruges in Belgium and did not return to England until 1922.

Gilbert and George
1943– and 1942–

The English multimedia artists Gilbert and George—Gilbert Proesch and George Passmore—met at St Martin's School of Art, London, in the 1960s. Calling themselves "living sculptures", they soon established a reputation for their performance art: in *Living Statues* (late 1960s), for example, they painted their hands and faces with bronze paint, and, dressed in the ill-fitting suits that became their trademark, stood motionless for hours. Their preoccupation has been the creation of a single persona—they call their works "one-man shows"—in which a parody of middle-class Englishness, formal and old fashioned, contrasts ironically with their provocative, avantgarde strategies. Later works include large photoworks (a single image being made up of separately taken photographs) whose ambiguous political significance and increasingly explicit homoeroticism have helped to make them controversial figures. Seen by some as subversive ironists, they are regarded by others as banal and nihilistic self-publicists.

Gill Eric 1882–1940

The English sculptor and typographer Eric Gill was born Arthur Eric Rowton Gill in Brighton. He studied at Chichester and Central Schools of Art, and from 1903 worked as a letter-cutter and lecturer. From 1907 to 1924 he lived at Ditchling, Sussex, where, following his conversion to Roman Catholicism, he established a community of craftsmen.

In 1918 he completed *The Stations of the Cross* in Westminster Cathedral, London. In the 1920s he became involved with book design and illustration and designed the "Perpetua" and "Gill Sans" typefaces. Three carvings commissioned from Gill in 1929 for St James' underground station led to his receiving the commissions for *Prospero and Ariel* for the facade of Broadcasting House, London. He died at Harefield, Middlesex.

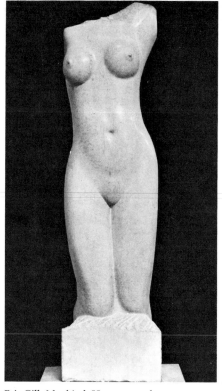

Eric Gill: Mankind; Hoptonwood stone; 242×61×48cm (95×24×18in); 1927–8. Tate Gallery, London

Gillot Claude 1673–1722

The French painter Claude Gillot was born in Langres, near Dijon and trained by his father, Jean, and then in Paris by Jean-Baptiste Corneille (1649–95). He became an associate of the Académie in 1710 and Director of Costumes and Decoration at the Opéra from 1715. His importance in French art is due not so much to his qualities as a painter, which are not very high, but to his subject matter and influence. It was Gillot who introduced theatrical scenes, in particular those from the *commedia dell'arte*, into French painting, as in *The Tomb of Maître André* (c1707; Louvre, Paris). His pupils, Watteau and Lancret, adapted those scenes to advantage. Gillot's own paintings are crude, but his drawings have more vivacity; with those of Claude III Audran, his drawings for ornaments formed a repertoire of Rococo designs.

Claude Gillot: A scene from "The Tomb of Maître André"; oil on canvas; 100×139cm (39×55in); c1707. Louvre, Paris

Gillray James 1757–1815

The English caricaturist and engraver James Gillray was born in Chelsea, London. At an early age he was apprenticed to the metal engraver Henry Ashby (1744–1818), and he produced his first caricatures in 1775. He was a contemporary of Rowlandson, and like Rowlandson was greatly influenced by Mortimer's pen-and-ink satires. He attempted some serious engravings in the 1780s, including a series of illustrations to Henry Fielding's *Tom Jones*. After 1790 he worked almost exclusively as a freelance satirist, disseminating his extravagant designs through etchings tinted with watercolors. In an age that relished the wit of vituperative social and political commentary, Gillray stands out as the supreme master of this art.

Giordano Luca 1632–1705

The Neapolitan artist Luca "Fapresto" Giordano opened a new era in grand decorative painting. His early style was influenced by Jusepe de Ribera (1591–1652). Later he traveled widely, studied deeply the works of Pietro da Cortona (1596–1669) and Veronese (1528–88), and imitated many other styles. Based in Naples, he was much in demand. Between 1680 and 1682 he painted frescoes in the Palazzo Medici-Riccardi in Florence; for ten years, from 1692 to 1702, he was court painter in Spain. His output was immense and his speed of execution proverbial (hence his nickname, *fa presto*). He excelled in covering vast spaces with brilliantly improvised compositions; his touch is light and airy and the spirit of his work anticipates the Rococo.

Giorgione 1477/8?–1510

Giorgio Barbarelli, called Giorgione, was an Italian painter born in Castelfranco on the Venetian mainland; in the space of a short career he brought about many of the changes that were of crucial importance for the development of Venetian art in the High Renaissance.

SHAKESPEARE - SACRIFICED; _ or _ The Offering to AVARICE.

Above: James Gillray: Shakespeare Sacrificed or the Offering to Avarice; engraving; 47×37cm (19×15in); 1789. British Museum, London

Below: Luca Giordano: Commerce and Navigation from the series of allegories of Medici rule; fresco; c1680–2. Palazzo Medici-Riccardi, Florence

There are very few documents concerning Giorgione's career, and only one signed and dated work, *Laura* (Kunsthistorisches Museum, Vienna) although a group of others has by tradition been attributed to him. His date of birth is unknown but Vasari suggests 1477 or 1478. The first certain dates do not occur until the first decade of the 16th century. The panel of *Laura* has the date 1 June 1506 inscribed on the reverse; in 1507 and 1508 there are payments for work (destroyed later in the century) in the Doge's Palace, and records of the frescoes on the facade of the Fondaco dei Tedeschi (now the Venetian Post Office). Late in 1510 Giorgione died of the plague in Venice; he left behind him a fine reputation and a small number of exquisite works, many of which were seen and recorded in the private homes of Venetian collectors by 16th-century connoisseurs, especially Marcantonio Michiel and Vasari.

The difficulty of placing Giorgione in a historical context is partially helped by our knowledge of his collaboration with other artists. Early commentators, including Vasari, record Giovanni Bellini as his master. The inscription on the back of *Laura* records his collaboration with Vincenzo Catena in this small work. Michiel relates that Sebastiano del Piombo completed the *Three Philosophers* (Kunsthistorisches Museum, Vienna) and that Titian completed and altered the *Dresden Venus* (Gemäldegalerie Alte Meister, Dresden), while we know from a variety of evidence that Titian as well as Giorgione worked on the Fondaco frescoes.

From this slender documentation generations of art historians have attempted to piece together some notion of his artistic development. There are, however, other important factors to be taken into consideration. Firstly, Leonardo's visits to Venice in 1500 and 1503: Vasari noted their importance for Giorgione; a Leonardesque *sfumato* and softness of outline is one of the characteristics of Giorgione's style. Secondly, in the absence of fuller documentation we cannot afford to ignore remarks such as that made by Vasari that "by about 1507 Giorgione had begun to show a greater softness and depth in his work".

Laura is perhaps the best documented of Giorgione's works. It is dated 1506, but there are complications—principally in size—for using it to provide a touchstone for dating other works. It is generally

Giorgione: Tempesta; canvas; 82×73cm (32×29in); c1506–10. Gallerie dell'Accademia, Venice

agreed that those paintings on which Titian and Sebastiano collaborated—the *Three Philosophers*, the *Dresden Venus*, and probably *Tempesta* (Gallerie dell'Accademia, Venice)—date from after 1506; while the *Allendale Nativity* (National Gallery of Art, Washington D.C.) and the Castelfranco Altarpiece (Castelfranco Cathedral) are earlier. They both suggest a prior knowledge of Leonardo's art. Vasari states that early in his career Giorgione painted a large number of panels representing the Madonna and Child: the *Madonna Reading* (Ashmolean Museum, Oxford) may be one of these, although the technique suggests that it is probably a mature work. There is, in fact, no painting among the generally accepted works of Giorgione which dates from before Leonardo's influential visits to Venice.

The Castelfranco Altarpiece has been connected with the date 1504; a young member of the family that commissioned the painting died in that year. This work

owes much (including the pose of St Francis) to Giovanni Bellini; but the setting is entirely external and the placing of the figures does not resemble Bellini's. The Virgin is enthroned high above the other figures to introduce us to a beautiful landscape background behind the foreground wall. Giorgione consistently preferred to set his compositions in landscape, where the relationship of one figure to another is consequently blurred. The figures are rarely involved in action or dialogue—they are usually resting, or engaged in contemplation.

That is certainly the case with the *Tempestà* (Gallerie dell'Accademia, Venice). The painting is probably the one described by Michiel in 1530 in the house of Gabriele Vendramin in Venice. This enigmatic work has been the subject of numerous studies arguing a variety of interpretations: whatever the answer, the preponderance of landscape and atmospheric conditions in the painting set it apart as a new type of picture. Other works by Giorgione seen by Michiel in private houses in Venice have similarly puzzling subject matter and novelty of purpose: such is the case with the *Three Philosophers*, the *Dresden Venus*, and to a lesser extent with *Laura* as well. It is significant that Vasari could not identify the subject of Giorgione's frescoes on the Fondaco dei Tedeschi, and suggested that perhaps no meaning was intended.

Apart from *Laura* these frescoes are the only documented works by Giorgione to survive even in part: the fragments of painted plaster in Venice (Gallerie dell'Accademia), plus Zanetti's engravings, combine to give us a rough idea of their original appearance. Giorgione's frescoes were on the side of the Fondaco facing the Grand Canal; they consisted of individual figures, nude or seminude, either standing in fictive niches or seated in quasi-Classical poses. They introduce us to a branch of Renaissance painting that has almost disappeared, and which is governed by different factors to those determining the appearance of panel paintings or canvases.

The innovatory elements of Giorgione's art were taken up and developed by his followers. Palma Vecchio continued to paint faithfully in the Giorgionesque vein, as did Sebastiano del Piombio until his move to Rome. For Titian, features such as Giorgione's technique and the importance given to landscape were of prime importance until the end of his days.

Further reading. Coletti, L. *Tutta la Pittura di Giorgione*, Milan (1955). Pignatti, T. *Giorgione*, London (1971). Richter, G.M. *Giorgio da Castelfranco, called Giorgione*, Chicago (1937). Venturi, L. *Giorgione e il Giorgionismo*, Milan (1913). Zampetti, P. (ed.) *Giorgione e i Giorgioneschi*, Venice (1955).

Giotto di Bondone 1266–1337

A Florentine, born in Colle di Vespignano, Giotto was the supremely influential painter of the 14th century. His is the most remarkable individual achievement in the stylistic revolution that took place in Italy in the latter part of the 13th century and the first part of the 14th century. In this revolution towards greatly increased naturalism, Giotto's name is linked with those of Cavallini and Cimabue in painting, and the Pisani in sculpture.

While much of his life is obscure, it seems clear that Giotto was in Rome early in his career and he may have been a pupil of Cimabue; it was probably between 1295 and 1300 that he created the mosaic of *La Navicella* (St Peter's, Rome; much restored), and the Stephaneschi Altarpiece (Vatican Museums, Rome) which contains a considerable amount of assistants' work. During the same period he executed a series of frescoes in the apse of St Peter's, of which only a minute fragment has survived (private collection, Assisi). It is in Rome rather than in Florence that we now look for the development of the new naturalism of late-13th-century painting. For it was in Rome at this time that the richest and most active patronage was centered in the hands of the church. In Rome, too, there still survived a number of Early Christian fresco cycles; these were beginning to be restored and studied anew, creating a direct link with the Antique. The important position of Rome was maintained until the Pope's removal to Avignon in 1309; thereafter, Rome was excluded from any place in the history of 14th-century painting.

Not the least of the achievements of the Roman Church patronage before the papal exile was the fresh impetus given to the decoration of the new Basilica of St Francis at Assisi. The work was ordered by Pope Nicholas IV in a bull of 1288. Here we come to one of the main problems in the history of western art: was it in fact Giotto who painted the famous *Legend of St Francis* in the Upper Church of St Francis at Assisi? While for many centuries it was popularly supposed to be the work of Giotto, opinion in this century has tended steadily towards denying him the authorship of the *Legend*. The basic reason for this is the difficulty in reconciling the style of the *Legend*, both its execution and design, with that of the frescoes in the Capella dell'Arena in Padua. These are universally accepted as Giotto's, painted c1303–6. It is increasingly felt that the date of the Arena Chapel frescoes is far too close to that of the Assisi frescoes (probably late 1290s) for the difference in style to be explained by the changes wrought on Giotto's style by time. The *Legend* is certainly executed by a number of different masters, perhaps to the design of one of them, who is sometimes called "the Master of *The Legend of St Francis*". The idea that the work was probably done by a Roman school of painters is entirely in keeping with previous artistic activity in Assisi, and

its connections with the church of Rome.

In order to explain the popular connection of Giotto with Assisi, attempts have been made to identify his hand in other parts of the Basilica, particularly with the Master of the Isaac Frescoes who painted some frescoes higher up on the wall above *The Legend of St Francis*. The Basilica at Assisi is a double church; and in the Lower Church there are a number of works by painters close to Giotto, one of whom (the painter of the Magdalen Chapel, c1320) is perhaps identifiable with Giotto's chief assistant in Padua.

The Scrovegni Chapel, S. Maria Annunziata dell'Arena, Padua, is Giotto's greatest surviving work; the chapel itself may have been designed by him for his own frescoes. These are a series of paintings covering the walls and roof of the nave of a small chapel, which was built by Enrico Scrovegni in expiation of his father's usurious activities. They are designed to be read from the center of the chapel, descending clockwise from the top right near the chancel to bottom left at the same end. In three rows they tell *The Story of Joachim and Anna* and *The Early Life of the Virgin* (both top row) and *The Life and Passion of Christ* (lower two rows). On the chancel arch is *The Sending of Gabriel* by God the Father to the Virgin, and the *Annunciation* itself (the Chapel is dedicated to the Virgin Annunciate). Below, on either side of the chancel arch, are scenes from the stories mentioned above, together with two remarkable illusionistic chapels which are probably meant to represent tombs. The whole west (entrance) wall is covered by a *Last Judgment*. Along either side of the nave below the other frescoes are, on the left, seven *Vices*, and on the right, seven *Virtues*. These allegorical figures are in grisaille, set among illusionistic marbling. Indeed the light falls on the marbling in the frames of all the frescoes in every detail so as to be consistent with a point of view in the center of the Chapel.

The 39 narrative scenes are distinguished by their extraordinary dramatic intensity, in which the weight and three-dimensionality of Giotto's figures and the naturalism of the draperies play a decisive part— notably in the famous *Kiss of Judas* and *Lamentation*. Both these pictures demonstrate Giotto's compositional power and control in the creation of his essentially human drama.

Giotto's major surviving panel-painting is the huge *Ognissanti Madonna* (c1307;

Giotto di Bondone: The Lamentation from The Life and Passion of Christ; fresco; 200×185cm (79×73in); 1304–6. S. Maria Annunziata dell' Arena (Scrovegni Chapel), Padua

tempera on panel; Uffizi, Florence). This is the last of the great Tuscan panels of the Madonna and Child of the kind typified by Duccio's *Rucellai Madonna* (1285) and Cimabue's *S. Trinità Madonna* (*c*1285; both in the Uffizi, Florence). In Giotto's work the central group of the Madonna and Child retains a hierarchical difference in scale from the surrounding angels, saints, and prophets, but the careful arrangement of the architecture and figures

creates a realistic space. The naturalism of the drapery in the central group, and the feeling of real limbs and bodies beneath the clothes, helps to create the sensation of a far more human relationship between Mother and Child than had been usual. Yet the sense of grandeur is undiminished in this altogether monumental work.

The Bardi Chapel (*c*1312–*c*17) and the Peruzzi Chapel (*c*1320–*c*28), both in S. Croce in Florence, present problems of

dating, and to some scholars problems of authorship. Both chapels are typical Florentine commissions of the 14th century. The Bardi and the Peruzzi were great international banking families who like other wealthy Florentines bought and decorated private chapels in the new building of S. Croce. The condition of the frescoes is very bad owing to the maltreatment of centuries, not least that of the 19th century when they were rediscovered and then repainted. Both chapels have recently been restored. One reason for the poor condition of the Peruzzi Chapel (*Stories of St John the Baptist and St John the Evangelist*) is that Giotto, contrary to his usual custom, painted it not in *buon fresco* (on patches of wet plaster) but in *fresco secco* (on a complete area of dry plaster)—a far less durable method. There are certain advantages in using *fresco secco*, especially the way it enables the painter to see the whole scene taking place at once. In view of the extraordinary artistic advances Giotto was making in the Chapel, the decision to use this exceptional technique must have been a deliberate one.

It is only reasonable to suppose that the Peruzzi Chapel follows the Bardi Chapel in date, and that both represent stages of Giotto's response to a problem very different from that of the Arena Chapel. Both S. Croce chapels are tall and very narrow; not only are the scenes difficult to see, but the shape of the picture field is an awkward lunette or rectangle, unlike the regular squares of the Arena Chapel.

In the Bardi Chapel *Life of St Francis* Giotto seems to have concentrated on a mainly frontal viewpoint, and in the Peruzzi to have exploited instead a viewpoint from the entrance to the Chapel. In the Bardi, the architecture is everywhere confined by the picture frame, while in the Peruzzi the architecture often disappears behind the picture frame, much more as if the scene were a hole in space. The execution of the Bardi Chapel was largely left to assistants, which has further complicated the attitude of scholars to these two chapels. But even in its sad state of repair, the Peruzzi Chapel still shows us a shadow of the breadth and magnificence of the late achievement of Giotto. It explains why Michelangelo at the height of the Renaissance wished to learn from a study of the figures in *The Ascension of St John*, and why Masaccio learnt so much from Giotto in the early 15th century. In *The Raising of Drusiana*, for example, there is an entirely new naturalism in the relationship of figures to architecture, and a new richness in figure and drapery style.

The same richness, and great elegance, can be seen in the soft, repeated folds of the robe of the *Madonna and Child* in the Kress Collection (*c*1320; National Gallery of Art, Washington, D.C.). Here the Gothic influence of such sculptors as the Pisani has been taken to new heights. If we could imagine the Kress *Madonna* full-length, we would surely see a figure with a pronounced Gothic S-curve, the weight on one leg, the Child on one hip. It is not too difficult, allowing for the passage of 20 years, to see the identity of authorship between this panel and the Badia Altarpiece (*c*1295–1300; Uffizi, Florence). That was an early work painted for the high altar of the Badia in Florence where Giotto also painted some frescoes, only fragments of which survive. Unfortunately the Badia Altarpiece is in rather poor condition.

None of the works so far mentioned is signed. Curiously, it is signed altarpieces, such as *The Madonna and the Saints* from S. Maria degli Angeli, Bologna (*c*1328; Pinacoteca Nazionale, Bologna), and *The Coronation of the Virgin* in the Baroncelli Chapel (*c*1328; S. Croce, Florence), which are held to be the work of assistants and not of Giotto, as though they required some such guarantee of authenticity.

Towards the end of his life (*c*1328–32) Giotto was called to Naples; all works from this period have since been lost. In 1334 he was back in Florence, appointed chief of works at the cathedral. The most famous testimony to his skill as an architect is the Campanile of Florence Cathedral, which does seem to have been initially designed by him though altered later.

There are several works traditionally connected with Giotto, particularly *The Dormition of the Virgin* (Staatliche Museen, Berlin), which was painted for the same church of the Ognissanti as the *Madonna* in the Uffizi, the very fine *Crucifix* in S. Maria Novella, Florence, while the *Crucifix* in Rimini (Tempio Malatestiano) seems typically derivative from a Giottesque model. The Museo Civico at Padua contains Giotto's small *Crucifix* from the Arena Chapel. Workshop products include *The Stigmatization of St Francis* in the Louvre, Paris, probably dating from the early 1300s, and an interesting group of seven panels of *The Life of Christ*. These are separated between Museums in London, Munich, Boston, New York, and Florence.

Our view of Giotto must be based upon his small core of certain surviving works, especially the Arena Chapel, the *Ognissanti Madonna*, the Bardi and Peruzzi Chapels. It is a tribute to Giotto's stature that so many other outstanding works of the period should be associated with his name—not least, of course, *The Legend of St Francis* at Assisi.

Further reading. Meiss, M. *Giotto and Assisi*, New York (1960). Previtali, G. *Giotto e la sua Bottega*, Milan (1967). Smart, A. *The Assisi Problem and the Art of Giotto*, Oxford (1971). Stubblebine J.H. (ed.) *The Arena Chapel Frescoes*, London (1969). Tintori, L. and Meiss, M. *The Painting of "The Life of St Francis" in Assisi, with Notes on the Arena Chapel*, New York (1962). White, J. *Art and Architecture in Italy: 1250–1400*, London (1966). White, J. *The Birth and Rebirth of Pictorial Space*, London (1957).

Giovanni Bologna *c*1524–1608

Giovanni Bologna (or Giambologna) was a Flemish sculptor active in Italy. His original name was Jean Boulogne. He trained in his native Flanders under a major sculptor, Jacques Dubroeucq, mastering the techniques of modeling and carving, and learning the Italianate, classicizing style which Dubroeucq had evolved after a visit to Rome. Giambologna himself journeyed to Rome some time between 1553 and 1555 and made models of Greco-Roman and Renaissance sculpture.

When Giambologna met the elderly Michelangelo, the latter criticized one of Giambologna's models for displaying too high a finish, before the basic pose had been properly established. This was a fault characteristic of Northern Renaissance sculpture as a whole. The young sculptor never forgot this lesson, and became an assiduous maker of sketch-models in wax or clay while preparing his compositions. Several of these have survived (examples in the Victoria and Albert Museum, London). He was deeply impressed by the technical and anatomical virtuosity of Hellenistic sculpture, with its ambitious groups of figures in action—for example *The Farnese Bull*, excavated *c*1546 (Museo e Gallerie Nazionali di Capodimonte, Naples).

On his way homewards Giambologna visited Florence, to study the sculpture of the early Renaissance and of Michelangelo. Bernardo Vecchietti, a rich patron of the arts, offered him accomodation and financial support and soon introduced him to Francesco de' Medici (later Grand Duke). This encouraged the artist to settle in Florence: by 1561 he was being paid a monthly salary by the Medici. He produced ephemeral sculpture for public spectacles, made bronzes and marbles for Medicean gardens, and explored the medium of the small bronze statuette, destined for collectors' cabinets.

From the work of Michelangelo and his Florentine followers Tribolo and Pierino da Vinci, Giambologna evolved a style of composing figures using a contrapposto exaggerated far beyond the Classical norm, with a serpentine axis and a flame-like contour. This instilled new life into Florentine sculpture, which had become academic and stilted in the middle of the century, in the hands of Baccio Bandinelli and Benvenuto Cellini.

Giambologna's developing powers were catalyzed in 1563 by a commission for bronze sculptures to decorate a Fountain of Neptune in Bologna (Piazza del Nettuno). The fountain is pyramidal in design, with a host of lively and sensuous subsidiary figures below. These lead the eye up to the mighty Neptune, who has an energetic spiral pose, momentarily arrested by the gesture of the arm and sharp turn of the head. Hellenistic and Michelangelesque motifs are amalgamated into a brilliant, original composition. Possibly during his stay in Bologna, Giambologna produced the earliest of several versions of a "flying" figure of Mercury. This was to become his most celebrated composition: a statuette initialled "I B" (Kunsthistorisches Museum, Vienna) was sent as a diplomatic gift from the Medici to the Holy Roman Emperor in 1565; a larger bronze version in the Museo Nazionale, Florence was cast later. The vigorous but beautifully balanced pose owes much to earlier bronzes, such as Verrocchio's *Boy with a Dolphin* and Rustici's *Mercury*, both of which were in the Medici collections. The subject may have been inspired by the Mercury statuette on the base of Cellini's *Perseus with the Head of Medusa* (1554; Loggia dei Lanzi, Florence).

On Giambologna's return to Florence, Francesco de' Medici commissioned his first major sculpture in marble, a political allegory of *Florence Triumphant over Pisa* (Museo Nazionale, Florence). This was intended as a pendant to Michelangelo's *Victory*, which had been released from the studio after the master's death in 1564. The young Giambologna was forced to seek a means of uniting two figures into a satisfying action group. The problem had been first posed by Michelangelo in his designs for the tomb of Pope Julius II, and it was later attempted by most of the sculptors in Florence in the middle of the century. Giambologna resolved it with the help of preliminary models in wax and

Giovanni Bologna: Mercury; cast bronze; height 180cm (71in); 1580. Museo Nazionale, Florence

plaster; the final composition is an amalgamation of spiraling curves and zigzag lines, working within a conical volume. Next he carved a group showing *Samson slaying a Philistine* (Victoria and Albert Museum, London) as the centerpiece for a large fountain. Both subject and treatment recall a project of Michelangelo's from the 1520s, which is known only from a number of casts in bronze recording a lost original wax model (examples are in the Museo Nazionale, Florence, and the Louvre, Paris).

Giambologna's third great marble group was the *Rape of the Sabines* (1579–82; Loggia dei Lanzi, Florence). It represented the climax of his career as a figure sculptor, combining three figures into a cohesive group. This was an idea that had obsessed Michelangelo without his ever having brought himself to realize it in marble.

Giambologna's first thoughts are embodied in a bronze group with a standing man and a woman raised in his arms, which he produced in 1579 for Ottavio Farnese. The subject, he wrote to this patron, was chosen to give scope to the knowledge and study of art—it was a conceptual rather than a narrative composition. The sculptor's contemporaries subsequently compelled him to identify the particular episode shown in the full-scale marble version by adding a bronze relief below, showing the Romans and Sabines fighting over the Sabine women. The development from a group of two to one with three figures is plotted in preliminary wax models (Victoria and Albert Museum, London). The three figures are linked psychologically, by the directions of their glances, as well as formally, by the arrangement of their limbs and bodies. The spiral composition means that the group cannot be fully comprehended from any single viewpoint. In technical terms, the sculpture is a masterpiece of virtuosity, carrying to the furthest limits the technique of undercutting which Giambologna had observed in Hellenistic carving, and the use of which distinguishes his work so sharply from Michelangelo's.

In monumental sculpture, his other major achievement was the equestrian statue in bronze of *Cosimo I* (Piazza della Signoria, Florence), which set a precedent soon to be copied by virtually every monarch in Europe.

There are few points of reference in the enormous production of bronze statuettes by Giambologna and his principal assistant, Francesco Susini: most were original, small compositions rather than reductions from full-scale statuettes. Apart from the *Mercury* of 1565 mentioned above, the gilt-bronze female allegory of *Astronomy* (Kunsthistorisches Museum, Vienna), also signed, is probably an early masterpiece. The closed composition and spiral axis given to the figure is characteristic, appearing, for example, in the larger statuette of *Apollo* that he contributed to the Studiolo of Francesco de' Medici (Palazzo Vecchio, Florence). Apart from the human figure, his repertoire included animals, particularly horses, bulls, and groups showing animals attacked by lions. He also sculpted life-size bronzes of birds, which were used to decorate garden grottoes (examples include the *Turkey*, *Owl*, and *Peacock* in the Museo Nazionale, Florence). For his bird sculptures he invented an "impressionistic" rendering in wax of their plumage, which was faithfully translated by skillful casting into the final bronze versions. His animals pointed the way for the 19th century French school of "animaliers".

The Counter-Reformation created a demand for religious scenes with a clear exposition of narrative. For this purpose Giambologna developed a logical relief style that owed much to Donatello in its sense of perspective. Giambologna's immediate predecessors, Bandinelli and Cellini, had been fascinated by Mannerist surface patterns, which had resulted in a loss of clarity in their work.

Giambologna exerted great influence during his lifetime and for some years afterwards, both in Italy and in the North. His statuettes made handsome gifts and were rapidly distributed through the courts and studios of Europe, disseminating an enthusiasm for his elegant style far beyond Italy. Later, his many pupils, often Flemings or Germans, were in demand to serve these very courts, thus reinforcing his influence, though with personal variations on his basic style (for example the sculptors Adrian de Vries, Hubert Gerhard, and Hans Reichle). Giambologna occupies a crucial position in the history of sculpture in between the better known figures of Michelangelo and Bernini; his style was only superseded by the advent of the Baroque in Rome.

Further reading. Avery, C. *Florentine Renaissance Sculpture*, London and New York (1970). Avery, C. *Giambologna*, London (1987). Dhanens, E. *Jean Boulogne*, Brussels (1956). Holderbaum, J. "Giambologna" in *Maestri della Scultura* vol. 13, Milan (1966). Pope-Hennessy, J. *Italian High Renaissance and Baroque Sculpture*, London and New York (1970).

Giovanni di Paolo 1403–83

Giovanni di Paolo di Grazia was a Sienese painter and miniaturist whose work in Siena is documented from 1426 to 1475. Although he experimented with Florentine innovations, he remained within the Sienese Gothic tradition.

Like his contemporaries Sassetta, Sano di Pietro, and Vecchietta he was inspired by the eloquent moral preaching of the reformer San Bernardino of Siena (1380–1444), which also encouraged Sienese families and institutions to commission altarpieces for their chapels. This provided

Giovanni di Paolo: detail of The Expulsion of Adam and Eve from Paradise and the Annunciation; tempera and gold on wood panel; full size 40×46cm (16×18in); c1445. National Gallery of Art, Washington, D.C.

the basis for Giovanni's work, and many of his altarpieces are still in Siena.

Few of his works are signed and dated, but his style is unmistakable. It shows his sympathy for the natural world, particularly for landscape, and it also displays a profound identification with the religious stories and saints he portrays with such meticulous detail. The major figures of the polyptychs contrast with the small-boned participants of the lively *predella* narratives.

The male faces have peaked eyelids, a rim of white under the iris, sunken cheeks, and depressive mouths. Unlike Sassetta's serenely spaced features, Giovanni's are compressed, particularly in the female saints and the small figures of the *predellae*. His technique in handling drapery shows the exquisite skill of the miniaturist. Each hair is delineated against a darker ground. He sometimes paints or incises outlines on gold leaf.

In his landscapes he leaves the Byzantine conventions he used in the late 1420s (as in *Christ, Suffering and Triumphant*, Pinacoteca Nazionale, Siena; Pecci Altarpiece, 1426, 4 *predella* panels in the Walters Art Gallery, Baltimore); those of the 1430s become more specifically Sienese (*Flight into Egypt*, c1436?; Pinacoteca Nazionale, Siena). Of all the varieties of the Sienese countryside, he preferred the dream world of the *crete*, to the east of Siena: miniature deserts next to cultivated land, with crevassed clay hills (seen in *St John in the Desert*, c1454; Art Institute of Chicago).

Giovanni's altarpiece of 1463 for the church of the humanist Pope Pius II in Pienza had a Renaissance frame with a dead Christ based on a Classical relief in the lunette. But this experiment in Renaissance taste did not have a lasting effect on his style. In his last works, in Gothic frames, the major figures become massive and distorted. The *predellae*, however, continue to show his sense of wonder at the natural world, making use of topographical landscapes.

Paradoxically the most traditional and the most adventurous of Quattrocento Sienese painters, Giovanni di Paolo's vision was too personal to be developed by others.

Girardon François 1628–1715

François Girardon was the favorite sculptor of Louis XIV during the period in which the classical ideal and the direction of Colbert were the controlling influences in French art.

Born at Troyes, he studied in Rome and at the Académie before being received as a member in 1657. The decoration of Versailles offered abundant opportunities, and the marble group *Apollo Served by the Nymphs* (1666–72, made for the grotto of Thetis at Versailles, but dismantled and rearranged in the late 18th century) shows the spirit in which he worked; it is almost the translation into stone of a pictorial composition. For his group, Girardon copied the Greek *Apollo Belvedere* (Vatican Museums, Rome), with Apollo's heroic pose only slightly adjusted; Apollo is now shown (rather incongruously) laved and pomaded by the nymphs of Thetis who surround him. The principles of the composition are Poussinesque but a certain dandified virility is Girardon's own.

Girardon's *Rape of Proserpina* (1677–9), also made for the gardens at Versailles, recalls Italian models. It is significant that statuettes attributed to the school of Giambologna (Giovanni da Bologna) and casts after Giambologna and Bernini, as well as from the Antique, formed part of Girardon's large private collection of sculptures.

The tomb of Richelieu (church of the Sorbonne) is considered Girardon's masterpiece. It originally stood in the choir on the main axis of the church. The three-figure freestanding group was begun in 1675. Careful consideration was given to its position in the church, which afforded two main views of the sculpture, one from the altar and one from the north. In the middle of the 18th century it was still regarded by authorities as the most perfect monument in France.

Other important works include *Le Bain des Nymphes* relief (1668–70) and the Pyramid fountain of 1668 for the gardens at Versailles. His bronze equestrian statue of Louis XIV (1683–99) was destroyed in the Revolution.

After Colbert's death in 1683 Girardon lost favor. He died in Paris in 1715, having completed his most important work before the end of the 17th century.

François Girardon: Apollo Served by the Nymphs; marble; 1666–72. Grotto of Apollo, Versailles

Girodet-Trioson: Joseph Recognized by his Brothers; oil on canvas; 120×155cm (47×61in); 1789. École des Beaux-Arts, Paris

Girodet-Trioson 1767–1824

The French painter Anne-Louis Girodet de Roucy, known as Girodet-Trioson, was born at Montangis. He was later a pupil of J.-L. David, entering David's studio in 1786. After two attempts, he won the Prix de Rome in 1789 with *Joseph Recognized by his Brother* (École des Beaux-Arts, Paris). A *Deposition* (church of Montes-quieu-Volvestre, Haut-Garonne) dates from the same year. The shadowy emotion of this work prefigures the fuller Romanti-cism of his *Funeral of Atala* (1808; Louvre, Paris), inspired by the popular novel by Chateaubriand.

Girodet's versatility in this period of great stylistic change—even confusion—meant that he could paint in a "straight" Neo-classical manner when required. He did this in his *Hippocrates Refusing the Pre-sents of Artaxerxes* (painted in Rome, 1792; now Faculty of Medicine, Paris). He could also adopt a blatantly mannerist approach, as in *Mlle Lange as Danaë* (1799; Minneapolis Institute of Arts). He painted bright, brash battle scenes, like *The Riots in Cairo, 21 October 1798* (Versailles), again with mannerist ele-ments. Perhaps the key to his work is a sense of poetry, as in his Ossianic *The Apotheosis of the French Heroes* (1801; Malmaison, Rueil).

Girtin Thomas 1775–1802

The English watercolorist Thomas Girtin was born at Southwark, London. In 1789,

after training with a drawing-master, he was apprenticed to the topographer Edward Dayes. Girtin's earliest drawings date from around this time, and bear witness to the strong influence that Dayes exerted on his apprentice. Dayes' influence continued to predominate during the period that he and Girtin were employed by the antiquarian James Moore, from 1792 to 1794.

There is reason to believe that Girtin was well acquainted with his exact contempo-rary J.M.W. Turner, since for three years, from c1794, Girtin worked for the ama-teur and collector Dr Thomas Munro. Joseph Farington reports in his diary that Girtin was chiefly employed by Dr Munro in copying the outlines or unfinished draw-ings of J.R. Cozens, while Turner washed in the effects.

During the next few years, Girtin fre-quently toured north Wales, the west country, Yorkshire, and Northumberland. He embarked on the first of these many sketching excursions in 1796. At this point he began to develop a highly original style, perhaps partly as a result of his contact with the work of Cozens. Recording a subjective response to nature, Girtin began to interpret subjects in optical terms, using loose, broad color washes to reduce the detail of a landscape to its formal elements.

Girtin's chief source of inspiration ap-pears to have been found in the north of England, and the works of the last two or three years of his life reflect a sensitive interpretation of atmospheric values that undoubtedly paved the way for the "poetic" landscape of English Romantic painting. Girtin's *Eidometropolis* was a vast panorama of London, almost 2,000 ft (609 m) square. It was exhibited in 1802 and is now lost, but studies for it remain in the British Museum, London, along with a good collection of watercolors. Subject to asthmatic illness, Girtin died in the November of 1802. He spent the last few months of his life preparing a set of soft etchings of Paris, after a visit there late in 1801 for health reasons.

Thomas Girtin: Kirkstall Abbey on the Banks of the River Aire; watercolor; 32×52cm (13×20in); c1800. Victoria and Albert Museum, London

Gislebertus of Autun 12th century

The name of the French sculptor Gislebertus of Autun is known from an inscription on one of the masterpieces of Romanesque art, the tympanum of the Cathedral of St Lazarus at Autun. He is one of the very few sculptors of the Romanesque period whose career can be reconstructed with some accuracy, not with the help of documents, but exclusively from the study of his surviving works.

It is almost certain that young Gislebertus was employed on the decoration of the celebrated abbey of Cluny in Burgundy at the turn of the 11th and 12th centuries. He subsequently worked in the Abbey of St Mary Magdalene at Vézelay, where several of his reliefs on capitals can be seen. He left Vézelay in order to take charge of the sculptural decoration of the cathedral of St Lazarus at Autun. Working there from c1125 for at least ten years, he carved a large number of capitals for the interior, and two external portals. When the church was completed, Gislebertus was no doubt engaged on making the furnishings; but of these only one wooden statue of the Virgin survives, possibly intended for an altar (Metropolitan Museum, New York).

The capitals show Gislebertus as an artist with a great range of expressive moods, from the lyrical in *The Infancy of Christ* series, to the dramatic in the two *Temptations of Christ*. From the north portal comes the relief of Eve (now in the Musée Rolin, Autun): a frank, if not openly sensuous portrayal of the female nude, probably unique in Romanesque art. The west portal contains a huge tympanum, framed by carved ornamental molding. The subject is the *Last Judgment*, dominated by Christ in a mandorla: a severe, awe-inspiring creation. The composition includes scenes of the elect being led to heaven, a group of humble apostles worshiping Christ, and the horrifying details of the torments of the damned. It is a work of wonderful technical skill, great piety, and a supreme power of expression.

Giulio Romano c1499–1546

The Italian painter Giulio Pippi, called Giulio Romano, is one of the outstanding artists of Mannerism in the range of his work, in the elegance and wit of his style, and in his inventive relationship with the Antique. Born in Rome, he trained in Raphael's workshop, executing his master's designs in the Villa Farnesina and in

Giulio Romano: the architect's house in Mantua; facade reconstructed probably c1540–4

the Stanza dell'Incendio in the Vatican Palace. At Raphael's death in 1520 Giulio, together with G.F. Penni, was appointed executor of his will and completed a number of commissions begun by Raphael. Notable among these was the *Transfiguration*, now in the Vatican Museums, Rome.

In the Sala di Costantino, Raphael had initiated a brilliant decorative scheme where the story of the life of Constantine is shown on frescoes painted to resemble tapestries; these are framed by Popes seated on complex thrones, flanked by allegorical figures. He had also left drawings for the major narrative fresco, *The Battle of the Milvian Bridge*. Giulio was responsible for both the design and the execution of the remaining frescoes of the series. *The Allocution of Constantine* is based on Classical reliefs of an *adlocutio* (in which a general exhorts his troops before battle). Giulio echoes Raphael's interest in 'antiquarian' details of costume and setting. These are combined with a close study of Michelangelo's figure-style in the second half of the Sistine Ceiling, from which Giulio develops the contrapposto of his figures.

Giulio helped to complete the decoration of the loggia of the Villa Madama, de-

signed by Raphael. His work there was combined with stucco decorations by another of the artists from Raphael's workshop, Giovanni da Udine. Giovanni's rediscovery of the ancient technique of stucco, and his elegant reinterpretation of Roman ceilings, are important as the inspiration for later designs by Giulio.

During the Renaissance, architecture was often designed by painters and sculptors, and Giulio conformed to this practice by designing the Villa Lante on the Janiculum in Rome. Its severe entrance facade, with its Doric and Ionic pilasters, contrasts with the Salone at the back where the rhythmic interplay of the windows opens out on to a view of the gardens.

In 1524 Giulio was invited to Mantua as court artist for the Gonzagas. His acceptance of the invitation had profound effects on painting, sculpture, and architecture in Venice, the Veneto, and northern Europe; it offered him the opportunity to develop to the full the talents he had established in Rome. He made many drawings for items such as decorative plates and jugs; prepared a set of tapestries of *The Triumph of Scipio* for the King of France; and designed the frescoes of the *Assumption of the Virgin* in Verona Cathedral, which were executed by his studio.

His outstanding achievement in Mantua was his architecture, whose wide range reveals both his response to differing commissions and his sense of decorum. The navè of Mantua Cathedral is a brilliant revival of the Early Christian basilican church carried through with a sense of harmony and of proportion, and a brilliant control over lighting; while his rebuilding of S. Benedetto Po reveals his skill in modernizing an older structure, much of which he had to retain. The villa of Marmirolo outside Mantua that he designed and decorated no longer survives, but the facade of his own house in Mantua shows his inventive approach to tradition.

The Palazzo del Tè is one of the crucial works of Mannerism in North Italy; its influence extended from the Veneto to Germany and Fontainebleau. The Palace was set on the island of the Tè, outside Mantua, where the Gonzagas had their stables; it was used for hunting and for entertainment after the hunt. Because it replaced older structures it was not built all at one time; the old foundations that remained forced upon Giulio many slight irregularities in the handling of the facades, which are most notable in the first block to have been built, the one to the north. These irregularities were corrected in the other later blocks, which completed the square design around the courtyard (which once had a maze), and also in his plan of the palace, which we know from a near-contemporary copy.

The palace is an extension of the earlier design of the Villa Lante. The severe and massive rustication of the three main facades, which are articulated by Doric pilasters and triple openings in the doorways, is contrasted with the open garden facade. Here the triple rhythm of the doorways was to have been combined with a massive Classical pediment derived from Roman triumphal arches. (The pediment was not executed but is recorded in drawings after the original project). The courtyard is lighter and more playful in character than the forbidding facades, and in his design for the fallen triglyphs of the pediment Giulio quotes the Antique with characteristic wit and invention.

Giulio directed a large workshop to execute the decoration. The combination of stucco and frescoes both in the Palace and in the small grotto continued the pattern of the work of Villa Madama. The horses in the Sala dei Cavalli reflect the interests of the patrons, and the illusion that they stand in front of the architecture in the spectator's space derives from Mantegna's frescoes in the Camera degli Sposi in the Ducal Palace at Mantua. This new interest in illusionism also influenced the daring foreshortening of the scenes from the story of Cupid and Psyche. It culminated in the Sala dei Giganti: here Jupiter and the Olympian gods throw down massive, Michelangelesque giants who seem to fall on to the spectator—in their struggles, they even appear to pull the building down on top of him. The effect was much enjoyed by Vasari, who visited the Palace with Giulio, and who gave an enthusiastic description of the room in his *Lives of the Artists*. The illusion was repeated by Zelotti in his frescoes at Villa Thiene, and by Battista Franco at Villa Malcontenta, both probably dating from the 1550s.

Further reading. Hartt, F. *Giulio Romano* (2 vols.), London and New Haven (1958). Jestaz, B. and Bacou, R. *Jules Romain: l'Histoire de Scipion*, Paris (1978). Shearman, J. "Giulio Romano, Tradigione, Licenze, Artifice", *Bollettino del Centro Internazionale di Studi di Archittetura "A. Palladio"* vol. IX, Rome (1967). Verheyen, E. "Bemerkungen zu einer Zeichnung aus Giulio Romanos Mantuaner Studio", *Mitteilungen des Kunsthistorischen Institutes in Florenz* vol. XIII, Florence (1968). Verheyen, E. *The Palazzo del Te in Mantua: Images of Love and Politics*, Baltimore and London (1977).

Glackens William 1870–1938

William James Glackens was an American painter and illustrator, and a member of the group of artists known as The Eight. He was born in Philadelphia and studied at the Pennsylvania Academy of the Fine Arts, and later in Paris. His first employment was as a newspaper illustrator for the *Philadelphia Press*, but he moved to New York in 1896. With the encouragement of his fellow artist Robert Henri he turned increasingly to painting. Glackens' Manet-inspired café picture *Chez Mouquin* (1905; Art Institute of Chicago) was shown at The Eight's only group exhibition in 1908. He continued to work as a much admired illustrator for *Life* and other magazines, while producing paintings of everyday New York life in an increasingly bright colored palette. He died in Westport, Connecticut.

Glarner Fritz 1899–1972

The Swiss-American painter Fritz Glarner was born in Zurich. He studied art in Naples and in Paris, and in 1933 became a member of the Abstract artists' group *Abstraction-Création*. He moved to New York in 1936 and subsequently became an American citizen, without ever relinquishing his close ties with Paris and Switzerland.

It was in New York during the years 1943 and 1944 that Glarner became closely associated with Mondrian. He introduced a new style which he called "Relational Painting". This involved the use of the slanted line, and frequently, of the tondo format.

Fritz Glarner: Relational Painting no. 70; oil on canvas; 71×41cm (28×16in); 1954. Galerie Louis Carré et Cie, Paris

Godefroid de Claire 12th century

Godefroid de Claire, also known as Godefroid de Huy, is often described as one of the outstanding goldsmiths of the 12th century. He worked in the valley of the River Meuse in Belgium, the "Mosan region". A large number of reliquaries and enamels have been attributed to him, but he remains a difficult figure to establish historically. His death is recorded in the late-12th-century register of the monastery of Neufmoûtier near Huy. A mid-13th-century addition in the margin says that Canon Godefroid, citizen of Huy, had "no equal as a goldsmith and he made many shrines in many places and objects for Kings".

We only know of two reliquaries certainly made by him, the house-shrines of St Mangold and St Domitian, made at the order of Bishop Raoul of Zähringen in 1173 for the church of Notre Dame of Huy. (These were recorded in an inventory of 1274.)

On the basis of this information Godefroid has been identified as the goldsmith to whom some letters were addressed as "My dear son G." by Abbot Wibald of Stavelot (born 1098, Abbot 1130, ob. 1158). "Master G." was responsible for making the Head Reliquary of Pope Alexander in 1145 (now in the Musées Royaux des Beaux-Arts de Belgique, Brussels) and the Remaclus Retable (known only from a 17th-century drawing) mentioned as being under construction in 1148.

It seems likely that Master G. engraved some Imperial seals for the Emperor Frederik Barbarossa, through the mediation of Abbot Wibald. It is still not proven that Master G. is identical with Godefroid de Claire. An analysis of the two Huy shrines, although these are poorly preserved, makes it seem distinctly possible. The rather indiscriminate attribution to Godefroid of a very large number of enamels and other goldsmith's work produced in this area between 1145 and 1173 has not helped our understanding of the development of Romanesque metalwork.

Goeritz Matthias 1915–

The architect, sculptor, and painter Matthias Goeritz was born at Danzig, Germany. Goeritz studied in Berlin where he obtained a doctorate in art history; he was greatly affected by the 1920s international avant-garde. He left Germany for Morocco in 1940 and moved to Spain at the end of the Second World War. In 1949 he left Spain to take up a teaching post at a new school of architecture in Guadalajara, Mexico.

In Mexico, where Goeritz has lived ever since, his output in all branches of art and design has been prolific. His visionary, "emotional" architecture has taken shape in a series of remarkable projects, notably

Hugo van der Goes: The Fall of Man; panel: 36×23cm (14×9in); c1467–77. Kunsthistorisches Museum, Vienna

the El Eco Museum of Experimental Art (1952–3) and the Five Towers outside Mexico City (1957). Goeritz has also held major teaching posts in architecture and visual education.

Goes Hugo van der c1436–82

Hugo van der Goes was the most remarkable Flemish painter of the second half of the 15th century. He became a master in the Painter's Guild in Ghent in 1467, and was Dean of the Guild from 1473 to 1475. More than any other Flemish painter of his time, van der Goes felt at home working on a large scale, as he shows in his

Portinari Altarpiece (c1475; Uffizi, Florence). By a quirk of history, the fame of the great Flemish artist largely rests upon this altarpiece in Italy. His most important work, the altarpiece exerted a considerable influence on Italian painters of the 15th century, while it must have remained all but unknown in the Netherlands. The story of the altarpiece helps to explain this.

Tommaso Portinari was the agent of the Medici bank in Bruges, where van der Goes' presence is documented in 1468. When Portinari commissioned a painting from a famous artist of the country he was living in, he must have wanted it to suit its surroundings back in his own city of

Florence. As the altarpiece was for the family chapel in the church of S. Egidio, Portinari no doubt specified that the work should be the size of the usual Florentine altarpiece. There were certainly Netherlandish paintings (and even painters) in Italy by the time the Portinari Altarpiece arrived there; a similar realism of portraiture and heightened naturalism of observed detail was known from other works. But the Portinari Altarpiece is distinguished not only by its exceptional quality, but by its size, which is unusual for a Flemish picture of this period. The altarpiece is in the form of a triptych, with the Nativity in the center panel and portraits of the donor and his wife on either wing. When closed, the shutters show an Annunciation in grisaille.

The work had both iconographical and technical significance for the Florentine painters who saw it *c*1475. The Child lies on the ground surrounded by adoring figures—a particularly Northern iconography of the Nativity which became popular in Italy. An influential group is that of the three shepherds, who are shown in a markedly unidealized study of three peasants. Apart from its iconographical importance, the altarpiece serves as a superb demonstration—in such details as the glass of water—of the Northern technique of oil painting. The technique was known in Italy by this time, but there was no oil painting in Florence on this scale, and no work that could give such a consummate demonstration of the advantages of oil painting over tempera. There is a rich luminosity about the rather cool colors which is very attractive.

The composition of the Portinari Altarpiece has a certain looseness about it which contrasts with another large work by van der Goes, *The Adoration of the Kings* (the Monforte Altarpiece, *c*1463–75; Staatliche Museen, Berlin). This is a much more compact picture, earlier in date, and closer in spirit to the work of van der Goes' great predecessors: artists such as Rogier van der Weyden. A painting later than the Portinari Altarpiece is the *Death of the Virgin* (State Museum, Bruges), a work which displays the rather unsettled grandeur characteristic of van der Goes.

It is easy to project into all these paintings our knowledge of van der Goes' final insanity. There is a remoteness in his work, which is especially evident in the rather haunting *Death of the Virgin*. His working life must have been fairly short as he went into semiretirement in a monastery near Brussels in 1478. From this time he became increasingly subject to fits of madness. The rather self-satisfied account of van der Goes' suffering left by a fellow monk suggests that these fits took the form of religious mania, with a conviction of his own eternal damnation. While in the monastery, van der Goes continued to receive visits from his rich and powerful admirers; but he succumbed to a distressing attack on a visit to Cologne *c*1481, and died in the following year.

Further reading. Friedländer, M.J. *Early Netherlandish Painting* vol. IV, Leiden (1967). Winkler, F. *Das Werk des Hugo van der Goes*, Berlin (1964).

Gogh Vincent van 1853–90

The Dutch artist Vincent van Gogh is one of the most popular artists in the world today, but much of his fame may be due to his sensational life history and the drama and pathos of his short creative span. His work, his personality, and his intellectual interests, so articulately expressed in over 600 surviving letters, claim a more profound consideration. He was a man of great intelligence, sensitivity, and determination. He read widely in contemporary literature, philosophy, and history, and responded to the many exciting currents in 19th-century art and society. He is a touchstone for our understanding of many of these ideas and experiences, and his appeal for us today may be that he seems to epitomize modern man.

Before Van Gogh died at the age of 37, his short life had centered around three focal points: religion, art, and literature. He was born at Zundert in Holland. His father was an evangelical pastor, and he had uncles who were art dealers, admirals, and booksellers. It was natural that he should start work at 16, in 1869, in the family art-dealing firm in The Hague; this had been merged with a French company and was known as Goupil and Cie. He loved his work in the gallery and was absorbed in art. He visited museums and exhibitions wherever he went—his list of admired artists was almost endless—and he read widely the current literature, in magazines such as *Gazette des Beaux-Arts*.

His first acquaintance with art was from the standpoint of dealer and amateur critic, and his judgment was shrewd and sure. He loved the 17th-century Dutch artists, Rembrandt, Hals, and Jacob Ruisdael, and the French 19th-century landscape painters of the Barbizon School, Millet, Rousseau, and Dupré. He also promoted and supported the newly formed Hague School, the work of a group of Dutch artists, many of whom he got to know personally during his stay in the Hague from 1869 to 1873. He carried these tastes with him throughout his life. In 1888 he wrote to his friend and fellow artist Émile Bernard, "As for me, when I'm in the Louvre, I still go, with a great love in my heart, to the Dutch, Rembrandt first of all".

Van Gogh worked for Goupil and Cie in London (1873–5) and in Paris (1875–6), but he became depressed after an unhappy experience with the daughter of his London landlady, and was finally dismissed from the firm in April 1876. He turned more and more to religion, and to the Bible. He spent a few months working for a bookseller in Dordrecht in 1877. His love of literature expressed itself in wide reading and varied tastes. Among the authors he admired were the French historian Michelet, English authors like George Eliot, Dickens, and Carlyle, and French novelists such as Zola, the de Goncourt brothers, and de Maupassant. He later included his favorite books in paintings. In the late portrait of *Dr Gachet* (1890; private collection) the doctor leans his elbow on novels by the de Goncourt brothers, *Germinie Lacertueux* and *Manette Salomon*. Books also inspired his paintings directly. The important painting in the Kröller-Müller Museum, Otterlo, Holland, of Madame Roulin, wife of the Arles postman is entitled *La Berceuse*, the cradle-rocker: Vincent had been reading Pierre Loti's *Pêcheurs d'Islande* ("Fishermen of Iceland") and felt that sailors would need to take to sea just such an image of maternal comfort.

Van Gogh became more and more religious in the late 1870s. He spent nine months in England helping Methodist ministers, and even composed and delivered a lengthy sermon. By the middle of 1877 he had decided to follow in his father's footsteps and train for the church. With this intention he studied in Amsterdam and then in Brussels, and was able in November to go as a probationary evangelist to the poverty-stricken mining district of Belgium, the Borinage. This was a crucial period, for here Van Gogh lived out the practice of the Gospel, dedicating himself to the miners, giving away his clothes and food, and nursing the injured after fire-damp explosions in the mines. But his zeal and his willingness to carry out the commands of the Gospel in a literal manner found no support among the respectable churchmen. His behavior contradicted the accepted conventions of his class and profession, and he was dismissed.

Van Gogh became deeply suspicious of the hypocrisy of the established church and of so-called respectable people. Time and again he found himself rejected for conducting his life too closely in accord with his religious theory. In The Hague, for example, he took in a destitute and abandoned woman, and was dropped by many of the artists in the town. In Nuenen, in 1884, his friendship with Margot Begemann was the subject of such slander that the woman attempted to kill herself. To his brother, Theo, Van Gogh exploded:

> But for heaven's sake, what is the meaning and standing of that absurd religion which respectable people maintain?—oh they are perfectly absurd, making society a kind of lunatic asylum, a perfectly topsy-turvy world ...

At the age of 26 Van Gogh had tried many professions and had failed in each of them. He wandered around the Borinage in bitter desperation, which he described most movingly to Theo in a letter written in July 1880. All his interests began to be synthesized into one activity: art. He turned to the art he knew, Rembrandt, Delacroix, Millet; and to the books of Dickens, Hugo, and Michelet; he wrote:

> There is something of Rembrandt in Shakespeare, ... of Delacroix in Victor Hugo; and then there is something of Rembrandt in the Gospel, or something of the Gospel in Rembrandt.

In his footsore wanderings in the Borinage, Van Gogh had made an abortive journey to Courrières to meet an artist he admired, Jules Breton. There he made a decision:

> Well, even in that deep misery I felt my energy revive, and I said to myself—In spite of everything I shall rise again: I will take up my pencil, which I have forsaken in my great discouragement and I will go on with my drawing. From that moment everything had seemed transformed for me.

Van Gogh had drawn before 1880. He had drawn skillfully in his youth, produc-ing fine copies of engravings and prints. He drew tiny sketches and caricatures for a small girl in The Hague in 1872 and 1873. He has left us images of most of the houses he lived in. Now he took up his pencil with a clearer idea of what he wanted to produce. He would make strong drawings of working people, in a rugged style matched to his subject matter, in order to express his feeling about "the people": first the miners, then the weavers, and then the peasants of Brabant and Provence.

His subsequent career falls easily into periods marked by the places in which he lived: Etten in 1880, The Hague from 1881 to 1883, Drenthe in 1883, Nuenen from 1883 to 1885, Antwerp from 1885 to 1886, Paris from 1886 to 1888, Arles in 1888, St Remy from 1889 to 1890, Auvers in 1890. He spent the first half of his active life as an artist in Holland, studying and finally bringing his own individual touch to the current style of the Hague school. It would be a mistake to dismiss the earlier works of his short career as a beginner's studies. The somber colors, the richly applied paint, the loving depiction of peasants in their cottages or at work in the fields echo the work of Josef Israels (1824–1911) and Anton Mauve (1838–88).

Van Gogh was related to Mauve by marriage and had become a personal friend. He turned to him for advice and encouragement when he undertook to become an artist. Mauve was his only real teacher in the conventional sense; Van Gogh remained devoted to him. When he heard of his death in 1888, Vincent inscribed on one of his best paintings of a tree in blossom, "Souvenir de Mauve" and sent it to his widow.

Van Gogh was drawn to figure-painting in these years and felt the highest form of modern art was the depiction of the peasant figure in action. Some of his best drawings are inspired by the men and women of Nuenen engaged in agricultural tasks. His most important figure-subject is of these peasants at rest, *The Potato Eaters* (1885; Rijksmuseum Vincent van Gogh, Amsterdam), which shows a family of five around the table in the dim light of their old oil lamp, eating the potatoes they have sown and dug. This subject was depicted many times by other Dutch artists of the period and entitled "The Frugal Meal" or "Potato Eaters"; Josef Israels particularly loved the theme. Van Gogh's painting, however, is stripped of all sentimentality, anecdote, or obvious social comment. The handling is more vigorous, the color more resonant, and the painting is alive with the powerful feeling Van Gogh had for these peasants. He saw how their way of life was being gradually undermined by the encroachments of industrialization on to the simple existence in which man lived by the soil.

Van Gogh felt isolated in the country far from other artists and left for Antwerp, where he enrolled in an Academy in order to draw from the model. Suddenly, however, he decided to leave for Paris and sent Theo this note: "Dear Theo, Do not be cross with me for having come all at once like this ... Shall be at the Louvre from midday or sooner, if you like."

Paris was alive with new ideas, and movements to stimulate the imagination of a young artist. Van Gogh could see the Impressionist exhibition, the annual Salon, the new Salon Nationale exhibition, a retrospective of his favorite artist, Millet, a show of Monet and Renoir at Petit's gallery, Symbolist works by Gustave Moreau and Odilon Redon. He went to study at the studio of an established artist Ferdinand Cormon, where he met Henri de Toulouse-Lautrec. The work of the Impressionists, particularly that of Claude Monet, affected his work enormously; it produced new, brighter colors, a gayer, freer choice of subject, and an interest in landscapes and views of Paris. But he soon began to experiment with the ideas of the Neo-Impressionists through Paul Signac. Dots of broken color begin to run across his canvas, and urgent trails of hurried dashes.

Van Gogh arrived in Paris when a new growth of ideas among younger artists was developing beyond Impressionism, and when the older men, Monet and Renoir, were themselves exploring fresh ideas. Van Gogh digested all this, but began to find his own direction under the powerful influence of the Japanese colored woodcuts that were then the rage in Paris. Their use of bold areas of pure, bright color, and their popular subject matter made them for Vincent more than lively decorations. They represented a golden paradise of color and light.

The tensions of Paris and the battles waged between artists of differing persuasions proved too much for Van Gogh, so he decided to go south to find his own Japan, in the sun and color of southern France. He hoped to found there a cooperative community of artists, similar

Vincent van Gogh: Self-portrait with Bandaged Ear; oil on canvas; 60×49cm (24×19in); 1889.
Courtauld Institute Galleries, London

part of his left ear with a razor.

This first fit of insanity led to Van Gogh's incarceration and release, then a reincarceration requested by the people of Arles, and finally his voluntary entry into the mental asylum of St Paul at St Rémy. Van Gogh's illness was characterized by numerous attacks, followed by periods of lethargy and inability to work, followed in turn by complete lucidity and amazingly concentrated activity. It has been variously explained as schizophrenia, as epilepsy, or as an inherited family weakness. The inadequacy of medical records and the crudity of diagnosis in mental illness make it difficult to be certain, but it seems likely that Van Goth suffered from a form of temporal lobe epilepsy whose symptoms often mirror the features of schizophrenia. It is possible that his "madness" did not directly affect his art; but the experience and fear of attacks, and the ensuing depression would inevitably have had a disturbing and distressing effect on his equilibrium.

Van Gogh was able to paint in St Rémy but there is a change in his style: the tone of the color is more somber and the forms seem convulsed by their own energy, which seems now beyond Van Gogh's control. Clouds twist and swirl through a disturbed sky, cypresses lick the skies like flames. Significantly, Van Gogh turned back to the inspirations of his early years: to Millet, to Rembrandt, and to Delacroix, whose work he translated into his own color. He asked Theo to send him earlier drawings, and he produced a series of peasants, cottages, and landscapes which are called "Memories of the North". He even drew a version of *The Potato Eaters* from memory.

One of the most important works of this period is his rendering of Rembrandt's etching *The Raising of Lazarus* (1890; Rijksmuseum Vincent van Gogh, Amsterdam). In black and white etching, Rembrandt used the fall of light to symbolize the emanating power of Christ. Van Gogh eliminates the figure of Christ and replaces it with a huge yellow sun whose light, embodied in the pervasive gold of the paint, represents the force of life itself. Rembrandt is transformed by the sun; north and south are joined; religion, art, and nature are combined in one single statement.

Van Gogh went north again in May 1890. He passed through Paris, saw a few exhibitions, and met his sister-in-law and

to groups of the Barbizon School, The Hague School, and the workshops of the Japanese printmakers.

Van Gogh was charmed by the South, and felt he had found his Japan; but it also brought back strong memories of his native Holland. He wrote to his sister that what he had learned in Paris was leaving him; and in his letters to Theo he wrote how the Provençal countryside reminded him of the works of Ruisdael and Hobbema. The landscapes he painted there recall the wide flat plains of 17th-century Dutch landscapes, and he repeated the Dutch motif of drawbridges, which had actually been built by Dutch engineers in Provence.

In 1888 Paul Gauguin had been persuaded to join Van Gogh in Arles as the beginning of their planned artists' society, "Studio of the Tropics". The two painters differed dramatically in their views about art, and this led to tremendous arguments

which Van Gogh described as "electric". Gauguin wanted to free art from a dependence on nature, while Van Gogh was dedicated to the reality of the natural world. He had written to Émile Bernard: "We can—and this was done by the old Dutchmen … we can paint an atom of chaos, a horse, a portrait, your grandmother, apples and a landscape …" Such subjects could, he believed, be transformed with color and feeling into powerful symbols. For instance, the simplest bowl of flowers that Van Gogh painted, *The Sunflowers* (1888; National Gallery, London), is as potent an evocation of the sun—its light, its power, its energy—as anything in the history of art. Yet it remains an "atom of chaos" observed with humility and love. The tension with Gauguin culminated in Van Gogh's violent attack on his friend followed by a horrific self-mutilation when Van Gogh cut off

Vincent van Gogh: Group of Houses seen against a Hill (View at Auvers); oil on canvas; 50×100cm (20×40in); 1890. Tate Gallery, London

infant nephew for the first time before going to Auvers. At this village near Paris he was able to stay under the sympathetic eye of Dr Gachet, physician, painter, and friend of the Impressionists. Van Gogh worked incredibly hard, producing drawings and paintings often at the rate of two or more a day. In the light of the knowledge of his suicide in July of that year, one is tempted to read this period backwards and endow the often sunny and powerful paintings of these months with a meaning and menace born of further knowledge. Vincent was worried about his brother Theo, who had provided his only financial support for the past ten years. The strain of dependence, his lack of success, fear for the future, failure of his cooperative schemes, and anxiety about recurring breakdowns and possible inability to work weighed understandably heavily on him. In one of his last letters, Van Gogh is acutely concerned about the vulnerability of artists to the commercial art world. Undoubtedly some of his paintings are desolate and harrowingly empty.

On 27th July 1890 Vincent tried to kill himself with a revolver; he died from his wounds two days later, in Theo's arms, at the age of 37. The tragedy of his death has overshadowed his life, and his work often seems accompanied by an invisible label,

"This was painted by a man who was 'mad' and who committed suicide."

Van Gogh was both a brilliant colorist and an equally consummate draftsman. He began his career as an artist by drawing for almost two years, and some of his most satisfying work is to be found in the drawings of the peasants of Nuenen at their labors, and in the panoramic landscapes of Provence. At first, he worked in a vigorous style emphasizing the outline, but he gradually broadened his range when he came to draw landscapes. For these he developed a wonderfully varied and energetic technique made up of a myriad of different types of graphic marks—dots, dashes, and swirls. Everything combined to create a sense of energetic movement and heat-filled vibration. The best-known period of Van Gogh's work, in terms of paintings, is the creative time he spent in Arles, during 1888 and 1889. Here he combined his technical knowledge of new color theories, his love of strongly colored Japanese prints, his understanding of the work of Eugène Delacroix, and the effect of the southern sunflowers, sowers, harvesters and seascapes. He was acutely sensitive to color itself, but he wanted to use it to express something more than appearance. He wrote to Theo: "... instead of trying to reproduce exactly what I

have before my eyes, I use color more arbitrarily, in order to express myself forcibly."

To this end he used almost symbolic combinations of color, as in the portrait of a friend where he placed an exaggeratedly blond head against a deep blue ground in order to create the "mysterious brightness of a pale star in the infinite". He wanted to incorporate into his paintings the energy he was able to create in his drawings. So he applied his brilliant gemlike colors with graphic brush strokes, which curled around forms, ran in radiating haloes round bright stars and suns, and licked the flamelike branches of the cypresses. He used the direction of the strokes in painting and drawing alike to help to create space and perspective and to fill the whole canvas of paper with pulsating light. Sometimes, towards the end of his life, this energy seems beyond his control; forms break out and spread, or the figures bulge and buckle at the joints. In his greatest works, however, Van Gogh was able to express form, energy, and light by the marriage of line and color through which he recreated his intense perceptions of the natural world.

Van Gogh is rare among artists for he has left such a fascinating and revealing picture of his interests, and his acute responses to art, literature, music, and politics in his letters. But he searched above all for visual expressiveness. He brought into a new synthesis streams from all aspects of culture and of the history of art, and expressed them in a way accessible to anyone who cares to look or read. He is, paradoxically, one of the most comprehensible of modern artists and also one of the most profound.

Further reading. Faille, J.B. de la *The Works of Vincent van Gogh: his Paintings and Drawings*, Amsterdam and London (1970). Gogh, V. van *The Complete Letters of Vincent van Gogh*, London and New York (1958). Pollock, G. and Orton, F. *Vincent van Gogh, Artist of his Time*, Oxford (1978). Wadley, N. *The Drawings of Van Gogh*, London (1969). Welsh-Ovcharov, B.M. (ed.) *Van Gogh in Perspective*, Englewood Cliffs, N.J. (1974).

Goltzius Hendrick 1558–1617

The Dutch engraver and painter Hendrick Goltzius was born in Mulbrecht. He was at first the pupil of his father, Jan Goltz. In 1577 he followed his second master, Dirck Volckertsz. Coornhert, to Haarlem where he was influenced by the Flemish Mannerist Bartholomaeus Spranger. The slender and agitated forms of his chiaroscuro woodcut of *Proserpine* is typical of his style at this time. A consummate master of

the engraver's art, his skill with the burin is well exemplified in *The Standard Bearer*.

In 1590, a visit to Rome caused him to abandon this extravagant style, in favor of a more classical approach. His panoramic landscapes and forceful portraits indicate both versatility and acute powers of observation. However, it was Goltzius' technical virtuosity that most impressed his contemporaries.

Goltzius also produced brilliant drawings, some on a life-size scale. His *Venus, Ceres, and Bacchus with a Self Portrait* in the Hermitage Museum, St Petersburg, was the most prodigious of these. He also produced some paintings in a Mannerist style, but these lack the verve and immediacy of his graphic work.

A complex artist, Goltzius' wit and audacity reflect contemporary Mannerism, and his technical mastery typifies the Northern tradition.

Golub Leon 1922–

After military service during World War Two, the American painter Leon Golub studied at the Art Institute of Chicago. He moved to Paris in 1959 and returned to the United States in 1964. An overtly political artist, Golub is concerned to make painting relevant and disturbing at a time when the endless flow of mass media images of brutality has made people insensitive to the

moral and political complexities of events. His large, imposing works typically show scenes of torture or interrogation, the explicit violence balanced by an ambiguity, and even a grace, that encourages an unsettling identification with both the victims and the perpetrators of violence. *Interrogation II* (1983; Art Institute of Chicago) is typical, both in its subject and its technique, the canvas painted, scraped and repainted many times to create a tense, skinlike surface.

Gonçalves Nuno *fl.* 1450–71

The history of Portuguese painting in the 15th century is dominated by one man, Nuno Gonçalves. His reputation rests on the splendid altarpiece of *The Veneration of St Vincent* (National Museum of Art, Lisbon), from the monastery of São Vicente de Fora in Lisbon. Relatively little Portuguese painting from before the middle of the 15th century has survived; much of it shows strong Italian influence and none of the frescoes or portraits can be regarded as a convincing native source for Gonçalves' style.

The life of Nuno Gonçalves is thinly documented. As painter to Alfonso V he was active between 1450 and 1472. In 1471 he replaced the decorative artist João Anes as official painter to the city of Lisbon. Franciso de Olanda, friend of Michelangelo, reckoned Gonçalves among the "eagles"—the foremost painters of his age. According to Olanda, Gonçalves was the painter "who painted the altar of St Vincent in the Cathedral of Lisbon".

The polyptych of *The Veneration of St Vincent* (c1460) has six panels; the figure of the Saint appears twice, suggesting that the work stood in two sections on either side of a statue. In front of St Vincent—patron saint of the Portuguese Royal Family and the Army—are Alfonso V, Henry the Navigator, and a retinue including nobles, knights, clerics, and fishermen.

Gonçalves' style has often been compared with that of the early Florentine fresco painters, and also with that of Jan van Eyck, who worked in Portugal in 1428. Yet this altarpiece has its individual character: it is essentially a composition of human figures, from which Italianate or Flemish notions of decorative detail have been eliminated. There is neither architectural perspective nor landscape to distract the eye; it is even doubtful whether the setting is interior or exterior. Gonçalves

Hendrick Goltzius: The Fat Kitchen; pen and ink with brown wash on paper; 20×33cm (8×13in); 1603. Print Room of the University of Leiden

used color with restraint; gold is largely replaced by yellow, while the strong reds and greens of the fabrics are the more effective for the somber tones of the background. The faces suggest carved wood—long, fine-boned, and brooding, they are characteristically Portuguese.

No other painting can be safely attributed to Gonçalves. Works depicting St Theotonius and St Francis, and a portrait of a young man, indicate a vigorous following among his contemporaries and successors: he began a flourishing tradition, which lasted well into the 16th century.

Gontcharova Natalia 1881–1962

The Russian painter and stage designer Natalia Gontcharova was born at Ladyzhino near Tula, the daughter of an architect of noble family. She studied at the Moscow School of Painting, where she met her husband and lifelong associate, Michail Larionoff. Together they were active in the Moscow avant-garde until 1913, participating in such exhibitions as "The Golden Fleece", "The Knave of Diamonds", "Donkey's Tail", and "The Target", and inventing the new Abstract style of Rayonnism. In 1913 Gontcharova met Diaghilev, and designed the opera Coq d'Or for his 1914 Paris production. She settled in Paris in 1915, and lived there until her death. Her later work was almost exclusively devoted to ballet and opera designs, and her reputation rests mainly on the Cubist-Primitivist and Rayonnist paintings she produced between 1908 and 1918.

Further reading. Chamot, M. Natalia Gontcharova, Paris (1972). Gontcharova, N. Les Ballets Russes de Serge Diaghilev et la Decoration Theatricale, Belves (1930). Gray, C. The Russian Experiment in Art 1863–1922, London (1971).

González Julio 1876–1942

The Spanish sculptor Julio González was born in Barcelona in 1876. Both his father and grandfather were goldsmiths and metalworkers, and it was in the craftsman's tradition that Julio and his elder brother, Joan, grew up. They attended painting classes at the School of Fine Arts in Barcelona; among the young artists they met at this time was Pablo Picasso, who became Julio's lifelong friend.

In 1900 the González family moved to

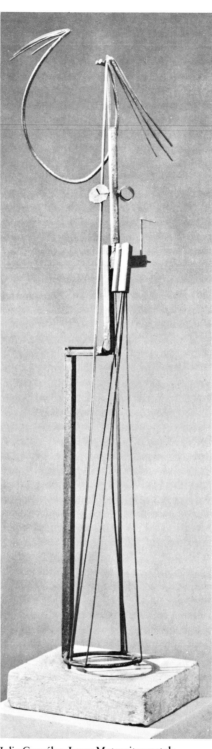

Julio González: Large Maternity; metal; 130×41×23cm (51×16×9in); 1934. Tate Gallery, London

Paris, producing decorative metal work that was shown at international exhibitions there and in Chicago. Julio was active in the family workshop; at the same time, with little success, he attempted to establish himself as a painter. He was at

this period in the shadow of his brother, Joan, whose premature death in 1908 was a very serious blow that extinguished Julio's creative gifts for many years. He retired from the art world altogether; during the First World War he worked at the Renault car factory where he learned the technique of oxyacetylene welding.

Slowly Julio González returned to art, concentrating now on sculpture rather than painting; he worked in relief, coloring some of his metal sculptures. He gave much technical advice in metal sculpture to his friend Picasso (1930–1), and his renewed contact liberated his own imagination. From 1930 until his death 12 years later González produced a succession of iron sculptures that showed the formal possibilities of this intractable but powerfully eloquent material. Some, like Montserrat (1936–7; Stedelijk Museum, Amsterdam), were directly realist in style and subject; but others made use of metaphor, for example The Kiss (1930) and several Cactus Men (1939–40). These works displayed a new attitude to sculptural space that has made González one of the most influential of 20th-century sculptors.

Further reading. Descargues, P. Julio González, Paris (1971). Julio González: Les Matériaux de son Expression, Zurich (1969). Tucker, W. "The Sculpture of González", Studio International, London (December 1970).

Gorky Arshile 1904–48

Gorky was an American painter who played a key role in the merging of abstraction and Surrealism to prepare for the new style of Abstract Expressionism.

He was born Vosdanik Manook Adoian in Khorkom, a village near Lake Van in Turkish Armenia, the son of a wheat farmer and trader. Victims of the Turkish persecution of Armenians, the family emigrated to the United States in 1920; they lived first in Boston then in Providence, Rhode Island, where Gorky began his art studies. About 1925 he moved to New York, and adopted the name Arshile Gorky. Befriended by the painter Stuart Davis in 1929, his first important paintings were Cubist still lifes; but the most charac-

Arshile Gorky: Waterfall; oil on canvas; 155×114cm (61×45in); 1943. Tate Gallery, London

teristic early works are the portraits, especially *The Artist and his Mother* which was based on a photograph taken in 1912 (1926–35; Whitney Museum of American Art, New York).

In 1933 Gorky got to know another young emigrant painter, Willem de Kooning, and his work changed under the influence of the Surrealist Picasso and the abstraction of Arp and Miró. He drew and painted certain subjects repeatedly: for example *Garden in Sochi* (1940–2; one version of 1941 in the Museum of Modern Art, New York). Such paintings used Gorky's memories of childhood to create a composition of suggestive forms.

By 1944 Gorky had met André Breton, Matta, and other Surrealist refugees in New York, and the final phase of his art began. His paintings now displayed the open fluid qualities of 1914 Kandinsky; and they became more Abstract. As Gorky faced such private disasters as the destruction by fire of his studio and an operation for cancer in 1946, his paintings became increasingly anguished and tragic in form and color. Such paintings as *Agony* (1947; Museum of Modern Art, New York) and *Betrothal II* (1947; Whitney Museum of American Art, New York) stand out among his hundreds of drawings. The period ended with Gorky's tragic suicide, after he had suffered an incapacitating motor accident in July 1948.

Further reading. Jordan, J. *The Paintings of Arshile Gorky*, New York (1982). Waldman, D. *Arshile Gorky*, New York (1981).

Goshun Matsumura 1752–1811

Matsumura Goshun was the founder of the *Shijo* School of Japanese painting. The *Shijo* was based on a mixture of the realistic *Maruyama* School with the neo-Chinese *Nanga* School; its name derived from the location of Goshun's studio on Fourth Street in Kyoto. It became a major style of painting and printed book illustration in the 19th century.

Goshun was born in Kyoto in 1752. He was not the son of a professional painter, and at first he worked as a letter writer in Shimbara. He studied painting under Onishi Suigetsu; and, even more important to his subsequent career, learned to write *haiku* under the great painter and *haiku* poet, Yosa Buson. He became a monk in 1782, when he took the name of Goshun

Jan Gossaert: Jean Carondelet, from the Carondelet Diptych; panel; 43×27cm (17×11in); 1517. Louvre, Paris

(of his many other names, the best known is Gekkei). Presumably he found the *Nanga* style unsuited to his taste, for in the early 1780s he asked Maruyama Okyo if he could become his pupil. Knowing of his skill as a painter, Okyo instead took him into his studio as an equal.

After he set up his own studio (some time after 1788) in Shijo-dori, Goshun's style, later to become the *Shijo* style, was formed. He had many famous pupils in-

cluding his younger brother Keibun, Okamoto Toyohiko, and Sato Suiseki.

Despite its *Nanga* ancestry, the style is essentially the least calligraphic of the later Japanese styles. Its abbreviation of realism is never so precise as to become formal, but in the hand of a lesser painter it can seem merely pretty. In the mid 19th century some members of the school veered back towards *Nanga* and away from realism, especially in figure-painting.

Gossaert Jan *c1478–1532*

The Flemish painter Jan or Jennyn Gossaert is also known as Mabuse, this name deriving from Mauberge in Hainault, where he was born. From *c*1516 he usually signed his name in the Latin form of "Joannes Malbodius". He is recorded in the Antwerp guild records from 1503. By 1507 he had become court painter to Philip of Burgundy, an illegitimate son of the Burgundian ducal house who was Governor of Gelderland and Zutphen.

When Philip headed an embassy to Rome on behalf of the Emperor Maximilian in 1508, Mabuse traveled in his entourage. He stayed in Rome for some months after his patron had left; but he was back in the Netherlands, at Middelburg, by the end of 1509. He continued to serve Philip when the latter became Bishop of Utrecht in 1517, and he is also known to have worked at the court of Margaret of Austria, Regent of the Netherlands, at Malines.

The *Adoration of the Magi* (National Gallery, London) is the masterpiece of his early style. The work has the richly detailed quality of an elaborately carved altarpiece. There are debts to Hugo van der Goes in the angels, and to Dürer's prints in the careful perspective of crumbling walls and archways. The dog in the right foreground is a direct quotation from Dürer's *St Eustace* print of 1501. The complicated theme of the work matches its elaborate textural detail, for here the kings are joined in adoration by the shepherds, and the Trinity is also included.

On his visit to Italy Mabuse drew extensively after the Antique, showing more interest in this than in Renaissance art. His style became increasingly sculptural as a result. The *St Luke Painting the Virgin* (1515; Kunsthistorisches Museum, Vienna) is set in a Classical interior with applied antique ornament.

More unusual, however, is a series of small mythological paintings, many of them probably painted for Philip. Before this period the painting of nude figures had been almost exclusively confined to the subject of Adam and Eve. With paintings of *Neptune and Amphitrite* (1516; Staatliche Museen, Berlin), *Hercules and Deianeira* (Barber Institute of Fine Arts, Birmingham), and *Venus and Cupid* (1521; Musées Royaux des Beaux-Arts de Belgique, Brussels), Gossaert introduced a new range of subject matter. The nudes seem to be sculpture come alive. The figure-style shows the influence of the later works of Dürer and the engraved nude figures of Jacopo de' Barbari, with whom Mabuse collaborated on the decoration of Castle Souburg for Philip of Burgundy in 1516.

His portrait style is more conservative and he retains the traditional Flemish format of placing figures behind a ledge. His *Children of King Christian II of Denmark* (1526/7; Hampton Court Palace, London), is one of his more lively studies.

Gossaert's crucial role in the development of Netherlandish painting won early recognition. Guicciardini noted in his *Descrittione di tutti i Paesi Bassi* (1567) that "he was the first who brought from Italy to these lands the skill of painting histories and poetical subjects (*poesie*) with nude figures".

Gottlieb Adolph *1903–73*

The American painter Adolph Gottlieb was born in New York City. He had some lessons from John Sloan at the Art Students league, but he was essentially a self-taught artist. As a young man he worked on mural projects for the W.P.A. (Works Progress Administration), decorating the post office at Yerrington, Nevada, and the Millburn Synagogue, New Jersey. Later, his profound interest in ancient hieroglyphs and American Indian art led to a radical change in style.

He remained in New York for the rest of

Adolph Gottlieb: Counterpoise 1959; oil on canvas; 276×228cm (108×90in); 1959. Private collection

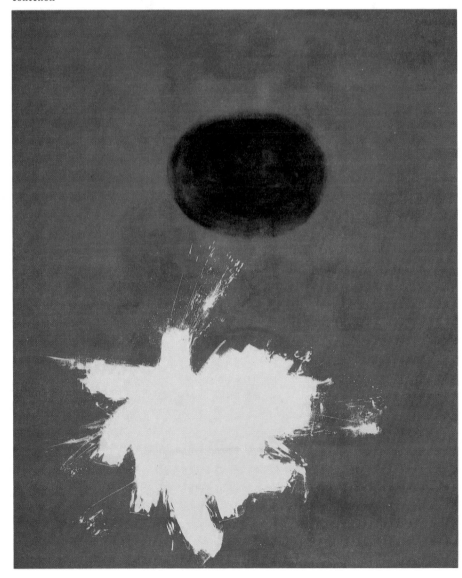

his life, and his close association with Rothko and Newman in the 1940s was an important element in the so-called New York School.

From 1941 Gottlieb called his paintings pictographs: he wanted to create visual images that would convey feeling without recourse to any kind of descriptive language. His work began with comparatively complicated structures such as *The Seer* of 1950 (The Phillips Collection, Washington, D.C.). A later development was the simplicity of the *Burst* series (begun 1957; for example, *Expanding*, 1962; Art Institute of Chicago).

Further reading. Doty, R. and Waldman, D. *Adolphe Gottlieb*, New York (1968).

Goujon Jean c1510–c65

Jean Goujon dominated French sculpture in the middle decades of the 16th century; he belonged to the group of native artists who emerged at the end of the period when France had owed both art and artists to Italy. His sculptural style owed much to the first generation of Italian artists working at Fontainebleau. Taking Mannerist characteristics from such artists as Rosso and Primaticcio, he added a delicate classicism that is typically French.

Information on his birth and early career is sparse. The earliest works attributed to him in Rouen include the cathedral tomb of Louis de Brézé, husband of Diane de Poitiers. Certainly the caryatids of the tomb anticipate those he executed in 1550 as part of the interior decoration of the Louvre. He worked much of the time as a decorator of architecture in collaboration with the architect Pierre Lescot. In an appendix to the 1547 French edition of Vitruvius, Goujon is referred to as an architect and he discusses the optical problems involved in the positioning of sculptured reliefs in architectural frameworks.

His first commission in Paris, the decoration of the rood screen in St Germain-L'Auxerrois (and particularly the *Deposition* relief of 1544) is evidence of the influence of such Italian Mannerist artists as Rosso. Indeed much of his work was in the form of shallow-relief panels, with a stressing of the surface plane not unlike the strong emphasis on surface in many Mannerist paintings.

In his famous piece for the Rue aux Fers, the Fontaine des Innocents of 1550 (rebuilt in 1776 in the square that replaced the Cemetery of the Innocents), the typically French treatment of the combined classical and Mannerist features is obvious; this is especially true of the six tall narrow reliefs of nymphs bearing urns, who strike a variety of poses. In the middle of the 18th

century, the critic A.N. Dézallier d'Argenville wrote that they could not be admired too much, and in the 19th century they were still being copied by Renoir and Cézanne.

The most famous French sculpture of the middle of the 16th century, *Diana and the Stag* (Louvre, Paris), from the Château d'Anet, was traditionally attributed to Goujon. Its authorship is now uncertain.

Goujon worked at the Louvre from 1550 to 1562, producing work for both the exterior and the interior; but there is no further trace of his presence there after 1562. He died c1565.

Govardhan 17th century

Govardhan was a Mughal court artist under the Emperors Jahangir (1605–27) and Shah Jahan (1628–58). His earliest surviving work is probably that in the *Akbar-nama* (1605–10; Chester Beatty Library, Dublin). Other early works are among the margin drawings of the Jahangir Album leaves in the Gulistan Palace Library, Teheran. On one of these is a painting of Govardhan by his fellow miniaturist Daulat. He later kept abreast of the times in his painting of genre scenes, especially those depicting fakirs and other religious figures (in the Minto Album, divided between the Chester Beatty Library, Dublin, and the Victoria and Albert Museum, London). There is also an album containing his work in the Hermitage Museum, Leningrad. In the Minto Album there is a pair of facing equestrian portraits of Timur and of Shah Jahan. He excelled in facial expression, as in the portraits of courtiers painted during the 1630s, now in the British Museum, London.

Goya 1746–1828

The Spanish artist Francisco José de Goya y Lucientes, known as Goya, was born in Fuendetosdos, a small village outside Saragossa. His father was a master gilder. Goya's career as an artist was decided by the age of 14 when he was apprenticed to José Luzan, a busy church decorator. Spanish art had been for a long time in a state of decay, until Charles III remedied this by inducing Mengs and G.B. Tiepolo, the two finest artists working in Europe, to come to Madrid. It was under their shadow that Goya developed his own style. Some of Goya's earliest work survives, from a visit to Italy in 1771, and

Jean Goujon (attrib.): Diana and the Stag; marble; 211×258×135cm (83×102×53in); c1550–4. Louvre, Paris

these pictures show how far he was expected to bend to contemporary taste. The Goya we know from the late works does not emerge until after 1775.

Upon returning from Italy he won the first of a series of church commissions which began with the cathedral of El Pilar, in Saragossa, his home town. While working there he married Josepha Bayeu. She was the sister of Francisco Bayeu, who was Mengs' first assistant and the most respected native artist of his day.

Charles III had put Mengs in control of the Royal Tapestry Factory in Madrid; through the recommendation of Francisco Bayeu, Goya was employed to work on designs for the tapestries. These "cartoons", preserved in the Prado, Madrid, offer an illuminating account of Goya's rapid mastery of the medium, from the first oil sketch in 1774 to the last, in 1792. Apart from their painterly skills, Goya's designs outclass any decorative works done in Europe at this time. *The Parasol* (delivered in 1778; cartoons in the Prado, Madrid), strikes such a perfect balance between the ornate outlines of Tiepolo and the classical solidity of Mengs that it could be called one of the last great achievements of the Baroque school.

Goya's contact with the court led to the next important step in his development. In 1777–8 he made a series of etchings of Velazquez's paintings in the royal collection. This gave him his first experience of the technique of etching with aquatint, in which he soon emerged one of the world's masters. It also introduced him to Velazquez, who more than any contemporary influence helped Goya make a final step into complete maturity.

In 1779 Goya's application for the post of Court Painter was turned down; but his *Christ on the Cross* (1780; Prado, Madrid), a restrained diploma piece, gained him the title of Academician. During the next ten years Goya strove to be recognized as Spain's foremost artist. His winning of the royal commission to paint *San Francisco el Grande* in Madrid, his work for great Spanish families like the Osunas, the leading politicians such as the chief minister, Floridablanca, were all part of this steady uphill climb. That Goya was aware of his shifting position in society can be seen in the self-portraits included in the paintings that span these years, *Floridablanca*, 1783, *San Francisco el Grande*, 1781–3, and *The Family of Charles IV* 1800–1 (all in the Prado, Madrid).

Goya: Portrait of King Ferdinand VII of Spain in the Uniform of a General; detail; oil on canvas; **full size 207×140cm (81×55in); 1814. Prado, Madrid**

Goya was at last made Court Painter when the new King, Charles IV, succeeded to the throne in 1789. The new reign brought Goya an increasing burden of work. Besides continuing the tapestry designs and now-popular portrait commissions, he was expected to produce a whole new set of royal portraits. This period was also one of the darkest in Spanish history. Under the threat of the French Revolution, and dominated by the Queen (and her ally, the first minister, Godoy), Charles IV collapsed into a state of panic reaction. Two of Goya's pro-French liberal friends were banished and it was probably such anxieties, coupled with overwork, that brought on the illness Goya suffered during 1792 and 1793. Its exact nature remains a mystery, but we know it was a

traumatic experience from which he emerged stone-deaf, and that it marks a change in his work. He became more isolated, and suddenly aware of the depths of his own mind. On a more practical level, the collection of paintings and prints of Sebastian Martinez (with whom he stayed during his illness) suggested a new range of imagery and subjects, and the period of convalescence allowed him a new freedom from the restraints of patronage.

A fascination with scenes of cruelty and affliction emerges in the small paintings on copper of 1794, but, at the same time, Goya's broad mastery as a painter remains intact, perhaps even augmented. Begun as the more idiosyncratic *Suenos* ("Dreams") *Los Caprichos* of 1797 became the first fruit of these new ideas. Many of the 80 captioned plates reflect the ideas of the liberal movement of the day, particularly of its leader, Jovillanos. The dome of S. Antonio de la Florida, Madrid, shows that this mastery was not confined to etching or oils but applied to fresco as well. Painted in 1798, when the artist had little sympathy for the rituals of the church, it makes its subject the common people of Madrid rather than the miracle they witness. All Goya's work of this period is marked with the same daring and intensity. *The Family of Charles IV* (1800–1; Prado, Madrid) with its delight in ornament and its disarming naturalism, is in part a celebration of his own position as First Painter to the Court. By the time the short-lived liberal

regime collapsed, by which time Goya had lost more friends through banishment and other intrigues, his own position was so well established that he could negotiate with both Godoy and the King. The two versions of the *Majas* (now Prado, Madrid), clothed and unclothed, were painted before 1805 and appear in an inventory of Godoy's estate in 1808.

From 1808 until the end of his life Goya was strongly affected, emotionally rather than physically, by political events. Napolean had become increasingly involved in Spanish affairs; in 1808 he not only forced the abdication of Charles IV but abducted his heir, Ferdinand, to imprisonment in France. In their place he appointed as King

his brother Joseph. For the next six years Spain suffered the "War of Independence", marked by Wellington's Peninsular Campaign and the first incidences of guerilla warfare. After violent civilian suffering and famine, this culminated in the reinstatement of Ferdinand VII in March 1814.

Apart from a brief visit to Saragossa in 1808, Goya spent the whole of this period in Madrid, in growing isolation. His portrait commissions from the Spanish nobility diminished; his wife died in 1812; and he concentrated largely on personal work. He did consent to paint such portraits of the conquerors as his splendid *General Nicolas Guye* (1810; Marshall Field Collection, New York) which demonstrates his continuing skill in portraiture in the grand manner: and official commissions such as the *Allegory of Madrid* (1810; Ayuntamiento (City Hall), Madrid), which originally included a portrait of the usurping king, Joseph Bonaparte. His personal reaction to the war is, however, recorded in his *Disasters of War*, a series of 80 plates in etching and aquatint designed to illustrate "the fatal consequences of the bloody war against Bonaparte in Spain" (1808–1814). The spectacular horror of these scenes, with their depiction (accompanied, like *Los Caprichos*, by ironic captions) of the inhumanity to which all classes in Spain had been reduced, contrasts with the self-confident sentimentality of official military art in Napoleonic France (for example, the works of Gros and Horace Vernet). In his scenes of murder, rape, and famine, executed with spectacular use of mass and grouping, Goya offers not a glimmer of hope. The *Disasters* were not published until 1863. At this period he also painted some small oils and, unusually, still lifes.

The Government that succeeded Joseph's disappointed liberal expectations. The new King initiated a series of purges of liberals and reintroduced the Inquisition; but Goya was not censured for his work for the previous regime, and remained Painter to the Chamber. He painted a series of portraits of the new King in which his disillusionment is rendered in the increasing repulsiveness of the monarch.

The end of the war was marked by some notable commissions. In England are the two portraits of Wellington, both painted in 1812 after the briefest of sittings (National Gallery, London, and Wellington Museum, London): the subject is

Goya: Lady in a Black Mantilla; oil on canvas; 54×43cm (21×17in); 1815–24. National Gallery of Ireland, Dublin

characteristic of Goya's flexible attitude to those in power. In 1814 he proposed to the Council of Regency a series of "the most notable and heroic events" of the war. *Madrid, the Second of May* (1808; Prado, Madrid), was painted to commemorate a revolt by the people of Madrid in favor of their Spanish king, which had been brutally suppressed by the French. The painting influenced Delacroix by its use of startling bright color and vigorous movement. His most revolutionary work at this period, however, is the *Third of May 1808* (1814; Prado, Madrid). Its stark composition is characteristic of Goya's increasing simplicity of style; so is its use of black priming and its violent coloring (compare with Manet's *Execution of the Emperor Maximilian*, 1867; Städtische Kunstalle, Mannheim).

Goya's unease is apparent in *The General Assembly of the Company of the Philippines* (1815; Staatliche Museen, Berlin), which shows his ability to introduce powerful emotion, in this case boredom and fear, into an apparently straightforward subject (a meeting chaired by the King). Goya conveys a sensation of space by his treatment of light. By this time, however, his work was not receiving such general acceptance. The blander academic manner of Vicente Lopez (1772–1850) was increasingly admired. Although in such works as *Seated Lady with a Fan* (1815; Louvre, Paris), Goya attempted to emulate this charming rectilinear style, he was never deeply in sympathy with the aspirations of Neoclassicism. His diminished official reputation is demonstrated by the inclusion in the Prado Gallery, on its opening in 1820, of only two of his works: the equestrian *Charles IV* and *Maria Luisa*.

During the last ten years of his life, Goya moved into retirement. In 1819 he bought a country house, the Quinta del Sordo ("House of the Deafman"), which in the next four years he decorated with the "Black Paintings", a series of 16 works on canvases of various dimensions, now in the Prado, Madrid. His program is now obscure: the works include literary, biblical, and genre subjects. The dark colors and the distortion of form and scale produce powerful and at times horrifying images, as in the *Saturn Devouring one of his Children*, demonstrating his increasing preoccupation with the darker side of human nature.

The liberal government which had forced Ferdinand to accept the Constitution of Cadiz in 1820 was overthrown three years later by a French army in conspiracy with the Spanish King. Goya, many of whose friends had already left the country, applied for permission to travel to France. In 1824, after a visit to Paris, he settled in Bordeaux, where he died. In his old age his activity did not diminish; he continued to paint portraits, with a new economy of brushwork and simplified composition, and the use of a narrow, dark palette. He experimented both with the recently evolved technique of lithography and with painting on ivory. These last years were marked by loneliness and despair.

The development of Goya's style can be seen in his treatment of figure-painting: in an early work such as his portrait of *José Moniño, Count of Floridablanca* (1783; Urquijo Bank, Madrid) the 18th-century French *grand style* is still dominant. The painting shows stiff treatment of a man in an official position, and it lacks the penetrating sense of character which becomes apparent later in works like *Manuel Godoy in the Field* (1801; Academy of San Fernando, Madrid). Here Goya suggests the worldliness and superficiality of Godoy's character through the arrogant pose and gaudy coloring, and the illusion of depth is created through color rather than perspective. Goya's portraiture is at its most powerful in paintings like *The Countess of Chinchon* (1800; Collection of the Duke de Sueca, Madrid). The lady was married against her will to Godoy. Her wistful isolation is conveyed not only by the delineation of her features and the nervous clutching of her fingers, but also by the startling juxtaposition of the flimsy gilt chair and the surrounding blackness.

Goya's style is characterized by his method of building up his coloring through several thin glazes. This is first apparent in *Francisco Bayeau* (1795; Prado, Madrid). After his work on the engravings (*Los Caprichos* and *The Disasters of War*) a more Rembrandtesque awareness of chiaroscuro emerges. His self-proclaimed masters were Nature, Velazquez, and Rembrandt.

Goya achieved an enormous reputation in 19th-century France. He was praised by Baudelaire, Hugo, and Gautier for his prefiguring of Romanticism and Impressionism, and he inspired artists like Delacroix, Guys, Daumier, and Manet. The English, on the whole, showed little interest in him until the end of the century, when in 1896 the National Gallery acquired three of his paintings. Today he has come to be recognized as the greatest artist of the period c1800, not only in Spain but probably in the whole of Europe.

The best view of his work can be obtained in the Prado, Madrid; he is also represented in most other European and American major collections.

Further reading. Gassier, P. and Wilson, J. *Goya*, London (1971). Gudiol, J. *Goya*, Barcelona (1971). Harris, T. *Goya's Graphic Work*, Oxford (1964). Sanchez Canton, F.J. *Goya*, Paris (1930) and Madrid (1951).

Goyen Jan van 1596–1656

Jan Josephsz. van Goyen was a prominent Dutch landscapist who was born at Leiden. Studying under six different teachers from 1606 onwards, he spent a year in Harlem with Esaias van de Velde, who was to have the most decisive influence. His earliest works date from 1620 and are often circular in shape. They are close in character to those of Esaias van de Velde in their use of *coulisse*-type compositions, strong colors, and richly illustrative detail, depicting small panoramic views of country roads and Dutch villages. At this stage atmospheric treatment remains insignificant, and the figures seem detached from the landscape.

Van Goyen settled in Leiden in 1618. In the late 1620s, he abandoned his early style in favor of a simpler subject-matter. Concentrating on a closely observed section of landscape, a few peasant cottages along a road or in the dunes, he developed a monochromatic palette. He used tonal treatment in browns, pale yellows, and greens to subdue local color and present atmospheric effect. At this stage he introduced such devices as the leading diagonal, or a dark strip of shadow along the foreground, lending unity and a sense of depth to the work.

In 1634, van Goyen moved to The Hague. During the 1630s, he introduced water into his scenes. In yellowish and gray-green tones, his fluid brush strokes depict settlements beside canals, or broad silhouettes of towns by rivers, dominated by vast skies that lend a transparent airiness to the horizon. In the 1640s winter landscapes predominate, with people skating or riding in sleds, as well as city views, river scenes, and seascapes.

Jan van Goyen: The Sea at Haarlem; oil on canvas; 39×54cm (15×21in); 1656. Städelsches Kunstinstitut, Frankfurt am Main

Van Goyen's late work is enlivened by a deepening tonality, warmer browns, stronger contrasts of luminous skies and water against dark foregrounds, with a thin and vibrant quality to the paint. Van Goyen visited France as a young man and later traveled frequently and extensively in the Netherlands and the regions of the Lower Rhine: he has left many sketchbooks filled with rapid black chalk drawings.

As in the case of his contemporaries, van Goyen's financial position was insecure. He supplemented his income through work as a picture dealer and valuer, as well as speculating in property and tulip bulbs. Despite these efforts, he died insolvent in 1656. A respected member of the Painters' Guild, he had a profound influence upon many artists, notably Salomon van Ruys-dael, Nicolaes Berchem, and Aelbert Cuyp. A prolific worker, he left over 1,000 pictures which are well distributed among major galleries, such as the Rijksmuseum, Amsterdam; Smith College Museum of Art in Northampton, Mass; Royal Museum of Art (Mauritshuis), The Hague, and many private collections.

Graf Urs c1485–1527

The Swiss draftsman, engraver, and goldsmith Urs Graf was born in Soleure in 1485. He frequently left his goldsmith's shop in Basel to fight as a mercenary soldier, making many sketches of camp life as well as drawing horrifying studies of battle and its aftermath. He is revealed by legal documents as a lusty bully and cutthroat, and his work, immensely popular in his day, reflected the same unbridled force.

Graf's characteristic subjects were coarse variations on themes of love and death. The late Gothic style took on a fierce vitality in his hands. His capricious exuberance led him naturally to etching, traditionally a part of the craft of the armorer. It had probably been used as a graphic medium in the armorer's shops at Augsburg soon after 1500; but the first dated etching, of a typically salacious subject, was made by Urs Graf in 1513. He disappeared from Basel in 1527; he may have died in the Italian campaigns of that year.

Gran Daniel 1694–1757

Born in Vienna, Daniel Gran was one of the leading fresco painters employed in the decoration of the great Austrian Baroque buildings. He was taught by Gregor Werle, whose patron, Adam Schwarzenberg, enabled him to travel to Italy. He studied under Ricci in Venice and Solimena in Naples.

After his return to Vienna, he painted the ceiling frescoes of Schwarzenberg's palace (1724–5) and of the Imperial Library (1726–30). The latter work, an allegory of Charles VI as patron of the arts and sciences, established his reputation; it brought him numerous commissions for ceiling frescoes and altar paintings, mainly in Lower Austria.

Gran's style, though displaying the joyful splendor of the Austrian Baroque, departs from the exuberance and illusionism of the main Baroque tradition. His figures hover rather than soar, and express a feeling of serene composure and dignity. Like his compatriots, Fischer von Erlach and Raphael Donner, he thus achieved a synthesis of Baroque and Neoclassical values.

Grant Duncan 1885–1979

The British painter Duncan Grant was born at Rothiemurchus in Invernesshire. He studied briefly at the Slade School of Fine Arts and with Jacques-Émile Blanche in Paris. In the years before 1914, Grant was a member of the Bloomsbury circle: a group of friends that included the economist John Maynard Keynes, the novelist Virginia Woolf, the critic Clive Bell, and the painter Vanessa Bell. Grant's association with the last two was an intimate one, and from 1916 the three lived together at Charleston in Sussex.

Grant's painting was adventurous in color and form in the years between 1910 and 1920, when the influence of Picasso and Matisse can be discerned. His later work consisted of landscape, still life, and portraiture, in a more conservative impressionistic idiom. His talents as a large-scale decorator never had the opportunities they seemed to demand.

Further reading. Shone, R. *Bloomsbury Portraits*, Oxford (1976).

Grasser Erasmus c1450–1518

The German sculptor and architect Erasmus Grasser seems to have been trained in Munich. In 1480 he executed his first known work, 16 *Morris Dancers*, for the town hall in Munich. These exciting, freestanding figures are full of movement and character; even in their comic *grotesquerie* they express the tendency of contemporary German sculpture to evolve from the late Gothic style. Grasser's much more profound achievement, extremely characteristic of Renaissance sculpture in Germany, is his masterpiece, the sculptured St Peter Altarpiece for the church of St Peter's in Munich (1492). The life-sized figure of St Peter has a great air of solemnity and realism of characterization. Grasser is recorded as architect in 1484 in Kloster Mariaberg near Rorschach. Among his other works is the signed and dated Aresinger tomb in St Peter's, Munich (1482). (*See* overleaf.)

Grassi Giovannino de' *fl.* 1389–98

Giovannino de' Grassi was an Italian illuminator, sculptor, and painter. He was a leading representative of the internationally influential Lombard school of miniaturists, which flourished under Visconti patronage. These artists were distinguished for their vivid representation of the natural world; Giovannino's achievement in this field can be seen in those pages he executed in a model-book in the Biblioteca Communale, Bergamo (MS. Delta VII. 14). His studies of birds in this volume are delightful not only for their scientific accuracy but also for their lovely coloring. Giovannino's was a courtly art, and with

Duncan Grant: Portrait of a Woman; oil on canvas; 72×58cm (28×23in); 1927. Tate Gallery, London

his son Salamone he made the highly decorated *Uffiziolo* (Book of Offices) for Gian Galeazzo Visconti (Visconti di Modrone Collection, Milan). He was involved in many aspects of work on Milan Cathedral. His single documented work as a sculptor is the relief of *Christ and the Samaritan Woman* (1391–6) in the northern sacristy of the building.

Gravelot 1669–1773

The French designer and engraver Hubert François Bourguignon was commonly known as Gravelot. A native of Paris, he achieved distinction for his book illustrations and his *rocaille* designs for cabinetmakers, upholsterers, and metalworkers. From 1732 to 1745 he lived in London where his sophisticated illustrations of contemporary manners and costumes considerably influenced English artists. Thomas Gainsborough and Francis Hayman were his pupils, and the style of Joseph Highmore's literary illustrations is clearly related to that of his colleague Gravelot. Exacting in his standards, he revitalized illustrative engraving in England; an accomplished school of native engravers continued to work in his manner well after his return to Paris. The descriptive precision and elegance of his line and the inexhaustible variety of his inventions can be seen in the drawings for two of his more important commissions, the second volume of Gay's *Fables* (1738; 13 drawings in the British Museum, London) and the second edition of L. Theobald's *The Works of Shakespeare in Eight Volumes* (1740; 28 drawings in the Graphische Sammlung Albertina, Vienna, and the Huntington Library and Art Gallery, San Marino).

Graves Morris 1910–

Morris Graves is one of the American West Coast painters whose work has been deeply affected by Oriental art and thought. He was born in Fox Valley, Oregon. He taught himself and traveled extensively in the East, though he settled in Seattle and in later years spent more and more time in Ireland.

In the late 1930s he met Mark Tobey,

Erasmus Grasser: the tomb of Dr Ulrich Aresinger; stone; 1482. Church of St Peter, Munich

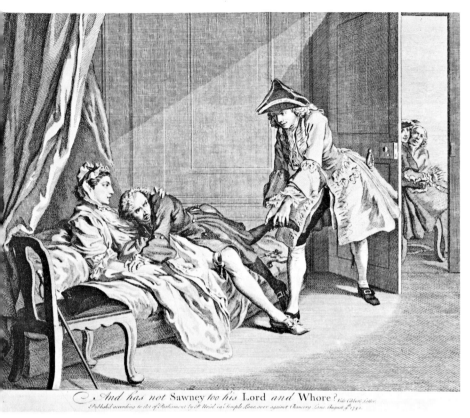

Gravelot: "And has not Sawney too his Lord and Whore?"; engraving; 28×33cm (11×13in); 1742. British Museum, London

whose so-called "white writings" Graves adapted to his own technique. Working mainly in gouache and watercolor, Graves paints strange landscapes and creatures that belong to dreams and visions rather than to the everyday world. *The Bird Singing in the Moonlight* (1938/9; Museum of Modern Art, New York) is a characteristic example of his work.

Greco El 1541–1614

The Spanish painter Domenico Theotokopouli was commonly known as El Greco. He was born in Crete, which was then a Venetian possession, but little information exists about his early life. It is likely that he is to be identified with a master painter recorded in Crete in 1566. According to the contemporary miniaturist Giulio Clovio, he had been trained at Titian's workshop in Venice before traveling to Rome in 1570. A few years later he visited Madrid, possibly to obtain commissions from Philip II to paint pictures for the Escorial. In 1577 he went to Toledo to paint the altarpieces and design the architectural framework and sculptural decoration for the church of S. Domingo el Antiguo. He remained in Toledo until his death.

El Greco's interest in literature, history, philosophy, and theology is reflected in the inventory of his library, and corroborated by the intellectuals whose company he frequented in Italy and Spain. During his stay in Rome he met Fulvio Orsini, antiquarian and librarian of the Farnese Palace, and Pedro Chacon, the Toledan employed to reform the Gregorian calendar. In Toledo he seems to have gained the favor of the sophisticated and cosmopolitan Mendoza family. He was also a close friend of the clerics Luis and Diego da Castilla, the antiquarian Antonio Covarrubias, and the historian Salazar de Mendoza. The celebrated poets Góngora and Paravicino sang his praises.

Contemporary philosophical and theological ideas in Spain had a profound influence on the art of El Greco. From the 1580s onwards his paintings appear to express Christian doctrine according to the concepts of Neoplatonism. He rejected the notion of seeing the manifestation of God in naturalistic forms and sought to create abstract forms as an aid to religious contemplation. The dazzling brightness of El Greco's light and color is intended to be a reflection of divine light which will illuminate the mind of the beholder. The soaring movement from naturalistically described forms to heavenly beings of superhuman proportions will enable the viewer's soul to reascend to God. This combination of light metaphysics with the ascent from the material to the immaterial was derived from the c 6th-century *Celestial Hierarchy* of Pseudo-Dionysius the Areopagite, and was a concept shared by contemporary spiritual writers.

In his early work in Italy El Greco strove after naturalistic representation. For instance *The Purification of the Temple* (1560s; National Gallery of Art, Washington, D.C.) is a bold but abortive attempt to emulate the achievements of the great Venetian painters Titian, Jacopo Bassano, Tintoretto, and Veronese. The composition is loosely organized, the treatment of space confused, and the drawing imprecise. Yet his handling of iridescent colors and flickering highlights, together with the rhythmic outline of his forms, anticipate the style of his Toledan masterpieces. Under the impact of the works of Michelangelo and Raphael in Rome, his second version of *The Purification of the Temple* (Minneapolis Institute of Arts) achieves greater clarity in the treatment of space by the elimination of superfluous anecdote. It reveals a more accurate observation of the structure of forms, with a more carefully modulated tonal range.

This style reaches its climax in his earliest works in Toledo, the altarpieces for S. Domingo el Antiguo (1577–9) and the *Espolio* (1577–9) painted for the cathedral sacristy. In the former he adapted Vignola's design for the facade of the church of the Gesù in Rome to the architectural framework of the high altar, thereby imposing on the native Plateresque style a sense of classical harmony and restraint. This is echoed in the central canvas, the *Assumption of the Virgin* (Art Institute of Chicago), in which a knowledge of Roman draftsmanship and design is coupled with a Venetian sensibility to color, to express the glorification of the Virgin.

In the *Espolio* (the disrobing of Christ before the Crucifixion) he created, by means of precise drawing, convincing three-dimensional forms that suggest polychrome sculpture. The jostling crowd presses down on Christ while the executioner, unmoved by his plight, bores a hole in the Cross which seems to lie at our

El Greco: Lady in a Fur Wrap; oil on canvas; 62×50cm (24×20in); c1577–8. Pollok House, Glasgow

feet. But this claustrophobic space, with its grim foreboding of death, is pierced by the scarlet robe of Christ. Faceted like a jewel, its intensity reassures the beholder of the triumph of Christ. The Cathedral authorities objected to the inclusion of the three Marys, as well as to the placing of the heads of the crowd higher than that of Christ. However, the picture remained unaltered. El Greco probably defended his interpretation by referring to the *Meditations on the Life of Christ* by Pseudo-Bonaventura. This late-13th-century text,

with its vivid description of the Passion of Christ, was in vogue during the Counter-Reformation.

El Greco's imaginative response to subject matter is best illustrated by *The Martyrdom of St Maurice* (1582; Escorial, near Madrid) commissioned by Philip II. The picture was rejected, and a substitute painted by a mediocre Italian artist, Romulo Cincinnato. The latter painted decapitated bodies almost spilling out of the picture, in true orthodox fashion, whereas El Greco had removed them to the

background. He abandoned the carnage of Cincinnato's version and the blatant emotion of his own *Espolio* in favor of a polemic on the theme of martyrdom. St Maurice and his generals are presented as graceful, attenuated beings set against a backcloth of cool and restrained colors: lemon, pale gray, pale blue, and pale pink.

From now on El Greco virtually confined himself to patrons in Toledo, and during the 1580s he developed a style characterized by flatter, more elongated forms compressed into a shallow space and woven into a pattern of rhythmic curves. Colors are more expressive, less descriptive, and there are distinct tonal transitions from light to dark.

The Burial of the Count of Orgaz (1586) for the church of S. Tomé, Toledo, is his most dazzling essay in this style. The picture commemorates the burial in 1323 of the Lord of Orgaz, a benefactor of Santo Tomé. St Augustine and St Stephen were said to have miraculously appeared at the ceremony and to have placed him in his sepulcher. The reality of the miracle is expressed through such naturalistic details as the damascened armor of the Lord and the diaphanous surplice of the priest, and by the depiction of contemporary Toledans.

Among the other figures who have been identified with certainty are El Greco's young son, Jorge Manuel, and the humanist Antonio Covarrubias. The figure of the dead man may be a portrait of Alvar Perez de Guzman y Mendoza, the 10th Lord and the Count of Orgaz. As the body is being lowered into the tomb (depicted in a fresco beneath the canvas which has since disappeared), an angel holds the soul of the Lord—portrayed in insubstantial form as a child—and spirals upwards to "an open heaven in glory". The celestial vision is evoked by a pronounced elongation of form, by abstract clouds, and by the exceedingly bright light emanating from Christ. No longer the embodiment of physical beauty and power as in the *Espolio*, Christ is now conceived of as a radiance of light. This vision of the divine is enhanced by the real light flooding downwards from the window above the painting.

After this painting El Greco's style

El Greco: Portrait of Brother Hortensio Félix Paravicino; oil on canvas; 113×86cm (44×34in); 1609. Museum of Fine Arts, Boston

changes. He no longer observes the structure or appearance of material but creates abstract forms to convey ideas. Light is more intense and seems to emanate from these forms. There is a greater variety of colors and these are juxtaposed so that they vibrate. Contours are no longer so clearly defined, and seem to release light and color from their confines. Thus the flat surface design characteristic of the 1580s is disrupted by the vertical thrust of forms and the projection of incandescent light and brilliant color.

His supreme technical skill and the conceptual handling of color, light, and form is evident in his portraiture as well as in his religious compositions. His portrait of the Inquisitor General, Cardinal Fernando Niño de Guevara (c1600–1; Metropolitan Museum, New York), has all the ingredients of a splendid state portrait, with its dazzling light flashing across folds of sumptuous drapery. But the acid color, spatial tension, and taut, sharp-edged contours create an atmosphere of restlessness. Guevara seems to fidget in his chair, his feet askew. His expression is furtive and he grips one arm of the chair uneasily. El Greco's ability to transcend physiognomy and conjure up the idea of the man is beautifully recorded in the portrait of his friend *Brother Hortensio Félix Paravicino* (1609; Museum of Fine Arts, Boston). With consummate skill he conveys the sophistication and spiritual intensity of the poet by sweeping red, black, and white paint into a pattern of rhythmic shapes.

This total concern with the realm of the spirit is conveyed in his decorative schemes for the Augustinian Church of Doña María de Aragón, Madrid (1596–1600), S. José Chapel, Toledo (1597–9), the Hospital of La Caridad, Illescas (1603–5), Oballe Chapel in S. Vicente, Toledo (1607–13), and the Hospital of Tavera (begun in 1608 and completed after El Greco's death by his son Jorge Manuel).

The Immaculate Conception (Santa Cruz Museum, Toledo) from the Oballe Chapel in S. Vicente is possibly the most splendid example. The painting originally rested on the altar. At the bottom there is a cluster of roses and lilies (symbols of the Virgin) naturalistically rendered so as to mirror real flowers placed on the altar. Elsewhere in the painting El Greco has distorted light, color, and form: heavenly beings of immense proportions soar effortlessly heavenwards; garments of bright blue and red and yellow are juxtaposed to create a

dazzling effect. Although the light originates from above, it is reflected off these garments with such intensity that each seems to have its own source of light. A vision of heavenly beings flares upwards from the naturalistic flowers, illuminating the dark night. The inclusion of naturalistic details at the bottom of the painting thus provides the beholder with a stepping stone from the "sensible to the intelligible"; that is, to the realm of heavenly beings. He will continue his ascent with their aid until ultimately he will reattain union with God. The function of El Greco's religious paintings is "to raise the soul of man heavenwards with its movement of spirit".

El Greco's art reflects his response to the spiritual climate of Toledo at the time of the Counter-Reformation. Even his painting of *Laocoön* (c1610; National Gallery of Art, Washington, D.C.) is almost certainly allegorical. As in a dream, the wooden horse trots towards the Visagra Gate of Toledo, the sky is ominous, and Toledo seems doomed. In subject matter, El Greco's pictures run the gamut of Counter-Reformation themes, such as the purification of the Temple, the Passion of Christ, the Immaculate Conception, the martyrdom of saints, the contemplation of death, and acts of charity. But his stylistic interpretations, especially after the 1580s, conflict with those proposed in the decrees of the Council of Trent with their emphasis on clarity and verisimilitude. It is not surprising that at a time of strict religious orthodoxy his art should find no successors. As Paravicino aptly remarked, "future ages will admire his genius, but none will imitate it".

Further reading. Cossio, M.B. *El Greco* (2 vols.), Madrid (1972). Goldscheider, L. *El Greco*, London (1949). Troutman, P. *El Greco*, London (1971). Wethey, H.E. *El Greco and his School* (2 vols.), London and Princeton, N.J. (1962).

Greuze Jean-Baptiste 1725–1805

Jean-Baptiste Greuze was the most important French painter of the mid 18th century. His most appreciated works today are his portraits, such as the superbly commanding *J.G. Wille* (1763; Musée Jacquemart-André, Paris). His true significance, however, lies in the contemporary success of his genre paintings. These, although superficially related to the Dutch

tradition, are in fact history paintings; but they are not couched in the usual aristocratic milieu. His subjects are peasants, the working class, and the lower bourgeoisie. Unlike a straightforward genre painter, Greuze is not interested in quaintness of detail, prettiness of color, or whimsicality of emotion. He neither pokes fun at the lower classes nor adopts an attitude of condescension towards them. Rather, like a traditional history painter, he is concerned with mankind in general, and with representing the balance or imbalance between the passions and the intellect.

His works are therefore moralized and idealized, since they seek to provide an exemplar of virtue. Often his scenes provoked the spectator to tears. Sensibility was very much *à la mode* then, as it is not now, and this forms a barrier to our comprehension of the dividing line between true and touching sentiment, and chocolate-box sentimentality.

His first great success was *The Village Bride* (1761; Louvre, Paris), which, like *The Paralytic tended by his Children* (1763; Hermitage Museum, Leningrad), eulogized the virtues of family life and *pietàs*. Both works are classical in style: a restrained color scheme parallels the restrained gestures and expressions, and the simple frieze of players on the "stage" is backed by plain walls, any details of which help to tell the story. *The Paralytic* may be considered as a reinterpretation of the classical deathbed scene, as used by Poussin in his *Testament of Eudamidas* (c1660; State Art Museum, Copenhagen) which was soon to be popular with Neoclassical artists.

In fact Greuze's manner, which owes much to the example of Raphael and Poussin (whom he was the first to revive), lays the foundations for Neoclassicism. Diderot did not live to see David's *Oath of the Horatii* (1784; Louvre, Paris), but he helped form the Neoclassical *credo* by his constant encouragement of Greuze, whose bourgeois genre painting is the counterpart of Diderot's plays. Both tell a story, and tell it with feeling, and these elements of narrative and sentimentality are the essence of early Neoclassicism. Details like the weeping women in *Oath of the Horatii* may derive partly from Greuze's example, although they have antique sources as well.

Greuze once attempted the full Neoclassical manner himself, in his *Septimius Severus rebuking Caracalla* (1769; Louvre, Paris), which was his reception piece to the

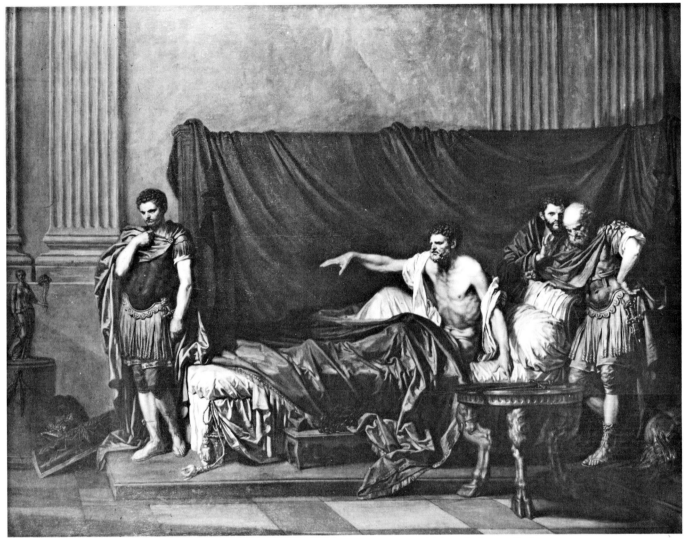

Jean-Baptiste Greuze: Septimius Severus rebuking Caracalla; oil on canvas; 124×160cm (49×63in); 1769. Louvre, Paris

Academy. Unfortunately, this was judged unacceptable as a history painting, and Greuze—to his chagrin—was received only as a genre painter. The work was quite rightly criticized for poor drawing, but it is indeed a history painting. It may have failed through a mixture of jealousy and an awareness of the applicant's immense vanity.

Although Greuze lived through the Revolution, his early Neoclassicism fell from favor during the 1780s when the sterner, antique manner of David came to the fore. He then made his money on the type of single-figure, mawkish, and broadly painted moralistic work represented by *The Broken Jug* (late 1770s; Louvre, Paris), in which the jug is a metaphor for the beginnings of the sexual experience of the sad-looking girl who carries it.

Greuze's quality as a painter is variable, and his coloring is sometimes monotonous; so is his repetition of subject matter, often popularized through engravings. The fact that the Marquis de Marigny, Directeur des Bâtiments, bought *The Village Bride*, and that it subsequently went to Louis XVI, demonstrates the official policy of morality in painting—a program that was to nurture quite deliberately a Neoclassical style.

Gris Juan 1887–1927

The Spanish painter José Victoriano Gonzalès was known as Juan Gris. He was born in Madrid, studied at the School of Industrial and Applied Arts, and worked as a draftsman for satirical magazines. In 1906 he moved to Paris, where he spent the rest of his life. In his early years in Paris, he continued to work as a freelance illustrator. As a friend and neighbour of Picasso in Montmartre, he mixed in the avant-garde circle of painters and writers and by 1911 had turned seriously to painting. He rapidly became a central figure in Cubist painting.

He had not participated in the early experimental phases of Cubism, but with remarkable fluency he now accepted a highly sophisticated modern idiom as the normal vocabulary available to a painter. The fragmentation, dislocation, and near monochrome palette of Analytical Cubism feature in paintings like *Oil Lamp* (*Lampe à pétiole*, c1912; Kröller-Müller Museum, Otterlo). Characteristic qualities of his art are the dense immutable sense of surface, the almost austere clarity of the image, and the rhythmical structure in which lines and edges blend into a lyrical, disciplined architecture. There are no soft atmospheric

Juan Gris: Figure seated in a Café; oil and collage on canvas; 99×72cm (39×28in); 1914. Collection of Mr and Mrs Leigh B. Block, Chicago

edge with interlocked fragments of newspaper, wallpaper, and labels with fragments of painting and of drawing and of writing. In their choice of *collé* headlines and other materials (mirror, glass, reproductions, and so forth), they are packed with witty allusions to the reality and the artifice of art.

During the First World War Gris formed close friendships with Matisse, who supported him financially, and with Lipchitz.

He also worked as stage-designer (notably for Sergei Diaghilev) and book illustrator (for his friend Réverdy, for Jacob, Gertrude Stein, and Tzara).

His mature works were an extension of his own Cubist paintings: broader and softer in drawing, color, and mood. Subject matter is restrained. They are mainly still lifes such as *The Virgin* (1916; Öffentliche Kunstsammlung, Kunstmuseum Basel), and interiors, apart from a group of figure-paintings (*Pierrots and Harlequins*, c1919–22) and an impressive series of portrait drawings (such as his 1920 *Self-portrait*; Galerie Louise Leiris, Paris). The angularity of his linear Cubist constructions gave way in the 1920s to a broader, continuous curvilinear idiom linking muted color areas.

Further reading. Cooper, D. *Letters of Juan Gris 1913–1927*, London (1956). Gaya-Numo, J.A. *Juan Gris*, Barcelona and Paris (1974). Kahnweiler, D.-H. *Juan Gris: his Life and Work*, London and New York (1947).

Gropius Walter 1883–1969

The German architect Walter Gropius was born in Berlin. His career as an architect and teacher was intimately associated with the development of modern architecture. Between 1903 and 1907 he studied architecture at university in Berlin and Munich. He then spent three years as assistant to Peter Behrens, who was employed as an industrial designer and architect by the German electrical company, A.E.G.

Gropius set up in practice in Berlin in 1910 and in 1911 was engaged with his partner Adolf Meyer (1881–1929) to design the Fagus shoe-last factory at Alfeld, the layout of which had already been determined. Gropius' design was free from historic ornament of any kind, and crisply cuboid; he exploited the building's steel frame in an imaginative way by treating the walls as a glass membrane,

allusions as in early Cubism. The two-dimensional integrity of the surface seems impregnable. Yet the painted objects have an extraordinarily physical reality and identity.

This first idiom closely anticipated the form and theory of Synthetic Cubism. Gris produced many outstanding works in the next few years, between 1912 and 1915; later he articulated some of the clearest statements of Synthetic Cubism's intent, stressing the authenticity of painting's new reality. "Cézanne turns a bottle into a cylinder, but I begin with a cylinder and create an individual of a special type: I make a bottle—a particular bottle—out of a cylinder" (1921).

His paintings of these years, mostly intimate still lifes, have a strong sense of the particular. They are tightly organized but sumptuous relationships of luminous color, texture, and pattern. The collages of 1913 and 1914 such as *Breakfast* (1914; Museum of Modern Art, New York) have a similar, meticulously organized precision. The surface is crowded from edge to

apparently unsupported at the corners.

Dramatic use of glass also characterized the model factory and administrative building which Gropius and Meyer designed for the *Deutscher Werkbund's* 1914 exhibition in Cologne, although here the formal effect was somewhat indecisive. At this time Gropius also had the experience of designing a variety of furniture and industrial products, including a railway locomotive (1913) and a railway sleeping car (1914).

In 1918 Gropius was appointed head of the School of Arts and Crafts and the Fine Art Academy in Weimar, which he amalgamated as the Bauhaus. Here the skills of artist, craftsman, and architect were developed as specializations of a common approach to design, and the fine and applied arts were seen as "inseparable components of a new architecture". This approach, which derived from Arts and Crafts ideology, was strongly advocated by left-wing Expressionist architects. Gropius' sympathy for Expressionism at this time can be seen in the jagged outline of the memorial at Weimar that commemorated the victims of a 1920 uprising. It is also apparent in the angular forms of the Sommerfeld house, Dahlem, Berlin (designed in 1921 by Gropius and Meyer, with collaboration from Bauhaus students).

However, Gropius gradually turned from this very personal manner to a more rational and generally more cubic architecture. His *Internationale Architektur* (the first *Bauhausbuch*) was almost a guidebook to the emerging International style. Its publication in 1925 coincided with the removal of the Bauhaus from Weimar to Dessau, where new buildings were erected to Gropius' designs. Its clean white concrete forms, the large expanse of glass walling in the workshop wing, and the carefully balanced asymmetry of the whole made the new Bauhaus building a potent symbol of 20th-century rationalism.

This return to the regularity of industrial forms was perhaps partly motivated by the realization that individually commissioned houses and handmade goods could only be afforded by the rich. Gropius' desire to provide working people with well designed homes and furnishings led him to explore the possibilities of standardization. The housing he designed for the Törten estate in Dessau (1926) and for the Werkbund's Weissenhof exhibition in Stuttgart (1927) was prefabricated. The furniture he de-

signed for the Feder stores (1927) was mass produced from standard components which could be combined in various ways. Other important designs of these years were Gropius' plan for a "Total Theater" for proletarian drama productions (1927), and the Dessau employment exchange (1927), on which a number of Bauhaus students assisted with furniture and fittings.

In 1928 Gropius resigned from the Bauhaus. During the next few years he continued to design prefabricated houses, mass-produced furniture, and industrial products (including car bodies and cast-iron stoves). He also planned a variety of schemes for multistory blocks of flats, since he believed that high building density was imperative in cities. The most ambitious of these schemes actually to be carried out was for four-story blocks of workers' flats at Berlin-Siemensstadt (1929). These were much lower than the 8 to 12 stories he advocated. The long white blocks were separated by generous expanses of lawn and trees which he saw as a major virtue of such developments.

With Hitler's assumption of power in Germany, political pressure on Gropius increased; in 1934 he emigrated to England, where he worked for three years with Maxwell Fry (1899–). The most important outcome of this association was Impington Village College (1936), a school community centre in rural Cambridgeshire. It was informally laid out and designed to make the most of fine weather: a predominantly single story building in brick, less purely geometric than much of Gropius' previous work.

Shortly after plans for the college were completed, Gropius was invited to be Professor of Architecture at Harvard University, and so left for America in 1937. In America he designed a number of private houses with a former Bauhaus colleague, Marcel Breuer (1902–70).

In 1941 the partnership planned a low-cost workers' housing scheme in New Kensington, Pittsburgh, devising a system of standardized timber frames for the 250 houses which were placed in short terraces about a hillside site. The possibilities of standardized wooden components were further exploited in the Packaged House System which Gropius developed with Konrad Wachsmann. This was the first of Gropius' schemes for prefabricated houses to go into large-scale mass-production (1943–5).

In 1941 Gropius' partnership with Breuer came to an end. Four years later Gropius joined forces with a group of younger men to create The Architects' Collaborative (T.A.C.), with which he worked until his death. Among the many products of this enterprise were the Harvard University Graduate Centre (1949), the United States Embassy in Athens (1956–61), and the Rosenthal china factory at Selb, Germany (1965).

Gropius wanted to design buildings that were as representative of the 20th century as the Gothic cathedral was of medieval Europe. He strove to reconcile technology with human needs, and gave sophisticated formal expression to this, most notably in the Fagus factory and the Bauhaus building. He believed that design involved the interplay of technical considerations and artistic creativity, and saw no reason why its advantages should be available only to the enlightened rich. Through his teaching in Germany and America, several generations of architects and designers were inspired by his ideals.

Further reading. Fitch, J.M. *Walter Gropius*, New York (1960). Giedion, S. *Walter Gropius, Work and Teamwork*, Zurich (1954). Gropius, W. *Apollo in the Democracy: the Cultural Obligation of the Architect*, New York (1968).

Grosz George 1893–1959

Born in Berlin, Grosz studied art in Dresden and Berlin. His first works were caricatures in the style of *Die Jugend*; but in Berlin and in Paris, where he lived in 1913, his drawing matured under the influence of the French graphic tradition. He established a powerful style of drawing and painting, which incorporated the formal devices of Expressionism and Futurism (seen in *Metropolis*, 1917; Museum of Modern Art, New York). After settling in Berlin in 1918, he became a founder of the Berlin Dada movement and attacked the bourgeois supporters of the Weimar Republic with his bitingly satirical drawings (for example, *Couple*, 1930; Tate Gallery, London). He left Germany for New York in 1933 and focused his attention on urban America before returning to Berlin in 1958. (*See* overleaf.)

Further reading. Hess, H. *George Grosz*, New Haven (1985). Schneede, U. *George Grosz*, London (1979).

George Grosz: Fit for Active Service; india ink on paper; 51×36cm (20×14in); 1916–17. Museum of Modern Art, New York

Grünewald 1470/80–1528

The German painter, Matthias Gothardt Neithardt (or Nithardt) has been generally known as Grünewald ever since that name was given him by the 17th-century historian, Joachim von Sandrart. His name appears in the rate books of the Town of Seligenstadt, near Würzburg, from 1501 to 1525. He became court painter to Uriel van Gemmingen and Albrecht of Brandenburg, successive Archbishops of Mainz; and he seems also to have advised on architectural and engineering schemes in the diocese. It is likely that he lost his place at court at the time of upheaval during the Peasants War of 1526; the 12 articles of faith found among his effects at his death suggest Protestant sympathies. He moved to Frankfurt and then to Halle, where he is recorded as in charge of the municipal waterworks and where he died in 1528.

Since much of Grünewald's work has been lost and there is a monogram signature on only three of his surviving paintings, chronology is problematical. His modern reputation has rested on one major work, the Isenheim Altarpiece, still in its complete state. There are also several smaller works, fragments of altarpieces, and about 40 drawings. Although so few of his works have survived, he emerges nevertheless as one of the most remarkable painters of his age, indeed of all time.

The small *Mocking of Christ* (1503; Alte Pinakothek, Munich), is probably his earliest surviving work and its features are characteristic of much that is to come. The religious drama is played out against a dark background, and the figures are highly expressive to accentuate the torment of the scene. There is a highly individualistic use of color, which suggests an

artist whose concern for painterly effects allows the brush to draw and describe in place of detailed preliminary preparation.

The Isenheim Altarpiece, dated 1515, was painted for the choir of the Antonite monastery at Isenheim, Alsace (the altarpiece, dismembered for display purposes, is now in the Musée d'Unterlinden, Colmar). Grünewald worked at the behest of Guido Guersi, the preceptor of the Order, whose coat of arms appears on the altarpiece. The Grünewald paintings were commissioned for the enlargement of a wooden altarpiece of 1505 which has carved figures of St Anthony, St Augustine, and St Jerome. His paintings turned the work into a polyptych in three stages. By means of three pairs of wings, two movable and one fixed, the altarpiece could be opened and reopened to show different sets of religious representations for weekday, Sunday, and Holy Day services.

The first stage shows the *Crucifixion*, flanked by fixed wings of St Anthony and St Sebastian, with a Lamentation on the *predella* below. The Christ of the Crucifixion dominates the scene, his body racked with pain, the flesh torn and turning green. His figure is larger than those of his mourners, fulfilling the prophecy of the pointing St John at the right as inscribed on the picture: "He will increase whilst I decrease". The dark setting throws the figures into relief and heightens the emotion of the scene. *Pentimenti*, or changes in brushwork, revealed by X rays, show how Grünewald accentuated the expressive content as he painted; the fingers of the Magdalene have been lengthened and the Virgin originally stood upright.

The second stage shows angels making music before the Virgin and Child and is perhaps best described symbolically as *The Incarnation of Christ and the Glorification of the Mother of God*. The angels show the artist at his most inventive coloristically, as they materialize before our eyes in pinks and yellows, sharp blues and greens. This visionary quality is matched by the building in which they appear, which seems itself to be in a state of metamorphosis with leaves and tendrils springing from the columns. This scene is flanked by the *Annunciation* and the *Resurrection of Christ*. In the latter scene the halo of Christ is the only source of light. The unearthly

Grünewald: The Meeting of St Erasmus and Maurice; oil on pine panel; 226×176cm (89×69in); 1517–23. Alte Pinakothek, Munich

quality of this celestial light is especially evident in the trailing drapery where shades of white and blue turn to deep pinks and grays in the folds.

The third stage of the altarpiece consists of the original carved structure with Grünewald's painted wings of *The Hermit Saints Anthony and Paul in the Desert* to the left and *The Temptation of St Anthony* to the right. Here are the most overt references to the duties of the Antonite Order in caring for the sick, by the presence of the medicinal plants in the *Hermit Saints* and the diseased figure in the *Temptation*.

The chief iconographical source for the altarpiece as a whole has been identified as the mystical *Revelations of St Bridget of Sweden*, written in the 14th century and first published in Germany in 1492.

Grünewald painted three smaller versions of the *Crucifixion* (Öffentlich Kunstsammlung, Basel; National Gallery of Art, Washington, D.C.; and Staatliche Kunsthalle Karlsruhe). Fragments remain of two other major altarpiece commissions. *The Madonna in the Garden* (now in the parish church, Stuppach) and *The Miracle of the Snows* (Augustinermuseum, Freiburg) probably each formed a part of the altarpiece in the collegiate church at Aschaffenburg (1517–19). Grisaille panels of saints (Fürstenberg Collection, Donaueschingen, and Städelsches Kunstinstitut, Frankfurt am Main) are from the Heller Altarpiece at Frankfurt. Some of Grünewald's drawings can be connected with lost works, including three paintings for the cathedral at Mainz. Many of his drawings are taken from the life and are highly unusual for their period. He used black chalk, often with a watercolor wash, to obtain softened, painterly effects. He is interested in the palpability of forms rather than line and contour; studies for the arms of the St Sebastian of the Isenheim Altarpiece are concerned less with the construction of the human form than with light playing over the surface of the flesh.

Grünewald was almost the exact contemporary of Albrecht Dürer (1471–1528), against whom all German art of the period is inevitably judged. Dürer's surviving work bears witness to the fact that despite the range of his accomplishment he remains primarily a graphic artist; whereas the work of Grünewald shows an inspired quality of painterliness that Dürer never matched.

Further reading. Pevsner, N. and Meier, M. *Grünewald*, London (1958). Ruhmer, E. *Grünewald*, London (1958). Ruhmer, E. (ed.) *Grünewald Drawings*, London (1970). Zulch, W.K. *Der Historische Grünewald, Mathis Gothardt-Neithardt*, Munich (1938).

Guardi: View of the Grand Canal, Venice (the Church of the Salute and Customs House); oil on canvas; 71×94cm (28×37in); c1770–80. Wallace Collection, London

Guardi brothers
17th and 18th centuries

Compared with Canaletto, Tiepolo, and Pittoni, the Guardi brothers were almost unheard of in 18th-century Venice. Their family came from the South Tyrol, and it was at first from there, and from other districts far from Venice, that the Guardi received commissions. Giovanni (Gian) Antonio (1698–1760) was the eldest of three painter brothers, and until his death it was he who ran the family workshop; it was under his name (if any were mentioned at all) that paintings were produced. This practice of coproduction has made it difficult to evaluate the individual merits of Gian Antonio and Francesco (1712–93) until c1750, when Francesco branched out on his own as a painter of views. The youngest brother, Niccolò (1715–85), is almost totally unknown as an artist.

The type of painting that the workshop produced is seen at its best in the altarpiece in Belvedere di Aquileia, Italy, where flimsy figures are painted in pretty pinks, pale greens, and light blues. In Venice their work may well have seemed bizarre; indeed, until Gian Antonio's death broke up the workshop, their art had more in common with Austrian Rococo painting than contemporary Venetian work.

Francesco Guardi seems to have taken up view painting 10 years or so before his elder brother's death. The early 1750s was an opportune time for a new specialist. Canaletto had left Venice for England in 1746, and except for a short break of a few months he remained there for a decade. Canaletto's rival Michele Marieschi had died in 1744. Not surprisingly, Francesco leaned heavily on both these artists; their influence, particularly that of Canaletto, is evident in the robust composition and feeling of space of his early works (for example, *Piazza San Marco*; National Gallery, London). Francesco may also have improved his technique by his study of Canaletto's works, for the latter was technically by far the better painter.

During his development as a view painter Francesco steadily freed himself from Canaletto's straightforward realism. His later views were not so much views of particular places as paintings of mood. Some of his most intimate works are scenes of the backwaters of Venice and the Lagoon; for instance the *Rio dei Medicanti* (Galleria dell'Accademia Carrara, Bergamo). This was one of the views etched by Luca Carlevaris at the beginning of the century; but unlike Carlevaris, Francesco Guardi was not interested in accurate topography—rather in the flickering sunlight on the gondoliers, and the passing shadows. His late views are nostalgic; his figures seem cocooned in a world of their own, oblivious of the decaying buildings that surround them.

Ironically it was the very qualities that caused Francesco Guardi's lack of success that were appreciated after his death. His wistful views of a city in decline, with their sketchiness and inaccuracies, have always appealed to a public that enjoys the idea of Venice as much as Venice itself.

Guarini Guarino 1624–83

The Italian architect Guarino Guarini was born at Modena in 1624. He entered the order of the Theatines in 1639, studied architecture in Rome along with theology, philosophy, and mathematics. Ordained in 1647, he settled in Messina in 1660. His membership of the Theatine Order, and his position as the Theatine's Professor of Mathematics in Messina were the keys to his architectural career. Through his connection with the Order he built the façade of the Theatine Church of SS. Annunziata dei Catalani in Messina c1661, and in Paris he built the church of Ste Anne-la-Royale some time after 1662. Neither of these buildings survive and it is only in his works in Turin that his mature style can be fully appreciated.

His two notable Turinese churches, S. Lorenzo (1668–87) and the Capella della SS. Sindone (1677–90), perfectly express his concern for the inside rather than the exterior of his buildings, and his fanatical passion for vaulted construction. In his structural daring, and his undisguised preference for Gothic rather than classical solutions, he echoed the Roman work of Borromini. The Palazzo Carignano of 1679, in Turin, repeated in secular form these aspects of his religious architecture. His *Architettura Civile* was published posthumously by Vittone in 1737 and influenced much 18th-century Turinese architecture. (*See* overleaf.)

Guas Juan fl. 1459–?97

The Spanish architect Juan Guas was born in France, at Lyons. He moved to Spain c1450 and by 1459 was working with his father on the Door of the Lions at Toledo Cathedral. He was master mason at Segovia Cathedral from 1473 to 1491 and at Toledo Cathedral c1483 to 1495. He was partly responsible for the richly carved screen surrounding the Toledo Cathedral sanctuary. In the years 1479 to 1480 he designed for Queen Isabella the church and monastery of S. Juan de los Reyes in Toledo. The church is his masterpiece, and combines elements from several architectural traditions. The wide single nave with recess-like lateral chapels is of southern French type; the star vaults and the decorative carving are Flemish, while underneath the capitals of the crossing hang miniature stalactites in Islamic fashion.

Guercino 1591–1666

The Italian painter Giovanni Francesco Barbieri was known because of his squint as Guercino. He came from Cento, where he studied under Benedetto Gennari. More important to his early stylistic development were the painters Lodovico Carracci and Ippolito Scarsella. Between 1615 and 1617 he painted frescoes at the Casa Pannini, Bologna. In 1618 a visit to Venice encouraged his absorption of the painterly traditions and lyrical poetry of Venetian art. A dusky, flickering light, sweeping diagonals, and rich color and texture distinguished his early altarpieces; this phase culminates in *St William of Aquitaine Receiving the Cowl* (1620; Pinacoteca Nazionale, Bologna).

In 1621 the newly elected Bolognese Pope Gregory XV called Guercino to Rome. In that year he painted the huge *The Burial and Reception into Heaven of St Petronilla* (Palazzo dei Conservatori, Rome), and also, between 1621 and 1623, the ceiling fresco *Aurora* for the Casino Ludovisi. Above an illusionistic architectural framework Dawn in her chariot sweeps across the sky; on the end walls are figures representing Night and Day. This dramatic work, with its creation of a unified pictorial space, its sense of dynamic movement, and its boldness of handling, marks the beginnings of the High Baroque. Yet Guercino's own style, in response to the prevailing tendencies of Roman art, became more classical.

In 1623 he returned to Cento; he visited Piacenza in 1626 to fresco the cathedral dome, and went to Modena in 1633. On Guido Reni's death in 1642 Guercino moved to Bologna. He continued to paint many altarpieces and easel pictures. His late style conforms to the classical stan-

Guercino: Ermina and the Shepherd; oil on canvas; 149×178cm (59×70in); c1618–20. City of Birmingham Museums and Art Gallery

Guarino Guarini: interior of the church of S. Lorenzo, Turin; 1668–87

dards of Reni, and lacks his earlier powerful originality.

Guglielmo of Pisa 12th century

Guglielmo of Pisa was the most prominent Romanesque sculptor in Tuscany. His pulpit for Pisa Cathedral (1157–62) provided a model for the more famous Tuscan pulpits by Nicola Pisano and his son Giovanni. It was, in fact, the pulpit by the latter that made Guglielmo's earlier version redundant; so it was shipped to Sardinia in 1311 and is now in the cathedral at Cagliari. Guglielmo was not trained in Provence, as has often been claimed; he evolved his classicizing style out of Italian Romanesque and, above all, Roman sculpture. He worked on the decoration of the facade of Pisa Cathedral, and his followers carried his style to many centers, not only in Tuscany but as far away as Roussillon in the Pyrenees.

Guido da Siena 13th century

Guido da Siena was the almost legendary founder of the Sienese School of painting. Little of the legend has survived the probings of modern scholarship; but the nature of his true contribution to early Italian painting remains impressive.

For centuries, Guido's fame and reputation depended on a mystifying inscription on a painting of the *Madonna and Child* now in the Palazzo Pubblico at Siena. This not only identifies him as the artist responsible for the work, but goes on to state quite explicitly that it was painted in 1221. Since the painting exhibits characteristics that are not found in Tuscan art until the second half of the 13th century, the inscription, if taken at face value, would mean that Siena preceded Florence in the development of 13th-century painting. Not only Florentines have found this theory unacceptable. Modern criticism has demonstrated beyond all reasonable doubt that a painting with the particular stylistic features displayed by the *Madonna and Child* could not have been produced much before the 1260s and that it is probably a work of c1280.

Of the many ingenious theories that have

Guido da Siena: Madonna and Child; panel; 283×194cm (111×76in); c1280. Palazzo Pubblico, Siena

Child, first became established in the city.

The attribution of the *Madonna and Child* to the period c1280 makes possible a more convincing reconstruction of Guido's artistic personality. Modern criticism now accepts as Guido's work a number of other panels which appear to have come originally from the same altarpiece as this picture. Also accepted are a pair of reliquary shutters, a polyptych of the *Madonna and Child with Saints*, and a Lenten hanging painted on linen, all three of which are now in the Pinacoteca Nazionale, Siena. These appear to be earlier than the *Madonna and Child* and were perhaps painted in the 1260s and 1270s.

Guido's works reveal him as an artist whose great achievement was to transform Florentine spatial and formal innovations into a style now regarded as specifically Sienese. The delicacy and refinement which are so marked a feature of the great Sienese masterpieces of the next century make their first appearance in Guido's paintings.

Further reading. Stubblebine, J. *Guido da Siena*, Princeton (1964).

Guimard Hector 1867–1942

The French architect Hector Guimard was born in Paris. He studied at the École des Beaux-Arts and the École des Arts Décoratifs, where he later taught. He was the most assured Art Nouveau architect working in France, and his early building was influenced by the Belgian Victor Horta. Guimard's achievements include several spectacular entrances to the Paris Métro with their serpentine forms in ironwork (1898–1901). Before this, he built the block of flats in Paris known as the Castel Béranger. Finished in 1897, the building uses metal in an extraordinarily imaginative way: the asymmetrical design on the gates seems like Rococo gone mad. He also made original use of glass and faience.

Günther Ignaz 1725–75

The German sculptor Ignaz Günther was born at Altmannstein (Oberpfalz). He learned sculpture from his father, a cabinetmaker and wood-sculptor. In 1743 he went to Munich, where he entered the workshop of the court sculptor Johann Baptist Straub. From 1750 he moved around southern Germany and Austria, working in Salzburg, in Mannheim with the sculptor Paul Egell, and in Vienna,

been advanced to account for the appearance of the date 1221 on what is demonstrably a later painting, none is entirely satisfactory. Only two need be noted. It has been suggested that the *Madonna and Child* might be a copy of a painting executed in 1221, and that, for reasons of his own, Guido decided to incorporate the date of this older image into his own inscription. Other scholars have drawn attention to the fact that the *Madonna and Child* was substantially repainted by a Sienese follower of Duccio early in the 14th century, and have gone on to speculate that the inscription as a whole might have been added by the same hand. According to this theory, some allusion to the year 1221 would not have been out of place in the new inscription, because it was in that year that the Dominicans, for whose principal church in Siena Guido originally executed the *Madonna and*

Hector Guimard: an entrance to the Paris Métro: c1898–1901

where he came under the influence of Donner. Returning to Munich in 1754, he established himself there, eventually becoming the outstanding Bavarian Rococo sculptor.

Most of Günther's work is in the traditional South German form of altarpieces of painted wood. He was prolific, and his work is to be found in churches all over southern Germany. His sculptures stand out forcefully from their elaborate settings. Günther combined a graceful elongation in his figures, derived from a close study of late-16th-century Mannerist sculpture, with a hard realism recalling late Gothic. He produced powerfully religious images within the light and colorful convention of the Rococo.

Among Günther's early works the most impressive is the altar in the church at Kopřivná in Czechoslovakia (1752–3), in which his personal style is already quite recognizable. A characteristic work from his middle period is the great *Annunciation*

group in the church at Weyarn in Upper Bavaria. He can be seen at his most serious and expressive in his last known work, dated 1774, a superbly simple group of the *Virgin with the Dead Christ* in the cemetery chapel at Nenningen.

Günther Matthäus 1705–88

Born in Upper Bavaria, the German painter Matthäus Günther received his formative training in the studio of C.D. Asam in Munich during the years 1723 to 1728. He became a master in Augsburg in 1731, and the remainder of his artistic career was based on that city. In 1740 he purchased the contents of the studio of J.E. Holzer and was influenced by him, on several occasions making use of his sketches. The leading Rococo fresco-painter of the Augsburg school, Günther worked all over southern Germany and the Tyrol; he succeeded J.G. Bergmüller as Catholic Director of the Augsburg Academy in 1762.

Guston Philip 1913–80

Born in Montreal, Canada, the American painter Philip Guston moved with his family to Los Angeles in 1919. Until the mid 1940s, he worked in a figurative style, partly influenced by the Social Realist murals he had seen in Mexico in 1934, and partly by Surrealism. He worked on murals himself for the W.P.A. (Works Progress Adminstration) Federal Arts Project in New York from 1936 to 1940. After the Second World War, however, Guston was caught up in the Abstract Expressionist movement. By the early 1950s he was producing large canvases in which texture is as important as the shape of the forms. The pictures of the 1950s are often relatively light in tone and atmospheric in feeling (for example *The Return*, 1956–8; Tate Gallery, London). In the 1960s the forms became heavier, the coloring darker, and the mood often more somber. (*See overleaf.*)

Philip Guston: The Return; oil on canvas; 178×199cm (70×78in); 1956–8. Tate Gallery, London

Guttuso Renato 1912–

The Italian painter Renato Guttuso was born in Palermo, the son of a land surveyor. He gave up his law studies and began to paint seriously in 1931. While living in Milan between 1935 and 1937 he met a number of artists and writers, among them Manzu, Fontana, Moravia, and Roberto Longhi. He was a member of the *Corrente* movement (1940–2) which opposed official Italian cultural policy. From 1943 to 1945 Guttuso was in the Italian Resistance movement. In 1947 he was a founder member of the *Fronte Nuovo delle Arti*.

A social realist, Guttuso has since the 1930s been influenced by the work of Goya and Picasso (particularly by Picasso's *Guernica*). This influence is evident stylistically, as well as in his choice of subject, for example his polemics against war and social injustice. From the early 1960s his works have contained artistic quotations from paintings by Picasso and others (for example *Das Totenmahl*, 1973; Neue Galerie, Sammlung Ludwig, Aachen).

Guys Constantin 1805–92

Born in Holland, but of French blood, Constantin Guys was essentially an illustrator. He worked for the *Illustrated London News* during the Revolution of 1848 and the Crimean War (1854–6). He traveled extensively in Italy, Spain, Germany, England, and the Orient. His work—in watercolor as well as drawing—was greatly admired by Manet, the Goncourt brothers, and, above all, by Baudelaire. He himself thought little of it ("these sketches have no value"), but Baudelaire's essay "The Painter of Modern Life", published in 1863, produced a deserved recognition of his talents.

Gyokudo Uragami 1745–1820

Admired in his circle as a man of general culture, and remembered after his death mainly as a master of the *koto* (zither), the painter Uragami Gyokudo has only in the mid 20th century been recognized as one of Japan's greatest artists. He now ranks among the Japanese as one of the four great *Nanga* masters; the others are Ike no Taiga (1723–76), Yosa Buson (1716–83) and Tanomura Chikuden (1777–1835). His *Frozen Clouds and Shifting Powdery*

Constantin Guys: The Promenade in the Woods; pen and ink and watercolor; 19×25cm (7½×10in). Private collection

Snow (hanging scroll, *c*1810; Collection Yasunari Kawabata, Kanagawa Prefecture) has the rare distinction of being listed as a Japanese National Treasure.

Although he undoubtedly belonged to the school called *Nanga*, which in the 18th and 19th centuries based its work on the ideals and theories of the *Bunjinga* "scholar-painters" of China, his painting was intensely eccentric. It was no doubt this quality that delayed his recognition until the 20th century, which has come to value individualism very highly.

The artist's life and circumstances explain much about his work. He was born Uragami Heiemon in 1745 of a samurai family in the house of his father's feudal lord, the head of the Okayama clan. Thus he was born into a class brought up to rigid self-discipline based on military virtues. This discipline accounts for his single-minded absorption in exploring in ink one aspect only of *Nanga* painting: landscape.

The religion of his class had for centuries been Zen Buddhism, which placed great importance on intuitive action and understanding. We must look to this for the immediate, white-hot intensity of his brushwork. At this period the totalitarian Tokugawa government had seen fit to promote Confucian doctrines, since their endorsement of a feudal order in society was politically convenient. Hence Confu-

cian studies, the doorway to the culture of China itself, became part of Gyokudo's education. Confucianism led him to the studies of a Chinese gentleman—music, literature, painting, and calligraphy—and so to the *Nanga* School.

As a young man he became an official Confucianist to his master Ikeda, received government appointments, and moved in intellectual circles in Kyoto and Edo (modern Tokyo). At this time he devoted himself to literature and the study of the *koto*. What paintings he did in his early and middle years must have been unexceptional, and they have not survived. His earliest dated paintings were done between 1787 and 1792; while pleasant, they show little of his later force. In 1779 he acquired his famous *koto* on which was the inscription *Gyokudo* ("Jade Hall"). Thereafter he called himself Gyokudo Kinshi (Gyokudo the *Koto* Master).

His life as an official came to an end for two main reasons. Firstly, in 1790 the Wang Yangming branch of Confucianism was found politically suspect by the government and suppressed. Gyokudo seems to have embraced its unorthodox doctrines and so to have been under a cloud. Wang Yangming's strong emphasis on intuition and on the unity of different ways of thought can be felt in Gyokudo's landscapes. There is no strain in them

between intent and expression. Every painting looks as though it came direct from his brain on to the paper, and as though the scenes he saw had all their disparate parts rendered into a whole by the strength of his vision.

Secondly, in 1792 his wife died. Adopting, perhaps consciously, the proper Confucian role, he resigned his post in 1793 and retired from the world of affairs. Taking his two sons Shunkin ("Spring *Koto*") and Shukin ("Autumn *Koto*"), his *koto*, and his artist's materials, he began a life of wandering around Japan, living simply, drinking heavily, playing on his instrument, and now more and more, painting. He returned occasionally to city exhibitions and literary gatherings, but he never settled down again. To these years belong the masterpieces of landscape painting for which he is remembered. He died in Kyoto in 1820.

The great majority of Gyokudo's paintings are done on paper. Silk had a more academic flavor which appealed to some painters of the *Nanga* School, but the material has the effect of slowing up the brush. It requires greater care from the painter and inhibits his freedom. Gyokudo's impetuous visions were clearly dashed down in a spirit of exaltation, or even drunkenness, and for them paper was the only suitable vehicle. The best Japanese paper is tough but alive, setting up its own relationship with the brush. It absorbs wet ink deeply, but allows the almost dry brush to skate lightly over its surface. These opportunities for exciting texture were fully grasped by Gyokudo, as in the intensely vibrant and bewilderingly complex welter of strokes and washes that make up the foreground trees in *Twin Peaks Embracing the Clouds* (*c*1805; Idemitsu Art Museum, Tokyo).

The medium of his art, as in nearly all Far Eastern painting, was the brush loaded with Chinese ink. Loaded in different ways, with wash or thick ink, or with one side wetter than the other, it was perhaps the most comprehensive vehicle for painting ever devised. Gyokudo found black ink alone almost enough for his purposes. Many of his most impressive landscapes have no color in them at all. He appears to have found that the adding of color obstructed the directness of his painting.

When he does use color it is brilliantly effective, although often arbitrary. In *Frozen Clouds and Shifting Snow*, for example, a majestic and bleak vision of a frozen gray mountain world is enlivened by a few apparently random spatters of blood-red ink on the trees and rocks. They represent nothing, yet they pull the eye into themselves and make the looker feel the inherent force of life in the dead terrain. Gyokudo's use of color, indeed, is almost limited to red inks in a few paintings. But so subtle is his use of them that in the famous page from the *Album of Mists* (1811) called *Green Mountains and Red Woods* (c1811; Umegawa Memorial Hall, Tokyo) the whole scene seems to glow with the varied colors of a Japanese autumn, although only red and black are used. (See also *Mountains Stained by Red Leaves*, a hanging scroll, c1815–20; Teizo Kimura Collection, Aichi prefecture.)

There were five main formats available to the Japanese artist: screens, handscrolls, hanging scrolls, albums, and fan-leaves. Gyokudo did not paint screens, nor did he do more than a very few handscrolls. The reasons are practical. Both these formats need careful organization; in the case of screens it would scarcely be possible with so large a form to paint direct from nature. The often inebriated Gyokudo needed to paint directly. The handscroll was designed to unfold slowly, a few feet at a time, in the hands of the connoisseur. It was a leisurely journey through changing scenes and even changing styles. It was therefore popular among the more scholarly *Nanga* painters; but for Gyokudo it would not do. The handscroll *Old Age in the Southern Mountains* (an approximate translation of a typically cryptic title; private collection) in the style of the Chinese master Mi Fu is one of his tamest works. It is also one of his earliest (1787).

Gyokudo preferred the simple unity of the hanging scroll, the fan-leaf, and the album-leaf. It was in the field of the large hanging scroll that his greatest triumphs were won. Because of his ability to transcend the scholarly restraints of his school, he became the grandest of its masters. He is unequaled in it for his ability to expand his technique and his vision into a really large surface. Such a work as *Idle in the Mountains* (c1807; Kyoto National Museum) has the exceptional length of painted area of 5 ft 9⅜ in by 3 ft 1⅚ in (1.76 by 0.95 m) yet it never collapses into its component sections as do the works of even such a master as Taiga.

Most of Gyokudo's works are landscapes painted in the last 20 years of his life, during which he was traveling almost constantly round the mountainous areas of Japan. There can be no doubt that his pictures—nearly all of which consist of round-topped mountains, covered nearly to their peaks by vegetation and rising out of thickly wooded valleys—are at heart portraits of his own land, however distorted the artist's vision may have been. This has to be emphasized, because the *Nanga* painters of Japan very often adapted or copied the landscapes of the Chinese scholar-painters, who themselves usually painted a highly idealized scene.

The Confucian idea laid down by the great Chinese theorist of painting Tung Ch'i-ch'ang (1555–1636) was that pure landscape, devoid of any but tiny human figures, was the proper practice of the scholar-painter. It was in reality a form of self-portrait. Gyokudo must have subscribed to this, for his works conform to the idea very closely; but to it he added the dimension of his passionate love of his own countryside. In many of his works we find the repeated idea of a tiny traveler on a bridge, among trees, looking up at the mountains which are majestic and yet close-by, not remote as in the Chinese masters. It is a scene he himself must have acted out many times.

In this sense, Gyokudo's landscapes are uncontrived. The mountains usually form a center to the picture, and are not artificially placed to one side, while below them the woods spread out naturally. The artifice added by Gyokudo is the wildly irrational welter of brush strokes imposed over the basic shapes. Sometimes a whole painting will be covered in apparently meaningless horizontal strokes, as in *Mountains Wrapped in Rain* (hanging scroll, c1805; Ohara Art Museum, Okayama prefecture), giving an intense feeling of nature in movement, in perpetual change.

This impression of flux is something that goes deeper than official Confucianism, for it is one of the basic doctrines of the Buddhism that had so affected the Japanese character since the 6th century AD. The intuitive nature of Zen Buddhist perception was something Gyokudo grew up with, and which must have attracted him to the Wang Yangming branch of Confucianism, the suppression of which led to his departure from official life. Wang Yangming had taught intuition and the unity of things and ways of thought.

As he grew older, Gyokudo's vision became more and more distorted. Strange circular shapes appear on his mountain-sides, dominating the eye with peculiar force, as in *Quiet View in the Cloudy Mountains* (private collection). The mountains themselves become more and more fluid until in *High Wind, Slanting Geese* (1817; private collection) they resemble an explosion. At the same time, his mountain-tops tend to shapes so overtly phallic (as in *Retreat in Winter Woods* or *Leisured Spot in the Frozen Woods* (private collection) that one realizes there are more primitive forces behind his violent brushwork than mere philosophies.

Gyokudo's strength ultimately lies in his individual view of nature and the sheer visual excitement of the brushwork that expressed it. It is the achievement as much of a Zen painter as of a *Nanga* painter. His ability to suggest the violent energy of nature and of his own mind has appealed strongly to 20th-century man, particularly in the West.

His sons Shunkin and Shukin were conventional *Nanga* painters, the former admired more than his father in his day. They handed down nothing of his spirit, and he left no school. Only the last *Nanga* master, Tomioka Tessai (1836–1924), approaches his extraordinary insight into nature and his visual tensions. Uragami Gyokudo should not be confused with Kawai Gyokudo (1873–1957), an excellent lyrical nature-painter of the present century who belonged to an entirely different school.

Further reading. Akiyama, T. *Japanese Painting*, Cleveland (1961). Cahill, J. *Scholar Painters of Japan: The Nanga School*, New York (1972). Yonezawa, Y. and Yoshizawa, C. *Japanese Painting in the Literati Style*, New York (1974).

Gyosai Kawanabe 1831–89

Kawanabe Gyosai was a Japanese painter, often called Kyosai. Of precocious gifts, he trained with *Ukiyoe* and *Kano* artists as well as studying more ancient Japanese styles. He emerged as perhaps the most accomplished copier of other artists, in a country where copying traditionally formed the basic artistic training. His personal genius was for *giga* (cartoon-like comic sketches) and for *diablerie* of a joyous vitality; these were often inspired by indulgence in drink, like the splendid series of hell scenes in the British Museum, London. He was also a serious painter and print artist of nationalist themes in the Revival-*Yamatoe* style. The British architect Josiah Conder became his pupil.

H

Hakuin Ekaku 1685–1768

The Japanese Zen painter, calligrapher, and mystic Ekaku Hakuin was born in Hara (Shizuoku Prefecture). He became a Zen monk at an early age and spent most of his life traveling in Japan and trying to popularize the sect. His writings on Zen experience are vivid, and he also developed a very powerful and heavy style of calligraphy which broke all the classical rules. His work was deliberately clumsy in appearance, often painted against an inked-in background. Its aim was to convey Buddhist truths to the common people through simple, effective images of figures like Boddhidarma and Kannon. Hakuin's semi-popular style has nonetheless great spiritual strength and confidence.

Hals Frans c1581/5–1666

The Dutch painter Frans Hals was second only to Rembrandt in portraiture. He was born in Antwerp, the son of a Flemish clothmaker. His parents emigrated to the Northern Provinces in 1585 (the year Antwerp fell to the Spanish) and settled in Haarlem. Apart from one or two visits to Flanders, Hals remained in Haarlem (an important center of early-17th-century Dutch art) for the rest of his life.

Almost nothing is known of Hals' youthful years. There are no dated paintings earlier than a portrait from 1611, when the artist was between 25 and 30 years old. In this and other extant paintings from c1611 to 1615, the tendency is towards relatively detailed execution, with bright colors set off against dark backgrounds. Hals' professional success dates from 1616, the year of the first of his large group portraits: *The Banquet of the Officers of the Militia Company of St George* (Frans Hals Museum, Haarlem, where the artist's work can best be studied).

The Company of St George was one of Haarlem's two civic guards: bodies of men whose defensive role during the war against Spain had been reduced by 1616 to a purely social one. Following their three-year term, officers frequently commissioned portraits of themselves to hang in their company's headquarters. The costs of these portraits were borne equally by all the sitters—who therefore expected equal prominence, a consideration also demanded by the need to present adequate individual likenesses. Hals' innovation was to break up the customary monotonous rows of expressionless faces into differentiated groups of men whose varied facial expressions, gestures, and postures reveal his gift for individual characterization and desire for greater informality.

The immediacy Hals achieved in this first ceremonial scene was enhanced in the dazzling *Officers of the Militia Company of St Hadrian* (c1627; Frans Hals Museum, Haarlem), where varied directional movements in the figures are emphasized by the bold diagonals of sashes and banners. The lack of a clear focus of attention that would arrest this picture's excessive animation is corrected in a later version, the daringly assymmetrical *Officers of the Militia Company of St Hadrian* of c1633 (Frans Hals Museum, Haarlem). Here the diagonals are replaced by more architectonic vertical and horizontal elements. Certain figures are now subordinated to background positions, but although this contributed to greater formal unity, convincing psychological unity in such paintings was not achieved until Rembrandt's *Night Watch* of 1642

Frans Hals: Portrait of Isabella Coymans; detail; oil on canvas; full size 116×86cm (46×34in); 1648–50. Rothschild Collection, Paris

(Rijksmuseum, Amsterdam).

The majority of Hals' portraits are half- or three-quarter-length single-figure paintings, usually of professional men, merchants, and their wives. The celebrated *Laughing Cavalier* (1624; Wallace Collection, London) is typical of commissions from the 1620s, with their casual informality and brilliant but increasingly cool color. These portraits invariably suggest incipient changes of posture and expression, and rarely look posed.

Hals can be criticized for not penetrating his sitters' inner characters, but his intention was to extend the scope of a portrait from a visual likeness to something approaching a "speaking" likeness, particularly through the animation of the face by a smile, a laugh, or intimations of conversation. Hals heightened the sense of presence he sought by establishing emotional links between sitter and spectator. This is achieved by glances towards us, and also by such illusionistic devices as movements and gestures made in our direction: the raising of a glass is a favorite technique.

Genre pictures are frequent during the first half of Hals' career. The earliest examples are richly detailed, brightly colored, and boisterous. Typical of this period is *Merry Company* (c1615–17; Metropolitan Museum, New York), a theatrical scene in which Shrove Tuesday is being celebrated. The iconography and light tonality of several exuberant life-size musicians, drinkers, and harlots from the 1620s and early 1630s reveal the influence of the Utrecht School, with the difference that Hals' genre pieces invariably have a distinctly portrait-like character (for example, *Yonker Ramp and his Sweetheart*, c1623; Metropolitan Museum, New York; *The Merry Drinker*, c1628–30; Rijksmuseum, Amsterdam).

Hals was much in demand as a portraitist in the 1620s and 1630s, and had to rely on the help of assistants. But he received fewer commissions in the 1640s, perhaps because the informality of his work was unsuited to the more sober mood of the now well-established republic. His later portraits show a marked tendency towards monochromatic colors and darker tones: a development only partially explained by the move towards greater sobriety in Dutch costume after c1635. But his palette, although limited to blacks, whites, grays, yellowish browns, and flesh tints, was still rich in variety; Van Gogh remarked that Hals had no less than 27 different blacks.

Panache and movement disappear in Hals' later paintings; plain, frontal poses are common and the mood is quiet. His handling of paint, on the other hand, becomes increasingly broad and free; angular, vigorously applied brush strokes are capable of summarizing forms with the greatest economy. This direct approach made preliminary studies superfluous (no drawings survive). In his final paintings Hals even dispensed with underpainting, applying his oils straight on to the bare canvas. This spontaneous handling of paint gave vitality and animation to Hals' figures, heightened the sense of the momentary, and conveyed an impression of sparkling light effects. But it was incapable of distinguishing between different textures, and although suited to the dashing, extrovert character of young male sitters, was less appropriate to women and older models.

Hals' culminating works are the two great group portraits of the *Regents* and *Regentesses of the Haarlem Old Men's Alms House* (both c1664; Frans Hals Museum, Haarlem). These, painted when Hals was 80 years old and himself destitute, convey a sense of austere, solemn dignity with utmost simplicity of means. Their pathos is unprecedented in the artist's work.

Hals had little influence during his lifetime, nor was he properly appreciated after his death (only about 250 paintings have been preserved). The sketchiness of his virtuoso technique contributed to Hals' neglect by later generations. His rediscovery dates from the mid 19th century—when the Impressionists, Manet in particular, emulated his brilliant brushwork.

Further reading. Slive, S. *Frans Hals* (3 vols.), London (1970–4). Trivas, N.S. *The Paintings of Frans Hals*, London (1941). Valentiner, W.R. (ed.) *Frans Hals*, Stuttgart (1923).

Hamilton Gavin 1723–98

Gavin Hamilton was a Scottish history and portrait painter. An associate of Stuart and Revett, Winckelmann and Mengs, and an early supporter of Canova, he has been regarded as a seminal figure in the development of international Neoclassicism.

Born in Lanarkshire, he went to study painting in Rome in 1748 and for a short time was a pupil of Agostino Masucci.

Gavin Hamilton: detail of Hector's Farewell to Andromache; oil on canvas; 315×399cm (124×157in); 1788. Hunterian Museum and Art Gallery, Glasgow

Duane Hanson: Bowery Bums; fiberglass, polyester, found materials; 1969–70. Museum Ludwig, Cologne

Except for two brief visits to London, he remained in Rome for the rest of his life. His earliest recorded history painting, *Dawkins and Wood Discovering Palmyra* (1758; on loan to the Hunterian Museum and University Art Collections, Glasgow), anticipates in theme his own archaeological efforts. These resulted in the discovery of several pieces of antique sculpture. His two series of compositions based on Homer (1760s and 1782/4) received wide circulation in the form of engravings.

Hamilton's most important single painting, *The Oath of Brutus*, exists in several versions (one *c*1763; Paul Mellon Center for British Art, New Haven). This novel and grand conception of an incident recorded in Livy was a direct source for a number of Neoclassical pictures, the best known of which is David's *Oath of the Horatii* (1784; Louvre, Paris). In general, Hamilton's style reflects the eclectic tastes of the early Neoclassicists, combining as it often does elements from diverse antique and Baroque sources.

Hamilton Richard 1922–

The British painter Richard Hamilton was born in London. He studied at the Royal Academy (1938–40; 1946–7) and at the Slade School of Fine Art (1948–51), and in 1952 was a founder member of the Independent Group. Hamilton was a pioneer figure in the development of Pop art in Britain in the 1950s. A friend of Marcel Duchamp, by whom he has been much influenced, Hamilton works in collage. He uses fragments of popular culture—such as magazine photographs—to create new images that are both a tribute to their sources and successful as partially abstract works of fine art.

Hanson Duane 1925–

The American Super-Realist sculptor was born in Alexandria, Minnesota. He finished his studies with a year at the Cranbrook Academy of Art, Michigan, where he had his first solo exhibition in 1951. By the time he came to prominence in the late 1960s he had developed a technique of casting figures in fiberglass and dressing them in real clothes. He used this process to create tableaux from contemporary life, usually of a violent emotive subject such as *Vietnam Scene* (1969; Wilhelm-Lehmbruck-Museum, Duisberg). He then abandoned these so-called "Expressionist" groups for mostly single figures representing American types, such as *Supermarket Lady* (1970; Neue Galerie, Sammlung Ludwig, Aachen).

Richard Hamilton: Swingeing London 67 II; screenprint, oil on canvas; 67×85cm (26×33in); 1967. Museum Ludwig, Cologne

Harnett William 1848–92

The American painter William Michael Harnett was born at Clonakilty, County Cork, Ireland. Taken to Philadelphia as a child, he was apprenticed to an engraver. He studied at the Pennsylvania Academy, and at the National Academy, New York, then visited Germany between 1871 and 1881. His still lifes are noted for their extraordinarily convincing *trompe-l'oeil* effects. They show groups of objects, pinned on to, and hung from, walls and doors. They are similar to those of John F. Peter; between them these two artists established a style which forms an important part of the American tradition. Harnett's are superior to Peter's in that they use a wider variety of objects and textured surfaces.

Hartley Marsden 1877–1943

Marsden Hartley was an American painter whose artistic ancestry stemmed from American Romantics such as Albert P. Ryder. Hartley was associated with the earliest modern art in New York, inspired by Alfred Stieglitz. Stieglitz helped him to visit Berlin, where he exhibited with the *Blaue Reiter* group. Works such as *Portrait of a German Officer* (1914; Metropolitan Museum, New York) are in a European Expressionist manner; but already Hartley's passionate identification with his native Maine had appeared in claustrophobic and menacing paintings such as *The Dark Mountain* (1909; Art Institute of Chicago). Hartley's mature style was a mixture of European Expressionism and a personal interpretation of the life and landscape of the northeastern American seaboard.

Hartung Hans 1904–89

Hans Hartung was a German-French painter and graphic artist. He went to the Gymnasium in Dresden (1915–24) and the University and Academy of Fine Arts in Leipzig (1924–5), where he studied philosophy and art history. He was advised to go to the Bauhaus but chose instead the academies of Fine Arts in Dresden and Munich, studying with Feldbauer, Dorsche, Wehlte, and Dörner. By this time he had received inspiration from Rembrandt and Goya and discovered the German Expressionists, particularly Oskar Kokoschka and Emil Nolde. He spent the years 1927 to 1935 traveling and living in Minorca and Paris. Returning to Berlin in 1935 to sort out his finances, Hartung was forced to flee Nazi Germany. He went to Paris, with help from Will Grohmann and Christian Zervos. In Paris in 1936 he exhibited at the Galerie Pierre with Kandinsky, Arp, and Hélion; in 1937 he met Julio Gonzàlez, whose work he admired. Between 1939 and 1945 Hartung was in the French Foreign Legion. In 1945 he was made a French citizen, and thereafter lived and worked in Paris, exhibiting widely.

By the mid 1930s Hartung's work was developing the characteristics for which it came to be known in the 1950s: a rhythmic calligraphic style and automatism preceded by a period of meditation on the canvas (*Painting T 54–16*, oil on canvas; 1954; Musée National d'Art Moderne, Paris). By the early 1960s the brisk brush strokes had given way to scoring the paint while wet, and by the end of the decade dark stains on the canvas had gained over the graphic element.

Further reading. Apollonis, U. *Hans Hartung*, Paris (1967). Rousseau, M. *Hans Hartung*, Stuttgart (1949).

Harunobu Suzuki 1725–70

The Japanese print artist Suzuki Harunobu worked in Edo (Tokyo); but stylistically he seems to have been a follower of the Kyoto *Ukiyoe* artists, and particularly of the book illustrator Nishikawa Sukenobu

Suzuki Harunobu: Interior with a Girl and her Maid; woodblock print; 27×20cm (11×8in); c1750–70. British Museum, London

(1682–1752). He came to prominence in 1764, when groups of connoisseurs first commissioned multicolored woodblock prints, the so-called "brocade prints" of which Harunobu was the first master.

He established a style of varied but delicate color, sensitive line, and mock-innocent romanticism, putting his women and their lovers in convincing domestic or outdoor settings which give unity to the compositions. He also introduced classical allusions and subjects into these basically bourgeois works, thus linking them more strongly with older artistic traditions.

Hassam Childe 1859–1935

The painter and printmaker (Frederick) Childe Hassam was one of the leading American Impressionists. He began as a wood engraver in Boston, and spent the years 1886–89 in France, where he acquired a thorough knowledge of Impressionism. On his return to the United States he settled in New York, and in 1898 became a member of a group of American Impressionists known as "The Ten". His pictures, often of the streets of Boston and New York under snow, display a sensitive use of color and light, though their Impressionism is tempered by a strain of American realism. Among his best-known works are *Boston Common at Dusk* (1885–86; Museum of Fine Arts, Boston) and *Flag Day* (1919; County Museum of Art, Los Angeles).

Further reading. Hoopes, D.I. *Childe Hassam*, New York (1988).

Haussmann Baron 1809–91

Baron Georges-Eugène Haussmann was born in Paris, although his family came from Alsace. In 1853 he was appointed by Napoleon III as Prefect of the Department of the Seine. It is to Haussmann, who held this post for nearly 20 years, that we owe the transformation of Paris from an essentially medieval city to the modern metropolis of today. Long, straight, and wide boulevards were cut through and around the city. At major intersections, or *rond-points*, important monuments and public buildings were erected (for example, the Opéra), thus opening out superb vistas. Haussmann was influenced in his choice of layout by military and political considerations, as well as by the requirements of hygiene and circulation.

Nicholas Hawksmoor: the Codrington Library (left) and the towers in the north quadrangle of All Souls College, Oxford; built 1716–35

Hawksmoor Nicholas *c1661–1736*

Nicholas Hawksmoor was an English architect. His precise contribution to English Baroque architecture is surrounded by mystery and may never be completely understood. Introspective, with a marked lack of faith in his own talents, Hawksmoor spent much of his career as an assistant to his two most illustrious contemporaries, Sir Christopher Wren and Sir John Vanbrugh.

The extent to which these architects relied on Hawksmoor's genius is not fully known. The masterly assurance of his first completely independent commission (and only country house) Easton Neston, Northamptonshire (1696–1702), strongly

suggests that his cooperation with Wren at Greenwich hospital (1696–1702) extended to more than merely supervising the Surveyor General's designs. It was undoubtedly Hawksmoor who transmitted Wren's late style to Vanbrugh at Castle Howard and Blenheim Palace.

His six London churches—St Alphege, Greenwich (1712–14), St Anne, Limehouse (1714–30), St George, Wapping (1715–23), St Mary, Woolnoth (1716–27), St George, Bloomsbury (1716–31), and Christchurch, Spittalfields (1714–29)—reveal the full extent of his inventive brilliance. Medieval in silhouette, Imperial Roman in detail, they form the culmination of the tradition of Wren's city churches. Their adventurous composition-

al massing—anticipated by the bold spatial contrasts of Hawksmoor's (planned but never completed) forecourt of Easton Neston—clearly relates to Vanbrugh's experiments in the field of country house architecture.

Outside London his work is best represented in Oxford, where he was responsible for the Clarendon Building (1712–15), Queen's College front quadrangle (1709–38), and the north quadrangle and towers of All Souls College (1715–40). The latter is in an austere Gothic style that anticipated his west towers of Westminster Abbey (1734), and found a classical counterpart in the gaunt silhouette of the mausoleum at Castle Howard (1729–36).

Francis Hayman: The Artist at his Easel; oil on canvas; 69×59cm (27×23in); c1745–50. Royal Albert Memorial Museum, Exeter

Hayman Francis 1708–76

The English painter Francis Hayman was first employed in London as a scene-painter at Drury Lane. In the 1740s he collaborated with Gravelot in the designs and engravings for a number of literary illustrations, and in the ornamental decorations at London's Vauxhall Gardens. His depiction of the Wrestling Scene from *As You Like It* in *The Works of Shakespeare* edited by Sir T. Hanmer (c1744) is one of the most original early illustrations to Shakespeare. He offered his most ambitious history painting, *The Finding of Moses* (1746), to the Foundling Hospital in London. Conversations and theatrical portraits also figure prominently in his work at this time. Hayman's blend of realism with elements of French Rococo style was an important influence on Gainsborough. He played a key role in the founding of both the Society of Artists and the Royal Academy.

Heartfield John 1891–1968

John Heartfield was a German graphic designer. In protest against German nationalistic fervor, he anglicized his name from Helmut Herzefelde during the First World War. He joined the Communist Party in 1918 and remained a committed political artist for the rest of his life. Prominent in the Berlin Dada group, he was one of the inventors—perhaps the greatest exponent—of the photomontage technique. This became in his hands a supremely effective satirical method. He was scenic director of the Max Reinhardt theaters in Berlin from 1921 to 1923, edited the satirical magazine *Der Knüppel* from 1923 to 1927, and produced some of his finest photomontages for the German Communist press in the early 1930s. Harassed by the Hitler regime, he lived as a refugee in London between 1938 and 1950. He died in East Berlin.

Heckel Erich 1883–1970

Born in Döbeln (Saxony), Erich Heckel studied architecture at Dresden. Together with Fritz Bleyl, Ernst Ludwig Kirchner, and Karl Schmidt-Rottluff, he founded the *Brücke* artists association in 1905. Self-taught, his admiration for medieval German woodcuts and African sculpture is shown in his own powerful woodcuts. These were in advance of his painting style until c1907, when the influence of Van Gogh begins to appear in his work. After his move to Berlin in 1911, the wilder Post-Impressionist colors yield to an angular crystalline structure, reflecting Cubist influences. In Berlin he became a founder of the New Secession. His work was proscribed by the Nazis in 1937. After the Second World War he was a member of the Karlsruhe Academy from 1949 to 1955.

Heemskerck Maerten van 1498–1574

Maerten van Heemskerck was a Dutch artist who trained in Haarlem and Delft. He was a pupil of Jan van Scorel whose influence is evident in the *Virgin and St Luke* (1532; Frans Hals Museum, Haarlem). On a journey to Rome during the years 1532 to 1535 he produced a series of drawings of the city which show a keen archaeological interest, acknowledged in the background of his *Self-portrait* of 1553 (Fitzwilliam Museum, Cambridge). His re-

Maerten van Heemskerck: Torso, the Apollo Belvedere; ink on paper; c1532–6. Staatliche Museen, Berlin

sponse to Michelangelo was also profound, even as late as the *Erythræan Sybil* (1564; Rijksmuseum, Amsterdam), whose costume, turning position, and crossed legs are indebted to the figures on the Sistine Chapel ceiling.

Hemessen Jan van *c1500–?66*

The Flemish painter Jan Sanders van Hemessen trained at Antwerp but moved north to Haarlem after 1550, probably for religious reasons. It is likely that he traveled to Italy. A knowledge of Italian Mannerist painting is evident in his *Judith* (c1540–5; Art Institute of Chicago), where the powerful nude form is accommodated within the picture space only by the turn of her body and the foreshortened arm. His biblical and genre paintings usually show figures close to the foreground plane with landscape purely as a backdrop to the action, as in the *Tobias Healing his Blind Father* (1555; Louvre, Paris).

Henri Robert *1865–1929*

The American painter and teacher Robert Henri was born in Cincinnati, Ohio. He studied at the Pennsylvania Academy of Fine Arts, and in Paris at the Académie Julian and at the École des Beaux-Arts. He returned to Philadelphia in 1891 and became friendly with Glackens, Shinn, Luks, and Sloan. He continued to travel, and he taught in New York, first at the Chase School and later, after becoming disenchanted with Academic methods, in his own establishment. Henri remains an important figure. This is not so much for his own art, which is an adroit but not original blend of Impressionism and older influences such as Hals and Courbet (seen, for example, in *Woman in White*, 1904; Joseph Hirshhorn Museum, Washington, D.C.), but for his influence as a teacher. In particular he encouraged the development of new aesthetic ideas. For example, after a rejection by the New York Academy he was involved in the independent exhibition of The Eight at the Macbeth Gallery in 1908. He was also involved in the Armory Show.

Henriques Francisco *fl. 1500–19*

Francisco Henriques was a Portuguese painter, probably of Flemish origin, originally named Frans Hendricks. His only attributed work is a number of panels in the National Museum of Art, Lisbon, and in the Solar dos Patudos, Alpiarça, surviving from retables executed during the years 1509–11 for São Francisco, Evora. Here his Flemish heritage is evident in the folds of the robes, the tiled floors, interior views, and detailed backgrounds of town and landscape. The monumentality of the figures recalls Nuno Gonçalves. The expressions on the faces are, however, softer and the gestures more awkward. In the *Passion* series, some compositions are reminiscent of Schongauer's engravings.

Henry of Reyns *fl. 1243–53*

The English master mason Henry of Reyns is first documented in 1243 working for Henry III at Windsor Castle. Here a wall arcade in the King's Chapel has stylistic affiliations with his greatest achievement, Westminster Abbey, begun in 1245.

As Master of the King's Works at the time, it is likely that Henry designed the Abbey. Controversy exists over whether he was from England or from Reims in France, as his name suggests. Westminster Abbey incorporates architectural features from both countries. The obvious similarities to Reims Cathedral, begun in 1211, are the plan and proportions of the polygonal apse with radiating chapels, the ambulatory wall passage, bar tracery, the pier forms, and the use of naturalistic foliage carving for the first time in England. Additional French influence, from the more recently built Amiens Cathedral (begun in 1218) and from the Sainte Chapelle (begun in 1243) is revealed in the window tracery, particularly in those windows shaped like spherical triangles. It has also been suggested that the plan and elevation of Westminster derive from the now ruined Royaumont Abbey, dedicated in 1236.

English features, however, include the gallery instead of triforium, the vault ridge rib, and especially the polygonal plan of the chapter house on the Lincoln Cathedral model of the 1240s. It is possible that Henry of Reyns was English, but visited France where he studied the latest architectural developments, or else that he was French but had English masons working with him in the traditional English style.

A masonry break can be detected at Westminster, one bay west of the crossing, so it is assumed that at this stage John of Gloucester, first mentioned in the documents in 1253, took control as master mason, due no doubt to his predecessor's death.

Henry of Reyns is also documented as having worked on Clifford's Tower in York in 1244 and the Tower of London in 1250, and he may have designed Hayles Abbey in Gloucestershire.

Hepworth Barbara *1903–75*

The English sculptor Barbara Hepworth was born in Wakefield, Yorkshire. As a child the beauty of the Yorkshire dales made a deep impression on her, and memories of this unspoiled countryside remained with her throughout her life. The importance of man in the landscape, and the unity of man and nature, were to become the basic impulses of her sculpture.

In 1920 Hepworth won a scholarship to the Leeds School of Art. There she met Henry Moore, with whom she was closely associated for the next 20 years. The following year she entered the Royal College of Art in London. Like Moore she was interested in direct carving, respecting the characteristics of stone or wood, letting the material dictate the forms of the sculpture. Although from the mid 1950s she also worked in bronze and other materials, Hepworth remained primarily a carver.

After she was awarded the Diploma of the Royal College of Art in 1924, she went

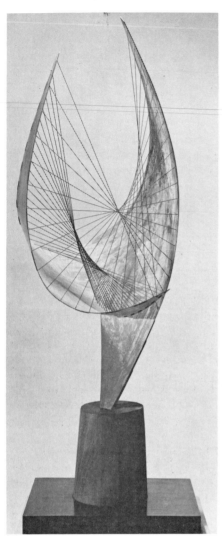

Barbara Hepworth: Theme on Electronics (Orpheus); second maquette; brass with strings on wooden base; 115×43×41cm (45×17×16in); 1956. Tate Gallery, London

to Italy, where she studied Romanesque and early Renaissance sculpture and architecture. The following year she married the sculptor John Skeaping, and moved from Florence to Rome. They returned to London in 1926.

Hepworth's interest in the art of the past centered on Egyptian, Cycladic, and Archaic Greek sculpture. Several naturalistic carvings of the late 1920s are stylistically related to the life drawings of the period. Four sculptures of birds, shown at her first one-woman exhibition at the Beaux-Arts Gallery, London, in 1928, reflect the influence of Epstein and Gaudier-Brzeska. In 1928 she moved to Parkhill Road, Hampstead, where she lived until 1939.

In *Pierced Form* of 1931 (destroyed in the Second World War) a hole was carved through the alabaster, an innovation which was to have far-reaching effects in the development of her work. She has written of "the most intense pleasure in piercing the stone in order to make an abstract form and space".

In that same year Hepworth met the painter Ben Nicholson, who was to become her second husband. In 1932 Hepworth and Nicholson visited the Paris studios of Picasso, Braque, Brancusi, and Arp, and of Mondrian in 1933. Contact with these artists, particularly with the formal purity of the work of Brancusi and Mondrian, revealed the possibilities of Abstract art. Although Hepworth's sculpture of 1931 to 1934 was becoming more Abstract, it still retained tenuous references to the human figure. By 1935 her sculpture had become completely Abstract. She became a member of the *Abstraction-Création* group in 1933 and of Unit One in 1934, and contributed to *Circle: International Survey of Constructive Art*, published in 1937. She began using color and strings in her sculpture in 1939, and these were to remain lasting features of her work. Color in the concavities suggests water and caves; the strings express the tension between herself, and the sea, wind, or hills.

A week before the outbreak of the Second World War, Hepworth and Nicholson moved to St Ives, Cornwall, with their three children (triplets, born 1934). She grew to love the Cornish landscape (reminiscent of her native Yorkshire), with its rugged coastlines and cliffs, brilliant light, the blues, greens, and grays of the sea, the movement of tides and waves. A number of her sculptures reflect the influence of this landscape: *Figure in Landscape* (*Zennor*) (1952; private collection), *Hollow Form* (*Penwith*) (1955; Museum of Modern Art, New York), *Pelagos*, of 1946 (Tate Gallery, London) were inspired by the curve of St Ives Bay and the waves of the sea.

In 1949 Hepworth bought Trewyn Studios in St Ives. She lived there from 1951, when her marriage to Nicholson was dissolved, until her death. During the 1950s her work was exhibited at the 25th Venice Biennale (1950) and at the 5th Sao Paulo Bienale (1959) where she won the Grand Prix. In 1954 she visited Greece. A subsequent series of wood carvings attest to the tremendous impact the Greek landscape had made on her (they include *Curved Form* (*Delphi*), 1955; Ulster Museum, Belfast). As worldwide recognition grew she received important commissions: these produced, among others, *Meridian* (bronze; 1958–9; State House, London), *Winged Figure* (aluminum; 1962; John Lewis Building, London), and *Single Form* (bronze; 1962–3; for the United Nations Building, New York, as a memorial to her friend Dag Hammarskjöld). Major exhibitions were held at the Kröller-Müller Museum, Otterlo (1956), and at the Tate Gallery, London (1968). In June 1965 Hepworth was created Dame of the British Empire.

Hepworth died in a fire in her St Ives studio in May 1975. In April 1976 Trewyn Studios and garden, now the Barbara Hepworth Museum, were opened to the public. Carvings, bronzes, and drawings—embodying geometric purity, classical calm, grace and tenderness—are displayed in the town where Barbara lived and worked for 36 years.

Further reading. Hepworth, B. *Barbara Hepworth: a Pictorial Autobiography*, London (1970). Hepworth, B. "The Sculptor Carves because he Must", *The Studio*, London (December 1932). Hodin, J.P. *Barbara Hepworth: Life and Work*, London (1961).

Herbin Auguste 1882–1960

The French painter Auguste Herbin was born at Quiévy. He studied at the École des Beaux-Arts and at the Atelier Winter, Lille, from 1898 to 1901. He moved to Paris, and in 1909 took a studio at the Bateau-Lavoir. In 1931 he was one of the co-founders of the *Abstraction-Création* group. He died in Paris in 1960.

From 1903 to 1907 his work consisted of Fauvist still lifes, landscapes, and figures. In 1909 contact with Picasso, Braque, and Gris caused him to turn to Cubism. He produced his first Abstract paintings in 1917, and between 1919 and 1921 produced symmetrical paintings and reliefs. In the period from 1922 to 1926 he returned to rigorously architectonic paintings from nature. In 1926 he began to create Abstract structured compositions of flat colored forms implying movement with arabesques and eccentric hard-edged shapes. During the 1940s he developed a system of Abstract painting, published in his book *L'Art Non-Figuratif Non-Objectif* in 1949 in which pure geometric shapes and colors were disposed against monochrome grounds and allied to musical notes.

Francisco Herrera the Younger: detail of The Triumph of St Hermengeld; c1654. Prado, Madrid

Heron Patrick 1920–

The British painter Patrick Heron was born in Leeds, and spent a part of his childhood in Cornwall (where he was to return later in life). He studied at the Slade School of Fine Art (1937–9) and between 1945 and 1958 published art criticism (in *The New Statesman* and other journals). He has exhibited widely since 1947 and was awarded the Grand Prize at the second John Moores Liverpool exhibition (1959) and the Silver Medal at the 1965 Sao Paulo Bienal. Heron's earlier work was Abstract, but with a strong landscape association. He later developed a large-scale, wholly Abstract idiom, partly as a result of the influence of the New York School, and particularly of painters such as Rothko. In the paintings of the 1970s, large cut-out shapes—sometimes resembling pieces of a jigsaw, and strongly colored—are contrasted and combined. The jagged edges contribute a note of tension to the otherwise lyrical effects produced by the bold poster coloring (examples include a series of canvases painted between 1971 and 1975 and shown at the Waddington Galleries II, London, in May 1975).

Herrera family
16th and 17th centuries

The Spanish painter Francisco Herrera the Elder (*c*1589/91–*c*1657) was active in Seville, working in a vigorous naturalistic style with occasional traces of Mannerism, before moving to Madrid *c*1640. His best works include the series of scenes from the life of Saint Bonaventura (1626) painted for various religious communities in Seville (*Healing* and *Communion* are now in the Louvre, Paris), *The Vision of St Basil* (1639; Provincial Museum of Fine Arts, Seville), and *Miracle of the Loaves and Fishes* (1647; Archbishop's Palace, Madrid).

His son Francisco Herrera the Younger (1622–85) studied in Italy and worked in Seville and Madrid, painting in a dynamic and colorful Baroque style. His masterpieces are the *St Francis* (1660; Seville Cathedral), and *The Triumph of St Hermengeld* (*c*1654; Prado, Madrid); but none of the still-life compositions that gained him contemporary fame are identifiable today.

Herrera Juan de *c*1530–97

Juan de Herrera was a Spanish architect

who worked for Philip II in a heavy, monotonous, and unimaginative classical style which was named Herreran after him. After study in Italy he at first assisted, and then in 1572 succeeded, Juan Bautista de Toledo as architect of the monastery-palace at El Escorial. From Herrera's modified design, its church was executed from 1574 to 1582 as a centrally-planned aisled building, with a large entrance vestibule, and a mausoleum below a sacramental chapel behind the main altar. The granite facade is cold and austere.

At Valladolid Cathedral, Aranjuez, and Seville, Herrera later adapted the same style and proportions to different needs.

Hesse Eva 1936–70

Although she had a very short career, the American sculptor Eva Hesse was one of the leading Conceptual artists of the 1960s. She was born in Germany, her parents emigrating to the U.S.A. in 1939. She studied at the Pratt Institute, at the Art Students League, and at Yale under Joseph Albers. In 1964 she turned from painting to sculpture, exploring the potential of a wide range of materials such as rubber, fiberglass, cloth and string. Essentially a "process artist", she was more concerned with her spontaneous response to materials, allowing their characteristics to

suggest forms, than with a finished product. Works formed from latex or rubber, for example, often suggest fleshy, organic forms (reminiscent of the sculptures of Louise Bourgeois), while others have the austerity of Minimalist sculpture: *Addendum* (1967; Tate Gallery, London) consists of 17 cords hanging from a row of small, breast-like domes, while *Contingent* (1969; Australian National Gallery, Canberra) features hanging sheets of cheesecloth treated with latex and fiberglass. Her innovative use of materials influenced many later artists.

Heyden Jan van der 1637–1712

Jan van der Heyden was the first and most important townscape painter of Amsterdam. His town views (mostly from the 1660s) are characterized by precise rendering of details such as brickwork, but this is combined with simplicity in the disposition of light and shade, atmospheric unity, and structural balance and clarity. Some of the townscapes are *capriccios* or imaginary views (for example, *An Architectural Fantasy*, c1667–9; National Gallery, London), and even the paintings purporting to be of particular places are not always topographically correct. Van der Heyden also painted a few *vanitas* still lifes: pictures containing symbols of life's transience.

Hicks Edward 1780–1849

The landscape, religious, and historical painter Edward Hicks was the best known of those 19th-century American artists who worked in a "primitive" style. He was born in Bucks County, Pennsylvania, and spent most of his life there. He began to practice art as a trade, decorating coaches and signs. An active Quaker, he led his community and gave much of his time to depicting religious scenes. His *Peaceable Kingdom* (of which there are over 100 versions) is the most successful of these.

Highmore Joseph 1692–1780

The English painter Joseph Highmore was born in London. Although a nephew of Thomas Highmore, Sergeant-Painter to the Crown, he was essentially self-taught. By 1730 he had gained a reputation in London as a painter of single-figure portraits and conversation pieces. The success of Hogarth's serial pictures probably persuaded Highmore to paint 12 illustrations for the novel *Pamela* by Samuel Richardson in the 1740s (now in the Tate Gallery, London). His painting with its nonchalant attitudes of pose, natural coloring, and slightly precious refinement, epitomizes the French influence on English artists towards the middle of the 18th century. Like Francis Hayman, Hogarth, and others, he contributed a history painting to the Foundling Hospital, London, in 1746. Dating from the end of this decade are some of his finest portraits, such as *Mr Oldham and his Friends* (c1750; Tate Gallery, London). This is an inventive, life-size composition, which represents an inspired digression from the dainty urbanity of his earlier works.

Hildebrandt Johann von 1668–1745

The son of a German captain in the Genoese army, the architect Johann Lucas von Hildebrandt was born in Genoa and was educated there until c1690, when he went to study in Rome under Carlo Fontana. Trained initially as a town planner

Jan van der Heyden: The Huis ten Bosch at The Hague; oil on oak panel; 22×29cm (9×11in). National Gallery, London

Above: Edward Hicks: Peaceable Kingdom; oil on canvas; 83×105cm (33×41in); 1826. Philadelphia Museum of Art

Below: Joseph Highmore: Mr Oldham and his Friends; oil on canvas; 105×130cm (42×51in); c1750. Tate Gallery, London

and military engineer, Hildebrandt served under Prince Eugene in his Piedmontese campaigns (1695–6) and by 1698 was firmly established in Vienna when he was appointed an Imperial Councillor. In 1700 he became Architect to the Court, and eventually succeeded Fischer von Erlach as Surveyor General after the latter's death in 1723. Unlike Fischer von Erlach, however, von Hildebrandt received little direct Imperial patronage and his style is in considerable contrast to Fischer von Erlach's Imperial Baroque. Northern Italy left a deep impression on him, and he inherited from Italian Mannerist architecture his predilection for richly decorated surfaces, and his lack of interest in structure.

The important church of sv. Vavřinec at Jablonné v Podještědí in Northern Bohemia, begun by Hildebrandt in 1699, reveals in its ground plan his debt to Guarino Guarini. It is closely related to S. Lorenzo in Turin, but the church was completed by other hands and bears little resemblance to his later work. On the basis of comparisons with this ground plan the Piaristenkirche in Vienna (plan of 1698) is attributed to Hildebrandt; but again the church was substantially modified during construction. Shortly afterwards, Hildebrandt was himself responsible for modifying G. Montani's designs for the Peterskirche in Vienna (probably 1702/7), and he subsequently employed the longitudinal oval plan again for his Priesterseminarkirche in Linz (1717–25).

Hildebrandt's principal activity, however, was as a designer of palaces. His Schwarzenberg Palace in Vienna (begun 1697), with its restrained low relief treatment before Fischer von Erlach modified it c1720, illustrates his early secular style. His mature style is well revealed by the brilliant facade of the Daun Kinsky Palace in Vienna (1713–16). Here plain pilasters give way to elegant tapered forms for the three central bays, and the bizarre Borrominesque pediments add a rich counterpoint.

The decorated surface of the palace and the painterly qualities sought after by Hildebrandt reach a triumphant climax in the Upper Belvedere, built for Prince Eugene just outside the center of Vienna in 1721–2. The gardens rise up steeply to it and the richly orchestrated pattern of roofs crowning the separate units of the long narrow summer palace are always seen silhouetted against the sky.

In Germany Hildebrandt was called in by Lothar Franz von Schönborn to solve the problems of the staircase hall of Schloss Pommersfelden (1711). For the Elector's nephew, Friedrich Carl, Hildebrandt collaborated with Balthasar Neumann until 1744 in the design of the Würzburg Residenz. His rebuildings of the abbeys of Göttweig and Louka were never fully finished, but plans attest to his magnificent conceptions.

Hill Anthony 1930–

The English constructivist, sculptor, and painter Anthony Hill was born in London. He studied at St Martin's School of Art and at the Central School of Art between 1948 and 1951. During 1951 and 1952 he visited Paris, meeting Picabia, Kupka, and Vantongerloo. He taught at Chelsea School of Art from 1957. He was Leverhulme Research Fellow in Mathematics at University College London from 1970 to 1972, and Research Associate thereafter.

By 1954 Hill had abandoned Surrealism. He began to make geometric paintings of straight black lines on white grounds, tentatively exploring kinetic effects. About this date he made his first relief constructions in perspex and aluminum. From 1960 he became increasingly concerned with symmetry and the physical and optical properties of light, reflection, space, and movement. From the late 1960s his freestanding aluminum sculptures and his two-dimensional paintings on perspex exploit the same mathematical structures, in which he explores the boundaries between aesthetic and mathematical concepts.

Hilliard Nicholas c1547–1619

The miniaturist and goldsmith Nicholas Hilliard is the first English painter of whose career we possess a certain amount of knowledge. He was born in Exeter, the son of a goldsmith, and by the age of 13 had taken up miniature painting. At an early date he became goldsmith and limner to Queen Elizabeth I, and by the 1580s was well established in Court circles. In 1583/4 he was granted the right to make portraits of the Queen, and in 1584 designed and executed her second Great Seal. He may have visited France about 1577, and was certainly familiar with the work of French painters such as the Clouets, although he stated that he modeled himself on Holbein.

Nicholas Hilliard: Portrait of a Young Man; watercolor on card; 13.5×7cm (5½×2¾in); c1588. Victoria and Albert Museum, London

By 1572 Hilliard had completed a series of works, including his first dated portrait of the Queen (National Portrait Gallery, London), which showed his full mastery of miniature painting. His style is characterized by a craftsman's knowledge of line in defining form, but details such as hair and costume are expressed in a broad, flowing calligraphic manner. His most striking works are portraits of young men—painted in the period when Shakespeare was composing his sonnets—which reflect the virtues of the Elizabethan age.

By the turn of the century his style had become tighter, but his last years marked a return to mastery with his portraits of young ladies. In his *Treatise Concerning the Arte of Limning*, composed c1600, Hilliard shows himself very much the Renaissance man, true to the precepts of the humanists. His greatest pupil was Isaac Oliver who, by the mid 1590s, was working in a similar style.

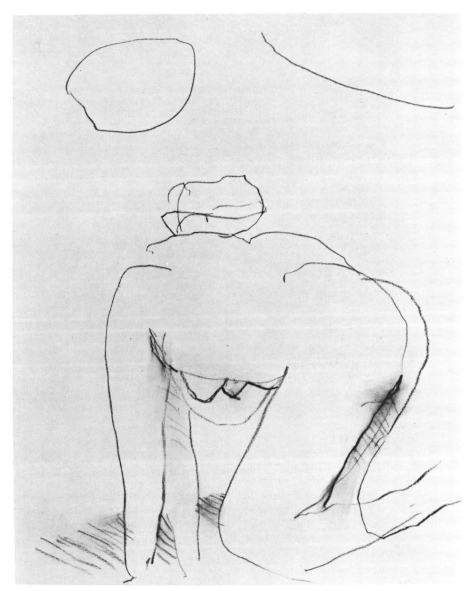

Roger Hilton: Nude (Nude on All Fours); charcoal on paper; 27×21cm (10½×8in); 1962. Private collection

which was settled in 443 BC and where he is known to have lived for a while. There is clearer evidence that he laid out Piraeus, the harbor town of Athens, in the middle of the 5th century. Examples of the application of his principles can be seen in the excavated plans of cities such as Olynthus, founded in north Greece towards the end of the 5th century, and Priene, near Miletus, founded after his death, in the mid 4th century. He acquired a reputation as an eccentric, and also as a political thinker. This may have dictated his plans for the physical accommodation of new city states in the Greek world.

Hiroshige Ando 1797–1858

The Japanese artist Ando Hiroshige is well known in the West for his landscape prints. He studied with the *Ukiyoe* artist Utagawa Toyohiro, but was also influenced by the *Shijo* School. This became clear after his master's death in 1828, when he began to produce his great series of woodblock landscapes, notably *Fifty-three Stations of the Tokaido Road*, which are full of *Shijo*-inspired poetry and brought him recognition. (See, for example, *Downpour at Shono*, 1833, from the series *Fifty-three Stations*, a copy of

Ando Hiroshige: The Iris Garden at Horikiri, from "One Hundred Views of Yedo"; woodblock print; height 27cm (10½in); 1857. British Museum, London

Hilton Roger 1911–75

The English painter Roger Hilton was born in Northwood. He studied at the Slade School of Fine Art from 1929 to 1931, and at the Académie Ranson, Paris, with Roger Bissière. He taught at the Central School of Art from 1954 to 1956 and began to visit Cornwall, where he lived at St Just from 1965. By 1950 Hilton had painted his first Abstracts. In 1953, influenced by Mondrian, his paintings were of flat, rough-edged shapes in a few pure colors, black and white. He soon turned again to using figurative allusions, in works where nude or landscape are implied in sensuously painted earthy smudged color masses and loose drawing. In the early 1960s he produced some frankly figurative works in bright colors. He drew—particularly the nude—throughout his life, but especially after 1972, when he ceased oil painting because of illness.

Hippodamus 5th century BC

The Greek town-planner Hippodamus came from Miletus. He was reported to have invented the grid plan for towns, with roads intersecting at right angles, laid out without regard to the contour of the site. The general idea of a grid for a new city had been known earlier in Greece, but he probably codified the practice and had several opportunities to impose it on new or ruined sites. Much probably depended on his layout of the relative positions of important areas of assembly, entertainment, marketing, and worship in relation to walls and gates, and the allocation of blocks or groups of blocks to larger complexes. His home town, sacked by the Persians in 494 BC, may have been instructive, and the final plan may be his work.

Hippodamus acted as traveling consultant to other states, probably including the Athenian town at Thurii in south Italy

which is in the Museum of Fine Arts, Boston.) Before his retirement in 1858, Hiroshige had designed about 5,000 prints. No popular artist had ever before depicted the Japanese landscape with such realism and sensitivity. He is at his best in scenes of snow, rain, and mist.

Hitchens Ivon 1893–1979

The English painter Ivon Hitchens studied at the Royal Academy Schools, London, intermittently during the years 1911 to 1919. He came away from his studies with a profound respect for the classical tradition, which helped to predispose him towards Cézanne, Matisse, and Cubism. The latter enabled him to break away from naturalism, and briefly—in the mid 1930s—Hitchen painted in a nonfigurative style. In 1940 he moved to Sussex where he lived and painted until his death. Here in relative isolation Hitchens developed his characteristic form of abstracted landscape, which was rich in color, broadly applied yet carefully structured. While a part of the English landscape tradition, these paintings possess much of the ordered clarity of French *belle peinture*.

Ivon Hitchens: Poppies in a Jug; oil on canvas; 103×69cm (41×27in); 1943. Sheffield City Art Galleries

Hobbema Meyndert 1638–1709

Meyndert Lubbertsz. Hobbema was a Dutch painter from Amsterdam whose importance in the sphere of realist landscape is exceeded only by that of his teacher, Jacob Ruisdael. Hobbema studied under Ruisdael in the late 1650s. The two artists remained friends; they appear to have sketched together, and sometimes painted the same views. Hobbema's earliest dated pictures are from the late 1650s: small, lightly-colored river scenes in which his fondness for trees is already evident. During these early years Hobbema imitated Ruisdael's paintings, occasionally even using his teacher's drawings as studies.

Hobbema's greatest paintings were produced in the 1660s; these are larger, have fresher and more varied colors, and convey effects of sparkling sunlight in clear, luminous air. It is sometimes difficult to distinguish Hobbema's work from Ruisdael's. Hobbema's landscapes are more sunny and open than Ruisdael's brooding, melancholy scenes, and there is less sense of solitude. They give little hint of the power and majesty of nature suggested by the massive trees and dramatic style of his teacher. His range of motifs, too, is more limited, being largely confined to forest and river scenes.

At the age of 30 Hobbema married and found employment as a wine gauger with the Amsterdam Excise. Thereafter he painted less, and his increasingly schematic work lost much of its vividness, the major exception being *The Avenue, Middelharnis* (1689; National Gallery, London). Hobbema's genius was only properly recognized in the 18th and 19th centuries, especially in England—where he had a significant influence on the development of landscape painting.

Hockney David 1937–

The British painter David Hockney is also an etcher, draftsman, and designer. Born in Bradford, Yorkshire, Hockney studied at the Bradford School of Art (1953–7) and at the Royal College of Art (1959–62), and soon gained critical attention with a series of Pop art paintings. These were extremely well designed, and light—almost jokey—in mood. Towards the end of the 1960s, however, Hockney became interested in a relatively straightforward kind of naturalism (seen in *Mr and Mrs Clark and Percy*, 1970–1; Tate Gallery, London), and this

Meyndert Hobbema: A Woody Landscape with a Cottage; oil on canvas; 99×130cm (39×51in). National Gallery, London

has been the basis of his art since then. Hockney is also a brilliant draftsman, and among his best works are the etched illustrations to Cavafy's *Poems* (1966) and Grimm's *Fairy Tales* (1969). He has also emerged as a successful designer for the theater (his work here includes sets and costumes for *The Rake's Progress*, Glyndebourne Opera, 1975). A strong flair for public relations has made Hockney by far the best-known of younger British painters. (*See* overleaf.)

David Hockney: Man taking Shower in Beverley Hills; acrylic on canvas; 167×167cm (66×66in); 1964. Tate Gallery, London

Further reading. Finch, C. *Images as Language: Aspects of British Art*, London (1969). Hockney, D. *David Hockney by David Hockney*, London (1976). Livingstone, M. *David Hockney*, London (1981). Lynton, N. "London Letter: Hockney", *Art International*, Lugano (March 1964).

Hodler Ferdinand 1853–1918

The Swiss painter Ferdinand Hodler was born in Bern. After serving as an apprentice to a minor painter in Thun in 1872 he moved to Geneva, which became his lifelong home. He studied under Bar-thelemy Menn at the École des Beaux-Arts for five years. In the late 1870s and early 1880s Hodler's financial situation was desperate due to poor critical reception of his work in Geneva. In addition he went through a religious crisis in 1880, and was greatly affected by the deaths of his parents, brothers, and sisters between 1860 and 1885. Hodler painted over 30 self-portraits in the early and late periods of his life. *The Angry Man* (1881; Berner Kunstmuseum, Bern) boldly shows his emotions at the time. It was the first painting he exhibited in the Paris Salon, and was also the first of his works to be bought for a public institution, in 1887.

In 1886 Hodler undertook his first commission for a cycle of historical scenes in Geneva, and had his first solo exhibition in Bern. Competition entries and commissions for decorative historical paintings, mostly of national and patriotic subjects, formed a large part of his work throughout his career. They include the fresco *The Retreat from Marignano* (1890; Schweizerisches Landesmuseum, Zurich) and *The Rising of the Jena Students* (1908; Schiller University, Jena).

Hodler's style developed with little contact with the modern art movement in

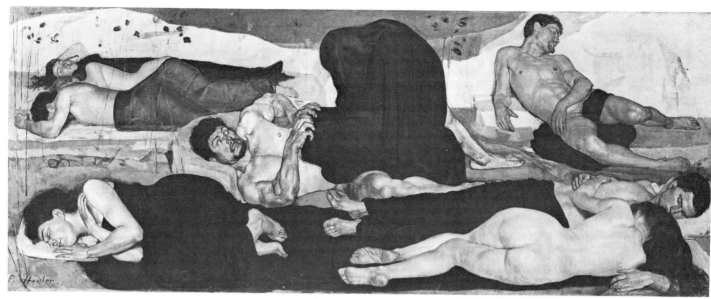

Ferdinand Hodler: Night; oil on canvas; 116×299cm (46×118in); 1890. Berner Kunstmuseum, Bern

Paris. His early landscapes reflected the influence of Corot. An example is *On the Shore of the Manzanares River* (1879; Musée d'Art et d'Histoire, Geneva) painted on a visit to Spain in 1878–9. His portraits and figures revealed knowledge of the works of Manet and Degas.

In the mid 1880s Hodler began to express his theory of Parallelism in landscapes like *Beech Forest* (1885; Museum der Stadt Solothurn) which illustrate a formal structure and the unity rather than diversity that Hodler found in nature. In 1890 Parallelism found expression in his great figure-painting *Night* (Berner Kunstmuseum, Bern) which marked the beginning of his international recognition.

Autobiographical, symbolic, *Night* combined themes of eros, sleep, death, and dream, and evokes feelings rather than depicts events. Paradoxically his first new work looks back to Raphael and Michelangelo. In 1891 the painting was enthusiastically received in Paris at the Salon du Champ-de-Mars where Hodler began to exhibit regularly. These large figure-paintings eventually went beyond the allegorical decoration of *Jugendstil* after the turn of the century when Hodler introduced a new realism combined with forceful color.

In 1892 *The Disillusioned* (Berner Kunstmuseum, Bern) was shown at the Salon de la Rose et Croix-Esthétique of which he became a member. In 1904 an exhibition of 31 paintings at the Vienna Secession, which he had joined a year earlier, established his European reputation, and he was acclaimed by Klimt with whom he exhibited. Hodler taught at the Fribourg Museum of Decorative Arts (1896–9), and was awarded an honorary doctorate by Basel University in 1910. In 1913 he was featured at the Salon d'Automne and made an officer of the Légion d'Honneur. In 1916 he was given an honorary professorship at the Geneva École des Beaux-Arts where he taught drawing for a year.

However, without doubt Hodler's modern reputation is based on his landscapes and portraits from after the turn of the century. The landscape views of Lake Thun and Lake Geneva and the mountains became increasingly symmetrical from the late 1890s. Possibly the greatest among them is *Eiger, Mönch, and Jungfrau in Moonlight* (1908; Museum der Stadt Solothurn), visionary, mysterious, and pan-

Ferdinand Hodler: A Poor Soul; 72×94cm (28×37in); oil on canvas; 1890/1. Öffentliche Kunstsammlung, Kunstmuseum Basel

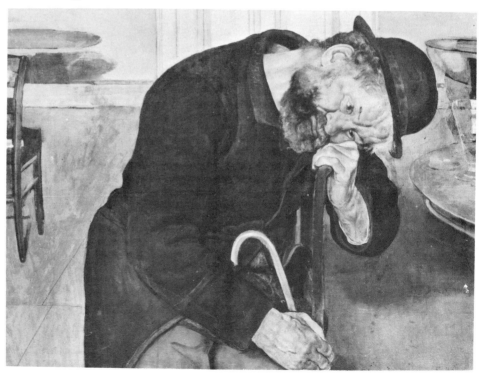

theistic, painted almost entirely in blues.

From 1908, when they first met, Valentine Godé-Darel was the subject of numerous drawings, studies, and paintings. From 1914 until her death in 1915, Hodler recorded her in her sickbed in a unique and moving cycle, and he painted her even after death, as in *The Dead Valentine Godé-Darel* (1915; Museum der Stadt Solothurn)—as he had also painted his first mistress, Augustine Dupin, in 1909.

In the last years of his life Hodler continued his landscapes, especially sunrises and sunsets painted in vivid, loosely brushed colors. *Landscape near Caux with Rising Clouds* (1917; Kunsthaus, Zurich) no longer displays clear contours; instead Hodler has allowed the features to dissolve. In 1917 he had a large retrospective exhibition in Zurich.

Further reading. Hirsh, S. *Ferdinand Hodler*, London (1982).

Hoffmann Josef 1870–1956

The Austrian architect and designer Josef Hoffmann was a pupil of Otto Wagner and one of the founders of the Vienna Secession. Hoffmann's work is noted for its elegance and attention to detail. Except for the Sanatorium at Purkersdorf (1904–5), his buildings are not so "modern" looking as those of his more radical contemporary Adolf Loos, who scorned Hoffmann's indulgence in expensive and exquisite design. Luxuriousness dominates his most famous work, the Palais Stoclet in Brussels (1905–11), a collaborative effort with the painter Klimt and the Wiener Werkstätte. The latter was a workshop for applied art, based on English craft ideals and encouraged by Charles Rennie Mackintosh, which Hoffmann and others started in 1903.

Hofmann Hans 1880–1966

The painter Hans Hofmann was a Bavarian who worked in Paris and Munich, and moved to America in 1932. He became the most influential teacher of modern art in the United States where he founded his own school in New York and Providence; his structured yet tolerant teaching was

William Hogarth: The Artist with the Pug; oil on canvas; 90×70cm (35×28in); 1745. Tate Gallery, London

Hans Hofmann: Effervescence; oil, india ink, casein, and enamel on plywood panel; 138×91cm (54×36in); 1944. University Art Museum, Berkeley

one of the prime factors in the emergence of the New York School. Hofmann's paintings in 1940 such as *Spring* (oil; private collection) presage the automatism and the technique of Jackson Pollock. His later works such as *Blue Rhythm* (oil; 1950; Art Institute of Chicago) are major works of the New York School.

Further reading. Hunter, S. *Hans Hofmann*, New York (1963).

Hogarth William 1697–1764

The English painter, engraver, and satirist William Hogarth was born in London, where he lived and worked all his life. When he was 10 his family was put in a debtors prison, and this experience provided William with a chance to develop the keen observation of human foibles that he was later to use in his art. At 16 he was apprenticed to a silversmith, and learned to engrave armorial designs on gold and silver work. But his frustrated artistic ambition led him to take up unorthodox methods of self-instruction, which ultimately contributed much to his originality as an artist. He set up in business as an engraver in 1720 and in the following year he produced his first dated engraving, a satire on the government's "South Sea Company" investment crisis.

In his "conversation pieces" Hogarth developed tentatively as a painter; but after joining the Free Academy of Sir James Thornhill (whose daughter Jane he married in 1729) he began to evolve a type of subject painting entirely new to English art, which the novelist Henry Fielding described as "comic-history". These concerns are already apparent in Hogarth's first major work, a series of 12 plates based on Samuel Butler's *Hudibras*.

His first public success was the launching of a subscription for engravings of *The Harlot's Progress* paintings. Instead of issuing them through a printseller he published them himself, and reaped a handsome profit. In 1735 the engravings of *A Rake's Progress* (Sir John Soane's Museum, London) appeared; and in 1736 he painted two large religious scenes—inspired by his father-in-law's work—for St Bartholomew's Hospital.

At the time Hogarth was also illustrating Shakespeare, and deriving inspiration from the theater. In his portraits—such as that of his friend *Thomas Coram* (1740; Foundling Hospital, London), founder of the Foundling Hospital—Hogarth also attempted to compete with his Continental rivals. No further satirical prints were issued until 1745 when the *Marriage à la Mode* paintings (National Gallery, London) were engraved; the pictures themselves remained unsold until 1750/1.

In the later 1740s Hogarth's reputation began to wane, and he turned to producing prints from drawings rather than paintings. The subject matter of his prints became more popular (for example *Gin Lane, Stages of Cruelty*, 1751), and the organization of his paintings much simpler, as in *The Wedding Banquet* (c1745; County Museum and Art Gallery, Truro), possibly painted as part of a projected series concerning a "happy marriage", where incident is reduced to a minimum and the paint takes on a purely expressive function.

In 1753 Hogarth published *The Analysis of Beauty*, the first formalist English art treatise, in which he related his experiments in form to their expression and meaning. Hogarth had done much to further the cause of English art, opening an art academy and urging the passing of an act to protect engravers from piracy, but his essentially anti-academic attitude made him unpopular in later life. In the 1750s the feeling of disillusionment in English politics brought on by the Seven Years War was reflected in a falling off in Hogarth's productivity, and his last years were marked by ill health and political quarrels.

Further reading. Antal, F. *Hogarth's Place in European Art*, London (1962). Baldini, G. and Mandel, G. *L'opera Completa di Hogarth Pittore*, Milan (1967). Hogarth, W. (ed. Burke, J.) *The Analysis of Beauty* (*1753*), Oxford (1955). Paulson, R. *Hogarth: His Life, Art and Times* (2 vols.), London and New Haven (1971).

Hoitsu Sakai 1761–1828

Sakai Hoitsu was a Japanese painter of the *Rimpa* School. A son of the rich Lord of Himeji he learned painting in the *Kano* School, but finally turned to the decorative style of Ogata Korin. He made a big colllection of Korin's works and published illustrated works on him.

Hoitsu was a "feminine" painter, elegant and soft, but rarely forceful. His screens on gold and particularly on silver backgrounds, like those of a *Stream Amid Summer and Autumn Flowers* (Tokyo National Museum) are exquisitely delicate and harmonious. His long scroll *Birds and Flowers of the Four Seasons* (1808; Tokyo National Museum) is perhaps his masterpiece.

Hokusai Katsushika 1760–1849

The painter and print designer Katsushika Hokusai is the most famous of all Japanese artists in the West, though not in his own country. He is best known for his woodblock print series *Thirty-Six Views of Fuji* (published *c*1823–31; it contains 46 plates—it was so popular he added 10 new scenes) in which he virtually invented the landscape print, and made the first recorded use of Prussian blue in Japan. He used color to convey mood and light as never before in Japan. He is also celebrated for his woodblock books called *Manga* (1814–19), a huge series of endlessly inventive sketches, and for the monochrome *One Hundred Views of Fuji* (1834–5) which had enormous influence on Western design.

Despite his great output of prints and books, Hokusai remained basically a painter. Nearly all of his own works were destroyed in a fire in 1839. Most extant paintings and drawings are therefore of his rather wild old age, and his reputation as a painter has suffered.

Born in Tokyo, he studied with Katsukawa Shunsho, and for 20 years produced *Ukiyoe* prints of actors and beauties. He gradually developed an eclectic, rather eccentric style using Chinese landscape elements and a characteristic broad, somewhat Chinese face. These characteristics can be seen in his painting *Tametomo and the Demons* of 1811 (British Museum, London). They also appear in the brilliantly bold series of landscape prints which made his reputation—the *Fuji* series, the *Waterfalls*, and the *Bridges*, all of them depending on a powerful central subject.

Yet he was always capable of delicacy, especially in his deluxe *surimono* prints and his brush studies of birds. There are a great many ink sketches dating from his late years. Some of these are very successful, but many are by his large studio of followers.

Further reading. Hillier, J. *Hokusai*, Oxford (1978). Lane, R. *Hokusai and Hiroshige*, Tokyo (1976). Yasuda, G. *Gwakyo Hokusai*, Tokyo (1971).

Holbein family
15th and 16th centuries

The Holbein family workshop dominated painting in Augsburg at the beginning of the 16th century and produced, in Hans the Younger, an artist of major European importance. Hans the Elder (1460/5–1524) seems to have traveled widely during his formative years as an artist. That he was familiar with the work of Martin Schongauer on the upper Rhine, and with paintings by leading Flemish artists, is shown by his earliest works. *The Death of the Virgin* (*c*1490–5; Öffentliche Kunstsammlung, Kunstmuseum Basel) is indebted to Rogier van der Weyden, though the linearity of Rogier is here softened both in contour and color.

Apart from his work at Augsburg, Holbein the Elder is recorded at Ulm, Frankfurt, and Isenheim, where he probably painted *The Martyrdom of St Sebastian* altar (*c*1515–17; Alte Pinakothek, Munich). This shows the increasing Italian influence upon him both in the pose of the archers on the main panel, and in the decorative panels of classical ornament which frame the monumentalized forms of Saints Elizabeth and Barbara on the wings.

The style of Hans Holbein the Younger (1497/8–1543) was at first close to that of his father, though at an early age he moved out of the Augsburg workshop. In 1514 he went to Basel with his brother Ambrosius, also a painter, and entered the shop of Hans Herbster as a journeyman-apprentice. For more than a decade he found employment at Basel on a variety of commissions: he painted frescoes for the Town Hall, illustrated books (including a woodcut series of *The Dance of Death* in 1523–6) and painted many altarpieces.

Katsushika Hokusai: Fuji in Clear Weather, from the series "Thirty-Six Views of Fuji"; woodblock print; 26×38cm (10×15in); c1823–9. British Museum, London

Hans Holbein the Younger: Portrait of Desiderius Erasmus; oil on panel; 43×33cm (17×13in); 1523. Louvre, Paris

An extended visit to Lucerne in 1517 and 1518 may have included a trip to Italy. The shutters of an altarpiece showing scenes from the *Passion of Christ* (c1520; Öffentliche Kunstsammlung, Kunstmuseum Basel) have quotations from the work of Mantegna, and a hard, enamel-like finish that seems influenced by Lombard painting. His virtuosity as a master of the decorative arts found scope on the facade of the *Haus zum Tanz* ("House of the Dance") in Basel, now known only through surviving designs; here he revived the antique style of house decoration with illusionistic reliefs and figures.

The stark realism of the *Dead Christ* (1521; Öffentliche Kunstsammlung, Kunstmuseum Basel), where the figure is stretched out in a long, narrow panel, displays the sharpness of observation and detachment from subject matter that made Holbein the Younger one of the most successful portrait-painters of the 16th century. The pendant portraits of the first identifiable patrons, the Basel Burgomaster *Jacob Meyer and his Wife* (1516; Öffentliche Kunstsammlung, Kunstmuseum Basel) typify the finely drawn quality of all his portraiture. A certain animation in the *Jacob Meyer* portrait was suppressed in later court portraits.

For the same patrons, Holbein painted *The Meyer family in Adoration of the Virgin and Child* (begun 1526, finished

Hans Holbein the Younger: Portrait of Sir John Godsalve; detail; black and red chalk, india ink, body color and watercolor on paper; full size 36×30cm (15×12in); c1532. Collection of H.M. Queen Elizabeth II

1528–30; Hessisches Landesmuseum, Darmstadt). Here a Northern concern for detail in the carpet and costumes is offset by Italian influences in the firm modeling of form and the shell niche that encloses the Madonna. It is one of Holbein's last religious pictures, for by this date the market for religious pictures in post-Reformation Basel had contracted sharply.

The European fame of Holbein the Younger came as a result of his contact with humanist, literary circles. While Erasmus was living in Basel Holbein painted his portrait several times, the most famous examples being those in the Louvre, Paris, and in Longford Castle, near Salisbury, England. The latter was probably presented to Sir Thomas More, and thus gained Holbein an entry into More's circle on his first visit to England from 1526 to 1528. He painted a large group portrait of the More family, now known only from a preparatory drawing (Öffentliche Kunstsammlung, Kunstmuseum Basel) and from copies. The depiction of a family group in domestic surroundings on this scale was unprecedented in Northern art.

Holbein's careful preparatory work for portraits is apparent from the many single-figure drawings in colored chalks that survive both for this work and later single portraits. The attention to surface texture and the high degree of finish in his work at this time can be seen in the single *Portrait of More* (Frick Collection, New York) where the tactile qualities of the curtain, the velvet sleeves, the fur of the cloak, and the sitter's beard are carefully rendered.

On his second visit to London in 1532 Holbein's success with portraits of foreign merchants and diplomats brought him to the notice of the Court. *The Ambassadors* (1533; National Gallery, London) represents the young Frenchmen Jean de Dinteville and Georges de Selve and demonstrates Holbein's ability—crucial to the success of any Court portraitist—to place his sitters in a context that flatters their social and intellectual pretensions. The figures are accompanied by symbols of the arts of learning and music in which they were accomplished. Even so, the reminders of death are also here, notably in the distorted skull of the foreground.

Holbein became Court Painter to Henry VIII in 1536, at a time when the King sought to establish his image as religious and temporal head of the new commonwealth, separated from the Church of Rome. Holbein first produced his standard

form for the King's portrait in an allegorical mural painting of the monarch, his parents, and his third wife, painted for the Palace of Whitehall. The mural is lost, but a fragment of the original cartoon survives (National Portrait Gallery, London) showing the formalized, hieratic image of the King. Holbein was also prolific as a designer of pageants, ceremonial dress, book-bindings, and jewelry for the Court.

Other portraits of his last years in England have the common characteristics of a half-length figure against a neutral ground, and care for detailed physiognomy at the expense of lively character description. The attention to details of dress, the placing of the hands, and sometimes an inscription identifying the sitter and his status, emphasize the rather withdrawn character of the image (for example, *Anne of Cleves*, 1539–40; Louvre, Paris). If the technical quality of his work was never matched, this formula for the portrait was to have a profound impact on English portraiture for more than half a century after Holbein's death from the Plague in 1543.

Further reading. Ganz, P. *The Paintings of Hans Holbein*, London (1956). *Holbein and the Court of Henry VIII*, London (1978). Parker, M.T. *The Drawings of Hans Holbein at Windsor Castle*, Oxford (1945). Strong, R. *Holbein and Henry VIII*, London (1967). Von der Osten, G. and Vey, H. *Painting and Sculpture in Germany and the Netherlands: 1500–1600*, Harmondsworth (1969). Waterhouse, E.K. *Painting in Britain: 1550–1790*, Harmondsworth (1978).

Hollar Wenzel 1607–77

Wenzel Hollar, a widely traveled watercolorist, book-illustrator, and printmaker, was the most important topographical artist working in England during the 17th century. He was born in Prague, and trained in the Frankfurt studio of the famous engraver of biblical illustrations and publisher of topographical prints Mathäus Merian (1593–1650). While working in Cologne in 1636 he met the Earl of Arundel, a connoisseur with whom he traveled around Europe making views and studies of works of art. Hollar then traveled to England, where, after an interval in Antwerp between 1645 and 1652, he eventually settled in London. Following the Restoration, Charles II appointed him "His Majesty's Scenographer and Designer

Wenzel Hollar: The Realm of Venus; etching after a painting by Adam Elsheimer; 9×15cm (4×6in); 1646. National Gallery of Scotland, Edinburgh

of Prospects". In England he produced many etchings and engravings depicting contemporary events, maps, costumes, views of London before the Great Fire of 1666, and works of art.

Homer Winslow 1836–1910

The American painter and illustrator Winslow Homer was born in Boston in 1836. He was apprenticed to a lithographer for three years and in 1857 began a career as a freelance illustrator. In 1859 he moved to New York and studied painting part-time. His first oil paintings were of the Civil War which he covered for *Harper's Weekly* (1862–5). In 1866 he spent ten months in France. His paintings in oil during the 1860s and 1870s and in watercolor after 1873 resembled early Impressionism in their concern for light and the direct rendering of motifs. He depicted mostly rural scenes and figures in outdoor settings, such as *Croquet Scene* (1866; Art Institute of Chicago). During 1881 and 1882 Homer visited Tynemouth, England, where he became attracted to the sea. On his return to America in 1883 he settled in Prout's Neck on the lonely Maine coast where he lived until his death. His main theme was the ocean—its grandeur, beauty, and power, and its dangers to those who sailed on it and lived by it, especially the fishermen. The late oils of sea rescues, such as *The Life Line* (1894; Philadelphia Museum of Art), and many other sea pictures, for example *Eight Bells* (1886; Addison Gallery of American Art, Andover, Mass.), became famous during his lifetime. They are painted in a bold

Winslow Homer: Snap the Whip; oil on canvas; 56×91cm (22×36in); 1872. Butler Institute of American Art, Youngstown, Ohio

naturalistic style, with strong formal qualities and color harmonies.

His watercolors make him one of the leading naturalistic painters in 19th-century America. His many views include scenes of his hunting and fishing trips in the Adirondacks and Quebec, for example *Adirondack Guide* (1894; Museum of Fine Arts, Boston), as well as the Maine coast. In the last ten years of his life he produced paintings of the Bahamas, Cuba, and Florida, where he spent his winter months. His style was original, fresh and strong in design, with brilliant colors.

Further reading. Hendricks, G. *The Life and Work of Winslow Homer*, New York (1979). Scott Atkinson, D. and Wierich, J. *Winslow Homer in Gloucester*, New York (1991).

Honoré Master *fl.* 1280–1310

The French illuminator Master Honoré was possibly born in Amiens, but lived in Paris during the late 13th century. He is one of the first Gothic illuminators to emerge as a distinct personality, and his innovations provide a basis for subsequent developments in 14th-century Paris.

Honoré lived in the quarter of Paris favored by scribes and illuminators and close to the University. He owned his own house in the Rue Erembourc-de-Brie (now Rue Boutebrie) and worked there with his son-in-law, Richard of Verdun, and a valet. He must have been the most successful artist of his time; the Poll Tax register in 1292 informs us that he paid more tax than any other miniaturist in the Paris guild. From the royal accounts for 1296 he is known to have worked for Philip the Fair, King of France, and a royal Breviary of the same year is generally regarded as one of his key works (Bibliothèque Nationale, Paris; MS. Lat. 1023).

Honoré's personal style is best seen in the frontispiece of the Breviary of Philip the Fair and in a sumptuous copy of a moral treatise in French known as *La Somme le Roy* (British Library, London; Add. MS. 54180). In illustrating scenes from the life of David in the Breviary, or of Moses in the moral treatise, he aims at a dramatic presentation not intended simply to illustrate the text but to have pictorial value in its own right. His subtly modeled figures have a sturdy volume that contrasts sharply with the flat decorative treatment found in other court manuscripts of the

Gerrit van Honthorst: Christ before the High Priest; oil on canvas; 269×183cm (106×72in); c1617. National Gallery, London

mid 13th century. Their emergence from the picture-plane draws attention to the need for an independently created illusion of space; this must have encouraged later experiments in perspective such as those of Jean Pucelle in the 1320s.

Honoré is recorded only in Paris and his style must have developed there; but connections with northern France and with England have also been noted. He appears in some documents as "Maître Honoré d'Amiens". A Psalter and Book of Hours (Pierpont Morgan Library, New York, MS. 729) made for Yolande of Soissons, probably in Amiens, has some miniatures in a related style which may precede the

Paris works. On the other hand, there is a Book of Hours (Stadtbibliothek, Nuremberg; No. 4), where calendar and litany suggest an English owner. The style is that of Master Honoré's workshop, and it introduces an international element for which no complete explanation has been forthcoming.

A number of manuscripts have been attributed to Honoré on stylistic grounds and his probable lifespan is of relevance here. By 1318 his son-in-law, Richard of Verdun, had inherited the workshop. The absence of any mention of Honoré or the house he had inhabited when an extraordinary tax was levied on the citizens of Paris in 1313, suggests that he was then already dead. It seems probable that Richard, who was associated with him for many years, carried on the same workshop tradition, and that in the early 14th century products of the original workshop and its continuation become inextricably interwoven.

Honthorst Gerrit van 1590–1656

A leading member of the Utrecht school, Gerrit (or Gerard) van Honthorst was one of the few Dutch painters of his day to acquire an international reputation. His historical importance lies mainly in his popularization of the chiaroscuro effects of Caravaggio and his followers, and his involvement in the development of early-17th-century Dutch genre painting. Honthorst began his career as a pupil of Abraham Bloemaert. This was followed by a period in Italy from c1610 to c1620, where he painted religious pictures for churches in Rome, and acquired several wealthy patrons and considerable celebrity.

The influence of Caravaggio's work in Rome (which he copied) was crucial during these years, and can be seen in the abrupt conjunctions of extreme lights and darks and the dramatically illuminated facial expressions in the *Christ before the High Priest* (1617; National Gallery, London). Honthorst (nicknamed "Gherardo della Notte") continued to exploit nocturnal effects, particularly candle light, long after his return to Utrecht. This can be seen in several of his large genre pictures of light-hearted, dissolute revelry—a central theme in the development of Dutch genre painting. These pictures may have been known to the young Rembrandt, who adopted their darkly silhouetted figures and concealed light sources in his *Money-Changer* painting (1627; Staatliche Museen, Berlin). Honthorst's later years were occupied with conventional portraits, and also with historical and allegorical pictures for the courts of northern Europe—paintings completed with the help of many assistants and pupils.

Hooch Pieter de 1629–c85

The Dutch genre painter Pieter Hendricksz. de Hooch is second only to Vermeer in the complex spatial organization and feeling for light of his small-scale interiors. Born in Rotterdam, he began his career with paintings of stable scenes and guardrooms. In 1654 he moved to Delft (where Carel

Pieter de Hooch: Figures Drinking in a Courtyard with an Arbor; 67×57cm (26×22in); 1658. On loan to the National Gallery of Scotland, Edinburgh

Fabritius and Vermeer were working) in the service of a rich clothmaker to whom he was "Painter and Manservant". There he concentrated on domestic pictures of courtyards, gardens, and interiors: scenes in which orderly middle-class homes are the settings for women and maidservants going about their household tasks, burghers sampling a bottle of wine, and occasionally a family portrait.

These intimate pictures with their multiplicity of domestic details are much less intellectual than Vermeer's austere paintings, but their underlying formal organization is almost as complex. A typical preoccupation is with the walls and pictures that

surround, and often frame his figures. (De Hooch usually began his pictures by painting the architectural framework, placing his figures within it afterwards.) The spatial organization very often involves a continuous series of cubic spaces. These provide vistas through open doors, in which depth is underlined by alternations of light and shade and the perspective of receding flagstones.

There is a less perfect balance between de Hooch's somewhat slight figures and their surroundings than is found in Vermeer's work. This is compensated for by the stillness, tranquillity, and sense of suspended movement in his interiors. De

Hooch shared Vermeer's interest in light as it streamed through a window or fell in a sunny courtyard, but he differentiated more between the textures of the objects on which the light fell, whether fabrics, furniture, brickwork, plaster or tiles. The quality of de Hooch's light is itself also different from Vermeer's: like his colors, in which reds and golden browns prevail, it is much warmer. The pictures painted during de Hooch's Delft period are generally considered his best; after settling in Amsterdam c1666/7 there is a decline, perhaps accounted for by his removal from the inspiration of Vermeer.

Further reading. Sutton, P.C. *Pieter de Hooch*, Oxford (1980).

Hopper Edward 1882–1967

The painter and graphic artist Edward Hopper was one of the most important American realists of the 20th century. Born in Nyack, New York, he trained as an illustrator before studying with Robert Henri at the New York School of Art. He made four brief trips to Europe between 1906 and 1910, and though some influences are discernible (such as Manet and Degas) he remained unaffected by avant-garde developments, preferring to develop the potential of American realism. He exhibited at the Armory Show 1913, and between 1915 and 1923 concentrated on graphic works in which he quickly discovered his characteristic subjects and techniques. His vision of everyday American life—typically of empty streets, isolated buildings and solitary, remote figures—is dominated by a profound sense of loneliness and boredom. Major works include *Early Sunday Morning* (1930; Whitney Museum of American Art, New York) and *Night Hawks* (1942; Art Institute of Chicago). Hopper's concern with structure is emphasized by his skillful use of strong verticals, horizontals and diagonals, a simplification of forms and the use of oblique sunlight. At times—as in *Rooms by the Sea* (1951; Yale University Art Gallery), which is dominated by a blank wall and an open door framing a view of the sea—Hopper's work acquires a Surrealistic tone.

Further reading. Hobbs, R. *Edward Hopper*, New York (1987). Levin, G. *Edward Hopper: The Art and the Artist*, New York (1987).

Horta Victor 1861–1947

Victor Horta was the original architect of European Art Nouveau. Born at Ghent, he studied in Brussels under the Neoclassical architect Alphonse Balat (1818–95). His first work of importance was the Hotel Tassel (1892–3) in Brussels, whose interior was revolutionary in almost every respect: spaces flow into one another organically off an octagonal hall and a staircase, thus abandoning the conventional division into stories. In its use of iron, both structurally and decoratively (in the staircase for example), the Tassel house was the first of its kind. In his use of curvilinear forms derived from nature—the "whiplash" line which entwines itself round and over every surface—Horta initiated a style that gripped European architects for the next 10 years.

Exactly how he arrived at this style is something of a mystery. Familiarity with English design, with Continental Post-Impressionist and Symbolist painting, and with the theories of Viollet-le-Duc (1814–79) and Owen Jones (1809–74) all probably contributed to Horta's invention of a new architectural means of expression.

Next in Horta's domestic oeuvre came the Hotel Solvay (1895–1900), perhaps his most mature Art Nouveau building. A bold use of iron and glass characterizes his public commissions: for example, the Maison du Peuple (1896–9) and the Innovation store (1901) in Brussels.

Further reading. Borsi, F. and Portoghesi, P. *Horta*, New York (1991).

Houdon Jean-Antoine 1741–1828

The sculptor Jean-Antoine Houdon was born in Versailles and brought up in the Académie Royale de Peinture et de Sculpture where his father became doorkeeper. He studied there under Michel-Ange Slodtz, obtained one of its Rome scholarships in 1764, and exhibited there regularly from the year of his return in 1768.

Houdon's first commission had been for the *St Bruno* in S. Maria degli Angeli in Rome (1766), an image of withdrawn and silent meditation. He also began the companion *St John the Baptist*. The latter work was never completed and was destroyed in 1894, but from it derives the *Ecorché* casts, which are to be found in many art academies, and which Houdon regarded as his most outstanding contribution to art. His experience of the Classical and Baroque masterpieces of Italy inspired such works as *The Priest of the Lupercals* (1768; Schlossmuseum, Gotha), the *Vestal* (1767–8; Metropolitan Museum, New York) and the naked, running *Diana* balanced on one foot (1776; Schlossmuseum, Gotha). Many of his religious works were destroyed at the Revolution, but these mythological sculptures and the *Tourville* (1781; Versailles) prove his capacity to create imaginative historical statues. Works such as the *Baiser Donné* and the *Baiser Rendu* (c1774), or the *Frileuse* (or *Winter*, 1781; marble of 1783 in the Musée Fabre, Montpellier) shivering in her inadequate covering, show him in the lighter vein of Rococo eroticism.

However, it is as a portraitist that Houdon ranks as one of the world's greatest sculptors. No intellectual, he had a profound respect for reality, never losing an opportunity to take a cast from the face of a dead celebrity, and inventing a machine as an aid to accurate drawing from nature. The quality of his work came from the life he could instil into these images, from the virtuosity of his carving of flesh, hair, and costume, from the inventiveness of his treatment of the eyes (often contrasting the shadow of a deeply cut pupil with a cube of projecting marble or bronze which flashes like a highlight), and from the taste with which he disposed the draperies round that artificially dismembered form, the portrait bust. A good businessman, he ensured that his works were produced in many examples, often in variant forms.

One of his earliest successes was the bust of *Denis Diderot* (c1771; terracotta in the Louvre, Paris), an admirer who secured for him powerful patrons in Germany and Russia. Houdon portrayed the aristocrats of Europe, the statesmen of France, the intellectuals of the *Encyclopédie*, and the leaders of republican America. He was justly proud of his bronze foundry, but his ambition to cast an equestrian statue of George Washington remained unfulfilled. However, he carved a standing figure of Washington as the new Cincinnatus (1788; Capitol, Richmond, Va.). His portraits of Voltaire, above all the seated figures in the Hermitage, St Petersburg, and in the Comédie Française in Paris (both 1781), have proved the most enduring visual images of the writer's intellectual vigor and mordant wit. Besides his busts of eminent men and beautiful women, Houdon created a number of the most charming but totally unsentimental portraits of children and babies ever produced.

Hoyland John 1934–

The English nonfigurative painter John Hoyland was born in Sheffield. During a long and thorough training at the Sheffield College of Art (1946–56) and the Royal Academy Schools, London (1956–60), Hoyland gradually developed his nonfigurative style, at first by abstracting from landscapes and still lifes. From *c*1957, under the impact of the work of Rothko and Turnbull, he experimented with pure forms and colors. In order to achieve a greater integrity of the picture-surface, Hoyland began in 1963 to stain his canvases with acrylic paint. However, concerned with the richness as well as the unity of visual experience, he continued to paint independent forms (usually squares) on top of this ground. Encouraged by the work of Hans Hofmann, Hoyland further developed this aspect of his art in the 1970s; the shapes increased in number until they filled the whole of the canvas with a rich profusion of impastoed colors.

Hsia Kuei *fl.* 1180–1230

Born in Ch'ien T'ang, the Chinese artist Hsia Kuei was an Academy painter of the later Southern Sung Court. He was a follower of Fan K'uan and Li T'ang and with his contemporary Ma Yuan, de-

Jean-Antoine Houdon: Madame de Serilly; marble; height 62cm (24in); 1782. Wallace Collection, London

veloped a style influential in Chinese painting known as the Hsia-Ma School. He often used ink and paper and composed pictures with the elegance associated with the Sung Court Academy.

His virtuosity of brushwork allowed him many dramatic effects ranging from the marvelously simple evocation of distance by controlled tone washes to effects of texture achieved by a bravura use of the "axe cut" brush stroke. Hsia Kuei liked to use a worn brush which, used with thick ink and dragged across the surface of the paper, produces an expressive stroke when painting rocks and bare landscape. Figures and animals appear as inhabitants of Hsia Kuei's landscapes, often painted with humor and always in a lively manner.

Hsia's most famous surviving painting is the long handscroll in the National Palace Museum collection, Taipei, *Ten Thousand Li of the Yangste*. This is in ink on paper and is 34 ft (10.1 m) long. It takes the viewer through many aspects of the course of the great river—from the rapids of Szechwan, where the boatmen struggle, to the wide flood plain of the lower reaches, where it is not always easy to see the other bank of the river. This masterpiece epitomizes all Hsia's characteristics: his daring composition, and directness of the brushwork combined with great sophistication.

John Hoyland: 17.3.69; acrylic on canvas; 198×366cm (78×144in); 1969. Tate Gallery, London

Huang Chun-pi 1899–

Huang Chun-pi is Cantonese and a leading member of the *Ling-nan* School. Between 1929 and 1935 he was Professor at the Canton City Art School, but moved north to Nanking as a professor at the National Central University, Nanking. He is a traditional painter who depicts mountain landscapes in a rich ink style. In common with his school he favors the use of slight color with the rich dark ink, and so produces a heavy decorative effect. The Canton School of painters have a distinctive style of which Huang Chun-pi's work is a good example.

Huang Kung-wang 1269–1354

The Chinese painter Huang Kung-wang was born the son of the Lu family, his original name being Lu Chien. He was very early adopted into the Huang family, when he was given the name by which he is now known (and also the name Tzu-chiu, indicating that he was a child for their old age). He was very gifted and soon reached a high standard in his studies in history and philosophy. He was to become a revered scholar, poet, musician, and painter. He served for a while as a clerk in the office of the Provincial Judge of Chekiang but retired early to live as a Taoist recluse in the Hangchow area, where his friend Ts'ao Chih-p'o also lived in retirement.

Huang wandered all over the Wu district and spent the last seven or eight years of his life in the Fu Ch'un mountains. During this time he painted the famous *Fu Ch'un*

Mountain handscroll of which two versions remain in the National Palace Museum, Taipei, Taiwan. One of these bears the date 1338, the other, regarded as genuine, is dated 1354. This latter, longer scroll bears an inscription:

In the 7th year of Chih-chang [1347] I went back to the Fu Ch'un mountains and stayed there with Master Wu Yung. In the days of leisure, while living in the South Pavilion, I played with the brush and painted this scroll whenever I felt inspired. I did not weary myself; [yet] the composition grew gradually. I work as if filling in documents. In this way three or four years passed but the picture was not finished because I left it in the mountains when I went rambling about like a floating cloud. Then I brought it back in my bag and whenever I could spare the time in the morning or in the evening I worked on it, though without anxiety.

This describes the tempo of such painting by a man regarded by Tung Ch'i-ch'ang as the first to use painting both as a means of expression and for his own pleasure. He is also recorded as having gone about with paper and brush in his sleeve making sketches when he came upon a beautiful scene. He noted the effects of time of day and the seasons, working from nature but clearly with a very scholarly brush. He is noted for his extremely subtle ink tone and texture.

Huang Kung-wang: Dwelling in Fu Ch'un Mountains, a detail of the second Fu Ch'un Mountain handscroll; ink on paper; full size 33×637cm (13×251in); 1354. National Palace Museum, Taipei

Huber Wolfgang c1490–1553

The Swiss painter Wolfgang Huber was born at Feldkirch in the Vorarlberg district of Austria. For several years from c1505 he traveled through the Hapsburg lands, visiting Innsbruck and Salzburg. The Danube school of landscape painting and the graphic works of Albrecht Dürer, especially his *Life of the Virgin* series, were the major sources of his early work. *The Flight into Egypt* (Staatliche Museen, Berlin), from an altarpiece of the *Life of the Virgin*, is a good example of his combination of these influences. Huber settled at Passau some time between 1510 and 1515 and there established a large workshop. Between 1515 and 1521 he painted an altarpiece for the Stadtpfarkirche at Feldkirch in which the color and linear quality of his earliest work have given place to a less assertive style. In portraiture he at first adopted the style of the Augsburg school and of the Holbein workshop in particular, placing the sitter against a setting of Classical architecture. In later works he favors a sky background, as in the portrait of *Jakob Ziegler* (c1544–9; Kunsthistorisches Museum, Vienna).

Much of his painted work appears to be lost, however, and he now emerges at his most original through surviving landscape drawings. In the early drawing of the *Mondsee* (1510; Germanisches Nationalmuseum, Nuremberg) he already declares his independence of the Danube school in the economy of line and description. The foreground is left bare, the background suggested only by a thin, jagged line of mountains, and the effect of distance is created by the placing of the horizontals of the bridge against the line of receding pollarded trees. Later his conception of landscape becomes more subjective; the *View of Feldkirch* (1523; British Museum, London) concentrates less on the city than on the strange and fantastic tree in the foreground, which by the loosening and thinning of the pen-work appears to be growing in front of the spectator's eyes.

Hughes Arthur 1832–1915

The English painter Arthur Hughes was influenced by the work of the Pre-Raphaelite Brotherhood. After training in London at the Government School of Design and the Royal Academy Schools, he came into the orbit of first D.G. Rossetti, then Millais. Sharing the Pre-Raphaelite desire to depict intensely emotional incidents in mi-

Arthur Hughes: Ophelia; oil on canvas; 105×52cm (41×20in); 1859. City of Birmingham Museums and Art Gallery

nutely observed natural settings, Hughes produced works of a distinctive luminous coloring and soft handling (*April Love*, 1855–6; Tate Gallery, London; *Home from Sea*, 1856–62; Ashmolean Museum, Oxford). Later his style became more diffuse; with a lightening of palette and change in landscape mood (seen in *The First Easter*, 1896; William Morris Gallery, London) his works lost their impact.

Hugo of Bury St Edmunds
fl. early 12th century

Hugo of Bury St Edmunds was an illuminator whose birthplace is not known, but who worked in England. There are documentary references to four of his works for the Abbey of St Edmund at Bury. He carved a crucifix with statues of John the Baptist and Mary flanking it, he cast a bell, he made the bronze doors for the Abbey's main entrance (the only bronze doors recorded in medieval England), and he illuminated a Bible now identified as one in Corpus Christi College Library, Cambridge.

The Bible was probably commissioned *c*1135: the Sacrist, Herveus, who found the money to pay for it, was apparently out of office by 1138. Herveus became sacrist in the mid 1120s but so early a date is scarcely possible given the advanced nature of the work's early Gothic script. The main illuminations are on separate sheets of vellum pasted into the manuscript. This vellum had to be specially imported from Scotland, presumably because locally prepared skins were not of high enough quality for the perfect finish that Hugo gave to his paintings. The illuminations have a richness and originality of figure-style and foliage decoration that fully account for the praise lavished on the artist in contemporary records. Furthermore, they embody a style that was of paramount importance for the development of English art in the middle of the 12th century. This so-called "damp fold" style is characterized by areas of drapery that cling to the body, and are divided from each other by single pipe folds which both model and articulate the forms. By *c*1150 the style had spread to Winchester, Canterbury, and Durham and had been transmitted to the Abbey of Liessies in Hainault. Artists working in Winchester particularly felt the influence, not only of Hugo's figure-style, but also of his vocabulary of foliage forms.

Hugo's other remarkable contribution was technical. Not only are his figures wonderfully graceful in pose, but the pigments with which they are painted are almost unbelievably refined and the color is of marvelous intensity and purity. His work is one of the most important manifestations of the concern for craftsmanship which found contemporary expression in the often quoted "materiam superabat opus": "the workmanship surpassed the material" (Abbot Suger of St-Denis). Hugo's art owes a great deal to Middle Byzantine and Ottonian sources and also has certain affinities with contemporary art from the Meuse Valley. In addition, there are clear late Anglo-Saxon elements, for example the small swirls of drapery on the shoulders. Although his exact origins are obscure, his work has all the liveliness and grace of the best English art of the period. The only other work almost certainly from his hand is the seal matrix of St Edmund's Abbey, of which several impressions survive.

Hugo Victor 1802–85

Victor Hugo was not only the leader of the Romantic movement in French literature but also an artist who produced an important body of drawings. His early drawings record his travels in France and Belgium and on the Rhine during the years 1834 to 1843. These at first show a meticulous style influenced by contemporary illustrated travel books (for example, *View of Lierre*, 1837; Bibliothèque Nationale, Paris), and later become more imaginative and Romantic in conception (for example, *Le Tour des Rats*, 1840; Maison Victor Hugo, Paris). His work was visionary, using remembered or imaginary subjects floating in an empty space (seen in *Hanged Man*, 1859; Louvre, Paris). He anticipates Surrealism in his exploitation of chance effects and "automatic" drawing.

Further reading. Barbon, A. *Victor Hugo and his Times*, New York (1976). Richardson, J. *Victor Hugo*, London (1977).

Huguet Jaime c1415–92

The Spanish painter Jaime Huguet was born in Valls, Tarragona. He worked at first in Saragossa and Tarragona, but by 1448 he had established his own workshop in Barcelona; he was the last painter in a Catalan tradition that extended from Ferrer Bassa to Bernardo Martorell. One phase of his activity suggests the Flemish influence of Dalmau; but his masterpieces—the altarpiece of SS. Abdon and Sennen (1460), and the altarpiece of the Chapel Royal of Santa Águeda (1464)—show a naturalistic concern with movement, with light and shade, and with facial expression which exceeds the limits of Gothic formalism and owes more to Martorell. He had numerous collaborators.

Hui Tsung and the Academy
early 12th century

Hui Tsung (reigned 1101–26) was the eighth and last Emperor of the Chinese Northern Sung dynasty. His court at Kaifeng is remembered as one of China's most cultured. Though ineffectual as a ruler, and officiating over the loss of over half of his kingdom, the Emperor was a man of sensitivity and culture and was himself a painter and calligrapher of distinction. The Imperial Academy, which had already reached a position of respect in the time of his predecessors, was raised to a status equal to that of the bureaucratic Boards, thus giving artists an unprecedented standing in court society. Hui Tsung gathered around him the most gifted painters of his time; from contemporary accounts it would seem that the Emperor took a keen interest in their work, and indeed participated in the competitive painting that played a part in the life of this unique Academy.

This elite group developed a school of painting, particularly of bird and flower subjects in a small format, for which they evolved a sophisticated system of composition (for example, *Five-colored Parakeet on Apricot Branch*; Museum of Fine Arts, Boston). The surface pattern becomes dominant and depends on a nice judgment of balance, and near imbalance, of space, form, and line. Their quite unashamedly decorative style of painting, with its exquisite drawing and jewel-like coloring, is diametrically opposed to the aesthetic of the scholar painter. However, the painters of the Academy were also scholars; they developed an allusive quality in their paint-

Holman Hunt: The Lady of Shalott; oil on canvas; 188×146cm (74×58in); 1886–1905. Wadsworth Atheneum, Hartford, Conn.

ing similar to the poetic reference so important in literature. A good example of this is the reported incident of a prize-winning painting of butterflies fluttering around a horse's hoof to illustrate the couplet "The scent of trampled flowers follows the hoofs of the returning horse". The allusive character and poetic content of their paintings and a concern with very carefully controlled surface composition almost to the exclusion of a composition in depth, were characteristics of the Northern Sung Academy of Hui Tsung. These qualities are retained to this day in various schools and styles of Chinese painting.

Although its chief products were decorative works, the main line of landscape painting was also influenced by the Academy. The major landscape painter was Li T'ang (1049–1130), a traditional artist who followed Li Ssu-hsun. He and Chao Ta-nien led the way in adapting the old "master mountain" style to the smaller format requiring a simpler composition and encouraging a more self-conscious use of brush strokes. Thus the Academy was the bridge between the classical landscape painting of the 10th and 11th centuries and that of the stylized Southern Sung. This connection is personified in Li T'ang himself: he outlived the Northern Sung and was persuaded to move to Hangchow to lead the new Academy established for the court of the Southern Sung.

Hundertwasser Fritz 1928–

The Austrian painter Fritz Hundertwasser was born and named Friedrich Stowasser in Vienna in 1928. Largely self-taught, he has always worked on a small scale, mainly in watercolor. He has been influenced by his many travels, especially by a journey to Tunisia in 1951. A wide range of art—including Oriental miniatures, the *Jugendstil* of Klimt and Schiele, and the imagery of Klee—has provided the basis for his unique, imaginative, and poetic style. Unashamedly decorative, and tending towards the abstract, he used many bright colors, often incorporating gold and silver leaf, in flat patterns that frequently dominate the ostensible subject. In 1981 he was appointed a Professor at the Vienna Academy. Hundertwasser has also produced many prints, including woodblocks—inspired by Japanese prints—of great technical complexity.

Hunt Holman 1827–1910

The English painter William Holman Hunt was the son of a London warehouse manager. He left his job as a clerk for an artistic career in spite of strong parental objections, and was accepted into the Royal Academy Schools aged 17; but neither technical confidence nor financial security were to come easily. One of Hunt's fellow students was John Everett Millais. Hunt and Millais discussed the artificiality of contemporary art and, following the aesthetic of Ruskin, determined to "go back to Nature". In their enthusiasm for the naivety of art before the revered Raphael they were joined by another dissatisfied youth, D.G. Rossetti, and in 1848 the "Pre-Raphaelite Brotherhood" was formed.

The principles contributed particularly by Hunt to this short-lived association are embodied in *Rienzi* (1848–9; private collection). Each element of the painting was executed before the motif, "abjuring altogether brown foliage, smoky clouds, and dark corners, painting the whole out of doors, direct on the canvas itself, with every detail I can see, and with the sunlight brightness of the day itself". The subject is characteristically high-minded: an Italian patriot and revolutionary, modeled by Rossetti, swearing an oath over the dead body of his young brother.

Hunt's painting *A Converted British Family Sheltering a Christian Priest from the Persecution of the Druids* (1849–50; Ashmolean Museum, Oxford) received critical derision when shown at the Academy exhibition. Though rich in biblical symbols such as vines, corn, and fishing nets, it retains credibility on a factual level, thus exemplifying Hunt's aim in all his religious works. The frames of these works are often inscribed with scriptural quotations; here they refer to the theme of persecution. Hunt achieved an almost preternatural luminosity by painting over a wet, white ground in a laborious, piecemeal manner reminiscent of fresco. The overall sharpness of focus and his casual-looking disposition of figures offended prevalent canons of centralized composition, while the angularity of his poses seemed willfully unattractive.

When *Valentine Rescuing Sylvia from Proteus* (1850–1; City of Birmingham Museums and Art Gallery) was attacked in the Press, the greatly respected Ruskin came to its defence with heartening praise for its "truth" and "finish". *The Hireling Shepherd* (1851–2; City of Manchester Art Gallery) derives partly from the pastoral imagery of Ruskin's ecclesiastical *Notes on the Construction of Sheepfolds*, published in 1851. The landscape was painted in summer near Ewell, Surrey, where Millais worked simultaneously on *Ophelia* (Tate Gallery, London). Flirting with a shepherdess whom he teases with a death's-head moth, and neglecting his flock, the hireling is intended to symbolize clergymen preoccupied by esoteric theological issues. The picture can be interpreted more specifically in terms of the topical dispute between High Church and Low Church Anglicans. Its purchase by a naturalist testifies to the "scientific" precision of Hunt's observation.

Executed by moonlight, *The Light of the World* (1851–3; Keble College, Oxford) shows Christ knocking at the weed-choked door of the human soul. As usual, Hunt insisted on the painting of every detail from an actual object, having Christ's lantern, for instance, specially manufactured for the purpose. *The Awakening Conscience* (1853–4; Tate Gallery, London) is a modern life counterpart to the last-mentioned work. A kept woman remembers the innocence of her childhood and is stirred to repentance. Light—for "Enlightenment"—is again the central symbol; the "light of other days" in the lyric of a song on the piano is actualized in the sunny brilliance of the garden out into which the girl stares through a window. The hallucinatory clarity of Hunt's technique befits her state of heightened awareness, while her predicament is epitomized in the detail of a cat tormenting a trapped bird beneath the table of the gaudily furnished room. Such subject matter, tackled also by Millais and Rossetti about this time, parallels social concerns in contemporary literature, notably Dickens's novels.

His desire for historical accuracy in sacred subjects led Hunt to paint *The Scapegoat* (1854–5; Lady Lever Art Gallery, Port Sunlight) entirely beside the salt-encrusted shores of the Dead Sea. Bearing away in its death the burden of sin, the scarlet-filleted animal is a symbol of Christ. The violently dazzling colors of sunset on the distant mountains are rendered with an uncompromising fidelity that well demonstrates Hunt's moral integrity as an artist, his devotion to emotional expression rather than pleasing visual effect.

He scored the great popular success of his career with another work done in the Holy Land: *The Finding of the Saviour in the Temple* (1854–60; City of Birmingham Museums and Art Gallery). Thematically less abstruse than *The Scapegoat*, which was poorly received, it appealed to the public's sentimental attitude towards children as well as to its liking for fact and detail, for instance in the use of genuinely Jewish costumes and faces. It was bought by the dealer Gambart for an unprecedented £5,500 including copyright, became enormously well known as an engraving, and established Hunt as the foremost religious painter of the age.

The Shadow of Death (1869–73; City of Manchester Art Gallery) and *The Triumph of the Innocents* (one version 1876–87, Walker Art Gallery, Liverpool; another 1880–4, Tate Gallery, London) constitute the mainstay of his unprolific later career. In the first, Jesus is seen in an accurately reconstructed carpenter's shop. Stretching out his work-weary arms, he casts an ominous cruciform shadow on the wall. Less ingeniously, the second depicts an apparition to the fleeing Holy Family of the far-from-ethereal spirits of the children martyred at Bethlehem. Its overloaded iconography is explained by Hunt in a long pamphlet.

The principal painting of his old age was *The Lady of Shalott* (1886–1905; Wadsworth Atheneum, Hartford), an early design expanded to allegorize "the failure of a human Soul towards its accepted responsibility". He also produced a life-size replica of *The Light of the World* (c1900; St Paul's Cathedral, London).

His eyesight failing, Hunt was now turning to the written word to propagate the artistic creed he had followed unflinchingly and in increasing isolation since the first days of the Pre-Raphaelite Brotherhood—that is, the exposition of religious ideas in terms of the minutiae of Creation, and, as far as possible, without the intervention of style.

Further reading. Bennett, M. *William Holman Hunt*, Liverpool and London (1969). Fredeman, W.E. *Pre-Raphaelitism: A Biblio-Critical Survey*, Cambridge, Mass. (1965). Gaunt, W. *Painting in Britain 1800–1900: The Restless Century*, London (1972). Hunt, W.H. *Pre-Raphaelitism and the Pre-Raphaelite Brotherhood*, London (1905). Landow, G. *William Holman Hunt and Typological Symbolism*, London and New Haven (1979).

Hurley William *fl.* 1320–54

The English carpenter William Hurley (or Horlee, Hurlee, or Hurlegh) was already well established by 1320 when he was employed at St Stephen's Chapel, Westminster Palace, where he later made the timber vault (1345–8). In 1336 he was appointed chief carpenter for the King's Works south of the Trent. With the exception of the Ely Cathedral choir-stalls his only surviving work is the timber vault (1328–40) of the octagon there, constructed to replace the crossing tower that collapsed in 1322. This immense structure, imitating a stone vault, shows Hurley to have been an outstanding engineer in timber, and indicates the virtuoso quality of his lost work for the court. He died in 1354.

Hyakusen Sakaki 1697–1752

Sakaki Hyakusen was the pioneer Japanese painter of the *Bunjinga* School. He was a skilled *haiku* poet, but his artistic origins are unknown. Earlier artists like Gion Nankai (1676–1751) had genuinely tried to follow the life-style of the Chinese amateur gentleman-scholar painters; but the low born Hyakusen merely followed Chinese styles as a full professional. This became the usual Japanese attitude, as was Hyakusen's eclectic mixture of varied Chinese styles. He was the first to transfer Chinese literary painting to the screen format, as in *Visit to the Red Cliff* (private collection) and the boldly eccentric *Banana Plants and Taihu Rocks* (private collection).

I

Ictinus 5th century BC

Ictinus was a Greek architect of the 5th century BC who worked principally in Athens. A striking feature of all the works attributed to him, which were regarded as the masterpieces of the Classical period, is his originality of design and ornament in a craft that tended to stereotype design. With Callicrates, he was the leading architect of the Parthenon in Athens. The Parthenon is the prime example of the Doric Order, but incorporates novel features such as the Ionic frieze. He also collaborated in the planning of the Hall of the Mysteries (Telesterion) at Eleusis, being responsible for its remarkable span of roof. He was alleged to have been the architect of the Temple of Apollo at Bassae in Arcadia, a Doric building which includes an Ionic colonnade within and the earliest known examples of Corinthian column capitals. Ictinus also wrote a treatise on the Parthenon.

Inayat *fl.* late 16th–early 17th century

The Mughal artist Inayat was born in the Imperial household and worked in the reigns of three Mughal emperors, Akbar (1556–1605), Jahangir (1605–1627), and Shah Jahan (1628–1658). His early works, which are to be found in the British Museum, London, include the *Babur-*

Robert Indiana: The American Dream; oil on canvas; 183×153cm (72×60in); 1961. Museum of Modern Art, New York

nama done in collaboration with Bishndas, and the *Akbar-nama*. Two other works, *Muzaffar Khan Taking Leave of Akbar* and *Sayyid Abd Allah Khan Brings News of Bengal Conquest* are both in the Chester Beatty Library Dublin. An animal drawing by Inayat (a wild goat or a *Markhor*, c1607) is in the Victoria and Albert Museum, London. He showed special skill in rendering night scenes and figures illuminated by firelight. Typical of these is *Ascetics Study by Firelight* in the British Museum, London (dated 1630).

Indiana Robert 1928–

The American painter Robert Indiana was originally called Robert Clarke but changed his surname to that of his native state. Indiana uses road signs and other public signs and symbols with altered lettering to make a stark and challenging visual statement. *The Red Diamond Die* (1962; Walker Art Center, Minneapolis) and *The Black Yield Brother 3* (1963; private collection) demonstrate obsessions with motoring, sex, and food that the artist has turned into a powerful commentary on modern American life. Indiana moved to New York in 1956 and settled in lower Manhattan. His friendship with Elsworth Kelly, Jack Youngerman, and James Rosenquist placed him in a group of Hard Edge abstractionists at a time when Action Painting was the style of the majority in New York.

Ingres J.-A.-D. 1780–1867

The French history, portrait, and genre painter Jean-Auguste-Dominique Ingres is conventionally seen as the upholder of Neoclassicism in France, in opposition to Delacroix and Romanticism. This view has been fostered by Ingres' own teachings on art, which assert a strict classical aesthetic, the supremacy of line over color. However, his painting in fact shows a variety of styles and a number of influential stylistic innovations. His subject matter includes the conventional classicist depictions of Greek and Roman scenes, and traditional Raphaelesque religious painting, but also genre scenes of French medieval history and exotic Near Eastern subjects. Today, Ingres is most appreciated for his portraiture which he saw as an inferior genre, rather than for the large works with which he fought his battle against the Romantics.

Born in Montauban, Ingres was guided towards the arts by his father (himself a minor artist), and entered the Academy of Toulouse in 1791. In 1797 he went to Paris to study in the studio of J.-L. David. He won the Grand Prix de Rome in 1801, but was unable to take it up until 1806. He remained in Italy until 1824, returning to Paris as an established artist. Though he received official recognition at this time, and had a flourishing teaching studio, his dogmatism and sensitivity to criticism led him into conflict with the critics. He withdrew to Rome again in 1835, this time as Director of the French Academy. He felt isolated from and misunderstood by his contemporaries, and abstained from showing his work in public for many years. On his return to Paris in 1841 he received a warm welcome; he remained there, holder of many high official honors, until his death in 1867.

His student years in Paris (1797–1806) exposed Ingres to a number of radical tendencies which later left their mark on works he saw as classical and orthodox. The archaic linear quality advocated in David's studio by the Primitifs led by Maurice Quay, and also seen in Flaxman's engravings, is vividly reflected in the early *Venus Wounded by Diomedes* (c1803; formerly, Collection of Baron Robert von Hirsch, Basel), and returns later in a subdued form as linear distortion for formal or expressive purposes. Archaic hyperrealism is seen in another early work, *Napoleon I on the Imperial Throne* (1806; Musée de l'Armée, Paris). Critics characterized it as "Gothic", referring to a van-Eyckian precision of detail. Thus Ingres before his first trip to Rome was in many senses an artistic revolutionary, in ways that affected his supposedly orthodox mature style.

Ingres remained in Rome after the end of his four-year term at the French Academy. He became acquainted with the French officials living in Rome under the Napoleonic occupation, who became the subject of a series of portraits. The early portraits are often set against a background of landscape, a device used in the portrait of *Mademoiselle Rivière* (1805; Louvre, Paris), where a fresh green landscape with a calm silvery river serves as the backdrop for a portrait of a 15-year-old girl. From the Italian period, the portraits of *Granet* (c1807; Musée Granet, Aix-en-Provence) and *M. Cordier* (1811; Louvre, Paris) are set against a background of a Roman hillside on a stormy evening and use the setting to bring out moods and personality characteristics in the sitter. Also from the Roman period date a group of exquisite pencil drawings of French officials and English tourists, commissions accepted by Ingres because of financial necessity (for example, *Sir John Hay and his Sister Mary*, 1816; British Museum, London).

Ingres' later portraits are usually set in interiors, and are characterized by the use of a rich material setting, in which luxurious fabrics and jewels are used to bring out the social position of the sitter. Painted with minute realism, they recreate for us the opulence of the Second Empire. An example is *Madame Moitessier Seated* (1856; National Gallery, London). This painting uses the device of reflection of the sitter in a mirror—one of Ingres' favorite techniques—to give a profile as well as a three-quarter view. The pose of Madame Moitessier is based on an antique model, a Roman fresco at Herculaneum. These portraits often have a compelling psychological presence, as in the *Portrait of Louis-François Bertin* (1832; Louvre, Paris).

The paintings that embody Ingres' doctrinaire views about art are less accessible to us today because their rigid conformity to classical rules seems formal and dogmatic. *The Apotheosis of Homer* (1827; Louvre, Paris) is based on Raphael's *School of Athens*, and uses a pyramidal composition placed frontally before a Greek temple. The carefully documented figures of artists and writers are arranged symmetrically around Homer, moving in a hierarchy from the ancients near the apex to the moderns at the base. In religious painting, a Raphaelesque prototype is often used, as in the *Virgin with the Host* (1854; Louvre, Paris). In many of these works, such as *The Martyrdom of St Symphorien* (1834; Autun Cathedral), the intellectual scheme is so heavily worked and apparent to the eye that the painting is a failure.

One of the richest themes of Ingres' genre painting was the exoticism of the harem, which he paints with voluptuous sensuality. *Odalisque with Slave* (William Hayes Fogg Art Museum, Cambridge, Mass.) contrasts the richly patterned setting with the fluid, linear contours of the body of the odalisque. Ingres does not attempt to render the precise anatomical line of the body, but to create an arabesque of abstract beauty which translates the grace

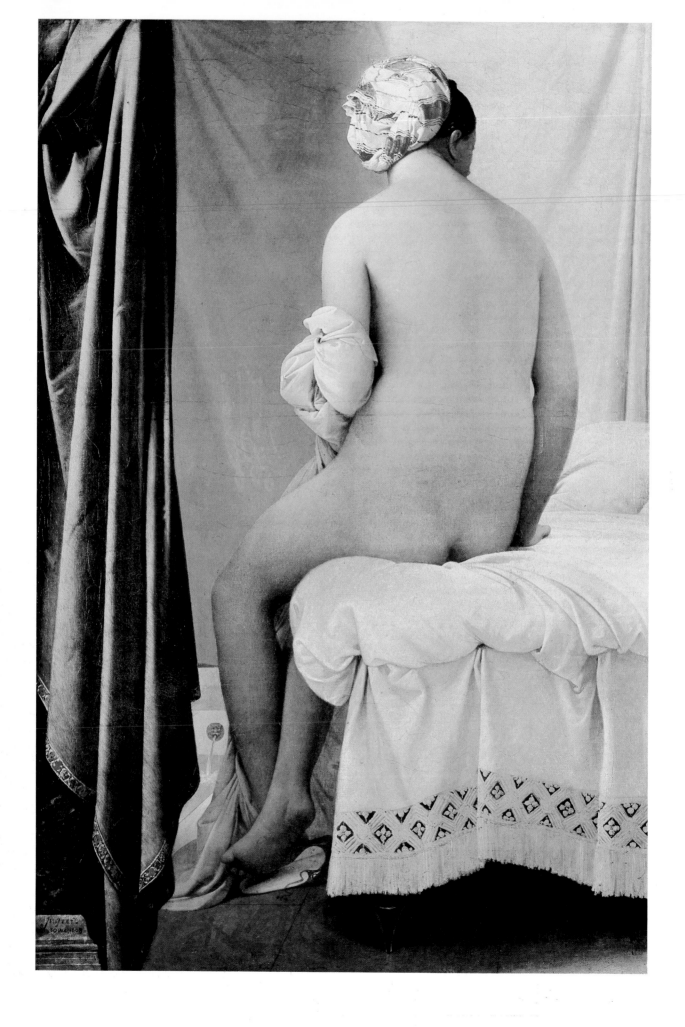

and abandon of the odalisque. He also painted genre scenes drawn from literature or from French history; these, like the larger works, are perfectly finished in every detail, and show the clear brilliant color that Ingres preferred to the chiaroscuro of Delacroix. He adapted his style to his subject, using an archaic, box-like space for a medieval subject, as in *Paolo and Francesca* (1819; Musée des Beaux-Arts, Angers).

Ingres' immediate influence among his pupils was strong, but, with some notable exceptions such as Théodore Chassériau, it led to insipid painting, since Ingres' official doctrines were not always successful when carried out by other hands. His stylized, schematic qualities influenced later artists such as Renoir, Degas, and Picasso.

Further reading. Friedländer, W. *David to Delacroix*, Cambridge, Mass. (1952). Rosenblum, R. *J.A.D. Ingres*, London (1967). Wildenstein, G. *Ingres*, London (1954).

Inness George 1825–94

The American landscape painter George Inness was born on a farm in New York State. He spent his youth in New York City, first exhibiting at the National Gallery when aged 19. He was made an Academician in 1853. His early works are broad, bright, and idealized landscapes in the manner of the Hudson River School (for example, *The Old Mill*, 1849; Art Institute of Chicago). Inness evolved his mature works through the influence of the Barbizon School during his visits to France and Italy between 1870 and 1874. His late works (for example, *Rainbow over Peigigia*, 1875; Museum of Fine Arts, Boston) reflect the soft forms of J.-F. Millet and Corot, as well as the pantheistic teachings of Emanuel Swedenborg. Innes eventually settled at Montclair, New Jersey, and died while in pursuit of the Picturesque at Bridge-of-Allan, Scotland.

Ipoustéguy Jean 1920–

The French sculptor Jean Ipoustéguy was born in Dan-sur-Meuse. In 1938 he studied with Robert Lesbounit in Paris. He was commissioned to execute frescoes and stained glass windows for the church of St

J.-A.-D. Ingres: The Valpincon Bather; oil on canvas; 146×98cm (57×39in); 1808. Louvre, Paris

Jacques de Montrouge, Paris (1947–9). Ipoustéguy designed tapestries as well, but since 1949 has concentrated entirely on sculpture. His sculpture has been both Abstract and figurative, with bodies emerging from the mass of material (an example is *Man Pushing the Door*; bronze; 1966; Hirshhorn Museum and Sculpture Garden, Washington, D.C.). Frequently emphasizing sexual organs, Ipoustéguy's sculpture is brutal and aggressive with a strong element of the surreal.

Israels Jozef 1824–1911

The Dutch painter, etcher, and watercolorist Jozef Israels was the leading figure painter of the Hague School. His humanitarian treatment of peasant subjects and his richly colored and painted style earned him comparison with Rembrandt. Born in Groningen, he was destined for the Rabbinate, but instead he studied art in Amsterdam and Paris, producing Romantic works in the style of Ary Scheffer (1795–1858). After 1855, his personal contact with the peasants at Zandvoort inspired him to change both style and subject and he slowly came to maturity in the 1870s. He settled permanently in The Hague in 1871 and produced there series of works on the themes of bereavement (such as *Alone in the World*, 1880; Hendrik Willem Mesdag Museum, The Hague) and peasants eating (such as *Frugal Meal*, 1876; Glasgow Art Gallery and Museum). He influenced a whole generation of Dutch painters, the most important of whom is Vincent van Gogh.

Itcho Hanabusa 1652–1724

Hanabusa Itcho was a Japanese painter whose real family name was Taga. He used many pseudonyms until he adopted the invented name Hanabusa Itcho late in life. He studied with Kano Yasunobu (1613–85) from whom he learned both the firm *Kano* line, and Yasunobu's own skill in misty washes. He worked in Edo (Tokyo) in a personal genre style that is often compared with *Ukiyoe* but which is in fact much livelier in line and less idealistic in subject. An outspoken satirist, he was exiled in 1699 for political reasons to Miyake Island where he remained for many years. A notable stylistic feature of his work is the varied and eccentric series of viewpoints from which he paints his genre subjects.

George Inness: Short Cut, Watching Station, N.J.; oil on canvas; 96×74cm (38×29in); 1883. Philadelphia Museum of Art

Jean Ipoustéguy: The Death of the Father; marble; 600×310×125cm (236×122×49in); 1967–8. National Gallery of Victoria, Melbourne

J

Jacobsen Arne 1902–71

Born in Copenhagen, the architect Arne Jacobsen reacted strongly to certain aspects of the Danish Neoclassical tradition, which survived into the 20th century. He emerged in the early 1930s as an architect of the International style. An important influence upon him was the Swede Gunnar Asplund (1885–1940) who designed the Stockholm Exhibition of 1930, contributing a lightness and elegance that had not hitherto been special characteristics of modern architecture.

Jacobsen really came into his own after the Second World War with the Munkegard School at Gentofte (1952–6), a milestone in school architecture, and the Town Hall at Rodovre (1955–6), an architectural statement of extreme purity.

Jacobsen Robert 1912–

The Danish sculptor Robert Jacobsen was born in Copenhagen. He lived in France from 1947, returning to Denmark in the late 1960s. Self-taught, he began to make wood carvings in 1931, influenced by German Expressionism. He joined the Danish "Host" group in 1940, and made his first Abstract pieces, a direction confirmed by meeting French sculptor Jean Arp, who advised him to carve in stone. He soon developed his mature style, working in metal from the late 1940s. He welded scrap iron to make small-scale open-form pieces, sometimes painted, in which space is carefully enclosed and defined. In the 1960s he also made larger sculptures and imaginative figures cut from sheet iron. He was a prizewinner in the 1966 Venice Biennale.

Jakuchu Ito 1716–1800

The Japanese painter Ito Jakuchu was the son of a Kyoto greengrocer. He soon gave up the family business to become a Buddhist priest, and devoted the rest of his life to the study and practice of painting. His grounding was probably with the *Kano* School, but he studied the Sung and Yuan works in Kyoto temples, and also contemporary Chinese and possibly Korean works. He painted in two original but contrasting manners: dashing calligraphic ink studies mainly of cocks and hens, and extremely detailed flower and bird works in an expanded Nagasaki School manner. His masterpieces are the great series of paintings of the animal and vegetable kingdom (Imperial Collection, Tokyo).

Janco Marcel 1895–

The Rumanian artist Marcel Janco was born in Bucharest. In 1915 he went to Zurich where he met Tzara and Arp. Both architect and painter, he was one of the original participants in the "Cabaret Voltaire" when it opened in 1916 as a center for the Dada movement; the savage masks he made for performances there were impressive in their provocative power. His work as an artist, though not aggressively iconoclastic, had a Dada inconsequentiality in its crude painting of plaster relief. These were sometimes Abstract, and sometimes based on Cubist still life. In 1922 he returned to Rumania; deprived of Dada stimulus, his work quickly declined into decorative slackness.

Janssens Abraham c1573/4–1632

The Antwerp artist Abraham Janssens painted religious pictures, allegories, and portraits. The turning point in his career was a visit to Italy c1598–1601. Here, in Rome and possibly also in Bologna, his early predilection for a Mannerist idiom ultimately deriving from Bartholomaeus Spranger gave way to a more classicist style. His stylistic development can be traced from the elegant distortions of the early *Diana and Callisto* (1601; Museum of Fine Arts, Budapest) to the sculpturally conceived classicism of *Scaldis and Antwerpia* (1609; a commission for the States Chamber of Antwerp Town Hall, now in the Royal Museum of Fine Arts, Antwerp). Some writers see Caravaggio's influence in the latter, and suggest that Janssens may have made a second trip to Italy c1604.

Jawlensky Alexei 1864–1941

The Russian painter Alexei von Jawlensky studied in St Petersburg with Ilya Repin, a member of the Realist "Wanderers" group. He moved in 1869 to Munich where he abandoned realism for Jugendstil. With Kandinsky he founded the *Neue Künstlervereinigung* in 1909 and was closely associated with the *Blaue Reiter* group. Influenced by Van Gogh and Gau-

Alexei Jawlensky: Portrait of Clothilde Sacharov; lithograph; 55×43cm (22×17in); c1909

guin, and by Matisse with whom he worked in 1907, he painted simplified forms rendered with flat areas of contrasting colors and heavy blue contours. In his series of *Heads* begun in 1910, Russian folk elements are combined with a mystical conception of painting. In 1924 he joined Kandinsky, Klee, and Feininger as "The Blue Four". His series of *Têtes Mystiques* of 1917 led him to abstraction.

Works can be seen in the Kunsthaus, Zurich, Nationalgalerie, Berlin, Art Institute of Chicago, the Solomon R. Guggenheim Museum, New York, and others.

Jean de Liège fl. 1361–82

Described in 1361 as "faiseur de tombs demeurant à Paris", the sculptor Jean (Hennequin) de Liège had been a pupil and assistant of Jean de Huy in the Netherlands. The principal sculptor of Charles V of France, he carved an uncomplimentary effigy of Queen Philippa of Hainault (1367; Westminster Abbey, London). Later he executed the monument for the head of Charles V in Rouen Cathedral (1368). His simple, severe style and conventional draperies influenced English sculpture. The effigies of the Black Prince (Canterbury Cathedral) and Edward III

(Westminster Abbey, London), both *c*1377–80, are probably the products of his workmanship in Paris. He died in 1382.

Jean d'Orbais 13th century

Jean d'Orbais was a French master mason. He was depicted in the now destroyed labyrinth of Reims Cathedral, which he designed after its Carolingian predecessor had burned down in 1210. The choir and transepts were unusually spacious in design, to cater for coronation ceremonies. He actually built these, and the first few nave bays, although he may not have completed the vaulting. At Reims he introduced bar tracery, a development from the slightly earlier plate tracery at Chartres. He also pioneered the use of *tas-de-charge*: bonding the lowest courses of the vaults into the wall, and also began linking clerestory mullions to the triforium. All these innovations are hallmarks of the mature Gothic style.

Jenkins Paul 1923–

The American painter Paul Jenkins is, like Sam Francis, a second generation Abstract Expressionist who has become associated with art in Paris. His work has moved away from the claustrophobic density of Abstract Expressionism toward the considered open spaces of "color-field" painting. Born in Kansas City, Jenkins studied at the Art Students League in New York from 1948 to 1951. From 1953 he has lived in New York and Paris and developed an Abstract romantic style based loosely on the observation of nature. An example is *Phenomena in Heaven's Way* (acrylic; 1967; Martha Jackson Gallery, New York). His work has been widely exhibited and appreciated in Europe.

Joan Pere *fl.* 1418–55

Pere Joan was the outstanding Gothic sculptor of Cataluña. Little is known about him, however. By 1418 he had completed the fine statue of St George on the facade of the Generalidad in Barcelona. In 1426 he carved, in alabaster, at least a part of the *Lives of St Tecla and the Virgin Mary* for the principal altarpiece of Tarragona Cathedral. His work in the church of the Espírito Santo in Saragossa has been lost, though the contract still exists. His confident and fluent style, possibly Burgundian in background, gives an im-

Augustus John: Portrait of W.B. Yeats; oil on canvas; 50×46cm (20×18in); 1907. Tate Gallery, London

pression of movement and depth which brings to life his essentially narrative subjects.

Johannes von Valkenburg
*fl. c*1299

The German miniature and manuscript painter Johannes von Valkenburg was a Franciscan friar in Cologne. He illustrated two graduals (one is now in the Universitätsbibliothek, Bonn, the other in the Erzbischöflisches Diözesanmuseum, Cologne). Both include inscriptions naming Johannes, and the date 1299.

The graduals are important early examples of Rhenish Gothic work. The initial letters are usually composed within painted rectangles, and contain scenes with figures illustrating the text. The rectangles are filled with diaper pattern and sometimes contain a Gothic architectural framework. The borders of the text are also decorated with abstract or foliated patterns which sometimes tail off with stylized

flourishes. Both initials and borders are often enlivened by animals and birds that perch and leap about them.

The colors of the intial letters themselves are usually dark blue with the architectural decoration in gold. Other colors used were reds, green, and pale blue. The style of the painting is related to north French illumination but with characteristic Rhenish features in the bold, rather heavy rendering of the figures. Numerous later manuscripts have similarities to Johannes' work, particularly within the area of the Rhine and the Moselle.

John Augustus 1878–1961

Augustus John was a British painter and printmaker. He trained at the Slade School of Fine Art, where he was thought to be the greatest draftsman since Rembrandt. However, his facility, spontaneity, and superficial brilliance were no substitute for the profounder virtues. John led a bohemian existence, painting gypsies and also his own rapidly growing family. He sought to emulate Puvis de Chavannes (1824–98) in his large decorative paintings. Some of his most successful early works are landscapes of his native Wales and of the south of France, where he produced his own version of Post-Impressionism. He painted many portraits of members of the official *nouveau riche* and literary establishment, (for example, *Sir William Nicholson*, 1909, Fitzwilliam Museum, Cambridge; and *Lady Cynthia Asquith: Portrait of a Lady in Black*, 1917, Art Gallery of Ontario, Toronto). His portraits of *W.B. Yeats* (1907; Tate Gallery, London) and *Dylan Thomas* (1938; National Museum of Wales, Cardiff) are among his most successful, as are many studies of his family (for example, *Robin*, c1912; Tate Gallery, London).

Further reading. Easton, M. and Holroyd, M. *The Art of Augustus John*, London (1974). Lewis, W. *Blasting and Bombardiering*, London (1967). Shone, R. *Augustus John*, Oxford (1979).

Johns Jasper 1930–

The American painter Jasper Johns was born in Augusta, Georgia, and later studied at the University of South Carolina (1947–8). He moved to New York in 1949, and worked closely with Robert Rauschenberg in the mid 1950s. Johns became one of the leading exponents of the first phase of American Pop art. He took commonplace subjects—flags, targets, numbers, alphabets—but painted them in such a way that they acquired surprising overtones. He would use encaustic paint, applied very thickly, almost in relief, or introduce an unexpected element (such as the face masks above the board in *Target with Four Faces*, 1955; Museum of Modern Art, New York). The painting thus becomes no longer a reproduction of a flag or target, but a unique object in its own right in which the image of a target or flag happens to play a part.

Johns took the idea further with a series of everyday objects cast in bronze and painted, such as beer cans, light bulbs, flashlights, and even a can filled with paintbrushes. In works such as these, Johns suggests an underlying influence from both Marcel Duchamp and the Surrealists.

In the early 1960s, Johns entered a new phase. He began to create large and very

Jasper Johns: Zero through Nine; oil on canvas; 137×104cm (54×41in); 1961. Tate Gallery, London

painterly abstracts to which he affixed various objects—numbers, rulers, letters, even part of an old chair or a cast of a human leg (for example, *Fool's House*, 1962; private collection). These large-scale works are characteristic of John's art as a whole: witty, teasing, allusive, and intended to challenge the spectator. His works can be seen in the Tate Gallery, London, Whitney Museum, New York, Stedelijk Museum, Amsterdam, and in many other public and private collections.

Further reading. Field, R. *Jasper Johns' Prints 1960–1970*, London and New York (1970). Huber, C. *Jasper Johns Graphik*, Berne (1970). Kozloff, M. *Jasper Johns*, New York (1969). Orton, F. *Figuring. Jasper Johns*, London (1994).

Johnson Cornelius 1593–1661

The Anglo-Netherlandish painter Cornelius Johnson was born in London of Flemish parents. His early work combines the influence of Dutch portrait painting with attention to detail derived from English miniature painting. By the 1620s his style had broadened and his painting became more vigorous and atmospheric. Although his work was never as bold and assured as that of his contemporary Daniel Mytens, his later work (for example, *The Family of Arthur, Lord Capel*, c1640; National Portrait Gallery, London) was on a grander scale and reveals the influence of van Dyck in composition and accessories. In 1643 he left for Holland, where his work was much in demand among Englishmen traveling in the Low Countries.

Cornelius Johnson: The Family of Arthur, Lord Capel; oil on canvas; 160×259cm (63×102in); c1640. National Portrait Gallery, London

ling the styles of Sotatsu (*fl. c*1600–30) and Shoi (1578–1651). In 1660 he was appointed official painter to the Sumiyoshi Shrine and adopted its name. Like his successors, he worked for the Shogunal government in Edo (Tokyo). He specialized in conventional illustrations to classical poetry and prose, but his style was more robust and colorful than that of the *Tosa* family.

Jones Allen 1937–

The British painter Allen Jones was born in Southampton and studied at the Hornsey School of Art (1958–9) and at the Royal College of Art (1959–60). In the early 1960s, he was involved in the development of Pop art, though in his case figurative imagery is often overlaid with a rich and

Allen Jones: Man Woman; oil on canvas; 215×189cm (85×74in); 1963. Tate Gallery, London

Johnson Philip 1906–

The American architect Philip Cortelyon Johnson was born at Cleveland, Ohio, and later studied at Harvard. With Henry-Russell Hitchcock he wrote the book which for the first time outlined the characteristics of modern architecture and gave it its name: this was *The International Style: Architecture Since 1922*, published in 1932 to accompany an exhibition at the Museum of Modern Art, New York.

Johnson did not actually start to train as an architect until the early 1940s. He began as a convinced pupil of Mies van der Rohe, as can be seen in the "Glass House" he built for himself at new Canaan, Connecticut, in 1949. Variations on the theme of the glass box followed. In 1958 he collaborated with Mies van der Rohe on the Seagram Building, New York. But the influence of Mies gave way to a more personal brand of neoclassicism (for example the Sheldon Art Gallery, Lincoln, Nebraska, 1962), nurtured by Johnson's academic interest in architecture.

Jokei Sumiyoshi 1599–1670

The Japanese painter Sumiyoshi Jokei, founder of the *Sumiyoshi* School, was also known as Hiromichi. The son of Tosa Mitsuyoshi, he learned the traditional *Yamatoe* techniques. In 1626 he began a copy in 19 handscrolls of the original work of the Heian period, *Events of the Year*; but with many decorative features recal-

abstract use of color (as in *Sun Plane*, 1963; Sunderland Museum and Art Gallery). Since *c*1964, he has been concerned primarily with a type of erotic imagery based on "pin-ups", dressed in fetishistic shiny stockings and high heels (for example, *Wet Seal*, 1964; artist's collection). Details such as the shine on materials or the creases in cloth are often treated almost illusionistically, but the general effect of the pictures is wholly artificial.

Jones Inigo 1573–1652

Inigo Jones was England's first Renaissance architect. He was born in Smithfield, London, the son of a clothmaker. Very little is known of his early career, but he certainly traveled to Italy *c*1600, and lived (perhaps for several years) in Venice. He had returned to England by 1603, when a payment recorded by the Duke of Rutland refers to him as "a picture maker". It was in this capacity—as a designer of elaborate masques—that he was first employed by the English court.

His earliest architectural drawings—executed with a precision and delicacy that immediately distinguish him from his Jacobean predecessors—date from 1608. The following year he was in France, examining the Château of Chambord, and in 1610 he received his first specifically architectural appointment, the post of Surveyor to Henry, Prince of Wales. No buildings survive from this period, but when, in 1613, Jones returned to Italy it was primarily to study architecture. He traveled widely, visiting Rome, Naples, and Florence. Most important of all, he went to Vicenza and Venice. Here in the Veneto he met Vincenzo Scamozzi, and made an exhaustive study of the palaces and villas of Palladio, whose architectural treatise, *I Quattro Libri dell'Architettura*, he had bought as early as 1601.

On his return to England in 1615 he was appointed Surveyor General. Soon afterwards, Jones produced his revolutionary designs for three buildings: the Queen's House, Greenwich (1616–18 and 1629–35), the first completely Renaissance building in England; The Prince's Lodging, Newmarket (1619–22, now destroyed); and the Banqueting House, Whitehall, London (1619–22).

"Solid, proporsionable according to the rules, masculine and unaffected", they broke decisively with England's lingering medieval traditions. They demonstrated his complete assimilation—and highly personal interpretation—of Palladian theory, and also his stubborn resistance to the proto-Baroque innovations of his Roman contemporaries Giacomo della Porta and Carlo Maderno.

Few of his late works have survived. The colossal Corinthian portico added (1634–42) to the west end of St Paul's Cathedral was demolished shortly after the Great Fire, while his plans (*c*1638) for a Royal Palace at Whitehall were never carried out. Of his solitary experiment in town planning, Covent Garden Square (1631–40), only St Paul's Church remains (1631; heavily restored 1795): a remarkable attempt to recreate Palladio's interpretation of the Vitruvian Tuscan Order.

Despite numerous optimistic attributions, Jones probably never designed a country house. However, he appears to have worked in an advisory capacity at Stoke Bruerne, Northamptonshire (*c*1629–35), at Chevening, Kent (*c*1630), and, especially at Wilton House, Wiltshire (*c*1632). The latter exemplifies his rich, but heavy style of interior decoration which had already, at the Banqueting House, provided a suitably grandiose setting for Rubens' *Apotheosis of James I* (1634–5).

Further reading. Allsopp, B. (ed.) *Inigo Jones on Palladio* (2 vols.), London (1977). Orgel, S. and Strong, R. *Inigo Jones: the Theatre of the Stuart Court* (2 vols.), Berkeley, Calif. (1973).

Inigo Jones: the Queen's House, Greenwich; built 1616–18 and 1629–35

Jongkind Johan 1819-91

The Dutch painter and printmaker Johan Barthold Jongkind was born near Rotterdam, but from 1846 onwards he spent most of his time in France. His early landscapes tend to be dark in tone and deliberately composed. From the 1860s, however, his touch became lighter, his composition freer, and his exploitation of light and atmosphere more pronounced. He became friendly with Boudin and the young Claude Monet, who always acknowledged his debt to Jongkind. His views of Honfleur and of Notre-Dame of Paris certainly influenced Monet. He was also an accomplished watercolorist: his achievements were much praised by the Neo-Impressionist painter, Paul Signac. He contributed, too, to the revival of etching in the 1860s.

Johan Jongkind: The Harbour at Honfleur; etching; 25×33cm (10×13in); 1866. Rijksmuseum, Amsterdam

Jordaens Jacob 1593-1678

The Flemish painter Jacob Jordaens was born in Antwerp and spent most of his working life there. He studied under Adam van Noort, whose daughter he married. At the time of his admission to the guild, in 1615, he was described as a "water scilder"—an artist who painted on tempera. As far as we know, Jordaens was primarily an oil painter, although he designed numerous tapestries, which entailed the preparation of large watercolor cartoons.

During the period when Jordaens began to work on his own account, Rubens was firmly established as the leading master in Antwerp, and the precocious van Dyck was just beginning to paint. Although Jordaens never studied directly under Rubens, he could not but be strongly influenced by the older man. Early studies suggest a certain amount of collaboration between Jordaens and van Dyck in the years before 1620, while the two were working as Rubens' assistants. All three seem to have had a hand in *Christ in the House of Simon the Pharisee* (c1618–20; Hermitage Museum, Leningrad).

The forms of an early Jordaens, such as the *Allegory of Fruitfulness* (or *Fertility*, c1617; Alte Pinakothek, Munich) indicate an obvious debt to Rubens. The sinuous interplay of line around which the composition has been constructed owes a debt to the Mannerist tradition, whereas the presence of certain realistic physical details suggests the work of Caravaggio. Several years later, the artist painted a second version of this theme, now in Brussels

(c1625; Musées Royaux des Beaux-Arts de Belgique). In composition this is a much tighter work, with the inevitable luxuriousness of the subject matter held in play by a system of dominant verticals. Later he returned to this subject again (one example c1645, now in the Wallace Collection, London).

This compositional tendency continued in other works of the 1620s, such as the Florida *Judgment of Paris* (c1620–5; Samuel H. Kress Collection, Lowe Gallery of the University of Miami, Coral Gables). Although the picture contains a large number of figures, dominant centralizing motifs impose a curiously restrained atmosphere. Jordaens worked once more beside van Dyck and Rubens in 1628, when each of the younger men provided an altarpiece to flank the older man's *Mystic Marriage of St Catherine* (1628) for the Augustijnenkerk in Antwerp. Jordaen's contribution, *The Martyrdom of St Apollonia* (1628), is a much more animated work than his earlier pictures, mentioned above. However, the abundance of varied forms is not lucidly organized, which has an extremely disruptive effect on the essential narrative of the composition. The slightly later altarpiece of *The Church Triumphant* (National Gallery of Ireland, Dublin) is rather more coherent, although it seems anecdotal by comparison with the grand religious pictures of Rubens.

Jordaens seems to have been happier when working within a narrower format. In his picture *The Fruit Seller* (c1625;

substantially reworked c1635; Glasgow Art Gallery and Museum), the main figure stands out in contrast to the artificially lit couple within the doorway, which provides a firm central accent to the composi-

Jacob Jordaens: Study of a Bearded Man with a Censer Descending a Step; ink, wash, and body color over chalk on paper; 52×29cm (20×11½in). Boymans-van Beuningen Museum, Rotterdam

tion. The florid Mannerist decoration of the door frame prevents the architecture from dominating the scene, enlivening the surface and amplifying the cheerful mood of the figures. This sort of picture reaches its high point of development in Jordaens' Flemish genre pieces, *The King Drinks* (*c*1638; Musées Royaux des Beaux-Arts de Belgique, Brussels) and *As the Old Sing, So the Young Twitter* (1636–40; Royal Museum of Fine Arts, Antwerp).

Both depict a festive gathering grouped around a table. Each composition is anchored by a frontal figure, placed slightly off-center, retaining the cohesion of the richly varied groups without mitigating the rumbustious and festive air of either.

Owing to Rubens' increasing infirmity, more and more work came Jordaens' way during the later 1630s. In 1635 he helped paint the triumphal arch of Philip IV, and in 1637 executed the *Apollo and Marsyas*, now in the Prado, Madrid. Both these works had been designed by Rubens. In 1639 Jordaens began a series of decorations for the Queen's House in Greenwich: another commission which had originally been given to Rubens. When the great man died the following year, it was apparent to the English agent at Antwerp that Jordaens was now the "prime painter here". He remained so for the next 30 years.

During the 1640s a vast number of commissions kept Jordaens and his assistants busy, often working on huge oil paintings and tapestry cartoons. Such pressure was not conducive to high quality. One of the most impressive of the monumental pictures executed during these years was *The Triumph of Frederick Henry* covering the walls of the Huis ten Bosch ("House in the Woods", a Royal country retreat near The Hague). Entirely the work of Jordaens himself, it was completed in 1652. The work is filled almost to bursting point with figures, swamping the architectural setting. In *Christ Among the Doctors* (1665; Mittelrheinisches Landesmuseum, Mainz), the rigidly symmetrical disposition of the numerous figures echoes that of the architecture. As a result, Jordaens' characters are powerless to animate the composition, despite their variety of dress and expression.

Jordaens also painted portraits. The painting of his younger daughter Anna Catherina (undated; Collection of the Marquess of Bute, Mt Stuart, Island of Bute, Scotland) reveals a remarkable lightness of touch when contrasted with the artist's more usual subject matter. Similarly, the *Portrait of a Girl and a Boy with a Dog and Sheep in a Landscape* of the late 1640s (formerly in the Hallsborough Gallery, London) is a radiant picture, which avoids potential sentimentality by a well-chosen balance of figures, landscape, and decorative motifs.

Jordaens apparently designed a set of tapestries as early as 1620, although these have not survived. In the 1620s he executed the suite of *The History of Alexander the Great* (for example, *Alexander Wounded at the Battle of Issus*, Holyrood House, Edinburgh) and the very popular *Scenes from Country Life* (for example, *Huntsman Resting with Hounds*, 2 versions; Kunsthistorisches Museum, Vienna). *The Story of Ulysses* series (for example, *Ulysses Threatening Circe*, Palazzo del Quirinale, Rome) dates from the 1630s. After Rubens' death, he contributed two designs to the *Achilles* series (for example, *Thetis Leading Achilles to the Oracle*, Museum of Fine Arts, Boston), begun by the older man and, in 1644, he began a suite of eight *Flemish Proverbs*. His last known essay in this field was *The History of Charlemagne* (Palazzo del Quirinale, Rome) which dates from the 1660s.

There are a great many surviving drawings by Jordaens, in a variety of techniques. In addition to ink and chalk, he used watercolor extensively in the preparation of preliminary sketches. As one might expect from his broad manner of execution, he was little interested in print-

Jacob Jordaens: The Four Evangelists; oil on canvas; 133×118cm (52×46in); c1620–5. Louvre, Paris

making. The seven etchings he made himself are not technically outstanding. During his lifetime, 31 engravings were made by other men after Jordaens' drawings.

It cannot be said that Jordaens' compositions compare with those of Rubens in their sense of mass and movement, nor with those of van Dyck in pathos. He was most successful with a less elevated subject matter, such as his festive genre scenes, which build creatively upon the Flemish tradition of the 16th century. For this reason, his productions are often criticized as vulgar, pedestrian, and anecdotal. However, he could certainly work effectively enough in the Grand Manner even though it was not his forte: to be rated second only to Rubens and van Dyck in this respect hardly betokens inferior status. While his more illustrious associates were frequently absent from the Netherlands, Jordaens never traveled far from Antwerp, throughout a long career, spanning 60 years. His art constitutes what is probably the single most important thread of continuity in the history of Flemish Baroque painting.

Further reading. Hulst, R.A. d' *Jordaens Drawings* (4 vols.), Ghent (1974). Gerson, H. and Ter Kuile, E.H. *Art and Architecture in Belgium: 1600–1800*, Harmondsworth (1960). Jaffe, M. *Jordaens*, Ottawa (1968). Puyvelde, L. van *Jordaens*, Paris (1953). Puyvelde, L. van (trans. Kendall, A.) *Flemish Painting in the Age of Rubens and van Dyck*, London (1971).

Jorn Asger 1914–73

The Danish painter, sculptor, and ceramist Asger Jorn was born at Vejrum. He moved to Silkeborg in 1929, and from 1936 to 1937 studied at Léger's Académie Contemporaine, Paris. In 1937 he helped to decorate Le Corbusier's Pavilion des Temps Nouveaux, Paris. Throughout the period of the Nazi occupation of Denmark during the Second World War Jorn published a banned periodical. He founded CoBrA in 1948. From 1953, Jorn lived in Paris and Albisola. He was cofounder of the International Situationist movement in 1957. He died in Copenhagen.

The years 1937 to 1953 were marked by intense creativity and experiment, moving away from Purist influences and Surrealism. In 1940 he developed a calligraphic automatist technique, controlled by linear contours, creating an iconography of crea-

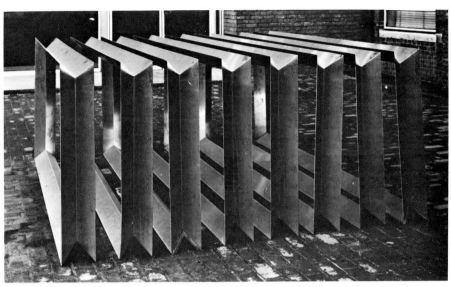

Donald Judd: untitled (eight-modular unit, V-channel piece); steel; 120×313×318cm (47×123×125in); 1966–8. Museum Ludwig, Cologne

tures and figures. From 1951 onwards, a greater luminosity, gestural freedom, and improvisation heralded his mature style. This showed an intense vision, embracing both figuration and abstraction. Jorn made a giant ceramic mural for Aarhus in 1959, tapestries in 1960, and several series of paintings in consciously contrived styles: examples are *The Sun Wearies Me*, 1961, and *Les Enfants*, 1962, both in Galerie Rive Gauche, Paris. He published many books and articles and a large number of graphic works.

Jouvenet Jean-Baptiste 1644–1717

Born in Rouen, the French painter Jean-Baptiste Jouvenet joined the studio of Charles Lebrun after moving to Paris in 1661. In 1675 he became an Academician, and rose to be Director of the Académie. He was, after the deaths of Lebrun and Pierre Mignard, the premier painter of France.

An artist of great facility, he painted decorative cycles for the Salon de Mars, Versailles, the Parlements at Rennes and Rouen, and many altarpieces for Paris churches. *The Miraculous Draft of Fishes* (1706; Louvre, Paris), one of four altarpieces for St Martin-des-Champs, illustrates his debt to Lebrun and to the late work of Raphael. The painting displays the naturalism that set him apart from his contemporaries: the piles of fish given prominence in the foreground were sketched at Dieppe, where Jouvenet had gone to watch the catch being landed.

Judd Donald 1928–94

The American Minimalist sculptor Donald Judd was born in Excelsior Springs, Missouri. Arguably his work was related to the sculpture of Anthony Caro, and to the painting of Barnett Newman on the one hand and Frank Stella on the other. But Judd himself denied any relation to previous or contemporary Minimal art, claiming his works were complete in themselves, excluding all outside references and even excluding the viewer. Made of galvanized iron or aluminum, Judd's sculptures are composed of series of mathematically related identical solids, which became increasingly subtle in their disposition throughout the 1960s.

Further reading. Judd, D. *Complete Writings 1959–1975*, New York (1975).

Junge Johannes fl. c1406–?c30

The leading sculptor in Lübeck between 1406 and 1428, the Hanseatic artist Johannes Junge also worked for patrons in Denmark and Sweden. His delicate, serene figures from Niendorf (St Annenmuseum, Lübeck) are International Gothic in character, and the origins of his style are to be sought in the southern Netherlands. Johannes Junge also executed the alabaster carvings on the tomb of Queen Margaret of Denmark (completed 1423; Roskilde Cathedral) and the elegant alabaster *Pietà* for the church at Sønder-Alslev (National Museum, Copenhagen). It is uncertain whether he was responsible for the deeply impressive oak figures in the convent church at Vadstena, Sweden.

Justus of Ghent *fl. 1460–c80*

Between 1473 and 1475 an artist named "Giusto da Guanto" (Justus of Ghent) is documented as the painter of the *Communion of the Apostles* altarpiece in Urbino. This man is clearly identical with a Flemish master named Joos van Wassenhove, active at Antwerp in 1460 and recorded at Ghent from 1464 to 1469. A Flemish document of 1475 states both that he was an associate of Hugo van der Goes and that he had gone to Rome some time previously.

A handful of pictures such as the *Adoration of the Magi* (*c*1460–5; Metropolitan Museum, New York) have been attributed to Justus from the period before he left the Netherlands, by stylistic comparison with his only documented work, the *Communion* altarpiece. The most substantial of these is the *Mount Calvary* triptych in St-Bavon Cathedral, Ghent. Like the Urbino painting, it reveals points of contact with northern Netherlandish art, especially that of Dieric Bouts. The *Communion of the Apostles* (Galleria Nazionale delle Marche, Urbino) was produced for a confraternity (for the church of St Agatha in Urbino) under Montefeltro patronage (Federico da Montefeltro is actually portrayed in the painting). Joos is usually identified with

Justus of Ghent: Communion of the Apostles; panel; 331×335cm (130×132in); 1473–5. Galleria Nazionale delle Marche, Urbino

Filippo Juvarra: castle of Stupinigi, near Turin; begun 1729-33

the anonymous painter of a large group of pictures in a Netherlandish style executed for the Urbino court. These consist of 28 portraits of *Famous Men* (philosophers, writers, and poets) which were probably painted *c*1473–6 for the ducal study in Urbino. Four fragments from a series of *The Seven Liberal Arts*. These, together with a portrait of *Federico da Montefeltro Attending a Lecture*, were also painted *c*1476–80 for a similar study in Gubbio. The *Famous Men* group is divided between Paris (Louvre) and Urbino (Galleria Nazionale delle Marche) and the *Liberal Arts* between London (National Gallery and Hampton Court Palace), and (until their destruction in 1945) Berlin. It has often been suggested that Pedro Berruguete assisted Joos with both schemes. This seems probable, although it is clear that the Spaniard could only have played a very subordinate role in the work.

Joos is the only Flemish painter of the 15th century some of whose surviving works are actually known to have been produced in Italy. These paintings reveal his steadily increasing mastery both in the handling of illusionistic perspective and in the representation of Italianate subject matter. For these reasons he is a highly interesting forerunner of the rapprochement between Flemish and Italian art which took place during the early 16th century.

Juvarra Filippo 1678–1736

The Italian architect Filippo Juvarra (or Juvara) was born in Messina. As a young man, he was trained in Rome under Carlo Fontana. The vast quantity of designs that survives from this early period in his career proves that he was already a prolific artist.

His great opportunity came in 1714, when King Vittorio Amadeo II of Savoy asked him to enter his service. He designed an immense number of buildings for this patron. Among the most important of these are the sanctuary of the Superga (1715–27), the Palazzo Madama (1718–20), and his masterpiece, the castle of Stupingi (begun 1718), all in or near Turin. Juvarra designed a number of projects for Rome, but few of these were carried out.

These works establish Juvarra as the most important Italian architect of the 18th century. They indicate the artist's know-

ledge of the Italian tradition stretching back to the Quattrocento, as well as the north European tradition exemplified in the great churches of Melk in Austria and Einsiedeln in Switzerland. Their characteristic scenic quality recalls his early experience as a stage-designer.

Other important works by Juvarra are the churches of S. Filippo Neri, Turin (1715), S. Croce, Rome (begun in 1718), and the Carmine, Turin (1732–6; restored after war damage, 1950–3), the Palazzo Birago della Valle, Turin (1716), the house built for Signor Rica di Convasolo, Turin (1730), the Palazzo d'Ormea, Turin (1730), the royal chapel and other works of the Veneria Reale palace complex in the Po Valley (1714–26), and the Castello in Rivoli (1718–21). He visited Portugal, London, and Paris, as well as Madrid, where he died while engaged on work for Philip V.

Juvarra was not so much an innovator as an extremely sophisticated composer of current ideas, with which he achieved novel and distinctive results. In this respect he is justly comparable with Tiepolo, his near-contemporary in the pictorial arts.

K

Kahlo Frida 1910-54

The Mexican painter Frida Kahlo was born in Coyoicoán, Mexico City; her mother was Mexican, her father German. She began painting at the age of 15 while recovering from a road accident that condemned her to a life of pain and increasing disability. Kahlo sent her works to the painter Diego Rivera, who encouraged her, and in 1928 they married. Drawing in some degree on Surrealism, but more importantly on popular Mexican art (such as painted votive images), she created a series of highly original, often harrowing, self-portraits that are, in part, an ironic adaptation of traditional images of the Madonna. Though their immediate subject is her own physical and emotional suffering—her relationship with Rivera was stormy—they also explore political issues and the complex nature of Mexican identity. Well-known paintings include *The Broken Column* (1944; Delores Olmedo Collection, Mexico City) and *Self-portrait on the Borderline* (1932; Mr and Mrs Manuel Reyero, New York). One of her earliest supporters, the Surrealist André Breton, described her work as "a ribbon around a bomb".

Further reading. Herrera, H. *Frida*, New York (1983). Zamora, M. *Frida Kahlo: The Brush of Anguish*, London (1990).

Kandinsky Wassily 1866-1944

The Russian painter Wassily Kandinsky was born in Moscow. In 1871 his family moved to Odessa. From 1886 to 1889 he studied law in Moscow and in 1889 he researched into peasant law in Vologda where he also made a study of folk art. In 1896 he went to Munich to study art, and in 1901 he founded the Phalanx group, the main purpose of which was to introduce advanced French painting to the backward Munich art world.

His paintings of the early 1900s include landscapes executed in impasto with the palette knife, at first somber in color, later acquiring an almost Fauve intensity. At the

Wassily Kandinsky: Panel III (Summer) of the four Campbell panels; oil on canvas; 162×92cm (64×36in); 1914. Museum of Modern Art, New York

same time he painted fantasies based both on old Russia and on an idealized view of the German Middle Ages. These works reflect a rejection of 19th-century materialism which at this point could only be expressed in terms of picturesque evocations of a past age.

This period was also marked by technical experimentation. In particular he used tempera against a dark paper so giving the impression of a transparent surface lit from behind. By painting in colored light against a consistent dark he united every part of the picture in an overall, flat pattern. At the same time he made a number of woodcuts in which the light areas form the positive of the image against a hard black. The very tonal consistency of both light and dark emphasizes pattern, undermining the distinction between the figures and their setting, and so bringing the composition closer to abstraction.

Towards the end of the decade Kandinsky's painting tended still further towards flatness by giving each area of color an equal intensity and creating a shimmering surface that destroyed all illusion of depth. In the series of paintings of mounted riders in combat begun in 1909, the line of the horizon is gradually eradicated, together with other indications of space. In *Composition IV* (1911; Kunstsammlung Nordrhein-Westfalen, Düsseldorf) a residual relationship to this theme survives but the figures have become so simplified, the colors so arbitrary, and the space so confused that it is impossible to read the subject without reference to the earlier paintings.

Kandinsky's preference during these years was for violent apocalyptic themes, originating in the religious imagery of German and Russian folk art. Examples of Kandinsky's works were published in *Der Blaue Reiter*, the almanac he edited with Franz Marc in 1912, by which time his work had gone through many productive changes. These represented an alternative tradition to classical "High Art" and the materialistic view it stood for. Complex scenes involving many figures in violent action allowed him more scope for juggling with representational conventions. By 1913 when Kandinsky painted *Black Lines* (Solomon R. Guggenheim Museum, New York) one can no longer speak of abstraction from the subject. Color and line have taken on a life of their own, with a vitality and expressiveness that avoid mere

pattern making. Works like this are among the earliest nonrepresentational paintings.

Kandinsky's development towards abstraction found a theoretical justification in the influential book *Abstraction and Empathy* by Wilhelm Worringer, published in 1908. It argued that the present hierarchy of artistic values, based on the High Renaissance, was invalid for the consideration of art emanating from other cultures. Many artists created from an impulse to abstract from reality, as opposed to wanting to invoke within the spectator an empathy towards the subject.

At the same time Kandinsky was interested in the ideas of Theosophy, which sought a fundamental truth behind the externals of doctrine and ritual in all the world's religions. The belief in an essential reality underlying appearances provides an obvious rationale for Abstract art. Kandinsky was certainly influenced by Theosophy when in his book *On the Spiritual in Art*, published in 1912, he spoke of "a new epoch of great spirituality" and of the contribution of painting to this. The new art would be based on a language of color, and Kandinsky gave indications as to the emotional properties of each tint. Unlike previous color theorists such as Goethe, he was not concerned with the spectrum but only with the response of the soul.

At the outbreak of the First World War, Kandinsky returned to Russia. Such was the importance of the stimulus he had received from the avant-garde in Germany—not only from the painters Franz Marc and Paul Klee, who were also working towards abstraction, but also from the composer Arnold Schoenberg, whose struggle to liberate music from tonality mirrors Kandinsky's revolt against the subject—that there now followed a hiatus in his work: in 1915 Kandinsky painted nothing, although later in Russia he resumed his activity as an Abstract painter.

After the 1917 Bolshevik coup Kandinsky was kept busy by administrative work, including the foundation of museums throughout Russia and attempts to reform the art school system. His plans for educational courses based on the theoretical analysis of color and form met opposition from the majority of artists: they were more concerned with the pressing problems of production, so Kandinsky's ideas were never put into practice. This convinced him that post-Revolutionary Russia would prove an unsympathetic environment for the development of pure painting,

and in 1921 he returned to Germany.

In 1922 he began teaching at the Weimar Bauhaus. At this stage there were no painting classes. Kandinsky taught the foundation course, based on an investigation of the properties of form; this was the type of art education he had hoped to establish in Russia. The work of his Bauhaus years was more disciplined than that of the prewar period. While he was certainly influenced by the Russian avant-garde (there were strong parallels with works by Malevich and Lissitzky in the floating geometric shapes he painted in the early 1920s), Kandinsky's development had its own internal logic. He was concerned with building up his compositions from the tensions created by each form. This was a concept he tried to codify in his book *Point and Line to Plane*, published in 1926. He sought a theoretical basis for painting as strong as that existing for music. It was inevitable that he should now abandon the amorphous shapes he had used when his theoretical concerns were with color alone.

When the Bauhaus was closed by the Nazis in 1933, Kandinsky went to live in Neuilly near Paris. The biomorphism of Miró and Arp made a strong impact on him, and in the painting of his last years certain passages remind the spectator of living creatures, admittedly impossible to identify. This was no backsliding, for Kandinsky was still concerned with extracting the essential energy of the forms, as opposed to making an abstraction from natural appearances. At its best, his late work achieves an emotional force, through nonreferential means, genuinely analogous to music.

Further reading. Grohmann, W. *Wassily Kandinsky: Life and Work*, New York (1958). Hahl-Koch, J. *Kandinsky*, New York (1993). Roethel, H.K. *Kandinsky*, Oxford (1979).

Kaprow Allan 1927–

The American painter Allan Kaprow is the founder of the modern "Happening". Happenings, as spontaneous, erratic, and mildly delinquent theatrical evenings, were first engineered by the Dada artists during the First World War. Kaprow recreated them as the theatrical and total environmental extensions of Pop art in the late 1950s in New York. He maintains that the idea first came to him in an exhibition of

Jackson Pollock's painting which created a total and all-embracing environment. Kaprow's Happenings range from stage-managed, theatrically constructed environments to such events as *Household*, commissioned by Cornell University in 1964, in which students eat jam smeared all over the body work of an automobile.

Further reading. Kaprow, A. "Happenings in the New York Scene" in Kerman, A. (ed.) *The Modern American Theater: a Collection of Critical Essays*, New York (1967). Kirst, M. *Happenings*, New York (1965). Kostelanetz, R. *The Theater of Mixed Means*, New York (1968).

Kauffmann Angelica 1741–1807

Maria Anne Angelica Catherina Kauffmann's portraits and Classical subjects were much sought after in her lifetime, and she worked in both England and Italy. She first trained under her father in Milan, and went to Rome in 1763 where she painted her *Portrait of Winckelmann* (1764; Kunsthaus, Zurich). In England from *c*1765 she became a society portrait-painter, exhibited regularly at the Royal Academy, and decorated the interiors of several Robert Adam houses. By the early 1780s she had returned to Italy with her second husband, the painter Antonio Zucchi. Kauffmann's portraits were painted in the Reynolds manner, and her highly decorative history paintings were widely known through engravings.

Kazan Watanabe 1793–1841

The Japanese artist Watanabe Kazan painted in both the *Bunjinga* and "Western" styles. Born in Edo (Tokyo), he rose to become an adviser on coastal defence to the local lords of Tahara, and thereby came to study the forbidden Western science and learning. For this he was arrested in 1839; he killed himself while under confinement.

Kazan inherited an eclectic attitude from his painting master Tani Buncho. In native styles he is at his best in his lively sketchbooks, as in the *One Hundred Figures* (Tahara Local Museum). He is best known for his essays in Western realistic portraiture, done with native techniques but using light and shade, as in the *Portrait of Takami Senseki* (Tokyo National Museum).

Keene Charles 1823–91

The British humorous graphic artist Charles Samuel Keene was born near Ips-

Angelica Kauffmann: The Despair of Achilles; oil on canvas; 79×95cm (31×38in); 1789. Private collection

Charles Keene: Southwold Harbour; etching; 10×15cm (4×6in); 1867. Victoria and Albert Museum, London

wich. After training and working for various periodicals including the *Illustrated London News*, Keene joined *Punch*, where he made his name. He also worked for serious magazines like *Once a Week*, illustrating stories by Charles Reade, Douglas Jerrold, George Meredith, W.M. Thackeray, and George Eliot. His popular comic works are witty but never unkind. He was a retiring, shy man, and remained a bachelor. Recognition of his brilliance, and of "black and white" work generally, came late; but he lived to receive the Gold Medal at the Paris Exhibition of 1890.

Keibun Matsumura 1779–1843

The Japanese painter Matsumura Keibun was born in Kyoto. He studied with his elder brother Goshun, founder of the *Shijo* branch of the *Maruyama/Shijo* School. Gentle in temperament, he took easily to the atmospheric and lyrical side of his brother's style, excelling in landscape and bird-and-flower studies, done in soft ink washes with light color. This side of his work represents the standard style of the *Shijo* school. He also developed a decorative manner using black outline with colors on gold background. This can be seen in the interiors of a princely palanquin in the Myohoin, Kyoto. Keibun was buried at the Kompukuji, Kyoto, where his brother and the painter Buson also lie.

Kelly Ellsworth 1923–

The American Minimalist painter Ellsworth Kelly was born in Newburgh, N.Y. He studied at the Boston School of Fine Arts, then at the École des Beaux-Arts in Paris from 1948 to 1954. He returned to Paris to work there from 1958 to 1964. As early as 1953, Kelly was making serial paintings such as *Atlantic* (oil; 1956; Whitney Museum of American Art, New York). His style was a cross between the mathematical series of Josef Albers and the imprecise, emotional "color-field" painting of Rothko. Kelly's work at that period was essentially "hard-edged" and preoccupied with the shape itself rather than its containment. More recently his interest in serial formulae have led him to series of color progressions in which the dominant personalized shape has been subordinated to a routine formula, as in *Blue, Green, Yellow, Orange, Red* (acrylic; 1956; Solomon R. Guggenheim Museum, New York).

Kemeny Zoltan 1907–65

Zoltan Kemeny was a Hungarian/Swiss sculptor born in Banica, Transylvania. From 1921 to 1923 he was an apprentice joiner. He then studied in Budapest, architecture at the School of Decorative Arts (1924–7) and painting at the School of Fine Arts (1927–30), and settled in Paris, working as a fashion designer among other occupations (1939–40). From 1940 to 1942 he was in Marseilles, moving in 1942 to Zurich and working as fashion designer and editor of a Swiss magazine. Then he

Ellsworth Kelly: Green, Blue and Red; oil on canvas; 185×254cm (78×100in); 1964. Whitney Museum of American Art, New York

started to paint again. By 1946, he was working on collages and reliefs, and by 1951 he was making translucent reliefs, designed to be set up in front of electric lights. The metal reliefs that Kemeny has come to be known for started to appear in 1954.

His reliefs give an impression of rhythmic movement through the interlinking of metal objects, either "ready-made" or "found" (for example, *Shadow of the Miracle*; copper T-sections mounted on wood; 1957; Museum of Modern Art, New York). Kemeny acquired Swiss nationality in 1957, and died in 1965 in Zurich.

Kent Rockwell 1882–1971

The American painter and illustrator Rockwell Kent was born in 1882 in Tarrytown, New York. He first studied architecture at Cornell University and then painting under Robert Henri at the New York School of Art (1903–4). His paintings, mainly landscapes and marine subjects, were influenced by the Ash Can School; they were freely painted, expressing the vitality of contemporary rural American life and the grandeur of nature. His popular reputation was founded in the late 1920s and 1930s on his wood-engraved illustrations of the classics, including Shakespeare and the Decameron, and also on his illustrated travel journals. His left-wing political stance is apparent in much of his work from the late 1940s. He died in 1971 in New York.

Kent William c1685–1748

William Kent was an English architect, painter, and landscape gardener. He is chiefly remembered as an architect, one of the major Palladian revivalists; but his early career was spent solely as a painter, working in the Baroque illusionistic style of Sir James Thornhill (1676–1734) and Louis Laguerre (1663–1721).

Born in Bridlington, Yorkshire, he trained in Italy for eight years, returning to England in 1719 in the company of his close friend and lifelong patron Richard Boyle, third Earl of Burlington. It was as a result of Burlington's influence that he turned his talents to architecture, although it was not until the mid 1730s and later that he designed his major works: Holkham Hall, Norfolk (begun 1734), the Treasury Building, Whitehall (1734–6),

William Kent: Rousham House, Oxfordshire; garden landscaped by Kent c1738–40

and the Horse Guards, Whitehall (1751–8), his last building.

As befitted an architect with little or no formal training, Kent interpreted Vitruvian canons with greater flexibility than the other major Palladians. If his exteriors exemplify the restraint, order, and discipline demanded by Burlington as the quintessence of English Palladianism, his interiors are less formal; they are characterized by a richness of ornament that found a historical precedent in the architecture of Inigo Jones, whose *Designs* Kent edited and published in 1727.

Kent's contribution to landscape gardening has long been recognized. According to Walpole, he was the first to have "leap'd the fence and seen that all nature is a garden". Many of his "innovations" had in fact been anticipated by Charles Bridgeman. But it was Kent who broke decisively with Baroque formality. At Rousham, Oxford (c1738–40), and Stowe, Buckinghamshire (c1740), he provided the inspiration for the apparently casual (but in fact carefully composed) landscapes popularized later in the century by Capability Brown.

Kiefer Anselm 1945–

The German artist Anselm Kiefer came to prominence as one of the leading figures of the Neo-Expressionist movement of the 1970s and '80s. A student of Joseph Beuys, he shares the older artist's concern with broad political issues and also his belief that the artist has an almost shamenistic function in modern society. Kiefer's paintings, sculptures and books of photographs reveal a deep concern with Germany's recent past, in particular with Nazism; one of his aims has been to "bring to light things that are covered, that are forgotten". Early works showed somber images of architecture, scorched landscapes, and symbols of German history and myth. Typical works are the painting *Sulamith* (1983; Saatchi Collection, London) and the sculpture *Das Buch* (1985; Los Angeles County Museum), which comprises a huge pair of wings—a recurrent image—attached to a lectern.

Kienholz Edward 1927–

The Californian artist Edward Kienholz is the most savage and powerful of the American Pop sculptors. His art is one of assemblage: the creation of works of sculpture from everyday "found" objects and three dimensional settings; these are peopled by plaster-cast characters to create environments of a ghostly and frequently hideous realism. Although the method derives from Dada, and in particular from Duchamp, the aim is a satirical environmental realism. This is sometimes almost surrealistic, as in the life-size recreation of a lunch counter, *The Beanery* (1965; Stedelijk Museum, Amsterdam), in which all the figures have the faces of clocks. Much more frequently the sculptor's satire is horribly pointed, as in *The State Hospital* (1964–6; Modern Museum, Stockholm) or *The Illegal Operation* (1966; Whitney Museum of American Art, New York).

King Phillip 1934–

The British sculptor Phillip King was born in Tunis. He settled in England in 1945. After reading languages at Cambridge, he studied at London's St Martin's School of Art under Anthony Caro. He then became one of Henry Moore's assistants—and it is symptomatic of the conditions of 20th-century art that he was not influenced by the work of the great British sculptor. Instead, he became one of the first sculp-

tors in Britain to develop the possibilities of glass fiber and polyester, in a series of Abstract creations that are sometimes painted in bright colors.

Kinkoku Yokoi 1761–1832

A Japanese painter of the *Bunjinga* School, Yokoi Kinkoku was born near Otsu on Lake Biwa. A man of many parts, he was Buddhist priest, sword-fighter, painter, poet, musician, and had many less reputable occupations. He made his living in early life by painting for temples and shrines in the *Yamatoe* style. Later he became a follower of Buson, though not his pupil. In his last years he painted in a more forceful, less poetic transformation of his earlier style, specializing in landscape. His works have great visual excitement, using one ink stroke over another, or spattered ink washes in the Chinese manner. His best landscapes have a monumental power rare in the *Bunjinga* School.

Kirchner Ernst 1880–1938

Generally regarded as the leading spirit and most gifted member of the *Brücke* group, the German painter Ernst Ludwig Kirchner was born at Aschaffenburg. After living in Chemnitz he studied architecture in Dresden from 1901. By 1904 he had met Fritz Bleyl, Erich Heckel, and Karl Schmidt-Rottluff. From 1903 to 1904 he studied under Hermann Obrist in Munich, and assimilated the spirit of *Jugendstil* line. It was his sympathy for Post–Impressionism—particularly the work of Gauguin, Van Gogh, Toulouse-Lautrec, and Valloton, which he first saw in Munich—that influenced his early paintings and graphics.

If Kirchner's paintings before 1905 seem to reflect somewhat hesitantly different Post-Impressionist styles, his work in succeeding years became more forceful in color and form than that of his Fauvist contemporaries. His figurative paintings acquired the high-key color and brushwork of Van Gogh and the visionary aspect of Munch, whose influence is apparent in Kirchner's woodcuts of the period. By 1907 he was using line in his paintings to describe their form, in a manner he later described as his "hieroglyph" and which still relate his work to *Jugendstil*. In his *Self-portrait with Model* (1908; Hamburger Kunsthalle, Hamburg), violent, brash colors are combined in a flattened picture plane that recalls the distorted

perspective of Munch.

Kirchner's mature style and his liking for metropolitan subject matter reached fullfilment when, with the other members of the *Brücke*, he moved to Berlin. He became a cofounder of the New Secession in 1910. His woodcut style seems to have been responsible for an increased sensitivity to the expression of color and form in his paintings (as in *Nude with Hat*, 1911; Wallraf-Richartz-Museum, Cologne). Most of Kirchner's energies at this time were expended in formulating his reactions to city life, and in describing the rhythms and relationships of anonymous figures in urban streetscapes. In contrast to the curvilinear rhythms of his Dresden period, his Berlin paintings use jagged lines and angular forms set in uptilted perspectives to accentuate the tensions of his figures (for example, *The Street*, 1913; Museum of Modern Art, New York).

In Berlin, Kirchner's strong personality and his criticism of the work of his fellow *Brücke* artists was largely responsible for the break-up of the group when the *Brücke Chronik* was published in 1913, a personal statement by Kirchner which his friends objected to. He grew increasingly antagonistic towards his former associates, suf-

Ernst Kirchner: Self-portrait with Cat; oil on canvas; 120×85cm (47×33in); 1920. Busch-Reisinger Museum, Cambridge, Mass.

fered from a cycle of depressive illnesses, and retired to Switzerland in 1917 to recover from a nervous breakdown. His paintings became more peaceful in expression (for example, *Moonlit Winter Night*, 1918; Detroit Institute of Arts), but by 1922 he again displayed something of the strength and dynamism of the former period (seen in *The Amselfluh*, 1923; Öffentliche Kunstsammlung, Kunstmuseum Basel). In 1926 he depicted himself in the midst of his former *Brücke* colleagues in a group portrait (Wallraf-Richartz Museum, Cologne). The painting is outwardly calm but nonetheless suggests the tense dominance of his artistic personality. Kirchner committed suicide in 1938.

Further reading. Dube, W.-D. *The Expressionists*, London (1972). Gordon, D.E. *Ernst Ludwig Kirchner*, Cambridge, Mass. (1968). Selz, P. *German Expressionist Painting*, Berkeley (1972).

Kitaj R.B. 1932–

The American painter R.B. Kitaj was born in Cleveland, Ohio. He studied at the Cooper Union Institute, New York (1950), in Vienna (1951), and, after a phase as a seaman and in the U.S. Army, at the Ruskin School of Drawing and Fine Art, Oxford (1958–9) and the Royal College of Art, London (1959–61). Between 1961 and 1967, Kitaj taught in London at the

Paul Klee: Fire in the Evening; oil on board; 34×33cm (13×13in); 1929. Museum of Modern Art, New York

Ealing School of Art, Camberwell School of Art, and at the Slade School of Fine Art. He became an important contributor to the development of Pop art in Britain, with a series of canvases that combine brilliant

draftsmanship, compositions with overtones of Cubism and Surrealism, and deliberately *recherché* subject matter (see *The Ohio Gang*, 1964, Museum of Modern Art, New York; *Walter Lippmann*, 1966, Albright-Knox Art Gallery, Buffalo). Retrospective exhibitions were held in Los Angeles, Hanover and Rotterdam.

Further reading. Haftmann, W. and Kitaj, R.B. *R.B. Kitaj: Complete Graphics: 1963–1969*, Berlin (1969). Kitaj, R.B. *First Diasporist Manifesto*, London (1989). Livingstone, M. *R.B. Kitaj*, London (1985). Ríos, J. *Kitaj: Pictures and Conversations*, London (1994).

Klee Paul 1879–1940

In a massive output of paintings in oil and watercolor, drawings and etchings, the Swiss artist Paul Klee combined a multiplicity of Expressionist and other modern styles to convey, often in a humorous and satirical manner, a personalized vision of 20th-century man's inner imagination, fears, and fantasies. Klee was born at Münchenbuchsee near Bern into a middle-class cultured family. Both his parents were musicians. He soon became an ac-

R.B. Kitaj: From London (James Joll and John Golding); oil on canvas; 152×244cm (60×96in); 1975–6. Private collection

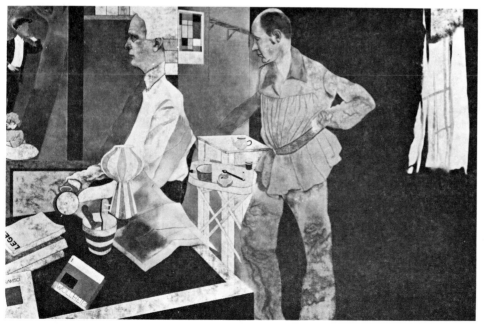

complished poet and musician and played the violin in the Bern municipal orchestra. He had a lifelong interest in the formal aspects of literature and music, both of which stimulated his art.

Although Klee was equally talented at an early age as a painter and draftsman, it was not until he was 35 that he came to fully regard himself as a painter. After his formal education had been completed he studied art in Munich from 1898 to 1900, first under Knirr and then under Franz von Stuck; he received a formal training in figure-drawing under the latter but devoted little attention to color. By this time he had decided to become a painter, and after traveling in Italy in 1901, where he became acquainted with the Western Renaissance tradition, he devoted himself on his return to Bern to a series of 17 grotesque satirical etchings. They reveal his admiration for the visionary symbolism of Blake and Goya, as well as for Ensor and Redon whose work he saw in Paris in 1905.

Klee's interests during this period included early Renaissance paintings and German woodcuts. The literary subject matter of his first etchings also reflects his wide reading, particularly Baudelaire and the French Symbolist writers. Ten of the etchings were exhibited at the Munich Secession in 1906; Klee moved to Munich that year and became familiar with Impressionist and Post-Impressionist painting, including the work of Van Gogh, Cézanne, and Matisse. Under the influence of French Impressionism he began to work from nature, and although his drawing now included color and reflected something of the flat planar distortions of Cézanne and Matisse, he did not abandon the intuitive approach to subject matter that characterized his early work.

Klee's first one-man exhibition in Munich in 1911 brought his work to the attention of the *Neue Künstlervereinigung*, and to Alfred Kubin, whose art Klee's superficially resembled at the time. Through Kubin, Klee was introduced to the circle of Kandinsky and Marc. Klee felt strong affinities with Kandinsky's theories of the spiritual essence of art, and he exhibited his work in the second *Blaue Reiter* exhibition of paintings and drawings in 1912. Franz Marc's interpretation of the rhythmic relationship of animal life also strongly appealed to him, and provided him with a basis for the exploration of the creative life-force which he was later to pursue.

In 1912 Klee visited Robert Delaunay in Paris. Delaunay's individual brand of Orphic Cubism, and his chromatic series of window pictures built up with overlapping color rectangles, further opened his eyes to the potential use of color. The following year he translated Delaunay's *Sur la Lumière* into German. However, it was not until 1914, when he journeyed to Tunisia with August Macke, that the strong light and intense color of North Africa prompted him to write in his diary: "Color has taken hold of me ... once and for all.... Color and I are one. I am a painter". In this, Macke, for long a strong colorist himself, proved a decisive influence.

Although Klee's art after 1914 is clearly indebted to Cubism, and particularly to Delaunay, it never became Abstract but was deeply rooted in nature. Between 1914 and 1920, in landscapes and cityscapes, Klee built up a tapestry of rectangles in prismatic colors resembling mosaics; they were strengthened by the grid-like structures of Cubism and painted with all the intensity of Expressionism. The theme of the city and tower in his work is imbued with the mystical qualities of a new Jerusalem, and as such still carries Symbolist and literary and mythological associations (seen in *City of Towers*, 1916; Philadelphia Museum of Art). In his immediate postwar work Klee was concerned with capturing not just the visual world as he perceived it, but with the processes of creation, genesis, and motion. It was these themes that he analyzed in pictorial terms in his teaching in the following decade.

In 1920 Walter Gropius invited Klee to join the staff of the Bauhaus at Weimar, where he taught at first in the departments of stained glass and weaving. Later he conducted his own course in the theory of forms. In 1925 his *Pedagogical Sketchbook*, which outlined his fundamental theories of points, lines, and planes, was published by the Bauhaus. He produced paintings during these years in a bewildering variety of different styles which he adapted to suit the requirements of content and subject matter. His subject matter included architecture, plant, animal, and human life, and incorporated reference to child art, primitive, medieval, and folk art. At times the strict geometry of his paintings is reminiscent of Constructivist form. In other instances he departed from the structural basis of Cubism to explore the inner world of the subconscious, although

his art in this decade is only tangentially connected to that of the Surrealists, who nevertheless admired his work (for example, *Fish Magic*, 1925; Philadelphia Museum of Art). In 1924 he exhibited with Kandinsky, Jawlensky, and Feininger as "The Blue Four".

It is possible to see in Klee's work during these years two distinct lines of enquiry. First there were his formal exercises in pictorial form, expressing growth and movement through line and plane. But there was also Klee's combination of mythological or philosophical truths expressed in more complex language, which are much indebted to concepts in poetry and literature as they are to visual art. Humor and fantasy are often used to explore deeper meanings, as are subjects depicting pain and grief, an approach Klee described as a "synthesis of outward sight and inner vision". In 1930 Klee left the Bauhaus for a teaching post at Düsseldorf, from which he was dismissed by the Nazis in 1933. His late works increased in size, and the symbolism became more graphic and prophetically doom-laden—yet humor and irony still often lie quite close to the surface (as in *Death and Fire*, 1940; Paul-Klee-Stiftung, Berner Kunstmuseum, Bern). Klee's art continued to bear out his belief that "art does not reproduce the visible, but makes visible".

Further reading. Grohmann, W. *Paul Klee*, London (1955). Klee, F. (ed.) *The Diaries of Paul Klee 1878–1918*, Berkeley (1964). Klee, P. *Notebooks* (2 vols.), London (1961 and 1973). Klee, P. *On Modern Art*, London (1966). Klee, P. *Pedagogical Sketchbooks*, London (1953). Lynton, N. *Klee*, London (1975). Pierce, J.S. *Paul Klee and Primitive Art*, New York (1976).

Klein Yves 1928–62

The career of the French painter Yves Klein was short but fairly sensational. He was born in Nice and received very little academic training. He originally came into prominence with a series of paintings consisting of a single color, at first applied rather thickly but later put on more smoothly. Many of these pictures were blue, which he regarded as the most significant color. Klein was always antiacademic and soon extended his interests to gestural and performing arts. A show in Paris in 1958 (Galerie Iris Clert) simply consisted of the empty wall of the gallery,

Yves Klein: I.K.B. 79; paint on cotton scrim over plywood backing; 140×120cm (55×47in); c1959. Tate Gallery, London

while in the following years he concocted his *Anthropometries*, which had an audience and consisted of nude models, painted blue, rolling around on bare canvas and leaving chance imprints of form. It was a kind of Action Painting through body contact. Although his work was not always well received during his lifetime, Klein was commissioned to produce mural decorations for an opera house at Gelsenkirchen in Germany.

Further reading. Restany, P. *Yves Klein*, New York (1982).

Kleophrades Painter
fl. c500–470 BC

The Kleophrades Painter was the greatest Athenian painter of large vessels of his generation. He was the pupil of Euthymides, and was the last red-figure painter to use the black-figure technique with any proficiency. Some of his early works have subsidiary zones in black-figure. Like the Berlin Painter, he painted a series of prize Panathenaic *amphorae*.

Early in his mature period he painted the wonderful pointed *amphora* in Munich (Staatliche Antikensammlungen; Inv. 2344). There we see Dionysos surrounded by satyrs and maenads, huge figures filled with power and life. Two maenads on the reverse show the painter's great gift for "mood-figures". One dances ecstatically,

head flung back, feverishly pulling at her *thyrsos* rod, a raucous cry on her lips. In contrast, the other maenad sways gently, her expression detached and serene, her lips parted in transcendent joy.

A later piece of his mature years is the *hydria* showing the sack of Troy by the Greeks (Museo Archeologico Nazionale, Naples; Inv. 2422). Here despair and resistance, flight and ruthless violence fill the eye. The simplicity of the woman seated beneath the drooping palm and her companion in despair at the foot of Athena's statue rival Giotto's hooded mourners of Christ (*Mourning of Christ*, c1306; Capella dell'Arena, Padua). The quality of quiet grandeur and lofty seriousness in his figures seems not unlike that attributed to the famous Classical wall-painter Polygnotus.

His last pieces, however, show signs of fatigue. His style had burned itself out and his only follower, the Boot Painter, continued his late weak work on a series of rather poor cups.

Klimt Gustav 1862–1918

The Austrian painter Gustav Klimt was born at Baumgarten, a suburb of Vienna, the son of an engraver. Between 1876 and 1883 he studied at the School of Decorative Arts in Vienna. His early large-scale decorative works were followed in 1894 by a commission to produce designs for a painted ceiling at the Vienna University Hall. Klimt presented his designs for *Philosophy, Jurisprudence,* and *Medicine* in 1896. Two years later he was asked to carry out the work in conjunction with Franz Matsch, who was to paint the centerpiece and *Theology*.

By this time Klimt had already been made president of the Vienna Secession. His art had undergone a radical change, partly as a result of his assimilation of *Jugendstil* and the work of the Munich painters. *Pallas Athene* (1898; Historisches Museum der Stadt Wien, Vienna), shown at the second Secession exhibition, marks this new style. It is characterized by frontality, interest in surface pattern, and the use of gold and other metal. Its inclusion of a tiny naked female figure in the lower lefthand part of the canvas looks forward to paintings and decorative schemes in which sexuality was a predominant theme—one that often caused offence. Klimt's use of a variety of exotic materials was an important device. His interest in ornament was

further stimulated by a visit to see the Byzantine mosaics at Ravenna in 1903; it reached a climax in the huge mosaic frieze Klimt designed for the Stoclet Palace, known as the Stoclet Frieze (1905–11; Palais Stoclet, Brussels; working drawing for the Stoclet Frieze in the Österreichisches Museum für Angewandte Kunst, Vienna).

Philosophy was exhibited in March 1900 at the Secession; it aroused great controversy amongst Viennese academics, the public, and the press. *Medicine* had a similar reception the following year. *Jurisprudence*, shown at the Secession's Klimt retrospective in 1903, was the most decorative of the three but also the most stylized and abstract in design. The influence of the Symbolist painter Jan Toorop is distinctly shown in this work. In 1905 Klimt resigned his commission for the University paintings.

His large allegorical frieze for the Secession's *Beethoven* exhibition of 1902 was as controversial as the University paintings, and accusations of pornography were leveled against it. The motif of the embracing couple was taken up again in *The Kiss* (1908; Österreichische Galerie, Vienna), probably his most famous work. This was exhibited at the first Kunstschau (1908), together with some fine landscapes and female portraits. Portraiture and landscape preoccupied Klimt after the second Kunstschau (1909): both genres show the artist adopting a simpler, more painterly style, devoid of dazzling ornamental effects. It was not until 1917 that his art appeared to be ready to make another stylistic turn—possibly influenced by his knowledge of Schiele's work. But Klimt did not live long enough to explore any new directions fully. He died in 1918.

Further reading. Bouillon, J.-P. *Klimt: Beethoven, Frieze for the Ninth Symphony*, New York (1987). Comini, A. *Gustav Klimt*, London (1975). Nebehay, C.M. *Gustav Klimt: Dokumentation*, Vienna (1969). Vergo, P. *Art in Vienna 1898–1918*, Oxford (1981).

Kline Franz 1910–62

The American painter Franz Kline was born in Wilkes-Barre, Pennsylvania. He studied painting at Boston University (1931–5) and then in London, returning to New York in 1939. His earlier work, which includes landscapes, portraits, and

Franz Kline: Painting no. 7; oil on canvas; 146×208cm (57×82in); 1952. Solomon R. Guggenheim Museum, New York

was designed as a sequence of changing scales and viewpoints, creating dream worlds populated by nightmarish or surreal figures. His paintings included both decorative panels and large easel works. *The Judgment of Paris* (1885–7; Kunsthistorisches Museum, Vienna) combines the spatial unease and veiled symbolism of his engraving series with Klinger's growing interest in sculpture, to which he devoted himself almost exclusively after 1900.

Koetsu Hon'ami 1558–1637

Calligrapher, potter, and designer, Hon 'ami Koetsu was the greatest all-round figure in Japanese art. He was a member of

murals (for the Bleeker Street Tavern, New York, 1940) was relatively traditional in character. But from 1947 onwards, Kline became increasingly preoccupied with abstraction. He is best known for his large black and white paintings, in which a rugged and powerful structure of black forms is imposed on a white ground. These are among the most distinguished productions of Abstract Expressionism (for example, *Mahoning*, 1956; Whitney Museum of American Art, New York).

Klinger Max 1857–1920

Max Klinger was a German painter, printmaker, and sculptor. His pictorial images haunted the imaginations of Symbolists and Decadents, and his innovations in sculpture (for example the polychrome marble monument of a Jupiter-like *Beethoven*, 1902, which he left to the Museum der Bildenen Künste in Leipzig) paralleled those of Sir Alfred Gilbert, Fernand Knopff, and Sir George Frampton. Born in Leipzig, Klinger trained in Karlsruhe (1874), Berlin (1875), and briefly with Arnold Böcklin. He traveled extensively during his life (Brussels, Vienna, Paris, Rome, Leipzig), finally settling in Grossjena near Naumberg, where he died.

Success first came to Klinger through his engravings. Issued in series (such as *On Death*, 1889; *Brahms Phantasy Opus XII*, 1894) between 1879 and 1903, each set

Max Klinger: To Beauty, from the series of etchings "Of Death"; 41×32cm (16×13in); 1898. Graphische Sammlung Albertina, Vienna

Oskar Kokoschka: The River Elbe near Dresden; oil on canvas; 81×112cm (32×44in); 1919. Art Institute of Chicago

the Hon'ami family, who for generations had been appraisers of sword blades—the most astringent form of aesthetic appreciation in Japanese life. Like many artists of his time, he was an adherent of the nationalistic and practical Nichiren Buddhist sect.

Koetsu first came to notice in the early 17th century with his *Saga-bon*, sumptuously printed texts of *No* plays and old poetic anthologies done on high quality paper. His basic mission was to revive the arts of Kyoto's glorious past, and to make them better known to the merchant class to which he belonged. In this he partly resembled the 19th-century Englishman William Morris. Like Morris, Koetsu was very much a man of his age, as can be seen in his wonderfully liquid calligraphy. This recalls Heian *hiragana* works, but is done on top of motifs, either printed or painted, designed by the flamboyant artist Sotatsu.

In 1616 he was given land by the govern-

ment at Takagamine in northwest Kyoto, and there set up a village of artists, potters, lacquerers, papermakers, and other craftsmen. He did designs for the lacquerers and papermakers, the most famous being his *Boat-Bridge* ink-box (Tokyo National Museum), inlaid with his calligraphy in mother-of-pearl. He also set up a pottery and produced powerfully astringent teabowls used in the tea ceremony, among them the very celebrated *Mount Fuji*. Through his association with Sotatsu he is often thought of as the founder of the *Rimpa* School, and his influence on later design was great.

Kokan Shiba 1747–1818

Shiba Kokan was both artist and scientific writer. Born in Edo (Tokyo) he studied with a *Kano* artist; after the death of Harunobu in 1770 he spent a few years making prints in his style. He then studied

with the Nagasaki School artist So Shiseki. He revived European copperplate engraving and pioneered etching, producing prints of Japanese scenes using Western shading and perspective, like the *Ryogoku Bridge* (British Museum, London). He also painted landscapes in imitation of European oils, using chalk pigments mixed with oil or wax. As a writer on European science he was very influential.

Kokoschka Oskar 1888–1980

The Austrian painter Oskar Kokoschka was born at Pöchlarn on the Danube in Lower Austria. His father's family were goldsmiths from Prague. He studied at the Kunstgewerbeschule (School of Applied Art) in Vienna and in 1907 began working for the Wiener Werkstätte, designing fans and postcards. In 1908 a group of artists and architects, who had resigned from the Vienna Secession with Klimt three years earlier, put on a large and important exhibition, the Kunstschau. Here Kokoschka showed tapestry designs, illustrations for his Expressionist drama *Murderer, Hope of Women* and for his fairy-tale *The Dreaming Youths*, and a painted plaster bust—a savage self-portrait—which was bought by Adolf Loos. He also designed the poster for the exhibition.

It was Loos who persuaded Kokoschka to leave the Werkstätte and embark upon a painting career. His many portraits of this period, in which tactile, free brush strokes are used to convey intense emotion, are powerful examples of Expressionist art. They have a penetrating, analytical quality which has caused people to link the artist metaphorically with the name of Freud, Kokoschka's Viennese contemporary.

In 1910 Kokoschka went to Berlin where he was employed by Herwath Walden to draw for his avant-garde Expressionist periodical *Der Sturm*. During this period he also recorded his stormy relationship with the beautiful and seductive Alma Mahler (the widow of the composer Gustav Mahler and later the wife, in succession, of Walter Gropius and Franz Werfel) in two outstanding paintings: *Self-portrait with Alma Mahler* (1912; Horstmann Collection, Hamburg) and the great, symbolic *The Tempest* (1914; Öffentliche Kunstsammlung, Kunstmuseum Basel).

Kokoschka was severely wounded in the First World War. He settled in Dresden in 1917. The famous life-size doll that was specially made for him dates from this time: it became the model for the painting *Woman in Blue* (1919: Staatsgalerie, Stuttgart). Although it depicts an inanimate object, the painting is vibrant with color and pulsates with a life of its own. He continued to paint portraits of great intensity, including many self-portraits. His landscapes and townscapes of many of the great European cities were noted for their visionary power (for example, *Jerusalem*, 1929–30, Detroit Institute of Arts; *London, Large Thames View I*, 1926, Albright-Knox Art Gallery, Buffalo).

In 1934 Kokoschka emigrated to Prague. He painted a symbolical portrait of Tomás Masaryk, President of Czechoslovakia, a man with whose humanist views he felt he had much in common (completed 1936; Carnegie Institute, Pittsburgh). At the 1937 exhibition of "Degenerate Art" in Munich, organized by the Nazis, eight of Kokoschka's paintings were shown. His

Philips Koninck: An Extensive Landscape with a Road by a Ruin; oil on canvas; 137×168cm (54×66in); 1655. National Gallery, London

reply was to paint a large and tragic self-portrait which he called *Portrait of a "Degenerate Artist"* (1937; private collection).

He spent the years of the Second World War in England—years marked by a series of allegorical pictures, and by writings in which he fought for humanist principles. In 1953 he gave his first course at the International Summer School for the Visual Arts at Salzburg under the title "The School of Vision". He then settled in Switzerland. His autobiography—a fascinating story—was published in 1971.

Further reading. Hodin, J.P. *Kokoschka: the Artist and his Time*, London (1966). Kokoschka, O. *Der Expressionismus Edvard Munchs*, Munich and Vienna (1953). Whitford, F. *Oscar Kokoschka—a Life*, London (1986).

Kollwitz Käthe 1867–1945

Born Käthe Schmidt, the German artist Käthe Kollwitz came from a nonconformist background and lived for most of her life in a poor district of Berlin. Her graphics and her sculpture—which resembles that of Barlach—are Expressionist; but her work is more concerned with objectifying social ills than with conveying an inner response. Her early etchings and lithographs are in an illustrative tradition, but her postwar woodcuts are in the expressive Gauguin-Munch technique of the *Brücke* group. In 1919 she was elected the first woman member of the Prussian academy, and in the 1920s depicted the social consequences of the First World War in an emotive, figurative idiom.

Further reading. Klein, A. and N. *Käthe Kollwitz: Life in Art*, New York (1975). Kollwitz, K. (ed. Kollwitz, H.) *The Diaries and Letters of Kaethe Kollwitz*, Chicago (1955). Nagel, O. *Kaethe Kollwitz*, New York (1971). Shikes, R.E. *The Indignant Eye: the Artist as Social Critic in Prints and Drawings*, Boston (1969).

Koninck Philips 1619–88

The Dutch landscape painter Philips Aertsz. Koninck was a pupil of Rembrandt during the early 1640s. He initially modeled his work on his teacher's imaginary landscapes. Later he turned to more realistic views of Dutch scenes which have their origin in Rembrandt's drawings and etchings. Increasingly he developed a speciality in large, luminous panoramas seen from high vantage points, in which the sense of limitless space is heightened by the introduction of tiny figures. Dark cloud formations frequently scud across Koninck's skies, throwing immense patches of transparent shadow over fields, dunes, and winding rivers, and adding a note of melancholy to his work.

Koninck Salomon 1609–56

The Dutch painter Salomon Koninck studied under David Colijns and Nicholas Moeyaert. Based in Amsterdam he was one of the most able imitators of Rembrandt's style. He specialized in biblical subjects, incorporating Oriental costumes and powerful facial types (for example, *The Idolatry of King Solomon*, 1644; Rijksmuseum, Amsterdam). He was also highly successful in his imitation of Rembrandt's effects of light and texture. The measure of his ability is reflected in the fact that Rembrandt's so-called Sobieski portrait in the Hermitage Museum, Leningrad, was once attributed to him.

Since Koninck excelled as an imitator, the limits of his oeuvre are difficult to define. There are signed works by him in Amsterdam, Dresden, Frankfurt, and Rotterdam.

Kooning Willem de 1904–

The American Abstract Expressionist painter, Willem de Kooning was born in Rotterdam and apprenticed as a commercial painter and decorator. In 1926 he went to New York, initially with no idea of becoming an artist. There he met Arshile Gorky and John Graham, founding the nucleus of a Greenwich Village group of artists who experimented with and adapted all that they could learn of modern European art in the 1930s. De Kooning was painting extremely well by 1940. Unlike Pollock and Gorky, he made no radical break in the 1940s from his work of the previous decade.

De Kooning was interested in the separation and overlapping of objects and in emphasizing the space that contains them. These preoccupations are apparent in *Two Men Standing* (oil on board; c1938; private collection) in which the spatial ambiguity adds an element of disquiet to an otherwise straightforward figure study. *Seated Woman* (c1940; Collection of Mrs Albert Greenfield, Philadelphia) introduces a series of studies of women that, growing in intensity of expression and execution, characterizes de Kooning's work of the 1940s and 1950s and provides the perfect subject matter for the Abstract Expressionist technique (for example, *Woman I*, 1950–2; Museum of Modern Art, New

York). In *Pink Angels* (c1947; private collection) the human figure is dismembered, and any corporeal identity is blotted out by miscellaneous linear shapes and an almost ubiquitous pink: a color that was a leitmotiv of early Abstract Expressionist painting. The quality of blotting out is taken further in *Excavation* (oil on canvas; 1950; Art Institute of Chicago), a monumental statement of de Kooning's Abstract Expressionism, achieved after a period of severe retrenchment and study in black and white only. *Excavation* is built up of layers of overlapping forms. Fragments of dismembered sensuous shapes float against a cream background upon which shape is imposed by black lines and enlivened by patches of strong color.

The multiple interests of de Kooning as a painter were fused again in a further series of *Women* (mostly in private collections) in the 1950s. These were increasingly violent, becoming almost monstrous in physiognomy and crude physical reference. The vast scale, and the control of the slashing brush stroke nevertheless achieved the same sort of equilibrium that is found in the best of Pollock. The later works of de Kooning return to a landscape theme which emphasizes the ambiguity of intervening space, one of the painter's most enduring preoccupations.

De Kooning has painted far longer and with more consistently high-quality results than any other Abstract Expressionist painter.

Further reading. Rosenberg, H. *De Kooning*, New York (1973). Waldman, D. *Willem de Kooning*, New York (1988). Zilczer, J. *Willem de Kooning*, New York (1993).

Korin Ogata 1658–1716

The Japanese painter Ogata Korin was the second great master of the *Rimpa* School. He was the son of a rich Kyoto textile designer who had connections with Koetsu's artistic village at Takagamine, hence his interest in Sotatsu's work. But he trained in the *Kano* School, and did not become a professional painter until the ruin of the family fortunes in the 1690s. He moved to Edo (Tokyo) for a while, and developed a style based on the decorative work of Sotatsu, but less powerful and more elegant. His younger brother Kenzan (1663–1743) was a celebrated potter, and Korin painted sharply characteristic designs on some of his dishes.

Korin's monochrome ink style is strange and spiky, as in his twofold screens of plum and bamboo (private collection), where the blossoms are reduced to almost circular design-motifs, a habit which grew in the *Rimpa* School. These shapes appear in red and white in his famous *Red and White Plum Blossom* screens (Atami Art Museum). Here the distorted trees, their trunks covered with gold, green, and blue patches, their roots reduced to a horizontal line on the gold, flank the astonishing silver-and-brown river. This is perhaps the greatest example of the Japanese tendency to treat natural objects as pure decoration. The same can be seen in the *Waves* screens (Metropolitan Museum, New York).

Korin was also a master of the small, delicate fan-painting, based on the Kyoto traditions of the Heian court. There is a fine example of court nobles pasted on a box in the Yamato Bunkakan, Nara.

Kossoff Leon 1926–

The English painter Leon Kossoff was born in London. He studied at St Martin's School of Art and in evenings with David Bomberg at the Borough Polytechnic from 1949 to 1953, and at the Royal College of Art, from 1953 to 1956. He taught at the Regent Street Polytechnic and Chelsea School of Art from 1959 to 1964, and at St Martin's School of Art from 1966 to 1969. Kossoff's Expressionist style, marked especially by very thick impasto, is directly related to Bomberg's teaching. His subject matter is restricted to figures in interiors and the London cityscape of excavations, demolition and building sites, and railways. His paintings are made very rapidly *alla prima*. Somber dense colors gave way to a brighter palette in 1975.

Kosuth Joseph 1945–

The American Conceptual artist and theorist Joseph Kosuth was born in Toledo, Ohio. Combining analytical philosophy, aesthetics, and linguistics, Kosuth investigates the nature of the art object in relation to its context. While a student at the School of Visual Arts, New York (1965–7), and as a faculty member in 1968, he worked on his photoenlargements of dictionary definitions and words in neon. Later he used magazine and billboard advertisements to remove the work from the art context. From the early 1970s photocopies of his *Investigations* (begun in

Willem de Kooning: Woman and Bicycle; oil on canvas; 194×124cm (76×49in); 1952–3. Whitney Museum of American Art, New York

Utagawa Kunisada: Moonlight; woodblock print; each section 37×25cm (15×10in); 1857. British Museum, London

1966) have been displayed in special gallery installations. In 1971 and 1972 Kosuth studied philosophy and anthropology at the New School for Social Research, New York. He had a major retrospective exhibition in Lucerne in 1973 and one-man shows at the Leo Castelli Gallery, New York, from 1969 onwards.

Further reading. Kosuth, J. *Art Investigations and Problematics since 1965*, Lucerne (1973). Kosuth, J. *Concept-Théorie*, Paris (1970). Lippard, L. *Six Years: the Dematerialization of the Art Object*, New York (1973).

Ku K'ai-chih 345–406

The painter Ku K'ai-chih came from Chin Ling, Wu Hsi, and was the son of an official of the Chin State of East China. He became an official himself early in his life and died in office. His reputation, which was considerable in his own time, rested at least as much on his poetry as on his painting; indeed he is mentioned under the literati heading in the *Chin Shu* (Chin dynastic history) biography section. Amongst his poetry, of which little remains, his most famous work is the *Lightning and Thunder fu*. As a courtier the assessment of Ku K'ai-chih's success is problematical. He was notably skilled at getting along with sworn enemies and is reputed to have been naive to the point of

foolishness. It has been suggested that he may have acted the fool and thereby retained his position throughout a period of unrest, much as a court jester protects himself. His reputation as an eccentric is clearly not unkind and is a matter for admiration.

His fame as a painter rested in his own time largely on his portraiture, recorded as vivid and lifelike. His technique of "putting the highlights in the eyes last" is remarked upon with some wonder. He was a master of the "Red and Green" style, an old-fashioned style both rich and decorative. Our own experience of Ku K'ai-chih's painting, however, is of a different aspect. Although those works known to us today must be later copies of copies, we have three major works in the *Admonitions of a Preceptress to a Girl about to enter the Palace*, a hand scroll in the British Museum, London; another handscroll, *The Fairy of the Lo River*, now in the Freer Gallery of Art, Washington, D.C.; and the *Landscape* in the Royal Ontario Museum, Toronto. The last two scrolls, appearing in their copied form as somewhat stiff and lacking in life, retain a hint of the fascination the magical world of the Taoist had for Ku K'ai-chih. The fairies float above and into a delicate and simple landscape of groups of trees and trailing streams.

The *Admonitions* scroll, regarded as perhaps a 10th-century copy, is of separate figure-scenes. Each one represents a situa-

tion likely to be met by the young girl entering the palace as a concubine. The short script introducing each scene advises the girl on the proper attitude: to be kind to her children and get on well with her fellow palace women, to be dutiful to her husband, and so forth. The final scene of a huntsman in landscape seems to give a clue to the mountain landscapes which came into the painter's repertoire and were developed over the years to become his major art. Here the figures are lively and gracefully painted. Even in their copied state they retain something of the character with which Chinese genre painting at its most lively abounds.

While these works give us some hint of the late-4th-century landscape style, it is interesting to note also that Hsieh Ho in the *Ku Hua P'in Lu* rates Ku low among painters, regarding him as far from being the greatest artist of his day.

Kunisada Utagawa 1786–1865

The Japanese print artist Utagawa Kunisada was a pupil of Utagawa Toyokuni. From 1844 he signed himself "Toyokuni", claiming to be the second of that name, though the true Toyokuni II was Toyoshige who died in 1835. Kunisada is therefore often called Toyokuni III. Kunisada's importance lies in his dominance of the figure print in the mid 19th century. He produced over 20,000 compositions and his long, rather ugly and tortured faces and his dark, hard colors became the standard for the period. In his youth, however, he had produced actor prints of some power in Toyokuni's tradition, and even a few sensitive landscapes. His prints are encountered more frequently than any other's.

Kuo Hsi 1020–90

The Chinese painter Kuo Hsi was born in Honan; very little is known of his family. He was a Taoist. He was appointed early in his career to the Imperial Academy of painting of the Northern Sung, and became one of its most illustrious members, later becoming a member of the Imperial Council with various honorary offices. Kuo Hsi was a teacher in the Imperial Academy and was considered by his contemporaries to be the greatest master of landscape painting. As a court painter he undertook a wide variety of work, particularly fresco paintings. These have all perished with the palaces. The large landscape attributed to Kuo Hsi, *Early Spring* (National Palace Museum, Taipei, Taiwan) shows a masterly baroque composition, rich in detail and expressing great depth of distance and atmosphere. Clearly Kuo Hsi followed the styles of Li Ch'eng and Fan K'uan. But he added the dimension of his own breadth and articulation of form, to give his mountains not only the static grandeur of his predecessors' works, but also that quality of a landscape "in which one can take a walk" that his patrons and contemporaries so much admired.

Kupezký Jan 1667–1740

Probably the greatest central European portrait painter of the early 18th century, Kupezký was Bohemian by birth, but worked all over Europe. He was trained in Vienna and was later active in Venice and Rome before returning to Vienna in 1709. However, he never felt secure in Catholic states, and he finally settled in Protestant Nuremberg in 1725. In his portraits Kupezký brought together Italian Baroque patterns and a Northern sharp eye for detail, often giving his sitters a brooding intensity and an extraordinary sense of immediacy. This psychological penetration was deepened further by the exploitation of still-life elements in sharp focus, which emphasized the personality of the sitter.

Kupka Frank 1871–1957

The Czech painter Frank Kupka was born in Opocno in eastern Bohemia and studied in Prague and Vienna. He came to Paris in 1895 and worked there for the rest of his life. At first he made his living as an illustrator, his work for the satirical magazine *L'Assiette au Beurre* expressing his own anticlerical and anarchist beliefs.

The precise chronology of his development is difficult to establish, but it is certain that in the autumn of 1912 he exhibited one of the earliest nonfigurative paintings, his first entirely Abstract work, *Amorpha, Fugue for Two Colors* (1911–12; National Gallery, Prague). In this painting the arabesques created by intersecting arcs were the result of a process of abstraction from movement that Kupka had begun in 1908 with a naturalistic painting of his stepdaughter with a ball. Probably inspired by the multiexposure photographs of figures in motion made by Marey in the 1880s, Kupka made a series of drawings in which an abstract rhythm gradually replaces the subject. The movement of the ball acquires connotations of planetary orbits; it is likely that Kupka, who had a lifelong interest in the occult, believed he could depict an all-embracing cosmic motion.

The *Vertical Planes* (1913; National Gallery, Prague) exhibited in 1913 anticipate Malevich and Lissitzky in their depiction of floating rectangles. The emphasis on verticals stretching from top to bottom, destroying the opportunity to see a horizon, derives from a painting of piano keys of 1909. In drawings of the same year, the depiction of motion is aided by breaking up the surface continuity to suggest distinct moments of time.

Kupka has often been classed with Robert Delaunay as an "Orphist", although the opaque and labored handling of the Czech painter militates against the effects of space and light achieved by the Delaunays. After 1931, when he joined the *Abstraction-Création* group, his painting became absorbed into international geometric abstraction.

Further reading. Cassou, J. and Fedit, D. *Frank Kupka*, London (1965). Heath, A. *Abstract Painting: its Origin and Meaning*, London (1953). Mladek, M. and Rowell, M. *Frantisek Kupka: a Retrospective*, New York (1975).

L

Lachaise Gaston 1882–1935

The Franco-American sculptor Gaston Lachaise was born in Paris and studied there. He worked at the production of Art Nouveau objects for Réné Lalique. In 1906 he emigrated to the United States where he began work as an assistant to H.H. Kitson, a designer of military monuments. Lachaise quickly became a prominent sculptor whose vast bulbous women in bronze are in the tradition of Maillol and Matisse. Casts of his most famous work, *Standing Woman* (1912–17; Albright-Knox Art Gallery, Buffalo), are in galleries throughout America. Lachaise was also an accomplished portraitist whose subjects include notable American artists and writers such as Marianne Moore and e e cummings.

Lafosse Charles de 1636–1716

The French painter Charles de Lafosse trained under Charles Lebrun. He spent the years from 1658 to 1663 in Italy, starting his studies in Rome where he examined the works of Pietro da Cortona, and spending three years in Venice where he studied the works of Paolo Veronese. He brought back to France a coloristic Venetian style, but was also much influenced by Rubens. Venetian and Flemish influences made him the leading *Rubéniste*, softening the classicism of Lebrun and preparing the way for the painterly grace of Watteau and the Rococo. He executed altarpieces and Baroque decorative schemes for the provinces, but worked mainly for projects in Paris (for example, the dome of the church of the Invalides, Paris, 1692) and for Versailles (mythological scenes for the Trianon, 1688). He was favored by the influential collector Pierre Crozat.

Laguerre Louis 1663–1721

The French-born decorative painter Louis Laguerre was a pupil of Charles Lebrun. He came to England in 1684, and worked with Antonio Verrio at Windsor and Whitehall. He was also employed extensively in decorating the interiors of important country houses with grand illusionistic and allegorical mural and ceiling paintings.

Louis Laguerre: C. Dubosc's engraving after Laguerre's painting The Battle of Tanieres, near Mons, 1709, in Marlborough House, London; 48×73cm (19×29in); c1712–33. British Museum, London

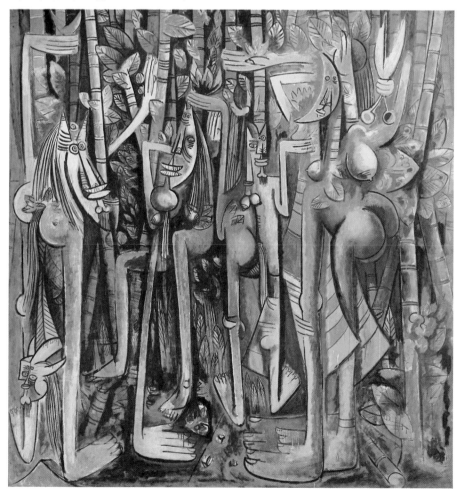

Examples of these can be seen in Chatsworth House (1689–97) and Sudbury Hall (1691) in Derbyshire, at Burghley House in Lincolnshire (1698), and in various London houses. These schemes show the influence of Lebrun and Baroque decorative painting, tempered with a dull classicism. His masterpiece is the Saloon at Blenheim Palace, Oxfordshire (c1720), with its allegorical ceiling and illusionistic terraces on the walls crowded with the peoples of all nations. During the last decade of his life, his reputation was overshadowed by that of Sir James Thornhill.

Lam Wifredo 1902–82

The Cuban painter Wifredo Lam (Wifredo Oscar de la Conception Lam y Castilla) was born in Sanga la Grande, Cuba, and studied first at the Havana School of Fine Arts (1920–3) and then in Madrid and Paris. In Paris in 1938 he met Picasso, André Breton, Max Ernst, and Victor Brauner. His first major one-man exhibition was in Paris at the Galerie Pierre in 1939. Lam fled from Europe in 1941 on the same boat as André Breton, André Masson, and Claude Lévi-Strauss. From

Wilfredo Lam: The Jungle; gouache on paper mounted on canvas; 239×230cm (94×91in); 1943. Museum of Modern Art, New York

1947 to 1952 he lived in Cuba, New York, and Paris, visiting Italy and England. In 1952 he left Cuba for Paris, where he has lived practically ever since. While Lam was never formally a member of the Surrealist group, his work—with its tortured human-like imagery (for example, *The Jungle*, 1943; Museum of Modern Art, New York)—indicates a close kinship with Surrealism and Cubism. (See also *Rumblings of the Earth*, oil on canvas; 1950; Solomon R. Guggenheim Museum, New York.)

Further reading. Jouffroy, A. *Lam*, Paris (1972). Lewis, M. *Wifredo Lam*, Milan (1970). Tarnaud, C. "Wifredo Lam et la Bestiaire Ambigu", *XXᵉ Siècle*, Paris (May, 1963).

Lancret Nicolas 1690–1743

Nicolas Lancret was a French painter and draftsman. A student at the Académie de Peinture and of Claude Gillot, he was essentially a painter of *fêtes galantes*; as such, he was the chief follower of Watteau, continuing this mode into the 1740s. An early example of this is *Italian Comedians by a Fountain* (Wallace Collection, London), with colors less saturated than those of Watteau. A member of the Académie in 1719, he was soon established as a popular artist, particularly in court circles. As well as working for Versailles, he attracted many of Watteau's former patrons. His sense of observation was acute and often humorous, as in *The Cup of Chocolate* (National Gallery, London), shown at the Salon of 1742.

Landseer Sir Edwin 1802–73

The sporting, genre, and portrait painter Sir Edwin Henry Landseer was born in London, the son of an engraver. He exhibited at the Royal Academy from 1815. He was taught by B.R. Haydon, beginning his studies by dissecting animals. Landseer became Royal Academician in 1831. It was on visits to the Scottish Highlands that he found his most popular subjects. Fine examples of his work include *The Hunted Stag* (c1833; Tate Gallery, London), *The Old Shepherd's Chief Mourner* (1837; Victoria and Albert Museum, London), *The Monarch of the Glen* (1851; Dewar House, London), and *Man Proposes, God Disposes* (1864; Royal Holloway College, London). He was admired by Queen Victoria, who employed him to paint royal

Nicolas Lancret: A Lady and Gentleman with Two Girls; oil on canvas; 89×98cm (35×39in); 1742. National Gallery, London

portraits and pets. He also modeled the lions for Trafalgar Square (1858–63), and was offered the presidency of the Royal Academy but turned it down because of failing health; he exhibited there for a total of 58 years.

Lanfranco Giovanni 1582–1647

A painter of the transition from early to High Baroque, Giovanni Lanfranco was active mainly in Rome and Naples. Born in Parma, he was probably trained there by Agostino Carracci. In 1602 he went to Rome to work with Agostino's brother Annibale, perhaps as an assistant on the Farnese gallery; this experience is clearly reflected in his own ceiling of the Villa Borghese (1624–5). A brief return visit to his native town from 1610 to 1612 seems to have stimulated a new interest in Correggio, and in a work such as the *St*

Sir Edwin Landseer: Wild Cattle of Chillingham; oil on canvas; 229×155cm (90×61in); c1867. Laing Art Gallery and Museum, Newcastle upon Tyne

Giovanni Lanfranco: The Miracle of the Loaves and Fishes; oil on canvas; 229×426cm (90×168in); c1620–3. National Gallery of Ireland, Dublin

Margaret of Cortona (1618–20; Palazzo Pitti, Florence) the swirling movement, the flicker of light and shade, and the emotional expressiveness all anticipate the style of Bernini.

By this date Lanfranco's increasingly Baroque tendencies had already brought him into conflict with Domenichino, who was the leading representative of Bolognese classicism in Rome. The rivalry between the two artists was to reach a climax with their respective decorations in S. Andrea della Valle (1624–8). Lanfranco's illusionistically conceived *Assumption of the Virgin* in the dome, successfully updating Correggio's domes in Parma, and ingeniously exploiting the real light source of the lantern for dramatic effect, was to exert a profound influence on later Baroque dome decoration. By the mid 1630s, Lanfranco was beginning to lose his preeminent position in Rome to Pietro da Cortona. In 1634 he moved to Naples, where his many fresco decorations quickly established the High Baroque as the prevalent style. He returned to Rome in 1646 for the last year of his life.

Lanyon Peter 1918–64

The English painter George Peter Lanyon was born at St Ives, Cornwall, where he lived all his life, though traveling widely. He studied with Borlase Smart at St Ives, at the Penzance School of Art in 1937, and at the Euston Road School in 1938. He died in 1964 after a gliding accident. Primarily a landscape painter, Lanyon's originality lay in his combination of a Cubist vision ordered by an Abstract Expressionist technique. Under the influence of Ben Nichol-

Peter Lanyon: Thermal; oil on canvas; 183×152cm (72×60in); 1960. Tate Gallery, London

son and Naum Gabo, he spent a period making constructions. Later he returned to landscapes which were based on his subjective response to appearances rather than on overt description. After 1959, gliding added a further dimension to his style, especially in the use of brighter colors. Some of his paintings were preceded by studies in painted wood and collage.

Largillière Nicolas de 1656–1746

The French painter Nicolas de Largillière was born in Paris but trained in Antwerp. In 1674 he went to England, where he worked in the studio of Lely. Working in Paris from 1680, he was the leading portraitist outside court circles, where Rigaud was supreme. He was received into the Académie in 1686 with a portrait of *Charles Lebrun* (Louvre, Paris), a suitably grand and autocratic image of Louis XIV's chief painter. For the *Échevins* (magistrates) of Paris he made large group portraits in a somewhat Baroque manner, tempered by knowledge of Dutch corporation portraits. The masterpiece of this genre shows *The Échevins of Paris before St Geneviève* (1696; St Étienne-du-Mont, Paris), a cross betwen sober group portrait and Baroque altarpiece. He also painted still lifes and landscapes.

Larionoff Michail 1881–1964

The Russian painter Michail Larionoff was born in Teraspol, Ukraine. His work at first went through Symbolist and Impressionist phases. In 1909 he adopted a "primitivist" manner based on Russian popular art. His paintings used strident and often bawdy imagery as a deliberate affront to Western pictorial conventions, an effect reinforced by the artist's unconventional behavior, designed to ruffle the complacency of the Moscow bourgeoisie. With his lifelong friend and associate Natalia Goncharova, he was the originator and principal exponent of Rayonism, a style that entailed the presentation of objects through reflected rays of light. By 1913, the schematic application of this method had led him to abstraction. He left Russia for Switzerland in 1915 to design for Diaghilev, and never returned.

Lastman Pieter 1583–1633

Pieter Pietersz. Lastman was a Dutch painter of multifigure historical and mythological pictures. The dramatic impact of his glossy, sumptuously colored narratives—achieved largely by animated gestures and facial expression—tends to be diminished by distracting genre and still-life details. He is nowadays chiefly remembered as Rembrandt's teacher in Amsterdam for about six months c1624–5. Lastman worked in Italy in his youth, and it was through him that Rembrandt became acquainted with Italian Renaissance art.

Nicolas de Largillière: Self-portrait; oil on canvas; 79×63cm (31×25in); c1710. Musée Fabre, Montpellier

Michail Larionoff: Woman Walking on the Boulevard; oil on canvas; 116×86cm (46×34in); 1912. Private collection

Latham John 1921–

The British artist John Latham was born on the Zambesi River in Mozambique in Africa. He trained at the Chelsea School of Art (1946–50). His infamous *Distillation* (1967; Museum of Modern Art, New York), a reduced and bottled copy of Greenberg's *Art and Culture*, led to his dismissal from St Martin's School of Art, London where he taught part-time (1966 to 1967). Latham has been a respected if poorly understood British avant-garde artist since the late 1950s when he produced his first book sculptures, which were seen at the time to be part of the Assemblage movement. His aesthetic theories developed over two decades are based on an interpretation of time, space, and events. They were published in a treatise, *Time-base and Determination in Events* (Düsseldorf, 1975), at the time of his major retrospective in the Kunsthalle in Düsseldorf. Since 1968 he has been active in the Artist Placement Group, of which he was a founder member, and through which he undertook several environmental projects in Scotland in the mid 1970s. In 1976 his work was shown at the Tate Gallery in London.

La Tour Georges de 1593–1652

The son of a baker at Vic-sur-Seille in Lorraine, the French artist Georges de La Tour was of respectable but undistinguished origin. He is first recorded as a painter in Vic in his marriage contract of 1617. In 1620 he moved to his wife's town of Lunéville, where he remained for the rest of his life. La Tour's first known painting, probably dating from 1615–16, is a genre piece, *The Payment of Dues* (Lvov State Picture Gallery). It shows an interior scene, lit by a solitary candle, with figures gathered around a ledger while one man counts out money; its meaning is not wholly clear. The candlelit interior presages much of La Tour's later work. *The Fortune Teller*, in the Metropolitan Museum, New York, is known from its signature to have been painted in Lunéville, and with it may be associated *The Cheat with the Ace of Diamonds* (Louvre, Paris). In these pictures both the subject matter—with its covert sexuality and moral ambivalence—and the technique derive directly from Caravaggio; La Tour must have become familiar with his work, possibly through copies. However, the differences between the two artists are significant; in La Tour the earthiness and vigor of Caravaggio have become formalized, bland, and mysterious.

If La Tour declines to make a moral statement in these detailed depictions of conspiracy and deceit, he is more explicit in a series of mainly half-length figures of saints, some of which survive only through copies. In these paintings La Tour's minute realism is used to point a moral. His saints are bearded, compelling peasant figures, withdrawn in their concentration but no longer distant or frozen in some other world. The most important of the series is the *St Jerome* (1621–3; Musée de Peinture et de Sculpture, Grenoble). Here the aging Saint is shown almost naked, his thin wiry arms contrasting with his sagging old man's belly; the blood-caked knot of the rope with which he beats himself hangs from his hand, lying on the floor with sharp stones and a skull. Against this apparently dispassionate portrayal of the ravages of old age and the mortification of the flesh is set the absorbed concentration of the head as the Saint looks at the Cross clenched in his left hand.

The technique too has changed. The fluid luminous tones of *The Fortune Teller* have given way, most noticeably in the flesh areas, to a drier, almost clay-like handling; this probably derives from the artist's firsthand knowledge of the work of Hendrick Terbrugghen, a Dutch Caravag-

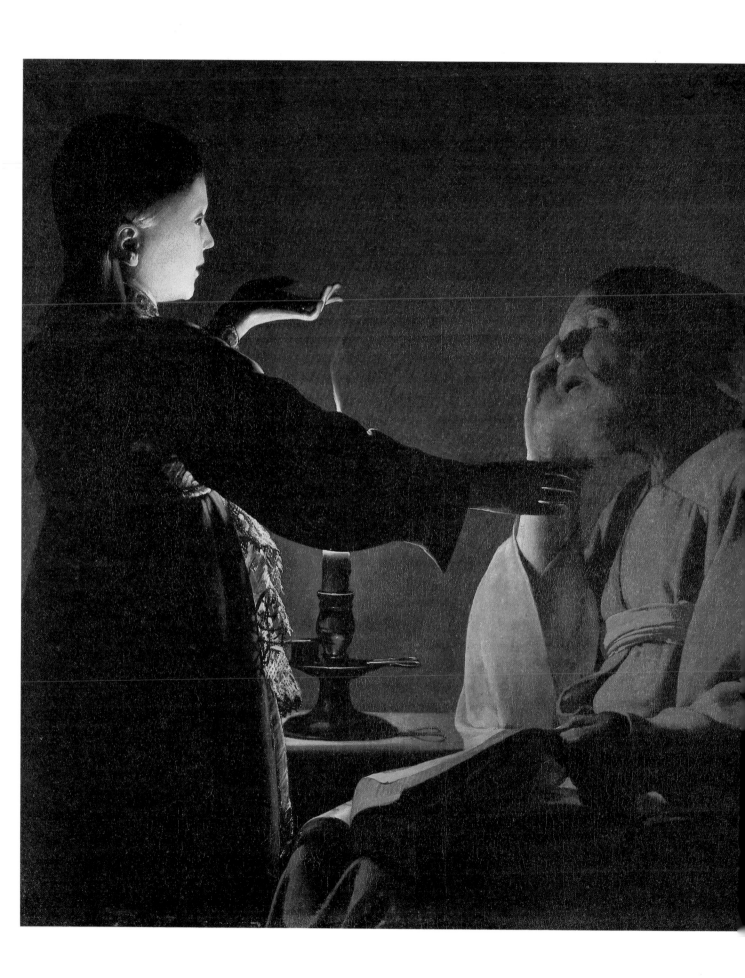

gesque working in Utrecht. Paralleled with the series of saints are a number of genre scenes, more loosely painted and more immediate than the earlier pictures. In these, beggars and musicians predominate, culminating in *The Beggars' Brawl* (c1627–30; J. Paul Getty Museum, Malibu), where the inaudible scream of the woman who looks out from the left of the picture gives the key to the viewer's response.

With *The Flea Catcher* (c1635; Musée Historique Lorrain, Nancy) La Tour reverts to the candlelit interior, a trick or perhaps an obsession that remains with him for the rest of his life. An extraordinary, intimate scene, the subject matter has parallels with "Susannah" subjects. But here, there is no sense of voyeurism; the figure is ungainly, self-absorbed, undressed rather than nude. A series of paintings of the Repentant Magdalene, datable to the late 1630s, shows possible evidence of a second visit to the Netherlands. In 1627 Terbrugghen had painted the *Magdalene Contemplating a Skull* (Schloss Weissenstein, Graf von Schönbornsche Kunstsammlungen, Pommersfelden) and the close parallels between this painting and La Tour's *Magdalene* are very close. They are alike in their candlelit interiors, in virtuoso effects of light and shade, and in their props: the mirror and the skull. They display a new, coppery tone which may derive from an acquaintance with the work of Honthorst.

Candlelit interiors of increasing virtuosity and religious intensity occasionally give way to genre scenes, such as *The Boy Blowing on a Charcoal Stick* (c1638–40; Musée des Beaux-Arts, Dijon). Despite the clear religious intensity of his work, there is substantial evidence that by this time La Tour had become an extremely difficult, aggressive, and conceited man, much given to self-aggrandisement. In 1639 he is referred to in a document as "Georges de La Tour Peintre Ordinaire du Roy", an honor that probably marked La Tour's presentation of a picture of St Sebastian to King Louis XIII.

In the paintings of the 1640s La Tour's technique becomes broader. Ostensibly simple, composition and lighting are in fact rigidly controlled; superfluous detail is

Georges de La Tour: The Dream of St Joseph; oil on canvas; 93×81cm (37×32in); c1640. Musée des Beaux-Arts, Nantes

eliminated, and forms reduced to almost geometrical terms. In the *St Sebastian Tended by St Irene*, painted for the church of Bois Anzeray in 1649 (Louvre, Paris), a variant of the painting presented to the King, this reduction to essentials of composition, lighting, form and gesture is clearly marked. The saint is transfixed by only one arrow, one drop of blood serving to indicate his martyrdom. St Sebastian is conventionally depicted bristling with arrows, running with blood, yet alive and radiant with faith; here he is seen motionless, apparently dead; the implicit violence and horror are replaced by an economy of movement, each figure expressing only one emotion: love, compassion, tears, and prayer.

His last years dogged by illness, La Tour died in 1652. His oldest surviving son had qualified as a painter in 1646 but he seems to have done little to prevent the almost total lapse into obscurity of the work and even the name of his father. Much of his work survived unrecognized, unidentified, or else ascribed to other artists. Many of his compositions exist in two or more versions, some autograph replicas, some copies. Few of his works are signed and fewer are securely datable. While much is known of La Tour's daily life in Lunéville, there survives no contemporary assessment of his work. The rediscovery of La Tour as a painter in 1915 and the gradual piecing together of his oeuvre has been described as a triumph of art history, but the triumph is not yet total. There remains much that is still guesswork.

Further reading. Arland, M. *Georges de la Tour*, Paris (1953). Nicolson, B. and Wright, C. *Georges de la Tour*, London (1974). Periset, G. *Georges de la Tour*, Paris (1948).

La Tour Maurice de 1704–88

The French pastellist Maurice Quentin de La Tour was born in Saint-Quentin. After a visit to London, he settled in Paris. His first visit to the city had probably been in 1720–1, when he realized how he could benefit from the vogue for pastel portraits begun by Rosalba Carriera. He entered the Académie in 1737, and exhibited at the Salon that same year, achieving a success which was to be lasting. He specialized in portraits of the face alone, and made his sitters seem larger than life and very vivacious, with a twinkle in the eye and a direct

Maurice de La Tour: Portrait of Jean Restout; oil on canvas; 41×31cm (16×12in); c1738. Musée A. Lecuyer, St-Quentin

and open expression. His ability to make almost anyone seem attractive in spirit if not in face, and to grasp a sitter's character in that difficult yet sensitive medium, made his fortune.

Lauber Diebold fl. 1427–69

Diebold Lauber was a German illuminator. Based at Hagenau in Alsace, he was the head of a large atelier of about 16 illuminators known as the Hagenau School. Although this workshop has a distinctive style, it is extremely difficult to identify the contributions of the individual members of the atelier. It seems to have specialized in large Bibles and popular treatises and chronicles. About 50 manuscripts from the Hagenau school are known, 12 of which are in the Library of Heidelberg University. The illuminations in these books are in general sketchily drawn and crudely colored. While they lack finish, they are often highly vivacious. Lauber worked for the Bishop of Strasbourg and for Count Ludwig IV of Heidelberg. He also produced manuscripts on his own account as speculative ventures for general sale. In this respect, his business practice foreshadows that of the later publishers of printed books.

Laurana Francesco c1430–?c1502

The Italian sculptor Francesco Laurana was born in Vrana, Dalmatia. He is first

recorded in 1453 working on the Triumphal Arch of Alfonso I at Castelnuovo, Naples, where he is usually said to have carved the high-relief panel depicting Alfonso and his court. This shows a number of figures cramped beneath a loggia of classical design, with friezes of classically-inspired nereids, mermaids, and swag-bearing *putti* above and below. He also worked in Sicily (c1470) and in Provence from the 1460s, returning several times afterwards. There he produced medals for René d'Anjou and important work in Avignon and Marseilles (for example the Chapel of St Lazarus, Old Cathedral, Marseilles), demonstrating a peculiarly late-Gothic character. Apart from these excursions abroad, he worked mainly in Naples, where he produced several female bust portraits carved in smoothly polished marble with a calm and simple naturalism. Famous works are to be seen in the Kunsthistorisches Museum, Vienna, the Bargello in Florence, the Louvre in Paris, and in the Staatliche Museen, Berlin.

Laurana Luciano 1420/5?–79

The Dalmatian architect Luciano Laurana was born at Zara. He was one of the most distinguished architectural designers of the 15th century in Italy. His most famous surviving work is at Urbino where he designed a considerable part of the existing Palazzo Ducale (c1465–72), in particular the main *cortile* and numerous doorways, chimneypieces, and other interior fittings. Laurana was much influenced by previous Florentine architectural practice; but his own work, with its clarity, precision, and restraint, has its own individual character. It seems likely that in the acquisition of this taste he was influenced by the work of the resident court painter, Piero della Francesca. Laurana also served as a military engineer in Naples; he was working on the fortification of Pesaro when he died.

Laurencin Marie 1885–1956

Marie Laurencin was a French painter and theater designer. She was largely self-taught, but during the years 1908–12 was the mistress of Guillaume Apollinaire which enabled her to move in the Cubist

Francesco Laurana (attrib.): the Arch of Alfonso I, Castelnuovo, Naples; c1453

circles of the Bateau-Lavoir group, where she met Picasso and Braque. However, she never produced a Cubist picture herself; her *métier* was pictures of young, graceful girls, in subdued colors, living out their delicate idylls. She was much influenced by Rococo art and by Persian miniatures. She produced designs for Poiret and in the 1920s and 1930s, "Laurencin-girls" abounded; she answered a period need. She also designed Poulenc's ballet *Les Biches* for Diaghilev in 1924 and illustrated many books.

Laurens Henri 1885–1954

The French sculptor Henri Laurens was born and died in Paris. He was originally trained as a decorative craftsman. Working and exhibiting in Cubist circles from 1911, he rapidly emerged as one of the most inventive Cubist sculptors: first in simple architectural stone pieces, then in a succession of polychrome constructions using a variety of improvised materials (for example, *Mask*, 1918; Museum of Modern Art, New York).

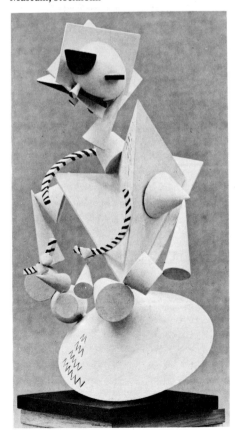

Henri Laurens: Clown; paint on wooden shapes; height 64cm (25in); 1915. Modern Museum, Stockholm

What they have in common with the great bronzes of his maturity (1920 onwards) is a generous sense of vitality and humor. "I aspire to ripeness of form", he said in 1951. His bronzes, usually of female nudes, and often with an aquatic theme, are characterized by a fruity opulence and sensuality. They have a natural skin-like surface, and they marry playful intimacy with a sense of the monumental. The largest collection is in the Musée National d'Art Moderne, Paris.

Laurens was also a fluent draftsman and worked extensively as a theater designer (for Diaghilev in the 1920s) and as an illustrator.

Lawrence Thomas 1769–1830

The English portrait-painter Sir Thomas Lawrence was born in Bristol. His father, a bankrupted innkeeper, was not slow to exploit the boy's precocious natural facility, notably in Bath, where in his early teens he earned the main part of the family income making likenesses in pencil and pastel. In 1786 he moved to London, entering the Royal Academy Schools, and the following year sent seven oils to the Academy exhibition. Abundant official recognition lay ahead: succeeding Reynolds, he became Painter-in-Ordinary to the King in 1792; and at the Royal Academy he was elected Associate in 1791, full member in 1794, and President in 1820.

Seventeen hundred and ninety saw the exhibition of his *Queen Charlotte* (National Gallery, London). This glittering performance confirmed Lawrence's fashionable status, but he was disastrously tempted into accepting more commissions than he could well handle. His early career was thus something of an anticlimax, probably worsened by financial and emotional troubles. His works were criticized for their exaggerated highlighting effects and for their theatricality. Following ideas in Reynolds' *Discourses*, he believed that a painter's aspirations should lie beyond portraiture, in the realm of subject painting; but his most ambitious subject picture, the muscle-bound *Satan Summoning up his Legions* (1797; Royal Academy of Arts, London), lacks the romantic power of works such as the *Kemble as Hamlet* (1801; Tate Gallery, London), which bridge the gap between the two genres. The latter work also exemplifies Lawrence's fascination with the stage.

His declining reputation was revived by a

Thomas Lawrence: Charles William Lambton (The Red Boy); oil on canvas; 137×112cm (54×44in); first exhibited 1825. Private collection

strong showing at the Royal Academy exhibition of 1807, featuring the *Sir Francis Baring and his Associates* (Collection of Lord Northbrook, Winchester, Hampshire). This highly animated picture—the subjects are engaged in a business discussion—contrasts with the static Reynolds group portrait for which it was intended as a pendant, yet avoids the mannerisms to which the artist's style was prone.

Ceremonial or military costume lent itself especially well to the brilliance of Lawrence's treatment: *The Third Marquess of Londonderry* (1813; Marquess of Londonderry Collection, Cleveland) invites comparison with works by Gros and Géricault. In 1815, he was knighted as a prelude to undertaking an important royal commission to commemorate in portraits the sovereigns, soldiers, and statesmen associated with the overthrow of Napoleon: the Waterloo Chamber series at Windsor Castle. From 1818 to 1820 he worked

abroad from the sitters themselves—and thereby established an international reputation—leaving last touches for his return home. Some of the portraits in fact remained unfinished at the artist's death, when they were finally delivered up to George IV. The *Pius VII*, which alludes to the restoration to the Vatican of antique sculpture plundered by the French, is the most vital of the series. Lawrence seems to have been particularly attracted to the 77-year-old Pope, whose features, he felt, were "animated with benevolence and a sort of mild energy".

Lawrence's apparently dashing manner belies his careful working method; he always drew in features before painting. His work is nonetheless strikingly uneven in quality, owing partly to his use of assistants. This, and the glossy vulgarization of his style that became popular in the 1830s and 1840s, have provoked unjust defamations of his art.

Lebrun Charles 1619–90

The French artist Charles Lebrun was the principal painter for much of the reign of Louis XIV. He created a style intended to glorify that monarch's prowess—a manner much imitated by the court painters of other European rulers and princelings with similarly absolutist ambitions.

Born in Paris, Lebrun received his training first from his father, Nicolas, a minor sculptor, and then from François Perrier and Simon Vouet. In 1643 he was sent by his patron, the Chancellor Séguier, to Rome; there he studied the works of Antiquity and of modern masters, and learned above all from the example and counsel of Nicolas Poussin. Returning to Paris in 1646 he received numerous commissions for altarpieces, designs for engravings, and ceiling paintings. Among the latter are those for the Hôtels de Nouveau (1650–1) and de la Rivière (1652–3), both now in the Musée Carnavalet, for the Hôtel Lambert, and for a room in the Louvre. From 1658 to 1661 he was employed by Nicolas Foucquet at his château of Vaux-le-Vicomte, not only on the decoration of the rooms, but also as a designer of sculpture for the park, of furniture, and of tapestries.

On the fall of Foucquet he passed into the service of the King, and for him he controlled the decoration of Versailles. He selected and in some cases guided the other painters, himself painted the Escalier des Ambassadeurs (1674–8) and the Galerie des Glaces with the Salons at either end (1678–87), provided drawings for sculpture, and directed the Gobelins factory which produced both furniture and tapestries.

In this work he had the support of Colbert, who was the *Surintendant des Bâtiments*. Colbert also favored the development of the Académie Royale de Peinture et de Sculpture, of which Lebrun had been a founder in 1648 and became Chancellor for Life from 1663. Lebrun used this forum to propound his ideal of narrative painting, in which the story was depicted by carefully studied facial expressions and gestures, supported by color. His lecture on the Expression of the Passions was his most influential single contribution. His approach, so important for the development of academic art in other countries and later centuries, is best exemplified by his painting of *Alexander at the Tent of Darius* (1660–1; Versailles).

After Colbert's death in 1683 Lebrun's

Charles Lebrun: Eberhard Jacob and his Family; oil on canvas; 275×325cm (108×128in); c1650. Formerly Kaiser Friedrich Museum, Berlin

power waned, and the failing economy of the court added to his troubles. His later years were devoted to producing smaller biblical paintings in a revived Poussinesque manner.

The traditional accusation that Lebrun exercised an artistic dictatorship is an exaggeration, and underestimates his tolerance of the variety of styles employed by his followers. Nonetheless, his influence was very considerable, and strongly affected many lesser talents, while the authority of his position ensured a basic unity in French court art of the period.

Leck Bart van der 1876–1958

Bart Anthony van der Leck was a Dutch painter, book-illustrator, and designer. He studied at the State School for Decorative Arts, Utrecht. His early painting was in the tradition of the Hague landscape school. He was then influenced by the Dutch Monumentalists art movement, whose aim was to attain a simplified mural art. Gradually from 1912 his work, which was socially concerned, became more simplified and stylized, and extremely two dimensional: for example *The Tempest* (1916; Kröller-Müller Museum, Otterlo).

Reducing forms to rectangles, triangles, and their combinations, and using only primary colors, his stylization led to abstraction, exemplified in *Leaving the Factory* (Boymans—Van Beuningen Museum, Rotterdam). Leck's work influenced Mondrian, van Doesburg, and the artists of *De Stijl*. He joined the group in 1917 but soon left. His subsequent work became less abstract.

Le Corbusier 1887–1965

The career of Charles-Édouard Jeanneret, known as Le Corbusier, is inextricably linked with the fate of 20th-century architecture; the same triumphs and defeats, the same hopes and frustrations were shared by both. To pin down this many-sided, controversial genius is as difficult as charting the twists and turns of a creative spirit like Picasso—an artist with whom Le Corbusier liked to be compared.

Born at La Chaux-de-Fonds in Switzerland, the son of an engraver of watches, Charles-Édouard Jeanneret was encouraged to take up architecture by his local art school teacher, Charles L'Eplattenier. The years from 1906 to 1912 were spent in self-education and travel. He made contact

with many of the pioneers of modern architecture: Josef Hoffmann and Adolf Loos in Vienna, Tony Garnier in Lyons, Auguste Perret in Paris, who taught him about reinforced concrete, and Peter Behrens in Berlin, then involved with industrial design. From his eye-opening tour of Greece and Turkey in 1911 he brought back some important sketches.

In 1917 he left Switzerland to settle in Paris, after the construction of his first major building, the Villa Schwob at La Chaux-de-Fonds (1916). Already the ideals of his later work are present: geometrical simplicity, perfect proportional harmony, a rational method of planning and construction, and an ability to sculpt fluid, plastic spaces.

In 1918 Le Corbusier and the painter Amadée Ozenfant launched the movement known as Purism. Le Corbusier began to paint, an activity he never gave up. In 1920, the year he adopted his pseudonym, they began publishing the magazine *L'Esprit Nouveau* in which he formulated his aesthetic and architectural ideas. These were collected in 1923 in what was to become the most influential book by any 20th-century architect, *Vers Une Architecture*.

In a series of private houses between 1923 and 1930 Le Corbusier put these ideas into practice. The Villa Savoye at Poissy (1927–31) was a poetic demonstration of the elements of the clean white cubic style first shown to the public at the Weissenhof Exhibition at Stuttgart (1927). It used a reinforced-concrete support system, developed from earlier projects for skeleton-framed, mass-produced housing (Dom-ino, 1914; Citrohan, 1921). It also abolished the load-bearing wall, permitting long uninterrupted strips of window, and fluid internal spaces that were often composed like the primary geometrical shapes of Purist painting, and were similarly colored. Thin columns ("pilotis") lift up the box-like living area, giving the house a weightless appearance. The roof is flat, with terrace or garden. The use of standard industrial components, given prominence in the Pavillon de l'Esprit Nouveau (1925), completes the streamlined, "machine aesthetic" finish.

In the early 1930s Le Corbusier worked on large-scale projects that were of great influence. Of the few actually built, the most important were the Salvation Army Hostel (1931; Paris) and the Pavillon Suisse (1932; Paris). Both works show their architect conceiving of a building in terms of a complex of interlocking but clearly defined parts, each with a different function, lending weight to his much-quoted proposition that "Architecture is the masterly, correct, and magnificent play of volumes assembled in light."

A crucially important but now largely discredited aspect of Le Corbusier's whole output, especially during the 1930s, was town planning, The smallest unit or cell of his many schemes for collective housing was the Immeuble-Villa (1923) or Pavillon de l'Esprit Nouveau, a flat on two floors with double-story living-room. His prototypes, the Contemporary City for three million (1922) and the Plan Voisin (1925), owed much to Sant'Elia's drawings for a Futurist New City (1914) and to Tony Garnier's Cité Industrielle (1901). Multilevel circulation, a cluster of enormous skyscrapers for business in the center, and multistory villas set in parkland, were the main features of these and numerous other designs for cities throughout the world.

In the 1930s Le Corbusier also renounced the somewhat inhuman, "precision-instrument" idiom of the previous decade; he began to incorporate solid, earthy materials—stone, brick, timber—and more willful forms into his buildings. The first hint of this came in the Pavillon Suisse, with its curved rubble wall; it was confirmed in a tiny, picturesque Maison de Weekend at La Celle-de-Saint-Cloud (1935). But it was not until the postwar, monumental Unité d'Habitation at Marseilles (1947–52) that crude concrete became an aesthetic end in itself, later to be imitated by the architects of Brutalism.

With the Unité, which was followed by others at Nantes and Berlin, Le Corbusier was at last able to put into effect his schemes for mass-housing, although even this was only one part of a proposed suburb made up of similar massive blocks. Some of the themes of his earlier work were taken up—giant "pilotis" (Pavillon Suisse) and sunbreaks (Salvation Army Hostel)—but the extraordinary sculpted roofscape was the most daring thing of its kind to date. The Unité was composed of 350 apartments in eight double-stories and based on a proportional system which Le Corbusier called "Modulor". In the two little Maisons Jaoul at Neuilly (1954–6) he continued his exploitation of rough concrete and natural materials; the brick walls and barrel vaults were again widely copied.

The pilgrimage church of Notre Dame du

Le Corbusier: Notre Dame du Haut, Ronchamp; 1950–4

Haut at Ronchamp (1950–4) was visually his most exciting postwar work and undoubtedly one of his masterpieces. Its shape suggests some huge bird poised for flight, a moving, living being. Every detail of this expressive, sculptural building appears arbitrary, but its irregularity is the result of a complete reassessment of the requirements of worship. It is a potent symbol of the wonder of religion; to visit it is a profoundly moving experience.

From 1951 Le Corbusier was busy with plans for the new city of Chandigarh, capital of the Punjab, where, in addition to designing the Law Courts and Secretariat, he was able to try out many of his solutions to problems of urban living. The Dominican convent of Sainte-Marie-de-la-Tourette at Eveux-sur-Arbreste (1957–60) was perhaps his strongest single statement in the years preceding his death. In stark contrast to the smooth white curves of Ronchamp, but no less dramatic, it is a predominantly rectilinear building in exposed concrete: it is rich in sculptural forms, with two identical strips of precast cells raised high on three sides above a central courtyard overlooking a valley.

Le Corbusier not only worked in Europe, he practiced on a world scale—in India, South America, North Africa, U.S.A., and Japan. Like Gropius and Mies van der Rohe, he helped to ensure the universal recognition of a new architectural language which he believed spoke for the rapidly changing patterns of 20th-century

life. He was the most internationally admired—and hated—of them all.

Further reading. Besset, M. *Who was Le Corbusier?*, Geneva (1968). Curtis, W. et al. *Le Corbusier, History of Architecture and Design 1890–1939*, Milton Keynes (1975). Le Corbusier *The Complete Architectural Works*, London (1966). Moos, S. von *Le Corbusier, L'architecte et Son Mythe*, Paris (1971).

Ledoux Claude-Nicholas
1736–1806

The French architect Claude-Nicholas Ledoux was born at Dormans (Maine) and trained under J.F. Blondel. His first professional work was as a decorative designer, but by 1770 he had risen to fame with plans for several Parisian hotels. Although some of his early designs for churches and bridges foreshadow his mature work, he was best known before the French Revolution for his houses for the French nobility such as the château de Benouville (1768) and the Hotel Thélusson, Paris (1783).

In 1771 Ledoux was appointed *Inspecteur des Salines* for the saltworks at Arc-et-Senans, for which he drew up two projects: a design for the factory and workers' living accommodation, and the plan for an ideal city outside the saltworks. In the former elliptical plan, the rugged utilitarianism of the remaining buildings echoes the grandeur of Piranesi. For the city, Ledoux planned a wide range of buildings, in which the occupants' function was expressed by entirely original iconographic allusions: a woodcutter's house composed of a pile of logs, a cooper's house in the form of a barrel, and so forth. This visionary approach of *architecture parlante* was revalued in functional terms for civic schemes such as the Théâtre at Besançon, 1780 (destroyed in the 19th century).

In the 1780s Ledoux produced a number of plans, in many styles, for the new toll and guard houses encircling Paris; many of these *barrières* were destroyed during the Revolution. Ledoux's architectural theories were embodied in his treatise *L'Architecture considérée sous le rapport de l'Art, des Moeurs et de la Législation*, published in 1804, which, though badly written, had artistic and social significance.

Léger Fernand 1881–1955

The French painter Fernand Léger was born of peasant stock at Argentan, Normandy. He first studied architecture at Caen in 1897 and then went to Paris where he worked as an architectural draftsman from 1900 to 1902. After military service he studied painting in the studios of Gêrome and Ferrier at the École des Arts Décoratifs in 1903, having failed to gain a place at the École des Beaux-Arts. Like many Parisian painters he was deeply affected by the Cézanne retrospective exhibition of 1907. His first major work, *The Seamstress* (1909; Kahnweiler Collection, Paris), demonstrates this influence in its boldly faceted relief, although its gray tones may derive from Douanier Rousseau.

After noticing from his studio window how billows of smoke enlivened the rooftop scenery, he painted *Smoke over the Roofs* (1910; R. Weil Collection, St Louis), in which large areas of pale grays bounded by taut curves are mingled with darker areas of small angular shapes, recognizable as roofs.

In the large canvas *Nudes in a Forest* (1909–11; Kröller-Müller Museum, Otterlo), Léger extended his explorations into the new Cubist forms, although his Cubism differs in significant respects from that of Picasso and Braque. This picture caused a stir at the first "Cubist" Salon des Indépendants, probably because in contrast to the flatness of much Cubist painting at the time it is made up almost entirely

of cylindrical forms in aggressive relief. It also maintains the spacial integrity of a scene viewed from a single point, unlike the multiviewpoints and ambiguous shallow spaces implied in work of Picasso and Braque. The figures are merely geometricized, and the picture is still a scene rather than an object in its own right.

This anchor in reality is used by Léger as a dynamic quality. He begins to use the abstract pattern of smoke, first seen in *Smoke over the Roofs* and then developed in *The Smokers* (1911; Solomon R. Guggenheim Museum, New York), and *The Wedding* (1911–12; Musée National d'Art Moderne, Paris), as a contrast to the detailed areas containing references to reality such as faces, hands, and roofs. In *The Woman in Blue* (1912; Öffentliche Kunstsammlung, Kunstmuseum Basel), the large abstract shapes are distributed regularly over the surface, their edges as sharp as the cut paper inventions (*papier collés*) of Picasso and Braque, with the fragments of reality reduced to mere clues to the identity of the subject.

In 1913, the year in which Kahnweiler offered him a contract and bought the contents of his studio, Léger followed the logic of this development by producing a number of completely Abstract works. Called *Contrasts of Forms*, perhaps as a

conscious parallel to Delaunay's ideas about color contrasts, these pictures maintain the fierce three-dimensional character of Léger's earlier works; thrusting cylinders and cones of roughly equal size are suggested by schematized reflections and shadows in crude primary colors and white. The rough, frequently incomplete, black outlines create a sense of restlessness by their repetition and diagonal orientation.

This phase did not last long, however, perhaps because Léger felt that the contrast between reality and abstraction was too dynamic to dismiss. *The Staircase* (1914; Öffentliche Kunstsammlung, Kunstmuseum Basel), returns to the depiction of the figure and its surroundings, but it is built out of the forms of the previous Abstract works.

Léger's military experience from 1914 to 1917 revealed to him the visual possibilities of machines as the representatives of modernity. His earlier style was predisposed to development along these lines, and he now used his cylindrical and geometrical forms to suggest a mechanized world. Unlike the Futurists he did not romanticize or worship machines; his preoccupation was to reconcile their hard, metallic, regular shapes to the organic forms of life, to build a humanistic vision.

Fernand Léger: The City; oil on canvas; 231×297cm (91×117in); 1919. Philadelphia Museum of Art

The horizontal *The City* (1919; Philadelphia Museum of Art), while being part of a general awareness of urban life shared by Delaunay, Mondrian, and the Futurists, differs from their work in its pragmatism, and also in the glimpse of the workers who have had a hand in the construction of the city.

As in his prewar paintings, Léger plays off large abstract forms against areas of detail; but now the detail is redolent of cogs and cranes, without actually depicting them, while the abstract forms tend to the geometrical. Frequently the contrast is made more poignant by the use of a landscape invaded by the man-made forms of buildings.

Léger was extraordinarily open to the stylistic developments of the 1920s and 1930s. Some of his paintings of these years bear the impressions of Kandinsky's more relaxed work, of the vertical and horizontal discipline of the *de Stijl* movement, and of Surrealism's juxtapositions of unlikely objects. His most characteristic works of this period, however, are figure-studies, from *The Mechanic* (1920; Louis Carré Gallery, Paris), to *The Beautiful Cyclists* (1943–8; Musée Fernand Léger, Biot), in which calm monumental, expressionless contemporary faces boldly confront the spectator.

He worked in many media, illustrating books, designing sets and costumes for ballet (including *The Creation of the World* in 1922), and contributing to several films, before collaborating with Man Ray, Dudley Murphy, and G. Antheil to make *The Mechanical Ballet* in 1924. 1925 saw his first murals, at the Exhibition of Decorative Art in Paris, and he later designed his first mosaic, to decorate the facade of the church at Assy (1946–9), as well as various stained-glass windows. He visited the United States three times, in 1931, 1935, and 1938, before taking refuge there from 1940 to 1945 when he became a professor at Yale.

His lifelong allegiance to the people is demonstrated by his acceptance of large-scale public commissions, his attendance at the Wroclaw Peace Congress in 1948 and the Sokols Congress in Prague in 1955, but most of all by the ordinary working men and women who are the heroes of his art.

Further reading. Cooper, D. *Fernand Léger et le Nouvel Espace*, London and New York (1949). De Francia, P. *Fernand Léger*, New Haven (1983). Francis, P. de *Léger, the Great Parade*, London (1969). Kuh, K. *Léger*, Urbana, Ill. (1953).

Lehmbruck Wilhelm 1881–1919

The German sculptor and printmaker Wilhelm Lehmbruck was born near Duisburg, the son of a miner. He trained at the School of Arts and Crafts, Düsseldorf, then visited Italy from 1905 to 1906 and again in 1912, and Paris in 1908. From 1910 to 1914 he lived in Paris, where he produced a series of larger-than-life-size statues in bronze and artificial stone (for example, *The Kneeling Woman*, 1911; Museum of Modern Art, New York). In his work, Expressionistic elongations were allied to an elegiac mood, conceivably influenced by medieval prototypes and also by Rodin. In 1914 he returned to Germany, his work becoming increasingly spare and tragic, and in 1919 he committed suicide.

Further reading. Hoff, A. *Wilhelm Lehmbruck*, New York (1969).

Leibl Wilhelm 1844–1900

The German painter Wilhelm Maria Hubert Leibl studied at the Munich Academy (1864–9) where he concentrated on chiaroscuro portraiture. In 1869 he came under the influence of Courbet, whom he met in Munich, and he went to study in Paris (1869–70). Subsequently he became the head of a group of Realist artists in Munich known as the Leibl Circle, but in 1873 he moved to the Dachau moors. There he developed a flat, monumental Realism, based on a tight, detailed style and starkly silhouetted figures (for example, *Three Women in Church*, 1878–82; Hamburger Kunsthalle, Hamburg). Leibl was the first of many German artists to seek simple values in peasant communities.

Leighton Frederic 1830–96

Frederic, 1st Baron Leighton, was the most esteemed English painter of the later 19th century. Born in Scarborough, Yorkshire, he spent much of his early life abroad, particularly in Frankfurt where he trained with the Nazarene Eduard Jakob von Steinle at the Städel Institute, and in Rome, where he executed his first major work, *Cimabue's celebrated Madonna is Carried in Procession through the Streets of Florence* (1855; Collection of H.M. Queen Elizabeth II). Widely acclaimed, its mixture of Italian Renaissance anecdote and contemporary German style, plus its high technical competence, made it an ideal antidote to the Pre-Raphaelites.

Moving to Paris, where he lived from 1855 to 1860, Leighton developed a heightened sense of coloring, based on contemporary French practice and 17th-century Italian masters. He displayed a preference for Classical subjects—at first emotionally tense and *mouvementé* (as in *Orpheus and*

Wilhelm Lehmbruck: Fallen Man; synthetic stone; 72×239cm (28×94in); 1915–16. Private collection

Frederic Leighton: Winding the Skein; oil on canvas; 100×161cm (39×63in); first exhibited 1878. Art Gallery of New South Wales, Sydney

Eurydice, 1864; Leighton House Art Gallery and Museum, London) but later more dispassionate.

In London from 1860, Leighton rapidly achieved a high position: Royal Academician in 1868, President of the Royal Academy in 1878, in 1896 he became the unique English painter-Peer. Though undoubtedly aided by tactful diplomacy and immense personal charm, Leighton's position owed much to consistent output of high-principled works. It is true he exhibited many seemingly slight studies of feminine beauty and charm (for example *Weaving the Wreath*, 1873; Sudley Art Gallery and Museum, Liverpool). But his serious works, their subject matter drawn from the Bible or Classical mythology, consisted of extended studies of form, composition, and color (for example, *The Return of Persephone*, 1891; City Art Gallery, Leeds). His masterpieces were vast; usually consisting of frieze-like arrangements of figure-groups in architectural and landscape settings, they embody a complex orchestration of the basic ele-

ments of painting (for example, *The Daphnephoria*, 1876; Lady Lever Art Gallery, Port Sunlight). Seeming too deliberate, these works lack the free handling and vital coloring of Leighton's sketches. But a sublimated color vibrancy remains, and the studied artistry is of permanent value, even though currently unfashionable.

Further reading. Newall, C. *The Art of Lord Leighton*, London (1990).

Leinberger Hans c1480–c1535?

The sculptor Hans Leinberger was born in Landshut in southern Germany. His earliest works display the exaggerated pose of the figure and deeply-cut drapery style characteristic of the late Gothic. This is found both in his wood sculpture, such as the high altar for the collegiate church of Moosburg (1511–14) and in the armored bronze figure of *Albrecht von Hapsburg* for the funerary monument of the Emperor Maximilian in the Hofkirche, Innsbruck (1514–18). His awareness of contempor-

ary art, however, is evident, in the *Crucifixion* relief of 1516 (Bayerisches Nationalmuseum, Munich) which has affinities with the style of the Danube School.

Lely Peter 1618–80

Sir Peter Lely was the foremost painter in England during the Commonwealth and Restoration. Born Pieter van der Faes in the town of Soest, Westphalia, Lely adopted a family nickname about the time that he became a student of Frans Pietersz. de Grebber in Haarlem, in 1637. Around 1641 he moved to London, where he remained most of his life. He practiced first as a history and landscape painter in the Dutch-Italianate manner of Cornelis van Poelenburgh, but receiving little encouragement for this type of picture he turned to portraiture. He modeled his early portrait style on that of van Dyck, although his vigorous handling of paint, strong local coloring, and richly atmospheric landscape settings were entirely his own. In 1661 Lely was made Principal Painter to Charles

II, and in 1668 he was knighted. His best known late pictures, the series of *Flagmen* (National Maritime Museum, Greenwich) and *Windsor Beauties* (Hampton Court Palace, London), evoke fully the swagger and voluptuousness of the second Caroline court.

Lemercier Jacques c1585–1654

The son of a Parisian master mason, the French architect Jacques Lemercier studied in Rome from c1607 to 1614. With Louis Levau and Jules-Hardouin Mansart he may be credited with the formation of the French classical style. Less talented than they, his essential contribution was the introduction of the academic, Classical Roman tradition stemming from Giacomo della Porta (c1533–1602), although he himself was unable to fuse this successfully with his native tradition. Commissioned in 1624 by Louis XIII to extend the Louvre, his most significant contribution was the Pavillon de l'Horloge. For his principal patron, Cardinal Richelieu, he designed the château and church of Rueil, the château and town of Richelieu (begun 1631), the Sorbonne, Paris (begun 1626), and the Palais Cardinal (Palais Royal, begun 1633). He was an ingenious planner of townhouses and his Hotel de Liancourt (1623) was an influential prototype.

Lemoyne François 1688–1737

The French decorative artist François Lemoyne was for a short time the master of François Boucher. He was received at the Académie Royale in 1718 and made First Painter to the King in 1736. He worked at Versailles, decorating the Salon de la Paix in 1736 with his highly praised ceiling, *The Apotheosis of Hercules*. He continued the 17th-century tradition of historical painting practiced by his predecessor, Charles Lebrun. Such classicism and love of allegory was still upheld by the Académie in preference to the gayer, more intimate approach of Watteau. Lemoyne was influenced by Veronese and Rubens. He killed himself, probably through overwork.

Lemoyne Jean-Baptiste 1704–78

The French sculptor Jean-Baptiste Lemoyne was the son of the sculptor Jean-Louis Lemoyne. Born in Paris, he was the most distinguished member of a family of sculptors. In 1725 Lemoyne won the Prix de Rome; but, at his father's request, he never

Sir Peter Lely: Two Ladies of the Lake Family; oil on canvas; 127×180cm (50×71in); c1660. Tate Gallery, London

François Lemoyne: Perseus and Andromeda; oil on canvas; 184×151cm (72×59in); 1723. Wallace Collection, London

made the journey to Italy. Perhaps because of this, his art is quite untouched by classicism, and he is the great representative of Rococo in the French sculpture of his day. Lemoyne was the favorite sculptor of Louis XV. He produced some superb monumental sculpture, much of it mutilated or destroyed during the Revolution, but he is best remembered for his vividly expressive portrait busts.

Lenain family
16th and 17th centuries

The French painters of the Lenain family were Antoine (c1588–1648), Louis (c1593–1648), and Mathieu (c1607–77). All three were born in Laon in northeast France close to what was then the frontier with Flanders. All three died in Paris. Their

work was rediscovered in the middle of the 19th century by Champfleury and has been a source of continuous speculation. The whereabouts and extent of their artistic education is still unknown. Antoine was known to have specialized in small genre scenes while Louis concentrated on larger figure-compositions, some of which had a religious or mythological content. Mathieu is supposed to have been responsible for the rest, the portraits in particular.

Some 15 or so signed works survive. All the signatures take the form "Le Nain" and are sometimes followed by a date—usually in the 1640s. It would be absurd to suppose that all their surviving work dates from the 1640s and therefore even a tentative dating is difficult. The formation of their style, like their individual personalities, is a mystery. Their subject

matter—peasant genre and down-to-earth religious scenes—conforms to the Netherlandish type, and their work has sometimes even been confused with that of Jan Molenaer.

Too little is known about the artistic context of the Paris of Louis XIII to say whether their work is typical of a general taste which does not happen to have survived, or whether they catered for a rather specialized patron familiar with Netherlandish art.

Peasants at Supper (c1642–5; Louvre, Paris) illustrates both the strengths and weaknesses of their style. There is an unerring eye in the observation of each figure, but there is a certain gaucheness in the composition. The artist is not always sure where to place the figures and is equally uncertain of their relationships with each other. This picture could almost be described as the seven ages of man, as each figure is clearly in a different age group.

In the *Charette* (1641; Louvre, Paris) the figures are integrated with some care into the landscape. It is this aspect of their art that has been neglected by many critics. French landscape is inevitably seen in terms of Claude and Poussin and the contribution of the Lenain brothers is often ignored. The *Group of Peasants* (Victoria and Albert Museum, London) shows figures both seated and standing with perfect naturalness in a flat (northeastern French ?) landscape with a low line of hills in the distance. This landscape belongs to the tradition—or indeed is its beginning in France—of the observation of landscape without the intervention of theory or artifice. This approach is taken even further in the *Peasants in a Landscape* (Wadsworth Atheneum, Hartford, Conn.) where the picture is almost a landscape in its own right; it is painted in a direct manner which makes the work of many Dutch landscapists appear composed.

In their religious and mythological pictures the artists used conventional Baroque subject matter, but interpreted it in an original way. The *Venus at the Forge of Vulcan* (Musée des Beaux-Arts, Reims) is a strange mixture of heavy peasant realism and a none-too-happy Venus in a semiformal pose. The mythological element is eliminated in *The Forge* (Louvre, Paris) where the rapid brush strokes and direct vision make it difficult to conceive of such a work as the product of collaboration.

The religious pictures are equally varied.

Louis Lenain: The Donkey; oil on canvas; 51×59cm (20×23in); c1641. Hermitage Museum, St Petersburg

The *Nativity* (National Gallery, London) has a sentimental sweetness befitting the subject—indeed the artists did not seem to be at home with a subject they could not observe. This is particularly true of the *Birth of the Virgin* (Notre Dame, Paris) where St Anne in bed in the background seems perfectly observed from nature while much of the rest of the picture is composed in a conventional Baroque way.

It is to be hoped that one day the problem of the extent of the collaboration of the three brothers will be solved. They seem a little out of place in the context of the Paris of Vouet, Lesueur, and Philippe de Champaigne. Yet all three brothers were elected founder members of the Academy in 1648. Parisian art had not yet settled down to the conventions that were to inhibit individuality in the latter half of the century.

Leochares 4th century BC

The Greek late Classical sculptor Leochares was probably Athenian. He collaborated with Scopas and Bryaxis in the Mausoleum, and with Lysippos in the bronze group of *Alexander's Lion Hunt* at Delphi. He also made portraits of the orator Isocrates in bronze and of the family of Philip of Macedon in ivory and gold. His bronze group of *Ganymedes Being Raised to Heaven by the Eagle of Zeus* is probably represented by a copy in the Vatican Museums, Rome; his *Apollo* in Athens by the striding *Apollo Belvedere* (Vatican Museums, Rome) which has fascinated European artists since the Renaissance. Leochares' style combines Attic grandeur with the elongated proportions, limbs moving into space, and restless stance first explored by Lysippos.

Leonardo da Vinci 1452–1519

Leonardo da Vinci was a painter, sculptor, architect, engineer, and investigator of nature. He described painting as the "sole imitator of all the visible works of nature" and as "a subtle invention which with philosophy and clever speculation considers the natures of all forms". This elevated aspiration provided the basis for his claim that the painter was superior to the practitioners of all other disciplines, particularly the poets who were so highly respected in the court circles he frequented.

Most of the first 30 years of his life were spent around Vinci, the small Tuscan town near which he was born, the illegitimate son of a notary, and in Florence, largely under the care of the sculptor Andrea del Verrocchio. Leonardo's continued residence with his accomplished master, four years after his matriculation in 1472 as independent painter, suggests that the versatile studio provided a congenial environment.

His first dated work is a pen drawing of *The Arno Valley* (1473; Uffizi, Florence) which possesses a remarkable sense of atmosphere and flickering vitality. These qualities provide ample grounds for attributing to him the suggestive beauties of the distant landscape in Verrocchio's *Baptism* (Uffizi, Florence), in addition to the foreground angel ascribed to him in early accounts. The inner nervous life of this angel, the vibrant filaments of hair, and the naively obtrusive folds of angular drapery provide uneasy contrasts with the more orthodox modeling and conventional piety of Verrocchio's figures.

His earliest surviving painting, the *Annunciation* (c1472–3; Uffizi, Florence), contains splendid passages, but the overall organization is gauche, in spite of its pedantically correct perspective. The same combination of vivacious detail and stiff presentation characterizes his portrait of *Ginevra de' Benci* (c1474; National Gallery of Art, Washington, D.C.)

Greater compositional fluency first appeared in his drawings (for example, *Madonna, Child, and Cat*, c1480; British Museum, London). He developed a highly original technique of passionately energetic scribbling which both suggests new arrangements and captures complex movements in a spontaneous manner. His *Madonna with a Vase of Flowers* (c1476; Alte Pinakothek, Munich) and *Virgin and Child (Madonna Benois)* (c1478–80; Hermitage Museum, St Petersburg) are lively examples of his developing design methods. His growing reputation is reflected in his commissions in 1478 and 1481 for altarpieces in the Palazzo Vecchio (the Florentine seat of Government) and S. Donato a Scopeto. The former probably did not progress beyond the design stage, and the latter remained unfinished as the magnificent underpainting of the *Adoration of the Kings* (Uffizi, Florence). He has transformed the pageant spirit of Florentine Adorations into a crowd scene of disturbing urgency, in which awed figures gesticulate tumultuously around

Leonardo da Vinci:
Virgin and Child
(Madonna Benois);
wood transferred to
canvas; 50×31cm
(20×12in); c1478–80.
Hermitage Museum,
St Petersburg

Leonardo da Vinci: Self-portrait; red chalk; 33×21cm (13×8in); c1512. Royal Library, Turin.

the tranquil virgin, while in the background unbridled animal passions are given free rein in ruined architecture. In his interpretation, the replacement of the old world with the new was not to be an easy process of benign inevitability.

He moved to the Sforza court at Milan, probably in 1482. The draft of his introductory letter to Duke Ludovico indicates that he intended to establish himself as an engineer specializing in military matters. His range of activity at the court embraced the roles of architect, engineer, inventor, theatrical designer of court spectaculars, sculptor, musician, scientist, art theorist, pundit and painter; but little remains to show for his industry. His damaged Sala delle Asse (1498; Castello Sforzesco, Milan) gives some idea of the elegant inventiveness with which he fulfilled his court duties. From rock-embedded roots at the base of the wall painted tree trunks ascend on each side towards the vaults of the ceiling, where leafy branches interlace with a golden cord to form an incredibly complicated canopy.

In contrast to the witty conceit of transforming a room into a forest bower is the high spiritual seriousness of his contemporary Last Supper (c1497; S. Maria delle Grazie, Milan), in which Christ's terrible announcement of the impending betrayal, and the institution of the Eucharist provide profoundly interwoven themes. Within a

contrived and ambiguous space, which extends the end wall of the refectory, the figures are arranged behind the table with a cunning that conceals their crowding. The meaning is made fully apparent through his unrivalled command of expression and gesture. Judas is differentiated by psychological means—the guilty disciple is shocked rigid, not galvanized into innocent action—rather than by traditionally isolating him on the opposite side of the table.

Leonardo's scientific studies during the 1490s gave him an increasingly profound understanding of natural law as it was then understood. He demanded that painting should express the principles of light, space, anatomy, psychology, geology, and the other sciences, all of which he infused with his special sensitivity to nature as a living force. He filled his notebooks with variations upon medieval scientific themes; he also planned his treatise on painting, which was to contain uncompromising statements on art as the depiction of natural effects through an understanding of their causes.

His studies of light are reflected in the vivid modeling of the Virgin of the Rocks (c1483–6; Louvre, Paris) and the second version (finished 1508; National Gallery, London), which shows the meeting in the wilderness of the Virgin and Christ with the infant St John and the the archangel Uriel. The contours are softened, given the effect he called sfumato ("smoked") by means of softly veiling shadows, some of which he blended with his hands rather than with the brush. The progressive dominance of shadow over the individual colors created a new tonal unity, which is nowhere more apparent than in the pools of light and shade in his portrait of the Duke's mistress Cecilia Gallerani, Lady with an Ermine (c1483–4; Czartoryski Museum, Krakow). An ermine, the animal symbolic of purity, lies sinuously in her arms as she turns, smiling slightly, to greet an implied companion.

The major artistic project of his Milanese years, the huge equestrian statue of Ludovico's father, Francesco, became a victim of historical circumstance. Towards the beleaguered end of his reign the Duke could not afford the bronze for the horse, and when the French expelled him in 1499 they destroyed the full-scale clay model which had been unveiled in 1493. Leonardo left the city and wandered to Mantua and Venice before returning to Florence in 1500.

For two years he strove to reestablish himself, painting the Madonna with a Yarnwinder (lost, but known through drawings, copies, or studio versions) and completing a cartoon of the Madonna, Child, and St Anne (lost). These works introduced Florentines to a new narrative method of integrating symbols into Madonna compositions. The painting showed the young Christ surging across his mother's lap to grasp the cross-shaped yarnwinder (a reference to the future crucifixion), while the Virgin watches with anxious compassion. The lost cartoon was the distant prototype for the Madonna, Child, and St Anne in the Louvre, Paris (c1508–15). It involved a complex interplay of emotions between the child who innocently tried to play with a lamb (a sacrificial animal signifying the coming Passion), and the Virgin who restrained him as if wishing to forestall her son's fate; meanwhile, St Anne's expression knowingly implied that what must be, must be. The composition of the surviving painting, based upon a compelling diagonal, brilliantly conveys the ebb and flow of human relationships.

In 1502–3 he spent some months traveling as military engineer to Cesare Borgia, who was rampaging on the Pope's behalf in central Italy. Appropriately, when Leonardo returned to Florence he was commissioned to paint a scene of war, The Battle of Anghiari, in the Grand Council Hall of the Palazzo Vecchio. Michelangelo was to be asked soon afterwards for a companion piece, The Battle of Cascina. Leonardo began painting in 1504, but he seems to have run into difficulties with his experimental oil technique and the work was never completed. Copies and his own drawings assist in reconstructing the appearance of the central group, which consisted of a writhing knot of Florentine and Milanese cavalry. The interlocked motion set new standards in the depiction of violent action, which were to be as deeply respected by Rubens in the next century as they were influential upon Leonardo's contemporaries.

At the other extreme, during this period, he began his studies for Leda and the Swan, culminating in a lost painting of Leda in mutual embrace with the swan (Jupiter in disguise). The seductive curves of her serpentine pose provided a rhythmical counterpoint to the sinuous neck of the bird. Leonardo's fascination with the processes of generation, birth, growth, and motion pervaded the whole painting, from the total design to the smallest details—such as the springing spirals of Leda's hair, for which compelling drawings survive (Royal Library, Windsor Castle).

The Florentines, under pressure from the French king, Louis XII, were forced to grant Leonardo leave to visit Milan in 1506. None of his subsequent periods in Florence lasted as long as a year, and in July 1508 he resumed more or less permanent residence in Milan, in the service of the French governor. Shortly after his arrival he planned, but never executed, an equestrian statue of General Trivulzio.

Henceforth, he devoted much of his energy to scientific investigations, which gained new authority as he mastered medieval science and refined his methods. In his anatomy he aimed to discover a perfect functional explanation of every small facet of natural form. His studies of sight passed beyond painter's perspective and into the realms of illusions, distortions, and unstable variables. The more he investigated nature, the more he revered the complexity and subtlety of man and his world.

This awe is expressed in the background of the so-called *Mona Lisa* (Louvre, Paris), where rivers descend from high lakes, continuously and inexorably eroding the mountains. The sitter has not been satisfactorily identified, whatever popular myths and hopeful historians may have suggested to the contrary. The earliest reference (1517) records that it was "the portrait of a certain Florentine lady made at the request of the late Magnificent Giuliano de' Medici" (therefore finished in Rome after 1513 when he worked for Giuliano, rather than in 1503–4 as is generally assumed); but this is by no means definite. Never before had a portrait made such an open attempt to communicate with the spectator; but it is a consciously ambiguous communication, the elusive forms defying precise reading of her expression.

His conception of a portrait as an archetype of nature's inner power is utterly consistent with his transformation of *St John the Baptist* (c1509; Louvre, Paris) into an archetype of spiritual insight which is evocative of the creative forces behind and beyond the visible surfaces of forms. *St John*, disconcertingly bisexual in a way that may reflect Leonardo's homosexuality, looms from the shadows to mesmerize the spectator with his message of Christ's coming. The Saint's expression conveys the same ineffable knowingness as the *St Anne* and *Mona Lisa*.

After his move to Rome in 1513, he was increasingly concerned with the mathematics of nature in dynamic action. Sheets of geometrical conundrums are interspersed with beautiful demonstrations of nature in movement, whether it be the turbulence of blood in the heart, the spiraling flight of birds, or the destructive maelstroms of his *Deluge* drawings (c1515; Royal Library, Windsor Castle). In the *Deluges*, the vortex patterns which formed the basis of his hydrodynamic science have been reformed into terrifying visions of cosmological flux.

Alongside these largely private works, he continued his public career in the service of the Medici in Rome. After 1516 he lived in France under the patronage of François I, for whom he undertook many of the same court tasks he had performed in Milan. Honored in France as a venerable seer, he died at Amboise.

Only a small number of his relatively few finished paintings have survived. No extant sculpture or architecture can be definitely assigned to him, and none of his writings was published until 1651. But his impact upon almost every aspect of art was enormous. His immediate pupils were unworthy, but he found true successors in Raphael, Bramante, and even the apparently hostile Michangelo. His inventions became part of the standard currency of European art.

Further reading. Clark, K. *Leonardo da Vinci*, Harmondsworth (1967). Clark, K. *The Drawings of Leonardo da Vinci at Windsor Castle*, London (1969). Goldscheider, L. *Leonardo da Vinci, Landscapes and Plants*, London (1952). Goldscheider, L. *Leonardo, Paintings and Drawings*, London (1959). Heydenreich, L.A. *Leonardo da Vinci* (2 vols.), Basel and New York (1954). Kemp, M. *Leonardo da Vinci: the Marvellous Works of Nature and Man*, London (1981). McCurdy, E. *The Notebooks of Leonardo da Vinci* (2 vols.), London (1959). McMahon, A.P. (ed.) *Leonardo's Treatise on Painting*, Princeton (1956). O'Malley, C.D. (ed.) *Leonardo's Legacy: an International Symposium*, Berkeley (1969). Pedretti, C. *Leonardo*, London (1973). Pedretti, C. *The Literary Works of Leonardo: Commentary to Jean Paul Richter's Edition* (2 vols.), London (1977). Popham, A. *The Drawings of Leonardo da Vinci*, London (1946). Reti, L. (ed.) *The Unknown Leonardo*, London (1974). Richter, J.P. (ed.) *The Literary Works of Leonardo da Vinci*, London (1970). Zubov, V.P. *Leonardo da Vinci*, Cambridge, Mass. (1968).

Leoni family 16th and 17th centuries

Leone Leoni (1509–90) and his son Pompeo (c1533–1608) were Italian sculptors. Born at Menaggio (Como) of Aretine stock, Leone Leoni is first known as a medalist at Padua in 1537 and was one of the most brilliant exponents of the art of the medal of his time. He seems to have come comparatively late in his career to sculpture, in which he perhaps had no formal training, and of which he became a highly idiosyncratic practitioner. Engraver at the Papal Mint in Rome from 1537 to 1540, he caused the imprisonment of Benvenuto Cellini in 1538, and was himself sent to the galleys in 1540 for a brutal assault on a colleague. Freed the following year, he became Master of the Imperial Mint in Milan in 1542, holding this post initially for three years, and then again from 1550 to 1589.

Although his finest work as a sculptor is the monument to Gian Giacomo de' Medici, Marquis of Melegnano, in Milan Cathedral (1560–3), he is best known for his great series of sculptures, mostly in bronze, for the house of Hapsburg (Prado, Madrid). These were the fruit of visits to the Court of the Emperor Charles V in Brussels in 1548–9 and 1556 and Augsburg in 1551. His collaborator in these was his son Pompeo.

Shortly after Charles V's abdication in 1556, Pompeo entered the service of the regent Juana of Austria in Madrid, later working for Philip II. Father and son collaborated on Pompeo's important commission of 1579 for 27 massive gilt-bronze statues for the high altar of the Escorial, cast in Milan between 1582 and 1589.

Pompeo's own most memorable achievements in sculpture are the splendid gilt-bronze monuments to Charles V and Philip II, commissioned by Philip in 1591 for the Escorial, and made entirely in Spain. Pompeo remained in Spain until his death in 1608; his many other works there prove him to have been a sculptor of great ability in his own right, who in the shadow of his brilliant father has never quite received the recognition he deserves.

Le Parc Julio 1928–

The sculptor Julio Le Parc was born at Mendoza, Argentina, and studied in Buenos Aires. In 1958 he moved to Paris and in 1960 was a founder member of the *Groupe de Recherches d'Art Visuel* (*GRAV*, Paris 1960–8). He also took part in the activities fof the *Nouvelle Tendance* movement.

Le Parc's optical-kinetic constructions, made usually from polished metal, often exploit internal reflections. They rely upon air currents or the spectator's moving eye and body for their distorting, disorienting, and transient effects. As well as reliefs and mobiles (for example *Continuel Mobile, Continuel Lumière*, 1963; Tate Gallery, London) Le Parc has made light-reflecting machines, and works using mirrors and translucent plastic. He was awarded the first prize at the Venice Biennale in 1966.

Lescot Pierre c1515–78

Unlike the master masons who preceded him, the French master mason Pierre Lescot came from a prosperous legal family and was a man of learning and liberal education. His reputation rests mainly on the rebuilding of the Louvre, Paris, begun under his direction in 1546. His other works are the Hotel Carnavalet (c1545–50), the Fontaine des Innocents (1547–9), and the screen at St Germain L'Auxerrois (1554), all in Paris. His buildings are striking in their classicism and accuracy of antique detail; but their lack of monumentality and their emphasis on surface decoration are both quite un-Italian: they are the antithesis of the work of his contemporary Philibert Delorme. In all his buildings, Lescot worked in close collaboration with Jean Goujon, the greatest sculptor of his day.

Lesueur Eustache 1616/17–55

The French painter Eustache Lesueur was born in Paris. In 1632 he became a pupil of Simon Vouet, whose work at first greatly influenced him. He worked at the Hotel Lambert, on a *History of Cupid* for the Cabinet d'Amour (1646–7), and on paintings of the Muses for the *Cabinet des Muses* (1647–9). These works are markedly more independent than the commission

Leone Leoni: Ferrante Gonzaga Triumphant; bronze cast; 1564. Piazza Roma, Guastella

for tapestry designs which Vouet had passed on to him c1637. Illustrating scenes from the *Hypnerotomachia Polifili*, an antiquarian love-story printed at Venice in 1499, these designs show the popularity of humanist themes in France at that time.

As Lesueur grew older, his style became more austere: the *Cabinet des Muses* paintings already suggest Raphael's work in the Villa Farnesina—if only by hindsight. Like his later series of *The Life of St Bruno* (for the Charterhouse at Paris, c1648; Louvre, Paris) they show a strong influence from Poussin, whom Lesueur may well have met during that master's visit to Paris from 1640 to 1642. Lesueur's late works show a reappraisal of Raphael, particularly Raphael's tapestry cartoons. Lesueur imitated these in works of grandeur, such as his *St Paul at Ephesus* (1649; Louvre, Paris).

Le Sueur Hubert *fl. c1610–51*

Between 1610 and 1619, the sculptor Hubert Le Sueur was in the French royal service. By 1626 he was in England, making figures for the catafalque of James I. He executed a number of tombs, the only ones of real consequence being those of Sir Thomas Richardson and Lady Cottington, both at Westminster. From 1631 he was in the service of Charles I, for whom he designed his best-known work, the equestrian statue of the King at Charing Cross, London. He also made a series of busts of the monarch.

Although Le Sueur was a second-rate artist, he is important for introducing contemporary Continental ideas into English sculpture, helping to break the hold of the moribund style of the previous century.

Le Tavernier Jean *fl. 1434–67*

The Flemish painter Jean Le Tavernier was one of the principal illuminators working for Philip the Good. A stylish and technically assured artist, he was not associated with any single publishing house; he presided over an independent illuminator's shop in Oudenaarde, near Ghent, where he is documented from 1454 until his death. The earliest extant work attributable to him is the Book of Hours for Philip of 1454 (Royal Library, The Hague; MS. 76. F. 2). His masterpiece is the *Chroniques de Charlemagne* (1458; Bibliothèque Royale Albert I, Brussels). Both are executed in grisaille, a medium in which the artist

specialized. In his late period, exemplified by the *Miracles de Nostre-Dame* (Bibliothèque Nationale, Paris) made for Charles the Bold, his work shows the influence of the style associated with the name of Philippe de Mazerolles (c1420–79).

Levau Louis 1612–70

The architect Louis Levau was a Parisian, and a contemporary of François Mansart. His career was, however, very different from that of Mansart—he was successful with his patrons, careless and impatient with the finer rules of classicism, and deeply committed to the Italian Baroque. His château at Vaux-le-Vicomte (1658–61), for the royal financier Fouquet, and his Parisian Hotel Lambert (1640–4) both show the full and dramatic use of that style. The gallery and staircase of the latter were remarkable for their ingenuity and magnificence. In the commissions that followed, the Collège des Quatres Nations (1662), the East Front of the Louvre (1667), and Versailles (begun in 1669), the lessons of these two buildings were repeated, with almost the same group of craftsmen in charge. At Versailles, the ingenuity with which Levau masked the old château of Louis XIII, and the lively grandeur he gave to his new garden facade, show him responding brilliantly to a problem that demanded both skill and imagination.

Levine Jack 1915–

Jack Levine is an American painter, born in Boston. Brought up in the Depression and employed on W.P.A. (Works Progress Administration) mural projects, Levine became an artist of social protest, building on the legacy of the Ash Can School. His art is one of character exposure, in an Expressionistic technique that owes much to Daumier, Rouault, Soutine, and George Grosz. The objects of his satire are the gangsters, mobsters, and perverters of American justice. His paintings, such as *Gangster Funeral* (oil; 1952–3; Whitney Museum of American Art, New York) and *The Trial* (oil; 1953–4; Art Institute of Chicago), are elaborately worked out in both composition and symbolism.

Levni 18th century

The Turkish artist known as Levni was

court painter to the Ottoman Sultan Ahmet III (1703–30). His real name was Abdulcelil Chelebi. He was born in Edirne and brought to Istanbul by the Sultan in 1718. Here he enjoyed the Sultan's favor through the Tulip period of lavish patronage of the arts, especially the arts of the book. He directed the illustration of the *Sur-nama* of Vehbi with 137 miniatures (1720–1; Topkapi Saray Museum, Istanbul; A. 3593) and also a set of portraits of the Sultans to Ahmet III (A. 3109). These are icon-like and conservative; but he also drew a large set of single figures from life, including Europeans, in realistic style.

Lewis Wyndham 1882–1957

The painter and writer Percy Wyndham Lewis was born at sea off Nova Scotia, Canada, son of an American father and a British mother. He moved to London with his mother, and studied at the Slade School of Fine Art from 1898 to 1901. From then until 1909 he often traveled and worked abroad, in particular in Paris and Munich. His companions included Spencer Gore, Augustus John, and Ambrose McEvoy. In 1909 and 1910 the influence of early Cubism and German Expressionism became apparent in his work, while his designs for the portfolio *Timon of Athens* exhibited at the Second Post-Impressionist Exhibition in 1912 revealed his assimilation of Futurist idioms, and the beginnings of a personal style.

In 1913 Lewis arrived at an original Abstract style derived from a synthesis of Expressionist, Cubist and Futurist ideas that was subsequently termed "Vorticism"; *Composition* (1913; Tate Gallery, London) and his folio of 20 drawings on modern life entitled *Timon of Athens* (1913) are typical works. His paintings of 1913 to 1915 were the first sustained body of Abstract work to be produced in England. In 1913 he also joined Roger Fry's Omega Workshops, but withdrew with others amidst controversy later in the year, to found the rival Rebel Art Center which became the seedbed of Vorticism. Most of the "rebels" contributed to the first issue of the Vorticist magazine *Blast* in 1914.

Lewis' verbal and visual concerns came together in this publication, not least in the aggressive typography and design. *Blast*, inspired by Futurist publications and intended to shake up the English art establishment, was very largely the expression of Lewis' attitudes. His were practically

Wyndham Lewis: A Battery Shelled; oil on canvas; 183×318cm (72×125in); 1919. Imperial War Museum, London

the only works illustrated in the magazine to match the strident prose; indeed Ezra Pound, a fellow-contributor, considered Vorticism itself to be "nine-tenths Lewis". His paintings of 1913 to 1915 were so individual and assertive, and of such clarity and dynamism, that it was inevitable that his work should shape the style of the other Vorticists.

By 1915 the conviction of his Abstract works began to wane. *Workshop* of 1915 (New York Public Library), for example, has lost much of the tightness and internal rhythm of the paintings of 1913 and 1914, such as *Man of War* and *Red Duet* (private collection). In 1916 Lewis eventually joined the Army, and was seconded as a war artist in 1917. The paintings that resulted, such as *A Battery Shelled* (1919; Imperial War Museum, London), were figurative but tightly organized, and were some of the finest works of their kind. Apart from a brief episode in the early 1920s he never approached total abstraction again.

Lewis' linear gifts were subsequently evident in an increasing number of uncompromising portraits, both drawings and oils, from *Ezra Pound* (1914–15; now lost; 1938 version in the Tate Gallery, London) to *T.S. Eliot (II)* (1938; Durban Museum and Art Gallery). He also painted some ambitious but rather unsuccessful literary and historical compositions in the 1930s. The general tendency of his work after the crystalline Vorticist paintings was towards a more organic kind of composition. The latter can be linked with English neo-Romantic art of the Second World War. Lewis' vision deteriorated, and he finally went blind in 1950. Thereafter he concentrated all his energies upon writing, with which he had been engaged spas-

modically for over 40 years. He died in London.

Further reading. Cork, R. *Vorticism and Abstract Art in the First Machine Age*, London (1976). Handley-Read, C. *The Art of Wyndham Lewis*, London (1951). Rothenstein, J. *Modern English Painters: Lewis to Moore*, London (1962).

LeWitt Sol 1928–

The American sculptor Sol LeWitt was born in Hartford, Connecticut. He attended Syracuse University from 1945 to 1949. He then taught at the Museum of Modern Art School, New York (1964–7), at Cooper Union (1967–8), at the School of Visual Arts (1969–70), and at New York University. In the years 1962 to 1965, LeWitt's Abstract sculptures and reliefs in painted wood explored repeated square motifs and modular proportions. From 1965 to 1969, all his sculptures in wood or white enameled steel were variations and permutations of open-frame cubes, or cube boxes with open and closed sides, sometimes rising from square grid bases. In 1968 he created his first wall drawings, made by the artist or to his instructions, consisting of combinations of straight, curved, or random black or colored lines. From 1973 these gave way to simple lines and geometric figures based on the dimensions of a given wall space. In 1970 he began to make prints based on the same principles.

Sol LeWitt: untitled; etching; 18×17cm (7×6½in); 1971. **Museum of Modern Art, New York**

sociated with the Ch'an artists.

Liang K'ai's name is often linked with that of Mu Ch'i; but from the evidence of the very few paintings attributed to him, Liang painted with a wry humor and witty brush. His two most famous works are of figures, each making a comment which is both succinct and good-humored. They each show the hand of a consummate draftsman used in a way quite unusual in Chinese figure-painting. Although Liang K'ai is an unusual genius in his treatment of his subject, he is one of the many elegant handlers of brush and ink working in the 12th and 13th centuries.

Liberale da Verona *c*1445–1526/9

Liberale was, as his name indicates, a Veronese painter. Besides undertaking the usual commissions—altarpieces, fresco cycles, and devotional Madonnas—Liberale also displayed skills as a miniaturist. He worked in Tuscany from 1467 to 1476 illustrating graduals for Monte Oliveto Monastery (now at Chiusi Cathedral) and Siena Cathedral (Piccolomini Library, Siena), the latter with Girolamo da Cremona. His later work mainly centered around Verona; for example, the frescoes he painted in S. Anastasia. The dominant influence upon his style was Andrea Mantegna (1431–1506). Liberale used vivid coloring, particularly in his miniatures. He often gave his figures mournful eyes and pained expressions, such as those in the Berlin *Madonna and Saints* (1489; Staatliche Museen, Berlin).

Liberale da Verona: St Martin and the Beggar; a miniature on folio 76 of Graduale no. 12. Piccolomini Library, Siena

Liang K'ai: The Sixth Patrician Chopping Bamboo; hanging scroll, ink on paper; height 74cm (29in). Tokyo National Museum

Liang K'ai *c*1140–*c*1210

The Chinese painter Liang K'ai came from Tung P'ing and started his career as a court painter of the late Southern Sung. He was therefore thoroughly trained in the Hsia-Ma School and his work bears all the qualities of skilled and controlled brushwork. Later in his life Liang K'ai retired to the Liu T'ung temple, although there is no evidence that he ever became a monk. It seems that he lived a retired but congenial life painting, drinking, and meeting friends. He was in sympathy with Ch'an painting, and was a fine exponent of the expressive style of direct and explosive brushwork which had already become as-

Li Ch'eng *fl. 940–67*

The Chinese painter Li Ch'eng was a descendant of the T'ang royal house. Certainly educated in the Confucian scholarly tradition, he moved from Ch'ang An to Ying Ch'iu in Shantung Province. He is recorded to have been an overbearing and unsuccessful official who made a reputation as a landscape painter. However Mi Fei (1051–1107) records that Li Ch'eng's paintings were very rare by his time. He painted, in ink with slight color, winter landscapes of majestic mountains with bare trees which he depicted distinctively with "crab claw" branches. It is said that his brush strokes seem a thousand *li* away, emphasizing his skill in expressing distance. Although now a shadowy figure, he stands at the head of the school of great mountain painters, following the still more shadowy Kuan T'ung.

Lichtenstein Roy *1923–*

The American painter Roy Lichtenstein was born in New York. He studied under Reginald Marsh and at Ohio State College from 1940 to 1943. He served in the Second World War, taught at Ohio State College, and subsequently lived in Cleveland, Ohio (1951–7). During the 1950s, he worked in an Abstract Expressionist style; but after *c*1957, he became absorbed in imagery based on mass-market advertising and cheap comic strips, which he enlarged to heroic size. *Whaam!* (1962; Tate Gallery, London) is over 13 ft (3.96 m) wide. As well as incorporating wording, Lichtenstein imitates the dots that are part of the screened images from which comics were printed. This style was fully de-

Roy Lichtenstein: Takka Takka; acrylic on canvas; 143×173cm (56×68in); 1962. Museum Ludwig, Cologne

veloped by the beginning of the 1960s and has remained the basis of his art. He has often applied it to more sophisticated sources, such as derivations from Cubism and Picasso, and views of Greek temples.

Further reading. Alloway, L. *Roy Lichtenstein*, London (1983).

Liebermann Max *1847–1935*

Max Liebermann was a German genre painter of the Realist school. He studied in Weimar and Paris from 1872 to 1878. He was influenced in his youth by Millet and Courbet and spent one important summer at Barbizon, in 1878. His Munich paintings depict daily life and people at work in interiors. After 1884 his works became increasingly Romantic, not only in their treatment of paint but also in choice of subject (for example, *The Parrot's Walk at the Amsterdam Zoo*, 1902; Kunsthalle Bremen). This reflected the later influence of the French Impressionists, who encouraged him to select open-air scenes, and to lighten his palette.

Liédet Loyset *fl. c1454–78*

Loyset Liédet was a Flemish illuminator who apparently came from Hesdin. He worked in the atelier of Jean Wauquelin at Mons and with Simon Marmion at Valenciennes, before returning to set up his own atelier in Hesdin, where he is documented in 1460. Shortly afterwards, he collaborated with the scribe David Aubert, perhaps at Brussels. In 1469 he was admitted to the illuminators' guild at Bruges, where he remained until his death. He illuminated a number of manuscripts for Philip the Good, including the *Histoires Romaines* (Bibliothèque de l'Arsenal, Paris; MSS. 5087 and 5088), the *Vita Christi* (Bibliothèque Royale Albert I, Brussels; MS. IV. 106), and the *Histoire de Charles Martel* (Bibliothèque Royale Albert I, Brussels; MSS. 6–9). One of the leading Flemish illuminators of his day, Liédet was the head of a large and extremely prolific atelier.

Lievensz. Jan *1607–74*

The Dutch painter and etcher Jan Lievensz. was born in Leiden, where he was first apprenticed. Later he became a pupil of Pieter Lastman in Amsterdam. He shared a studio with the slightly older but less

Max Liebermann: The Parrot's Walk at the Amsterdam Zoo; oil on canvas; 88×73cm (35×29in); 1902. Kunsthalle Bremen

precocious Rembrandt between 1625 and 1631. The two artists often collaborated on the same picture: the *Portrait of a Child* (Rijksmuseum, Amsterdam) is signed "Lievens retouched by Rembrandt". The early works of both painters exhibit a minute technique, dark tones, and dramatic mood (for example Lievens' somewhat theatrical *The Raising of Lazarus*, 1631; Art Gallery and Museum, Brighton); the attribution of paintings from their workshop is therefore sometimes a problem. Constantin Huygens, the Secretary of Prince Frederick Henry and a patron of both artists, regarded them as equals at this stage; he considered Rembrandt to be more emotionally expressive, but Lievensz. superior in "grandeur of invention and boldness".

The early pictures are genre scenes (often life size), religious subjects, and portraits. Lievensz. was in England between *c*1632 and 1634, and is reputed to have painted the Royal Family. On his return his portraits were influenced by the courtly style of van Dyck, while a small group of landscapes reveal his study of Rubens and Brouwer. Between 1644 and 1674 Lievensz. lived mainly in Amsterdam, where he was a popular portraitist and successful painter of large-scale historical and allegorical subjects (for example, his paintings from 1656 and 1661 for the new Amsterdam Town Hall).

Limburg brothers late 14th–early 15th century

The Limburgs were a family of French illuminators. There were at least three brothers: Paul (Polequin), Jean (Jacquemin), and Herman. There may also have been a fourth brother, Arnold. They are exceptionally well documented for their period: between 1399 and 1416 some 35 records are preserved, which refer to them and their activities. We know their parentage and origin: their father was a sculptor in Nijmegen (Netherlands), who called himself "Limburg", where he came from. Their mother was the sister of the well known painter Jean Malouel.

Early in 1399 two of the brothers, Jean and Herman, were apprenticed to a Parisian goldsmith, when they are called "jonnes enfans". Because of an epidemic in Paris, they were sent back to their native country, but a conflict between Brabant and Guelders delayed them; they were imprisoned and held for ransom in Brussels. The Duke Philip the Bold of Burgundy advanced the money to free the boys after they had been in prison for about six months. Early in 1402 another document records that Philip the Bold engaged Paul and Jean to illuminate a "très belle et notable Bible" for him. They are now called "enlumineurs" and are requested to paint the miniatures in this codex as quickly as possible.

After the death of their first patron in 1404, the brothers entered the service of Duc Jean de Berry, for whom they undertook the illuminations of two splendid books of hours: the *Belle Heures* (Cloisters, New York) which were completed in 1408 or 1409 and are described in the inventory of the Duc de Berry of 1413; and the most famous *Très Riches Heures du Duc de Berry* (Musée Condé, Chantilly). This manuscript was only half finished when the Duc de Berry died in 1416. The brothers died in the same year.

Although not recorded, from internal evidence it can be deduced that one or two, perhaps all three of the brothers, visited northern Italy, most likely Florence, Padua, and possibly Siena. *The Presentation of Christ* in the *Très Riches Heures*, modeled after the well known fresco in S. Croce, Florence, by Taddeo Gaddi, is one of the undeniable proofs of such a voyage. The first recorded work by the Limburgs, made for Philip the Bold between 1402 and 1404, is a *Bible moralisée* (now in the Bibliothèque Nationale, Paris, MS. Fr.

166). The Limburgs completed only the first three gatherings of this manuscript and started on the fourth. Their model is preserved: a *Bible moralisée* of c1350–70 (now also in the Bibliothèque Nationale, Paris; MS. fr. 167) which was then owned by Philip the Bold. The Limburgs followed the prototype closely; they also framed the miniatures in quatrefoils alternating with architectural borders as in the earlier *Bible moralisée*. The same texts in Latin, followed by a French translation, are inscribed in the wide margins.

The miniatures reproduce the compositions of the earlier Bible faithfully, but, as is usual in such cases, the Limburgs updated the style into that of their own period and altered details. Notable differences in the execution of these make it possible to distinguish two "hands", the two brothers Paul and Jean. Paul, the more gifted, displays a remarkably subtle range of colors; he often models his rather voluminous figures in delicate white on a light background. Jean, whose figures as a rule are slimmer, is inclined to fill his scenes with a greater number of people.

The *Bible moralisée* was far from being finished when Philip the Bold died in 1404. The brothers later entered the service of the Duc de Berry; at what exact date is not known. Jean, Duc de Berry was the greatest French patron of the arts at this period and he proved to be a most appreciative and inspiring Maecenas to the Limburgs. The first commission the brothers undertook for him is a Book of Hours, the so-called *Belles Heures* (Cloisters, New York). It is conjectured that the brothers—in this case all three of them were involved—started on this manuscript c1405. About the ownership of the Duc there can be no doubt. There are two portraits of him and one of his wife in the manuscript, as well as a superb inscription on the first folio by Jean Flamel, the Duc's secretary, which states explicitly that the Duc commissioned this Book of Hours. Furthermore, the script is mentioned in the fourth account of the Duc's collection drawn up by Robinet d'Estampes in 1412/13.

In contrast to the *Bible moralisée*, where the Limburgs had to follow closely an existing model, this Book of Hours provided ample opportunity for fresh innovations. No less than seven novel cycles are included in the manuscript. After the calendar it starts with 11 scenes from the legend of St Catherine; this unusually extended length can be attributed to St

Catherine's being one of the patron saints of the Duc de Berry's wife, Jeanne of Boulogne. The 11 scenes chosen leave out some of the best known incidents from her life, such as her mystical marriage to Christ, in favor of others that are only rarely shown—such as Catherine in prison tended by angels and visited by Queen Faustina, who in the next miniature is beheaded for her devotion to Catherine.

This cycle is followed by a shorter one, which is not only unprecedented in a Book of Hours, but is altogether new in art: four miniatures illustrate the Great Litany, of which only one scene, that of St Michael sheathing his sword, is at all customary. The third exceptional cycle tells in nine scenes the story of the 11th-century theologian Raymond Diocrès and of the foundation of the Carthusian Order by his pupil St Bruno: no earlier representations of Diocrès exist and of St Bruno only a few single scenes. Perhaps the most impressive of the nine miniatures is the last one, depicting from above, at an odd angle, the building of the Grand Chartreuse, while monks are fishing in a pool in the foreground.

The story of St Jerome is told at even greater length in 12 scenes. This cycle stresses Jerome's scholarship. Again the last one is of special interest: during the Saint's burial procession hermits emerge from caves to pay homage, and the blind and lame approach to be healed by touching the corpse. The hermits Paul and Anthony are the subjects of the next cycle with eight illustrations. Among them are some very attractive scenes, especially those in the "wilderness": in one scene St Anthony is looking for St Paul's hermitage and encounters a snake, while in the next one he is guided by a centaur to the Saint, who is sitting in front of his hut. The inventiveness of the brothers in these new cycles is matched by their unsurpassed delicate handling of color and contour, including some early attempts at perspective.

The last and the most important commission the brothers undertook for Jean de Berry is the *Très Riches Heures*, now in the Musée Condé at Chantilly. At the death of the patron and the artists in 1416 the manuscript was still unbound, and only about half finished. All three brothers worked on this, their masterpiece. The book starts, as Books of Hours do, with calendar pictures, though it is likely that the miniaturists did not begin their work

with this cycle. The calendar is normally illustrated with 24 small medallions, one each for the zodiac sign and the occupation of the month. The Limburgs for the first time combined these two, enlarged them and filled the entire space of the page, incorporating an equally wide arch above, enclosing in addition to the usual zodiac sign, astronomical information such as the days of the week and phases of the moon. In the inner lobe Apollo, holding the blazing sun, rides in his chariot drawn by winged horses.

The 11 pictures underneath (November was not finished by the Limburgs but by Jean Colombe) show four courtly scenes: January, a banquet with the Duc de Berry presiding; April, the betrothal of a courtly pair; May, an outing on horseback; and August, hawking. The other seven depict peasant activities such as plowing in March, haymaking in June, sheepshearing in July. January and February show indoor scenes. The other nine portray, as a backdrop against a brilliant blue sky, contemporary buildings such as castles, ones either in the possession of the Duc de Berry or of the King or of a nephew, Louis II of Anjou. Of these buildings only one is still in existence, but all can be identified with the help of early drawings and etchings. The one for June with the Sainte Chapelle on the right and the Palais de la Cité on the left is perhaps the most enchanting. To these should be added the Mont St Michel illustrating the Mass for St Michael towards the end of the book, as well as some smaller background silhouettes.

These unique backdrops are combined with minutely observed representations of seasonal work on the land which are rendered with delicate precision. Outstanding single pictures such as the Zodiac Man and the Map of Rome are rarities in a Book of Hours. Even the customary sequence of the Life of the Virgin and the Passion of Christ are presented with new and unexpected touches: Christ in Gethsemane stands against a black sky, relieved only by stars and a couple of torches; and the Crucifixion is plunged, as the biblical text describes, into an overall bluish-gray haze. In all these the Limburgs surpass any contemporary Italian—and herald Netherlandish—panel painting. The *Très Riches Heures* is a masterpiece of the first order,

and as such fully deserves the popularity it has recently acquired thanks to color reproductions.

Further reading. Meiss, M. and Beatson, E.H. *The Belles Heures of Jean, Duke of Berry*, New York (1974). Meiss, M. with Longnon, J. and Cazelles, R. *The Très Riches Heures of Jean, Duke of Berry*, New York (1969). Meiss, M. with Smith, S.O.D. and Beatson, E.H. *The Limburgs and their Contemporaries*, London (1974).

Lindner Richard 1901–78

The German-American painter Richard Lindner developed fairly late in his career the style by which he is best known. After studying music, he took up painting in 1922 and studied in Nuremberg and Munich. He lived in Germany until 1933, but fled after the Nazi rise to power. After a period in Paris, where he met Picasso, he settled in America in 1941. He worked as an illustrator for magazines such as *Harper's Bazaar* and *Vogue*, and for editions of the classics, including *Madame Bovary* and *The Tales of Hoffmann*. In 1951 he began to devote all his time to painting and teaching. Influences from Cubism, Léger, and Surrealism can all be felt in his shiny, hard-edged figure-style, with its frequently erotic, even fetishistic, overtones (for example *New York City IV*, 1964; Joseph Hirshhorn Museum, Washington, D.C.).

Further reading. Ashton, D. *Richard Lindner*, New York (1969).

Lipchitz Jacques 1891–1973

The French sculptor Jacques Lipchitz (originally Chaim Jacob) was born in Druskieniki in Lithuania. He settled in Paris in 1909 and lived there until emigrating to America in 1941. For the last ten years of his life he also lived in Italy.

Lipchitz was one of the major sculptors associated with Cubism. His response to Cubism in this early formative period was not unlike that of his friend Juan Gris: sober and with a tight-lipped discipline. Made in stone or bronze, Lipchitz's Cubist sculptures consisted of figures and still lifes composed from simple, rather static inclined planes and curves, enlivened by simple changes of texture (for example, *Man with Mandolin*, 1917; Yale University Art Gallery, New Haven). They reflect their origins in Cubist painting in their

Richard Lindner: Disneyland; canvas; 203×127cm (80×50in); 1965. Museum Ludwig, Cologne

Jacques Lipchitz: Mother and Child; bronze; 120×73×72cm (47×29×28in); 1940. Wilhelm-Lehmbruck-Museum, Duisberg

concern with shallow surface relationships and frequent use of the low-relief form.

He later recalled a period of crisis c1916 to 1918 when he had to struggle free from "ossification". Although a few later sculptures (like *Figure*, 1926–30; Museum of Modern Art, New York) echo the frontal solemnity of the Cubist pieces, most of his subsequent works are dramatically different in form and mood. They are more muscular than architectural, with a baroque sense of drama and scale and a full-blooded expressive romanticism.

In 1925 he invented some small maquettes which he called "Transparents" (for example, *Pierrot Escapes*, 1927; Kunsthaus, Zurich). A few inches high, they are pierced-form pieces made of thin sheets or ribbons, modeled in wax then cast in bronze. Whimsical in mood (pierrots, harlequins, acrobats) and increasingly open and curvilinear in form, they liberated his own thinking and anticipated the linear iron constructions of Picasso and González in the 1930s.

Their vitality and energetic arabesque quality was assimilated into the scale and mass of his early work, producing the characteristic, restless heavyweight rhythms of his mature style (seen in *Song of the Vowels*, 1932; private collection).

In the early 1950s he evolved another small-scale idiom: the "semi-automatic". Hand-size improvisations in warm wax were allowed to suggest a theme or configuration that was then consciously developed. These often inspired the monumental public sculptures that he had made from the 1940s onwards. Some of them are on an enormous scale.

He thought that the smaller works were the real power-house behind his own sculpture and considered modeling as his natural technique. It is the smaller pieces, fingered and squeezed by the hand, that best express that characteristic Lipchitz energy, vitality, and spontaneity; qualities that are sometimes diluted in the transfer to the massive public scale of his many commissions. The typical form of his mature work is Baroque and muscular, with a complex of heavyweight forms, curves, and hollows caught up in restless interaction—often streaming out laterally in a manner reminiscent of Daumier's figure groups.

He never became involved in modern art's inbred self-analysis and by the time of his death was firmly established as one of the century's major figure-sculptors.

Further reading. Hammacher, A.M. *Jacques Lipchitz, his Sculpture*, New York (1961). Lipchitz, J. and Arnason, H.H. *My Life in Sculpture*, New York (1972).

Lippi 15th and 16th centuries

Fra Filippo (c1406–69) and Filippino Lippi (c1457–1504) were Italian painters of the Florentine school, Filippino being the illegitimate son of Fra Filippo, a monk in holy orders. Filippo Lippi was placed as an orphan in the care of the monks of the Carmine, Florence, in 1421. He is first mentioned as a painter in 1431. Masaccio's presence in the Carmine during the 1420s, while he was decorating the Brancacci Chapel, meant that Filippo had closer contact with this artist than any other painter of his generation. Filippo's first

Fra Filippo Lippi: Virgin and Child; panel; 80×51cm (32×20in); 1440–5. **National Gallery of Art, Washington, D.C.**

Filippino Lippi: Tobias and the Angel; oil on panel; 33×23cm (13×9in); c1480. National Gallery of Art, Washington, D.C.

of *St Bernard* (Badia, Florence), we can easily trace the mystical and delicate quality of his father's late works. The style achieved great popularity in the patrician circles of Rome and Florence; and in 1498 Filippino signed important contracts to decorate the interiors of two private chapels—the Caraffa Chapel in S. Maria sopra Minerva, Rome (completed 1493) and the Strozzi Chapel in S. Maria Novella, Florence (completed 1502). Each has an elaborate decorative system, incorporating walls, ceiling, and altarpiece into one program, with many tricks to deceive the beholder. In these schemes and in the great *Adoration of the Magi* (1496; Uffizi, Florence), the influence of his father and of Botticelli, to whom his earlier work is so close, recedes. Filippino develops a more substantial portrayal of the human form, with close and brilliant attention to detail.

Lipton Seymour 1903–86

The American sculptor Seymour Arthur Lipton was born in New York. His original profession was dentistry. A self-taught artist, he turned seriously to sculpture in 1932 but continued to practice as a dentist for some years. His early works were Expressionist figurative wood carvings; but from 1945, when he began working sheet lead, his sculptures became more abstract. In the early 1950s he developed his mature style, working with bronze on sheet metal and Monel alloy, for which he invented a unique brazing process to texture his surfaces. His sculptures derive from natural imagery and the human figure, in which rounded skins of metal often enclose other forms. Lipton was a pioneer of direct-metal sculpture, and his many public commissions include *Archangel* (1964) for the Lincoln Center, New York.

Liss Johann c1590–1629

The German painter Johann Liss (or Lys) was a native of Oldenburg (Holstein), but was active in Venice for most of his short career. After an early visit to the Netherlands, where he was in contact with Jordaens, Liss moved to Italy, and established himself in Venice before 1624. Like his friend Domenico Feti, he did much to infuse new vigor into local tradition with his warm palette and animated brushwork. He first painted small-scale cabinet pictures, and later larger-scale altarpieces,

dated work, the *Tarquinia Madonna* of 1437 (Galleria Nazionale, Florence), reveals the additional influences of the sculpture of Donatello, and of the contemporary Flemish paintings that were then making their way to Italy. The Barbadori Altarpiece (Louvre, Paris), commissioned in 1437, shows a mastery of spatial construction; in the virtual elimination of framing divisions, it marks an important step in the development of the *sacra conversazione*.

Filippo's frescoes in the choir of Prato Cathedral (1452–65) show a new feature: a prettifying and sweetening of forms which was probably derived from a study of Fra Angelico's works. In Filippo's late works—particularly the group of panels representing the *Adoration of the Christ*

Child (Staatliche Museen, Berlin; Uffizi, Florence; etc) a new mystical interpretation of the subject matter is adopted. With this, any attempt at relating in depth the scales of the major figures to one another is abandoned. Filippo's last commission was for a series of frescoes in Spoleto Cathedral, on which he was involved at the time of his death in 1469. These were completed by his assistants, who probably included Filippino and Botticelli.

Filippino's earliest certain independent work does not occur until 1483. His first major commission came a year later, when he was asked to complete Masaccio's unfinished frescoes in the Brancacci Chapel, S. Maria del Carmine, Florence. In this work, and in paintings such as *The Vision*

developing towards the end of his life a style that anticipates the Rococo in its extreme freedom of handling, and its lightness and softness of color.

Lissitzky El 1890–1941

The Russian artist and architect El Lissitzky was born Eleazar Markovich Lissitsky in Polschlindk, Smolensk. He studied architecture at the Technische Hochschule, Darmstadt, Germany (1909–14) and engineering and architecture in Riga and Moscow (1914–15). He qualified as an engineer in Germany and as an architect in Moscow. Invited by Chagall, Director of the Vitebsk School of Art, he joined the School as Professor of Architecture and Graphic Arts (1919–21). He painted his first *Proun* painting in Vitebsk in 1919, after contact with the ideas of Malevich. In the several *Proun* paintings he combined Suprematist and Constructivist elements to link art and architecture (as in *Construction—Proun 2*, 1920; Philadelphia Museum of Art). By 1920 he used these elements in experimental typographical design, as in his *Story of Two Squares* (six drawings published in Holland in 1922). He moved to Moscow to become professor at the State Art School, Vkhutemas. During the 1920s he was extremely important in propagating new Russian art in Western Europe, through visits, writings, and organizing exhibitions. He collaborated with Jean Arp on *The Isms of Art* (published 1925) and created the ingeniously adaptable exhibiting rooms in the Landesmuseum, Hannover (1924; destroyed by the Nazis in 1936). His activities during the 1930s were limited by ill health.

Further reading. Barr, A.H. *Cubism and Abstract Art*, New York (1936). Gray, C. *The Great Experiment: Russian Art 1863–1922*, London (1962). Lissitzky, El. *Russia: an Architecture for World Revolution*, Vienna (1930). Lissitzky, El. and Arp, J. *Die Kunstismen*, Zurich (1925). Lissitzky-Küppers, S. *El Lissitzky: Life, Letters, Texts*, London (1968). Malevich, K. *The Non-Objective World*, Chicago (1959).

El Lissitzky: a reconstruction of the artist's "Abstract Room", an exhibition room of Abstract paintings originally arranged in Hanover in 1927; Niedersächsische Landesgalerie und Städtische Galerie, Hannover

Lochner Stefan c1400–51

The German painter Stefan Lochner was probably born at Meersburg, south Baden. He was the most distinguished master of the Cologne school, and it is in Cologne that many of his surviving paintings can now be seen. A new naturalism in his style of painting anecdotal subjects, peopled with soft featured figures in glowing colors on a gold ground, implies that he served his apprenticeship in the Low Countries. The influence of the Master of Flémalle and of Jan van Eyck is very likely.

Lochner is first documented in Cologne in 1442; he later represented his guild as a City Councillor in 1447 and 1450. Most of his works are attributed to him merely by stylistic comparison, and only two are dated: *The Presentation in the Temple* (1447; Hessisches Landesmuseum, Darmstadt) and *The Adoration of the Child* of 1447, also at Darmstadt.

Lochner's earliest paintings, *St Jerome in his Cell* and the *Madonna in the Rose Bower* still betray the influence of earlier miniature painters such as the Limburg brothers, particularly in his treatment of space. However, already they hint at the greater animation of the figures and the keen observation of nature that Lochner developed in his later works. About 1440 he probably began the *Last Judgment*, a triptych altarpiece for the church of St Laurence, Cologne, the panels of which are

Stefan Lochner: Madonna in the Rose Bower; panel; 51×40cm (20×16in); c1440. Wallraf-Richartz-Museum, Cologne

Lohse Richard 1902–88

The Swiss painter Richard Paul Lohse was born in Zurich. Although he was little known to the wider public, his view of geometric abstraction as a progressive attempt to systematize the elements of art had a decisive influence on artists working in this field. His paintings after 1943 were based on a horizontal-vertical grid, the proportions of which were determined mathematically, diagonal rhythms being introduced by predetermined progressions of color. Unlike many earlier geometric abstractionist painters, he did not wish to enter the field of applied art; the paintings were justified as the manifestation of an internal law.

Lombardo family

1 5th and 16th centuries

Born and trained in Lombardy, Pietro Lombardo (c1435–1515) was a sculptor and architect who moved to Venice in the

Pietro Lombardo: an angel in the vaulting of S. Giobbe, Venice; marble; c1475

now separate and dispersed (center panel, Wallraf-Richartz-Museum, Cologne; inner wings, Städelsches Kunstinstitut, Frankfurt am Main; outer wings; Alte Pinakothek, Munich). The central inner panel has all the drama of Bruegel or Bosch as the myriad little naked resurrected figures are led by angels to the Gate of Heaven or by demons to the Gate of Hell. Above them, the larger figure of Christ presides with the intercessors, John the Baptist and the Virgin Mary. The side wings depict the martyrdom of saints in 12 separate scenes, while their outer sides are painted with six saintly figures and two kneeling donors.

Another triptych, the *Patron Saints of Cologne* (painted before 1447), now in Cologne Cathedral, is Lochner's masterpiece. The outside of the wings shows the Annunciation in a domestic interior set against a richly brocaded curtain, reminiscent of van Eyck. The inside of all three

panels portrays figures offering homage to the Christ Child, seated on the Virgin's knee. The Magi occupy the center panel, to the left is St Ursula and her escort of Virgins, and to the right St Gereon with his men-at-arms. These two are the patron saints of the city. The figures are composed into a solemn semicircle around Christ, those at the back in darker shades to highlight the main characters. They are an elegant group, with faces full of individuality. The soft forms of their features contrast with the brilliant detailing of their clothes and the ground on which they stand.

The Cologne triptych is closely related to the Darmstadt *Adoration* in style, indicating that it was a product of Lochner's maturity. Albrecht Dürer wrote how it cost him two silver pennies to have the painting shown to him in the cathedral; he regarded it as the city's most important panel picture.

mid 1460s and was responsible for introducing a Renaissance style into the city. A series of wall tombs of Doges establishes the new architectural forms, which also appear in the frames of paintings by Giovanni Bellini and the Vivarini, creating, for the first time, a Renaissance context for their work. Working on a large scale Pietro, with his contemporary Codussi, gave a Renaissance reformulation to the traditional Venetian palace facade, and built the marble-encrusted church of S. Maria dei Miracoli (1481–9): the most perfect example of coloristic, neo-Byzantine, Venetian Renaissance architecture.

His sons developed their father's work as a monumental sculptor (for example the Vendramin Monument, SS. Giovanni e Paolo, Venice) in a more Classical direction, imitating the Antique. Tullio (c1460–1532) was a major sculptor in this "Neoclassical" mode, and the humanist cast of his work can be seen in his now scattered reliefs of antique subjects executed for Alfonso d'Este c1508 (Hermitage Museum, St Petersburg).

Long Richard 1945–

The English artist Richard Long was born in Bristol. He studied at Bristol School of Art (1962–4) and St Martin's School of Art, London, from 1966 to 1968, the year of his first solo exhibition in Düsseldorf. He represented Britain in the 1976 Venice Biennale. The foremost British "land artist" from 1968 onwards, Long has made art works during, or in response to, walks through the countryside in Britain and throughout the world. The pieces can take the form of captioned photographs, sometimes combined with maps, or else sculptures made in the country or on the gallery floor from natural materials—for instance stones or wood, arranged in simple forms such as circles, lines and spirals (for example, *119 Stones*, 1976; Tate Gallery, London).

Further reading. Seymour, A. *Richard Long: Walking in Circles*, London (1991).

Longhena Baldassare 1598–1682

Baldassare Longhena was the only architect of the Venetian Baroque to create a

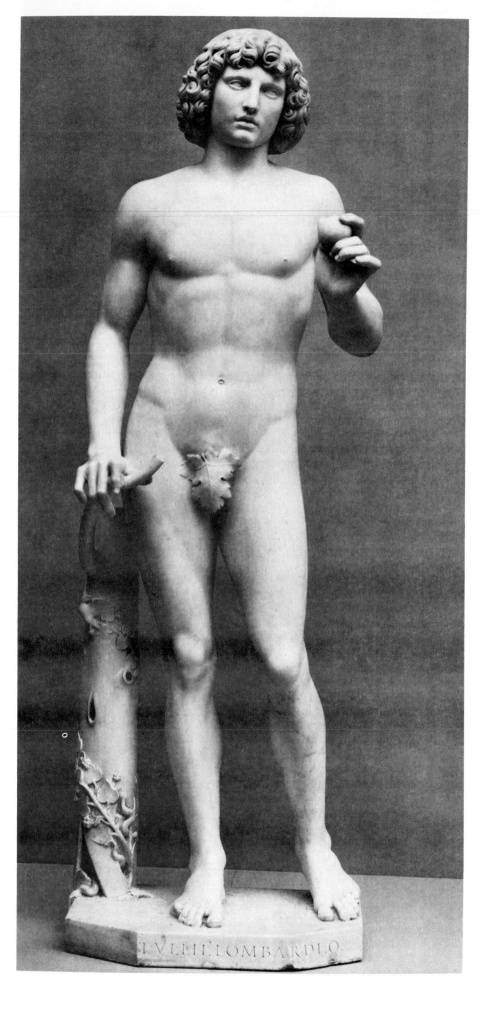

Tullio Lombardo: Adam from the Vendramin Monument, SS. Giovanni e Paolo, Venice; marble; height 193cm (76in); c1493. Metropolitan Museum, New York

style comparable in quality to the great Baroque architecture of Rome. Trained by the neo-Palladian Vincenzo Scamozzi, he quickly moved to a style more or less antithetical to that of his master; but the influence of Sansovino and of Palladio himself is ever present in his buildings, and it was to this specifically Venetian tradition that he gave Baroque expression.

Thus the sumptuous plastic richness of his palace facades on the Grand Canal (Ca' Pesaro and Ca' Rezzonico, both begun in the 1630s) comes from a magnificent marriage between the rather flat, three-tiered facade of Sansovino's already monumental Palazzo Corner Ca' Grande and the same architect's deeply cut, sculpturally enriched Library. From the Library, Longhena learned the importance of light as a means of giving substance and warmth to architecture. By means of ever richer variations of texture (including colossal rustication) and a vigorous profusion of forcefully carved sculptural detail, he intensified the chiaroscuro effects of Sansovino's building. Interacting with the changing light and the reflections from the Canal, his facades thus became full of movement and drama.

Longhena's main monument is the church of S. Maria della Salute (begun 1631), which was commissioned by the State as an ex voto offering for deliverance from the plague. The church is now so essential a feature of Venice that it is almost impossible to imagine the entrance to the Grand Canal without it; Longhena's domed octagonal structure perfectly fits its triangular site, spreading outwards by means of a patterned pavement to the very steps of the canal.

The plan of the church has been brilliantly analyzed as a fusion between the centralized, geometric plans of the Renaissance and the progressive scenographic space of the Baroque. Longhena's design owes something both to the Baroque theater and to Palladio's Redentore.

Theatrical too is the use of sculpture. Giant figures of Apostles placed above the columns enliven the space of the central octagon. On the exterior the volutes, which make the dynamic transition between the octagon and the dome, are topped by statues who ride above them as on the crest of a wave and seem about to bowl outwards into space.

The greater exuberance of Longhena's architecture as a whole shows the increasing tendency towards display in both public and private patronage in Venice from 1600: a grandiloquence that is perhaps a symptom of a city in decline.

Longhi Pietro 1702–85

The Italian painter Pietro Longhi was born Pietro Falca, the son of the silversmith Alessandro Falca, in Venice. He was apprenticed to Antonio Balestra (1666–1740). He visited Bologna in 1719; there he studied under Giuseppe Maria Crespi, who exerted a great influence upon him as a genre painter. It is possible that he also came into contact there with the genre painter, Gamberini. Longhi's early genre paintings reflect Crespi's manner in color range and in subject matter.

Before 1730 Longhi was back in Venice where he became successful as a painter of small-scale canvases showing everyday Venetian life. Human activities, such as the taking of afternoon tea, a visit to nearby friends, or a game of blind man's buff, were recorded with laconic fidelity. His attention was drawn equally to the daily lives of both the aristocracy and the peasantry; he depicted the whole social hierarchy of Venice and recorded his subjects dispassionately, without condemnation or comment, recording life as a photographer might today, highlighting the spontaneity of ordinary events.

Only rarely did Longhi paint major religious compositions for churches. His art received official recognition nonetheless, and he was a founding-member of the Accademia; in 1763 he was made Director of the Academy in the Palazzo Pisani. Longhi's genre paintings may be compared with those by Hogarth in England and by Lancret and de Troy in France; Longhi would have known these works through prints. A large number of paintings by Longhi still survive in Venice: important groups are to be found in the Museo Correr, the Galleria Querini Stampalia, and in the Gallerie dell'Accademia.

Loos Adolf 1870–1933

The Austrian architect and polemicist Adolf Loos was born at Brno, Moravia. An early visit to the U.S.A. made a lasting impression upon him. He worked mainly in Vienna, where he became Chief Architect of the Housing Estates Movement (1920–2), but also in Paris (1923–8) and Prague.

Loos was an ally of the moralist and critic

Pietro Longhi: A Lute-Player; chalk and pencil on paper; 1752. Museo Correr, Venice

Karl Kraus and a friend of other revolutionary artists and intellectuals—the painter Oskar Kokoschka, the composer Arnold Schoenberg, and the philosopher Ludwig Wittgenstein. He also wrote on a variety of social and cultural topics, but is remembered for his crusade against decoration in such essays as "The Poor Rich Man" (1900) and the notorious "Ornament and Crime" (1908). He attacked the Vienna Secession, the Wiener Werkstätte (run by Josef Hoffmann), and later the Bauhaus, for their concept of total design. He believed in the unselfconscious, anonymous products of the ordinary craftsman, as opposed to the artist-craftsman—a theme that Le Corbusier later adopted. As an architect, his most important building for the modern movement and its apologists was the deliberately plain-looking and cuboid Steiner house (Vienna, 1910).

Loos' particular type of multilevel open planning, which can be experienced in his houses of the 1920s (for example the Moller house, Vienna, 1928), was arguably his most significant contribution to modern architecture. But this aspect has been overlooked in favor of an image of him as a pioneer father of the International style—a label he would have despised. He was a classicist, and he had a passion for using luxury materials like marble in his buildings. Building without ornament was a doctrine which, Loos wrote in 1924, "the purists have pushed to absurdity".

Lorenzetti brothers
13th and 14th centuries

The Lorenzetti brothers Pietro (c1280–1348) and Ambrogio (c1290–1348) were Italian painters of the Sienese School. With Simone Martini, the Lorenzetti brought Sienese painting to its finest flowering and European renown. While Pietro's earliest works show Ducciesque influence, Ambrogio's *Madonna of S. Angelo* of 1319 (in Vico l'Abate, near Florence) reveals an independence of both Duccio and Pietro. Pietro's early activity took him to Assisi (Passion Cycle, lower church of S. Francesco) and to Arezzo (polyptych, 1320; church of S. Maria della Pieve). Ambrogio is twice documented as being in Florence (1321 and 1327).

The brothers' respective experiences undoubtedly formed their artistic personalities. Their periods of collaboration, first in the mid 1320s (when they produced frescoes in the church of S. Francesco, Siena; now mainly lost) and then in 1335 (to paint frescoes in the Spedale di S. Maria della Scala, Siena; now destroyed) account for the influence of one upon the other. Late in their careers they may have had a joint workshop.

Pietro's development increasingly emphasized the realization of volumes in space. Throughout his work there is a continuing exploration of the psychological states of his figures which was the special mark of his genius. He had a fine feeling for discursive narrative (seen in the Assisi frescoes and his predella, the Carmelite Altarpiece, 1329; Pinacoteca Nazionale, Siena). He shared with his brother an interest in problems of pictorial space (*Birth of the Virgin*, 1342; Museo dell'Opera del Duomo, Siena).

Ambrogio, by temperament calmer and more speculative, produced a body of work remarkable for its variety of innovations. His *Maestà*, painted for the cathedral of Massa Marittima (c1330) is the first work of his mature style; spatially and iconographically it elaborates Duccio's prototype (1308–11; Museo dell'Opera del Duomo, Siena). His *Scenes from the life of Saint Nicholas of Bari* (c1332; Uffizi, Florence) display great sensitivity for setting narrative within convincing spaces. *The Presentation in the Temple* (1342; Uffizi,

Pietro Lorenzetti: Deposition from the Cross; fresco; c1329. Lower church of S. Francesco, Assisi

Pietro Lorenzetti: The Last Supper; fresco; c1329. Lower church of S. Francesco, Assisi

Florence) and the *Annunciation* (1344; Pinacoteca Nazionale, Siena) combine monumentality and perspectival experiment. For its developments in composition, the evocation of space, and its realization of landscape, his political *Allegory of Good and Bad Government* (fresco, 1338–9; Palazzo Pubblico, Siena) is his best known work and certainly his masterpiece.

Further reading. Starn, R. *Ambrogio Lorenzetti: the Palazzo Pubblico, Siena*, New York (1994).

Lorenzo di Credi 1459?–1536

The Florentine painter Lorenzo di Credi trained under Verrocchio whose workshop, the most important in its day, also included the young Leonardo da Vinci. About 1485 Credi completed to Verrocchio's design an altarpiece for Pistoia Cathedral; in 1486 he took charge of his master's workshop, inheriting it on Verrocchio's death in 1498. For the period from 1491 until he entered a hospice in 1531, documents give a good picture of the activities of an unexceptional but professionally respected painter of his time. He restored paintings, sat on committees supervising and valuing the work of other artists, and arbitrated in disputes between them and their patrons. He died in 1536.

Many paintings are ascribed to him but few are documented. Essentially a workshop painter producing for the market, his paintings tend to be repetitions of particular types. Thus there are Madonnas for private devotion of which the London (National Gallery) version is typical, *tondi* showing the Virgin adoring the Child (Metropolitan Museum, New York), paintings of single saints, and a number of *sacra conversazione* altarpieces. Several portraits have been attributed to him, including a self-portrait (1488; National Gallery of Art, Washington, D.C.), and many drawings, including preparatory studies of heads of youths and old men (for example in the Louvre, Paris).

Credi's style changed little during his lifetime. Formed while a pupil of Verrocchio, and deeply influenced by the early work of Leonardo, it was largely unaffected by the advances of Leonardo, Raphael, and Sarto in the early 16th century. His compositions and figure-poses are monotonously conventional. However, the paintings are technically competent, their colors pleasantly bright, and their

Lorenzo di Credi: Self-portrait; panel; transferred to canvas; 46×32cm (18×13in); 1488. National Gallery of Art, Washington, D.C.

linear qualities typically Florentine. His figures can lack characterization, a shortcoming compensated for by the clarity of perception and delicate beauty of his drawings. Credi had a large number of pupils, none of whom became artists of significance.

Lorenzo Monaco c1370–1425

The Italian artist Lorenzo Monaco was born Piero di Giovanni. Although he had been born in Siena, he was considered a Florentine painter and miniaturist in his mature period. In 1391 he took vows in the Camaldolese monsastery of S. Maria degli Angeli, Florence. We have no certain information about his training but his first

works display a fusion of Sienese and Florentine elements, the latter deriving from the tradition of the Cioni and Gaddi. There is also a striving to assimilate Giottesque ideals of composition and figure-painting as interpreted by the late Trecento (for example, *Agony in the Garden*; Galleria dell' Accademia, Florence).

After 1400 both the plasticity of his figures and the gracefulness of his compositions increase, in a fashion that suggests renewed contacts with Sienese art and the possibility that he had learned about the late Gothic International style from Ghiberti. His works begin to show a greater sense of linear design and calligraphic beauty (seen in his *Annunciation*,

Galleria dell'Accademia, Florence). His *Coronation of the Virgin* (1413; Uffizi, Florence) seems to mark a return to aspects of his early work as forms take on increased volume and density. Late works such as the S. Trinità *Annunciation* (1422–4; Bartolini Chapel, S. Trinità, Florence) embody a more realistic description of figures and space.

Lorenzo's genius lay in his personal vision of a world in which natural and supernatural were convincingly united by calligraphic means, a world at once lyrical, exotic, and strangely compelling (seen in his *Adoration of the Magi*, *c*1410; Uffizi, Florence). Although he produced many impressive large works, it is perhaps in the small panels of his *predellae* and in his miniatures that his poetic imagination found its most vivid expression. Florence's chief exponent of the International Gothic style, he had many assistants and immediate followers; but his style was not to have long-term influence. The new preoccupations of the early Quattrocento led in other directions.

Lotto Lorenzo *c*1480–1556

The painter Lorenzo Lotto was born in Venice and presumably had his artistic training there. Bernard Berenson has plausibly suggested Alvise Vivarini (*c*1446–1503/5) as his primary master, but he was influenced, like all his generation in Venice, by Giovanni Bellini. He was also influenced by Jacopo dei Barbari and by contemporary German work. He was little employed in Venice itself, and the main fields of his activity were Bergamo and the district of Treviso, and such cities of the Marches as Jesi, Recanati, and Ancona. he is recorded as working in Rome in 1509. In 1554 he entered the Holy House at Loreto as an oblate.

Lotto was, after Giorgione, the most sensitive painter of his generation in Venice. Time and again we find passages in his work where the brushwork and the handling of light and color are a sheer delight. Yet in many of his larger paintings and in the impression given by his work as a whole he disappoints; in spite of the advocacy of devoted admirers, he retains the status of a minor master.

The *Madonna and Child with St Peter Martyr* (1503; Museo e Gallerie Nazionali di Capodimonte, Naples) is composed of Bellinesque elements but shows individual sensibility, especially in the landscape. The

Lorenzo Lotto: Portrait of a Gentleman in a Black Silk Cape; oil on canvas; 94×82cm (37×32in); 1546. New Orleans Museum of Art

Bishop Bernardo de' Rossi (1505; Museo e Gallerie Nazionali di Capodimonte, Naples) reveals at once, in its vivid characterization, Lotto's outstanding qualities as a portrait-painter. The enchanting cover of this work, the *Allegory* and the related *Maiden's Dream* (both 1505; National Gallery of Art, Washington, D.C.) have a magic akin to—though quite distinct from—that of Giorgione's almost contemporary *Tempesta* (Gallerie dell'Accademia, Venice). German influence is clearly to be seen in the *Bernardo de' Rossi* and also in the wooded landscape of the little *St Jerome* (1506; Louvre, Paris). The *Virgin Enthroned with Four Saints* (1506; S. Cristina al Tiverone, Treviso) is a dazzling variation on the theme of Giovanni Bellini's *Madonna Enthroned with Four Saints* (1505; S. Zaccaria, Venice). This period, in which Lotto experiments with the Venetian heritage of the Quattrocento, ends with the splendid polyptych of the *Madonna and Saints* (1508; Pinacoteca Civica, Recanati).

Lotto's visit to Rome in 1509 seems to have thrown him off balance, and the *Deposition* (1512; Museo e Pinacoteca Communali, Jesi, Ancona) is a turgid exercise in the Raphaelesque. Back in north Italy in the middle of the decade, he combines Raphaelesque elements with the Bellinesque tradition in the *Madonna Enthroned with Saints* (1516; S. Bartolomeo, Bergamo), achieving a style close to the contemporary work of Correggio.

The *Christ Taking Leave of His Mother* (1531; Staatliche Museen, Berlin) has a marvelous setting—a dark basilica giving on to a brightly lit garden—painted with a deftness that looks forward to Guardi (18th century). This technical bravura finds its fullest development in the main panel and the *predella* of the St Lucy Altarpiece (1532; Museo e Pinacoteca Communali, Jesi, Ancona), and is still to be seen in his last work, *The Presentation in the Temple* (*c*1555; Palazzo Apostolico, Loreto). Throughout his career he continued to paint fine portraits.

Morris Louis: Vav; acrylic on canvas; 262×359cm (103×142in); 1960. Tate Gallery, London

Louis Morris 1912–62

The American painter Morris Louis was born Morris Louis Bernst, in Baltimore. After studying at the Maryland Institute of Fine Arts he spent four years in New York (1936–40). He returned in 1940 to Balti-more, exhibiting there regularly until he moved to Washington, D.C. in 1952. In 1953, Louis became friendly with Clement Greenberg, who was to encourage and support his work. Although Louis was to exhibit throughout the 1950s, he was often discouraged by the reception of his pic-tures and destroyed many canvases.

His mature style, expressed in large-scale works, is Abstract in character and often lyrical in feeling. In the series of "Veil" paintings the color is almost floated on to the canvas in wedges and splashes, creating an effect sometimes reminiscent of silk-screen printing or even of watercolor (seen in *Point of Tranquility*, 1958; Joseph Hirshhorn Museum, Washington, D.C.). In the final phase of his career the colors are separated and applied either in rough parallel groupings across the corners of white canvases, or in vertical stripes and bands straight down the canvas, which is otherwise left plain.

Loutherbourg Philip de
1740–1812

The place of Philip James de Louther-bourg's paintings in the history of English landscape painting is between the classi-cism of Richard Wilson and the naturalism of Turner and Constable. A native of Alsace, he studied under the battle painter Francesco Casanova, and in 1767 was made a member of the French Academy. He was living in London by 1771, and worked as David Garrick's stage and scenery designer until 1785. Although the detailing in his landscapes is derived from Philips Wouwermans (1619–68), Nicolaes Berchem (1620–83), and the Dutch school, his somewhat contrived composi-tions reflect an over-exaggeration of the classical tradition in landscape painting.

Lowry L.S. 1887–1976

The British painter Laurence Stephen

Philip de Loutherbourg: Coalbrookdale by Night; oil on canvas; 68×107cm (27×42in); 1801. Science Museum, London

L.S. Lowry: Flowers in the Window; oil on canvas; 50×60cm (20×24in); 1956. Private collection

Lowry was born in Manchester. He studied painting and drawing at the Manchester Municipal Art College between 1905 and 1915 and also studied at Salford School of Art. It was not until c1916 that he developed an interest in the artistic possibilities of the bleak Northern industrial landscape, which he depicted in a "naive" style outside the general trends of his time. From 1909 until 1948 he lived and worked at Pendlebury; he was hardly known until his first one-man show in London in 1939.

This lateness of recognition rankled long after he had achieved fame and fortune. By the end of his life, Lowry was widely recognized as one of the leading British painters. At his best he went far deeper than the "naive" tone of his work initially suggests (for example, *An Accident*, 1926; City of Manchester Art Gallery). There is a satiric edge to his imagination, an ambiguous fondness for the grotesque, a darkness at the center of his vision (for example, *In a Park*, 1963; Whitworth Art Gallery, University of Manchester).

Further reading. Levy, M. *The Paintings of L.S. Lowry*, London (1975). Mullins, E.

L.S. Lowry, R.A., London (1966). Rothenstein, J. *Modern English Painters* vol. 2, London (1956). Spalding, J. *Lowry*, Oxford (1979).

Lucas van Leyden 1494–1533

The Flemish painter Lucas Hugensz. van Leyden trained under both his father Hugo Jacobsz. and the Leiden artist Cornelis Engelbrechtsz. He remained a member of the guild of painters at Leiden after also registering as a painter at Antwerp in 1522. Unlike many Netherlandish artists of the early 16th century, Lucas never became tied to the conventions of court art; he was one of the most original artists of his age in Northern Europe, despite the hardship of persistent ill-health throughout his life.

His earliest religious paintings, such as the *Adoration of the Kings* altarpiece (c1500–10; Barnes Foundation, Merion, Pa.) are close in style to late-15th-century Flemish works, and especially to the paintings of Geertgen tot Sint Jans. In later, more ambitious works such as *The Healing of the Blind Man of Jericho* (1531; Hermitage Museum, Leningrad), the hor-

izon line is lowered, the figures are more monumental, and the landscape is more spatially convincing, with subtle use of light and shade between the trees. Even where he retains the traditional triptych form, as in the *Last Judgment* of 1526–7 (Stedelijk Museum "De Lakenhal", Leiden), the continuous landscape across the three panels and the bell-shaped top lend the work a fluency of narrative and a spaciousness new to Flemish art.

He is also important for the development of Flemish genre painting. His scenes with half-length figures, such as the *Card Players* (c1514; Wilton House Collection, near Salisbury, Wilts.) are not only new in Flemish art by their size and relation of figures to picture-field, they also take a significant step toward the true genre picture, free of all moral connotations. Such works as these lack only the vital humorous ingredient to prefigure the finest 17th-century Dutch genre painting.

Lucas van Leyden's graphic works were much admired in his lifetime, especially in Italy, where Vasari judged his achievement as equal to Albrecht Dürer's in technique and composition. Certainly his prints had a profound impact on Florentine artists of the generation after the High Renaissance. He is said to have issued his first engravings at the age of nine, but the first securely dated work is the *Mahomet and the Monk Sergius* of 1508. This exemplifies the qualities that Vasari praised, for the skillful fading of distance and softening of tone are

Bernardino Luini: Virgin and Child; oil on panel; 74×53cm (29×21in). Wallace Collection, London

Lucas van Leyden: Card Players; oil on wood; 36×46cm (14×18in); c1514. Wilton House Collection, near Salisbury, Wiltshire

painterly in treatment. The *Ecce Homo* of 1510 is innovatory in its composition. The figure of Christ, hitherto in Northern art placed at the left of the scene in front of the crowd, is here moved to a place right of center and in the background, amid a vast scenario of buildings and landscape. Its format was to influence Rembrandt in his etching of this subject in the following century.

Luini Bernardino 1480/5–1532

The Milanese painter Bernardino Luini was a follower of Leonardo da Vinci. His earliest known works date from c1512 (for example, his *Annunciation*, c1512; Pinacoteca di Brera, Milan), by which time his style was already strongly Leonardesque, although this may have been preceded by an earlier phase influenced by Bramantino. Luini's understanding of Leonardo was to remain superficial. He tended to borrow external mannerisms, such as the famous enigmatic smile, rather than anything essential; but his ability to simplify and popularize Leonardo's style, without unpleasantly distorting it, won him great local success. His talents were much in demand both as a large-scale decorator and as a painter of small devotional panels.

Luks George 1867–1933

The American painter George Benjamin Luks was the most flamboyant and garrulous but technically unsound member of the New York group of The Eight of 1908, the nucleus of the Ash Can School. His style reflected the dark tones and slashing brush stroke that was popular in Munich, Paris, and America at the end of the 19th century. Luks' interest in realism, and his speed of execution, were the products of his work as a graphic journalist on *The Philadelphia Bulletin*, *The Philadelphia Press*, and the New York *World*. He was a member of the group of journalists seeking to become realist painters who gathered around Robert Henri in Philadelphia and later in New York. He was at his best with genre scenes and portraits of slum life in New York, such as *The Spielers* (oil on canvas; 1905; Addison Gallery of American Art, Andover, Mass.) and *The Wrestlers* (oil on canvas; 1905; Museum of Fine Arts, Boston).

Lurçat Jean 1892–1966

The French painter and tapestry designer Jean Lurçat studied painting under V. Prouvé in Nancy until 1912. He then went to Paris, becoming a pupil of B. Naudin at the Académie Colarossi. He belonged to the Paris circle of the poets Vildrac and Elie Faure, and knew artists such as Marcoussis and Picasso. He was in the French armed forces (1914–17), traveled in Spain (1923), North Africa, the Sahara, Greece, and the Near East (1924–9). He settled in Switzerland in 1931, traveling widely from 1936. He lived in Paris from 1955 until his death.

Lurçat is best known for tapestry designs which were first realized in 1939. With Marcel Gromaire, Henri Matisse, Marc Saint-Saens, and others, he revitalized the tapestry workshops at Aubusson. His own work had a brief association with Surrealism, but he found major inspiration from the designs of 14th-century French tapestries as well as Pre-Columbian textiles (seen in *Le Corton*, tapestry; 1947; Peter Stuyvesant Foundation, London).

Lutyens Edwin 1869–1944

The English architect Edwin Landseer Lutyens was born in London. After working briefly with George & Peto he set up his own architectural practice in 1889. He soon established a reputation for distinguished country houses, many of which had gardens laid out by Gertrude Jekyll (for example, Munstead Wood, Surrey, 1896; The Orchards, Godalming, 1899; Deanery Gardens, Sonning, Berkshire, 1901). These houses combined a display of craftsmanship and vernacular materials (such as brick, tile, and woodwork) with a Voysey-like massing of the parts.

Gradually Lutyens moved from this Arts and Crafts manner to a more formal and symmetrical style, adopting details that were Queen Anne (as at Great Maytham, Kent, 1910) or Palladian (as at Heathcote, Ilkley, 1906) in origin. This formality can also be seen in his axial plan for the centerpiece of Hampstead Garden Suburb (1908–10), which included two powerfully composed churches and a neo-Georgian Institute. In his designs for the enormous Viceroy's House at New Delhi (1913 onwards) he created a genuinely imposing effect by his highly competent handling of a fully classical vocabulary, with ranges of columns and a central dome.

The confidence Lutyens derived from his New Delhi work inspired him to undertake a number of monumental schemes: in central London alone these include the Cenotaph (1919), the Midland Bank headquarters (1924), the Britannic House, Finsbury Circus (1924–7). But in many ways his smaller commercial buildings, like the Midland Bank's Piccadilly branch in the style of Wren (1922), are more fitting monuments to Lutyens' skills, to be set beside the achievement of his more famous country houses.

Lydos *fl. c560–540 BC*

Lydos was an Athenian-trained painter of uncertain birthplace. He signed two vases "painted by the Lydian", so was therefore either an immigrant from the East or born in Greece of Lydian parentage. Whatever his origins, he learned his trade in Athens, and took his place in the dazzling generation of black-figure masters headed by Exekias and the Amasis Painter.

Lydos began his career at an awkward moment in the history of 6th-century painting. He and his contemporaries had not yet abandoned their infatuation with the conventional figures and lumbering animal friezes they had learned from their competitors in Corinth. On the other hand, the quest for narrative painting had already been initiated by Sophilos; Kleitias had proclaimed its manifesto on his François Vase, and by the 550s it was the prime concern of almost every painter.

A neck-*amphora* in Florence belonging to Lydos' early days illustrates the confrontation of these two conflicting traditions. The main scene is devoted to *The Judgment of Paris* and on the reverse, to a symposium. Above and below are animal friezes in the time-worn Corinthian style. The figures are painted in a bold, broad style quite unlike the diminutive tribe of Kleitias, and incised with a clean and steady hand unknown to Sophilos.

A signed work belonging to Lydos' prime is the fragmentary *dinos* from the Acropolis, Athens. The upper frieze is dedicated to the *Battle of Gods and Giants*, set in an intricate composition of fierce, overlapping figures. Helmets, thigh-armor, and sword-handles are incised with great care and there are some exceptionally fine shield-devices: a Gorgon head, a great winged bee, and a hairy satyr face in profile relief. In the middle zone, a cow, a sow, and a sheep are led to sacrifice by two robust men with trim red beards and hair. One of them wears a kilt with a case of knives slung over his shoulder and must be the slaughterer. The large somber animals are painted in clean-edged strokes and

incised with patterns to suggest the contrasting textures of sheepskin, pigskin, and cowhide. The rendering of these doomed beasts is exceptional and of a rare sensitivity that anticipates the procession of sacrificial animals along the north and south friezes of the Parthenon. The lower zone contains a frieze of unexpectedly sturdy animals.

Another mature work is his column-*krater* in New York, which is almost as large as the François Vase. But whereas Kleitias had relied upon six narrow friezes (depicting no less than eight mythological subjects and one animal brigade) to cover the *krater* and its foot, Lydos needed only one frieze and this was dedicated exclusively to a monumental rendition of *The Return of Hephaistos*. It is a riotous procession of loose bouncy satyrs and their companions, the maenads. The satyrs are corporeal creatures with knees sagging beneath their body-weight as they plod along. There are incidents of bottom-slapping, tail-pulling, and shoving; one large-headed satyr steals a drink from his friend's wine-skin. On the reverse comes Hephaistos—the *raison d'être* of the procession—riding on his mule and holding a drinking horn, the source of his undoing.

The New York *krater* gives eloquent testimony to the importance of Lydos as a master of large-scale narrative painting. The mouth of the *krater*, however, is decorated in a fine miniaturist style with tidy florals on the side, animals on the top, and a gorgoneion on each handle-plate. It should serve as a reminder of the numerous small vases that have also been attributed to his hand.

Lysippos 4th century BC

Lysippos was a Greek late Classical and early Hellenistic sculptor from Sicyon who specialized in bronze. His impact on Greek sculpture was comparable to that of Pheidias. He marked the transition from the Classical to the Hellenistic, as his style gradually developed in the direction of greater naturalism.

He was said to acknowledge no masters but Nature and the *Doryphoros* of Polycleitos, whose stance and proportions he altered drastically by adapting the innovations of his predecessors. The heads of his figures he made small and the bodies long and slim so that they looked taller than they were; in this way, the optical distortions of figures placed at an elevation were

reduced. Lysippos also converted the carefully balanced Classical pose to a restless momentary impression, truer to nature.

The sculptor's most famous work (known through Roman copies, now in the Vatican Museums) seems to have been a rather late work, the nude *Apoxyomenos* (*Youth Scraping Oil off his Body with a Strigil*; there is a copy in reverse in the Terme Museum, Rome). The youth stands tense in the process of shifting his weight from one foot to the other; one arm is brought across the body to be scraped by the other hand. This revolutionary protrusion of the arms breaks the frontal plane of the statue and invites the spectator to walk around it, thus realizing its third dimension. The *Apoxyomenos* was later taken to Rome.

Lysippos lived long and was reputed to have produced 1,500 statues. His large repertory looks forward to Hellenistic taste. Besides the traditional gods, heroes, and athletes, he created *colossi*, large groups, animal allegories, chariots, and portraits. His works stood all over the Greek world from southern Italy to Asia Minor. The School of Sicyon flourished until late in the Hellenistic period, developing his innovations.

A new process of making portraits from life masks and another of making copies from casts taken from statues were ascribed to Lysistratos, brother of Lysippos. The continuous spiral torsion of the figure in movement seems to have developed among that group of artists: one of the earliest specimens, a *Dancing Girl* known from fragmentary copies, may derive from Lysippos' *Drunken Flute Player*.

Lysippos was favored by the royal house of Macedon. He produced portraits of Alexander as a boy and as King which combined the fierceness and sensitivity of the subject. He also made a bronze group of Alexander among the 25 of his nobles who fell at Granicus, all on horseback; a portrait of Seleucus; and, in collaboration with Leochares, a bronze group of *Alexander and Craterus Hunting*, dedicated at Delphi by Craterus' son after his death in 321.

Closest to Lysippos' early style comes the marble statue of the athlete *Agias*, part of the Daochus family dedication at Delphi (337–332 BC; Delphi Museum). This seems to be a contemporary copy of his bronze *Agias* in Thessaly. The relief base of his statue of the athlete Pulydamas survives in the Museum at Olympia.

M

Macdonald-Wright Stanton
1890–1973

The American painter Stanton Mac-Donald-Wright was born in Charlottesville, Va. He studied at the Los Angeles Art Students' League (1905–6). From 1907 to 1913 he lived in Paris, at first studying color theory with the Canadian painter Percyval Tudor-Hart (1873–1954). He then developed the principles of Synchromism with Morgan Russell. The Synchromist paintings they exhibited together were Abstract and based on the juxtaposition of shapes whose colors came from different parts of the spectrum. After his return to California in 1919 he lost interest in Synchromism; he taught painting until the early 1950s, then took up Abstract painting again, continuing until his death in 1973.

Stanton Macdonald-Wright: Synchromy in Purple; oil on canvas; 91×71cm (36×28in); 1917. Los Angeles County Museum of Art, Los Angeles

Machuca Pedro *fl.* 1520–50

Pedro Machuca was a Spanish painter, architect, and sculptor, born at Toledo. With Alonso Berruguete (1486–1561), Machuca shared the distinctions of being the greatest Spanish representative of Renaissance artistic versatility and contributing to the birth of Florentine Mannerism in painting (with, for example, *Virgin of Suffrage*, 1517; Prado, Madrid).

After studying under Michelangelo, he returned to Spain in 1520 and designed the Palace of Charles V in the Alhambra, Granada: basically a square block with a raised circular courtyard within. Begun in 1527 in an Italianate style recalling Bramante, it was slightly influenced by contemporary Plateresque details. Machuca also contributed stone reliefs in a purely classical style. He died in 1550.

Mack Heinz 1931–

The optical-kinetic artist Otto Heinz Mack was born in Loller, Germany. Between

Pedro Machuca: the Palace of Charles V in the Alhambra, Granada; begun in 1527

C.R. Mackintosh: Preliminary Design for Mural Decoration of the First Floor Room of Miss Cranston's Buchanan Street Tearooms; pencil and watercolor on tracing paper; 36×75cm (14×29in); 1896/7. Mackintosh Collection, Glasgow University

1950 and 1953 he studied at the Academy of Art in Düsseldorf, and in 1956 at the University of Cologne. With Otto Piene he founded the "Zero" group in 1957. In 1960 he began an important series of rotating reliefs and "light dynamos".

Mack's constructions are concerned primarily with movement, light, and dissolution of form. They involve the use of reflecting surfaces (mirror, glass, aluminum), beams of light, and motors, and thus affect the entire environment in which they are placed. Institutions that own his work include the Museum of Modern Art, New York, the Niigata B.S.N. Art Museum, Japan, and the Victoria and Albert Museum, London.

Mackintosh C.R. 1868–1928

The Scottish architect Charles Rennie Mackintosh was born in Glasgow. He attended evening classes at the Glasgow School of Art, and from 1884 to 1889 was articled to a local architect. In 1890 he joined the firm of Honeyman & Keppie (becoming a full partner in 1904), received his first commission, and won a traveling scholarship which enabled him to spend several months sketching buildings in Italy.

While pursuing his architectural career he also took an interest in graphic design and furniture. He was one of a group ("The Four") whose work was shown in a London Arts and Crafts exhibition, illustrated in *The Studio*, and exhibited in Vienna and Turin. Much of The Four's work was marked by an attenuated, almost Art Nouveau stylization, which was considered decadent by the English public and which figured in many of the remarkable decorative schemes Mackintosh designed for a series of Glasgow tearooms for Mrs Cranston.

But in most of his work this element was only a complement to plainer and more rational forms. Thus the emphatic austerity of large studio windows dominates his most famous building, the Glasgow School of Art (1897–9), despite the discreet elegance of the external ironwork. Mackintosh's dependence on vernacular building traditions can be detected in the asymmetrically arranged features around the Art School's entrance. It is to be seen more clearly in his domestic buildings (for example, Windyhill, Kilmacolm, 1899; Hill House, Helensburgh, 1902; and his entry for the German "House of an Art-Lover" competition, 1901), though these buildings are outstanding for their freedom from historical detail.

The impression of solidity given by large areas of plain masonry in Mackintosh's later buildings is often counteracted by expansive spatial effects, such as the dramatically glazed stair towers of Scotland Street School, Glasgow (1904). In his designs for the 1907-9 extension to the Glasgow School of Art, the forbidding castle-like exterior, with its tall oriel windows, conceals the rich and exciting space of the library, based on a robust but ingenious wooden framework.

The Art School extension was Mackintosh's last major architectural work. His relations with colleagues and clients were not easy, and the strain of his fastidious working methods eventually began to tell. He resigned from Honeyman & Keppie in 1913, moved to Suffolk in 1914, and thence to London. His alterations to No. 78 Derngate, Northampton (1916), show that his imaginative flair did not diminish, but he was unable to reestablish an architectural practice and in 1923 moved to the south of France. There he produced a number of powerful landscape paintings before illness overcame him and forced his return to London, where he died in 1928.

McWilliam F.E. 1909–

The British sculptor Frederick Edward McWilliam was born in Northern Ireland. From 1928 to 1931 he studied painting and drawing at the Slade School of Fine Art, London. His sculptural imagination was fired by a visit to Brancusi's studio in Paris in 1931. This made him receptive to the smooth shapes and human references in Henry Moore's work, and pushed him

F.E. McWilliam: Portrait of Elizabeth Frink; bronze; height 183cm (72in); 1956. Harlow New Town, England

Carlo Maderno: the facade of S. Susanna, Rome; 1603

away from pure abstraction towards Surrealism. He joined the British Surrealist Group in 1938. In his first one-man exhibition at the London Gallery in 1939, his series of carvings called *The Complete Fragment* clearly showed his debt to Picasso, Arp, and Magritte: they represented parts of the head that the observer was invited to complete (for example *Eye, Nose, and Cheek*, 1939; Tate Gallery, London). McWilliam's postwar sculptures are mainly cast in bronze; in style and temperament they reflect the move away from Surrealism towards Existentialism, as championed by Alberto Giacometti, Lynn Chadwick, and Kenneth Armitage.

Maderno Carlo 1556–1629

The Italian architect Carlo Maderno was the most important practitioner of the early Baroque style in Rome in the early 17th century. Born at Capolago, he was in Rome by 1588 where he was a pupil of his uncle, Domenico Fontana. In 1603 he was made architect of St Peter's, and from 1607 to 1612 he added the nave and facade to the existing centralized structure by Michelangelo. His other important works in Rome include the facade of S. Susanna (1603), the dome of S. Andrea della Valle (1622), and the Palazzo Barberini (from 1621, later completed by Bernini).

Further reading. Donati, U. *Carlo Maderno, Architetto Ticinese a Roma*, Lugano (1957). Hibbard, H. *Carlo Maderno and Roman Architecture 1580–1630*, London (1971).

Maes Nicolaes 1634–93

A Dutch painter originally from Dordrecht, Nicolaes Maes studied under Rembrandt from c1650 to 1654. His earliest works have much of the rich, warm, reddish colors of Rembrandt's paintings from the 1640s, and also something of their subtle light and shade effects. Some of them are biblical pictures, but Maes' forte

was household interiors with large figures (particularly old women praying, sleeping, or engaged in household tasks), and intimate anecdotal genre scenes (for example, *Saying Grace*, 1648; Louvre, Paris). These, showing the domestic life of women and children, occasionally have the tenderness of the drawings of such themes made by Rembrandt in the 1640s.

Maes' subject matter and style changed after his return c1665–7 from Antwerp, which he visited in order to see pictures by Rubens, van Dyck, and Jordaens. He subsequently became a fashionable portraitist, producing large numbers of small, brightly colored pictures of elegantly dressed sitters (for example, *Portrait of a Man*, c1675; Niedersächsiche Landesgalerie und Städtische Galerie, Hannover). These paintings are mostly from after 1673—the date of Maes' move to Amsterdam. They have a much lighter tonality than the Rembrandtesque early works.

Maffei Francesco c1620?–60

The Vicentine painter Francesco Maffei was also active in Venice, Brescia, Rovigo, and Padua. Despite the provincial character of his origins and career, Maffei is one of the most impressive artists of the Venetian 17th century. He derived from his study of the great masters of the previous century a freshness and vigor absent from the academic Mannerism of his metropolitan contemporaries. He was also influenced by the works of earlier visitors to Venice, such as Johann Liss and Bernardo Strozzi, though he preserved a very personal taste for loose brushwork and dissonant color schemes, creating effects that often verge on the fantastic.

Magnasco Alessandro 1667–1749

Born in Genoa, the painter Alessandro Magnasco moved to Milan between 1680 and 1688. In the early 18th century he visited Florence and in 1735 returned to Genoa. He specialized in small figures in wild landscapes, influenced by Salvator Rosa (1615–73) and by the elongated figure style of the late Mannerist etchings of Jacques Callot (1592–1635). Magnasco's fragmented and rapid brush strokes

Nicolaes Maes: Portrait of a Woman; oil on canvas; 90×72cm (35×28in); 1667. Musée d'Arras

Alessandro Magnasco: A Scene of the Inquisition; oil on canvas; 44×83cm (17×33cm); c1710–20. Kunsthistorisches Museum, Vienna

Francesco Maffei: The Israelites Gathering Manna; oil on canvas; c1658–60. S. Giustina, Padua

René Magritte: Memory; gouache and watercolor on paper; 35×26cm (14×10in); c1942. Private collection

and ghostly, bizarre figures are frantic and psychologically disturbing. He chose strange subjects—witches and magic, obscure religious sects, quack doctors, scenes of trial and torture, saints and monks in ecstasy. Whether these are intended to be satire or farce, or whether they are the outpourings of a religious fanatic, remains unclear.

Magritte René 1898–1967

The Belgian Surrealist painter René Magritte was born in Lessines, Hainaut. He studied at the Académie des Beaux-Arts, Brussels (1916–18). His work from 1920 to 1924—in its treatment of themes of modern life, its bright color, and its exploration of the relationship of three-dimensional form to flat picture plane—shows the combined influence of Cubism,

Orphism, Futurism, and Purism. But in 1925, Magritte was profoundly moved by reproductions of the Metaphysical paintings of de Chirico and abandoned his earlier manner. In such works as *The Robe of Adventure* (1926; private collection), which owe much to de Chirico and to Ernst's work of 1921 to 1924, he expressed his sense of the mystery of the world by means of abrupt, irrational juxtapositions of objects and the evocation of a silent, trance-like atmosphere.

An active member of the Surrealist group in Brussels from 1925, Magritte remained unaffected by the emphasis on automatism in the Parisian group during the mid 1920s. In September 1927, he moved to the Parisian suburb Le Perreux-sur-Marne, where he lived for three years; his example contributed to the resurgence of illusionism in Surrealist painting in the late 1920s.

Unlike Dali, Magritte does not use painting to express his private obsessions or fantasies: wit, irony, and a spirit of intelligent debate rather than self-revelation characterize his work. Thus, in the word-paintings of 1928 to 1930 he explores the ambiguous relationship between words and images and the objects they denote. In such works as *The Human Condition I* (1933; private collection) where a canvas on an easel exactly reproduces the "real" landscape beyond the window, he probes the relationship of art to nature. There is a studied objectivity—Magritte liked to pose as the average bourgeois. But the frequent repetition of themes of suffocation, and the sense of claustrophobia induced by the extreme shallowness of the pictorial space, seem to correspond to some personal anxiety. These themes have been interpreted as reflecting Magritte's unconscious memory of his mother's suicide by drowning when he was 14.

In many paintings, Magritte questions our assumptions about the world—for instance, he disturbs normal scale or defies the laws of gravity—and implies that nothing is sure, everything is mysterious. The force of the image always depends upon the impersonality of the style, which resembles that of a sign-painter and forbids disbelief. It was a style that remained virtually unchanged throughout Magritte's mature work, except during the 1940s. From 1943 to 1946 he adopted an Impressionist brushwork and palette, apparently in order to alleviate the gloom of the war years. In the winter of 1947 to 1948—his so-called "Fauve" or "Vache" period—he painted a series of works remarkable for their violent color and grotesque imagery. The critical response to these experiments was generally hostile, and Magritte reverted to his accustomed manner. In his later work, despite a number of masterpieces, he was too often content to repeat successful themes or images; inevitably, a certain blandness entered his work.

Magritte's influence on Pop art was significant; the cerebral quality of his work also makes it relevant to other recent avant-garde developments.

Further reading. Calvocoressi, R. *Magritte*, Oxford (1979). Gablik, S. *Magritte*, London (1970). *Rétrospective Magritte*, Brussels (1978) and Paris (1979). Sylvester, D. *Magritte*, New York (1969). Waldberg, P. *René Magritte*, Brussels (1965).

Mahmud Muzahhib *fl. c1538–c60*

The Persian illuminator Mahmud Muzah-hib came from Herat but worked at Bukhara from *c*1538 to *c*1560. He is said to have been a pupil of Shaykh Zadeh, a Safavid master who may himself have gone to Bukhara. Mahmud Muzahhib preserved the style of Herat of the 1490s, especially in manuscript illustration, a particular feature of his work being a preference for illuminated double-page openings (seen for example in the *Bustan* of Sa'di, *c*1548; Gulbenkian Foundation, Lisbon). He also painted single figures or pairs of figures.

Maillol Aristide 1861–1944

The French sculptor, painter, and graphic artist Aristide Joseph Bonaventure Maillol was born in the southern town of Banyuls-sur-Mer. In 1893 he established a tapestry workshop, and his early paintings reflect in their flatness and formalization both tap-estry design and the influence of Gauguin. He began making sculpture in 1895, but only in 1900, after a temporary blindness, did he fully devote himself to it. His austere bronzes of the female nude, compactly designed and lacking in surface appeal, were in strong contrast to the fluid Impressionism of Rodin. Although they corresponded to a movement towards classicism and against anecdote among younger French sculptors, the robust female types owe more to local beauty than to the Greek ideal. His late sculptures such as the *Seated Figure* (1930) or *The River* (1939–43; both in the Museum of Modern Art, New York) avoid monumentality in favor of a dynamic relationship between figure and base.

Maitani Lorenzo *c1275–1330*

Lorenzo Maitani was a Sienese architect and sculptor. From 1310 until his death in 1330, Maitani was "Capomaestro" of the cathedral at Orvieto. Although documents reveal Lorenzo's supervision of every aspect of the cathedral fabric, the assumption that he was the creator of any of the facade sculptures rests on a single document of 1330. This refers to bronze supplied to Maitani for the casting of *The Eagle of St John*, one of the *Four Symbols of the Evangelists* on the cornice that runs across the facade just above the three main doors. Over the center door is a freestanding bronze group of the *Madonna and Child with Angels*, and there are stylistic similarities between these bronzes and the reliefs on the facade.

The four piers that divide the three doorways are covered with carved reliefs up to the level of the cornice. From the left they contain *The Creation and the Fall*, *The Tree of Jesse* and *Prophecies of Christ's Coming*, *The Life of Christ*, and *The Last Judgment*. Apart from its extraordinary

Aristide Maillol: Profile of a Young Girl; oil on canvas; 74×103cm (29×41in); c1895–6. Musée Hyacinthe Rigaud, Perpignan

quality, often seeming to possess a French Gothic lyricism, this extensive series contains fascinating evidence about the collaborative methods of a large 14th-century workshop. The sculptures are in varying stages of completion, and from these it can be seen that a sequence of operations was carried out by different workmen over the whole surface of the reliefs. This operation would have been done to the design of Maitani who might be assumed to have intervened at any time, especially on the final stage. While Maitani's workshop can be regarded as responsible for the majority of the reliefs, those in the lower part of the two central piers were done by someone else altogether.

If Maitani's precise role as sculptor is a matter of some guesswork, his role as architect of the cathedral facade as a whole is less open to dispute. There survive two designs for the facade, in pen on parchment. The later of these, much closer to the facade as it appears today, is probably that by Maitani referred to in an inventory of 1356. Comparison with the earlier, anonymous design reveals a change to a broader, less vertical effect; but the salient features of a triple, gabled portal, a rose window, and mosaic and sculptural decoration are retained. The first of the designs, which shows knowledge of French Gothic architecture, probably reflects the influence of

Lorenzo Maitani: detail of The Last Judgment; marble; c1310–30. Orvieto Cathedral

the transept ends of Notre Dame in Paris. This is combined with a regard for decorative and pictorial elements, especially evident in the siting of the mosaic *Coronation of the Virgin* in the main gable. Maitani's changes towards a broader, more spread-out effect emphasize this rather Italian element in the design, and the result is a profusion of architecture, sculpture (in bronze and stone), and mosaic that forms a splendid whole.

Malevich Kasimir 1878–1935

The Russian painter Kasimir Malevich was born in Kiev; he came to Moscow in 1902 to study art. In the 1900s he painted Impressionist-influenced landscape and figure scenes. In 1907 he met Michail Larionoff, and over the next few years shared a strong primitive manner employing popular art conventions, particularly the depiction of uncompromisingly frontal figures. However, Malevich's paintings are far more intense in color, the technique of gouache on paper lending itself to a broad treatment; they reflect the influence of Matisse, whose work he saw in the private collection of Sergei Shchukin.

In 1912 Malevich showed his paintings of peasant subjects at the "Donkey's Tail" exhibition in Moscow. The most recent of these *Taking in the Rye* (1912; Stedelijk Museum, Amsterdam) showed a turning away from the crudely graphic manner that had linked him to Larionoff, towards massive, tubular forms owing something to Picasso's paintings of 1908–9.

Malevich's paintings showed an increasing absorption of Western avant-garde influences, so placing him in strong opposition to the anti-European bias of Larionoff. *The Knife Grinder* (1912; Yale University Art Gallery, New Haven) combines Cubist fragmentation and Futurist multiplication of the image. The Cubist *Head of a Peasant* (1912; Stedelijk Museum, Amsterdam) is arbitrary in its relation to the subject, compared with the classic paintings of Picasso and Braque.

After breaking with Larionoff, Malevich came into contact with a new intellectual circle including the writer Kruchenykh and the composer M.V. Matyushin. The group subscribed to the concept of "alogism" which, as its name implies, was an attempt to break free from the bounds of casual connection. An "alogical" painting, such as *An Englishman in Moscow* (1914; Stedelijk Museum, Amsterdam) superim-

poses varied words and images in a way that cannot be resolved in the way most intricate Cubist pictures can; it undermines any kind of representational logic. Malevich's interest in popular art persists in the emblematic representation of everyday objects, reminiscent of sign painting. In *Woman at a Poster Column* (1914; Stedelijk Museum, Amsterdam), simple abstract shapes are as important to the composition as the vestigial references to the outside world in the form of collage and lettering.

The culmination of "alogism" was the production in St Petersburg in December 1913 of the opera *Victory over the Sun* with a libretto by Kruchenykh, music by Matyushin, and designs by Malevich. The title suggests a disturbing reversal of established values. The cancellation of the sun and its imprisonment in a box, achieved by the hero, can be equated with the partially deleted *Mona Lisa* in a painting of 1914. Malevich's designs included a curtain with a black square, which for him symbolized the zero, full of the new potentialities that arose from the passing of the old order.

This square was to acquire the significance of an icon for Malevich. As a painting on a white ground it occupied a central position—hung high up and straddled between two walls—when in December 1915 at the "0.10" exhibition at St Petersburg he showed, for the first time, his "Suprematist" paintings. These were nonfigurative compositions based on compositions of simple geometric forms, generally deriving from the square. By confining himself to such elementary means and a small predefined repertoire of "Suprematist" colors he was able to arrive at an independence from the subject which had evaded earlier Russian avant-garde painters. Occasional titles in the exhibition catalog, such as *Boy with Knapsack* (probably the painting now known as *Supremus no. 56*, in the State Russian Museum, St Petersburg) should be seen as indicating an attempt to represent in geometric terms the interaction of forces and masses, rather than an abstraction of the visible form.

Malevich justified his Suprematism by condemning representational art as a theft from nature, and said that the artist must construct "on the basis of weight, speed, and the direction of movement". In these paintings he conveyed strong impressions of floating or falling by placing shapes against a plain background which permitted no spatial interpretations. How-

Kasimir Malevich: An Englishman in Moscow; oil on canvas; 88×57cm (35×57in); 1914. Stedelijk Museum, Amsterdam

ary Russia who renounced painting as a speculative activity. Although a supporter of the Revolution and not conventionally religious, Malevich's thinking was of a mystical bent. He was concerned with presenting a new vision which, though not possible outside the context of a scientific and industrial society, was not directly related to the problems of functional design. In *The Non-Objective World* published in Munich in 1927 he stated that the artist would always be in advance of society. This being the case, he could not willingly suppress his own ideas for the sake of socially defined concepts of utility.

Malevich's principal activities during the 1920s seem to have been as a teacher. Invited by Chagall in 1919 to Vitebsk to teach at his school, he formed among his pupils the "Unovis" group (1920) which became a sufficiently powerful force to lead to the resignation of the former artist when the two quarreled. In 1921 the group itself was ousted, and after 1922 was based in St Petersburg (then Petrograd). Under Malevich, who had virtually given up painting, the group made a number of models that attempted an investigation of his theories of "planity" and "arkhitektory" (basic architectural form).

After 1930 Malevich began painting again. He returned to the peasant themes that had occupied him in his early years, employing basic shapes as if trying to establish a new grammar of form in terms of the human body. This partial return to figuration may have been an attempt to come to terms with the newly established official doctrine of "socialist realism", with its demand that art be comprehensible to the masses; but on the basis of the material available in the West, any assessment of Malevich's last phase must be tentative.

Further reading. Anderson, T. *Malevich*, Amsterdam (1970). Gray, C. *The Great Experiment: Russian Art 1863–1922*, London (1962). Haftmann, W. *Kasimir Malevich*, Cologne (1962). Karshan, D.H. *Malevich: the Graphic Work*, Jerusalem (1973). Malevich, K. *Essays in Art, 1915–33* (2 vols.), London (1969). Malevich, K. *From Cubism and Futurism to Suprematism*, Moscow and St Petersburg (1915). Moholy-Nagy, S. "Constructivism from Kasimir Malevich to Laszlo Moholy-Nagy", *Arts and Architecture*, New York (June 1966). Zhadova, L. *Malevich*, London (1982).

ever, relationships can sometimes be inferred from overlappings, so that while volume is rarely hinted at there is no suggestion of purely two-dimensional pattern.

Most of the early Suprematist paintings take their cue from *Black Square* in the austerity of their conception. Later, superimpositions and the incorporation of irregular quadrilaterals create a more complex image. Malevich faced the dilemma that to develop Abstract images through formal elaboration increased the associative content of the painting, so impeding

its ability to communicate pure sensation. In paintings after 1917 he returned to a simple structure, often basing his paintings on no more than a cross. Elsewhere he worked on the edge of perception by painting in white on white, confounding spatial readings by emphasizing the fact of the pigment. When in 1918 he painted *White Square on a White Background* (Museum of Modern Art, New York) this was a virtual admission that his researches had come to a dead end.

At the same time he was out of sympathy with advanced artists in post-Revolution-

Mallarmé Stéphane 1842–98

The French poet and art and theater critic Stéphane Mallarmé was a close friend of Manet, and the center of an avant-garde Parisian salon. A devotee of British and American culture, he popularized translations of Edgar Allen Poe and his friend Whistler's *Ten O'Clock Lecture* (1888) in France as well as information about Tennyson, Swinburne, and London art exhibitions. Born in Paris, he earned his living teaching English in *lycées* in Tournon, Besançon, Avignon, and, from 1871, in Paris. He established his famous "Tuesday" *salon* in 1875; here writers such as Huysmans and Verlaine met and mixed with such artists as Manet, Pissarro, Gauguin, and Redon.

His poetic output was small and sporadic but of seminal importance to Symbolist writers and artists. Following a spiritual crisis during the winter of 1864–5, Mallarmé rejected his earlier style—reminiscent of Baudelaire's—to evolve a radically new poetry whose aim was to intimate the Objec-

tive Ideal. The Ideal, defined by Mallarmé as the void left vacant by the dethronement of God, could not be defined in concrete, finite language; its existence could only be suggested by the ambiguity of words with multivalent meaning and the random placing of stanzas across a page. This new poetry received its complete expression in his poem, *Le Coup de Dés* (1897).

Malouel Jean *fl.* 1396–1415

The Netherlandish artist Jean Malouel was born in Nijmegen. He became Court Painter and *Valet de Chambre* to the Dukes of Burgundy. He belonged to a family of artists who were active in Nijmegen in Guelders in the late 14th century, and was uncle to the Limburg brothers, whose careers he helped to establish. He is recorded in Paris in 1396, when he was working for the Queen of France; but in 1397 he was called to Dijon by Philip the Bold to become his official painter in Burgundy. The remainder of his life was

spent in the service of the Burgundian court.

Although he traveled for the Duke to Conflans, Paris, and Arras, and numerous documents testify to his varied activities in Burgundy, attempts to identify his individual style focus on works commissioned for the Carthusian Monastery on the outskirts of Dijon known as the Chartreuse de Champmol. This foundation of Philip the Bold's was a major center of artistic activity *c*1400, and there Malouel was associated with Claus Sluter, whose sculptures in the large cloister were painted by him.

The Chartreuse was demolished after the French Revolution and its works of art dispersed. Five large altarpieces for it were commissioned from Malouel in 1398, but the only relevant identifiable work from the Chartreuse is an altarpiece now in the Louvre, Paris, known to have been completed in 1416, after Malouel's death, by his successor Henri Bellechose. Its complex iconography shows the martyrdom and mystic communion of St Denis dominated by the crucified Christ and the other two Persons of the Trinity (to whom the Chartreuse was dedicated). Stylistically it appears to involve two artists. An apparently earlier work in a related style bearing the arms of Burgundy on the reverse (Louvre, Paris) is attributed by most scholars to Malouel and is the key work in his identification. One of the earliest surviving circular paintings, it combines the Trinity with a poignant rendering of mourning over the dead Christ.

Further attributions include a *Pietà* (Musée des Beaux-Arts, Troyes) and a *Madonna with Angels* (Staatliche Museen, Berlin). It is possible that the latter painting (in tempera on cloth) once formed part of a diptych. An 18th-century drawing of John the Fearless (Bibliothèque Nationale, Paris; Coll. Bourgogne xx fol. 308) is thought to be derived from an original portrait by Malouel.

Jean Malouel (attrib.): Pietà; panel; diameter 64cm (25in); c1400/10. Louvre, Paris

Manessier Alfred 1911–

The French artist Alfred Manessier was born in Saint-Ouen. He studied architecture at the École des Beaux-Arts in Amiens, and went to Paris in 1929 to continue architectural studies at the École des Beaux-Arts, with extra classes at the Louvre and various academies in Montparnasse. He met and studied with the painter Roger Bissière in 1935, joining the group around him. From 1936 to 1938 he

Alfred Manessier: And I Saw the Glory of the Resurrection; 230×200cm (91×79in); 1961. Private collection

lived in Saint-Ouen, returning to Paris in 1939. After military service from 1939 to 1940, he resumed his studies with Bissière in 1940. In 1943 he spent some time in a Trappist Monastery at Soligny-la-Trappe, Orme—a period important to the development of his work.

Manessier is a member of the School of Paris. Besides painting, he designs stained-glass windows, tapestries, stage-sets, and costumes. His mature works, especially those of the 1950s, consist of abstract symbols in glowing colors, with figurative, often religious titles (for example, *Près d'Harlem*, oil on canvas; 1953; Musée des Beaux-Arts, Dijon).

Manet Édouard 1832–83

Édouard Manet was born in Paris in 1832, and it was at the annual Paris Salon that, for over 20 years, he sought academic and public acceptance for his original, brilliant, and enigmatic canvases. Because of the furore that his works created at the Salons, he became the first major artist in whose career the journalists and the general public played vital roles.

Intended for the law by his father, head of staff at the Ministry of Justice, Manet chose the navy; he voyaged to South America as a naval cadet in 1838. But after twice failing his entrance examinations to naval college (in 1848 and 1849), he was allowed to enroll at the École des Beaux-Arts, in the studio of Thomas Couture, then highly respected for his academic historical compositions. Manet is said to have quarreled frequently with Couture, but nevertheless studied with him for six years and acquired the basis of his later technique.

Manet was 26 when he first submitted to the Salon. His *Absinthe Drinker* (1858–9; Ny Carlsberg Glyptotek, Copenhagen), a cloaked, top-hatted bohemian figure, was rejected in 1859. But in 1861 his large *Spanish Singer* (1860; Metropolitan Museum, New York) was accepted, given

Édouard Manet: Study of a Woman; charcoal on paper; 55×41cm (22×16in); 1881. Rijksmuseum Vincent van Gogh, Amsterdam

an honorable mention, and was widely acclaimed. An admirer said that it stood between Realism and Romanticism. Manet worked throughout 1862 and began 1863 by showing 14 canvases at a dealer's art gallery and sending three major works to the Salon. All three were rejected. But that

Édouard Manet: Races at Longchamp; oil on canvas; 44×85cm (17×33in); 1864. Art Institute of Chicago

Édouard Manet: A Villa at Rueil; oil on canvas; 92×72cm (36×28in); 1882. National Gallery of Victoria, Melbourne

year artists were allowed, by Imperial decree, to show their rejected works separately at a Salon des Refusés. There Manet's large composition *Le Déjeuner sur l'Herbe* (or *Luncheon on the Grass*, originally called *Le Bain* (Bathing) 1863; Musée du Jeu de Paume, Paris) in which women were shown undressed beside clothed men in a wood, created a scandal; it became the object of press ridicule and attracted crowds of sightseers.

From that time, Manet's new canvases were the focus of popular attention. When, in 1865, the Salon did show his *Olympia* (1863; Musée du Jeu de Paume, Paris) an even greater outcry followed. The following year, his *Fifer* (1866; Musée du Jeu de Paume, Paris) was rejected. So in 1867, when he was not invited to exhibit at the Paris World Fair, Manet erected his own pavilion to show 50 works. Later that year the authorities forbade him to exhibit *The Execution of the Emperor Maximilian* because of its topical political relevance. (Several versions of *The Execution of the Emperor Maximilian* survive; the most complete is in the Städtische Kunsthalle Mannheim.)

If, like Chardin before him, Manet had confined himself to still life and small subject pictures, he might have been excused or even accepted. But his canvases of the 1860s were large, challenging comparison with the great art of the past. And Manet was aware of the great masters: he had spent six years copying them. He did not simply paint what he found around him; he painted modern versions of old subjects. *Le Déjeuner sur l'Herbe* was a version of Giorgione's *Fête Champêtre* (c1510; Louvre, Paris), *Olympia* was based on Titian's *Venus of Urbino* (1538; Uffizi, Florence), and almost every canvas of the decade had its precedent in earlier art. But in Manet's variations, traditional motifs became enigmatic, even ambiguous. Giorgione's naked nymphs and Titian's Venus looked frankly indecent in modern settings.

Nor did Manet just set up his models in traditional poses. His vision was itself original. He analyzed and simplified his motifs, eliminating half-tones, using a frontal light that flattened planes and reduced shadows to outlines, and so created bold patterns of colored patches.

In this he was guided by an odd range of earlier examples: the works of Frans Hals and Velazquez, but also Japanese woodcuts. His broad simplifications at last led to the *Fifer* in which the flat heraldic colors of the boy's uniform are set off by an almost blank background.

For almost a decade, Manet challenged the Salon with a sequence of heroic versions of works by artists ranging from Mantegna to Goya. He was controversial, which meant he had his supporters. By 1860, he had been befriended by Baudelaire, and for a time the poet and painter seem to have shared a vision of modern heroism, as Baudelaire described in his essay "The Painter of Modern Life". Manet met Degas in 1862, and soon afterwards Pissarro, Renoir, and the other painters later to become the Impressionists. In 1867, he was championed by the novelist Émile Zola.

With the end of the Franco-Prussian war and the coming of the Third Republic, the tide had turned for Manet. His work was usually, though not always, accepted for the Salon; and in 1873 his *Le Bon Bock* (*Portrait of Émile Bellot*, 1873; Philadelphia Museum of Art), a portrait of a jovial beer drinker, enjoyed a real popular success. But public attention had been diverted to the new artistic scandal: Impressionism.

Although Manet was respected by the

Impressionists, who were sometimes called "la bande à Manet", he never exhibited with them or painted a truly Impressionist work. Nevertheless, his paintings of the early 1870s do seem influenced by Impressionism, or perhaps by Berthe Morisot, who had become his pupil in 1868, was later his model and, in 1874, his sister-in-law. His canvases became smaller, his motifs less monumental, and his touch more broken. There are fewer set pieces, and even the largest of these do not match the scale of his earlier works.

It was in the second half of the decade that Manet developed his latest style. This was a sequence of portraits of contemporary life, which developed hints of his own earliest canvases and of some of Degas' portraits. These paintings showed characteristic types of the period in their settings. They included *The Prune* (1877; Paul Mellon Collection, Upperville, Virginia), a woman drinking alone in a bar; *Nana* (1877; Hamburger Kunsthalle, Hamburg), a prostitute and her client; and compositions based on cafés, concerts, and beer halls (for example, *Waitress* or *La Servante de Bocks*, 1878–9; National Gallery, London). That Manet was following a conscious program is confirmed by his letter of 1879 offering to decorate the new Town Hall with scenes showing the heart of Paris.

In 1881, at the age of 49, Manet had his triumph at the Salon. His portrait of the big-game hunter *Pertuiset* (Museum of Art, Sao Paulo) was awarded a second class medal, and with it the right to exhibit at future Salons without the approval of the jury. Unfortunately he was already suffering from locomotor ataxia. He was in pain, walked with difficulty, and worked more and more with pastel as his condition deteriorated. But he painted a final masterpiece: *The Bar at the Folies-Bergère* (1881–2; Courtauld Institute Galleries, London) which in its motif, a radiant young woman typifying contemporary life, in its monumental composition, and in its new brilliant technique, unifies the various strands of his earlier works. It was a success in the Salon of 1882.

Early in 1883, Manet, already bedfast, had a leg amputated and died soon after the operation, on 30 April, at the age of 51.

Further reading. Bataille, G. *Manet*, Geneva (1955). Guérin, M. *L'Oeuvre Gravé de Manet*, Paris (1944). Hansen, A.C. *Édouard Manet*, Philadelphia (1966). Rewald, J. *History of Impressionism*, London and New York (1973). Richardson, J. *Édouard Manet: Paintings and Drawings*, London (1958). Zola, É. *Édouard Manet, Étude Biographique et Critique*, Paris (1867).

Manohar c1565–c1628

Manohar was a Hindu painter at the Mughal court. Born in the Imperial household, he was the son of Basawan, and served as his father's apprentice in 1581. He collaborated with Basawan, Mukund, and Anant on the *Akbar-nama* (Victoria and Albert Museum, London), and at an early age was entrusted with illustrating a *Gulistan* (Royal Asiatic Society, London); the manuscript contains a youthful self-portrait. He rose to eminence during the reign of Jahangir (1605–27). The Emperor gave a portrait of him by Manohar to Sir Thomas Roe, the English ambassador at the Mughal court; the original has been lost. He painted a number of Christian subjects and was influenced by European art. The Leningrad Album in the Hermitage Museum, Leningrad, contains several of his works: a coronation scene on which he collaborated with Mansur, two portraits of Jahangir, and European allegorical and religious subjects. He ceased to work c1628.

Mansart François 1598–1666

In many ways the French architect François Mansart followed the French classical style created by Salomon de Brosse (1571–1626). He remained loyal to its traditions and was deeply suspicious of the Baroque style championed by Louis Levau. It is worth comparing the formality, subtlety, and classical integrity of his château of Maisons-Lafitte (1642–6), with Levau's château at Vaux-le-Vicomte (1658–61). It is easy to see in Mansart his development from the conservative if not vernacular style in the château at Berny, through the less complex and more compact manner of Balleroy (c1626), to the final classical maturity of his rebuilding of the château of Blois (1635–8) and his schemes of 1664 for the Louvre. Yet he did not entirely turn his back on the Baroque. In the staircase hall at Blois, in the dome of his church of the Visitation, Paris (begun as a centralized plan in 1632), and in his projected staircase for the Louvre, he showed a dramatic use of light and a structural ingenuity worthy of the Baroque.

In many respects Mansart continued the nationalistic classical style evolved in the 1550s. He disliked the Italianate manner eagerly taken up by Levau at Vaux-le-Vicomte. Mansart's refusal to leave France or even stray too far from Paris isolated him and threw him back on his own resources. His lack of success at court heightened this, and his bids for favor with the schemes for the Louvre of 1664 and the Bourbon Mausoleum at St-Denis were unsuccessful.

His influence in France after his death was more apparent than real. The practical, perhaps slipshod, classicism of his nephew J.-H. Mansart would have pleased him little, and it was only with the classical revival of the mid 18th century that he was once again appreciated and understood in France.

Mansart J.-H. 1646–1708

Great-nephew of the more distinguished architect François Mansart, Jules-Hardouin Mansart was the perfect example of the court architect. His entire career was spent in the service of Louis XIV, beginning with his work with Le Notre at the château for Mme de Montespan at Bosquet des Domes in 1675, and closing with his designs for the chapel at Versailles of 1689, which was completed after his death in 1708 by his pupil Robert de Cotte.

At Versailles, where he was heir to the work of Levau and François d'Orbay, his most dramatic, and at the same time unfortunate, contribution was the filling in of the center of the park facade with the sumptuous Hall of Mirrors (1678–81). He worked there and on the adjoining *Salon de la Guerre* and *Salon de la Paix* in a particularly fruitful partnership with Charles Lebrun. His success repeated what he had undertaken at the château at Clagny in 1676 for Madame de Montespan, and was itself repeated on a more intimate scale for his Grand Trianon (1678) in the park at Versailles.

The Trianon was followed by the now destroyed château of Marly, which developed the pavilion or *trianon* principle, laying out a parallel row of them on either side of the main block of the palace. In this as in some other designs, he showed a Baroque inventiveness which counteracted his rather pompous classicism. The former

J.-H. Mansart: the Hall of Mirrors in the Palace of Versailles; 1678–81

was obvious in the twin stables built at Versailles in 1678 and 1686, which completed a grand forecourt to the palace and echoed the layout and scale of the Roman Piazza del Popolo. Apart from his royal commissions, his most distinguished buildings were the rebuilding of the chapel at the Invalides (1680–91), and the layout of the Parisian Place Vendôme (1698) and Place des Victoires (1685) which did much to set the tone of urban planning in the city. Their influence was felt in the provinces in a scheme such as the Place des États at Dijon of 1686, and ultimately in Gabriel's Place de la Concorde in Paris.

Perhaps one of the most notable aspects of his career was his ability both to delegate and cooperate. At Versailles, his vital association with Lebrun continued that formed by Levau; it stretched to sculptors and stuccoists like Coysevox, Tubi, and Cucci, and more significantly to the gardener Le Notre. He worked with Le Notre at Versailles, Trianon, and at Chantilly.

His method of giving much of his work to assistants, especially to talented ones like L'Assurance and Pierre le Peintre, helped to foster the style of the Rococo.

Mansur *fl.* late 16th–mid 17th century

The Muslim painter Ustad (master) Mansur received from the Emperor Jahangir the title "Nadir-al-Asr" ("Wonder of the Age"). He started work in the Akbar period (1556–1605) painting in the *Akbar-nama* (Victoria and Albert Museum, London) and the *Babur-nama* (divided between the British Museum, London, and the National Museum of India, New Delhi). Although famous for natural history subjects he was no mean portraitist, as is evident from *The Vina Player* (*c*1600; Edward Croft-Murray Collection, London). The St Petersburg Album (Hermitage Museum) contains a fine portrait of Jahangir by Mansur and Manohar.

Mansur was instructed by Jahangir to paint the flowers of Kashmir; he recorded some 100 specimens. His reputation rests chiefly on his portrayal of exotic and domestic animals, painted with meticulous accuracy and with frozen, stylized grandeur—including a zebra, a turkey cock, a cheer pheasant, and a hornbill.

Mansur: An Abyssinian Zebra; gouache on paper; 18×24cm (7×9in). Victoria and Albert Museum, London

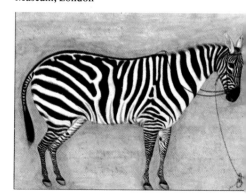

Mantegna Andrea 1431–1506

Andrea Mantegna was an Italian painter and engraver and, according to his contemporaries, also a sculptor. The adopted son and apprentice of a Paduan painter and antiquary, Francesco Squarcione, Mantegna's first big commission was for frescoes of scenes from *The Lives of SS. James and Christopher* (1448–52; Eremitani, Ovetari Chapel, Padua; destroyed in the Second World War). Their success no doubt inspired the commission for the San Zeno Altarpiece (1456–9; S. Zeno, Verona). In 1457 he accepted the invitation of Lodovico Gonzaga, Marquis of Mantua, to be his court painter, and settled by 1460 in that humanistic court.

Documents record the variety of his tasks: portraits, designs for buildings, tapestries, vases and cups, and frescoes both religious and profane. He also created stage designs on canvas (the newly restored *Triumphs of Caesar*, c1486–c94; Hampton Court Palace, London) and painted panels of *Parnassus* and *The Triumph of Virtue* (c1497; both in the Louvre, Paris) for Isabella d'Este's Studiolo, which housed her antiquities. He visited Venice in 1448, and in Ferrara, in 1449, may have met Piero della Francesca whose monumentality probably affected his style. He was in Florence in 1466, and from 1488 to 1490 Marquis Francesco "lent" him to the Pope to fresco a chapel in the Vatican Belvedere.

Florentine art and the antiquarianism of the Paduan *milieu* (his father had visited Greece, and had a large collection of antiquities) were decisive influences on Mantegna's style. He knew the vigorous and sculptural frescoes by Andrea del Castagno in Venice (1442; S. Zaccaria). Another Florentine, Filippo Lippi, had worked in Padua c1434 (in the Capella del Podestà; now destroyed), and Mantegna learned through his example the gravity of style and three-dimensionality of Masaccio, whose pupil Filippo may have been. Furthermore, Giotto's frescoes in the Capella dell'Arena in Padua proclaimed essentially similar qualities.

More important to the young man than any of these was the arrival of Donatello and his assistants in 1443 to make an altar for the Basilica of St Anthony (the Santo Altar), and the statue of *Gattamelata* which stands, like Marcus Aurelius reborn, near the Basilica. Uccello came also, and painted monochrome frescoes (now lost) which probably showed his intense involvement with problems of perspective. Echoes of Donatello's art, steeped in antique grandeur, occur throughout Mantegna's career; and his concern with the excitement of perspective is continuous.

Mantegna's importance derives from his evocative antiquarianism, his sculptural figure-style, and his startling illusionism. In *The Martyrdom of St James* (?1554–7; Ovetari Chapel, Padua), we look up at the scene, with its background of Roman ruins and town. A soldier leans over the foreground fence, but that fence is attached to the frame of the fresco at the left, and so the soldier obtrudes into our own space, and the head of the executed saint will soon roll down towards us.

The San Zeno Altarpiece again profits from perspective to draw together into an airy loggia those elements of the *sacra conversazione* that were usually marooned in separate panels. He may have taken the concept from Filippo Lippi's Barbadori Altarpiece (commissioned 1437; Louvre, Paris) or from the original figure arrangement and architectural canopy of Donatello's Santo Altar. Mantegna's loggia resembles an antique shrine, with its columns and pillars with antique friezes, and garlands of fruit and flowers. As is frequently the case, humor tempers and therefore underlines the high seriousness of this monumental work: for the Anatolian carpet below the Virgin's throne hides the upper part of the two putti, while their fellows (brothers to those on the bronze panels of the Santo Altar) concentrate on their singing.

In Mantua, in the Camera degli Sposi (1472–4; Palazzo Ducale), Mantegna created another "loggia" with scenes of court life. Two walls were hung with actual gold-painted leather curtains, and these Mantegna continues on his painted walls, hanging them behind the scene of the Gonzaga court on one wall, and swept back (somewhat twisted over the door) to reveal on the adjacent wall the meeting of the Marquis with his son, Cardinal Francesco Gonzaga. Behind them lies a landscape strewn with evidence of the Romans—a colosseum, pyramid, great statue, mausoleum—and thus evidence, too, of the court's scholarly inclinations. We then look up past spandrels with scenes from Classical mythology, past cofferings wherein putti hold roundels with the heads of Roman emperors, to a central oculus with elaborate balcony, over which people stare down and around which putti

edge precariously. Painted ceiling and painted people seem real because they are apparently in our space, and hence we are in their space and share their life. This room deliberately confuses the real with the painted; Correggio, in his work in the Camera di San Paolo (1518–19; S. Paolo, Parma) was later to imitate elements from it. And it is, indeed, from the Camera degli Sposi that the illusionistic ceiling decoration of the Baroque ultimately derives.

Mantegna's figure-style, popular in his day in northern Italy, was too brittle and linear to appeal to the High Renaissance, but his vision of Antiquity continued to hold great fascination. He never copied antiquities exactly, but sought to recreate an antique spirit, as in the nine monumental *Triumphs of Caesar*, painted in tempera on canvas (an early use of this support), which imitate Roman triumphal monuments and sculpture, and parallel Mantuan ceremonial.

Mantegna's influence was wide-ranging. He had begun to engrave c1465, and works by him and an extensive school further popularized his paintings. He was partly responsible for transmitting Florentine ideas to his brother-in-law, Giovanni Bellini, including the idea of the unified altarpiece. His works in Mantua increased Titian's interest in the Antique when he visited the city in 1523. They also impressed Giulio Romano when he settled there in 1524 and built the Palazzo del Tè (which one early commentator claimed was built just to house *The Triumphs of Caesar*). Rubens' period as court painter (1600–8 with interruptions) converted him, so to speak, to the Italian language of painting.

With the impoverishment of Mantua, Charles I bought the *Triumphs*, together with other paintings and Antique sculptures, in 1629; Richelieu eventually bought the paintings from the Studiolo after the Sack of 1630. The Camera degli Sposi remains a reminder of the Mantuan passion for Antiquity in plays, processions, ceremonial, scholarship, and art. Its illusionism might well derive from antique fresco decoration, just as the Palazzo del Tè imitates Roman villa design, and Alberti's churches in Mantua are based on antique temples and triumphal arches.

Further reading. Kristeller, P. *Andrea Mantegna*, London (1901). Levenson, J.A., Oberhuber, K., and Sheehan, J.L. *Early Italian Engravings from the National Gal-*

Andrea Mantegna: The Agony in the Garden; panel; 63×80cm (25×32in); c1455. National Gallery, London

lery of Art (sections VIII and IX), Washington, D.C. (1973). Martindale, A. and Garavaglia, N. *The Complete Paintings of Mantegna*, London (1971). Martindale, A. *The Triumphs of Caesar: Mantegna Paintings in the Collection of* *H.M. The Queen at Hampton Court*, London (1979). Paccagnini, G. *Andrea Mantegna*, Venice (1961). Paccagnini, G. and Mezzetti, A. *Andrea Mantegna*, Venice (1961).

Maratti Carlo 1625–1713

Carlo Maratti was the leading exponent of High Baroque Classicism in later 17th-century Rome. His achievement was based mainly on the production of altarpieces in the grand manner. A pupil of Andrea

protégé, Baciccia, during the 1670s, Maratti's classicizing and somewhat academic style was to dominate Roman painting for the rest of his long life.

Marc Franz 1880–1916

In his mature work the German painter Franz Marc pursued a mystical relationship between form and color using animals as his subjects. Like Kandinsky, with whom he organized the first *Blaue Reiter* exhibition in Munich in 1911, he adopted a spiritual attitude to the color and content of his paintings.

The son of a minor genre and landscape painter, Marc studied theology and then received a full academic training in art in Munich (1900–3), visiting Paris in 1903 and again in 1907. In his early work, most of which he destroyed, animals had already assumed a place of importance. The flat decorative patterns of *Jugendstil* liberated him from a servile study of nature, and his early decorative paintings are enlivened by the light in Impressionist art and the color of Van Gogh, whose paintings had particularly impressed him in Paris.

After his second visit to Paris in 1907, he applied himself to a rigorous study of animal anatomy, and painted in a number of Post-Impressionist styles, including Di-

Carlo Maratti: Self-portrait; red chalk on paper; 37×27cm (15×11in); 1684. British Museum, London

visionism. He developed a rhythmic approach to animals in landscape which he later described as "the anatomization of art". By 1910 he had adopted a theory of symbolic colors, and the flat strong color

Franz Marc: Two Cats: oil on canvas; 74×98cm (29×39in); 1912. Öffentliche Kunstsammlung, Kunstmuseum Basel

Sacchi and a friend of the theorist Pietro Bellori, he shared their admiration of Raphael and Annibale Carracci, and their disapproval of the more radically Baroque styles of Bernini and Pietro da Cortona. After a period of rivalry with Bernini's

of his paintings, reminiscent of Fauvism and the *Brücke*, brought him to the brink of Expressionist abstraction (in, for example, *House in Landscape*, 1910; Museum Folkwang, Essen). These works were intended to convey in symbolic color the rhythms of nature and of animal life.

In February 1911, when he joined the *Neue Künstlervereinigung* with Kandinsky, he wrote: "there are no 'subjects', and no 'colors' in art, only expression'". He later admitted that it was Kandinsky's painting that allowed him to use color to liberate and communicate his emotions. His paintings became more expressive and his color intense, with animals and landscape interlocked in a continuous rhythmic space (for example, *Blue Horses*, 1911; Walker Art Center, Minneapolis).

After participating in the *Blaue Reiter* exhibition and editing the *Blaue Reiter* almanac with Kandinsky, he went to Paris in 1912 with Macke (whom he had met in 1910) and visited Robert Delaunay, whose chromatic series of window-pictures made a strong impression on him. The interpretation of subject and surroundings in Marc's work after 1912 owes something to Delaunay's theories of Orphic "simultaneity", and to his contact with Cubism, which he described as a "mystic-inward construction".

The planar rhythms of Futurist painting also appealed to Marc and pushed him further towards abstraction. By 1913 the animals in his paintings assume a lesser importance and are dominated by swirling geometric forms in brilliant colors (for example, *Tyrol*, 1913–14; Neue Pinakothek, Munich). After participating in Walden's *Erster Deutscher Herbstsalon* in Berlin in 1913, Marc abandoned altogether the use of the subject. From then onwards he occupied himself almost exclusively with Abstract compositions, to which he gave titles such as *Struggling Forms*, *Broken Forms*, and *Cheerful Forms*. After moving to Ried (Upper Bavaria) in 1914, he was called up for military service and was killed at Verdun in 1916.

Further reading. Gerhardus, M. and D. *Expressionism*, Oxford (1979). Kandinsky, W. and Marc, F. *Der Blaue Reiter*, Munich (1965).

Hans von Marées: Self-portrait with Franz Lenbach; oil on canvas; 54×62cm (21×24in); 1863. Neue Pinakothek, Munich

Marca-Relli Conrad 1913–

Corrado di Marca-Relli (or Conrad Marca-Relli) was one of the earliest of the second generation of American Abstract Expressionists. Born in Boston, he studied at the Cooper Union in New York (1930). He worked in the Federal Art Project, New York, from 1935 to 1938 and served in the U.S. army from 1941 to 1945. His favored technique is a painted collage with cut-out pieces of canvas laid on the canvas itself. His art in the 1950s owed something to Arshile Gorky, Willem de Kooning, and Robert Motherwell. His compositions ranged from the expressive and classical to the more Expressionist *The Battle* (1956; Metropolitan Museum, New York), a theme that was nonetheless inspired by Uccello's *Rout of San Romano* (c1456; panels in the Uffizi, Florence; National Gallery, London; and Louvre, Paris). Marca-Relli has developed a luminous and lyrical style of Abstract painting.

Marées Hans von 1837–87

The German painter Hans von Marées studied under Carl Steffek in Berlin (1853–5) and Carl Piloty in Munich (1857–64). In the early 1860s he began to work from nature under the influence of the Barbizon School, and painted landscapes in which the figure groups were integrated with their setting. In 1864 Count Schack sent him to Italy to copy Old Master paintings. This led to a more richly painted, but less realistically detailed style: a development strengthened in Paris in 1869, when he probably saw works by Puvis de Chavannes.

From this time onwards, Marées' work became more Symbolist in subject matter (for example *The Golden Age*; 1879–85 version and *Garden of the Hesperides*, 1884–5, both in the Neue Pinakothek, Munich) and more monumental in style (for example *Friends of the Artist in a Pergola*, 1873; part of the fresco done for the Stazione Zoologica, Naples). Influenced by the aesthetic ideas of Konrad Fiedler and Adolf von Hildebrand, Marées attempted to reconcile the tactile feeling for the third dimension with the two-dimensional demands of the picture plane: the constant reworking of his later canvases is evidence of his failure to achieve this goal.

Margaritone d'Arezzo 1216–93

The Tuscan Romanesque painter Mar-

Margaritone d'Arezzo: The Virgin and Child Enthroned, with Scenes of the Nativity and the Lives of the Saints; panel; 93×183cm (37×72in); c1262? National Gallery, London

garitone d'Arezzo worked in a style similar to that of Coppo di Marcovaldo and Guido da Siena. Our information about this artist comes mostly from Vasari's *Lives*, where he appears to have been given prominence not because of artistic quality, but because he and Vasari shared the same birthplace. Of one of his works, Vasari says that it was executed "with diligence and grace ... the little figures in it are so carefully finished that they resemble the work of an illuminator". This agrees with surviving works, such as his *Virgin and Child Enthroned* (National Gallery, London), where the figures are contained within a delicate mandorla. Again according to Vasari, Margaritone was also a sculptor in wood, an experimenter with canvas as a support, and an architect.

Marin John 1870–1953

An American painter, promoted by Alfred Stieglitz, John Marin developed a style based on a combination of a Futurist shorthand interpretation of New York and a romantic appreciation of the landscape of New England. He trained as an architect, traveled (though was relatively untouched by his European experiences), and had reached a personal expression by 1912 with *Movement: Fifth Avenue* (water-color; Art Institute of Chicago). Later, his fragmented but painterly style was applied to landscape, as in *Maine Islands* (water-color; 1922; The Phillips Collection, Washington, D.C.). As a watercolorist and etcher he was at his best; he achieved a personal vision, developed from Futurist sources, combined with a poetic identification with a particular landscape, and forged by an artistic single-mindedness.

Marinetti Emilio 1876–1944

Emilio Filippo Tommaso Marinetti was an Italian poet and writer, editor of *Poesia* from 1905, and founder of the literary Futurist movement. He became dissatisfied with the "passivity" of literature, and used the political manifesto as an instrument of artistic innovation in the *First Futurist Manifesto* published in the Paris *Figaro* of 20 February 1909. In 1910 the *Technical Manifesto of Futurist Painting*, signed by Carlo Carrà, Giacomo Balla, Umberto Boccioni, Gino Severini, and Luigi Russolo, embodied Marinetti's love of destruction and speed. In 1912 he proposed a poetry of "free words" in which the text is freely disposed on the page; *Zang-tumb tuum* (1914) was his first work in this style. He later became an apologist of Fascism (*Futurisimo e fascismo*, 1924).

Marini Marino 1901–80

The Italian sculptor and painter Marino Marini was born in Pistoia and studied at the Academy of Art in Florence with Domenico Trentacosta. He taught at the School of Art at the Villa Reale in Monza

Marino Marini: Horseman; bronze; 163×155×68cm (65×61×27in); 1947. Tate Gallery, London

(1929–40) and in 1940 he was appointed Professor of Sculpture at the Brera Academy in Milan. In Paris he became acquainted with Kandinsky, Maillol, and Picasso, and in Switzerland (1942–6) he met Fritz Wotruba and Alberto Giacometti. Later he lived and worked in Milan.

Marini's best known works—sculpture, painting, and graphics—deal with portrait heads and the themes of "Pomona" and the "Horse and Rider" (for example, *Horse and Rider*, 1957; Peggy Guggenheim Collection, Venice). After the Second World War the development of the latter theme reflected Marini's ideas on the tragedy of human existence (for example, *Horse and Rider*; bronze; 1947; Tate Gallery, London). He is also famous for his portrait busts (for example *Igor Stravinsky*, 1950; San Francisco Museum of Art).

Further reading. Finn, D. and Hunter, S. *Marino Marini*, New York (1993).

Marinus van Reymerswaele
c1493–c1567

Marinus Claesz. van Reymerswaele was a Flemish artist, probably born in Roymerswaele, Zeeland, trained at Antwerp. He painted several versions of the *St Jerome in his Study* theme (1521 version; Prado, Madrid), which is loosely derived from a composition by Albrecht Dürer and influenced by the fashion for caricature painting established by the Massys workshop. The usual humanistic portrayal of the Saint is here replaced by strong asceticism. His style became increasingly exaggerated and linear; the elaborate headgear of the *Tax Gatherers* (National Gallery, London) may be a satirical comment on official dress of the period. In 1567 he participated in the destruction of images in Middelburg Cathedral (Zeeland) and was exiled.

Marisol 1930–

Marisol Escobar, who never uses her second name, is an American Pop sculptor. She is a Venezuelan, born in Paris, who studied at the École des Beaux-Arts, Paris, in 1949, and later with Hans Hofmann in New York. Her art is one of Pop assemblage, in a style more refined and whimsical than that of Claes Oldenburg and less savage than that of Edward Kienholz. Marisol creates wooden groups of figures, such as *The Family* (1961; Museum of Modern Art, New York), from carving, assemblage, drawing, and stencil work. Her own face frequently appears in her work, which, despite its sophistication, has a self-conscious naivety that links it with the craft tradition in American art.

Marmion Simon *c1420–89*

Simon Marmion was a French painter active in Flanders at the time when the munificent Philip the Good (Duke of Burgundy 1419–67) afforded such liberal patronage to artists. Marmion was born in Amiens, where he still lived in 1454. He subsequently moved to Valenciennes, where he is recorded from 1458 to 1484. There he worked in the publishing house of the scribe and historian Jean Mansel; the so-called "Mansel Master", a painter in the tradition of the Master of the Duke of Bedford, was his collaborator and may have been his teacher. Some miniatures in the Mansel Master's sumptuous *La Fleur des Histoires* (Bibliothèque Royale Albert I, Brussels; MS. 9231–9232) may be by the young Marmion. More than 50 manuscripts and panel paintings formerly attributed to him are now regarded as the work of several hands; it is not certain which, if any, should be attributed to Marmion himself.

Marisol: The Family; painted wood and other materials in three sections; 210×166cm (83×65in); 1962. Museum of Modern Art, New York

Simon Marmion: St Jerome with a Donor; panel; 65×49cm (26×19in). John G. Johnson Art Collection, Philadelphia Museum of Art

The first work to be hypothetically associated with his name was the fragmentary St Bertin Altarpiece (Staatliche Museen, Berlin, and National Gallery, London). Surviving panels depict scenes from the life of the Saint; the narrative is expertly controlled and exquisitely detailed. The same hand contributed to the *Grandes Chroniques de France* (State Library, St Petersburg), another copy of the *Fleur des Histoires* (Scottenstift, Vienna; MS. 139–140), and a number of devotional books. These show the artist to have been influenced by Jan van Eyck and Rogier van der Weyden, but his ability to tell a story is unprecedented.

Many of the "Marmion" miniatures illustrate historical texts that had no established iconographic tradition: the inventiveness shown in devising appropriate images is unfailing. Various individual hands have been distinguished among these manuscripts, including that of the Louthe Master, named after a book of hours in Louvain (Library of the Catholic University; MS. A. 2), and the Tondal Master, named after the *Vision du Chevalier Tondal*, a moralizing tract in Cambridge, Mass. (Houghton Library, MS. 235H).

The palettes of the "Marmion" painters differ widely, but all the artists share a competence in linear perspective that is suavely manipulated to avoid destroying the essentially flat surface of the manuscript page. Their landscapes are elegant and fanciful, their figures individually characterized, and their subject matter is often original. Their influence can be seen in the work of contemporaries like Loyset Liédet, and their effect on the next generation of illuminators was profound. Although there is no solid evidence to link Marmion himself with any extant paintings, he is extensively documented in legal and fiscal records. He was evidently regarded as the most important of the Valenciennes artists, and was described by a contemporary poet as "prince d'enluminure".

Martin John 1789–1854

John Martin was an English history and landscape painter and engraver. Born in Haydon Bridge, Northumberland, he exhibited his first major history painting, *Joshua Commanding the Sun to Stand Still Upon Gibeon* (Grand Lodge Museum, London), at the Royal Academy in 1816.

John Martin: The Assuaging of the Waters; oil on canvas; 132×203cm (52×80in); 1840. General Assembly of the Church of Scotland, Edinburgh

He specialized in painting catastrophic history subjects in which multitudes of figures were convulsed in turbulent landscapes or dwarfed by elaborate architectural fantasies. *Joshua* was followed by a succession of equally sensational canvases: *Belshazzar's Feast* (1821; Mansion House, Newcastle-upon-Tyne), *The Fall of Nineveh* (1827/8), and trilogies on the themes of the *Deluge* (1826–40) and *Last Judgment* (1851–4).

Martin became a bitter opponent of the London art establishment, by whom he was treated badly, and in the 1820s took to promoting his pictures by publishing his own mezzotint reproductions. His paintings and engravings, and his published illustrations to *Paradise Lost* (1825) and the Old Testament (1831–5) were immensely successful with the public, both in England and France, influencing painters and writers from Thomas Cole to Victor Hugo.

Further reading. Feaver, W. *The Art of John Martin*, London (1975).

Martin Kenneth and Mary
20th century

The British painters and sculptors Kenneth and Mary Martin were married in 1930. Kenneth Martin (1905–) was born in Sheffield, studying at the city's School of Art and at the Royal College of Art in London (1929–32). During the 1930s he painted landscapes but after the mid 1940s turned to Abstract styles. He is best known for his mobiles and sculpture in metal, often small in scale, severe in style, and

made, seemingly, with mathematical precision (for example, *Rotary Rings (4th version)*, 1968; Tate Gallery, London).

Mary Martin (1907–69) was born in Folkestone and studied at Goldsmiths' School of Art and at the Royal College of Art. Landscape and still life were her favorite themes, but she also produced constructed Abstract reliefs and was associated with the constructivist group that included Anthony Hill, Victor Pasmore, and her husband.

Martini Arturo 1889–1947

The Italian sculptor Arturo Martini was born in Treviso. He studied under Adolf von Hildebrand in Munich in 1909. Hildebrand's belief that the parts of a sculpture should be instantaneously visible was an influence on the later art of Martini. Therefore he often used high relief evoking an interior space, as did Italian Renaissance sculptors. In 1921 he joined the *Valori Plastici* ("Plastic Values") group which advocated a return to classicism. The geometric treatment of the figures in many of Martini's sculptures recalls the painting of another member of the group, Carlo Carrà. Martini believed that sculpture was an impersonal, universal art. He executed many public commissions in Italy (for example, *Corporate Justice*, 1937; Palace of Justice, Milan), including *Italian Pioneers of America* (1927–8; Worcester, Mass.) in collaboration with Maurice Sterne (1878–1957). His complex, turbulent, and always original work has been influential on subsequent Italian sculpture.

Martins Maria 1900–73

The Brazilian sculptor Maria Martins (also known simply as Maria) was born in Campanha, Brazil, and studied painting at the Academy in Rio de Janeiro and with Catherine Barjanski in Paris, before turning to sculpture in wood in 1926. In the 1930s in Japan she worked in ceramics, then in 1939 studied under the sculptor Oscar Jespers in Brussels. Eventually she turned from wood and stone to work in bronze. She was represented at the "Surrealist International Exhibition" in Paris in 1947. Her work, which refers to her memories of the tropical vegetation of her home country, was inspired by Surrealism and approaches abstraction (for example, *The Impossible III*; bronze; 1946; Museum of Modern Art, New York).

Masaccio: Study of a Student; pen and ink on paper. Uffizi, Florence

Masaccio 1401–28?

The Italian painter Tommaso Cassai is known to us by his nickname. "Masaccio" is a shortened form of "Tommasaccio", today the Italian for something equivalent to "big ugly Tom"; the name Masaccio may have been adopted to distinguish him from his older colleague, Tommaso di Cristoforo Fini, nicknamed "Masolino" (1383–1440/7), "little Thomas", with whom Masaccio worked. Masaccio died at the early age of 26 or 27 but managed to paint a few pictures of such enormous impact as to affect not only the whole future course of Florentine painting but also that of European painting in general.

He was born on 21 December 1401 at Castel San Giovanni, the modern San Giovanni Valdarno. Located in the upper Arno valley, San Giovanni lies some 28 miles (45 km) from Florence and about 18½ miles (30 km) from Arezzo. Masaccio's father was a young notary, his mother, Mona Jacopa di Martinozzo, the daughter of an innkeeper from a nearby town. Masaccio's father died young, but his mother remarried, this time a rich apothecary in San Giovanni. This second husband, Tedesco del Maestro Feo, died in 1417. Masaccio had one brother, the painter Giovanni di Ser Giovanni (1406–?) nicknamed "Lo Scheggia". One of their step-sisters, Caterina, married in 1422 the painter Mariotto di Cristofano.

Beyond what can be gleamed from his paintings, very little is known of Masaccio's life. From documents it is, however, known that on 7 January 1422 he became a member of the Florentine painters' guild, the Arte de' Medici e Speziali, while living in the parish of San Niccolò Oltrarno. In 1424 he joined the Compagnia di San Luca, to which painters often belonged. Eight payments towards an altarpiece painted for the Carmelite church in Pisa attest to the fact that he was in that city during much of 1426, that he knew Donatello, and employed Andrea di Giusto. There is a mention of Masaccio and his brother in the 1426 *Estimo* for San Giovanni Valdarno. In 1427 Masaccio made, in his own handwriting, his tax declaration to the newly instituted *Catasto*: he was then living in what is now the Via dei Servi and had his shop near the Badia. This same source gives us the approximate date of his death: next to his name for the returns of 1429 is written, "Dicesi è morto a Roma", that is: "He is said to have died in Rome".

Nothing is known of Masaccio's training. The apprentice system was such that he was probably learning a trade as early as 1410. This may have begun in a local painter's shop, or else in a family workshop. (Masaccio's paternal grandfather was a maker of *cassoni* or wooden chests; these were often painted.) Or he may have been sent to train in a *bottega* in Arezzo, in Florence, or elsewhere—but there is no evidence to show his early training was necessarily in the painter's craft.

Masaccio's earliest known extant painting, an altarpiece of the *Madonna and Child with Two Angels and Four Saints* (1422; from S. Giovenale di Cascia, near S. Giovanni; now in the Uffizi, Florence) does give us some idea of what his training as a painter must have been. Masaccio was 20 years old when this picture was dated. It shows us that he is already interested in space: not only do the lines in the floor indicate an attempt to grasp the laws of linear perspective, but so does the structure of the throne, with its slanted sides and curved back. The sense of space is heightened both by the apparent modeling of the robes and faces and by the use of alternating light and dark colors. Wherever Masaccio trained, it can hardly have been in the strongly International Gothic atmosphere prevalent in Florentine painting in the first two decades of the 15th century, where a sinuous elegant surface line was more important than depth within the picture. On the contrary an interest in modeling, in flesh tones, in space, and in light is much more characteristic of Marchigian painters. Both Arcangelo di Cola da Camerino (*fl.* 1416–22) and Gentile da Fabriano (*c*1370–1427) show particular interest in these things, and both were in Florence, the former *c*1419–22, the latter first in 1419–20 and then again in 1422–5. It is possible that Masaccio was influenced by one or both of them. There is also one Florentine painter who shows much of Masaccio's interest in modeling and space, Giovanni Toscani, and it is not unlikely that Masaccio was trained by him. Other possible masters to Masaccio were Bicci di Lorenzo and Francesco di Antonio. Masolino, who came from near San Giovanni, and with whom Masaccio worked on at least three commissions, was almost certainly not Masaccio's master. Masolino probably hired Masaccio to help him with important commissions; but it was the much younger painter, Masaccio, who then influenced his senior.

The whole of Masaccio's authenticated extant work, besides the San Giovenale painting, derives from only five other commissions: the so-called "Matterza" *Madonna and Child with St Anne* (*c*1424; Uffizi Florence), the Pisa Altarpiece (panels now dispersed), a fresco of *The Trinity* in S. Maria Novella, Florence, frescoes in the Brancacci Chapel, S. Maria del Carmine, Florence, and *SS. Jerome and John the Baptist* from an altarpiece originally in S. Maria Maggiore, Rome.

The first of these, the Uffizi *Madonna and Child with St Anne*, was executed with the help of Masolino *c*1424 for the church of S. Ambrogio in Florence. Masolino painted St Anne, plus all the angels except the middle one on the right; Masaccio did the Virgin, Christ Child, and remaining angel. In spite of the difference between Masolino's more orthodox approach and Masaccio's strong volumes, the picture is remarkably harmonious. Masaccio has placed his Madonna extremely low, emphasizing the light and shade falling on her knees, on the folds in her robes, and on the Infant Christ. As in the S. Giovenale painting, he has painted the Christ Child nude; but here the figure seems so solid and is so Classical in flavor that the painter must have drawn it after an antique statue. There are, in fact, many extant antique statues of babes in just this pose.

The chronology of the other known works is not clear, although they seem all to have been painted between 1425 and the artist's death, probably some time in 1428. It seems possible that Masaccio painted *The Trinity* in S. Maria Novella, Florence, in 1425 or 1426, perhaps for the feast of Corpus Domini in one of those years, although stylistically the painting is so advanced that it may well date after the painter's earliest work in the Brancacci chapel. Masaccio probably helped Masolino to plan the frescoes in the Brancacci Chapel in S. Maria del Carmine during 1425, and then began himself to paint there some time after Masolino's departure for Hungary in September of the same year. Masaccio must have worked at them during 1426, as well perhaps as during 1427. The Pisa Altarpiece is, as mentioned above, documented during much of 1426; while the panel of *SS. Jerome and John the Baptist* (National Gallery, London) from the S. Maria Maggiore altarpiece was probably painted during Masaccio's trip to Rome in 1427/28.

From the tentative converging lines of the San Giovenale triptych, right through all his subsequent works, Masaccio developed two themes that were to remain central to the history of Western painting. The first is the successful portrayal of a natural world within the painting, with convincing space, light, air, and objects. The second is part of this, but at the same time independent of it: the portrayal of a convincing replica of man, who dominates and gives order to that world. This is, of course, a visual version of the more general search for a correct scientific definition of man's place in the natural world, which occupies the Renaissance in all its facets.

Masaccio's *Trinity* terminates the Middle Ages by expressing the essence of medieval Christian belief in Renaissance terms. His *The Tribute Money* in the Brancacci Chapel, on the other hand, stands clearly beyond the threshold, in the light-filled world of the Renaissance.

Nothing could be more traditional to the waning Christian age than Masaccio's *Trinity* theme of a predominant God the Father, supporting his crucified human Son, joined by the white dove of the Holy Spirit: the universal, the human, the spiritual. But nothing could be less traditional in its expression. Vaulted by a magnificent Renaissance triumphal arch, the divine trio appears almost suspended before a pierced wall. This coffered Brunelleschian space seems to be a mortuary chamber, a holy sepulcher from which the Christ is shown resurrected by His Father, Savior to a waiting world, presented by the Virgin and St John; this world is symbolized by the two donors just outside. The worldly spectator is also included in the painting by association with the skeleton under the altar; unlike the human body of Christ, which rose intact, our worldly bodies decay. Above the skeleton are written some words to warn the passerby; "I was that which you are, you will be that which I am". Inside the sepulcher, the space has been constructed according to the laws of linear perspective, so that the eye appears to be looking into the interior of a magnificent Renaissance building.

Masaccio set the background to *The Tribute Money*, in the Brancacci Chapel at S. Maria del Carmine, in a light-filled landscape, dominated (as is the countryside at San Giovanni Valdarno) by high hills. The painter, using newly established laws of perspective, created an infallible illusion of air, light, and space. But whereas in *The Trinity* God is the theme, here it is Man who dominates. Masaccio places in the natural scene classical statuesque figures, also apparently modeled after the Antique, who are above all human and free to move within their own natural world.

The Tribute Money emerges as, historically, the most important single picture in Florence today. Each individual in the painting stands, for the first time, strong and solitary, on a natural and benevolent earth, sustained by real air, bathed in light, master of the world stretching all around. Masaccio threw off the gloom and mystery of earlier times, resurrecting the forms of an ancient pre-Christian world. In the painting Christ stands equal to Man, not dominating him: a human being Himself, giving good advice to His followers. In *The Tribute Money* we already witness a Reformation—clearly evident too in the humanistic work of Donatello and Brunelleschi—in which Man does not cease to believe in Christ, although he may cease to believe the infallibility of the Roman Church. Rather, Man ceases to believe in a triumphal Christ-God and begins to believe in a human Christ-Man.

The frescoes in the Brancacci chapel, of which *The Tribute Money* is one, relate scenes from the life of St Peter. The whole cycle seems to have been begun by Masolino *c*1425, and then continued by Masaccio. The chapel was not actually finished until much later in the 15th century, by Filippino Lippi. *The Tribute Money* itself alludes in some way to Man's separate duties to the State and to the Church. In it St Peter is instructed by Christ to pay a tax to the civil authority. This must certainly be a reference to the obligations of the Roman Church towards secular authority; it probably also refers to each individual man's obligation to render separately to God and to Caesar that which is due to them.

The other paintings by Masaccio in the chapel seem to confirm this message: St Peter is seen preaching, baptizing, healing, and distributing alms: all corporal works of mercy. What then is the meaning of Masaccio's stupendous fresco of *The Expulsion from Paradise* on the entrance arch to the chapel? Perhaps Masaccio meant simply to point out that the anguish of Man over his loss of paradise can be solaced by the good works of Holy Mother the Church; the Church is the source of grace, through which Man can be saved.

The only two other extant, autograph works by Masaccio have already been

Masaccio: Madonna and Child with Angels, from the Pisa Altarpiece; panel; 136×73cm (54×29in); 1426. National Gallery, London

else, he introduces the greatest innovation of Renaissance painting: light defined as coming from a single source, by the shadows it casts. In this painting too, one is aware of the great sensitivity and delicacy of the painter's brushwork—the angels playing lutes are of such a simplicity and craftsmanship as to make them seem to sing. Two other remarkable paintings from this altarpiece are the small panels of the *Crucifixion* now in Naples (Museo e Gallerie Nazionali di Capodimonte), and the *Nativity* in Berlin (Staatliche Museen). In the former the animal-like figure of the crouched Magdalene gesturing towards the anguish of St John and of the Virgin is of such a simple expressive force as almost to defy analysis. Christ's stark, shadow-struck body, meant to be seen from below, is also intensely expressive. As for the small *Nativity* panel, its lifelike Kings, the animals, the Holy Family—all are bathed in a dawn light, clearly defining the spaces involved, throwing sharp shadows.

The London panel of *SS. Jerome and John the Baptist* was once part of a triptych painted on both sides for the Roman basilica of S. Maria Maggiore. This painting, which represents the founding of that church, flanked by saints, is predominantly by Masolino; for some unknown reason, however, Masaccio executed this one panel. Since Masaccio and Masolino worked together on the Uffizi Madonna, in the Brancacci Chapel, as well as perhaps in other places, it is not so surprising that they collaborated here too.

Masaccio's contribution to the development of Western painting is enormous. During the first two decades of the 15th century, both sculpture (primarily through the work of Jacopo della Quercia and Donatello) and architecture (through that of Brunelleschi) began to be cast in a new Renaissance idiom. In the course of a few years during the 1420s, Masaccio managed to set Western painting on a Renaissance course, similar in essence and language to that taken by those other expressions. Whereas Giotto had created, over a century earlier, an ideal world in which Christian myths were acted out, Masaccio secularized that world by filling it with space, light, and air, and by placing a Classical sort of man within it, surrounded by nature. This idea of man as central to a logical natural world, and master of it, was to remain the principal source of imagery for Western painting until very recent times.

mentioned: the various panels from the Pisa polyptych, and the panel of *SS. Jerome and John the Baptist* from Masolino's S. Maria Maggiore altarpiece. The former group includes the strongly rendered *Madonna and Child with Four Angels*, now in London's National Gallery, the central panel of the original altarpiece. Here, even within the most traditional late medieval *schema*, the painter introduces strong volumes for the Madonna's robes, and space all around the throne. Above all

Further reading. Berti, L. *Masaccio*, London and University Park, Pa (1967). Berti, L. *Masaccio*, Milan (1964). Gilbert, C. *Masaccio*, New York (1969). Meiss, M. "Masaccio and the Early Renaissance", *Studies in Western Art: Acts of the XXth International Congress* vol. II, Princeton (1963). Procacci, U. *The Complete Paintings of Masaccio*, New York (1962). Wald, E.T. de *Italian Painting 1200–1600*, New York (1961).

Masanobu Kano c1434–c1530

The Japanese painter Kano Masanobu was the founder of the *Kano* School, whose members were official painters to the government and court for 400 years. His appointment as leader of the academy was a major innovation, since he was of lowly birth and not a Zen devotee (though he learned landscape in the Chinese monochrome style). His few surviving works show the exaggerated contrast between strongly outlined, hatched rocks and trees, and misty washes and patches of color, that became the standard *Kano* style.

Maso di Banco *fl.* 1340–50

The Florentine painter Maso di Banco was a pupil of Giotto. (Vasari identified him with an artist named "Giottino", but modern critics do not accept this and there is some doubt whether Giottino ever existed.) Little is known of Maso di Banco apart from documentary references between 1341 and 1350. In 1341 his painting equipment was confiscated by Ridolfo dei Bardi, probably because he failed to finish the frescoes in the Chapel of S. Silvestro, S. Croce, Florence, by the stipulated time. These frescoes form the basis for attributing to him two altarpieces, one in S. Spirito, Florence, and the other formerly divided between a private collection and Berlin (the Berlin panels were destroyed in the Second World War). To these works can be added a fragmentary fresco of *The Coronation of the Virgin* (entry to the cloister, S. Croce, Florence) and a small panel in Budapest.

Although the S. Silvestro frescoes have been repainted, they show Maso to be a highly original artist as well as a logical and supremely able follower of Giotto. In *St Sylvester Reviving a Bull* the absence of decorative framing round the scene is part of a general breaking down of the division between real and pictorial space. Over a tomb in the same chapel is a powerful fresco portrait of Ridolfo dei Bardi praying to Christ the Judge while the Last Trump is sounded over a deserted landscape.

Maso's S. Spirito Altarpiece contrasts with the vigor of the S. Silvestro frescoes, and shows a gentle refinement of design and execution. The figures on either side of the Madonna and Child are shown in rather more than half-length, helping to emphasize the effect of each figure turning inwards. Despite the gold background of each compartment, the final impression is of a row of sculptural niches with three-dimensional figures. Typically, his achievement here is founded on a deep knowledge of Giotto's work, together with a sensitivity to the contemporary influence of Sienese art on Florentine painting.

Maso di Banco: St Sylvester Restores to Life Two Sorcerers; fresco; c1340. Chapel of S. Silvestro, S. Croce, Florence

Masolino: detail of St Peter raising St Tabitha; fresco; 1424/5. S. Maria del Carmine, Florence

Masolino 1383–c1447

The early work of the Florentine painter, Tommaso di Cristoforo Fini, called Masolino, was rooted in the 14th century, as for example his *Madonna* of 1423 (Kunsthalle Bremen). But while engaged on frescoes in the Brancacci Chapel (S. Maria del Carmine, Florence) during the years 1424 and 1425 he momentarily adopted the grander, weightier figure-style of the young Masaccio, with whom he shared the project. Masolino's later work, such as the fresco cycles in Rome (1427–31?; S. Clemente) and in the Baptistery at Castiglione d'Olona near Milan (1435), show a reversion to the softer, more decorative style associated with International Gothic. This can look incongruous against his occasional virtuoso displays of perspective.

Further reading. Roberts, P. *Masolino da Panicale*, Oxford (1993).

Masson André 1896–1987

André Masson was a French painter who was associated with the Surrealist movement. At first influenced by Cubism (as in *Card Players*, 1923; private collection) he began to frequent the Surrealist group in 1923 and 1924, having attracted André Breton's attention, and produced, in a remarkable series of drawings, some of the earliest essays in pictorial automatism. With his sand-paintings of 1926 onwards, they epitomize the Surrealist doctrine of obedience to chance and the unconscious. He broke with the Surrealists in 1929, but reestablished contact in the late 1930s. From 1941 to 1945 he lived in Connecticut, where his work was a formative influence on Abstract Expressionism.

Masson's work underwent many stylistic changes. Influenced by philosophy and myth, he concentrated on rendering symbolically man's relationship to nature and the urgency of human passion. His work is frequently erotic and violent (for example, *Massacres*, 1932–3; a pen and ink drawing in the Galerie Louise Leiris, Paris) characterized by expressionistic line, color, and brushwork (for example, *Nioke*, 1947; Galerie Louise Leiris, Paris), and agitated composition *(Wave of the Future*, 1976; private collection). He executed sculptures and Surrealist objects, illustrated books (for example, Malraux's *Conquerors*, 1948) and designed sets and costumes for the theater.

Further reading. Clebert, J.-P. *Mythologie de André Masson*, Geneva (1971). Hahn, O. *Masson*, Paris (1965). Leiris, M. and Limbour, G. *André Masson and his Universe*, London (1947). Rubin, W. and Lanchner, C. *André Masson*, New York (1976).

Massys family
15th and 16th centuries

The Massys were a family of Flemish painters, which included Quentin (1465/6–1530), Cornelis (c1508–c60), and Jan (c1510–75). Quentin Massys was born at Louvain in the southern Netherlands. There is no record of his training in any specific workshop. His early style suggests a grounding in the current Flemish idiom of such painters as Hans Memling and Gerard David, with the additional knowl-

edge of current trends in the High Renaissance painting of Italy.

His *The Betrothal of St Catherine* (c1500; National Gallery, London), painted on canvas, shows a three-quarter-length Madonna and Child, flanked by saints in an architectural setting. The format and courtly style of dress parallels other Flemish pictures, but the scale of work is Italian and the soft treatment of the features reminiscent of Leonardo. In 1511 Massys completed a life-size triptych of *The Family of St Anne* for S. Pierre, Louvain (now Musées Royaux des Beaux-Arts de Belgique, Brussels). Again the figures are placed before an architectural screen, which here gives on to landscape. Softness of line and color is accentuated by the diffusion of light so that the forms appear almost shadowless.

The other important triptych of these years, the Lamentation Altar (1507–9; Royal Museum of Fine Arts, Antwerp), reveals a close study of Rogier van der Weyden's *Deposition* (Prado, Madrid), then in Louvain. But it substitutes a landscape background, and suppresses the heightened emotion of the earlier work. The top of the altarpiece when opened is shaped as a double curve, a form that Massys helped introduce to Flemish art.

Later works show a certain sentimentality, as in the entwined gestures of the *Madonna and Child* of c1520 (Staatliche Museen, Berlin). Massys came closest to Leonardo's figure-style in the *Virgin and Child* (National Museum, Poznan) which directly reflects Leonardo's concern with a pyramidal grouping of figures in a land-

André Masson: Battle of the Fishes; mixed media including sand on canvas; 36×73cm (14×29in); 1926. Museum of Modern Art, New York

Quentin Massys: The Banker and his Wife; panel; 74×68cm (29×27in); 1514. Louvre, Paris

scape setting. It is significant that the chief attraction of Italy for Massys was the work of Leonardo and the Lombard school; he seems less interested than other Netherlandish artists in Rome and the Antique. He was always aware of the Flemish 15th-century tradition; works such as *The Banker and his Wife* (1514; Louvre, Paris) are a conscious revival of the techniques and style of dress of the age of Jan van Eyck.

Quentin Massys' influence was profound,

not only technically and stylistically but in the creation of new fashions in pictures; he is credited, for example, with the invention of the theme of the "ill-matched couple" that became a popular subject in northern Europe.

Cornelis Massys, the elder son of Quentin, was chiefly a painter of landscape subjects. In *The Arrival of the Holy Family at Bethlehem* (1543; Staatliche Museen, Berlin), the landscape takes precedence over the religious subject.

Jan Massys, the younger son, was banished from Antwerp as a Protestant and worked mainly in France and Italy. His *Flora Meretrix* (1561; National-museum, Stockholm), while close to Quentin Massys in countenance, has the elegance and courtliness of the painting style of the School of Fontainebleau. His choice of religious subjects is often determined by this style, as in *Susanna and the Elders* (1567; Musées Royaux des Beaux-Arts de Belgique, Brussels).

Further reading. Bosque, A. de *Quentin Metsys*, Brussels (1974). Friedländer, M.J. *Early Netherlandish Painting* (vol. 7), Leiden (1971).

Master Bertram *c*1345–1415

The German painter Master Bertram, apparently a native of Minden, is first recorded in Hamburg in 1367. His name appears in the town accounts in connection with official commissions until 1387. From 1379 to 1383 he painted the great altarpiece for the high altar of St Peter in Hamburg (Hamburger Kunsthalle, Hamburg) known as the Grabower Altarpiece. The realism he exhibits in this work anticipates certain qualities of 15th-century Flemish painting and provides a parallel to contemporary painting in Bohemia. Master Bertram's later activity, and the status of the Buxtehuder and Harvestehuder Altars (Hamburger Kunsthalle, Hamburg) is less certain, though he died in Hamburg having been the most important painter there.

Master of Cabestany

fl. mid–late 12th century

The Master of Cabestany was a sculptor trained either in Tuscany or Roussillon, whose career spanned the years from the middle to the end of the 12th century. His works can be found in two areas: either in churches on both sides of the modern frontier between France and Spain (some fragments from works in this area are to be found in the Fitzwilliam Museum, Cambridge, and in the Cloisters, New York) or else in Tuscany, most notably in the abbey church of S. Antimo. The tympanum of the church at Cabestany near Perpignan (hence the Master's name) is decorated with scenes of the Death and Assumption of the Virgin, whose girdle is held by St Thomas. This may indicate that the Master was of Tuscan origin—Prato in Tuscany was the most famous of several places to claim possession of the Virgin's girdle. But whether the Master was Italian, French, or Catalan it is impossible to say.

His highly charged emotional figures with massive heads are swathed in toga-like garments etched into deep drilled channels. It was probably from a study of late Roman or Early Christian sarcophagus sculpture that he developed a highly idiosyncratic use of the drill. He also liked working in marble.

Master of the Duke of Bedford

fl. 1405–35

The Master of the Duke of Bedford was head of one of the major illuminators' shops in Paris. He was named after his patron, the Regent of France, for whom he produced his two masterpieces: the Bedford Hours (British Library, London; Add. MS. 18850; *c*1423) and Breviary (Bibliothèque Nationale, Paris; MS. Lat. 17294; *c*1435). These profusely illustrated books, in which the miniatures are surrounded by smaller scenes set in medallions in the ornamental borders, reveal a sophisticated sense of color. He collaborated with the Boucicaut and Rohan Masters; compared with theirs, this technique is more "painterly". A panel-painting of the *Last Judgment* (Louvre, Paris) has been attributed to him.

Master of the Duke of Bedford: The Building of the Ark, from the Bedford Hours; 41×28cm (16×11in); *c*1423. British Library, London

Master ES *c*1430–67

The father of true copperplate engraving, the Master ES is named from the signature "E" or "ES" on a group of 18 engravings, some of which are also dated 1466 and 1467. The "S" could possibly stand for Strasbourg since some engravings include Alsatian coats of arms; around them an oeuvre of more than 300 plates has been assembled. The Master ES was responsible for a technical revolution when he developed an intricate repertoire of short flicks of the burin combined with dots and crosshatching to model his forms. His most sophisticated works are the dated plates of 1466 and 1467. Scholars have concluded that he probably died soon after completing them. Examples of his work may be seen in the Graphische Sammlung Albertina, Vienna.

Master of Flémalle *c*1375–1444

The Flemish painter known as the Master of Flémalle takes his name from a group of panel-paintings at Frankfurt which allegedly come from a putative abbey at Flémalle-lez-Liège. This artist is now usually identified with Robert Campin. Although the latter has no surviving documented works, this identification appears secure, because the pictures of artists known to have been Campin's pupils reveal an intimate knowledge of the style of the Master of Flémalle. A significant number of paintings have been attributed to the composite personality Flémalle/Campin, but the general lack of documentation inhibits unanimity of opinion on the precise nature of his oeuvre.

Campin may have been born in Valenciennes. By 1406 he had moved to Tournai, where he remained until his death. He enjoyed various influential posts in the painters' guild and in the city. From 1423 until 1428 the guilds held political power in Tournai, and Campin became a councillor. After the return of the patriciate he was victimized by the authorities, being prosecuted for alleged immorality in 1429 and 1432. In spite of this, he continued to receive municipal commissions, maintained a large workshop, and seems to have remained extremely prosperous. His most famous pupil was Rogier van der Weyden.

Campin's earliest surviving work is probably the *Entombment* triptych in the Home House Collection, London. Although this altarpiece retains the gold

Master of Flémalle: Virgin and Child before a Firescreen; oil on oak panel; 64×49cm (25×19in); c1430. National Gallery, London

ground typical of earlier panel-paintings, the conception of the figures represents a dramatic break with the International Gothic tradition. The voluminous draperies of Campin's weighty figures relate more closely to the sculpture of Claus Sluter than to any previous pictorial models. As the motif of the angel wiping his eyes with the back of his hand appears to derive from Sluter's *Well of Moses* for the center of the great cloister of the Charterhouse of Champmol in Dijon, the possibility of direct contact is all the more

likely. On iconographic grounds the double-faced panel *The Betrothal of the Virgin* (c1420–30; Prado, Madrid) is equally revolutionary: the main composition incorporates Romanesque and Flamboyant Gothic buildings to symbolize the distinction between the Old and the New Testaments, and the reverse side features simulated statues painted in grisaille. Both ideas soon became characteristic of the Early Netherlandish school.

Campin's Dijon *Nativity* (Musée des Beaux-Arts) includes an impressively naturalistic landscape. Although derived from earlier illuminated manuscripts, this represents a substantial improvement upon its models, and appears to be the earliest depiction of such a view in the larger format of panel painting. Paintings such as the Mérode Altarpiece (Cloisters, New York) and the *Virgin and Child before a Firescreen* (National Gallery, London) are among the very first large-scale representations of another theme borrowed from manuscript illumination: the so-called "Bourgeois Interior".

It seems probable that the large Frankfurt panels of the *Virgin and Child*, *St Veronica*, the *Trinity*, and the fragmentary *Thief on the Cross* (Städelsches Kunstinstitut, Frankfurt am Main), from which Campin acquired his pseudonym, ought to be placed late in his career. They are solemn and monumental conceptions which nevertheless reveal a superb delicacy of touch. The huge dismembered altarpieces of which they once formed a part must have counted among the grandest conceptions of the first generation of Early Netherlandish painting.

As the contemporary of Jan van Eyck and the master of Rogier van der Weyden, the Master of Flémalle/Robert Campin belongs with the pioneers of the new naturalistic style in the Netherlands. He was a fearless innovator, and it is difficult to understate the significance of his art for his generation.

Master Francke *fl.* 1405–25

Master Francke was a German painter who is documented as having worked in Hamburg. He may have trained in France, possibly in Paris, since his style indicates a knowledge of French manuscript illumination.

Although one of the most important German painters of his time, his reputation rests on only a few paintings, of which the St Thomas Altarpiece (Hamburger Kunsthalle, Hamburg) is his major work. It was commissioned in 1424 by the Hamburg merchants who traded with England, for their chapel in St John's church. Although the eight scenes of the wings of the altar are complete, only one fragment of the center panel survives. The two scenes on the outside of the wings represent the Flight and Martyrdom of St Thomas à Becket while the remainder depict scenes from the Life of Christ. Originally the Crucifixion filled the center panel.

Master Francke: The Nativity, a fragment of the St Thomas Altarpiece; 99×89cm (39×35in); 1424. Hamburger Kunsthalle, Hamburg

Francke was a painter in the elegant International Gothic style. His colors are cleverly graded and his details realistically portrayed. He is exceptional in the way he has carefully contrived the composition in each panel. In some, he has successfully achieved an impression of spatial depth by attempting perspective in the architecture and by foreshortening objects. The Flagellation panel in particular combines all these qualities, and the figures also add drama by their contrasting expressions and poses. The men with whips are violent and brutal, the seated Pilate luxuriously robed and shifty eyed, as is his adviser, while the bowed body of Christ is as expressive as his anguished face. The Martyrdom of St Thomas is an equally powerful composition, with the kneeling Saint a horrific blood-bespattered figure. In such pictures, Francke appears to have been influenced by harsh Netherlandish realism as well as by French delicacy.

His other great work is the St Barbara Altarpiece (*c*1410; Amos Anderson Art Museum, Helsinki). It contains eight scenes from the legend of the Saint's life. Again the characteristics of the International Gothic style are displayed. The charming rural scene—in which the ragged shepherds betray the Saint, while their sheep turn into grasshoppers—has been compared to miniatures by the Limburg brothers. This link, and the less adventurous composition of the scenes compared to those in the St Thomas Altarpiece, suggest that it is an early work.

The contrast between Francke's early and late work is well illustrated by two panels depicting the same subject, *The Man of Sorrows*, or Christ displaying his wounds. The first, in the Museum der Bildenden Künste, Leipzig, shows Christ supported

by angels in an angular awkward pose holding the instruments of the Passion, which together form a confused tableau on a gold ground. The latter work, in the Kunsthalle in Hamburg, has a more monumental figure of Christ dominating the panel with the five angels placed in subordinate roles. Most striking are the features of Christ's face, which have been softened to have a chiaroscuro effect.

Francke's influence was widespread and can be traced in numerous altarpieces throughout north Germany and the Baltic countries.

Master of the Housebook
*fl. c*1475–90

The German artist known as the Master of the Housebook was formerly called "The Master of the Amsterdam Cabinet", because the collection in the Rijksmuseum Print Room in Amsterdam houses 82 of his 91 known drypoints, and additionally as "The Master of 1480" from the date on one of his engravings. The Master of the Housebook takes his name from a volume of drawings called the *Hausbuch* in Schloss Wolfegg near Antendorf (Lake Constance, Switzerland). He was active as a draftsman and painter, as well as as an engraver, in the central Rhine area and probably around Lake Constance. He may have used pewter plates rather than copper, since most of his surviving drypoints are unique. The velvety quality of his lines and his pictorial technique mark a complete break with the traditions of silver engraving and woodcutting.

Master of the Isaac Frescoes
fl. late 13th century

The Master of the Isaac Frescoes, probably a Roman painter, was active in the last quarter of the 13th century. It is a measure of his enormous originality and power that attempts have been made to identify the Isaac Master with the young Giotto, or to identify him as Giotto's teacher. While he probably did influence Giotto, his work is that of an individual, mature artist. He is named after the frescoes of *Isaac and Esau* and *Isaac and Jacob* in the second bay on the right-hand wall of the Upper Church of St Francis at Assisi. His workshop also painted the *Four Doctors of the Church* in the entrance vault of the nave, and other scenes in the upper register of the first two bays of the nave. The Isaac Master's sense

Master of the Isaac Frescoes: Pietà; fresco; late 13th century; Upper church of S. Francesco, Assisi

of dramatic composition is profoundly like Giotto's, as is his understanding and use of Classical models for his figures. He takes his place with Cimabue, Cavallini, and Giotto as a founder of the new naturalistic style in painting that developed in Italy at the time. He is only less famous because anonymous, and because so little of his work survives.

Master of Liesborn

fl. mid 15th century

The Master of Liesborn takes his name from the now dismembered high altarpiece of the Benedictine Abbey of Liesborn in Westphalia, of which the most important surviving panels are in the National Gallery, London. Nothing is known of the location of the studio of this Westphalian painter and the documentary evidence concerning his activity is minimal. The Liesborn high altar was dedicated by Abbot Heinrich von Kleve in 1465, together with four other altars, and he is recorded as having commissioned the paintings for all five. Since he was enthroned as abbot only in 1464 and did not die until 1490, the year 1465 can be interpreted in the light of

the abbey chronicle written between 1515 and 1520 as the earliest likely date for the Liesborn high altarpiece.

Apart from this celebrated work, which remained in situ until the suppression of the abbey in 1803, there are no other certain autograph works by the Master of Liesborn. The tentative reconstruction of his oeuvre depends upon the variations in quality acceptable to historians, and upon any development that can be postulated. The influence of the 15th-century Cologne school of painters is self-evident. The strongly Netherlandish character of the *Annunciation* from the Liesborn high altarpiece (National Gallery, London), with its unusually detailed interior, may even indicate direct contact with Netherlandish prototypes. Based on the style of the furniture, a case can be made for dating the *Annunciation*, and by implication the whole high altarpiece, to as late as *c*1480; but it was presumably completed by 1490.

Master of Mary of Burgundy

*fl. c*1470–90

The Master of Mary of Burgundy was the leading Flemish book-illuminator, work-

ing probably in Ghent in the 1470s and 1480s. Various attempts have been made to identify him, for instance with Sanders Bening. He receives his name from two Books of Hours made for Mary of Burgundy, daughter of Charles the Bold and Margaret of York (1457–82). One is in Berlin (Kupferstichkabinett; MS. 78 B. 12) the other in Vienna (Nationalbibliothek; MS. 1857). Outstanding among the other works attributed to him are the Hours of Engelbert of Nassau (Bodleian Library, Oxford; MS. Douce 219–20) and a book of Hours in Madrid (National Library; MS. Vit. 25–5). A group of manuscripts, some of which were made for Margaret of York, appear to be earlier works that he did in the 1470s (St John's College, Cambridge; H. 13, Breviary, etc).

A master of the depiction of space and light, responsible for "the first example of plein-air painting in Northern art" (Pächt), he also introduces original solutions to the problem of relating the picture to the surface of the page. His scenes appear as though viewed through a window, and his borders are exquisitely painted with *trompe-l'oeil* flowers and insects.

Further reading. Alexander, J.J.G. *The Master of Mary of Burgundy*, London (1970). Schryver, A. de and Unterkircher, F. *Stundenbuch der Maria van Burgund*, Graz (1969).

Master of Moulins *fl. c*1480–*c*1500

The French painter known as the Master of Moulins takes his name from the triptych in Moulins Cathedral, an altarpiece of the Virgin and Child surrounded by Angels commissioned by the Duke of Bourbon which is datable to *c*1498. This painting is

Master of Moulins: Nativity, with Cardinal Rolin; panel; 55×73cm (22×29in); c1480–3. Musée des Beaux Arts, Autun

stylistically analogous to a *Nativity* at Autun (Musée des Beaux-Arts) painted for Cardinal Jean Rolin which cannot be later than 1483. Both works indicate a clear debt to Hugo van der Goes, so it seems likely that their author was trained in the Netherlands. A number of other pictures have been attributed to this Master. Some of them, such as the fragment of *Charlemagne and the Meeting at the Golden Gate* (National Gallery, London) include Italianate architectural details which probably derive from the studio of Jean Fouquet. 'Monumental clarity of form and a delicate but rich use of color distinguish the style of the Master of Moulins. He was the last great French painter of the 15th-century tradition.

Master of Naumburg *fl. c1230–70*

The German sculptor known as the Master of Naumburg takes his name from the superb series of sculptures in the west choir of Naumburg Cathedral. His style as revealed there is so clearly defined that his activity can be traced for some 40 years. Such a distinct artistic personality is most exceptional during the 13th century, and thus the reconstruction of his career must be treated with caution.

The hand of the Master of Naumburg has been detected at Noyon, and he also seems to have worked in Metz (fragments from the Portal of the Virgin, Metz Cathedral). It is much more certain that by c1239 he was active in Mainz, where he was responsible for the figurative sculpture decorating the west rood screen of the cathedral. Dismembered and scattered, the relief of *St Martin and the Beggar* (the so-called *Bassenheim Rider*), now in the parish church of Bassenheim, probably comes from Mainz Cathedral together with the equally expressive *Head with a Bandeau* and fragments of a *Last Judgment* (Bischöfliches Dom- und Diözesanmuseum, Mainz).

The west choir of Naumburg Cathedral was built by Bishop Dietrich from 1249 onwards, and the interior is decorated with life-size figures of princes and princesses of his family, the House of Wettin. Together with the *Bamberg Rider* (Bamberg Cathedral) these dignified figures not only embody the noblest ideals of medieval chivalry, but also portray within closely defined limits their individual personalities. Internal evidence suggests that they were completed a few years before the death of Bishop Dietrich in 1273, and that the highly expressive *Passion* reliefs and figures on the west rood screen date from his last years.

Master of the Playing Cards
fl. c1430–60

Probably active in the Upper Rhineland, and possibly in Basel, the Master of the Playing Cards seems also to have worked as a painter and goldsmith. He takes his name from a series of engraved playing cards. The animals he includes in them are copied from the decorations painted in Mainz in the margins of a group of Bibles dating from the 1450s. His modeling of forms by means of massed strokes and occasional crosshatching is closely based on the technique of pen-and-ink drawings. The importance of the Master of the Playing Cards lies in his growing independence from the techniques of the silversmiths.

Master of Naumburg: Hermann and Reglindis, from the series of sculptures on the west choir of Naumburg Cathedral; c1249–70

Master of St Cecilia: the St Cecilia Altarpiece; panel; 85×181cm (33×71in); before 1304? Uffizi, Florence

Master of the Rohan Hours
fl. c1410–25

The Master of the Rohan Hours was a French miniaturist and painter, to whose workshop some 35 manuscripts can be assigned, mainly Books of Hours. A few of these were made for the use of Troyes, but the majority were for the use of Paris; not all of them have miniatures by the hand of the Master. He is named after the most important of these Books of Hours (Bibliothèque Nationale, Paris; MS. Lat. 9471), which at some later date in the 15th century belonged to a member of the Rohan family, whose coat-of-arms was then added. This manuscript contains the most impressive miniatures by the Master. He knew and made use of a number of compositions and single figures by the Limburgs and by the Boucicaut Master, which helps to date and locate his works.

He is an extraordinary artist, who has rightly been called an "expressionist". He often covers the entire parchment with compositions, leaving no room for the customary borders; he fills the space with a few large figures in profile, with heightened tension between them. He has a strong predilection for macabre subjects: the *Lamentation*, the *Dying Man in Front of Christ*, and the *Last Judgment* are all presented with stark simplicity. By including enlarged figures (such as that of a corpse) which up to then had been displayed only in small size in the borders, he enhances them

and invests them with new intensity.

The Rohan Hours is a late work and his most accomplished and substantial one. The much smaller Giac Hours, now in Toronto (Royal Ontario Museum), is one of his earliest works, but already displays similar tendencies. Another speciality of his studio is long additional series in the margins of the front and back of each page, carrying on their independent story regardless of the main text and of the main illustrations. The *Bible moralisée* is added in this manner to the Rohan Hours, and the *Pèlérinages* of Guillaume de Digueville to the Cambridge Hours.

There is evidence that the Rohan Master worked not only as a miniaturist, but also as a panel-painter. The fragment of an altarpiece in Laon with a donor portrait and apostle figures has been ascribed to his hand; a single parchment sheet with a drawing of *The Miracle of Bethesda* (Herzog Anton Ulrich Museum, Brunswick) is undoubtedly his.

Master of St Cecilia   *fl. c1290–1304*

The Italian painter known as the Master of St Cecilia may have come from Florence. He takes his name from the St Cecilia Altarpiece (Uffizi, Florence) painted in the years shortly before 1304. He was one of the major masters who collaborated on *The Legend of St Francis* at Assisi (Upper Church of St Francis) of which he painted

the first and the last three scenes. (All four were painted after the completion of the rest of the cycle.) In addition he painted two altarpieces in S. Margherita a Montici near Florence, and a panel of *St Peter Enthroned* (S. Simone, Florence). All his narrative scenes are characterized by figures with elongated bodies, small heads, and rake-like hands. Apart from these eccentricities, he possessed a remarkable feeling for architecture, often including portraits of appropriate Classical buildings in Rome. His drapery has soft, naturalistic folds. He made a significant contribution to artistic development in Italy at the beginning of the 14th century.

Master of Wittingau   *fl. c1380–95*

The Bohemian painter known as the Master of Wittingau was the greatest middle European artist of his time. He is named after the winged altarpiece created for the church of St Giles at the Augustine monastery in Třeboň (formerly Wittingau). This probably consisted of five panels, with a large central Crucifixion scene. Only three panels from the wings remain: *Gethsemane, The Resurrection* and *The Entombment* (c1380–5; National Gallery, Prague). On the reverse of each panel is a group of three apostles or saints. The altarpiece was dismantled during the 18th century, and dispersed to various neighboring churches.

Mateo of Santiago: the Portico of Glory; St James Cathedral, Santiago de Compostela; completed c1188

Mateo of Santiago *fl. c1168–1217*

Mateo of Santiago was a Spanish sculptor whose gigantic main entrance to St James Cathedral, Santiago de Compostela, is signed and dated 1188. The work was started in 1168, and in 1217 Mateo was still employed by the cathedral chapter. The triple entrance, known as the "Portico de la Gloria", is within the narthex. The central doorway, with the Christ in Majesty on a huge tympanum, has a trumeau on which is carved the Tree of Jesse and the figure of St James, patron saint of the cathedral and of Spain. All three doorways have column-figures, a clear indication of the influence from France. There are still traces of polychromy.

Mathieu Georges 1921–

The French painter Georges Mathieu was born in Boulogne-sur-Mer. He studied English, law, and philosophy, and moved to Paris in 1947. There he organized exhibitions of "lyrical abstraction" (his own term), becoming a major publicist for antigeometric painting, including American Abstract Expressionism. In 1953 he founded the *United States Lines Paris Review*.

He created his first Abstract-Surrealist paintings in 1944. Influenced by Wols, in 1947 he began to develop his unique calligraphic style; this relies upon spontaneous improvisation, so that speed minimizes conscious control. His works display open dynamic arabesques in thick lines sitting on the surface of the canvas; lattice-like complexes, layered and blotched, contrast vividly with expansive monochrome grounds.

Further reading. Charpentier, J. *Georges Mathieu*, Paris (1965).

Georges Mathieu: Danâ; oil on canvas; 65×100cm (26×39in); 1958. Museum Ludwig, Cologne

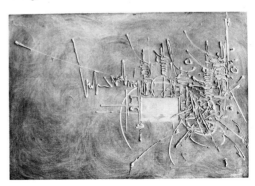

The Wittingau Master was undoubtedly responsible for introducing the so-called "beautiful" style which reached its apotheosis in Bohemia c1400. The source of his singular authority is not easily traceable to Bohemian forerunners. Towards the end of the 14th century the court of Charles IV in Prague provided an international *milieu* for artists, which may partly account for Italian and Franco-Flemish influences in his work. It cannot explain his advanced technique, in which older Gothic conventions are combined with an understanding of chiaroscuro, which was revolutionary in his time. His altarpiece panels display a visionary conception, while an unearthly radiance illuminates the figural focus of the composition.

Some paintings, once attributed to assistants, are now assigned mainly to his own hand. These include the *Crucifixion* from the chapel of St Barbara near Třeboň (c1380–5; National Gallery, Prague) and the *Roudnice Madonna* (c1390–5; National Gallery, Prague). This Madonna compares closely with the St Catherine on the reverse of the *Gethsemane* panel. It is an important work, demonstrating the "beautiful" style at its finest. No contemporary artist developed immediately from the Wittingau Master, and it was some years before his innovatory genius was understood in Bohemia. His influence on the painting of central and western Europe and on manuscript-illumination was profound, and can be traced by c1400.

Matisse Henri 1869–1954

Henri Matisse, born at Le Cateau-Cambrésis (Nord, France), was one of the leaders of avant-garde art before the First World War. He was famous for his brilliant and expressive use of color, and his bold innovations. His artistic identity evolved slowly and with apparent difficulty. Although he was 30 at the beginning of the century, it was not until 1905 that he discovered his own vision. Thereafter he rapidly became notorious as the leader of the group of painters known as the Fauves. He lived to become, in his old age, internationally honored as a master.

At 17, Matisse was set to study law by his father, a corn merchant. It is said that when he was 20 and convalescing from an appendectomy his mother gave him a paintbox and so he began painting. His earliest works, still lifes of 1890, are strikingly assured in a conventional academic manner. He quickly became technically skillful and for several years was able to supplement his meager allowance by making official copies in the Louvre.

He was never officially accepted as a student at the École des Beaux-Arts. In 1891, he was allowed to leave the lawyer's office in St Quentin and go to Paris where he attended the Académie Julian under Bouguereau, but he soon transferred unofficially to Gustave Moreau's classes at the École des Beaux-Arts. Among his fellow students were Marquet, Manguin, and Rouault, all younger than him.

In 1896, Matisse appeared to be on the threshold of his professional career. His painting of a woman reading in a lamplit interior, in the tradition of Henri Fantin-Latour, was shown at the Salon de la Société Nationale des Beaux-Arts, and was bought by the State for Rambouillet; the Société Nationale itself elected him an associate member, and he was introduced to Pissarro and Rodin. The following year, he showed The Dinner Table (private collection) at the Salon. This large canvas, depicting a servant arranging flowers on a table sumptuously spread for a large family meal, was painted in brilliant impressionist colors. His first major composition, it was badly hung and harshly criticized.

Henri Matisse: The Swan; etching; designed for Skira's edition of the poems of Stéphane Mallarmé, 1932. Victoria and Albert Museum, London

From that time onward, the course of Matisse's career changed radically. For seven years he worked constantly. But his canvases were researches rather than achievements, being either sketches roughly laid in and then abandoned, or labored exercises killed by overworking. He developed no consistent style but conducted a variety of experiments in the use of brilliant color.

In 1898 he married, and the following year bought with money from his wife's dowry a small painting, Three Bathers, by Cézanne. Though he never directly imitated Cézanne's style, this painting became a talisman for him which he cherished for many years, until in 1936 he presented it to the Musée d'Art Moderne de la Ville de Paris.

But the years of study and hardship continued. In 1900 Matisse attended evening classes in sculpture, and in later years sculptured many important works in bronze. He painted exhibition decorations for a living, and in 1902 Mme Matisse opened a millinery shop.

In 1904 Matisse worked with Paul Signac at St Tropez, and adopted his own, intuitive version of pointillisme. In this technique he painted an idyllic fantasy of women bathing on a beach (1905; private collection). Its title, Luxe, Calme et Volupté, he took from Baudelaire's poem "The Invitation to the Voyage", an invitation to a loved one to a dream land where

all is harmony and beauty, "luxury, tranquillity and delight". The picture and its title announce Matisse's arrival at his own vision of art.

But his own version of pointillisme was too rigid for him. In 1905 at Collioure, where he spent the summer with the much younger Derain, he painted small canvases with an apparent careless abandon he had never dared before. Open Window, Collioure (1905; Collection of John Hay Whitney, New York), bold in its calligraphy and indifferent to the original colors of the motif, captures the sparkle of light glancing off the ripples of the harbor alive with bobbing boats. He painted two portraits of Mme Matisse (Woman with the Hat, Walter A. Haas Collection, San Francisco; Madame Matisse: the Green Line, State Art Museum, Copenhagen) that were no less bold, and he vied with Derain as they painted each other's portraits (André Derain, 1905; Tate Gallery, London).

At the Salon d'Automne that year, Matisse's new canvases and works of similar violence by Derain, Vlaminck, Marquet, and others, were hung together in one room. The public was appalled by such crude daubs and the painters were called "Fauves"—wild beasts. The Woman with the Hat (1905; Walter A. Haas Collection, San Francisco) caused a particular sensation.

But this new style had admirers too, and a wealthy American brother and sister living in Paris, Leo and Gertrude Stein, met Matisse and bought this work. The following year, at the Salon des Indépendants, Matisse showed an ambitious composition, Joy of Life (1906; Barnes Foundation, Merion, Pennsylvania). It was an Arcadian scene with naked nymphs and shepherds, drawn with a new calligraphic boldness and with the clear coloring of an Oriental rug. Leo Stein bought it immediately.

Leo remained Matisse's friend, admirer, and patron (Gertrude favored Picasso) and soon other collectors began to vie for Matisse's new works. From 1906 his patrons included the Cone sisters of Baltimore, after 1908 the Russian merchant Sergei Shchukin, and from 1912 another Russian, Morosov. In 1909, Shchukin commissioned two important works, Dance (study, 1909, Museum of Modern Art, New York; oil, 1910, Hermitage Museum, St Petersburg) and Music (1910; Hermitage Museum, St Petersburg). Between them the Russians bought almost 50

Mateo of Santiago: St Peter, St Paul, St James and St John, on the Portico of Glory; St James Cathedral, Santiago de Compostela; stone; completed c1188 (see page 435)

works; these were acquired by the Russian state in 1923.

With this patronage, Matisse was able to visit Algeria in 1906. In later years he traveled widely, to Italy, Spain, Germany, Russia, and the U.S.A.; but his most significant visits were to North Africa in 1906, 1911, and 1912, and to Tahiti in 1930.

In 1908 Matisse was encouraged to open a small school, the Atelier Matisse, where he taught for a short time. In that same year he published his first theoretical essay "Notes of a Painter", in *La Grande Revue* (25 December 1908).

He was rejected for military service in 1914; he spent the War years painting, at Issy, Paris, and Nice. For the rest of his life he was to spend much of his time either in Paris or Nice.

With the return of peace, Matisse became more and more widely recognized as the master of the École de Paris and of modern painting. In 1925, he was made a Chevalier of the Legion of Honor. He worked in a growing variety of media. In addition to painting and sculpture, he designed for the ballet and designed illustrated editions: of Mallarmé's poems for Skira (1932), Joyce's *Ulysses* (1935),

Baudelaire's *Fleurs du Mal* (1943), and the *Florilège des Amours de Ronsard* (1941). His most important book was *Jazz* (1947) which combined his colored designs and a poetic essay on art in his own script.

In 1931 the great American collector, Dr Albert C. Barnes commissioned murals for the hall of the Barnes Foundation, Merion, Pa. When Matisse had completed the panels in his Paris studio they were found to be to wrong measurements, so he painted completely new versions which were successfully installed.

Matisse's last commission, despite his earlier lack of religious conviction, was the small Chapel of the Rosary of the Dominican nuns, Vence, begun in 1948 and consecrated in 1951.

After 1941, the aging Matisse suffered increasing ill health and often worked in bed. He died on 3 November 1954 at Nice, shortly before his 85th birthday.

Matisse first wrote about his art in 1908, in "Notes of a Painter", and 44 years later, when he was 82, he insisted that in spirit he had remained unchanged, because "all this time I have sought the same ends, which perhaps I have achieved in different ways". His end was always expression. Expression was a strenuous, paradoxical

achievement, the result of the artist's intuitive pictorial response to his experience of the object. Thus he painted in many different ways that at first sight show little consistency, modeling forms heavily in one canvas and painting with the flat simplicity of a child in another. He avoided any system of representation that depended on applied skills, but sought the pure spontaneous expression of each unique experience. Nevertheless, the metamorphoses of his style may be seen to follow a broad sequence of development.

Immediately after the sophisticated abstractions of *The Joy of Life*, he painted a number of canvases (notably *Le Luxe I*, 1907, Musée National d'Art Moderne, Paris; and *Le Luxe II*, 1907, State Art Museum, Copenhagen) in which he developed a childlike or primitive simplicity of line. (Matisse was among the first to collect Negro art.) This search for uncompromisingly "pure" form and color culminated in the Hermitage Museum's *Dance* and *Music* (1909–10). Drawn with a stark primitive outline and painted in the three basic colors of blue sky, green earth, and scarlet flesh, they are as theoretical as any later canvases by Kandinsky or Mondrian, but remain representational. The other single work with a similar doctrinaire spirit is a still life of 1914 entitled *Lemons: Still Life of Lemons the forms of which correspond to that of a drawing of a black vase on the wall* (Museum of Art, Rhode Island School of Design, Providence, Rhode Island).

The austere abstractions of *Dance* and *Music* were followed shortly afterwards by the fruits of his first visit to North Africa, a series of large scenes of Islamic life glowing with sensuous color. They appear effortlessly spontaneous, and their simple outlines could be mistaken as genuinely naive. These were followed by a further advance towards abstraction in *Open Window, Collioure* (1914; private collection) in which vertical bands of green, gray, and pale blue that are the window shutters frame a plain black rectangle, an entirely opaque night sky. *Composition: Yellow Curtain* (1915; private collection) is too big to be its pendant, yet is, formally, its daytime equivalent.

About the beginning of the War, Matisse showed the influence of Cubism. In *Mlle Yvonne Landsberg* (1914; Philadelphia Museum of Art) the negroid mask and expanding arcs scratched in the paint appear unconvincing. But *Moroccans*

Henri Matisse:
Seated Nude;
woodcut; 58×46cm
(23×18in); 1906.
Scottish National
Gallery of Modern
Art, Edinburgh

(1916; Museum of Modern Art, New York), though undoubtedly reflecting post-Cubist abstraction, is one of the most mysterious and powerful of his images. Its boldly silhouetted shapes anticipate the qualities of his own cut paper compositions of 20 years later.

As the War continued, Matisse in the isolation of his Paris studio painted a number of large canvases: somber, noble images of the studio, with Paris glimpsed through the window; they recall in their scale and spatial quality some of the great canvases of Manet.

In a hotel room in Nice in 1919, Matisse painted a totally different kind of *Artist and his Model* (Collection of Dr and Mrs Harry Bakwin, New York). The artist, by the quality of his line and the tentative washes of color, might be an elderly amateur faced with his first nude model. But ironically this naive gentleman is included in the picture; and the picture itself, despite its sketchy brushmarks, is taut and delicately precise in its spatial relationships. For another ten years, Matisse painted a sequence of such small genre scenes of the hedonism of sunlit Mediterranean hotels, in which the qualities of Impressionism or the intimate vision of his friend Bonnard were matched with an enigmatic simplicity.

In contrast, the Barnes murals were perhaps the most mannered inventions of Matisse's career. The flat shapes of the dancers, anticipating his later use of cut paper, leap into and out of the lunettes with a brittle vitality. Nevertheless, they point towards the painter's return to a more monumental imagery. Over the last 20 years of his long life, Matisse perfected his last, most consistent, mode of representation. He worked with thin, fluid paint, washing off unacceptable essays and starting afresh on the cleaned canvas, so preserving the vital quality of spontaneity. He drew with broad gestures, avoiding foreshortenings, and filling the canvas with grand arabesques which he charged with dazzling combinations of glowing color. Though many of these canvases are small they have a monumental quality.

After the Second World War, Matisse began to work increasingly in cut paper. He had immense sheets of paper washed over with gouache colors and then cut out his shapes and stuck them together (for example, *The Snail*, 1953; Tate Gallery, London). He said: "Cutting into living color reminds me of the sculptor's direct

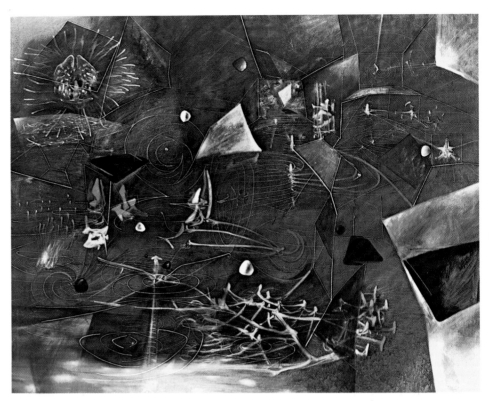

Roberto Matta: Eros Precipitate (Le Vertige d'Eros); oil on canvas; 196×251cm (77×99in); 1944. Museum of Modern Art, New York

carving." Though he cut often trite vegetable shapes, he composed them into splendid harmonies that are a fitting climax to his career.

His last masterpiece was the Dominican chapel of Notre-Dame du Rosaire (1947–51) at Vence, a small spare space made large and noble by the subtle balance of simple elements: the deliberately schematic black outline drawings on the white tiled walls, illuminated by the abstract colors flooding exultantly through the windows.

Further reading. Aragon, H. *Matisse: a Novel* (2 vols.), London (1972). Barr, A.H. Jr *Matisse: his Art and his Public*, New York (1951). Diehl, G. *Henri Matisse*, New York and Paris (1958). Elsen, A.E. *The Sculpture of Henri Matisse*, New York (1972). Escholier, R. *Matisse: a Portrait of the Artist and the Man*, London and New York (1960). Flam, J.D. *Matisse on Art*, London (1973). Gowing, L. *Matisse*, London (1979). Reverdy, P. and Duthuit, G. *The Last Works of Matisse*, New York (1958). Schneider, P. *Henri Matisse: a Retrospective Exhibition at the Grand Palais*, Paris (1970).

Matta Roberto 1912–

The Chilean painter Roberto Echaurren Matta enrolled in 1934 to study architecture in Le Corbusier's Paris office. He joined the Surrealists in 1937 and began to paint in 1938. In 1939 he emigrated to

New York where his friends Duchamp, Ernst, Tanguy, and André Breton exerted an enormous influence on his work. He traveled to Mexico in 1941, and after 1949 paid long visits to Italy, England, and France where he now lives.

Matta's personal brand of Surrealism dealt in its early years with the morphology of shapes in an ever-changing dream world. By the mid 1940s there appeared the tortured humanoid creatures that have dominated his work ever since, seen, for example, in *Eros Precipitate* (or *Le Vertige d'Eros*; oil on canvas; 1944; Museum of Modern Art, New York).

Matteo di Giovanni c1430?–95

The Italian painter Matteo di Giovanni was also known as Matteo da Siena. He was Siena's dominant painter during the second half of the 15th century. He was trained by Vecchietta, from whom he inherited interests in naturalism and in rigid sculptural forms, and was subsequently influenced by Antonio Pollaiuolo. From 1475 onwards his work saw an increasing assimilation of Antiquity with his naturalistic tendencies. About 1490 he reverted to a less innovative style, and thereafter placed emphasis on decorative effects of flat pattern. Representative works by Matteo include *Assumption of the Virgin* (c1470/5; National Gallery, London), *Massacre of the Innocents* (1482; S. Agostino, Siena), and *Madonna*

and Child with SS. John the Baptist and Michael (*c*1490; Barber Institute of Fine Arts, Birmingham, England).

Matyushin Mikhail 1861–1934

The Russian artist Mikhail Vasil'evich Matyushin was originally a musician. His artistic training, begun in 1898, included studying with Leon Bakst and Mstislav Dobuzhinsky. He was a cofounder of the Union of Youth group (1909) and in 1913 wrote the music for the opera *Victory over the Sun* (prologue by Khlebnikov, libretto by Kruchenykh, decor by Malevich). As head of the Organic Culture department at the Institute of Artistic Culture in Leningrad (*c*1920–6), he elaborated his concept of *Zorved* ("see-know"), devising exercises in cognitive (intuitive) and physical vision towards a perception of the fourth dimension. His theoretical and practical work on color was published in 1933, and his color investigation tablets (Stedelijk Museum, Amsterdam) were until recently attributed to Malevich.

Maulbertsch F.A. 1724–96

Franz Anton Maulbertsch (or Maulpertsch) was the outstanding monumental painter active in the Hapsburg territories during the second half of the 18th century. He was born at Langenargen on the Bodensee. He was first trained by his father, the painter Anton Maulbertsch, and may have been subsequently in contact with F.J. Spielgler. In 1739, under the patronage of Count Ernst von Montfort, he was sent to study in Vienna under Peter van Roy; he also came into contact with the Vienna Academy.

In 1745 Maulbertsch became a master in Vienna and his early style reveals the impact of Paul Troger. Although primarily a fresco painter, he also executed altarpieces and smaller special commissions, and the superb quality of his oil sketches for these has always been recognized. The chronology of Maulbertsch's work is based on the long series of documented frescoes, but study of the oil paintings is greatly complicated by the large number of his pupils and imitators.

Major commissions came early. The swirling clouds and figures in the vaults of

Matteo di Giovanni: Assumption of the Virgin; panel; 332×174cm (131×69in); c1470/5. National Gallery, London

F.A. Maulbertsch: Self-portrait; oil on canvas; 119×93cm (47×37in); c1790. Österreichische Galerie, Vienna

the Piaristenkirche, Vienna (1752–3), are a prelude to the brilliant series of frescoes in the abbey church of Heiligenkreuz-Gutenbrunn (Lower Austria, 1757), the parish church of Sümeg (Hungary, 1757–8), and the Feudal Hall of the Residence of Kroměříž (Moravia, 1759). During the 1760s Maulbertsch began to move away from this exuberance. The frescoes in Schloss Halbturn (Burgenland, 1765) reveal a growing clarity of lighting and the use of sculptural forms; these were to lead inexorably to the classicism of the frescoes at Strahov (Prague, 1794).

Ma Yuan 1190–1224

Ma Yuan, the great-grandson of the famous bird painter Ma Fen, was a member of a scholarly family that produced many painters. Ma Yuan himself was an Academy painter of the late Sung Court who was noted for his lyrical use of the brush strokes of Li T'ang, and the exaggerated "one corner" composition developed in the Sung Court style. He often chose to paint on silk and used soft colors.

Although he used the same vocabulary of brush strokes as Hsia Kuei, Ma Yuan seems to have softened the effect, partly by the use of silk as a base and partly by his own characteristic elegance of brush. The two painters' treatment of subject matter is also contrasting, for Ma Yuan's figures set the atmosphere of the scene and indeed are

often courtly people. This is evident in the small painting of the poet in the garden with his servant. This gentleman seems to be a forerunner of Shen Chou's scholar walking in his landscape and speaking through his poem to the viewer.

Ma Yuan's son, Ma Lin, was a painter and has left a tiny masterpiece in a fan painting (now in the National Palace Museum, Taipei) *Waiting for Guests by Candlelight*.

The school that has linked Hsia Kuei and Ma Yuan is one of elegant decorative painting in which both brushwork and composition are of refined sophistication. There have been a number of fine exponents of this style, which has also been regarded as the progenitor of decorative bird and flower painting.

Mazerolles Philippe de c1420–79

Philippe de Mazerolles was an illuminator working in Paris (1454) and Bruges (from 1467), where he was court painter to the Dukes of Burgundy. He is credited with the introduction of a new kind of manuscript illumination in which the figures are smaller than before, landscapes more extensive, and the importance of the decorative borders is reasserted. Calligraphic flourishes in the margins are particularly distinctive, as in the prayer book of Charles the Bold (Nationalbibliothek, Vienna). Recent scholarship has attributed his extant oeuvre to an artist from Ghent named Liévin van Lathem, who worked in Bruges from 1468 and also in Antwerp. He too is documented as having made a prayer book for Charles (Durrieu Collection, Larivière). Whatever the actual identity of the artist of the works associated with the name of de Mazerolles, he was a major figure in the history of Flemish illumination.

Meadows Bernard 1915–

The English sculptor Bernard Meadows studied at the Norwich School of Art (1934–6) and the Royal College of Art (1938–40 and 1946–8). He was studio assistant to Henry Moore from 1936 to 1939 and was one of the young generation of sculptors who came to prominence after the Second World War. Like Moore and Sutherland, Meadows used organic forms to express aspects of the human condition. One of his favorite motifs in the 1950s was the crab, which became a metaphor for tense excitement with a threat of ag-

Ma Yuan: Egrets on a Snowy Bank; ink and light color on silk scroll; 95×38cm (37×15in). National Palace Museum, Taipei

gression (for example, *Black Crab*; bronze; 1954; Clare Picture Guild, London). In the 1960s and 1970s he turned his attention increasingly to the human figure, which he suggests in anthropomorphic terms reminiscent of Moore and Arp. Meadows has always preferred casting in bronze to carving.

Meckenem Israhel van, the Younger *fl.* 1450–1503

A pupil of Master ES, Israhel van Meckenem the Younger was a goldsmith and prolific engraver active in Bocholt and Cleve in Westphalia. More than 600 plates bear his initials or signature, and as the first of the large-scale producers of prints he appears to have used factory methods. As might be expected, he did not hesitate to copy designs from a wide range of sources, including the productions of other printmakers, and he reworked at least 41 plates by Master ES.

Further plates were copied from the Master of the Berlin Passion (Israhel van Meckenem the Elder), the Master of the Housebook, and Hans Holbein the Elder, among others; but most of his composi-

J.-L.-E. Meissonnier: The Emperor Napoleon III at Solferino (24 June 1859); oil on wood panel; 44×76cm (17×30in); 1863. Louvre, Paris

Israhel van Meckenem the Younger: The Artist and his Wife Ida; copperplate engraving; 12×17cm (5×7in); c1490. Staatliche Museen, Berlin

tions are original, if uninspired. Clearly he must have employed many assistants, including possibly his wife Ida, and many of the editions were sufficiently large to require reworking of the copper plates.

The artist's late plates, such as *The Madonna on the Crescent Moon Surrounded by Six Angels*, dated 1502, are in their technique highly competent; but the stereotyped facial expressions and drapery patterns, and the lack of energy, belong to the final phase of late Gothic engraving.

Meidias Painter *fl. c420–400 BC*

The Meidias Painter was a Greek vase-painter who worked in Athens. His name is short for "the painter of the vase in London with the potter-signature of Meidias". Vase-painting in the second half of the 5th century BC owed much to the freer art of panel and wall painting. From these sources come the Meidias Painter's use of different levels within his pictures, three-quarter views with quite successful foreshortenings, and personified abstractions.

He was a follower of the Eretria Painter. The stately figures of the previous generation, however, have now become more effeminate, the drapery more luxurious, and the drawing more mannered. His style also reflects contemporary sculpture, especially the Nike Balustrade, but utterly lacks its dignity. The Meidias Painter's world is full of scented bowers, clinging drapery, pouting lips, and soulful glances: a gilded world of love and daydreams. His favorite subjects are from the realms of Aphrodite and Dionysos. Such themes were perhaps an attempt to escape the agonies of a Greece wracked by the Peloponnesian War.

Two *hydriae* found in the same tomb in Populonia show the Meidias Painter at the height of his rich mannerism. Both depict figures from Aphrodite's exploits: on one is Adonis; on the other, preserved intact, is Phaon. Phaon was an aged boatman to whom Aphrodite gave youth and external beauty. Here he plays the lyre to Demonassa under a gilded laurel canopy (Museo Archeologico, Florence; 81947). On the left two nymphs watch longingly, but on the right Leto has eyes only for her son Apollo. Above, Aphrodite circles in a chariot drawn by Desire and Longing, while other symbolic figures look on— Health, Happiness, All-Night Feasting, and Spring Time. Wavy incised lines, as usual in this painter's works, give an impression of the rocks on which some of the characters sit.

The Meidias Painter had much influence on the painters of small vases, both during his own period and later.

Meissonier J.-L.-E. 1815–91

Jean-Louis-Ernest Meissonier was a French genre and military painter. He worked as an illustrator early in his career, and showed his first Salon painting in 1834. He specialized in genre scenes on a very small scale, depicting such figures as painters, cardplayers, and Flemish burghers, using carefully documented historical settings (for example, *The Lost Game*, 1858; Wallace Collection, London). These works of Dutch inspiration, acquired immense popularity. In 1859 he joined Napoleon III's staff on the Italian campaign, which inspired a group of larger works based on the Napoleonic epic (for example, *The Emperor at Solferino*, 1863; Louvre, Paris). His scrupulous craftsmanship and anecdotal qualities made him highly popular among his contemporaries.

Meissonnier Juste-Aurèle 1695–1750

Although little of the work of the French goldsmith and architect Juste-Aurèle Meissonnier survives, he was highly influential in creating the Rococo style in Paris and, through engravings after his designs, in its spread throughout Europe.

Meissonnier was born in Turin and was much indebted to the work of the late Baroque artist Filippo Juvara. He was in Paris by c1720, and in 1725 or 1726 he was given an influential court appointment where his responsibilities ranged from silver designs to firework displays.

In the mid 1720s he put forward a plan for the facade of St-Sulpice, Paris; but like many of his architectural projects, it was never built.

Meit Conrad c1480–c1550

Conrad Meit was a German sculptor. Originally from Worms, he worked for Frederick the Wise at Wittenberg and for Margaret of Austria at Malines before ending his career at Antwerp. A colleague of Lucas Cranach and Jan Gossaert, he also met Jacopo de' Barbari and Albrecht Dürer. While the tombs at Brou reveal his skill at large-scale work, Meit is best known for his small sculpture. His most famous piece is the exquisite little alabaster

Judith in the Bayerisches National-museum, Munich. Other statuettes indicate that he was equally expert in the handling of boxwood and bronze.

Meit's work is outstanding both for its plasticity and for its luscious surface finish. A pioneering figure in German Renaissance sculpture, his long career spans the period between the break up of the late Gothic and the consolidation of Northern Mannerism.

Melozzo da Forlì 1438–94

Melozzo da Forlì was an Italian painter from Forlì in the Marches. His most important works were executed in Rome for Pope Sixtus IV (1471–84). His fresco in the Vatican Museums, showing the ceremonial appointment of Platina as Vatican Librarian (1477), originally decorated the main wall of Sixtus' library. The scene takes place within a Classically-inspired and marble-faced room; and the figures, which are probably all portraits, have a solemn monumentality clearly inspired by Piero della Francesca, who may have been Melozzo's master.

Contemporaries such as Giovanni Santi (and later Vasari) acclaimed Melozzo for his skill in perspective; but his most ambitious schemes, in vaults and domes of churches in Rome, Loreto, and Forlì (where he spent his last years), are now largely destroyed. The frescoes in the dome of the Capella del Tesoro in the Sacristy of St Mark, Loreto (1480s), use a sophisticated *trompe-l'oeil* technique. They show angels floating in front of each of the eight compartments of the dome behind which the sky is visible, while eight prophets sit below on the cornice of the dome.

Melozzo da Forlì: An Angel Musician; fresco; c1480. Vatican Museums, Rome

Probably the most influential of Melozzo's schemes was the fresco of the Ascension in the choir apse of SS. Apostoli in Rome (by 1480). The surviving fragments (the figure of Christ in the Palazzo del Quirinale; musical angels and heads of Apostles in the Vatican Museums) show clearly how Melozzo's scientific interest was combined with a love of decorative detail, to create an understandably popular idiom.

Memling Hans c1440–94

Although the painter Hans Memling was born at Seligenstadt near Frankfurt am Main, his style is Flemish rather than German. Active in Bruges, he may have been trained in the workshop of Rogier van der Weyden, although the influence of Dieric Bouts is also apparent in his work. Memling enjoyed a wide circle of patronage and several of his most important pictures were produced for foreign clients. The finest collection of his work is in the Memling Museum (Hôpital St-Jean) in Bruges. His numerous altarpieces and portraits are painted in a highly accomplished but rather bland and conservative manner.

Memmi da Siena c1285–c1361

Lippo Memmi da Siena, also known as Filippo di Memmo, was a Sienese painter of religious panels and frescoes, son of the painter Memmo di Filippencio. In 1317, he signed the *Maestà* in the Palazzo Nuovo del Podestà in San Gimignano. This work is in the manner of Simone Martini, and particularly of his *Maestà* of 1315: the two men were, in fact, brothers-in-law, and there is some argument as to how to apportion their works. Obviously a painter of quality, Memmi is documented as having collaborated with his relative on the *Annunciation* now in the Uffizi, Florence (1333); they certainly both signed it. But the extent of his involvement is hotly debated. His other works are devotional pictures which, reflecting the manner of Simone, become increasingly elegant and decorative. He may have accompanied his brother-in-law to Avignon, but was certainly back in Italy by 1361, when he worked on the Sala del Consiglio in the Palazzo Pubblico in Siena.

Hans Memling: The Presentation in the Temple; detail; oil on panel; full size 60×48cm (24×19in); c1463. Kress Collection, Washington, D.C.

Mena Pedro de 1628–88

The Spanish sculptor Pedro de Mena was born in Granada, the son of the sculptor Alonso de Mena. At his father's death in 1646, Mena, aged only 18, became the master of the workshop. When Alonso Cano arrived in Granada in 1652 Mena became his pupil and principal assistant; he collaborated with him on a number of important works until 1656, when Cano left for Madrid. His statue of St Francis in Toledo Cathedral, probably to a design by Cano, gained him the appointment as sculptor to the cathedral in 1653, although he remained working in Granada.

In 1658 Mena moved to Malaga, where he settled for the rest of his career, producing there his most original work on the 40 high-relief figures for the choir of the cathedral. A brief visit to Madrid in 1662–3 brought him under the influence of the great Castilian sculptor Gregorio Fernandez. A fruit of this visit is the famous statue of St Mary Magdalene (National Museum of Sculpture, Valladolid) carved at Malaga in 1664 for the Jesuit Congregation of St Philip Neri at Madrid.

Mena was a wood-carver of outstanding subtlety and technical virtuosity. His art displays an unidealized naturalism, and an emotionalism that is firmly restrained. It is to be seen at its best in the half-lengths of the quietly sorrowing Virgin, of which the finest, carved in 1673, is in the Descalzas Reales in Madrid.

Anton Mengs: Self-portrait; oil on canvas; 98×73cm (39×29in); 1774. Uffizi, Florence

Mendelsohn Erich 1887–1953

The German architect Erich Mendelsohn was associated with Expressionism, and with the use of new building techniques and materials (such as concrete and steel) to produce curvilinear buildings with an expressive organic quality. The dramatic curves of the Einstein Tower, Potsdam (1917–21), were preserved in his later, more functionally determined International style designs for the Schocken stores at Stuttgart (1926) and Chemnitz (1928). In 1933 he moved to England and in partnership with Serge Chermayeff (1900–) designed the De La Warr Pavilion, Bexhill (1934). He went to Israel in 1934 and designed several hospitals there (including one at Haifa, 1937). In 1941 he moved to America where he designed the Maimonides Hospital, San Francisco (1946).

Mengs Anton 1728–79

Anton Raphael Mengs, the purest exponent and theorist of Neoclassical painting, was named by his father, the Dresden court painter, after Antonio Correggio and Raphael. Mengs studied the work of Michelangelo and Raphael in Rome during the 1740s, and on his return to Dresden in 1751 was appointed chief court painter. By 1775 he had met J.J. Winckelmann, in Rome, who praised him and influenced his work.

His finest fresco in Rome was the ceiling of S. Eusebio (1757–8), which is painted in the Baroque style. However, by 1761 he had completed the *Parnassus* fresco on the ceiling of the Villa Albani, Rome, which in contrast shows a careful study of the antiquities at Herculaneum. *Parnassus* rejects the Baroque illusionism of the past and follows the convention of a low relief derived from the Antique.

After this he went to Spain, where he was appointed court painter to Charles III, returning to Rome in 1769. In Spain he painted three mythological cycles on ceilings in the Royal Palace, the last of which was completed on a second visit in 1775. He was elected Principal of the Academy of St Luke in Rome in 1770. In 1772 he worked for Pope Clement XIV on the decorations in the Camera dei Papiri at the Vatican, the program of which is a historical allegory on the function of the Camera.

Mengs' most accomplished work was as a portrait painter; his influential style prefigures much of the Neoclassicism of Jacques-Louis David.

Adolf von Menzel: Studies of a Worker Eating; pencil on paper; 27×37cm (11×15in); c1870–5. Staatliche Museen, Berlin

delicately executed and intimate depictions of domestic middle-class life, and a few market scenes. *Mother and Sick Child* (c1660; Rijksmuseum, Amsterdam) shows him at his best: it is a carefully balanced composition revealing an awareness of Pieter de Hooch and Vermeer, though with added sentiment. Materials and textures are carefully imitated in Metsu's genre pictures, and also in the portraits painted after his move to Amsterdam sometime between 1655 and 1657. In the latter, Metsu sacrificed study of character and psychological relationships to the painstaking transcription of the silks, tapestries, rich carpets, and heavy furniture of the ostentatiously prosperous Dutch bourgeoisie of the 1660s.

Menzel Adolf von 1815–1905

Adolf Friedrich Erdmann von Menzel was a German Realist painter and draftsman. Largely self-taught in his father's lithographic workshop in Berlin (1830–3), Menzel adopted the graphic style of local Biedermeier artists. His woodcut series illustrating the life of Frederick the Great (1839–42) inaugurated an atmospheric style akin to etching.

As a self-taught painter, Menzel was influenced by the painterly techniques of John Constable (whose works were exhibited in Berlin in 1839) and K. Blechen. The works he painted in the 1840s are very advanced, both in their freely handled use of pure color and in their documentation of contemporary reality (for example, *The Berlin–Potsdam Railway*, 1847; Neue Nationalgalerie, Berlin). But Menzel never exhibited them. His contemporary fame rested on his paintings of Frederick the Great.

Metsu Gabriel 1629–67

Gabriel Metsu was a Dutch painter from Leiden who spent most of his working life in Amsterdam. He produced religious, mythological, and allegorical pictures in his youth, but is principally known for

Gabriel Metsu: A Man and Woman Seated by a Virginal; oil on oak panel; 38×32cm (15×13in); c1658–60. National Gallery, London

Meunier Constantin 1831–1905

The Belgian artist Constantin Émile Meunier first trained to become a sculptor, but abandoned this in 1851 and turned to painting. At the Atelier Navez in 1854 he met Charles de Groux, whose Social Realism was later to influence him. Between 1857 and 1875 Meunier painted mainly religious subjects, but in 1878 his discovery of Belgium's industrial area turned his attention to the life of modern working man. He took up sculpture again in 1884, and glorified (in heroic poses) figures symbolizing trades such as *The Porter* (c1900, Kunsthistorisches Museum, Vienna) or *The Longshoreman* (1905; Royal Museum of Fine Arts, Antwerp). Meunier's unfinished *Monument au Travail* (1893–1905; Musée Constantin Meunier, Brussels) borders on Symbolism in its attempt at universal synthesis.

Michael Astrapas and Eutychios
fl. 1295–c1325

Michael Astrapas and Eutychios were Byzantine painters active in Macedonia and Serbia. Their autographed work is in the Peribleptos church at Ohrid (1295), Bogorodica Ievíška at Prizren (1306), St George at Staro Nagoričino (1313–18), and Sveti Nikita at Čučer. Their style exhibits two phases—a provincial and a metropolitan.

The style of the Peribleptos and of several icons at Ohrid, notably St Matthew, is often called "cubist" because of its multiple perspective and fractured surfaces. The compositions are crowded with agitated figures and heavy architecture. The figures are bulky with drooping shoulders, and enveloped by voluminous, angular drapery. Faces are broken into jagged planes. The intense colors are highlighted so as to create sharp edges.

The second phase of work is seen in their other churches, as well as the Joachim and Anna church at Studenica (1314), and the Protaton of Mt Athos, attributed to them by scholars on stylistic grounds. Under influences from Constantinople, there is a trend towards elongated figures, softer modeling, and a more subdued palette.

Michaux Henri 1899–1984

The Belgian-French painter and author Henri Michaux was born in Namur, Belgium. It was in writing that Michaux first expressed himself artistically, in Brussels in 1922. In 1924 he moved to Paris, where the shock of seeing the nonnaturalistic, semiautomatic approach of Klee and Ernst awakened his interest in painting. He began intermittently to draw and paint signs and personal ideograms from 1925, because he felt writing could not express all he had to say. From 1937 onwards both activities were complementary, and he occasionally published books containing both writing and paintings.

Michaux always sought to tap the unconscious mind by allowing his fantasy to develop random blots and squiggles. In the late 1950s he even experimented with hallucinogenic drugs, in an attempt to free his mind from conscious control and facilitate his search for a personal language capable of expressing more directly the movement of his inner being.

Michelangelo 1475–1564

The Italian painter, sculptor, and architect Michelangelo Buonarroti was born at Caprese near Arezzo, the son of a minor official. As a child he was taken to Florence, where he was apprenticed to the painter Ghirlandaio; he seems to have found his master's somewhat bland style uncongenial, preferring the more austere and monumental art of Giotto and Masaccio. He appears to have taken up sculpture almost immediately. Among his earliest works is a relief of the *Battle of Lapiths and Centaurs* (c1492; Casa Buonarroti, Florence), which is clearly inspired by Classical sarcophagi and also reflects the antiquarian interests of the sculptor Bertoldo di Giovanni. The latter was closely associated with Lorenzo de' Medici ("Il Magnifico"), then the virtual ruler of Florence; Lorenzo seems to have allowed the young Michelangelo free access to his collection.

After a brief sojourn in Bologna, in 1496 Michelangelo was in Rome, where he was able to study far finer examples of Classical art than he could have found in Florence. His first work there, a life-sized *Bacchus* (c1496–7; Museo Nazionale, Florence), is an entirely convincing imitation of an antique statue. Its success led to the commission for the *Pietà* (1498–9; St Peter's, Rome). This at once established his reputation as the foremost living sculptor, both because of the exceptional beauty and pathos of its composition, and because of the amazing virtuosity of its technique.

Shortly afterwards Michelangelo returned to Florence, where he began work on a colossal statue of *David* (1501–4; Galleria dell'Accademia, Florence). This was the largest marble statue to be carved in Italy since the end of the Roman Empire and the first to bear comparison, in its mastery of human anatomy, with the finest achievements of Antiquity. However, the tension of the figure—and the mood of suppressed energy—is wholly un-Classical.

While he was in Florence Michelangelo also produced four devotional works for private patrons, namely the *Bruges Madonna* (1501–6; Notre Dame, Bruges), a freestanding group; the *Pitti Tondo* (c1503–5; Museo Nazionale, Florence) and the *Taddei Tondo* (c1504–5; Royal Academy of Arts, London), both unfinished marble reliefs; and also the *Doni Tondo* (c1504–6; Uffizi, Florence), his only known completed oil painting. This last work is wholly sculptural in feeling. The principal group, the Holy Family, is shown as if carved from a single block, with hard, absolutely clear contours and bright unrealistic colors; the poses are deliberately complex, with an exaggerated use of contrapposto, suggesting that Michelangelo's interest lay almost exclusively in the exploration of formal problems, rather than in the content.

These preoccupations are equally apparent in his last major work of this period, a cartoon for a fresco of *The Battle of Cascina*, commissioned for the Great Council chamber of Florence in 1504. The cartoon, known only through copies (a copy by Bastiano da Sangallo is in Holkham Hall, Norfolk), constituted the central section of a much larger composition and showed a group of soldiers surprised by the enemy while bathing. Michelangelo seems to have regarded the subject merely as a pretext for showing the heroic male nude in a great variety of poses of outstanding beauty and originality, which were to provide a constant source of inspiration for later Florentine artists.

In 1505 he was summoned to Rome to make a gigantic tomb for Pope Julius II in St Peter's; the project was to obsess him for more than three decades, as successive powerful patrons demanded his services for other commissions. In the next year, for example, he was forced to make a colossal bronze statue of Julius in Bologna, which was destroyed soon afterwards. Then in 1508 the Pope ordered him to paint the vault of the Sistine Chapel in the

Michelangelo: The Creation of Man, a detail of the ceiling of the Sistine Chapel, the Vatican, Rome; 1508–12

Vatican: the result was the most influential single work in the history of European art.

The original project consisted simply of frescoes of the 12 Apostles, but Michelangelo soon replaced this with a much more elaborate scheme. In the center of the vault there are nine scenes taken from Genesis, flanked by pairs of naked youths (the *Ignudi*), who are in fact angels. Towards the sides of the ceiling there are 12 large seated Prophets and Sibyls, and then, lower still, the Ancestors of Christ. The various separate elements are arranged within an elaborate painted architectural framework. As Michelangelo proceeded his draftsmanship became even more assured, the poses increasingly varied and bold, and the figures endowed

with ever-greater energy and nobility. His frescoes are the most perfect visual embodiment of the then-current Neoplatonic belief, to which he was deeply committed, that physical beauty, and especially that of the human figure, is a reflection of the Divine.

After completing the ceiling in 1512 Michelangelo was able to resume his work on the tomb. The initial plan had involved a freestanding two-story monument with more than 40 large sculptured figures. He now decided on a three-sided structure projecting from a wall, but the quantity of sculpture required was not substantially reduced. Michelangelo was only able to carve two figures of *Slaves* (c1513; Louvre, Paris) and the seated *Moses* (1515–16; San

Pietro in Vincoli, Rome). Then in 1516 Julius' successor, Leo X, a member of the Medici family, ordered him to return to Florence (now once again under Medici rule), in order to design a new facade for the church of S. Lorenzo. This commission, like the ceiling and the tomb, involved an elaborate combination of figures and architecture, and it was conceived on an equally ambitious scale. For much of the next three years Michelangelo remained in the mountains near Carrara, making arrangements for the quarrying and transportation of the enormous blocks of marble required for the facade. But in 1519 Leo lost interest in the commission, which was canceled in the next year, and instead ordered Michelangelo to begin

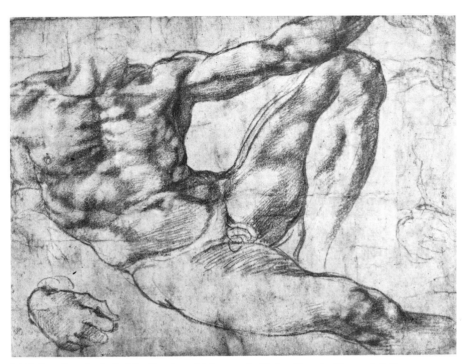

Michelangelo: a Study for The Creation of Adam on the Sistine Chapel ceiling; red chalk on paper; 19×26cm (7½×10in); 1510/11. British Museum, London

namely the four unfinished *Slaves* (1519–34; Galleria dell'Accademia, Florence) and the *Victory* group (*c*1532–4; Palazzo Vecchio, Florence). The *Slaves* very clearly illustrate his conception of sculpture as a process of revealing the underlying form concealed within the block of marble; but it would be unjustified to infer, as many critics have done, that he left so many of his works unfinished by choice, as a way of demonstrating this idea.

In 1534 Michelangelo moved to Rome, where he remained for the rest of his life. His first work there, commissioned by Pope Paul III, was the gigantic fresco of the *Last Judgment* on the altar wall of the Sistine Chapel, which was painted between 1536 and 1541. By now the optimistic Neoplatonism of his earlier years had been replaced by a more austere piety typical of the new climate of the Counter-Reformation, and in this fresco the figures have none of the ideal beauty of those on the ceiling. Instead, the anatomy is often grossly exaggerated, with deliberately inelegant, distorted poses and violent foreshortening. Deviations from the Classical norm of an equally extreme kind are to be found in the work of many of Michelangelo's contemporaries, whose style would now be described as Mannerist; but no other artist was capable of matching the intense expressive power of his composition, the

work on a mausoleum for the Medici family to be built at the other end of the church.

The mausoleum, usually known as the New Sacristy, is a square structure surmounted by a cupola; one wall is broken by a deep niche containing an altar. As usual with his major projects, Michelangelo only gradually reached his final solution, which in the event was never carried out in its entirety. Opposite the altar there was to have been a double tomb for Lorenzo il Magnifico and his brother Giuliano; but the only tombs actually built were those on the side walls, for two of Lorenzo's sons. Each consists of a highly idealized seated effigy of the deceased in a narrow niche, framed by an elaborate architectural setting, in front of which there is a huge sarcophagus surmounted by a pair of reclining figures symbolizing the times of day. The precise meaning of the scheme is not entirely clear, but it seems to have some kind of Neoplatonic theme, with the oppressively crowded lower zone of the building symbolizing the material world, and the more brilliantly illuminated and simpler architecture of the cupola representing the ideal world of the spirit. Even in its present uncompleted form, the Sacristy conveys an unparalleled impression of solemnity; it exists as a complete and consistent environment, in which the normal boundary between reality and the work of art is dissolved.

While he was in Florence Michelangelo also undertook one other project for the Medici, the construction of the Laurentian

Library in the monastery of San Lorenzo, begun in 1524. The most remarkable feature of the design is the small vestibule, in which the conventional language of Renaissance architecture is distorted in a seemingly almost perverse way for expressive effect. During this period, and especially from 1527 to 1529 when the Medici family temporarily lost control of the city, he was also able to work on additional figures for the tomb of Julius II,

Michelangelo: Joel, a detail of the Sistine Chapel ceiling, the Vatican, Rome; 1508–12

quality defined so succinctly by his friend and biographer Vasari as "terribilità".

Soon after finishing the *Last Judgment* Michelangelo began two much smaller frescoes in the Pauline Chapel, also in the Vatican: these were *The Crucifixion of St Peter* (1542–5) and *The Conversion of St Paul* (1545–50). In the total elimination of any suggestion of physical beauty, and in the extreme simplicity of pose and gesture, they represent the final development of his figure-style. The only concession to conventional aesthetic standards is in the treatment of color, which has an unexpected delicacy and luminosity.

The austerity of these paintings is matched in the late sculpture. In 1542 the "tragedy of the tomb", as Michelangelo himself described the fiasco of the Julius monument, was finally ended by an agreement with the Pope's heirs. They were now prepared to accept an extremely modest structure in S. Pietro in Vincoli, containing only the *Moses* and some other statues executed by pupils. The only major sculptures of Michelangelo's old age are two *Pietà* groups, one intended for his own tomb and then abandoned (*c*1550–61; Florence Cathedral), and the other, the *Ronadanini Pietà* (1560s; Castello Sforzesco, Milan), also produced for his own satisfaction and still unfinished at his death. Both bear eloquent witness to his inability to give concrete physical expression to his by now virtually abstract conceptions.

Michelangelo's growing disillusionment with the figurative arts was matched by an increasing interest in architecture, especially after he was put in charge of the reconstruction of St Peter's in 1546. He totally rejected the proposals of his predecessor Antonio da Sangallo the Younger, which involved a consistent system of proportion and an accumulation of individual elements. He favored a much more unified and simple scheme, relying for its effect on an undulating exterior wall articulated by a few massive pilasters, which created a strong upward emphasis and led the eye directly to the huge cupola. The style is dynamic and overtly dramatic, and anticipates the Baroque. His other late Roman projects—notably the reconstruction of the Capitol (probably designed in 1538), the completion of the Palazzo Farnese (late 1540s) and the Porta Pia (1561–5)—are equally subjective, and no less radical in their rejection of Renaissance and Classical norms.

In his own lifetime Michelangelo enjoyed greater fame and prestige than any artist before him, thanks in part to the efforts of his contemporary biographers Condivi and Vasari. The scale of his projects, the difficulties he encountered, his total single-mindedness, and his solitary and austere personality established the concept of the creative genius that has become a fundamental element of the European consciousness. Works such as the Sistine Chapel ceiling, the *Moses*, and the New Sacristy provided standards that later artists might reject, but which they could not disregard. Thus it was almost entirely through Michelangelo's efforts that for three centuries the heroic male nude should have been considered the major challenge open to painters and sculptors, the one indispensable characteristic of great art.

Further reading. Ackerman, J.S. *The Architecture of Michelangelo*, Harmondsworth (1970). Beck, J., Paolucci, A., and Santi, B. *Michelangelo: The Medici Chapel*, London (1994). Ramsden, E.H. *The Letters of Michelangelo* (2 vols.), London (1963). Tolnay, C. de *Michelangelo* (5 vols.), Princeton (1947–60).

Michelozzo di Bartolomeo
1396–1472

The Florentine architect and sculptor Michelozzo di Bartolomeo was the son of an immigrant Burgundian tailor. He appears as a die-caster at the Florentine mint in 1410. From 1419 to 1424 he assisted Ghiberti, presumably as a bronzecaster and chaser. Thereafter he worked in partnership with Donatello for a decade, carving the Madonna and Child and the figures of the Virtues for the Coscia monument in Florence Baptistery (*c*1424–7), most of the marble figures for the tomb of Cardinal Brancacci in S. Angelo a Nilo in Naples (*c*1426–30), and substantial parts of the outdoor pulpit at Prato Cathedral (*c*1428–38). The Aragazzi monument in Montepulciano Cathedral (*c*1430–8) is entirely his own work. During the years 1430–3 he and Donatello worked in Rome.

As early as the period from 1420 to 1427 Michelozzo was already working as an architect, on the little church of S. Francesco al Bosco in the Mugello near Florence. After his return from Rome he turned increasingly towards architecture. In the 1430s, he redesigned the church of S. Marco in Florence, one of the earliest of

Michelozzo di Bartolomeo: a Virtue, part of the tomb of Cardinal Brancacci in S. Angelo a Nilo, Naples; *c*1426–30

the many commissions he received from the Medici. He began the rebuilding of SS. Annunziata in Florence in 1444 for the Marquis of Mantua. This daring design incorporated an east rotunda closely based upon the temple of Minerva Medica which caused a storm of controversy in architectural circles. The church was still incomplete when Michelozzo withdrew from the project in 1455, and it was subsequently finished under the supervision of Alberti. Michelozzo's most important architectural commission was the Palazzo Medici, begun in 1444. With its boldly rusticated ground story and its massive raking cornice, this building became a model of Renaissance *palazzo* design. He received many other commissions for buildings in and around Florence and as far afield as Venice, Milan, and Dubrovnik.

Michelozzo's reputation has suffered as the result of comparison with his more illustrious contemporaries Brunelleschi and Donatello. While he had a less inquiring mind than either, he was second only to Brunelleschi as an architect. He was also a very distinguished sculptor who played a crucial role in the development of the Quattrocento wall tomb.

Mies van der Rohe 1886–1969

The German architect Ludwig Mies van der Rohe was born in Aachen. The son of a mason, he was apprenticed as a stone-cutter between 1900 and 1902, a training that probably influenced his lifelong attention to detailing in his buildings. In 1907 he traveled to Italy and was impressed with the work of Brunelleschi (1377–1446) and Palladio (1508–80), in particular the manner in which they articulated their buildings while confining themselves to few means.

Mies entered the office of Behrens in 1908 (Gropius and Le Corbusier also spent a period working with Behrens) and was introduced by him to the German classical tradition of K.F. Schinkel, whose Altes Museum in Berlin Mies particularly admired—from which, he was later to state, one could learn everything in architecture. Behrens placed him in charge of the building of the German Embassy in St Petersburg (1909). The German publishing house, Wasmuth, introduced the work of Frank Lloyd Wright to European architects in 1910, an event that was to clarify Mies' thinking. He left Behrens in 1911 and set up his own practice. In 1912 he was engaged on a project for Madame H.E.L.J. Kröller for the Kröller-Müller house at the Hague.

His first major postwar undertakings were the projects for Berlin's Friedrich-strasse (c1921) and a skyscraper (c1922), both of which were to be glass-walled, a revolutionary idea on this scale. Expressionist in ambition and concept, these may possibly have been influenced by the writing of Scheerbart and the architecture of Bruno Taut—for instance Taut's use of glass in the Glass Pavilion, in the Cologne Werkbund Exhibition, 1914. The chief determinants for Mies were the provision of sufficient illumination of interiors, the play of reflections, and the revealing of structure. In 1921 he became Director of Architectural Exhibitions for the Novembergruppe in Berlin, a group loosely Expressionist, sympathetic to socialism, whose aim was to exploit the possibilities for cooperation between art and society.

Mies' 1922 project for a concrete office block still shows some Expressionist qualities, for example the tapering outward of floors towards the top; but compared with his glass tower projects, the emphasis is now more horizontal. The weight is carried by an internal post and slab system, allowing alternating continuous bands of windows around the building. His work became increasingly Elementarist and less Expressionist in nature, the emphasis being placed upon the skeletal structure. His move towards an Elementarist position is manifested in his 1923 brick-villa project (where there are elements reminiscent of some De Stijl work and of El Lissitzky) and in his membership of "G" (Gestaltung, creative force) a group of Abstract artists. In 1925 he joined the Ring, a loose association of Berlin architects, Expressionists, and Elementarists, including Gropius, Mendelsohn, and the Tauts; and by the late 1920s he was among the leading architects in the city.

The Deutscher Werkbund, the official German Design authority, invited Mies to take charge of overall planning for a big architectural exhibition of modern residential buildings to be held in 1927, at the Weissenhof Siedlung (housing estate) in Stuttgart. Although modified by practical constraints, his planning of the site, and the relationship of buildings to the landscape, was striking. Mies, who was responsible for an apartment block, did not confine participation to German architects; J.J.D. Oud, Mart Stam, and Le Corbusier took part.

Another official undertaking, the German Pavilion at the Barcelona International Exhibition of 1928–9, was the occasion for one of his most famous and contentious buildings. Rich in the materials used—marble, onyx, tinted glass, chromium glazing bars, steel and leather chairs—the design is spare and in the Elementarist manner, with echoes of Frank Lloyd Wright (the emphatic roof line) and possibly Adolf Loos (rich materials combined with severe design). The Pavilion had no doors. Each room was only partially enclosed by three partitions on three sides, made from large tinted glass sheets, with some walls faced with marble or onyx. These walls reached to the roof but it was, in fact, supported by regularly placed freestanding columns. Two large pools were set into the extensive marble floor. Critics were divided: within its rationalist tradition it did not seem functional.

Towards the end of the decade and into the 1930s Mies was engaged on a number of projects which were to prefigure clearly his later buildings in America. In 1928 he planned the remodeling of the Alexanderplatz in Berlin. Here the structural regularity of the steel skeleton determines the strict rectangular shapes; metal framing and glass curtain walls emphasize the effect. In 1928–30 the "Tugendhat" house was built in Brno, Czechoslovakia. The 1933 Reichsbank project, more horizontal in its emphasis, also uses the curtain wall. Between these dates he became involved with the Bauhaus. As a result of political pressures, the Marxist Hannes Meyer, a Swiss architect, was removed from his post as Principal of the Bauhaus in 1930 and Mies was appointed in his place. Under Nazi pressure Mies finally moved the Bauhaus from Dessau to Berlin, being forced to close it in 1933 because of its alleged "Kultural Bolshevismus". He received a number of offers from America. In 1938 he became Director of Architecture at the Illinois Institute of Technology, a position he held until 1958, when he resigned to allow himself to give more time to his practice.

His American work shows the development of ideas already implicit in his work of the 1920s and 1930s, for example his apartment blocks at Lake Shore Drive, Chicago (1948–51), through to Lafeyette Towers, Detroit (1955–63). However, the works that have probably claimed most attention are the Farnsworth house (1945–50), a simply designed steel-and-glass residence, slightly raised above the ground, suspended on steel beams, isolated and open to nature on all sides; his Seagram building (1954–8), with its attention to detailing, its facade of bronze sections and glass tinted to match; and his work for the Illinois Institute of Technology (started 1940, completed 1962). Among his European work of the later period is his Gallery of the Twentieth Century, Berlin (1962–8).

Central to an understanding of Mies' development and work are arguments concerning functionalism, rationalism, and idealism as determinants on his style. He himself claimed an indifference to style. According to him there is an unfolding of the great form in each epoch: this is not invented by a particular architect but is contributed to by the individual. His emphasis was on structural architecture, as he felt this was based on reason, an architecture for a technological society, an architecture that anybody could practice.

Further reading. Blaser, W. *Mies van der Rohe: the Art of Structure*, London and New York (1965). Carter, P. *Mies van der Rohe at Work*, Chicago (1972). Drexler, A. *Ludwig Mies van der Rohe*, London and New York (1960).

Mignard Pierre 1612–95

The French painter, Pierre Mignard trained at Bourges and in Paris under Simon Vouet. From 1636 to 1657 he worked in Italy, where he was influenced by Poussin and by Bolognese classicism. He was to be more a practicing classicist than his rival Charles Lebrun, whom he was to succeed in all respects in 1690. In Paris he painted a number of decorations for private houses and churches. But he is best remembered as a portraitist in a rather stiff Italian manner, reviving the 16th-century allegorical/mythological type.

His brother, Nicolas (1606–68), worked mainly as a religious painter at Avignon, in a dry manner derived from Vouet, Poussin, and the Roman Seicento.

Mikon *fl.* early 5th century BC

Mikon was an Athenian painter of the early 5th century BC. He suffered in Antiquity by comparison with his greater contemporary and part-time collaborator Polygnotus. His most famous works were in Athens: battles against the Amazons were in the Stoa Poikile (the Painted Stoa, which gave its name to the Stoic school of philosophy) and probably also in the sanctuary of Theseus, where he certainly painted exploits of the Athenian hero; and the expedition of the Argonauts was in the Anakeion.

Millais J.E. 1829–96

The English painter John Everett Millais was born in Southampton. His family, having lived for some time in Jersey and northern France, moved in 1838 to London, where Millais' precocious talent could be properly developed; between the ages of 11 and 17 he attended the Royal Academy Schools. His first exhibited oil was the conventional romantic *Pizarro Seizing the Inca of Peru* (1846; Victoria and Albert Museum, London).

He was one of the young and dissatisfied artists who banded together in 1848 as the Pre-Raphaelite Brotherhood. Exhibited the following year, his *Lorenzo and Isabella* (Walker Art Gallery, Liverpool) shows the minute detailing, the pristine color, the symbolism, and the use of friends as models seen in contemporary works by Holman Hunt and Rossetti. *Christ in the House of His Parents* (1850; Tate Gallery, London) applied the same principles to religious subject matter. It was attacked for its unidealized depiction of the Holy Family, while its stylized, almost ritualistic quality associated it disastrously with the dreaded encroachment of the Roman Church and "popish" asceticism. The paintings he exhibited in 1851 were also badly received.

J.E. Millais: A Dream of the Past, Sir Isumbras at the Ford; oil on canvas; 124×170cm (49×67in); 1856–7. Lady Lever Art Gallery, Port Sunlight

A Huguenot (1851–2; private collection) won great popularity, however, and its pathetic theme of lovers parted by historical circumstances recurred in *The Proscribed Royalist* (1852–3; private collection), *The Black Brunswicker* (1860; Lady Lever Art Gallery, Port Sunlight), and others. The two-figure formula removed the need for more complex compositions, which Millais seems to have found difficult. His best-known picture, *Ophelia* (1851–2; Tate Gallery, London), illustrates his working method at this period, the setting painted painstakingly from nature in summer and the figure added from a model in the studio during the winter, ready for the Academy exhibition in May.

While painting John Ruskin's portrait, staged on a Scottish waterfall (1853–4; private collection), Millais fell in love with his sitter's wife, Effie. Soon after her divorce from Ruskin they married, and the first of eight children was born in 1856. Family commitments inevitably made Millais conscious of the need to sell his work, which he did with mounting success, earning by the 1880s some £30,000 a year.

In the later 1850s he produced a series of pictures whose power lay in the evocation of a general mood rather than the description of a particular situation. The most atmospheric is *Autumn Leaves* (1855–6; City of Manchester Art Gallery), in which the budding youth of some girls is set against the cyclical decay of natural things: dead leaves burning at dusk. The conjunction was calculated to induce, he claimed, "the deepest religious reflection". Landscape and figures interact similarly in other works, including *The Blind Girl* (1854–6; City of Birmingham Museums and Art Gallery), in which the beauty of the scenery intensifies the subject's pathos, and *The Vale of Rest* (1858–9; Tate Gallery, London), a strange image of nuns digging a grave in the gathering gloom of evening.

Millais had always shown himself a gifted draftsman and his many finished pen-and-ink drawings of the earlier 1850s, for example *The Race-Meeting* (1853; Ashmolean Museum, Oxford), a scene reminiscent of contemporary novels, led naturally on to his illustrative work, which begins with the edition of Tennyson's poems published by Moxon in 1857. Throughout the 1860s he was a prolific illustrator, both for magazines, notably *Once a Week*, and for novels, especially those of Trollope.

His painting technique, already losing its Pre-Raphaelite meticulousness, became increasingly broad from now on, enabling him to work more quickly and on larger canvases. He admired English 18th-century portraitists and the Old Masters, calling his presentation picture as an Academician *Souvenir of Velazquez* (1867–8; Royal Academy of Arts, London).

First in a line of studies of single children—often his own—was *My First Sermon* (1862–3; Guildhall Art Gallery, London), depicting a little girl in a pew. The Reynolds-like *Cherry Ripe* (1879; private collection), the much more painterly manner of which exemplifies the evolution of Millais' style, was published as a color reproduction, selling 600,000 copies. He also dealt in historical child-subjects such as *The Boyhood of Raleigh* (1870; Tate Gallery, London). Another category was the young lady in 18th-century costume; *Clarissa* for instance (1887; private collection), modeled by his daughter Sophie, imitates Gainsborough's portrait *The Honourable Mrs Graham* (c1777; National Gallery of Scotland, Edinburgh).

His first major pure landscape was *Chill October* (1870; private collection). Autumn and winter visits to Scotland, during which he did much hunting and shooting as well as landscape-painting, came to provide a welcome escape from the increasing pressures of his London portrait practice. His depictions of often rather bleak scenes were intended to suggest human sentiments, especially loneliness and a sense of the impassivity of Nature. They show technical subtlety in rendering effects of wind, dew, and mist, and sensitivity in capturing the mood of a certain season or time of day, as for example in *Lingering Autumn* (1890; Lady Lever Art Gallery, Port Sunlight).

Hearts are Trumps (1872; Tate Gallery, London), showing three ladies around a card-table, is an early example of his society portraiture. Such luxuriously dressed female sitters exercised Millais' now bold and rich handling of paint. With male subjects he concentrated on the delineation of strong character in the features: in the two portraits of Gladstone, for example (1879, National Portrait Gallery, London; 1884–5, Christ Church, Oxford). Outline is a particularly telling aspect of his work, seen to effect in *Mrs Jopling* (1879; Collection of L.M. Jopling, on loan to the Ashmolean Museum, Oxford). With its three-quarter-length figure depicted

against a plain background, this compares in simplicity of statement with contemporary work by Manet.

Of several studies of old age, the patriotic *North-West Passage* (1874; Tate Gallery, London), which shows a retired sea-dog, is the most attractive, especially in its coloring. *The Ruling Passion* (1885; Glasgow Art Gallery and Museum), depicting a bedridden ornithologist, typifies Millais' later preference for dark tones and an overall impression of brownness. This is also seen in the late religious paintings, for instance *St Stephen* (1895; Tate Gallery, London).

Created a baronet in 1885, and elected President of the Royal Academy in 1896, Millais commanded the highest personal popularity and professional esteem.

Further reading. Bennett, M. *P.R.B. Millais P.R.A.* (London 1967). Gaunt, W. *The Restless Century*, London (1972). Lutyens, M. *Millais and the Ruskins*, London (1967). Millais, J.G. *Life and Letters of Sir John Everett Millais* (2 vols.), London (1899).

Milles Carl 1875–1955

The Swedish sculptor Carl Milles was renowned for his fountains. Born near Uppsala and trained in Stockholm, he settled in Paris in 1897. He made his debut at the Salon of 1899 and met Rodin in 1900. After living in Munich and Rome, he returned to Sweden in 1908 to work on monumental commissions. His studio at Lidings eventually became the Millesgarden (Milles Museum) famous for its terraces and waterfalls. His early works in the style of Rodin and Maillol brought him international acclaim at the 1914 Malmö Baltic Exhibition. Around 1917 he came under the influence of the German sculptor and theorist, Adolf Hildebrand, and his style changed dramatically. *The Meeting of the Waters* (1940; Aloo Plaza, St Louis, Missouri) illustrates Milles' new-found belief that sculpture can be monumental and architectural without being contained within an architectural framework; the freestanding figures are grouped into a balanced composition and movement is provided by the play of the water. Milles moved to the United States in 1931. Major works include *Man and Nature* (1940; wood; Rockefeller Center, New York) and *The Hand of God* (1954, Eskèltsuna, Sweden).

Jean-François Millet: The Gleaners; oil on canvas; 84×111cm (33×44in); 1857. Louvre, Paris

Millet Jean-François 1814–75

A leading painter of the Barbizon School, Jean-François Millet was noted for his portrayal of peasant themes. He was born into a Norman farming family, and received his earliest artistic instruction in Cherbourg. In 1837 he went to Paris, where he studied under Paul Delaroche. His first Salon exhibit, a portrait, was shown in 1840. After years of penury in Paris, he moved in 1849 to Barbizon, where the peasant stream of his art developed, and where he remained for the rest of his life.

His earliest surviving works are portraits, for example that of his first wife, *Pauline Ono* (1841–2; Musée Thomas Henry, Cherbourg). In the early 1840s he painted in a Rococo manner, producing erotic nudes and *scènes galantes* reminiscent of Diaz de la Pena (for example, *Reclining Nude*, 1844–5; Louvre, Paris). A more forceful style emerged *c*1847 as can be seen in *The Quarrymen* (1846–7; Toledo Museum of Art, Toledo, Ohio). The dynamic poses of the workers reflect Michelangelo and Daumier, but the style is still related to earlier works.

Millet turned to peasant subjects as he became aware of the changes brought about by urbanization and the industrial revolution. The immediate stimulus was the Revolution of 1848, which brought social questions to the fore. Millet exhibited a peasant subject, *The Winnower* (1848; private collection) in the Salon of 1848, and *The Sower* (1850; Provident National Bank, Philadelphia), a monumental figure of rustic labor, in 1850.

The stark portrayal of the peasant, on a large scale and without an element of humor or anecdote, was new in France; it was not considered a worthy pictorial motif. In the sensitive political climate of the day, such works were also seen as revolutionary statements. However, Millet seems to have intended to express only his fatalistic conception that man was doomed to unremitting labor. *The Gleaners* (1857; Louvre, Paris), and *The Man with the Hoe* (1860–2; private collection) aroused much criticism over their supposed political content.

Although seen as a revolutionary, Millet shows continuity with traditional Western art in some themes and compositions. *The Harvester Meal* (1851–3; Museum of Fine Arts, Boston) refers to the biblical story of Ruth and Boaz, and reflects some compositions of Poussin. His *Peasant Grafting a Tree* (1855; private collection) evokes Virgil. He uses a somber palette to depict the rough faces and ungainly figures of his peasant subjects (for example, *Woman Grazing her Cow*, 1858; Musée de l'Ain, Bourg-en-Bresse). His melancholy, idealized settings often exploit the diffused light of dawn or dusk (for example, *The Angelus*, 1855–7; Louvre, Paris). After 1863, under the influence of Rousseau, he painted more pure landscapes (such as *L'Hiver aux Corbeaux*, 1862; Kunsthistorisches Museum, Vienna).

Millet produced many drawings and pastels, which are among his most attractive works, being simple depictions of ordinary life and everyday tasks (for example, *Shepherdess Resting*, 1849; Fitzwilliam Museum, Cambridge.)

Milow Keith 1945–

The English artist Keith Milow was born in London. He studied at the Camberwell School of Art (1962–7) and at the Royal College of Art (1967–8). He was appointed Gregory Fellow at Leeds University (1970) and subsequently awarded a Harkness Fellowship to the United States.

Working in series, each one characterized by strikingly different materials and approaches, Milow's works are always based on images of real objects which are manipulated by the creative process. Since the late 1960s he has produced reliefs that explore the nature of both painting and sculpture.

Earlier works, for example *Improved Reproductions* (1970; Tate Gallery, London) were in resin, based on photographs. The *Split Definitives* in the mid 1970s were painted on panels set at right angles to the walls, as were the *Cenotaphs* (1979), based on the famous London monument. Since 1974 Milow has produced over a hundred *Crosses* in various materials and sizes. In them he explores the form of the cross through variations in an attempt both to acknowledge and deny its powerful symbolism.

Mincho Kichisan 1352–1431

The Japanese painter Kichisan Mincho was also known as Cho Densu. A priest of the Tofukuji Temple in Kyoto, he was the major artist in the change from brilliantly colored figure-painting of *rakan* (saints) and famous priests, with mixed ink and color landscape backgrounds, to pure ink paintings of mythical figures and almost unpeopled landscapes. His skill in the former style is seen in the *tour-de-force* of the *Five Hundred Rakan* (Nezu Museum of Art, Tokyo). This was painted in the Takuma figure-style, of which he was the last great exponent. His painting in pure ink is more tentative, like the attributed *Hut by a Mountain Stream* of 1413 (Nanzenji Temple, Kyoto); but it has great historical importance.

Mino da Fiesole 1429–84

Mino da Fiesole was an Italian sculptor. He is said by Vasari to have been trained by his near-contemporary Desiderio da Settignano, though there is little sign of it in his early work. He was a less gifted carver of marble than Desiderio or Antonio Rossellino, though he was strongly influenced by their style. His earliest dated work is a portrait bust of Piero de' Medici of 1453 and he carved six other good busts. He produced several large tombs and tabernacles in and around Florence, and also worked extensively at Rome in the 1460s and 1470s. He may be identical with a sculptor active there and in Naples who signed himself Mino del Reame.

Mino da Fiesole: Portrait of Astorgio Manfredi; marble; 52×54×28cm (20×21×11in); c1456. National Gallery of Art, Washington, D.C.

Mino's cutting of drapery is slick and linear, his faces are bland stereotypes, and his compositions naive. While superficially attractive, his sculpture is devoid of emotional involvement and degenerates into sentimentality.

Mirak Naqqash late 15th century

The Persian painter Mirak Naqqash was a Sayyid of Herat. A versatile artist, he was

Joan Miró: Women and Bird in the Moonlight; oil on canvas; 81×66cm (32×26in); 1949. Tate Gallery, London

in turn calligrapher, illuminator, and painter. He became head of the library of Sultan Husayn Bayqara (1469–1507). He is said to have designed inscriptions for all the principal buildings of Herat, no doubt in tile mosaic. He was the painting master of Bihzad. Six miniatures in a *Khamsa* of Nizami (British Library London; MS. Or. 6810), datable to 1494–5 but old-fashioned for that date, have been plausibly attributed to him. He also gained a reputation as an athlete and pugilist. He died in 1507. He should not be confused with Aqa Mirak, an early Safavid court painter.

Mir Musavvir *fl.* 1520–60

The Persian painter Mir Musavvir of Badakhshan contributed three miniatures to the royal Safavid *Shah-nama* of Tahmasp (one dated 1527/8; private col-

lection) and one dated 1540 to the *Khamsa* of Nizami in the British Library, London. About 1540 he succeeded Sultan Muhammad as head of the Library of Shah Tahmasp in Qazwin. He excelled in figure drawing. His son, Mir Sayyid Ali, was a founder of the Mughal court school under Humayun (c1549), who offered to buy him from the Shah; shortly afterwards, Humayun retook Delhi (1555) and founded the Mughal School of Indian painting. Mir Sayyid's father joined him in India and died there.

Miró Joan 1893–1983

Joan Miró was a Spanish painter, ceramist, and sculptor, and a leading member of the Surrealist movement. Born in Barcelona, he at first hesitated between art and business studies, but in 1912, after a serious breakdown, he enrolled in Francesco Galí's School of Art in Barcelona, where he was introduced to avant-garde French art. His paintings of 1914 show a highly original amalgam of Post-Impressionist, Fauve, and Cubist influences. Several landscapes painted in 1918 are reminiscent of Persian miniatures in their precision of line, decorative treatment of flat areas of color, and patterning of forms.

On his first visit to Paris in 1919, Miró sought out his countryman, Picasso, with whom he developed an enduring and mutually stimulating friendship. In 1920 he took a studio in Paris, and through André Masson—a neighbor—he met the Dada and Surrealist poets. Henceforward he divided his time between Paris and Spain.

Although still anchored in the "real" world, Miró's paintings of 1918 to 1923 became increasingly strange, due to an almost manic attention to detail, a hallucinatory vision of ordinary objects, and an expressive intensity. In works such as *The Tilled Field* (1923–4; Solomon R. Guggenheim Museum, New York), the element of fantasy and irrationality is pronounced. In 1924 he joined the Surrealists, who encouraged him to rely on imagination and dreams for his imagery (as in *The Harlequin's Carnival*, 1924–5; Albright-Knox Art Gallery, Buffalo). During the years 1925 to 1927, responding to Surrealist theories of automatism, Miró produced a large number of spontaneously and rapidly executed "dream" paintings, which border on abstraction. In these he began to develop the sign-language—cosmic and sexual in its subject matter—characteristic of much of his later work.

In 1928, Miró reverted to his detailed manner in the *Dutch Interiors*, which were based on Old Master paintings. From that time until his death his work alternated between freedom and precision, the two extremes occasionally being combined in the same work. During the 1930s, his distress at the political situation in Europe was reflected in the savage subject matter and mood of such paintings as *Seated Woman* (1932; private collection).

In 1940 and 1941 Miró painted his *Constellations*—a series of gouaches which demonstrates his dazzling command of overall pictorial design and linear rhythm. He made his first ceramics in 1944, in collaboration with Llorens Artigas, abandoning painting from 1955 to 1959 in order to explore this new medium with characteristically radical inventiveness. In the 1960s, he devoted much time to huge sculptures based on the biomorphic personages in his paintings, and to sculptures created from found objects.

Miró's paintings after 1960 were large, simple, bold abstractions, employing his personal sign-language with great expressive inventiveness. He enjoyed experimenting with a wide variety of unconventional techniques such as tearing and burning. His influence on postwar painting—especially Abstract Expressionism—was considerable.

Further reading. Dupin, J. *Joan Miró: Life and Work*, London (1962). Dupin, J. *Miró Engravings Vol. III 1973–1975*, New York (1989). Gimferrer, P. *The Roots of Miró*, New York (1993).

Mir Sayyid Ali *fl. c*1530–80

Mir Sayyid Ali was a Persian painter born in Tabriz. As the son of the painter Mir Musavvir he worked at the Safavid court from early youth, contributing one miniature to the *Nizami* of Tahmasp (1539–43), and probably also to his *Shah-nama* (78 of its 258 illustrations are in the Metropolitan Museum, New York). He joined the Mughal emperor in exile in Kabul (1545), and went with him to India. There he painted for him a large imaginary group portrait of his ancestors reaching back to Timur, at a picnic in a garden (British Museum, London). The painting is in pure Safavid style, but on cloth 45 in (114 cm) square. With Abd al-Samad he founded the Mughal School of Indian painting.

Mitsunobu Tosa *c*1430–*c*1521

Tosa Mitsunobu was a Japanese *Yamatoe*-style painter, the greatest of the family who dominated the Kyoto *edokoro* (painting office). Later he became an official painter to the Shogun's government. This, and the marriage of his daughter to Kano Motonobu, began the 16th-century union of the Japanese and Chinese styles.

In Kyoto temples, many sets of screens of figure-subjects against gold backgrounds are attributed to Mitsunobu. His major certified works are the sets of handscrolls *Kitano Tenjin Engi* (1502; Kitano Shrine) and *Kiyomizudera Engi* (1517; Tokyo National Museum). In both these works, the traditional narrative style is given power and cohesion by an extremely forceful personality.

Mochi Francesco 1580–1654

The Italian artist Francesco Mochi was the most idiosyncratic of the great sculptors of the Roman Baroque. His *St Veronica* (1629–40; St Peter's, Rome) displays his violent dramatic power through an abstract play of near-geometric forms and taut linear rhythms. His monuments in Piacenza to Ranuccio (1612–22) and Alessandro Farnese (completed 1625) are the most forceful and inspired equestrian statues of the 17th century, while the scenes on their bases (completed 1629) perfect the pictorial low-relief style originated by Giovanni da Bologna in Mochi's native Tuscany. The psychological intensity of Mochi's vision, and the increasingly unrealistic forms in which he embodied it, found little favor in 17th-century Rome.

Modersohn-Becker Paula 1876–1907

After studying in London and Berlin, the German artist Paula Becker moved in 1898 to the artists' colony of Worpswede in northern Germany, where she met and married the painter Otto Modersohn. Increasingly dissatisfied with the naturalism and sentimentality of the Worpswede painters, she visited Paris several times, where she discovered the works of Van Gogh, Cézanne, and Gauguin (she was one of the very first German artists to respond to Post-Impressionism). Painting mostly women, children and herself, she used bold colors and flat, simplified forms, with leaves and flowers as recurrent motifs. The themes of nature, motherhood and female identity play a major role in her work. She met with little understanding or success, even at Worpswede, though she was encouraged by the poet Rainer Maria Rilke, whose portrait she painted. A characteristic work from her maturity is her nude *Self-Portrait with Amber Necklace* (1906; Roselius Collection, Bremen). In her use of form and color she was an important precursor of Expressionism.

Further reading. Perry, G. *Paula Modersohn-Becker*, New York (1979).

Modigliani Amedeo 1884–1920

The Italian painter and sculptor Amedeo Modigliani was born at Livorno. He was encouraged in his early talent by his mother, before studying at the Academies of Rome, Florence, and Venice. During his

Francesco Mochi: equestrian monument to Alessandro Farnese; cast bronze; completed 1625. Piazza Cavalli, Piacenza

stay in Venice from 1903 to 1906, the Biennale introduced him to the current Art Nouveau and Impressionist trends; he traveled to Paris in 1906.

He quickly joined the artists in Montmartre and showed seven works at the 1907 Salon d'Automne, a remarkable success for a recently arrived young man. The Cézanne retrospective was mounted in the same exhibition. Modigliani's work, however, was nearer to Lautrec or early Picasso in style, with an elegance of line that betrays his Art Nouveau tendencies.

He turned to sculpture in 1910. While continuing to paint, he became fascinated by primitive sculpture, probably under the influence of Brancusi and Matisse. He carved heads directly in stone; some have rudimentary features that respect the original block to such an extent that they have been called unfinished. Others are elegant, mannered versions of ethnographic types, extravagantly elongated, with stylized features (for example, *Head*, 1911–12; Tate Gallery, London).

After 1910, these features began to show themselves in his paintings, from now on almost exclusively figures and portraits. He seems to have worked out the formal aspects of this style in his imaginative work first, developing a series of *Caryatids*; these began quite close to their ethnographic models in 1911 but their style became increasingly arabesque by 1913.

In 1914 or 1915 he made the acquaintance of the English poet Beatrice Hastings, who lived with him until 1916 and looked after him irregularly as his health deteriorated. In this short period he produced his most powerful paintings, including portraits of *Juan Gris* (1915; Metropolitan Museum, New York), *Beatrice Hastings* (1915; Art Gallery of Ontario, Toronto), *Picasso* (1915; private collection), *Jean Cocteau* (1916; Pearlman Foundation, New York), *Paul Guillaume* (1916; Galleria d'Arte Moderna, Milan), and *Chaim Soutine* (1916–17; National Gallery of Art, Washington, D.C.). When confronted by a sitter he modified his stereotype and produced extraordinarily perceptive studies; his portrait of *Picasso* (1915; George Moos Collection, Geneva), seems to have been taken over by the vitality of the subject.

Amedeo Modigliani: Head of a Woman Wearing a Hat; watercolor; 35×27cm (14×11in); 1907. Collection of William Young and Co., Boston, Mass.

After Modigliani had taken part in a successful group exhibition in 1916, the dealer Leopold Zborowski furnished him with models and a studio. However, he continued his irregular mode of life, shared after 1917 by Jeanne Hébuterne, who bore him a child in 1918. Increasingly his figures, particularly his nudes, take on a lassitude that is both voluptuous and melancholic. The day after he died of tuberculosis Jeanne Hébuterne, who was seven months pregnant, killed herself.

Further reading. Fifield, W. *Modigliani, a Biography*, London (1978). Hall, D. *Modigliani*, Oxford (1979). Lanthemann, J. *Modigliani: Catalogue Raisonné*, Barcelona (1970). Soby, J.T. *Modigliani*, New York (1954).

Laszlo Moholy-Nagy: Light-Space Modulator; reflecting metals and transparent plastics; height 151cm (59in); 1923–30. Busch-Reisinger Museum, Cambridge, Mass.

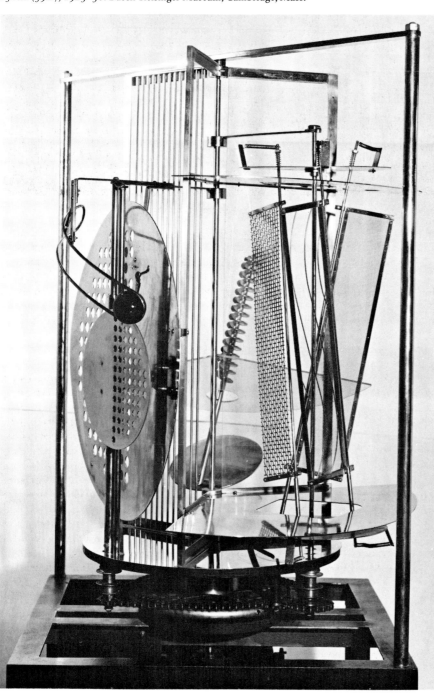

Moholy-Nagy Laszlo 1895–1946

Laszlo Moholy-Nagy was a Hungarian painter, theorist, and maker of constructions. He first studied law, but by the end of the First World War he had begun to paint, influenced by the contemporary Hungarian painters Janos Uitz and Jozsef Nemes-Lamperth, both associates of the politically engaged MA circle. In 1921 he moved to Berlin, and in the same year was a signatory to the short manifesto "A Call for Elementarist Art", published in *De Stijl*. Essentially Moholy-Nagy opposed individualism in style—on which he made common cause with Theo van Doesburg and El Lissitzky.

Moholy-Nagy's early painting uses Suprematist elements of circle, cross, and square. In 1924 he exhibited at the Sturm Gallery, Berlin, three factory-made works of identical composition but varying sizes; painted on porcelain enamel these were made by the factory supervisor from his instructions. By this time he was interesting himself in modern materials, for instance transparent plastics, which allowed him to experiment with light, and in photography.

He was appointed to the Bauhaus in 1923, when the emphasis there shifted from Expressionism to Constructivism, and was put in charge of both the metalwork shop and the preliminary course. His Constructivist ideas were also to change the direction of typography and its layout, towards greater order and clarity. With Gropius he coedited a series of Bauhaus books, and was also responsible for the layout and design of some of them. These set out the ideas of leading artists and architects, including Klee, Mondrian, and Malevich. *Von Material zu Architektur*, his own contribution, dealt with various artists and photography, with kinetic sculpture, and with illuminated advertising. An important part of his theory was concerned with the creation of "virtual" volume by light: to realize this he created his "Light-Space Modulators". He resigned from the Bauhaus in 1928, after a policy change.

In 1934 he left Germany for Holland, then lived in London from 1935 to 1937, before emigrating to America. In 1937 the New Bauhaus was established in Chicago (it became the Institute of Design in 1958) with Moholy-Nagy as its head until his death. He was a prolific writer and theorist and in 1946 published *A New Vision and Abstract of an Artist*.

Further reading. Fawkes, C. *Moholy-Nagy and the Bauhaus*, London (1973). Kostelanetz, R. *Moholy-Nagy*, New York (1970). Moholy-Nagy, L. *Painting, Photography, Film*, London (1969). Moholy-Nagy, S. *Moholy-Nagy: Experiment in Totality*, Cambridge, Mass. (1972).

Mokubei Aoki 1767–1833

Aoki Mokubei was a Japanese painter and potter of the *Bunjinga* School. He was born in Kyoto, where he acquired a taste for things Chinese. He became a maker of Chinese-style pottery and porcelain, especially for the *sencha* form of tea ceremony favored by the literary, and opened kilns in Kyoto, Wakayama, and Kaga. His painting consists mostly of landscapes in a superficially *Bunjinga* style, but with a light delicacy of touch and a predominantly pink and blue palette which are all his own. Sometimes of real Japanese scenes, they have a quality of dreamy fantasy, as in his *Sunny Morning at Uji* (Tokyo National Museum).

Mola Pier 1612–66

The Italian painter Pier Francesco Mola was a native of Coldrerio, near Como; by 1616 his family had moved to Rome. From 1633 to 1640 and again from 1641 to 1647 he worked in Venice and northern Italy, studying for two years (1645–7) with Albani in Bologna. His earliest known works are frescoes at Coldrerio. In these years he was deeply influenced by Venetian art and by Guercino (1591–1666). A group of small-scale landscapes show the development of an intensely romantic style; his palette is dark and his chiaroscuro rich and warm.

Under the influence of Albani, Mola's landscapes became more classical. In 1647 he returned to Rome, where he painted frescoes and altarpieces that continue the traditions of Bolognese classicism. In his major official commission, *Joseph and his Brethren* (1636–7; Palazzo del Quirinale, Rome) he moves towards the grandeur of the High Renaissance and the vivid colors of Pietro da Cortona. In 1658 he began frescoes in the Palazzo Pamphili at Valmontone, but a dispute with his patron led to their destruction.

Mola remained a romantic, most successful in the exotic *Barbary Pirate* (1650; Louvre, Paris) and in a beautiful series of hermits in Venetian landscapes. After 1660

Pier Mola: Joseph and his Brethren; fresco; 475×475cm (187×187in); 1656–7. Palazzo del Quirinale, Rome

he again sought inspiration in 16th-century Venetian art. His highly dramatic paintings of anchorite saints—*St Bruno* (1665, Jannetti Collection, Rome) and *St Jerome* (Buscot Park, Faringdon, Oxfordshire)—and his tender and idyllic treatment of poetic subjects—*Bacchus and Ariadne* (Wilton House, Salisbury, Wiltshire) and *Erminia tending the wounded Tancred* (M.H. de Young Memorial Museum, San Francisco)—are perhaps his most personal and attractive contributions to the Baroque.

Momper Joos de 1564–1635

Joos de Momper was a Flemish painter from Antwerp. Taught by his father, Bartholomeus de Momper, he also trained his sons Phillips and Gaspard. Although he spent most of his life in his native Antwerp, Momper visited Italy in 1581 and 1591. In 1594 he worked beside Cornelis Floris on the decorations for the triumphal entry of Archduke Ernest.

Momper's fanciful mountain panoramas (examples in many European public galleries) earned him great success during his lifetime. Strictly a landscape specialist, he developed Pieter Bruegel the Elder's investigations of this genre to their ultimate degree. The figures in his paintings were generally executed by other painters, notably Jan Bruegel. His work occupies an important place in the development from the Flemish Mannerist landscape to the more naturalistic style of the 17th century.

Mondrian Piet 1872–1944

Pieter Cornelisz. Mondriaan, the eldest child of a schoolmaster in Amersfoort, Holland, is ranked among the greatest pioneers of Abstract art. His austere compositions of horizontal and vertical lines and primary colors, taken with his theoretical writings, have had a profound influence on 20th-century art and aesthetics.

Intended by his Calvinist father to become a schoolteacher, Mondriaan completed his training and was 20 before he determined to enrol at the Amsterdam Academy of Fine Arts, in 1892.

For the following 15 years, though he worked assiduously, he had little success. He taught, and did portraits, copies, and technical drawings, in order to continue his own work. He became a landscape painter in the manner of such Dutch contemporaries as Jozef Israels and Maris. The early work of Van Gogh inspired him to live at Uden, in Brabant, throughout 1904.

Piet Mondrian: Composition with Yellow; oil on canvas; 46×47cm (18×19in); 1930. Kunstsammlung Nordrhein-Westfalen, Düsseldorf

Returning to Amsterdam in 1905, he began to respond to Modernist ideas. He met the painter Jan Toorop in 1908 on the island of Walcheren. From this time he began to paint a succession of series—studies of a lighthouse, a windmill, a church tower, of sea and dunes, and especially of an apple tree—in which he experimented with the innovations of the Divisionists and the Fauves.

In 1909 came two significant events. In January, at the Stedelijk Museum, Amsterdam, with Jan Sluters and Cornelis Spoor, he exhibited work that conservative critics attacked as being unbalanced. And he joined the Theosophical Society of Holland. Theosophy became an alternative to Calvinism and gave him a metaphysical theory out of which he later developed his theory of art. In the following two years his reputation grew. In 1911, he became a Director of Amsterdam's *Moderne Kunstring*, and at the Society's October exhibition his canvases were hung beside works by the Fauves, the Cubists, and

Cézanne. It was then that he began to sign his name "Mondrian".

In December 1911 he settled in Paris, where he remained, apart from the years of the First World War, until 1938. Although Paris was one of the centers of early modernism, Mondrian lived alone, seldom mixing with other painters. His work, however, showed the influence of Cubism. His exhibits at the Salon des Indépendants of 1913 were noticed favorably by Apollinaire. By 1914, his representations of trees, building facades, and still life had become patterns of staccato verticals and horizontals with occasional arcs, tinted in pale pastel colors. Nevertheless, like other Cubist works, they remained essentially based on individual motifs.

Mondrian returned to Holland in 1914 to attend his father's deathbed. The outbreak of war compelled him to stay in Holland for five crucial years. He returned to painting the sea, and his sequence of studies *Pier and Ocean* confirmed for him the need to abandon the individual motif for a more

universal expression. At the same time, he discovered three friends and a patron, Salomon Slijper.

His first friend was a younger painter, Bart van der Leck, who was also exploring abstraction. Together, they developed a system restricted to rectangular shapes. The second friendship was with M.H.J. Schoenmaekers, a philosopher, whose book *New Image of the World*, almost the only volume Mondrian owned, profoundly influenced his theory of art. The third friendship was with C.E.M. Kupper (also known as I.K. Bonset among Dadaists). As "Theo van Doesberg" Kupper founded with Mondrian the movement and the periodical *De Stijl*, in 1917. *De Stijl* stood for abstraction, the unification of the arts, and the creation of new values for humanity.

In *De Stijl* Mondrian began to publish his theory of art. In 1919 he wrote: "the truly modern artist is aware of abstraction in an emotion of beauty; he is conscious of the fact that the emotion of beauty is cosmic, universal". Therefore, he argues, modern art will ignore "natural form and color. On the contrary, it should find its expression in the abstraction of form and color, that is to say, in the straight line and clearly defined primary color".

He justified his extreme abstraction, saying "we find that in nature all relations are dominated by a single primordial relation which is defined by the opposition of two extremes". In painting, this primordial relation should be represented by horizontals and verticals "which form the right angle. This positional relation is the most balanced of all ... and contains all other relations". He believed that his austere system did contain all other relations and express universal harmony. So when, in 1925, van Doesberg based his compositions on diagonals, Mondrian denounced them and left *De Stijl*.

Theory preceded his mature practice. In 1919, when he returned to Paris, he did adopt a severe rectilinear form. But it was not until 1921 that he settled for the ultimate primordial relationship of intersecting horizontal and vertical bands of black on white—spare grids to which he added occasional rectangles of primary red, yellow, or blue. In these severely restricted forms he found a theme capable of infinite variations, which he developed with austere integrity for another 20 years.

In 1925 (the year of his break with *De Stijl*) his essay on "Neo-plasticism", originally published in French in 1920, was translated into German and published by the Bauhaus in Weimar. Mondrian was thus established as one of the leaders of modernism. More practical recognition came the following year when the American collector, Katherine S. Dreier, bought one of his works. From that time, Mondrian acquired the patronage of a few Americans and Germans that sustained him for the rest of his life.

Mondrian's final years were among the most eventful. In September 1938, disturbed by the prospect of war, he left Paris for London, where he was befriended by the circle of Abstract artists around Ben Nicholson and Barbara Hepworth. In 1940, a bomb falling close to his London studio drove him to New York. There he established another bare, cell-like studio, identical in its essentials to those he had abandoned in Paris and London.

The experience of New York was stimulating. The skyscrapers were like the realization of his art. This, and the jazz music he had loved for years, led him to a transformation of his art so extreme as to verge on the rejection of his own tenets. It produced some of his most brilliant compositions, including *Broadway Boogie Woogie* (1942–3; Museum of Modern Art, New York) and *Victory Boogie Woogie* (1943–4; Tremaine Collection, Meridien, Connecticut), *Trafalgar Square* (1939–43; Museum of Modern Art, New York), and *New York City I* (1942; Sidney Janis Gallery, New York). In January 1942 he had his first one-man show at the Valentin Dudensing Gallery, New York.

On 1 February 1944 he died of pneumonia at Murray Hill hospital, New York, a month before his 72nd birthday.

Further reading. Elgar, F. *Mondrian*, New York (1968). Fauchereau, S. *Mondrian*, New York (1994). Mondrian, P. (ed. Holzman, H.) *The New Art; the New Life; the Collected Writings of Piet Mondrian*, New York (1972). Mondrian, P. (trans. Welsh, R.P.) *Two Mondrian Sketchbooks: 1912–14*, Amsterdam (1969). Tomassoni, I. *Piet Mondrian*, Florence (1969) and London (1970). Welsh, R.P. (ed.) *Piet Mondrian*, Toronto (1966).

Monet Claude 1840–1926

The French Impressionist painter Claude Oscar Monet was born in Paris but spent his childhood on the Channel Coast at Le Havre. In his teens, he won a local reputation as a caricaturist; but he was converted to the art of landscape painting by Eugène Boudin, who was then living locally, and whom he met in c1856. On Boudin's advice, Monet visited Paris in 1859 and 1860, and there met Camille Pissarro. After a spell of military service in Algeria, he returned to the Le Havre area, where in 1862 he met the Dutch landscapist Johan Barthold Jongkind. Boudin and Jongkind were to have a strong influence on his early artistic development. From 1862 to 1864, Monet studied in Paris in the studio of Charles Gleyre, where he met Pierre-Auguste Renoir, Frédéric Bazille, and Alfred Sisley; Renoir and Bazille became particularly close friends.

Monet made his public debut at the Salon exhibition of 1865; he showed two large seascapes (including *La Pointe de la Hève*, Kimbell Art Museum, Fort Worth, Texas), whose fluent yet concise brushwork shows a debt to Jongkind. Inspired by the success of these pictures, he undertook a vast project in the summer of 1865, an outdoor picnic scene measuring about 15 ft by 20 ft (approximately 6 m by 8 m). In this *Déjeuner sur l'Herbe* he aimed to reinterpret the theme of Manet's notorious *Le Déjeuner sur l'Herbe* (Musée du Jeu de Paume, Paris) of 1863, by treating the figures more naturally than Manet had, and by putting them into a more convincing outdoor setting and lighting. He was unable to complete this huge canvas (oil sketch, 1865; State Pushkin Museum of Fine Arts, Moscow) but realized a similar aim in *Women in the Garden* (1866–7; Musée du Jeu de Paume, Paris), a painting 8 ft 5 in by 6 ft 10 in (2.56 by 2.08 m) much of which was actually painted in the open air. *Women in the Garden* was rejected at the 1867 Salon, and Monet never again painted on such a scale out of doors.

At the same time, he was making important experiments on smaller canvases. In *Terrace at Sainte-Adresse* (1867; Metropolitan Museum, New York) and in three views of Paris, all of 1867, he adopted a high viewpoint; he avoided a single central focus in his compositions in order to suggest the animation and multiplicity characteristic of the way we see the scenes around us. Monet's subject matter at this period sets him firmly among the painters who were focusing on city life and fashionable figures, in their attempt to become painters of modern life. The detached mood of Monet's scenes allies them with the ideas of Baudelaire's essay "Le Peintre de la Vie Moderne" ("The Painter of Modern Life"; published in 1863); while the crisp individual strokes of paint that he used to define forms show his debt to Manet. In *Terrace at Sainte-Adresse*, the structured grid-like composition is an early example of the impact of Japanese color prints, which had such a wide influence on younger painters from the 1860s onwards.

In the late 1860s, Monet was also pursuing his observation of light and color, seeking ways of translating natural effects quickly and directly on to the canvas. His studies of La Grenouillère of 1869, though he did not at the time regard them as finished paintings, show how freely he could use paint and color. During the Franco-Prussian War of 1870–1 Monet lived in London, and there he first saw the art of Joseph Mallord William Turner. However, his paintings from immediately after his return to France in 1871 show no clear sign of Turner's influence; rather, they continue one facet of his work of the late 1860s—his concern with variations of weather and lighting. In this respect, the La Grenouillère paintings of 1869 anticipate the ensuing developments in his art.

Monet concentrated on smaller-scale landscapes during the 1870s. Many of them showed scenes around Argenteuil, a village on the Seine a few miles downstream of Paris, where he lived between 1872 and 1878. The handling and coloring of these paintings varies greatly in response to the varied natural scenes he had in front of him. By 1873, his technique had become a type of representational shorthand, so adaptable that he could convey the most diverse effects of weather and light. One example of these preoccupations is the rapidly executed *Impression: Sunrise* (Musée Marmottan, Paris), whose title gave the Impressionists their name when it was included in their first group exhibition in 1874. However, canvases as summary as this were not the principal focus of Monet's work at the time. Alongside this painting, which he titled *Impression* to indicate that it was only a sketch, Monet also exhibited more highly finished pictures, such as *Boulevard des Capucines* (State Pushkin Museum of Fine Arts, Moscow).

He kept to the same pattern in the group exhibitions later in the 1870s, including the occasional rapid notation of nature, but only side by side with more fully worked canvases. He wanted his audience

Claude Monet: The Seine at Lavacourt; oil on canvas; 98×149cm (39×59in); 1880. Dallas Museum of Fine Arts

to witness the directness of his response to nature, but also to see how he transformed this into more complete works of art. He even continued to punctuate his exhibits with large pictures of a type suitable for the Salon exhibitions, such as *La Japonaise* of 1876 (Museum of Fine Arts, Boston). Though sketches such as *Impression: Sunrise* gave Impressionism its public reputation, and Monet was prepared to sell his less-finished paintings when short of money, his art in the 1870s can only be fully understood when these are seen beside his more fully completed statements.

During the 1870s, Monet's fluent and varied brushwork was accompanied by an increasingly bold use of color. In his sunlit scenes of the 1860s, such as *Terrace at Sainte-Adresse*, he had begun to introduce color into areas of shadow—generally soft blues; the lessons of Eugène Delacroix's coloration were important for this development. In the following decade, he came to use nuances of color with increasing subtlety to suggest light effects. In some sunlit scenes, such as *Autumn at Argenteuil* (1873; Courtauld Institute Galleries, London), the contrast between dark and light tones is almost entirely abandoned in

favor of a rich play of varied high-key colors which suggest the forms in the picture. Even in overcast scenes that retain strong tonal contrasts, such as *Men Unloading Coal* (c1875; private collection), he used soft touches of varied color to convey atmosphere. This development—towards the suggestion of forms by the use of variations and contrasts of color rather than by tonal modeling—was at the center of the Impressionists' ideas on color.

Monet's subject matter remained essentially modern and man-made throughout the 1870s. Sometimes, as in *Men Unloading Coal* and in his paintings of the Gare

Claude Monet: The Port of Zaandam; oil on canvas; 47×74cm (19×29in); 1871. Private collection

Saint-Lazare of 1877, his subjects overtly reflected industry and mechanization. More often, they showed life at Argenteuil: originally a country village, Argenteuil was becoming industrialized at the time, and was also a center for sailing and rowing, fashionable pastimes of the day.

The pattern of Monet's life, and his choice of subject matter, changed in the 1880s. He moved away from the Paris area, further down the Seine Valley, finally settling in 1883 at Giverny where he spent the rest of his life. At the same time, he took less part in the Impressionists' group exhibitions, apparently feeling that their notoriety had harmed his commercial prospects. From 1881 onwards he had, for the first time, a regular if not wholly secure source of income from sales to dealers—at first mainly to Paul Durand-Ruel.

Monet traveled widely in the 1880s seeking dramatic natural subjects and extreme effects of weather and light. He painted the cliffs of Normandy, the Atlantic storms on the island of Belle-Isle off Brittany, the rocky hills of the Massif Central, and the luminous atmosphere of the Mediterranean coast. Instead of the horizontality that dominates his pictures of the Seine Valley, he often adopted high viewpoints, and chose subjects with dramatic contrasts of scale and jumps in space. In paintings such as *Varengeville Church* (1882; Barber Institute of Fine Arts, Birmingham, England) the off-center composition and silhouetted trees have close parallels in Japanese color prints, of which Monet was an avid collector. However, their influence on him was not a matter of direct imitation: their example helped him to select viewpoints for his landscapes which revealed the full drama of his subjects.

Varengeville Church also shows a richer and more elaborate color scheme than his previous work. Even the shadows are rich in color, and the whole painting is based on an opposition of oranges and pinks against greens and blues. His later experience of working beside the Mediterranean in 1884 and 1888 showed him further possibilities of using color harmonies as a means of expressing light and atmosphere; in the South, he favored high-key contrasts of rose and blue, as seen in *The Corniche de Monaco* of 1884 (Stedelijk Museum, Amsterdam).

Equally, in the 1880s his brushwork became more elaborate. In the 1870s it had varied greatly from part to part of the same picture; but in the 1880s he came to link whole paintings together by recurrent rhythms, as in *Storm on Belle-Isle* (1886; Musée du Jeu de Paume, Paris) in which sweeping brush strokes convey the violence of the storm and at the same time create a rich surface pattern in the picture.

During this period, Monet came increasingly to rework his paintings in the studio. In part, this was for practical reasons. As his eye became more and more sensitive to minute changes in natural effects, he could spend less time on a picture before the effect he was painting was compromised by changes in the lighting; so he was forced to paint in the studio in order to finish any work at all. However, he came to see a more positive value in studio work, realizing that he could better judge his paintings away from their subject. He could thus more easily add those final touches that recreated nature's effects in pictorial terms—not by direct imitation of individual forms, but by emphasizing unifying effects of color and pattern on the picture surface.

Studio work became still more important after 1890, when he embarked on a succession of series of paintings of single subjects in different lightings. The first of these was the group of 15 paintings of haystacks exhibited in 1891 (three in the Art Institute of Chicago; two in the Museum of Fine Arts, Boston; one each in the Musée du Jeu de Paume, Paris, National Gallery of Scotland, Edinburgh, Metropolitan Museum, New York). In their rich color harmonies, these continue his work of the 1880s, but in two ways they are very different: in their subjects, and in the way they were exhibited. In place of his dramatic scenes of the 1880s, the *Haystacks* are a wholly unpicturesque subject, seen near his home; the prime focus is on their atmospheric effects. They were exhibited together as a unit, gaining, Monet said, "their full value only by the comparison and the succession of the whole series". Previously, Monet had deliberately included diverse paintings in his exhibitions, to show the range of his work.

In later series, such as that of *Rouen Cathedral* (1892–4; five in the Musée du Jeu de Paume, Paris), Monet's color schemes became still more elaborate, and only distantly related to the initial effect of light on the cathedral's stone facade. The encrusted colored surfaces of these paintings, no longer animated by the dynamic brushwork that Monet had used during the 1880s, evoke the harmonizing effect of sunlight, but also bear witness to long periods of work in the studio.

After 1900, Monet focused on a new subject, one that bridged the gap between art and nature—the elaborate water garden, with trees and water lilies, that he had built near his house at Giverny. He painted it first in series of individual canvases, and then, after 1914, embarked on a long-held plan to make the pond the subject for a continuous decoration to run around a room. This project was finally realized in the two oval rooms of Water Lily decorations, installed after Monet's death in the Orangerie in Paris according to his precise instructions. The large canvases which make them up, over 6 ft high (approximately 2 m), were painted in a studio, but developed from outdoor studies. They form a continuous frieze of water, without horizon, and cut by occasional trees. The water surfaces are punctuated by lily pads and by the reflections of trees and sky beyond. To suit their scale, Monet enlarged his brush stroke.

The lilies are conveyed by bold calligraphic strokes which, seen from close to, float freely across the picture surface. From a distance, though, all become part of the continuous effect of light and atmosphere, which is enhanced by their unified color scheme, dominantly in soft greens and blues. Other versions of his Water-Lily paintings and many canvases may be seen in the Musée Marmottan in Paris. More *Water Lilies* are in the National Gallery, London.

Even at the end of his life, Monet's basic aim remained, as he described it in 1926, to "render my impressions in front of the most fleeting effects"—a phrase he could equally have used 50 years earlier. His development as an artist lay in his evolving ways of realizing this aim—from his direct sketches of nature of the 1870s, through a gradual process of elaboration and interpretation, to the rich color harmonies and densely worked surfaces of his later paintings. In these, he found a way of going beyond his immediate experience of nature, of recreating visual experience in purely pictorial terms.

Further reading. *Hommage à Claude Monet*, Paris (1980). Isaacson, J. *Claude Monet, Observation and Reflection*, Oxford (1978). Levine, S.Z., *Monet and his Critics*, New York and London (1976). Petrie, B. *Claude Monet, The First of the Impressionists*, Oxford (1979). Rewald, J. *History of Impressionism*, London and New York (1973). Spate, V. *Claude Monet, Life and Work*, New York (1992). Wildenstein, D. *Claude Monet, Biographie et Catalogue Raisonné* (3 vols.), Lausanne and Paris (vol. I, 1974; vols. II and III, 1979).

Montañés Juan 1568–1649

The Spanish sculptor Juan Martínez Montañés was born at Alcalá la Real (Jaen). At the age of 14 he went to Seville, where he was to be based for the rest of his life, becoming the head of the school of sculpture at Seville. Probably initially a pupil of Juan-Bautista Vázquez the Elder, he worked for a short time (1598–1602) in Granada with Pablo de Rojas, whose pupil he claimed to be. Returning to Seville, he set up his own workshop, which soon became the busiest and most important in Andalusia. It is only from 1603, when he was aged 35, that his own distinct artistic personality began to emerge. Known in his

day as the "God of Woodcarving", Montañés enjoyed a reputation that has never been eclipsed in Spain.

To the powerful realism of Andalusian sculpture he united a classical sense of composition. His sculpture, always in wood, was in many cases painted by the erudite painter Francisco Pacheco, the master of Velázquez. In 1635 Montañés was invited to Court by Velázquez to model the bust of Philip IV for the great bronze equestrian statue to be cast in Italy by Tacca. Velázquez' portrait of him (Prado, Madrid) dates from this time. His output, some of which was exported to Spanish America, was vast. His major works are in and around Seville; they include his great masterpiece, the high altar in S. Isidoro del Campo, Santiponce.

Monticelli Adolphe 1824–96

Adolphe Joseph Thomas Monticelli was a French painter. Born in Marseilles, he is sometimes classed with Cézanne and Daumier as a purveyor of a Provençal style. He worked in Paris between 1856 and 1870, when he achieved some kind of recognition for subjects drawn from Boccaccio and from the 18th-century French tradition of *fêtes galantes*, as seen in the works of Watteau. Monticelli's versions, however, were painted in a strongly handled, often violent, occasionally high-colored manner, partly influenced by Delacroix and Diaz. He also produced portraits and still lifes in the same style. He died, allegedly, of alcoholism. Van Gogh greatly admired his paintings, often producing works as a gesture of homage to Monticelli.

Moore Albert 1841–93

Albert Joseph Moore was an English painter of decorative color harmonies, born at York. He first painted biblical works (for example, *Elijah's Sacrifice*, 1863; Art Gallery and Museum, Bury) and architectural decorative schemes. In the mid 1860s he began to merge the decorative aesthetic into his easel paintings, using classically-draped women in various postures as the basis of his compositions. Without ostensible subject-matter they were used simply to portray elaborately worked-out color schemes (for example, *Apricots*, 1866; Public Library, Fulham, London). Much admired by the Aesthetic Movement, this type of draped female figure scarcely

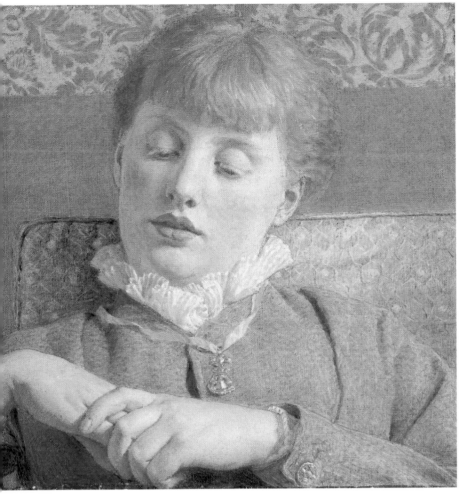

Albert Moore: Portrait of a Girl; oil on canvas; 25×25cm (10×10in). Private collection

changed during Moore's remaining career, featuring both in major compositions (such as *Reading Aloud*, 1884; Art Gallery and Museum, Glasgow), and in simpler works (for example, *Birds*, 1878; City of Birmingham Museums and Art Gallery).

Moore Henry 1898–1986

Henry Moore, long considered England's greatest sculptor, was largely responsible for the gradual emergence of British art from provincialism into the mainstream of modern art. Ironically it was during the 1930s, when Moore's work was so violently attacked in the press, that he and his contemporaries Ben Nicholson and Barbara Hepworth were laying the foundations of modern art in England. By 1946, with his first major retrospective exhibition at the Museum of Modern Art, New York, the art of sculpture in England was fully established, and Moore had become one of the most admired and influential sculptors in the world.

Born in Castleford, Yorkshire, the seventh child of a miner, Henry Moore by the age of 10 or 11 had decided that he wanted to become a sculptor. He received

his first lessons in drawing at the Castleford Grammar School from the art mistress, Alice Gostick, whose support and encouragement meant a great deal to him. After serving two years in the Army, Moore was awarded an ex-serviceman's grant to the Leeds School of Art, and enrolled in the two-year course in September 1919. He was joined there in 1920 by Barbara Hepworth, who became a friend and close associate during the next 20 years. While at Leeds he met Sir Michael Sadler, whose remarkable collection included paintings by Cézanne, Gauguin, and Matisse, the first examples of modern art that Moore saw. At the time he read Roger Fry's *Vision and Design* and was particularly influenced by the chapters on "Ancient American Art" and "Negro Sculpture".

In 1921 Moore began the three-year diploma course at the Royal College of Art in London. A conflict soon developed between the academic course-work and his desire to follow his own direction in sculpture, based on knowledge gained from numerous visits to the British Museum. There he studied sculpture of many periods: prehistoric, Egyptian, Assyrian,

Sumerian, Archaic Greek, African, and Oceanic; but he was most attracted to Mexican art, which was to become the major influence on his work during the 1920s. He managed a compromise, drawing and modeling from life during term time, with evenings and holidays free to pursue his own interests.

In 1922, on the first of many trips to Paris, he saw the Pellerin Collection, which included Cézanne's *Grandes Baigneuses* (now in the Philadelphia Museum of Art). He has written: "Seeing that picture, for me, was like seeing Chartres Cathedral. It was one of the big impacts." In 1924 he was awarded a traveling scholarship, and was also appointed instructor in sculpture at the Royal College of Art for a period of seven years. He left for France and Italy in January 1925. He greatly admired the monumentality of the Masaccio frescoes in the Brancacci Chapel, S. Maria del Carmine, Florence.

On his return to London in the summer of 1925 he completed the Hornton stone *Mother and Child* of 1924–5 (City of Manchester Art Gallery). Almost all his sculptures between 1921 and 1939 were carvings. Like Modigliani, Gaudier-Brzeska, Brancusi, Epstein, and Hepworth, Moore was interested in direct carving; he believed in the doctrine of truth to materials, of understanding and being in sympathy with the qualities of wood or stone. In the Manchester carving, the forms have not been freed from the material, and remain somewhat buried in the blockiness of the stone. The carving is, like the kind of sculpture Moore most admires, "not perfectly symmetrical, it is static and it is strong and vital, giving off something of the energy and power of great mountains." Unlike Hepworth, for example, Moore is not concerned with an ideal, classical beauty and purity. He aims at the power of expression, giving his sculpture a pent-up energy, a life of its own.

Moore's first one-man exhibition was held at Warren Gallery, London, in 1928. That same year he received his first public commission, a relief entitled *North Wind* for the new London Passenger Transport Board headquarters.

Reclining Figure of 1929 (Leeds City Art Gallery), undoubtedly Moore's most important sculpture of the 1920s, was the first work to reflect the tremendous influence of the Mexican Chac Mool reclining figure. Although the Leeds carving has the same massiveness and weight that he admired in the Mexican prototype and the alert, mask-like head turned at right angles to the body, the reclining pose is quite different. The figure rests on its side, with the left arm raised behind the head, and the left leg looming above the right one. In the reclining figure Moore had found a subject that allowed him to experiment with new formal ideas, to explore infinite variations on a single theme. By the late 1920s the mother-and-child theme and the reclining figure had become the two principal obsessions in Moore's work.

In 1929 Moore married Irina Radetsky, a student at the Royal College of Art School of Painting. They moved to Parkhill Road, Hampstead, London, where they lived until 1940. The first of two country cottages in Kent, for use during vacations, was bought in 1931.

The enigmatic carved *Composition* of 1931 marked a radical new departure that allied Moore's work to the biomorphic abstractions current in the work of Arp, Miró, Tanguy, and above all Picasso. The sculpture and drawings Picasso created during the late 1920s exerted a direct influence on Moore's sculpture and drawings of the early 1930s. Like Hepworth and Nicholson, Moore visited the Paris studios of Picasso, Braque, and Brancusi. *Composition* illustrates how quickly and intuitively Moore had assimilated the visual imagery of Picasso's work.

In 1932 he established the Department of Sculpture at the Chelsea School of Art. The following year he was elected a member of "Unit One". The first of his two-, three-, and four-piece compositions appeared in 1934 and are related to the work of Arp and Giacometti. He often used the Surrealist idiom of the found object, and made several carvings using ironstone pebbles. In 1932, he did a series of drawings of bones and shells, transforming shapes in nature into human forms. In the multipart sculptures of 1934 the human body was divided into fragments and reassembled. It was not until the late 1950s and 1960s that he returned to the two- and three-piece figure theme.

Moore's square-form carvings of 1935 and 1937, among his most abstract works, reflect the influence of Ben Nicholson's reliefs of the period. During these years, when he was living in Hampstead near Hepworth, Nicholson, and the critic Herbert Read, there was a fruitful exchange of ideas among these artists with broadly similar aims. Moore's work never became

totally Abstract; there is always some reference to human or organic forms. He participated in the "International Surrealist Exhibition" in London in 1936, and in the following year contributed to *Circle: International Survey of Constructive Art*.

The idea of the reclining female figure as a metaphor for landscape first appeared in the *Reclining Figure* of 1929 (City Art Gallery, Leeds) and then in the *Reclining Woman* of 1930 (National Gallery of Canada, Ottawa). The landscape idiom, in which breast and knees are like hills or mountains, and holes like caves in a hillside, is beautifully resolved in *Recumbent Figure* of 1938 (Tate Gallery, London). The gently rising and falling rhythms echo the Sussex Downs, where the sculpture was originally sited.

From 1937 to 1939 Moore executed a series of stringed figure-drawings and sculptures, a brief interlude in his work. His first "helmet sculpture" appeared in 1939–40.

Between 1921 and the mid 1950s the genesis for almost all Moore's sculptures is to be found in the sketchbooks and larger drawings. The drawings for sculpture were a means of generating ideas for sculpture, of recording the overflow of ideas too numerous to explore directly in wood or stone.

In September 1940 Moore began work on his shelter drawings, scenes of Londoners sheltering from the Blitz in the London Underground stations. The following month his Hampstead studio was badly damaged by a bomb, and the Moores moved to a 17th-century farmhouse at Much Hadham, 30 miles north of London. As a war artist, he spent the next year working on the shelter drawings. He visited the shelters once or twice a week, and did the drawings from memory on his return home. In 1942 he did a series of drawings of miners at work at the coalface.

The *Madonna and Child* of 1943–4, commissioned for the Church of St Matthew, Northampton, reflects the influence of the shelter drawings in the use of drapery and in the humanist emphasis. The Mediterranean tradition, which on his Italian trip in 1925 had been in conflict with his interest in primitive art, had come once more to the surface.

In 1946, the year of his first retrospective at the Museum of Modern Art, New York, his daughter Mary was born. Two years later he won the International Sculpture Prize at the 24th Venice Biennale. His first

retrospective at the Tate Gallery was held in 1951. Moore's worldwide reputation was now firmly established.

During the 1950s the two most important commissions were for a screen for the facade and the bronze *Draped Reclining Figure* (1952–3) for the new Time-Life Building in London, and the large Roman travertine marble *Reclining Figure* (1957–8) for UNESCO headquarters in Paris.

Although Moore's interest in carving continued throughout his life, many of his best-known postwar sculptures—such as *Family Group* (1948–9; Museum of Modern Art, New York), *King and Queen* (1952–3; Joseph Hirshhorn Museum and Sculpture Garden, Smithsonian Institution, Washington, D.C.), *Warrior with Shield* (1953–4; Art Gallery of Ontario, Toronto), *Reclining Figure* (1963–5; Lincoln Center, New York), and *Nuclear Energy* (1964–6; University of Chicago)—were made in plaster and cast in bronze. A fine collection of the plasters can be seen in the Art Gallery of Ontario, Toronto.

Among the most impressive sculptures of the past two decades are the two- and three-piece reclining figures of 1959–62 (examples can be seen in the Albright-Knox Art Gallery, Buffalo; the Museum of Modern Art, New York; etc). The landscape metaphor, a source of Moore's inspiration since the late 1920s, is reversed: the sculptures are more landscape than human. Fragmentary elements of a rugged landscape of rocks, cliffs, and caves become the female figure.

By the mid 1950s, as his sculpture was becoming more three-dimensional, having an organic completeness from every point of view, drawing no longer served as a way of developing ideas for sculpture. The point of departure for most of his subsequent sculpture has been the bones, shells, and flint stones that abound in the maquette studio at Much Hadham.

After 1968 Moore showed a renewed interest in drawing as an activity independent of sculpture, and in printmaking, and produced more than 260 lithographs and etchings, including the *Elephant Skull, Auden, Stonehenge*, and *Sheep* portfolios.

The major retrospective at the Tate Gallery in 1968 was followed in 1972 by the magnificent exhibition at the Forte di Belvedere in Florence. Many large bronzes and fiberglass casts were placed on the terraces; the architecture of Florence and the hills beyond made this one of the most splendid sites in the world to exhibit

Henry Moore: Reclining Figure; plaster; 105×227×89cm (42×90×35in); 1951. Tate Gallery, London

sculpture on the enormous scale of Moore's late work. October 1974 saw the opening of the Henry Moore Sculpture Center in Toronto; the Center houses Moore's gift to the Art Gallery of Ontario of more than 500 original plasters, bronzes, drawings, and prints.

Moore continued to work for most of the year in Much Hadham, and spent a month or two each summer in Italy, carving at the Querceta marble works of Messrs Henraux. From his small house nearby at Forte dei Marmi he could see the Carrara Mountains where Michelangelo is said to have selected large blocks of marble for his carvings.

The essential humanism of Moore's art has been nourished by sources as disparate as Paleolithic sculpture and the work of Picasso. With the human figure as the central subject of his work, he used elements of landscape, the shapes of bones, shells, and pebbles to enlarge the three-dimensional language of sculpture. Henry Moore takes his rightful place among the greatest sculptors in Western art, having built on and extended the tradition to which his work belongs.

Further reading. Bowness, A. (ed.) *Henry Moore, Sculpture and Drawings 1949–1954*, London (1965). Bowness, A. (ed.) *Henry Moore, Sculpture 1955–1964*, London (1965). Clark, K. *Henry Moore, Drawings*, London (1964). Cramer, G., Grant, A., and Mitchinson, D. *Henry Moore, the Graphic Work 1931–1972*, Geneva (1973). Cramer, G., Grant, A., and Mitchinson, D. *Henry Moore, the Graphic Work 1973–1975*, Geneva (1976). Hall, D. *Henry Moore, the Life and Work of a Great Sculptor*, London (1966). Hedgecoe, J. (ed.) *Henry Moore*, London (1968). James, P. (ed.) *Henry Moore on Sculpture*, London (1966). Melville, R. *Henry Moore, Sculpture and Drawings 1921–1969*, London (1970). Read, H. *Henry Moore*, London (1965). Read, H. *Henry Moore Sculptor*, London (1934). Russell, J. *Henry Moore*, London (1968). Seldis, H. *Henry Moore in America*, New York (1973). Sweeney, J.J. *Henry Moore*, New York (1946). Sylvester, D. *Henry Moore*, London (1968). Sylvester, D. (ed.) *Henry Moore, Sculpture and Drawings 1921–1948*, London (1957). Wilkinson, A.G. *The Henry Moore Sculpture Centre*, Toronto (1974).

Mor van Dashorst Anthonis
*c*1517–76/7

Born at Utrecht, the Netherlandish painter Anthonis Mor van Dashorst was probably a pupil of Jan van Scorel. He joined the Antwerp guild in 1547, but worked mainly as a portrait-painter at several European courts, and visited Rome from 1550 to 1551. His portraits combine the elegance of the three-quarter length form, influenced by Italian art, with the minute description of surface texture common to Northern painting. This is best seen in his portraits of *The Duke of Alba* (1549; Hispanic Society, New York) and of *Mary Tudor* (1554; Prado, Madrid); the latter was painted on the occasion of the English Queen's marriage to Philip of Spain.

Morales Luis de c1520–86

The Spanish painter Luis de Morales was probably born at Badajoz. It is not known with certainty whether he ever traveled outside his native region of Extremadura, but Morales undoubtedly absorbed a strong influence from Flemish painting, particularly from the work of Quentin Massys, and also from Leonardo da Vinci, perhaps via Flanders.

Often known as *El Divino* because of the predominance of religious subjects in his work, Morales frequently painted Passion scenes, especially *Ecce Homo*, *Pietà*, and *Christ at the Column*. He also painted many Madonnas (for example, *Virgin and Child*, National Gallery, London) in a highly finished, smooth style, with little variation or development throughout his career. Among Church patrons in Extremadura and neighboring Portugal, his success was considerable.

Morandi Giorgio 1890–1964

Giorgio Morandi was an Italian painter and etcher. His paintings of 1918 to 1920 were influenced by the metaphysical painting of Carlo Carrà. They depict precisely delineated groups of objects, their metaphysical element arising out of an extreme formalization combined with visual paradox. His career after 1920 was marked by the intensity he applied to the still life. He achieved an extraordinary monumentality within a small scale, by means of the idealization of simple objects, using light to make an abstraction of their shapes without recourse to distortion. The unswerving path followed by Morandi reflects his isolation from the contemporary art world. He spent all his life near Bologna, travelling seldom, and never leaving his native Italy.

Moreau Gustave 1826–98

Born the son of an architect in Paris, Gustave Moreau became an eminently successful painter. He was an influential figure in the move away from Realist attitudes that occurred in the 1880s, and showed himself sympathetic to originality, as a teacher at the École des Beaux-Arts in Paris. He had studied there himself as a young man under Picot; Théodore Chassé-

Giorgio Morandi: Still Life; oil on canvas; 30×35cm (12×14in); 1942. Private collection

riau, with whom Moreau became friendly, and Eugène Delacroix, were also important formative influences upon him, as the painterliness of his mature style suggests. His exhibits at the Salons of 1852 and 1853 reflected his respect for the imaginative force of their work.

No hint of Courbet's Realist school is evident in Moreau. He returns in contrast to erudite antique themes, rich in narrative and emotional expression, echoing and even quoting directly from the Italian Renaissance painters he admired. Moreau studied in Rome between 1857 and 1859, painting landscapes and copying works by

Gustave Moreau: The Unicorns; oil on canvas; 115×90cm (45×35in); c1885. Musée Gustave Moreau, Paris

Anthonis Mor van Dashorst: Mary Tudor; detail; oil on canvas; full size 109×84cm (43×33in); 1554. Prado, Madrid

Carpaccio, Mantegna, and Michelangelo. Subsequently many of his paintings were to reveal in addition a debt to Leonardo da Vinci. His circle of friends in Rome included Puvis de Chavannes, Élie Delaunay, and Degas.

Success at the Paris Salon followed, with a sequence of sumptuous paintings on mythological themes. *Oedipus and the Sphinx* (Metropolitan Museum, New York), strongly reminiscent of Ingres' treatment of the subject, was shown at the Salon in 1864. Its success was consolidated in the following year when Moreau exhibited *Jason* (Louvre, Paris). In 1866, Moreau's *Orpheus* (Louvre, Paris) was purchased by the State. He returned to the Salon in the 1870s, reestablishing his reputation as an erudite, original, and talented painter with *Hercules and the Hydra* (1876; Art Institute of Chicago), paintings of *Salomé* and *The Apparition* (one example *c*1876; William Hayes Fogg Art Museum, Cambridge, Mass.), and a tempera painting of *St Sebastian* (1876; William Hayes Fogg Art Museum, Cambridge, Mass.). He exhibited further at the *Exposition Universelle* in Paris in 1878 and for the last time at the Salon in 1880 with *Helen* and *Galatea* (Collection of Robert Lebel, Paris).

As a man of private means, Moreau did not need to court financial success, yet recognition had come through the Salon and had established his reputation. His independence did mean, however, that he could give free rein to his imagination. He was absolved from a need to be either explicit or popular. The densely worked, scratched, glazed, and impasto surfaces of his paintings, their lavish textures and otherworldly subjects, gave vent to an extraordinary imagination, as if his canvases were illumined by a light that was beyond the here and now.

It is curious to consider Moreau's success at the Salon of 1876 in contrast with the emergence of Impressionist painting, particularly in view of his friendship with Degas. Indeed, when the Symbolist movement evolved during the mid 1880s, it was the obsessive, emotive, and suggestive qualities of Moreau's paintings that attracted and excited Symbolist painters and writers. The novelist and critic Joris-Karl Huysmans in *À Rebours*, published in 1884, had described Moreau's shimmering and supernatural *Apparition* among the possessions of Des Esseintes, the central figure of his novel. Together with Redon

Moretto: Portrait of Count Sciarra Martinengo-Cesaresco; oil on canvas; 114×94cm (45×37in); c1516–18. National Gallery, London

and the poet Mallarmé, Moreau was emulated by Symbolists as a precursor of their demands for an art of imagination and ideas, and also as an honorary member of the multifarious Symbolist groups. In 1886, the year that Jean Moréas published his *Symbolist Manifesto*, Gustave Moreau gave his last public exhibition: 65 illustrations to the *Fables* of La Fontaine shown at the Goupil Gallery, Paris.

Moreau had attracted many younger admirers. In the face of growing interest in the depiction of the daily world, he had asserted the effectiveness of erudition in subject matter and of suggestive handling of his paint as vehicles for emotional and imaginative expression. His individuality itself provided an influential and an encouraging example. When Moreau's friend Élie Delaunay died in 1891, Moreau assumed his teaching atelier at the École des Beaux-Arts, Paris (1892–8). His influence upon the individual development of younger painters extended to many later

associated with the Fauves: Matisse, Manguin, Marquet, and Rouault were all pupils at the Beaux-Arts under Moreau. Rouault became the Keeper of the Musée Gustave Moreau in Paris where Moreau's studio and many of his works are still preserved. The studio became in due course a place for pilgrimage for the Surrealists, as it had been earlier for Symbolists.

Further reading. *French Symbolist Painters, Moreau, Puvis de Chavannes, Redon and their Followers*, London (1972). Mathieu, P.-L. *Gustave Moreau*, Oxford (1977). Paladilhe, J. *Gustave Moreau*, Paris (1971).

Moretto c1498–1554

Alessandro Bonvicino, known as Moretto, was a Brescian painter whose style, more eclectic than that of his slightly older contemporary Romanino, shows evident

Central Italian influences, particularly from Raphael; these reached him through the engravings of Marc Antonio Raimondi and others. His elevated, monumental style has hard outlines and clear sharp forms, which give to his figures some of the qualities of sculpture. Although, on occasion, he uses deep chiaroscuro and painterly effects of texture, his works are always more conceptualized than those of Romanino or the Venetians, and further away from visual experience. He lacks entirely the earthy realism of Romanino, and the factual detail always characteristic of Brescian painters sometimes sits rather oddly on his idealized forms.

Moretto's most individual quality is a personal range of low, muted color, often dominated by a gray-violet, which more than anything else sets the key of contemplative melancholy typical of his work. His art shows considerable development. A first phase may be seen in the varied canvases he painted alongside Romanino for the Chapel of the Sacrament in S. Giovanni Evangelista, Brescia. Roman, Venetian, Flemish, and Brescian elements mingle and contrast in the different subjects, while in the *Coronation of the Virgin* from SS. Nazaro e Celso, one of his numerous altarpieces for Brescian churches, he combines a more specifically Romanist vein with Correggesque sentiment and silvery color.

In Moretto's work the coldness of the color, while emphasizing the still detachment of his figures, often seems at variance with the sentimental ardor of their expressions. This tension is not really resolved even when, as in many of his later works, he adopted a more Venetian chiaroscuro. To this later period belongs his elegaic *Crucified Christ with a Mourning Angel* in the Pinacoteca Civica "Tosio Martinengo", Brescia, which shows him at his most painterly.

Moretto also practiced as a portrait-painter. His lovesick member of the Martinengo-Cesaresco family in the National Gallery, London, is in a sense, halfway between Titian and Holbein. The generalized poetic mood, characteristic of so many Giorgionesque portraits of young men, is given an emotional context as specific as the veristically painted details of costume and accoutrements. Also in the National Gallery is a swagger, full-length portrait of a Brescian nobleman, which is dated 1526 and is therefore the first full-length portrait known to have been

Berthe Morisot: In the Dining Room; oil on canvas; 62×50cm (24×20in); 1886. National Gallery of Art, Washington, D.C.

painted in Italy. The full-length portrait seems to have originated in Germany, and the type may have reached Moretto from the north. Certainly his portraiture shows a fusion between Italian idealization and Northern verism, typical of Brescian painting as a whole.

Morikage Kuzumi *fl. c1680*

The Japanese painter Kuzumi Morikage was the most independent of the pupils of Kano Tan'yu. He is said to have been expelled from Tan'yu's studio for lack of orthodoxy. Little of his life is known, but many of his works are concentrated in the Kanazawa area where he probably worked for the Maeda family. He was mainly an ink painter, though he used pale color washes with great charm, specializing in powerful, economical sketches of people, animals, and birds and in larger-scale misty landscapes peopled with real farmers and peasants. Of these, his masterpieces are the sixfold screens of agricultural scenes in the Ishikawa Prefectural Art Museum, Kanazawa.

Morisot Berthe 1841–95

The French painter Berthe Marie Pauline Morisot was taught by Corot in the early

George Morland: Ferreting; oil on canvas; 29×38cm (11×15in); 1792. Private collection

1860s. She met Édouard Manet c1868, and married his brother Eugène in 1874. After exhibiting at the Salon in the 1860s, she showed at most of the Impressionists' group exhibitions between 1874 and 1886. From the later 1880s onwards, she gave regular dinners, bringing together painters such as Monet, Renoir, Degas, and Puvis de Chavannes with Mallarmé and other poets and writers. Her painting owes much to Manet in its free, delicate brushwork, and in the 1870s she adopted the light and varied color of Impressionism. Her favorite subjects were garden scenes with figures.

Morland George 1763–1804

George Charles Morland was an English genre painter, the son of a minor artist and art dealer, to whom he was apprenticed before entering the Royal Academy schools in 1784. He set up as a portrait-painter in London in 1785, but soon discovered a more lucrative practice in painting sentimental fancy pictures of the type popularized by Francis Wheatley. About 1790 his interests shifted to rustic and picturesque themes. His best compositions date to the early 1790s and include a variety of farmyard and hunt scenes, coastal views with smugglers, and gypsy en-

campments, to which he was apparently no stranger during the course of his dissolute life. His debt to the 17th-century Dutch landscapists is most evident in his winter landscapes, which are often rich in texture and masterly in design. Morland's promising development was halted by the rapid decline of his health and powers after 1800.

Morone Domenico c1442–c1517

Domenico Morone was a Veronese painter. Many of his works, including fresco cycles, have not survived. The influence of Gentile Bellini is apparent in three of his earliest extant paintings: two *cassone* panels decorated with tournament scenes (*c*1490; National Gallery, London) and *The Fight between the Gonzagas and Buonaccolsi* (1494; Palazzo Ducale, Mantua). Between *c*1498 and 1503 he was engaged on frescoes in S. Bernardino, Verona (Chapel of S. Antonio and Old Library) which are Mantegnesque in style. Domenico was a leading figure in Veronese art of the later Quattrocento. His son Francesco (*c*1471–1529) was also a painter.

Moroni Giambattista *c*1525–78

Moroni was an Italian painter, trained by Moretto, who worked both in Brescia and in his native city of Bergamo. While he painted numerous monumental altarpieces in the manner of his master, he is most individual and important as a portrait-painter. Although he was influenced by Lotto as well as Moretto, his portraits are less romantic than theirs: his approach to character is more detached, and his treatment of costume and accoutrements dryly realistic.

The elegance of his portraits (particularly the emphasis on the silhouette) allies him to central Italian Mannerist court portraiture, for example to Bronzino. But the low-keyed color and the precise detail are typically Brescian, evoking a sense of reality, objectively observed and coolly apprehended, that at its best anticipates Velázquez.

Moroni's portraits cover an unusually wide social range for the period, and some of the best of them, for example *The Tailor* (National Gallery, London) are of plebeian or middle-class sitters.

Domenico Morone: detail of the frescoes in the Old Library, S. Bernardino, Verona, Lionello Sagramoso Presented to the Virgin by St Francis; c1498–1503

Moronobu Hishikawa *c*1625–*c*94

The Japanese artist Hishikawa Moronobu stabilized the *Ukiyoe* School. He was born near Edo (Tokyo), was the son of a textile-designer, and his work always showed an interest in fashion and fabrics. Some of his over 100 printed books are in fact pattern-books, but in others he established the picture-book of the gay world of Edo as an important genre. These, like his sheet prints, were in ink monochrome, brilliantly exploiting the lustrous Japanese ink and

Left: Hishikawa Moronobu: A Riverboat Party; color woodblock print; 19×17cm (7½×6½in); 1683. British Museum, London

Giambattista Moroni: Portrait of a Man ("The Tailor"); oil on canvas; 97×74cm (39×30in); c1571. National Gallery, London

receptive paper. He was also a fine painter, giving the Edo *Ukiyoe* movement a distinctive style of restrained modishness. His best works are the handscroll of Yoshiwara scenes (Tokyo National Museum), and his sixfold screens of Edo life (Freer Gallery of Art, Washington, D.C.).

Morris Robert 1931–

The American sculptor Robert Morris was born in Kansas City. He first studied engineering at the University of Kansas City, and then art at Kansas City Art Institute (1948–50), California School of Fine Arts (1951), and Reed College, Oregon (1953–5). He later studied art history at Hunter College, New York (1962–3).

Morris was initially a painter. From his first sculptures in 1961, the great variety of his sculptural modes allies him closely with Conceptual art. From 1964 to 1966 he made simple, minimal geometric structures in wood, fiberglass, and metal, devoid of formal expressive qualities. These were followed by randomly placed felt wall and floor sculptures, mixed media "scatter" pieces, and process works involving natural phenomena, such as growth and steam. In 1970 he began to make environmental sculptures in timber and concrete, and earthworks. His concern for active involvement with art-making is manifested in his choreography, performances, films, participation pieces, and writings.

Morris William 1834–96

The English artist William Morris was born in Walthamstow into a wealthy family; he enjoyed a private income from the time he came of age. As a child, riding in Epping Forest, he began to develop his lifelong love of the English countryside, together with the habit of imagining what it was like in the Middle Ages. In 1853 he went up to Oxford intending to enter the Church, but he found himself increasingly attracted to the architecture, literature, and life of the medieval past. At Oxford he met Edward Jones (later Sir Edward Burne-Jones) and together they studied illuminated manuscripts, Dürer prints, and brass rubbings, and read ancient and modern authors such as Chaucer, Malory, Scott, La Motte-Fouqué, Carlyle, Kingsley, and Ruskin.

In 1855, on his second visit to the cathedrals of northern France, Morris decided to become an architect and for a short time worked in the office of G.E. Street. But early in 1856 he met the Pre-Raphaelites' leader D.G. Rossetti, and was persuaded to become a painter. Rossetti was in turn impressed by Morris' poems and stories, which appeared throughout 1856 in the *Oxford and Cambridge Magazine*. These works and the poems published in his first book *The Defence of Guenevere* (1858), dedicated to Rossetti, strongly convey Morris' intense awareness of the vitality, landscape, pattern, and color of the Middle Ages but also his awareness of the period's brutality.

Rossetti involved Morris in painting the Oxford Union in 1857, and partly through this work Morris realized that his genius lay in pattern design. His fondness for the Middle Ages and his hatred of industrialization led him to recreate the spirit of the past. In 1856 he had massive medieval furniture built for his rooms in London. Four years later, after his marriage to Jane Burden, he moved into Red House, Bexleyheath, designed for him by his friend Philip Webb. This was a simple red brick house, Gothic in style; Morris furnished it with furniture painted by himself and his friends, embroidered hangings, stained glass, and wall paintings, so that it became a richly colored medieval palace of art.

Morris' experience at Red House led him and his friends to set up the firm Morris, Marshall, Faulkner and Company in 1861. With Rossetti, Madox Brown, Jones, Arthur Hughes, and other painters working for it, this firm showed how the rift between the "fine arts" and the "minor arts" could be healed. At the International Exhibition in 1862 they showed painted furniture and stained glass. Stained glass was to provide much of the firm's income and Morris himself was responsible for a few complete cartoons (in the early days), the foliage backgrounds to many figures drawn by the other artists, and always for the coloring.

He also designed wallpapers, at first (c1862–4) simple, naively naturalistic ones such as *Daisy*; and then, from the early 1870s, papers such as *Jasmine*, full of growth, controlled depth, and a suggestion of mysterious abundance. In deliberate opposition to the theories of the South Kensington School of Design, Morris wanted his designs to provide a substitute for nature, with familiar plants and believable patterns of growth. He also designed chintzes (from 1873), carpets (from 1878), tapestries (from 1879), and embroideries, always taking great care to use natural processes and often reviving forgotten methods such as dyeing with vegetable dyes. Because of the time and skill needed to execute his designs the firm's work was always expensive, but in the 1870s and early 1880s it was taken up by the Aesthetic Movement and sold well.

Morris continued to write poetry, publishing *The Life and Death of Jason* (1867), *The Earthly Paradise* (1868–70), and *Sigurd the Volsung* (1876), perhaps his finest poem. With the help of E. Magnusson, whom he met in 1868, he translated Icelandic sagas and in 1871 and 1873 made visits to Iceland, which impressed him deeply. He had in 1871 leased Kelmscott Manor on the Upper Thames; from about this time, vernacular buildings made from local materials by local craftsmen began to interest him as much as, if not more than, the famous monuments. In 1877 he was instrumental in founding the "Society for the Protection of Ancient Buildings": an attempt to prevent the overzealous restoration of historic buildings that often destroyed their surface, and with it, the hand of the original craftsman.

At the same time, and with the growing realization that art and society were indivisible, Morris began to play an active role in politics and the tackling of social problems. Ruskin's belief (expressed in the chapter "The Nature of Gothic" in *The Stones of Venice*), that the division of labor in industry prevented the workers from using their imagination and enjoying their work, formed the keystone of Morris' thinking. With its "profit mongering", the capitalist system had killed the practice and appreciation of art except for the privileged few. Morris, like Ruskin, believed that "Art is Man's Expression of his Joy in Labour".

In January 1883 Morris joined the Social Democratic Federation, and in the following year formed his own Socialist League. He continued to play an active part in this until 1890, editing and financing its paper *The Commonweal*, and lecturing up and down the country to foment discontent among the lower classes, and encourage an educated, directed revolution.

William Morris: Queen Guinevere; oil on canvas; 71×51cm (28×20in); 1858. Tate Gallery, London

Shortly before anarchist domination of the League forced him to withdraw and establish the Hammersmith Socialist Society, Morris published his utopian socialist novel *News from Nowhere* in *The Commonweal* (1890). Here he clearly expresses his hope for the future, when the English population would have left the large towns for small holdings in the revivified countryside; men and women would develop freely in beautiful surroundings, enjoying varied manual and intellectual work, and producing unconsciously, in everything they did, beautiful works of art. From 1890 until his death in 1896, Morris put his theories into practice, in the production of fine books at the Kelmscott Press and in his presidency of the Arts and Crafts Exhibition Society. His influence was immense and cannot be overestimated. Followers concerned about the crafts and their place in society included Walter Crane, Arthur Mackmurdo, Ernest Gimson, C.R. Ashbee, Henri van de Velde, and, for a short time, Walter Gropius; while poets like W.B. Yeats and socialists like Clement Attlee also acknowledged their debt to him.

Further reading. Briggs, A. (ed.) *William Morris: Selected Writings and Designs*, London (1962) and New York (1964). Gaunt, W. *The Restless Century*, London (1972). Henderson, P. *William Morris*, New York (1967). Thompson, E.P. *The Work of William Morris*, London (1967).

Moser Lukas *fl. c1431*

The German painter Lukas Moser is known only from the pioneer Magdalene Altar in the parish church of Tiefenbronn near Pforzheim, which he signed and dated in 1431. He is one of the key artists in Germany in the move away from the International Gothic towards a more realistic style. The figures of *Mary Magdalene* and *St Lazarus* on the inside of the wings, represented against patterned gold grounds, display a new monumentality, while the scenes on the outside are represented in naturalistic settings with a wealth of closely observed details. The spatial relationships, nevertheless, remain tentative and unconvincing when compared to the work of the Master of Flémalle (Robert Campin).

Motherwell Robert 1915–91

Robert Burns Motherwell was the youngest of the group of Abstract Expressionist painters in New York in the early 1940s. A student of philosophy and art history, he was a link between the exiled Surrealists in New York and modern American painters. His art, however, fits neither into the expressionist category of Jackson Pollock and Willem de Kooning nor into that of the Color field paintings of Mark Rothko and Barnett Newman. Motherwell's works consist of series of powerful images, often derived from semiautomatic doodlings but subsequently highly controlled, such as *Pancho Villa, Dead and Alive* (gouache and oil with collage on cardboard, 1943; Museum of Modern Art, New York) and his series of *Elegies for the Spanish Republic* (begun in 1947; for example, *Elegy for the Spanish Republic XXIV*, 1953–4; Albright-Knox Art Gallery, Buffalo). His themes and symbols seem to be endlessly expanded, contracted, and juxtaposed until they finally appropriate the entire picture plane.

Further reading. Carmeau, E.A. Jr *The Collages of Robert Motherwell*, Houston,

Robert Motherwell: Je t'aime; oil on canvas; 183×137cm (72×54in); 1955. Sidney Janis Gallery, New York

Tex. (1972). Greenberg, C. "Art", *The Nation* vol. 159, New York (1948). Krauss, R. "Robert Motherwell's New Paintings", *Artforum*, New York (May 1969). Motherwell, R. *Collages 1943–1949*, New York (1949). Raynor, V. "A Talk with Robert Motherwell", *Art News*, New York (April 1974).

Motonobu Kano 1476–1559

The Japanese painter Kano Motonobu was the second master of the *Kano* School, succeeding his father Masanobu as official government artist. He married the daughter of Tosa Mitsunobu, leader of the court painters, and thus started over a century of close cooperation between the schools and mutual influence between their styles. Motonobu studied Zen, but like his father he was a lay adherent of the more popular Amidist Buddhism. He became a freelance decorator-painter, specializing in large-scale compositions over sliding doors and panels in palaces and temples. His vast output has assured the survival of a fair body of his work.

Motonobu's achievement was to devise a genuinely Japanese style suitable for decorative sets of doors while retaining some of the elevated seriousness of the 15th-century monochrome tradition. In his magnificent set of doors from the Daisen'in of the Daitokuji Temple, Kyoto, foreground elements are given great prominence—a huge twisted tree-trunk, a highly stylized waterfall that owes much to *Tosa* style, carefully selected and placed birds. The line is so thick, firm, and varied that it is in itself decorative rather than expressive. Color is used selectively on plants, animals, and birds—not symbolically as in Chinese painting, but solely for visual impact. A landscape background is retained, misty and deep and rather undefined. This series was done before 1513, and is a little lacking in movement, but it remains one of the peaks of Japanese screen painting. His series for the Reiun'in in the same temple, done some 20 years later, is more fluid and assured, especially in its handling of rocks, water, and mist.

Mu Ch'i c1200–70

Little is known of the identity of the painter Mu Ch'i. Although he worked in China, it is sometimes claimed that he was in fact Japanese. However it is known that he was an abbot (sometimes called Fa-

Kano Motonobu: Pheasants and Paeonies. Daisen'in, Daitokuji Temple, Kyoto

ch'ang) who was influential in the revitalized monasteries of the Hangchow area in the early 13th century. Here he practiced painting which, despite a pronounced Ch'an (Zen) outlook, shows an elegant and disciplined brushwork indicative of a Chinese academic training. As a Ch'an Buddhist painter Mu Ch'i's choice of subject is unorthodox, and many of his finest paintings have been preserved in Japan. His characteristically daring composition and ink tone is seen at its best in the *Six Persimmons* where color is evoked by tone.

The triptych now in the Daitokuji Temple, Kyoto, Japan, presents some of the most elegant and moving painting by this artist. The goddess Kuan Yin (seated on a rock by a stream) is flanked by a scroll of gibbons and one of a walking crane; they may not have been intended to hang together but now complement each other. Here the portrayal of the figure of the white-robed Kuan Yin seems to reach unusual expressiveness in the context of Chinese Buddhist iconographic painting. The use of fluent brushwork, well within the style of the period, is most imaginative and inventive. A comparison between this painting and the work of the contemporary artist Ma Yuan is instructive in assessing their related styles. (*See* overleaf.)

Mu Ch'i (attrib.): A Wild Goose; ink on paper (hanging scroll); 87×34cm (34×13in). Staatliche Museen, East Berlin

Muhammadi *fl.* late 16th century

Muhammadi, *ustad* (master) of Herat, was a leading Persian painter during the 1570s. He was reputedly a son of Sultan Muhammad, who died *c*1540. Muhammadi probably trained in Qazwin in the 1550s. After the death of Shah Isma'il II in 1576, he returned to Herat and worked for Ali Quli Khan Shamlu who was Governor from 1576 to 1587. His masterpiece is the sensitive *Pastoral* (or *Country*) *Scene* dated 1578 (Louvre, Paris). He made other tinted drawings, of dervishes dancing (Public Library, Leningrad; Freer Gallery of Art, Washington, D.C.) and elegant figure-paintings including a self-portrait (Museum of Fine Arts, Boston). Both of these types were later copied and imitated in Isfahan.

Muhammad Nadir 17th century

The Indian painter Muhammad Nadir came from Samarkand. Working at the Mughal court, he continued to paint in the style of the Jahangir period (1605–27) during the period of Shah Jahan (1628–58). One of the finest painters of the era, he was specially known for his animal painting. The falcon attributed to him recalls the work of Chinese artists in its finesse. There are six portraits attributed to Nadir in the British Museum, London. These show restraint and economy, strong drawing, and the use of a new idiom, *siyahi qalam*. With Muhammad Murad, he was the last foreign painter to work at the Mughal court.

Muhammad Zaman
fl. late 17th century

Muhammad Zaman was the son of Hajji Yusuf of Isfahan. A painter in the European style, he was active in the court of Shah Sulayman from *c*1671 to 1695. For Shah Sulayman he added two miniatures each to the *Khamsa* of Nizami of 1539–43 (British Library, London; Or. 2265) and to the *Shah-nama* of Shah Abbas I of *c*1590 in the Chester Beatty Library, Dublin. He also contributed to a *Nizami* dated 1675/6 in the Pierpont Morgan Library, New York (M. 469). These and album paintings in the Hermitage Museum, Leningrad, are based on the work of Hendrick Goltzius and other northern artists of the school of Caravaggio. His identification with a student sent to Rome by Abbas II and converted there to Christianity is incorrect. His son Muhammad Ali was also a painter, active from 1700 to 1722 at the court of Sultan Husayn Safavi.

Mu'in Musavvir *c*1617–*c*1700

The Persian painter Mu'in Musavvir was a pupil of Riza Abbasi. A prolific draftsman and miniaturist he was active in the city of Isfahan from 1635. He worked for the Shah Sulayman, probably designing the figured tile panels—including a confronted pair of peacock-bearing angels—over the gate in the Hasht Bihisht palace (1677). He also painted many miniatures in a life of Shah Isma'il I. His style is easily recognized by the dashing calligraphic line, and is usually signed. When full color is added in his work it is strong but harmonious, and always free from Western influence.

Müller Otto 1874–1930

Born in Liebau (Saxony), the German painter Otto Müller studied in Dresden (1894–6) and Munich (1898–9). He destroyed his own early work which had been influenced by Arnold Böcklin, and the *Jugendstil*. His mature style was formed by 1908, when he moved to Berlin; there he painted a series of nudes in landscapes which were influenced by Matisse, primitive art, and Egyptian painting. His work was rejected by the Berlin Secession in 1910. He joined the *Brücke* group, whose members were attracted by his use of flat distemper colors. After he had worked with Ernst Kirchner, Müller's nudes became more angular and geometric (for example, *Three Nudes*, *c*1912; Neue Pinakothek, Munich). From 1920 onwards he mostly painted gypsy subjects.

Multscher Hans *c*1400–67

The German sculptor and painter Hans Multscher was the most important late Gothic sculptor in Swabia. He ran a large and influential workshop at Ulm. In common with workshops in other prosperous south German towns, Multscher's undertook a wide variety of commissions including stone tomb monuments, single limewood figures, and large elaborate altar retables. The latter involved both painting and sculpture and Multscher made at least two of them.

He was born *c*1400 in Allgäu but became a citizen of Ulm in 1427. Documentation and authenticated works survive for only two periods of his life, the 1430s and 1450s. Some time between 1427 and 1433 he carved a number of stone figures for the principal window of Ulm Town Hall (now in the Ulmer Museum) representing the Emperor and various princes with their pages. Two works in Ulm Minster also date from this time, a statue of the *Man of Sorrows* (1429) on the west portal, and inside, a stone altar (largely destroyed) produced for the Karg family, dated 1433. For a tomb (projected but never carried out) for Duke Ludwig the Beardless of Bavaria, he made a model of the lid (Bayerisches Nationalmuseum, Munich) showing the Duke dressed as a knight kneeling before the Trinity. However, the major work of this period was probably the so-called "Wurzach" Altar, signed and dated 1437, from which remain the painted wings (Staatliche Museen, Berlin). They consist of four scenes from the Pas-

Otto Müller: Two Female Nudes in the Open Air; canvas; 175×110cm (69×43in); 1915. Städtische Kunsthalle, Mannheim

sion and four depicting the life of the Virgin. It is likely that they once enclosed a central compartment containing sculpture.

A gap of more than a decade follows before Multscher's next surviving works in the 1450s. Among these are a bronze monument to Countess Mechthild of the Palatinate (Stiftskirche, Tübingen) and

some wood carvings including a Palmesel (Dominikanerinnenkloster, Wettenhausen) of 1456. Palmesel sculptures depict Christ riding an ass; they were led in procession through the streets of south German towns on Palm Sunday.

In 1456 Multscher contracted to supply an altarpiece to the Stadtpfarrkirche at

Sterzing (now Vipiteno) in the South Tyrol. He supervised its erection from 1458 to 1459. Now dismembered, it originally consisted of a central shrine containing limewood sculptures of the Madonna and Child and four saints. The painted wings and decorated finials were the work of assistants. Flanking the altarpiece were two freestanding figures of Saints George and Florian.

Munch Edvard 1863–1944

Edvard Munch was the most internationally important Scandinavian artist of the early modern movement. Born of a doctor's family in Løten, Norway, he grew up in Oslo (known as Kristiania until 1924) where he received his initial art training. Early in the 1880s he became influenced by two older compatriots, Christian Krohg and Frits Thaulow, who were then enlivening the conservative Norwegian art scene with paintings based on French naturalism. In 1886, after a brief first visit to Paris, he discovered his own direction with The Sick Child (1885–6; National Gallery, Oslo). With impressionistic simplification, he fused an observed experience with recollections of the earlier death of a sister from tuberculosis, creating a haunting tragedy of doomed youth.

From 1889 to 1892 State scholarships enabled him to live mainly in France, although he established the habit of returning to Norway for the summers. In Paris he explored the new French painting, while formulating his intention to replace naturalism with an art symbolizing man's deepest emotions. His new works, based mostly on variations of French Impressionist technique, were included in his large exhibitions in Oslo and Berlin during the autumn of 1892. In both cities they were disliked, but in Berlin they provoked a scandal which caused the exhibition's closure after a week, and split the host organization, the Berlin Artists' Association. However, this notoriety earned Munch further exhibitions in Germany and he decided to base himself there. The Portrait of the Artist's Sister Inger (1892; National Gallery, Oslo) marks a decisive turning point in his career.

In Berlin he developed a series of subjects linked by the sequence of love, suffering, and death—the Frieze of Life, which dominated his work for many years. He publicly initiated this cycle in 1893 by exhibiting the six related paintings of the

Edvard Munch: Self-portrait in Blue Suit; oil on canvas; 100×110cm (39×43in); 1909. Bergen Art Gallery

Love series, including those today entitled *The Kiss* (1892), *Madonna* (c1893), and *The Scream* (1893; all in the National Gallery, Oslo). Factual experiences were still synthesized into an expression of emotional forces, but impressionistic treatment was now replaced by a dramatic yet decorative symbolism, recalling Gauguin or Van Gogh. Munch's tortured self-portraits reveal that the feeling of uncontrollable life forces which grip his figures arises from personal emotional insecurity. These works found appreciation among the Berlin avant-garde, writers like Strindberg, Przybyszewski, and Dehmel, who were equally intensely preoccupied with man's psychic condition.

It was during his years in Berlin that Munch started to make prints. Etching, lithographs, and woodcuts became as important to him as painting. He spent 1896 and 1897 in Paris where he developed color printing, working with the master printers Lemercier and Clot (who printed for Bonnard and Vuillard). He saw woodcuts by Gauguin and the Japanese: woodcuts were to become his own most consis-

tently original graphic achievements. His boldly cut images, often with complex color combinations and wood-grain overprinting, were to have a strong influence on German Expressionist printmaking. In Paris Munch moved in literary Symbolist circles, portraying Mallarmé, and designing programs for productions of Ibsen (whose plays fascinated him) at the *Théâtre de l'Oeuvre*. He exhibited at Bing's Art Nouveau gallery and the Indépendants.

During the next few years Munch lived more in Norway, expanding the *Frieze of Life* in paintings and prints, his ambition for large-scale projects stimulated by visits to Italy. Several new subjects, such as *Mother and Daughter* (c1897; National Gallery, Oslo), *Girls on the Jetty* (c1899–1901; National Gallery, Oslo), and the impressive portraits he executed (for example, *The Four Sons of Dr Max Linde*, 1903; Behnhaus-Museum, Lübeck), imply a less pessimistic philosophy; while some magnificent Oslo Fjord landscapes (for example, *View of Oslo Fjord from Nordstrand*, c1900; Städtische Kunsthalle,

Mannheim)—always Munch's favorite scenery—and paintings such as *Winter* (1899; National Gallery, Oslo) and *The Dance on the Shore* (1900–2; National Gallery, Prague) demonstrate a renewed interest in the external forces of nature.

The year 1902 proved to be a crisis year. The violent end of a protracted love affair and subsequent quarrels with Norwegian artists aggravated Munch's insecurity, convincing him of persecution at home and causing him to live increasingly in Germany. There, recognition was growing. A major selection from the *Frieze of Life* was well received at the 1902 exhibition of the Berlin Secession, and frequent exhibitions followed in Germany and central Europe. Wealthy patrons were forthcoming, art dealers offered contracts, and commissions for stage designs and decorations came from Max Reinhardt's Berlin theater. Munch now started changing his painting style from the somber tonalities and swirling patterns of the 1890s (which he felt might become mannered) to staccato brush strokes of brilliant, high-keyed colors, appropriate to his new, more frequently extrovert subjects.

In 1908 Munch's nervous condition finally reached complete breakdown and he retired to a Danish nursing home. There he took stock of himself and his art and the following spring he felt able to settle again in Norway, where his art was now increasingly appreciated.

From then until 1916 Munch's major works were the murals for the Great Hall of Oslo University. As if symbolizing his recovery, their theme was human life as part of nature's continuity ("the great external forces" as Munch expressed it), and it was to complement the *Frieze of Life* ("the suffering and joys of the individual as seen from close at hand"). Many of the motifs were developed from the more optimistic paintings he had created from the late 1890s onward. The brightly colored figures in their Oslo Fjord setting seem, as Munch intended, both typically Norwegian yet universal, and opposite to the Hall's Neoclassical architecture.

Despite increasing fame, Munch continued to live quietly outside Oslo, working hard. Motifs included landscapes, figure compositions, and subjects from the past, often reworked in his new color range. He also painted decorative murals for a factory canteen, and among the new prints he made at this time were subjects from Ibsen. The quality of his late works is less even than before, but to the end he could still paint new masterpieces like the remarkable *Self-portrait Between the Clock and the Bed* (1940–2; Munch Museum, Oslo).

Munch's most obvious importance lies in his uniquely powerful synthesis of northern *fin-de-siècle* ideas with French Post-Impressionist styles; his famous paintings of the 1890s link Gauguin and Van Gogh with modern German Expressionism. The best work of his later years, although no longer avant-garde, can contribute equally personal images that enlarge his total artistic personality.

Further reading. Benesch, O. *Edvard Munch*, London (1960). Boulton-Smith, J. *Munch*, New York and Oxford (1977). Deknatel, F.B. *Edvard Munch*, New York (1950). Heller, R. *Edvard Munch: The Scream*, London (1973). Langaard, J.H. and Revold, R. *A Year by Year Record of Edvard Munch's Life*, Oslo (1961). Stang, R. *Edvard Munch: the Man and the Artist*, London (1979). Timm, W. *The Graphic Art of Edvard Munch*, London (1969).

Münter Gabriele 1877–1962

The German artist Gabriele Münter was one of the leading figures in the development of German Expressionism. After studying briefly at the Women Artists' Association in Munich, she moved (1902) to the progressive Phalanx Art School, where she met Wassily Kandinsky. Living together from 1903 to 1914, they first traveled widely and then settled in Murnau, becoming the leading figures in the New Artists' Association and *Der Blaue Reiter* (The Blue Rider) group. Despite their closeness, Münter developed an independent style, drawing inspiration from Van Gogh, Jawlensky and Bavarian folk art (in the form of religious images painted on glass). She painted mainly landscapes and still lifes, her colors bold, expressive and often somber, her simplified forms bounded by strong, flowing outlines. Her works include *Man Listening (Portrait of Jawlensky)* and *Still Life with Chair* (both 1909; both Städtische Galerie im Lenbachhaus, Munich). She did little work after her relationship with Kandinsky ended in 1917.

Further reading. Hoberg, A. *Wassily Kandinsky and Gabriele Münter*, New York (1994). Lohnstein, P. *Gabriele Münter*, New York (1971).

Murillo Bartolomé 1617–82

The Spanish painter Bartolomé Esteban Murillo was born and died in Seville. Probably apprenticed there to Juan del Castillo, he produced a large number of religious compositions in Seville for churches and monasteries. These were painted in a graceful and colorful late Baroque style, full of movement, his handling steadily becoming freer and his outlines more diffused. His command of tonal values and of light exceeded from the beginning anything that his master could have taught him.

Although they were only a small part of his large output, his portraits in simple but effective full- or half-length poses reached a high level of technical accomplishment.

They may have owed something indirectly to Velázquez (whom Murillo could not have met before visiting Madrid in the late 1650s). His scenes of everyday life, particularly those of beggar-boys (a fine example, undated, is in the Louvre, Paris) have always been among his most popular works (see also *Grape and Melon Eaters*, Alte Pinakothek, Munich).

Murillo's first large commission was a series of 11 compositions of Franciscan subjects (including the *Miracle of S. Diego of Alcalá* or *Angel's Kitchen*, Louvre, Paris). Painted in 1645 and 1646 for the Franciscan monastery in Seville, these are now widely dispersed in Europe and America. Though less impressive than Zurbarán's earlier Hieronymite series at

Bartolomé Murillo: The Beggar-boy; oil on canvas; 137×115cm (54×45in). Louvre, Paris

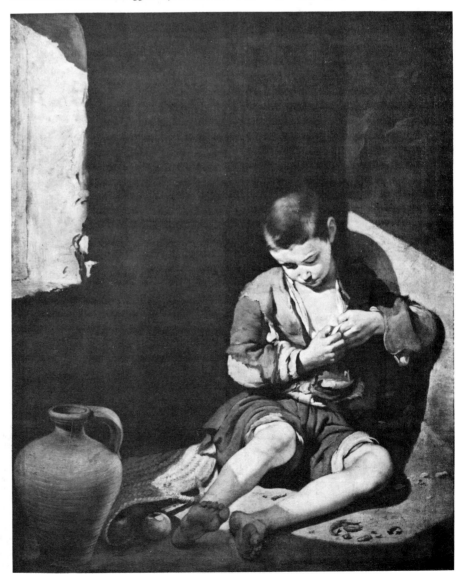

Guadalupe, and equally lacking in movement, these compositions immediately gained him fame; thereafter, Murillo's popularity began to overtake Zurbarán's.

From this period also date the earliest representations of the *Virgin and Child,* at Pollok House, Glasgow, and the Palazzo Pitti, Florence. Many others date from the 1650s, as do his depictions of such popular subjects as the *Adoration of the Shepherds,* the *Holy Family,* and the *Annunciation* (Prado, Madrid).

In 1656 Murillo painted one of his largest works, *The Vision of St Anthony of Padua* (Seville Cathedral). This skillfully contrasts the supernatural light of the celestial vision above with the sunlight seen through the doorway below, while on the saint's table a glass jar of lilies demonstrates the painter's mastery of still life details.

Although he never painted landscapes without figures, Murillo was a fine landscapist, as in the freely handled backgrounds of the large series of canvases of the *Story of Jacob* of the late 1660s (Cleveland Museum of Art; Meadows Museum and Sculpture Court, Texas; and the Hermitage Museum, St Petersburg).

The half-length *Self-portrait* (*c*1672; National Gallery, London) is of superb quality. So is the slightly earlier *Flower-Girl* (Dulwich College Picture Gallery, London) which is notable for its crisp handling and toneful color scheme. Murillo's best-known works are the series of enormous biblical subjects painted during the years 1667 to 1674 for the Charity Hospital, Seville (some still *in situ*); and the many versions of the Immaculate Conception, in widely varying poses, that he painted from 1652 onward. Like some of his Virgins and compositions of the youthful St John the Baptist, a few of these verge on the sentimental: they have thus contributed to the decline of Murillo's popularity in the 20th century, unduly obscuring the brilliant painterly qualities of most of his work.

Murillo's pupils and collaborators included the landscape specialist Ignacio Iriarte and the genre-painter Pedro Núñez de Villavicencio.

Further reading. Abbad Rios, F. *Las Inmaculadas de Murillo: Estudio Critico,* Barcelona (1948). Angulo Íñiquez, D. *Murillo* (3 vols.), Madrid (1981). Brown, J. *Murillo and his Drawings,* Princeton (1977).

Myron 5th century BC

Myron was a Greek bronze sculptor from Eleutherae, a border town between Boeotia and Attica. He was a reputed pupil of Ageladas and an older contemporary of Pheidias and Polycleitos. The most interesting part of his career falls within the early Classical phase, as he experimented in the rendering of motion, aiming at a higher degree of naturalism than his successors. The ancient critics noticed that he employed a greater stock of positions than Polycleitos and was also more consistent in his use of the rule of proportions.

The high point of Myron's career is the statue of the *Discobolus* (*Discus-thrower*), described in detail by Lucian (2nd century AD) and identified in copies (the best in the Terme Museum, Rome). It represents the moment of back-swing, the athlete looking back at the hand holding the discus. In a second he will lunge forward, pivoting on his right leg. Myron captures the dynamic moment of suspended action. His statue is composed in a system of triangles around the central sweeping S-curve of the body; it depends entirely on its animated outline to express movement, because the anatomy does not respond to the action. It is conceived as a figure in relief and probably owes its inspiration to contemporary painting. Its artificiality had impressed the Romans who saw it as "distorted and elaborate".

Myron's naturalistic tendencies were demonstrated in his bronze *Cow* on the Acropolis, which a calf was said to have mistaken for its mother. He worked mostly in Athens and may have been involved in the Parthenon; his style is recognized on some of the metopes of the south side. A type of quiet standing *Herakles* copied in statuettes is thought to derive from his colossal group of *Herakles, Zeus, and Athena* on Samos. His group of *Athena and Marsyas* has been reconstructed, not without controversy, on the evidence of vases and coins.

Mytens Daniel c1590–1647

Before the arrival of Anthony van Dyck in England in 1632, the work of the Dutch painter, Daniel Mytens, exerted an important foreign influence on English portrai-

Myron: Discobolus (Discus-thrower); height 125cm (49in); a Roman copy after an original of the 5th century BC. Terme Museum, Rome

Daniel Mytens: Portrait of the Duke of Hamilton; oil on canvas; 216×135cm (85×53in); 1629. Scottish National Portrait Gallery, Edinburgh (on loan from the Duke of Hamilton)

ture. Mytens was trained in The Hague, and came to London c1618. He became a royal portraitist on the accession of Charles I. His portraits show a marked break with the Jacobean convention of spectacular patterning and rich detail, and instead concentrate on the sitter's person-ality. Mytens' realism, an aspect of his work inherited from the art of the Low Countries, gradually became more ambitious and assured. In his late work he produced some of the most elegant and powerful full-length portraits of the 17th century.

N

Nadelman Elie 1882–1946

Elie Nadelman was a Polish sculptor who emigrated to America in 1914. He had already achieved great success in Paris (especially through his famous one-man show at the Galerie Druet, 1909) and had exhibited in London, Barcelona, and Berlin. Helena Rubinstein was an early admirer and supported him by buying much of his work. He went to New York (where his work was included in the 1913 Armory Show) and his almost clinical search for the basic structures of plastic form led him to a style of curvilinear Abstract sculpture which was well received in avant-garde and fashionable circles.

Elie Nadelman: Relief; 1912–13.

Later he also produced painted terracotta figures and miniature doll-like carvings. Nadelman's style, primarily transmitted through the early patronage of Helena Rubinstein, was one of the formative ingredients of the style of design later known as Art Deco.

Nainsukh c1725–c90

Nainsukh was a Hindu Pahari artist, the second son of the Brahman *pundit* Seu Raina, and brother of the painter Manaku. A native of Guler, he was responsible for introducing the Mughal style in the Pahari courts, either through being trained by an immigrant Mughal artist, or being trained at the Mughal court. His portraits and animal paintings show the influence of the Muhammad Shah style. Much has been discovered about Nainsukh and his family through recent important researches into temple records at the pilgrim site of Hardwar. There are a number of signed paintings by him of his first patron, Balwant Singh. There is also a self-portrait. After the death of Balwant Singh in 1763, he entered the service of Amrit Pal of Basohli (1757–76). This was a crucial period, when through the influence of Nainsukh a new graceful naturalism entered Basohli painting. His works show a flair for capturing movement and depicting people in action.

Nanni di Banco c1375–1421

The Italian sculptor Giovanni di Antonio di Banco was known as Nanni di Banco. He was born in Florence, the son of a stonemason. Together with Jacopo della Quercia and Lorenzo Ghiberti, he belongs to the first generation of artists who determined the style of the early Renaissance. Though his works are small in number, they excel by their typical interweaving of Gothic reminiscences and neo-antique Classicism, thus showing the transitional period at the beginning of the 15th century.

Two large commissions dominated Nanni's life: the decoration of the Porta della Mandorla, one of the side entrances of Florence Cathedral, and the sculptural adornment of the niches at Orsanmichele, the Florentine guilds' church. He started his career in the first decade of the 15th century by carving the reliefs of the inner arch of the Porta della Mandorla. About 1413, the Chapter of the cathedral as-

signed to Nanni, Donatello, and two lesser known sculptors the execution of the seated marble figures of the Evangelists, destined for the cathedral's facade. Nanni di Banco's *St Luke* (Museo dell'Opera del Duomo, Florence) not only reveals close study of Roman Antiquity, but also shows a new monumental style, which compares with Donatello's early sculptures.

For the niches at Orsanmichele he executed the almost antique statue of *St Philip* (c1412), the important group of Four Crowned Saints called *Quattro Coronati* (c1414), and *St Eligius* (c1417–18), who strongly recalls late Gothic tradition. The four monumental statues of the *Quattro Coronati*, the first attempt to combine several freestanding figures within the architectonic frame of a niche, decisively influenced later generations. His most important work is the relief of the Virgin in the tympanum of the Porta della Mandorla. The dynamic, unique conception is only formally related to Andrea Orcagna's relief of the Virgin in Orsanmichele (1359). Moreover, it shows Nanni's comprehension of the vocabulary of Roman Antiquity.

Nardo di Cione fl. 1343–65/6

The Florentine painter Nardo di Cione was the brother of Orcagna. While Orcagna painted the altarpiece in the Strozzi Chapel in S. Maria Novella, Florence (dated 1357), Nardo painted the fresco decora-

Nardo di Cione: Christ, a detail from the fresco of Heaven in the Strozzi Chapel, S. Maria Novella, Florence; c1354–7

tion on the walls: the *Last Judgment*, *Heaven*, and *Hell*. These probably date from the same period as the altarpiece, (*c*1354–7). It seems likely that Nardo was Orcagna's usual assistant and collaborator, and although he was the lesser artist, his own style can be identified as a less rigorous version of his brother's. The higher quality of the figures of Christ and the Virgin in Heaven, for example, supports the probability that Orcagna was actually responsible for the design and some of the painting of these frescoes.

Nash John 1752–1835

John Nash was the leading architect of the English Regency period. He trained under Sir Robert Taylor. His early career, spent mainly in Wales, was undistinguished, and included a bankruptcy in 1783. In 1796 he formed a highly profitable partnership with the landscape gardener Humphry Repton. Their association ended in 1802, but not before it had established Nash's reputation as a fashionable country house architect.

Talented, self-confident, and enormously ambitious, Nash was assisted by more than a measure of good fortune. The premature death of James Wyatt, in 1813, removed his only serious rival as a country house architect, while his marriage to a mistress of the future George IV introduced him to court circles, enabling him to benefit from the vast expansion of royal patronage that took place in the second and third decades of the 19th century. It was as a result of his close friendship with the Regent that he was awarded two of his most important commissions: Buckingham Palace, London (1825–30) and the Royal Pavilion, Brighton (1815–21).

His success owed little to stylistic integrity. He was prepared, when occasion demanded, to submit designs for classical, castellated, Gothic, or even "Hindoo" buildings, while his notorious indifference to detail forced him to rely heavily on the skill of assistants, including J.A. Repton and A.C. Pugin. His strength was in composition. The partnership with Repton had instilled an appreciation of the Picturesque, and it was Nash, more than any other early-19th-century architect, whose buildings exemplified the Picturesque

Nanni di Banco: Four Crowned Saints with workshop scenes below; stone; c1414. Orsanmichele, Florence

ideal—whether it was in the ragged skyline of Ravensworth Castle, County Durham (1808), the daring asymmetry of Cronkhill, Shropshire (1802), or the interaction of landscape, villas, and terrace facades of The Regent's Park (1821–30).

Further reading. Mansbridge, M. *John Nash: A Complete Catalogue*, New York (1991). Summerson, J.N. *John Nash, Architect to King George IV*, London (1949).

Nash Paul 1889–1946

The English painter Paul Nash was born in London. After initial training in illustration, he studied at the London County Council School (1908–10) and at the Slade School of Fine Art, London (1910–11). Unsuccessful in figure-drawing, he turned increasingly to landscape to express personal feelings. The breakthrough came when as an Official War Artist he painted *We Are Making a New World* (1918; Imperial War Museum, London), which conveyed a sense of desolate outrage by color and form alone. From 1919 to 1925 Nash continued this development in his Cubist-influenced Dymchurch landscapes.

The impact of Surrealism from 1928 onward made his art more openly Symbolic, and led him to use ancient landscape features (such as megaliths) to express the spirit of place and the continuity of history. Both aspects are important to the English landscape tradition, and make Nash one of its central 20th-century figures.

Further reading. Bertram, A. *Paul Nash: the Portrait of an Artist*, London (1955). Causey, A. *Paul Nash*, Oxford (1980). Eates, M. *Paul Nash: the Master of the Image, 1889–1946*, London (1973). Postan, A. *The Complete Graphic Works of Paul Nash*, London (1973). Rothenstein, J. *Paul Nash 1889–1946*, London (1967).

Nattier Jean-Marc 1685–1766

The French painter Jean-Marc Nattier was the son of parents who were themselves both painters. He began life as an engraver, with his father and brother, of Rubens' *Marie de Medici* cycle (the paintings are now in the Louvre, Paris). He then turned to historical portraiture, and finally became a favorite painter of the women at the Court of Louis XV. Those ladies he presented in flights of Rococo splendor as,

for example, his *Duchesse d'Orléans as Hebe* (1745; Nationalmuseum, Stockholm), where the conceit is that the Duchess is a goddess, floating on powder-puff clouds in no earthly paradise. A critic underlined the painting's artificiality by wondering how many women in France actually tamed eagles by feeding them white wine. Nattier's works have charm and delicacy, as well as being likenesses; but, as the criticism intimates, they failed to please the severe demand of nascent Neoclassicism.

Neel Alice 1900–84

The American portrait painter Alice Neel studied at the Philadelphia School of Design for Women, and lived briefly in Cuba before settling in New York. Following a period in a psychiatric hospital in her 20s, she developed an intense, stark form of portraiture reminiscent of German Expressionism: typically her contours are tense and the sitters' features strongly emphasized, while large areas of the canvas are left lightly sketched in. Neel lived in Greenwich Village and then for 25 years in Spanish Harlem, her portraits of friends and neighbors expressing an unsentimental compassion for the physical and psychological effects of poverty—she described herself as a "collector of souls". Uninfluenced by the many avant-garde developments in American 20th-century art, she remained neglected until the late 1960s.

Characteristically frank and incisive portraits include *Andy Warhol* (1970; Whitney Museum of American Art, New York) and her nude *Self-portrait* (1980; Robert Miller Gallery, New York), painted when she was 80.

Further reading. Hills, P. *Alice Neel*, New York (1983).

Neer Aert van der 1603–77

The Dutch landscape painter Aert van der Neer settled in 1630 in Amsterdam, where he specialized in nocturnal and winter scenes. The nocturnal landscapes (usually imaginative interpretations of the countryside around Amsterdam) are sometimes lit by flames from burning buildings, but more usually by the pale, transparent beams of a full moon. These create a melancholy mood as they fall on water, ice, and land, and reflect back to cloudy

skies. The poetic content of these pictures was admired by 19th-century German Romantic painters. Van der Neer's spacious, multifigured winter landscapes are in the manner of Avercamp's skating scenes. Through the subtle coloristic and tonal modulation of a limited palette of whites, silvery-grays, and pale blues, they brilliantly convey the crisp, cold atmosphere of a winter's day. Van der Neer achieved little success as a painter. A venture into tavern-keeping was also unsuccessful, and the artist was declared bankrupt in 1662.

Nervi Pier Luigi 1891–1979

Pier Luigi Nervi, a structural engineer and architect born in Lombardy, is considered the modern master of concrete construction. His success at vaulting large areas with reinforced concrete, as in his various aircraft hangars of the 1930s, was greatly admired, and led to important cooperative projects after the Second World War. Among these were the UNESCO Building in Paris (1953–6), the Palazzetto dello Sport in Rome (1957), and the Pirelli Skyscraper in Milan (1955–8), where Nervi's structural answer to the problem of the skyscraper block was dazzlingly demonstrated. Nervi is one of the many engineer "heroes" of modern architecture.

Neumann Balthasar 1687–1753

Balthasar Neumann was one of the two leading German architects of the 18th century, the other being J.M. Fischer. Neumann was a native of Eger, and was originally trained as a cannon- and bell-founder. Throughout his career he retained an intensely practical approach to problems, and was a superb technician. In 1714 he enlisted in the Würzburg palace guards as a lieutenant of artillery; he served as an engineer in the Belgrade campaign of 1717, visiting Milan and Vienna in 1718. On his return to Würzburg in 1720, he and Johann Dientzenhofer were appointed by the Prince Bishop, Philip Franz von Schönborn, to be joint surveyors of a vast new palace that was planned. Most of his major architectural commissions were to be closely connected with the Schönborn family.

Aert van der Neer: A Landscape with a River at Evening; oil on canvas; 79×65cm (31×26in); c1650–3. National Gallery, London

Work on the Würzburg Residenz began in earnest under Friedrich Carl von Schönborn (who reigned from 1729 to 1746) and the final designs were influenced by Robert de Cotte and Gabriel-Germain Boffrand as well as by Lucas von Hildebrandt. In the dynamic composition of the Hofkirche in the south wing the architecture is by Neumann (1730); the decoration was designed by Hildebrandt, and much of the strength of the Bohemian-inspired vaulting is dissipated. The design for the staircase was finally approved in 1735; together with the Weissersaal and Kaisersaal which lead from it, it was completed during the 1750s.

Hildebrandt also advised Neumann in the building of the Prince Bishop's summer residence, Schloss Werneck in Schweinfurt (1734–45). Neumann's personal style is best seen there in the dynamic design of the chapel, a type of composition first worked out by him in the Schönborn Chapel attached to Würzburg Cathedral, where he revised the plans of M. von Welsch (1723–36). Unfortunately his great abbey church of Münsterschwarzach (1727–42) was demolished during the 19th century. In it Neumann developed his complex vaults, supported by pillars set obliquely, which break down the traditional spatial divisions of his church interiors, and lead to the almost willful complexity of Vierzehnheiligen.

For other members of the Schönborn family, Neumann was active further west. From 1733 he worked for Franz Georg, Archbishop Elector of Trier, reconstructing the abbey church of St Paulinus there (begun 1734). For Damian Hugo, Bishop of Speyer, he began work on Schloss Bruchsal in 1728. The twin ascending flights of the staircase (1731–2), enfolding the central oval area that links the state rooms, was one of his greatest triumphs. The building was later partially destroyed.

During his later years Neumann's greatest successes lay in his church designs—his projects for vast palaces remained unexecuted. In the pilgrimage church of Vierzehnheiligen, interpenetrating vaults are exploited to the full, in order to focus attention on to the shrine in the nave. In Neumann's last important church, at Neresheim (1747–92), calm reigns again and the interior is dominated by the central rotunda.

Further reading. Freeden, M.H. von *Balthasar Neumann: Leben und Werk*, Munich (1953). Knapp, F. *Balthasar Neumann*, Berlin (1937).

Barnett Newman: Covenant; oil on canvas; 122×152cm (48×60in); 1949. Joseph Hirshhorn Museum, Washington, D.C.

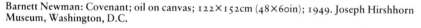

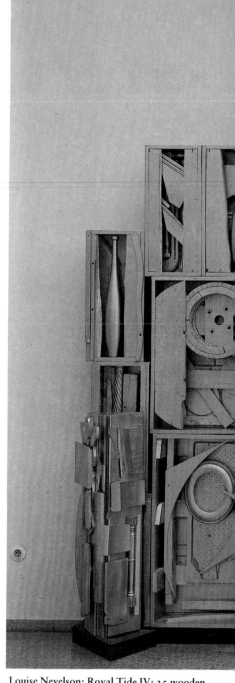

Louise Nevelson: Royal Tide IV; 35 wooden chests painted gold; 335×427cm (131×166in); 1959–60. Wallraf-Richartz-Museum, Cologne

Neutra Richard 1892–1970

The Austrian architect Richard Neutra was a Viennese, and a pupil of Adolf Loos before the First World War. He then worked in Switzerland, and in 1922 in Germany with Eric Mendelsohn, before emigrating to the U.S.A. In 1926 he joined his compatriot Rudolf Schindler in Los Angeles. Both architects were inspired by, and worked with, Frank Lloyd Wright.

Neutra's first work of note, the Lovell

house, Los Angeles (1927–9), is usually seen as the first building in an American "International style". He continued designing in this manner, attaining ever greater heights of elegance and finish, throughout the 1930s and 1940s. The Kaufmann Desert house, Palm Springs (1946–7), is remarkable, like all of Neutra's houses, for its dramatic siting.

Nevelson Louise 1899–1988

Louise Nevelson was an American sculptor born Louise Beliawsky in Kiev, Russia. Her family emigrated to Rockland, Maine,

in 1905. She studied painting and drawing in New York, first with Theresa Bernstein and William Meyerowitz (1920), and then at The Art Students League, with Kenneth Hayes Miller and Kimon Nicolaides (1929–30). She also worked briefly with Hans Hofmann in Munich (1931), and assisted Diego Rivera on a mural for the New Workers' School, New York (1932). Her first one-woman show came in 1941 (Nierendorf Gallery, New York).

Nevelson's work has been influenced by a wide variety of sources such as Futurism, Cubism, and the work of Brancusi. Her most characteristic works have come to be

"sculptural walls": a series of wooden boxes or "pigeon holes" filled with forms which are usually abstract but which have overtones of ordinary objects.

Further reading. Glimcher, A.B. *Louise Nevelson*, New York (1972).

Newman Barnett 1905–70

The American painter Barnett Newman was, with Mark Rothko, one of the leading New York painters of the 1950s. He moved away from the free brushwork of Abstract Expressionism towards a cerebral, restrained yet lyrical Color-field painting. In 1944 and 1945 Newman was working in Abstract Surrealist "automatic" style. By 1948, as in *Onement I* (oil on canvas; 1948; private collection), the Surrealist symbols were eradicated, to be replaced by a flat rectangularly divided picture-plane, the ingredient for all his later work. Vast areas of color are meticulously applied and, perfectly articulated, move horizontally across his canvases, as in *Vir Heroicus Sublimis* (oil on canvas; 1950–1; Museum of Modern Art, New York). Such paintings are early and seminal examples of hard-edge Minimal art.

Further reading. Hess, T. *Barnett Newman*, New York (1971). Newman, B. "Studio 35" in Motherwell, R. and Reinhardt, A. (eds.) *Modern Artists in America*, New York (1952). Restany, P. "Barnett Newman: a Value of Civilization", *Domus*, Milan (Feb. 1973). Rosenberg, H. "Barnett Newman and Meaning in Abstract Art", *Art International*, Lugano (1972).

Niccolò *fl. c1120–c50*

Niccolò was a Romanesque sculptor whose first signed work is the Zodiac Portal of the Abbey of Sagra di S. Michele in Piedmont (1122–30). Subsequently, he carved the south portal of Piacenza Cathedral (*c1130*) and the west portals of Ferrara Cathedral (*c1135*), of S. Zeno's church at Verona (*c1138*), and of Verona Cathedral (*post* 1139). In contrast to the expressive and powerful style of his predecessor Wiligelmo, his reliefs are delicate, almost lyrical, and are carved with great attention to detail.

Niccolò played an important role in the development of portal design. His portals consist of numerous recessed orders of colonnettes (small decorative columns) and arches, a large tympanum (hitherto rare in Italy), and a projecting porch resting on columns carried on the backs of lions or griffins. At Ferrara and the cathedral at Verona, there are in addition figures attached to the jambs, thus providing a design similar to that used at the abbey of St-Denis, which revolutionized portal design for many centuries to come by the use of column-figures. At S. Zeno in Verona, flanking the main portal, are reliefs with scenes from Genesis (south side) and the life of Christ (north side), thus extending the sculptural decoration well

Niccolò: Six Scenes from Genesis, a detail of the south side of the main portal of S. Zeno, Verona; c1138

beyond the portal.

It is often claimed that Niccolò must have known sculpture in France, especially in Languedoc; this is quite feasible, for some elements in his style could have originated there. His influence on the development of sculpture in Italy was profound, but has been little studied. True column-figures in a style similar to that of Niccolò were employed in Ravenna, Ancona, and elsewhere in Italy—and it is tempting to think that Niccolò invented this device in a monument now destroyed. If that were indeed the case, then the column-figures at St-Denis would have been of Italian inspiration.

Niccolò Alunno *c1430–1502*

The Italian painter Niccolò Alunno was also known as Niccolò di Liberatore and as Niccolò da Foligno. He began as a pupil and imitator of Benozzo Gozzoli: his *Madonna dei Consoli* (signed and dated 1457/8; Pinacoteca Comunale, Deruta) is close to the master's fresco style in S. Francesco at Montefalco, Umbria (finished 1452). Later he moved away from the manner of Gozzoli to that of Alvise Vivarini and Carlo Crivelli, as in the *Coronation of the Virgin, with Saints* (1466; Vatican Museums, Rome) and the *Virgin and Child Enthroned* (1482; Pinacoteca Nazionale, Bologna). His color becomes brighter, his design harder, and he makes great use of expressive gestures.

Towards the end of the 15th century, in *The Nativity* (1492; central panel of a polyptych, Pinacoteca Comunale, Foligno), heroism is coupled with an assured handling of perspective and natural details clearly located in space. The expressive use of drapery contrasts the vigor of the St Joseph with the pious gentleness of the Virgin as she worships the Child.

Niccolò's style was popular in the Marches, where he was active from *c*1466. Vasari praises his work as "natural", saying that "all his heads were portraits and seemed alive".

Nicholas of Verdun *fl.* 1181–*c*1205

Nicholas of Verdun is not the earliest medieval artist who can be established historically, either by signed surviving work or documents; but he is the first whose development as an artistic personality can be traced through early, mature, and late work.

He is first established by the great enameled pulpit he made for Klosterneuburg near Vienna, which is signed by him and was completed in 1181. A later addition to the inscription records that after a fire in 1330, the pulpit was reconstructed in 1331 by the addition of six enameled figure-scenes, and painted scenes on the back, to create the present altar retable.

Nicholas' pulpit, originally part of the choir screen of the church, was decorated with 45 large champlevé enameled panels. These were arranged in three horizontal rows, with scenes from the life of Christ in the center; above and below each scene are Old Testament prefigurations from before and after the Law of Moses. Each scene is surrounded by texts, and set under a triple arch carried on paired columns, with half-length angels in the spandrels. Although the whole is clearly the work of one hand, it is possible to see a development within it, ranging from a softer, more static style, with the scene arranged in parallel to the surface in the earlier scenes on the left leaf of the retable, to much more vividly drawn and composed scenes in the center and on the right wing—such as the Sacrifice of Isaac, with strong compositional diagonals, rich use of massed lines of drapery, and expressive heads.

After the pulpit, Nicholas undoubtedly worked on the Shrine of Three Kings in Cologne, although his presence is not recorded by documents. The great silver-gilt figures of Prophets and Apostles are perfect translations of the late expressive style of Klosterneuburg into a powerful three-dimensional presence. A late work, documented by inscriptions, is the Shrine

Ben Nicholson: November 11, 1947 (Mousehole); oil and pencil on canvas mounted on wood; 46×58cm (18×23in); 1947. Collection of the British Council

of Our Lady at Tournai, completed in 1205. Although it has suffered much from later restorations, enough survives to see Nicholas' late style—much less classical in proportion, more fluid in form, flatter, more linear, but of almost visionary intensity.

Both in technique and in iconography—especially at Klosterneuburg—his art is derived from a Mosan background (from the art of the Meuse River Valley area of the 11th and 12th centuries). But his originality as a creative artist is exceptional, and his work marks a new phase in the history of art called the "Transitional style". Nicholas clearly knew both antique and, more especially, contemporary Byzantine works of art; there is more than a suspicion in his work that he was among the first artists working *c*1200 to seek to imitate nature. However that may be, he certainly made use of his many and varied sources in a personal way, not simply by imitating them, but by studying them, and by absorbing them into a self-conscious creation of an individual style.

Nicholson Ben 1894–1982

Ben Nicholson, who has done more than any other artist to introduce and nurture nonfigurative art in England, was the son of the painter William Nicholson. He studied briefly at the Slade School of Fine Art (1910–11), but was largely self-taught;

very little of his early work remains. After the war, stimulated by early Italian painting and by Cézanne and Cubism, Nicholson began to examine methodically—without preconception of what a picture ought to look like—ways of representing his feeling for space and light. This brought him close to abstraction by 1924. In the later 1920s, living chiefly in Cumberland, he painted simplified, carefully crafted landscapes and still lifes, which became more conceptual after his discovery of the Cornish primitive painter Alfred Wallis in 1928.

From 1931 to 1939 Nicholson lived in Hampstead, as part of the group of avant-garde artists who committed themselves wholeheartedly to links with Paris. With Barbara Hepworth, whom he married as his second wife, Nicholson visited the studios of many Paris artists; he profited from meeting Picasso and Braque and, among the nonfigurative painters, Piet Mondrian. The more abstract Surrealists, such as Miró, helped a new range of cursive forms to emerge in his art. A series of paintings of 1932 allude to France and Nicholson's interest in Cubism, and display his visual humor and sense of enigma at their most developed. From these Nicholson progressed quickly to his first Abstract reliefs (1933) and to the first all-white paintings (1934). His introduction of primary colors shortly afterwards can be taken as a tribute to Mondrian; but a feeling for tonal relationships and a taste for muted color, which Nicholson inherited from his father's generation, were deeply rooted, and he never succumbed to the more extreme severities of Mondrian's art.

Nicholson was a member of the Parisian nonfigurative artists' group *Abstraction-Création* from 1933 to 1935. He showed with the avant-garde Unit One group in London in 1934; and in 1935 he led the Seven and Five Society (of which he had been a member since 1924 and chairman since 1926) to exhibit nonfigurative work only. He was coeditor in 1937 of the publication *Circle*, which acted as a manifesto for the Abstract group in England.

In 1939 Nicholson and Hepworth settled in Cornwall. There, living in the country for the first time since the 1920s, he partly reverted to figurative themes and his colors became closer to nature even in his abstractions. The underlying strength his work had gained in the 1930s made it possible to endure the relative isolation. When research into abstraction in England was reopened towards 1950, Nicholson's experience was of immeasurable value to younger artists—he provided them with the example he had himself lacked after the First World War.

Nicholson won several international prizes in the 1950s, and had major retrospective exhibitions in the United States (1952–3), in Europe (1955), and at the Tate Gallery (1955 and 1969). The lyrical abstractions he made in the 1950s were among the most impressive achievements of his career. After his third marriage, Nicholson lived in Switzerland from 1958 to 1971. He later lived near Cambridge and in Hampstead, London, and continued to paint and exhibit regularly.

Further reading. Harrison, C. *Ben Nicholson*, London (1969). Nicholson, B. *Paintings, Reliefs, and Drawings* (2 vols.), London (1955 and 1956). Read, H. *Ben Nicholson*, London (1956). Sausmarez, M. de *Ben Nicholson*, London (1969). Summerson, J. *Ben Nicholson*, Harmondsworth (1948).

Nicholson William 1872–1949

The English artist William Newzam Prior Nicholson was a painter in oil of portraits, still lifes, and landscapes; he also worked as both graphic artist and stage designer. Born at Newark-upon-Trent, he studied at Bushey School of Art under (Sir) Hubert von Herkomer, and in Paris at the Académie Julian (1889–90). In 1893 he married Mabel Pryde, sister of the painter James Pryde. He collaborated with James Pryde under the name J. and W. Beggarstaff on a revolutionary series of poster designs. It is for these that he remains most famous, but his later works include many other paintings in oil. He was a sensitive portraitist. He visited the U.S.A., India, and South Africa, and also traveled widely in Europe. He was knighted in 1936.

Niemeyer Oscar 1907–

The leading Brazilian architect Oscar Niemeyer Soares Filho began his career in 1936 when, under the direction of Lucio Costa, he worked with Le Corbusier on the design for the Ministry of Health and Education, Rio de Janeiro (1936–43). Le Corbusier was a powerful influence on Niemeyer; but the latter's own qualities of expressiveness are unique and almost unmatched in 20th-century architecture.

A repertory of exciting forms in reinforced concrete and expansive spaces characterizes Niemeyer's dramatic architecture. The buildings he designed at Pampulha (1942–3) were his first important commission. Many others followed, but Niemeyer is best known for his spectacular work at Brasilia, the new capital planned by Lucio Costa (for example the Parliament Buildings, 1957–60).

Further reading. Niemeyer, O. *The Work of Oscar Niemeyer*, New York (1950). Underwood, D. *Oscar Niemeyer and the Architecture of Brazil*, New York (1994).

Nikias *fl. c*340–300 BC

Nikias was an Athenian painter. Descriptions of his works, which are all lost, suggest a sober Classical style in which the figures are clearly delineated and stand out from their backgrounds in a sculptural manner. He advocated massive composi-

William Nicholson: The Hill above Harlech; oil on canvas; 53×59cm (21×23in); c1917. Tate Gallery, London

tions, in which this technique would have been essential. He also collaborated with the sculptor Praxiteles, painting his statues. He had a special reputation for his depiction of women. Of his works, the *Perseus with Andromeda* and the *Io* were perhaps the inspiration for versions that have been preserved in Roman wall painting.

Ni Tsan 1301–74

The Chinese painter Ni Tsan was the son of a wealthy merchant family. He showed his cultivated tastes early, making collections of painting and books. He was a fastidious man who, it is related, had an obsession with cleanliness. He was a young friend of Huang Kung-wang in Chiangnan, but at the time of the troubles in that region he dispersed his property among his family and took to a wandering life with his wife. Ni Tsan was a limited painter of lake landscapes and bamboo, with a strangely haunting and ascetic style. He built up his landscapes of interlocking spurs and spaces of water to create a deserted, still picture into which no human being ever steps, although there is often an empty pavilion. These repetitive compositions, painted with a dry pale ink and sparing brushwork, have fascinated many painters; however, no follower has ever recaptured the special quality of his work.

The fine example in the C.C. Wang Collection, New York (*Trees in the Valley of the River at Yu-chan*, 1371) is typical of this very personal style. The "stretched" surface composition is delicately bound together and tied to the picture frame, while the recession is expressed by daring spaces of calm water defined with slips of land and a distant hill. The use of ink is such as to create a sense of illumination by soft sunlight.

Noguchi Isamu 1904–88

Isamu Noguchi was an American sculptor born in Los Angeles of mixed Japanese and American parentage. He spent 12 years in Japan (1906–18) before returning to the U.S.A. to finish school in Indiana. After two years of medical school at Columbia University he studied sculpture at the Leonardo da Vinci Art School and at the East Side Art School—both in New York (1924–6). He went to Paris on a Guggenheim Fellowship and spent the years 1927 to 1929 in Brancusi's studio. Be-

Isamu Noguchi: Sign of Peace, engraved on the fountain of the Japanese garden, UNESCO, Paris; 1962

tween 1929 and 1939 he returned to the U.S.A. and then traveled to China and Japan, England and Mexico, studying brush drawing (with Chi Pai Shi in Peking) and pottery (with Uno Junnatsu in Kyoto).

Noguchi's concern was to integrate sculpture with man and his environment. This led him to design dance and theater sets: he began a collaboration with Martha Graham in 1935 which led to more than 20 sets. He also designed playgrounds, gardens, and fountains. Works of his are owned by the Metropolitan and Whitney Museums and the Museum of Modern Art, New York.

Further reading. Ashton, D. *Noguchi*, New York (1992). Altshuler, B. *Noguchi*, New York (1994).

Nolan Sidney 1917–

The Australian painter Sidney Robert Nolan was born in Melbourne, where he studied art (*c*1934–6). He took up painting full-time *c*1938. His first phase was Abstract, but he turned to representational painting at the beginning of the 1940s. He served in the Australian Army from 1942 to 1945, and first visited Europe in 1951, the year of his first London exhibition.

Sidney Nolan: Glenrowan, from the additional paintings for the second Ned Kelly series; acrylic on board; 91×122cm (36×48in); 1956–7. Tate Gallery, London

Kenneth Noland: Gift; acrylic on canvas; 183×183cm (72×72in); 1961–2. Tate Gallery, London

Nolan became well-known through the two series of paintings inspired by the career of the late-19th-century Australian outlaw, Ned Kelly. The first series (1945–7) was painted in Melbourne; the second (1954–5) in Europe, with a few additional canvases dating from 1956–7 (for example *Glenrowan*, 1956–7; Tate Gallery, London). The Ned Kelly pictures, his finest achievement to date, are characterized by a strong sense of atmosphere interacting with a cunning use of Abstract and quasi-Abstract forms. Nolan is a good landscape painter, with a powerful feeling for the heat and emptiness of the Australian scene.

Since Ned Kelly, Nolan has turned to other themes, such as the legend of Leda and the Swan, and the image of Shakespeare. He has traveled a great deal, visiting Greece, Italy, Africa, Mexico, and Japan.

Further reading. Bonython, K. (ed.) *Modern Australian Painting and Sculpture 1950–1960*, Adelaide (1960). Lynn, E. *Sidney Nolan: Myth and Imagery*, London (1967). Neville, R. *Ned Kelly: Twenty-Seven Paintings by Sidney Nolan*, London (1964); U.S. edn *The Legend of Ned Kelly, Australia's Outlaw Hero*, New York (1964). Reed, J.R. *Australian Landscape*

Painting, Melbourne (1965).

Noland Kenneth 1924–

Kenneth Noland is one of the best known contemporary American Minimalist painters. He works within a range of 1960s styles collectively named "post-painterly abstraction" by Clement Greenberg. The aim is purely optical, and the practice avoids any drawing, line, value, or depth; the painting is therefore reduced to the "hue" on the surface of the canvas.

Born in Asheville, North Carolina, Noland studied in 1946 at Black Mountain

College in North Carolina. In 1948 and 1949 he worked with Ossip Zadkine in Paris, and in the early 1950s met Morris Louis in Washington. In 1953 Clement Greenberg introduced both artists to the work of Helen Frankenthaler, whose "soak-stain" technique, using thin washes of paint, made a great impression on them. Louis and Noland worked closely together for the rest of the decade, using diluted acrylic paints and bright colors in fluent lyrical shapes on unprimed, unsized canvases.

Noland's preoccupation with the relationship of the image to the containing edge of the picture led him in 1958 away from the freedom of Louis, to a series of studies of concentric rings, or bull's-eyes, using unlikely color combinations. Since 1962 he has, like Frank Stella, pioneered the "shaped" canvas, initially with a series of symmetrical and asymmetrical diamonds or chevrons. In these paintings the edges of the canvas become as structurally important as the center.

In 1964 Noland occupied half the American pavilion at the Venice Biennale, and in 1965 his work was exhibited at the Washington Gallery of Modern Art. In the same year he had a major exhibition at the Jewish Museum in New York. He has remained among the best-known internationally of contemporary American painters. His "shaped" canvases are highly irregular and asymmetrical, resulting in increasingly complex structures of great control and integrity.

Nolde Emil 1867–1956

Born Emil Hansen, the painter Emil Nolde took his name from his birthplace in Schleswig, northern Germany. He first worked as an apprentice wood carver and furniture draftsman. After studying in Munich, Karlsruhe, and Paris, he developed an Impressionist style of painting. He continued in this style until 1904, when his work began to reflect the brilliant flat colors and spontaneous brushwork of Gauguin and Van Gogh. This brought him to the attention of the *Brücke* group which he joined in 1906; he was thus alerted to their interest in primitive art, an influence reflected in his woodcuts.

After 1908, his figure-paintings combine the simplified areas of strong color of his *Brücke* colleagues with the intensity of Ensor, whom he visited in 1911. This influence is apparent in his mask and religious paintings after 1909 (for example, *Last Supper*, 1909; Stiftung Seebüll Ada und Emil Nolde, Seebüll). One of these was rejected by the Berlin Secession in 1910, thus provoking Nolde's attack on the Secession and the foundation of the New Secession. In 1912 he participated in the second *Blaue Reiter* exhibition in Munich, and the *Sonderbund* exhibition in Cologne. Controversies over his work encouraged his isolation, but his interest in primitive art did not wane.

After an extended visit to Asia and the South Seas in 1913 and 1914, he returned to northern Germany, eventually settling at Seebüll in 1926. His late works in watercolor, particularly the "Unpainted Pictures" after 1941 when he was forbidden to paint by the Nazis, were done from memory and are remarkable for their luminous, gently floating colors (Stiftung Seebüll Ada und Emil Nolde, Seebüll).

Nollekens Joseph 1737–1823

The English sculptor Joseph Nollekens was the son of a Flemish painter working in London. He was apprenticed in 1750 to the sculptor Peter Scheemaeckers. A brilliant student, he won three prizes at the Society of Arts. In 1760 he went to Rome, where he practiced very successfully for ten years, making busts and restoring and copying Classical sculptures. On his return to London he established a large and prosperous practice in portraiture and monumental sculpture. Nollekens was a hard-headed businessman, and amassed a great fortune from his work; but he was also a sensitive and highly intelligent artist. Among his own works he preferred his ideal statues, but these were in fact his weakest point, and he is remembered chiefly today as an outstandingly fine portrait sculptor.

Nötke Bernt c1440–1509

Bernt Nötke was a German sculptor and painter. Born in Lassan in Pomerania (Poland), he was the greatest sculptor of his day in the Baltic area. For much of his life he lived in Lübeck, where the majority of his works may now be seen in the St Annen-Museum. In 1467 it is recorded that he was exempted from the Guild regulations, indicating the elevated status he enjoyed over contemporary German artists. In 1477 he carved a magnificent cross in polychromed wood for Lübeck Cathedral.

Nötke did not work only in Germany. He was one of several Lübeck artists of the period who went to Scandinavia, where some of his greatest works survive. For Aarhus Cathedral, Denmark, he produced the altar triptych between 1478 and 1482. The precise authorship of the several parts of the work is not certain, but it seems likely that Nötke was responsible for the paintings and his assistants for the sculpture. In 1483 he painted the triptych for the high altar at Reval Cathedral, Sweden; and then in 1484 he traveled to Stockholm, where he remained for the greater part of the next 13 years. During that time he carved in wood his best-known work, the great 10 ft (4 m) high polychrome statue of *St George and the Dragon*, for the church of St Nicholas in Stockholm. It was an important work, commissioned by the Swedish Chancellor to commemorate victory over the Danes on St George's day, 1471.

Stylistically, a number of other works in Scandinavia have been attributed to Nötke and his pupil Henning von der Heide, among them the *St John the Evangelist* in Roskilde Cathedral, Denmark. However, he had returned to Lübeck by c1500. He then produced his great panel painting, the only one firmly attributed to him, of *The Mass of St Gregory*, for the Marienkirche (it was destroyed in 1942). About 1508 he began his last known work, the incised bronze tomb slab in memory of Herman Hutterock, also in the Marienkirche.

At a time when other artists had lapsed into depicting the detailed trivialities so characteristic of the High Gothic style, Nötke never lost sight of the underlying spiritual content in the subject matter of his works. They also display an easy elegance and a fastidious eye for realism, not least in his use of materials. These qualities are most striking in the *St George and the Dragon*. The tableau has an overall bristling Gothic appearance, but through it emerges the divinity of St George and the demonism of the dragon. In his quest for realism, Nötke gave the saint's horse real horsehair, while the dragon boasts elk horns. *The Mass of St Gregory* is equally skilled. The picture displays an awareness of the ritualistic meaning of the scene, which is witnessed by several realistically portrayed faces. Behind them a rugged landscape appears through the window. Nötke's colors, though strong, were nevertheless applied with restraint.

O

Oderisi da Gubbio 1240–99

The Italian painter Oderisi da Gubbio was mentioned by Dante as an artist whose reputation rests on his skill as an illuminator. In Dante's famous comparison of how Giotto was now considered better than Cimabue, the poet said that Oderisi was in his turn outshone by Franco Bolognese. No one has identified any of his work with certainty, but manuscripts at Modena (a Gradual in the Este Library; 'R.I.6) and Turin (the *Informatium of Justinian*, Biblioteca Nazionale; E.I.8.) are often connected with either Oderisi or Franco. Dante's comparison is telling: for the Bolognese school of illumination, and the manuscripts mentioned, show a developing classicism; this can be paralleled by the art of Giotto, whose style finds ready acceptance in Bologna in the 14th century.

O'Keeffe Georgia 1887–1986

The American painter Georgia O'Keeffe was born in Wisconsin. After 1949 she lived in Abiquiu, New Mexico. Distinctive features of her work are the ambivalence of its imagery, and the breadth of its artistic language; this ranges from abstraction to representation, but always has its origins in nature. O'Keeffe studied at the Art Institute of Chicago (1905–6) and the Art Students League, New York (1907–8). She worked for four years as a commercial artist before returning to painting. At this period she was inspired by the ideas of Arthur Dow, with whom she later studied at Columbia University (1914–15). From 1912 to 1918 she taught

art. In 1915 O'Keeffe made her first self-consciously original works. These were shown to Alfred Stieglitz, who gave her a solo exhibition in 1917 at the 291 gallery. She gave up teaching in 1918 and moved to New York.

Until 1924, when she married Stieglitz, O'Keeffe's drawings and paintings in watercolor and oil were predominantly Abstract. Works such as *Blue and Green Music* (1919; Art Institute of Chicago) were unique in form, expressive power, and chromatic range. O'Keeffe is probably best known for her large, close-up views of flowers, such as *Black Iris* (1926; Metropolitan Museum, New York) with their sexual associations—she never painted the human figure as such. After the 1920s she often painted in series, such as the six versions of *Jack-in-a-Pulpit* (1930). In 1929 she made her first visit to New Mexico; thereafter she visited the State every year, buying a house in Abiquiu in 1945, the year before Stieglitz's death.

In the 1930s and 1940s she added new imagery to her range—animal bones, the New Mexico landscape, her adobe house. A surrealist feeling emerges in some of the bone pictures. For example, a skull hovers above a desert landscape in *From the Faraway Nearby* (1937; Metropolitan Museum, New York). In 1953 she visited Europe for the first time and began to travel widely. Flying introduced more new imagery—skyscrapers with clouds, views of the land from above. O'Keeffe won numerous awards, and exhibited often in the United States.

Further reading. Castro, J. *The Art and Life of Georgia O'Keeffe*, London (1986). Eldredge, C.C. *Georgia O'Keeffe: the Development of an American Modern*, Minnesota (1971). Goodrich, L. and Bry,

D. *Georgia O'Keeffe*, New York (1970). O'Keeffe, G. "Letters to Alfred Stieglitz" in *Georgia O'Keeffe Catalogue*, New York (1938). O'Keeffe, G. *Georgia O'Keeffe*, New York (1976).

Okyo Maruyama 1733–95

The Japanese painter Maruyama Okyo was the founder of the *Maruyama* School, and has been a major influence on Japanese painting since. His original synthesis of native brushwork with Chinese and Western elements created a manner that came to dominate over others and that formed the basis for the modern *Nihonga* style.

He was born of farming stock near Kameoka, not far from Kyoto. The accident of birthplace was important in his work. He retained throughout his life an affection for the gentle agricultural landscapes of his home area, for the more dramatic Hozu Gorge through which he would have passed on the way to Kyoto, and for farming people and the ordinary townspeople of Kyoto, among whom he lived as a boy when working there in the toy industry.

Okyo was little educated in an age of increasing prestige for scholarship and his calligraphy was never more than barely competent; as a result his genius was purely visual. His painting was unpretentious, done joyously for its own sake, and these features he passed on to his School.

At 16 Okyo went to study with the *Kano* artist Ishida Yutei. The *Kano* School had by then reached a low point of academic dullness and resistance to innovation, and Okyo was soon looking for more vigorous attitudes. His grounding in *Kano* monochrome brushwork remained with him and he always stayed half a *Kano* artist, but he was so much more talented than his orthodox contemporaries that his style appears completely new.

By the time he reached his mid thirties he had studied Western perspective, through designing copperplate prints for the recently imported *camera oscura*. He had also studied the works of the Japanese and Chinese old masters in the Kyoto collection, and the contemporary decorative Chinese painting practiced in Nagasaki, and from all of these he fashioned a new style.

Okyo's most important innovation was his insistence on painting from nature, exemplified in his detailed sketchbooks of insects in the Tokyo National Museum. It

Georgia O'Keeffe: White Canadian Barn no. 2; oil on canvas; 30×76cm (12×30in); 1932. Metropolitan Museum, New York.

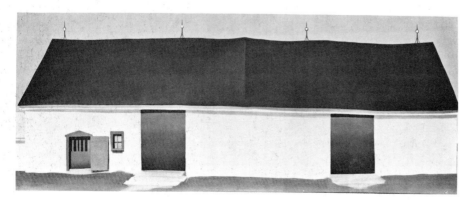

was this above all that breathed new life into Japanese art. From this time he became the most celebrated artist of his day.

Okyo pioneered or revived a number of painting styles which were taken up by his followers. They include the following six types: dramatic decorative screens influenced by Western perspective and sense of space (*Hozu Rapids*, Nishiyama Collection; *Snowy Pines*, Mitsui Collection); studies of nature in free, relaxed brushwork (*Wisteria Screens*, Nezu Museum of Art, Tokyo); unidealized genre paintings (*Seven Happinesses and Seven Misfortunes*, handscrolls, Eman'in, Otsu); formal portraits of Chinese beauties and bird-and-flower paintings in the Chinese style (*Peacocks and Paeonies*, Eman'in, Otsu); displays of ink monochrome of extraordinary virtuosity (*Dragon Screens*, Tokyo National Museum); and soft and misty landscape (screens of *Spring* and *Summer*, Yamato Bunkakan, Nara). Okyo's direct pupils included Matsumura Goshun, Nagasawa Rosetsu, Komai Genki, Watanbe Nangaku, Yamaguchi Soken, and Mori Tessan.

Olbrich Josef Maria 1867–1908

The career of the Austrian architect and designer Josef Olbrich was brief but full of inspiration. He worked as chief draftsman for Otto Wagner and contributed designs for the Vienna Stadtbahn project. One of the cofounders of the Vienna Secession, he designed its exhibition building in 1898. His brilliant *Jugendstil* graphics for *Ver Sacrum*, the magazine of the Secession, were extremely influential; more than anyone else involved, Olbrich's work came to be identified with a Secession style.

In 1899 Olbrich left Vienna for Darmstadt. There he built a large part of the Duke of Hesse's new colony for artists, including his own house (1901) and the transitional and prophetic Hochzeitsturm (1908).

Oldenburg Claes 1929–

Claes Oldenburg is a Swedish-born sculptor and environmentalist. The son of a diplomat, he traveled a great deal during his childhood. After graduating from Yale University, and working as a reporter, he studied at the Chicago Art Institute with Paul Weighardt (1952–4). After moving to New York he worked for a while as a

Claes Oldenburg: Proposed Monument for Thames River, Thames Ball; crayon, ink, watercolor on postcard; 9×14cm (3½×5½in); 1967. Private collection

painter. With a group of New York artists that included Jim Dine, he became involved in a new kind of participatory art known as the "happening". He then turned to painted plaster replicas of food (*Two Cheeseburgers, with Everything*, 1962; Museum of Modern Art, New York). Oldenburg's involvement with popular products (including ice creams, pies, baked potatoes) was an important aspect of the first phase of Pop art.

Further reading. Baro, G. *Claes Oldenburg: Drawings and Prints*, London and New York (1969). Kramer, H. *The Age of the Avant-Garde*, London (1974). Oldenburg, C. *Notes in Hand: Miniatures of my Notebook Pages*, New York (1971). Oldenburg, C. *Claes Oldenburg and Coosje van Bruggen: Large-Scale Projects*, London (1994).

Olitski Jules 1922–

The American painter and sculptor Jules Olitski was born in Snovsk, Russia. He studied in New York at the National Academy of Design, the Beaux-Arts Institute, and New York University (1940–2), and at the Zadkine School of Sculpture, Paris (1949), before teaching at Post College, Conn. and Bennington College, Vt. until 1967. In the 1960s Olitski made large Abstract stained paintings. In 1965 he began his distinctive spray paintings, in which he emphasized the edges and colored surface with hand-painted features.

During the 1970s he came to rely upon thick gestural paint surfaces. Since 1968, when he made his first painted steel sculptures, Olitski has worked with equal critical acclaim in both media. He represented the U.S.A. in the 1966 Venice Biennale.

Jules Olitski: Thigh Smoke; acrylic on canvas; 424×235cm (167×93in); 1966. Collection of the First National Bank, Seattle

Further reading. Greenberg, C. *Three New American Painters: Louis, Noland, Olitski*, Regina, Sask. (1963). Moffett, K. *Jules Olitski*, Boston (1973). Olitski, J. "On Sculpture", *Metropolitan Museum of Art Bulletin*, New York (April 1969).

Oliver Isaac, the Elder
fl. 1568–1617

The English miniaturist Isaac Oliver was born in Rouen of Huguenot parents. He lived in London from 1568, and was apprenticed to Nicolas Hilliard *c*1580. Although he was influenced by Hilliard, Oliver showed a strong preference for Flemish masters and the Italian Mannerists, whose works he copied in Italy in 1596. By 1595 Oliver had become a rival to Hilliard, and in 1604 was appointed limner to Queen Anne of Denmark. Unlike the work of Hilliard, Oliver's limning often resembles a reduction of full-scale portraiture, and his dramatic lighting and shadows in the Flemish manner show a taste for composition on an ambitious scale.

Opicinus de Canistris
1296–*c*1350

The Italian author and draftsman Opicinus de Canistris produced a remarkable series of visionary drawings after a mental breakdown. He was born near Pavia and trained for the priesthood, but poverty forced him to work as a teacher and, from 1315, as a professional illuminator of manuscripts; he also studied medicine. In 1329 he was appointed to the Papal Chancery at Avignon in recognition of his activities as a political writer. His breakdown in 1334 left his right hand paralyzed. This ended his Chancery work, but he was still able to draw—though he claimed that the pictures were not produced by any normal human means.

Certainly, these works (preserved in two manuscripts in the Vatican) are unlike anything else in medieval art. Although his style is typically Lombard and unremarkable, and although the drawings are made up of conventional features derived from cartography, medical illustrations, and schemata, these elements are combined to create grotesque images which are both fantastic and didactic—and also uniquely personal for a Trecento artist.

The biography of Opicinus is known from a pictorial composition consisting of

Isaac Oliver the Elder: Frances Howard, Countess of Somerset and Essex; watercolor on vellum; diameter 13cm (5in); *c*1595. Victoria and Albert Museum, London

40 concentric circles, one for each year of his life, divided into 365 segments; on this "calendar" Opicinus inscribed important events in the appropriate place. He surrounded the whole with busts of the evangelists and four self-portraits, each showing him at a different age.

Many of this artist's drawings are based on the map of Europe, reflecting recent developments in cartography; but the land-masses and seas are, with the addition of a few extra lines, transformed into deformed human figures. Copious inscriptions explain the symbolism of these pictures. Other drawings employ familiar Christian motifs—the Crucifixion, the Virgin and Child—but the scale of the figures varies enormously, creating a hallucinatory effect: tiny bodies are superimposed on gigantic ones, suggesting contemporary medical illustrations of the foetus in the womb. Indeed, a marked sexual ele-

ment pervades Opicinus' work; this, with his mental history, has made him of special interest to students of psychotic art.

Orcagna 1308?–*c*68

Andrea di Cione, known as Orcagna, was a Florentine painter, sculptor, and architect. His signature on his magnificent sculptured *Tabernacle* (1359) in the church of Orsanmichele, Florence, suggests that he thought of himself primarily as a painter. But owing to the loss of many of his frescoes, such as those in the Florentine churches of S. Croce and S. Maria Novella (fragments of which survive), his chief fame in this respect rests on his signed and dated Strozzi Altarpiece (1357) in the Strozzi Chapel, S. Maria Novella, Florence. Our knowledge of his position as "capomaestro" in both Orsanmichele (by 1356) and Orvieto Cathedral (1358–*c*62) as well as his advice on Florence Cathedral (1366), means that, paradoxically, there is more evidence of his work as sculptor, architect, even as mosaicist (at Orvieto), than as a painter.

The Strozzi Altarpiece, however, is enough to show that Orcagna is the most important Florentine painter of his time. It acted not only as chapel altarpiece but also as a focus for the fresco decoration on the chapel walls, which consists of the *Last Judgment, Heaven* and *Hell*, painted by Orcagna's brother, Nardo di Cione.

The theme of the Last Judgment, which also formed the subject of Orcagna's frescoes in S. Croce, can be seen as typical of the age, and probably reflects the experience of the 1348 Black Death. While the first half of the 14th century is marked by an increasing humanity and tenderness in the painting of sacred subjects in Tuscany, the period of Orcagna's activity sees this replaced by an emphasis on the supernatural, hieratic relationship of God to Man, more typical of the previous century. The change in attitude is embodied in a change in style. The creation of three-dimensional realistic space, so characteristic of Giotto and his followers, is not the dominating concern of Orcagna. Instead he contrasts the realistic painting of bodies and drapery with an equivocal space, and stresses the surface pattern formed by severe silhouettes and an unforeshortened ground.

In the centre of the Strozzi Altarpiece is the figure of Christ the Judge surrounded by seraphim, with two pairs of saints at either side. The gold background has vestigial columns incised upon it which connect the back of the ground ("behind" the figures) and the pendentives of the frame ("in front of" the figures). The result is a highly sophisticated spatial tension. This is only clearly resolved in the powerful figure of Christ who, in contrast with the other figures of the altarpiece, is seen in a starkly uncompromising frontal pose.

As well as Nardo di Cione, Orcagna had another brother, Jacopo, who also worked with him. Under Orcagna's leadership, the three together formed the most influential Florentine workshop of the period.

Ordóñez Bartolomé *fl. 1517–20*

The Spanish sculptor Bartolomé Ordóñez was born in Burgos. He was the first of the so-called "Four Eagles" of Spanish Renaissance sculpture. First documented at Naples in 1517 (where he worked on the Carraciolo Altar in S. Giovanni a Carbonara), he was in Barcelona in 1518 (where he worked on the *trascoro*—the front part on the choir screen—in the cathedral). While in Barcelona, in 1519, he was given the commissions for the tombs of Philip the Handsome and Joan the Mad (Royal Chapel, Granada) and of Cardinal Cisneros (Magistral Church, Alcalá do Henares) by Charles V. The commissions had originally been given to Domenico Fancelli, who died in 1519 and who may have been Ordóñez's master. In order to carry out these commissions Ordóñez moved his workshop to Carrara, where he died in December 1520. One of his last works was the tomb of Bishop Fonseca, in Coca (1520).

Orley Bernaert van 1491/2–1542

The Flemish painter Bernaert van Orley worked mainly at the court of the Regent of the Netherlands, Margaret of Austria, at Brussels. Unlike many of his Flemish contemporaries, who simply incorporated Italian motifs into painting, van Orley had a profound knowledge of the principles of Italian High Renaissance design. The Altarpiece of the Visions of Job (1521; Musées Royaux des Beaux-Arts de Belgique, Brussels) is indebted to Raphael, whose compositions he knew both through engravings and through the original cartoons for the Sistine tapestries, then in the Netherlands. Van Orley himself was highly successful as a designer of tapestry and stained glass. His portraits (for example *Dr Zelle*, 1519; Musées Royaux des Beaux-Arts de Belgique, Brussels) are more schematic, less individually characterized than those of his contemporary, Gossaert.

Orozco José 1883–1949

The Mexican mural painter José Clemente Orozco was one of the three major Mexican muralists of the 20th century, the other two being Diego Rivera and Siqueiros. Born in Ciudad Guzman, Jalisco, Orozco first trained as an agronomist (1895–9), then from 1908 to 1914 he studied art sporadically at the Academia San Carlos in Mexico City. During the Mexican Revolution he worked as a political caricaturist and propagandist (1911–17). From 1923 he painted in public buildings large murals whose thematic content is derived from his Mexican Revolution and Civil War experi-

Bernaert van Orley: Portrait of Emperor Charles V; panel; 72×52cm (28×20in); c1516. Museum of Fine Arts, Budapest

ences (for example, *Prometheus*, 1950; Pomona College, Claremont, California). He spent the years 1930 to 1934 in the U.S.A. and Europe. In his work Orozco angrily criticizes the futile struggles in which people are needlessly sacrificed. His use of color is sober and austere, his forms often tormented (*Man in Flames*; fresco; 1938–9, Hospicio Cabañas, Guadalajara), **and he treated his subjects with a blend of unsentimental social criticism and compassion.**

Further reading. Charlot, J. *An Artist on Art: Collected Essays of Jean Charlot*, Honolulu (1972). Helm, M. *Man of Fire: José Clemente Orozco*, New York (1953). Orozco, J.C. *An Autobiography*, Austin, Tex. (1962). Orozco, J.C. *The Artist in New York: Letters to Jean Charlot and Unpublished Writings 1925–1929*, Austin Tex. and London (1974). Reed, A. *J.C. Orozco*, New York (1956). Reed, A. *The Mexican Muralists*, New York (1960).

Ostade Adriaen van 1610–84

Adriaen Jansz. van Ostade was a Dutch painter and etcher from Haarlem who specialized in low-life genre scenes. He was probably a pupil of Frans Hals about the same time as Adriaen Brouwer, a painter whose pictures influenced his subject matter, style, and content. Ostade's pictures from the 1630s are painted in subdued brown tones with little local color, and generally depict boisterous tavern or

Adriaen van Ostade: The Alchemist; detail; oil on wood panel; full size 34×45cm (14×18in); 1661. National Gallery, London

hovel scenes of drunken, dancing, or brawling peasants. The treatment of such themes is good-humored and without satire.

In the 1640s Ostade's work acquired deepening contrasts of light and shadow and a greater sense of atmosphere. After *c*1650 his peasants became less rowdy and more respectable, his colors richer, his tonality lighter, and his technique more refined (for example, *The Alchemist*, 1661; National Gallery, London). The lessening of vulgarity (which is accompanied by a certain loss of vitality) may be related to changes in the artist's clientele, his financial success, and his marriage to a woman from a higher social class than himself.

Isaack van Ostade (1621–49) was the brother and a pupil of Adriaen. His early pictures are similar to his brother's low-life scenes but he later inclined towards landscape, notably atmospheric silvery-gray winter scenes with many figures.

Oud J.J.P. 1890–1963

The Dutch architect Jacobus Johannes Pieter Oud was born at Purmerend, near Amsterdam. He completed his studies at the Technical University, Delft. In 1917 he was a cofounder of the *De Stijl* movement. His early projects (terrace houses at Scheveningen and a factory at Purmerend) were inspired in part by *De Stijl* principles. After he was appointed City Architect of Rotterdam in 1918 he designed standardized workers' dwellings for the city's Spangen settlement. Oud left *De Stijl* in 1921 but continued partly to apply its principles, emphasizing social context, in designing large housing developments at the Hook of Holland (1924), Kiefhoek, and Rotterdam (1925). His book, *Dutch Architecture*, was published in 1926 by the Bauhaus, where he had lectured in 1922. He built a terrace of small houses at the International Exhibition, Stuttgart, in 1927. Throughout his long career Oud completed many important architectural projects.

Oudry Jean-Baptiste 1686–1755

Jean-Baptiste Oudry was a French painter of hunting and still-life subjects. The pupil first of his father, then of Michel Serre, and especially of Nicolas de Largillière, he continued the tradition of still life and animal painting already well established by Desportes. The type and style of these pictures derive from painters of the Rubens school, such as Frans Snyders and Jan Fyt, or the Dutch Jan Weenix; but Oudry's art is more decorative and Rococo in form and color than the earthier art of Desportes.

A member of the Académie in 1719, he began as a history painter, and also painted portraits. His favorite subjects were of the hunt, and his chief patron Louis XV. For the King, he designed a celebrated series of large tapestries, *The Hunts of Louis XV* (1733–46; cartoons at Fontainebleau), to be executed at the Gobelins works. These skillfully reconcile the older stylized perspectives of decorative tapestries with a more acute sense of realism. Oudry made many studies in the royal forests of Compiègne and Fontainebleau.

In 1726 Oudry became a designer at the Beauvais tapestry works, rising to Director in 1734. Here he employed the young François Boucher, and completely reorganized the works. He introduced more intimate, simple and natural forms, styles, and colors into tapestry design. In 1736, he was made Superintendent of the Gobelins works. As in the case of Boucher, working on tapestry designs had a profound effect on the decorative aspects of Oudry's painting. He also worked for the courts of Denmark, Sweden, and especially Mecklenburg-Schwerin. Oudry's interest in realism is also seen in his very fine landscape drawings, and he seems to have encouraged other artists in this.

Ouwater Albert van *fl. c*1445–*c*80

Albert van Ouwater was a Dutch painter, apparently based in Haarlem. Apart from a solitary documentary reference of 1467, we are entirely dependent upon Carel van Mander's *Schilderboek* of 1604 for information about him. This states that Geertgen tot Sint Jans was his pupil and that he excelled in the painting of landscape. It also describes what is today his only surviving identified work, *The Raising of Lazarus* in the Staatliche Museen, Berlin. This painting implies a degree of association with Bouts and a knowledge of

Jean-Baptiste Oudry: The Farm; oil on canvas; 130×212cm (51×83in); 1750. Louvre, Paris

southern Netherlandish art. *The Raising of Lazarus* is iconographically unprecedented in that it depicts this scene within an interior, rather than out of doors. Ouwater was the dominant artistic personality active in the northern Netherlands in the middle of the 15th century. He is doubly important as the master of Geertgen tot Sint Jans.

Overbeck Johann 1789–1869

Johann Friedrich Overbeck was a German painter and draftsman born in Lübeck. He studied at the Vienna Academy (1806–9), but preferred to frequent the circle around Eberhard Wächter. His friendship with Franz Pforr led to the formation in 1809 of the St Luke Brotherhood (also known as the Nazarenes), one of whose aims was the revival of Christian art. Overbeck was particularly dedicated to this ideal, which he sought to realize by painting religious subjects in the style of Raphael and Perugino (for example, *The Entry into Jerusalem*, 1809–24; formerly Marienkirche, Lübeck, destroyed 1942). Besides the sweetness of expression thereby achieved, the strict use of local colors and the emphasis on line and contour give these works the clarity and flatness of frescoes.

Overbeck's move to Rome in 1810 allowed him to study the Vatican frescoes of Pintoricchio and Raphael and greatly increased the Italianate influence in his work. He acknowledged this debt in the painting *Italia and Germania* (1811–23; Neue Pinakothek, Munich), which expresses not only his own love of Italian art but Germany's constant yearning for the South. Pforr's death in 1812 precipitated a spiritual crisis in Overbeck's life, which he surmounted by becoming a Catholic in 1813. It was probably Overbeck who suggested the religious subject of *Joseph in Egypt* for the frescoes painted in the house of the Prussian Consul in Rome, Salomon Bartholdi (1815–16; now in the Nationalgalerie, East Berlin). His own contributions to the decorations are remarkable for the degree to which he created a personal idiom out of his Italian models. The balance he achieved between a lyrical expression of nature and a humane view of man is truly Romantic in spirit.

These same qualities are evident in the work he did for the Casino Massimo frescoes (1818–27; Casino Massimo, Rome). Typically, Overbeck chose to treat the subject, Tasso's *Gerusalemme Liberata*, undramatically, emphasizing the Christian rather than the heroic aspects of the epic. In 1829 he painted the highly persuasive fresco *The Miracle of the Roses* (Portiuncula Chapel, S. Maria degli Angeli, Assisi). In this painting religious fervor is tempered by a simple, warm humanity; but

his later works, like *The Triumph of Religion in the Arts* (1840; Städelsches Kunstinstitut, Frankfurt am Main) are marred by a dogmatic Catholicism. His line hardened and his color often became cold and enamel-like.

Overbeck became celebrated in his later years. He only returned twice to Germany, but was visited in Rome by statesmen and artists alike. He was particularly influential in England on artists such as W. Dyce and Ford Madox Brown. His frescoes were cited as a model for the decorations of the Houses of Parliament.

Ozenfant Amédée 1886–1966

The French painter Amédée Ozenfant was born at Saint-Quentin. He published the magazine *L'Élan* (1915–17) and, with Charles-Édouard Jeanneret (later called le Corbusier), *L'Esprit Nouveau* (1920–5) and *Aprés le Cubisme* (1919). These expounded the ideas of Purism embodied in his paintings: the removal of the romantic element from Cubism and the use of classically calm, architectonic principles of composition. His mural designs of the 1920s and 1930s culminated in an enormous composition called *Life* (1931–8; Musée National d'Art Moderne, Paris). His theoretical writings include *Art* (1928) and a diary of the period 1931–4. He lived in New York from 1939 to his death.

P

Pacheco Francisco 1564–1654

The Spanish painter, writer, and theorist Francisco Pacheco was born in Sanlúcar de Barrameda. He studied in Seville under Luis Fernández, and then briefly in Flanders. As a painter his methods were painstaking, his style rooted in 16th-century Mannerism, and his achievement mediocre. Nevertheless he had the satisfaction of being the master of Diego Velázquez, who married his daughter.

Pacheco's most important paintings were a series of Mercedarian scenes for the Merced Calzada, Seville (1601–11). He also painted the *Immaculate Conception* many times. He was more influential as a writer than as a painter; his artistic theories and iconographical precepts were set out in his *Arte de la Pintura* ("Art of Painting"; 1649).

Pacher Michael c1435–98

The greatest sculptor and painter of the late Gothic in Austria, Michael Pacher is documented as a citizen of Brunico (Bruneck) in the Val Pusteria (Pustertal) from 1467 until 1496. He then transferred his center of activity to Salzburg. A now-lost altarpiece is recorded as having been signed and dated 1465, and the contract for the altarpiece in the old parish church of Gríes (Gries) outside Bolzano (Bozen) is dated 27 May 1471. In it Pacher was instructed to follow the pattern of the high altarpiece of the parish church of Bolzano (by Hans von Judenburg, 1422–3), and the composition is accordingly conservative.

On 13 December 1471 Pacher signed the contract for the large-scale altarpiece in the pilgrimage church of St Wolfgang in the Salzkammergut, which he signed and dated 1481, and presumably work on the Gríes Altarpiece continued well after 1471. Similarly, although the documentary evidence suggests that the altarpiece for the parish church of S. Lorenzo in Pusteria (St Lorenzen) was donated in 1462–3, the actual execution of that altarpiece, of

Michael Pacher: altarpiece of The Fathers of the Church; center panel 216×196cm (85×77in), wing paintings 206×93cm (81×37in); c1483. Alte Pinakothek, Munich

which only the carved *Madonna Enthroned* survives (in situ), stretched over many years.

The painted panels depicting scenes of *The Life of St Lawrence* (Alte Pinakothek, Munich, and Österreichische Galerie, Vienna) probably formed part of the S. Lorenzo Altarpiece, but they reveal contacts with Italian 15th-century painting, especially the works of Mantegna, not detectable in the carved figures.

This contrast is even more apparent in Pacher's masterpiece, the St Wolfgang Altarpiece. His tentative attempts, in the Gríes Altarpiece, to give a greater illusion of depth by adding painted angels behind are replaced in the St Wolfgang Altarpiece by a fully three-dimensional composition.

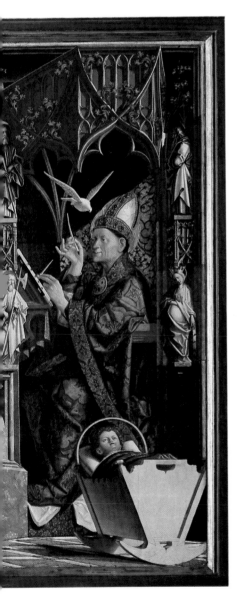

Again depicting *The Coronation of the Virgin*, the figures and the architecture are completely integrated: the principal protagonists of the *tableau vivant* grow out of the dark, mysterious recesses of the shrine, and the intricate web of pierced canopies is extended up into the elaborate cresting of figures and pinnacles. In this carved and gilt complex there are no echoes of the Italian Renaissance; the evolution of Pacher as a sculptor reveals instead contact with the sculptural traditions of the Upper Rhine, and possibly with Nikolaus Gerhaert van Leyden at Constance, as well as with the engravings of the Master ES.

On the other hand the style of Pacher as a painter, in the wings of the St Wolfgang Altarpiece, shows such a depth of understanding for rationally constructed spaces that direct experience of Italian Renaissance painting, probably in Padua, must be postulated. These opposing developments are brought together in the altarpiece of *The Fathers of the Church* from Novacella (Neustift), now in the Alte Pinakothek, Munich, which dates from c1483. Pacher was active in Salzburg in 1484, and for longer periods during the years 1496 to 1498. The last payment to him for the destroyed altarpiece formerly in the Franziskanerkirche is dated 7 July, 1498. By 24 August 1498 Pacher was dead.

Further reading. Hempel, E. *Michael Pacher*, Vienna (1931). Rasmo, N. *Michael Pacher*, London (1971) and Milan (1969).

Padarath *c1550–c1650*

Padarath was a Mughal painter in the reigns of Akbar (1556–1605) and Jahangir (1605–27). Very little is known about him. One of his most remarkable works is *The Mountain Sheep* from the Royal Albums in the Chester Beatty Library, Dublin. The drawing is subtle, the colors are restrained yet richly glowing with a dominant dark red. It rivals some of the finest animal paintings of Mansur and Abul Hasan. In the Chester Beatty *Akbarnama* album, *Himu Brought Before Akbar* is by Padarath. Another of his works is in the *Anwar-i-Suhayli* (British Library, London).

Pajou Augustin *1730–1809*

The French sculptor Augustin Pajou was born in Paris. He was a pupil of J.-B.

Padarath: The Mountain Sheep; vellum; 28×19cm (11×7½in); c1610–20. Chester Beatty Library, Dublin

Lemoyne. An accomplished draftsman and designer, his greatest achievement is the sculptural decoration of the Opera House at Versailles (1768–70). Favored by Madame du Barry, Pajou enjoyed a number of royal commissions, but survived the Revolution unaffected. He made many portrait busts, those of his friends being much more successful than the well-known but insipid ones of du Barry herself. His most celebrated work is the statue of *Psyche Abandoned* (1791; Louvre, Paris), a sentimental piece with a Neoclassical overlay that anticipates French 19th-century Academic sculpture.

Palladio Andrea *1508–80*

Andrea Palladio was perhaps the most distinguished architect working in northern Italy during the 16th century. Certainly to contemporary eyes he was the most famous. Although he was also a builder of churches and palaces, it is his villas that have attracted greatest attention. The villas provided much of the inspiration for the style called Palladianism which rapidly gained currency in England and the United States during the 17th and 18th centuries. The understanding of the work of Inigo Jones, Lord Burlington, or Thomas Jeffer-

Andrea Palladio: the Villa Rotunda, near Vicenza; built 1566–7

son is impossible without an appreciation of Palladio and his book *I Quattro Libri dell'Architettura* ("The Four Books of Architecture").

The life of Palladio is well documented. He was born as Andrea di Pietro in Padua in 1508. His family had moved to Vicenza—not very far away—by 1521, and there Palladio continued his apprenticeship as a mason. He remained in Vicenza and later Venice until his death in 1580. By the accident of birth, he was therefore two things that are of considerable importance in understanding his career and later reputation: he was northern and provincial. Because he chose to remain as such, visiting only briefly the artistic magnet of Rome, success was the greater struggle and fame had perforce to be captured rather than sought.

Palladio was lucky. His translation from di Pietro to Palladio in 1540 marked the real start of his architectural career, and simultaneously his encounter with what may be termed the Vicentine Enlightenment, particularly with Gian Giorgio Trissino. In his work at Trissino's villa at Cricoli in 1538 he was a mason rather than designer, but his latent talents were sufficiently displayed to impress his patron. Trissino took him to Rome the following year and introduced him in 1542 to the important Thiene family. He was involved with their Vicentine palace, and on the death of the designer Giulio Romano in 1546 he took over as architect. He revisited Rome in 1547, and in 1549 won the important commission in Vicenza for the rebuilding of the basilica.

The basilica was a 15th-century building whose surrounding loggias had partially collapsed in 1446; to rebuild them was Palladio's commission. His solution was an outrageously modern one for Vicenza, redolent of Classical ideas, and closely inspired by his visits to Rome. He built a system of what were really small triumphal arches, loosely based on the arch at Aquino, and derived in scale from a structure such as the Theater of Marcellus in Rome. In more contemporary terms it showed a familiarity with Sansovino's Library at S. Marco, Venice (begun in 1537), and a more than diligent reading of Serlio's *Architettura*. This harmonious blending of antique and modern was totally successful, both in visual terms and—of more importance for Palladio's career—with his scholarly patrons in the Vicentine Council.

Close on the heels of his basilica commission followed three villas: the Villa Pisani (now Placco) in Montagnana (1552), the Villa Cornaro at Piombino Dese (c1560–5), and the Villa Chiericati (1554). Of the three, the Villa Chiericati at Vancimuglio near Vicenza was perhaps the most notable, because of its large freestanding portico of the Ionic order. This appeared here for the first time in Palladio's work and cast a long shadow over his later villas, and indeed the whole Palladian school. It was built for Giovanni Chiericati, the brother of Girolamo (for whom Palladio designed the Palazzo Chiericati in Vicenza;

1551–4) and one of his supporters in the basilican scheme.

In 1554 Palladio again visited Rome, this time in the company of another Vicentine oligarch, Daniele Barbaro. One important result of the visit was the publication in Venice in 1556 of Barbaro's edition of Vitruvius's *De Architectura* which was strongly influenced by Palladio in more than just the illustrations. This collaboration was more solidly expressed in the building of the Villa Barbaro at Maser, before 1558, for Daniele and his brother Marc' Antonio. While the villa—with its cruciform hall similar to that of the Villa Pisani, and its flanking ranges of farm buildings—was typical of Palladio, the extraordinary mannered form of the *nymphaeum* in the rear of the villa, and the windows and balconies of the first floor, were quite untypical. It was possibly a cooperative venture between Barbaro and Palladio, strongly influenced by the Roman architecture of Michelangelo. It was certainly at variance with the other villas of the period: Repeta (c1566), Badoer (1566), and the incomplete Thiene at Cicogna. These villas possibly fix the high watermark of Palladio's reputation in Vicenza, and it is significant for Palladio's growing fame that the builders of both the Villa Pisani and the Villa Cornaro were Venetians.

Palladio's reputation had spread. During the 1560s his most notable work was in Venice, where he built the facade of S. Francesco della Vigna (1562), and began work in 1565 at S. Giorgio Maggiore. At the former his design, with its application of the giant order and incidental theme of smaller columns, was considered sufficiently novel to supersede the earlier scheme of Sansovino. It was repeated by Palladio at S. Giorgio—more obviously in the exterior, more subtly in the nave, where the columns on pedestals and the pilasters in the ground make a decisive unity. His plan was a longitudinal one, with a dome at the crossing, typical of Tridentine church architecture, but with the more startling innovation of the choir ending in a screen through which the church extended into the presbytery. Moreover it synthesized the conflicting forms of the Greek Cross, as at Bramante's

Andrea Palladio: the facade of S. Giorgio Maggiore, Venice; begun in 1565

St Peter's, and the longitudinal plan favored by the Catholic reformists. At the same time, the visual extension of the nave into the presbytery gave an axial drive to the church from the very moment it was entered.

In the secular sphere at this time, Palladio designed two contrasting villa types. The Villa Emo at Fanzolo, begun c1562, followed the Villa Barbaro in the use of the flanking farm buildings to make the villa visually more impressive, and to provide a foil to the style of the main building. The latter was typical of what was to become the villa motif: a pedimented portico—in this case, three bays set flush with the walls rather than projecting—with a window bay on either side. As a facade it was a simpler and more successful version of the one Palladio had used some six years earlier at the Villa Badoer, and this spartan quality well became its role as little more than a farmhouse.

Its companion of 1566–7, the famous Rotunda, was a villa of a very different sort. It was foremost a suburban building on a hillside site just outside Vicenza, where the landscape was to be admired rather than farmed. The building, with its central dome and hall and four projecting porticos, was a reworking of his drawings of the ruined temple of Fortune at Palestrina. (The temple's inspiration is again obvious in the grandiose project for the Villa Trissino of c1566.) The Villa Rotunda existed on its own terms as the sophisticated setting for the social life of a retired clergyman. In this way, it belonged with similar but grander Roman villas such as the Madama (which Palladio had seen and drawn) and the Villa Giulia.

The last decade of Palladio's career was dominated by public commissions. With the death of his Venetian rival, Jacopo Sansovino, in 1570, Palladio ruled Venice as he had done Vicenza. In 1571, he built the Loggia del Capitaniato in Vicenza as a public commission from the City Council. Its function as a sort of secular Benediction Loggia dictated its design. His composition for the facade facing the piazza was three bays of the giant order with balconies in between which served to emphasize the center. It was an impressive design, but one achieved at the expense of classical orthodoxy. For the Venetians, he worked at the Doges' Palace in San Marco, and more spectacularly in 1577 at the church of the Redentore.

The Redentore followed roughly the plan of S. Giorgio except that the emphasis on the longitudinal was substantially increased, and the perforated screen walls at the east end became all the more dramatic. The main facade was a fuller and more sophisticated rendering of the temple front found at S. Giorgio. It was composed according to the formula of the Pantheon: portico against abutment, abutment against dome. Although this was a flatter design, it was amazingly successful as a piece of sculpture when seen from the Piazza of San Marco across the lagoon. It had been conceived as a monument to the terrible plague of 1575–6, and as such this scenographic effect was wholly appropriate.

One of the last of Palladio's works was the eye-catching Teatro Olimpico in Vicenza, begun in 1580. It was completed by Scamozzi in 1583. Its semicircular auditorium was based on the antique amphitheater (of which Verona contained a good example), with a permanent scene front in the form of a triumphal arch decorated with statues of the richer and more distinguished members of the Olympic Academy. This was derived appropriately enough from his own illustration in Barbaro's edition of Vitruvius's *De Architectura*.

Palladio died in August 1580. His memorial was the buildings he had built in and around Vicenza and Venice, and more durably his book, *I Quattro Libri dell'Architettura* of 1570. In Books II and III of this he gave a vivid kaleidoscope of his architectural achievements, made the more catching and influential by the series of woodcut plans, elevations, and sections that accompanied and explained most of his schemes. Of the two other parts, Book I was devoted to the Classical orders and Book IV to antique temples. Palladio, like Serlio, intended to continue with further installments, but none was ever published. It was left to Lord Burlington in 1730 to pick up where he had left off, and to publish his drawings of the Roman baths as *Fabriche Antiche disegnate di Andrea Palladio Vicentino* ("Antique Buildings drawn by Andrea Palladio of Vicenza").

By his contemporary, Vasari, Palladio was extolled as "a man of singular judgment and brain", a summary of whose buildings would make "too long a study to seek to recount the many particulars of the strange and lively inventions and fantasies that are in them". To the succeeding centuries, Palladio's claim was much the same: an architect who balanced classicism and imagination, the grand and the utilitarian, and who appealed widely at a variety of levels. It was the extraordinary range of his talents that made him perennially popular, so much so that even the arch-Romantic Goethe wrote in 1795: "The more one studies Palladio, the more incredible one finds the man's genius, mastery, richness, versatility, and grace."

Further reading. Ackerman, J. S. *Palladio*, Harmondsworth (1966). *Andrea Palladio 1508–1580*, London (1975). Puppi, L. *Andrea Palladio*, London (1975).

Palma Vecchio 1480?–1528

The Venetian painter Jocopo d'Antonio Negretti adopted the name of Palma. He is known as Palma Vecchio, "Old Palma", to distinguish him from his great-nephew, Palma Giovine, "Young Palma" (1544–1628). He came from the Province of Bergamo but was settled in Venice by 1510. We know nothing of his training. If Vasari is right in saying he died aged 48, he will probably have been a little younger than Giorgione and a little older than Titian, and we can see his free and rather luscious style as a parallel development to that of those painters from the later style of Giovanni Bellini.

Palma painted religious pictures and straightforward portraits, but his speciality was pictures of blond women of somewhat ample charms, such as the *Portrait of a Lady* (c1520; Museo Poldi Pezzoli, Milan). Good examples of this are the *Girl with a Lute* in the collection of the Duke of Northumberland at Alnwick Castle, Northumberland, and the *Three Sisters*, or *Three Graces* in the Gemäldegalerie Alte Meister, Dresden, an intimate group in which the Bellinesque formula of an oblong picture of the Madonna flanked by two saints is ingeniously adapted to a secular role (unless these in fact represent the Cardinal Virtues). There is also the splendid *Venus and Cupid* in the Fitzwilliam Museum, Cambridge, with its lovely landscape of blue, green, and gold.

His finest religious painting is the *St Barbara* in S. Maria Formosa, Venice. The beautiful *Holy Family with Saints* in the Gallerie dell'Accademia, Venice, was completed by Titian, who defeated Palma in the year of his death in the competition for the altarpiece of *The Death of St Peter Martyr* in SS. Giovanni e Paolo, Venice.

Palma Vecchio: Portrait of a Gentleman; oil on panel transferred to canvas; 70×56cm (27×22in). Philadelphia Museum of Art

Further reading. Mariacher, G. *Palma il Vecchio*, Milan (1968). Rylands, P. *Palma Vecchio*, Cambridge, England (1992).

Palmer Samuel 1805–81

The English painter and printmaker Samuel Palmer was born in London, where he received his first training with a topographical painter of mean talent. His earliest landscapes, which he began exhibiting at the Royal Academy in 1819, show an admiration for Turner and a studied appreciation of the leading watercolor painters of the period. About 1822 he met his future father-in-law, the landscape and **portrait painter John Linnell (1792–1882), who encouraged him to study the engravings of Northern Renaissance artists and to approach painting with attention to nature's minute details.**

The immediate impact of Linnell's tuition is apparent in Palmer's 1824 sketchbook (British Museum, London, and Victoria and Albert Museum, London). His development of a more unorthodox landscape style was greatly facilitated by his introduction to William Blake in the same year. Devoutly religious, with a keen poetic sense, Palmer enthusiastically embraced Blake's visionary conception of nature; he was especially wrought up by the "mystic and dreamy glimmer" of Blake's woodcut designs for Thornton's *Virgil*. Some of his finest extant drawings, the six sepia landscapes of 1825 (Ashmolean Museum, Oxford), were the first fruits of this intoxicating friendship. These tightly compacted drawings present a completely private view of a nature that is numinous in its rich details.

Between 1826 and 1832 Palmer lived at Shoreham, where he adopted a rustic lifestyle and entertained a small group of like-minded Blake devotees who called themselves "The Ancients". The almost artless style of his earlier drawings gave way to a more fluid treatment of landscape, and towards the end of this intensively productive period he began to introduce more conventional pastoral imagery.

The Reform Bill of 1833 brought turmoil to Palmer's sheltered retreat, and by 1836 he was permanently resettled in London. The following year he married Hannah Linnell, and in the company of George Richmond left for Italy where he studied the old masters and the landscape terrain that had inspired Claude. In 1839 he returned to London. Concerned with developing a market for his pictures, he began exhibiting regularly with the Society of Painters in Watercolors from 1843; he became a full member of that society in 1854.

Palmer's finished watercolors during the 1840s and 1850s consisted of topographical views in Italy and England, episodes of English history, and literary illustrations, with Milton providing a recurrent inspiration. Calculated to appeal to a public rapidly becoming accustomed to the scientific naturalism and bright colors of Pre-Raphaelite painting, these exhibition pictures lack the elemental simplicity and spirituality of his earlier works; however, they can be very impressive technically, especially in their light effects, and they have their own unique poetic charm. During this period he also learned etching, a medium he found most congenial to lyric expression.

In the early 1860s Palmer left London for Reigate. From 1864 he worked on illustrations, some of which he etched, for Milton's *Minor Poems*; he left unfinished at his death his illustrated translation of Virgil's *Eclogues*. The diverse and often conflicting aims that plagued Palmer's art throughout his later career are resolved in the twilight reveries and tranquillity of these last designs.

Further reading. Grigson, G. *Samuel Palmer's Valley of Vision*, London (1960). Grigson, G. *Samuel Palmer: the Visionary Years*, London (1947). Melville, R. *Samuel Palmer*, London (1956).

Panini Giovanni 1691–1765

Giovanni Paolo Panini, an Italian painter of ruins, public festivals, and historic

Samuel Palmer: Ruth Returned from Gleaning; pen and ink wash heightened with white chalk on paper; 29×39cm (11×15in); 1828. Victoria and Albert Museum, London

Giovanni Panini: Imaginary Gallery of Ancient Roman Art; oil on canvas; 171×231cm (67×91in); 1757. Metropolitan Museum, New York

events, was born in Piacenza. By 1711 he was in Rome, where he trained with scenographic architects and landscape painters. He became both an architect and a painter of large-scale illusionistic designs (in, for example, the Palazzo Albani, 1720, and the Palazzo Quirinale, 1722, both in Rome). Popular with French patrons, he participated in decorations for the *Fête* held in Rome in 1729 to commemorate the birth of the Dauphin. From *c*1725 Panini painted numerous views both of the modern city and of the ruins of Rome, which were often bought by foreign tourists.

Paolozzi Eduardo 1924–

The Scottish sculptor and printmaker Eduardo Paolozzi was born in Edinburgh of Italian parents. He studied at Edinburgh College of Art (1943–4) and at the Slade School of Fine Art (1944–7). From 1947 to 1949 he lived in Paris, returning to London to teach at the Central School until 1955 and at St Martin's School of Art (1955–8). He was visiting professor at Hamburg School of Art (1960–2) and at the University of California, Berkeley (1968). Since 1967 he has been a lecturer in ceramics at the Royal College of Art, London.

Throughout his career, Paolozzi has been inspired by modern technology and has explored its relationship to art and society in many prints and sculptures. Paolozzi's early contact with Surrealism in Paris has influenced all aspects of his work, mainly through collage techniques. Giacometti is reflected in the open, linear wire and bronze sculptures made between 1947 and 1955. Later he made Pop-related fantastic figures and heads, cast from junk, with richly detailed surfaces. These led to anthropomorphic painted aluminum pieces cast from stock machine parts. Until the early 1970s he made a group of Abstract "futuristic" organic and extremely reductive sculptures in chromed steel and aluminum.

In the 1970s Paolozzi worked mainly in relief both in wood and cast materials. Though such works are Abstract, they are built up of a multiplicity of often repeated elements which are based on one central idea or image. Among his many commissions are the Four Doors for the Hunterian Art Gallery, Glasgow (1979).

Paolozzi has an equally great reputation as a printmaker. His major contribution was to the development of silkscreen and photolithography as fine art media with his Pop art prints, for example *As is When* (1964–5).

Eduardo Paolozzi: Jason; bronze; height 168cm (66in), base 37×29cm (15×11in); 1956. Museum of Modern Art, New York

Paris Matthew *c1200–59*

Matthew Paris was an English historian and illuminator. One of the few named medieval artists to whom a substantial body of work can be attributed with some certainty, Paris spent his career at St Albans, England. In 1217 he made his profession as a monk, and *c*1235 succeeded Roger of Wendover as the Abbey's historian. His interests were wide, including cartography, heraldry, and cosmography, but his main achievement consists of the chronicles and lives of the saints which he both wrote and illustrated. He was probably also involved in practical administrative duties, in connection with which he visited Norway from 1248 to 1249.

Although a monk, Paris had close contact with the lay nobility, including the court at Westminster. Richard Earl of Cornwall (brother of Henry III, whom he also knew) was an important source of information about events described in the chronicles. The inferred format of his saints' lives, with continuous bands of illustration placed above the Anglo-Norman French texts, indicates that they were intended for nobility like the Cornwalls. A note in the *Life of St Alban* (Trinity College Library, Dublin) refers to another saint's life "which I translated and illustrated and which the lady countess of Cornwall may keep till Whitsuntide".

Most of his illustrations are tinted drawings—a technique often favored by English medieval artists—and Paris was possibly familiar with Anglo-Saxon illustration in this medium. Although his work is accomplished, it is not especially advanced in style. The weight and the firm outlines of the figures in the *Life of St Alban* (*c*1240), probably his earliest surviving work, indicate a considerable debt to the transitional style of *c*1200. In the scene of Aracle's conversion, however, the agile poses of the soldier's attackers and the slender proportions of the saint are characteristic of early Gothic art. The grotesque faces reveal Paris' interest in striking characterization.

A similar concern with dramatic incident is found in the many marginal drawings of the *Chronica Maiora* (1241–51; Corpus Christi College Library, Cambridge) where unusual, often contemporary subjects are depicted in witty and sharply observed compositions. These freshly executed scenes are frequently new inventions. Typical in its lively, anecdotal quality is the battle between William Mareschall and Baldwin of Guisnes, in which Baldwin

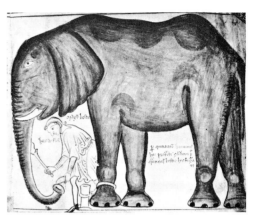

Matthew Paris: An Elephant and its Keeper, an illustration in the "Chronica Maiora"; 14×18cm (5½×7in); c1240–50. Corpus Christi College Library, Cambridge

tumbles from his mount, casually watched by a passing figure leading two horses.

A drawing of the Virgin and Child from the *Historia Anglorum* (British Library, London), with the artist himself at the Virgin's feet, is probably among his last works (1250–5). The delicate faces and the tender relationship between mother and child are characteristic of the developed Gothic style. Although the seated figure still has considerable weight, her rippling drapery has an elegance commonly found in the art of the mid 13th century.

Several manuscripts with illustrations in the St Albans style, though not by Paris himself, show his influence, while the pictures in a copy of his *Life of St Edward* (*c*1255; University Library, Cambridge), in the style of the Westminster Court School, were probably based on his original.

Parler family   14th and 15th centuries

The most celebrated of the numerous medieval mason families, the Parler family worked chiefly in an area that is now south Germany and Czechoslovakia. About 12 members of the family have been identified as masons or sculptors, or both, in the 14th and early 15th centuries; but attributions have to be treated with caution, since the word *Parlier* is German for foreman-mason and can be confused with the Parlers.

Heinrich I is one of the most distinguished of the Parlers. From being a *Parlier* at Cologne he went to Schwäbisch-Gmünd in 1351, and built the Heiligenkreuzkirche, an early example of the south German hall church. It has a nave and aisles of similar height, giving the interior an unusually spacious appearance flooded with light. The hall church design is one of the most important German contributions to Gothic architecture. Schwäbisch-Gmünd is also notable for the way in which its circular columns rise uninterrupted to join the rib system of the vault, which is a complex pattern described as the *Sondergotik* style. It was probably the same Heinrich who planned the chancel of Ulm Minster *c*1377.

His son Peter was the greatest of the Parlers. In 1356, aged only 23, he went to Prague to continue building the cathedral for the Emperor. It had been started in 1344 by the French mason, Mathias of Arras, and Peter completed the choir from the triforium level. It is a strange synthesis of the French rayonnant style and English early-14th-century features. The latter include a massive triforium level balustrade, like the one at Exeter Cathedral, diagonal arches across the lower part of the clerestory, as at Wells Cathedral choir, and a net vault on the English West Country pattern, as are also the skeleton vaults of Prague's sacristy and south porch. The stellate pattern of the choir vault became usual for churches in Bohemia, for example at St Barbara, Kuttenburg, which may have been built by Peter Parler after 1388.

Like his father, Peter was a sculptor as well as a stonemason. At Prague, his workshop produced the royal tombs and the 21 portrait busts in the choir triforium, including one representing Peter himself together with an inscription that lists his works. These busts are notable for their realism; the style was influential throughout the area of south Germany and environs, where several members of the Parler family are recorded as sculptors.

Another branch of the Parlers may have been based at Freiburg. Johann was master mason there from 1359 and was probably responsible for rebuilding the Minster's choir with its elaborate *Sondergotik* vaults. It was a Michael Parler of Freiburg who drew an elevation, which survives, for Strasbourg Cathedral's west front in the 1380s. He intended to create a huge rose window with a single central tower and spire rising above it in the German manner. The same Michael also worked on the southwest tower of Cologne Cathedral.

Two other Parlers, Heinrich of Gmünd and Hans of Freiburg, were both advisors at Milan Cathedral in the 1390s—although, like other invited foreign masons, they failed to persuade the Italians to accept their plans.

Parmigianino 1503–40

The real name of the artist known as Parmigianino was Girolamo Francesco Maria Mazzola or Mazzuoli. He was an Italian painter and etcher whose canons of suave beauty played a key role in the formation of Mannerist style throughout Europe. His reputation as the artist who developed artificial elegance to a bizarre extreme does less than justice to the emotional complexity of his art, and the increasingly unsettled brilliance of his mind. Gifted with incredible facility and prodigious inventive powers, he was hailed at the age of 21 as Raphael reincarnated, only to end his career in acrimony, imprisonment, flight, and disgrace.

The young man's talent was carefully nurtured in Parma by his painter-uncles. (His father, also a painter, had died when Francesco was two years old.) His *Marriage of St Catherine* (S. Maria, Bardi), probably painted as early as 1521, is remarkably accomplished for a painter still in his teens. His precosity was such that he was asked to decorate a chapel in Parma Cathedral before he was 20; probably at about the same time, he embarked upon frescoes in S. Giovanni Evangelista. Strongly influenced by Correggio (1490–1534), Parmigianino's sophisticated skill was ideally suited to the courtly decoration of a room in the fortress of Fontanellato for Gian Galeazzo Sanvitale, whose portrait he painted in 1524 (Museo e Gallerie Nazionali di Capodimonte, Naples). The vault is envisaged as an airy trellis; winged cherubs look down on the story of Diana and Acteon, which is displayed with fluent elegance and velvety color, belying the violence of the narrative.

In 1524 he arrived in Rome, accompanied by an uncle and some sample pictures, including a meltingly beautiful *Holy Family* (Prado, Madrid) and a consciously clever *Self-portrait in a Convex Mirror* (Kunsthistorisches Museum, Vienna). These paintings exude a confident air of sparkling intelligence and wit. In Rome his drawings, some of which were engraved, show the growing complexity of his figure draftsmanship. Of the few paintings from this period, *The Marriage of St Catherine* (c1526; National Gallery, London) demonstrates his ability to create intimate delicacy on a small scale, while *The Vision of St Jerome* (1527; National Gallery, London) makes a haunting emotional impact in a large, unusually lofty altarpiece. In front of the diminutive, sleeping figure of St Jerome, the hypnotically staring St John kneels and pivots, directing our attention to a radiant Madonna and Child inspired by Raphael.

After the sack of Rome in 1527, Parmigianino found employment in Bologna and entered upon the most productive phase of his career. The mannered grace of his figures was increasingly combined with a highly charged atmosphere of transcendental spirituality. The contrast between the ethereal saint and the sober donor in his *St Roch* (c1527–8; S. Petronio, Bologna) reveals his aspiration to evoke the otherness of divine power by creating an attenuated beauty remote from natural proportions.

In 1530 he completed an elaborate and influential *Allegorical Portrait of Charles V* (now lost) and probably also the *Madonna della Rosa* (Gemäldegalerie Alte Meister, Dresden), which represents the extreme point in his identification of sensual with spiritual beauty.

Returning to Parma in 1531, he received the important commission to paint the apse of S. Maria della Steccata. The sad story of the Confraternity's slowly exhausted patience with the dilatory artist can be traced through surviving documents. Between 1532 and 1534 Parmigianino seems to have ceased work. A new contract was drawn up in 1535. A further extension was granted in 1538, but the following year he was imprisoned for nonreturn of advances. After his release he took refuge in Casalmaggiore; finally, in 1539, he was irrevocably dismissed. The only section of the painting to be completed was that on the underside of the crossing arch, where two groups of three graceful maidens, carrying vases and the oil lamps of the wise and foolish virgins, glide across the cornice.

During this period, his reported obsession with the mystical science of alchemy appears to have devoured much of his time. The drawings for the Steccata suggest an additional reason for his delays, namely that his boundless ability to design apparently effortless alternatives for each figure resulted in paralyzing indecision.

His progress on the *Madonna del Collo Lungo* ("Madonna of the Long Neck", Uffizi, Florence), commissioned in 1534, was rather better; but this too remained incomplete. The remarkably slender proportions of the unfinished portico in the background are shared by the sinuous Virgin and seductively pretty angels, who rival the sensuous appeal of his earlier *Cupid* (c1531; Kunsthistorisches Museum, Vienna). The jar of oil held by the nearest angel prefigures Christ's anointment after death, while the Child lies ominously in deathly sleep.

In exile he completed the *Madonna with Saints Stephen and John the Baptist* (1539–40; Gemäldegalerie Alte Meister, Dresden). In this painting his exaggerated system of proportion, already less apparent in the Steccata maidens, has been superseded by monumental forms circumscribed by grand curves, and heavy shadows are used as a foil for the divine radiance of the Madonna and Child. The spaniel-like devotion of the donor suggests a transformation in the painter's own attitude towards spiritual expression, but his early death prevented further development of this more soberly devotional manner.

His European influence was substantially due to his own etchings and the prints after his works by others. His own productions, most notably *The Entombment* (c1528), translate the feathery touch of his sketches into prints of unrivaled evocativeness, in which etching received its first full liberation from the imitation of engraving. The chiaroscuro (3 or 4 tone) woodcuts after his work, particularly those by Antonio da Trento, go far towards capturing the vitality of his brilliant drawings. These have themselves survived in sufficient numbers to have exercised a considerable influence in their own right.

Further reading. Freedberg, S. J. *Parmigianino: his Works in Painting*, Cambridge, Mass. (1950). Popham, A. E. *Catalogue of the Drawings of Parmigianino* (3 vols.), London and New Haven (1971). Quintavale, A. O. *Il Parmigianino*, Milan (1948).

Parrhasios *fl.* late 5th century BC

The Greek painter Parrhasios came from Ephesus and worked in Athens. He prepared drawings that were used by the engraver Mys on the shield of Pheidias' bronze statue of *Athena Promachos* on the Acropolis. His painting was notable for the subtlety of its contour, and for the successful depiction of features and bodies in

Parmigianino: The Vision of St Jerome; panel; 343×149cm (135×59in); 1527. National Gallery, London violent action or under the stress of emotion—for example Odysseus pretending madness, and a characterization of the fickle people (*demos*) of Athens. Parrhasios acquired a reputation for arrogance and extravagance. Xenophon has him discuss with Socrates the possibility of rendering emotion and character in painting.

Pasiteles 1st century BC

Pasiteles was a Greek sculptor and silversmith from south Italy. He became a Roman citizen *c*90 BC. He was involved in the invention of mechanical means for copying the sculptures of earlier periods for Roman clients. The antiquarianism of Pasiteles was manifested in his book on the masterpieces of the ancient world. He was known to have made an ivory statue of *Jupiter* for the temple of Metellus in Rome, and to have drawn a lion from life for use in a relief. Statues and groups in the manner of the early and late Classical periods signed by members of his school survive in Rome.

Pasmore Victor 1908–

The British painter Victor Pasmore was born in Chelsham, Surrey. Until 1938 he was able to study art only part time. He first exhibited in 1930, at the Zwemmer Gallery, and had his first one-man show in 1933. He joined the London Group in 1934 and was a founder-member of the Euston Road Group, which consciously rebelled against the "escapism" of the School of Paris. Pasmore's work of this period is representational in character, and serious in tone.

In the mid 1940s, he concentrated on landscape. His sense of atmosphere derives from a deep study of late Turner and, to a lesser extent, Whistler; but already Pasmore has begun to concentrate on certain objects and shapes within the picture that he evidently valued for their abstract qualities. Note the pattern of branches, for example, in the 1944 *Chiswick Reach* (National Gallery of Canada, Ottawa).

By 1946 the abstract emphasis is even stronger, as in *Chiswick: Sun Shining Through Mist* (1946/7; National Gallery of Victoria, Melbourne), with its strong horizontal elements and areas of pointillist technique. In 1947, Pasmore turned to a fully-fledged Abstract style. From 1947 to 1950 he concentrated on a mixture of oils and collage. From 1949 to 1951 he experimented in oil studies of spiral motifs. From the mid 1950s onwards he painted

far less and began working on three-dimensional reliefs of great austerity.

Further reading. Bowness, A. *Victor Pasmore*, London (1980).

Patenier Joachim *c*1480–*c*1525

The Flemish painter Joachim Patenier may originally have worked at Bruges before registering as a master at Antwerp in 1515. Only a handful of works by this artist survive, but he had a profound impact on the development of landscape painting in 16th-century northern Europe.

Patenier specialized in scenes where the figure subject is dominated by a vast surrounding landscape. In these his sense of perspective remained empirical; in most of his works, mountains seen from below are placed on a ground plane seen from above. However, his application of color—from brownish foregrounds to green in the middle distance and blue in the background—gives an impression of atmosphere that was innovatory.

In paintings such as the *Landscape with St Jerome* (National Gallery, London) the crags and precipices of the artist's imagination take on a life of their own, and dwarf the true subject of the picture. The *Charon Crossing the Stygian Lake* (Prado, Madrid) restates, with Patenier's more poetic sense of landscape, the juxtaposition of paradise and hell found in the paintings of Hieronymus Bosch. Patenier sometimes painted the backgrounds of figure subjects by his Flemish contemporaries; *The Temptation of St Anthony* (Prado, Madrid) is a joint work with Quentin Massys.

His compositions were reproduced by Herri met de Bles, the chief copyist of his style. Historically Patenier's chief influence was on the painting of Pieter Bruegel the Elder (1525–69), whose vision of landscape, especially in his early years, is particularly indebted to this artist.

Pater Jean-Baptiste 1695–1736

The French painter and draftsman Jean-Baptiste Pater was a pupil of Antoine Watteau for a short time *c*1713, and again in 1721. Pater continued Watteauesque military subjects and *fêtes galantes* into the 1730s, along with artists such as Lancret (for example, *Women Bathing*, *c*1735; Musée de Peinture et de Sculpture, Grenoble). His works are rather poor and eclectic imitations of his master's, and less richly

Victor Pasmore: The Thames at Chiswick: Sun Shining through Mist; oil on canvas; 76×100cm (30×39in); 1946–7. National Gallery of Victoria, Melbourne

Joachim Patenier: Landscape with St Jerome; panel; 36×34cm (14×13½in); c1520. National Gallery, London

to stone or wood. Some of his subjects were remembered for their special effects, for example a frontal view of an ox painted black and making no use of shading or highlights, and a figure of Drunkenness (Methe) with her face appearing through the glass cup. His florals were especially admired and may have inspired the distinctive floral patterns on later mosaic floors in Macedonian palaces and on Italian vases.

Paxton Joseph 1801–65

The English gardener and architect Sir Joseph Paxton was born at Milton Bryant, Bedfordshire. His rise from garden-boy to knighthood was a paradigm of 19th-century self-improvement. As superintendent of the gardens at Chatsworth, Derbyshire, Paxton laid out the estate village (Edensor, c1839). He designed several horticultural buildings, including the Great Conservatory (1836–40) whose "ridge and furrow" glazing system, with light structural supports, was the basis of his successful scheme for the Crystal Palace, London (1851). Prefabrication of the glass and iron elements enabled this, the largest building in the world, to be erected in nine months, bringing world fame to its designer.

colored. Towards the end of his life his art took the more incisive turn first suggested by his engraved illustrations to Paul Scarron's *Roman Comique* (1729–36; published in Potsdam), but he died too young to realize fully the implications of this. Some of his landscapes, with pretty little figures, anticipate the art of François Boucher. His largest and most individual work is *The Fair at Bezons* (c1735, Metropolitan Museum, New York).

Pausias mid 4th century BC

The Greek painter Pausias came from Sicyon and was a leading artist of the influential Sicyonian school of painting. He was said to have introduced the practice of painting panels for ceilings, and he was an early exponent of the "encaustic" technique, using heated wax to bind colors

Jean-Baptiste Pater: Fête Champêtre; oil on canvas; 75×93cm (30×37in); c1730. National Gallery of Art, Washington, D.C.

Peale Charles 1741–1827

The American painter Charles Wilson Peale was born in Maryland, Pa. He was originally apprenticed to a saddler, and briefly entered that trade. At the age of 21 he took lessons in painting, and left for London to study under Benjamin West. He returned to America in 1769 to travel the East Coast, painting portraits. He fought in the War of Independence and painted portraits of many of its prominent figures, including a number of George Washington. Having settled in Philadelphia he opened first a picture gallery in 1782, and then the Peale Museum, containing scientific exhibits and portraits of the leading figures of American history. He was Founder of the Academy of Fine Arts, and became a regular exhibitor. Important collections of his paintings can be seen in Philadelphia, in Independence Hall and at the Historical Society of Pennsylvania. Peale married three times and fathered 17 children, all of whom became artists.

Pearlstein Philip 1924–

The American artist Philip Pearlstein was one of the leading figures in the return to figurative painting in the 1960s. He studied at the Carnegie Institute of Technology. In the 1950s Pearlstein painted in the Abstract Expressionist idiom, but by the early 1960s, attempting to "rescue the human figure" from the distortions of the "Expressionists and Cubists", he had developed a distinctive style of unidealized nude painting. Dubbed perceptual realism, his approach focuses on the depiction of bodies exactly as they appear, without psychological, social or sexual interpretation. *Female Model on Eames Stool* (1978; Metropolitan Museum of Art, New York) is typical of his precise, objective approach. Unusual angles and compositions, highly finished surfaces, and hidden or cropped faces stress the abstract qualities of his works, though ironically they often also tend to raise rather than dispel questions of interpretation.

Pei Ieoh Ming 1917–

Born in China, the American architect Ieoh Ming Pei emigrated to the United States in 1935 and studied at Massachusetts Insti-

Charles Peale: Staircase Group; oil on canvas; 226×100cm (89×39in); 1795. Philadelphia Museum of Art

tute of Technology and at Harvard (under Walter Gropius). A prolific architect, he has worked on a broad range of public projects in the United States, his buildings often large scale and sharply geometrical. Pei is noted for the skill with which he relates design and materials to a specific environment. His work on urban renewal projects, such as Denver's Mile High Center (1952–56) illustrated his awareness of urban environments, while his design for the National Center for Atmospheric Research in Colorado (1961–67) demonstrated a sensitivity to a dramatic natural setting. He firmly established his career with innovative and confident buildings such as the John F. Kennedy Library, Boston, (1964–79) and East Building of the National Gallery, Washington, D.C., (1968–78), though it was with his controversial glass pyramid over a new entrance to the Louvre in Paris (1983–89) that he achieved international fame. Other works include the Xiangshan (Fragrant Hill) Hotel in Peking (1979–83) and the characteristically extrovert 70–story Bank of China building in Hong Kong (1990).

Further reading. Suner, B. *Ieoh Ming Pei*, Paris (1984)

Permeke Constant 1886–1952

The Belgian Expressionist painter and sculptor Constant Permeke was the son of an Antwerp marine painter. He studied at the art academies of Bruges (1903–6) and Ghent (1906–8). During the years 1909 to 1912 he stayed in Laethem-Saint-Martin with the painters Gust and Leon de Smet, Fritz van den Berghe, and Albert Servaes. Although he was still struggling with Impressionism at this time, he and his friends were apparently aware of German Expressionism. It was in England, where he had been evacuated during the First World War, that he finally broke through to his characteristically robust and earthy form of Expressionism (seen in *The Stranger*, 1916; Musées Royaux des Beaux-Arts de Belgique, Brussels). He returned in 1919 to Belgium, where he painted fishermen, peasants, and landscapes. These works are full of human sympathy, painted in somber colors with a broad impasto technique; the figures attain monumental proportions. He began to sculpt figures, mostly in plaster and clay, in 1936 (for example *Marie-Lou*, 1935–6; Middelheim Open Air Museum of Sculpture, Antwerp).

Perrault Claude 1613–88

Claude Perrault was a French doctor with an amateur interest in architecture. In 1667 he was appointed by Louis XIV to collaborate with Louis Levau and the painter Charles Lebrun on a design for the east front of the Louvre, Paris, to replace the scheme prepared by Bernini. Perrault's part in the final design is not clear. The Baroque rhythm of the coupled columns is probably Levau's, but the strict application of Roman forms, which made it a seminal work for the 18th century, reflects Perrault's archaeological interests. These led in 1673 to his edition of Vitruvius's *De Architectura*. He also designed the Paris Observatoire (1667) and a château at Sceaux for Colbert (1663–4; demolished). His brother Charles (1626–1703) was a theorist and chief assistant to Colbert in the *Surintendance des Bâtiments*.

Perréal Jean c1460–c1530

The French artist Jean Perréal has been identified (with little justification) both with the "Jehan de Paris, enlumineur" active in Bourges before 1480, and with the Maître de Moulins. He may have been born in Paris. By 1483 he was certainly in Lyons, where he held the post of painter, decorator, and *valet-de-chambre* to Charles VIII. He organized Charles' solemn entry into the city in 1489, and Anne de Bretagne's in 1493. Between 1499 and 1502 he followed the armies of Louis XII in Italy (where he met Leonardo da Vinci). His job was apparently to paint battles, but also, according to the chronicler Jehan Lemaire de Belges, to record "les villes conquises en Italie".

On his return to France in 1502, Perréal designed the tomb of François II and his wife Marguerite de Foix, commissioned by their daughter, Anne de Bretagne. The work, in Nantes Cathedral, is the masterpiece of the sculptor Michel de Colombe. In 1504 Perréal was appointed artistic adviser to Margaret of Austria, for whom he supervised at least part of the decoration of the splendidly exuberant monastery church at Brou (the fruit of a vow made by Margaret's mother-in-law, Marguerite de Bourbon). He also drew up plans for the tombs of Marguerite, and of Philibert II "Le Beau" de Savoie, Margaret of Austria's husband. He visited England at least once, in 1514.

Perréal's status as a painter is obscured by the circumstance that only three paintings—portraits of Charles VIII, of Anne de Bretagne, and of Pierre Sala—can safely be attributed to him. It has been suggested that he also illustrated the *Illustrations de Gaule et Singularitez de Troye* (1509) of Jean Lemaire de Belges, who was an admirer of Perréal and who also lived in Lyons.

Perret Auguste 1874–1954

The architect Auguste Perret was born in Ixelles, near Brussels. He studied at the École des Beaux-Arts in Paris but left in 1895 to join his father's building and contracting firm. His importance for the Modern Movement rests upon a handful of buildings in which he established reinforced concrete as an aesthetically acceptable material for architecture, as well as hinting at its structural potential. Nevertheless, Perret never overturned the academic tradition but preferred to fit concrete into it. He based his use of the material upon a system of columns and beams derived from wooden construction.

His first notable work was the block of flats at No. 25b Rue Franklin in Paris (1903), which displays its frame explicitly; it is also novel in plan, since the lightwell required by law is incorporated in the front of the building. In the Garage Ponthieu (1905) Perret left the structural concrete exposed. The structure that he conceived for the Théâtre des Champs Élysées (1911–14; with Henry van de Velde) anticipates the skeleton frames of the architecture of the 1920s.

The church of Notre Dame du Raincey (1922–3) was Perret's last influential work. It presented little that was daring in structural terms, except for its tall, attenuated columns; but it made a considerable impact upon younger architects in the utterly frank use of precast concrete units, and in the patterning of surfaces by means of the shuttering used to contain the concrete.

Perronneau J.-B. 1715–83

The French portrait painter Jean-Baptiste Perronneau was born in Paris and studied under Charles-Joseph Natoire and the engraver Laurent Cars. During his lifetime his reputation as a pastel portrait painter was overshadowed by that of Maurice-Quentin de La Tour (1704–88), whose greater virtuosity appealed more to Parisian taste. Perronneau found his patrons in the French provinces, and also abroad, in Italy, England, Russia, and especially Holland, where he died. Unlike La Tour, Perronneau was a successful painter in oils. His *Portrait of a Man* (National Gallery of Ireland, Dublin), for instance, has a directness and lack of flattery very rarely found in the French portraiture of his day.

Perugino *c*1448–1523

The Italian painter Pietro Vannucci was born at Città della Pieve, and was known as Perugino. In the late 1460s he may have been a pupil of Piero della Francesca; he then seems to have moved to Florence, where he worked in the studio of Verrocchio. Perugino's early career is somewhat obscure, but he was certainly an established master by 1479, when he was recorded as working in the Vatican. His earliest paintings in Rome are lost, but his frescoes in the Sistine Chapel of the Vatican, dating from 1481–2, already reveal the major characteristics of his mature style. The finest of them, *The Delivery of the Keys to St Peter* or *Christ's Charge to St Peter*, is notable for its spacious and clearly defined setting, which obviously shows the influence of Piero. But compared with those of Perugino's teacher the figures are rather timid and insubstantial, with gentle, rhythmic, and slightly monotonous poses.

J.-B. Perronneau: Portrait of Jacques Cazotte; oil on canvas; 92×73cm (36×29in); c1760–4. National Gallery, London

Perugino's style is always decorative rather than monumental or expressive. Virtually all his pictures have the same kind of sweetness of mood: the figures are stereotyped in pose and physical type, with an unvarying expression of vapid mildness, and they are set in ample landscapes which recall the work of Flemish artists such as Hans Memling. At his best, as for example in the fresco of the *Crucifixion with Saints* (1496; S. Maria Maddalena dei Pazzi, Florence) Perugino's supreme craftsmanship enabled him to produce an image of genuine power, in which the sense of subdued piety is entirely appropriate to the pathos of the subject. But the repetition of a well-worn repertoire of devotional formulae, for which he could always find a ready market, reveals the poverty of his invention as well as the excellence of his technique, especially in the rendering of space and light. Vasari's comment that "he always refused to accept the immortality of the soul" may be no more than malice, since it is not supported by any other evidence; but it is an understandable response to Perugino's apparent complacency.

In the later part of the 15th century Perugino enjoyed an immense reputation, not only in his native Umbria and in Tuscany, but even as far afield as Venice. He somewhat surprisingly undertook to paint a battle picture for the Doges' Palace, though he never actually delivered it. He was even employed by Isabella d'Este, the Marchioness of Mantua and one of the foremost patrons of the period, for whom he painted a *Combat between Love and Chastity* (1503–5; Louvre, Paris). During the 16th century his work began to seem old-fashioned beside the achievements of artists such as Leonardo, Michelangelo, and Raphael, who was for a time his pupil; but until his death Perugino remained singularly impervious to the influence of the younger generation.

Peruzzi Baldassare 1481–1536

Baldassare Tommaso Peruzzi was born in Siena, and may have trained as an architect and painter with Francesco di Giorgio. Before 1505, he designed for Sigismondo Chigi the Villa Le Volte, just outside Siena. He then moved to Rome, where he began the design of the Villa Farnesina for the rich papal banker, Agostino Chigi. The articulation of the walls, with doric pilasters, reflects Peruzzi's response to Rome.

Perugino: The Delivery of the Keys to St Peter; fresco; 335×550cm (132×217in); 1482. Sistine Chapel, the Vatican, Rome

The two loggias, which look out on to the Tiber and the garden, develop the Renaissance interest in opening buildings to the landscape. (This was a conscious revival of the effects described by Pliny the Younger in his account of his villas.) The "U" shape of the villa, which has its roots in the Quattrocento, was not continued in 16th-century Italy.

By contrast with his architecture, Peruzzi's paintings were provincial, and Agostino Chigi preferred Raphael's. Nevertheless, in 1517 Peruzzi returned to the Farnesina to enlarge the Sala delle Prospettive on the first floor. He decorated it with doric columns and pilasters (with a frieze above). They support the cornice, and extend the room to the balustrades that are set in front of the brilliantly conceived views of Rome. The illusionism of these views has no direct precedent in the Renaissance.

Baldassare Peruzzi: the Sala delle Prospettive; c1517. Villa Farnesina, Rome

Peruzzi's skills as an architectural painter were given full expression in his designs for the theater. This aspect of his work, together with his study of the Antique, influenced the treatise of his pupil, Sebastiano Serlio. Peruzzi's late work is best represented by the Palazzo delle Colonne, Rome, begun in 1532. The curve of the facade was suggested by the irregular site. The restriction of the pilasters and columns to the ground floor, with the mass of rustication above broken only by the window aedicules, shows his development of an inventive and expressive Mannerism, comparable to that of Giulio Romano and Michelangelo.

Pesellino Francesco c1422–57

Francesco di Stefano Pesellino was a Florentine painter. In 1455 he was commissioned to paint an altarpiece of *The Trinity with Saints* for a Pistoian church. Now in the National Gallery, London, it was unfinished at his death in 1457. Its completion, notably the painting of the *predella*, was entrusted to Filippo Lippi and his workshop. Pesellino's style owes much to Lippi, as seen in, for example, a *Madonna and Child with Saints* in the Metropolitan Museum, New York. Some *predella* panels attributed to him (for example, *A Miracle of St Sylvester*; Worcester Art Museum, Worcester, Mass.) and several *cassone* paintings (for example, *The Story of Griselda*; Galleria dell'Accademia Carrara, Bergamo), reveal skills in painting on a smaller scale.

Pettoruti Emilio 1895–1971

The Argentine painter Emilio Pettoruti studied in 1913 in Florence where he associated with the Futurists. From 1916 to 1917 he studied in Rome, where he became acquainted with Giacomo Balla, Enrico Prampolini, and Giorgio de Chirico. He spent 1919 in Milan, and 1921 in Vienna and Munich. In 1923 he exhibited at Herwarth Walden's center, "Der Sturm", in Berlin. He then went to Paris where he met Juan Gris and Gino Severini. In 1924 Pettoruti returned to Argentina where he remained for nearly 30 years, becoming director of the Museo Nacional de la Plata in 1930. Under Peron's dictatorship he was removed from his post, in 1947; he moved back to Paris in 1951.

Pettoruti's earliest work reflects his interest in Balla's Abstract pictures. After 1917 he painted figurative works in a late Cubist style (for example, *The Verdigris Goblet*, 1934; Museum of Modern Art, New York). He reverted to abstraction after 1950.

Pevsner Antoine 1886–1962

The Russian painter and sculptor Antoine Pevsner was born in Orel, Russia, and went to Paris in 1912 to paint; in 1915 he joined his brother Naum Gabo in Oslo. In 1917 they both returned to Russia, which was in a state of artistic as well as political ferment. In 1920 they published the *Realistic Manifesto* as their contribution to the debate about the future of art. During these years Pevsner's painting developed from a curvilinear Cubism to geometric abstraction.

In 1923 he moved to Paris, and began working in three dimensions. His earliest ventures are figures in relief, built up from curved sheets of plastic. He followed his brother in the use of synthetic materials and engineering techniques, although unlike Gabo he did not devote himself

Francesco Pesellino: The Triumph of David over Saul; detail; oil on panel; full size 45×180cm (18×71in). National Gallery, London

entirely to abstraction until the early 1930s. For all the superficial similarities between the work of the two brothers, Pevsner's sculpture is marked by a far more expressive quality. Even at his most abstract, the interplay between concave and convex surfaces gives form to sensations of stress and strain which inevitably become associated with muscular tensions.

After 1936 Pevsner began to construct his sculptures from bronze and copper rods, closely welded together. This gives rise to a richly textured surface that draws attention to itself, rather than, as with Gabo, to the void it delineates. The result impedes the apprehension of internal spatial relationships, reversing the principles of the *Realistic Manifesto* in favor of the traditional sculptural treatment of volume as mass.

Further reading. Duchamp, M. *Antoine Pevsner*, Paris (1947). Pevsner, A. *A Biographical Sketch of my Brothers, Naum Gabo and Antoine Pevsner*, Amsterdam (1964).

Pheidias 5th century BC

Pheidias was a Greek sculptor of the high Classical period from Athens, the son of Charmides, and related to the painter Panaenus. He was a pupil of Ageladas and a contemporary of Polycleitos. The Greeks considered him their greatest sculptor; he was also undoubtedly fortunate in being given the opportunity to realize his intentions. Supported by the Athenian statesman Pericles, Pheidias became the artistic agent of the political, financial, and cultural supremacy of Athens as head of a maritime empire.

He was appointed supervisor of the sculptural decoration of the temple of Athena (the Parthenon) on the Acropolis of Athens, employing some of the leading sculptors of the time, among them Agoracritus, Alcamenes, Cresilias, and Myron. In the Parthenon sculptures (448–432 BC) the naturalistic tendencies of the early Classical were invested with idealism, and the Classical style emerged as the expression of the conservative ideals of the enlightened aristocracy of the city. The forms created on the Parthenon lived to the end of the Classical world, and the temple itself has served as a model of imperial monuments both ancient and modern. The hand of Pheidias cannot be identified on the remaining fragments of Parthenon sculpture (British Museum, London; Acropolis Museum, Athens; Louvre, Paris), but his influence is manifest in their excellence.

The Greeks were much impressed by the colossal cult-statue of *Athena Parthenos* (Virgin) made by Pheidias for the *cella* of the Parthenon in ivory and gold (the gold in removable plating deposited by the state treasury). Although its significance was more political than religious, it settled the image of Athena for all time. The helmeted goddess was standing with her shield at her side, the snake Erichthonius curling within its concavity. She held a spear in the right hand and a flying Victory on the palm of the left hand, which was supported by a column. The statue was decorated with mythical scenes, like a temple: its base with the birth of Pandora, the first woman, and the sandals and shield with battle scenes. Popular tradition claimed that Pheidias had included portraits of himself and Pericles among the combatants on the shield.

Shortly after the statue's dedication in 438, Pheidias was indicted for embezzlement of some of the state gold from the *Parthenos* and fled to Olympia. There he created his second masterpiece in ivory and gold: a colossal cult-statue of *Zeus* for his temple at Olympia, financed from the spoils of the war between Elis and Pisa. The sublime figure carved by Pheidias had a deep theological significance and was acknowledged as a contribution to traditional religion. Zeus was shown as the benevolent king and father of gods and men, allegedly inspired by the imagery of the Homeric *Iliad*. He sat in an elaborate throne, holding a Victory in his right hand and a scepter crowned by an eagle in the left. Some of the clay molds used for sections of the golden drapery and other accessories (datable to the 430s) have been found in the workshop of Pheidias at Olympia, together with a mug incised with his signature as owner (Archaeological Museum, Olympia).

Before his work on the Parthenon, Pheidias had made a bronze colossus of *Athena Promachos* (Guardian) for Athens; it was erected on the Acropolis *c*456 BC, and financed by the spoils of the battle of Marathon. The top of her crest and spear were supposed to have been visible to sailors at Cape Sunion. His smaller bronze *Athena Lemnia* was dedicated on the Acropolis by the Athenian colonists of Lemnos, and was admired for the detailed treatment of the face (for once not covered by the helmet): she was not a warlike goddess but a graceful maiden. This statue has been reconstructed from copies as a bare-headed Athena holding her helmet in her right hand. The knowledge of the original is based on a head in the Museo Civico, Bologna, and on a torso in the Skulpturensammlung, Dresden.

Pheidias presented his own solution to the problem of stance and proportions by developing the quietly standing figure with both feet on the same level, one leg bent with the knee pointing to the side. He did not cultivate the animated rhythmical outline of Myron and Polycleitos, but achieved an effect of grandeur by means of elaborate drapery or detailed musculature combined with an idealized head. His ideas were at the root of a great many subsequent innovations. His experiments with statues, shifting their weight on to an external support, as in his *Amazon* in Ephesus, proved particularly fertile; they influenced Alcamenes, Cresilias, and Praxiteles. However, despite the enormous impact made by Pheidias on Greek and Roman art and taste, we know very little about his personality.

Further reading. Brommer, F. *Athena Parthenos*, Bremen (1957). Hekler, A. *Die Kunst des Phidias*, Stuttgart (1924). Richter, G. M. *A Handbook of Greek Art*, London and New York (1974).

Phillips Tom 1937–

The English painter and composer Tom Phillips was born in London. After reading English at Oxford University (1957–60) he studied painting at Camberwell School of Art with Frank Auerbach (1961–4). He taught art history at Ipswich School of Art (1965–6), painting at the Bath Academy of Art (1966–7), and then taught at Wolverhampton College of Art (1967–70). He has also been an instructor at the Royal College of Art and at the Slade School of Fine Art (1975).

Most of Phillips' imagery is derived from specially selected color postcards which he interprets in paintings made according to a preconceived program which combines figuration and abstraction. Since 1969 the paintings have included color catalogs of all the colors used in their making, painted in lines around the image, for example, *Benches* (1970–1; Tate Gallery, London). Other independent paintings called *Terminal Greys* are made from mixtures of

Tom Phillips: Benches; acrylic on canvas; 122×276cm (48×109in); 1970–1. Tate Gallery, London

colors used. A major series of paintings made between 1971 and 1975 reconstructs a wall of paintings shown in an old museum postcard. Since 1972 some of the paintings have been politically motivated by subjects like apartheid.

From 1966 Phillips has created many works, including paintings, prints, and an opera and ballet scenario from the pages of an obscure English novel, *A Human Document* (1892) by W. H. Mallock. Their collective title, *A Humument*, is also the title of a book published in 1980 in which every page of the novel has been painted over to produce a blend of painting and poetry.

Piazzetta Giovanni 1683–1754

In many ways the Italian painter Giovanni Battista (or Giambattista) Valentino Piazzetta stands apart from his Venetian contemporaries in his Bolognese training, in his slow working method, and in the fact that after 1711 he does not seem to have painted outside his native Venice.

His training under G. M. Crespi in Bologna was of fundamental importance. He inherited that city's famous tradition of fine academic drawing, becoming one of the greatest draftsmen of the 18th century. His use of strong chiaroscuro, especially in his early works, shows that he studied Guercino's paintings while in Bologna.

Piazzetta's early career in Venice is not clear. He was back in the city by 1711, but no dated paintings are known from before 1717 when he provided *The Martyrdom of St James* for S. Stae, Venice. With its harsh realism and zigzag composition, this work was one of the best of the similar canvases painted for the church by several prominent Venetian artists between 1717 and 1721. It is a measure of Piazzetta's success that when G. B. Tiepolo came to paint his own *Martyrdom* for S. Stae he followed Piazzetta's closely.

Realism remained throughout Piazzetta's career a hallmark of his art, and during the 1720s another became evident. This was his magnificent use of color, first apparent in the ceiling of a chapel in SS. Giovanni e Paolo, Venice, where pinkish browns, pale blues, greens, and grays lighten towards the center. Piazzetta was always reluctant to use too much color. At the end of the 1730s, a time when Venetian painting in general was getting lighter and brighter, he produced the altarpiece in the Gesuati, Venice. Here in complete contrast with contemporary fashion he carefully controlled his austere range of colors.

The slowness of his working method also set Piazzetta apart from his fellow artists and explains why he never tried fresco painting. His deliberations would also have proved disadvantageous in work at foreign courts and capitals. However, although he remained in Venice, many of Piazzetta's commissions came from abroad: not from the "advanced" centers of Rococo patronage like Paris, London, and Düsseldorf, but from the Electors of Saxony and Cologne, and other more conservative patrons.

During the 1740s Piazzetta produced several genre paintings where the subject matter and gentle afternoon light were unexceptional for contemporary painting. What sets these apart from mainstream Rococo work is their feeling of mystery and uncertainty. From the 1740s until his death, assistants became more and more important in his workshop, especially after 1750, when Piazzetta was made Director of the Venetian Academy. It was probably then, for the Academy, that he made most of his splendid nude drawings (most of which are now dispersed between private collections though a few remain in the Gallerie dell'Accademia, Venice). He remained the Director until his death four years later.

Picabia Francis 1879–1953

Francis Picabia was a painter and writer of mixed Spanish, Cuban, and French descent, who was one of the leaders of the Dada movement. He was born in Paris and began studying painting there in 1894. From 1898 to 1910 he worked with considerable success in an Impressionist style, but already by c1907 he had begun to experiment with abstraction. In 1911 he entered a Cubist phase, participating in the *Section d'Or* group and receiving encouragement from Apollinaire, who termed his type of Cubism "Orphic".

In 1913, under Duchamp's influence, Picabia embarked on a remarkable series of canvases—including *I See Again in Memory my Dear Udnie* (1913; Museum of Modern Art, New York). In these, within a basically Cubist structure, he expressed erotic themes by means of veiled, ironic allusions to mechanistic and natural forms.

Picabia lived in New York in 1915 and 1916 and, with Duchamp, was the center of a Dadaist group. In the dry, objective style of technical drawing, he produced works like *Machine, Turn Quickly* (1916; Galleria Schwarz, Milan), in which machine imagery is used with iconoclastic and satiric intent. From 1917 to 1921 Picabia was an active promoter of Dada in Barcelona, New York, Zurich, and Paris,

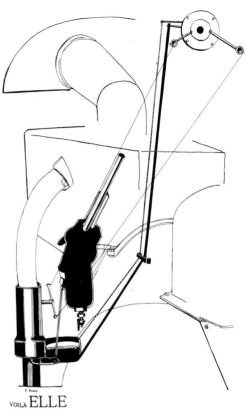

VOILÀ ELLE

Francis Picabia: Violà Elle!, the photograph of the original work (now lost) that appeared in "291"

editing his own Dada review, *291*.

Withdrawing from Dada in 1921, Picabia abandoned his machine style in favor of the expressionistic, figurative manner of *The Kiss* (1924; private collection). This phase was succeeded in 1927 by the so-called "Transparencies"—superimposed, transparent silhouettes of figures scattered over the picture. In the 1930s, he was associated sporadically with the Surrealists.

Further reading. Camfield, W. *Francis Picabia: His Art, Life and Times*, Princeton (1979).

Picasso 1881–1973

Born in Málaga, Spain, Pablo Ruiz Picasso was the son of a painter and art teacher, José Ruiz Blases. After active participation in the early-20th-century avant-garde—first in Barcelona and then in Paris—Picasso emerged as perhaps the most influential and vital single creative force in modern art. He remained at the forefront of European painting from the 1900s at least until the Second World War, if not until his death.

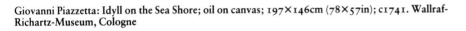

Giovanni Piazzetta: Idyll on the Sea Shore; oil on canvas; 197×146cm (78×57in); c1741. Wallraf-Richartz-Museum, Cologne

His prodigious ability was recognized in the Academies of Coruña, Barcelona, and Madrid (1895–6) and his personable originality led to his teenage entry into the bohemian avant-garde circles of Spain in the 1890s. He first went to Paris in 1900 and continued to pay visits there until 1904, when he finally settled in the city, taking a studio in the Montmartre tenement known as "le Bateau-Lavoir".

His early works of 1898 to 1905, full of adolescent eclecticism, are also powerfully individual. With remarkable facility and vivacity he assimilated ideas and techniques from Post-Impressionist and other *fin-de-siècle* art, as well as from older painting (for instance Classical art, Catalan art, and the works of El Greco). It was as though he were measuring himself against all available artistic terms of reference. (His friend Max Jacob remarked that Picasso made conscious pastiches after everyone, to make sure that he didn't do it unconsciously.) What distinguished him from the French avant-garde, with whom he became associated, was that he cast his net of inquiry so wide. He was not inhibited by the Parisian *belle peinture* tradition, and felt no allegiance to any one tradition of painting. He was more concerned with the making of things and images than with painting as such.

Picasso wrote later that he wanted "to get to the stage where nobody can tell how a picture of mine was done. What's the point of that? Simply that I want nothing but emotion given off by it." He did not want Parisian concerns for the painterliness of the activity to obstruct the power of the image. He was more involved as a painter with concepts and faiths than with the act of looking. He felt strong affinities with French Symbolist literature (with Mallarmé, Rimbaud, Verlaine). He had been closely associated with the Barcelona literary avant-garde, and his significant early contacts in Paris were also with writers (Apollinaire, Jacòb, Gertrude Stein, Jarry). By 1905 his studio was known as "le rendezvous des poètes".

The content of Picasso's early work is about the reality of life more than art or nature. The intense melancholia of his "Blue Period" (c1901–4) is infected with *fin-de-siècle* obsessions with life and death, images of energy and the lack of energy. In art, he was interested in Munch, Van Gogh, and Gauguin. The *Tragedy* (1903; National Gallery of Art, Washington, D.C.), *The Old Guitarist* (1903; Art Insti-

tute of Chicago), and the etching *Frugal Repast* (1904; National Gallery of Art, Washington, D.C.) exemplify the period. *La Vie* (1903; Cleveland Museum of Art), perhaps the most ambitious, is typical in its dense blue palette and the brooding pessimism of its oblique allegory.

In the "Rose Period" (1904–6), his palette lightens towards pinks, grays, and ochers and the mood sweetens to a poignant sadness. Subjects come from circus and theater, the Montmartre acrobats and strolling players (many of them Spanish) that he had befriended. The autobiographical association of artist with isolated entertainer (especially with Harlequin) was to recur throughout his work. In *The Family of Saltimbanques* (1905; Art Institute of Chicago), the passive group in a desolate landscape has a muted pathos and dignity. It reflects Picasso's lifelong concern as man and artist with humanitarian values and with social and political inequality, but in a quiet understatement.

Subsequently, under the pervasive influence of French art, he concentrated more on formal problems and this muting of subject matter continued. Still monochromatic, but now less emotive in color (using browns and ochers), the paintings of 1906 seem devoid of sentiment (for example, *Portrait of Gertrude Stein* and *Two Nudes*, both in the Museum of Modern Art, New York). His concern is with sculptural and tonal oppositions, and he experiments with formal devices from various traditions, classical and archaic.

This conscious formal confrontation reaches a climax in *Les Demoiselles d'Avignon* (1907; Museum of Modern Art, New York). It is both a summation of his early work and the start of a revolutionary new phase in Picasso's art. The painting started in the mood of refined, stylized resolution that had made his early reputation. Its barely disguised allusions to the late works of Cézanne and to those of his contemporary, Matisse, suggest that it was some sort of conclusive answer to French traditions of monumental figure painting. But both the savageness of its change of mood and technique (apparently inspired by African tribal art) and Picasso's dramatic alterations to the work display the radical degree of enquiry to which he was to submit painting during the next decade.

Other 1907–8 works (*Landscape*, 1907, Musée Picasso, Paris; *Nude with Drapery*, Hermitage Museum, St Petersburg; and

Nude with Raised Arms, Thyssen-Bornemisza Collection, Lugano, Switzerland) reflect the same aggressive urgency, and the same attack on the sanctity of European traditions of naturalism. Ritualistic art was uninhibited by either the High Art tradition of easel painting or Classical traditions of ideal beauty. Picasso was the first Western artist to bring this liberated vision to bear on the problems of European image-making.

In collaboration with Braque, whom he met in 1907, Picasso conducted an intensive overhaul of the practice of painting. The conceptual objectivity of his approach and the imaginative, often playful level of his improvisation and assimilation were the driving force behind each stage in the development of Cubism between 1907 and 1914. Once he had been drawn by Braque into an investigation of French traditions of painterliness and visual analysis—particularly of Cézanne's late work—Picasso produced a series of increasingly refined variations on the theme of Post-Impressionism. His portraits of the dealers Vollard, Uhde, and Kahnweiler (1909–10) are among the masterpieces of Analytical Cubism. They exploit a fine poise between the painting as a physical image (elusive but potent) and as an autonomous structure (a subtle monochrome fabric, lit like a crystal by internal reflection).

In his collages and in Synthetic Cubism (from 1912 onwards), Picasso's sharp and opportunist instincts for images and materials again came to the fore. After the almost classical reserve of Analytical Cubism, the latent Expressionism of his early art also reemerged. In a wide range of media—paintings like *Green Still Life* (1914; Museum of Modern Art, New York), constructions like the wooden *Still Life* (Tate Gallery, London), and sculptures like the painted bronze *Absinthe Glass* (edition of 6), all 1914—he improvised generously with the expressive and animistic properties of dislocated Cubist imagery. At the same time he revived a highly realistic idiom in a series of pencil portrait drawings: *Portrait of Vollard* for example (1915; Metropolitan Museum, New York). Such abrupt shifts as well as the range of simultaneous manners remained characteristic in his mature art.

Picasso: Three Dancers; oil on canvas; 215×142cm (85×56in); 1925. Tate Gallery, London

In 1917 Picasso visited Italy, invited by Jean Cocteau to design for Diaghilev's *Ballet Russe* in Rome. He worked on *Parade* in collaboration with Cocteau, Erik Satie, and Léonide Massine; he also met Igor Stravinsky. The drop curtain (Musée National d'Art Moderne, Paris) was in a naturalistic manner, but among the costumes the two Stage Managers wore enormous Cubist constructions, 10 ft (3.5 m) high. Picasso later designed for Diaghilev's *Le Tricorne* (1919), *Pulcinella* (1920), and *Cuadro Flamenco* (1921). While in Italy Picasso visited Naples and Pompeii and this may have precipitated the classical flavor that pervades his paintings of the early 1920s.

These include the large-scale "neoclassical" figure-paintings such as *Seated Woman* (Tate Gallery, London), and *Pipes of Pan* (Musée Picasso, Paris), both from 1923. He also painted some monumental and equally classical examples of late Synthetic Cubism, such as *Three Musicians* (1921; Philadelphia Museum of Art). The sense of menace or tragedy that seems to lurk behind even the calm somber simplicity of these images breaks out violently in others of the period. Finally, the *Three Dancers* (1925; Tate Gallery, London) relinquish all classical serenity for a ritualistic violence. Here the language of

Picasso: Three Figures in an Interior; gouache; 40×80cm (16×31in); 1933. Private collection

Picasso: Nude Woman in a Red Armchair; oil on canvas; 130×97cm (51×38in); 1932. Tate Gallery, London

Synthetic Cubism is openly converted into a vehicle for surreal fantasy.

This phase of his work coincides with the birth of the Surrealist movement. He met André Breton, became a close friend of Paul Éluard, and often contributed to Surrealist exhibitions and periodicals. To some extent he shared the political aspirations of the movement, but the connection is largely by virtue of the Surrealists' admiration for and assimilation of Picasso's inventive imagery. Paramount examples are the invented anatomies of Picasso's paintings and drawings in the early 1930s (*Seated Bather*, Museum of Modern Art, New York). Alongside such fantastic images he also painted the intimately beautiful *Woman in a Red Armchair* (1932; Tate Gallery, London). Here again are the two poles of life and death, love and violence.

In 1931 he moved south of Paris to Boisgeloup where he set up a sculpture studio and an etching workshop. With the technical help of a friend, the sculptor Julio González, he made a series of iron constructions that were often very linear in character, as well as a number of pieces incorporating *objets trouvés*. Others were carved in wood, and there are a few plaster heads. During this period he was active as an illustrator (for Balzac's *Chef d'Oeuvre Inconnu*, 1931; Ovid's *Metamorphoses*, 1931; and Bouffon's *Histoire Naturelle*, 1942). He also made the great series of etchings, *The Sculptor's Studio* (1933–4), in which the Minotaur succeeds Harlequin

as the artist's symbolic self-portrait.

In 1937 Picasso was invited to contribute to the Spanish section of the International Exhibition in Paris. *The Dream and Lie of Franco* etchings of 1936 had already shown the strength of his sympathies over the Spanish Civil War. The total devastation of the ancient Basque capital of Guernica by three hours' bombing focused his feelings and was the subject of the great mural *Guernica*, exhibited in the Spanish Pavilion in 1937 (now in the Prado, Madrid). Considered by many to be his masterpiece, it brings together not only many of the symbols and allegories he had evolved in the 1920s and 1930s, but also the expressive potency of his post-Cubist visual language. Monochromatic, and extraordinarily direct and simple in composition, it is one of the great symbolic images of European art. His later images of political protest (*The Charnel House*, 1945, Museum of Modern Art, New York; *Massacre in Korea*, 1951, Musée Picasso, Paris) do not achieve the same universality.

Picasso spent most of the Second World War in occupied Paris, making paintings and sculptures; many of these were exhibited at the first Salon d'Automne after the Liberation, in 1944, and in London in 1945. These exhibitions showed him at 63 to be the painter most capable of evoking massive public reaction and formed the basis for the remarkable popular reputation of his later years.

He devoted considerable time and energy in the late 1940s and early 1950s to a series of Peace Conferences around Europe. He had joined the Communist Party in 1944. Despite repeated condemnation of his art as degenerate by Communist leaders, he was suddenly awarded the Lenin Prize by Moscow in 1961. He said that his sympathy with Communism was "the logical outcome of my whole life"; it was humanitarian rather than political.

In 1945 he moved to the South of France, where he was to live for the rest of his life. He was in Antibes in 1946, moved to Vallauris in 1948, to Cannes in 1955, to Vauvenargues in 1958, and finally to Mougins in 1961. In this last long period between the Second World War and his death in 1973—he outlived most of his great friends and contemporaries by many years—he remained prolifically, if erratically, productive. An exhibition held in the Palais des Papes, Avignon, in 1970 of his previous year's output included 165 paintings and 45 drawings.

As always, he worked in many media concurrently. In the ceramics workshop that he set up in Vallauris he produced a large number of works, relaxed and joyful and full of the obvious relish he felt for the novelty of the medium. He spent several periods making linocut prints, equally light and inventive, and displayed continuous concern with sculpture. This concentrated in the 1950s on further improvisations with found objects (*She-Goat*, 1950, Museum of Modern Art, New York; *The Bathers*, 1956, National Trust for Historic Preservation in the United States, Washington, D.C.). In the 1960s he turned to freely-painted sheet iron works, again picking up a lead from the fertile period of 1912 to 1915. Several of these were enlarged—usually in sand-blasted concrete—for public sites in Europe and America (for instance the great *Head* in the Civic Center, Chicago, 1965–7).

He also undertook a few painting commissions: the *War* and *Peace* panels for the deconsecrated chapel in Vallauris (1952) and the mural for the UNESCO Building, Paris (1957–8). Other paintings include several sets of variations on motifs from other artists (from, for example, Delacroix's *Femmes d'Alger*, Velazquez's *Las Meninas*, works by Poussin, El Greco, Cranach, Courbet, and Manet). These are full of the dazzling virtuosity and improvisation displayed so clearly in Henri-Georges Clouzot's film of the artist at work, *Le Mystère Picasso* (1953).

His late work is epitomized in *The Artist and his Model* engravings (1968) and the many related paintings and drawings of the last years. They combine intimate autobiography with universal human allegory, as had his earliest paintings. They have an exuberant sensuality: sometimes lyrical, always erotic. Subtleties of facial and bodily expression are nailed with a sharp, almost caricatural perception. Above all they exude the energy and radiant lifeforce that is at the heart of Picasso's art and influence.

Major exhibitions of Picasso's work were held in Paris (1955), London (1960), New York (1962), and Paris (1966–7), as well as memorial exhibitions in 1973 and a major retrospective at the Museum of Modern Art, New York (1980). There are several museums devoted to his work in France (including the Musée Picasso in Paris) as well as the Museo Picasso in Barcelona which contains the complete *Las Meninas* variations. The enormous collection of his works still in his own possession at his death were bequeathed to the Louvre, Paris.

Further reading. Ashton, D. (ed.) *Picasso on Art*, London and New York (1972). Barr, A. H. *Picasso: Fifty Years of his Art*, New York (1946). Berger, J. *Success and Failure of Picasso*, Harmondsworth (1965). Blunt, A. *Picasso's "Guernica"*, Oxford (1969). Gilot, F. *Life with Picasso*, New York and Paris (1964). McCully, M. (ed.) *A Picasso Anthology: Documents, Criticism, Reminiscences*, London (1981). Penrose, R. *Picasso: his Life and Work*, London (1971). Rubin, W. (ed.) *Pablo Picasso: a Retrospective*, London and New York (1980).

Piene Otto 1928–

The German Kinetic artist Otto Piene was born at Laasphe, Westphalia. After studying in Munich and Cologne he founded the utopian "Zero" group in 1957 with Heinz Mack, and in 1958 he produced a magazine of the same name which included a contribution from Yves Klein on monochrome painting.

Piene's work has concentrated on the phenomena of movement, space, and the articulation of light. Much of his time has been taken up with events and performances, for example those of his *Luminous Ballet*, developed in 1959 and 1960. Light projections, smoke, fire, and inflatables are

some of the means and materials he employs. Piene has written and lectured extensively and his public commissions are many.

Piero della Francesca c1410/20–92

The Italian painter Piero della Francesca responded to a wide range of influences: the elegance of the International Gothic, the monumentality and control of light of Masaccio, and the innovations in landscape and technique of Flemish painting; but no artist of his generation combined these interests with such a mastery of clear, luminous color.

He was born Piero da Benedetto de' Franceschi in Borgo San Sepolcro, near Arezzo. We know neither his date of birth nor the reason why he was called Piero della Francesca. His early training is equally uncertain: the only document is the record of his presence in Florence in 1439 with Domenico Veneziano, who was working in S. Maria Novella. The disappearance of these frescoes means that we can only decide on Piero's status at this time by reference to his earliest work, the polyptych of *The Madonna of the Misericordia with SS. Sebastian, John the Baptist, Andrew, and Bernadino of Siena*, commissioned by the Confraternity of the Misericordia in Borgo in 1445. The contract specified it was to have been finished within three years. The comparative immaturity of the style suggests both that this was done and that in 1439 Piero had been an assistant of Domenico Veneziano: his influence can be seen in the bright, clear colors, in the drapery of the Madonna, and in her face with the swept-back hair and plucked eyebrows. The crumpled drapery of Saints John and Andrew reflect the influence of another Florentine artist, Andrea del Castagno, whose *Resurrection* provided the starting point for the *Resurrection* that Piero painted in Borgo (probably in the 1450s).

The immaturity of the Borgo polyptych can be brought out by comparing the exaggerated and clumsy contrapposto of St Sebastian with the refined and balanced pose of Christ in the center of *The Baptism of Christ* (National Gallery, London), probably painted in the early 1450s. The other flanking saints are developed in later works. St Andrew recurs in more solid and monumental form as St Sigismund in the 1451 *Pandolfo Malatesta before St Sigismund* in the Tempio Malatestiano, Rimini;

Piero della Francesca: The Baptism of Christ; panel; 167×116cm (66×46in); early 1450s. National Gallery, London

he is seen again, with a new range of color and richness of drapery, in the saint from the S. Agostino Altarpiece (1454–69) in the Frick Collection, New York. He is one of the four flanking saints in a polyptych commissioned for the main altar in S. Agostino, Borgo in 1454, but only executed at the end of the 1460s. The central *Virgin and Child* from this polyptych are lost. The other saints that survive are *St Augustine* in the National Gallery, Lisbon, *St Michael* in the National Gallery, London, and *St Nicholas of Tolentino* in the Museo Poldi Pezzoli, Milan.

This account of the Misericordia polyptych has so far failed to mention the

directness with which the light falls (the source is to the right), and the strength of the shadows cast. Piero looks beyond his immediate models in Florentine painting of the 1430s to the achievement of Masaccio. This interest is made explicit in the small Crucifixion on the top of the polyptych which is closely modeled upon that from Masaccio's polyptych formerly in the Carmine, Pisa, now in the Museo e Galerie Nazionali di Capodimonte, Naples. The link is important for Piero's greatest achievement, the Arezzo frescoes, but also for other later works; *The Madonna of Senigallia* (Galleria Nazionale delle Marche, Urbino), from the end of Piero's

career in the early 1470s, is a last tribute to Masaccio. The interest in projecting the massive forms of the Virgin and Child in space is combined with a new sophistication in the contrasting costumes worn by the two flanking angels. The setting, with a view through to a window in a vestibule on the left of the panel, reveals a debt to Flemish painting. Flemish influence had transformed his handling of landscape from that in the National Gallery *Baptism*, where the green in the foreground is the same as that in the far distance, to that of the Portraits of *Federico da Montefeltro* and *Battista Sforza* (c mid 1460s; Uffizi, Florence) where there is an atmospheric handling of the misty distance behind the profile portraits (the format is Flemish).

Flemish painting served to transform the medium in which Piero painted from tempera in his early pictures, through a mixed medium with a combination of tempera and oil, to a full oil technique in his latest work. In the *Madonna Enthroned with Saints and Adored by Federico da Montefeltro* (Pinacoteca di Brera, Milan), the influence of Flemish painting is linked with Piero's mastery over perspective. This culminated in two treatises written at the Court of Urbino at the end of his career, when his sight had failed. Neither the Misericordia polyptych, nor that in Perugia, had afforded the opportunity to elaborate the settings. The *Madonna Enthroned* breaks with the Italian tradition of the *sacra conversazione*, and follows Flemish models by placing the figures in the nave of a church in front of the crossing and apse (which is dominated by a curious large egg, probably that of an ostrich). Such is the skill with which the figures are placed within the rich marble of the church that we overlook the discrepancy in scale—with the head of the seated Virgin on a line with that of the standing saints and angels.

Much about the picture remains uncertain. It cannot have been painted for S. Bernardino in Urbino, where it was first recorded, because that church was only built after 1483 and before 1491. The Brera altar must be earlier, because Piero gave up painting at the end of his career (when his sight failed), and because Federico da Montefeltro is not depicted with the ermine and the garter, both of which he was awarded in 1474, and which he wore in later portraits. Speculation connecting the ostrich egg in the background with the birth (after a number of daughters) of a son and heir for the Duke in 1472 seems misplaced: tradition records that the Duchess prayed at the shrine of S. Ubaldo, who is not included among the saints around the Virgin's throne.

The still calm that prevails in so much of Piero's work leaves us unprepared for the vividness with which he handles the narrative of *The History of the True Cross* in the fresco cycle in the main chapel of the church of S. Francesco, Arezzo. The decoration had been provided for by the Bacci family in 1416; but work was only begun in 1447 when Bicci di Lorenzo began the ceiling, most of which he had completed by his death in 1452. The date at which the commission was given to Piero is not known. He is referred to as the artist who had painted the cycle in a document of 1466, and it is possible that he only began it after 1459, a year he is documented as working in Rome. The debts to the Antique which suggest this dating occur both at the

bottom in *The Defeat of Chosroes*, where the leaping horseman on the right derives from a relief on the Arch of Constantine, and in *The Death of Adam* in the lunette of the south wall.

The frescoes are arranged in traditional manner on the side-walls of the chapel, with smaller frescoes flanking the lancet window. The light, which is taken as falling from this source, models the forms with an intensity that looks back to Masaccio, although Piero works with a brighter palette.

There may well have been a change in the original program. Both the choice of subject (from *The Golden Legend*) and its treatment connect with the call for a crusade against the Turks, made after the fall of Constantinople in 1453. This would explain why the narrative on the north wall is disrupted to show *The Defeat of Chosroes* (in a form not found in *The Golden Legend*). This is opposite *Constan-*

tine's Victory at the Milvian Bridge, where the introduction of the previous Byzantine Emperor, John Paleologus, as Constantine reinforces the reference to Constantinople. The contemporary overtones are brought out by the eagle of the Empire which flutters over the victors, and by the mixture of contemporary and classical armor. The notables of Arezzo crowd in to watch *The Meeting of Solomon and Sheba* and *The Death of Chosroes*.

The frescoes combine a feeling for variety with a sense of control. The courtly ritual of Sheba and her attendants is contrasted with the struggle of the laborers who have to bury the huge beam; and the night scene in which the angel appears to Constantine is set beside the clear, limpid morning light of his subsequent *Victory at the Milvian Bridge*. The perspective in *The Discovery of the Three Crosses* section of the S. Francesco frescoes is not an end in itself, but is used to differentiate between the discovery of the three crosses outside Jerusalem and the miraculous cure effected by the true cross within the city. Piero's achievement in S. Francesco can be compared with the outstanding monumental frescoes of the Quattrocento, those by Pisanello and Mantegna in the Palazzo Ducale, Mantua, and by Masaccio in the Brancacci Chapel, S. Maria del Carmine, Florence.

Further reading. Aronberg-Lavin, M. *Piero della Francesca's "Flagellation": the Triumph of Christian Glory*, Harmondsworth (1971). Clark, K. *Piero della Francesca*, London (1971). Fasola, N. (ed.) *Piero della Francesca: de Prospectiva Pingendi*, Florence (1942). Mancini, G. (ed.) *Piero della Francesca: Libellus de Quinque Corporibus Regularibus*, Rome (1915). Meiss, M. "Once again, Piero della Francesca's Montefeltro Altarpiece", *Art Bulletin*, New York (1966). Shearman, J. "The Logic and Realism of Piero della Francesca" in Kosegarten, A. and Tigler, P. (eds.) *Festschrift für Ullrich Middeldorf*, Berlin (1968).

Piero di Cosimo 1462–1521

The Florentine painter Piero di Cosimo was, as his name indicates, the pupil of Cosimo Rosselli. He was in Rosselli's shop by 1480, but it is not known when he left. According to Vasari, who provides the only documentation for his life and works, his early experience was with Rosselli in

Piero della Francesca: the train of the Queen of Sheba, a detail of The Meeting of Solomon and the Queen of Sheba; fresco; 1452–65. S. Francesco, Arezzo

Piero di Cosimo: The Forest Fire; panel; 71×203cm (28×80in); c1487–9. Ashmolean Museum, Oxford

Rome, where he helped his master with landscapes, and introduced portraits into the work on the walls of the Sistine Chapel (1481/2).

Piero was a strange man, who seems to have left his garden unkempt, saying that "nature ought to be allowed to look after itself …" A mean man, he lived on hard-boiled eggs, cooking several days' supply at once in his glue-pot, to save on fuel costs. As an artist, he was certainly interested in the bizarre and the unusual. Vasari says "he stopped to examine a wall where sick persons had used to spit, imagining that he saw there combats of horses and the most fantastic cities and extraordinary landscapes … He cherished the same fancies of clouds …" Such Leonardesque ideas appear also in his work, and his style sometimes imitates that of his great compatriot. Although his portraits can be hard, in the manner of Baldovinetti, they often show Leonardo's delicacy and intimate intensity.

The best-known of Piero's works are a series of panels on *The Early History of the World*, including *A Fight between Lapiths and Centaurs* (National Gallery, London), *The Hunt* (Metropolitan Museum, New York), and *Prometheus* (Musée des Beaux-Arts, Strasbourg), based on stories deriving from Ovid. Although the exact meaning of these works is often unclear, their style is startlingly vital, resting partly on the example of Luca Signorelli, who was also working in the Sistine Chapel in the 1480s. Piero's art might be used as an example of the variations that are possible within the Renaissance manner of art, which concentrates on the human body and shows great interest in Classical mythology. Instead of being monumental or heroic, Piero conjures up a poetic atmosphere which the intricacy and Flemish-style detailing of his landscapes helps to remove further from everyday life. His bodies are muscular and exciting in their sharp outline, but they do not blend with the landscape in any kind of unified perspective. Perspective is certainly present, however, as in *The Hunt*: here, a corpse dripping blood is placed in steep perspective, head lolling out of the picture—very much in the manner of Uccello's battle scenes, whose style Piero's work resembles.

Very different are works like his *Madonna and Child with a Dove* (Louvre, Paris), which attains a moral weight and physical dynamism most unlike his *poesie* (as the genre was to be called in the time of Titian). Like Leonardo (traces of whose *sfumato* are visible, in hardened form, in the *Madonna and Child with a Dove*), Piero was also apparently popular as a designer of festival ephemera. Possibly his morbid imagination was enhanced by Si-gnorelli's scenes of death and damnation in *The Last Judgment* (c1499; Orvieto Cathedral). These may have inspired a particularly nasty triumphal chariot (in the Renaissance tradition, taken over from the Middle Ages, of Triumphs of Love, Fame, Chastity, Honor, and so forth). This is *The Triumph of Death* (1511) as described by Vasari: a "most realistic but a horrid and terrible sight … this lugubrious spectacle, by its novelty and tremendous character … at once terrified and amazed the whole city …" This was only one of several contraptions he designed.

The importance of Piero, then, is twofold: his interest in the early history of the world was a reflection of contemporary appreciation of the notion of the Golden Age and its variations. Yet his landscapes, full of poetry, and described by Vasari as "very lovely and the coloring soft, graceful, harmonious and well blended", were well on the way to an interest in landscape for its own sake—to the creation of a new genre, which was to appear among the Venetians.

Pierre de Montreuil *fl.* 1231–67

Pierre de Montreuil was a French master mason. In 1231 he began rebuilding the Carolingian nave and transepts of the royal mausoleum of St-Denis, Paris, to link

the 12th-century choir, also partly rebuilt, and the narthex erected by Abbot Suger. The work is an early example of the Rayonnant style, characterized by a glazed triforium, large clerestory windows, transept rose windows, and tall, slim, vertical shafts from floor to vault. About 1265, he continued in this style at Notre Dame, Paris. He completed the additional bay of the south transept, with its rose window, as part of the enlargement of the cathedral that had been begun by Jean de Chelles.

Pietro da Cortona 1596–1669

Pietro da Cortona, one of the most influential artists of the Roman High Baroque, was architect, painter, decorator, and designer of monuments. He became the leading fresco painter in Rome; his superb control of complex iconographical schemes and richly diverse, large-scale compositions realized the full potential of the Baroque style.

His real name was Pietro Berrettini; he was known as da Cortona from the place of his birth, where his first teacher was Andrea Commodi. In 1612 he arrived in Rome and there developed his personal style from a study of Raphael and the Antique. He was also profoundly moved by a love for Titian, which was to make him a founder of the Neo-Venetian move-

ment. His earliest known works are frescoes in the Villa Muti at Frascati and in the Palazzo Mattei, Mantua (1622–3).

Cortona rapidly attracted powerful patrons such as the Sacchetti family and Cardinal Francesco Barberini, through whom he was commissioned to paint frescoes in the church of S. Bibbiana (1642–6). These paintings of the life of the saint reveal his profound response to the Antique; they include a profusion of meticulously observed classical ornament and backgrounds of grandiose imperial architecture. These are the result of Cortona's many drawings of vases, sarcophagi, arches, and Roman archaeological remains which he undertook for the famous antiquarian Cassiano dal Pozzo. Yet the boldness and drama of his style are new; his compositions depend on thrusting diagonals, and his touch is spirited.

For the Sacchetti family, Cortona decorated the chapel at the Chigi Palace at Castel Fusano with brilliant, freely painted landscape frescoes. A series of large mythological and historical paintings culminate in 1629 with *Rape of the Sabines* (Palazzo dei Conservatori, Rome). The powerful, almost sculptural groups of figures are organized in an energetic flow of movement both into and across the canvas; the color has a Venetian brilliance.

Between 1633 and 1639 Cortona frescoed the ceiling of the great hall of the Palazzo Barberini in Rome. The central theme is the glorification of Pope Urban VIII as the agent of Providence; the program was devised by the poet Francesco Bracciolini. An illusionistic architectural framework is created from a variety of intricate decorative details painted in simulated stucco. The ceiling is divided into five distinct areas. Painted figures float above and below the framework, giving the illusion of an airy space open to the sky. The rich diversity of subjects that subtly elaborate the central theme, and the swirling mass of brilliantly foreshortened figures, are orchestrated into a composition of overwhelming power focusing on the personification of Divine Providence. In 1637 Cortona had visited Florence and Venice; both in composition and in the beautiful effects of flickering light and atmosphere, his achievement owes much to a study of Veronese's ceilings. Between 1634 and 1638 his preeminence was recognized in Rome and he was elected *principe* of the Accademia di San Luca.

In Florence Cortona had begun to deco-

rate the Sala della Stufa in the Palazzo Pitti with frescoes of the Four Ages. In 1640 he returned to finish these frescoes, and between 1641 and 1647 he decorated a sequence of rooms in the grand ducal apartment. These rooms are unified by a vast iconographical program relating the virtues of Cosimo I to the signs of the planets. The painted scenes are framed by luxuriant stucco decoration; in them the artist reveals a new, highly sophisticated elegance. He also frescoed two small rooms in the Palazzo Pitti for Gian Carlo de' Medici.

Cortona's late compositions develop away from the passionate exuberance of the 1630s towards a calmer and more classical style. In the 1650s he painted many altarpieces and easel pictures and between 1647 and 1665 frescoed the dome, nave, and apse of S. Maria in Vallicella; the dome frescoes are a reworking of the illusionism of Giovanni Lanfranco and Correggio. Between 1651 and 1654 he decorated with fresco the ceiling of the long gallery in the Palazzo Pamphili Navona for Pope Innocent X. The ceiling shows a variety of scenes from *The Aeneid*. Influenced by Raphael and the Antique, it is a work of great elegance and delicacy, whose pale yet radiant colors anticipate the lightness of the Rococo.

Throughout his career Cortona was also occupied by large architectural commissions. The Villa del Pigneto near Rome was built for the Sacchetti family before 1630: here concave lateral wings framed a high central structure with a monumental niche, an idea that derived from the Belvedere in the Vatican. Between 1635 and 1650 Cortona was concerned with the rebuilding of SS. Martina e Luca, Rome. The plan is a Greek cross with apsidal endings, surmounted by a dome. The upper part of the church is richly decorated with a variety of different motifs that ultimately derive from Florentine Mannerism. In the dome, ribs are superimposed upon highly idiosyncratic and undulating recessed panels (coffers). The external facade is curved, seemingly in response to the pressures of internal space. This suggested movement is firmly halted by paired pilasters.

This contrast of concave and convex forms, a theme characteristic of the Roman Baroque, is further developed in Cortona's remodeling of the facade of S. Maria della Pace, Rome (1656–7). Here he placed a bold semicircular porch in front of the lower part of the facade. He emphasized its

Pietro da Cortona: The Apotheosis of Aeneas; detail; ceiling fresco; 1651–4. Galleria Doria Pamphili, Rome

outward thrust by setting it against a convex upper tier, framed by deep concave wings that seem to transform the whole area of the *piazza* into a stage. Yet in other ways the church is more sober than SS. Martina e Luca, and this tendency towards Roman grandeur and simplicity is further developed in the facade of S. Maria in Via Lata, Rome (1658–62). Here two stories are separated by a wide projecting entablature. In the lower story a Corinthian colonnade opens into a portico, in the upper story into a loggia. In the upper colonnade a round arch, enclosed by a triangular pediment, breaks into the entablature—a motive borrowed from Hellenistic or Roman Imperial sources.

In 1664 Cortona submitted plans for the completion of the Louvre. The most important project of his final years was the dome of S. Carlo al Corso, Rome, where the classic simplicity of the motifs contrasts sharply with the Mannerist intricacy of the dome of SS. Martina e Luca.

Further reading. Briganti, G. *Pietro da Cortona e la Pittura Barocca*, Florence (1962). Waterhouse, E. K. *Baroque Painting in Rome*, London (1937). Waterhouse, E. K. *Italian Baroque Painting*, London (1962). Wittkower, R. *Art and Architecture in Italy: 1600–1750*, Harmondsworth (1973).

Pigalle Jean-Baptiste 1714–85

The French sculptor, Jean-Baptiste Pigalle was born in Paris, the son of a joiner. He was to become the leading French sculptor of the mid 18th century, and the chief representative in sculpture of the Enlighten-

ment. The pupil first of Robert Le Lorrain and then of Jean-Baptiste Lemoyne, his beginnings were not auspicious. He failed to win a scholarship to Rome, and went there at his own expense. In his three years there (1736–9) he seems to have been little influenced by either Classical or Baroque sculpture. His phenomenal rise to fame began in 1744, when he exhibited his celebrated *Mercury* (Louvre, Paris) at the Academy: it was the most successful of all sculptural reception pieces.

Pigalle was a highly individual sculptor, whose style steers a middle course between classicism and the Baroque and is characterized by its regard for truth. An intellectual who avoided the seductive, he was closely associated with Voltaire and the Philosophes. He was a favorite sculptor of Madame de Pompadour, and received through Marigny in 1755 the commission for the great equestrian statue of Louis XV for Reims.

Pigalle's most original work is his extraordinary statue of the nude Voltaire (1770–6; Louvre, Paris) which caused a scandal in its day. His finest achievement is the monument to the Maréchal de Saxe at Strasbourg (1753–76; St Thomas), the outstanding French monument of the 18th century.

Jean-Baptiste Pigalle: the monument to the Maréchal de Saxe; marble; 1753–76. Church of St Thomas, Strasbourg

Pilon Germain *c1525/30–90*

The French sculptor Germain Pilon was born in Paris. In his early years he may have been responsible for the most famous and most mysterious of French Renaissance statues, *Diana of Anet* (Louvre, Paris), first mentioned in 1554. The first record of Pilon is in 1558, when he completed figures (now lost) for the tomb of Francis I. In 1560 he was working for Primaticcio, carving the well-known group of the *Three Graces* for the monument for the heart of Henry II (Louvre, Paris).

Between 1563 and 1570, as a member of Primaticcio's workshop, he provided most of the sculpture for the tomb of Henry II and Catherine de Medici (abbey of St-Denis, Paris), including two of the great bronze Virtues and the marble effigies and kneeling figures in bronze on the top. In these Pilon's individual mature style is first foreshadowed. From the 1570s date some superb portrait busts, of which the finest is perhaps that of the shifty-eyed *Charles IX* (Wallace Collection, London).

In the last ten years of his life, from 1580, Pilon emerged as the most powerfully emotive sculptor of the time. He reflected in his work the upheavals, the anxieties, and the strong religious feeling of the closing years of the Valois dynasty. From these years come sculptures for the never-completed royal mausoleum at St-Denis, including *The Virgin of Pity* (terracotta in the Louvre, Paris; marble in the church of St Paul and St Louis, Paris), which shows a return to the spirit of the late Gothic. Also from this period are the works that stand as his supreme masterpieces: the tombs of Chancellor René de Birague and his wife Valentine Balbiani, together with the associated bronze relief of *The Entombment*, all now in the Louvre, Paris.

Pintoricchio *c1454–1513*

The Italian painter Bernardino di Betto, known as Pinturicchio or Pintoricchio, was born in Perugia. His frescoes are his most important works, though he also painted altarpieces and portraits. He came to Rome in 1481 as Perugino's assistant, one of the group of Umbrian and Florentine artists (including Ghirlandaio, Rosselli, Signorelli, and Botticelli) Sixtus IV had summoned to fresco the Sistine Chapel.

Pintoricchio later secured important fresco commissions in Rome: for the decoration of the Bufalini Chapel in S. Maria in Aracoeli (*c*1485), the Borgia apartments in the Vatican Palace (1492–4), and Julius II's presbytery chapel in S. Maria del Popolo (1509–10). He also painted two important series outside Rome: the frescoes of the Baglioni Chapel in Spello (1501; S. Maria Maggiore) and those of the Piccolomini Library in Siena (1502–8).

Pintoricchio's many frescoes, and the many painted by contemporaries such as Ghirlandaio, show that increased opportunities for large-scale painting arose during the late 15th century. These stimulated Pintoricchio and other artists to try new approaches to mural decoration.

Pintoricchio's paintings often flamboyantly honor his patron. The Piccolomini Library in Siena was built to honor Aeneas Sylvius Piccolomini, the humanist Pope Pius II (1458–64), by preserving his collection of Classical texts. Pintoricchio's frescoes depict triumphant moments in the Pope's career, which he had recorded in his autobiography. (This was based squarely upon an ancient text: Julius Caesar's *Commentaries*.) References to Aeneas Sylvius extend even to the ceiling, where the Piccolomini *stemma* is at the center of the decoration.

Those paintings and others by Pintoricchio are effective decoration because of the charm of his seemingly naïve approach to monumental narrative. His paintings, both early and late, are stilted versions of those by his early master, Perugino. The space is more fragmented and the figures stiffer than in Perugino's suave creations. But Pintoricchio's awkwardness actually complements his pursuit of narrative pageantry. His paintings are tableaux in which he sought neither Peruginesque harmony nor dramatic intensity. Instead, he consistently transmuted events into innocent, beguiling pageants performed by pretty figures who pose before numerous picturesque props.

He developed a system of painted frames, fitting the narrative scenes into architectural settings in such a way that the scenes become illusionistic extensions of the room. For instance, he framed the scenes of the Piccolomini Library with fictive arches which seem to project forward. They thus make the narrative scenes appear to take place outside the room. Those painted arches also transform the room into an open loggia, reminiscent of the antique painted loggias described by Pliny the Elder (*c* AD 23–79).

Such Classical motifs pervade Pintoricchio's work. The rediscovery of the *Domus Aurea* (the "Golden House" of Nero) in Rome spurred him and other late-15th-century artists to imitate the painted and stucco ornament of its rooms. Patrons encouraged the development of such decoration *all'antica*. Pintoricchio's contract for the Piccolomini Library required him to include *grotteschi* in the decoration. He obliged, covering the applied pilasters of the Library's walls and its ceiling pendentives with polychrome grotesque ornament, copied from the decoration of the *Domus Aurea*.

Pintoricchio was a popular artist; he was innovative as well as prolific. The unfolding of his career in Rome, then the new artistic capital of Italy because of the Pope's return from Avignon, is in itself significant. His career established the pattern for later ambitious artists, from Raphael to Pietro da Cortona, who also came to Rome to paint monumental murals in its churches and palaces (*See* overleaf.)

Piranesi G.B. *1720–78*

The Italian printmaker and architect Giovanni Battista Piranesi was born at Mogliano. He first trained with his uncle,

G.B. Piranesi: A Staircase before a Vaulted Hall; pen, brown ink, and wash over red chalk on paper; 38×26cm (15×10in); c1755. British Museum, London

the architect Matteo Lucchesi, then with another architect, Giovanni Scalfarotto, and with the engraver Carlo Zucchi. In 1740 Piranesi traveled to Rome as draftsman to Marco Foscarini, ambassador to the Papal Court of Benedict XIV. In Rome he was taught etching by Giuseppe Vasi, and took an interest in Roman Antiquity, history, and literature. In 1743 he visited Naples and the excavations at Pompeii and Herculaneum, then went on to Venice.

Returning to Rome, Piranesi began a successful series of print publications: the *Carceri* ("Prisons"), 1745; the *Vedute* ("Views"), 137 etchings of ancient and modern Rome, from 1745; *Le Antichità Romane*, 1756. He was supported by Pope Benedict XIV, and also by an Englishman, James Caulfield, Earl of Charlemont. His prints were popular among English connoisseurs; in 1757 he was made Honorary Fellow of the Society of Antiquaries, London.

Piranesi wrote an impassioned defence of the Etruscan (as opposed to the Greek) origin of Roman Antiquities in his *Magnificenza ed Architettura de' Romani* ("Magnificence and Architecture of the Romans"), 1761. His architectural works include improvements to the Papal Palace, Castel Gandolfo; S. Maria del Priorato, and the Piazza de' Cavalieri, Rome, 1764–9.

In his topographical prints, Piranesi infused a somber, even menacing, scale to the buildings he portrayed by the exaggerated use of perspective. By heavily shading certain areas of his compositions, he reinforced this dramatic mood.

Pisanello 1395–1455

The Italian artist Antonio Pisano, called Pisanello, was a fashionable court painter and medalist; he was a follower of Gentile da Fabriano, exponent of the International Gothic style.

Brought up in Verona, he was probably first trained under Stefano da Verona, whose influence distinguishes the early *Madonna della Quaglia* (c1420; Museo di Castelvecchio, Verona). Between 1415 and 1422 he worked in Venice, where he continued Gentile da Fabriano's fresco cycle (now destroyed) in the Grand Hall of the Doges' Palace under Gentile's direction. Later he is documented in Verona

Pintoricchio: Pius II arrives at Ancona for the Crusade, a fresco scene in the Piccolomini Library, Siena; c1506–8

and Mantua, and in 1423 may have traveled to Florence to help Gentile in the painting of his Strozzi Altarpiece (Uffizi, Florence).

From 1424 to 1425 Pisanello worked at the Gonzaga court in Mantua; during the same period he frescoed a signed *Annunciation* over the tomb of Niccolò Brenzoni in the Veronese church of S. Fermo. He either accompanied or followed Gentile da Fabriano to Rome in 1426, remaining there until 1432, and completing the fresco cycle in the Lateran Basilica left unfinished on Gentile's death (now destroyed). He also made drawings of Roman antiquities.

On returning to Verona, he frescoed the Pellegrini Chapel in the church of S. Anastasia (1436–8); only the *St George and the Princess* survives, demonstrating his predilection for animals. Indeed, in *The Vision of St Eustace* (1436–8; National Gallery, London) animals usurp all religious purport. Several preparatory drawings for both works exist among the numerous animal drawings attributed to Pisanello, many of which are in the Codex Villardi in the Louvre, Paris. They reveal him as one of the most observant depicters of fauna in Western art.

Pisanello went to Ferrara in 1438. It was at the Congress of Ferrara, attended by John VIII Paleologus, Emperor of Constantinople, that his career as a medalist began. His medallion of the Emperor (the first cast Renaissance medal made in Italy) must belong to the same year. It inaugurated a series of superb portrait medallions commissioned by the reigning tyrants of Italy, including those of Gianfrancesco Gonzaga (1439–40), Filippo Maria Visconti (1440), Francesco Sforza (1442), Lionello d'Este (1441–3), Sigismondo Pandolfo Malatesta (1445), Ludovico III and Cecilia Gonzaga (1447), and Alfonso of Aragon (1449). Pisanello's distinction as a portraitist is equally revealed in his paintings. These include the *Portrait of a Princess* (1435–40; Louvre, Paris), in which the subject is depicted against a background of pinks and columbines among which butterflies flit, and the similar profile *Portrait of Lionello d'Este* (1441; Galleria dell'Accademia Carrara, Bergamo).

In 1439 Pisanello returned to Mantua. During the following decade he moved between its Gonzaga court, the Este court in Ferrara, and his native Verona. In the Palazzo Ducale in Mantua he painted murals which were long believed to have

Above: Pisanello: Madonna and Child with St George and St Anthony Abbot; tempera on panel; 47×29cm (19×11in); c1445. National Gallery, London

Below: Pisanello: Study of Two Horses' Heads; pencil on paper; 29×19cm (11×7½in). Louvre, Paris

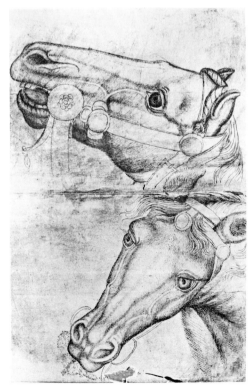

disappeared. But in 1969 the Sala del Pisanello was rediscovered. Extensive portions of *intonaco* painting (*Tournament Battle*) and *sinopie* (*Landscape with Episodes of Chivalrous Legend*) were revealed (*c*1436–42). The murals, commemorating King Henry VI's bestowal of the English Royal Livery on Gianfrancesco Gonzaga, were presumably abandoned on Pisanello's banishment from Mantua in 1442.

In 1448 Pisanello went to the Neapolitan court of Alfonso of Aragon, for whom he worked as a medalist. After 1449, we have no documentary evidence of his activities or whereabouts. He died in 1455.

Pisani 13th and 14th centuries

The group of Italian sculptors known as the Pisani included Nicola Pisano (*fl.* 1258–78) and his son Giovanni (*fl.* 1245/50–1314); Andrea da Pontedera, known as Andrea Pisano (*fl. c*1290–1348/9), and his son Nino (*fl.*1349–?68). The two families were not related.

Their name indicates their origins, and it was at Pisa that they founded and maintained the Pisan School which dominated Tuscan and to a lesser extent Italian sculpture over the century 1250 to 1350. Other artists of great accomplishment such as Arnolfo di Cambio and Tino di Camaino came from that circle. Their combined talents produced innovations in style, iconography, and sculptural programs that mark a major peak in the history of European art.

Pisa, at its heyday *c*1250, was one of several Tuscan city states (Florence, Siena, and Lucca being most notable among the others) that were in continuous rivalry during the later Middle Ages. Their rivalries, fueled by Guelph or Ghibelline loyalties, often spilled over into open warfare. But it was not a situation that prevented the movement of artists. Thus Nicola and Giovanni Pisano worked in Siena, the latter being a Sienese citizen for a number of years, and Andrea worked extensively in Florence.

An important factor in assessing the art of the Pisani is the presence in Naples from the 1260s onwards of the French Angevin monarchy. It prompted the appearance of French culture in Italy, particularly the Gothic style, of which there were to be many instances in the work of the Pisani. But this powerful influence was never able to extinguish the innate echoes of Classical Antiquity in Italian art, echoes that were to reverberate with great clarity in the sculpture of Nicola and Giovanni Pisano.

Knowledge of the lives of both Nicola and Giovanni is patchy, but much of their sculpture has survived in good condition, particularly the famous series of pulpits. These are the keystones of their work. Because of the advances they show in naturalistic representation—advances that precede the great achievements of Giotto—they are the basis for the claim that Nicola and Giovanni were the first Renaissance artists.

Nicola Pisano's date of birth is unknown, and his origins uncertain. While most documents refer to him as being "from Pisa", two say that he is from Apulia. Evidence to substantiate this possible south Italian origin is provided by his first pulpit, that at Pisa: the abundance of its quotations from antique art may have been inspired by work, deliberately Classical in style, carried out in southern Italy for the Emperor Frederick II (*ob.* 1250).

Nicola is first documented in 1258, and again in 1260 when he signed the pulpit in the Baptistery at Pisa. This hexagonal structure has three parts. The lower consists of seven columns. Their foliated capitals support the middle section, an archivolt of trilobe arches with prophets and evangelists in the spandrels, and statuettes of Virtues and St John the Baptist at the corners. The upper level, the casket, is decorated with five reliefs depicting incidents from the life of Christ and the Last Judgment, these being divided by clusters of three columns. The hard, solid forms of the reliefs are the result of Nicola's study of the Antique, and several figures can be traced to Roman sarcophagi that still survive. Though elements of the shape and arrangement follow south Italian and Tuscan traditions, the pulpit's originality lies in the new and highly sophisticated way these elements are handled.

After completing the Pisa pulpit, Nicola probably undertook two reliefs for Lucca Cathedral. These are neither documented nor signed, and the extent of his contribution is disputed. In 1265 he contracted to make a pulpit for Siena Cathedral. It was finished in 1268. Larger and more elaborate than the Pisa pulpit, it is octagonal, and has statuettes at the angles of the casket instead of columns. The relief scenes are smaller in scale than those at Pisa and their figures more numerous. In several places, particularly the angle figures of the casket, a softening of form and line introduces a Gothic flavor that was largely absent at Pisa. The pulpit's variety of styles and uneven quality is the result of workshop participation. Documents refer to four assistants, notably Giovanni Pisano and Arnolfo di Cambio. One reason for their involvement was the fact that Nicola was simultaneously supervising another major commission, the tomb of St Dominic at S. Domenico in Bologna. That work was finished by 1267, and again there is much evidence of studio participation.

The last documented work of Nicola's is the *Fontana Maggiore* at Perugia, undertaken with Giovanni and completed in 1278. It is on three levels: the lower basin is a 25-sided polygon decorated with 50 reliefs; above is a smaller 12-sided basin interspersed with statuettes. The upper level, all in bronze, consists of a column, surmounted by a basin and a caryatid from which gushes the water. The marble reliefs read like a medieval encyclopedia with carvings of, for example, the Labors of the Months and the Liberal Arts. The statuettes range from saints and prophets to city officials and personifications of local places. Style and iconography show French influence in parts, and may indicate Giovanni's hand.

Nicola's greatness lay in his ability to formulate large-scale sculptural programs, and his creation of a naturalistic relief style based on borrowings from Antiquity and northern Gothic. Suggestions that the latter are the result of a visit to France are entirely hypothetical.

Giovanni's date of birth is also unknown, though he was born a Pisan. After the completion of the Siena and Perugia projects he may have remained in Nicola's workshop, helping his father with the sculptural decoration of the outside of the Pisa Baptistery, a scheme that is not documented but is confidently assigned to this circle.

By 1285 he was resident in Siena and undertaking the design and decoration of the cathedral facade, though there is no direct documentary proof for this and he is first referred to as "capomaestro" (chief architect) only in 1290. By the time he left, probably in 1297, he had completed six animals and 14 large full-length biblical prophets and sages of Antiquity, all for the lower part of the facade. The badly weathered figures are now in the Museo dell'Opera del Duomo, Siena. Unlike such schemes in northern Europe, they were not incorporated in a rigid architectural framework,

Giovanni Pisano: the pulpit in Pisa Cathedral; marble; 1302–10

pulpit than he was commissioned in 1302 to make another, this time for Pisa Cathedral. Completed in 1310, it is much larger than the other three and is octagonal in shape. The iconography of the upper sections is the same, though necessarily expanded. The main departure is the replacement of some columns by caryatids, two being accompanied by elaborate figure sculpture around the bases. Just as in Nicola's Siena pulpit, Giovanni's second version shows variations in quality that point to workshop participation, particularly in the angle figures. Some of the finest work—certainly done by Giovanni himself—is to be found in the caryatids. One, the "Prudence" figure, exemplifies the reappearance of Classical motifs in this pulpit. Other motifs, such as the acanthus-leaf brackets replacing the pointed arches of Pistoia, help to emphasize the contrast with the earlier pulpit. The springy lightness of Pistoia has given way to a heavier, monumental, almost Baroque splendor.

In 1311–12 Giovanni carved his only surviving tomb sculpture, the monument to Margaret of Luxembourg, wife of Emperor Henry VII (fragments at the Palazzo Bianco, Genoa, and elsewhere). Other works that survive include some wooden crucifixes and a number of Madonna and Child groups, including one carved in ivory (Pisa Cathedral treasury). Most are undocumented and unsigned but are ascribed on firm stylistic evidence to various periods in Giovanni's life.

There is no concrete evidence for the claim, sometimes made, that Giovanni visited France, though the Gothic elements in his work are certainly considerable. Along with the borrowings from Antiquity, they are well assimilated in a way that his father's are not. Moreover, his work is marked by an easy confidence in the handling of gestures and groups of figures, and his narrative reliefs are extremely vivid. Giovanni's hallmarks include the long necks and jutting heads of his figures.

The massive achievements of Nicola and Giovanni Pisano overshadow the work of their namesakes in the 14th century. In the case of Andrea Pisano this is particularly regrettable, for his bronze doors for the Baptistery of Florence Cathedral are among the major monuments of Italian art. The doors, signed and dated 1330, provide the first mention of Andrea. Subsequent documents refer to various assistants and casting arrangements. The work was completed in 1336. Together the doors

but seem to move around and interrelate with one another. To ensure that their powerful gestures and expressions were visible from the ground, Giovanni cut deeply into the marble and distorted both poses and features. The effect is awesomely impressive.

Probably soon after his return to Pisa, Giovanni began the third in the great series of pulpits, that for the church of S. Andrea at Pistoia. Completed in 1301, the pulpit differs little in arrangement and iconography from Nicola's at Siena, but returns to the hexagonal shape of that at Pisa. The

angle figures are larger in scale and now are carved to be seen from a number of viewpoints. Their thrusting, vigorous poses recall some of the Siena facade statues. In the five reliefs Giovanni stresses the human side of the stories, such as the tenderness of the Nativity or the violent emotions of the Massacre of the Innocents. In style the pulpit is in marked contrast to Nicola's works. It is essentially Gothic, with its pointed arches supporting the casket, its figure-style, and its general air of lightness and delicacy.

No sooner had Giovanni finished this

contain 20 scenes from the life of John the
Baptist and eight personifications of virtues, each contained in a quatrefoil, a
decorative element that enlivens the surface of the doors. There is no obvious
source for the general arrangement though
the quatrefoils, a French motif, were used
by Giotto in the Capella dell'Arena, Padua.
Giotto's figure and drapery style is employed
with great beauty and gracefulness by
Andrea, some of whose brilliant compositions are adapted from the painter's Peruzzi Chapel frescoes (in S. Croce, Florence).
Where these fail to provide a prototype,
Andrea uses the mosaics in the dome of the
Baptistery. The format of the doors was
copied by Ghiberti in his first set of doors
for the same building.

In 1340 Andrea is mentioned as
"capomaestro" of Florence Cathedral, a
post he held until 1343. He was responsible for extending the campanile as far as
the second main cornice. He is also generally held to have designed and executed
most of the reliefs surrounding the lower
half of the base, where again the style
shows Giotto's influence. Some of the
statues in the niches above have also been
attributed to him on stylistic evidence.

He was appointed "capomaestro" at Orvieto Cathedral in 1347, being succeeded
by his son in 1349. He may have died
either then or at Florence in the following
year.

Surviving references to Andrea's son
Nino are very sparse. By 1353 he had left
his post at Orvieto. In 1357–8 he is
recorded as a silversmith at Pisa. By 1368
he was dead. His three surviving signed
works are undated. Two of these, a
Madonna and Child (S. Maria Novella,
Florence) and some figures, including a
Madonna and Child, surmounting the
Cornaro monument (SS. Giovanni e Paolo,
Venice), indicate a Gothic style close to
contemporary French art. Their charm is
exemplified by the sweet smiles of the
Madonnas. On these works is hung a
whole collection of homeless mid-14th-
century sculpture. Few can be either attributed or dated with any certainty. Two of
the more definite are a *Madonna and Child*

Left: Andrea Pisano: the south door of the
Baptistery, Florence; bronze; height 564cm
(222in); 1330–6

Right: Nino Pisano: Madonna and Child;
marble; c1348. S. Maria Novella, Florence

where the Virgin is suckling the Child (Museo Nazionale di San Matteo, Pisa) and a pair of marble figures, *The Virgin and the Annunciatory Angel* (S. Catherina, Pisa) that were to be influential on later Annunciation groups.

Further reading. Crichton, G.H. and E.R. *Nicola Pisano and the Survival of Sculpture in Italy*, Cambridge (1938). Mellini, G.L. *Giovanni Pisano*, Milan (1970).

Pissarro Camille 1830–1903

The Impressionist painter Camille Jacob Pissarro was born on the island of St Thomas in the West Indies, the son of a Jewish father and a Creole mother. He settled in France in 1855, and studied landscape under Corot *c*1860; he met Monet at this time, and Cézanne in 1861. His early landscapes are in the tradition of the Barbizon School, quite subdued in color and simple in structure, for instance the large *Banks of the Marne at Chennevières*, shown at the 1865 Salon (National Gallery of Scotland, Edinburgh). The execution of this painting, largely by the palette-knife, shows a debt to Courbet. By 1870, Pissarro was painting smaller pictures, whose varied touch conveys the differing textures and effects in his landscape subjects, such as *The Diligence at Louveciennes* (Musée du Jeu de Paume, Paris).

In 1870 Pissarro took refuge from the Franco-Prussian War in London, where he found Monet, and had a chance to study the work of Constable and Turner. However, his paintings of London, and those painted between 1871 and 1873 after his return to France, show no direct influence of British painting. They continue the traits of his 1870 work, in their response to the variety of nature, as in *The Louveciennes Road* (1872; Musée du Jeu de Paume, Paris). Pissarro's concerns in this period were particularly close to those of Sisley.

Around 1874 Pissarro began to look for a greater surface unity in his paintings, perhaps as a result of his contact with Cézanne, with whom he worked regularly during the years 1872 to 1874. In paint-

Camille Pissarro: The Diligence on the Road from Ennery to L'Hermitage, Pontoise; oil on canvas; 47×55cm (19×22in); 1877. Musée du Jeu de Paume, Paris

Camille Pissarro: The Boieldieu Bridge at Rouen; oil on canvas; 74×91cm (29×36in); 1896. City of Birmingham Museums and Art Gallery

ings such as *Quarry at Pontoise* (c1874; Öffentliche Kunstsammlung, Kunstmuseum, Basel) he used the palette knife to give this unity, by comparatively broad strokes of paint. However, in 1876 and 1877 he began to seek homogeneity with small juxtaposed brush strokes, varied in color but often parallel in direction; these unified the picture surface but at the same time permitted him to introduce the varied atmospheric color he was increasingly seeking. This development, seen in a marked form in *Landscape at Chaponval* (1880; Musée du Jeu de Paume, Paris), is closely paralleled by the so-called "constructive stroke" adopted by Cézanne during the same years.

Pissarro lived in the Pontoise area, north of Paris, from 1872 to 1884; he then moved further north to the village of Eragny, and lived there for the rest of his life. He was a central figure in the organization of the Impressionist group exhibitions of 1874 to 1886, and was the only

artist to exhibit in all eight shows. Landscape, often with peasant figures, was his prime subject, apart from a sequence of townscapes of Rouen and Paris, which he began in 1896. His peasant subjects reflected his anarchist political beliefs; he felt that the future of society should lie in decentralization and in a return to the land.

Several members of the Neo-Impressionist group in the later 1880s were also anarchists, notably Paul Signac and Maximilien Luce. These shared beliefs, together with the increasing systematization in Pissarro's technique of 1877 to 1895, encouraged him in 1886 to adopt the Divisionist technique pioneered by Seurat, and to redefine the bases of his art in terms of the color theories of writers such as Michel-Eugène Chevreul and Ogden Rood. However, by 1888 Pissarro found that the rigors of pointillist execution prevented him from responding directly to the diversity of nature. *View from my Window,*

Eragny, completed in 1888 (Ashmolean Museum, Oxford), shows great variety of touch, though the individual brush strokes remain very small. Pissarro's handling and color effects became much broader in later paintings such as *The Boieldieu Bridge at Rouen* (1896; City of Birmingham Museums and Art Gallery). The rich color scheme of this work suggests that it was in the 1890s, rather than the 1870s, that Turner's color became relevant to Pissarro's art, when, in the works of his last decade, he sought to give his paintings an overriding unity of effect.

Further reading. Adler, K. *Camille Pissarro: a Biography*, London (1978). Lloyd, C. (*et al.*) *Camille Pissarro 1830–1903*, London (1980). Pissarro, C. (ed. Rewald, J.) *Letters to his Son Lucien*, London (1943). Rewald, J. *Camille Pissarro*, London (1963). Shikes, R.E. and Harper, P. *Pissarro, his Life and Work*, New York (1980).

Giambattista Pittoni: St Jerome and St Peter of Alcantara; oil on canvas; 275×143cm (108×56in). National Gallery of Scotland, Edinburgh

Pittoni Giambattista 1687–1767

The reputation of the Venetian artist Giambattista Pittoni was high in his lifetime, but has justifiably declined. His style. an amalgam of the styles of many earlier artists, was seldom infused with the sparkle of originality that distinguished his contemporaries G.B. Tiepolo and G.B. Piazzetta. He is seen at his best in the early altarpieces in the parish church at S. Germano dei Berici, Vicenza (*Madonna and Child with Saints*) and in the National Gallery of Scotland, Edinburgh, where the succulent paint and rich coloring are allied with excellent draftsmanship. Like most of his Venetian contemporaries, he received many commissions from outside the city.

Pleydenwurff Hans c1420–72

A native of Bamberg, the painter Hans Pleydenwurff became a citizen of Nuremberg in 1457. Apart from a brief stay in Breslau in 1462, he worked in Nuremberg until his death. He also supplied designs for glass painters, and his style was developed from the Early Netherlandish painters, in particular Rogier van der Weyden.

Pleydenwurff's *The Descent from the Cross*, painted for the High Altar of the church of St Elizabeth in Breslau (1462; Germanisches Nationalmuseum, Nuremberg), is the artist's earliest surviving major commission; the exact means by which he developed his mature style remains little understood. However, his superb *Portrait of George, Count of Löwenstein* (Germanisches Nationalmuseum, Nuremberg) can be dated to c1456. It reveals the depth of Pleydenwurff's understanding of the Master of Flémalle/Rogier van der Weyden tradition of portrait painting. Indeed, this portrait is a major landmark in the evolution of portraiture in Germany.

It is possible that Pleydenwurff spent some time in the Netherlands. The clear spatial organization and the detailed treatment of figures and landscape elements in his *Crucifixion* (c1470; Alte Pinakothek, Munich) demonstrate his continued debt to Netherlandish models at the end of his life. The town in the background is clearly intended to be a realistic view of Bamberg; the *Crucifixion* was probably painted for Löwenstein, and formerly hung in Bamberg Cathedral.

After Pleydenwurff's death in 1472 Michael Wolgemut took over the workshop, and thus the traditions of Pleydenwurff's studio would have been transmitted to the young Albrecht Dürer.

Poelenburgh Cornelis van c1586–1667

Cornelis van Poelenburgh, a painter from Utrecht, was one of the first early-17th-century Dutch landscapists to visit and work in Rome. There he copied the small, poetic landscapes of Adam Elsheimer (1578–1610), and also admired the pictures of the Flemish landscapist Paul Bril (1554–1626). During his Italian visit, and after his return to Utrecht c1626, Poelenburgh painted much-admired and influential Italianate landscapes on copper, in cool, enamel-like colors. These are often arcadian in character, and exploit ancient ruins and mythological personages to evoke the Classical past. Poelenburgh painted a few small-scale portraits, and sometimes added the figures to the landscapes of other artists, for instance to those of Jan Both (c1618?–52).

Poliakoff Serge 1906–69

The French painter Serge Poliakoff was of Russian background. In 1919 he traveled with his aunt, the singer Nastia Poliakoff, as her accompanist. They went to Constantinople and from there via Sofia, Bel-

Cornelis van Poelenburgh: A Roman Landscape; oil on panel; 44×60cm (18×24in); c1620. Toledo Museum of Art, Toledo, Ohio

grade, Vienna, and Berlin, to Paris. He settled in Paris in 1923, making his living playing the guitar, and studied painting at the Académie Frochot, Grande Chaumière. In 1935 he moved to London, studying at the Slade School of Fine Art. He returned to Paris, and in 1937 met Kandinsky. In the following year Poliakoff was a regular attender at the artists' gatherings at the home of Sonia and Robert Delaunay.

His mature work, from 1949 onwards, is characterized by the use of decisive abstract shapes and strongly contrasting color (for example, *Composition*; oil on plywood, 1950; Solomon R. Guggenheim Museum, New York). His work may be compared with that of other members of the School de Paris.

Polidoro da Caravaggio
1496/1500–43

Polidoro da Caravaggio was an Italian painter. His early years in Lombardy are obscure; Vasari says he began painting in the loggias of the Vatican under the influence of Giovanni da Udine. It was probably here that he discovered the type of *all'antica* fictive relief for the development of which he is perhaps best known. His resourcefulness lay in adapting it to the long, narrow areas on the facades of houses and palaces, mainly in Rome. The owners of such palaces required painted decorations whose subject matter would reflect the culture of ancient Rome. An example of his work is to be seen in the Palazzo Ricci, Rome. Most of these decorations have now faded away. After the Sack of Rome (1527) Polidoro went south, where the requirements of patronage led him to paint mostly altarpieces.

Pollaiuolo brothers 15th century

Antonio Pollaiuolo (1431/2–98) was a Florentine goldsmith, sculptor, painter, engraver and designer; his brother Piero (1441–94/6) was a painter. The brothers were sons of Jacopo di Giovanni Benci, a Florentine poulterer. According to tradition, Antonio trained under Lorenzo Ghiberti, and Piero under Andrea del Castagno. In 1466 Antonio entered the goldsmiths' guild. Both belonged to the Compania di San Luca, Piero being listed in 1472 as a painter and Antonio in 1473 as a goldsmith and painter. The two ran a joint workshop in which Antonio seems to have been the senior partner. As they

Piero Pollaiuolo: The Coronation of the Virgin; tempera on panel; 1483. S. Agostino, San Gimignano

frequently collaborated, it is often difficult to distinguish the work of one from that of the other. Antonio was undoubtedly a much more significant and versatile artist than Piero; but the common practice of attributing all the better productions of their workshop to the elder brother and all the worse to the younger is arbitrary and possibly misleading.

Several of Antonio's most important works were commissioned for Florence Baptistery and are still preserved in the Museo dell'Opera del Duomo, Florence. They are a large silver reliquary cross (1457–9; made with the assistance of Betto Betti), a silver relief of *The Birth of the Baptist* for the altar of S. Giovanni (1478–80), and a series of vestment embroideries of *The Life of St John the Baptist* (1469–80; executed by a team of embroiderers to Antonio's designs). Almost all of his numerous other pieces of goldsmith's work, parade armor, and jewelry have been lost.

As early as 1460 the two brothers collaborated on a series of large canvases of *The Exploits of Hercules* for Piero de' Medici for the Medici Palace, Florence.

Pallaiuolo brothers: The Martyrdom of St Sebastian; tempera on panel; 292×203cm (115×80in); c1475. National Gallery, London

of the human body in motion. It proved enormously influential.

The large *The Martyrdom of St Sebastian* (c1475; National Gallery, London) was almost certainly a collaborative enterprise, and is the most impressive surviving painting produced by the Pollaiuoli. Its strangely rigid composition may reveal a deliberate exercise in the precepts of Alberti. The painting is particularly memorable for its representation of the human body from a wide variety of viewpoints, so it seems likely that Antonio played the more important part in its conception.

Although Antonio executed a number of small bronzes, it was only towards the very end of his life that he received large-scale sculptural commissions. These are the two bronze tombs of Pope Sixtus IV and Pope Innocent VIII at St Peter's in Rome. The former (c1484–93) is a freestanding monument, of a form unusual in Italy. The latter (c1492–8) is a more traditional type of wall tomb. It incorporates the interesting innovation of representing the Pope twice: as a recumbent corpse, and triumphantly enthroned, as if alive. Although Piero accompanied his brother to Rome (where both subsequently died), it is virtually certain that he played no part in the design of either monument. Both tombs indicate Antonio's training as a goldsmith—they are skillful assemblages of small bronzes arranged around dominant motifs, rather than truly monumental designs. However, his superb standards of craftsmanship and his profound interest in characterization and the human physique are equally apparent.

A number of other panel paintings, frescoes, and drawings survive, demonstrating the wide range of the Pollaiuoli's activities. Antonio's drawings are usually very vivacious and were clearly highly influential. In particular, they reveal his profound scientific knowledge of human anatomy. It was this aspect of his art that most impressed Antonio's contemporaries.

Further reading. Ettlinger, L.D. *Antonio and Piero Pollaiuolo*, Oxford and New York (1978).

Although these are now lost, smaller variants record two of the compositions. They appear to have been the first monumental Florentine mythological compositions in the antique manner. The altarpiece of *St James between St Vincent and St Eustace* in the Uffizi was also a joint project, executed in 1466–7 for the chapel of the Cardinal of Portugal in S. Miniato al Monte.

Piero undertook a series of *Virtues* in the Uffizi for the Florentine Mercanzia in 1469 and an altarpiece of *The Coronation of the Virgin* in San Gimignano in 1483 (in the church of S. Agostino). These works are monumental and quite accomplished, although rather dry and monotonous in conception. A comparison of them with Antonio's large signed engraving of *The Battle of the Ten Nudes* (c1471–2) aptly demonstrates the superiority of the elder brother's powers of invention. This superb print has no apparent subject matter and was presumably intended as an illustration

Pollock Jackson 1912–56

The American painter Jackson Pollock was the leading figure of the New York School of the 1940s. Brought up in California, he moved to New York in 1929 and studied at the Art Students' League under Thomas

Antonio Pollaiuolo: Apollo and Daphne; panel; 30×20cm (12×8in). National Gallery, London

Graham, a Russian émigré who talked and wrote of Picasso, African art, symbolism, and the role of the unconscious in artistic creation. Pollock assimilated these elements to a great extent. They colored the obsessive symbols that appeared when he began drawing under psychoanalysis, as part of a psychiatric cure for alcoholism. The emphasis on the role of the unconscious was of particular importance for Pollock, who was to take the Surrealist principle of automatism to its furthest physical and artistic limits.

Pollock's work matured suddenly in 1943, aided by the example of Hans Hofmann, by the émigré artists in New York, and by the patronage of Peggy Guggenheim. The next decade saw the creation of all his most important work. *The Guardians of the Secret* (oil on canvas; 1943; San Francisco Museum of Art) synthesized Pollock's interests of the 1930s and looked forward to even more expressionist works. In this painting the "guardians", images both zoological and abstract, lurk around a central rectangle unified by a web of bright colors against a dark background, diversified by contradictory and frequently

Jackson Pollock: Don Quixote; oil on canvas; 74×46cm (29×18in); c1944. Peggy Guggenheim Foundation, Venice

Hart Benton, the American Regionalist. *Going West* (oil on gesso ground on composition board; 1934–5; private collection), with its exaggerated simplification of a folk subject, reflects Benton's championship of the American heartland as opposed to the artistic ideals of a decadent Europe.

For Pollock, as for all the New York School, the 1930s were years of vital experimentation and assimilation. Pollock's career was saved by employment in the easel division of the Works Progress Administration from 1935 to 1943, years during which his work was in crisis and he was also suffering from acute alcoholism. Through Benton, Pollock met David Siqueiros, the Mexican muralist, who was running an experimental workshop in Union Square, New York. Siqueiros' influence introduced Pollock to a new scale of execution, and to new techniques such as spray painting and the use of enamel paint.

He also learned much from John

canceled depth.

The images disappear in *Mural* (oil on canvas; 1943; University of Iowa, Iowa City), commissioned by Peggy Guggenheim for her New York apartment. *Mural* is the essential Pollock: large scale, fluent and consecutive in execution, eliminating image in favor of an elaborate swirling web of inscription. At his best Pollock produced an overall rhythmic structure with an automatic intuitive technique. The process was intensified by the "drip" method of paint splashed over a canvas stretched on the floor. It was seen at its most grandiose in *Cathedral* (enamel and aluminum paint on canvas; 1947; Dallas Museum of Fine Arts). Here the intensity of the web of lines and color, consciously flattened by the enamel, produces a final stillness. *Cathedral* was the furthest point to which Pollock's Abstract Expressionist style could be taken. After six years of its practice, coupled with experimentation in various directions, the impetus went out of his work in 1953.

Pollock, the greatest of the Abstract Expressionists, was widely copied in America and Europe in the 1950s. But his followers, lacking his personal struggle and his innate control, rapidly reduced his style to a formula and a cliché.

Further reading. Greenberg, C. "Jackson Pollock", *Evergreen Review*, New York (1957). O'Hara, F. *Jackson Pollock*, New York (1959). Tomassoni, I. *Pollock*, London (1968). Wolfe, T. "Jungian Aspects of Jackson Pollock's Imagination", *Artforum*, New York (1972).

Polycleitos 5th century BC

Polycleitos was a Greek sculptor of the high Classical period who came from Sicyon. He was a pupil of the Argive Ageladas, reputed master of Pheidias and Myron. He perfected the technique of bronze casting, and was the most distinguished representative of the Argive School, which specialized in bronze nudes of victorious athletes for the sanctuaries of southern Greece.

His contribution to sculpture consisted in the invention of the contrapposto. This was a pose suspended between walking and resting, with one side of the statue relaxed, the other tense, and the weight carried by one leg. He also devised a system of proportions aiming at the perfect scale, based on the quadrifacial nature of

Polycleitos: Doryphoros; marble; height 198cm (78in); a Roman copy of the 5th-century BC original. Museo Archeologico Nazionale, Naples

the Classical statue. He thus created a model type which exerted a formative influence on Greek and Roman sculpture. Its beauty depended on two apparently incompatible principles: the commensurability of parts, and a rather loose application of mathematical rules. This coincided with similar practices in architecture (for instance in the Parthenon) and was a development of earlier experiments.

Polycleitos explained his theory in a treatise, one of the first of its kind, and applied it to a statue: both treatise and statue are known as the *Canon* (Rule). The statue is a

boyish *Doryphoros* (spear-bearer) standing on the right foot, the left drawn back on its toes. His left hand carries the spear on his shoulder, its line harmoniously incorporated into the balanced composition. (The best copies are in the Museo Archeologico Nazionale, Naples.) Roman critics complained that all the figures by Polycleitos were cut to one pattern. His works included a *Herakles* and a *Hermes* that have been identified in copies; and a figure with raised arms, the *Diadumenus* (*Youth tying his hair with a Band*), best known from a Hellenistic copy from Delos (National Museum, Athens; another marble copy is in the British Museum, London).

Like his contemporaries, Pheidias, Cresilas, and Phradmon, Polycleitos entered the competition to make a wounded *Amazon* for the temple of Artemis in Ephesus. According to the story about their competition, each of the other three sculptors ranked Polycleitos' *Amazon* second only to his own, so that he won the first prize. (Such stories were common in Antiquity, and have been told of Agoracritus and Pheidias, among others.) His *Amazon* is perhaps represented in copies showing her leaning on a spear while she uncovers her wounded breast (Museo Capitolino, Rome). The distribution of weight of the statue departs slightly from the *Canon*; it corresponds to that of the *Westmacott Athlete* (British Museum, London), a work thought to derive from Polycleitos' statue of the boy boxer Cyniscus. In both, the emphasis is shifted to one side, as they raise the right arm and bend the head under it.

Polycleitos also made a gold and ivory cult-statue of *Hera* for her temple at Argos, rebuilt after the fire of 423 BC. She was seated with a pomegranate in one hand and a scepter in the other, topped by a cuckoo, personifying her husband Zeus. She was accompanied by a standing *Hebe*, also in gold and ivory, by Naucydes, a member of Polycleitos' School. Naucydes was the brother of Polycleitos the Younger (4th century BC) who was both a sculptor and the architect of the Tholos and the theater at Epidaurus.

Polygnotus *fl.* 475–447 BC

The Greek artist Polygnotus, of Thasos and Athens, was the most famous painter of Antiquity. His name was borrowed by two vase painters in Athens, and in the

Jacopo Pontormo: Joseph in Egypt; oil on panel; 97×110cm (38×43in); 1517–18. National Gallery, London

view of Theophrastus he was the founder of the art of painting. His work represents a break with the Archaic tradition and the inception of the Classical, comparable with that of the master of the Olympia sculptures. Like the sculptures, his figures were remembered for the ethos and dignity that they portrayed. This was achieved by a technique of simple outline drawing with washes of color and effects of transparent dress, but no extensive use of shading, highlights, or any true perspective.

Polygnotus specialized in massed compositions for walls, dispersing the figures up and down the field to render depth. The device was copied on some Athenian vases and it is to these that we have to look for echoes of his compositions and figures, since no original works have survived. He painted *The Sack of Troy* and *The Underworld* for the Lesche (clubhouse) dedicated by the Cnidians at Delphi, with careful characterization of the individual heroes, described in detail by Pausanias. In Athens he executed another *Sack of Troy* in the Painted Stoa and his panels were long exhibited in the picture gallery in the north wing of the Propylaea on the Acropolis. He was a friend of the statesman Cimon and the poet Sophocles. Several of his themes were those also treated by the 5th-century dramatists, and he clearly played an important role in the intellectual life of early Classical Athens.

Pontormo Jacopo 1494–1557

The Italian painter Jacopo Pontormo was born Jacopo Carucci in Pontormo near Empoli outside Florence. Around 1507 he moved to Florence, and finished his training there in the workshop of Andrea del Sarto during the years 1512–14. His first work, the *Madonna and Saints* of c1514 painted for S. Rufillo, Florence (now in the Capella di S. Luca of SS. Annunziata), reveals his absorption of Andrea's figure-types, fluent grouping, and expressive gestures.

Pontormo's *Visitation* of 1515–16 (SS. Annunziata, Florence) is more personal in the figure-style and more independent in the use of the niche, which derives from Fra Bartolommeo (1472–1517). Andrea had experimented with the pyramidal grouping introduced by Leonardo, but none of his monumental works achieve the variety of Pontormo's fresco, where the spectators to the left are intended to distract attention from the Virgin in the center. The asymmetry is reinforced by the contrast between the small naked boy sitting on the second step and the large woman sitting on the other side of the step. She is closer to the spectator and suggests, in the elegance of her S-shaped curve, a distant derivation from the Libyan Sybil on the Sistine Chapel ceiling, Vatican, Rome. The ambiguities with which the figures interlock are developed by Pontormo in

the Visdomini Altar of 1518, whose dark tonality is conceived as a reaction against the brighter colors of Andrea's work (as also is the range of saints).

The drawings from this period and the drawings for the lost *St Michael* (c1519; Galleria della Collegiata, Empoli) reveal his profound study of Michelangelo. This underlies Pontormo's achievement in the years 1520 to 1530. His work ranges widely, from the light-hearted *Vertumnus and Pomona* of 1520 in Lorenzo de' Medici's villa at Poggio a Caiano, to the combination of emotional intensity and elegance in the *Deposition* of 1526–8 (S. Felicita, Florence). There is an expressive reinterpretation of Dürer in the frescoes at the Certosa di Val d'Ema (1523–4), where the grouping of the figures recalls Michelangelo's early *Entombment* (National Gallery, London).

The originality of these paintings is matched by that of his portraiture where, as in the portrait of the young man thought to be Alessandro de' Medici (Museo Nazionale di Villa Guinigi, Lucca) the stiffness of the pose and of the sitter's robes emphasize his effortless superiority. Other portraits combine this stiff elegance with an architectural setting that serves as an attribute, rather than as a space within which the figures are placed (for example, *Portrait of a Lady*, c1532; Städelsches Kunstinstitut, Frankfurt am Main). Pontormo's involvement with Michelangelo led, in 1530, to the commission to paint two pictures (neither of which has survived) from Michelangelo's cartoons. The contact with Michelangelo's work contributed to a change in his style: this is best documented in his drawings, since few of the paintings from this later period have survived. (The decoration of the Medicean villas at Careggi and Castello, and the frescoes in the choir of S. Lorenzo are all destroyed.) His studies for S. Lorenzo, where he was working from c1548 to 1557, show that the figures are still piled into the space with the intentional lack of logic of the *Deposition* in S. Felicita. But in style they combine the breadth and block-like form of late Michelangelo with the complexity of movement of earlier Pontormo, in a personal form of Mannerism—one that was very alien to Vasari.

Further reading. Berti, L. *L'Opera Completa del Pontormo*, Milan (1973). Nicco-Fasola, G. *Pontormo o del Cinquecento*, Florence (1947). Pontormo, J. *Diario*

INRI

1554–1556, Florence (1956). Reanek, J. C. *The Drawings of Pontormo*, Cambridge, Mass. (1964).

Poons Larry 1937–

Larry Poons is one of the leading American Post-Painterly Abstractionists, a group that includes Kenneth Noland, Jules Olitsky, Ellsworth Kelly, Jack Youngerman, Al Held, and Frank Stella. Poons' art demonstrates a tendency towards systems: his color-shapes—dots in ellipses floated on a field of strong, contrasted color—are worked out mathematically on graph paper. The sensation created by the pattern, and the contrast achieved, is intended to be more than merely optical: Poons aims to produce the maximum feeling of intensity commensurate with the retention of the integrity of the picture plane.

Pordenone Giovanni da
*c*1484–1539

Born in the Friulian town from which he took his name, Giovanni Antonio da Pordenone was a painter, formed in Venice, who—according to Vasari—consciously sought to rival Titian. About 1516 he seems to have visited Rome. His mature style combines a somewhat exaggerated apprehension of plastic form, derived from Michelangelo and Raphael, with Venetian color and bravura brushwork.

Uniquely among Venetian 16th-century artists he worked extensively in fresco. He painted major cycles in the Cappella Malciostro of the Duomo, Treviso (1520), in Cremona Cathedral (1520–2), where he displaced Romanino, and in the Pallavicini Chapel at Cortemaggiore, near Piacenza. All these, and particularly the last, show an extreme delight in illusionistic effects, which was not at all Venetian, but was related to his contemporary, Correggio. They also display a violent, aggressive emotionalism, conveyed through sweeping rhythms, large gestures, and contorted expressions.

His *Pietà* at Cremona Cathedral is typical of this style—the feet of Christ, for example, are thrust out at the spectator. The vast *Crucifixion* on the west wall above is a measure of both Pordenone's ambitions and his failure to realize them. Ill-drawn and hastily executed, its effect is over-inflated rather than truly grand.

His altarpieces in oil (for example, the *Madonna of Mercy with Saints and Donors*, 1516; Pordenone Cathedral) are gentler and more carefully executed than his frescoes, but show the same love of monumental effects. Their dark, smoky colors seem to reflect the light and tone of Pordenone's native Friuli. There are sometimes landscape backgrounds, although in his later works these are usually replaced by an imposing apparatus of columns.

The emotionalism as well as the illusionism of Pordenone's art were unusual in Venice, and had considerable influence in the second, "Mannerist" half of the century; notably on some of the works of Tintoretto. His synthesis of Roman and Venetian styles also appealed naturally to early Baroque artists, and his influence can be felt in the youthful work of Rubens.

Porta Giacomo della *c*1533–1602

The Roman architect Giacomo della Porta was a pupil of Michelangelo, and succeeded him as surveyor of works on the Capitol. He was also influenced by Vignola, whom he followed as architect in charge of St Peter's and the Palazzo Farnese. He also executed the facades of the Gesù, S. Maria ai Monti, and began S. Andrea della Valle.

By comparison with that of Vignola, the work of della Porta emerges as sober and simplified, much more in the tradition of late Michelangelo. Through his sympathetic understanding of his master's style, della Porta emerged as the most important Roman architect of the late 16th century. Competent rather than original, his genius lay in his ability to complete successfully the conceptions of greater men.

Porta Guglielmo della *fl.* 1534–77

The origins of the Italian sculptor Guglielmo della Porta are obscure. He was the most distinguished member of a Genoese family of sculptors, and is first recorded in Genoa in 1534. He worked there with his uncle, Gian Giacomo della Porta, on the sculptural decoration of the chapel of the Apostles Peter and Paul in the Cathedral. According to Vasari, he moved to Rome in 1537, although he is not recorded there until 1546, when he was working in the Vatican. In Rome he was profoundly influenced by Michelangelo. On the death of Sebastiano del Piombo in 1547 he succeeded to the papal sinecure of the "Piombo", and remained in Rome for the rest of his life. His most important surviving work is the tomb of Pope Paul III in St Peter's (1549–75).

Guglielmo della Porta: the altar in the chapel of Peter and Paul, Genoa Cathedral; marble; 1534–7

Giovanni da Pordenone: The Crucifixion; fresco; 1520–1. Cremona Cathedral

Paulus Potter: The Young Bull; oil on canvas; 236×339cm (93×133in); 1647. Royal Museum of Art (Mauritshuis), The Hague

Frans Pourbus II: Portrait of Claude de Lorraine, Duke of Chevreuse; oil on canvas; 198×123cm (78×49in); 1610. Althorp, Northants.

Portinari Candido 1903–62

The son of Italian immigrants, the Brazilian artist Candido Portinari was born in Sao Paolo. He began painting when he was eight, and in 1918 entered the Fine Arts School in Rio. In 1928 he won a journey to Europe, with an academic portrait of the poet Mariano, shown at the National Salon. In Europe his style was transformed, and he returned to Rio in 1930 to become the leader of the modern school. His monumental realism, indigenous subject matter, and prolific output, which have affinities with Mexican muralists like Diego Rivera, quickly won international recognition. In 1935, *Coffee* was exhibited at the Carnegie Institute, New York. From 1936 he executed a number of frescoes, including *War and Peace* (1953) for the United Nations General Assembly Building in New York. He also collaborated on the decoration of the Ministry of Education and Culture in Rio. In the 1940s he experimented with Cubism, but he never abandoned figuration.

Potter Paulus 1625–54

Paulus Pietersz. Potter was the most celebrated of Dutch animal painters. He devoted his short career almost exclusively to depictions of herds of cows, sheep, goats, and horses grazing in the lush green pastures of Holland. He painted a few subject

pictures, but these are mainly of themes such as Orpheus taming the animals which allowed Potter to concentrate on his favorite motifs. Potter's most famous work is the life-size *The Young Bull* in The Hague (1647; Royal Museum of Art, Mauritshuis). His smaller pictures are superior, however, with their less labored detail, serene brownish-gold and light green landscape backgrounds, delicate light effects, and more thoughtful groupings. Potter produced the life-size *Equestrian Portrait of Dirk Tulp* (1653; Six Collection, Amsterdam) and a number of etchings of animals.

Pourbus family
16th and 17th centuries

The Pourbus were a family of Flemish painters active in the later 16th and early 17th centuries. Pieter Jansz. (1520–84) moved from his native Gouda to Bruges. There he executed religious works in a manner related to, but less florid than, that of his father-in-law, Lancelot Blondeel. He also produced portraits. He taught his son, Frans I (1545–81), who worked mainly in Antwerp. Frans I was an admirer of Frans Floris, whose niece he married. In addition to religious works, which reveal Floris' influence, he produced portraits, which owe a debt to Anthonis Mor. His son, Frans II (1569–1622), was the most inter-

national of the family. He painted portraits of the aristocracy throughout Europe.

Poussin Gaspard 1615–75

Gaspard Poussin was originally called Gaspard Dughet. A French landscape painter active in Italy, he was born in Rome. He was the brother-in-law of Nicolas Poussin, in whose studio he served and whose surname he adopted. In 1635 he set up as an independent landscape painter; his classically structured views were strongly influenced by the compositions of Annibale Carracci and Domenichino. During the 1630s he visited Naples, Perugia, and Florence. The frescoes he painted between 1647 and 1651 in S. Martino ai Monti, Rome, made him famous, and led to commissions to decorate the Palazzo Colonna and the Palazzo Pamphili (Piazza Navona), Rome. He also painted numerous landscapes on canvas.

Poussin Nicolas 1594–1665

Nicolas Poussin was the greatest representative of Baroque classicism. His austere and profoundly moving style was the fruit of many years of intense intellectual effort. Imposing order and discipline on an ardent temperament, he sought to attain an ideal of beauty that he thought would be revealed by a passionate study of the laws of reason. He took as his guides the art of the ancients, and of Raphael (1483–1520), and of Annibale Carracci (1560–1609). He was a learned painter, unusually concerned with literary and philosophical problems. His art has none of the exuberance and extravagant emotion of his Baroque contemporaries, but is characterized above all by an attempt to appeal to the intelligence.

Poussin was born in a village in Normandy. He studied painting first in Rouen, and then in Paris from 1612 to 1624, where his masters were Ferdinand Elle and probably Philippe Lallemant. His earliest known works are a series of drawings illustrating Ovid's *Metamorphoses* (c1623); these were commissioned by the Italian poet G. B. Marino, whom he may have met at the Court of Marie de Medici. They show a gift for capturing, with directness and simplicity, the most dramatic moment in the classical stories. In 1624 Poussin arrived in Rome, after a few months in Venice on the way.

Later in the 1620s, after undergoing extreme poverty, Poussin was patronized by Cardinal Francesco Barberini. He experimented freely with different styles and subjects, military, religious, and mythological. He learned a great deal from other artists—from Domenichino, in whose studio he worked, from Raphael and Veronese, and from antique sculpture. His most important work from this period is a group of large religious paintings, in which the light and glowing color and rich, free handling of the paint suggest the influence of Titian and Veronese. In 1628–9 Poussin obtained a commission for an altarpiece in St Peter's, Rome, *The Martyrdom of St Erasmus* (Vatican Museums, Rome) and in 1629–30 he painted *The Virgin Appearing to St James the Greater* (Louvre, Paris) for the city of Valenciennes in Flanders. These two large altarpieces were the closest he ever came to the Baroque. *The Virgin appearing to St James* uses dramatic contrasts of light and shade, the composition depends on an ascending diagonal, and the dirty feet of the figure kneeling in the foreground was imitated from Caravaggio's *Madonna di Loreto* (Sant'Agostino, Rome).

More significant for the future than Baroque visions and ecstasies was Poussin's first fully mature work, the *Death of Germanicus* (c1627; Minneapolis Institute of Arts). The subject, from Roman history, is tragic and elevated; the color and texture have a Venetian brilliance and warmth; yet the composition, derived from an ancient relief, is austere and restrained. The space is shallow and figures and architecture are clearly arranged, in layers parallel to the picture plane. The gravity of the work introduced a new attitude to the stern ethics of the Romans, anticipated only by the austere classicism of Domenichino.

After his recovery from a serious illness in 1629–30, Poussin gave up his early attempts to secure public commissions for

Nicolas Poussin: Et in Arcadia Ego (The Shepherds of Arcadia); oil on canvas; 85×121cm (33×48in); 1638–9. Louvre, Paris

churches and palaces in Rome, and began to paint smaller pictures for a circle of learned connoisseurs who encouraged his study of Antiquity. Perhaps the most important of these was Cassiano dal Pozzo, who had commissioned a team of artists to make for him a large reference library of drawings after the Antique.

From 1629 to 1633 Poussin concentrated on themes from Classical poetry, particularly Ovid's *Metamorphoses*, and from Tasso. He painted the well-known stories of Diana and Endymion, Narcissus and Echo, Cephalus and Aurora, and subjects connected with Bacchus. At this period the dominant influence on his work was that of Titian. Poussin had studied Titian's great Bacchanals, which were then at the Villa Ludovisi: it is from them that he derived his wonderfully poetic light and color, his use of landscape motives, his Bacchic emblems, nymphs, satyrs, and river gods. Yet Poussin's treatment of the loves of the gods is tinged with a melancholy and pathos unknown to Titian. His ethereal figures are aware of the unhappiness and dangers of love, and of the ephemeral nature of human happiness; the dusky twilight and stormy light create an intensely elegiac mood.

Although many of these paintings contain allegorical allusions, the treatment of human emotion is direct and passionate. *Narcissus and Echo* (Louvre, Paris) shows with deep pathos the dying Narcissus, exhausted by desire for his own reflection. In *Diana and Endymion* (Detroit Institute of Arts), perhaps the most poetic of all 17th-century mythological paintings, Endymion kneels, desperate and pleading, at the feet of the departing Diana. Poussin seems to have been particularly attracted by Ovid's stories of metamorphoses into flowers. In *The Realm of Flora* (1631; Gemäldegalerie Alte Meister, Dresden) the goddess of flowers dances amid lovers, who, victims of their own tragic desires, have been turned into flowers. Her gaiety and serenity tempers the tragedy of their loves, from which a new form of beauty has sprung.

Poussin's *Adoration of the Magi* (1633; Gemäldegalerie Alte Meister, Dresden), indebted to Raphael rather than to Titian, presages another change in Poussin's style. After completing a series of Titianesque Bacchanals for Cardinal Richelieu in 1635–6, he had turned increasingly to Roman sculpture and ancient reliefs, and also to Raphael (1483–1520), particularly

the later Raphael of the tapestry cartoons. In this period Poussin was particularly interested in the problem of expressing emotion by means of gesture and facial expression. He tended to prefer scenes that showed many figures, each reacting in different ways to some dramatic crisis.

In 1639 he wrote of the *Israelite Gathering the Manna* (1638–9; Louvre, Paris) "I have found a certain distribution and certain natural attitudes ... which show the misery and hunger to which the Jewish people have been reduced, and also the joy and happiness which have come over them, the astonishment which has struck them, and the respect and veneration which they feel for their law giver ..." In *The Rape of the Sabine Women* (c1635; Metropolitan Museum, New York) the scene takes place in the carefully reconstructed forum of a Roman city. We are meant to study each group and each figure, and to appreciate the desolate grief of the old nurse, the terror of the abducted women, and the helplessness of the Sabine men. Each gesture and expression is held and crystallized at a moment of violent intensity. The light is cool and clear, and the figure groups, many indebted to ancient sculpture, are sharply and precisely modeled. By this date, the moral gravity and solemn stylization of Poussin's works were in open conflict with Pietro da Cortona's warm and romantic Baroque treatment of the fables of ancient Greece and Rome.

From 1640 to 1642 Poussin was in Paris, having at last succumbed to increasingly pressing invitations from Richelieu and Louis XIII. The kind of work they demanded from him was not suited to his talents. He was asked to decorate the long gallery of the Louvre, and to paint altarpieces and large allegories for Richelieu. The unhappy interlude was aggravated by the intrigues of threatened French artists, and Poussin must have left again for Rome with some relief.

In Paris he had made a new circle of intellectual friends and patrons—civil servants, bankers, and merchants—and it was for them that he painted after his return to Rome. They encouraged his interest in the philosophy of Stoicism, and after 1640 Poussin began to concentrate on themes that illustrated serious ethical problems. Many of his subjects are taken from Stoic writers, and he painted scenes from the life of Phocion, Diogenes, Scipio, and Coriolanus. Stylistically, he sought to

purge his works of their early sensuous charms, and to progress towards a greater clarity and intellectual precision. In 1642 he wrote, "My nature leads me to seek out and cherish things that are well ordered, shunning confusion which is as contrary and menacing to me as dark shadows are to the light of day".

In the period from 1642 to 1650 Poussin's art attained a new magnificence and gravity. His compositions tend to be clear and direct. There is little movement, and a few figures, whose gestures and expressions are full of significance, are arranged as if in a bas relief; space is exactly defined. Perhaps the most perfect embodiment of Poussin's classical style is the series of the *Seven Sacraments* painted for Chantelou between 1644 and 1648 (Collection of the Duke of Sutherland; on loan to the National Gallery of Scotland, Edinburgh). A scene from the life of the Virgin or Christ symbolizes each sacrament, and Poussin paid great attention to questions of archaeological accuracy. The architectural settings are restrained and severe, and the weighty figures, draped in long togas, have the gravity of ancient sculpture. The solemnity of the scenes is heightened by an aura of silence and stillness; each emotion is analyzed with great intellectual precision.

In these years Poussin sought for dramatic rhetoric and narrative vivacity. He was particularly indebted to the late works of Raphael, whose influence may be felt in *The Judgment of Solomon* (1649; Louvre, Paris) which Poussin considered to be his most perfect work. Violent emotion is communicated with heightened dramatic power, and the movement is extremely formalized. Solomon is enthroned in the center of the painting between the two mothers who claim the living child as their own. The two mothers respond to his judgment with wide-flung rhetorical gestures, and the onlookers with horror, conveyed by sharply turned heads and shoulders and emphatic use of the hands.

Between 1648 and 1651 Poussin created a new type of Holy Family, in which his principles of composition at this central period may be most lucidly appreciated. *The Madonna on the Steps* (1648; National Gallery of Art, Washington, D.C.) although indebted to Raphael and Andrea del Sarto, emphasizes the geometric structure of the composition in a new way: the figure-group is set into an elaborate architectural setting. The great beauty of the

Andrea Pozzo: The Apotheosis of St Ignatius; fresco; 1691–4; S. Ignazio, Rome

painting depends on the careful balance of horizontal and vertical, of cylindrical and rectangular blocks, of solid and void. Glowing fruits and foliage, rich draperies, and shining metal are set against the perfect forms and clear, hard surfaces of the stone. In Poussin's last decade the somber gravity that characterizes the Holy Families is developed still further; the colors become paler and softer.

In the same years Poussin turned his attention to landscapes; in these, space is as clearly and mathematically ordered as in his figure-paintings. Indebted initially to Venetian traditions, and, later, to the ideal landscapes of Annibale Carracci and Domenichino, he organized and controlled the world of nature. His most severe and elaborate landscapes are a pair, *The Ashes of Phocion Collected by his Widow* (1648; Collection of the Earl of Derby, Knowsley Hall, Lancashire) and *The Funeral of Phocion* (1648; Collection of the Earl of Plymouth, Oakly Park, Shropshire); Phocion was a Stoic hero unjustly executed for treason. In both works, a Classical city is spread out across the background, and the geometrical forms of the architecture set the pattern for his organization of trees, rocks, and clouds. Each detail is placed with care, and a sharp, bright sunlight

defines the forms. The world of nature is dominated and formed by man.

Towards the end of his life, in the mid 1650s, Poussin's style changed yet again. Landscape became still more important, but nature is wilder and more luxuriant, and Man is dwarfed by its immensity. Poussin returned to the Ovidian themes that had attracted him earlier in his career, but transformed them into symbols of cosmic significance. Many of them are iconographically very obscure. In *The Birth of Bacchus* (William Hayes Fogg Art Museum, Cambridge, Mass.) Mercury delivers Bacchus to Dirce, who, accompanied by a graceful group of naiads, sits before a cave overgrown with dense ivy and grapevines. In sharp contrast to this gaiety and fertility, Poussin included the pallid figures of the dead Narcissus and grieving Echo. The painting contrasts fertility and sterility, life and death; the theme fascinated Poussin, particularly in his last years. Between 1660 and 1664 he painted four canvases of *The Seasons* (Louvre, Paris) in which he uses an historical episode to symbolize each season. Marvelously clear and simple in form, they contain complex layers of meaning, and allude also to the four stages of Man's history and to pagan ideas of the seasons. Poussin's late works

no longer depend on the rational principles that had guided him in the 1640s; they attain a new and mysterious grandeur and sublimity.

Further reading. Blunt, A. *Nicolas Poussin*, London and New York (1967). Friedländer, W. *Nicolas Poussin*, London (1966).

Pozzo Andrea 1642–1709

The Italian painter Andrea Pozzo was born in Trent. He was educated by the Jesuits, whose Order he entered in Milan in 1685. He decorated many Jesuit churches, including the Gesù, Genoa; the Chiesa dei Gesuiti, Mondovì; and SS. Martiri, Turin. Called to Rome in 1680, he designed the high altar and the altar of St Ignatius in the Gesù, Rome, both of which were completed by 1700. His masterpiece, *The Apotheosis of St Ignatius* (S. Ignazio, Rome) was begun in 1691. His grandiose illusionistic decorations were inspired by those of Pietro da Cortona and Giovanni Battista Gaulli.

Praxiteles *fl. c370–330 BC*

A Greek late Classical sculptor from Athens, Praxiteles was the foremost representative of the Attic School in the middle years of the 4th century BC. He may have been either a son or a son-in-law of Cephisodotus. He spent most of his life in Athens, but is known to have traveled to Ephesus to decorate the altar of the temple of Artemis, rebuilt after 356 BC.

Praxiteles preserved the high Classical tradition of the Polycleitan stance and proportions; but he favored the languid variant, and tilted his statues a little off-balance by thrusting the hips sideways, creating an S-shaped body contour. His figures were often supported by a tree-trunk conceived as an element of landscape.

The surface treatment of Praxiteles' sculptures was famous for its luminosity and delicacy, and he was well-known for his rendering of emotion. His sculptures had a pictorial quality akin to the developments of painting. Significantly, he seems to have preferred those of his statues that were colored by Nikias, a diligent painter of the female form. Praxiteles represented certain aspects of the gods in a playful spirit tinted with eroticism; some of the deities he rejuvenated. The loveliness he imparted to his figures of boys and women had a perennial influence on Hellenistic and Roman art.

He had no special interest in portraiture, but he was reputed to have modeled his statues of Aphrodite on the courtesan Phryne. His only recorded portraits are of Phryne, one gilded in Delphi, another at her native Thespiae in Boeotia. He was responsible for the first major female nude that had any impact in the development of Greek sculpture, the marble *Aphrodite of Cnidos* (one Roman copy in the Vatican Museums, Rome). The goddess was shown placing her clothes on an urn in anticipation of a bath. She was described as smiling softly with inviting eyes. The Polycleitan proportions were here adapted to the female form, with broader hips and narrower shoulders; the knees were closer together. The statue made Cnidos a center of pilgrimage; it was placed in a temple with a back entrance in order to be visible from behind. The type was adapted by Praxiteles himself, emulated by Scopas, and later repeated with endless variations.

The *Hermes and the child Dionysos* (Archaeological Museum, Olympia) was found in the temple of Hera at Olympia in 1877. It had probably been brought there from another building, and had suffered reworking at the back. Whether it is in fact an original work of the sculptor is still a

Mattia Preti: St Andrew Bound to the Cross; fresco; c1651. S. Andrea della Valle, Rome

matter of dispute, but the style is unmistakably Praxitelean. The composition of adult and child is indebted to Cephisodotus' *Peace and Wealth*, with the weight of both here carried by a tree-trunk. The artist exploits textural contrasts between the delicate face of Hermes and his roughly blocked out hair, between the naturalistic drapery and his radiant skin.

The largest part of the relief base of his cult statues of Leto, Apollo, and Artemis at Mantinea survives in Athens (National Museum), carved by assistants to represent the musical contest of Apollo and Marsyas. The merging of the figures with the background illustrates the pictorial tendencies of Praxiteles' sculpture.

Further reading. Bieber, M. *The Sculpture of the Hellenistic Age*, London and New York (1961). Richter, G.M.A. *The Sculpture and Sculptors of the Greeks*, London and New Haven (1950).

Préault Antoine 1809–79

The French artist Antoine Augustin Préault was one of the most original sculptors of the Romantic school, a pupil of David d'Angers. He attempted to sculpt figures undergoing violent emotions; but he was cramped by insufficient technical knowledge, and by the difficulty of applying the Romantic doctrine of spontaneous expression to the slow creative process of sculpture. His work attracted official opposition, and he was excluded from the Salon between 1837 and 1849. His best-known works are *Massacre* (plaster; 1834; Musée Municipal, Chartres), *Silence* (marble; 1848; Père Lachaise, Paris), the *Gallic Horseman* (stone; 1853; Pont de Iéna, Paris) and *Ophelia* (bronze; 1876; Musée des Beaux-Arts, Marseilles).

Preti Mattia 1613–99

Born in Calabria, the Italian painter

Mattia Preti was in Rome by 1630. Later he worked in Venice, Rome, Modena, and Naples (1656–60), and in Malta (1661–99). He was a Caravaggesque painter of vigorous originality. His frescoes, with their restless, flickering movement, and vibrating light and shade, herald the stylistic change from High to late Baroque. For a period, notably in the frescoes in the apse of S. Andrea della Valle, Rome (1650–1), he was influenced by Bolognese classicism. His most powerful works were done in Naples, where he fused influences from the Neapolitan Caravaggisti with colors and compositions deeply indebted to Tintoretto and Veronese.

Primaticcio Francesco 1504–70

The Italian painter, decorator, and architect Francesco Primaticcio was born at Bologna, and brought up there in the surroundings of a minor Raphaelesque cult. Probably by 1527 he had joined the team of artists employed on the decoration of the Palazzo del Tè at Mantua, to designs by Giulio Romano. Recommended to Francis I of France, he joined Rosso Fiorentino at Fontainebleau in 1532. His first work as a decorator there (now lost) may have been prescribed by Giulio; he was Rosso's adjutant in the decoration of the Gallery of Francis I, and was responsible for the execution of the stucco work.

On the death of Rosso in 1540, Primaticcio came into his own as the leader of the enterprise at Fontainebleau under four successive kings. He created the essential figurative style of that place—one of finely cadenced physical grace (psychologically almost vacant), Raphaelesque by extraction, and influenced by Parmigianino and the Hellenistic Antique.

Little of his finished work survives; the best, if fragmentary, sample is in the stuccoes and frescoes for the *Chambre de la Duchesse d'Étampes* at Fontainebleau (c1541–4). Most is known through a substantial number of fluent chalk drawings (in the Louvre, Paris, and elsewhere). These are chiefly of mythological subjects, intended for translation into fresco, or sometimes into sculpture, by collaborators. One of these, Niccolò dell'Abbate, brought particular refreshment to his style.

Primaticcio worked occasionally and eclectically as an architect, his largest piece being the Vignolesque Aile de la Belle Cheminée at Fontainebleau (1568). He died at Paris.

Francesco Primaticcio: The Rape of Helen; oil on canvas; 155×188cm (61×74in); c1530–9. Bowes Museum, Barnard Castle, County Durham

Procaccini Giulio 1574–1625

Giulio Cesare Procaccini, one of a family of Bolognese artists who moved to Milan, was trained as a sculptor, but by c1602–9 was working as a painter on the decorations for S. Maria presso S. Celso, where he developed a dramatic and highly emotional style. In 1610 he was commissioned, as one of the three leading painters in Milan, to paint six scenes from the life of S. Carlo Borromeo (Milan Cathedral): his style now became more exaggerated and bombastic.

Later, probably in 1618, he visited Genoa. By 1612 the influence of Parmigianino became obvious in his elegant figure-style, dazzling colors, and crowded yet shallow compositions, as in *The Mystic Marriage of St Catherine* (Pinacoteca di Brera, Milan). His later work was stiffer and more academic.

Prud'hon Pierre-Paul 1758–1823

The French painter Pierre-Paul Prud'hon studied under François Devosge at the École de Dessin of Dijon. After spending three years in Paris he returned to Dijon, where he won the Prix de Rome of the États de Bourgogne in 1784. His stay in Rome was decisive in the formation of his

highly individual style. Prud'hon absorbed the graceful art of Raphael (1483–1520), Leonardo (1452–1519), and Correggio (1490–1534), and was only minimally affected by the prevailing influences of J.-L. David and revolutionary Neoclassicism; he has, therefore, little in common with his contemporaries. Although he became an

Giulio Procaccini: The Mystic Marriage of St Catherine; oil on canvas; 145×149cm (57×59in). Pinacoteca di Brera, Milan

enthusiastic supporter of the Revolution, his allegories such as *The Union of Love and Friendship* (1793; Minneapolis Institute of Arts) and *Wisdom and Truth Come to Earth* (1799; Louvre, Paris), reveal a sentiment and harmony totally out of keeping with current expressions of heroism and Stoic morality.

His portraits show a grasp of the individual that heralds the psychological accuracy of Romanticism (for example, *M. Georges Anthony*, 1796, Musée des Beaux-Arts, Dijon; *Madame Anthony and her Children*, 1796, Musée des Beaux-Arts, Lyons). Although his art went against prevailing trends, Prud'hon attracted support and commissions. In 1799 he painted the decorations for the Hotel de Lanois. Napoleon commissioned the melancholy portrait of *The Empress Josephine* (1805; Louvre, Paris) and Prud'hon was later appointed drawing master and decorator to the new Empress Marie-Louise. His masterpiece was *Justice and Divine Vengeance Pursuing Crime* (1808; Louvre, Paris). Destined for the Court Room at the Palais de Justice, the painting shows a moonlit scene of grandeur and violence.

Puget Pierre 1620–94

The French sculptor Pierre Puget was born in Marseilles. He spent the years 1640 to 1643 in Rome and Florence working under Pietro da Cortona, largely on the decoration of the rooms in the Palazzo Pitti, Florence. From 1643 to 1656 he worked in Marseilles and Toulon, where he divided his time between designing the decoration of warships and producing paintings for local churches. In 1656 he gained his first important commission, the door of the Hotel de Ville at Toulon. The scheme of two supporting herms was current in Roman Baroque, and here perhaps derives from similar, painted supporters by Cortona on the ceiling of the Palazzo Barberini (now Galleria Nazionale), Rome. The figures are charged by Puget with an anguish far removed from the usual image of burden.

In 1659 Puget was called to Paris to execute two statues for Claude Girardin, who was assistant to Nicholas Fouquet, the *Surintendant des Bâtiments*. Following

Pierre-Paul Prud'hon: The Union of Love and Friendship; oil on canvas; 146×114cm (57×45in); c1793. Minneapolis Institute of Arts

Pierre Puget: Self-portrait; marble

this commission Fouquet himself commissioned a *Hercules Resting* (Louvre, Paris). Puget sensed the possibility of real success, but his hopes were dashed by Fouquet's fall from power before the statue was completed. Under Colbert, Fouquet's successor at the Surintendance, Puget received no Royal commissions for 20 years. His Baroque, individual, and Italianate style was alien to the hybrid, but carefully orchestrated classicism that had become the official Court style under the direction of Charles Lebrun.

Following this setback, Puget settled in Genoa, establishing a local reputation as a sculptor. His most important works during this period were two statues, *St Sebastian* and *The Blessed Alessandro Sauli*, for niches at the crossing of S. Maria di Carignano, Genoa. In these works Puget approaches Bernini more closely than ever before, but resists the full three-dimensionality of the High Baroque. Returning to Marseilles and Toulon in 1667, Puget resumed work on the decoration of ships and on architectural work in Marseilles; but he continued to produce sculpture. In 1670, with Colbert's permission, he carved the relief of *Alexander and Diogenes* and the *Milo of Crotona* (both Louvre, Paris) from two blocks of marble abandoned in the dockyards at Toulon.

The *Milo* is Puget's most significant work. It represents the moment when Milo, an athlete of the 6th century BC, has

become caught in the cleft of a tree while attempting to rend it asunder; he is attacked and eaten by wild animals. The anguish already seen in the Hotel de Ville at Toulon is restated. Puget's sources for the *Milo* are not unusual, though they are perhaps revealing. The head and mask are quotations from the *Laocoön*, the most baroque of all antique prototypes for physical torment, but important in this context for its restraint in terms of contemporary Roman Baroque. Puget again rejects the three-dimensionality of Bernini, choosing a single frontal viewpoint with rigidly controlled axes of movement, to create a style at once Baroque and classical. Taken to Versailles in 1683, the statue was approved by the King and placed prominently in the Gardens.

On Colbert's death some months later, Puget was given more commissions for Versailles by Colbert's successor Louvois; but the sculptor's last years were clouded by further failures at Court. The *Alexander and Diogenes* never reached Versailles; and his last work, a relief of *St Charles Borromeo in the Plague at Milan* (Musée des Beaux-Arts, Marseilles), was refused by the King.

Pugin A.W.N. 1812–52

Augustus Welby Northmore Pugin was an English architect, born in London. His father was Augustus Charles Pugin (1762–1832), an emigré Frenchman. The young Pugin attended his father's drawing school, where he developed as a skilled and sensitive draftsman, and helped to illustrate his father's books on Gothic architecture. In his teens, Pugin designed furniture for Windsor Castle, worked as a stage carpenter at Covent Garden, set up a short-lived cabinet-making enterprise, and designed stage-settings.

During the years 1832 to 1835 he was converted to Roman Catholicism, and established himself as an architect. He designed his own house (St Marie's Grange, near Salisbury; 1835), undertook architectural work for Charles Barry, and broadened his experience of medieval art. In 1835 his book of Gothic furniture designs appeared, and in 1836 he published a volume of the *Examples of Gothic Architecture* which his father had begun.

But it was *Contrasts* (1836) that established Pugin as an outstanding architectural critic. The book's reception foreshadowed the controversy that came to surround his career. The illustrations devastatingly satirized the meager standards of contemporary architecture, always using medieval buildings as the basis for comparison; while the text associated Christianity with Gothic architecture, and condemned all classical styles as pagan. The book's expanded second edition (1841) compared the fortunate social conditions of the Christian Middle Ages with grim images of 19th-century England. These extraordinary drawings and Pugin's radical argument were tremendously persuasive, and gave the Gothic Revival henceforth a distinctive sense of moral purpose.

After the success of *Contrasts* Pugin received an increasing number of commissions. Moving to London in 1837 he immersed himself in a frenzy of activity, designing numerous Roman Catholic churches, colleges, and convents. The cathedrals of St Chad, Birmingham (1839), St Barnabas, Nottingham (1841), and St Mary, Killarney (begun 1842) are impressive products of this period. All are correctly Gothic and boldly massed, tending to be plain externally and emphatically vertical within.

St Giles' Church, Cheadle (1841–6), is notable for its rich decorative scheme, and for heralding the change to asymmetry in church design. This asymmetry of plan and elevation is a feature of Pugin's later work (for example, St Augustine's Ramsgate; 1846). It was an extension of ideas that he formulated in *True Principles of Pointed or Christian Architecture* (1841), in which he employed rationalist arguments of "fitness for purpose" to justify the irregular or picturesque.

During the final years of his life Pugin received fewer commissions for churches, as younger Catholic architects gained success. But his consummate skill as a designer was given wide scope when, in 1844, Barry asked him to design most of the fittings and furnishings for the Houses of Parliament: this is one of Pugin's best-known memorials.

Pugin's last years were marked by recurring illness and eventual madness. He could not sustain the assertiveness of his earlier public encounters, and almost disowned some of his finest buildings. But of his enormous influence as a critic and theorist, even he had no doubt: he had "revolutionized the taste of England".

Puvis de Chavannes Pierre
1824–98

A contemporary of Gustave Moreau, Pierre Puvis de Chavannes admired the achievements of Théodore Chassériau as much as did Moreau himself. Puvis was born in Lyons and traveled to Italy to convalesce after illness in 1847. By the following year he had decided to become a painter. Chassériau's murals at the Cours des Comptes, which were destroyed in 1870, impressed Puvis with the possibility of reviving mural painting in 19th-century France. Puvis was to dedicate the greater part of his professional life as a painter to this pursuit, gathering to him in the process public success, civic commissions, and the admiration of a diverse number of younger painters.

Puvis first exhibited at the Salon in 1850, yet his work was frequently rejected during the following decade. Success was inaugurated with the showing of his allegorical paintings *Bellum* and *Concordia* at the Salon of 1861. These works were subsequently acquired for the Musée de Picardie, Amiens, and the Museum made further acquisitions from the Salons of 1864 (*Work* and *Rest*) and of 1865 (*Ave Picardia Nutrix*).

His paintings combined a mythological ambience with allegorical references that could be quite specific. His paintings were often colossal, consisting of canvases attached to the walls of buildings rather than murals painted upon the walls themselves. The composition of such huge paintings was evolved from numerous preparatory drawings. The design was established by focal figures or groups placed along the canvas according to a precise and rhythmic sense of interval. It was an influential achievement of Puvis' large paintings that they made full recognition of the flatness of

A.W.N. Pugin: design for a flagon; 1827. Victoria and Albert Museum, London

Puvis de Chavannes: The Sacred Wood; canvas mural; 460×1041cm (181×410in); 1884–6. Musée des Beaux-Arts, Lyons

the wall surface: as a result, areas of color were flattened and the color remained unmodulated and pale. Puvis' allegorical and mythological tendencies removed the daily world from the range of his subject matter. Within the fields and meadows of his large, bland paintings each element could be made to contribute towards the harmony of the whole. He was able to control minutely the shifts of hue and interval in his paintings. His paintings were so finely tuned in the relations of their parts one to another that he greatly impressed painters concerned with comparable questions of picture construction. His work was particularly admired by Post-Impressionists and Symbolists during the 1880s and 1890s.

His mural commissions continued throughout the Symbolist period. After showing paintings for Marseilles Museum (1869) and Poitiers (1872–5), Puvis undertook murals on the theme of St Geneviève for the Panthéon in Paris. Murals followed for, among others, the Palais des Arts at Lyons (1883–6), the Sorbonne (1887), and the Paris Hotel de Ville (1891–4). He painted a second series of murals for the Panthéon between 1896 and 1898. A major foreign commission also fell to

Puvis, for paintings to decorate the Boston Public Library (1894–6).

His paintings fulfilled a civic as well as a decorative role. They were much in demand, and his studio in Place Pigalle in Paris was extremely busy. Yet Puvis' reputation and achievement extends beyond the provision of public work, for his paintings impressed painters and writers as much as mayoral committees. If, on the one hand, public recognition led to a grand banquet in his honor in 1895, on the other he had received many homages from painters (among them Gauguin, Seurat, and the Symbolists Alphonse Osbert and Henri Martin), and from writers (including the Symbolists Mallarmé and Charles Morice).

To the Symbolists, his otherworldly love of the Antique, his rejection of the depiction of daily life, and his astute control over line, color, and rhythm to expressive and emotive effect, all made him a pioneer of the principles they embraced. Like Moreau, Puvis was adopted as both precursor and contributor to Symbolist art, and in this respect his easel paintings were of particular importance for their role as vehicles of emotional expression. Hope (1871; Louvre, Paris), dating from the Franco-Prussian War, and The Poor

Fisherman (1881; Louvre, Paris) were convincing examples of the art of ideas and of feelings that Symbolists were seeking.

Further reading. Brown Price, A. *Pierre Puvis de Chavannes*, New York (1994). *French Symbolist Painting: Moreau, Puvis de Chavannes, Redon and their followers*, London (1972). Vachon, M. *Puvis de Chavannes*, Paris (1895).

Pythagoras 5th century BC

The Greek early Classical sculptor Pythagoras of Rhegium was a contemporary of Myron and Calamis. The ancient sources sometimes divide his career between two artists, but in all probability there was only one. He was active in south Italy and Sicily, and also at the sanctuaries of Olympia and Delphi, for which he provided monuments to victorious athletes. He worked primarily in bronze, and was interested in the problems of the stance and proportions of the male nude in movement. His works included an *Apollo shooting Python with his Arrows*, a winged *Perseus, Eteocles and Polynices* killing each other, and a *Philoctetes* limping.

Q

Quarenghi Giacomo 1744–1817

The Italian Neoclassical architect Giacomo Quarenghi is best known for the buildings he designed in St Petersburg for Catherine the Great. He was born near Bergamo, and from 1763 lived in Rome working as a painter. He was influenced both by the work of Anton Mengs and by the buildings of Antiquity. After reading Palladio's *I Quattro Libri dell'Architettura* ("The Four Books of Architecture") he produced his only major work in Italy, the Benedictine Church at Subiaco (1772). Between 1779 and 1796 he was in Russia, where he designed important buildings in St Petersburg, such as the Hermitage Theater and the State Bank. His architecture combines Palladian concepts of Antiquity with Neoclassical detail.

Further reading. Reau, L. *L'Art Russe*, Paris (1922).

Quay Maurice c1779–1804

The French painter Maurice Quay was a pupil of J.-L. David. He was the leader of a group of fellow students known as the Barbus. Their aim was to return to the most ancient sources of inspiration, and to this end they cultivated an interest in Italian painters before Raphael (1483–1520). Though he died quite young, Quay's theories remained a strong influence on his companions. Their interest in "Primitivism" or "Etruscanism" eventually became respectable, and influenced the work of painters such as J.-A.-D. Ingres.

Quellinus Artus 1609–68

The Flemish sculptor Artus Quellinus was trained by his father, a sculptor in Antwerp. His first major works were paid for by the Stadholder of the northern Netherlands in 1634. He then traveled to Rome and spent five years there, probably as an associate of his elder countryman François Duquesnoy. He picked up many of the latter's stylistic traits and was impressed by Hellenistic sculpture, but was scarcely affected by the Baroque style of Bernini. In 1639 he was again working in Antwerp; he joined the guild there in the following year, falling under the strong influence of Rubens. An ivory *Sleeping Putto* dated

Artus Quellinus: the Royal Palace (formerly the Town Hall), Amsterdam; sculpture carved c1650–61 (architect: Jan van Campen)

1641 (Walters Art Gallery, Baltimore) betrays his continuing fascination with Duquesnoy and his modes of sculptural expression.

By 1646/7 Artus was engaged on the projected new Town Hall for Amsterdam, designed by Jacob van Campen, and from 1650 to 1664 he contracted to stay in that city, joining the guild there in 1651. In the ensuing decade he delivered a vast amount of sculpture in relief for the interior and exterior of the Town Hall which is still the glory of that building, now the Royal Palace. Artus' original models in terracotta (preserved in the Rijksmuseum, Amsterdam) betray a Rubensian amplitude and tactile quality in the modeling of naked flesh, while the drapery is loosely hung in a fashion derived from Duquesnoy. The types of figure are Hellenistic, but their implied movement is slow and gentle, lacking the verve and drama produced by Bernini. There is a typically Netherlandish interest in incidental details—flora, fauna, and marine motifs, frequently composed into "still lifes". Artus also executed a few excellent portrait busts, based in format on Bernini's, with hands included among the lower drapery.

Under Artus the Elder, the sculptor Rombout Verhulst (1624–98) and Artus' nephew, Artus Quellinus the Younger (1625–1700), also worked on the Amsterdam Town Hall. The latter had a successful career in his native south Netherlands, specializing in religious sculpture and particularly in wood carving for church furnishings such as pulpits and confessionals.

Quercia Jacopo della 1367–1438

The Italian sculptor Jacopo della Quercia was born in Siena, the son of a goldsmith and wood carver. A singular genius, he belongs, together with Donatello and Ghiberti, among the founders of early Renaissance statuary and imagery. Nothing is recorded about his early training, but there are plausible reasons to believe he worked as an assistant in the Bologna workshop of Pierpaolo and Jacobello dalle Masegne, and that he was strongly influenced by the Northern Gothic sculpture.

Between 1401 and 1403 he participated unsuccessfully in the competition for the door of the Florentine Baptistery (his entry has been lost). A small marble *Madonna of Humility* (National Gallery of Art, Washington, D.C.) seems to date from these early years. His first documented and preserved work is the monumental marble *Silvestri Madonna* (Ferrara Cathedral), finished in 1406. The massive entity of this block-like, majestic figure marks a strikingly new aspect of sculpture in its relation to human space. The monument to Ilaria del Carretto (Lucca Cathedral) must have been executed shortly afterwards (*c*1408) and shows a significant interweaving of antique motifs, such as the frieze of winged putti ornamenting the sarcophagus, with the almost Burgundian recumbent figure of Ilaria.

In 1408 Quercia was commissioned to execute the city fountain, *Fonte Gaia*, in Siena (now replaced by a 19th-century copy; the original is in Palazzo Pubblico, Siena). Because of several interruptions, this enterprise lasted until 1419. The fountain forms an open trapezoid, surmounted at its ends by two freestanding statues of Acca Larentia and Rea Silvia (the latter carved from Quercia's model by Francesco da Valdambrino). Each of them is represented with the twins Romulus and Remus, elected by the proud city of Siena as its founders, in order to compete with Rome. The walls are decorated with shallow reliefs, depicting the creation of Adam and the expulsion from paradise, together with representations of the Virtues, with the Virgin in the center. Iconographically unique, the program of the *Fonte Gaia* shows a peaceful mingling of paganism and Christian salvation.

A freestanding, double-life-sized marble Apostle (*c*1420; S. Martino, Lucca) displays a new self-consciousness and a new comprehension of man as independent being, comparable only to the contemporary statuary of Donatello. Shortly afterwards, Quercia finished the marble altar for Lorenzo Trenta (S. Frediano, Lucca), probably executed with a great deal of assistance from his workshop. His only surviving wooden sculpture is an Annunciation group (*c*1421–5; Museo di Arte Sacra, S. Gimignano); executed for the Collegiata at S. Gimignano, it still bears the original polychromy. Between 1417 and 1431, della Quercia contributed towards the erection of the Siena baptismal font by providing the gilt-bronze relief of *The Annunciation to Zacharias*.

His last and most important work is the decoration of the *Porta Magna* at S. Petronio in Bologna (1425–38). This is one of the great landmarks of early Renaissance sculpture. Its lunette shows the freestanding figures of SS. Petronius and Ambrosius, the latter added in the 16th century. The jambs depict the history of the creation, including the sacrifice of Abraham, flanked by busts of prophets in the inner jambs. Here the new perception of man, already formulated in the goddesses from the *Fonte Gaia*, is brought to an unique culmination—one that greatly influenced Michelangelo.

Further reading. Pope-Hennessy, J. *Italian Gothic Sculpture*, London (1972). Seymour, C. Jr *Sculpture in Italy: 1400–1500*, Harmondsworth (1966). Supino, I.B. *Jacopo della Quercia*, Bologna (1926).

Jacopo della Quercia: Madonna and Child (Silvestri Madonna); marble; height 210cm (83in); 1406. Ferrara Cathedral

R

Raeburn Henry 1756–1823

The leading portrait painter of his generation in Scotland, Henry Raeburn was born at Stockbridge, near Edinburgh. He taught himself miniature painting before studying briefly with the portraitist David Martin. Two years of study in Rome, 1785 and 1786, had little effect on his subsequent development. After settling permanently in Edinburgh in 1787, his productivity increased dramatically. He developed a broad style of painting that relied on strong chiaroscuro for modeling and for the integration of figures and settings. He maintained this style, with only slight modifications, throughout his career. In 1815 he was elected Royal Academician, in 1822 he was knighted, and in 1823 appointed His Majesty's Limner for Scotland.

Raimondi Marc-Antonio c1480–c1534

The Italian engraver Marc-Antonio Raimondi probably learned metalwork in Bologna under Francesco Francia. The uncertainty of style of his engravings before 1505 is resolved during the period he spent in Venice, where he fell under the spell of Albrecht Dürer. He reproduced Dürer's woodcut series of *The Life of Mary* in copper (1506), also making signed copies of *The Small Passion*. Moving to Rome in 1509, he entered the circle of Raphael who provided designs for such engraved masterpieces as *The Massacre of the Innocents* and *The Judgment of Paris*. After the Sack of Rome in 1527, he probably passed the remainder of his life in Bologna.

Henry Raeburn: Portrait of Sir John Sinclair; oil on canvas; 238×154cm (94×61in); c1794–5. National Gallery of Scotland, Edinburgh

Rainaldi Carlo 1611–91

The Italian architect Carlo Rainaldi was born in Rome. He was trained by his father, Girolamo Rainaldi (1570–1655), a mediocre architect. Father and son collaborated in the design of a number of buildings in north Italy and later, in 1652–3, in the design of S. Agnese, Rome (later completed by Borromini). Carlo's principal work is the church of S. Maria in Campitelli, Rome (1663–7), a Baroque masterpiece in which influences from Bernini are combined with qualities that derive from Mannerist and north Italian architecture. Carlo also designed the facade of S. Andrea della Valle, Rome (begun 1661).

Ramsay Allan 1713–84

The Scottish portrait painter Allan Ramsay was born in Edinburgh but practiced mainly in London. His first style was influenced by Imperiali and Francesco Solimena (1657–1747), with whom he studied in Italy from 1735 to 1737. His early full-lengths, such as *Dr Mead* (1746; Foundling Hospital, London), exhibit strong characterization and a robust dignity. Returning to Italy in 1754, he renewed his friendship with the fashionable portraitist Pompeo Batoni, whose sophisticated style suggested the course of Ramsay's subsequent development. His recognized masterpiece, *Portrait of Margaret Ramsay* (1754–5; National Gallery of Scotland, Edinburgh), was painted during this visit. Its intimacy, graceful

Above: Marc-Antonio Raimondi: Raphael's Dream; engraving after a design by Raphael(?); 23×33cm (9×13in). British Museum, London

design, and delicate modeling introduce the traits of his best mature works.

In 1767 he became principal painter to George III, but after 1770 he virtually abandoned his profession, in order to write political essays and pamphlets. Ramsay was well educated, and numbered among his acquaintances the leading philosophers and writers of the period. He issued one important treatise, *Dialogue on Taste* (1754), but took no students and remained somewhat aloof from his colleagues. As a painter, he ranks with the best British portraitists of the 18th century and helped to inaugurate the Grand Style of English portraiture.

Raphael 1483–1520

Raphael was the common name of the Italian painter Raffaello Sanzio or Santi. He was born in the small hill town of Urbino, then ruled by the Montefeltro family, whose court was famous throughout Italy as a center of artistic and intellectual activity. His first teacher was presumably his father, Giovanni, a successful if mediocre local painter and a man of some cultural pretensions, who died in 1494.

Raphael was evidently a precocious artist: his first major altarpiece, *The Coronation of St Nicholas of Tolentino*, painted for a church in Città di Castello when he was only 17, is already extremely assured (1500–1; fragments in the Museo e Gallerie Nazionali di Capodimonte, Naples, and in the Pinacoteca Civica "Tosio Martinengo", Brescia). Throughout his career he showed himself exceptionally responsive to the work of other artists. His early style is a synthesis of the achievements of the major figures of the previous generation in central Italy—Melozzo da Forlì, Luca Signorelli, Pintoricchio, and above all Perugino, with whom he is known to have collaborated for a time soon after 1500.

By 1504, when he painted the masterpiece of his early period, *The Marriage of the Virgin* (Pinacoteca di Brera, Milan), Raphael had fully assimilated all these influences. His picture is closely based on another version of the same subject by Perugino (*c*1500–4; Musée des Beaux-Arts, Caen), but it is superior to its prototype in virtually every respect. The composition is much more spacious, with a

Left: Allan Ramsay: Portrait of Margaret Ramsay; oil on canvas; 76×64cm (30×25in); 1754–5. National Gallery of Scotland, Edinburgh

less rigid and schematic arrangement of figures; the poses are freer, more graceful and more varied; the color is richer and more harmonious; even the architectural background is an original creation, in contrast to the purely conventional design adopted by Perugino.

Raphael spent most of the period from 1504 to 1508 in Florence, where he had his first experience of the work of Leonardo da Vinci and Michelangelo, both of whom were then active in the city. As a result of his contact with Leonardo, drawings now began to play an increasingly important role in his creative process. Instead of attempting to give his ideas a definitive form at the first draft, as he had done previously, Raphael now learned to develop them gradually through a series of

sketches. He used the different techniques of pen and chalk with an astonishing virtuosity, but virtually dispensed with the more precise and delicate medium of silverpoint. This new method of working enabled him to produce much more complex and unified compositions than he had achieved before. Michelangelo's influence was less significant. The two men seem to have been personally antipathetic, and Raphael never shared Michelangelo's single-minded obsession with the male nude—even though his figures now acquired something of the tension and vigor so characteristic of the latter's work.

While Raphael was in Florence his reputation was still insufficient to gain him important commissions. Most of the pictures that he produced in this period were

relatively small compositions showing the Madonna and Child, often with one or two other figures, based on works by Leonardo and Michelangelo. Among the finest are the *Madonna of the Meadow* (1505/6; Kunsthistorisches Museum, Vienna), *Madonna of the Goldfinch* (c1506; Uffizi, Florence), and *La Belle Jardinière* (1507; Louvre, Paris). These Florentine *Madonnas* are probably Raphael's most famous works. They were particularly admired in the 19th century, when they were often reproduced in versions that exaggerated their somewhat sentimental religiosity. Indeed, their popularity as devotional objects has tended to obscure their real quality as an exceptionally brilliant and original series of variations on a single restricted theme. It was

Raphael: The Liberation of St Peter; detail; fresco; width of base of entire fresco 660cm (260in); 1513–14. Stanza di Eliodoro, Vatican, Rome

precisely the limitations of the subject that stimulated Raphael's powers of invention.

These paintings show that by 1508 he had fully mastered the problems involved in compositions with two or three figures. When he tried to produce an equally coherent design on a larger scale, in the *Entombment* (1507; Museo e Galleria Borghese, Rome), painted for a chapel in Perugia, the result was not entirely successful. The difficulties that he encountered in attempting to organize ten figures and to give them a sense of movement are all too evident. Despite the beauty of some of the individual poses, the composition as a whole is labored, frozen, and artificial.

Late in 1508 he was summoned to Rome by Pope Julius II, apparently at the suggestion of the papal architect Bramante, who was, like Raphael, a native of Urbino. He was employed in the redecoration of a series of rooms in the Vatican (known as the "Stanze"), at first merely as one of a team of artists, but very soon entirely on his own. He began work in the Pope's private library, now known as the Stanza della Segnatura. Besides a number of small scenes on the ceiling, the decorative scheme included a large fresco on each of the four walls symbolizing one of the four main topics of literature: theology, philosophy, poetry, and jurisprudence. For example, the so-called *School of Athens* shows Plato and Aristotle surrounded by a large number of other philosophers engaged in discussion or contemplation; while in the *Parnassus*, Apollo and the Muses are accompanied by the most famous ancient and modern poets.

In these frescoes Raphael succeeded in creating an ideal world, peopled with figures of superhuman nobility and grace, who were arranged in perfectly balanced compositions and linked to one another by a complex play of glances and gestures. His achievement was not just the culmination of a steady process of development, but to a great extent the reflection of his discovery of classical art, which he was able to see in quantity only after his arrival in Rome. Raphael's response to the Classical world was immediate, intense, and decisive. To a more marked degree than any artist before him, including even Michelangelo, he possessed the desire as well as the ability to recreate the style and the spirit of antique and especially of Hellenistic art with complete fidelity and consistency. This was an enterprise that was perfectly in tune with the contempo-

rary intellectual climate; it was just at this period that the Papacy was attempting to restore Rome to something of its former status by means of a conscious evocation of its Imperial past.

Immediately after completing the Stanza della Segnatura in 1511, Raphael began work in the next room, the Stanza d'Eliodoro. Here, during the next three years, he painted four large scenes showing instances of God's miraculous intervention on behalf of His Church, together with four smaller scenes on the ceiling. The style is different from that of the earlier frescoes, with more complex poses, a greater sense of movement, and a darker, more dramatic tonality. By now Raphael was a complete master of the fresco technique. He exploited it here with unprecedented brilliance, obtaining effects of color and lighting almost comparable to those of oil paintings.

From *c*1514 onwards, as a result of the pressure of commissions, he was forced increasingly to make use of assistants in carrying out his designs. This is first noticeable in the third of the Vatican Stanze, the Stanza dell'Incendio, painted between 1514 and 1517. Here the general quality is markedly lower than in the earlier rooms, and only one of the frescoes, *Fire in the Borgo*, seems to be substantially by Raphael's hand. Although he was usually able to exercise a high degree of control over the activities of his pupils, it must be admitted that in comparison with his best work, the actual execution of the majority of his later paintings leaves something to be desired. The extent of his participation varied greatly, depending on the nature of the commission. For instance, the series of nine large cartoons for tapestries to be hung in the Sistine Chapel was a highly important project in which Raphael found himself in direct competition with Michelangelo, who had already decorated the vault with frescoes. In this case he not only took immense pains with the compositions but was also personally responsible for much of the actual painting. On the other hand, the decoration of two large loggias in the Vatican, dating from *c*1518–19, was carried out almost entirely by assistants, who even provided some of the designs.

The tapestry cartoons, of which seven survive (1515–16; Victoria and Albert Museum, London, on loan from H.M. Queen Elizabeth II), are among Raphael's greatest and most influential works. They

established a pictorial convention that was to remain the norm for the presentation of historical narrative until the 19th century. The subjects were taken from the Acts of the Apostles. In each scene the content was expressed with absolute clarity and immediacy by a composition of monumental calm and simplicity, and by a highly rhetorical yet dignified vocabulary of gesture derived from Classical sculpture.

The major decorative projects for the Papacy comprised only a part of Raphael's artistic activity in Rome. His most important private patron was the banker Agostino Chigi. His villa, now known as the Farnesina, contained Raphael's fresco of *Galatea*, dating from 1511, as well as a series of scenes illustrating the story of Cupid and Psyche, which were painted by pupils from the artist's designs in 1518. Both works were imaginative recreations of Classical wall-paintings. They were to prove just as influential as models for the depiction of mythological subjects as the tapestry cartoons were for biblical and historical themes.

Raphael also designed two chapels for Agostino Chigi, one in the church of S. Maria della Pace, the other in S. Maria del Popolo. The latter, completed in 1516, was his first architectural project. It was remarkable both for the accurate rendering of motifs taken from Classical sources, notably the Pantheon, and for the lavish use of rich materials such as bronze and marble, which also followed antique precedents. In the later part of his career, and especially after he was put in charge of the reconstruction of St Peter's in 1514, Raphael became increasingly preoccupied with architecture. His buildings reflect his interest in the Classical world even more strongly than his paintings. Unfortunately, few of his projects have survived in the form that he intended.

One other particular noteworthy aspect of Raphael's immense output is portraiture. In Florence his portraits were still relatively stereotyped in pose and scarcely differentiated in mood, but in Rome he learned how to vary his compositions to express the personality and status of the sitter. For example, the apparent spontaneity of the portrait of his friend *Baldassare Castiglione* (*c*1514–15; Louvre, Paris), who is shown as if pausing momentarily in conversation, conceals the rigor and complexity of the pyramidal design. It is a perfect visual embodiment of the qualities of grace and facility that Castiglione defined as ideals in his book *The Courtier*. This and other Roman portraits, such as that of *Julius II* (1512; National Gallery, London) and that of *Leo X with Cardinals Giulio de' Medici and Luigi de' Rossi* (?1518; Uffizi, Florence), were imitated by countless later artists.

Raphael's last major work, the altarpiece of the *Transfiguration* (1518–20; Vatican Museums, Rome), was still not quite finished at his death. The design, however, is entirely his responsibility, as is most of the execution. Compared with his earlier pictures, there is a greater use of chiaroscuro, a more complex narrative structure, and a more dramatic, artificial vocabulary of gesture. These are the essential characteristics of Mannerism, the style developed during the 1520s by his pupils, particularly Giulio Romano. Until recently, Raphael's Roman works up to the time of the tapestry cartoons were conventionally regarded as constituting a standard of perfection, while the late paintings such as the *Transfiguration* were seen either as symptomatic of a decline in his powers, or else as embodying a deliberate reaction against his ideals on the part of his pupils. This analysis no longer seems convincing. There is no indication that he had reached an impasse *c*1515. On the contrary, his creativity was undiminished in his last years, and his work of this period established the direction taken by the next generation of artists in Rome and indeed throughout most of Italy.

Further reading. Dussler, L. *Raphael*, London (1971). Fischel, O. *Raphael* (2 vols.), London (1948). Golzio, V. *Raffaello nei Documenti*, Vatican City (1936). Pope-Hennessy, J. *Raphael*, London (1970).

Rauschenberg Robert 1925–

The American painter Robert Rauschenberg was born in Texas. He served in the Second World War before studying at the Kansas City Art Institute (1946–7), the Académie Julian in Paris (1947), and at Black Mountain College, North Carolina (with Josef Albers). His early paintings were Abstract and conventional in technique, but in the 1950s he became increasingly interested in collage and assemblage. For example, *Bed* of 1955 incorporates real bed-linen and a quilt (Leo Castelli Gallery, New York). Some of those works are most easily categorized as sculpture: *Monogram* (1955–9), shows a goat with a

Robert Rauschenberg: Almanac; silkscreen and oil on canvas; 244×152cm (96×60in); 1962. Tate Gallery, London

tire round its middle (Modern Museum, National Museum, Stockholm).

Rauschenberg also developed a method of combining oil paint with silk-screen techniques (seen in, for example, *Barge*, 1963; Leo Castelli Gallery, New York). The imagery often incorporates newspaper photographs and reproductions of well-known paintings: for instance in *Barge*, Velazquez's *Rokeby Venus* merges into shots of a truck and a road junction seen from the air.

A winner of the First Prize for Painting at

the 1964 Venice Biennale, Rauschenberg has also been involved in the dance, designing sets and costumes for the Merce Cunningham Dance Company since 1955, and even dancing himself (with the Surplus Dance Theater).

Further reading. Ashton, D. *The Unknown Shore*, New York (1962). Battock, G. (ed.) *Minimal Art: a Critical Anthology*, New York (1968). Forge, A. *Rauschenberg*, New York (1972). Tomkins, C. *The Bride and the Bachelors*, London (1965).

Ray Man 1890–1976

Man Ray was the most important American Dada artist. Under the influence of Marcel Duchamp in New York, from 1915 onwards, he pioneered the construction of useless artifacts, such as *Object to be Destroyed* (destroyed), a metronome, and a painted eye. He also used the principles of chance in composition, as in *The Rope Dancer Accompanies Herself with Her Shadows* (1916); Museum of Modern Art, New York). By 1918 he was using a commercial airbrush in painting, 30 years before Abstract Expressionism or Tachisme. His main photographic achievement was the Rayograph, a technique for rendering a three-dimensional abstract world in a photographic print.

Further reading. Aragon, L., Arp, J., *et al. Man Ray: Sixty Years of Liberties*, Milan (1971). Bourgeade, P. *Bonsoir, Man Ray*, Paris (1972). Penrose, R. *Man Ray*, London (1975). Ray, M. and Eluard, P. *Les Mains Libres*, Paris (1937). Ray, M. *Self-Portrait*, Boston (1963). Schwarz, A. *Man Ray: the Rigour of Imagination*, New York (1977).

Above: Man Ray: Pisces; canvas; 61×73cm (24×29in); 1938. Tate Gallery, London

Read Herbert 1893–1968

Herbert Read was an English critic and poet, and a champion of modern art in the years between the First and Second World Wars. He became a neighbor of the painters Paul Nash and Ben Nicholson and the sculptors Henry Moore and Barbara Hepworth when he moved to Hampstead in 1933. With them he founded the group Unit One, "a point in the forward thrust of modernism in architecture, painting and sculpture". They were joined in Hampstead by Walter Gropius and other notable architects and artists who were refugees from the Continent. Read's most influential book of these years was the dogmatic *Art and Industry* (1934) which outlined a design aesthetic similar to that of Gropius and the Bauhaus. His other important works include *Education through Art* (1943) and *A Concise History of Modern Painting* (1959). He received a knighthood in 1953.

Redon Odilon 1840–1916

The French artist and printmaker Odilon Redon developed an intensely personal visual vocabulary. Although he was held in high esteem by Symbolist writers and ar-

Below: Odilon Redon: Woman with Outstretched Arms; watercolor on paper; 15×20cm (6×8in); c1910–14. Musée du Petit Palais, Paris

tists, he had few immediate followers.

Born in Bordeaux, he grew up on the family estate, Peyrelebade, amid the desolation of the flat, pine-covered Landes bordered by barren sand dunes and silent marshlands. This landscape haunted Redon throughout his life, providing a constant supply of visual images. Drawing lessons in Bordeaux were followed by studies in architecture and then painting in Paris. A mental breakdown forced him to return to Bordeaux, probably in 1862.

Apart from a careful study of Corot and Delacroix, it was his meetings with Rodolphe Bresdin, in 1863, and with Henri Fantin-Latour, in 1874, that were to shape the course of his artistic career. Bresdin taught Redon etching, enabling him during the 1860s to embark upon a series of small engravings whose subject matter consisted of memories of landscapes known in childhood, peopled with motifs taken from Corot and Delacroix. By 1870, however, Redon had discovered the more immediate technique of charcoal. Over the next nine years he evolved his own highly personal visual symbolism, which he translated into lithographs after 1879.

Redon was introduced to the lithographic technique by Fantin-Latour. Between 1879 and 1899 he produced 166 lithographs: 37 single plates (for example, *Brunnhilde*, 1886), 17 groups of book illustrations (for example, for Flaubert's *Tentation de St Antoine*, three sets 1888, 1889, 1896), and five groups of non-literary sequences of images (*Dans le Rêve*, 1879, and *Songes*, 1891). Most of the lithographs were complemented by deliberately ambiguous captions, usually invented by Redon himself.

In his diary-like autobiography, *À Soi-même* (1922; new edition 1961) Redon suggested that his lithographs summarized two concerns central to his art; the relationship between Man and Nature, and "suggestive" art. Influenced by his friend, the Bordeaux botanist Armand Clavaud, Redon frequently depicted images that expressed the interchangeability of Man and Nature, as in *The Marsh Flower* (plate II, *Hommage à Goya*, 1885). He proposed an alternative theory of evolution to that of Darwin, which he investigated more fully in his non-literary series, *Les Origines* (1883).

Like Mallarmé, who was his close friend and admirer from 1884 onwards, Redon believed in involving the spectator in the creative process. Rather than present a finite image or idea, he created a "suggestive art" in which the spectator was invited to enter into and complete the visual and mental images initially depicted by the artist. Redon achieved this by creating a world of visual ambiguities and absurdities, using for example an illogical juxtaposition of random objects and seemingly unrelated captions and images, a total disregard for unity of scale (*Sad Ascent*, plate 19 of *Dans le Rêve*, 1879) and a frequent reference to infinite space (*Blossoming*, plate 18 of *Dans le Rêve*).

Until c1895, Redon's life had not been happy. He was melancholic by nature, and the death of his first son and the tardiness of critical acclaim colored both the images and the media of his art. However, growing recognition of his work during the 1880s and early 1890s (from J.-K. Huysmans, Alfred Verhaeren and *Les Vingt*, Maurice Denis, and Émile Bernard), the sale of Peyrelebade, and the birth of another son caused light to flood into his work. He experimented with color in several ways. He translated the subjects of his lithographs into victorious images of explosive color (as in *Pegasus Triumphant*, 1905–10; Kröller-Müller Museum, Otterlo). He painted pastels of flower pieces and portraits in subtly balanced colors and textures. And he investigated the effects of mixed media in decorative cycles, screens, and easel paintings.

Redon's brilliant, non-naturalistic color presaged the art of the Fauves, and his use of illogical objects inhabiting an ambiguous world foreshadowed the art of the Surrealists.

Further reading. Bacou, R. *Odilon Redon* (2 vols.), Geneva (1956). Druick, D. (ed.) *Odilon Redon*, London (1994). Redon A. *Lettres de Gauguin, Gide, Huysmans, Jammes, Mallarmé, Verhaeren ... à Odilon Redon*, Paris (1960). Redon, O. *À Soi-même, Journal: Notes sur la Vie, l'Art, et les Artistes*, Paris (1961). Wilson, M. *Nature and Imagination: the Works of Odilon Redon*, Oxford (1978).

Reinhardt Ad 1913–67

Ad Reinhardt emerged as the most relentless of American Minimalist painters, working with a logic that takes every theory of diminution and purity to its logical end. He painted geometrical abstractions in the 1930s and worked in a calligraphic style, related to that of Mark Tobey, in the 1950s. From there he progressed from studies of multiplicities of squares, to simple sequences, to the simple sequences, to the uncompromising *Untitled (Black)* (oil on canvas; 1960–6; Jewish Museum, New York)—an all-black, square canvas. Reinhardt was a vigorous polemicist of purity in art. He was an inspiration to the Minimalists, to whom the irreducible fact of color or shape in its simplest form is an expression of mystical value.

Further reading. Bois, Y.-A. *Ad Reinhardt*, New York (1991). Lippard, L. and Hunter, S. *Ad Reinhardt: Black Paintings 1951–1967*, New York (1990). Lippard, L. and Hunter, S. *Ad Reinhardt: Paintings*, New York (1966).

Rembrandt van Rijn 1606–69

Rembrandt Harmensz. van Rijn was the greatest painter of the Dutch School. He was born in Leiden, the son of a miller. After seven years at grammar school he enrolled at Leiden University, but left a few months later to begin an apprenticeship with a local artist. His first teacher has not been identified; his second, between 1620 and 1623, was a now little-known painter named Jacob van Swanenburgh. He completed his training with six months in the Amsterdam studio of the then famous Pieter Lastman (c1624/5). It was Lastman's work that inspired him to become a historical painter, and familiarized him with narrative techniques deriving from Italian Renaissance art.

In 1625 Rembrandt returned to Leiden, where he set up as an independent artist. Some genre paintings date from these early years, for instance *The Money-changer* (1627; Staatliche Museen, Berlin), a work influenced by Utrecht School nocturnal pictures, but Rembrandt's principal interest was, and remained, biblical history. His earliest surviving painting, the large *The Martyrdom of St Stephen* panel (1625; Musée des Beaux-Arts, Lyons) is an attempt to master dynamic physical action in a multifigured composition. This quickly gave way to more detailed work on a smaller scale, as in *The Presentation in the Temple* (1631; Royal Museum of Art,

Rembrandt van Rijn: Lady with a Fan; oil on canvas; 127×101cm (50×40in); 1633. Private collection

Mauritshuis, The Hague), with its numerous tiny figures, vast spatial effects, and use of chiaroscuro for dramatic ends.

Concurrently, Rembrandt painted a number of single-figure pictures which reveal his attraction to old people. Several of these are of biblical characters, for example *The Prophetess Hannah* (1631; Rijksmuseum, Amsterdam), in which the artist's mother was the model. In others the iconography is problematic, notably in several pictures of elderly sages who sit reading in dimly lit rooms. These are often regarded simply as philosophers or scholars, but allusions to prophets or saints may sometimes have been intended. The most important work from the Leiden period is the 1629 *Judas Returning the Thirty Pieces of Silver* (Lady Normanby Collection,

Mulgrave Castle, Yorkshire). Rembrandt's success in conveying emotion through gesture and facial expression in this work was admired by Constantin Huygens, the Secretary to the Stadholder, Prince Frederick Henry of Orange, who observed that he had already equaled the greatest painters and would soon surpass them.

Around 1631/2 Rembrandt settled permanently in Amsterdam, where he quickly established himself as a fashionable portrait painter among the prosperous bourgeoisie. The ensuing half, three-quarter, and full-length likenesses, each immensely varied in conception, are painted in a detailed and highly-finished technique; as much attention is given to costume as to the sitter's features. This style was related to the demands of pat-

rons, for in other paintings from this period (such as the artist's studies of both old men and models dressed in exotic Oriental costume) his brushwork was already much bolder. In one of the double portraits from these years, *The Shipbuilder and his Wife* (1633; Collection of H.M. Queen Elizabeth II) the apprehension of momentary action echoes the preoccupation of Frans Hals at this date.

Rembrandt's fame was consolidated by group portraits, in particular *The Anatomy Lesson of Dr Tulp* of 1632 (Royal Museum of Art; Mauritshuis, The Hague). The intent listeners in this painting are members of the Guild of Amsterdam Surgeons. The so-called *Night Watch* (1642; Rijksmuseum, Amsterdam), which shows the militia company of Captain Frans Banning Cocq about to form ranks, marks Rembrandt's high point in public esteem. This huge canvas (11 ft 9 in by 14 ft 4 in, 3.59 by 4.38 m; originally even larger) was a revolutionary variant on traditional versions of the commemorative group portrait. It had been customary to give each individual equal prominence, but Rembrandt sacrificed this in favor of common action and psychological unity. This was an application to portraiture of the principles governing his historical pictures. The misleading title of the painting dates from the time when it was darkened by discolored varnish.

The most notable religious pictures from the 1630s are the Passion scenes painted for Prince Frederick Henry (1633–9; Alte Pinakothek, Munich). The pathos of the Calvary scenes in this series distinguishes them from the glorification of Christ found in Rubens' interpretations of the Passion. The explicitly narrative intention reveals that Rembrandt's sources were didactic prints of the 16th century. He was well aware of Rubens' achievements, however, and the gruesome *The Blinding of Samson* (1636; Städelsches Kunstinstitut, Frankfurt am Main), which exhibits his youthful delight in themes of horrifying brutality, was conceived in emulation of the Flemish painter. Rembrandt's expressive range at this date can be seen in the mythological painting of *Danaë* (1636; Hermitage Museum, St Petersburg. This is a particularly beautiful example of his sensuous treatment of the female nude, and of his exploration of the possibilities of light as an agent of the supernatural.

Rembrandt was a wealthy man by the late 1630s. In 1639 he moved to a large

Rembrandt van Rijn: Portrait of Rembrandt's Mother Reading; oil on canvas; 74×62cm (29×24in); c1631? Wilton House, near Salisbury, Wiltshire

house in the Jodenbreestraat, where he lived with Saskia van Uylenborch, a well-connected girl whom he had married in 1634. The artist's awareness of his improved social status and of his celebrity as a painter is apparent in self-portraits from these years. An important consequence of prosperity was that it enabled Rembrandt to build up an extensive art collection; this played a vital role in his work as a source of pictorial and thematic ideas. The inventory of the collection reveals an enormous quantity of prints and drawings by other artists, many of them from the 16th century or earlier.

During the 1640s the mood of Rembrandt's work became quieter and more contemplative, a departure from the urgent physical dramas of earlier years. The change was to some extent related to the death of his wife in 1642—a bereavement that followed the death of three of their four children in infancy. The altered mood is especially evident in such small-scale devotional pictures as the *Adoration of the Shepherds* (1646; National Gallery, London). Rembrandt's conceptions in these intimate, somberly colored works are unaffectedly realistic, and this is typical of his general tendency to humanize rather than idealize biblical figures and scenes. The mystery and spiritual quality with which such works are imbued is achieved largely through the subtle manipulation of light and shade. Rembrandt's religious narratives are firmly rooted in assiduous reading of the Bible, and this is evident in the many other scenes from Christ's life painted during the 1640s. Departures from the text usually only arose when there was a need to extend the narrative scope, as in the famous *Hundred Guilder Print* etching (*Christ Healing the Sick*, c1642–5), where Rembrandt illustrated the whole of St Matthew, chapter 19.

The artist turned to landscape in the late 1630s and 1640s. He made many landscape drawings and etchings, works of incomparable luminosity and atmosphere which are predominantly naturalistic portrayals of the countryside around Amsterdam. The relatively few landscape paintings, by contrast, are intensely imaginative: romantic visions in which bleak mountain ranges, deserted river valleys, and mysterious ruins are momentarily flooded with light bursting through dark storm clouds. No other Dutch painter dramatized nature to this degree. But Rembrandt's interests lay primarily with

humanity, and after the mid 1650s he abandoned landscape as a subject in itself.

Although he received fewer commissions in the 1640s and 1650s, Rembrandt did not, as is often supposed, fall out of favor with patrons. It was the cumulative effects of living beyond his means that resulted in his eventual insolvency. His house and goods were auctioned between 1657 and 1658, and he moved to the Rozengracht, a poorer district of Amsterdam. He never completely cleared his debts; but he was partially protected from his creditors by Hendrickje Stoffels, who was his mistress from c1649, and by Titus (his only surviving son by Saskia), who formed an art-dealing firm and made him its employee.

The Anatomy Lesson of Dr Deijman (1656; Rijksmuseum, Amsterdam) is one of the more important late commissions. The surviving fragment of this group, which shows the corpse and two figures, has a poignancy normally associated with the *Pietà* theme. *The Syndics of the Drapers' Guild* (1662; Rijksmuseum, Amsterdam) is remarkable for Rembrandt's reversal of the customary relationship between sitter and spectator; it is the latter, not the former, who is the object of scrutiny here. In 1652 Rembrandt received his first known commission from abroad: an *Aristotle* (1653; Metropolitan Museum, New York) for which Don Antonio Ruffo, a Sicilian nobleman, was charged 500 guilders. Ruffo paid up, but remarked that this was eight times as much as an Italian artist would have received. A contract in 1661 for a painting to decorate the new Amsterdam Town Hall confirms that Rembrandt's reputation remained high, although the picture (*The Conspiracy of Julius Civilis*, National Museum, Stockholm), was ultimately replaced by a pupil's work. The reasons for this are not known.

Rembrandt is unique for his time in his practice of producing work independently of commissions. This practice increases in later years, with a number of single-figure pictures of Jews, old men, and members of the artist's family. Little or no church patronage existed in 17th-century Holland, and many of his religious paintings (for instance *Bathsheba*, 1654; Louvre, Paris) may also fall into this uncommissioned category. The majority of his later drawings are also private works—musings on historical themes, which are dissociated from such traditional functions as collecting pictorial ideas or serving as preliminary studies for paintings. Rembrandt's draw-

Rembrandt van Rijn: A Girl Sleeping; brush and wash on paper; 24×20cm (9×8in); c1655–60. British Museum, London

ings (only 1,500 or so survive) were not widely known in his lifetime; his 300 etchings, on the other hand, were much more familiar to the public than his paintings. They were an important source of income; it was in fact among the 17th-century connoisseurs who admired them that the history of print-collecting on a widespread scale began.

The unorthodox technique of Rembrandt's last paintings, in which broken touches of thickly impasted paint are worked with the brush handle and even the fingers, is accompanied by a greater degree of brilliance and warmth of color than before. This can be seen in such portraits as *The Jewish Bride* (c1666; Rijksmuseum, Amsterdam) and the *Family Portrait* (c1668; Herzog Anton Ulrich Museum, Brunswick). The consummate tenderness of these essays on the theme of human love is also manifested in such late religious paintings as *The Return of the Prodigal Son* (c1669; Hermitage Museum, St Petersburg), where the artist's reflections on the nature of human forgiveness are unmatched in Christian art for their depth of feeling. The choice of this particular episode from the parable (as opposed to scenes of debauchery) is consistent with Rembrandt's later preference for subjects involving emotional crises, as against those based primarily on physical action, and which have strong elements of sensuality or violence. Other examples are found in his later representations of the story of

Joseph and Potiphar's wife. These concentrate on the accusation scene, rather than on the scene of attempted seduction which Rembrandt had treated in the 1630s.

Themes involving stress arising from moral dilemmas—as in Rembrandt's representations of Bathsheba, and Peter at the time of his denial of Christ—are also characteristic of this tendency. An exception is found in the dark and tragic *Three Crosses* etching (completed *c*1661). Here the cataclysmic events of Christ's last hours are expressed in a purely pictorial way, by arresting contrasts of deep blacks and piercing lights.

Rembrandt's closing years were clouded by personal tragedies: Hendrickje Stoffels died in 1663, Titus in 1668. But knowledge of such biographical details is not necessary in order to appreciate the profoundly moving portrayal of the artist's careworn face in the final self-portraits.

Changes in taste since the 17th century have not always accommodated Rembrandt, but his greatness has rarely been questioned. The admiration of his contemporaries centered on the narrative scope and invention of the history paintings, the verve and characterization of the early portraits, and Rembrandt's technical facility as an etcher. This is also true of later generations of critics, although they invariably expressed reservations about his apparent indifference to ancient sculpture and to Italian Renaissance art, his rejection of precise, linear draftsmanship, and a certain lack of decorum. Today we are inclined to emphasize the content of Rembrandt's work, although our critical language is rarely equal to the descriptive tasks this involves.

Further reading. Benesch, O. *The Drawings of Rembrandt* (6 vols.), London (1954-7). Bredius, A. (revised by Gerson, H.) *The Paintings of Rembrandt*, London (1969). Münz, L. *Rembrandt's Etchings* (2 vols.), London (1952). Rosenberg, J. *Rembrandt: Life and Work*, Oxford (1981).

Remington Frederic 1861–1909

Frederic Remington became famous for his heroic depictions of the American West. He studied at Yale University and briefly at the Art Students League, New York, achieving his first success with illustrations for journals such as *Harper's Weekly* and *Century*. Concentrating on heroic and glamorously rugged subjects, he made a major contribution to the myth of the Wild West, which was championed at the end of the 19th century by newspapers, dime novels and the Wild West shows featuring William F. "Buffalo Bill" Cody. Remington's paintings, spirited, colorful and full of authentic detail, became very popular. *Flight for the Waterhole* (*c*1895; Houston Museum, Texas) was one of the best known. His bronze sculptures, including *The Bronco Buster* (1895), were popular too, and often recast.

René of Anjou 1409–80

René of Anjou was the ruler of lands in southern France and Italy. He was also a patron of the arts, an author, and probably an illuminator—though there is no unequivocal evidence that René himself executed the illustrations to his writings. The artist's masterpiece is *Le Livre du Coeur d'Amour Épris* (1457; Nationalbibliothek, Vienna; MS. 2597) which employs dramatic lighting effects unprecedented in miniature painting. Other works by the same hand, like the *Livre des Tournois* (Bibliothèque Nationale, Paris; MS. Fr. 2695) and the *Mortifement de la Vaine Plaisance* (Bibliothèque Royale Albert I, Brussels; MS. 10308), are less striking and conform more to established genres of illumination. Nevertheless, they reveal an artist of originality, with elements of the mannered style of the Master of the Rohan Hours, whom René knew.

Rembrandt van Rijn: Self-portrait; oil on canvas; 53×44cm (21×17in); 1657. National Gallery of Scotland, Edinburgh (on loan from the Duke of Sutherland)

Guido Reni: St Cecilia; oil on canvas; 94×75cm (37×30in); 1606. Norton Simon Museum, Pasadena

Reni Guido 1575–1642

The Italian painter Guido Reni was born in Bologna, and from 1584 to 1593 was apprenticed to the Fleming Denys Calvaert (1540–1619). About 1595 he joined the Carracci Academy, where he was influenced by Annibale Carracci and by Raphael. He was essentially a classical artist who became increasingly devoted to the concept of ideal beauty. In his mature works, the inspiration of Classical sculpture and the importance of elegant line and flowing rhythms is clear. His classicism is personal and imaginative; it is sweeter, more nostalgic, and more melancholic than the classicism of the High Renaissance. Yet in one important way, Reni was a Baroque artist: he was concerned with the direct expression of charged religious emotion, an expression that modern spectators have often found distasteful.

Reni had already painted important altarpieces for churches in Bologna when he moved to Rome c1602. His early Roman works show the immediate influence of Caravaggio. He was patronized by Cardinal Scipione Borghese and by Pope Paul V, and a series of important commissions brought him immense success. These include frescoes in two rooms in the Vatican (1608–9), St Andrew led to Martyrdom in S. Gregorio, Rome (1608), frescoes in the Borghese chapel in S. Maria Maggiore (1610–12), and frescoes in the Cappella dell'Annunziata in the Palazzo del Quirinale (1609–12). The latter works reveal strongly the influence of the Florentine Renaissance. Their tenderness of feeling, and the radiant golden light that fills the painted dome, crowded with angels, make these some of the artist's most poetic works.

Between 1612 and 1614 Reni executed his famous fresco Dawn (Aurora), on the ceiling of the Casino Rospigliosi in Rome. This work, which makes no concessions to illusionism, shows how consciously Reni adapted the tradition of Classical art and of Raphael. It shows Dawn flying before Apollo in his chariot, accompanied by the maidens of the Hours, figures of ideal beauty who dance in graceful harmony. The colors are glowing and the landscape radiantly beautiful.

In 1611 Reni had visited Bologna and painted important works there. In 1614 he returned permanently to the city. He then painted a series of large altarpieces. In these his handling is broad, and his color rich, but the compositions are carefully balanced and even rigidly symmetrical. At this period he was also painting poetic reinterpretations of historical and mythological subjects for the nobility. In 1622 he went to Naples to fresco the Tesoro di S. Gennaro, but difficulties over the contract caused his departure for Rome. In his last years Reni developed a new style, distinguished by delicate silvery tonalities and ravishing combinations of oranges, pinks, and mauves.

Renier de Huy 12th century

Although the name of Renier de Huy has little historical foundation, it has been firmly connected with the creation of the 12th-century Mosan style of the Meuse River region of Flanders. The bronze font commissioned by Abbot Hellinus (1107–18) for his church of Notre-Dame-aux-Forts at Liège (now in the church of St-Barthélemy in Liège) has long been attributed to Renier. "Reinerus aurifaber" also appears as a witness on a charter of the church of Notre Dame at Huy, signed by Bishop Albero I of Liège in 1125—but the evidence for linking this goldsmith with the Liège font is very poor.

A contemporary rhymed chronicle written by a Canon of Liège Cathedral describes the font carefully, and states that it was made in the time of Abbot Hellinus and by him. It is not until the 15th-century chronicle of Liège that Renier's name is given as the craftsman responsible for the font ordered by Bishop Albero.

Renoir Auguste 1841–1919

The French Impressionist painter Pierre-Auguste Renoir was born at Limoges, but

Auguste Renoir: La Parisienne (Woman in Blue); oil on canvas; 160×106cm (63×42in); 1874.
National Museum of Wales, Cardiff

temporary, for example *Lise with a Parasol* (1867; Museum Folkwang, Essen). Others fuse a naturalistic treatment of the figure with a mythological subject such as *Diana* (1867; National Gallery of Art, Washington, D.C.). This combination of modernity and timelessness has close parallels with Courbet's contemporary work, and became Renoir's central preoccupation in the later part of his career.

Renoir's brushwork of the later 1860s owes a debt to Manet's bold handling of paint, but always retains a delicacy of touch reminiscent of the French 18th-century masters, notably Fragonard. This appears even in Renoir's direct studies from nature, as can be seen by comparing his 1869 view of La Grenouillère (National Museum, Stockholm) with Monet's more broadly handled treatment of the same subject (Metropolitan Museum, New York).

After his Salon submissions were rejected in 1873, Renoir abstained from the Salon for four years, and exhibited in the first three Impressionist group exhibitions, in 1874, 1876, and 1877. His exhibits at these shows reveal the diversity of his aims and his work during the 1870s. In his small-scale paintings, he developed an extremely summary, spontaneous technique, evoking the presence of objects by apparently formless dabs and dashes of paint, as in *The Harvesters* (1873; Stiftung Sammlung E. G. Bührle, Zürich). He applied a similarly abbreviated technique to a female nude in *Woman in the Sunlight* (1875; Musée du Jeu de Paume, Paris). He clearly felt that these experimental studies were worth exhibiting, but he only showed them alongside far more ambitious and fully finished canvases, such as *La Parisienne* (*Woman in Blue*) (National Museum of Wales, Cardiff). This was an almost lifesize full-length portrait of a woman in blue, closely related in type to the fashionable portraiture of the day.

In his genre scenes of modern life, Renoir combined something of the spontaneity of his outdoor studies with—in the principal figures—the interest in characterization shown in his portraits. This is seen in *La Loge* (Courtauld Institute Galleries, London), and in Renoir's most ambitious modern-life painting of the decade, *Moulin de la Galette* (Musée du Jeu de Paume, Paris). The shadow effects in *Moulin de la Galette* are treated in rich blues, and its forms are modeled by persistent variations of color. In other, smaller paintings of this

he spent his childhood in Paris, where he was to live until he moved to the south of France in 1902. In the later 1850s he worked as a painter on porcelain, and then painted blinds, studying at the same time in the Louvre, where he became devoted to French 18th-century art. In 1862 he entered Gleyre's studio, where he met Monet,

Sisley, and Bazille; Monet and Bazille became particularly close friends.

During the 1860s, like the other Impressionists-to-be, Renoir sought success at the annual Salon exhibitions. In his landscapes of the period, he was indebted to the painters of the Barbizon School. Some of his figure-pieces are wholly con-

period, such as *Woman Reading* (c1876; Musée du Jeu de Paume, Paris), the modeling of the figure is almost entirely suppressed in favor of bold strokes of varied color; the patterns of light and shade on the woman virtually dissolve into those of the background.

In the later 1870s, Renoir began to gain a wider practice as a fashionable portraitist. This was largely through his contacts with Madame Georges Charpentier who was a society hostess and the wife of a leading publisher. He exhibited at the Salon again between 1878 and 1883, winning his greatest success with his *Portrait of Madame Charpentier and her Children* (1878; Metropolitan Museum, New York), a picture tighter in handling and more conventional in color than *Moulin de la Galette*.

During the same years, probably as the result of the demands made on him by portrait commissions, he began to feel dissatisfied with the extreme formlessness of paintings such as *Woman Reading*. This dissatisfaction led him to a period of crisis in which he reexamined all the bases of his art, and began to seek ways of reintroducing tighter drawing and modeling into his paintings. He studied Ingres' oil paintings, for the clarity of their draftsmanship in paint. He also began to experiment with painting in thin, translucent glazes, on a dense white ground, instead of using a dense impasto; this can be seen in *Young Girl with a Falcon* (1880; Sterling and Francine Clark Art Institute, Williamstown). Then in autumn 1881 he traveled to Italy; he visited Florence, Venice, Rome, and Naples.

He was particularly impressed by the more informal of Raphael's frescoes—those in the Villa Farnesina in Rome—and by the Pompeian mural paintings in the Naples Museum. He wrote to Madame Charpentier that in his own paintings he was seeking to emulate the grandeur and simplicity by which these earlier works suggested sunlight, by concentrating not on details, but on broad harmonies. He also found a relevance in the treatment of subject matters of the Renaissance masters and the Greco-Roman artists of Pompeii, in the way they treated mythological stories as lively genre scenes, in contrast to the idealizations and archaeological reconstructions characteristic of French 19th-century Neoclassical painting. In the 1870s, Renoir had been preoccupied with the most ephemeral modern scenes. But in the 1880s he began to treat more timeless subjects, and the informal treatments of mythology that he found on his Italian trip helped him to give spontaneity to such themes.

In the aftermath of his trip to Italy, his handling of paint became drier, and his drawing of forms very crisp. Sometimes he even tried to emulate in oils the dryness of fresco, as in *Woman Arranging her Hair* (1885; Sterling and Francine Clark Art Institute, Williamstown). This period of experiment culminated in *The Bathers* (1887; Philadelphia Museum of Art). Here, Renoir derived the figures in part from a 17th-century relief by François Girardon in the park at Versailles; the picture invites comparison with the similarly timeless treatments of the Bather theme by Boucher (*Diana Resting after her Bath*) and Fragonard (*Women Bathing*; both in the Louvre, Paris). Renoir's outlines are harsh, and some details meticulously defined, but the figures are frozen in the middle of apparently fleeting movements.

Renoir soon found this style too tight, and sought ways of regaining his spontaneity of brushwork without losing the fuller modeling of form which he had reached. He achieved this by c1890, adopting a type of handling in which fluent brushstrokes followed the contours of the form. It was the technique of Fragonard, in

Auguste Renoir: Woman Reading; oil on canvas; 47×38cm (19×15in); c1876. Musée du Jeu de Paume, Paris

particular, that helped him to attain this. Some of Renoir's canvases of c1890 are particularly reminiscent of the French 18th century in feeling, as well as in handling, for example *In the Meadow* (Metropolitan Museum, New York). During the 1880s Renoir's color became richer and warmer; this was as a result of two trips to Algeria, in 1881 and 1882, and of spells working on the Mediterranean coast. In his last period, after he had settled at Cagnes on the Mediterranean in 1902, his color became still more lavish and his handling more fluid. In the finest of his last paintings, such as *The Bathers* (1918–19; Musée du Jeu de Paume, Paris), form and color are married with unprecedented freedom, to create an idealized vision of womanhood far from the modern Parisian girls who had dominated his art in the 1870s. Renoir's greatest achievements lie at these two poles: as the painter of the modern life of the 1870s, and in the timeless visions created by his brush in his last years.

Further reading. Daulte, F. *Auguste Renoir: I, Figures 1860–1890*, Lausanne (1971). Drucker, M. *Renoir*, Paris (1949). Renoir, J. *Renoir, My Father*, London (1962). Rewald, J. *The History of Impressionism*, London and New York (1973). Vollard, A. *Renoir*, Paris (1918).

Repin Ilya 1844–1930

Ilya Efimovich Repin was a Russian Realist painter. Trained at the St Petersburg Academy, he subsequently spent two years in Paris (1873–4) where he was influenced by the Impressionists' use of color. In 1874 he joined the Abramtsevo artists' colony founded by S. I. Mamontov, and also became a member of the *Peredvishniki* ("Wanderers"). Both groups believed that art should be socially useful, and should concentrate on those subjects likely to elicit sympathy. Repin embodied these ideals in works with a strong idea-content, though he never neglected painterly qualities (for example, *Volga Boatman Hauling*, 1872; State Russian Museum, Leningrad). He painted portraits of many prominent Russians, including several of Tolstoy.

Repton Humphry 1752–1818

Humphry Repton was an English landscape gardener whose early life was spent

as a country gentleman. It was not until 1788 that he turned an amateur interest into a profession and became a "landscape gardener" (he was the first to adopt the title). As such he fell heir to a tradition that had achieved, through the career of Lancelot ("Capability") Brown, a status equal to architecture, painting, and sculpture.

His first major publication, *Sketches and Hints on Landscape Gardening*, appeared in 1795. Criticizing the contrived informality of the Brownian setting, it argued the merits of a more rugged, natural landscape: one that his own enormous practice did more than anything else to popularize. He holds a prominent place in the development of the Picturesque aesthetic, although the emphasis he placed upon convenience and utility led him to preserve many features (including the balustraded terrace close to the house) that infuriated the more extreme exponents of the Picturesque.

Unlike Brown, Repton rarely practiced as an architect; but the list of architects with whom he worked includes Nash, Wyatt, Wilkins (senior), and his own sons, George and J.A. Repton. Despite his lack of practical experience, he held firm views on architecture. It was largely due to his writings that the "irregular Gothic style" of James Wyatt was popularized, as the architectural equivalent to the revolution that Repton had pioneered in landscape design.

No Reptonian landscapes have survived in an unaltered state, but good examples are still to be found at Tatton Park, Cheshire (1791), Cobham Hall, Kent (1790), and Corsham Court, Wilts. (1795).

Restout Family
17th and 18th centuries

The French painter Jean Restout the Younger (1692–1768) was born in Rouen. His father, Jean Restout the Elder (1663–1702), and his grandfather, Marguerin Restout (*fl.* 1624), had both been painters. Jean moved to Paris in 1707 to work under his uncle, Jouvenet. He was received at the Académie in 1720, rising to become its Chancellor in 1761. The severity and integrity that marked both his life and his work were atypical of his age. His religious works have a seriousness lacking in the work of his contemporaries Coypel and J.-B. Lemoyne; his manner seems to have stemmed, through the influence of Jouvenet, from 17th-century artists like Hubert Le Sueur. His mythological sub-

jects steer clear of the mildly erotic and the light-hearted, with an emotional commitment that presages J.-L. David. His son, Jean-Bernard Restout (1732–97), was also a painter, and his portrait of his father (*Portrait of Jean Restout*, Versailles) is revealing.

Rethel Alfred 1816–59

Alfred Rethel was a German painter and draftsman. He studied under the Nazarene artist W. von Schadow at the Düsseldorf Academy (1829–36). Schadow's style and ideals greatly influenced his early work, such as the Charlemagne Frescoes in the Kaisersaal, Aachen Town Hall (1840–7). Rethel is most famous for his drawings and for his woodcuts—a medium then enjoying a renaissance in Germany. Several of these show a medieval preoccupation with death (for example, *Death as Destroyer*, c1848); but the woodcut cycle *Also a Dance of Death* (1849) seems, more specifically, to be a reactionary answer to the Revolution of 1848. Their power lies in the matter-of-fact inclusion of the figure of Death into a realistic setting. Rethel was mentally ill from 1853 until his death.

Reynolds Joshua 1723–92

An artist of refined intellect and taste, Sir Joshua Reynolds was the most celebrated and influential painter in England during the second half of the 18th century. His preeminence as a portrait painter was challenged only by Allan Ramsay in the 1750s and by Thomas Gainsborough after 1774. Through his paintings, which figured prominently in public exhibitions from 1760 onwards, and his 15 *Discourses on Art* delivered to the students of the Royal Academy (1769–90), he dictated the canons of taste and the methods of practice for successive generations of English artists. His collection of Old Master drawings and prints was one of the finest ever assembled by an English connoisseur, and he numbered among his intimate acquaintances the literary and political elite of his age.

Reynolds was born at Plympton in Devonshire. In 1740 he was apprenticed to the London portrait painter Thomas

Jean Restout the Younger: The Adoration of the Shepherds; oil on canvas; 400×330cm (157×130in); 1761. Church of St-Louis, Versailles

Hudson, but in 1743 he set up his own practice, working in Devon and London until his departure for Italy in 1749. In Rome, from 1750 to 1752, he studied assiduously the art works of Antiquity and of the High Renaissance. He was particularly inspired by the Bolognese classicists, Reni, Guercino, and the Carracci. After returning to London in 1753, he formulated his own version of the grand style, in which he sought to extend the limits of history painting to include the less honored category of portraiture. The "history" portrait, based on a solid appreciation of the aesthetic principles of past masters, and frequently quoting the poses and motifs of Classical statuary and paintings, was Reynolds' primary contribution to English portraiture. It was in the class of the heroic full-length, such as *Commodore Keppel* (1753/4; National Maritime Museum, London) and *Captain Robert Orme* (1756; National Gallery, London), that he registered his initial successes in this field.

Reynolds was never more dogmatic in his classicism than during the years immediately surrounding his election as first President of the Royal Academy in 1768. To this period belong the innovative *Garrick between Tragedy and Comedy* (1762; private collection), *Lady Cockburn and her Three Eldest Sons* (1774; National Gallery, London), and *Daughters of Sir William Montgomery as the Graces Adorning a Term of Hymen* (1774; Tate Gallery, London). In addition to the more formal commissions of the 1770s, he also painted so-called "fancy pictures", and became popular as a portrayer of children. His late work *Master Henry Hoare* (1788; Toledo Museum of Art, Toledo, Ohio) is one of his most sensitive pictures in this category.

In 1781, Reynolds toured Flanders and Holland where he made a careful study of Rubens' paintings. His approach to characterization in portraiture tends to be less intellectual after this date, although in his *Sarah Siddons as The Tragic Muse* (1784; Huntington Library and Art Gallery, San Marino) and *Lieutenant-Colonel Banastre Tarleton* (1782; National Gallery, London), the classical idiom is reiterated with increased vigor and insight. In the late 1780s he contributed three paintings to John Boydell's Shakespeare Gallery (*Macbeth and the Witches*, 1788, and *The Death of Cardinal Beaufort*, 1788, now at Petworth House, Petworth, Sussex: *Puck*, 1789, Collection of Earl Fitzwilliam, Milton Park, Peterborough, Cambridge-

Francisco Ribalta: Christ Embracing St
Bernard; oil on canvas; 158×113cm
(62×44in). Prado, Madrid

Further reading. Cormack, M. *Exhibition
of Works of Sir Joshua Reynolds, P.R.A.*,
Birmingham (1961). Graves, A. and
Cronin, W.V. *A History of the Works of
Sir Joshua Reynolds* (4 vols.), London
(1899–1901). Hudson, D. *Sir Joshua Rey-
nolds*, London (1958). Wark, R.R. (ed.) *Sir
Joshua Reynolds: Discourses on Art*, San
Marino (1959). Waterhouse, E. *Reynolds*,
London (1973).

Ribalta Francisco 1565–1628

The Spanish painter Francisco Ribalta was
born in Solsona in Catalonia. In Madrid by
1582, he absorbed the style of the painters
at the Escorial, especially the tenebrism of
Juan Fernández de Navarrete (c1526–79).

By 1599 he was in Valencia, developing a
strongly naturalistic Mannerist style similar to that of Bartolomé Carducho (1560–
1680) in works for the church of Algemesí
(1603) and for the Colegio del Patriarca at
Valencia (1604–11).

Ribalta probably visited Italy between
c1613 and 1615. This is suggested both by
a signed copy of Caravaggio's *The Martyrdom of St Peter* and by the increasing
realism and tenebrism of his later work.
His masterpieces are luminous evocations
of Franciscan legends (examples in the
Prado, Madrid, and the Wadsworth
Atheneum, Hartford, Conn.).

Joshua Reynolds: Lt-Col. Banastre Tarleton; oil on canvas; 236×145cm (93×57in); exhibited 1782.
National Gallery, London

shire), and while he attempted serious
history painting at this time, his efforts in
this line were never entirely successful.
After losing the sight of his left eye in
1789, he virtually stopped painting. He
read his last *Discourses* to the Royal
Academy in 1790. His last two years were
not happy but he was given a sumptuous
funeral and was buried at St Paul's in 1792
with unparalleled ceremony for an artist.

Ribera Jusepe de 1591–1652

The Spanish painter Jusepe de Ribera was born in Játiva (Valencia). He is believed to have been a pupil of Francisco Ribalta in Valencia, but nothing more is known of his working life in Spain. He went to Italy at an early age. After visiting Emilia and Rome, where he became a member of the Accademia di San Luca, he had settled by 1616 in Naples, where he lived for the rest of his life and was one of the leading artists.

His early style was close to that of Caravaggio in its realism and tenebrism, but it was also typically Spanish in its depth of religious feeling. He was soon patronized by the Duke of Osuna, the Spanish Viceroy in Naples, who commissioned a group of religious works for the collegiate church of Osuna in Andalusia. These include his early masterpiece, the large *Crucifixion* (1616–20), in which the composition recalls Reni, though the style is strongly Caravaggesque. In addition to many Neapolitan patrons, Ribera frequently worked for the King of Spain and for Spanish religious orders, who channeled commissions to him through successive Viceroys. He proudly emphasized his

Jusepe de Ribera: The Club-footed Boy; oil on canvas; 164×92cm (65×36in); 1642. Louvre, Paris

Spanish origin in the wording of the signatures on his paintings, while his style retained a Spanish flavor throughout his career.

In the middle 1630s Ribera's palette became more colorful, as in the large *Immaculate Conception* (1635; center of the main altarpiece, Augustinian monastery, Salamanca). This work was commissioned by the Count of Monterrey, then Viceroy in Naples, for his newly founded convent of Augustinian nuns in Salamanca. It influenced painters of the School of Madrid from Juan Carreño de Miranda to Claudio Coello. After a few years during which Venetian color-schemes predominated, as in the *Isaac and Jacob* (1637; Prado, Madrid), Ribera returned c1640 to the darker tones of his early period. The increasing vigor and movement in his works were typical of the High Baroque, but his main figures were usually concentrated into a shallow area of foreground, with landscape relegated to an unobtrusive background role.

Ribera was best known for his rugged half-length philosophers, his usually bearded apostles and aged saints (particularly St Jerome), his scenes of *The Martyrdom of St Sebastian* (numerous versions) and *St Bartholomew* (1630; Prado, Madrid), and his sometimes gruesome mythological subjects like *Apollo and Marsyas* (1637; S. Martino, Naples). But he was not impervious to physical beauty, as in *The Penitent Magdalen* (c1640; Prado, Madrid) and *The Holy Family with St Catherine* (1648; Metropolitan Museum, New York). Outstanding among his rare portraits were the *Jesuit Missionary* (1638; Museo Poldi-Pezzoli, Milan) and the bearded woman *Magdalena Ventura* (1631; Duke of Lerma Foundation Museum, Toledo). He also executed a number of fine etchings.

Ribera's thick fleshy handling of paint was imitated briefly by his outstanding pupil, Luca Giordano. His influence had earlier affected most of the contemporary Neapolitan painters, from Massimo Stanzione onwards, of whom he remained to the end a keen and successful rival.

Further reading. Felton, C.M. *Jusepe de Ribera: a Catalogue Raisonné*, Pittsburgh (1971). Pérez Sánchez, A.E. and Spinosa, N. *L'Opera Completa del Ribera*, Milan (1978). Trapier, E. du G. *Ribera*, New York (1952).

Sebastiano Ricci: St Peter Released from Prison; fresco; 165×138cm (65×54in); 1722–3. S. Stae, Venice

Ricci family
17th and 18th centuries

The Ricci were painters born in Belluno, active mainly in Venice. The historical importance of Sebastiano Ricci (1659–1734) lies in his successful revival of the great tradition of Venetian history painting after a century of decadence, preparing the way for the achievements of G.A. Pellegrini, Piazzetta, and Tiepolo. After an early career that included visits to Bologna, Parma, and Rome, he established himself in Venice c1700, setting the pattern for his successors by making several further extended journeys abroad, visiting Vienna (1701–3), Florence (1706–7), London (1712–16), and Paris (1716). The breadth of his artistic experience is reflected in the eclecticism of his style, which variously reveals the influence of Antonio Correggio, the Carracci, Pietro da Cortona, and especially Paolo Veronese. At times, indeed, Ricci's paintings come dangerously close to becoming more pastiches of Veronese's, and he has been accused of lacking original inspiration; but quite apart from the novel gaiety and lightness of his palette, and the sheer brilliance of his painterly technique, his very choice of sources was to be of crucial importance for the next generation of Venetian painters.

Marco Ricci (1676–1730), Sebastiano's nephew and occasional collaborator, was by contrast a specialist in landscape painting. Within this genre, his historical position roughly parallels that of his uncle, and his early assimilation of a wide range of foreign influences, including Salvator Rosa, Claude Lorrain, and perhaps also the Dutch, was to help lay the foundations for the development of Venetian landscape and townscape painting in the 18th century.

Richard of Verdun *fl. 1288–1318*

Richard of Verdun was a French illuminator who lived in Paris. He was the son-in-law of Master Honoré, and as no work by his own hand has been identified his career is interwoven with that of the older master. He is first recorded in 1288, when he was witness to the sale of a manuscript by Honoré. Like him, he lived in the main residential quarter for lay illuminators in Paris (now Rue Boutebrie), and in 1292 the tax paid by him was substantial. He continued to enjoy the royal patronage accorded to Honoré, and is last recorded in 1318. This was in conjunction with an associate, Jean de la Mare, who had collaborated with him on the illumination of three Antiphonaries for the Sainte Chapelle. The attribution to him of various manuscripts, including *La Légende de Saint Denis* which was presented to Philip V in 1317, is purely hypothetical.

Richards Ceri 1903–71

The Welsh artist Ceri Giraldus Richards was born of Welsh-speaking parents near Swansea. He attended Swansea School of Art (1920–4) and the Royal College of Art, London (1924–7). Receptive to new visual ideas, he quickly assimilated the decorative economy of Matisse's portraits and the metamorphism of Picasso, Max Ernst, and other Surrealists. Such influences are discernible in his early reliefs (for example *Bird and Beast*, 1936; Scottish National Gallery of Modern Art, Edinburgh), but the whimsy and invention displayed in them are his own. They are among his finest achievements.

Throughout the 1930s and 1940s Richards often used the Surrealist techniques of free association and metamorphism to illustrate his favorite theme, the cycle of life. After the war he developed this further in many semi-abstract compositions, most notably perhaps in the series *Homage to Dylan Thomas* (1953–5; examples in the Tate Gallery, London; Cecil Higgins Art Gallery, Bedford; Glyn Vivian Art Gallery, Swansea). Here the richness of the forms themselves express the continual triumph of the life force over death.

Richier Germaine 1904-59

Germaine Richier was a French sculptor. During the 1930s she was influenced by the classicism of Charles Despiau and Aristide Maillol. *The Toad* of 1942, on one level a conventional nude, also refers obliquely to the title in its pose and is the first of her sculptures to use the human body as an analogy for animal life. While this penchant for visual metaphor relates her to Surrealism, her sinister zoomorphic images find parallels in the works of other postwar sculptors, notably César. So does her concern for richness of texture in her handling of bronze, sometimes emphasized by gilding or polychrome.

Richter Hans 1888–1976

The German painter, sculptor, and filmmaker Hans Richter was born in Berlin. He joined the Zurich Dada group in 1916. He never regarded Dada as purely nihilistic, but was strongly attracted to the idea of using dance as an element in his work. His Dada heads, created by a few strokes of black ink on white paper, had in their slightness the provocative quality sought by the movement; but they were also, for him, an exploration of musical rhythm. This concept was developed in the abstract films, the first of their kind, made by Richter and Viking Eggeling in 1920. Richter's book *Dada: Art and Anti-Art* (Cologne, 1964) is considered a classic on the subject.

Riemenschneider Tilman *c1460–1531*

First mentioned in Würzburg in 1478/9, the German sculptor Tilman Riemenschneider settled there in 1483 and became a citizen and master two years later. During his journeyman years he appears to have traveled extensively. Apart from absorbing the more recent developments in the Trier-Strasbourg-Ulm area, he reveals considerable Netherlandish echoes in his early alabaster *Annunciation* of 1484 (Bayerisches Nationalmuseum, Munich). His rise to fame was very rapid, and in a working career of over 40 years he produced at least 19 complex carved wooden retables, as well as a large body of stone sculpture.

In 1490 he was commissioned to carve the high altar (now dismembered) in the parish church of Münnerstadt, and the surviving parts reveal his characteristic gentle, naturalistic style. Contrary to the

Ceri Richards: Blossoms; oil on canvas; 51×61cm (20×24in); 1940. Tate Gallery, London

Tilman Riemenschneider: Virgin and Child; detail; limewood; full height 142cm (56in); c1490–3. Detroit Institute of Arts

maker. Before his association with the *De Stijl* group he began to work in primary forms and colors, producing his revolutionary open-construction "red and blue" chair in 1918. He joined the *De Stijl* group in 1919, with important consequences for its declared intention to unite architecture and painting. In 1923 he collaborated on an exhibition of architectural designs for the Galerie de l'Effort Moderne in Paris. His design for the Schröder house, which was built in 1924, realized *De Stijl* prin-

ciples, and is still regarded as a high point in the development of modern architecture. While practicing as an architect, Rietveld continued to design furniture. His later buildings included the Dutch Pavilion at the Venice Biennale of 1953.

Rigaud Hyacinthe 1659–1743

Hyacinthe Rigaud was a French portrait painter. Trained in the Midi, he came to Paris in 1681. His highly reputed career as

Hyacinthe Rigaud: Louis XIV; oil on canvas; 277×194cm (109×76in); 1701. Louvre, Paris

current practice in Germany he delivered this retable in natural wood, but in 1503 Veit Stoss was called in to "color, paint, and gild" it. Similarly, the tender *Adam* and *Eve* commissioned in 1491 for the Marienkapelle in Würzburg (Mainfränkisches Museum, Würzburg) show his exquisite sensitivity in exploiting the natural qualities of the sandstone. This novel approach to sculpture may owe something to earlier Netherlandish sculpture, but its closest spiritual ancestors are the sculptures of Nikolaus Gerhaert van Leyden. The same sensitivity and shy spirituality is characteristic of Riemenschneider's monument to *Konrad von Schaumberg* (c1500; Marienkapelle, Würzburg).

Above all, Riemenschneider and his large workshop were responsible for the great series of wooden retables culminating in the *Assumption of the Virgin* in the Herrgottskirche at Creglingen near Rothenburg (c1505–10). In this work the natural wood surfaces are treated with consummate delicacy. In his last sculptures, such as the *Deposition of Christ* in the parish church of Maidbronn (1520–5), his wistful melancholy deepens into a new intensity, reflecting his personal sufferings in the wake of the Peasants' War.

Rietveld Gerrit 1888–1964

The Dutch architect and designer Gerrit Thomas Rietveld trained as a cabinet-

a court painter began in 1688, when he painted a portrait of Monsieur, brother of King Louis XIV. He painted most people of note at Versailles, including generals, diplomats, and visiting princes. He developed a pattern for such portraits based on the elegance of Anthony van Dyck and the formality of Philippe de Champaigne. Typical military portraits show the figure in modern armor against a landscape with a distant battle. The State portraits can be typified by that of *Louis XIV* (1701; Louvre, Paris), with a tempered Baroque exuberance in its swirling draperies, complex curves, and rich color. Rigaud employed a large studio of assistants. He also painted some simple, direct portraits, which show his admiration for Rembrandt.

Rikyu Sen no 1521–92

Sen no Rikyu was a Japanese Tea Master (Tea Ceremony expert) whose influence as an arbiter of taste was unequaled. He trained in the Zen temple of the Daitokuji (Kyoto) and established the fully mature rules of taste for the Tea Ceremony. Deferred to in these matters even by the dictators Oda Nobunaga and Toyotumi Hideyoshi, he was finally forced to commit suicide by the latter, presumably because of his political influence.

Rikyu insisted on simple sobriety in architecture, in flower arrangement, and in the painting and calligraphy scrolls hung at a Tea Ceremony; and these austere tastes

have persisted since his time. He also patronized the simple, very tactile Black Raku pottery of Kyoto, which became the standard tea ware.

Riley Bridget 1931–

The British painter Bridget Riley was born in London. She studied at Goldsmiths' College (1949–52) and at the Royal College of Art (1952–5), and had her first one-woman show at Gallery One in 1962. She was given a large-scale retrospective at the Hayward Gallery, London, in 1971. Riley's art, influenced at first by Victor Vasarely, has always been concerned with pattern and optical effect. She creates elaborate abstract patterns, often markedly linear in feeling, that are deliberately intended to unsettle the eyes of the spectator. The patterns often give the impression of forms vibrating—almost like objects seen from a distance in a heat haze (for example, *Fall*, 1963; Tate Gallery, London). At first she worked exclusively in black and white, but she has since added color. The designs are worked out with enormous geometrical precision, the final canvases sometimes being executed by studio assistants on the basis of Riley's *modello*.

Further reading. Lucie-Smith, E. and White, P. *Art in Britain 1969–76*, London (1970). Vaizey, M. "For the Mind's Eye", *Sunday Times*, London (July 1976). Wolfe, T. *The Painted Word*, New York (1975).

Riopelle Jean-Paul 1923–

The Canadian artist Jean-Paul Riopelle was born in Montreal. He began to paint his first nonfigurative pictures in 1944 and 1945, then traveled to France and Germany, and then to New York in 1946, exhibiting in the International Surrealist Exhibition of that year. In 1948 he was a cosigner of the manifesto *Refus Global*, and cofounder with Paul-Emile Borduas of the *Automatistes* group, based in Montreal. He moved to Paris in 1946, becoming a close friend of Fernand Leduc and briefly an associate of Georges Mathieu. He is considered a member of the School of Paris.

Riopelle's mature work is based on his interest in Surrealist automatism. His best known paintings rely on much use of the palette knife, and the direct application of paint from the tube—creating a mosaic surface (for example, *Encounter*, 1956; Wallraf-Richartz-Museum, Cologne). Since the early 1960s he has also been sculpting in bronze.

Rivera Diego 1886–1957

Diego Rivera was a Mexican mural painter. From 1898 to 1904 he studied in Mexico City under Santiago Rebull (1829–1902). Receiving a grant in 1907 to study in Europe, he went first to Madrid and then to Paris, becoming friends with Modigliani and Picasso among others. He also traveled in Italy, Germany, and Russia.

Back in Mexico in 1921, he received his first commission for a fresco from the new socialist government. From then on he was the acknowledged leader of the new Mexican school of painting, which concerned itself with the portrayal of Mexican history through monumental wall painting in public buildings. At intervals between the years 1931 and 1941, Rivera painted murals in New York City, San Francisco, and Detroit which provoked considerable controversy. He sought to strengthen national consciousness and solidarity by depicting man in his social and working environment (for example, *Miner Being Searched*; fresco; 1923–8; Patio of Labor, Secretariat of Public Education, Mexico City).

Further reading. Arquin, F. *Diego Rivera: the Shaping of an Artist 1889–1921*, Norman, Okla. (1971). Rivera, D. *My Life, My Art*, New York (1960). Rivera, D.

Bridget Riley: Late Morning; acrylic on canvas; 89×142cm (35×56in); 1967–8. Tate Gallery, London

Diego Rivera: The Cafe Terrace; oil on canvas; 61×50cm (24×20in); 1915. Metropolitan Museum, New York

and Suarez, L. *Confesiones de Diego Rivera*, Mexico City (1962). Secker, H.S. *Diego Rivera*, Dresden (1957). Wolfe, B.D. *Diego Rivera: his Life and Times*, London and New York (1939).

Rivers Larry 1923–

Larry Rivers is an American painter born in the Bronx, New York, who studied both with Hans Hofmann and with William Baziotes. His style derived mainly from an admiration for Willem de Kooning's painting which led him out of the impasse of Abstract Expressionism. This reaction against Abstract Expressionism turned him towards both a stark realism, as in *Double Portrait of Birdie* (1955; Whitney Museum of American Art, New York), and towards a series of transcriptions of popular paintings such as *Washington Crossing the Delaware* (1953). The latter brought him close to the Pop Movement, although more in the sense of an interest in popular art as

kitsch than in the Pop image as developed by Andy Warhol or Claes Oldenburg.

Further reading. Hunter, S. *Larry Rivers*, New York (1972). Rivers, L. and Brightman, C. *Drawings and Digressions*, New York (1979). Rosenberg, H. *The Anxious Object: Art Today and its Audience*, New York (1964).

Riza c1565–1635

The Persian draftsman and miniaturist Riza was the son of Ali Asghar of Kashan. He received royal patronage from Shah Abbas I from the time of the latter's accession in 1587 and was in high favor during the 1590s, when he shared in the illustration of a large-scale *Shah-nama* (Book of kings) (surviving part is in the Chester Beatty Library, Dublin). By this time he was using the prefix Aqa ("Respected") but by 1606 he is said, by Qadi Ahmad, to have fallen in repute through keeping low company. By 1616 he had

fallen from royal favor and was in want. Probably c1610, when he needed to accept private commissions, he started to use the suffix Abbasi, which may have been granted to him by the Shah.

The use of two prefixes led scholars to attribute the work of Riza to two artists, but their common identity was demonstrated in 1964 by Ivan Stchoukine.

Even after 1610 Riza continued to produce some fully colored miniatures (examples in the Hermitage Museum, St Petersburg, 1610; and Seattle Art Museum) as well as some manuscripts (examples dated 1614 formerly in the Rothschild Collection; examples dated 1632 in the Victoria and Albert Museum, London). But he was now mainly occupied with separate drawings of figure subjects, in which he had always shown virtuosity. These range from the early finished portraits of young men

Riza: A Girl with a Fan; 16×7cm (6×3in); c1590. Freer Gallery of Art, Washington, D.C.

and girls to later brilliant, rapid sketches in line and wash. This kind of work continued until his death in 1635, a date given on a portrait of him by his ablest pupil, Mu'in. Characteristic figure drawings are in the British Museum, London; the William Hayes Fogg Art Museum, Cambridge, Mass.; Freer Gallery of Art, Washington, D.C.; and the Bibliothèque Nationale, Paris.

Robbia Luca della 1400–82

Trained in the workshop of Florence Cathedral as a marble carver, Luca della Robbia was a major Renaissance sculptor, whose career overlapped the second half of those of Ghiberti and Donatello. He is famed for an important technical innovation: the use of vitreous glazes to color sculpture modeled in terracotta. This rendered polychrome sculpture impervious to damp, and therefore durable in external architectural settings. He worked with his nephew Andrea (1434–1525), who introduced virtual mass-production of such sculpture. Their reliefs of the *Virgin and Child*, and coats-of-arms, in glazed terracotta, abound on buildings in Tuscany and in museums (for example, Museo Nazionale, Florence; Victoria and Albert Museum, London).

Luca's first documented commission, in 1431, was a marble Singing Gallery for Florence Cathedral: its child-musicians carved in low relief are famous. He also produced other works for the cathedral authorities: five stone reliefs, to complete a series carved a century before by Andrea Pisano for Giotto's Campanile (1437–9); lunettes showing the *Resurrection* (1442–5) and *Ascension* (1446–51) to set over the Sacristy doors—his first major works in glazed terracotta; and a pair of bronze doors for the North Sacristy (1445–68).

Elsewhere, Luca combined polychrome terracotta with marble. His first datable use of the two was for a sacramental tabernacle in S. Maria, Peretola (1441–3). He combined them again on the Federighi tomb in S. Trinità, Florence (1454). He produced several quasi-architectural projects including two for Piero de' Medici, the Chapel of the Crucifix in S. Miniato al Monte, Florence (1448), and a study in the Medici Palace (demolished; roundels from its vault now in the Victoria and Albert Museum, London). He also designed two chapels in the pilgrimage shrine of S. Maria at Impruneta near Florence and made the ceiling of the Chapel of the Cardinal of Portugal in S. Miniato, in collaboration with the Rossellino brothers (1462). Of his many reliefs in glazed terracotta inserted into architecture, the most famous are the roundels of *Apostles* in Brunelleschi's Pazzi Chapel, S. Croce, Florence (c1442).

Luca was an exponent of the "sweet style" in Florentine sculpture, avoiding the sort of violent emotion to be seen in the late work of Donatello. He preferred the calmer, even domestic, mood that suited his principal patrons, the Florentine bourgeois.

Further reading. Baldini, U. *La Bottega dei Della Robbia*, Florence (1965). Marquand, A. *Luca della Robbia*, Princeton (1914). Pope-Hennessy, J. *Italian Renaissance Sculpture*, London (1958). Pope-Hennessy, J. *Luca della Robbia*, Oxford (1980).

Luca della Robbia: The Stemma of the Arte dei Medici e degli Speziali; enameled terracotta; diameter 180cm (71in); c1464–5. Orsanmichele, Florence

Robert Hubert 1733–1808

The French artist Hubert Robert was sometimes nicknamed "Robert des Ruines". He was a painter of landscapes both imagined and real. Born in Paris, he went to Rome in 1754 under the protection of the future Duc de Choiseul, whom he knew because his father worked for the family. He spent some time at the French Academy there, but much more important was the friendship he made with Fragonard and with the Abbé de Saint-Non. The latter was a dilettante who was to patronize both artists, and with whom they visited southern Italy and Sicily.

Robert's drawing style can be so close to that of his friend that attribution is sometimes difficult. His main claim to distinction is for his revival of the tradition of the

Hubert Robert: The Finding of the Laocoön; oil on canvas; 119×163cm (47×64in); 1773. Virginia Museum of Fine Arts, Richmond, Va

architectural and landscape *capriccio* in the manner of Giovanni Paolo Panini, a painter at the height of his fame while Robert was in Rome. Robert used a bright palette and a dashing technique; he had a large, romantic imagination, which underlined the atmosphere of the scenes he wished to represent.

The *capriccio*—the representation of real places with ruins gathered from afar, or equally of imaginary sites with real monuments or ruins—thrives on the vision of past grandeur, subjected to the picturesque action of time. Robert's views of the Villa d'Este at Tivoli, long past its efficient best by the 18th century, show a sense of the power of nature, and the pleasurably melancholic sensation of ruins. Diderot praised these elements enthusiastically when the artist returned to Paris in 1765. He became both popular and prolific,

exhibiting 40 paintings and drawings at the Salon of 1769. Diderot sometimes reproached him for his sketchy manner, and his unwillingness to finish his work— but realized that this enabled the artist to make more money.

As well as depicting bizarre subjects like *Rome on Fire* (1771) or *The Grand Gallery of the Louvre in Ruins* (1796; Louvre, Paris), Robert began in later years to paint topographical views of Paris, which are now of value to architectural historians interested in that era of great change. He was interested in the notion of the museum, and in 1784 was appointed curator for the new French institution that was to educate the people in the glories of art—the Louvre. His interest in the Picturesque can be paralleled by the most forceful manner of Piranesi. His style sometimes approaches that of his rival C.-J. Vernet.

Roberti Ercole de' 1456?–96

Ercole de' Roberti was a Ferrarese painter. He was probably a pupil of Francesco del Cossa, following him to Bologna in 1470 and completing several of his paintings, including a *predella* (Vatican Museums, Rome). He succeeded Cosmè Tura as court painter at Ferrara in 1486. Although his activities are well recorded, only one painting can be authenticated, an altarpiece of 1480–1 (Pinacoteca di Brera, Milan). His many ascribed works, including a *Pietà* (Walker Art Gallery, Liverpool), show his indebtedness to Mantegna, Tura, and—in the soft, misty light effects—to Giovanni Bellini. His figures, with their expressive gestures and poses, convey intense emotions rare in the Ferrarese School. (*See* overleaf.)

Ercole de' Roberti: Portrait of Ginevra Bentivoglio; panel; 54×39cm (21×15in); c1480. National Gallery of Art, Washington, D.C.

Roberts William 1895–1980

The English painter William Roberts began his career in 1909 as a commercial artist, but his precocious talent for drawing won him a scholarship to the Slade School of Fine Art, London (1910–13). There he made increasing use of Cubist techniques, a development strengthened by a visit to France and Italy in 1913. In 1914 he joined the circle around Wyndham Lewis and signed the Vorticist Manifesto. Roberts always maintained an independent line, and his own form of mechanized abstraction developed naturally from his earlier Cubist works (for example *Study for Twostep II*, c1915; private collection).

During the First World War (spent partly as an Official War Artist) and thereafter, Roberts returned to figuration and painted groups of people engaged in communal activities. His works retained the expressive angularity of his Vorticist period; but after 1927 his figures assumed a wholesome rotundity reminiscent of Fernand Léger's classical nudes.

Rockwell Norman 1894–1978

Norman Rockwell was probably the most famous of all American illustrators. His warm, humorous depictions of everyday, small-town life in Middle America are bright, realistic and full of anecdotal detail. He created over 300 covers for the *Saturday Evening Post* and his "Four Freedoms" posters, based on a speech by F.D. Roosevelt, became some of the most familiar American images of the Second World War. With typical modesty and simplicity he wrote: "I do ordinary people in everyday situations, and that's about all I do." From the Depression to the Cold War, Rockwell provided affectionate and comforting images of an America that was innocent, untroubled and decent.

Further reading. Finch, C. *Norman Rockwell's America*, New York (1975). Walton, D. *A Rockwell Portrait*, New York (1978).

Rodchenko Alexander 1891–1956

Alexander Rodchenko was a Russian artist and designer, whose abstract paintings of 1915 onwards were based on simple geometric forms made using a pencil and pair of compasses. The images are often superimposed to suggest a relief structure, in contrast to the floating shapes of Malevich's Suprematism, the mystical basis of which Rodchenko rejected. In 1917 he began making constructions in wood and iron, under the influence of Tatlin. His hanging constructions of 1920, which could turn freely in space, were among the earliest sculptures to incorporate real motion, and are his most original contribution to Constructivism.

In the 1920s, Rodchenko, like most other Constructivists, rejected pure art as a parasitical activity, and concentrated on applied art and poster design.

William Roberts: The Cinema; oil on canvas; 91×76cm (36×30in); 1920. Tate Gallery, London

Auguste Rodin: The Eternal Idol; plaster; 74×40×52cm (29×16×20in); 1889. Musée Rodin, Paris

Rodin Auguste 1840–1917

François-Auguste-René Rodin was born in Paris and worked there for most of his life. After many years of hardship and neglect he was eventually recognized as the greatest sculptor of his age and, lionized by society, enjoyed international renown.

Rodin's father was a clerk in the Paris Prefecture de Police and the family was always poor. Rodin was sent away to school, however, as his uncle ran a boarding-school at Beauvais. He showed little academic ability, and at 13 returned to

Paris and entered the École Impériale Spéciale de Dessin et de Mathématiques. This was known as the Petite École, because it trained craftsmen and designers rather than artists, who studied at the Grande École des Beaux-Arts. But Rodin worked diligently (one of his teachers was Horace Lecoq de Boisbaudran) and at 16 confidently expected to be accepted by the École des Beaux-Arts. He was rejected by the examining board on three successive applications. This was the first of a sequence of defeats that continued for almost a quarter of a century.

Rodin began the long series of menial tasks that were to allow him to study and do his own work at night. He attended classes held by the animal sculptor Antoine-Louis Barye (1796–1875) at the Jardin des Plantes. And he completed his first surviving sculpture, a portrait bust of his father, on which he worked for three years from 1857 to 1860.

In 1862, shocked by the death of his beloved elder sister, Maria, Rodin abandoned sculpture and entered the religious order of the Fathers of the Holy Sacrament, taking the name of Brother Augustin. But Father Pierre-Julian Eymard recognized Rodin's true vocation, sat to him for a fine portrait bust, and persuaded him to leave the Order and to return to sculpture.

For Rodin, it was a return to hardship. His great skills were employed anonymously by other, more successful, sculptors and masons. In 1864, he entered the workshop of Ernest Carrier-Belleuse, and so contributed to the sculptural decoration of many of the buildings of Paris. In the same year, his own work, the bronze *The Mask of the Man With a Broken Nose* (Musée Rodin, Paris) was rejected by the Salon. It was at this time that he met Marie-Rose Beuret; she became his mistress, bore him a son in 1866, and, in the last months of his life, became his wife.

With the outbreak of the Franco-Prussian War in 1870 Rodin was drafted into the National Guard as a corporal, but was quickly discharged because of his weak eyesight. He accepted Carrier-Belleuse's invitation to work in Brussels. After a short time, Carrier-Belleuse left Brussels, but Rodin stayed on, in partnership with the Belgian sculptor Antoine Joseph van Rasbourg (1831–1902).

Very slowly, the tide began to turn. *The Mask of the Man With a Broken Nose*, remodeled as a bust and sculpted in marble, was accepted for the Brussels Salon of 1872; and, 11 years after its original rejection, it was accepted for the Paris Salon of 1875. In 1875, Rodin visited Italy for the first time, traveling to Turin, Genoa, Naples, Pisa and Venice, as well as to Florence and Rome.

Returning to Brussels, he hired a young soldier as a model and began 18 months' work on a life-size male nude. In January 1877, at the Brussels Salon, a plaster cast of this figure held a lance and was called *The Conquered*, in tribute to the fallen of the recent War; but later that year, at the Paris Salon, it was shown without a lance and called *The Age of Bronze* (Musée Rodin, Paris). It was Rodin's first major work and aroused controversy. Despite the statue's debt to Michelangelo 1475–1564) and Donatello (c1386–1466), the jury in Paris was unwilling to recognize that an unknown sculptor could have produced such a work, and suspected that it had been cast directly from the flesh of its model. But its merit could not be denied; and three years later, when a bronze cast was shown at the Salon, it was awarded a third-class medal and bought by the State.

Initial response, however, was disappointing. When Rodin returned to Paris in 1877 with his mistress and son, he continued as a journeyman working for other sculptors. In 1879, Carrier-Belleuse employed him as a designer for the Sèvres porcelain factory. At home, Rodin was working on his second male nude, the striding *John the Baptist* (Musée Rodin, Paris). The statue was exhibited in plaster beside the bronze *Age of Bronze*, at the Salon of 1880, and Rodin, who was almost 40, was recognized as the supreme master he had become.

His success was sealed when, in August 1880, he was invited to design doors for the projected Museum of Decorative Arts of Paris. He was given a handsome advance, and studios in the government Dépôt des Marbres. On a full-scale framework, he was soon developing an elaborate composition of several hundred figures. An early drawing shows that his original scheme followed the tradition established by Ghiberti's bronze doors for the Baptistery of Florence Cathedral, the Doors of Paradise. Rodin chose his imagery from Dante's great poem, the *Inferno;* and for this reason, and perhaps in contrast to Ghiberti's doors, his have become known as *The Gate of Hell* (now in the Musée Rodin, Paris). Rodin soon abandoned the regular panels of Ghiberti's design, in favor of a fluid open rhythm of writhing bodies recalling Michelangelo's fresco of the *Last Judgment* in the Sistine Chapel. In the center of the tympanum, where Christ in Majesty sits in the portals of Gothic churches, Rodin placed *The Thinker*, brooding over Man's folly and sin.

By 1884, the Gate was substantially complete; but when the enormous sum needed to pay for its casting was calculated, the project lapsed. In 1888 Rodin received a further advance, but the Gate remained unfinished until nine years after his death.

A bronze was finally made in 1926, a monument to the artist rather than to the unbuilt museum. Rodin never really stopped work on the doors. He made alterations and additions on several occasions, and took individual motifs from it that he elaborated into separate works.

In the following decade, Rodin received a number of important public commissions, and most of them led to controversy. In 1884, the city of Calais proposed a monument to its hero, Eustache de St Pierre, the leader of the six burghers who had given themselves as hostages to the besieging English in 1347. Rodin suggested that for the same fee he should represent all six burghers. He made numerous studies, including larger-than-life nude figures for three of the burghers. For their weighty limbs and gestures of despair he drew from Michelangelo, but also from the medieval Northern sculptor, Claus Sluter (c1350–1406). The final version is a noble, tragic image, a blend of individual characterizations and heroic rhythms. Although the work was completed by 1889, it was not until 1895 that it was erected, and then it was not at the height that Rodin had wished, nor in the site he had intended.

He received two state commissions for a monument to Victor Hugo for the Panthéon: in 1889, and again in 1892; but neither was considered suitable for the intended site. The pedestals of his monument to the painter Claude Lorrain for the town of Nancy (1889–92), and of his monument to the Argentinian President Sarmiento in Buenos Aires were both disliked. His sketch for a monument to the painter J.A.M. Whistler (1843–1903), intended for London's Chelsea Embankment, was rejected in 1908.

But it was the commission for a monument to the French novelist Honoré de Balzac that created the greatest scandal of Rodin's career. The Société des Gens de Lettres had originally given the commission to Henri-Michel-Antoine Chapu (1833–91); but on Chapu's death, the Society's President, Emile Zola, proposed Rodin. Balzac had died in 1850 and Rodin researched into his appearance and character with great thoroughness. He read the novels, looked for photographs, visited Balzac's home town, and even had a suit made up by the writer's tailor. After numerous preliminary studies, he created a strange, contorted image of the writer's enormous maned head emerging from a loose dressing gown; contemporaries cari-

catured it as a performing seal. When he exhibited the plaster at the Salon of 1898, the committee of the Society declared that it was unfinished and canceled the contract. Rodin was bitterly hurt, as he considered the *Balzac* (versions in the Sculpture Garden, Museum of Modern Art, New York; Musée Rodin, Paris) to be his most important work. (The Italian sculptor Medardo Rosso claimed that Rodin had stolen the unusual idea from him.)

None of these controversies interrupted the gradual rise of Rodin's fame. In 1887, the French State commissioned a large marble version of *The Kiss* (Musée Rodin, Paris). In 1888, it awarded the sculptor with the Cross of Chevalier de la Légion d'Honneur. In 1889, he shared an exhibition with the Impressionist Claude Monet at the Galerie Georges Petit. In 1893, he was made President of the sculpture section of the Société National des Beaux-Arts. And when, in 1900, he built his own pavilion in the Place de l'Alma for the Paris World Fair his exhibition was very successful.

By now his reputation was international. In 1902, on his visit to London, the art students of the Slade harnessed themselves to his carriage and drew him in triumph through the streets. In 1903, he was made President of the International Society of Sculptors, Painters, and Gravers.

His fame had not come simply from his official commissions: rather, he had received them because of his fame. His reputation had also been created by his portraits. Bernard Shaw, whose portrait bust was made by Rodin in 1906, said, "any man who, being a contemporary of Rodin, deliberately allowed his bust to be made by anyone else, must go down to posterity (if he went down at all) as a stupendous nincompoop". After 1900, Rodin could charge whatever sum he liked for his portrait busts.

But the ultimate source of his reputation lay in the sensuous nude figures he exhibited at the Salons. For years, many of these pieces were individual motifs extracted from *The Gate of Hell*. *The Kiss* was originally Dante's lovers, Paolo and Francesca, on the left-hand door. But although he gave his pieces traditional titles, these were afterthoughts, and even concealed his true subject. For example, *The Fallen Angel* has also been called *The Fall of Icarus*, but as in *Metamorphoses of Ovid* (before 1896), the motif is two women passionately embracing.

Auguste Rodin: Balzac (nude study);
bronze; 73×30×36cm
(30×12×14in); 1893. Musée Rodin,
Paris

**Auguste Rodin: Cambodian Dancer; pencil and
wash on paper. Musée Rodin, Paris**

Rodin's imagery had been frankly sexual
from the time that Camille Claudel (1856–
1943) became his pupil and his mistress, in
1882. But from the beginning, his true
theme had been the emotional significance
of the human body, the powerful sugges-
tiveness of a gesture, a pose, or even of a
muscular rhythm. His intuition of physical
rhythms enabled him to break with the
sculptural stereotypes that had been
handed down from the time of Bernini. He
developed new forms and a new vision of
the human body.

His sense of the expressiveness of his
inventions led him to the odd practice of
combining separate figures, or even limbs,
into new combinations; he would also, in
reminiscence of timeworn antique sculptures, exhibit fragments as whole works.

The foundation of his art was his prodigious skill as a modeler. He could be meticulously exact, but he worked with a fluency
that gives his bronzes an uncanny surface
at once like and also elusively unlike the
body it represents.

He continued working until his old age.
Some of his most original pieces are small
sketches of dancers made after 1910. In
1914 he published a book on one of his
early loves, *The Cathedrals of France*.

Further reading. Cladel, J. *Rodin*, London and New York (1967). Elson, A.E. *In Rodin's Studio*, Oxford (1980). Goldscheider, L. *Rodin Sculptures*, Oxford (1979). Sutton, D. *Triumphant Satyr: the World of Auguste Rodin*, London (1963). Tancock, J. *The Sculptures of Auguste Rodin, the Collection of the Rodin Museum in Philadelphia*, Philadelphia (1976). Thorson, V. *Rodin's Graphics*, California (1975).

Rogers Richard 1933–

The British architect Richard Rogers is one of the leading exponents of "high-tech" architecture. He studied at the Architecture Association, London, and at Yale University. In the 1960s he and Norman Foster (together with their wives, Sue Rogers and Wendy Foster) formed the Team 4 partnership, their most important work being the innovatory Reliance Controls Factory, Swindon (1966–67), which in its uncompromising use of technology as the basis of design set the keynote of their approach. Rogers achieved international fame with his flamboyant and controversial Beaubourg or Pompidou Center (1971–77), Paris, designed with Renzo Piano (1937–). A confident assertion of functionalism, it is built with its structure clearly visible, its services (such as escalators and brightly colored ducts) arranged on the outside to leave a large interior space open. Rogers took a similar approach in his equally confident, equally controversial, Lloyd's Insurance Building in London (1979–86).

Further reading. Appleyard, B. *Richard Rogers: A Biography*, London (1986).

Romanino c1484–c1559

Gerolamo da Romano, known as Romanino, was a prolific artist, born in Brescia, the leading master of the Brescian school of Renaissance painting. His native city, situated on the border between the Duchy of Milan and the Venetian Empire, changed hands several times during the 15th and 16th centuries, and Romanino's art was subject to both Lombard and Venetian influences.

Also important was a Teutonic strain which must have reached him through the Alpine valleys to the north. Romanino was an artist of the High Renaissance, working in the same mode as Giorgione or Titian;

Romanino: Madonna and Child with Saints, the great altarpiece painted for S. Giustina, Padua; oil on panel; 400×262cm (157×103in); 1513. Museo Civico, Padua

but at times there is a squat, peasant grotesqueness about his figures, more reminiscent of Conrad Witz or Grünewald than of the Italians.

He was Venetian in the central role he gave to color, in his free open brushwork, and in the importance of landscape in his paintings. But the smoky effects of light characteristic of his art were Lombard (they owed much to Vincenzo Foppa), and the particular visual qualities of the mountainous valley landscape behind Brescia were fundamental in his formation. Many of his paintings have wooded, mountain backgrounds. Often, as for example in his *St Alessandro* from the high altar of the Brescian church of that name (now National Gallery, London), the figure is seen from below, and is set directly against a vivid blue sky glimpsed through a patchwork of gray clouds. The light is stormy and the sense of space vertiginous.

Romanino used a network of loose brush strokes which convey, through their open structure, a sense of floating forms momentarily apprehended in a passing effect of light. Both his vision as a whole and his manner of recording it are, although Venetian in principle, entirely personal; they show him to be an original master of the first quality.

His career was chequered, and much of his most striking work was done for remote country villages. His early style can be seen in the great altarpiece, rich in color, texture, and largeness of form, that he painted for S. Giustina, Padua (1513; now Museo Civico, Padua). It can be seen, too, in the *Virgin and Saints* in Salò Cathedral, where the figures are placed in a stormy landscape and united with it by a tempestuous effect of light.

From 1519 to 1520 he painted in the Duomo, Cremona, continuing the cycle of frescoes begun by Boccacino and Altobello Melone. The scenes, which represent the Passion of Christ, are typical of this artist in the factual realism with which they narrate the stories; this clearly shows Northern influence, and here relates directly to Albrecht Dürer's engraved *Passion*. Romanino was, however, displaced by Pordenone, whose flashy illusionism had perhaps a more immediate appeal.

Romney George 1734–1802

The English painter George Romney was born near Dalton-in-Furness, Lancashire (now in Cumbria), and was apprenticed in 1755 to the itinerant portrait painter Christopher Steele. In the 1760s he gained prominence in London as a society portrait painter. He studied in Italy from 1773 to 1775. Shortly after returning to London, he met the poet William Hayley, who introduced him to a wide circle of literary figures and encouraged his interest in history painting. His most ambitious design in this vein, and one of the few to be realized on canvas, was *The Tempest* (now destroyed). It was commissioned by John Boydell in 1786 for his Shakespeare Gallery.

Romney remained a proficient, albeit reluctant portraitist throughout his career. In such pictures as *The Levenson-Gower Children* (1776–7; Abbot Hall Art Gallery, Kendal) he often achieved an incomparable lyricism and sensitivity. His genius as an artist, however, is more profitably measured by his oil sketches (many of which were inspired by Emma Hart, later Lady Hamilton, in the 1780s), and also by his profuse figure-drawings, which treat a wide range of horrific and sublime subjects from literature, history, and mythology.

Roriczer Matthäus *fl. 1486–c92/5*

Matthäus Roriczer was a German master mason and a member of a family of masons who were employed at Regensburg Cathedral for three generations. He is also recorded at work on other south German churches and from this experience he wrote a textbook *On the Ordination of Pinnacles*, published in 1486. It reveals, with diagrams, how medieval masons

worked according to a system of proportions. Once given the size of the pinnacle base, and the intended height as a multiple of the side of the base, they had sufficient information to erect the pinnacle. Significantly, the method could be applied to constructing other elements of a church.

Rosa Salvator 1615–73

The Neapolitan artist Salvator Rosa was taught by Francesco Fracanzano, Aniello Falcone, and possibly by Jusepe de Ribera. It was in Naples that he developed his predilection for a dark palette and for fiery battle scenes and violent subject matter.

In 1635 he went to Rome, where he painted small genre scenes. Then in 1640, having angered Bernini, he moved to Florence as court painter to the Medici. Here Rosa, a brilliant conversationalist, actor, and musician, became the center of a glittering array of intellectuals, and began to write satirical poetry deriding the decadence of the court. he painted seaports

George Romney: A Lady in a Brown Dress: "The Parson's Daughter"; oil on canvas; 65×65cm (26×26in); c1785. Tate Gallery, London

and pastoral landscapes (influenced by Paul Bril and by Claude Lorrain), portraits, and macabre scenes of witches. Also, with works such as *Moral Philosophy* (Palazzo Enzelberg, Caldaro), he introduced a new type of allegorical painting.

Rosa returned to Rome in 1649, and from this date became obsessed with a desire to paint great historical compositions. His subjects were erudite and often inspired by Stoic doctrines; the influence of Poussin is clear. The theme of vanity fascinated him. In his *Democritus* (National Museum, Copenhagen) he pours bitter scorn on human achievement, while the *Humana Fragilitas* (c1657; Fitzwilliam Museum, Cambridge) is an intensely poetic meditation on the brevity of human life. At this time Rosa made his most significant contribution to landscape: his scenes are wild and desolate, the skies dark and stormy, and the twisted, shaggy trees are swept by thundery wind.

Rebellious and "savage", Rosa fascinated the 18th century. His sublime landscapes and his etchings of bandits played an important part in early Romanticism.

Rosenquist James 1933–

The American Pop painter James Rosenquist was born in Grand Forks, North Dakota. He studied under Cameron Booth at Minnesota University (1952–4) and at the Art Students League, New York. While still a student he began working as an advertising billboard painter, and this became a full time occupation from 1957 to 1960. It proved the dominant influence on his paintings, which had previously been Abstract Expressionist in style. Since 1961, his style has remained relatively unchanged. He paints fragments of banal images of America, in contrasting scales, and especially in huge close-ups, derived from mass media and advertising. These are ironically and ambiguously juxtaposed, in a smooth photographic manner. Some of his paintings are extremely large (for example, *Flamingo Capsule*; Leo Castelli Gallery, New York), incorporating real objects and sheets of reflective materials. He began filmmaking in 1969.

Rosetsu Nagasawa 1755–99

The Japanese painter Nagasawa Rosetsu was a pupil of Okyo, whose ink monochrome style he learned; his works were

Salvator Rosa: Self-portrait; oil on canvas; 116×94cm (46×37in); c1641. National Gallery, London

even better than those of his master. Rosetsu's brilliant and vigorous originality in large-scale ink compositions, like the great tiger in the Okyo-Rosetsu Museum, Kushimoto, has given him the misleading label of eccentric. Much of his work is in fact done with a tightly controlled yet breathtaking technique, and in color work on silk he could paint with a clean precision rarely equalled (for example, his *Bird and Flower* handscroll in Kyoto National Museum). Rosetsu is Japan's finest animal and bird painter, imbuing his subjects—whether monkeys, tigers, toads, or sparrows—with an inner life partly humorous and partly pathetic.

Roslin Alexandre 1718–93

The Swedish born portrait painter Alex-

James Rosenquist: Marilyn; screenprint; 91×69cm (36×27in); 1974. Tate Gallery, London

andre Roslin worked mainly in Paris. After training in Sweden and traveling in Germany (1745–7), he went to Italy (1747–51) where he studied the portrait style of Francesco Solimena. He settled in Paris in 1752. A member of the Académie in 1753, he exhibited regularly at the Paris Salon throughout his life. His sober and sometimes stiff portraits were popular in court circles, in France and in northern European countries. Between 1774 and 1779 he traveled in northern and eastern Europe. His style lacks brilliance, wit, or excitement; but his virtues of solidity and observation maintained a steady though unfashionable reputation. His famous *Lady with a Fan* (1768; National Museum, Stockholm) is a portrait of his wife.

Rosselli Cosimo 1439–1507

Cosimo Rosselli was a Florentine painter. Though a pupil of Neri di Bicci from 1453 to 1456, he was much influenced by Benozzo Gozzoli. From 1481 to 1482 he was in Rome, painting four of the frescoes on the walls of the Sistine Chapel: these were scenes from the life of Moses and the life of Christ. At Florence he painted other frescoes, including *The Miracle of the Holy Blood* (1485–6; S. Ambrogio), and a

Cosimo Rosselli: Portrait of a Man; tempera on wood; 52×33cm (20×13in); c1481–2. Metropolitan Museum, New York

number of often large but usually conventional altarpieces. Rosselli, though competent, was never quite as good as his contemporaries, Botticelli, Perugino, or Ghirlandaio; his paintings were rather cluttered and his style lacked flair.

Rossellino brothers 15th century

The Italian sculptors Bernardo and Antonio Rossellino came from the quarry-town of Settignano. Although they were brothers, the separation in their birth dates consigned them to different generations. Bernardo (1409–64) trained Antonio (1427–79) and possibly also Desiderio da Settignano (c1428–64) in marble sculpture and architectural design. Bernardo's earliest known work, the facade of the Palazzo della Fraternita dei Laici at Arezzo (1433–6), shows his particular ability in combining sculpture with architecture. After executing a monument to the Florentine Chancellor Leonardo Bruni in S. Croce, Florence, and some distinguished sacramental tabernacles and other decorative sculpture, Bernardo devoted most of his time to architecture, erecting the Rucellai Palace in Florence (1446–51; designed by Alberti). He was subsequently appointed papal architect (holding the post from 1451 to 1453), built the new town of Pienza for Pope Pius II (1460–3), and ended his career as architect of Florence Cathedral.

Antonio's first signed work is a bust of Giovanni Chellini, Donatello's doctor (1456; Victoria and Albert Museum, London). Carved only three years after Mino da Fiesole's bust of Piero de' Medici (Museo Nazionale, Florence), it is one of the supreme portraits of the 15th century in Florence. Antonio collaborated with Bernardo on a number of projects, the most famous of which is the tomb-chapel of the Cardinal of Portugal at S. Miniato al Monte, Florence (1459–66), for which Luca della Robbia made the ceiling and the Pollaiuolo brothers the altarpiece. Antonio was active as a marble sculptor throughout the third quarter of the century and with Desiderio da Settignano was the principal exponent of the "Sweet" style. He specialized in reliefs, especially of the Virgin and Child, and he trained the sculptor and architect Benedetto da Maiano.

Bernardo Rossellino: monument to Leonardo Bruni; marble; c1444–7. S. Croce, Florence

Rossetti D.G. 1828–82

The Englishman Dante Gabriel Rossetti was both painter and poet. He came from a talented family: his father was a political refugee from Naples who became Professor of Italian at King's College, London; his sister, Christina Rossetti, became an important poet; and his brother, William Michael Rossetti, was an art critic. In his youth Rossetti (born Gabriel Charles Dante) vacillated between writing and painting; as no other English artist has done, with the exception of Blake, he achieved a marriage between the two arts.

After five years at King's College School, London, Rossetti joined Saas' Drawing Academy in 1841. At that time this was the traditional first step towards an artistic career; it led to a probationership and then studentship at the Royal Academy Schools. Here he met the young John Everett Millais and Holman Hunt; with four other associates they formed the Pre-Raphaelite Brotherhood in September 1848.

Although very much their inferior in painterly skill, Rossetti quickly became leader of the group: his conspicuous personality and fiery imagination inspired them in their choice of subjects for their pictures, as well as influencing their whole lifestyle and attitude to established society. Rossetti's first painting, *The Girlhood of Mary* (1849; Tate Gallery, London) was the first picture bearing the notorious initials "P.R.B." to be shown to the public. It was hung at the National Institution, which opened before the Royal Academy. This and *Ecce Ancilla Domini* ("Behold the Handmaid of the Lord"; Tate Gallery, London) were his only publicly exhibited works.

From 1851 Rossetti produced, almost exclusively, smaller works in watercolors and chalks. He found his subjects at first in the writings of Shakespeare, Dante, and Robert Browning; after 1856 he took them also from the Arthurian tales of Malory and Tennyson. These strongly worked, dramatically charged figure-scenes reflect the artist's inner life with an almost expressionist intensity. They create a world entirely different from the purely naturalistic one aimed at by Hunt and Millais, yet art historians refer to them all as "Pre-Raphaelite". Rossetti's naive style inspired the first phase of Pre-Raphaelitism in the late 1840s. It was then developed by him and imitated by admirers such as Burne-Jones and William Morris, and this new style also became known as Pre-Raphael-

Antonio Rossellino: Giovanni Chellini; marble; height 51cm (20in); 1456. Victoria and Albert Museum, London

ite; hence the confusion.

Rossetti was an imperious, generous, and enthusiastic man. His willingness to express himself in paint was not equaled by his facility of hand; compared to those of his friends, his works seem gauche. Yet the sheer frustration of the artist is part of their strength and magic. In them Rossetti developed a style out of naivety that influenced a whole generation; this was facilitated by the championship and protection of the critic John Ruskin. It is remarkable that Ruskin saw, and to the best of his ability nurtured, Rossetti's genius. Ruskin liked to dominate; Rossetti was beyond his control; but the critic was able to win him important new patrons among the collectors from the northern industrial towns.

As a result of Ruskin's appreciation of Rossetti's works in the press, Burne-Jones and William Morris, then graduates at Oxford, came to London in 1856 with the intention of becoming his disciples or students. This led to the decoration of the newly built Oxford Union Building Debating Hall with scenes from Arthurian legends. The young men who worked there with Rossetti, intoxicated by his charismatic influence, formed the second circle of Pre-Raphaelites, the first to have a distinctive style of its own, rather than a vague desire to challenge the Academy. The frescoes they painted quickly faded, since the ground had been most amateurishly prepared; but the ideas they formulated there lived on.

In 1861 Rossetti joined Morris and Burne-Jones as a founder-member of the

D.G. Rossetti: Ecce Ancilla Domini! (The Annunciation); oil on canvas; 74×41cm (29×17in); 1850. Tate Gallery, London

form. The most important model for these works was Elizabeth Siddal, with whom he lived at Blackfriars for ten years. They were finally married in 1860, and her death two years later from an overdose of laudanum was a blow from which he never recovered. He buried her with a sheaf of unpublished poems, and painted one last visionary portrait of her, as Dante's *Beata Beatrix* (*c*1863; Tate Gallery, London), perhaps his greatest work.

Those poems, which he was later persuaded to exhume and publish (as *The House of Life*, 1870), together with early writings for the P.R.B. journal *The Germ*, and translations from Dante, constitute the body of Rossetti's literary output.

After Elizabeth Siddal's death he continued to paint beautiful, idealized women, often in bust-length portraits, treated as historical or mythological figures such as Joan of Arc or Venus. A number of models posed for these works, but most of them are based on the features of either Fanny Cornforth, who lived with the artist at Cheyne Walk, or of Jane Morris, William Morris' wife, with whom Rossetti had a long and painful love affair. The pictures are frequently accompanied by verses from the artist's own pen; some explain the pictures while others are the pictures' sources of inspiration. The powerful women depicted by Rossetti relate strongly to the idea of the *femme fatale* evoked by the poet Algernon Charles Swinburne, who was included in the P.R.B. circle.

The style of these pictures is akin to the weighty classicism of George Moore, which was for a period in the 1860s an important source of ideas for many artists. Rossetti's frequent use of Japanese ephemera reflects another current phase, while his treatment of design and color is similar to that of J.A.M. Whistler and Frederick Sandys (1829–1904).

In the late 1860s his art entered its last period. Moving on to larger canvases, and working with darker colors, Rossetti painted new sinewy, swirling patterns around his symbolic figures. A work like *Astarte Syriaca* (1877; Manchester City Art Gallery) reflects his pursuit of the occult: Jane Morris' face is uplifted into a spiritual world, surrounded by the mannered forms of two attendants who press upwards against the top of the frame. The work has something of the naivety of the early watercolors, but there is also a lack of dexterity, a new attenuated curve of the lips, and a deadness in the eyes, which

decorating firm that became known as Morris, Marshall, Faulkner and Company. The influence of their designs for furniture and tapestries, and their bold emphasis upon weighty medieval forms, shaped

many of the first concepts of late Victorian aestheticism.

By the late 1850s the nervous tensions of Rossetti's earlier works began to give way to a more luxurious enjoyment of line and

were not there in *Beata Beatrix*. The familiar expression of longing for love has turned bitter. There is a cruel streak in the late pictures which, with their hard, mannered forms, leads directly on to the style of Art Nouveau and the Symbolist era, especially in a work like *La Piadé Tolomei* (1881; University of Kansas Museum of Art, Lawrence, Kansas) which also uses Jane Morris as its model.

At each stage of his career, from his early student days up to the last, when he wished to withdraw from the eyes of society, Rossetti's art was a constant source of inspiration for painters both older and younger than himself. From the mid 1860s his position as a leader-figure dwindled, but the style he had encouraged continued to flourish.

At his house in Cheyne Walk, Chelsea, he gathered around him a considerable group of admirers, and a strange collection of animals; but neither of these bolstered up his deepening depressions. He became addicted to chloral. Despite late efforts to wean himself from it, the support of his friend Ford Madox Brown, and a recuperative stay at Kelmscott House with the family of William Morris, he died in a deep state of paranoia.

Rossetti's works can be seen at the Tate Gallery, London, at Manchester City Art Gallery, at the City Museum and Art Gallery, Birmingham, and in other collections.

Further reading. Doughty, O. *A Victorian Romantic: Dante Gabriel Rossetti*, London (1949). Fleming, G. *Rossetti and the Pre-Raphaelite Brotherhood*, London (1967). Gaunt, W. *The Restless Century*, London (1972). Rose, A. *The Pre-Raphaelites*, Oxford (1977).

Rosso Fiorentino 1494–1540

The Italian painter Giovanni Battista di Jacopo was born at Florence. One of the originators of Florentine Mannerism, he became known as Rosso Fiorentino. Although nothing certain is known about his training—though he acquired at this early stage a reputation for contrariness—he probably studied under Andrea del Sarto together with the painter Jacopo Pontormo; his training was certainly complete by 1513.

His first major work was the fresco of the *Assumption* (1516–17; SS. Annunziata, Florence). His innovations in style may

have been encouraged by the example of Donatello's late reliefs. In his altarpiece *Madonna and Saints* (1518; Uffizi, Florence) Rosso proclaimed a counterassertion to Florentine classicism, replacing plastic and counterpoised forms with shapes that are angular, eccentric, dissonant, and nervous. His work displayed an anticlassical fragmentation and abstraction, in which unity is governed by highly pitched emotionalism rather than by formal relationships. He continued in this manner, even to the point of violence, in such works as the *Deposition* (1521; Pinacoteca Comunale, Volterra) and *Moses and the Daughters of Jethro* (c1523; Uffizi, Florence). His apparently willful pursuit of the unwonted was somewhat abated during his stay in Rome from 1524, where he encountered the decorative work of Michelangelo, and of Raphael and his followers. Little remains from this Roman period, during which he gathered materials he was to use at Fontainebleau.

The Sack of Rome (1527) drove him to the provinces. His emotionalism returned to a degree verging on hysteria in his *Deposition* of 1527–8 (S. Lorenzo, Borgo San Sepolcro). By 1530 he reached Venice and there met the humanist Pietro Aretino, who recommended him to Francis I of France. In the same year he entered the king's service at Fontainebleau.

Rosso's personal cultivation as well as his skill especially favored him with the French king. Francis appointed him as his principal painter, at the head of a team of artists and artisans gathered for the decoration of the newly built enlargements to the Palace of Fontainebleau. His adjutant, from 1532, was Primaticcio. Two pictures painted in France survive, both from the last years of his life: an unfinished *Madonna and Child with St Anne* (Los Angeles County Museum of Art, Los Angeles) and a monumental *Pietà* (Louvre, Paris).

His chief works, the decorations at Fontainebleau, have been largely destroyed. The exception is the Gallery of Francis I (1534–9), which has been recently restored. Its frescoes, containing recondite allusions to Francis, are set within fantasticated stucco framing of Rosso's design. The general arrangement is covertly dependent on the ceiling of the Sistine Chapel, while a number of the details openly allude to—or wittily pervert—Michelangelo's work. This variegated and striking scheme is particularly inventive in the stucco figures and ornaments. The latter offer the

Rosso Fiorentino (attrib.): Madonna and Child. Private collection

first examples of strap-work, a whimsical, abstract motif which was to become commonplace of Mannerist decoration in northern Europe.

Rosso, who lived in France "like a prince", is reported to have committed suicide.

Rosso Medardo 1858–1928

Medardo Rosso was an Italian sculptor, designer, and writer, who sought to find a plastic equivalent to the paintings of the Impressionists. Born in Turin, he moved to Milan with his family in 1870. After military service, he entered the Brera Academy, Milan, in 1882, only to be expelled the following year for disrupting classes. The next six years were spent in Milan, with brief visits to Rome, in 1883, for an exhibition of his work, and to Paris, in 1884, where he assisted the sculptor, Aimé-Jules Dalou. Rosso initially worked in clay and bronze, producing sculptures such as *The Last Kiss* (1882; now destroyed). This reflects the influence of the late-Romantic, avant-garde movement of Milan, the "Scapigliatura", with which Rosso was associated. By 1886, the year in which he executed *The Golden Age* (Galleria Comunale d'Arte Moderna, Rome), Rosso had not only adopted greater generalization in the handling of subject matter but had also employed the new technique of pouring wax over plaster. Both of these features were to characterize the rest of his work.

Rosso settled in Paris in 1889, remaining there until 1897. After a period of great physical privation, lack of recognition, and severe ill-health, he began to establish a reputation greatly helped by two exhibitions of his work held in 1893 at Charles Bodinière's Théâtre d'Application. It was here that he exchanged works with Rodin. The ensuing mutual admiration of the two sculptors has led to the suggestion that it was Rosso's influence that caused Rodin to clothe his nude *Balzac* in a dressing gown, and to alter the statue's stance.

For the last 3 r years of his life Rosso lived in Italy, producing no further original work apart from the *Ecce Puer* (1907; Musée de Luxembourg, Paris). Instead he devoted his energies to traveling across Europe organizing exhibitions of his works.

Rosso rejected all dependence upon the rules of antique sculpture, such as a constantly changing viewpoint and a clearly articulated silhouette. He was influenced by Baudelaire's belief that painting could alone qualify as "Ideal Art", because it was limited to one viewpoint and hence to the presentation of a finite image. So he sought to create sculpture that would approximate as closely as possible to this end. Furthermore, he saw the form of a sculptured figure as imprecise, its edges softened by the light emanating from the space the figure inhabits, thus fusing its form with its environment. These guiding principles in Rosso's art are illustrated in his mature work, *Conversation in the Garden* (1893; Collection of Dr Gianni Mattioli, Milan).

Roszak Theodore 1907–81

The American sculptor and printmaker Theodore Roszak was born in Poznan, Poland, and emigrated with his family to Chicago in 1909. He became an American citizen in 1919. In the late 1920s he studied at the Art Institute of Chicago, Illinois University, Urbana, Columbia University, and at the Academy of Design, New York. A fellowship for lithography enabled him to study in Europe between 1929 and 1931. He was exposed to European modernism first in Prague and then in Paris. From 1936 to 1945 he made geometric constructions in wood and plastic, while teaching at the New York Design

Mark Rothko: Red on Maroon, from the series of panels in the Tate Gallery, London; oil on canvas; 267×239cm (105×94in); 1959

Laboratory, guided by Laszlo Moholy-Nagy. Then he began working in welded and brazed metal, producing his characteristic sculptures with their free and often spiky forms alluding to nature. His public commissions include the eagle on the United States Embassy in London (1960).

Rothko Mark 1903–70

Mark Rothko was a Russian-born painter of the American School. He was born at Dvinsk in Russia, but in 1913 emigrated with his family to Portland, Oregon. In 1921 he went to Yale University to study the liberal arts, but left there in 1923 because of an insufficient interest in academic training. In 1925 he settled in New York and began to draw from the model. He also attended Max Weber's class at the Art Students League. He began to teach

children at the Center Academy, Brooklyn, in 1929, and continued to do so until 1952. In 1933 came his first one-man show at the Contemporary Arts Gallery, New York, while from 1936 to 1937 he worked on the Works Progress Administration Federal Arts Project in New York. In 1935 he had been cofounder of "The Ten", a group of artists with Expressionist sympathies who were to exhibit together for nearly ten years. In 1945, he had another one-man show, at Peggy Guggenheim's New York gallery.

Rothko's earlier work has Surrealist overtones (for example, *Baptismal Scene*, 1945; Whitney Museum of American Art, New York). It was not until the later 1940s that his most individual and characteristic style began to emerge. At first, it consisted of shapes with ragged edges loosely composed into an Abstract composition (for example, *No. 18*, 1948, Vassar College Art Gallery, Poughkeepsie, New York; *No. 24*, 1949, Joseph Hirshhorn Museum, Washington, D.C.). During the 1950s, Rothko refined his approach. The typical Rothko canvas is upright, and contains one, two, or three rectangular (or lozenge-shaped) areas of color set against a single-color background. The edges of the areas are blurred, and there is usually a variation in the density of both the areas and the background. The effect of the best Rothkos is luminous, serene, and grave. The Tate Gallery in London owns the series of panels that Rothko had at first intended for the decoration of a New York restaurant. There are examples of his work in most of the world's leading galleries of Modern Art, including the Art Institute, Chicago, and the Museum of Modern Art, New York.

Further reading. Ashton, D. *About Rothko*, New York (1983). *Mark Rothko*, Zurich (1971). Selz, P. *Mark Rothko*, New York (1961). Waldman, D. *Mark Rothko*, London and New York (1978).

Rottmayr von Rosenbrunn J.F.M. 1654–1730

The leading early-18th-century painter active in Vienna, Johann Franz Michael Rottmayr von Rosenbrunn spent 13 years from 1675 onwards working in the studio of J.C. Loth in Venice. After his return to Austria in 1687, Rottmayr first worked for the Bishop of Passau and the Archbishop of Salzburg before settling in Vienna, probably in 1696. He was ennobled in 1704. He was the first Germanic monumental painter to break the domination of the Italian painters in central Europe, and was active in Bohemia, Moravia, and Silesia, as well as in Pommersfelden. His dark, forceful early style subsequently gave way to more open compositions painted in lighter colors.

Rouault Georges 1871–1958

The French painter and printmaker Georges Rouault was born in Paris, the son of a carpenter. At the age of 14 he served an apprenticeship in two stained-glass workshops. The depth and purity of color and the heavy black enclosing lines in medieval glass were greatly to affect his later work. He was also much influenced by Gustave Moreau, whose pupil he

became in 1891. At about this time he met Matisse, and other painters who were later to be Fauves. After Moreau's death in 1898, he became curator of the Musée Gustave Moreau, Paris. In 1904, he met and was much impressed by the Catholic writer Léon Bloy.

The first unmistakable Rouault style appeared in 1903–4 in a series of "dark" gouaches devoted to acrobats, clowns, pierrots, and prostitutes. In Bloy's words, Rouault wished "to thrust at God the insistent cry of dereliction and anxiety for the orphaned multitude". Some of these were included in the Salon d'Automne of 1905. By 1908, he began his series of studies of judges and lawcourts. He also met the art dealer Ambrose Vollard who, in 1913, bought every picture in his studio and who, in 1917, provided Rouault with a room in his own house. During this collaboration with Vollard, Rouault began producing his extensive range of graphic and illustrative works, including the *Miserere* (60 etchings, completed in 1927, published in 1948), *Les Fleurs du Mal* (1926–7 and 1930s), and the 82 *Père Ubee* wood engravings and seven color etchings.

Most of his later work was concerned with religious themes. He often placed the events and parables of the New Testament in the blighted industrial suburbs of Paris. He is perhaps the last of the great religious artists.

Further reading. *Georges Rouault: Exposition du Centenaire*, Paris (1971). George, W. and Nouaille-Rouault, G. *Rouault*, London (1971). Rouault, G. and Suares, A. *Correspondance*, Paris (1960). Rouault, G. *Sur l'Art et sur la Vie*, Paris (1971). Soby, J.T. *Georges Rouault*, New York (1945).

Roubiliac L.-F. 1705–62

One of the most original sculptors of his day, the French artist Louis-François Roubiliac was born in Lyons of Huguenot parents. He is said to have served an initial apprenticeship in Protestant Dresden under Balthasar Permoser, later becoming a pupil of his fellow-Lyonnais Nicolas Coustou in Paris. At some time in the early 1730s, presumably because of his Protestant faith, he came to London, where he was to remain for the rest of his life.

He worked at first for the sculptor Henry Cheere, also of Huguenot stock, through whom he received in 1738 his first com-

Georges Rouault: Christ; stained glass; 1939–41. Musée National d'Art Moderne, Paris

mission, for a statue of George Frederick Handel for Vauxhall Gardens (now in the Victoria and Albert Museum, London). This highly original work, blending realism with allegory, is a landmark in Rococo sculpture. It established Roubiliac's reputation and gained him a practice in portrait sculpture, in which he far outshone his contemporaries in England. It was not, however, until 1746, with his monument to Bishop Hough (Worcester Cathedral) that Roubiliac obtained a commission for a major church monument. This clever design inaugurates a series of brilliantly original monuments by Roubiliac, in which he gradually broke down the architectural dominance in English monuments. His most important early monument is that to the Duke of Argyll (1746–9; Westminster Abbey, London), in which sculptural groupings dominate the design.

In 1752 Roubiliac visited Rome, where he was deeply impressed by the monuments of Bernini. From this time, his own works become even more dramatic and sculptural. The transition can be seen in the monuments to the Duke (1750–1) and Duchess (1753) of Montagu (Warkton, Northamptonshire). His later monuments, such as those to General Hargrave and Lady Elizabeth Nightingale (1757 and 1761; both in Westminster Abbey, London) surpass in originality and drama anything produced in France at the time.

Rousseau Henri 1844–1910

The French painter Henri Rousseau was born in Laval, of petty bourgeois parents. He served in the French army (he was a clarinettist in the regimental band at Caen). He never in fact went to Mexico, as he later claimed to have done. He settled in Paris in 1869, where he eventually obtained a post as gatekeeper in the customshouse at the city gate (his nickname "Le Douanier", "The Customs Officer", rather

elevates his office). In 1885, he resigned this post, took odd jobs such as painting inn-signs and devoted more time to his own painting.

Although his work was that of a primitive or "Sunday Painter", his own pretensions were to rival the Salon favorites of the day. Ironically, however, his work attracted the attention of the avant-garde: first Redon and Toulouse-Lautrec, then Alfred Jarry, and finally, in his last years, Picasso and

Apollinaire. What he possessed above all was a complete confidence in the value of his painting. He once told Picasso that they were the only great contemporary artists, "I in the modern manner and you in the Egyptian."

His decision to devote his life to painting coincided with the founding of the Salon des Indépendants in 1884. In that free, juryless exhibition, he showed between three and ten paintings almost every year from 1886 to 1910. The majority were landscapes and portraits. His earliest known works are local views (for instance, of the customs house), naive in their perception of reality and in their detailed descriptiveness. But such seemingly direct reportage was followed by inventive, imaginative, and dream-like works. However obsessed he was with exact and particular detail, he was able to control his composition, subordinating what might have been a host of minute and disparate observations into a rhythmical whole.

Rousseau's famous *Jungle Scenes* and *Exotic Landscapes* were not based on his mythical Mexican experiences, but on the tropical flora and fauna that he observed in the Jardin des Plantes in Paris. Equally, the exotic creatures inhabiting these forests—monkeys, water buffaloes, hunters, and dark-skinned natives—were reproduced from photographs, or from dolls and toys (for example, *Merry Jesters*, c1906; Philadelphia Museum of Art). One of his last works, *The Dream* (1910; Museum of Modern Art, New York) is a memory-image of his first love reclining on a sofa in one of his imaginary jungles. Its power and conviction, its sheer convincingness as dream-reality, foretell the best of Surrealist painting. Kandinsky called Rousseau the author of "new, greater reality", the complementary pole of the "new and greater abstraction". Rousseau remains the first and the greatest of the naive or primitive painters.

Further reading. Alley, R. *The Art of Henri Rousseau*, Oxford (1978). Apollinaire, G. (ed. Breunig, L.C., trans. Suleiman, S.) *On Art*, London (1972). Certigny, H. *La Verité sur le Douanier Rousseau*, Paris (1961). Delaunay, R. "Mon Ami Henri Rousseau", *Les Lettres Francaises*, Paris (7 Aug. 1952; 21 Aug. 1952; 28 Aug. 1952; 4 Sept. 1952). Tzara, T. *Henri Rousseau*, Zurich (1958). Uhde, W. *Five Primitive Masters*, New York (1949). Unde, W. *Rousseau le Douanier*, Lausanne (1948).

L.-F. Roubiliac: George II; marble; height 79cm (31in). Collection of H.M. Queen Elizabeth II

Henri Rousseau: The Snake Charmer; oil on canvas; 169×190cm (67×75in); 1907. Musée du Jeu de Paume, Paris

Rousseau Théodore 1812–67

The French landscape painter Pierre-Etienne-Théodore Rousseau was a leading figure in the Barbizon School. Born in Paris, he studied under Neoclassical teachers; but he was more influenced by the copies he made in the Louvre of Dutch masters. He began to paint plein-air landscapes around Paris in the 1820s.

He traveled widely in the French provinces in the early 1830s, visiting the Jura, the Auvergne, and Normandy. He developed a romantic manner of sharply contrasted light and shade, using energetic brushwork (for example, *The Jetty at Granville*, 1831; Wadsworth Atheneum, Hartford, Conn.). His Salon exhibits from 1831 onwards attracted the attention of progressive critics, and he soon had influential patrons including Delacroix, George Sand, and the critic T.-E.-J. Thoré. However the academic Salon jury refused

his *Descent of the Cattle* (Hendrik Willem Mesdag Museum, The Hague) in 1836; he was excluded from the Salon until 1847.

In the 1840s he began to paint more tranquil scenes in Berry and the Landes, and c1837 settled in Barbizon. He painted effects of weather and light (for example, *Edge of the Forest of Fontainebleau, Sunset*, 1851; Louvre, Paris). He also depicted woodland scenes, and liked to gain dramatic effects by placing trees, isolated

Théodore Rousseau: A Heath; pen, brown ink, and wash on paper; 20×28cm (8×11in). National Gallery of Scotland, Edinburgh

or in clumps, against a low skyline (for example, *The Oaks*, 1850–2; Louvre, Paris). The liberal Salon of 1849 brought his work once more into prominence, and he enjoyed a period of public and official recognition.

Though considered the Romantic landscape painter *par excellence*, Rousseau anticipated Impressionism in his dedication to plein-air painting, and in his portrayal of subtle changes of light and weather.

Rowlandson Thomas 1756–1827

Thomas Rowlandson, the English draftsman and etcher, was born in London. In 1772 he entered the Royal Academy Schools, and although he was awarded a silver medal in 1777, he had the reputation of being a capricious student. About 1774,

Thomas Rowlandson: A Club Subscription Room; pen and watercolor over pencil on paper; 32×45cm (13×18in); 1792. Victoria and Albert Museum, London

he made the first of several visits to the Continent. He exhibited watercolor drawings at the Royal Academy from 1775 to 1787, and from 1800 worked continuously for the publisher Rudolph Ackermann, for whom he illustrated *The Microcosm of London* (1808–10). *The Tours of Dr Syntax* (1818–21), and *The English Dance of Death* (1814–16).

Rowlandson's fame rests on his humorous watercolor depictions of Georgian life; however, he was a versatile artist and his repertoire of subjects included topography, rustic genre, and portraiture. His reputation has suffered from his own industriousness; yet within his prodigious graphic output there are many memorable designs. At his best, he organized large groups of figures, or described individual characters, with extraordinary facility, and with an elastic and calligraphic line that is ever varied and lively. There are fine collections of Rowlandson's drawings at the British Museum, London, the Boston Public Library, and the Huntington Library and Art Gallery, San Marino, California.

Further reading. Binyon, L. *English Watercolours*, London (1946). Falls, B. *Thomas Rowlandson: his Life and Work*, London (1949). George, M.D. *Hogarth to Cruikshank: Social Change in Graphic Satire*, London (1967). Grego, J. *Rowlandson the Caricaturist*, London (1880). Hayes, J. *Rowlandson, Watercolours and Drawings*, London (1972). Paulson, R. *Rowlandson: a New Interpretation*, London (1972).

Roy Jamini 1887–1974

Jamini Roy has been called the greatest modern Indian painter. He was able to resolve successfully the deadlock reached by the Nationalist Bengal School under Abanindranath (1861–1951) between the adoption of a pure European idiom and the self-conscious revival of ancient tradition.

Born in Bengal, he received training in the Western academic tradition at Calcutta Art School. Later he went through an inevitable sentimental revivalist "archaeological" phase, through the intervention of the Bengal School. Sensing the futility of trying to revive Ajanta or Mughal art, whose cultural values were so alien to the present age, he underwent a spiritual crisis. It was through a "great intellectual adventure" that he came to develop his highly personal style: robust,

Peter Paul Rubens: The Duke of Lerma on Horseback; oil on canvas; 289×205cm (114×81in); 1603. Prado, Madrid

simple, at once austere and sensuous, drawing upon popular Kalighat and folk styles.

Such primitivist borrowings were not self-conscious mannerism, for he deeply loved the Santal tribes he painted. Giving up commercial paints, he went back to the use of organic pigments. Later in life he renounced an "original" contribution to art, in favor of "mass" art that was within the easy reach of ordinary people. He shared its execution with his pupils and

assistants, thus making a serious social statement that sprang from deep conviction about the social function of art.

Rubens Peter Paul 1577–1640

Peter Paul Rubens was the greatest northern artist of the Baroque. His work was crucial to the genesis of that style, and his energy, versatility, and productivity have never been equaled in the history of art. He excelled in every kind of painting; his vast

output included altarpieces and other religious paintings, scenes from Classical history and mythology, portraits, and hunting scenes. He also produced designs for tapestry and silver, and book illustrations. He directed a large workshop, and designed and supervised the execution of many large-scale schemes of decoration. Moreover, he was a classical scholar and diplomat, and in the 1620s played an important part in international politics. The splendor of Rubens' art reflected and expressed the renewed confidence of the Roman Catholic church and the power and glory of the autocratic monarchs of the Counter-Reformation.

Rubens was born at Siegen in Westphalia. In 1587 his family returned to Antwerp where he studied painting with Tobias Verhaecht, Adam van Noort, and Otto van Veen. In 1598 he was enrolled as a master in the Antwerp Guild, and in 1600 went to Italy to study ancient and modern art. Here he entered the service of Vincenzo Gonzaga of Mantua; in the next eight years he traveled to Florence, Rome, Genoa, Venice, and Spain.

Rubens' years in Italy were crucial to his development. His knowledge of Classical civilization and literature was profound and he was inspired by the art of the Renaissance. He absorbed everything he saw in Italy, and throughout his life returned to this store of visual knowledge. He studied the glowing colors and opulence of the Venetians—of Titian (c1488–1576), Tintoretto (1518–94), and Veronese (1528–88)—and his sense of weight and volume clearly owes much to Michelangelo and to Classical sculpture. Among living artists he admired and copied Caravaggio, and emulated Annibale Carracci's large, bold drawings from life.

Rubens went to Spain on his first diplomatic mission in 1603. While he was there he made copies after paintings by Titian in the Spanish Royal collection. By 1608 he had already produced a series of important early Baroque masterpieces. The equestrian portrait of The Duke of Lerma (1603; Prado, Madrid), shows the horse head-on and boldly foreshortened. In 1606 he painted a series of portraits of the Genoese nobility. Their vitality of expression, the rustling movement and painterly surfaces of their elaborate costumes, and the terrace settings with columns and curtain, all broke with the stiffness of Mannerist portraiture and began a new tradition. The Madonna Adored by Saints (1607/8), the first version of an altarpiece painted for the Chiesa Nuova in Rome, heralds the Baroque; the colors and textures are decorative and glowing, the forms are powerful, and the mood ecstatic.

Rubens returned to Antwerp in 1608. In 1609 he was appointed painter to the Hapsburg Regents, the Infanta Isabella and the Archduke Albert, and in that same year he married Isabella Brant, daughter of an Antwerp lawyer. Between 1609 and 1621 an important series of paintings established him as the leading painter in northern Europe. The urgent movement and immediate sensuous appeal of his art must have amazed contemporary observers in Flanders. Rubens saw himself as heir to the great painters of the High Renaissance, and the monumentality of his work rivaled theirs.

The key works of this period were the Elevation of the Cross (1609–10; Antwerp Cathedral), the Descent from the Cross (1611–14; Antwerp Cathedral), and The Conversion of St Bavo (for St Bavon, Ghent, 1611–12; modello in the National Gallery, London). The Elevation of the Cross preserves the traditional triptych form; the composition of the central panel is based on a bold diagonal, and the powerfully modeled forms create a sense of violent overall movement. Rubens' early Antwerp style is restless and powerfully dramatic. This can be seen in a cycle of hunting scenes (c1615), and some battle paintings—The Defeat of Sennacherib, Alte Pinakothek, Munich, and its pendant, The Conversion of St Paul (1613–14; Courtauld Institute Galleries, London), and the Battle of the Amazons (c1618, Alte Pinakothek, Munich). These all show his unrivaled ability to convey in formally organized compositions the energy and power of struggling masses of men and animals. Yet his art at this period was also in a sense classical; the influence of his study of bas-reliefs and cameos is often apparent in his compositions. After 1615 he very rarely signed and dated his works.

In the 1620s Rubens was constantly involved with large-scale schemes of decoration. To fulfill these commissions he depended on the successful organization of a large workshop and on the brilliant use he made of preparatory sketches. He also began to supervise a team of engravers to popularize his work throughout Europe.

In 1620 he agreed to produce sketches for 39 canvases, to be executed with the help of assistants, for the ceiling of the Jesuit church in Antwerp (destroyed by fire in 1718). He had already painted altarpieces for the high altar. For these canvases Rubens produced two kinds of sketches: grisaille sketches, done on small panels, where the first ideas were brushed in hastily in brown tones with white highlights; and color sketches for his assistants to follow. The color sketches could also be used as contract models to show clients. He had begun to use sketches in 1605, and continued to follow variations of this procedure throughout his career; without it, the immense scope of his activity is unthinkable.

The ceiling paintings showed for the first time how deeply he had studied the great Venetian ceiling painters of the 16th century. The canvases were hung, in the Venetian manner, within wooden compartments; the individual compositions included derivations from Titian, Tintoretto, and Veronese.

Rubens also received important commissions from abroad. In 1622 Louis XIII commissioned 12 designs for tapestry of The Life of Constantine. Early in 1622, in 1623, and again in 1625, Rubens was in Paris to discuss and complete a cycle of paintings of The Life of Marie de Medici (Louvre, Paris) for the Luxembourg Palace. In this series he inaugurated a new type of political allegory. His task was not easy, as he had to commemorate several inglorious events in the life of the somewhat foolish Queen. Yet he transformed his delicate subject matter by the splendor of his allegory; ancient gods and Christian symbols work together to glorify the Queen: her birth is compared to the Nativity, and her education is presided over by the gods and goddesses of Antiquity. From 1626 to 1628 Rubens worked on designs for tapestries of The Triumph of the Eucharist for the Convent of the Descalzas Reales, Madrid.

The 1620s mark the climax of Rubens' Baroque style. The dramatic movement, bright light, and rhythmic force that bind the figures harmoniously together are exemplified in the Assumption (1626; Antwerp Cathedral) and the Madonna and Child adored by Saints (1628; Royal Museum of Fine Arts, Antwerp). A three-dimensional spiraling movement has re-

Peter Paul Rubens: the central panel of the St Idelfonso triptych; oil on canvas; 352×236cm (139×93in); 1630–2. Kunsthistorisches Museum, Vienna

placed the thrusting diagonals of the earlier period; Rubens' concept of dynamic movement, and his brilliantly fluent and expressive brushwork, were his most significant contributions to the Baroque.

This period was also, astonishingly, Rubens' most active time as a diplomat: he went on diplomatic missions to Spain, Holland, France, and England. His wife, Isabella Brant, had died in 1626 and Rubens was perhaps willing to distract himself with constant traveling. In 1628 he was in Spain and painted portraits of the Spanish Royal family. Accompanied sometimes by Velázquez, he again studied the Hapsburg Titians, and Titian is, in Rubens' late works, once more a profound source of inspiration.

In 1629–30, Rubens conducted peace negotiations in London. He was knighted by Charles I in 1630, and between 1630 and 1634 did paintings for the ceiling of the Banqueting House in Whitehall. These have a special importance because they are his only large decorative scheme that can still be seen in its original place. Their development may be traced through a series of exceptionally beautiful sketches. Here Rubens displayed his knowledge of classical allegory in the service of a heretic King: the theme of the ceiling was the Divine Authority of James I. As in the Jesuit ceiling, his deep indebtedness to the Venetian tradition is apparent both in the conception of the whole and in the individual canvases.

In the early 1630s Rubens was exempted from further diplomacy and in his last years enjoyed greater freedom from court duties. In 1636 he was appointed court painter to the Infanta's successor, the Cardinal Infante Ferdinand, brother of Philip IV. The Cardinal had made a state entry into Antwerp the previous year, and Rubens had supervised the lavish decorations of streets and squares. The theme was the decline in trade and other disastrous consequences of war against Holland.

Through Ferdinand, Rubens gained the contract for his last important commission, the decoration of the Torre de la Parada, Philip IV's hunting lodge near Madrid. The decorations were to include a series of scenes from Ovid and of other mythological subjects, a series of animal and hunting scenes ordered from Rubens' studio, and works by Velázquez. The mythological scenes were to be designed by Rubens himself and he did more than 50 oil sketches for them; in 1638, 112 paint-

ings, executed by assistants, were sent to Spain. Assistants played a larger part than usual in the finished products, and many are disappointing. The Torre sketches, however, are among the most spontaneous, personal, and economical of all his works; they are a warm and human interpretation of the loves of the gods.

In his last decade Rubens continued to paint the great religious themes, among them the *Adoration of the Magi* (1633–4; King's College Chapel, Cambridge) and the *St Idelfonso* triptych (1630–2; Kunsthistorisches Museum, Vienna). These works of his late style are calmer, more serene, and more radiantly spiritual than their powerfully Baroque predecessors. The *Ascent to Calvary* (c1634; Musées Royaux des Beaux-Arts de Belgique) is furiously Baroque, but the violence is tempered by the beauty of the silvery colors.

In 1630 Rubens had married the 17-year-old Hélène Fourment, daughter of a silk merchant. From this time, more of his works were painted purely for pleasure; his newfound domestic tranquillity and the beauty of his young wife inspired many of his late works. This tranquillity is the theme of a highly finished small work on panel, *Self Portrait with Hélène Fourment and his son Nicolas in their Garden* (1631; Alte Pinakothek, Munich). Beside an Italianate loggia and fountain the family enjoy their garden surrounded by tulips, orange trees, dogs, and peacocks.

Hélène Fourment also inspired his majestic renderings of the female nude. His most mellow and radiant mythological paintings, two versions of *The Judgment of Paris* (National Gallery, London, and Prado, Madrid) and also the splendid *Hélène Fourment in a Fur Wrap* (Kunsthistorisches Museum, Vienna) all date from this late period. No artist has surpassed Rubens' rendering of the sheen and glow of the surface of the skin.

In 1635 he purchased the country estate of the Château de Steen so that he could paint in peace and study landscape. His most important landscapes were all painted in the following years. They include the *An Autumn Landscape with a View of the Château de Steen* (National Gallery, London), the *Landscape with a Rainbow* (Wallace Collection, London),

Peter Paul Rubens: Hélène Fourment in a Fur Wrap; oil on panel; 175×96cm (69×38in); 1638. Kunsthistorisches Museum, Vienna

Peter Paul Rubens: Portrait of Isabella Brant; chalk and ink on paper; 38×29cm (15×11in); c1622. British Museum, London

and the *Landscape with Peasants returning from the Fields* (c1635–8; Palazzo Pitti, Florence). Rubens' landscapes, which owe much to those of his Flemish predecessor, Pieter Bruegel, start from a precise observation of the life around him: of birds, animals, fences, women carrying rakes and bundles of hay. But these details are included in compositions of solid grandeur that are controlled by Rubens' firm grasp of land masses, and irradiated by intensely romantic effects of light.

Rubens began to suffer from gout in 1627. In the late 1630s he began to have severe difficulties using his painting arm, and he died in 1640.

Further reading. Burckhardt, J. (trans. Hottinger, M.) *Recollections of Rubens*, London (1950). Fletcher, J. *Peter Paul Rubens*, London and New York (1968). Gerson, H. and Kuile, E.H. ter *Art and Architecture in Belgium: 1600–1800*, Harmondsworth (1960). Held, J.S. *Rubens: Selected Drawings*, London (1959). Jaffe, M. *Rubens and Italy*, Oxford (1977).

Rublev Andrei c1370–c1430

Andrei Rublev was a Russian painter. He entered a monastery at Zagorsk and later moved to another at Moscow, where he died. He produced both frescoes and icons; several of the latter are in museums in Moscow and St Petersburg. In Moscow Rublev collaborated with the older artist

Theophanes the Greek on the icons of the iconostasis of the Cathedral of the Annunciation in the Kremlin (1405); those of the *Nativity, Baptism*, and *Transfiguration* are generally attributed to Rublev.

Although he was influenced by Theophanes in his spiritual outlook and sense of composition, his teacher was probably Prokhor of Gorodets. Rublev developed a serene style distinctly different in its classically balanced forms, controlled draftsmanship, and purer palette from the nervous and asymmetric handling of Theophanes.

In the early 15th century, Rublev also worked on the cathedral of Zvenigorod, from which several frescoes survive, for instance *St Laurus*, and also icons, for instance one of the Savior. In 1408, in the Cathedral of the Dormition at Vladmir, he painted with the monk Deniil the extensive frescoes of the *Last Judgment* and several icons, one of which is *Christ in Majesty*. About 1411 he produced what is considered his masterpiece, the icon of the *Old Testament Trinity*. In 1422 he returned to his monastery at Zagorsk, where he and Daniil executed both frescoes and icons.

Further reading. Alpatov, M. *Andrej Rublev*, Milan (1962). Antonova, V. *The Rublev Exhibition*, Moscow (1960). Lebedeva, J.A. *Andrei Rubljow und seine Zeitgenossen*, Dresden (1962).

Rude François 1784–1855

François Rude was a French sculptor whose work is Romantic in conception, but expressed with Realist accuracy. He was apprenticed to his father, a metalworker, which gave him a strong technical grounding; he also received an academic training at the École des Beaux-Arts in Paris. He was an enthusiastic Bonapartist (see his *Awakening of Napoleon*, 1846; bronze, Fixin park, near Dijon), and spent 12 years in Belgium after the Restoration, where he had a workshop in Brussels. He sculpted a bust of the painter *J.-L. David* in exile (plaster, 1826; marble, 1831; both Louvre, Paris). His charming *Neapolitan Fisherboy* (marble; 1833; Louvre, Paris) shows the informality of his approach, while his famous *Marseillaise* (or *Departing of the Volunteers of 1792*) for the Arc de Triomphe, Paris (stone, 1836), combines expressive force with popular facial types despite its strongly classical conception.

Ruisdael Jacob van *c*1628/9–82

The painter and etcher Jacob Isaacksz. van Ruisdael is widely regarded as Holland's greatest landscapist. The son of a frame-maker and art dealer who also painted landscapes, Ruisdael may have studied under his father, and perhaps also with his uncle Salomon van Ruysdael, who influenced his early pictures. He was very precocious: the earliest dated works, views in the neighborhood of Haarlem done when he was not yet 20, show astonishing maturity, particularly in their contrasts of light and shadow and their vivid colors. Around 1650 Ruisdael visited east Holland and the regions of Germany that adjoined the Dutch border: hilly, forested areas which excited the romantic strain in him. He lived in Amsterdam from *c*1657 until his death, although he continued to travel about Holland.

Between *c*1650 and 1670 he tackled almost every kind of landscape: panoramas painted from 'the dunes overlooking the vast fertile plain around Haarlem, woodland scenes and the denser recesses of forests, country roads bordered by cottages and wheatfields, river scenes centered on picturesque watermills, stormy seascapes, calmer beach scenes, and pictures of villages in winter. From 1659 Ruisdael also painted a series of views of mountain streams and waterfalls inspired by the Scandinavian landscapes of Allart van Everdingen (1621–75).

Ruisdael's art is characterized by a sensitive response to the different moods of nature, whether in the elevating experience of vast, luminous panoramas of green meadows and golden wheatfields, or the image of dark, desolate winter scenes. The principal vehicle for the expression of mood in his landscapes is light and shade, particularly such dramatic and arresting devices as the fitful breaking of sunlight through massive clouds. Absence of light is also evocative, as in the melancholy forest interiors with their dead trees and stagnant pools. Many of Ruisdael's views are still recognizable, but he is not always a realist.

The conjunction of observation and imagination is illustrated by the two versions of *The Jewish Cemetery* (Gemäldegalerie Alte Meister, Dresden, and the Detroit Institute of Arts). In these paintings fictional mountains and ruins surround tombstones sketched at Ouderkerk, near Amsterdam. A degree of subjectivity is elsewhere evident in Ruisdael's majestic and powerful conception of nature—a

Jacob van Ruisdael: An Extensive Landscape with a Ruined Castle and a Village Church; oil on canvas; 109×146cm (43×57in); *c*1665–72. National Gallery, London

conception conveyed by giant oaks, foaming mountain torrents, and distant horizons. The question of realism is also complicated by occasional allusions to cyclical processes of decay, growth, and renewal. These are not necessarily of an explicitly allegorical kind. They are particularly evident in the *Jewish Cemetery* paintings, where a rainbow and new foliage are contrasted with such symbols of the transitoriness of life as tombs, ruins, and dead trees.

Although his influence on other Dutch artists (notably on his pupil and friend Meyndert Hobbema) was considerable, Ruisdael was much less popular in his lifetime than the painters of Italianate landscapes. There were many appreciative collectors of his work during the 18th century; but his importance was only fully recognized during the Romantic period, with the subsequent rise of naturalistic landscape in England and France during the first half of the 19th century. Works can be seen at the Hermitage, St Petersburg, the Metropolitan Museum, New York, the Rijksmuseum, Amsterdam, and the National Gallery, London.

Runge P.O. 1777–1810

Philipp Otto Runge was a German Romantic draftsman, painter, and theorist. He studied at the Copenhagen Academy (1799–1801), which was then one of the leading European centers for Neoclassicism. Under the influence of John Flaxman, William Blake, and Jacob Carstens, he developed a strong linear style, especially in his drawings. In 1801 he transferred to the Dresden Academy, hoping to find there a more profound approach to art, but he was disappointed. This, together with his failure in the Weimar Art Competition in 1801, caused him to question the whole basis of classical art and to seek inspiration in the literature of the Romantics (works by Tieck, Novalis, and Wackenroder), and the mystics (Jakob Böhme, etc).

He concluded that since art was the product of a particular age and country and the expression of the artist's inner self, a new art-form was needed to reflect the spiritual upheavals of the age. Landscape should supersede history painting, since idealistic philosophy had shown nature to be an extension of man's mind. Likewise, a revival of Christian art was required, not in its traditional historical form, but as the revelations of nature itself, interpreted by

P.O. Runge: Self-portrait; chalk on paper; 55×43cm (22×17in); 1801/2. Hamburger Kunsthalle, Hamburg

the divine spark within the artist.

This mystical pantheism found its greatest expression in his cycle *Die Tageszeiten* ("The Times of the Day"; drawings, 1802–3; engravings, 1805). Here, in four highly symmetrical, decorative compositions, Runge used an interrelated flower-and-child symbolism to represent the light or darkness at Morning, Noon, Evening, and Night. Several layers of meaning, involving Christian and cosmic symbolism, lie beneath this; but the detailed, linear style and complex allegorical framework fail to make them sensuously expressive. Color was needed. Runge devoted several years to color research (including a correspondence with Goethe), and in 1810 published his treatise *Die Farbenkugel* ("The Spheres of Color").

After his return to Hamburg in 1803, Runge took painting lessons, and painted several important portrait groups (for example, *We Three*, 1803; *The Artist's Parents*, 1806; both Hamburger Kunsthalle, Hamburg). In their stern realism and lack of idealization these works show the influence of Runge's Copenhagen teacher, J. Juel, and his Dresden mentor, A. Graff. But Runge's innovations lie in his almost plein-air treatment of landscape and his ability to combine an intense immediacy with symbolic meaning.

In 1808 Runge painted the first version of *Morning*, and in 1809 the second and larger version (both in Hamburger Kunsthalle, Hamburg). The greater visual impact

of the paintings compared with the drawing is due not only to the use of color but to the replacement of symbols by a real landscape. Runge had intended to paint even larger mural versions of all four *Tageszeiten* so as to create a total artistic environment, but ill health prevented this and he died in Hamburg in December 1810.

Ruskin John 1819–1900

The English critic, author, and artist John Ruskin was the most original and influential art theorist of his time. Born of prosperous parents (his father was a sherry merchant), he profited early from frequent trips to Italy. His experience of grand foreign scenery, coupled with a close, often scientific, study of nature formed the basis of his aesthetic. His early enthusiasm for the works of J.M.W. Turner widened this response.

Modern Painters, published between 1843 and 1859, began as a justification of Turner's vision; it became, in the course of five volumes, a general survey of art. The success of this, together with *The Seven Lamps of Architecture* (1851) and *The Stones of Venice* (1854), established Ruskin as a leading critic of the age.

In 1851 he became involved with the Pre-Raphaelites, defending their works in letters to *The Times*, and also in *Academy Notes*, a personal review of each year's display at the Royal Academy (1855–9). Ruskin's intervention on the behalf of Millais, Hunt, and Rossetti marks a turning point in their fortunes. In 1848 Ruskin married Effie Gray; she left him to become Millais' wife in 1854, but despite family battles, Ruskin continued to support Millais' work. He was also personally involved in Rossetti's life, giving him financial support, and winning him important patrons. In 1854, Ruskin began teaching drawing at the Working Men's College, and encouraged Rossetti to join him.

Ruskin exhibited at the Old Water Colour Society from 1873 to 1883; he completed over 2,000 drawings. His work consists mainly of watercolor and pencil studies of rocks, trees, plants, and architectural details.

In the 1860s he became increasingly involved with social problems, and his later writings are mainly economic and philosophical. In 1869 he was made Slade Professor at Oxford, and founded a drawing school there. He passed his last years at

John Ruskin: The Glacier des Bossons, Chamounix; bistre and brown wash on paper; 33×47cm (13×19in); 1849. Ashmolean Museum, Oxford

Brantwood on Lake Coniston, mentally troubled and often deeply depressed.

The best of Ruskin's critical writing is fired by a deeply personal response: his description of his visit to the Tintorettos in the Scuola di S. Rocco, Venice, is noteworthy. His passages in appreciation of the oils and watercolors of J.M.W. Turner remain unsurpassed.

Russell Morgan 1886–1953

Morgan Russell was a member of an American movement in Parisian painting called Synchromism, which was close to Cubism and Orphism. Born in New York, Russell trained first as an architect, and then with Robert Henri in New York. He absorbed the art of Monet and Cézanne in Paris; from 1908 to 1909 he worked as an assistant to Matisse, to whom he had been introduced by Gertrude Stein. His paintings, such as *Synchromy* (oil; c1913; Museum of Modern Art, New York) and

Synchromy in Orange: To Form (oil; 1913–14; Albright-Knox Art Gallery, Buffalo, N.Y.), are dense essays in the style of Delaunay. Despite vigorous polemics on the part of the American group, it is unlikely that their color theory and practice predated that of Robert Delaunay and Franz Kupka.

Ruysdael Salomon van c1600–70

Salomon Jacobsz. van Ruysdael was a Dutch painter of realist landscapes and seascapes; he came from Haarlem, and was an uncle of the more famous Jacob van Ruisdael. His early works show the influence of Esaias van de Velde; but those from c1630 to 1645 are more in the monochromatic style of the slightly older Jan van Goyen, and there are also similarities of motif. Ruysdael is best known for calm, expansive pictures of rivers and estuaries. These are usually cool in color, make use of diagonally receding

compositional axes, and have low viewpoints and horizons. His most characteristic motifs are ferries, sailing boats, and fishermen.

After the mid 1640s, Ruysdael introduced more compact and prominent features (such as groups of trees and windmills) into his paintings, and these served to integrate more fully the two main components of his work: land and sky. In the later 1640s and 1650s he used stronger color, and introduced more emphatic contrasts of light and shade. During this period he painted several seascapes, some of which are in a less usual vertical format. Ruysdael also painted some village scenes and winter landscapes with skaters.

Ryder Albert 1847–1917

The American painter Albert Pinkham Ryder was born in New Bedford, Mass., and moved with his family to New York in 1870. He was largely self-taught, although

Salomon van Ruysdael: Drawing the Eel; oil on panel; 75×106cm (30×42in); c1650. Metropolitan Museum, New York

he did study for a while at the National Academy of Design. He started by painting landscapes, but from c1880 he turned for inspiration to literary sources such as the Bible, Chaucer, Shakespeare, and the 19th-century Romantic poets. He is perhaps best known for his pictures of marine subjects (for example, *Toilers of the Sea*, 1884; Metropolitan Museum, New York). These are often shown by moonlight, and are painted in a very thick, sometimes even turgid technique. Between 1877 and 1896 Ryder traveled extensively in Europe but he was little influenced by the great tradition of European painting. His work sets him apart from the conventional schools of his day, just as his own somewhat eccentric character drove him to live the life of a hermit.

Albert Ryder (attrib.): Night and Clouds; oil on panel; 31×22cm (12×9in). Saint Louis Art Museum, Saint Louis, Mo.

Rysbrack John 1694–1770

John Michael Rysbrack was a Flemish sculptor who worked in England. He was born and trained in Antwerp, but in 1720 moved to England, and remained there for the rest of his life. Heir to the restrained Baroque of Francesco Duquesnoy, he developed a strong affinity with Roman sculpture, and was the sculptor most perfectly in tune with the English taste of the 18th century. He established a good and lasting practice in portrait sculpture, in which he excelled, and in monuments. He became the leading provider of monuments of his time in England, collaborating at first with the architect James Gibbs, and later with William Kent. More talented than his main rival, Peter Scheemaeckers, Rysbrack was so well established in English favor that he survived competition with the more brilliant and showy Louis-François Roubiliac, whose influence can, however, be seen in his later works.

S

Saarinen Eero 1910–61

The Finnish architect Eero Saarinen, son of the architect Eliel Saarinen (1873–1950), was born at Kirkkonummi. The family emigrated to the United States in 1923. Eero studied in Paris (1929–30) and at Yale University (1931–4) before briefly returning to Finland in 1935. From 1937 until after the Second World War he worked in partnership with his father. In 1949 he won the competition for the Jefferson National Expansion Memorial in St Louis, Mo. (completed in 1965).

The first significant works in Saarinen's brief career date from after his father's death in 1950. Initial designs for General Motors Technical and Research Center at Warren, Michigan, were done under Eliel's direction in the late 1940s, but the final project, with its highly individual water tower, is unquestionably Eero's work. The influence of Mies van der Rohe's plan for the Illinois Institute of Technology can be seen in Saarinen's solution for the General Motors complex: a number of glazed, box-like units assembled in interesting combinations around a large central lake.

He was not for long to remain a follower of van der Rohe. Surprise is the keynote of a career marked by what has been called a "bewildering eclecticism". There is little continuity between the various breathtaking achievements that came after General Motors. The Kresge Auditorium (1953–5) for the Massachusetts Institute of Technology, the Yale University Hockey Rink (1953–9), and the two airport schemes for which he is perhaps best known, the TWA Terminal, Kennedy Airport, New York (1956–62), and Dulles Airport, Washington, D.C. (1958–63), show Saarinen experimenting with dramatic forms to enclose vast interior spaces. In the case of the airport buildings, Saarinen confronted and attempted to solve some of the increasingly sophisticated problems connected with air travel.

Further reading. Saarinen, A.B. (ed.) *Eero Saarinen and his Works: a Selection of Buildings dating from 1947 to 1964*, London and New Haven (1968). Saarinen, E. *The City: its Growth, its Decay, its Future*, Cambridge, Mass. (1965). Temke, A. *Eero Saarinen*, New York (1962).

Andrea Sacchi: Hagar and Ishmael in the Wilderness; oil on canvas; 96×92cm (38×36in); c1630. National Gallery of Wales, Cardiff

Sacchi Andrea 1599–1661

The Italian painter Andrea Sacchi was born in Rome; he was a representative of the classical tendency in Roman painting of the mid 17th century. He was taught by Francesco Albani in both Rome and Bologna. He was in Rome again from 1621 and remained there for most of his life. From 1625 to 1627 he painted *St Gregory and the Miracle of the Caporal* (Vatican Museums, Rome) for St Peter's, a painting that shows his Raphaelesque manner and the restriction on the number of figures he used in a composition: only six. He developed this restrained approach in *The Vision of St Romuald* (c1638; Vatican Museums, Rome).

Artistically, Sacchi was the opposite of Pietro da Cortona, with whose work his has often been compared. Both artists were employed by the Barberini, and their differing approach to decorative fresco painting may be seen in the Palazzo Barberini, Rome. Here Sacchi painted *The Allegory of Divine Wisdom* (1629–33) which, muted in color, is composed of only 11 figures, and contrasts with Cortona's crowded *Divine Providence* (1633–9) in the same building. Sacchi's later works in Rome include *St Anthony of Padua Raises a Dead Man* (c1638; S. Maria della Concezione), *Stories of St John the Baptist* (1640–9; S. Giovanni in Fonte), and *The Death of St Anne* (1649; S. Carlo ai Catinari). With Poussin and Algardi, Sacchi maintained the classical tradition in the Baroque period; his later work leads directly towards the weightiness of the paintings of his pupil Carlo Maratti.

Further reading. Harris, A.S. *Andrea Sacchi: Complete Edition of the Paintings*, Oxford and Princeton (1977). Wittkower, R. *Art and Architecture in Italy: 1600–1750*, Harmondsworth (1973).

Sadiqi Beg 1533–1610

The Persian artist Sadiqi Beg was a soldier, poet and biographer, draftsman, and miniaturist. Born in Tabriz, he was a pupil of Muzaffar Ali. He was in the service of Shah Isma'il II (ruled 1576–7) and of Shah Abbas I from 1587 to 1598 as head of the Royal Library in Qazwin. His style was dynamic and colorful, his character overbearing, and his criticism outspoken. So he fell from office in 1598, his last royal work being on a large *Shah-nama* which survives in part in the Chester Beatty Library,

Dublin. In 1593 he was presented, probably by his pupils, with a book of fables, the *Anwar i-Suhayli* (private collection). This is illustrated with 107 miniatures attested as "prepared for Sadiqi Beg, the Rarity of the Age". Some scholars believe these to be by Sadiqi himself, but they seem to be the work of several hands.

Saenredam Pieter 1597–1665

The Dutch painter Pieter Jansz. Saenredam specialized in church interiors, although he also produced topographical views of architectural exteriors (for example, *The Old Town Hall of Amsterdam*, 1657; Rijksmuseum, Amsterdam). He sometimes depicted the interiors of churches in Amsterdam and elsewhere in Holland, but his views were more often of the Gothic churches in Utrecht and his native Haarlem. The development from his preliminary sketches to his finished oil paintings was usually a lengthy process, involving the preparation of detailed perspective drawings and other diagrams, with reference to architectural plans and measurements. The final result was invariably an accurate transcription of the view presented, although modifications were occasionally made for compositional reasons. In this respect his work differs from that of earlier architectural painters, in which the buildings tended to be imaginary structures.

Saenredam's paintings are of much more than architectural interest. Their colors are cool, delicate, and restful; there is a sensitivity to the effects of pale light reflected from whitewashed walls, and a subtle evocation of the stillness and silence enclosed beneath great vaults. The complex and harmonious geometry of flat, carefully balanced tones and colors Saenredam created from the architectural members and sparse decorations of Protestant church interiors looks forward to the formalism of certain 20th-century paintings.

Sagrera Guillen 1375?–1454

The Spanish sculptor Guillen Sagrera may have been born in Majorca. He was sculptor and architect to the Court of Aragon, although after 1420 his center of activity was Majorca. The figures of St Peter, St Paul, and a bearded man in Palma Cathedral are good examples of his work. His dramatic, almost Burgundian style is even better represented by the archangel on the

Pieter Saenredam: The Buurkerk at Utrecht; oil on panel; 60×50cm (24×20in); 1644. National Gallery, London

facade of the Lonja, or Commercial Exchange, of Palma—a building he was contracted to construct in 1426. In 1447 he was called to Naples by Alfonso the Magnanimous, to build the main hall of the Castel Nuovo; he died in Naples before the work was completed.

Saint-Gaudens Augustus 1848–1907

Augustus Saint-Gaudens was the most noted American sculptor of the late 19th century. As a boy he was apprenticed to a cameo-cutter, and studied at Cooper Union and the National Academy of Art and Design (both in New York), and at the École des Beaux-Arts in Paris. He established himself as a sculptor in New York in 1875, becoming famous both for his monumental sculptures (for example, his monument to Admiral Farragut, 1880; Madison Square Garden, New York), and for his bas-relief decorations. Saint-Gaudens belonged to one of the leading groups of late-19th-century American artists and architects, a circle that included Henry Hobson Richardson, Stanford White, and the painter John La Farge. A memorial collection of his works was made in Cornish, New Hampshire, after his death (the Saint-Gaudens National Historical Site).

Further reading. Cortissoz, R. *Augustus Saint-Gaudens*, Boston, Mass. (1967). Saint-Gaudens, H. (ed.) *The Reminiscences of Augustus Saint-Gaudens* (2 vols.), New York (1913). Taft, L. *The History of American Sculpture*, New York (1930).

Salviati: An Episode in the History of the Farnese Family; c1549–63. Palazzo Farnese, Rome

Salviati 1510–63

The Italian artist Francesco de' Rossi was known as Salviati; he was a leading Florentine Mannerist painter of the mid 16th century. Trained by Andrea del Sarto, he was active in Rome by 1530 under the protection of Cardinal Salviati, from whom he took his name. His mature style shows a typically Mannerist range of sources: it is reminiscent of works by both Raphael and Michelangelo but is endowed, however, with a new elegance, artificiality, and complexity. He specialized in large-scale multifigured mural decorations, usually packed with learned allegory and archaeological detail. He spent his career traveling restlessly between Florence and Rome; he also visited northern Italy from 1538 to 1541, and Fontainebleau in 1554.

Sánchez Coello Alonso 1531–88

The Spanish painter Alonso Sánchez Coello was born at Benifayó, Valencia. He was taken to Portugal when young and later sent to study under Anthonis Mor van Dashorst in Flanders. By 1555 he was in Castile, where he became court painter to Philip II and produced an extensive series of royal portraits in a stiff, Mannerist style with superbly rendered details of dress (examples in the Prado, Madrid; the Escorial, near Madrid; and Hampton Court Palace, London).

Although his reputation rests firmly on his portraits, Sánchez Coello also painted religious compositions, including many full-length pairs of saints over the minor altars of the monastery church at the Escorial (1580–2) and *The Martyrdom of St Sebastian* (1582; Prado, Madrid).

Sánchez Cotán Juan 1561–1627

The Spanish painter Juan Sánchez Cotán was born at Orgaz. At Toledo he studied under Blas del Prado (c1545–post 1592) and created the typical Spanish still-life composition; this consists of a few simple objects—mainly vegetables—spread out in precisely calculated rhythmical arrangement in a window opening or niche, or hanging on strings from above. Signed examples of his work are in the Museum of Art, San Diego and in the Hernani Collection, Madrid.

In 1603 Sánchez Cotán joined the Carthusian order as a lay brother and thereafter painted only religious compositions, sometimes in a tenebrist style. However, these works never rivaled his earlier still-life masterpieces, for example his *Still Life* of c1600 in the San Diego Museum of Art.

Sandby brothers

18th and 19th centuries

The British artists Paul Sandby (1725/6–1809) and his brother Thomas (1721–98) were important figures in the development of English landscape painting in watercolors. They worked in the Military Drawing Office of the Tower of London, and after 1745 were employed as draftsmen on a survey of the Scottish highlands. Thomas, who was not so accomplished as his brother, specialized in architectural details.

Paul worked extensively in Wales. He produced numerous landscape paintings that were remarkable for their spontaneity rather than for the conventions associated with the Picturesque. His varied technique included thin washes as well as work in gouache, and he also introduced the aquatint process to England. His landscapes were much admired by Thomas Gainsborough (1727–88).

Sangallo family

15th and 16th centuries

The Florentine Sangallo family was a large one and played a leading role in Italian architecture from the 1480s until the death of Antonio the Younger in 1546. Their practice was built around a family system and often several members were involved

Paul Sandby: A Milkmaid in Windsor Great Park; pen and watercolor; 30×24cm (12×9in); c1765–70. British Museum, London

Juan Sánchez Cotán: Still Life; oil on canvas; 69×85cm (27×33in); c1600. San Diego Museum of Art

in the same commission, as at the Villa Madama and S. Giovanni dei Fiorentini, in Rome. Their work included the whole range of architecture, including military architecture.

Giuliano (1445–1516) and Antonio the Younger (1483–1546) were perhaps the most distinguished members of the family. Giuliano's virtuoso performance in the 1480s, at the Villa of Poggia a Caiano, the fortress of Volterra, and the church of S. Maria delle Carceri, Prato, was most impressive. On his death in 1516, his mantle passed to his nephew Antonio the Younger; the stylistic contrast between them was that of the Quattrocento against the Cinquecento. Antonio the Elder (1455–1535), another uncle, also became more popular after his brother Giuliano's

Giuliano da Sangallo (architect): the gran salone of the Villa of Poggia a Caiano, Florence; c1485

death, producing his major works in the house of Montepulciano and the beautiful church of the Madonna di S. Biagio (1518–28; near Florence). Antonio the Younger, as a Florentine, enjoyed the patronage of the Medici pope Clement VII, and in 1520 he succeeded Raphael as *capomaestro* at St Peter's, Rome. He produced for this building a series of designs which culminated in the final model of c1534, engraved by Antonio dall'Abacco; this made an ambiguous compromise between a centralized and a longitudinal plan. Here, as at the Palazzo Farnese and S. Giovanni dei Fiorentini, his work was overtaken by the more dynamic style of Michelangelo. A vast collection of drawings by Antonio and by other members of the Sangallo family survives in the Uffizi at Florence.

Further reading. Clausse, G. *Les San Gallo*, Paris (1900–2). Giovannoni, G. *Antonio da Sangallo il Giovane* (2 vols.), Rome (1959). Loubouski, G.K. *Les Sangallo*, Paris (1934). Severini, G. *Architetture Militari di Giuliano da Sangallo*, Pisa (1970).

Sanmicheli Michele 1484–1559

Michele Sanmicheli was a Veronese architect, trained in Rome in the circle of Bramante, whose major works are in Venice and in his native city. He was, with Sansovino, one of the most original architects working in north Italy in the first half of the 16th century, and did more than anyone else to acclimatize the classical style to the Venetian *terra firma*. Earlier north Italian architects, like Gian Maria

Falconetto at Padua, had shown a somewhat timid and archaeological approach to classicism. Sanmicheli's architecture, by contrast, is plastic, vigorous, and highly imaginative. It gives an expressive and often specifically North Italian cast to the tradition of Bramante.

Early in his career, from 1509, Sanmicheli worked as architect to Orvieto Cathedral and advisor on papal fortifications. It was thus that he acquired his thorough knowledge of Classical and High Renaissance Roman architecture. Returning to north Italy by 1530, he embarked on a series of palace designs for his native city; they span his whole career and define the aims of his architecture. With their two-storied facades, the lower story rusticated, they are based on Bramante's Palazzo Caprini (the so-called House of Raphael). But they play complex variations upon it. These range from the Palazzo Bevilacque —with its complicated articulation of interlocking orders, its dramatic juxtapositions of solid and void, and its rich sculptural detail—to the more austere Palazzo Canossa, which has only a single order of half columns and shows a more restrained approach to surface texture.

The changes in Sanmicheli's facades are sometimes thought to reflect the general development of 16th-century Italian architecture, from the fantasy and elaboration of early Mannerism, in the 1530s and 1540s, to a more correctly classical style in the 1550s. But all Sanmicheli's architecture aims at giving imaginative expression to the function of the building, and the differences may equally be seen as varied interpretations of a central intention: that of displaying the grandeur and importance of the palace itself, and of the family who built it.

The same may be said of Sanmicheli's fortress architecture. Like most Renaissance architects, he built fortifications, and by 1530 was officially employed for this purpose by the Venetian Republic. His works are extensive, and are made particularly expressive by the use of very heavy rustication. His gateways, the Porta Nuova (1533–40), and the Porta Palio (c1555–60) in Verona, and the Castello di S. Andrea del Lido on the Venetian Lagoon, confront the onlooker with a firm statement of their intentions. In the most refined of them, the Porta Palio, we see a stylistic feature characteristic of Sanmicheli's architecture. It is a tendency to treat the facade in layers, cutting away sections of a wall to show another section behind it, often of a different texture. He also projects the facade outwards by means of pilasters, columns, and sculptural detail. This gives a great richness of light and shade to his architecture. The style can be seen in his Palazzo Grimani on the Grand Canal, Venice, where the forceful order of columns seems almost like a freestanding screen in front of the great arched windows behind.

Individual effects of this kind give Sanmicheli's buildings an air of inventive fantasy, which often seems to come from a fusion of Roman with North Italian modes. This is particularly true of his churches. Both the Pellegrini Chapel, attached to S. Bernardino, Verona, and the Madonna di Campagna outside the city, are centralized buildings in the tradition of North Italian votive chapels; but they are brought up to date by reference to Roman models: the Pantheon and Bramante's Tempietto. In the interior of the Pellegrini Chapel, the architectural articulation is richly complex, with its elaborate layers, discrete touches of color, and richness of texture in the individual features such as striated columns. It recalls the coloristic exuberance of 15th-century Lombard architecture, for example, Amadeo's Coleoni Chapel in Bergamo. It was Sanmicheli's mission to give the ornate and highly decorative tradition of north Italian architecture a new and more disciplined expression, through the classical vocabulary of the 16th century.

Further reading. Lagenskiöld, E. *Michele Sanmicheli, the Architect of Verona*, Uppsala (1938). Puppi, L. *Michele Sanmichele*, Padua (1971).

Sano di Pietro 1406–81

The Sienese painter and miniaturist Ansano di Pietro di Mencio was known as Sano di Pietro. He founded his style upon that of Sassetta (1392–1450), and concentrated on pleasing decorative effects. He was a popularizer of the Sienese preacher S. Bernardino (fresco, 1450; Palazzo Pubblico, Siena) and creator of the half-length Virgin with half-length saints and angels (Metropolitan Museum, New York). His work is easily recognizable by the sharp facial features of his figures, their large almond eyes, heavy forms, and hard outlines. He was a repetitive painter, but seems to have been popular with his con-

temporaries; his charm compensates for his rather monotonous style.

Sanraku Kano 1559–1635

The Japanese painter Kano Sanraku was the founder of the Kyoto branch of the *Kano* School. He was a retainer of the family of the dictator Hideyoshi, who apprenticed him to Kano Eitoku. Sanraku decorated Hideyoshi's Momoyama castle after his teacher's death. Although he was less brilliant than Eitoku, his technique was sound, and he embodies the change from the Momoyama style to the gentler early Edo manner.

This can be seen in the sliding doors of the Samboin, Hideyoshi's retreat at the Daigoji Temple, Kyoto, where waving grasses are set against gold-leaf backgrounds in elegantly complex patterns. It is also evident in the more famous set of doors at the Daikakuji Temple, Kyoto, where he sets big clumps of red or white peonies on a gold leaf ground, the foreground varied by a few simple rocks shaded in green. The ink outline is firm but not dashing, and the whole has the deceptive simplicity of the best Japanese decorative work.

However, Sanraku did not forget the boldness of his master's style. The room he decorated in the Nijo Palace, Kyoto, has a huge cypress tree spread across many panels, done with great grandeur but with a breathing liveliness which contrasts with the equally big but static pine compositions painted by the young Tan'yu in the same palace.

Sanraku continued the *Kano* ink-painting tradition, doing figure compositions on Chinese Confucian themes for the government, and also painting ink landscapes in a soft cursive style. In his last years his work took on the more tortured mood of a new age. He became a pioneer of distorted, leaning rock shapes and conflicting lines, which he passed on to his pupil Kano Sansetsu.

Sansetsu Kano 1590–1651

The Japanese painter Kano Sansetsu was the pupil of his adoptive father Sanraku. After the calm naturalism of the early Edo period, his work reflects the more tortured unnatural atmosphere that characterized the period of Japan's isolation from the outside world. In particular he adopted his master's tendency for conflicting pictorial

Sano di Pietro: The Madonna and Child; gold ground on panel; 60×46cm (24×18in). Private collection

planes. In the beautiful rooms of the Tenkyuin (*c*1635; Myoshinji Temple, Kyoto), the rocks are sloped and hatched to point in three different directions, and in the great *Plum Tree and Pheasant* composition, all pretence at naturalism is abandoned. His ink painting, also extremely skilled, showed the same tendencies to decorative drama. After the death of Sanraku, Sansetsu became head of the *Kano* School in Kyoto.

Sansovino Andrea c1467–1529

The Italian sculptor Andrea Contucci da Monte Sansovino was born in the Tuscan town of Monte San Savino or Sovino whence he derived his surname. He modeled altarpieces in terracotta in his native town. This bears out Vasari's statement that he was trained by Antonio Pollaiuolo, for the latter was primarily a modeler. Sansovino, however, found his *métier* in marble carving, which he probably learned in Florence, perhaps in the workshop of the Ferrucci family. He showed his prowess in his first documented commission in

Florence, the Corbinelli family altar in S. Spirito (1485–90). He was admitted to the sculptors' guild in 1491, and was then sent by Lorenzo de' Medici as an artistic emissary to Portugal, where he spent nine years.

Sansovino reappeared in Florence at the turn of the century and undertook two major commissions: a pair of marble statues (*Madonna and Child* and *St John the Baptist*), to complete a series in Genoa Cathedral left unfinished at the death of Civitali (1501), and a group of the *Baptism of Christ*, for the eastern doorway of the Baptistery in Florence (1502–5). Work on these was interrupted by a call to Rome in 1505, and it was not until 1569 that they were finished and erected, by Vincenzo Danti. The four marble statues from these two commissions are the epitome of High Renaissance sculpture in Florence, equivalent to paintings by Fra Bartolommeo (1472–1517) or Mariotto Albertinelli (1474–1515).

The sculptor was summoned to Rome by Pope Julius II to carve a pair of elaborate marble tombs in the choir of S. Maria del Popolo, for the Cardinals Ascanio Sforza and Basso della Rovere. They are designed like ancient Roman triumphal arches, containing eight nearly life-size statues, including the effigies. The angels and virtues are subtle variations on the classical themes of standing or seated female figures, and are

Andrea Sansovino: The Holy Family, a detail of Adoration of the Shepherds; marble; c1520–4. Basilica della Santa Casa, Loreto

some of the best High Renaissance sculptures. In 1512 Sansovino followed this success with a group of the *Virgin and Child with St Anne* (S. Agostino, Rome), deriving his composition from Leonardo's versions of the subject (cartoon in the National Gallery, London).

From 1513 until the end of his career Sansovino was in charge of the important Papal commission for a sculptural complex to be built in the Basilica della Santa Casa at Loreto. He carved two of the large narrative reliefs (1518–24)—the *Annunciation* and the *Adoration of the Shepherds*. He also supervised a group of younger sculptors, including important manifestations of the High Renaissance spirit, unaffected by the Mannerism that others were deriving from the later work of Raphael and Michelangelo.

Sansovino II 1486–1570

Jacopo Tatti, called Il Sansovino, was a High Renaissance sculptor and architect. He was born in Florence and trained in Rome by Andrea Sansovino, whose name he took. Before the Sack of Rome in 1527 he worked both there and in his native city, developing from his master a fluent, elevated style that was based on the grace and harmony of Raphael, rather than on the *terribilità* of Michelangelo. His *Madonna del Parto*, a Virgin and Child enthroned in a spacious, Bramantesque niche in S. Agostino, Rome, is close in style to Raphael's frescoed Isaiah in the same church. Like its model, it gives a gentler and more harmonious cast to the monumental figure-style that Michelangelo had evolved on the Sistine Chapel ceiling. The same is true of his *St James* for Florence Cathedral. This was carved during his stay there from 1511 to 1513, from a block originally intended for Michelangelo himself.

Jacopo Sansovino also worked as an architect in Rome. His work strives after an ideal balance between sculptural and architectural forms, seeking to translate into three dimensions what Raphael had achieved in paint in the Stanze of the Vatican.

In 1527, as a result of the Sack of Rome, Sansovino went to Venice. He had intended to go on to France, but the *Signoria* employed him to give advice on S. Marco, and in 1529 he was given an official position as architect to the Venetian Republic. He survived a temporary disgrace, when the vault of his new library col-

Il Sansovino: St John the Baptist; marble; height 120cm (47in); c1554–6. S. Maria Gloriosa dei Frari, Venice

lapsed, and held the post until his death.

As the first architect and sculptor to work in a High Renaissance style in Venice, he formed Venetian 16th-century taste in these fields. His major buildings—the Library, the Mint, the Loggetta for the Campanile of St Mark's, and the now-destroyed church of S. Geminiano at the end of Piazza S. Marco—were the first to give classical form to the city.

The settled political climate of Venice, her prosperity, self-confidence, and pride, formed an excellent basis for the development of the temperate and harmonious classicism of Sansovino's style—a style further enriched by the specifically Venetian experience of light and color.

This is apparent above all in the new

Library, one of the masterpieces of the High Renaissance. (The building was begun in 1537, and completed after Sansovino's death.) The long loggia of the Library faces those of the Doges' Palace on the other side of the Piazzetta. Its two-storied facade is lower than the three stories of the palace opposite. But Sansovino provides a contrast to the sheer, coloristically patterned surface of that 15th-century building, with his exceptionally deeply cut, sculpturally enriched structure; this is thrown into such rich and vibrant relief by the light that its weight perfectly matches the flat facade opposite. Most of the motifs are Roman, but the sensuous richness of the whole is Venetian. It is as original, in its way, as the pictorial style of Titian.

The neighboring Loggetta (1537–40), with its delicate use of colored marbles, again gives northern expression to central Italian ideas. Here, with bronze statues in niches elegantly incorporated into the design, Sansovino gives perfect expression to that harmonious relationship between sculpture and architecture which he had already sought in Rome. This ideal harmony is entirely in keeping with the iconography of the Loggetta, which, through figures such as Peace and Apollo, glorifies the harmony and virtues of the Venetian State.

Sansovino also worked in bronze in S. Marco, notably on the reliefs of the Sacristy door. He formed 16th-century Venetian tomb design through his Venice monument in S. Salvatore (1556–61); and he carved the colossal statues of Mars and Neptune which give the Sala dei Giganti of the Doges' Palace its name. With his friends Titian and Pietro Aretino, he became during the middle of the 16th century something of an arbiter of Venetian artistic taste.

Further reading. Howard, D. *Jacopo Sansovino: Architecture and Patronage in Renaissance Venice*, Yale (1975). Mariacher, G. *Il Sansovino*, Milan (1962). Tafuri, M. *Jacopo Sansovino e l'Architettura del 1500 a Venezia*, Padua (1969).

Sargent J.S. 1856–1925

John Singer Sargent was an American painter of portraits and landscapes. He was born while his parents were visiting Florence, and was educated in France, Italy, and Germany. He studied at the

J.S. Sargent: Carnation, Lily, Lily, Rose, oil on canvas; 174×154cm (69×61in); 1885–6. Tate Gallery, London

École des Beaux-Arts in Paris under Carlos Duran, and first exhibited at the Salon in 1877. His early portraits attracted harsh criticism in both London and Paris. His portrait of *Madame X (Madame Gautreau*, 1884; Metropolitan Museum, New York) caused a famous scandal in Paris, which provoked his move to London. He established a studio at Tite Street, London, and began a series of popular child portraits, the best known of which is *Carnation, Lily, Lily, Rose* (1885–6; Tate Gallery, London). He was perhaps equal to Joshua Reynolds (1723–92) and Thomas Gainsborough (1727–88) as a stylish portrait painter of his own era. The reputation that he established bridged the Atlantic. He was made a Royal Academician in 1897, he decorated Boston Public Library (1890–1921), and was appointed an official British War Artist in 1918.

Sarrazin Jacques 1588–1660

The most important French sculptor of the mid 17th century, Jacques Sarrazin, trained initially under Nicolas Gullain before spending the period from 1610 to c1617 in Rome. In Italy he worked at Frascati for Giacomo della Porta, and after his return the influence of the classicizing Roman style is evident. A more personal manner is apparent in his first royal commission—the decoration of Jacques Lemercier's Pavillon de l'Horloge, at the Louvre, Paris (1636). His caryatid figures on the attic story clearly derive from firsthand study of the Antique, and may claim to be the earliest examples of French classicism in sculpture. From 1642 to 1650 he directed the decoration of the Château de Maisons, Paris, for François Mansart. His last work was the monument to Henri Bourbon, Prince of Condé, in the church of St Paul, St Louis (begun in 1648, finished in 1663, and moved to Chantilly in the 19th century where it stands in the Musée Condé). It anticipates the Louis XIV style in its peculiar mixture of classicism and the Baroque. The style established by Sarrazin was to dominate the sculpture of Versailles for the next two decades.

Sassetta 1392–1450

Stefano di Giovanni, known as Sassetta, was the most important Sienese painter of the 15th century. He was probably born in Siena, and was certainly at work there by 1426. His first great work was an altarpiece for the Arte della Lana in Siena (1423–6), of which parts survive in Siena (Pinacoteca Nazionale), Budapest (National Gallery), the Vatican (Museums), and elsewhere. In 1426, he was working for Siena Cathedral, and the following year made a drawing for the baptistery font. He continued his architectural work, and in 1440 he made designs (which were not used) for the circular west window of the cathedral.

At first, Sassetta worked in an International Gothic style, much influenced by Taddeo di Bartolo. In his seven *Scenes from the Life of St Anthony Abbot* (c1436; some panels in National Gallery of Art, Washington, D.C., for example, *The Meeting of St Anthony Abbot and Paul the Hermit*), the influence of French illumination seems clear, placing the scenes far away from anything to do with ordinary life. Sassetta's art—and that of his contemporaries—is characterized by an intense awareness and imitation of the forms of the previous century. Whereas Florence was very conscious of the newness of her artistic style, and vaunted the break with the past occasioned by Masaccio and Donatello, Siena carried on using the gold backgrounds, brightly painted forms, and unreal settings until the end of the century.

Sassetta and his fellows did not, however, avoid absorbing some influence from Florence, seen, for example, in his splendid *Madonna of the Snows* (1430–2; Contini-Bonacossi Collection, Florence). Painted

Sassetta: St Francis renounces his Earthly Father; a panel from an altarpiece; 88×53cm (35×21in); c1437–44. National Gallery, London

for the Chapel of S. Bonifazio in Siena Cathedral, it depicts in the *predella* the miracle by which the plan of a church was marked out on the ground by a fall of snow. The carved and gilded scallops of the wooden frame overhang the painting as if it were formed of figures within an actual tabernacle; but there is little perspective, and the Virgin's robe is draped on to the floor in a slow elaboration of luscious folds. The saints at the back on either side are likewise flat and decorative. But the figures of the Baptist and St Francis of Assisi at the front are completely different. They are kneeling, and the artist has taken pains to indicate how the garment forms taut creases over the knees—and to impose those knees and also the slowly gesticulating hands almost into our space. In this work Sassetta has grafted the manner of Masaccio on to the traditionalism of Siena.

More characteristic of his style is the panel of the *Madonna and Child Crowned by Two Angels* (*c*1445; Frick Collection, New York), a late work in which a Virgin with all the sinuous delicacy of a Virgin by Simone Martini floats in a golden heaven, clutching her child warmly to her face. A similar gesture enlivens his *Madonna and Child with SS. John the Baptist, Michael, Nicolas and Margaret* (*c*1437; S. Domenico, Cortona). In this painting, the figures are not set within one unified space, as in *Madonna of the Snows*, but are separated from the central section by Gothic colonnettes, each housed within its own scalloped arch. Again, there is a distinction between the figure-styles: all the saints are flat and decorative, symbols of another world rather than elevated heroes from our planet, whereas the Virgin and the foremost of the two angels have some solidity—an indication of Florentine contact. Even after Sassetta's time, Florentine influence continued to pervade Sienese art in the work of painters like Matteo di Giovanni and Francesco di Giorgio.

Sassoferrato 1609–85

Giovanni Battista Salvi, called Sassoferrato from his birthplace, was active mostly in Rome and Umbria. He was one of a small group of painters in Rome who rejected the excitement and vivid color of the

Roelandt Savery: Alpine Landscape; black and red chalk with pale blue wash on paper; 40×39cm (16×15½in). British Museum, London

Sassoferrato: Self-portrait; oil on canvas; 38×33cm (15×13in). Uffizi, Florence

Baroque and sought instead a rigorous purity of design, and cold, clear colors. Sassoferrato's works are strikingly archaic, and reach for inspiration beyond Domenichino to the 15th century; they suggest a kind of 17th-century Pre-Raphaelitism. He painted some portraits of ecclesiastics, but most of his works are of sacred subjects. His many altarpieces and small devotional paintings of the Madonna and Child had widespread popular appeal.

Saura Antonio 1930–

The Spanish painter Antonio Saura began to paint in 1947, during a long illness. From 1953 to 1957 he lived in Paris. In 1956 he exhibited at the Spanish Museum of Contemporary Art in Madrid, and in 1957 became a founder member of the "El Paso" group of painters and writers, along with Rafael Canoger, Luis Feito, and

Manolo Millares. Early in his career he came under the influence of Surrealism, but by the late 1950s his work was concerned with an expressionistic, almost abstract, portrayal of figures (for example, *Crucifixion*; triptych; oil on canvas; 1959–60; Joseph Hirshhorn Museum, Washington, D.C.). From 1953 he used only black and white in his paintings, tempered later by the addition of brown contrasts. Saura moved towards more cartoon-like work with strongly emotional, political, and social subjects concerned to condemn the outrages done to man.

Savery Roelandt 1576?–1639

The painter Roelandt Savery was born at Courtrai of mixed Dutch and Flemish background. In 1591 he settled in Amsterdam, where he was probably taught by his brother. His combination of elegant artificiality and precise observation is characteristic of Flemish art in the early 17th century. He was most famous for his flower pieces—vast bouquets of an infinite variety of species set in niches. He specialized, too, in fantastic landscapes, crowded with exotic birds and animals. His work was influenced by Gillis van Coninxloo (1544–1607)—his many details are meticulously rendered, and the landscapes are sharply divided into planes of color (for example, *The Garden of Eden*, 1623; Kunsthistorisches Museum, Vienna). About 1604 he was called to Prague by Rudolph II; in 1619 he settled in Utrecht.

Savoldo Girolamo 1480?–1548

Giovanni Girolamo Savoldo was a Brescian painter, who settled in Venice *c*1520. He had visited Florence, where he must have seen the works of Michelangelo, and the grandeur of his large, monumental figures surely comes from this experience. In his *St Jerome* in the National Gallery, London, we can see the massiveness of the limbs and the expressive largeness of hands and feet. This is a feature common in Savoldo, and reminiscent of Michelangelo's *David*.

The ideal nobility of Savoldo's saints is always tempered by an earthy realism. They are peasants, and their garments, although they fall in grand, simplified folds, are homespun. This earthiness is typical of the Brescian school—we find it also in Romanino—and is one of the qualities that distinguishes Savoldo's style from Venetian painting proper. It is present even when, as in the *St Jerome*, he paints in a thoroughly Venetian manner, constructing his landscape in planes of intense blue in the manner of Titian.

Savoldo's chief contribution to the history of painting was a new apprehension of light. His settings are almost always dark, and he loved to paint the moment of dusk, when the local colors of the foreground forms stand out sharply against encroaching darkness.

This *contre nuit* (as opposed to *contre jour*) device is the main effect in his paintings. It is often enhanced by additional contrasts between different kinds of natural and artificial light—a fire, a candle, the remains of a sunset sky, moonlight, or the visionary light emanating from some spiritual being—as can be seen in the *St Matthew and the Angel* in the Metropolitan Museum, New York.

Girolamo Savoldo: St Mary Magdalen approaching the Sepulcher; oil on canvas; 86×79cm (34×31in). National Gallery, London

Such paintings evoke an intense, poetic mood and Savoldo was certainly influenced by Giorgione; but his careful recording of specific realistic effects is in the Lombard tradition. He influenced the later styles of his contemporaries Titian and Jacopo Bassano, and played an important role in the later 16th century in forming the artistic style of his fellow countryman, Caravaggio.

Johann Schadow: Self-portrait; height 41cm (16in); c1794. Nationalgalerie, Berlin

Scamozzi Vincenzio 1552–1616

The Italian architect Vincenzio Scamozzi is best known as the successor to Palladio and an early exponent of Palladianism. He completed several of Palladio's commissions, notably the Teatro Olimpico in Vicenza (1579–80; completed in 1583). The contrast between his style and Palladio's is shown in the more severe and geometric classicism of the Villa Pisani a Rocca (*c*1576), itself a chaste variation of Palladio's Villa Capra at Vicenza. In imitation of his master, he published in 1615 *L'Idea dell'Architettura Universale*, a longer, more detailed, but less effective version of Palladio's *I Quattro Libri*. About 1613 he sold a large collection of his drawings and those of Palladio to the Earl of Arundel and to Inigo Jones, which enormously advanced the standing of classical architecture in England.

Schadow Johann 1764–1850

Johann Gottfried Schadow was the greatest German Neo-classical sculptor, and a distinguished draftsman and graphic artist. He studied in Italy, where he befriended Antonio Canova, before returning to his native Berlin as court sculptor in 1788. His best period was from 1788 to 1797, when he produced the *Quadriga of Victory* for the Brandenburg Gate (1793), the double-portrait of *Princesses Louisa and Frederica of Prussia* (1797; Staatliche Museen, Berlin), and the statue of *General von Zieten* (1794). The latter was one of the first German monuments to a man who was not a ruler. He made a study-tour of French equestrian statues in northern Europe during 1791 and 1792, in preparation for a memorial to Frederick the Great; the commission was later canceled. From 1800 he depended chiefly on private commissions. He was Director of the Berlin Academy from 1816.

Scheemaeckers Peter 1691–1781

Peter Scheemaeckers was a Flemish sculptor who worked in England. Born in Antwerp, the son of a sculptor, he went to London at some time before 1721; he made his career there, retiring to Antwerp in 1771. By 1725 he had set up a practice in monumental sculpture in partnership with the Walloon Laurent Delvaux, with whom he went to Rome in 1728, to study Classical sculpture. Returning alone in 1730, Scheemaeckers became one of the most successful sculptors in England. He was more prolific than his rival Michael Rysbrack, whose prices he undercut, but he was less talented and flexible, and some of his work is mechanical and repetitive. In 1741 he briefly eclipsed Rysbrack with his monument to Shakespeare (Westminster Abbey, London).

Scheerre Herman *fl. c1403–19*

The illuminator Herman Scheerre was probably of Rhenish origin. He became master of a prominent English workshop early in the 15th century, with his associates, exercised a profound influence on native manuscript and illumination. Only one work bears his full signature: a small miniature of *St John the Evangelist*, in a simple select Missal (*c*1403–5; British Library, London). He may be identifiable with Herman Lymnour, who, in 1407, witnessed a London will connected with Cologne legatees. Certainly Scheerre's style shows affinity with the Cologne panel-painter known as the "Veronica Master". During 1388–9, William Duke of Gelder, close ally of Richard II, employed "Herman of Cologne"; this artist assisted Jean Malouel with work for the Duke of Burgundy in Dijon, between 1401 and 1403, and was in Paris, at court, in 1419. It seems probable that these Hermans are one and the same.

Scheerre was a versatile master-artist, rather than simply an illuminator. Although comparatively few miniatures are attributable to his hand with certainty, he brought a new approach to painting in England. He was no portraitist, but his figures convey a spiritual quality, with pallid faces and deep-set black eyes: their drapery is uncomplicated, the coloring harmonious and glowing. A courtly motto links a number of manuscripts like a workshop signature: *Omnia leuia sunt amanti. Si quis amat non laborat*. Part of this appears in the magnificent Great Bible (completed *c*1410; British Library, London) which employed many artists, English and foreign. The first illuminated initial of the Breviary made for Archbishop Chichele (*c*1408–14? Lambeth Palace, London), contains the second part of the motto, continuing *Quod Herman*.

The Bedford Hours and Psalter (*c*1419?; British Library, London) was commissioned for John Duke of Bedford, the younger son of Henry IV. It excels in variety; the rich border decoration in-

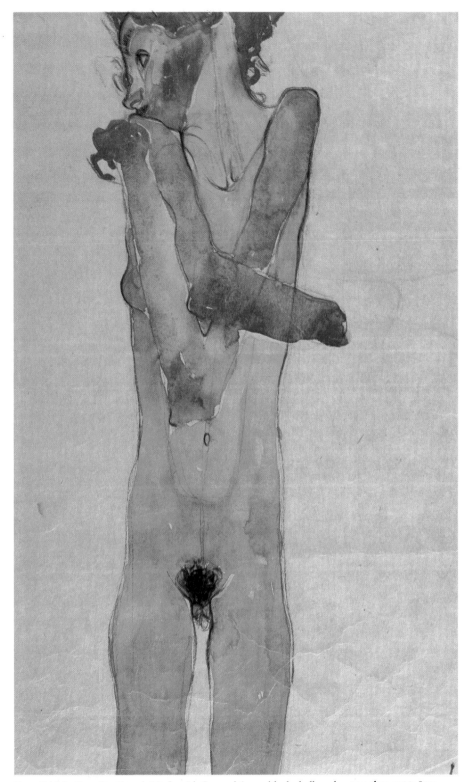

Egon Schiele: Standing Female Nude with Crossed Arms; black chalk and watercolor; 45×28cm (18×11in); 1910. Graphische Sammlung Albertina, Vienna

cludes fashionable French motifs. "Herman" is written in two line-endings. After this splendid work was finished Herman Scheerre apparently left England, but his School continued to produce manuscripts in a similar, if debased, style.

Schiele Egon 1890–1918

The Austrian painter Egon Schiele was born at Tulln, Lower Austria. After an unsatisfactory school career, he entered the Vienna Academy of Fine Arts in 1906. He soon came into contact with the avant-garde and exhibited at the second (*Internationale*) *Kunstschau* of 1909.

Gustav Klimt, whom Schiele met in 1907, had a formative influence upon his early work. Their admiration was mutual and Klimt was aware of the younger artist's powers of draftsmanship. Schiele quickly shook off his influence, and that of *Jugendstil* in general, and went on to produce oil paintings, watercolors, and drawings of great nervous intensity and an aggressive linear energy, often erotic in content. Sexuality was a theme that pervaded much radical Viennese thought and art of this time (for instance the works of Otto Weininger, Sigmund Freud, and Klimt), and Schiele's studies of nude girls and of his own body are no exception. They are explicit but at the same time tortured images of humanity, a fact that led people to label his work "Expressionist".

Just before and during the First World War, Schiele painted a series of major portraits, psychologically penetrating works such as the portraits of *Johann Harms* (1916; Solomon R. Guggenheim Museum, New York), *Albert Paris von Gütersloh* (1918; Minneapolis Institute of Arts), and *Edith Seated* (1917–18; Österreichische Galerie, Vienna). He also created some semiallegorical paintings, of which *The Family* (1917; Österreichische Galerie, Vienna) is the most forceful and moving. Schiele died in the notorious influenza epidemic of 1918—the year that also claimed Otto Wagner and Gustav Klimt, and saw the collapse of the old world of Austria-Hungary.

Further reading. Mitsch, E. *The Art of Egon Schiele*, London (1975). Vergo, P. *Art in Vienna 1898–1918*, London (1975). Whitford, F. *Egon Schiele*, London (1981). Wilson, S. *Egon Schiele*, Oxford (1980).

Schlemmer Oskar 1888–1943

The German painter and sculptor Oskar Schlemmer studied painting at Stuttgart under Holzel, and taught at the Bauhaus from 1920 to 1929 as form master in the metal and sculpture workshops. His most important contribution was as director of the stage workshop (1923–9). His designs for the *Triadisches Ballet* (performed in Stuttgart in 1922, and at the Bauhaus in 1923, to music by Paul Hindemith), accorded with his ideas of synthesis and universal art. He explored form and movement, reducing figures to precise profile, frontal, and rear positions. His Bauhaus staircase (Dessau, 1933) unified painting with architecture. He taught at Breslau (1929–32) and in Berlin (1932–3), before being classified as "degenerate" by the Nazis in 1933.

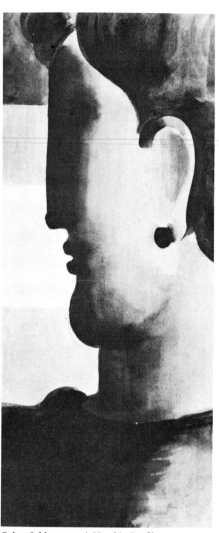

Oskar Schlemmer: A Head in Profile; watercolor over pencil on paper; 40×18cm (16×7in); 1931/2. Collection of Mrs Tut Schlemmer, Stuttgart

Schlüter Andreas c1660–1714

Trained in Danzig, the German architect and sculptor Andreas Schlüter is first documented as working on the decorative sculpture of the Krasiński Palace in Warsaw (1689–93). In 1694 he arrived in Berlin. His early work there is confined to sculpture, including the keystones for the Arsenal, commissioned in 1696. In the same year he began the bronze statue of *Frederick III* (1696–1709; Schloss Charlottenberg, Berlin). Between 1700 and 1706 he was the genius presiding over the commissions of Frederick III, including the ambitious, monumental Royal Palace in Berlin. His late style was revealed by his Kamecke house (1711–12; Berlin, destroyed). In 1714, after the death of his royal patron, he moved to St Petersburg, dying there in the same year.

Schmidt-Rottluff Karl 1884–1976

The German painter Karl Schmidt-Rottluff was born at Chemnitz, Saxony. He was an architectural student at Dresden, and founded the *Brücke* group in 1905 together with Fritz Bleyl, Erich Heckel, and Ernst Kirchner. After 1905 his paintings and graphics reflect the influence of Post-Impressionism, and also that of Emil Nolde, with whom he worked in 1906 (for example, *Self-portrait*, 1906; Stiftung Seebüll Ada und Emil Nolde, Seebüll). Unlike his *Brücke* colleagues he concentrated on landscapes, but in 1912 his expressive color brought him to the brink of Expressionist abstraction. His spiky figure paintings combined African influences in a semi-Cubist idiom (for example, *Woman Resting*, 1912; Staatsgalerie, Munich). Proscribed by the Nazis, he returned to Berlin after the war and taught art from 1947 in Berlin as a Professor at the Academy of Fine Arts.

Further reading. Brix, K. *Karl Schmidt-Rottluff*, Leipzig (1972). Dube, W.-D. *The Expressionists*, London (1972). Grohmann, W. *Schmidt-Rottluff, Aquarelle und Zeichnungen*, Munich (1963). Schmidt-Rottluff, K. "Brief über Munch und die Brücke", *Die Schanze*, Munich (1951).

Below: Karl Schmidt-Rottluff; Still Life. Private collection

Right: Martin Schongauer: Madonna in the Rose Bower; panel; 201×112cm (79×44in); 1473. Church of St Martin, Colmar

Schongauer Martin c1430–91

Descended from a patrician family of Augsburg, the German artist Martin Schongauer was best known in his lifetime as a painter, but his influence and his posthumous fame stem from his copper engravings. He was the son of a goldsmith who settled in Colmar c1440, and his name appears in the matriculation book of Leipzig University in 1465. Vasari records an old tradition that the young Schongauer studied under Rogier van der Weyden; he certainly knew the latter's *Last Judgment* Altarpiece in the hospital at Beaune. In 1469 he was mentioned as living in Colmar, but unlike his father he does not seem to have acquired citizenship there before his departure for Breisach.

Nothing certain is known about Schongauer's training as a painter. It seems probable that he studied under the minor Colmar painter Caspar Isenmann, who was himself greatly influenced by Netherlandish painting. No engravings can be dated to before 1465, but three drawings by Schongauer are dated 1469, and another 1470. These are clearly early works, and in them he is revealed to be the heir to the upper Rhine graphic tradition (that of Master ES and the Master of the Playing Cards).

His early *Adoration of the Magi* is inspired by Rogier van der Weyden's *St Columba* Altarpiece, a work which was then in Cologne (now Alte Pinakothek, Munich), and his early *Madonna and Child with the Parrot* is partially based on the *Madonna and Child* by Dieric Bouts (National Gallery, London). Although his technique has its origins in the Upper Rhine, the detailed treatment of the subject matter and the impeccable finish of his engravings stem from the sophistication of Netherlandish painting.

Presumably Schongauer traveled widely; his first known group of ten prints was executed shortly after 1470. His early work is characterized by vigorous and slightly uncoordinated hatching, as well as by vertical uprights to his initial "M"; his technical evolution parallels his stylistic development. In his mature years, the delicate hatching and soft transitions of light and shade have a poetic reticence and reach a climax in his late *Annunciation*. In the mature and late engravings, the uprights of the "M" in his initials are splayed. Although Schongauer initialed all his engravings and many drawings, no paintings that can be connected with him are signed, and only the *Madonna in the Rose Bower* is dated (1473; St Martin, Colmar).

In 1488, Schongauer moved to nearby Breisach to paint the enormous *Last Judgment* frescoes in the cathedral (these are now in ruinous condition). He died there in 1491, probably of the plague. The young Albrecht Dürer traveled to Breisach to visit him. He arrived after Schongauer's death, but acquired some of his drawings. The technical sophistication and clarity of Schongauer's forms deeply impressed Dürer, and the bizarre inventions of his *Temptation of St Anthony* engraving fascinated artists as different as Hieronymus Bosch and Michelangelo.

Schoonhoven Jan 1914–

The Dutch painter Johannes Jacobus (Jan) Schoonhoven was born in Delft. He studied at the Hague Academy from 1932 to 1936. Since 1946 he has worked for the Dutch Post Office. From 1957 to 1959 he was a member of the Netherlands Informal Group, and in 1960 he was a cofounder of "Groupe Null".

From 1940 to 1956 his works consisted of figurative drawings and gouaches inspired by Paul Klee. In 1957 he made his first formal, Abstract reliefs in papier-mâché which continued the linear and organic divisions of the picture surface of the earlier works. The white reliefs he made from 1960 onwards consisted of squares and rectangles, serial in form, gradually becoming more precise. Later, by using cardboard, he introduced inclined planes that produced changes in light and shade. All his reliefs—whether rectangular, in concentric circles, or spiral in form—are divided into identical, repeated elements, allying him to Minimal art. His freehand drawings display the same properties.

Schwitters Kurt 1887–1948

The German artist and poet Kurt Schwitters founded the Dadaist movement *Merz*. Born in Hannover, he studied art there and in Dresden. Towards the end of the First World War, abstract and expressionist tendencies emerged in his paintings, but his earliest independent works date from 1918–19, when he made his first collages and *Merz*-pictures. (The term *Merz* was derived from the name of a bank—*Kommerz und Privat Bank*—while making a collage from its newspaper advertisements, and was ultimately applied by Schwitters to all his art activities and to the magazine he founded in Hannover in 1923.)

The *Merz* pictures are composed entirely from rubbish—including wire, string, rags, newspaper, and tickets—which Schwitters had lovingly rescued. Although they are abstract in form, the choice of collage material ensures that many suggest identifiable themes or scenarios. His poems were composed into rhythmic patterns in a similar manner, from banal phrases, scraps of sentences, and fragments of words. The *Merz* pictures represent an implicit attack on the notion that art can be made only from fine materials, by someone possessed of special technical and creative gifts.

It was his insistence that *Merz* was an art, not an anti-art movement, together with his indifference to politics, that earned him the hostility of the leader of Berlin Dada, Richard Huelsenbeck, who debarred Schwitters from Dada activities in Berlin. But Schwitters had been friendly with Raoul Hausmann, a leading Berlin Dada artist, since 1918; he accompanied him on a Dada lecture tour to Prague in 1921, and his magazine, *Merz* (1923–32), was openly sympathetic to the Dada movement.

In 1922 he toured Holland with Theo van Doesburg. His subsequent *Merz* pictures—although still assembled from detritus—show the influence of *De Stijl* in their more rectilinear, less expressionistic compositions. In 1923, he began to work seriously on the conversion of his family home in Hannover into a complete *Merz* environment; over the years he transformed it into a series of grotto-like chambers by the accretion of an immense variety of objects. This, his first and most elaborate *Merzbau* (Merz house), was destroyed during the Second World War.

Increasingly involved in abstractionist and constructivist circles, Schwitters collaborated with El Lissitzky on various advertising projects in the mid 1920s, experimenting in a radical way with layout and typography. In 1932 he joined the *Abstraction-Création* group. Many of his *Merz* collages and constructions of this period reflect these contacts in their severe and simple compositions.

A refugee from Nazi Germany, Schwitters settled in Lysaker, near Oslo, in 1937, and there began work on a new *Merzbau*. (It, too, was destroyed—in 1951.) When the Germans invaded Norway in 1940, he fled to England. He spent a period in internment camps, and later lived in

Kurt Schwitters: interior view of the first Merzbau, Hannover; 1923–6; destroyed

London where he was welcomed by avant-garde artists; he finally settled in Ambleside in the Lake District. There he began work on a third *Merzbau*, but it was far from completion when he died.

Schwitters' ultimate ambition was to create a "total work of art". This *Merz-Stage* was never realized, but his collages and constructions have exerted a considerable influence on many artists since the War.

Further reading. Ades, D. *Dada and Surrealism Reviewed*, London (1978). Richter, H. *Dada: Art and Anti-Art*, New York (1965). Schmalenbach, W. *Kurt Schwitters: Leben und Werk*, Cologne (1967).

Steinitz, K. *Kurt Schwitters: a Portait from Life*, Los Angeles (1968). Tzara, T. "Merz Master: Kurt Schwitters 1887–1948", *Portfolio*, New York (Spring 1964).

Scopas 4th century BC

The Greek late Classical sculptor and architect Scopas came from Paros. He worked primarily in marble, and was active on the mainland as well as in east Greece and Samothrace. Around the middle of the 4th century he collaborated with Bryaxis, Leochares, and Timotheus in the sculptural decoration of the Mausoleum at Halicarnassus. While in Asia Minor, he carved one of the elaborate

columns of the Temple of Artemis in Ephesus. For Cnidos he executed an *Athena* and a *Dionysos*—works that were obscured by the glory of the *Aphrodite* of Praxiteles.

Scopas was the architect, and presumably supervisor of the sculptures, of the Temple of Athena Alea at Tegea. He also carved the marble statues of Asclepius and Hygeia on either side of the cult statue of Athena Alea in the *cella*. The temple was perhaps built after the Mausoleum; it was Doric, and had interior semidetached Corinthian columns with capitals of an individual design. The east pediment was decorated with *The Calydonian Boar-hunt*, the west with *The Battle of Achilles and Telephus*. The surviving heads of heroes offer an indication of Scopas' style: cubic, with deep-set eyes and half-open mouths, they are violently twisted to express emotion (examples in the Archaeological Museum, Tegea, and the National Museum, Athens).

The pathetic aspect of his art has long been emphasized. A *Maenad* in frenzy grasping a kid she had just killed was praised in verse and prose. We also hear of two statues of *Longing* (Pothos), one possibly copied in the figure of a winged effeminate boy, his body and gaze directed upwards and to the left, a goose at his feet.

His *Herakles* in Sicyon may be the prototype of the Lansdowne *Herakles* (J. Paul Getty Museum, Malibu, California), a Classical composition indebted to Polycleitos. Another Classical type attributed to Scopas is the *Meleager*, perhaps adapted by him from the east pediment of the temple in Tegea.

Scorel Jan van 1495–1562

The Dutch painter Jan van Scorel (or Schoorel) was born at Schoorl and studied at Amsterdam. Between 1519 and 1525 he traveled extensively through Germany, the Holy Land, and Italy, where he served for a time as conservator of the papal collections in Rome under the Dutch pontiff, Hadrian VI. He settled in Utrecht, where he became a canon. His *Rest on the Flight into Egypt* (1530; National Gallery of Art, Washington, D.C.) is highly Italian in format and style, with a classical mountainous landscape. The Madonna's dress is reminiscent of that of Michelangelo's *Madonna and Child* sculpture at Bruges (Notre-Dame). His portraits are more conventionally Northern, but with lively

Jan van Scorel: Alpine Landscape; pen and brown ink on paper; 21×16cm (8×6in); c1518. British Museum, London

characterization (for example, *Agatha van Schoonhoven*; Galleria Doria Pamphili, Rome).

Scott Tim 1937–

The English sculptor Tim Scott was born in London. He studied at the Architectural Association, London (1954–5), and with Anthony Caro at St Martin's School of Art, London (1955–9). From 1959 to 1961 he worked in Paris at the Le Corbusier-Wegenscky atelier. He has taught sculpture at St Martin's since 1962.

Since 1961, when he abandoned his cast-plaster techniques, Scott has favored combinations of contrasting materials. In the early 1960s he used painted fiberglass or wood and glass to create simple but eccentric shapes whose color emphasized mass.

From 1965 until the early 1970s he used colored acrylic sheets bolted to steel tubing to create large, open groups of flat planes. Smaller works constructed from clear acrylic sheets or blocks joined by steel elements, were followed in 1974 by sculptures in forged steel and bars, and later, by large, rugged works in steel and wood.

Scott William 1913–89

The British painter William Scott was born at Greenock, Scotland. He studied at the Belfast College of Art (1928–31) and at the Royal Academy in London (1931–5). For four years, from 1942 to 1946, Scott served in the Army and did no serious painting. His early work reveals the influence of both Cézanne and Picasso. His *Colander, Beans and Eggs* of 1948 (Al-

bright-Knox Art Gallery, Buffalo) reveals a strong interest in the flat, abstract qualities of shape and form. This continued as the basis of Scott's vision: a variation on some domestic theme, usually a simple still life, so treated that the main emphases fall on color, shape, and design (for example, *Deep Blues*, 1970–1; artist's collection).

Sebastiano del Piombo
c1485–1547

The Italian painter Sebastiano Luciani was called "del Piombo" from his keepership of the Papal seal, a sinecure for official artists that was conferred on him in 1531. He was a Venetian by birth, and his career until 1511 was closely paralleled by that of his near-contemporary, Titian. Like him, he passed from the studio of Giovanni Bellini to that of Giorgione, and participated in the completion of at least one unfinished work of that master's, the *Three Philosophers* (Kunsthistorisches Museum, Vienna). In 1511 he accepted an invitation to go to Rome and remained there, except for a visit to Venice during 1528/9, for the rest of his life.

His earliest certain works were a pair of organ shutters, of *St Lewis* and *St Sinibald* (1507–8; S. Bartolommeo a Rialto, Venice). These reflect the impression made on him by Giorgione's fresco figures on the Fondaco dei Tedeschi (now the main post office in Venice) and are painted with an extreme delicacy, and sensibility to subtleties of light and color, that derive from Giorgione. The altarpiece of *S. Giovanni Crisostomo and other Saints* (1509; S. Giovanni Crisostomo, Venice), and the unfinished *Judgment of Solomon* (c1510/11; Bankes Collection, Kingston Lacey, Dorset) show a monumental classicism beyond anything in Giorgione's authenticated work.

After his move to Rome, Sebastiano became a close friend of Michelangelo. It is widely accepted that some preliminary drawings for two of his major works are from Michelangelo's hand. The works are *The Raising of Lazarus* (c1517–19; National Gallery, London), painted for Narbonne Cathedral in rivalry with Raphael's *Transfiguration*, and the fresco of *The Flagellation of Christ* (1520–4; S. Pietro in Montorio, Rome). *The Raising of Lazarus* is a handsome picture, but the handling seems depressingly coarse and heavy.

Vasari regarded him as a portrait painter, and a number of powerful portraits have come down to us. The *Portrait of a Lady* (c1512; Staatliche Museen, Berlin) still retains much of the delicacy of his Venetian work, and a particularly fine example of his later style is the *Birth of the Virgin* (1532; S. Maria del Popolo, Rome).

Further reading. Dussler, L. *Sebastiano del Piombo*, Basel (1942). Hirst, M. *Sebastiano del Piombo*, London (1981). Palluchini, R. *Sebastiano Viniziano*, Milan (1944).

Sebastiano del Piombo: Portrait of a Lady; poplar panel; 76×60cm (30×24in); c1512. Staatliche Museen, Berlin

Segal George 1924–

Born in New York City, the American artist George Segal studied at Coopers Union, the Pratt Institute of Design, and Rutgers University. During the late 1950s he worked as a painter in an Abstract Expressionist style. Then in 1961 he turned to sculpture, making figure sculptures by taking plaster casts from life. Though rough, unfinished and starkly white, these fully dressed, life-size figures (reminiscent of the petrified figures from Pompeii) have an uncanny presence, and often evoke a mood of loneliness and isolation. Segal's stated concern is with the "presence of man in daily life" and he uses real objects to provide an everyday setting for his figures, who are captured performing the routine actions of anonymous, uneventful lives. In *The Diner* (1964–6; Walker Art Center, Minneapolis), for example, a stool, counter and coffee machine are used to create a setting for a waitress and a seated customer. From the mid 1970s he created part figures—concentrating, for example, on the head and an arm—and began experimenting with bright colors.

Further reading. Barrio-Garay, J.L. *The Private World of George Segal*, New York (1973). Hunter, S. and Hawthorne, D. *George Segal*, New York (1984).

Seghers Hercules 1589/90–c1635

Little is known of the life of Hercules Seghers, the first of the great 17th-century Dutch landscapists, and only about 15 of his paintings survive. He was born in Haarlem, and studied in Amsterdam under the Flemish-born landscapist Gillis van Coninxloo (1544–1607). Thereafter he worked in several Dutch centers, and may also have visited and worked in Flanders. His work seems to have found few buyers, and the artist died in poverty.

Seghers' paintings contain elements from 16th-century Flemish landscapes and also those of the German painter Adam Elsheimer (1578–1610), but they are otherwise highly individual works in which realistic detail is contained within visionary conceptions of awesome grandeur. His landscapes are typically horizontal, panoramic views of desolate valleys surrounded by vast mountain ranges. The few tiny figures emphasize the sense of solitude, and also underline the depth of space and the majesty of nature. A dramatic note is frequently added by the powerful interplay of light and shade in the sky and on land. Seghers' landscape paintings influenced the work of Philips Koninck, and also the landscapes of Rembrandt (who owned eight of Seghers' paintings).

A few of Seghers' paintings represent actual places (for example two views of Rhenen in the Staatliche Museen, Berlin), but it is fantasy that predominates in his work. Fantasy is also particularly characteristic of the artist's 50 or so etchings. In these the realistic detail found in paintings of mountain ranges and other motifs (which suggest that Seghers may have journeyed through the Alps) is subordinated to the unearthly appearance of wastelands filled with cold, crumbling rocks and water-filled craters. The power and individuality of Seghers' disturbingly eerie conceptions is such that his exploitation of traditional motifs (like the decaying pines of Danube School artists) is not at first apparent. The influence of Seghers' etchings is found in the prints of Jacob van Ruisdael rather than in those of Rembrandt, although the latter actually bought and reworked one of the artist's original copperplates. As an etcher, Seghers is historically important for his technical experiments, notably his use of colored inks, paper, and linen, and for his practice of tinting individual proofs. His prints have been admired by a number of 20th-century Surrealist artists.

Segonzac André Dunoyer de
1884–1974

The French painter and etcher André Dunoyer de Segonzac was born at Boussy-St-Antoine in the Île de France. He achieved international success between the Wars with paintings of the countryside of the Île de France and Provence. His somber browns and dark greens, and his vigorous use of the palette knife, owe much to Courbet. He views nature as a setting for leisure and repose. Figures are depicted boating or resting; the latter are sometimes mythological in style and are given a monumental quality by the use of foreshortening. He was acclaimed by conservative critics for presenting an undogmatic and characteristically French alternative to advanced art.

Semon Master *fl. c500 BC*

The Semon Master was a Greek gem-engraver. He is named for a gem in the Staatliche Museen, Berlin, showing a naked girl stooping to fill her jar at a fountain; the name Semon inscribed on it may be that of the owner. He is the best of the conventional late Archaic engravers, well able to combine the finest of Archaic patterning with decisive anatomical study on a small scale. He worked on scarabs and scaraboids of various colored quartzes, and the number of gems attributed to him and found on Cyprus suggests that he may have had his studio there for a time. The attributed stones include several with

winged figures—Eros seizing a girl (Metropolitan Museum, New York), a sphinx with a youth (British Museum, London), a griffin with a youth (Museum of Fine Arts, Boston), and a winged, man-faced bull (British Museum, London) which might be a Hellenized version of the Persian monster. A larger gem in the Museum of Fine Arts, Boston, has a subject rare for this date: a mythological study of Achilles killing the Amazon Queen Penthesilea.

Semper Gottfried 1803–79

The German architect and theoretician Gottfried Semper studied first law and then mathematics. He began his architectural studies in Munich with Friedrich von Gärtner (1792–1847), who influenced him towards classicism. A stay in Paris in 1826 further strengthened his interest in the architecture of Antiquity. Between 1830 and 1832 he visited Naples, Pompeii, Sicily, and Greece. In late 1833 he met the great German classical architect K.F. Schinkel in Berlin. At this time his attention turned towards the use of color in architecture, and in 1834 he published his first theoretical work, *Vorläufige Bermerkungen . . . (Provisional Remarks on the Polychrome Architecture and Sculpture of Antiquity)*. His first buildings were erected in Hamburg in 1834.

In the same year he was appointed Professor of Architecture at the Dresden Academy. The first famous building he designed was the Dresden Opera House (1837–41), which has been described as one of the epoch-making buildings of the 19th century. In accordance with his ideas on the polychrome architecture of Antiquity, his intention was a synthesis of all the arts of the decorator. Semper and Richard Wagner were friends, and it was intended that Semper be given the commission for designing the Festspielhaus in Munich. Caught up in the political activities of 1848, the Year of Revolutions, he was exiled in 1849 for his part in the May uprisings. He subsequently lived in Paris, England, Switzerland, and Vienna, and died in Rome.

His major theoretical work, *Der Stil* ("Style"), was published in 1860 during a Renaissance revival. In it he praises Roman architectural achievement above that of the Greeks, and especially emphasizes its realism—a style suitable for both churches and railroad stations. The book also advances a materialistic theory for the genesis

of an art based on utilitarian purpose, raw material, and technology. The impact of these ideas was to be felt in early contributions to the Modern period.

Sergel Johan 1740–1814

The Swedish Neoclassical sculptor Johan Tobias Sergel first worked for ten years under the French sculptor P.-H. Larchevêque. Between 1767 and 1778 he lived in Rome, where he met John Henry Fuseli and J.-A. Houdon. During his stay there Sergel was influenced by Antiquity, and by the work of Raphael, Michelangelo, and the Carracci. His most successful sculpture, of mythological groups, was made in Rome, but in 1778 he was recalled to Stockholm against his will, to become a portrait sculptor. Sergel's sculpture combines Neoclassical ideals with closely observed realism.

Serlio Sebastiano 1475–1554

Sebastiano Serlio was an Italian architect and decorative artist who worked in the circle of Peruzzi and Raphael in Rome. He left the city some time c1527. He was in Venice in 1528, and there began publication of a series of books on architecture planned as a complementary set of eight volumes. These are his chief claim to posterity. The idea of such a work evidently sprang from his association with Peruzzi, who had intended to produce some sort of publication on Classical architecture before his death in 1536. Serlio was the spiritual heir to this project, and several of his drawings were closely derived from those of his master. His third book, which appeared in 1540 with a dedication to Francis I of France, resulted in his arrival in Paris in 1541. He remained there, in court favor, until Francis' death in 1547, and thereafter eked out a living in France until he died at Lyons in 1554.

Serra Richard 1939–

The works of the American sculptor Richard Serra, who has worked almost exclusively with metal, combine Minimalism and Environmental sculpture. Born in San Francisco, he studied at Berkley and Yale, and then in Paris and Florence. In his early works there is often an element of precarious balance—in *One-Ton Prop (House of Cards)* (1968–69; Saatchi Collection, London) sheets of lead are leant against one another to form a cube. Later works, often constructed for a specific site, typically feature huge, gently curved sheets of untreated steel imbedded in the ground, Serra's intention being to create a "field force ... so that space is discerned physically rather than optically". One such work—*Tilted Arc* (1981), a sheet of steel 37m (120ft) long by 3.7m (12ft)—became the object of a bitter controversy when city officials had it removed from its site in Foley Square, New York, with politicians challenging the public funding of the arts, and the arts community defending artists' creative freedom.

Further reading. Serra, R. *Writings, Interviews*, Chicago (1994).

Sérusier Paul 1864–1927

Paul Sérusier was a French artist and theorist, and the intellectual leader of the Nabis. He was born in Paris, and studied at the Académie Julian. Visiting Pont-Aven, Brittany, in the summer of 1888, he was introduced by Emile Bernard to Gauguin, under whose tutelage he painted *The Talisman* (1888; Collection of J.F. Denis, Alençon). This was a brilliantly colored evocation rather than a literal transcription of a landscape. It became the pictorial manifesto for Sérusier's Académie Julian friends (Pierre Bonnard, Édouard Vuillard, Maurice Denis, Ker-Xavier Roussel, and Paul Ranson) who banded themselves together to form the Nabis. During the 1890s Sérusier was engaged in such "Nabi" activities as theater design (including designs for Alfred Jarry's play *Ubu Roi*, 1896), book illustration, and mural decoration. He also met Jan Verkade, a painter of the School of Beuron, under whose influence he became a Theosophist and embarked upon a search for an art based upon sacred proportions and color relationships. He published the fruits of these researches in *ABC de la Peinture* (1922).

Sesshu 1420–1506

The Japanese painter Sesshu was also known as Toyo. He was the greatest master of the Chinese-inspired ink monochrome style, and is considered by many of his countrymen to be their greatest artist. Like all the painters of that period who worked in pure ink he was a Zen monk, and his work is partly a conscious explora-

Paul Sérusier: Melancholia; oil on canvas; 71×57cm (28×22in); c1890. Collection of Mlle H. Boutaric, Paris

tion of the nature of reality.

Sesshu was born in Bitchu Province, near modern Okayama. He returned to live in western Japan later in his life, thus creating a precedent for great artists to work away from the capital. He was a pupil of Shubun at the Sokokuji Temple in Kyoto, then the center of Zen painting in the ink monochrome style. From Shubun he learned the subtle use of graded washes, which had originated in the Southern Sung school.

During the years 1467 to 1469 he visited China to seek more advanced masters, but he found none whom he considered worthy among the then-dominant Che School. However, the effect of his stay can be clearly seen in the four great landscape hanging scrolls of the seasons (Tokyo National Museum), which were done in China. They have the architectural power and rational organization that came naturally to even the weakest Che School

painter, but which was rarely achieved by the more emotional and decorative genius of the Japanese.

The majestic mountain landscapes of China, and no doubt the study of original Sung and Yuan period masterpieces in Peking, gave his later work a detached elevation. This is expressed in concise, exact ink strokes, to which ink washes are an adjunct, rather than of the essence—as they are among his contemporaries such as Bunsei, Gakuo, or Soami.

After his return, Sesshu traveled widely in Japan. Some of his later works show an admirable fusion of Japanese sentiment and detail with Chinese rational power—a synthesis never achieved by the later, Chinese-inspired *Kano* and *Nanga* schools. His masterpiece is the long handscroll of the four seasons (Mori Collection). This depicts a continuous, changing panorama, complex in detail but integrated in overall design, the brushwork varied almost in the manner of orchestration. Most of the individual details are Japanese, especially the series showing water with fishing boats. No other Japanese painting gives such a sense of intellectual power expressed through the brush.

Late in life, Sesshu developed from the depths of his confidence very abbreviated styles, where a few controlled but violent-seeming splashes of ink, and a few light washes, can suggest great mountains and vast distance (for example, *Haboku Landscape* or *Ink-Splash Landscape*, 1495; Tokyo National Museum). Even more startling is the *Snowy Landscape* (Tokyo National Museum) where the line of the side of a cliff is arbitrarily extended into the sky, like a crack in ice. No other Zen artist distorted apparent reality with such breathtaking and assured violence.

Sesson Shukei 1504–89

Shukei Sesson was an independent Japanese artist who painted in the Zen manner. An admirer of Sesshu, he followed his example by working in the provinces; his studio is preserved in Miharu, in the rugged northeast of Japan. The harshness of the area is reflected in the howling winds, scudding boat, and tongued waves of his famous ink sketch *Wind and Waves* (Nomura Collection, Kyoto), and in *The Immortal Lu Tung-pin on a Dragon in a Storm* (private collection). His technique was assured; but the directness and roughness of his approach, which is essentially Zen in spirit, tends to hide it. He had some followers, but was too individualistic to be greatly influential.

Seurat Georges 1859–91

The French painter Georges-Pierre Seurat was the leader of the Neo-Impressionist group. Born in Paris in 1859, he studied briefly at the École des Beaux-Arts (1878–9). He made many drawings after antique sculpture (for example of the Parthenon frieze), Renaissance masters (such as Piero della Francesca), and Ingres; he also did life drawings, often of a Holbeinesque naturalism. During his military service in Brest (1879–80), he drew more everyday subjects in his sketchbook.

On his return to Paris, he continued to draw, often using conté crayon on heavy-texture ("Michallet" or "Ingres") paper, from which he obtained an astonishing

Georges Seurat: A Small Man by a Parapet or The Invalid; oil on panel; 25×16cm (10×6in); 1881–2. Rothbart Collection, New York

range of texture and tone. Almost 500 drawings exist; from 1882, their subject matter was taken from the fields, from Parisian street-scenes, and from the urban poor, in which Daumier's influence can be detected. He also drew scenes from the circus and the café concert (the composition somewhat influenced by the work of Degas). Seurat deeply admired Rembrandt and Goya. From all these sources, he evolved a consciously considered, classical—and ultimately classic—style of drawing: it was a rigorously thought-out system rationally applied. His drawings alone would guarantee Seurat's place among the great artists.

In addition, he pondered deeply the problems of color. From early youth, he had been engrossed in scientific color theory. By 1881, he had read treatises on optical science by Michel-Eugène Chevreul,

Ogden Rood, and Hermann von Helmholtz; these eventually enabled him to move towards a systematic, methodical, and carefully analyzed application of color and brush stroke. He also looked hard at the paintings of Delacroix, as can be seen in his detailed color analyses of three of Delacroix's paintings. His early paintings were generally of small format, often on panel; most of them depict fragments of landscape around Paris. They show the influence of the Barbizon painters and, by 1882, of Impressionism. A drawing of his painter-friend, Edmond-François Aman-Jean, was accepted at the Salon in 1883.

In the spring of 1884, his large composition, *Bathing at Asnières* (reworked c1887; National Gallery, London), measuring 79 by 118 in (201 by 300 cm), was shown at the inaugural exhibition of the Salon des Artistes Indépendants. He met Signac in 1884; in the following year, Camille and Lucien Pissarro were converted to the Neo-Impressionist movement. At the last Impressionist exhibition in 1886, Seurat exhibited *Sunday Afternoon on the Island of the Grande Jatte* (1886; Art Institute of Chicago). This was an Impressionist subject *par excellence*, but the Impressionist technique was scientifically rationalized into a regular, dot-like brush stroke, and the seemingly haphazard Impressionist slice-of-nature was given a geometrically structured base. The picture created a scandal.

Divisionism and Pointillism were publicly denounced. Young Symbolist poets and critics—Félix Fénéon and Gustave Kahn in particular—wrote enthusiastically in their defence. At the exhibitions of the Salon des Artistes Indépendants, and in smaller venues like dealers' galleries, the group of artists who gathered around Seurat and Signac gave the movement a vital cohesiveness that lasted from 1886 until Seurat's death in 1891. Some of them were also invited to exhibit with Les Vingt in Brussels, and this helped to establish a group of Belgian Neo-Impressionists.

Seurat's own path, however, was masterfully and often secretively single-minded. He continued to draw; he continued to print small *pochades*; but fundamentally he aimed to produce at least one large "statement-picture" every year. He also painted a series of canvases that resulted from his summer stays in the Channel coast—Grandchamp (1885), Honfleur (1886), Port-en-Bessin (1888), Crotoy (1889), and Gravelines (1890). In these pictures an organized, finely filtered observation is married to an introspective, melancholic mood that is sometimes relieved by witty outbursts: for example, the "frozen" fluttering flags in *Sunday, Port-en-Bessin* (1888; Kröller-Müller Museum, Otterlo).

One further preoccupation found increasing outlets in his last works: his theory of the emotional character of linear directions. This was based to a large degree on the quasi-scientific writings of a brilliant young aesthetician, Charles Henry, whom both Seurat and Signac befriended. The theory is apparent in several of Seurat's "statement-pictures". These include *La Parade* ("Invitation to the Side-show", 1887-8; Metropolitan Museum, New York), which also reveals the workings of the system of proportion known as the Golden Section, and *Les Poseuses* ("The

Models", small version 1888; on loan to the Alte Pinakothek, Munich), which incidentally plays a skillful variation on the theme of picture-within-a-picture. In *Le Chahut* (1889-90; Kröller-Müller Museum, Otterlo) and *La Cirque* (1890-1; Musée du Jeu de Paume, Paris), the deliberately achieved stylization clearly gave a strong impetus to the emergence of Art Nouveau, especially through the Belgian *confrères* in Les Vingt.

Although Seurat himself wrote little, a few of his letters survive; one of these, to the writer Maurice Beaubourg (28 August 1890), provides a summary of his technique and his aesthetic. He was jealous of his discoveries, and it was left to Fénéon and Signac to explain them publicly. His secrecy extended to his private life. When Seurat died suddenly of angina in 1891, not even his closest friends were aware of his relationship with Madeleine Knobloch, who had borne him a son. She had been the model in his only large portrait, *Jeune Femme se Poudrant* (1889-90; Courtauld Institute Galleries, London).

Seurat is the epitome of the artist as laboratory scientist: analyzing, questioning, and seeking, fanatical and emotionally tense. He sought what he considered to be the universal laws of nature, and of art. His approach was essentially conceptual and rational, but it was never exclusively so. His method never dries up into a repetitive and lifeless formula, as happened to some of his lesser followers. Elements of his art have influenced the Fauvists, the Cubists, and the more geometrical exponents of Abstract art.

Further reading. Dorra, H. and Rewald, J. *Seurat*, Paris (1960). Hauke, C.M. de *Seurat et Son Oeuvre* (2 vols), Paris (1961). Herbert, R.L. *Seurat's Drawings*, New York (1963). Homer, W.I. *Seurat and the Science of Painting*, Cambridge, Mass. (1964). Russell, J. *Seurat*, London (1965).

Severini Gino 1883–1966

The Italian painter Gino Severini was born in Cortona, but lived in Paris from 1906. He signed the 1910 *Technical Manifesto of Futurist Painting* and was instrumental in bringing Futurism to Paris, London, and Berlin. He also introduced the Futurists to Cubism. He acknowledged the ideals of Futurism, but his paintings are decorative rather than aggressive (for example, *The Dynamic Hieroglyph of the Bal Tabarin*, 1912; Museum of Modern Art, New York), and he often aimed at reproducing the dynamics of movement and sensation. In the 1920s and 1930s Severini did many

Gino Severini: Still Life with "Lacerba"; papier collé, gouache, ink, and charcoal; 50×60cm (20×24in); 1913. Musée d'Art et d'Industrie, St-Etienne

murals and mosaics in Italy, France, and Switzerland. After he had published *Du Cubisme au Classicisme* in 1921, his style became Neoclassical, though he still experimented with Cubism.

Shafi Abbasi *fl. 1630–74*

Shafi Abbasi was a Persian draftsman and designer, the son of Riza. He imitated his father's work and signature, especially in an album from the Sarre Collection (Freer Gallery of Art, Washington, D.C.). His most original work was as a designer for textiles based on flower and bird studies, some of which derived from English engraved pattern books. The suffix Abbasi indicates that he must have served Shah Abbas II who reigned from 1642 to 1666, but by the latter date Shafi was at the court of the Mughal Emperor, where he died. Other works by him are in the St Petersburg Public Library, the Bibliothèque Nationale, Paris, and the Cleveland Museum of Art.

Shahn Ben 1898–1969

Ben Shahn was a Russian-born painter of the American school. His family emigrated to the United States in 1906. While studying at various New York colleges Shahn worked as a lithographer's assistant. In 1927 and 1929 he visited Europe, where he was deeply impressed by the work of the early Italian masters. Their "naivety" became part of his own very personal style, which he applied to subjects of serious social significance. Perhaps his best known works are the gouaches inspired by the Sacco and Vanzetti case (*The Passion of Sacco and Vanzetti*, 1931–2; Whitney Museum of American Art, New York). He often worked in tempera. His compositions are characterized by figures with enlarged heads in settings inspired by, but remote from, the world around him (for example, *Liberation*, 1945; private collection). Shahn was also involved in various large-scale decorative schemes, such as the frescoes in the Post Office, Bronx Central Annex, New York (1938–9), and the mural in the Washington Social Security Building (1940–2).

Further reading. Kuh, K. *The Artist's Voice: Talks with Seventeen Artists*, New York (1962). Moise, J.D. *Ben Shahn*, London and New York (1972). Pratt, D. (ed.) *The Photographic Eye of Ben Shahn*,

Cambridge, Mass. (1976). Shahn, B. *The Biography of a Painting*, New York (1966). Shahn, B. *The Shape of Content*, Cambridge, Mass. (1972). Shahn, B.B. *Ben Shahn*, New York (1975). Soby, J.T. *Ben Shahn: his Graphic Art*, New York (1957). Soby, J.T. *Ben Shahn: Paintings*, New York (1963).

Sharaku Toshusai *fl. 1794–5*

The Japanese artist Toshusai Sharaku was the greatest master of the *Kabuki* actor print, combining psychological subtlety with rare forcefulness of design. He is the most mysterious figure in Japanese art. He began making his 200 or so known prints in 1794, and they were published for only about ten months, into 1795. Nothing is known of his life or identity. His greatest prints are head-and-shoulders portraits of actors in specific roles, done with thick, flexible lines, and bright patches of color. They almost always have a plain background, often of mica, which emphasizes their artificiality. Yet they suggest both a dramatic moment in a play and the psychology of the actor.

Shaw Norman 1831–1912

The British architect Richard Norman Shaw was born in Edinburgh. He was articled to a London architect, won the Royal Academy Gold Medal and Traveling Studentship (1854), and published his sketches of continental Gothic buildings (1858). He succeeded Philip Webb as George Street's assistant, and in 1862 set up his own practice in London with William Eden Nesfield.

During the six years of this association, Shaw designed two churches (including the English church in Lyons, 1868) in a bold, early Gothic style, but he soon showed a preference for house design. He perfected a picturesque "manorial" type of country house (for example Leyswood, Sussex, 1868; and Grim's Dyke, Harrow, 1872) with tile hanging and half-timbering, far more ebullient than Webb's buildings. These did much to establish Shaw's international reputation.

For the many domestic and commercial buildings in London that he designed during the 1870s and 1880s, Shaw adopted an early-18th-century town-house style (generally, although inaccurately, called "Queen Anne"). At first he interpreted this most exuberantly (as in New

Toshusai Sharaku: Nakamura Konozo and Nakajima Wadgemon in Character; woodblock print; 38×23cm (15×9in); 1794. British Museum, London

Zealand Chambers, Leadenhall Street, 1872), but he later used decorative details more sparingly. He developed a versatile manner of building in red brick. This was suitable not only for the many artists' houses he built in Hampstead and Kensington, but also for the varied buildings of the first garden suburb (Bedford Park, begun 1875), and for larger buildings such as the Albert Hall Mansions (1879).

Shaw worked in this manner for some time, but gradually his enthusiasm for its picturesqueness waned; this can be seen in his more ordered designs for No. 170 Queen's Gate, London (1888), and Bryanston, Dorset (1890). He was by now one of the elders of British architecture. The formality of these buildings was the prelude to a period of overt classicism and monumentality, which Shaw adopted and which culminated in his designs for Regent Street and the Piccadilly Hotel, London (1905).

Sheeler Charles 1883–1965

The American painter and photographer Charles Sheeler was born in Philadelphia, where he studied under William Chase at the Pennsylvania Academy (1903–6). He saw works by modern French artists during a stay in Paris from 1908 to 1909, and showed in the Armory exhibition in 1913. In 1912 he took up photography. His commercial work for *Vogue* and *Vanity Fair* (1923–32) and the Ford Motor Company, particularly photographs of the River Rouge plant (1927), ensured his international reputation. Following the death of his friend and associate Morton Schamberg, Sheeler moved to New York in 1919. By the early 1920s his range of themes and his approach—from near abstraction to intense realism—had been defined. His paintings of the city, industrial landscape, and machinery, such as *Upper Deck* (1929; William Hayes Fogg

Art Museum, Cambridge, Mass.), contrast with his depictions of interiors and farm buildings, such as *Bucks County Barn* (1932, Museum of Modern Art, New York), but all may be considered outstanding examples of Precisionism.

In 1939, the year his biography was published, Sheeler had a retrospective exhibition at the Museum of Modern Art, New York. Throughout his career he alternated between photography and painting, but in both media he concentrated on structured, formal compositions with clearly defined features. His photographs were often the basis for, or an influence on,

his paintings, especially in the "double exposures" of the early 1950s such as *Architectural Cadences* (1954; Whitney Museum of American Art, New York).

Shen Chou 1427–1509

The Chinese painter Shen Chou was a native of Wu Hsien (today's Suchow), Kiangnan. The son of a landed family he was well educated. Just as he was about to take up an official career his father died. He remained at home, first for mourning and then to care for his mother, and never took up the career for which he was qualified. He became a painter and poet. He was the inspiration of the Wu School of painters, who felt themselves in contrast with, and sometimes in opposition to, the Che School of Chekiang, which consisted mostly of Academy and Court artists.

Shen Chou was a typical scholar-painter. By instinct an eclectic, he worked in many styles throughout his life. His position as a scholar-gentleman was such that he would have had access to many old masters; he was also personally popular with his contemporaries. There is a strong individual character to his works, which were often painted from his own experience. Many of his landscapes show places on his estate, and record specific occasions (for example, *Walking with a Staff*, Palace Museum Collection, Taichung) or feelings (for example, *Poetona Mountain*, Kansas City Album, William Rockhill Nelson Gallery, Kansas City, Mo.) which require the use of words. This use of simple poetry with a painting is beautifully done. Like all of Shen Chou's work, it shows a direct approach, unique to Far Eastern painting.

His handling of ink and color is both bold and sensitive. He follows the scholar's wish to handle his brush in an "unprofessional" style which will, nevertheless, show his undoubted knowledge of the old masters. His composition is inventive and daring, but in no way mannered, so that his paintings often appear very simple. His painting was highly thought of throughout the later periods of Chinese art, and was an inspiration to Shih T'ao (1630–1707) and some of the later-18th-century independent painters.

Many of Shen Chou's paintings have survived, often in handscroll and album leaf format, in ink or color on paper. His later work, from a period when he followed the ink style of Wu Chen, is still much admired. (*See* overleaf.)

Charles Sheeler: Upper Deck; oil on canvas; 74×56cm (29×22in); 1929. William Hayes Fogg Art Museum, Cambridge, Mass.

Shen Chou: Returning Home in the Autumn; ink and slight color on paper; 38×61cm (15×24in); c1495–1500. William Rockhill Nelson Gallery, Kansas City, Mo.

Shih T'ao 1630–1707

The real name of the Chinese painter Shih T'ao was Chu Tao-chi. He came from Honan, and was a relative of the Ming royal house. He retired to a monastery at the fall of the dynasty, but it is not recorded that he became a monk. After a period of wandering he finally settled in the Yangchow area. He was a well-educated intellectual, who was also a serious and individual painter. "When asked if I paint in the manner of the Southern School or Northern School, I reply with a laugh that I do not know whether I am of a School or the School of me, I paint in my own style".

Shih T'ao was a romantic painter who built upon his eclectic training, but who stressed the need to look at and to experience Nature. He also found inspiration in literature. His *Peach Blossom Valley* handscroll (Freer Gallery of Art, Washington, D.C.) is acutely evocative and displays something of the eclectic spirit that was very much alive in his day. Despite his independence of spirit, Shih T'ao was not out of touch with his fellow artists, and corresponded both with Chu Ta and with Wang Shi-min. He was engrossed in painting: he experimented with brushwork, with the use of color, and with composition, displaying such vitality that artists are building upon his work to this day.

Shih T'ao's range was enormous. It varied from large works on silk (which he disliked doing, and which must have been commissioned) through all sizes of work on paper, both in monochrome and in color, which he used to great atmospheric effect. His brushwork has a marvelous strength, although it is often delicate. In contrast to the works of Chu Ta, the paintings of Shih T'ao are in an additive style. He builds up his landscapes, covering the bones, however thinly, to create a sense of texture, light, and atmospheric distance.

Shiko Watanabe 1683–1755

A Japanese painter of the *Rimpa* School, Watanabe Shiko trained as a *Kano* artist, then changed to the style of Ogata Korin. His work combines *Kano* inkwork with Korin's brilliant decorative style, but adds a feeling for the real world that foreshadows Okyo's naturalism (he did a sketchbook of birds, that was copied by Okyo). His crowded screens, for example, *Flowers and Grasses of the Seasons* (Hatakeyama Collection) have a joyous exuberance lacking in the work of other *Rimpa* artists. His screens of the *Yoshino Cherry Blossom* (private collection) and his *Iris* screens (Cleveland Museum of Art) have the simple effectiveness of Korin or Sotatsu.

Shiseki So 1712–86

So Shiseki was a Japanese painter of the Nagasaki school who specialized in detailed bird-and-flower painting in the Chinese style. Born in Edo (Tokyo), he went to Nagasaki c1740 and studied under Kumashiro Yu, who had learned from the emigré Chinese artist Shen Nan-p'in. Later he studied under another Chinese artist, known in Japanese as So Shigan, from whom he adopted his new family name. Shiseki took the Nagasaki style back to Edo, where he popularized it in woodblock books, and also taught it, notably to Shiba Kokan and Tani Buncho. Shiseki added native sensuousness, poetry, and oblique design to his rather literal Chinese models.

Shohaku Soga 1730–81

Soga Shohaku was an eccentric and rebellious Japanese painter. He studied with the *Kano* School, but later claimed to be a *Soga* School artist, having adopted the dynamic *Soga* ink line. Little is known of his life, but the inscriptions on his paintings show that he worked in many different places. His favorite subjects were Chinese Buddhist and Taoist figures. These were usually painted with violent movement and grotesquely distorted faces (notably in the large hanging scrolls of *Kanzan* and *Jittoku* in the Kyoto National Museum). Most of his work is in ink monochrome. His landscapes can be surprisingly soft, but some are remarkable for their Cubist tendencies, the mountains being drawn as pure oblongs.

Shoi Iwasa 1578–1651

The Japanese painter Iwasa Shoi is better known as Matabei; he has been called, incorrectly, the founder of the *Ukiyoe* School. In fact, he was a *Tosa*-trained artist. Like his contemporaries Sotatsu and Jokei, he developed the traditional native styles into something both more dynamic and more decorative. His handscrolls, such as *Tokiwa in the Mountains* (Atami Art Museum, Atami), are vigorous in detail, often crowded, yet superbly organized; they convert the traditional *Tosa* cloud-bands into subtly shaded bands of mist. His faces have great vigor, and are distinguished by a strongly projecting chin. Shoi was also a master of dashing ink monochrome portraits, and also did decorative screens.

Shubun fl. c1420–c65

Shubun was a Japanese painter in the Chinese pure-ink style. The first major

Japanese artist in this school, he probably learned from Josetsu at the Sokokuji Temple in Kyoto; this was the headquarters of the government academy, and he later became its director. In the 1420s he visited Korea, which was apparently his principal source for the Chinese styles; it was here that he developed his interest in spatial depth. He was a Buddhist sculptor, and a painter of traditional images. He also painted many vertically constructed landscapes which were extremely influential, especially on Sesshu. No one surviving painting is certainly by his hand, but there is a consistency in the style of those works attributed to him.

Shunsho Katsukawa 1726–93

The Japanese painter and print designer Katsukawa Shunsho is the best-known member of the Katsukawa school, which specialized in prints of the *Kabuki* theater. He learned from Shunsui, the founder of the school, and also from the neo-*Kano* painter Sukoku. He is perhaps the most skillful of all the painters in the pure *Ukiyoe* style, combining strong composition, detailed and sensuous execution, and lyrical charm, as in *Airing Books* (Freer Gallery of Art, Washington, D.C.). In middle life he began to design prints of *Kabuki* actors (often in diptychs or triptychs), with a new realism and great subtlety of character, and an original use of simple blocks of powerful color. He is also notable as the teacher of Katsushika Hokusai.

Joannes Siberechts: Landscape with Rainbow (Henley-on-Thames); oil on canvas; 81×103cm (32×41cm); c1690. Tate Gallery, London

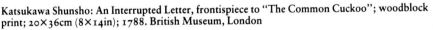

Katsukawa Shunsho: An Interrupted Letter, frontispiece to "The Common Cuckoo"; woodblock print; 20×36cm (8×14in); 1788. British Museum, London

Siberechts Joannes 1627–c1703

The Flemish painter Joannes Siberechts was born in Antwerp, but worked in Italy from 1648 to 1649. He painted peaceful landscapes with peasants and animals; his best pictures show fords and flooded roads, with carts, that suggest the influence of Rubens. Between 1672 and 1676 he lived in England, where he traveled extensively and pioneered the "portrait" of the English country house. He painted views of Longleat as early as 1675 and of Chatsworth in 1694. For Sir Thomas Willoughby he also painted landscapes of English scenery which show, for the first time in English art, a real awareness of the English countryside.

Sickert Walter 1860–1942

The English painter and printmaker Walter Richard Sickert was born in Munich. His father, an artist, was Danish, and his mother was Anglo-Irish. He was brought to England in 1868, educated at King's College, London, and, after a short period on the stage, studied briefly at the Slade School of Fine Art (1881–2). He then became a pupil of J.A.M. Whistler, and in 1883 met Degas in Paris. Whistler and Degas were the seminal influences on his work. In the 1880s and 1890s, he produced a series of music-hall pictures which explored fresh subject matter in late Victorian art, revealing new compositional devices and a mastery of low-toned color

(for example, *The Old Bedford*, *c*1897; Walker Art Gallery, Liverpool). For over 40 years, Sickert haunted Dieppe, observing its street architecture and depicting obsessively the medieval church of St Jacques. He has been called the "Canaletto of Dieppe"; but he banished ceremony and circumstance from his evocations of the Channel port.

In 1888 he joined the New English Art Club; in 1889, he helped organize an exhibition of the Club's more radical wing under the title of "The London Impressionists". His drawings and paintings were reproduced in *The Yellow Book*. He held his first one-man show in 1895. In the same year—and again in 1896—he visited Venice, producing a series of low-toned views that were not always of the tourist spots. From 1899 to 1905 he lived abroad, mainly in Dieppe and Venice. He held one-man shows in Paris in 1900, 1903, and 1907, also exhibiting there in the artists' societies. Had he chosen to stay in France, he could have continued to build up his reputation.

Instead, he returned to London in 1905, and gathered round him a new band of associates, including Harold Gilman and Spencer Gore; together they formed the Camden Town Group in 1911. He provided the group's theoretical justification and acted as its practical mentor. From a series of figures and nudes seen in fairly confined interiors, which he produced on his last stay in Venice from 1903 to 1904, Sickert evolved his characteristic Camden Town style. Based to a large extent on drawings, Impressionist in its fine observation of *contre-jour* effects, and asserting strong painterly qualities, this style marked the high point of his art.

Sickert had already written articles, reviews, and essays during the 1880s and 1890s; from 1908 to 1914, his literary output was virtually uninterrupted. He wrote about art from the inside, and was pungent and polemical, witty and idiosyncratic. He was also a prolific printmaker. In his late paintings, his palette lightened considerably, as can be seen in the series *Echoes*, based on Victorian illustrations.

Further reading. Bacon, W. *Sickert*, London (1973). Beil, I. *Victorian Artists*, London (1967).

Left: Walter Sickert: Boredom (Ennui); oil on canvas; 152×112cm (60×44in); c1914. Tate Gallery, London

Paul Signac: The Port of St Tropez; oil on canvas; 65×81cm (26×32in); 1899. Musée de l'Annonciade, St Tropez

Siferwas John *c*1360–*post* 1421

John Siferwas was an English illuminator of manuscripts. His workshop enlivened book-illumination during a period of changing styles and may have contributed to wall paintings in the Chapter House of Westminster Abbey. The Siferwas family was prominent in Herefordshire during the 14th century. John was ordained an acolyte at Farnham in 1380, and became a Dominican at Guildford Priory. His signature appears in two manuscripts: a massive missal executed for the Benedictine Abbey of Sherborne, Dorset (1396–1407; Collection of the Duke of Northumberland, Alnwick Castle), and a Gospel Lectionary (*c*1408; British Library, London) ordered as a gift for Salisbury Cathedral by John, 5th Lord Lovell of Tichmersh. A remarkable self-portrait shows Siferwas, wearing the Dominican habit, presenting the book to Lord Lovell.

The highly decorated Sherborne Missal measures 21 by 15 in (53 by 38 cm) even after an unfortunate trimming of the edges. The patrons of the work were Richard Medford, Bishop of Salisbury, and Robert Bruynyng, Abbot of Sherborne, both of whom are frequently depicted in its pages. Many birds are beautifully painted and named, and indicate a close connection

with a late-14th-century sketch book (in the Pepys Library, Magdalene College, Cambridge). This is evidently an atelier pattern-book, with human and animal figures. Pages of realistic birds recall the Sherborne Missal, and may be by Siferwas.

The great *Crucifixion* page in the Sherborne Missal, painted in the Italian style, is masterly though overcrowded. Drama is conveyed by rhythmic compositional stresses, but the faces of the mourning group lack the sensitivity of a painter like Herman Scheerre (*fl.* *c*1403–19). It has been suggested that the Italianate-English retable in Norwich Cathedral influenced the stye of Siferwas, and his ornate costumes are certainly similar. One assistant signed his name "Johannes" in the Marco Polo Manuscript (*c*1410; Bodleian Library, Oxford). He inherited the fantastical garments and headgear, with a cruder Siferwas style. Johannes apparently joined Herman Scheerre's workshop early in the 15th century, continuing the tradition in the absence of later known works by John Siferwas.

Signac Paul 1863–1935

The French painter and theorist Paul Signac was a close friend of Georges Seurat, and a propagandist for Neo-Impressionism. He was born in Paris, of well-to-do parents. His early paintings (*c*1880–4) show the influence of Monet and Armand Guillaumin. He met Seurat in 1884; both artists showed in the Salon des Artistes Indépendants, a juryless exhibiting society founded in Paris in May 1884. Signac introduced Pissarro to Seurat in 1885: the result was a strong group of Neo-Impressionist artists who showed at the last Impressionist exhibition and at the Salon des Indépendants of 1886.

From then until Seurat's death in 1891, the discoveries of the new movement were articulated and expanded. After 1891, Signac saw himself increasingly as the personification of Neo-Impressionism. The most lasting result of this was his book, *D'Eugène Delacroix au Neo-Impressionistes*, published in Paris in 1899, which influenced Matisse and Derain.

In Signac's own paintings, his early Impressionist phase was followed by his main Neo-Impressionist period (1884–1900), in which he exemplified the theoretical basis of the movement. His subject matter included views of Paris, of the Seine, of the Channel coast, and of the south of France. He settled in St Tropez in 1893. After 1900, the pointillist dots were enlarged into brush strokes that were predominantly square. He painted most of the harbors in France in this style (he was a keen yachtsman). He admired J.M.W. Turner, and the Dutch artist J.B. Jongkind, about whom he published a monograph in 1927. Signac's watercolors, more freshly convinced and spontaneously painted than his oils, show the influence of these two artists.

Signac maintained his allegiance to the Salon des Indépendants until his death, fulfilling the office of President with enthusiasm and tenacity.

Signorelli Luca *c*1450–1523

The Italian painter Luca Signorelli was born in Cortona. Little is known of his early years, but his surviving works support Vasari's claim that Piero della Francesca first taught him to paint. The pattern of Signorelli's career is similar to that of his teacher's. He, too, became an important provincial artist, who, though he visited Florence, set up a *bottega* in his small native town. During the half-century of Signorelli's activity, from *c*1470 to 1523, he produced a great many paintings; these were mostly for churches in and around

Luca Signorelli: Portrait of Dante; fresco; 1499–1504. S. Brizio Chapel, Orvieto Cathedral

Cortona, but also for important churches in more distant places, such as Loreto, Rome, and Orvieto.

In his early works, Signorelli was an important innovator who infused fresh dynamism into the monumental, sculptural style he had learned from Piero della Francesca. His *Flagellation of Christ* (*c*1480; Pinacoteca di Brera, Milan) and the Vagnucci Altarpiece (1484; Museo dell'Opera del Duomo, Perugia), show that he cultivated a new style at once grand and lively, as did his Florentine contemporaries Sandro Botticelli and Leonardo da Vinci. Signorelli is also important because he built upon the achievements of Antonio Pollaiuolo to develop a plausible formula for depicting the body in movement, and extending its expressive range.

Signorelli's frescoes in the S. Brizio Chapel (1499–1504; Orvieto Cathedral) secured his fame as a master of the nude figure. In eight large scenes Signorelli turned the Last Judgment into a narrative that begins with *The Preaching of the Anti-Christ* and ends with *The Crowning of the Blessed in Paradise*. Nude figures abound—twisted into *grotteschi* in the dadoes, contorted to express emotions of violent fear, pain, or joy in the Apocalyptic scenes. Those powerful, often brutal male nudes influenced not only Michelangelo but also, much later, Delacroix, Cézanne, and Max Beckmann.

Further reading. Kury, G. *The Early Work of Luca Signorelli 1465–1490*, New York (1978).

Siloe Gil de *fl.* 1475–*c*1505

Little is known of the origins or life of Gil de Siloe, one of the greatest sculptors of the Iberian peninsula, save that he was almost certainly Flemish by birth and training, and was possibly a native of Antwerp. It can only be said with certainty that by 1475 he was established in Burgos, and that his highly individual style was already well-formed and confident. By 1498 he was a property owner in Burgos. The apparent ending of his activities soon after the beginning of the 16th century suggests that he died *c*1505. He had one known son, Diego de Siloe, the architect of Granada Cathedral.

The works of Gil de Siloe are few, and are confined to the region of Burgos. At the time of his rather abrupt appearance in 1475, he was working on the tomb of Bishop D. Alonso de Cartagena in Burgos Cathedral. His two altarpieces in the cathedral may date from around the same period. His finest works were executed in the Cartuja de Miraflores between 1486 and 1499: there were the tombs of Juan II of Castille and Isabel of Portugal (1486), and of their son Don Alfonso (*c*1489). His masterpiece was the high altar of the same church (*c*1499), made with the collaboration of Diego de la Cruz. His last commission seems to have been the tomb of the page Juan de Padilla, in the monastery of Fresdelval (*c*1503).

The distinctive style of Gil de Siloe may reflect his northern origins. His delight in intricate but solid values, and especially in fabrics and embroidery, recalls the pleasure in textures to be found in Flemish painting. His concern with the expression of minute detail has invited comparison with gold- and silverwork, and is clearly related to the tastes that generated Plateresque architecture.

The tomb of Juan and Isabel is exceptionally complex. The richly dressed figures, separated by a grille of great intricacy and each with an equally intricate canopy, lie side by side on a geometrical base in the form of an eight-pointed star; they are attended by the Virtues and Old Testament figures. The monument to their son occupies a separate position on the wall; the boy kneels in prayer in the confines of a richly ornamental niche.

These works were executed in alabaster, but the high altar of Miraflores, in gilded wood, demonstrates the flexibility of Gil de Siloe's art. The work is dominated by an immense Christ, flanked by St Peter and St Paul. Yet, as with the tomb of Juan and Isabel, profusion is controlled by a strict geometrical and human structure. What might, in the hands of a lesser sculptor, have been a mass of sugary ornament, is always kept in check by an underlying strength of line. However great his delight in the richness of the superficial, Gil de Siloe was wholly conscious that his subject was the human form.

Simone Martini 1280/5?–1344

Simone di Martino, called Simone Martini, was an Italian painter of the Sienese school. His first certain work, the *Maestà* (1315) in the Sala del Mappamondo of Siena Town Hall or Palazzo Pubblico, suggests an apprenticeship in the studio of Duccio. It also reveals a knowledge of Florentine painting, both in the logical and unified treatment of space and light, and in specific features such as the kneeling angels bearing flower bowls at the foot of the Virgin's throne, derived directly from those in Giotto's *Ognissanti Madonna*. In this painting there are still clear Byzantine features, but during the course of Simone's career these are replaced by a feeling for line, decoration, and form which is derived rather from French Gothic art.

This French Gothic influence was introduced through a variety of channels, of which the French court in Naples was an important one. The King of Naples, Robert of Anjou, summoned Simone to Naples before 1317. He commissioned the artist to depict him kneeling at the feet of his elder brother, St Louis of Toulouse, who had abandoned the secular for the monastic life and resigned his dynastic rights and duties to Robert (*St Louis of Toulouse Crowning Robert of Anjou, King of Naples*; Museo e Gallerie Nazionali di Capodimonte, Naples). The *predella* panels show scenes from the life of St Louis, and in them for the first time the perspective of all five scenes is unified around a central axis.

By 1320 Simone had returned to Tuscany, painting altarpieces that are now in Pisa and Orvieto. In 1333 he signed and dated a panel painting depicting the *Annunciation* (Uffizi, Florence); according to the inscription, this was painted in partnership with his brother-in-law Lippo Memmi da Siera. Here the figure of the Virgin, suddenly disturbed by the Angel, is surrounded by an agitated line tracing the outline of her drapery, and her emotion is conveyed largely by means of this line.

At some time in the 1320s or 1330s Simone painted murals in the Chapel of St Martin in the Lower Church of St Francis at Assisi. As the result of another State commission, he depicted the figure of the commander of the recently victorious Sienese army, Guidoriccio da Fogliano (*c*1328), on the wall facing his *Maestà* in the Palazzo Pubblico, Siena. In these works Simone shows himself to be a skilled landscape painter, within the admitted limitations of the time.

The artist's last years were spent in Avignon, the seat of the Papacy for much of the 14th century. Petrarch, whom the artist met there, thanked him for a portrait of his beloved Laura in two Sonnets datable to before November 1336. This literary reference securely places Simone's first visit to Avignon before that date, although Sienese records put his final departure from Siena in late 1340. It also records, by referring to Simone's exact depiction of Laura's features in the now-lost portrait, Simone's interest at an early date in the precise imitation of facial features. His main works in Avignon, murals painted in the cathedral there, survive only fragmentarily although their appearance is known through copies. Simone, or more probably some French follower of his, has been held responsible for the highly ornamental hunting scenes decorating the walls of the Guardaroba in the Palais des Papes.

Among the surviving works from this time are the small but exquisite panel depicting *The Holy Family* (Walker Art Gallery, Liverpool), the six panels of the Antwerp Passion Polyptych (1340s; Royal Museum of Fine Arts, Antwerp, and Staatliche Museen, Berlin), and the frontispiece to Petrarch's copy of Virgil's *Aeneid* (Pinacoteca Ambrosiana, Milan). As in the Uffizi *Annunciation*, the later panel paintings make considerable dramatic use of the surrounding outline silhouetting the figures against the rich golden background. But the linear element in Simone's paintings never predominates to the exclusion of his sophisticated interest in spatial construction.

It was the combination of these talents, linear and spatial, together with an ability to imitate nature and to render and balance colors (inherited from Duccio), that ensured that his work would influence and inspire many later artists. In Italy and more especially in France, the school of miniaturists that developed in the Burgundian court during the 14th century often found their models in works by Simone.

Further reading. Edgell, G.H. *A History of Sienese Painting*, New York (1932). Paccagnini, G. *Simone Martini*, Milan (1955).

Sinan 1491–1588

Sinan was the greatest Ottoman architect, at a time when building was that culture's major form of artistic expression. He was born in 1491 in Kayseri, Anatolia. He was of Greek parentage, but was brought up in the Janissary school as a Muslim and a soldier. He fought in Rhodes (1520), and in the Hungarian campaign that culminated in Suleyman's great victory at Mohacs (1526). During this period Sinan served as a military engineer; he won notice from the Sultan for skilled bridging of the Danube and was promoted to the rank of captain. It was at this time that he first displayed his administrative gifts.

He was appointed Master of the Works in 1538 and held this post for 50 years, until his death in his 97th year. He remained a skilled military engineer as well as an architect. In 1539 he built his first mosque, at Aleppo, and in 1541 his first *türbe* (tomb chamber) for Barbarossa, at Besiktas on the Bosphorus. This was of classical octagonal form, in Marmara marble. At Usküdar, on a difficult site between shore and hillside, he built a mosque and madrasa for the Sultan's daughter Mihrimar, wife of Rustam Pasha (1548). It was erected on a podium, with a double portico facing towards the sea.

His greatest accomplishment was the building of the great complex round the Sultan's own mosque: *türbe*, bath house, caravansaries, and seven colleges, the whole completed in seven years by 1557. Here he showed his liking for the austere, with a limited use of tiles, but with clear articulation into 16 sections rising to a high dome with two semidomes and two great arches, as at St Sophia (Istanbul). The tiles used here in the mihrab and the *türbe* of Roxelana (1558) are superb examples of Iznik red and blue floral designs. Even more splendid are the tiles that cover the interior of the mosque of Rustam Pasha (1561), the building raised above the podium as an octagon set in a square.

His masterpiece is the great mosque at Edirne, built for Selim II. This was conceived in 1569, when Sinan was 78, and finished in 1575. Here the architect shows his genius in the organization of space and his skillful use of contrasts in stone and tiles, all with the finest detail.

Siqueiros David 1898–1974

The Mexican mural painter David Alfaro Siqueiros was born in Chihuahua and studied at the Academy of San Carlo in Mexico City. He played an active role in the revolutionary and economic struggles of his time as well as in the Mexican mural renaissance along with Orozco and Rivera. From 1919 to 1922 he traveled and studied in Belgium, France, Italy, and Spain. In 1932, and again in 1940, he was banished from Mexico because of his revolutionary politics. In 1936 he organized the Experimental Workshop in New York which was attended by Jackson Pollock.

Siqueiros was a technical innovator and attempted to revolutionize the materials, tools, and compositional forms of mural painting. This involved the use of spray guns and plastic paints, and led him to create the "New Realism" (with Surrealist elements), in order to convey his revolutionary message (for example, *Revolution against the Dictatorship of Porfirio Diaz: The Strike in Cananea*; pyroxilin; 1957; National History Museum, Mexico City).

Further reading. Charlot, J. (ed.) *An Artist on Art* vol. 2, Honolulu (1972). Charlot, J. *The Mexican Mural Renaissance 1920–5*, London and New Haven (1963). Reed, A.M. *The Mexican Muralists*, New York (1960). Rodriquez, A. *A History of Mexican Mural Painting*, London (1969). Siqueiros, D. *Art and Revolution*, New York (1975).

Sisley Alfred 1839–99

The Impressionist painter Alfred Sisley had English parents, but was born in Paris and spent his childhood there. He was in London from 1857 to 1861, preparing for a commercial career, and apparently studied the work of J.M.W. Turner and John Constable at that time. In 1862, having decided to become a painter, he entered the Paris studio of Charles Gleyre, where he met Monet, Renoir, and Frédéric Bazille. These friendships shaped the direction of his career.

In the later 1860s, he worked in the tradition of the Barbizon School landscapists, painting forest and village scenes in comparatively subdued color. One of these, *Avenue of Chestnut Trees near the Celle-Saint-Cloud* (Southampton Art Gallery) was shown at the 1868 Salon. In 1869 he began to paint Parisian scenes, and in 1870 exhibited at the Salon two small, informal views of the Canal Saint-Martin in Paris (*View of the Canal Saint-Martin*, Musée du Jeu de Paume, Paris; *Barges on the Canal Saint-Martin*, Sammlung Oskar Reinhart "Am Römerholz", Winterthur). These paintings are varied in brushwork and focus on atmospheric qualities; in many ways they anticipate the characteristic Impressionist landscapes of the early 1870s.

Between 1872 and 1880, Sisley lived mainly in the countryside west of Paris, around Marly and Louveciennes. In 1872, he worked with Monet at Argenteuil, and in 1874 spent four months in England, painting at Hampton Court. He exhibited in the first three Impressionist group exhibitions, in 1874, 1876, and 1877. More than any of the other Impressionists, he limited himself to landscape painting. He harnessed the varied touch and sensitivity to atmosphere of his 1870 canal scenes to the depiction of the Seine Valley, its villages and its countryside.

The paintings he did between 1872 and 1876 are of moderate size (rarely more than 30 in or 75 cm across), and show great responsiveness to the variety of natural lighting and textures. They share many features with Pissarro's work of 1871 to 1873. In these works Sisley sets off small, crisply painted accents against softer and broader areas of paint, to create subtle and carefully organized rhythms and patterns, as in *The Road to Sèvres* (1873; Musée du Jeu de Paume, Paris). Sometimes the rhythms are bolder, as in *The Weir at Molesey near Hampton Court* (1874; National Gallery of Scotland, Edinburgh). Like the other Impressionists, Sisley began in the early 1870s to introduce an increasing range of color to his landscapes; blues, in particular, are used to express shadow, and foliage is conveyed by a great variety of greens.

Later in the 1870s, Sisley began to adopt busier, more broken brushwork all over the picture, to animate the whole canvas —as in *The Seine at Suresnes* (1877; Musée du Jeu de Paume, Paris). In 1880 he moved to the area around Moret, near the junction of the Seine and Loing rivers, southeast of Paris and near the forest of Fontainebleau. Here he lived and painted for the rest of his life, in increasing seclu-

Alfred Sisley: View of the Canal Saint-Martin, Paris; oil on canvas; 50×65cm (20×26in); 1870. Musée du Jeu de Paume, Paris

sion; he traveled to paint only in 1894 (to Normandy) and 1897 (to the South Wales coast). In his later works, the touch is sometimes coarser and the color less sensitively used than in his best paintings of the 1870s, but at times his elaborate paint surfaces rival the richness of Monet's.

Further reading. Cogniat, R. *Sisley*, New York (1978). Shone, R. *Sisley*, New York (1979).

Škréta Karel 1610–74

A member of the aristocratic family of Šotnovský z Závořice, the painter Karel Škréta left Bohemia in 1628 to live with his mother in Saxony. As a Protestant, he spent ten years in exile, mostly in Italy, where he received his artistic training. He became a Catholic, and by 1650 was established as the leading painter in Prague. His portraits are distinguished by a sober realism expressed with extreme economy of color and strong chiaroscuro. The same qualities are apparent in his remarkable cycle depicting *The Legend of St Wenceslas* (1641–3; Mělník Castle). His later altarpieces, however, are more emotional and dramatic.

Sloan John 1871–1951

The American painter John Sloan was the leader of the group known as The Eight (of 1908), and of the Ashcan School in New York. He worked as a journalist in Philadelphia from 1871 to 1891, teaching himself to draw and to etch during these years. Encouraged by Robert Henri, he began to paint in 1897. Sloan was an illustrator, painter, and etcher, and organizer of the group exhibitions of the Ashcan School. He was a leading figure in the realist attack on the academy system's control of taste and patronage in America. Sloan's art was based on sympathetic observation rather than exposure or satire. It was at its best in his etchings, and in his paintings of the New York scene such as *Dust Storm, Fifth Avenue* (oil on canvas; 1906; Metropolitan Museum, New York) and *McSorley's Bar* (oil on canvas; 1912; Detroit Institute of Arts). (*See* overleaf.)

John Sloan: Southwest Art; oil on canvas; 53×64cm (21×25in); 1920. Collection of the Anschutz Corporation, Denver, Colo.

Slodtz family 17th and 18th centuries

The sculptor René-Michael Slodtz (1705–64) was also known as Michel-Ange Slodtz. One of the five sons of the sculptor Sebastien Slodtz (1665–1726), a Flemish-born sculptor and a former pupil of Girardon who settled in Paris, René-Michael won first prize for sculpture at the Académie in 1726, then left for Rome in 1728, returning in 1746. In Rome he developed a style that was full-bloodedly Baroque, yet sensitive to the germs of Neoclassicism. His chief Roman works were the St Bruno (for a niche at the crossing of St Peter's, Rome), and a bust for the tomb of Nicolas Vleughels in S. Luigi dei Francesi, Rome (1736; Musée Jacquemart—André, Paris). The monument to Archbishops La Tour d'Auvergue and Montmorin, (in St Maurice, Vienna) are among his other important works.

The St Bruno employs a variety of Baroque effects with consummate skill. The composition is at the point of apparent fragmentation—the saint's refusal of the crozier and miter of a bishopric, proffered by a child-angel, is expressed as much by the agitated twist of the drapery as by the gesture itself. The Montmorin monument (1740–4), and the monument to Languet de Glergy in St-Sulpice, completed in Paris in 1753, are equally Baroque. They borrow from Bernini not only their partly narrative, partly symbolic conception, but also the polychromy of differing metals and marbles. In sharp contrast is the Capponi Monument, S. Giovanni dei Fiorentini, Rome. Dating from the early 1740s, it shows Slodtz equally at home in a less rhetorical, more seriously classicizing style.

His brothers Sebastian-Antoine (c1695–1754) and Paul-Amboise Slodtz (1702–58) were also sculptors. They followed their father into the Menus-Plaisirs du Roi, producing pompes-funèbres and other ephemeral displays for the Court. Of the the two, only Paul-Amboise was a sculptor of merit, although his work is usually minor and decorative.

Sluter Claus c1350–1406

Claus Sluter was a Netherlandish sculptor whose career in the service of the Dukes of Burgundy left a permanent imprint on Burgundian art, and whose profound realism heralded a new phase in the art of northern Europe. His surviving works are concentrated in Dijon, where he was one of a number of distinguished artists engaged by Philip the Bold, Duke of Burgundy, to embellish the Carthusian monastery (the Chartreuse de Champmol) that he founded to house the tombs of the Burgundian dukes. The monastery was attacked during the French Revolution and later demolished, but the portal with Sluter's sculptures, and the remains of his monumental fountain in the large cloister remained in situ, and were incorporated into the design of the hospital built on the site. The ducal tombs were restored, and are now in the Musée des Beaux-Arts, Dijon.

Sluter's early career is obscure. Most of our information about him comes from the Burgundian archives, where he is documented from March 1385 until his death early in 1406. Various spellings of the name occur, but the form "Claus Sluter" was used by the artist himself for the design of his seal. He was born in Haarlem, in the county of Holland, but gravitated to Brussels, where he was inscribed in the stonemasons' guild c1380. He probably acquired some reputation in Brabant and Flanders at this time, and some of his contemporaries in the stonemasons' guild later came to work under his direction in Dijon. But apart from some statuettes of prophets from the Town Hall of Brussels (now in the Musée Communal de Saint-Lambert-Woluwe) no known surviving work relates very closely to his mature style.

In 1385 Sluter went to Dijon to join the workshop of Jean de Marville, who was then chief sculptor to the Duke of Burgundy. On Marville's death in 1389 he assumed contol of the workshop and was designated valet de chambre to the Duke. All the works stamped by his very individual style date from this time onwards. Apart from a few excursions made on behalf of the Duke (to Paris in 1392, to Mehun-sur-Yèvre in 1393, and to Dinant and Malines in 1395) he remained in Burgundy. A major work, known to have been done by him at this time but now lost, was the very original decoration of the château of Germolles (1396), where the Duke and Duchess were portrayed at its entrance in a pastoral scene.

The background to all Sluter's Burgundian activity was the sculpture for the Chartreuse de Champmol. Two of the major works associated with him at the Chartreuse were begun before he himself was in control of the workshop. The architectural framework of the Duke's tomb had already been completed, and the portal of the church (consecrated in 1388) had been built to a design by the Duke's architect Drouet de Dammartin. This was probably done in consultation with Marville, and was probably intended to include only three sculptures—standing figures of the Duke and Duchess, on either side of a *trumeau* figure of the Virgin. Sluter's dynamic transformation of this Parisian formula shows the independence of his creative approach. Huge consoles jut out and beyond the architectural framework, disregarding the limitations of the original design, to support additional figures of St John the Baptist and St Catherine. The two saints bend forward to present the kneeling figures of the Duke and Duchess to the Virgin. The drama of the presentation is intensified by the way in which the saints appear almost to surge forward towards the Virgin; she looks at the Child, who in turn looks up to where there was once a canopy of angels. The exaggerated scale of the saints in comparison to the Virgin suggests a type of stage perspective, in which the down-to-earth realism of the Duke and Duchess supply the human elements in a transcendental happening.

From 1395, Sluter was involved in the planning and execution of one of his greatest works. The *Puits de Moise* or *Well of Moses* is only a part of the monumental fountain that once dominated the large cloister of Chartreuse, which was also the monks' cemetery. It originally served as the hexagonal base for a tall Calvary—the whole being conceived as a "Fountain of Life". Only fragments of the Calvary, including the torso of Christ, survive (Musée Archéologique, Dijon). But the hexagonal base with its figures of six prophets (who predict the inevitability of the Crucifixion), and the angels (who mourn the sacrifice on the symbolic Mount Golgotha), are among the great sculptures of all time. Each of the prophets (Moses, David, Jeremiah, Zachariah, Daniel, and Isaiah) is interpreted with unprecedented realism, and with a psychological penetration that was only to be equalled later by Rembrandt. The fountain as originally painted and gilded must have been spectacular. Its deep religious significance and spiritual power were recognized by the granting of indulgences to pilgrims who visited it in the 15th century.

Although the tomb of Philip the Bold had been one of the first monuments to occupy Marville's workshop, Sluter seems to have been reluctant to bring it to a speedy completion. When the Duke died in April 1404, only two mourning figures (or *pleurants*) had been completed. They were the forerunners of the now-famous funeral procession that now surrounds the tomb. Sluter's own death in January 1406 undoubtedly frustrated the wishes of John the Fearless to have his father's tomb completed within a period of four years. But the final conception bears every mark of Sluter's personality, and it seems likely that his nephew, Claus de Werve, who finished the tomb by 1410, followed his uncle's designs.

As the tomb stands today the effigy of Philip is a modern restoration, but the *pleurants* survived the Revolution, and are remarkable for the range and depth of their expression. Sluter's idea of surrounding the tomb with a solemn liturgical procession was not new, but every detail of the procession is permeated by a new realism and a new sense of drama. Even when the facial expressions are concealed beneath heavy mourning garments, the attitudes of the figures and the fall of drapery can still emanate a profound emotional effect.

Sluter was a medieval artist with the

Claus Sluter: David and Jeremiah, two of the six prophets on the base of the Well of Moses; stone; 1395–1406. Musée Archéologique, Dijon

individuality of a Renaissance personality, and the patronage of Philip the Bold enabled him to express this. Contemporary painters and sculptors, caught in the decorative artificiality of the International Gothic style, found in his work the inspiration to explore for themselves a more deeply realistic approach to the problems of art.

Further reading. David, H. *Claus Sluter*, Paris (1951). Finn, D. *Claus Sluter*, London (1991). Liebreich, A. *Claus Sluter*, Brussels (1936). Monget, C. *La Chartreuse de Dijon* (3 vols.), Montreuil-sur-Mer and Tournai (1895–1905). Quarré, P. *La Chartreuse de Champmol*, Dijon (1960). Quarré, P. *Les Pleurants des Tombeaux des Ducs de Bourgogne*, Dijon (1971).

Smith David 1906–65

The American sculptor David Smith was born at Decatur, Indiana. He studied art first (by a correspondence course) at the Cleveland School of Art, and then at Ohio University (1924–5). In the summer of 1925, he worked in the steel frame assembly department at the Studebaker plant. The experience contributed to his lifelong skill as a worker in metal, and also left him with an equally long-lasting affection for machinery.

In 1926 he moved to New York, where he studied painting at the Art Students League of New York (1926–32). It was during this period that he became familiar with Cubism, which was to exert a considerable influence on his development. He also saw in a magazine reproductions of welded-steel sculpture by Picasso. Smith produced his first welded-steel piece in 1932; and throughout the 1930s and 1940s he created a whole series of sculpture in which the influence of both Picasso and Julio Gonzalez is apparent (for example, *Star Cage*, 1950; University of Minnesota, Minneapolis; *Aerial Construction*, 1936; Joseph Hirshhorn Museum, Washington, D.C.).

During the Second World War, he worked in a locomotive factory. The scale of the engines influenced his sculptural thinking and led, many years later, to the series of sculptures by which he will perhaps be best remembered. These are the very large-scale, freestanding pieces that he produced in the machine shop of his farm at Bolton Landing, New York State. They are sometimes still markedly linear in

character (for example, *Sentinal IV*, 1957; private collection).

The most striking of them, which were to influence the general development of Minimal art in America, are those of the so-called *Cubi* series. They are made out of cubes and cylinders of stainless steel, polished and then abraded; they are often balanced one on top of another in a seemingly precarious manner (for example, *Cubi XIX*, 1964, Tate Gallery, London; *Cubi XVII*, 1963, Dallas Museum of Fine Arts). Smith, who was the most original American sculptor of his

generation, was killed in an automobile accident in 1965.

Further reading. Baro, G. (ed.) "Some Late Words from David Smith", *Art International* vol. IX, Zurich (October 1965). Cone, J.H. *David Smith: a Retrospective Exhibition*, Cambridge, Mass. (1966). Greenberg, C. "David Smith", *Art in America* vol. XLIV, New York (1956–7). Hess, T.B. *David Smith*, New York (1964). Kramer, H. *David Smith: a Memorial Exhibition*, Los Angeles (1965).

Matthew Smith: Lilies in a Vase; oil on canvas; 74×53cm (29×21in); 1913–14. City Art Gallery, Leeds

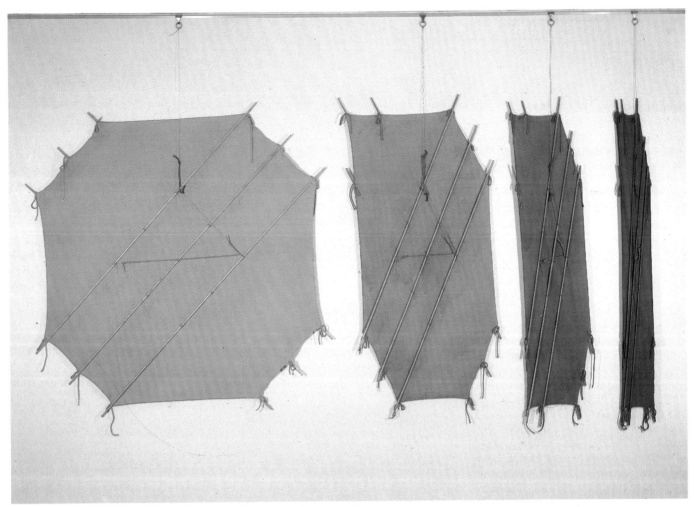

Richard Smith: The Pod; acrylic on canvas; 160×325cm (63×128in); 1976. Private collection

Smith Matthew 1879–1959

The English painter Sir Matthew Smith studied at the Manchester School of Art (1900–4), and the Slade School of Fine Art (1905–7), but drew his real inspiration from France. Between 1908 and 1912 he spent most of his time in Pont-Aven, Étaples, and Paris, slowly imbibing the influence of Gauguin and Matisse (he spent a month at Matisse's school). The resultant works, painted when he was back in London (for example, *Nude, Fitzroy Street, No. 1*, 1916; Tate Gallery, London), are related to paintings by the Camden Town artists, but are more Fauve in color. This boldness also characterizes the Cornish landscapes he painted in 1920. Thereafter his colors became less strident and took on a subdued sensuosity that matched the baroque richness of his nudes and still lifes.

Smith Richard 1931–

The English painter Richard Smith was born in Letchworth, Hertfordshire. He studied at Luton School and the St Albans School of Art (1948–54) and at the Royal College of Art (1954–7). He taught mural decoration at Hammersmith College of Art, London (1957–8), and spent the years 1959 and 1960 on a Harkness Fellowship in the United States. He taught at St Martin's School of Art (1961–3) and has held various teaching posts in the U.S.A. (1965–8). He was a prize winner at the Venice Biennale in 1966 and at São Paulo in 1967.

From 1961 to 1969 most of Smith's paintings were based on advertising images. In the early 1960s his loosely and elegantly painted pictures in heraldic colors were succeeded by large three-dimensional shaped relief paintings inspired by billboards. Smith's interest in the constructed supports then led to very long paintings made up of complicated modular sections, with blurred, spray-painted imagery, such as *Riverfall* (1969; Tate Gallery, London). In the early 1970s he reacted against the complexity of his earlier work and began painting on loosely stretched canvas on light, aluminum tube, in which strings and ties are left visible. These paintings may be in series or may combine two or more overlapping canvases. Smith has also made prints on the same theme using folded card or paper with ribbons.

Smith Tony 1912–80

The American sculptor, painter, and architect Tony Smith was born in South Orange, New Jersey. He studied part-time at the Art Students League, New York (1935–6), and at the New Bauhaus, Chicago (1937–8). In the following year he worked on architectural projects under Frank Lloyd Wright. Between 1940 and 1960 he designed houses, and also monuments that were not in fact built. He spent the years 1953 to 1955 in Germany. He taught at Bennington College, Vermont (1958–61), and at Hunter College, New York (1962–6).

Most of his work before 1960 was architectural, though he did some paintings and reliefs during the late 1930s that were influenced by Georges Vantongerloo. In 1961 he produced his first sculptures (for example, *Gracehoper*; Detroit Institute of Arts). These were constructed from pure geometrical modules, sliced, beveled, and truncated, and combined according to classical ratios with an architectural sensibility. Massive and austere, these intuitively controlled forms separate him from most Minimalist sculptors with whom he tends to be identified. In the late 1960s his structures became more complicated, based on multifaceted solids and repeated modules. His works originate as paper maquettes and plywood mock-ups, which are later executed in steel, welded bronze, or marble.

Smithson Robert 1938–73

Robert Smithson, the American "land" artist, writer, and visionary theorist, was born in New Jersey. He studied part-time at the Art Students League, New York (1953–6), and then at the Brooklyn Museum School. In the mid 1960s his sculptures were associated with Minimalism, but a group of transitional works, the *Mirror Displacements* and *Non-sites*, led him to make the large earth-works for which he is best known. Notable among these are *Spiral Jetty* (1970; Utah), a spiral of earth created in the Great Salt Lake, and *Amarillo Ramp* (1973; Texas). The latter work was completed after Smithson had been killed in a plane crash on the site. Few of his many large earthwork proposals were carried out.

Snyders Frans 1579–1657

Frans Snyders was a Flemish painter of animals and still-life subjects. He worked in Antwerp on his return from a visit to Italy between 1608 and 1609. He painted animals and still-life details in the pictures of Rubens and Jacob Jordaens. Rubens, in turn, painted the figures in a number of Snyders' hunting scenes. These are pictures of boar and stag hunts which, like those of fighting animals, contain exuberant color and vigorous movement. The vitality and freedom of style in these works was extended to Snyders' cornucopian still lifes. These blend the meticulous realism of the flower and fruit paintings of Pieter Bruegel the Younger (by whom Snyders was trained) with both formal and literal movement—the latter through the inclusion of animated cats, dogs, and birds.

Soami c1470–1525

Soami, also known as Shinso, was a Japanese ink painter who specialized in landscape. He was the third of the "three

Il Sodoma: St George and the Dragon; panel; 138×98cm (54×38in); c1516. National Gallery of Art, Washington, D.C.

-amis", his father and grandfather being the painters Geiami (1431–85) and Noami (1397–1471). Although all were ink painters, none were Zen devotees. They came from the artisan class whose names often ended "-ami" to indicate their belief in the savior Buddha Amida. All three painters worked at cataloging the Shogun's collection of paintings and *objets d'art* (nearly all of which were Chinese). Their influence as arbiters of taste probably caused the takeover of the Academy by the non-Zen *Kano* School.

Little is known of Soami's life, though a good many of his paintings survive. He is best known for his "wet" style, but he could paint in a number of other manners.

His versatility was derived from his study of the Shogun's Chinese collection, which he viewed in an aesthetic and nonreligious way. This is a very important transition in Japanese painting. His *Viewing a Waterfall in the Lu Mountains* (c1508; private collection) is done in the "square style" with firmly angled rocks and mountains and straight hatching, but the middle ground is filled with vaporous mists, giving an almost sensuous feeling of distance. This "hard and soft" mixture is very Japanese, and became a feature of the *Kano* School.

His greatest work is certainly the set of sliding doors of c1513 from the Daisen'in (Daitokuji Temple, Kyoto), now mounted as hanging scrolls. It is a great panorama done in wet wash (much influenced by Southern Sung) with almost no outline, combining grandeur with a credibly Japanese scale. Similar works with a feeling of total fluidity are the sixfold screens in the Metropolitan Museum, New York.

Sodoma Il 1477–1549

Together with Peruzzi and Beccafumi, Giovanni Antonio Bazzi, known as Il Sodoma, was one of the leading painters of early-16th-century Siena. Trained in his native Vercelli, he arrived in Siena by c1503, apparently already conversant with the Milanese works of Leonardo. He worked in Rome in 1508, and again from 1516 to 1518, as a large-scale decorator under the patronage of Agostino Chigi. He was only superficially influenced by the mature Raphael; and despite a certain response to Florentine Mannerism and to the art of Beccafumi, in his later career, after c1520, his style increasingly reverted to its provincial roots.

Solimena Francesco 1657–1747

Francesco Solimena, the Italian painter of the early Rococo, was born in Nocera. He was the leading Neapolitan painter during the first half of the 18th century. Having arrived in Naples by 1674, he was influenced by Luca Giordano, particularly in the frescoes of the sacristy of S. Paolo Maggiore, Naples (1690). After 1692 the influence of Mattia Preti is also discernible, and thereafter a darker color range is employed in his works: this quality is typical of his style. There are important frescoes of his late period in Naples, in S. Maria Donnaregina, S. Domenico Maggiore, and the Gesù Nuovo.

Sonderborg 1923–

The Danish-German artist Kurt R. Hoffmann, known from his place of birth as Sonderborg, was originally trained for a business career. He decided, however, to become a painter and attended the Landeskunstschule in Hamburg (1947–9). In

1951 he visited Italy. He studied graphics with S.W. Hayter in Paris in 1953 and became a member of the "Zen 49" group (1956–7). He began teaching at the Academy of Art in Stuttgart in 1965. From 1969 to 1970 he taught at the College of Art and Design in Minneapolis.

Automatism, speed, and movement are basic to Sonderborg's work. Through a drip technique, and the use of many different tools for scratching and digging at the surface of his canvases, he aims to catch fleeting impressions (for example, 13.11.58/2107–2156; gouache; 1958; Museum Bochum, Bochum).

Sophilos fl. c580–570 BC

Sophilos was an Athenian painter and potter. He is the first black-figure artist whose name is known, from four inscribed vases; three of these are signed by him as painter and one as potter.

His early career emerged from the old-fashioned school of Athenian artists,

Francesco Solimena: Dido Receiving Aeneas and Cupid Disguised as Ascanius; oil on canvas; 207×310cm (81×122in); 1720s. National Gallery, London

headed by the Gorgon Painter, whose major preoccupation was with the animal frieze style that they had learned from their rivals in Corinth. This involved covering the vase with numerous horizontal zones of animals (interspersed with florals), coursing monotonously round the pot. An *amphora* from Vourva (now in the National Museum, Athens) represents one of his many unsigned pieces decorated in this diehard style. The troop of animals and mechanical florals—weary and debased versions of the Gorgon Painter's more thoughtful and meticulous compositions—characterize the early achievement of Sophilos as a leading exponent of the conventional.

His important contribution to the history of black-figure painting came only after he had relegated the animal parades to an unobtrusive position on his vases. This done, he applied himself wholeheartedly to decorating vases with scenes from myth. A fragment of a *dinos* found in Thessaly (now in the National Museum, Athens) reveals Sophilos as an enterprising, if clumsy, proponent of early narrative art. The animals make an appearance on the lip and lower frieze; but the artist's prime concern is to depict a chariot race, with an animated team of horses galloping past a stand packed with gesticulating spectators. The artist proudly claims responsibility for the questionable draftsmanship—the vase is inscribed "Sophilos painted me". He goes on to say that this is no common race, but rather an excerpt from the *Iliad*.

A *dinos* resting on its own stand and signed by Sophilos as painter (British Museum, London), further illustrates his commitment to myth. Animals and florals occupy eight horizontal zones, while the upper frieze contains the main subject: the arrival of divine guests at the wedding festivities of Peleus and Thetis. The guests proceed round the vase to the house of the bridegroom, who stands before its closed doors, wine-cup in hand. There are fragments of another *dinos*, depicting the same scene and signed by Sophilos as painter, in the National Museum, Athens. The next painter to illustrate the celebrated wedding feast was Sophilos' younger and more fastidious follower, Kleitias, whose volute-*krater* is a true masterpiece of narrative painting: the animals are banished to a single subsidiary frieze, and five zones are devoted entirely to myth. This work, known as the François Vase, is in the Museo Archeologico, Florence.

Sophilos occupied a key position in Attic painting, as the last of a generation of animal frieze painters, and a pioneer in the formation of Greek narrative art. Although his enthusiasm as a story-teller usually surpassed his talents as a draftsman he had clearly paved the way for successors such as Kleitias.

Sosen Mori 1747–1821

The Japanese animal painter of the Edo period, Mori Sosen, worked mainly in Osaka. He learned painting from a *Kano* artist, but was clearly influenced by the naturalism of Okyo, though he was never his pupil. He became a specialist in painting monkeys, deer, and other furry animals. He is said to have studied wild monkeys in the mountains for three years. His animals are extraordinarily alive, whether done in the minute, detailed brushwork of his early style, or in the more free and dashing hand of his last years. Numerous forgeries have detracted from his reputation. His descendants (all called Mori), Yusen, Tessan, and Ippo, continued Sosen's tradition.

Sotatsu Tawaraya fl. c1600–30

The Japanese painter Tawaraya Sotatsu was the founder of the *Rimpa* School, influencing almost all movements after his time. The facts of his life are little known. He worked as a fan-painter in Kyoto, but rose to work for the court. As a producer of fine decorated papers for calligraphy, he absorbed much of Kyoto's old courtly culture. He met the great designer and calligrapher Hon'ami Koetsu, for whose elegant writing he painted under-designs in gold and silver.

Sotatsu excelled in works that needed careful placing—decorative screens and fans. He took to its highest level the Japanese genius for brilliant off-center composition. In his screens of *bugaku* dancers, for example (Daigoji Temple, Kyoto), the figures are placed thinly on a plain gold background, with no apparent organization, and yet with perfect effect. He pioneered a new boldness of color and line. Simple, bright colors are often applied in thick patches, as in his screens *God of Thunder* and *God of the Winds* (Kenninji Temple, Kyoto) and shapes are reduced to pure ornament. In his *Genji* screens (Seikado Foundation, Tokyo) the round, green hills are linked into one sweeping

thrust that runs diagonally across the six leaves. On his wooden doors in the Yogen'in, Kyoto, he made a virtue of necessity, producing on his massive elephant a line so thick that it became decorative in itself. He also popularized a technique of dropping one color on to another while the first was still wet (*tarashikomi*), and an original style of ink monochrome-painting where the ink was used sensuously, as if it were color.

Soto Jésus 1923–

Jésus Rafaël Soto, the Venezuelan optico-kinetic painter and musician, was born in Ciudad Bolivar. He studied at Caracas School of Fine Art (1942–7). After a period as Director of the Maracaibo School of Fine Art (1947–50), he moved to Paris. In 1954 he formulated the concepts of Kineticism, with Yaacov Agam and Jean Tinguely.

Between 1950 and 1952, influenced by Mondrian and the Constructivists, Soto made relief paintings of repeated geometrical elements and paintings of colored dots inspired by serial music. The paintings he did on superimposed sheets of clear plexiglass consisted of single colored motifs; dots and lines were his first exploitation of the "moiré effect", followed by spirals against striped grounds. In the early 1960s his informal, irregular constructions of twisted wires were succeeded by paintings in which metal plaques and rods appear to vibrate. Later reliefs made with moving elements led, in 1969, to "penetrables": sculptures of hanging rods, through which spectators may pass.

Soufflot Jacques 1713–80

The French architect Jacques-Germain Soufflot was the son of a provincial lawyer. He studied architecture in Rome between 1731 and 1738. His first major commission was the huge Hotel-Dieu, Lyons, begun in 1741. This made his reputation, and in 1749 he was chosen by Mme de Pompadour to accompany her brother, M. de Marigny, to Italy to prepare him for the office of *Surintendant des Bâtiments*. If this tour marks the birth of French Neoclassicism, Soufflot was to bring the style to maturity with the Panthéon in Paris. Designed as the Church of Ste-Geneviève in 1757, and unfinished at his death, it is Soufflot's masterpiece. Perhaps surprisingly, many of the structural techniques are borrowed from Gothic architecture. Soufflot did not attempt to conceal this fact, advocating in 1762 the combination of Greek orders with the admirable lightness of Gothic buildings. His later buildings, the École de Droit (1771–83), and garden buildings at the Château de Menars (begun in 1767) are less important.

Soulages Pierre 1919–

The French painter Pierre Soulages was born at Rodez. He developed an interest in local Romanesque and prehistoric art, and began painting while still at school. He visited Paris from 1938 to 1939 and there saw exhibitions of work by Cézanne and Picasso. In 1941, after serving in the French army for two years, he began work as a vineyard laborer. For the rest of the Occupation, until he settled in Paris in 1946, he did no painting, but he met Sonia Delaunay and became interested in Abstract art.

His first nonfigurative paintings, done in 1947, were graphically linked black brush strokes on a light ground. Rigorous avoidance of extra-pictorial references led to larger, denser, and more gestural forms. Later, blues, reds, and browns appear in his work, but the main architectonic structures are invariably black. The ground may be obliterated, or lights may permeate interlaced forms, but spatial readings of depth are always apparent. Soulages has designed for the theater, and since 1952 has also made etchings. His works are owned by many public collections around the world, including the Nationalgalerie, Berlin, the Musée National d'Art Moderne, Paris, the Art Institute of Chicago, and the Okara Art Museum, Kurashiki.

Soutine Chaim 1893–1943

The Russian painter Chaim Soutine spent most of his painting life in France. He was born near Minsk, the tenth son of a poor Jewish tailor who intended him to be a bootmaker. He attended art school at Vilna from 1910 to 1913, then from 1913 to 1918 he lived in Paris in extreme poverty. He paid his first visit to Cagnes, on the Mediterranean coast, in 1918, and the following year went to Céret in the Pyrenees. He spent much time in each of these places, until 1925. In 1922, he found a lavish patron in the American collector Dr Albert C. Barnes; from this time, the relationship guaranteed him some financial

security. In the early 1930s, he spent several summers near Chartres. The German occupation forced Soutine, as a Jew, to leave Paris. He moved to Touraine, but a stomach ulcer compelled him to return to Paris for an operation. He died in August 1943.

His early work in Paris was mainly still life. He also occasionally painted single figure portraits. The main influences on his

work were Cézanne, Van Gogh, and his friends Marc Chagall and Amedeo Modigliani. His southern landscapes were dense and somber: claustrophobic and almost two-dimensional at Céret, but more open, lighter, and airier at Cagnes. In paintings of both places, the landscape forms are turbulent and the brush strokes violent. His later landscapes of the Île de France are more controlled, but still belong to a kind

Pierre Soulages: Painting; oil on canvas; 194×130cm (76×51in); 1957. Musée National d'Art Moderne, Paris

Stanley Spencer: The Resurrection, Cookham; oil on canvas; 274×549cm (108×216in); 1923–7. Tate Gallery, London

of Slav-Jewish Expressionism. His best known single-figure portraits are of pastry cooks, page boys, valets, and waiters. Among his still lifes is a series done in 1925–6 influenced by Rembrandt's *The Flayed Ox* (1655; Louvre, Paris), for example *Side of Beef* (1925; Albright-Knox Art Gallery, Buffalo) and *Carcass of Beef* (*c*1925; Minneapolis Institute of Arts).

Spencer Stanley 1891–1959

The English painter Sir Stanley Spencer was born at Cookham, Berkshire. From 1908 to 1912 he studied at the Slade School of Fine Art, where his gift for drawing was strengthened by the teaching of Henry Tonks. From the beginning, Spencer's works showed a bold naiveté of vision that was the result of both study (particularly of the Italian Primitives and the Post-Impressionists) and a strong individuality. His experiences in the First World War heightened the visionary qualities of his work, and led to the murals he painted for the Memorial Chapel, Burghclere (1926–32). In these and in other paintings (for example, *The Resurrection, Cookham*, 1923–7; Tate Gallery, London) Spencer expressed his religious belief that all mankind's mundane activities partook

of the life eternal. In furtherance of this awareness he also preached sexual liberation, and painted several works whose explicit sexuality prefigures that of Francis Bacon and Lucian Freud.

Further reading. Carline, R. *Stanley Spencer at War*, London (1978). Robinson, D. (ed.) *Stanley Spencer 1891–1959*, London (1976). Robinson, D. *Stanley Spencer: Visions from a Berkshire Village*, Oxford (1979). Rothenstein, E. *Stanley Spencer*, London (1962). Rothenstein, J. (ed.) *Stanley Spencer, the Man: Correspondence and Reminiscences*, London (1979). *Stanley Spencer, R.A.*, London (1980).

Spinello Aretino *c*1345–1410

The Italian painter Spinello Aretino came from Arezzo, but he probably trained in Florence. His earliest documented work is a *Madonna* (1385; William Hayes Fogg Art Museum, Cambridge, Mass.). His most important surviving works are the sacristy frescoes in S. Miniato al Monte, Florence (*c*1387). Comparison of these with the work of Agnolo Gaddi (for instance his frescoes of *The Legend of the Cross* in the choir of S. Croce, Florence, *c*1380) suggest that Agnolo might have

been his teacher. The significance of Spinello's work is that it clearly restates the principles of Giotto (1266–1337). In his paintings, large, bulky figures move with monumental deliberation within simple compositions, sometimes backed by an architecture in almost-convincing perspective. Masaccio (1401–?28) must have learned much from Spinello's work.

Aretino Spinello: a detail of the scene St Benedict Expels the Devil from One of his Monks; fresco; *c*1387. Saeristy of S. Miniato al Monte, Florence

Spranger Bartholomaeus
1546–1611

The Flemish painter Bartholomaeus Spranger was the son of an Antwerp merchant. He studied under several local artists, including Jan Mandyn, Frans Mostaert, and Cornelis van Dalem, but his true apprenticeship was served in many years of travel through France and Italy. He is recorded at Paris, Lyons, Milan, and then at Parma, where the sensuous forms and colors of Correggio were to have a profound effect upon him.

By 1567 he was in Rome, where he stayed for several years. Most of his paintings for Roman churches are lost, but a *Last Judgment* painted for Pius V survives (now in the Museo Civico, Turin). He worked in the Zuccaro workshop for the Farnese family at Caprarola. In 1575 he was at the Imperial court at Vienna, and he finally settled in Prague in 1581 at the court of the Emperor Rudolf II. He married the daughter of a Prague jeweler.

As a result of his extensive travels, Spranger's style marks a highpoint of the International Mannerist style of the 16th century. His elongated, elegant forms, and bright, jewel-like colors are perhaps closest in type to the figure-style of the School of Fontainebleau. Works for Rudolf II such as the *Minerva Conquering Ignorance* (c1591; Kunsthistorisches Museum, Vienna) meet the demands of a circle of Court *cognoscenti*; they also convey the strong hint of eroticism demanded by the Emperor himself. The dark backgrounds of his pictures allow a highly contrived lighting, which accentuates the sweeping curves of figures and drapery.

Spranger's most successful religious works are those that give the opportunity for a flamboyance of dress and pose, as in the *Adoration of the Magi* (National Gallery, London). His influence was widespread in northern Europe, mainly through engravings after his work by Hendrick Goltzius (1558–1617).

Squarcione Francesco 1397–1468

Francesco Squarcione was an Italian painter of the Paduan school. In 1423 his profession was "tailor and embroiderer", and he is first mentioned as a painter in 1429. From the many paintings mentioned in documents, only two certain works survive: the Lazzara Altarpiece (1449–52; Museo Bottacin e Museo Communale, Padua) and a signed *Madonna and Child*,

also from the Lazzara family (Staatliche Museen, Berlin). The first of these is a polyptych, set within an elaborate Gothic frame, and with a surface richness similar to the work of the Vivarini. The Madonna shows a Tuscan influence (specifically that of Donatello), with the Virgin's face in sharp profile and the Child standing on a marble parapet before her.

Squarcione is chiefly important as the master of a large number of painters, including Andrea Mantegna. An early biographer records the artist's youthful travels through Greece and Italy, and his collection of sculpture, but the two works described above make no reference to such antiquarian interests.

Staël Nicolas de 1914–55

Nicolas de Staël was a French painter born in St Petersburg, Russia. Forced to flee after the Bolshevik coup of 1917, he was orphaned and grew up in Belgium. He studied with M. van Haelen at the Academy of Fine Arts in Brussels (1932–3). He visited Holland, and also Paris, where he was impressed by the work of Cézanne, Matisse, Braque, and Soutine. Between 1934 and 1938 he traveled and lived in Spain, North Africa, and Italy, before returning to Paris. After military service in the Foreign Legion (1939–40), he lived in Nice until 1942. He returned to Paris in 1943, and there, the following year, became a friend of Georges Braque. He obtained French nationality in 1948, and then traveled widely (1949–53), settling in Antibes in 1954.

De Staël's paintings are known for their luminous color, which was often laid on with a palette knife. His work in the early 1940s was abstract and geometric in design. It gradually shifted to a freer abstraction, and then—by the early 1950s—to figurative compositions of still lifes, figures, and seascapes (for example, *Le Bateau*; oil on canvas; 1954; Scottish National Gallery of Modern Art, Edinburgh).

Stankiewicz Richard 1922–83

The American sculptor Richard Stankiewicz was born in Philadelphia. He studied at the Hans Hofmann School, New York (1948–50), and in Paris under Fernand Léger and Ossip Zadkine (1950–1). In 1967 he became Professor of Art at New York State University, Albany, and settled in Massachusetts. Stankiewicz was a leading

Nicolas de Staël: Figure by the Sea; oil on canvas; 130×162cm (51×64in); 1952. Kunstsammlung Nordrhein-Westfalen, Düsseldorf

"junk" sculptor in the 1950s. He used mostly discarded machine parts such as pipes, gearwheels, cogs, boilers, and springs, to make witty parodies of human and animal figures, such as *Kabuki Dancer* (Whitney Museum of American Art, New York). In the 1960s the sculptures became lighter and nonreferential. Even more refined sculptures followed, made of fewer parts in limited forms such as "I-beams" and cylinders.

Steen Jan 1626–79

The Dutch artist Jan Steen painted humorous scenes showing the recreations of the middle and lower classes. His pictures are invariably categorized as genre, but they are often more complex, containing allusions to old proverbs and sayings. In this respect his mildly satirical work continues a tradition of which Hieronymus Bosch and Pieter Bruegel the Elder are two of the best-known exponents.

Steen was born in Leiden, the son of a brewer. He may have studied at Haarlem under Adriaen van Ostade and also at The Hague under the landscapist Jan van Goyen, in whose style he painted a few landscapes, and whose daughter he married. His *Game of Skittles* (c1660–3; National Gallery, London) reveals a more lyrical treatment of the kind of subject earlier popularized by both Ostade and Adriaen Brouwer. Steen simultaneously tackled portraits and biblical subjects (both of which are given genre-like treatment), but he is now best known for his tavern scenes and depictions of popular

festivals. In Haarlem during the 1660s he painted a number of pictures of this kind, full of animation and vitality. Notable among them are *The World Upside Down* (1663; Kunsthistorisches Museum, Vienna) and several versions of *The Feast of St Nicholas*. The paintings from this period are full of differentiations of character and expression in the figures. This, together with the profusion of detail, the multiplicity of incident, the frequent proverbial or literary basis, and an occasional theatrical element, requires them to be "read" rather than simply experienced as a visual whole. Subjects of this kind are complemented by a number of pictures of doctors' visits (to love-sick girls), and music lessons in respectable bourgeois settings. These are more tranquil works, which exhibit Steen's wide thematic range.

During his later years, when Steen combined the profession of painter and innkeeper at Leiden, he turned to a more idyllic vein, depicting scenes of amorous dalliance placed in park settings. These works look forward to the early 18th century *fête champêtre* paintings of Watteau. Steen apparently never gained popular esteem during his lifetime; he died with 500 unsold pictures in his house.

Steer Philip 1860–1942

The English painter Philip Wilson Steer was born in Birkenhead, Cheshire. He studied in Paris from 1882 to 1884, but without mastering the French language or familiarizing himself with avant-garde French painting. In 1886, however, after his return to London, he became a founder-member of the New English Art Club; this was a society led by Walter Sickert, which tried to import into English painting the lessons of Manet, Degas, and Monet.

Steer's landscapes of the late 1880s and early 1890s were beach scenes at Walberswick, often with young girls or children. They created a sharply individual note, in which high-keyed color, robust handling, and unexpected viewpoints aimed towards exciting new directions. In the same period, his figures in interiors were caught in offbeat, arbitrarily cut compositions, which he would also apply to his portraits (for example, *Mrs Cyprian Williams and her Children*, 1890–1; Tate Gallery,

Philip Steer: The Beach at Walberswick, Suffolk; oil on canvas; 60×76cm (24×30in); c1889. Tate Gallery, London

London). He held a one-man show at the Goupil Gallery, London, in 1894; he received critical support from D.S. MacColl, George Moore, and Walter Sickert; his work was illustrated in *The Yellow Book*; and he exhibited with Les Vingt in Brussels.

When Steer reached his mid 30s, his inventive searching began to flag. He never married. His life took on a repetitive pattern—he spent his summers in various parts of England and Wales, and his winters in London, where he taught at the Slade School of Fine Art from 1893 to 1930. His style became increasingly eclectic, echoing in turn the styles of François Boucher, of John Constable, and of Thomas Gainsborough. The handling in some of his landscapes showed an awareness of Adolphe Monticelli. He was an accomplished watercolorist, but his style became increasingly insular, accepting neither Post-Impressionism, nor any of the 20th-century art movements. He relapsed into an agreeable but fundamentally unadventurous picture-making that lasted from about 1910 until the mid 1930s, when blindness forced him to stop painting.

Stefano da Zevio c1375–1451

Stefano da Zevio was a painter from Zevio, near Verona; he was also known as

Stefano di Giovanni da Verona. He was a pupil of Altichiero (*fl.* 1369–90), and an exponent of the International Gothic style. His works have been described as "illuminated manuscripts on a larger scale". The *Madonna in the Rose Bower* (Museo di Castelvecchio, Verona) is typical of his works. They show the artist's fascination with the pretty details of nature, but lack any interest in pictorial depth of mass. This courtly style derives from Gentile da Fabriano. Vasari (who mentions Donatello's wonderment at the beauty of Stefano's work) says he was a pupil of Agnolo Gaddi, in Florence.

Stefano della Bella 1610–64

The Florentine etcher Stefano della Bella was early influenced by the art of Jacques Callot (1592–1635). As court artist to the Medici Dukes he etched scenes of lively popular holidays and of the lavish spectacles of Florentine court life. After a stay in Rome, he spent 11 years in Paris (1639-50), where his style absorbed something of the freer atmospheric effects of Rembrandt and the Dutch landscapists. He then returned to Florence. His etchings are technically superb—he produced over 1,000—in a subtle mixture of etching, drypoint, and engraving.

Left: Jan Steen: Game of Skittles; oil on panel; 33×27cm (13×11in); c1660–3. National Gallery, London

Steinbach Erwin von *fl. 1277–1318*

Erwin von Steinbach was a German master mason, eulogized by Goethe (in his essay "Von Deutscher Baukunst", "On German Architecture", published in *Von Deutscher Art und Kunst*, "On German Nature and Art", 1773). His name appears in documents and inscriptions at Strasbourg Cathedral where he designed the west facade, begun in 1277. He is probably the author of the surviving drawing, now known as "B", which was copied in the construction of Strasbourg Cathedral up to the level of the second gallery, where the design changes. The facade has been analyzed to prove the strict geometric basis for its plan, but it is chiefly remarkable for the skeletal effect˙ of the freestanding tracery that covers Erwin's work. The style suggests that he was influenced by French Gothic architecture, such as the facade of Reims Cathedral, and the church of St Urbain at Troyes.

Stella Frank 1936–

The American painter Frank Stella was born at Malden, Massachusetts. He studied painting at Phillips Academy, Andover, with Patrick Morgan, and also at Princeton with William Seitz and Stephen Greene. Since 1958 he has lived in New York. Although his earlier work has obvious links with Abstract Expressionism, he shared his contemporaries' distrust of that movement's potential self-indulgence.

The canvases Stella painted in the late 1950s, worked out in terms of stripes and patterns, are already characterized by the bold clarity of color and design that distinguishes his later and better known pictures. Since the early 1960s, the geometrical basis of his paintings has become even clearer; he uses many different shapes, sometimes cut out. The individual stripes of color are defined by hard edges. His color is often fluorescent in effect, creating a suggestion of hard, shiny machine-made surfaces.

Stella Joseph 1877–1946

The American painter Joseph Stella was born in Italy. In 1897, a year after arriving in New York, he enrolled at the Art Students League. He began his artistic career as an illustrator, but after two visits to Europe (1909–10, 1911–12), where he met Henri Matisse and the Futurist painter Carlo Carrá, he concentrated on painting.

Frank Stella: Sinjerli Variation I; fluorescent acrylic on canvas; diameter 305cm (120in); 1968. Private collection

Works by him were included in the Armory Show in 1913. His paintings from this period were in the Futurist idiom (for example, *Battle of the Lights, Coney Island*, 1913–14; Yale University Art Gallery, New Haven, Conn.). Later he developed his personal, more structured, illusionistic style, which was half abstract and half precisionist (for example, *Brooklyn Bridge*, 1917–18; Yale University Art Gallery, New Haven). In the early 1920s he made a group of very original Abstract collages. He continued to paint until his death in 1946.

Further reading. Jaffe, I.B. *Joseph Stella's Symbolism*, New York (1994).

Still Clyfford 1904–81

Clyfford Still, born in Grandin, North Dakota, was one of the earliest and most consistent of the American Abstract Ex-

pressionist painters. Unlike most of the group, he was not a New Yorker; he lived in the city only from 1950 to 1961. He made a single radical break with tradition in 1941 while doing war work in Oakland, California, far removed from the intellectual ferment of wartime New York. His paintings of this period demonstrate the formula of all his mature work. They reject the shallow, structured space of Cubism, and the literary overtones of Surrealism, in favor of a flat two-dimensional surface of almost-romantic, jagged shapes and colors (for example, *1957–D No. 1*, 1957; Albright-Knox Art Gallery, Buffalo).

Furthur reading. *Clyfford Still: Thirty-three Paintings in the Albright-Knox Art Gallery*, Buffalo, N.Y. (1966). Hess, T.B. "The Outsider". *Art News*, New York (December 1969). McCaughey, P. "Clyfford Still and the Gothic Imagination", *Artforum*, New York (April 1970).

Clyfford Still: 1953; oil on canvas; 236×174cm (93×69in); 1953. Tate Gallery, London

Stimmer Tobias 1539–84

The Swiss decorative artist Tobias Stimmer was born at Schaffhausen; his surviving work there includes the painted facade of the Haus zum Ritter (1568–70), now in the Museum zu Allerheiligen, Schaffhausen. Its illusionistic architecture, with mythological figures and cartouches, was much influenced by similar facade painting done by the Holbein workshop at Augsburg and Basel.

Stimmer spent later years in various German towns. He designed woodcut illustrations to biblical and Classical texts printed at Strasbourg, and decorated the astronomical clock at Münster (1571–4). He also did the ceiling paintings for the banqueting hall of the Castle of Baden-Baden (1578–9), which prefigure the German Baroque style. He was also noted for his large portraits, intimate in mood (for example *Jakob Schwytzer*, 1564; Öffentliche Kunstsammlung, Kunstmuseum Basel).

Stomer Matthias 1600–post 50

Matthias Stomer was a Dutch painter whose Caravaggesque manner is related to that of the artists of the Utrecht School. He is, deservedly, much less well known than his teacher Gerrit van Honthorst, whose style he imitated. After working in Utrecht in the 1620s, Stomer traveled in Italy: he is first recorded there in Rome, and subsequently in Naples. The remainder of his working life appears to have been spent in southern Italy and Sicily.

Stoss Veit *fl.* 1477–1533

A painter and printmaker as well as one of the greatest German sculptors of the late Gothic era, Veit Stoss was born at Horb in Swabia. Estimates of his birth date vary (from *c*1438 to *c*1447), but the first documented information is that in 1477 he resigned his citizenship of Nuremberg and moved with his family to Krakow. It can be deduced on stylistic grounds that his roots lie in the Upper Rhine area; he seems to have been influenced in particular by Nikolaus Gerhaert van Leyden. It is not known how long he had spent working in Nuremberg, but he must have been an experienced master by 1477 when he received the commission for the huge *Death of the Virgin* Altarpiece in the church of the Virgin at Krakow (completed 1489).

During nearly 20 years of activity in Krakow he also executed the red marble tomb of King Casimir IV Jagiello in Krakow Cathedral (1492), and other tombs at Włocławek and Gnesen. He returned to Nuremberg in 1496 a rich man, but lost his fortune through bad investments. He was convicted for forgery in 1503, and lost his rights as a citizen.

He carved the Volckamer memorial in the church of St Sebald, Nuremberg; it has three reliefs, and is signed and dated 1499. The *Christ Crucified* in St Lawrence, Nuremberg, dates from the same period (*c*1500). During 1503–4 he painted and gilded the figures in Tilman Riemenschneider's high altar for the parish church of Münnerstadt and added painted wings (now dismembered). In about 1508 the carved frame for Dürer's *Holy Family and Saints* was produced in his workshop.

His pair of figures of *Tobias and the Angel* were given to the Dominican church in Nuremberg in 1516 (Germanisches Nationalmuseum, Nuremburg) and the great *Annunciation* group for St Lawrence, Nuremberg, was carved in 1517–18. Among his important late works, the *Crucifix* in St Sebald, Nuremberg, was executed in 1520. The Reformation prevented the delivery of the *Altar of the Virgin* that had been intended for the Carmelite church in Bamberg (1520–3; unfinished and now in Bamberg Cathedral). Stoss died in 1533, having lost his sight.

The over-life-size figures in Krakow depicting the *Death of the Virgin* are polychromed and gilded. Their expressive qualities mark a high point in German late Gothic sculpture, and in the tomb of King

Casimir IV the veined, dark red marble is effectively used to evoke emotion. The Volckamer reliefs in St Sebald, Nuremberg, strike a more restrained note; the effect is entirely sculptural, since they were not polychromed. But in the brooding figure of St Andrew (c1505?) in the choir of the same church, the highly expressive, contorted folds reveal the intense spiritual energy of Veit Stoss' later sculptures.

Street George 1824–81

The English architect George Edmund Street was born at Woodford, Essex. He designed his first churches during the years 1845 to 1849 while he was working as an assistant to Gilbert Scott. He joined the Ecclesiological Society (as did Butterfield), was deeply religious, and was greatly interested in Gothic architecture. He had a preference for boldly massed forms, and the exploitation of the color or texture of building materials. The Village School at Inkpen, Berkshire (1850), is a characteristic early work; and St James the Less, Westminster (1860) with its simple brick tower is among the most famous of his many churches. Street's major secular work, the Law Courts, London, was still being built when he died.

Strozzi Bernardo 1581–1644

The Italian artist Bernardo Strozzi, born in Genoa, was the best and most influential painter working there in the early 17th century. From 1595 to 1597 he studied under the Sienese artist, Pietro Sorri. About 1597 he entered the Capuchin order. Although he remained a priest, from c1610 he was allowed to work as an artist, in order to support his destitute mother.

His early work shows the influence of Tuscan Mannerism, both in composition and in the delicate high-keyed colors. Around 1615 he developed a more expressive and naturalistic style. He responded to the works of Rubens that could be seen in Genoa, to the genre scenes produced by the Flemish artists working there (for example, *Old Woman at the Mirror*; private collection), and to paintings by visiting Caravaggesque artists. Strozzi's robust religious style has strong genre elements, and a new range of browns and reds and ruddy flesh tones; an example is the powerful *St Augustine washing Christ's Feet* (Museo dell' Accademia Ligustica di Belle Arti, Genoa). Between c1615 and 1620 he produced a

Bernardo Strozzi: Old Woman at the Mirror (An Allegory of Vanity); oil on canvas; 132×108cm (52×43in). Private collection

group of genre paintings. The most famous of these are *The Cook* (c1612; Palazzo Rosso, Genoa) with its elaborate still life, and *The Pipers* (Palazzo Rosso, Genoa), in which the figures surge forward with Rubensian vitality. He also painted frescoes and portraits.

In 1631 he settled in Venice, and shortly afterwards painted *Doge Francesco Erizzo* (Kunsthistorisches Museum, Vienna). He became one of the city's leading portrait painters. His admiration for the work of Veronese (1528–88) was unlimited. Among his important mythological and religious works are his *Rape of Europa* (National Museum, Poznan), and his *Martyrdom of St Sebastian* (c1635/6; S. Benedetto, Venice). They demonstrate how skillfully he continued the decorative and painterly qualities of the great 16th-century Venetian tradition.

Further reading. Milkovich, M. *Bernardo Strozzi: Paintings and Drawings*, Binghamton, N.Y. (1967). Mortani, L. *Bernardo Strozzi*, Rome (1966). Tietze, H. (ed.) *Three Baroque Masters: Strozzi, Crespi, Piazzetta*, Baltimore (1944).

Stuart Gilbert 1755–1828

The American painter Gilbert Charles Stuart was born in the colony of Rhode Island, of Scottish parentage. He came to London in 1775, and from 1777 to 1782 was a pupil of Benjamin West, one of the leading history painters of the day. Stuart stayed in London until 1787; he then lived for a period in Dublin before returning to America in 1793. He set up a studio in New York, and later worked in Philadelphia. There he painted several portraits of *George Washington*, which were much duplicated in his studio, and which are probably his best-known works. From *c*1805 until his death he lived in Boston.

Stuart's main practice was as a portrait painter. He combined a fluent sense of composition—influenced by what he had seen in London of the work of Thomas Gainsborough, Joshua Reynolds, and George Romney—with a straightforward approach to character. *Mrs Richard Yates* (1793–4; National Gallery of Art, Washington, D.C.), which shows a middle-aged lady seated at her needle-work, is among the finest of his portraits. The key images of George Washington are the so-called "Vaughan" portrait (1795; National Gallery of Art, Washington, D.C.), the "Athenaeum" Portrait (1796; Museum of Fine Arts, Boston), and the "Lansdowne"

Portrait (1796; Pennsylvania Academy of the Fine arts, Philadelphia).

Stubbs George 1724–1806

George Stubbs was an English animal and portrait painter. He was acknowledged during his lifetime as a master of the sporting picture, but the full scope of his talents has only recently been recognized. Born in Liverpool, he had little formal training in art. From the early 1740s until his departure for Italy in 1754, he studied anatomy in northern England while supporting himself by portraiture. He stayed only briefly in Rome, finding its artistic heritage of little interest. From 1756 to 1758 he lived in relative seclusion in Lincolnshire, where he dissected horses and made detailed anatomical studies. His *Anatomy of the Horse*, published in 1766 with his own text and illustrations, is one of the great achievements of 18th-century natural history.

By 1760 Stubbs had settled in London. His horse portraits and hunting and racing

pictures were immediately popular, and the next decade was the most productive of his artistic career. To this period belong such masterpieces as *The Grosvenor Hunt* (1762; Trustees of the Grosvenor Estate, London), *Gimcrack on Newmarket Heath* (1765; private collection), and the remarkable series of paintings of mares and foals. His earliest painting of a wild animal, the clinically observed *Zebra* (*c*1760–2; Paul Mellon Center for British Art, Yale University, New Haven), was followed shortly afterwards by the first of his animal paintings that depict the mortal combat of horses and lions. This last series anticipated specific themes that would be more fully exploited by the next generation of Romantic artists, both in England and in France.

Between 1770 and 1790 Stubbs complemented the successes of the previous decade with many of his most original conversation pieces and genre subjects. He also turned his inquisitive mind to experiments with printmaking techniques, and enamel painting on large ceramic plaques that were specially manufactured by Josiah Wedgwood. His second major investigation, *A Comparative Anatomical Exposition of the Structure of the Human Body with that of a Tiger and a Common Fowl*, was begun towards the end of his life. Although the book was never published, 142 delicate chalk and pencil studies for the illustrations have survived (Paul Mellon Center for British Art, Yale University, New Haven).

Further reading. Egerton, J. and Taylor, B. *George Stubbs: Anatomist and Animal Painter*, London (1976). Gaunt, W. *Stubbs*, Oxford (1977). Sparrow, W.S. *George Stubbs and Ben Marshall*, London and New York (1929). Tattersall, B. *Stubbs and Wedgewood: Unique Alliance between Artist and Potter*, London (1974). Taylor, B. *Stubbs*, London (1975).

Sugai Kumi 1919–

The Japanese painter Kumi Sugai was born in Kobe, and studied at the Osaka School of Art (1927–32). Little is known of his early work. He moved to Paris in 1952, where his reputation as one of the School of Paris tachist painters soon developed. His Abstract paintings of the 1950s were based on Oriental forms, painted in strong but luminous colors. Later he began to use quite different, linear forms with brighter

Gilbert Stuart: George Washington (the "Atheneum" portrait); oil on canvas; 122×94cm (48×37in); 1796. Museum of Fine Arts, Boston

George Stubbs: Whistlejacket; oil on canvas; 325×259cm (128×102in); 1761–2. Private collection

column-figures were invented in Italy or in France.

During the years 1140 to 1144 Suger built the choir of the abbey. This was the first Gothic structure in Europe, and one that was to have an enormous influence on the subsequent history of architecture. He was not the designer of this revolutionary building, but he had the foresight to allow the architectural experiment to be carried out.

Suger left an account of his work, devoting most space to a description of the metal objects he commissioned. These included altar frontals, a large cross, vessels of various kinds, candlesticks, and reliquaries—all made from precious materials and studded with jewels. Some of these still survive, and demonstrate that Suger was quite justified in using Ovid's phrase, "Materiam superabat opus" ("the workmanship surpassed the material"), when praising them. Suger also describes in some detail the stained glass windows he commissioned to be made "by the exquisite hands of many masters from different regions". Several of these also survive. It has been claimed that Suger invented some new iconographic representations, for instance the "Tree of Jesse", but these claims have since been disproved.

Further reading. Panofsky, E. *Abbot Suger on the Abbey Church of St Denis and its Art Treasures*, Princeton (1946).

Sullivan Louis 1856–1924

Louis Henry Sullivan was the most inventive member of the Chicago School of Architecture, and the first major American architect concerned with the aesthetics of the skyscraper. More than 100 of his most important city buildings were produced between 1879 and 1895, while he was in partnership with Dankmar Adler. These include the Auditorium Building, Chicago (1866–89), the Wainwright Building in St Louis (1890–1), and the Guaranty Building, Buffalo, New York (1894–5). Sullivan wanted to combine new techniques of construction and installation with a relevant and original decorative scheme. His writings, *Kindergarten Chats* (1901) and *Autobiography of an Idea* (1922), although subjective and frequently obscure, proclaim the stylistic and functional integrity in the commercial skyscraper. Among his pupils was the prominent architect Frank Lloyd Wright.

colors expressing energy and tension but carefully controlled. In 1968 he was included in the Japanese pavilion at the Venice Biennale and began to live in Tokyo again. During the 1970s he abandoned his earlier expressive, Abstact style, in favor of a slick, mechanical finish. This later work apparently expresses the conflicts between traditional and modern Japan. Sugai is also a notable printmaker.

Suger of St-Denis 1081–1151

Abbot Suger of St-Denis figures prominently in the history of medieval art, as a patron who commissioned the first Gothic building, sponsored a new type of portal design, and stimulated the development of stained glass windows and metalwork. In 1122 he was made Abbot of the royal abbey of St-Denis (now a suburb of Paris). He was a friend and advisor to two kings, Louis VI and Louis VII, also acting as Regent during the Second Crusade in 1146. Between 1137 and 1140 he added to the old Carolingian Abbey a two-towered west front which incorporated three portals with column-figures; it was the first time that such a feature had been used on a large scale in France. During the same period, the Italian sculptor Niccolò experimented with a similar portal design. Many features of Suger's portals are Italian, but it is not known whether the

Graham Sutherland: Devastation 1941: an East End Street; watercolor, gouache, pen and ink; 65×114cm (26×45in); 1941. Tate Gallery, London

Sultan Muhammad *fl. c1520–c40*

Sultan Muhammad of Tabriz, instructed the young Shah Tahmasp before his accession in 1524, and became head of his library. He must have both planned and contributed to the major royal manuscripts, including the "Houghton" *Shah-nama* of *c*1520–30 (Metropolitan Museum, New York, and private collections) and the British Library *Khamsa* of Nizami of 1539–43. There are two works signed by him in each manuscript. According to contemporaries, his masterpiece in the *Shah-nama* was *The Court of Gayumars* and this work can be identified in the "Houghton" manuscript. His training was at the Court of the Aqqoyunlu, but he was an artist with progressive ideas, as evidenced by his signed *Court Feast*; this work is in a *Hafiz* that was made for Sam Mirza, brother of the Shah, in about 1527. Sultan Muhammad's son Mirza Ali also joined the royal painting staff.

Sutherland Graham 1903–80

Graham Sutherland was an English landscape painter and portraitist. After abandoning an engineering apprenticeship, he went to Goldsmiths' College, London (1921–6), where he studied engraving. While there he became friends with the engraver F.L. Griggs, who shared Sutherland's enthusiasm for the work of Samuel Palmer (1805–81). This interest is reflected in the rich, dark etchings of pastoral subjects that Sutherland produced between 1925 and 1931. Palmer's romantic view of nature helped to stimulate Sutherland's imagination, but it also had a restricting effect. When the print market collapsed, he turned to landscape painting.

He taught himself to paint landscapes by copying objectively from nature, but in his drawings and watercolors he allowed his imagination freer rein. This approach (inspired by Paul Nash's poetic landscapes and *objets trouvés*) became dominant after his first visit to Pembrokeshire in 1934. He was captivated by the extraordinary richness of organic forms, and by the unexpected dramas of the landscape, and his paintings show this. They are romantic in mood, and Palmer's twilight colors linger on, but they are also often highly abstracted; his tree and rock forms have an anthropomorphic, malignant quality that presages his postwar creations.

During the Second World War Sutherland sketched armament factories and bombed cities as an Official War Artist: the experience heightened his Dantesque vision of the world, and renewed his interest in mechanical forms. In 1944 he was commissioned to paint a Crucifixion for St Matthew's Church, Northampton. This, his first major figure-painting, led to a renewed interest in anthropomorphic imagery. He saw Christ's crown of thorns as a "paraphrase" of the tortured human body. The related paintings of thorn trees and heads are more general metaphors of the underlying unity between Man and the natural world; and the hybrid, metamorphic forms that he developed in the 1950s (for example, *Head III*, 1953; Tate Gallery, London), express the predatory nature of all living things.

Although these works represent Sutherland's greatest contribution to postwar art, he is known popularly for his portraits, and for his tapestry of *Christ in Glory*, designed for Coventry Cathedral (1952–61). In both, he has shown that it is possible to give meaning to a debased genre, provided the artist is totally honest and committed.

Further reading. Cooper, D. *The Works of Graham Sutherland*, London (1961). Hayes, J. *The Art of Graham Sutherland*, Oxford (1980). Sackville-West, E. *Graham Sutherland*, Baltimore and London (1955). Sanesi, R. *Graham Sutherland*, Milan (1979). Tassi, R. *Graham Sutherland: Complete Graphic Work*, London (1978). Tassi, R. *Graham Sutherland: Parafese della Natura e Arte e Altre Corrispondenze*, Parma (1979).

T

Tacca Pietro 1577–1640

Pietro Tacca was a Florentine sculptor who worked during the period of the transition from Mannerism to the Baroque. The most distinguished of Giovanni da Bologna's pupils, he played an important role in the execution of the various equestrian monuments undertaken by his master in his late career. Tacca was particularly adept at working in bronze on a scale larger than life, and as official sculptor to the Medici Grand Dukes, he was responsible for two of the gigantic tomb statues of Ferdinand I and Cosimo II in the Cappella dei Principi, S. Lorenzo, Florence (1627–34). Among his independent equestrian statues, that of *Philip IV* of Spain in the Plaza de Oriente, Madrid (1634–40), is remarkable for its successful introduction of the motif of the prancing horse.

Taiga Ike no 1723–76

Ike no Taiga was a Japanese painter and calligrapher; he was one of the greatest masters of the *Bunjinga*, or scholar-painter's art. Born in Kyoto, he was educated at the Manpukuji Temple, where he learned Chinese-style calligraphy and acquired an interest in Chinese painting. As a young man he earned his living by painting fans, often with designs taken from Chinese painted manuals. He became famous for finger-painting—no mere party trick, as his great series of screens of *Five Hundred Rakan* (Manpukuji Temple, Kyoto) show. Finger-painting taught him his characteristic economy of means.

He traveled widely in Japan and transferred the Chinese idealistic landscape style to real views, as in his set of 12 ink landscapes (Kawabata Collection, Kamakura). He became so famous that his widow Gyokuran (1728–84), herself an original painter, set up the Taigado Museum in Kyoto in his memory. This may have been the world's first one-man art museum.

Taiga's styles were many, original, and unconventional. His techniques ranged from the simple monochrome album *Eight Views of the Hsiao-Hsiang* (Kumita Collection, Tokyo), each plate consisting of a few lines, to the refined and detailed album *Ten Conveniences and Ten Pleasures*, done with Yosa Buson, in which he shows his skill as a colorist. He could create dashing

Pietro Tacca: Slave; bronze; c1615–23. Piazza dalla Darsena, Leghorn

ink sketches, like the handscroll *Scenes of Mutsu Province* (Shimosaka Collection, Tokyo), or highly polished works such as his screens *Landscapes with Pavilions* (Tokyo National Museum), done in ink and splashes of bright color on gold. He also studied Western perspective, and adapted it to Chinese styles, thus extending the expressive range of his painting.

Taikan Yokoyama 1868–1958

The Japanese painter Yokoyama Taikan was the leading formulator of the Nihonga style. He entered the Tokyo School of Fine Arts in 1889, and in 1896 joined the theorist Okakura Tenshin, who inspired him to seek a new style of traditional painting. This was achieved by combining Western space, perspective, human naturalism, and some shading, with the bright colors, clear outline, and sense of design of *Yamatoe*.

The style is fully mature in his figure screens *Master Five Willows* (1912; Tokyo National Museum) and most splendid in *Cherry Trees at Night* (1929; Okura Shukokan Museum, Tokyo). Taikan also practiced virtuoso ink-painting without outline, notably in the landscape hand-scroll *The Wheel of Life* (1923; National Museum of Modern Art, Tokyo).

Talenti family 14th century

Francesco Talenti (*c*1300–69?) and his son Simone (*c*1340/5–81?) were Florentine architects. Francesco is first recorded in 1325 working in a minor capacity under Lorenzo Maitani at Orvieto Cathedral. In 1343 he succeeded Andrea Pisano as *capomaestro* of Florence Cathedral.

During the 1340s and 1350s he completed the Campanile, which had been started by Giotto in 1334 and continued by Andrea Pisano up to the second main cornice. Francesco adopted a more obviously Gothic style, with tracery windows and gables adorned with crockets. The whole is richly decorated with colored marble. The spire was never built.

While work on the Campanile proceeded, he drew up a scheme for the cathedral, which was accepted in 1357. This scheme was an enlargement of Arnolfo di Cambio's original plan. In the same year Francesco won the competition for the detailed design of the nave piers. In 1364 he was discharged from his post as *capomaestro*, though he was recalled in a much reduced capacity in 1366. The years 1366 and 1367 saw a revision of the plans amid many commissions and much public debate; Francesco took only a very minor part in all of this. Nevertheless the present interior—a very parochial Gothic style compared with contemporary building north of the Alps—is essentially the work of Francesco.

Simone Talenti was also involved in work for the cathedral. He helped his father to carve the prototype pier capital, and submitted (unsuccessfully) a design in the competitions of 1366–7. He was *capomaestro* briefly in 1376, and held a similar post at the church of Orsanmichele in Florence from 1379. From 1376, together with Taddeo Ristori and Benci di Cione, Simone oversaw the building of the Loggia della Signoria, employing a pier style similar to that of the Cathedral.

Tamayo Rufino 1899–

The Mexican painter Rufino Tamayo was born in Oaxaca in 1899, and studied at the Academia de Arte de San Carlos in Mexico City (1917–21). The most important influence on his art was his contact with Pre-Columbian and native artistic traditions, as a teacher of ethnographic drawing at the National Museum of Anthropology, Mexico City (1921–3). He experienced mainstream European art in New York and Paris, and his paintings are a synthesis of traditional Mexican styles with Cubist-derived figuration. In his Expressionist pictures of the 1940s and 1950s, such as *Animals* (1941; Museum of Modern Art, New York) he was influenced by Picasso. Since the late 1950s his single and paired figures have tended to depict archetypal and timeless themes; his colors and surface textures play an integral part in the expressive qualities of his work. He painted murals for the Palace of Fine Arts in Mexico City and the UNESCO headquarters in Paris, among others.

Tanguy Yves 1900–55

Yves Tanguy, a French Surrealist painter, was born in Paris. After several years in the Merchant Navy and in the Army he settled in Paris, and became a friend of the poet Jacques Prévert. In 1923, inspired by a painting by Giorgio de Chirico, he decided to become a painter. He joined the Surrealists in 1925. He was completely self-

Yves Tanguy: The Invisible Ones; oil on canvas; 99×81cm (39×32in); 1951. Tate Gallery, London

taught, and his earliest work is naive in execution and vision.

In 1927, he developed a precise and illusionistic style which altered little in later years (for example, *Mama, Papa is Wounded!*, 1927; Musum of Modern Art, New York). His mature work evokes a tangible but imaginary landscape, reminiscent of beach, desert, or sea-bed (for example, *Four Hours of Summer, Hope*, 1929; private collection). The deeply receding space is inhabited by three-dimensional biomorphic forms—owing much to Arp, Miró, and Picasso—which threateningly overcrowd the space of his late work. Restrained in color, his work combines a modern, abstract form-language with a labored, academic style.

Further reading. Tanguy, K. *Yves Tanguy: a Summary of His Works*, New York 1963).

Tan'yu Kano 1602–47

The Japanese painter Kano Tan'yu was the last great master of the *Kano* School. He was born in Kyoto, the son of Kano Takanobu (*ob.* 1618) and grandson of Kano Eitoku. With his brothers Naonobu (1607–50) and Yasunobu (1613–85) he was educated by Kano Koi (*ob.* 1636), who made them masters of the ink monochrome medium.

Tan'yu soon attracted official attention. At the age of 20 he was appointed painter to the Edo government, receiving a house at Kajibashi, and moving to the new capital. Thereafter, though much of his work continued to be in western Japan, his school was known as "Kajibashi Kano". His many official commissions included the decoration of the Nijo and Imperial palaces (Kyoto), and of Nagoya and Edo castles.

Like most great Japanese artists, Tan'yu painted well in many different styles. He is less successful as a decorative artist than as an ink-painter; his huge, many-paneled compositions of hawks on pine-trees in the Nijo palace are dull, compared with Sanraku's room there. Yet his folding screens of the *Four Seasons* from the Myoshinji Temple (Kyoto) have a charm equal to anything of the period, and his handscroll on the founding of the Toshogu Shrine is a masterpiece of delicate color in a *Tosa* idiom.

His strength lies in his ink-painting for temples, especially in his great landscapes

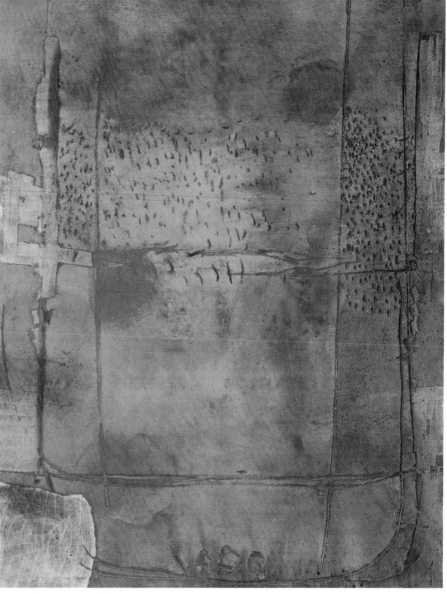

Antoni Tàpies: Gray Ocher LXX; oil on canvas; 262×196cm (103×77in); 1958. Tate Gallery, London

suggested in a few strokes and washes. Tan'yu's reputation reached such heights that later *Kano* artists spent much time copying his more academic works, to the great detriment of Japanese painting.

Tàpies Antoni 1923–

The Spanish painter and sculptor Antoni Tàpies was born in Barcelona. He read law at Barcelona University from 1943 to 1946, but as an artist he was largely self-taught. From 1945 to 1947 he made collages and impasted paintings. In 1948 he was a cofounder of *Dau al Set*, a late Surrealist group. During 1950 he lived in Paris on a French Government scholarship. After geometrical paintings and studies in pure color, he returned in 1953 to earlier techniques using plaster, collage, and

graffiti; he explored the formal qualities of banal materials, and incorporated real objects into his work. His later paintings are on or appear actually to be walls, doors, and windows. He made his first sculptures in 1970. Tàpies' work ranges from strongly gestural pure painting, through the random juxtaposition of common objects and materials, to contrived symmetrical images. He has also made murals, stained glass, and graphics.

Further reading. Permanyer, L. *Tàpies and the New Culture*, New York (1986).

Tassi Agostino c1580–1644

Agostino Buonamici Tassi was a painter of large-scale mural decorations in Baroque Rome. After an early career in Florence, where he was trained in the tradition of stage design, he returned to his native Rome, and then became a specialist in secular decoration involving perspective illusionism. Most of his major *quadratura* schemes in Roman palaces were executed in collaboration with important figure-painters such as Giovanni Lanfranco, Carlo Saraceni, Orazio Gentileschi, and Guercino. Tassi occasionally included within his decorative schemes landscapes and seascapes in the manner of Paul Bril (1554–1626), which were in turn to influence Tassi's pupil, Claude Lorrain.

Tatlin Vladimir 1885–1953

Vladimir Tatlin was a Russian artist who entered the Moscow School of Painting, Sculpture, and Architecture in 1910. Probably through Natalia Goncharova, his work was influenced by icon painting, especially in its use of color and flat curvilinear rhythm. But his greatest formative experience was his short visit to Paris in 1913, where he saw Picasso's Cubist constructions.

In late 1913 Tatlin began his "painting reliefs". These used what he termed "real materials [tin, wood, glass, plaster] in real space"; even at this early stage, they were more radical than the Cubist examples. The flat background of the relief imposed limits on real space. In 1915 he constructed the "corner relief", suspended on a wire attached to the walls in the corner. Now planes could move freely in all directions, released from the constraints of frame and background. He made studies of individual materials, and later used this "culture of material" in his teaching.

After the Bolshevik Revolution in Russia, Tatlin was appointed head of the Moscow section of the Department of Fine Arts (1918), which commissioned his project for a monument to the Third International. A large wooden model was exhibited in 1920, but the monument itself was not erected. Hugely ambitious, it was to have been twice the height of the Empire State Building. Its intention was both symbolic and functional: to house the many activities of the Revolutionary Government. His design consisted of three basic shapes constructed in glass—hemisphere, pyramid, and two cylinders—all revolving at different speeds. They were to be suspended on an asymmetrical axis within an iron spiral framework.

During the 1920s he designed practical objects such as workers' clothes. Another project was a self-propelled glider, based on a close study of insects and birds. He was for a time influential in the Constructivist movement in Russia and the West.

Further reading. Zhadova, L. (ed.) *Tatlin*, London (1988).

Tchelitchew Pavel 1898–1957

The Russian painter and stage designer Pavel Tchelitchew was born in Kaluga, Moscow. As a youth, he was influenced by the Romantic book illustrations of Gustave Doré and Mikhail Vrubel. He attended the Academy at Kiev and received encouragement from Léger's pupil, Aleksandra Exter. Tchelitchew lived in Berlin (1921–5) before settling in Paris, where he reacted against Abstract art and became a member of the group later known as the Neo-Romantics. He was much influenced by the early work of Picasso, painting clowns and acrobats, and often employing blue as the main color. He settled in America in 1934, but died in Rome.

Tchelitchew designed the scenery and costumes for Diaghilev's *Ode* (1928), and continued as a stage designer throughout the 1930s and 1940s. Much of his best work is Surrealist in mood and character

Vladimir Tatlin: Counter Relief 1915; wood and metal; 69×83×79cm (27×33×31in); a reconstruction. Private collection

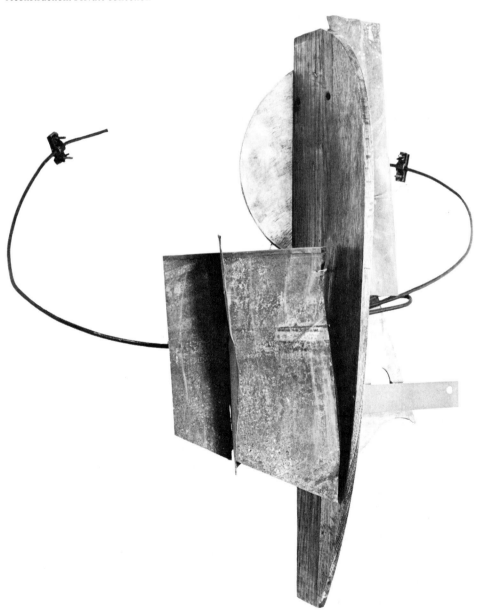

(for example, *Leaf Children*, 1939, and *Hide and Seek*, 1940–2; both Museum of Modern Art, New York). It was weakened by a certain theatrical artifice, an elegance tinged with *kitsch*, which he was never entirely able to banish from his art. He is often more interesting as a portrait painter, especially in the portraits of his friend, the poet Edith Sitwell (1937 version in the Tate Gallery, London).

Teniers David, the Younger
1610–90

The Flemish genre painter David Teniers the Younger was the most famous member of a family of artists. Born in Antwerp, he was probably trained by his father, David Teniers the Elder (1582–1649). He painted a wide range of subjects (including civic guard processions, landscapes, religious themes, and representations of the Witches' Sabbath) but is chiefly known for pictures of peasant life and some paintings of guardroom scenes. His work from the 1630s shows the influence of Adriaen Brouwer's low-life scenes, although it lacks Brouwer's vitality and coarseness. He later expanded his themes to include multi-figured depictions of rustic revelry, full of lively and amusing incident.

From 1651, Teniers was employed in Brussels as court painter by the Regent of the Netherlands, Archduke Leopold Wilhelm. His duties involved compiling a catalog of the Archduke's picture collection (published with engraved plates in 1660), and painting views of the galleries in which this collection was hung. Teniers made several small copies of paintings in the collection, notably of those by Venetian artists, but this practice had no visible effect on his other work. During these years in Brussels he also acted as an art dealer. The quality of Teniers' work declined in his later years, during which he relied much more than before on assistants.

Pavel Tchelitchew: The Composer Igor Markevitch and his Mother; oil on canvas; 91×74cm (36×29in); 1930. Tate Gallery, London (on loan from the Edward James Foundation)

Tenniel John 1820–1914

The English artist and draftsman Sir John Tenniel studied in London at the Royal Academy Schools and at Chipstone Street Life Academy. He joined *Punch* in 1850 as the magazine's second cartoonist. He became first cartoonist in 1864, and held the post until 1901. His political works won great respect for their fairness as well as their draftsmanship. He excelled in drawing beasts and allegorical figures, and his history paintings and serious illustrative work are also noteworthy. But it is usually for his illustrations to Lewis Carroll's *Alice's Adventures in Wonderland* (1866) and *Through the Looking-Glass and What Alice Found There* (1871) that he is remembered today. Tenniel was knighted in 1893.

Terborch Gerard 1617–81

Gerard Terborch (or ter Borch) was a Dutch genre and portrait painter. His early genre paintings show guardroom scenes, but he later abandoned these in favor of small pictures of genteel, expensively dressed Dutch families enjoying their leisure (for example, *The Concert*, c1675; Staatliche Museen, Berlin). These pictures are characterized by a minutely detailed technique, a limited color range of grays, blacks, and blues, and careful rendering of the textures of such materials as silk, satin, and velvet. The subtlety of Terborch's psychological relationships and the refined textures of his draperies are seen in *The Fatherly Admonition* (1654–5; Staatliche Museen, Berlin). The picture was long thought to represent a bourgeois family incident, but is in fact a depiction of a brothel scene.

David Teniers the Younger: A View of Het Sterckshof near Antwerp; oil on canvas; 82×118cm (32×46in); c1646. National Gallery, London

Terborch appears to have been fairly wealthy, and he traveled widely in Europe. In 1648 he was in Germany, where he painted one of the very few 17th-century Dutch representations of contemporary history: *The Swearing of the Oath of Ratification of the Treaty between the Dutch and the Spanish at Münster, 15 May, 1648* (National Gallery, London). This painting, which measures only 18 by 23 in (46 by 58 cm), contains over 50 full-length portraits. Few of the works Terborch saw on his travels influenced his style, although knowledge of Velázquez' paintings in Madrid is evident in a number of small full-length portraits.

Terbrugghen Hendrick
c1588–1629

The Dutch painter Hendrick Terbrugghen (or ter Brugghen) was the most important member of the Utrecht School. Born in Deventer, he is believed to have spent ten years in Italy as a young man, perhaps arriving in Rome as early as 1604. There he may have met Caravaggio, whose paintings had a decisive influence on him. His earliest surviving works, which date from after his return to Utrecht, sometimes echo Caravaggio's subjects, depicting such themes as *The Calling of St Matthew* (c1617; Nouveau Musée des Beaux-Arts, Le Havre). They frequently use Caravaggist chiaroscuro which, in Terbrugghen's paintings, creates rather hard, sculptural forms and throws sharply defined detail into relief.

Although Terbrugghen never completely abandoned Caravaggism, in his later work light falls more softly on figures and objects, conveying a more subtle sense of their forms and textures. Together with the rejection of harsh, raking light effects, there is a preoccupation with reflected light. This is particularly noticeable in such half-length single-figure genre paintings as the poetic *The Flute Player* (1621; Gemäldegalerie Alte Meister, Kassel). In these and in some later religious paintings the cool, clear colors, pale silvery tonality, and an air of silence and stillness look forward to Vermeer and the Delft School.

Terbrugghen was admired by Rubens, but he was much less well-known in his day than other Utrecht artists such as Gerrit van Honthorst, and was neglected until the present century.

Tessai Tomioka 1835–1924

The Japanese painter Tomioka Tessai was well-known in the West for the racy and individualistic style of the works he did in his old age. Born in Kyoto, he was deeply learned in Confucian and Taoist classics, Buddhist literature, and native Shinto studies, serving at times as a Shinto priest. He studied various painting styles, but finally developed a very strong neo-Chinese manner, specializing in the use of transparent color washes over a richly black and nervous line. His work exploits the traditional humor in the Chinese Immortals and Buddhist divinities. In the last 20 years of his life he produced many thousands of works, some of great power, but some merely eccentric.

Tessin family 17th and 18th centuries

The Swedish architect Nicodemus Tessin the Elder, lived from 1615 to 1681. He was born at Stralsund in Sweden, and trained as an architect under Simon de la Vallée. In 1651 and 1652 he toured Europe, and in 1661 was appointed City Architect of Stockholm, becoming one of the leading Baroque architects in Sweden.

His chief work is Drottningholm Palace (begun in 1662), built in an eclectic Baroque style which borrowed elements from Italy, France, and Holland. His other works include Kalmar Cathedral (1660) and Göteborg Town Hall (1670).

His son, Nicodemus Tessin the Younger (1654–1728), succeeded him as the leading Swedish architect, completing his father's work at Drottningholm. He traveled to England, France, and Italy between 1673 and 1680. His major building is the huge Royal Palace at Stockholm (begun 1697), which shows a knowledge of Bernini's unexecuted project for the Louvre. His son, Carl Gustavus Graf von Tessin (1695–1770), was an important patron of French 18th-century artists.

Further reading. Josephson, R. *L'Architecte de Charles XII, Nicodeme Tessin à la Cour de Louis XIV*, Brussels and Paris (1930). Kommer, B.R. *Nicodemus Tessin der Jungere und das Stockholmer Schloss*, Heidelberg (1974). Wiegert, R.-A. and Hern-Marck, C. *Les Relations Artistiques entre la France et la Suide 1693–1718: Nicodeme Tessin le Jeune et Daniel Cronstioni, Correspondance*, Stockholm (1964).

Testa Pietro 1611–50

Born in Lucca, the Italian artist Pietro Testa was in Rome by 1630; after a brief period in the studio of Domenichino he studied with Pietro da Cortona. His paintings and etchings, light and delicate in touch, were influenced by Titian's Bacchanals and by Poussin's lyrical reinterpretations of them.

Later in his career Testa's style became more classical and he concentrated almost exclusively on etching—a medium he considered most suitable for the expression of complex philosophical speculations. His compositions were crowded with emblematic and erudite symbolism. Testa's learning was in conflict with his melancholy temperament, and it is almost certain that he drowned himself in the Tiber.

Theodoric Master *fl.* 1348–86

Master Theodoric was an isolated figure in Bohemian painting of the 14th century. His surviving works are concentrated in the Chapel of the Holy Cross in the castle of Karštejn near Prague. He is recorded as court painter in Prague in 1359, with a house on the Hradčany, which he still owned in 1368. The dating of the decorations in the Chapel of the Holy Cross presents a number of problems.

The chapel was consecrated in 1357, and again in 1365. Master Theodoric was named as the artist responsible in 1367, when he was rewarded by the Emperor Charles IV. No other evidence is available to indicate whether the cycle of panels representing the *Crucifixion*, the *Man of Sorrows*, and 127 half-length saints, angels, and prophets, was executed between 1357 and 1365, or between 1365 and 1367.

Since the style of the panels by Master Theodoric marks such a sharp break with the earlier, Italian-inspired phase of Bohemian painting under Charles IV, the dating of 1365–7 is marginally the more probable. It is conceivable, however, that the differences in style between the inner and outer areas of the chapel are due to differences in date of execution, rather than to the employment of a studio assistant. Certain points of contact can be noted with the work of Master Bertram of Hamburg, but these are apparently generic rather than specific, and no direct links can be postulated.

The evolution of the style of the Master Theodoric can be satisfactorily explained in terms of Bohemian manuscript illuminations. Master Theodoric turned away from the earlier interest in relating figures to spatial constructions, by concentrating his entire attention on the physical bulk of the figures, and by allowing them to create their own space. His figures share a consistent canon of proportions, with massive heads set on short, thick necks, and fleshy faces and hands. Their draperies often extend over the integral frames, while the same diapered gold grounds extend over both.

These stylistic quirks reinforce the hypothesis that the Master Theodoric owed his origins, at least, to Bohemian miniature painting. However, outlines had little significance for him. Instead, the figures are built up of delicate transitions in tone, with occasional brilliant colors; the overall effect is one of extreme softness.

Master Theodoric appears to have been a technical innovator: his paint medium is close to oil paint, and in the *Holy Cross* cycle he exploited its relatively slow-drying characteristics. No other paintings can be attributed to him. Although he was a forerunner of the Soft style, his influence on Bohemian painting was very limited.

Theodorus of Samos 6th century BC

Theodorus of Samos was a Greek architect and artist, around whom legends grew up. He is an early example of the versatility that was probably common among Greek artists. With Rhoecus he planned the largest temple in the Greek world—the Temple of Hera on Samos. He was also consultant engineer for the Temple of Artemis at Ephesus.

As a sculptor, Theodorus had the reputation of being one of the first to cast major statuary in bronze. An anecdote tells how, by using Egyptian canons of proportion, he collaborated in the production of a statue with Telecles, who made one half in Samos while Theodorus made the other half in Ephesus. It was he who made the famous signet ring "encased in gold and made of an emerald", for Polycrates, tyrant of Samos. Polycrates threw the ring away, to demonstrate his renunciation of his most treasured possession and forestall the envy of the gods at his good fortune; the ring was returned in the belly of a fish.

Theophanes the Greek *c*1340–*c*1410

Theophanes the Greek was a Byzantine painter active in Russia. Probably born in Constantinople, he decorated about 40 churches there and in Russia, whither he emigrated in the 1370s. His only surviving frescoes are in the church of the Transfiguration in Novgorod (1378). They include the *Old Testament Trinity* (the three Persons of the Trinity, represented by the three angels entertained by Abraham).

His style was highly influential in Novgorod, where painters of his school decorated St Theodore Stratelates (*c*1380s), and the church of Volotovo (1380s). In Moscow, where he collaborated with Andrei Rublev, Theophanes painted two palaces, and three churches (in 1395, 1399, and 1405). A large icon of the *deesis* (1405) (the Virgin and John the Baptist flanking Christ as intercessors in the Cathedral of the Annunciation, Moscow) is attributed to him from this period.

Theophanes worked boldly, creating intense portraits with a silvery and terracotta palette and distinctive white linear highlights. The vigor of his style reflected his manner of painting as recorded by a contemporary: "No one ever saw him looking at models ... he seemed to be painting with his hands, while his feet moved without rest."

James Thornhill: a detail of the Painted Hall in Greenwich Hospital, London (Royal Naval College); 1708–27

Theophanes the Greek (attrib.): The "Virgin of the Don" Ikon; c1380. State Tretyakov Gallery, Moscow

Theophilus *fl.* early 12th century

The priest and craftsman Theophilus may have come from north Germany. He was the author of one of the most valuable texts to have survived from the earlier Middle Ages: the treatise on the arts entitled *De Diversis Artibus*. It contains instructions on the techniques employed in the arts in three parts, the second of which is incomplete. The first section is on painting, the second on glass working and enameling, and the third, the longest and most detailed, on goldsmith's work and bronze casting. It describes the refining of precious metals, how to make tools and dies, how to chase and emboss, how to design open and cast work, altar plate, frontals, bookcovers, reliquaries, and secular work like saddles and horse-trappings; it even gives detailed instructions for making an organ and casting church bells.

The earliest copy of the text to survive has been dated to the first half of the 12th century, and has at its beginning "Theophilus qui et Rugerus". This has led to the identification of the author as Roger of Helmarshausen, who is also known by a documented portable altar made in 1100 AD for Henry of Werl, Bishop of Paderborn. Dedicated to SS. Kilian and Liborius, it is now in Paderborn Cathedral. The techniques employed on this small altar provide almost an inventory of those described in Theophilus' text.

Because the internal evidence of the text also points to an early 12th-century date, and to a probable north German provenance, the identification of Theophilus as Roger is now often accepted, although it cannot be finally proved. Other work has been attributed to Roger, including the portable altar from the Abbey of Abdinghof, now in the Franciscan church, Paderborn, and the Gospels from Helmarshausen, in the Cathedral Library, Trier.

Roger's style of hard, linear Byzantine forms, with the human figure vividly articulated by panels of drapery, is probably derived from provincial Italian sources. It had an important influence in lower

Saxony until the end of the 12th century, especially at Hildesheim (Shrine of St Godehard; c1132) and at Fritzlar (chalice, church of St Peter; c1180).

Thornhill James 1676–1734

Sir James Thornhill was the only native artist to practice the Baroque style of decorative painting in England. His first major work was in the dome of St Paul's Cathedral, London, (1715–17), a reinterpretation of Raphael, but painted without the illusionistic bravura of the French Baroque. He reached his maturity with the walls and ceilings in the Painted Hall at Greenwich Hospital (1708–27), where he painted modern subjects in an allegorical manner, carried out in an Italianate illusionistic style. Thornhill also worked at Hampton Court (1717). He competed successfully with his many European rivals working in England, such as Louis Laguerre and Sebastiano Ricci, both of whom influenced his style.

Thornton John, of Coventry
fl. early 15th century

John Thornton of Coventry was an English glass-painter. His east window at York Minster (1405–8) contains scenes from Genesis, Exodus, and The Revelation of John, with individual figures above and below. Here he introduced a style of glass-painting new to York, which probably derived from the school working at Oxford and Winchester. The fine draftsmanship of his figures, in the International Gothic style, and the dramatic qualities of his extensive narrative scenes dominated York glass-painting for the following 50 years. He may also have supervised the painting of the *St William* window in York Minster (1422), and the *Fifteen Last Days* window in All Saints, North Street, York (c1410).

Thorvaldsen Bertel c1770–1844

Bertel Thorvaldsen was a Danish Neoclassical sculptor. He studied at the Royal Academy in Copenhagen with Johannes Wiedewelt and Nicolai Abildgaard. In 1797 he arrived in Rome, where he lived in a studio formerly occupied by John Flaxman. During his early years in Rome Thorvaldsen became an intimate of leading Neoclassicists, particularly Asmus Carstens and the Danish scholar Jörgen Zoëga. The artist's interest in Antiquity was fundamental to his sculpture, but he suffered from the overwhelming influence and rivalry of Antonio Canova.

Thorvaldsen developed a style of sculpture more severe and monumental than that of his great Italian contemporary. Canova himself considered that Thorvaldsen had founded a totally new style when he viewed the Dane's first large work, *Jason with the Golden Fleece* (1803–28, Thorvaldsen Museum, Copenhagen). It was bought by the rich Dutch banker Thomas Hope; his patronage, and that of other collectors interested in Neoclassicism, enabled Thorvaldsen to remain in Italy for most of his life.

He met many artists in Italy whose interest paralleled his own. They included J.-A.-D. Ingres, Joseph Koch, and John Gibson as well as the German Nazarenes, whose paintings and drawings Thorvaldsen often bought for his own collection. The sculptor's popularity increased, and he specialized in portrait busts, including one of his patron *Thomas Hope* (1817; Thorvaldsen Museum, Copenhagen).

In 1819 Thorvaldsen visited Denmark. He was received as a national celebrity and undertook several commissions to portray members of the Danish royal family. He moved to a large studio in Rome in 1822 and stayed in the city until 1838. After the deaths of Canova and Flaxman he was the greatest Neoclassical sculptor in Europe. His typical style is a static, heavy representation of Antiquity, but his drawings are lively and accomplished.

Tiepolo family 18th century

The Italian painter Giambattista Tiepolo (1696–1770) was the most important practitioner of the Rococo style in Italy during the 18th century. He combined the Venetian coloristic tradition of Titian and

Bertel Thorvaldsen: Brisëis Being Led away from Achilles; marble; height 116cm (46in); 1803. Thorvaldsen Museum, Copenhagen

Veronese with the art of Roman Baroque illusionism. He was born in Venice, and trained under Gregorio Lazzarini; his early work was influenced by the chiaroscuro manner of Federico Beneovich and Giambattista Piazzetta. He gradually moved away from these masters towards an independent, coloristic style, as in *The Sacrifice of Isaac* (1716; Chiesa dell'Ospedaletto, Venice).

With the return of Sebastiano Ricci—another influence on his work—to Venice in 1717, Giambattista turned towards Veronese's work for inspiration. His first monumental work, the *Madonna of the Carmelites and Saints* (1720–2; Pinacoteca di Brera, Milan) shows this influence in the open arrangement of figures, a compositional device he was to develop further. In his first ceiling decoration, *The Power of Eloquence* (1725; Palazzo Sandi, Venice), figures are seen foreshortened but their form is still suggested by means of light and shade rather than by pure color; a large expanse of sky sets off the figures.

The two masterpieces of Giambattista's early career are the decorations of the Cappella del Sacramento (1726; Udine Cathedral), and for Diomisio Dolfino's Palazzo Arcivescovado (formerly the Palazzo Dolfin) Udine (1726–7/8). The *Judgment of Solomon* in the latter shows the degree of luminosity he was able to obtain through modeling his figures by color alone, instead of using conventional chiaroscuro.

In 1731 Giambattista was commissioned to decorate the Palazzo Casati (now Dugnani) in Milan, returning to Venice in 1732. From then until his departure for Spain in 1760 he dominated Venetian painting. His decorative virtuosity was extraordinary, and his invention prodigious, as he covered huge areas of wall and ceiling with grandiose mythological or religious scenes. One of the most important works of his middle years is *The Institution of the Rosary* (1737–9; S. Maria dei Gesuati, Venice). The painting is Veronesian in its color and in its foreshortening; the fully-modeled figures emerge from a luminous background towards the spectator. Two other notable paintings from this period are *The Sacrifice of Melchizedek* and *The Gathering of the Manna* (1738–40; parish church of Verolanuova, Brescia).

In *St Simon Stock receiving the Scapular* (1740; Scuola dei Carmini, Venice), painted on canvas and placed in the center

Giambattista Tiepolo: The Banquet of Cleopatra; fresco; approx. 650×300cm (256×118in); 1743. Palazzo Labia, Venice

of a ceiling, most of the scenographic accessories that appeared so plentifully in the Gesuati ceiling have been abolished. The main theme is reduced nearly to its essentials. Color helps to unify the painting by evoking atmospheric luminosity. The most ambitious decoration of Giambattista's middle years in Venice was the painting of the *salone principe* of the Palazzo Labia, executed in 1743 in collaboration with Girolamo Mengozzi Colonna, who painted the architectural sections. *The Banquet of Cleopatra* is the most famous of its scenes; here the protagonists are portrayed with such realism that their

presence is almost palpable.

On 12 October 1750, Giambattista accepted the invitation of Prince-Archbishop Charles Phillip of Greiffenclau to decorate the dining-hall of his new palace, the Fürstbischöfliche Residenz in Würzburg. Later that year he arrived at Würzburg with his sons Giandomenico and Lorenzo Tiepolo. The two large scenes, *The Marriage of Barbarossa* and *The Investiture of Bishop Harold* are not framed with a painted architectural surround, but are set within actual stucco, which performs an abstract and decorative function. The treatment of the scenes themselves is also strongly illusionistic. Between 1752 and 1753 Giambattista painted the fresco above the stairway representing *Olympus*.

In 1753 Giambattista was back in Venice, where he painted *The Martyrdom of St Agatha* (Staatliche Museen, Berlin). One of his most complex works, it reveals the coloristic intensity of his late style. This magniloquence is also to be seen in the frescoes depicting mythological scenes from works by Tasso, Ariosto, and Virgil in the Villa and Foresteria of the Counts of Valmarana, Vicenza. These works date from the year 1757. Giambattista was assisted by Giandomenico, who decorated five of the rooms of the Foresteria. The last major work of Giambattista's late Venetian period was the ceiling of the *gran salone* of the Palazzo Pisani, Stra (Venice).

Giambattista was invited by Charles III of Spain to decorate the new Royal Palace in Madrid. He arrived on 4 June 1762, together with his sons Giandomenico and Lorenzo. Anton Raphael Mengs, the leader of the Neoclassical reform of European painting, was already in the city. In the Royal Palace, Giambattista painted three ceilings. *The Apotheosis of Spain* in the throne room, signed and dated 1764, is the most ambitious of these, but it also reveals the artist's declining powers. Giambattista died in Madrid on 27 March 1770. Faced with the competition of Mengs' purist approach, his exuberant Rococo had already begun to seem unfashionable.

The painter Giandomenico Tiepolo (1727–1804) was born in Venice. He worked as assistant to his father, Giambattista, and was deeply influenced by him, but did not possess his sublime vision, and was more attracted towards the realistic representation of contemporary life. Giandomenico's hand many be distinguished from that of his father, in the frescoes at Valmarana, by its more naturalistic style. Giandomenico was active as a printmaker, and 177 etchings by him are known. He was also a prolific draftsman. Among his independent works are the *Stations of the Via Crucis* (1748–9; Oratorio del Crocifisso, S. Polo, Venice), and *St Oswald prays for the Cure of a Sick Boy* (parish church, Merlengo). He went to Würzburg and Madrid with his father, and returned to Venice after the latter's death in 1770. There he found that the artistic atmosphere was much changed, and that his old-fashioned style, based on that of his father, was not in great demand.

Further reading. Knox, G. *Catalogue of Tiepolo Drawings in the Victoria and Albert Museum*, London (1960). Levey, M. *Giambattista Tiepolo: His Life and Art*, New Haven (1986). Morassi, A. *G.B. Tiepolo: his Life and Work*, London (1955). Rizzi, A. *The Etchings of the Tiepolos*, London and Milan (1971). Shaw, J.B. *The Drawings of Domenico Tiepolo*, London (1962).

Tinguely Jean 1925–

The Swiss sculptor Jean Tinguely was born at Fribourg and studied at the School of Fine Arts in Basel. In 1945 he began to construct in wire, metal, paper, and wood, and in 1948 experimented with motorized movement. In Paris, where he moved in 1953, Tinguely developed his "metamechanical" technique, which included the introduction of random and surprise elements into his constructions. In 1960 he founded, with Yves Klein and others, the *Nouveau Réalisme* movement.

There is much humor and irony in Tinguely's bizarre machines: the anarchic spirit of Dada lies behind his work. His fascination with the machine—his awareness of its obsolescence as well as its usefulness—led to a series of events in which his works exploded in a frenzy of self-destructive energy. The most famous of these took place in 1960 at the Museum of Modern Art, New York.

Tino da Camaino c1295–c1337

The Sienese sculptor Tino da Camaino was probably the pupil of Giovanni Pisano. His early work is in Pisa, where he was working by 1311 (and possibly as early as 1306). He was commissioned in 1315 to make the tomb of the Emperor Henry VII, of which only fragments survive (Camposanto, Pisa). He worked in Siena from 1319 to 1320. He probably spent the years 1321 to 1323 in Florence, making the tomb of Cardinal Orso (Florence Cathedral). From 1323 he lived at Naples, probably at the request of King Robert of Anjou, where he made the tomb of Margaret of Hungary with Gagliardo Primario (S. Maria Donna Regina, Naples), as well

Jean Tinguely: fragment from Homage to New York; painted metal; 204×224cm (80×88in); 1960. Museum of Modern Art, New York

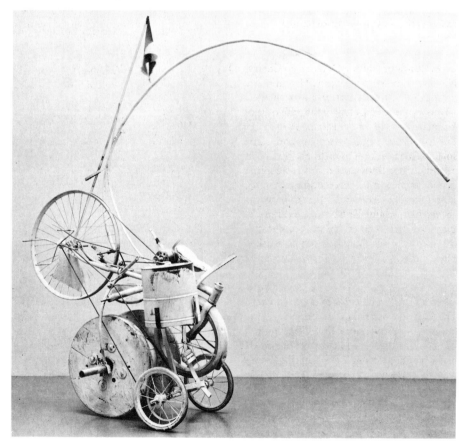

Tino da Camaino: Charity; marble; height 127cm (50in); c1321–3. Museo Bardini, Florence

states that Tintoretto spent a short time as a boy in Titian's studio, but that Titian expelled him through jealousy of his promise. He also tells us that Tintoretto wrote on the wall of his studio the motto: "The drawing of Michelangelo and the coloring of Titian". This is probably apocryphal, but reflects the fact that Tintoretto was deeply affected by contemporary develop-ments outside Venice, in northern and central Italy. In particular, his work shows the influence of Parmigianino as well as of Michelangelo. Tintoretto possessed copies of Michelangelo's Medici Chapel statues, and drew them from many angles.

The achievement of Tintoretto cannot, however, be expressed in any neat aca-demic formula of eclecticism. His powerful

Il Tintoretto: St George and the Dragon; oil on canvas; 158×100cm (62×39in); c1558. National Gallery, London

as the tomb of Mary of Valois (S. Chiara, Naples; 1333–7) and others. His influence on Neapolitan sculptors was extensive.

Tino's style derives from that of Giovanni Pisano, whose manner he helped to spread. But his work can have an additional solemn massiveness which at first sight relates to the classicism of Nicola Pisano. There is also the impression of contact with Giotto's example. The two artists surely met while Giotto was working in Naples from 1329 to 1333, but Giotto's influence on Tino's style must have taken place earlier.

Tintoretto Il 1518–94

The Italian artist Jacopo Robusti is always known by the nickname of "Il Tintoretto", "The Little Dyer", from the profession of his father. Second only to Titian, Tintoretto was the leading painter in Venice in the second half of the 16th century.

In *La Vita di Giacopo Robusti detto Il Tintoretto* ("The Life of Giacopo Robusti called Tintoretto"; 1648) Carlo Ridolfi

imagination dictated dynamic composition which he was able to realize on canvas through a unique mastery of light, and a brilliant technique of drawing directly with his pigment.

His earliest surviving work, *Apollo and Marsyas* (1545; Wadsworth Atheneum, Hartford, Conn.) was painted for a ceiling in the house of Pietro Aretino. It already shows his brilliance of handling but is rather flat and unexciting in design. It is in two pictures of the end of the decade, *The Last Supper* (1547; S. Marcuola, Venice), and *The Miracle of the Slave* (1548; Gallerie dell'Accademia, Venice) that we first encounter his genius. In this 1547 version of *The Last Supper*, Tintoretto places the figure of Christ in the conventional position in the center of the far side of the table, but four of the Apostles are seated at the near side, and some are rising to their feet, giving movement to the whole composition. In *The Miracle of the Slave*, St Mark hurtles down from the sky in bold foreshortening, the executioner displays his broken hammer to his master, and agitated spectators cling to the columns at the left. The color is strong, but clear and light, and the execution incisive and direct. Tintoretto's technique of building up forms through a series of clearly defined brush strokes is particularly well demonstrated in *The Four Evangelists* (1552; S. Maria Zobenigo, Venice).

At about the same time he produced *The Presentation of the Virgin* (c1552; Madonna del Orto, Venice). This picture originally formed the outer side of the organ shutters, and it is designed to be seen from below. Our gaze travels up the flight of curved steps to the point where Mary stands before the High Priest, silhouetted against the sky, while mysterious elders watch her from the shadows on the left. The emotive and symbolic character of the representation contrasts with the ordered rationalism of Titian's version of this subject (1534–8; Gallerie dell'Accademia, Venice).

Tintoretto's decoration of the choir of the same Gothic church of the Madonna del Orto survives intact, with its great canvases of *The Worship of the Golden Calf* and a *Last Judgment* on the side walls, reaching up into the pointed lunettes of the vault (c1560; Madonna del Orto, Venice). Comparison of the *Judgment* with the altar wall of the Sistine Chapel shows how little the fundamentals of Tintoretto's style, with its contrasts of light and shade and its re-

Il Tintoretto: Self-portrait; detail; oil on canvas; full size 61×51cm (24×20in); c1588. Louvre, Paris

cession into depth, owes to Michelangelo's example.

Shortly after his decoration of the Madonna del Orto, Tintoretto added two canvases to the series of the *Miracles of St Mark* which he had begun with *The Miracle of the Slave* in 1548: *The Finding of St Mark's Body* (c1562; Pinacoteca di Brera, Milan) and *The Transport of the Body of St Mark* (c1562; Gallerie dell'Accademia, Venice). These two paintings are distinguished by their deep perspective settings. In both, but especially the latter, this violent recession heightens the emotional impact of the picture.

The whole of the interior of the Scuola di San Rocco in Venice was decorated by Tintoretto between 1564 and 1587, and the decoration survives intact. Here, as nowhere else, we can appreciate the breadth of Tintoretto's genius. The canvas of *Christ before Pilate* (1564–6) shows the elongated, pale figure of Christ movingly isolated against the dark architecture. The *Ascension* (1576–81), with its rhythmical pattern of the cutting edges of the angels' wings in its upper part, and the open meadow with the Apostles below, is a splendidly imaginative creation. *The Flight into Egypt* (1583–7), with its extended landscape, reminds us how far Tintoretto anticipates the developments of the following century.

Almost all the pictures mentioned so far have been religious in content. They are

paralleled by a less extensive, but equally impressive, series of mythological paintings such as *The Origin of the Milky Way* (c1582, National Gallery, London). Another series of four paintings includes the *Bacchus and Ariadne* (1578; Sala del Anticollegio, Doges' Palace, Venice). He also painted historical scenes both for the Venetian Doges' Palace (Library) and for the Gonzaga family at Mantua (now in the Alte Pinakothek, Munich).

The great *Paradise* in the Sala del Maggior Consiglio in the Doges' Palace was begun after 1588 when Tintoretto was 70. It could only be carried out with the help of numerous assistants, and does not realize his idea as effectively as the sketch made for the original competition (1579; Louvre, Paris). A masterpiece of his last years is *The Last Supper* (1592–4; S. Giorgio Maggiore, Venice). With its receding diagonal perspective, it contrasts strikingly with this first version at S. Marcuola.

He was widely employed as a portrait painter, but his portraits lack the humane authority of Titian's and this remains a minor branch of his activity. However, his late *Self-portrait* (c1588; Louvre, Paris) is profoundly human, and at the same time splendidly abstract. Its icon-like quality is a reminder of the Byzantine substructure of all Venetian painting.

Tintoretto's son, Domenico (1562–1637), assisted him in his later work, and also worked independently. A daughter, Marietta, was also a painter.

Further reading. Berenson, B. *Venetian Painters of the Renaissance*, London and New York (1897). Bernardi, C. and Vecchi, P. de *L'Opera Completa di Tintoretto*, Milan (1970). Newton, E. *Tintoretto*, London (1952). Parlucchini, R. *La Giovanezza del Tintoretto*, Milan (1950). Pittaluga, M. *Il Tintoretto*, Bologna (1925). Rossi, P. *Jacopo Tintoretto*, Venice (1973). Tietze, H. *Tintoretto: the Paintings and Drawings*, London (1948).

Tissot James 1836–1902

The French painter James Tissot was born in Nantes. He went off to Paris in 1856 and became a friend of J.A.M. Whistler and Degas. He departed from his initial romantic-medieval style (seen, for example, in *The Two Sisters*, 1864; Louvre, Paris) and inaugurated a highly salable line in pictures of ladies wearing contemporary, exotic, and historical costumes. In

James Tissot: The Henley Regatta of 1877; oil on canvas; 46×95cm (18×37in); 1877. Leander Club, Henley-on-Thames

London, where he lived from 1871, his polished depictions of fashionable society (for example, *Ball on Shipboard*, 1874; Tate Gallery, London) soon gained middle-class popularity. On the death of his much-portrayed mistress in 1882, Tissot returned to Paris and took up spiritualism. His *Life of Christ* paintings (begun in 1886) received enormous acclaim for their factual quality (derived from studies and sketches made in the Holy Land, most of which are now in the Brooklyn Museum, New York). In 1896 he published the first volume of the *Tissot Bible*, illustrated with 865 compositions.

Titian *c1488–1576*

The Venetian painter Tiziano Vecellio is known in English as Titian. Contemporary sources indicate possible dates of birth as widely separated as 1473 and 1490. His earliest documented work is of 1511. He was born in the Alpine valley of Cadore and brought to Venice as a boy, where he was placed with the painter and mosaicist Sebastiano Zuccato. He passed through the studios of Gentile and Giovanni Bellini, and became associated with Giorgione *c1507*, completing a number of works that were left unfinished at Giorgione's death in 1510.

Titian remained based on Venice throughout his life, but worked for numerous outside patrons such as the Dukes of Ferrara, Mantua, and Urbino, the Emperor Charles V, his son Phillip II of Spain, and Pope Paul III. He visited Rome from 1545 to 1546 and Augsburg from 1548 to 1549 and again in 1550. He excelled as a painter of religious and mythological scenes and as a portraitist.

It is impossible to exaggerate Titian's importance in the history of Western painting. It was he, more than any other artist, who drew together the achievements of the earlier Renaissance and transmitted them to future generations as a living tradition. Unlike some other figures of the High Renaissance, he was essentially and exclusively a painter. The actual pigment plays as positive a part in the creation of his works as the marble does in Michelangelo's sculptures. Titian's feeling for the tangibility of pigment may owe something to his early contact with the art of mosaic. From Giovanni Bellini he would have learned the liberating possibilities of the oil technique.

Titian's earliest paintings, dating from the first decade of the century, such as *The Gipsy Madonna* (Kunsthistorisches Museum, Vienna) follow Bellinesque types of design, but are distinguished by their

freedom of handling and rich texture. The earliest of his altarpieces is the relatively small one, now in the sacristy of S. Maria della Salute in Venice, of *St Mark Enthroned*. The flanking saints, Cosmas and

Titian: The Tribute Money; oil on poplar panel; 75×56cm (30×22in); c1516. Gemäldegalerie Alte Meister, Dresden

Damian, Roche and Sebastian, are those invoked against the plague, and the picture is usually linked with the epidemic that carried off Giorgione in the autumn of 1510. The symmetrical disposition of the figures follows the traditional pattern. But the architecture is asymmetrical, and, by a bold stroke, the head of the principal figure is placed in shadow so that it is silhouetted against the light cloud behind.

This silhouetting reappears in the head of the central apostle in the great *Assumption of the Virgin*, painted for the high altar of S. Maria dei Frari between 1516 and 1518. In other respects, there is little in the quiet dignity of the *St Mark* to prepare us for this amazing work. Mary is borne up on a cloud crowded with boy angels, in a red robe, against an orange glory of light; the Father seems to take material form under our eyes as he prepares to receive her. The apostles, earth-bound, strain towards her and show her as humanity transfigured.

This work, painted when he was probably around 30, is a masterpiece, and sets Titian at once in the company of Leonardo, Michelangelo, and Raphael. He was to reach this level again, and by very different routes, but he could not surpass it.

We find this dramatic style in a very different context in the votive altarpiece of the Pesaro family, also in S. Maria dei Frari, painted between 1519 and 1526. Here Titian fused two earlier types: the votive picture, in which the donor kneels on one side before the holy figure enthroned on the other, and the conventional, centrally enthroned Madonna with saints. He produced a splendid asymmetrical but balanced design, which was to influence the future development of the altarpiece in Venice. It has been suggested recently that the great columns in the background of the painting, which echo the piers of the nave of the Gothic church, are a later modification of Titian's original

design. This theory is certainly mistaken. Titian's dramatic approach to altarpiece design culminated in the narrative scene of *The Death of St Peter Martyr*, painted for the church of SS. Giovanni e Paolo between 1528 and 1530. The picture was destroyed by fire in 1867.

Parallel with this development of religious themes we find a series of allegorical and mythological pictures. If *Fête Champêtre* in the Louvre, Paris, had been established as Titian's work it would be among the earliest of these. But its dreamy, indeterminate mood is remote from Titian's affirmative nature; it seems more probable that it is in part, if not wholly, the work of Giorgione. By contrast, the rich, incisive, and eloquent *Sacred and Profane Love* (c1515; Museo e Galleria Borghese, Rome) is the essence of Titian. It may be seen as the secular prelude to the *Assumption* begun in the following year, and is hardly less of a masterpiece.

Titian: The Venus of Urbino; oil on canvas; 120×165cm (47×65in); 1538. Uffizi, Florence

At about the same time, Titian began his series of Bacchanals for the Duke of Ferrara: *The Worship of Venus* and *Bacchanal of the Andrians* in the Prado, Madrid, and *Bacchus and Ariadne* in the National Gallery, London. The latter was completed in 1523. Its feeling for form and movement is close to the *Assumption* but is contained here in a frieze-like composition reminiscent of antique sculpture.

Bacchanal of the Andrians is probably the last of the series. It may be compared to another, smaller religious work, the *Entombment* in the Louvre, Paris, painted at about the same time for the Duke of Mantua. In his portraits of this period Titian gradually abandoned the restraint of his *Portrait of a Man* (National Gallery, London). This still used the containing parapet of the previous century, and may be dated, on grounds of costume, to c1512. He progressed towards the free movement of his *Man with a Glove* (1523; Louvre, Paris).

In the 1530s Titian's style became quieter. The *Presentation of the Virgin* (1534–8) still occupies the place for which he painted it in the Scuola della Carità, Venice, now part of the galleries of the Accademia. The picture reflects the Venetian tradition of civic pageantry and architectural fantasy (to be found about 40 years earlier in the work of Gentile Bellini and Carpaccio). It introduces us to a more subdued palette than that of the 1520s. For his *Venus of Urbino* (1538; Uffizi, Florence) he set the goddess awake, on a bed in a shaded room, with a lapdog and female attendants—no longer a goddess but a lovely woman.

Titian's first contacts with Charles V are commemorated in the full-length portrait of *Charles V with a White Dog* (1532–3; Prado, Madrid). Painted in Bologna in 1533, it is a sublime translation of the mediocre work done by Charles' Austrian court painter in the previous year. The portrait of *The Duke of Urbino* (Uffizi, Florence), painted at the same time as the Venus, is a dramatic presentation of the Duke in armor, as commander of a Papal league against the Turks. This probably reflects the martial spirit Titian infused into the great historical canvas of *The Battle of Cadore*. He was working on this at the time, for the Hall of the Greater Council in the Doges' Palace. The hall was destroyed by fire in 1577. Had Titian's work survived, it might have furnished a clear link with the work of the previous decade.

As early as the *Assumption*, Titian's work had shown knowledge and understanding of contemporary developments in central Italy, but it is not until his work of the 1540s that we begin to feel this as a determining influence. He was friendly with the sculptor and architect Jacopo Sansovino, who had come to Venice after the Sack of Rome in 1527. Titian had also known Giulio Romano and his work in Mantua, and he met Giorgio Vasari, who was in Venice in the early 1540s. We see the fruits of these contacts in such works as the ceiling panels now in the sacristy of S. Maria della Salute, painted between 1542 and 1544, with their more defined drawing, muted color, and bold use of foreshortening. Somewhat similar features distinguish the *St John the Baptist* in the Gallerie dell'Accademia, Venice, and *The Crowning with Thorns* of 1542–4 in the Louvre, Paris.

From 1545 to 1546 Titian made his only visit to Rome. The most important result of his stay is the *Danaë* in Naples (1545–6; Museo e Gallerie Nazionali di Capodimonte). In this painting Titian is measuring himself against Michelangelo, and has adopted for his figure a pose closely related to that of Michelangelo's *Notte* and his *Leda*. According to Vasari, Michelangelo admired the way this picture was painted, but regretted that the Venetian painters' training in drawing was imperfect.

This decade saw Titian's greatest achievements in portraiture. The trio *Clarissa Strozzi* (1542; Staatliche Museen, Berlin), *A Young Englishman* (1545; Pitti Palace, Florence), and *Paul III* (1546; Museo e Gallerie Nazionali di Capodimonte, Naples) shows childhood, manhood, and old age marvelously typified and at the same time individualized. Similar qualities distinguish the great group-portrait of *The Vendramin Family* (1543–7) in the National Gallery, London. The Pope wanted to establish Titian permanently in his service in Rome, but the painter rejected his offers and came to rely increasingly on the patronage first of the Emperor, and then of his son, Phillip II of Spain.

In 1548 Titian was summoned to the Imperial court at Augsburg, where Charles V was settling the affairs of Germany after the defeat of the Protestant princes at Mühlberg in the previous year. Titian was employed on the portraits of the principal actors in these events, and particularly on the equestrian portrait of *Charles V as the Victor of Mühlberg*, now in the Prado,

Madrid. This splendid composition provided the model from which, in the next century, the great equestrian portraits by Rubens, Anthony van Dyck, and Velazquez were to derive.

Titian had one more commission for the Emperor: the painting of the Imperial family in adoration of the Trinity (1551–4), known as *La Gloria* and now in the Prado, Madrid, which the Emperor took with him on his retirement from the world in 1556. The vertical composition with its screen of figures shows the impression made on Titian by Michelangelo's *Last Judgment* (Sistine Chapel, Vatican, Rome) but the functions of light, color, and pigment show how very differently he understood the painter's task.

At about the same time as he undertook this picture, Titian began a series of mythological paintings for Philip II. These are less frieze-like in composition than the Ferrara *Bacchanals*, and contain fewer figures on a larger scale. Their more open eroticism perhaps reflects a chord common to painter and patron. These works are distinguished by increasingly free handling of pigment and an overall use of broken color. The *Diana and Actaeon* of 1559 (on loan to the National Gallery of Scotland, Edinburgh, from the Duke of Sutherland) has a complex design in depth which may be contrasted with the frieze-like character of the *Bacchus and Ariadne*. We may also contrast the looser definition of forms in the *Diana and Actaeon*, and the more unified, less contrapuntal use of color.

The *Europa* (1559–62; Isabella Stewart Gardner Museum, Boston), finished a little later, is a singing, shimmering harmony of blue, silver, and pink. By contrast, the grim and vengeful picture of *The Death of Actaeon* in the National Gallery, London, which must have been painted c1559 is superficially almost monochrome in its effect, but is made up of the subtlest mingling of browns, greens, and reds. Similar but more silvery effects are seen in *Nymph and Shepherd* (1570; Kunsthistorisches Museum, Vienna). In the design for this, one of his last pictures, Titian seems to have gone back to the work of Giorgione, the companion of his youth. *The Flaying of Marsyas* (1570; Archiepiscopal Palace Museum, Kroměříž), another work probably in his studio at the time of his death, shows, like *The Death of Actaeon*, a sense of cruelty which seems to have formed part of Titian's understanding of the world.

Parallel to these mythologies is a splendid series of religious works, such as the swirling silvery *Annunciation* in S. Salvatore, Venice (early 1560s), and the recreation of the Louvre's *Crowning with Thorns* in terms of flickering lights and broken color. This painting (1570) is now in the Alte Pinakothek, Munich, and must have been among the last canvases on which he worked.

The whole of Titian's career seems to be summed up in the *Pietà* (1570–6) in the Gallerie dell'Accademia, Venice. He intended it for the altar in front of which he wished to be buried. The picture was unfinished at his death, and was tactfully completed by his pupil Palma Giovine. The scene is set before a symmetrical architecture, as in the altarpieces of his master, Giovanni Bellini. The central niche has a shimmering mosaic which may recall his apprenticeship with Sebastiano Zuccato. The gesture of the Magdalene recalls that of Sacred Love in *Sacred and Profane Love* (Museo e Galleria Borghese, Rome), and the central group of Mary and her Son derived from Michelangelo's *Pietà* in St Peter's, Rome. But Titian's *Pietà* points forward as well as looking back. This is the inheritance that Rubens, born in 1578 two years after Titian's death, was to take up and hand on to the future.

Further reading. Crowe, J.A. and Cavalcaselle, G.B. *Titian: his Life and Times* (2 vols.), London (1881). Pailucchini, R. *Tiziano*, Bologna (1953–4). Panofsky, E. *Problems in Titian, mostly Iconographic*, London and New York (1969). Wethey, H.E. *The Paintings of Titian* (3 vols.), London and Oxford (1969–75). Williams, J. *The World of Titian*, London and New York (1969).

Tobey Mark 1890–1976

The American painter Mark Tobey was born at Centerville, Wisconsin. His formal artistic training was restricted to a series of Saturday classes at the school of the Chicago Institute of Art (1908). He moved to New York in 1911 and worked there as a fashion designer and interior designer, and then did the same in Chicago, until 1917. In that year he had his first one-man show at Knoedler's, exhibiting charcoal portraits of a fashionable kind. He had already been impressed by the Armory Show, as well as striking up an acquaintance with Marcel Duchamp; but his own artistic aims were still confused.

In the months after the end of the First World War, Tobey became a convert to the Bahai faith, which preaches "A oneness of mankind, an indivisible reality that does not admit of multiplicity". He settled in Seattle (1922–30), but at the beginning of the Depression moved to England; until 1938, his base there was the advanced educational center at Dartington Hall, Devonshire.

Although Tobey had begun as a representational artist, he gradually moved towards a highly personal form of Abstract art. His development was influenced by his newly found religious faith, and by the art forms of the Far East (which he visited in 1934), especially calligraphy. He also became fascinated by Japanese woodcuts and American Indian art. A painting like *Broadway* (1936; Metropolitan Museum, New York) shows Tobey's art at a transitional stage: the perspective is still traditional, and it is possible to make out details of traffic and architecture, but the strongly textured calligraphic style is already beginning to absorb the forms into its own abstract scheme.

By the mid 1940s, the change to abstraction was complete. Tobey's mature style, with its elaborate buildup of tiny calligraphic signs and gestures, and its creation of effects that are both luminous and serene in appearance, can be seen in, for example, his painting *New York* (1945; private collection).

Further reading. Dahl, A. et al. *Mark Tobey: Art and Belief*, Oxford (1984).

Togan Unkoku 1547–1618

The Japanese painter Unkoku Togan was the founder of the Unkoku School. A Kyushu man of a Samurai family, he first studied with Kano Shoei (1519–92). Later he studied the style of Sesshu (1420–1506), with such success that he became official head of the Sesshu line, inherited the master's Unkokuan studio in western Honshu, and, moreover, adopted the name Unkoku.

Togan's greatest works are the set of ink monochrome sliding doors in the Daitoku-ji Temple, Kyoto; they are grave in feeling, soft yet detailed, and weighty in execution. Like his contemporary, Yusho, he favored the "boneless" style of figure-painting. His school continued into the 19th century with ink-painting in the Sesshu style.

Tohaku Hasegawa 1539–1610

The Japanese painter Hasegawa Tohaku was the founder of the Hasegawa School.

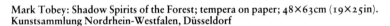
Mark Tobey: Shadow Spirits of the Forest; tempera on paper; 48×63cm (19×25in). Kunstsammlung Nordrhein-Westfalen, Düsseldorf

Above: Hasegawa Tohaku: Pine Woods; detail of a screen; full size 160×355cm (63×140in); c1570. Tokyo National Museum

He studied in the school of Sesshu and claimed to be his artistic heir, although this was disputed by Unkoku Togan. His talents as an ink-painter, however, did not need the authority of Sesshu behind them. Little is known of Tohaku's early life, but it is clear that he had access to Chinese paintings of the Southern Sung dynasty and the Zen works of Mu Ch'i.

His pair of screens depicting pines in the mist (Tokyo National Museum) represent the final absorption of Chinese techniques into a Japanese subject. The great foreground trees loom dimly in the smoky morning, and those further away almost disappear into the gray wash, with astonishing control. So real is this very Japanese scene that, on close inspection, the viewer is surprised by the powerful artifice of the ink work. Other mist-dominated, almost "empty" works, are the monkey and bamboo screens from the Sokokuji Temple, Kyoto. Tohaku was also a master of combining ink and gold washes.

He also attempted the Momoyama decorative style with great success, being the only challenger to Eitoku and his *Kano* successors. The sets of sliding doors at the Chishakuin, Kyoto, were done with his son Kyuzo (1568–93). They represent trees and plants of the four seasons done in ink and colors against gold leaf. Tohaku's naturalism in the famous maple-tree decoration, *Autumn* (Chishakuin, Kyoto), is allied with delicate coloring, powerful line, and dynamic composition to make it possibly the greatest of Momoyama screens.

Tomlin Bradley 1899–1953

Bradley Walker Tomlin, the American painter of the New York School, was born in Syracuse, New York. He studied painting at Syracuse University (1917–21) and then moved to New York, where he lived until his death. He worked as an illustrator, but his independent paintings took on a semi-Abstract, synthetic Cubist appearance. In the late 1940s, under the influence of his Abstract Expressionist contemporaries, he began to develop his mature Abstract style. This was initially calligraphic, with ribbon-like marks over a uniform ground. But his most memorable paintings resemble light colored petals; they consist of squared brush strokes floating over darker layers of loosely painted ground.

Tommaso da Modena 1325–79

Tommaso da Modena was an Italian painter. His style, unlike that of his fellow Modenese artist Barnaba da Siena, was thoroughly up-to-date; it may reflect a training in a center such as Bologna, and the influence of Siena. Much of his work looks like that of a miniaturist working on a large scale, and the confident, naturalistic figure-style is often at odds with the uncertain handling of perspective in surrounding details.

Most of Tommaso's work is to be found not in Modena, but further north, in Treviso. He is recorded there between

Below: Tommaso da Modena: Albertus Magnus, one of the Forty Dominican Worthies; fresco; c1352. S. Niccolò, Treviso

1349 and 1358, and painted frescoes in several Trevisan churches. His chief monument is the decoration of the chapter house of the Dominican church of S. Niccolò (frescoes signed and dated 1352). The subject matter, portraits of *Forty Dominican Worthies*, might have been repetitive and dull, but Tommaso enlivened the figures with many touches of characterization and detail, such as a pair of spectacles balanced on a nose, or the sharpening of a quill pen. On a pillar in the nave of the same church is a fresco of *St Jerome in his Study*, which cleverly adapts the subject to the curved picture surface. S. Margherita, Treviso, contains frescoes of *The Life of St Ursula*; these are believed to be by Tommaso, although the attribution has been questioned.

On the evidence of two signed panel paintings in Karlstein Castle, Prague, one of which includes St Wenceslas, it seems likely that Tommaso actually visited the city, which was then a considerable international center of court patronage. This is likely to have been late in his career, after his documented activity in Modena; he was painting in his native town between 1358 and 1368, but little of his work there has survived.

Toorop Jan 1858–1928

Born in Java, the Dutch painter Jan (Johann Theodorus) Toorop was a link between the late-19th-century avant-garde circles of Brussels, Paris, London, and Holland. He studied first in Amsterdam (1880–2), and then in Brussels (1883–5), where he met James Ensor and the poet Émile Verhaeren. In 1885 he was elected a member of Les Vingt for which he later organized two Dutch exhibitions (in 1891 and 1892). He traveled to Paris, and to London, where he met J.A.M. Whistler, and was impressed by the applied art of William Morris.

After he settled in The Hague in 1890, Toorop's painting moved from a socialist-inspired neo-Impressionism to the Symbolist, early Art Nouveau style of *The Three Brides* (1893; Kröller-Müller Museum, Otterlo). The works of Oscar Wilde provided some of his subject matter; Aubrey Beardsley, William Morris, and Javan shadow puppets were the prototypes for his use of two-dimensional space, his silhouetted figures, and his stylization of natural objects to create an abstract pattern. Toorop was converted to Roman Catholic-

ism in 1905, after which his painting became more traditional in style, and almost entirely devoted to religious subjects.

Torel William 13th century

William Torel was an English goldsmith. His gilded bronze effigies of Queen Eleanor and her father-in-law, Henry III (1293; Westminster Abbey, London) represent the earliest use in England of the *cire perdue* process for casting life-size figures. They were commissioned by Edward I for the Chapel of Edward the Confessor in the Abbey, in imitation of the French royal tombs at St-Denis. Although they are related in form to earlier English stone effigies, their delicate, idealized faces and rippling draperies are characteristic of the sophisticated style of Edward's court school. A second effigy of Queen Eleanor, made—probably from the same model—for Lincoln Cathedral, was destroyed in 1641.

Torres-Garciá Joaquin 1874–1949

The Uraguayan painter Joaquin Torres-Garciá was born in Montevideo. Between 1891 and 1934, when he returned to settle in his native city, he traveled extensively abroad. He went first to Spain; as a

Joaquin Torres-Garciá: Design with an Alien Figure; oil on canvas; 89×53cm (35×21in); 1931. Private collection

student, in Barcelona, he made contact with the Catalan architect Gaudí, who made a deep impression upon him. After a decade in Brussels (1900–10) Torres-Garciá returned to Spain. Ten years later he went to New York (1920–2), then to Italy (1923), and finally to France, where he stayed until 1932.

In Paris, Torres-Garciá was a founder member of the *Cercle et Carré* group of International Constructivists. Despite such geometrical-abstract tendencies, his work has affinities with Paul Klee's, and even with certain of the Surrealists', such as Joan Miró. Like them, Torres-Garciá was interested in the idea of painting as a language of signs, and sought inspiration in primitive art.

Torrigiano Pietro 1472–1528

Pietro Torrigiano was an Italian sculptor. He trained at Florence in the Medici sculpture collection under Bertoldo di Giovanni (c1490), and specialized in modeling statuettes and busts in terracotta. He was exiled from Florence by 1492, for breaking Michelangelo's nose in a quarrel. He went to Rome and produced a number of busts, three of which are now in the Ospedale di S. Fina, San Gimignano. In 1511 he contracted to make the tomb, in bronze and marble, of Lady Margaret Beaufort, and in 1512 that of King Henry VII and his Queen; both works are in Westminster Abbey, London. His terracotta busts of *Henry VII* (Victoria and Albert Museum, London) and of *Henry VIII* and *Bishop Fisher* (Metropolitan Museum, New York) also date from this period. After executing private commissions, and beginning a tomb for Henry VIII and Katherine of Aragon (1519), he went to Spain; there he modeled in terracotta a *Virgin and Child* and a *St Jerome* (Provincial Museum of Fine Arts, Seville). Torrigiano's sculpture is typical of the Florentine High Renaissance, evolving from the work of Benedetto da Maiano and Verrocchio, but not affected by Michelangelo. It played a crucial role in bringing Renaissance art to England.

Torriti Jacopo *fl.* 1287–92

Jacopo Torriti was an Italian painter and mosaicist. He is known for a signed mosaic in the apse of S. Giovanni in Laterano, Rome (c1291) and the mosaic of *The Coronation of the Virgin* in S. Maria Maggiore, Rome (c1296). The Lateran

Jacopo Torriti: The Coronation of the Virgin; mosaic; c1296. S. Maria Maggiore, Rome

work was, itself, probably a reworking or imitation of an original of the 4th or 5th century AD—demonstrating one of the sources of his style. In the mosaic of *The Coronation of the Virgin* in S. Maria Maggiore his manner is basically Byzantine. The mosaic resembles the work of Pietro Cavallini, and contains some naturalistic details from late Roman works; but it never attains the vigor of Cavallini, or his sense of monumentality.

Torriti may have worked on the fresco decoration of the Upper Church of St Francis at Assisi (c1290–2). The scenes of *The Creation* clearly recall the style of his Roman work, but the attribution has been disputed.

Toulouse-Lautrec Henri de
1864–1901

Henri de Toulouse-Lautrec was a French painter, printmaker, and poster artist. Born in Albi into the aristocratic family of Toulouse-Lautrec Monfa, he divided his early years between the family estates and school in Paris. His health was delicate, and he broke both femurs, one at 14, one at 15. These injuries left him with a normal torso, but stunted legs. He showed an early capacity for drawing and painting, and was encouraged by the animal painter René Princeteau (1843–1914). In 1882 he entered the atelier of Léon Bonnat, a strict academic teacher; he worked conscientiously and devotedly, and produced many drawings after the model. In 1883 he moved to Cormon's atelier, where he met Émile Bernard and Vincent van Gogh.

Among the influences on his early paintings were Manet, J.A.M. Whistler, and the Impressionists in general, but he reserved his greatest admiration for Degas. The influence of Japanese prints is also clear. In 1885 he finally settled in Paris; from then until his death, he was to observe urban life, especially that of the circus, theater, dance-hall, and brothel. His important paintings include the *Equestrienne of the Fernando Circus* of 1888, *At the Moulin Rouge* of 1892 (both Art Institute of Chicago), and the *Salon in the Rue des Moulins* of 1894 (Musée Toulouse-Lautrec,

Henri de Toulouse-Lautrec: The Salon in the Rue des Moulins; pastel; 112×133cm (44×52in); 1894. Musée Toulouse-Lautrec, Albi

Albi). He became a master of summary characterization, of tellingly abbreviated spatial effects, of the laconic line, and of heightened, non-naturalistic color. Most of his paintings were done with thinned oil-paint on unprimed cardboard; some were works in their own right; others, however, were rapid studies for his pictures and his posters.

It was in 1891 that Toulouse-Lautrec produced his first poster for the Moulin Rouge. Its large size, its eye-catching play of flattened and exaggerated shapes (for instance the continuous black silhouette of the onlookers in the background), and its simple and direct use of color revolutionized the art of the poster, transforming it from the Rococo-inspired extravaganzas

of Jules Cheret into the immediacy of Art Nouveau. Toulouse-Lautrec designed some 31 posters: in each, his exploitation of the resources of color lithography was skillful, idiosyncratic, and assured.

He began using lithography as early as 1885, but his greatest period of production was during the 1890s, coinciding with his work on the posters. Many of his lithographs were produced as series by the rapidly expanding print publishers. Among them are Le Café Concert (1893), 16 lithographs of the performer Yvette Guilbert (1894; text by Gustave Geoffroy), followed by a further set of the same (1898), Elles, a set of 11 lithographs (1896), and Les Histoires Naturelles of Jules Renard (1899).

Throughout his career, Toulouse-Lautrec used pastel and watercolor with brevity and wit. During a period of convalescence in a clinic in 1899, he worked on a series of drawings of the circus. His last paintings show a trend towards Expressionism, both in mood and in color.

Further reading. Adheman, J. Toulouse-Lautrec: his Complete Lithographs and Drypoints, New York (1965). Caproni, G. and Sugana, G.M. L'Opera Completa di Toulouse-Lautrec, Milan (1969). Cooper, D. Henri de Toulouse-Lautrec, London (1955). Toulouse-Lautrec, H. (ed. Goldschmidt, L. and Schimmel, H.) Unpublished Correspondence, London (1969).

Toyokuni Utagawa 1769–1825

Utagawa Toyokuni was a Japanese print artist of the *Ukiyoe* school. He was the true founder of the Utagawa figure-style which dominated the field for nearly a century. His master Toyoharu trained him in the *Ukiyoe* tradition and actually founded the Utagawa School. The style was characterized by a long face, hatchet chin, and tortured expression; although it suited heroic works, it killed the tradition of prints of beautiful women.

In his earlier years, Toyokuni had emulated the beauties of Utamaro and Eishi with some success, but his real talent was for the portrayal of actors, either full-length, or half-length, or "large head". In his last years, commercial considerations seemed to overcome his artistic scruples.

Traini Francesco *fl.* 1321–63

The Italian painter Francesco Traini came from Pisa. He is known both from documents and from a signed panel painting of *St Dominic* of 1345 (Museo Nazionale di S. Matteo, Pisa). This came from the same church as a panel painting of the Dominican *St Thomas Aquinas in Glory* (S. Caterina, Pisa) that can be attributed to him. It is clear from these two panels that Traini was strongly influenced by the Sienese painter Simone Martini (1280/5–1344), who painted an altarpiece in Pisa in 1320, and by the Lorenzetti. In 1321 we first hear of Traini in connection with the frescoes of the Camposanto, Pisa. Although it is still a matter of controversy, it seems likely that Traini painted the frescoes there of *The Triumph of Death, Last Judgment, Hell*, and *Legends of Hermits*. These were formerly dated to about the 1350s, but it is now believed that they were painted earlier.

The frescoes reflect the fear of God's judgment, which was so prevalent in the middle of the 14th century. The *Last Judgment* is accompanied by a vision of Hell far more dominant than any glimpse we are given of Paradise. In *The Triumph of Death*, Traini uses the emotional, Gothic elements of Sienese art to emphasize the cruel indifference of Death. The crippled and blind call out for deliverance from life, but Death instead strikes out at a group of young men and ladies enjoying a life of courtly pleasure.

The Camposanto frescoes have been damaged by war and the passage of time, but underneath them have been revealed *sinopie* of great beauty; these give a rare opportunity to study this usually hidden aspect of the art of the 14th-century painter.

Trdat of Armenia *fl.* 972–1036

The Armenian architect Trdat worked for the Bagratid court of Ani. His work marks a Renaissance of Armenian architecture. Although he used church plans and decorative elements from 7th-century Armenia, he made important modifications to the earlier style. He applied the pointed arch and the rib and colonnette in clustered piers, in vaulting, and in blind arcades to produce an effect resembling that of the Gothic architecture that came a century later.

His first commission was the cathedral of Argina (972–91). His renown is demonstrated by his employment in Constantinople to repair the damaged dome of S. Sophia (989). This direct contact with Byzantine architecture apparently left little

Above: Utagawa Toyokuni: The Festival Offerings; woodblock print; 38×25cm (15×10in); c1789. Private collection

Below: Francesco Traini: St Dominic and Scenes from his Life; panel; 1345. Museo Nazionale di S. Matteo, Pisa

mark on his subsequent work. For the cathedral of Ani (988–1000) he reused the 7th-century Armenian "cross in rectangle" plan which featured a dome supported by four piers. The church of St Gregory of Gagik (1001–10), also at Ani, is based on the aisled-tetraconch church of Zvartnots at Vagharchapat (641–61). A third church at Ani, the Holy Savior (1036), has a similarly centralized design.

Troost Cornelis 1697–1750

Cornelis Troost was a painter of the Dutch bourgeoisie in early-18th-century Amsterdam. He is associated with the development of the increasingly fashionable "Conversation Piece": a group portrait in which sitters are shown in their domestic setting and engaged in conversation, the playing of music, or some other leisurely or cultured activity. He also painted a number of humorous genre pictures, notably the series of five "NELRI" paintings in The Hague (Royal Museum of Art, Mauritshuis), which illustrate the debauchery accompanying a reunion supper party. Despite the absence of any moralizing intent, this type of work (done in pastel and gouache) earned Troost the designation of the "Dutch Hogarth". Troost, like William Hogarth (1697–1764), was interested in the theater. He painted pictures of contemporary theatrical performances, and also designed scenery for Amsterdam's municipal theater.

Cornelis Troost: The Dilettanti; oil on canvas; 66×56cm (26×22in); 1736. National Gallery of Ireland, Dublin

Trumbull John 1756–1843

The American painter and diplomat John Trumbull left his homeland in order to study under Benjamin West in London. During a visit to Paris he saw works by J.-L. David and Charles Lebrun and fell under their influence. On his return to the United States he painted scenes from the American Revolution. He made a second visit to London (1794–1804) as a commissioner for the Jay Treaty. Between 1816 and 1837 he worked on four of the eight canvases that decorate the interior of Capitol Rotunda, Washington. He played a leading role in the American Academy of Fine Arts, and was president of it from 1816 to 1835. He painted many portraits and modern history pictures, and also a fine group of American landscapes, mainly waterfalls.

Tucker William 1935–

The English sculptor William Tucker was born in Cairo. He read history at Oxford University (1955–8), then studied sculpture at the Central School of Art and Design and at St Martin's School of Art, London (1959–60). In 1961 he began teaching sculpture at Goldsmiths' College and at St Martin's School of Art. From 1968 to 1970 he was Gregory Fellow at Leeds University. He published *The Language of Sculpture* in 1974.

From 1960 Tucker worked with cut and welded iron, and created wood sculptures and reliefs. This led him to a concern with volume, contour, and symmetry; he began to use combinations of plaster, wood, polyester, and metal. From 1962 to 1969, his use of color added formal definition to his work. In 1964 he made symmetrical fabricated steel and fiberglass pieces, with repeated elements; later he turned to various permutations of a few cylindrical units. In 1970 he reacted against his former style, and made several series of works in wood, steel tubes, and bars; these were open, linear, complex, and intuitively constructed.

Tung Ch'i-ch'ang 1555–1636

The Chinese painter Tung Ch'i-ch'ang was a native of Hua T'ing. He was a successful graduate who rose to become an official in the Board of Rites, before retiring to live on his family estates. He was an accomplished painter with impeccable technique, and a great admirer of many old masters, particularly of Mi Fei (1051–1107) and Ni

John Trumbull: The Declaration of Independence, Philadelphia, 4 July 1776; oil on canvas; 51×76cm (20×30in); 1786–1819/20. Yale University Art Gallery, New Haven

Tsan (1301–74). His analytical nature led him to explore the construction and composition of landscape painting. He was a scholar of great erudition, and defined landscape in terms of the paintings of the old masters devoid of vulgarity or sentimentality, of spiritual significance. His own works follow the academic, eclectic tradition to which he was devoted.

With a group of artists known as the Nine Friends, but most notably with Mo Shih-lung, he undertook the study and classification of painting. The group's object was to point the right path for painting. They judged from a moral standpoint not only the painters of the past, but also their contemporaries. At the close of the Ming Dynasty, painting was moving towards a greater diversity of style. The Wu and Che schools had polarized two of the contrasting styles of the previous periods. Tung wished to point out the pitfalls of what he regarded as the superficialities of the Che School, and the painting from which it derived, which he termed the "Northern School". The corollary to this was his wish to evaluate the great line of landscape artists whose work had been inherited by the scholar painter tradition, described by Tung as the "Southern School".

Tung seems to have been the first art historian to do more than list and grade artists, and his classification is extremely perceptive. Unfortunately his strictures rather than his constructive comments have been remembered, and have sometimes inhibited lesser artists. After his day, the movement toward diversification continued; his classification, although preserved and still used, does not readily apply to many great works produced in the 17th century and later.

As a painter, Tung Ch'i-ch'ang shows a certain gracelessness, but he is an unusual Chinese painter in that he is above all a theoretician. His large compositions appear to be mere skeletons of Chinese classical painting. Explicitly working out the structure, he builds ever more convoluted mountains which strain the mechanisms of both surface and recessional composition. There is no place in Tung's large works for nuance or atmosphere. These are not abstractions, but they are analytical, and have the fascination of a com-plex structure. In his album leaves and his less formal painting one sees another side to this versatile artist. His small paintings are almost romantic in style; they are not original, but are more easily appreciated than his large compositions.

Tung Yuan *fl.* 947–70

The Chinese painter Tung Yuan came from the Chiangnan. He was called to the Court of the Southern T'ang during the Five Dynasties, and worked there for Li Hou-Chou, his ruler and patron. He held office as a court painter, and was a master of many styles. Tradition has it that he painted landscape in color in the style of Li Ssu-hsun, and that his figure-painting was meticulous and magically lifelike. It was his ink landscape painting, however, that established his reputation. He is said to have followed Wang Wei, and to have developed a style of soft ink tone, in which—according to contemporary critics—"only at a distance the object is clear". He created atmospheric effects of mist and rain and storm. Very little painting can be attributed as representative of his style. His immense influence on Chinese landscape painting rests on his depiction of soft southern landscape, in which a distant range of hills juts forward in a spur reaching to the foreground. He was also known for his fine painting of the trees, often making a group of contrasted trees form a focal point in a mountain landscape. This feature of his work was later to become an artistic cliché.

Tura Cosmè c1430–95

The Italian painter Cosmè Tura became the first great master of the Ferrarese school. He is recorded in the service of Duke Borso d'Este of Ferrara from 1451; in the following year he became a salaried employee, continuing as court painter until 1486, when he was succeeded by Ercole Roberti. A will made by Tura in 1471 shows that he had accumulated sufficient wealth to provide for the building and decorating of a church, and to bequeath a large sum of money to the poor of Venice. But less than 20 years later, in 1490, he described himself to Duke Ercole d'Este as poor, sick, and unable to work or support himself. The fashion for his idiosyncratic style of painting had evidently passed.

Tura's work for the Ferrarese Court (which included many items other than panel or mural painting) has mainly disappeared. That which survives shows that the most important influence on his style came from Padua, from the Squarcionesque painters, and from Mantegna and Donatello. In addition, Piero della Francesca's lost frescoes in Ferrara were certainly influential. His stylistic development cannot be accurately traced because of the scarcity of dated or datable works. Paintings that probably date from early in his career include *Madonna with the Sleeping Child* (Gallerie dell'Accademia, Venice), the dismembered altarpiece from the Ferrarese church of S. Maria della Consolazione (Musée Fesch, Ajaccio, and Italian public and private collections), and *Allegorical Figure* (National Gallery, London).

The Roverella Altarpiece (National Gallery, London) can be dated fairly precisely to 1474. In it we see many of the characteristic features of Tura's style, such as the wiry outline surrounding his firmly modeled figures, in which surfaces reflect rather

Cosmè Tura: Virgin and Child Enthroned (The Roverella Altarpiece); panel; 239×102cm (94×40in); c1474. National Gallery, London

than absorb light. We also notice his use of bright, flickering colors and of rich decorative details, most of which are derived directly from natural phenomena—especially shells, fish, and fruit. These are the distinguishing features of the Ferrarese school, which flourished during the second half of the 15th century and which included manuscript illuminators as well as panel painters. Other works by Tura, such as the damaged frescoes of the *Months* (Palazzo Schifanoia, Ferrara) and the *Lamentation* from the Roverella Altarpiece (Louvre, Paris), show the artist's abilities both in narrative painting, and in the depiction of pain and passion.

Turnbull William 1922–

The Anglo-Scots sculptor and painter William Turnbull was born in Dundee. He studied at the Slade School of Fine Art, London (1946–8), and then lived in Paris (1948–50). He worked at the Central School of Arts and Crafts, London, as a visiting instructor in Experimental Design (1952–61) and as a teacher of sculpture (1964–71). Since the late 1940s, his sculpture and paintings have emphasized cool simplicity and directness through a repetition of elements. His early stick or line sculptures led, through heads and masks, to stark, upright bronze "idols" and per-

William Turnbull: Head; bronze; height 20cm (8in); 1955. Collection of Mr D. Blinken, New York

J.M.W. Turner: A Scene on the Loire; body color and watercolor on blue-gray paper; 14×19cm (5½×7½in). Ashmolean Museum, Oxford

mutation pieces made of bronze and wood. His emphasis upon the vertical continued in the painted steel tube and zigzag sculptures that he made in the mid 1950s. Until the late 1970s his sculptures were permutations of identical elements, either upright on bases or lying, in metal, perspex, and wood. As a painter, he first produced Dubuffet-like heads, and tachist monochrome works. Later, pure color began to predominate, used in flat planes with borders or stripes, in one or two colors.

Turner J.M.W. 1775–1851

Joseph Mallord William Turner, born in London, was probably the greatest of all British painters, and the greatest landscape painter of the Romantic movement. Though firmly rooted in the academic traditions of the 18th century, his development was unmatched and his range covered all fields, including portraiture.

Turner's earliest artistic activity is said to have been the coloring of prints, which were sold in his father's barbershop. His first signed and dated watercolors were painted in 1786, and his first sketches from nature, in the "Oxford" sketchbook, probably dated from 1789 (British Museum, London). He became a pupil of the architectural topographer Thomas Malton (1748–1804) c1789 and entered the Royal Academy Schools the same year.

His first exhibit at the Royal Academy, the crude watercolor of *The Archbishop's Palace, Lambeth* (Indianapolis Museum of Art), was in 1790. In 1791 he began a series of annual sketching tours in Britain which provided material for highly accomplished topographical watercolors intended for exhibition, for landed patrons, or for engravings. These were in the traditional technique of the "tinted drawing": first a pencil outline, then monochrome washes establishing the broad areas of light and shade, and finally the local color, still restrained in tone.

From c1794 to 1797 Turner spent the winter evenings, together with Thomas Girtin and others, copying drawings by J.R. Cozens and other artists for the famous art connoisseur and collector Dr Monro. This introduced him to a different watercolor tradition, that of generalized, idealized landscapes. Although these depicted recognizable places, they conveyed atmosphere and mood in a freer technique than that of the earlier, topographical works. In 1799, the diarist Joseph Farington recorded that Turner had "no systematic process for making drawings ... By washing and occasionally rubbing out, he at last expresses in some degree the idea in his mind".

In 1796 Turner exhibited his first oil painting, *Fishermen at Sea* (Tate Gallery, London). This is a moonlight scene with

J.M.W. Turner: Snow Storm: Hannibal and his Army Crossing the Alps; oil on canvas; 145×236cm (57×93in); exhibited in 1812. Tate Gallery, London

contrasted warm light from a lamp in the manner of C.J. Vernet, P.J. de Loutherbourg, and Joseph Wright of Derby. In other oils of the later 1790s, such as *Buttermere Lake, a Shower* and *Morning amongst the Coniston Fells, Cumberland* (both Tate Gallery, London), the strongest influence is that of Richard Wilson, but Turner already surpasses his masters in the subtlety of his effects of weather and time of day—an interest echoed in his titles.

Turner was elected an Associate of the Royal Academy in 1799, and a full member in 1802. This early success was accompanied by a determined effort to make his mark with large pictures challenging the Old Masters. *The Fifth Plague of Egypt*, exhibited at the Royal Academy (R.A.) in 1800 (now Indianapolis Museum of Art), rivals Poussin; *Bridgewater Sea-piece* (or *Dutch Boats in a Gale*, R.A. 1801; private collection) brought new energy to the marine tradition that had been introduced into Britain in the 17th century by William van der Velde and his son.

In 1802, Turner's first journey abroad took him to the Savoy Alps. In Paris he visited the Louvre, where he made detailed studies of the Old Masters. His 1803 exhibits included the Titianesque *Holy Family* (Tate Gallery, London). Other works shown that year combined his ambitions more directly with the record of places seen. Among them were *Calais Pier* (National Gallery, London), based on his stormy crossing of the English Channel, the Poussinesque *Château de St Michael, Bonneville, Savoy* (Paul Mellon Center for British Art, New Haven, Conn.), and the Claudian *Festival upon the Opening of the Vintage at Mâcon* Sheffield City Art Galleries). A later example is *Snow Storm: Hannibal and his Army Crossing the Alps* (R.A. 1812; Tate Gallery, London), which combines his experience of the Alps with a dramatic storm he experienced in Yorkshire, a picture inspired by the Romantic interest in Hannibal (the series is described in Mrs Radcliffe's *The Mysteries of Udolpho*, 1794) and by David's *Napoleon Crossing the St Bernard Pass* (1800; Versailles). *Crossing the Brook* (R.A. 1815;

Tate Gallery, London) is an Italianate, Claudian view of the Tamar Valley in Devonshire. The two grand Claudian port scenes, *Dido Building Carthage* (R.A. 1815; National Gallery, London) and *The Decline of the Carthaginian Empire* (R.A. 1817; Tate Gallery, London), are early examples of Turner's preoccupation with the rise and fall of empires, and show the relevance of his painting to contemporary affairs.

His *Liber Studiorum* ("Book of Studies") engravings of landscapes categorized as "Historical", "Mountainous", "Pastoral", "Marine", "Architectural", or "Epic Pastoral", and issued in parts from 1807 to 1819, illustrate Turner's range, and his consciously didactic approach. At the same time, he continued sketching from nature; he produced more intimate landscapes for exhibition, lighter in tone and more atmospheric than his grander historical landscapes. The key works in this development are *Sun Rising through Vapour* (R.A. 1807; National Gallery, London), which also reflects Dutch models, and several groups of sketches on the Thames. Some of these are in pencil and watercolor, as in *The Thames from Reading to Walton* sketchbook (c1806–7; Tate Gallery, London); others are among his rare sketches from nature in oils, both on small mahogany panels and on larger canvases (these probably also date from c1806–7).

The more intimate style he developed appears in commissioned views of houses, such as the pair showing Tabley: *Tabley, the Seat of Sir J.F. Leicester, Bart.: Windy Day* (R.A. 1809; University of Manchester) and *Tabley the Seat of ... Calm Morning* (R.A. 1809; Petworth House, Sussex), *Petworth* (Petworth House, Sussex), and *Somer-Hill* (R.A. 1811; National Gallery of Scotland, Edinburgh). He also employed it in views of less specific locations, such as *Ploughing Up Turnips, near Slough* (1809; Tate Gallery, London) and *Dorchester Mead, Oxfordshire* (1810; Tate Gallery, London). The most considerable group of watercolors was that done for Walter Fawkes, in and around his Yorkshire home, Farnley Hall, between 1809 and 1818 (most of them are still at Farnley Hall). Similar in mood, though rather more finished, were the watercolors done for series of engravings, beginning with *The Southern Coast*, published from 1814 to 1826. In these works Turner's precise sense of locality extended to the depiction of the economic activities typical of each place.

In 1817, after the final defeat of Napoleon, Turner went abroad again, to the Low Countries, partly to gather material for *The Field of Waterloo* (1818; Tate Gallery, London). His journey resulted in a renewed interest in Dutch painting, particularly in the work of Aelbert Cuyp (1620–91); this led to a series of large pictures of harbors, beginning with the *Dort* (R.A. 1818; Paul Mellon Center for British Art, New Haven, Conn.). On the same trip Turner went up the Rhine as far as Mainz. He filled sketchbooks with small studies (in the Turner Bequest in the Tate Gallery, London), on the basis of which he completed, within three months, 51 finished watercolors (examples in the British Museum, London).

Turner's first visit to Italy, long anticipated in his paintings, occurred in 1819. He did a large number of drawings and watercolors in Venice, and in and around Rome and Naples; Venice in particular produced a new purity and delicacy in his colors. But in the next five years he only

exhibited four oil paintings, the lightweight *What you Will*, a pun on Watteau (R.A. 1820; Collection of Sir Michael Sobell, Englefield Green, Surrey), and three large Italian subjects: the artistic manifesto *Rome from the Vatican* (R.A. 1820; Tate Gallery, London), *The Bay of Baiae, with Apollo and the Sybil*, a grand panoramic landscape that set the pattern for several later works (R.A. 1823; Tate Gallery, London) and *Forum Romanum* (R.A. 1826; Tate Gallery, London).

However, it was in the later 1820s that Turner painted the first of the oil sketches, or unfinished pictures, that are now among his most admired works. One group is associated with Petworth House, where the unconventional Third Earl of Egremont even gave Turner a studio. Sketches of c1828 show Petworth Park and neighboring places such as Chichester Canal, more finished versions of which remain at Petworth. Also associated with Petworth, but probably dating from the mid 1830s, are the partly Rembrandt-inspired interiors such as *Music Party, Petworth* (c1835; Tate Gallery, London) and *Interior at Petworth* (c1837; Tate Gallery, London). These grew out of a group of small figure scenes done in body-color on blue paper—a technique developed from the drawings in pencil, pen and white chalk on blue paper, done while Turner was staying with the architect John Nash on the Isle of

Wight in 1827.

On that visit Turner also painted another group of delightful oil sketches. He used some of them for two pictures of *East Cowes Castle, the Regatta Beating to Windward* (R.A. 1828; Indianapolis Museum of Art) and *Starting for their Moorings* (R.A. 1828; Victoria and Albert Museum, London). All of these sketches were painted on two large rolls of canvas (only cut into separate pictures in 1905). This extraordinary procedure saved having separate stretchers, and made for ease of transport; Turner used the method again on his second visit to Italy (1828–9).

This second Italian visit was extremely productive of finished oil paintings, three even being exhibited at Rome: *Orvieto* (1828; reworked 1830; Tate Gallery, London) *Vision of Medea* (1828; Tate Gallery, London), and *Regulus* (1828, reworked 1837; Tate Gallery, London). All were exhibited again back in London, but only after considerable reworking. One of the oil sketches painted in Rome was used for *Ulysses Deriding Polyphemus* (R.A. 1829; National Gallery, London).

The remarkable feature of Turner's reworking was that, from as early as 1815, much of it was done after the paintings had been hung on the walls of the Royal Academy or the British Institution. It took place during the so-called Varnishing Days, which were allowed to members for

J.M.W. Turner: Petworth: Playing Billiards; watercolor on paper; 140×190cm (5½×7½in); c1827–30. Tate Gallery, London

minor adjustments necessitated by accidents of placing or lighting. Of *Orvieto* and *Pilate Washing his Hands* (R.A. 1830; Tate Gallery, London), a critic wrote that it was "difficult to define their subject" when they were first sent in; and of *The Burning of the House of Lords and Commons, 16 October 1834* (R.A. 1835; Philadelphia Museum of Art) E.V. Rippingille wrote that it was, when sent in, "a mere dab of several colors and 'without form and void', like chaos before the Creation". These and similar accounts show that what are now regarded as perhaps Turner's greatest works, the ethereal watercolor-like studies such as *Norham Castle, Sunrise* (c1835-40; Tate Gallery, London) are the chance survivors among oil sketches intended for later completion as pictures for exhibition.

In 1833 Turner exhibited *Bridge of Sighs, Ducal Palace and Custom-House, Venice: Canaletti Painting* (R.A. 1833; Tate Gallery, London), a typical tribute to an earlier painter. It was probably not until later the same year that he returned to Venice, for the first time since 1819. The Venetian pictures he continued to exhibit until 1837, and again from 1840 (the year of his third and last visit) until 1846, were among the most popular of his later works. His early aristocratic patrons had died, or had withdrawn support because of the hostile criticism of the connoisseur Sir George Beaumont. His chief patrons were now mainly *nouveau-riche* manufacturers or dealers. The critics, increasingly baffled by his later style, continued, however, to be impressed by the sheer impact of his work: "gorgeous" and "extravagant" are their most common adjectives. In 1843, Turner found a new champion with the publication of the first volume of John Ruskin's *Modern Painters*.

Turner's later output showed an increasing range of subjects and formats. There were industrial scenes such as *Keelmen heaving in Coals by Night* (R.A. 1835; National Gallery of Art, Washington, D.C.) and four pictures of *Whalers* exhibited in 1845 and 1846; one now in the Metropolitan Museum, New York, the others in the Tate Gallery, London). Pictures pairing ancient and modern Italy and Rome (*Ancient Italy, Ovid Banished from Rome*, R.A. 1838, private collection; *Modern Italy, the Pifferari*, R.A. 1838, Glasgow Art Gallery and Museum; *Ancient Rome...*, R.A. 1839, Tate Gallery, London; *Modern Rome, Campo Vaccino*,

R.A. 1839, private collection) led on to pairs, square or octagonal in shape, of contrasted coloring. These include *Peace—Burial at Sea* and *War—the Exile and the Rock Limpet* (R.A. 1842; both now in the Tate Gallery, London) and the experiments stimulated by reading Charles Eastlake's translation of Goethe's *Theory of Colours* (*Shade and Darkness—the Evening of the Deluge*, R.A. 1843, and *Light and Colour (Goethe's Theory)—the Morning after the Deluge—Moses Writing the Book of Genesis*, R.A. 1843; both Tate Gallery, London).

From c1840 Turner's compositions became rather less disciplined, his colors more broken, and his handling more fragmentary. In his best works the effect is more brilliant than ever, as in *Slavers Throwing Overboard the Dead and the Dying—Typhoon Coming On* (R.A. 1840; Museum of Fine Arts, Boston), *Snow Storm—Steam-Boat off a Harbour's Mouth* (R.A. 1842; Tate Gallery, London), and the apocalyptic *Angel Standing in the Sun* (R.A. 1846; Tate Gallery, London) perhaps intended as a deliberate "last work". In 1847 and 1849 he exhibited three pictures; all were from early in the century, though he repainted two of them. In 1850, in a final effort, he exhibited four pictures on the perennial theme of Carthage. In the exhibition of 1851 he showed nothing, and on 19 December of that year he died.

One great exception to this decline was the series of late Swiss watercolors. In 1842 and 1843 he painted 15 particularly highly finished examples on commission, including the *Red, Blue*, and *Dark Rigis* (National Gallery of Victoria, Melbourne, and private collections). He continued to paint further subjects until at least 1846.

During his lifetime, and for the rest of the 19th century, Turner was admired for his finished works. Only in the 20th century have the riches of his unfinished oils and watercolors become known, through the gradual bringing to light of the Turner Bequest, acquired by the British Nation as the result of his confused and disputed will. It is possible that Turner would have wanted to be judged solely on what he himself defined in his will as his "finished works". An essential part of these was their moral content, often based on mythological, historical, or literary sources—though he had received little academic education, and his reading was enthusiastic rather than thorough. It is a great part

of his achievement that he was able to enlarge the repertoire of his early Academic masterpieces to include scenes of less specific storms, fires, and glowing light, in which he gave expression to the forces of nature and their importance for mankind.

Further reading. Butlin, M. and Joll, E. *The Paintings of J.M.W. Turner* (2 vols.), London and New Haven (1977). Butlin, M., Wilton, A., and Gage, J. *Turner 1775–1851*, London (1974). Gage, J. *Colour in Turner*, London (1969). Gowing, L. *Turner: Imagination and Reality*, New York (1966). Lindsay, J. *J.M.W. Turner: his Life and Work*, London (1966). Wilton, A. *The Life and Work of J.M.W. Turner*, London (1979).

Twachtman John 1853–1902

John Twachtman was an American Impressionist painter who, with Childe Hassam, Theodore Robinson, and J. Alden Weir was part of the American Ten Exhibition in 1898. American Impressionists were among the most popular painters at the turn of the century, yet their art generally placed more emphasis on subject matter than on purely visual sensation, as with their French prototypes. Twachtman worked with Frank Duveneck in Munich during the 1870s. He went to Paris in 1883, and came closer than most of his contemporaries to the art of Monet, especially in late works such as *Hemlock Pool* (1902; Addison Gallery of American Art, Andover, Mass.).

Twombly Cy 1929–

After studying at the Museum of Fine Arts, Boston, the Art Students League, New York, and Black Mountain College, the American painter and graphic artist Cy Twombly moved to Rome in 1957. He developed a distinctive, calligraphic style, his surfaces being covered with seemingly random scribbles and marks, and with occasional scraps of text or diagram. With their emphasis on randomness—Twombly was strongly influenced by John Cage—and process, recording countless graffiti-like marks and erasures, his works reveal a fascination with the deepest sources of creativity. He was inspired by children's art, Surrealist automatism and, more directly, Abstract Expressionism, though his mood is lighter and more ironic.

U

Uccello 1397–1475

Paolo di Dono was a Florentine painter; he was nicknamed "Uccello" (bird) because of his paintings of birds and animals. Younger than Brunelleschi and Donatello, and older than Masaccio, Alberti, and Piero della Francesca, Uccello belonged to a generation of artists concerned with the general movement away from late Gothic forms, towards naturalism. His work is characterized by an obsession with perspective, blended with a passion for clear colors and tapestry-like compositions.

It is recorded that by 1407 Uccello was apprenticed to Lorenzo Ghiberti (1378–1455); he remained in the Ghiberti workshop until 1415, when he joined the guild of painters. Details of Uccello's early activity are not clear, but from 1425 until 1431 he was a master mosaicist at St Mark's in Venice, and was therefore away from Florence during the period when Masaccio was creating the important frescoes in the Brancacci Chapel (1425–8; S. Maria del Carmine, Florence).

Uccello's rapid absorption of new Renaissance ideas on his return to Florence in 1431 is demonstrated by his fresco of Sir John Hawkwood, painted in 1436 on the wall of Florence Cathedral. The foreshortening and modeling give the *trompe-l'oeil* impression that the fresco of this English *condottiere* is a statue—the painting was indeed a substitute for the sculptural effigy originally planned. Uccello's painting of *Four Prophets* of 1443 round the clock face of the cathedral further extends his experiments towards seemingly three-dimensional pictorial space.

In 1445 Uccello painted *The Flood* in the Green Cloister of S. Maria Novella in Florence; here modeling, architectural recession, and light and shadow play important parts. *The Flood* may be seen as a visual interpretation of the theories expounded by Alberti in his *Della Pittura* of 1436. Alberti's two basic art principles—beauty derived from geometry, and decorative form as ornament—are fully realized in this work. Uccello contrasts young, old, clothed, and naked figures, birds, and animals as though to satisfy Alberti's demands in *Della Pittura* for a copious and varied composition. Both the recession to one vanishing point, and the strange doughnut-shaped collar worn by one of the figures in the foreground are characteristic of Uccello's interest in geometrically constructed space.

Uccello's greatest work consists of three panels, painted *c*1456, representing *The Rout of San Romano* (now in the National Gallery, London; the Uffizi, Florence; and the Louvre, Paris). The work was commissioned by Cosimo de' Medici, and doubtless gave great pleasure to his seven-year-old grandson, Lorenzo, for it is a bloodless but action-packed battle scene depicting the triumph of the Florentine army over that of Siena in 1432. On another level, it serves to mark the power of the Medici banking family in Florentine finance and politics. Uccello's work is a magical combination of scientific perspective and festive love of incident and action. Broken lances serve both to suggest the melée of battle, and to act as perspective lines to lead the eye inward towards the horizon. In the London panel, a foreshortened, fallen knight and curved armor form part of the perspectival checkerboard of events. Uccello has neatly dovetailed the new linear perspective with existing rules relating to the visual impression that warm colors, like red, jump forward, and cold colors, like blue or green, recede.

Uccello: St George and the Dragon; tempera on panel; 52×90cm (20×35in); 1456–60. Musée Jacquemart-André, Paris

Uccello: A Hunt in a Forest; detail; tempera on wood; full size 65×165cm (26×65in); c1468. Ashmolean Museum, Oxford

St George and the Dragon (c1455–60; National Gallery, London) uses similar, but less obvious, perspective tricks; the profiled princess still retains an elongated, Gothic quality. The painting is on canvas, rather than the panel which had been more usual, indicating a change in taste: it is a portable possession of beauty, rather than a fixed devotional object. *A Hunt in a Forest* (c1468; Ashmolean Museum, Oxford), possibly Uccello's last work, is a veritable carnival in paint showing a hunting party. The movement of the animals is stylized, with their front legs raised and their back legs on the ground. This is a repetition of the formula used for the horses in *The Rout of San Romano* and *St George and the Dragon* paintings, and perfectly suggests their springiness.

Uccello's lasting achievement was his ability to overlay basic Quattrocento geometric structure with poetic detail, although the skull beneath the skin is always visible.

Further reading. Pope-Hennessy, J. *Paolo Uccello*, London (1969). White, J. *The Birth and Rebirth of Pictorial Space*, London (1957).

Ugolino da Siena *fl.* 1295–c1339

The Sienese painter Ugolino da Siena was sometimes called Ugolino di Nerio. According to Vasari, he was a pupil of Cimabue. He was active in Siena between 1317 and 1327. His only authenticated work is the high altar painted for S. Croce, Florence (c1320?; panels now scattered, between the National Gallery, London, the Staatliche Museen, Berlin, and the Philadelphia Museum of Art). The style of his painting, and even the details of composition, demonstrate how closely he followed Duccio, whose great *Maestà* (Museo del'Opera del Duomo, Siena) was painted between 1308 and 1311.

Ugolino di Vieri *fl.* 1329–85

Ugolino di Vieri was a Sienese goldsmith. His masterpieces are the Reliquary of the Holy Corporal (1338; Orvieto Cathedral) and the Reliquary of S. Savino (c1338; Orvieto Cathedral), the latter made in cooperation with the otherwise unknown Viva di Lando. The former work, nearly 5 ft (145 cm) in height, is formed like a miniature cathedral: it has pinnacles of amazing delicacy, gargoyles, and even a division of the body of the work into "nave" and "aisles". It is decorated with 32 scenes in enamel, of which the Passion subjects show the influence of similar scenes from Duccio's *Maestà* (1308–11; Museo del'Opera del Duomo, Siena). Ugolino's scenes of *The Miracle of Bolsena* and the early life of Christ in the Orvieto Reliquary of the Holy Corporal are close to the frescoes of Ambrogio Lorenzetti (S. Francesco, Siena).

Ulrich von Ensingen c1350–1419

Ulrich von Ensingen was a German master mason. His most important work, from 1392, was at Ulm Minster. Work on the Minster had been started in 1377 by the Parler family. He altered the design by lengthening the nave to ten bays, and broadening the aisles (since subdivided) to the same width as the nave. At the west end he began the huge tower with its triple bay porch. Its openwork masonry style is a typical German late Gothic feature; it was used by Ulrich in his other great work, at Strasbourg Cathedral, where he built the octagon stage of the north tower after 1399. In 1394 he went to Milan to advise on the building of the cathedral, but stayed there only briefly.

Utamaro Kitagawa 1753–1806

The Japanese artist Kitagawa Utamaro was the greatest master of the *Ukiyoe* print. He may have been the son of his teacher Toriyama Sekien (1712–88). Sekien was a *Kano* artist influenced by contemporary naturalism, which shows in his pupil's detailed and delicate printed picturebook of insects, *Ehon Mushi Erabi* (1788), and in the *Kano* and *Shijo* style landscapes in the printed albums *Kyogesubo* ("The Moon-Mad Monk"), and *Ginsekai* ("The Silver World"). These, and other albums and books, are among the world's most beautiful woodblock productions.

Utamaro's true genius, however, was developed in his sheet prints of the *Ukiyoe* world of women and their admirers. In the 1780s he followed the elegant, somewhat static style of Kiyonaga. During the 1790s his genuine obsession with women led him gradually to elongate his subjects into semi-goddesses; his interest in psychology added a new, electric force to the standard eroticism of this sort of print.

The new style, which soon put Kiyonaga out of fashion, first achieved maturity in the erotic masterpiece, the album *The Poem of the Pillow* (1788). Among his innovations were the half-length portrait, and the use of sumptuous mica backgrounds; both features can be seen in the portrait of the teahouse beauty *Ohisa* (British Museum, London). His figures reach an amazing elongation in the series of prints *The Twelve Hours of the Green Houses* (c1795; British Museum, London); the Green Houses were in fact brothels.

Utamaro's later works lack intensity, perhaps because of his dissipated life style, and the death of his mentor, the great publisher Tsutaya. In 1804 he was briefly imprisoned for a politically libelous print of the 16th-century dictator Hideyoshi.

Further reading. Goncourt, E. de *Outamaro: le Peintre des Maisons Vertes*, Paris (1891). Hillier, J. *Utamaro: Colour Prints and Paintings*, Oxford (1979).

Utrillo Maurice 1883–1955

The French painter Maurice Utrillo was born in Paris; he was the illegitimate son of the artist and model, Suzanne Valadon. He began to paint c1902, possibly as a therapeutic activity to counteract alcoholism. He is the epitome of the *peintre maudit*, his life being spent in and out of the sanatorium. His views of Montmartre, generally of a few buildings in sharp perspective, have topographical value; at their best, they also show a poetic sensibility to urban solitude. Utrillo's "White Period" (c1908–16) contains some of his finest work. In the 1920s his palette grew brighter, and hitherto deserted city squares were often enlivened by small figures.

Kitagawa Utamaro: Reclining Lovers; woodblock print; 25×37cm (10×15in). Victoria and Albert Museum, London

V

Valadon Suzanne 1867–1938

The French painter Suzanne Valadon (born Marie Clémentine Valadon) was a seamstress and circus performer before becoming, at the age of 16, a model for artists such as Renoir, Puvis de Chavannes and Toulouse-Lautrec. Renoir and Degas encouraged her to pursue her own talent for painting, and she developed a highly individual style that—combining the influences of Degas, Gauguin and the Nabis—is characterized by strong colors, emphatic contours and clear compositions. Although she painted some landscapes and still lifes, she was mainly a figure painter; her portraits and nudes give a frank and unsentimental view of women that subverts the male images of women found in both academic and avant-garde paintings of the period, as in her well-known *Blue Bedroom* (1923; Museum of Modern Art, Paris), and her nude self-portrait painted when she was 66 (1938; Museum of Modern Art, Paris). She was the mother of Maurice Utrillo.

Further reading. Warnod, J. *Suzanne Valadon*, New York (1981).

Valdés Leal Juan de 1622–90

The Spanish painter and etcher Juan de Valdés Leal was born in Seville, where he mainly worked, though he was also active at Cordoba. He was an outstanding colorist, whose vigorous handling and decorative Baroque style—full of movement—reflect a restless temperament. This can be seen in many religious compositions, for example *The Temptation of St Jerome* and *The Flagellation of St Jerome* (both 1657; Provincial Museum of Fine Arts, Seville). In other works he shows an interest in unusual iconography.

Valdés Leal's originality is most evident in his *Vanitas* subjects, notably those inscribed *Finis Gloriae Mundi* ("The end of the glory of the world") and *In Ictu Oculi* ("In the blinking of an eye"), the most gruesome and terrifying reminders of the transience of human life ever painted (1672; Charity Hospital, Seville).

Juan de Valdés Leal: St Jerome; oil on canvas; 211×131cm (83×52in). Prado, Madrid

Valentin de Boulogne 1594–1632

The Caravaggesque painter Valentin de Boulogne was active in Rome from c1614 until his early death. Despite his French origin, he seems to have received his entire training in Italy, and even his earliest works are marked by the uncompromising naturalism and powerful chiaroscuro effects of Caravaggio. His subject matter, like that of Bartolomeo Manfredi (c1580–c1620), was also inspired by the example of Caravaggio, in particular by that master's early works, depicting scenes from the low life.

Vallotton Félix 1865–1925

Félix Vallotton was a Swiss artist and engraver whose graphic work placed him among the leaders of the Parisian avant-garde during the 1890s. Born in Lausanne, he trained in Paris at the École des Beaux-Arts and at the Académie Julian. He formed a friendship with Charles Maurin, a Symbolist artist, pioneer woodblock engraver, and social critic. Maurin's influence, together with the 1890 Paris exhibition of Japanese woodblock prints, led Vallotton to reject the sober realism of his early paintings. In 1891 he embarked upon the production of radically simplified woodcuts and lithographs, such as *Burial* (1891), *Assassination* (1893), *The Demonstration* (1893). These depict everyday Parisian life, Swiss landscapes, portraits of leading politicians, writers, and artists, often with social and political satire. He was a friend of the Nabis group, exhibited with them, and collaborated with them on one of the leading avant-garde reviews, *La Revue Blanche* ("The White Review"). By 1901, he had virtually abandoned printed work; instead he began to paint nudes in the style of J.-A.-D. Ingres, such as *Reclining Nude on a Red Carpet* (1910; Petit Palais, Geneva), and landscapes that were indebted to Nicolas Poussin.

Vanbrugh John 1664–1726

The English Baroque architect Sir John Vanbrugh was born in London. He received an army commission in 1686, and was already a successful playwright before he turned his talents—"without thought or lecture"—to architecture. It is not certain when he did this, but by 1799 his reputation was sufficiently well established for him to replace the Comptroller General of the King's Works, William Talman, as the Earl of Carlisle's architect at Castle Howard; his subsequent career was almost exclusively that of a country-house architect working for the Whig aristocracy. It was through this connection that he was appointed Comptroller General in 1702, and received the commission for Blenheim Palace in 1704. He was knighted in 1714.

The speed with which Vanbrugh's mature style emerged belied his lack of formal training. It almost certainly reflected his early association with Nicholas Hawksmoor, Wren's assistant in the Office of Works. Hawksmoor's influence is discernible at Castle Howard, Yorkshire (1699–1726), where the open courtyard arrangement brilliantly paraphrased Christopher Wren's first plan for Greenwich Hospital. Blenheim Palace, Woodstock, Oxfordshire (1705–20), repeated the arrangement, but introduced the principle of compositional movement. This was probably inspired by the example of Elizabethan architecture, and was achieved by the bold massing of wings, pavilions, porticos, and colonnades; each feature varied in height and recession, to produce a theatrical effect that immediately distinguishes Vanbrugh's work from Wren's more cerebral Baroque.

Seaton Delaval, Northumberland (1720–8), Grimthorpe, Lincolnshire (1723–4), and the architect's own house, Vanbrugh Castle, Greenwich (1717), are the most impressive of his late works. The latter—castellated and (after the addition of a south wing in 1720) irregular—provided a remarkable precedent for the asymmetrical Picturesque castles popularized by John Nash early in the 19th century.

Further reading. Bingham, M. *Masks and Facades: Sir John Vanbrugh, the Man and his Setting*, London (1974). Downes, K. *Vanbrugh*, London (1977). Webb, G. *The Complete Works of Sir John Vanbrugh*, London (1928).

Van Loo family 18th century

Although they were of Flemish origin, the Van Loo family dominated French painting in the middle of the 18th century. Jean-Baptiste (1684–1745) was the oldest. He trained in Italy before settling in Paris with his brother Carle in 1719. Jean-Baptiste's two sons, Amédée (1715–95) and Louis-Michel (1707–71), as well as his much younger brother Carle (Charles-André, 1705–65) were all taught by him.

Carle was the most successful member of

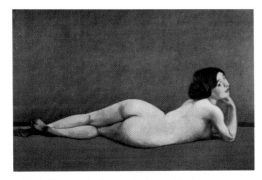

Félix Vallotton: Reclining Nude on a Red Carpet; oil on canvas; 73×100cm (29×39in); 1910. Petit Palais, Geneva

the family, though his work was insipid and dull compared with that of his contemporary and traveling companion, François Boucher. The dominating position of the family was not due to great originality or inspiration: it owed more to the wide range of their productions, which included huge altarpieces, royal portraits, and even exotic boudoir scenes.

Vantongerloo Georges 1886–1965

Born in Antwerp, the Belgian artist Georges Vantongerloo was primarily a sculptor, but also a man of many ideas. He joined the De Stijl group in 1917, its first year. His Abstract sculptures of this period, with their interlocking masses, often resemble three-dimensional jigsaw puzzles; they are explorations in the interpenetration of planes and solids (for example, *Construction*, 1917; Philadelphia Museum of Art). These enquiries into spatial relationships were of significance for later De Stijl architectural projects, such as those by Theo van Doesburg and Cornelis van Eesteren of 1923.

Vantongerloo left De Stijl in 1921. In the 1930s he was active in the Parisian Constructivist art circles centered round the magazines *Cercle et Carré* and *Abstraction-Création*.

Vanvitelli Luigi 1700–73

Although of Flemish origin, the architect Luigi Vanvitelli was born in Naples and brought up in Rome. "Vanvitelli" is an Italian rendering of his family name, van Wittel. After he had worked in Rome, Ancona, and Loreto, he was awarded an important commission in 1751 by Charles III: to build a palace in Caserta to house the large court. The facade of the palace is often criticized as monotonous, but it was not built with all the features that Vanvitelli had intended. Within, the palace is notable for the axial play by which the four courtyards are related, and for the monumental staircase. He also designed churches and various public works, including an aqueduct.

Vasarely Victor 1908–

The painter Victor Vasarely was born at Pecs, Hungary, and was trained in the design aesthetic of the Budapest "Bauhaus" from 1928 to 1929. In 1930 he left Hungary for Paris, where he worked as a graphic and commercial artist for a number of years. He made his first optical works in the 1930s, but did not evolve his characteristic, geometrical-abstract style until the early 1950s. His so-called "kinetic" works either involve actual movement by the spectator, or give an impression of movement (for example, *Ondho*, 1956–60; Museum of Modern Art, New York). This can be experienced either on a small scale, or in certain large environmental projects that Vasarely has carried out. In the 1960s he progressed from black and white to color and three-dimensional objects. He also moved into the field of mass-produced "multiples" in which a single picture is mass-produced by industrial method.

Further reading. Clay, J. "Vasarely: a Survey of his Work". *The Studio* vol. CLXXIII, London (May, 1967). Joray, M. (ed.) *Vasarely*, Neuchâtel (1965). Rotzler, W. "Victor Vasarely", *Graphis* vol. 27, Geneva (1972).

Vasari Giorgio 1511–73

The Italian painter, architect, and historian Giorgio Vasari was born in Arezzo. He began his training there before moving to Florence in 1524, first to the studio of Andrea del Sarto, then to that of Baccio Bandinelli. After journeys to Bologna and Arezzo, he made two visits to Rome. The first of these was in 1532, together with Francesco Salviati; the second was in 1538. It was during this visit that Vasari abandoned his early style, which had developed from Florentine painting of the 1520s, in favor of the Mannerism of Salviati's 1538 *Visitation* fresco (1538; S. Giovanni Decollato, Rome).

Vasari was an enormously prolific and popular painter, especially in Florence.

Victor Vasarely: Sirius II; oil on canvas; 30×20cm (12×8in); 1954. Galerie Denise René, Paris

The Sala dei Cento Giorni in the Cancelleria, Rome, gives an indication of his eclectic style. The scheme derives from that of Peruzzi's for the Sala delle Prospettive (in the Farnesina, Rome); like that work it is enriched with niches for the flanking allegorical figures. The figures seated above the cornice reflect those in Perino's Sala Paolina (Castel S. Angelo, Rome), begun the previous year. The episodes are extended into the spectator's space by steps that reflect those designed by Bramante for the Belvedere. The individual figures abound in artistic quotations, es-

Above: Giorgio Vasari: Self-portrait; oil on canvas; 101×80cm (40×31in); 1568–8. Uffizi, Florence

pecially from Michelangelo.

Vasari's major achievement was his *Vite* (*Le Vite dei più Eccellenti Architetti, Pittori, e Scultori Italiani . . .*, *The Lives of the Most Eminent Italian Architects, Painters, and Sculptors*), first published in 1550, revised and expanded version published in 1568. The work established a framework for all subsequent accounts of the Renaissance: its birth (Giotto and the Trecento), its growth (the Quattrocento), and its climax (the High Renaissance and Michelangelo).

Vasari's ability as a painter cannot match his talents either as an historian or as an architect. The end of the 16th century saw an unparalleled growth in the number of official buildings, as houses for new bureaucracies. Few of these new buildings can rival Vasari's Uffizi, designed in 1560. Its long facade is enlivened by motifs borrowed from Michelangelo and Peruzzi. It is further distinguished by the loggia on the ground floor (inspired by that of Sansovino's Library in Venice), which, together with the layout of the twin facades, distantly evokes a Roman forum.

Vecchietta c1412–80

Lorenzo di Pietro, known as Vecchietta, was an artist of the Sienese school; he worked as a painter, miniaturist, sculptor, and architect. He probably trained under

Vecchietta: The Virgin Receives the Souls of Foundlings (The Ladder of Paradise); fresco; c1446–9. S. Maria della Scala, Siena

Sassetta, but was influenced by contemporary Florentine art early in his career. Vecchietta's painting style combined naturalism with a talent for narrative description. Much patronized by Sienese institutions, such as the town government and the hospital of S. Maria della Scala, he left works in various media which were to have considerable influence on artists of the later 15th century. Among the most important of his surviving works are *The Ladder of Paradise* (fresco; c1446–9; S. Maria della Scala, Siena), *St Catherine* (fresco; 1461; Palazzo Pubblico, Siena), triptych (1461; Pienza Cathedral), and a bronze *ciborium* (1467–72; Siena Cathedral).

Velázquez Diego 1599–1660

The Spanish painter Diego Rodríguez de Silva y Velázquez was born in Seville. He was of aristocratic Portuguese descent on his father's side, but the surname he chose

to use was that of his mother. He was apprenticed to Francisco Pacheco in Seville from 1611 to 1617, and later married his master's daughter.

Some of Velázquez' earliest paintings were religious compositions, but most were of the type known as *bodegón* (the word means eating-house or tavern). They contain naturalistic figures in an interior, preparing or consuming food or drink. *Christ in the House of Martha* (1618; National Gallery, London) combines elements of both religious and *bodegón* types. The main incident takes place in the background, and is seen through an opening in the wall (or reflected in a mirror). The artist's skill in realistic representation of inanimate objects is apparent in the garlic, red pepper, fish, eggs, and simple utensils in the foreground.

In these early *bodegones*, a strong light from low on the left illuminates the scene, as in the *Old Woman Frying Eggs* (1618;

National Gallery of Scotland, Edinburgh) and *The Water-Seller* (c1620; Wellington Museum, London). These works are almost tenebrist in character. A similar light effect is seen in some early religious compositions, like the *Immaculate Conception* and *St John the Evangelist* (c1618; National Gallery, London). The effect is even more striking in the *Adoration of the Magi* (1619; Prado, Madrid), which is certainly tenebrist. This work is close to being Caravaggesque, whether by direct influence from works of Caravaggio or through parallel tendencies among Spanish contemporaries, is uncertain.

The earliest dated portraits by Velázquez date from 1620. That of the nun *Jerónima de la Fuente* (Prado, Madrid) shows a full-length monumental figure, firmly modeled in a brown habit against a dull green background. The painting is impressive in its characterization and in its simple pattern.

Recognizing his son-in-law's ability, Pacheco encouraged him to seek connections at court and to visit El Escorial. In April 1622, Velázquez went to Madrid for about two months. There he was received by fellow-Andalusians who moved in the circle of Philip IV's favorite, Don Gaspar de Guzmán (later Count-Duke of Olivares). Velázquez executed a portrait of the famous poet *Don Luis de Góngora* (Museum of Fine Arts, Boston), but did not realize his ambition to paint the sovereign. Nevertheless the portrait of Góngora had made a great impression, with its characterization and its subtle modeling in planes (not to be paralleled until Cézanne). Velázquez was soon recalled to Madrid by Olivares.

This time he went accompanied by Pacheco, in July 1623. A month later he painted a full-length portrait of Philip IV and in October was taken into the King's service. However, a bust of *Philip IV* painted shortly afterwards (Meadows Museum and Sculpture Court, Dallas, Texas) is close in its firm outlines and restrained color to the Boston *Góngora*, and is more realistic than the idealized portraits of the King painted in the early 1630s, such as the full-length in brown and silver in the National Gallery, London.

By this period Velázquez had progressed in his career, becoming an Usher of the Chamber in 1627, meeting Rubens in Madrid in 1628, and visiting Italy from 1629 to 1631. He had also executed an important large group of nine figures in *The Triumph of Bacchus*, popularly known as *Los Borrachos* ("The Topers"; 1628–9; Prado, Madrid). In spite of damage and cutting down, the picture is notable for its freedom of handling and its naturalistic conception. It depicts semi-nudes alongside a group of realistic figures, comparable with those in his early *bodegones*. Behind them lies a bleak, broad, windswept landscape of a type that Velázquez was to use in his outdoor portraits of the 1630s. *Los Borrachos* was not a mythological scene but a modern burlesque of one, a realistic piece of playacting on a popular level.

Half-nude figures appear again in two large compositions that Velázquez executed in Italy in 1630 and took back to Spain: *The Forge of Vulcan* (Prado, Madrid) and *Jacob's Coat* (The Escorial, near Madrid). Both are naturalistic; the placing of the figures in space is more skillful than in his earlier works, and the light effects more subtle. Particularly in *Jacob's Coat*, a Venetian refinement of color reflects the painter's widened experience.

On his first visit to Italy, Velázquez also probably painted two small views of *The Garden of the Villa Medici* (Prado, Madrid). In these he gave free rein to his sensitivity to landscape, the figures being subordinated to it for the first time. The vigorous handling and impasto of these atmospheric sketches recall the work of Titian; we know, from an account by Pacheco, that Velázquez imitated Titian's style in a lost self-portrait.

On returning to Madrid, Velázquez hastened to paint the King, and his son and heir *Baltasar Carlos* (1631; Museum of Fine Arts, Boston). In this first portrait of the Prince, at the age of 16 months, he is accompanied by a dwarf. The infant's superior status is emphasized by the more even light on him and the smoother handling of his face. The warm colors, dominated by deep red tones, seem to revolve round the highlight of his sash. Baltasar Carlos was painted again in a similar attitude, but this time alone and in a cooler color-scheme (1632; Wallace Collection, London). These two entrancing child portraits were to be followed by others, showing the Prince on horseback, in hunting dress, and in the riding school. They de-

monstrate Velázquez' unique flair for portraying the charms of childhood.

These outdoor portraits, and others of Philip IV, the Cardinal-Infante Fernando, and Olivares, were painted between 1633 and 1636. They were intended either for Philip's new Buen Retiro Palace, or for the reconstructed hunting lodge, the Torre de la Parada. For the Palace, Velázquez also painted the large group picture of *The Surrender of Breda* (1634–5; Prado, Madrid). Here the figures are arranged in balanced masses, parallel to the picture-plane in classical fashion, rather than with Baroque diagonal movement. They are seen against a magnificent atmospheric landscape background of immense depth. *The Boar Hunt* (c1636–7; National Gallery, London), from the Torre de la Parada, contains a colorful array of crisply painted figures on a smaller scale. They are in a more enclosed setting, but the landscape and the fresh air are a major feature of the work.

In 1631, Juan Bautista Martínez del Mazo became Velázquez' assistant, and in 1633 his son-in-law. In 1634, the master transferred to him his post of Usher of the Chamber. Velázquez himself continued to receive favors from Philip IV, who frequently visited his studio in the Alcázar to watch him paint. In 1636 he became Gentleman of the Wardrobe, and in 1643 Gentleman of the Bedchamber. Like his later promotions, however, these honors involved him in prolonged struggles with the exchequer officials, in attempts to obtain not only his increased salary, but earlier arrears.

Some outstanding works date from the late 1630s and 1640s, including *The Lady with a Fan* (c1638–9; Wallace Collection, London), the epitome of Spanish womanhood, brilliantly toneful and sensitively handled. The dignified *Philip IV in Military Dress* (1644; Frick Collection, New York) is a beautiful harmony of red, silver, gray, and black. The large *The Fable of Arachne* (c1644–8; Prado, Madrid) is popularly known as *Las Hilanderas* ("The Tapestry Weavers"). In this painting the varied depth of shadow and diffused light of the foreground are effectively contrasted with the brighter light that is concentrated on the figures representing the main incident in a background recess. The groups of figures are arranged symmetrically on central axes formed by the darkest figure in the foreground and the brightest of the group behind. Both groups recede so little

Diego Velázquez: Immaculate Conception; oil on canvas; 135×102cm (53×40in); c1618. National Gallery, London

in depth (in spite of some diagonal movement away from the central figures) that this is really a classical rather than a Baroque composition. Especially remarkable are the modeling of forms, by the imperceptible melting of tones into each other, and the skillful placing of the figures in depth, by subtly varied handling and the elimination of unnecessary detail.

Both *Las Hilanderas*, and *The Toilet of Venus* (c1644–8; National Gallery, London), Velázquez' only female nude, were probably executed for private patrons. The composition of the latter, based on a system of sweeping curves, is a triumph of discretion, with the model seen from behind and her face reflected imprecisely in the mirror. Her softly modeled body is in the center of the color scheme of unusual harmonies of crimson, gray, and blue.

Late in 1648, Velázquez left Madrid with his assistant, Juan de Pareja, on his second journey to Italy. His purpose was to ac-

quire paintings by Italian masters and casts of antique statues for the Royal Palace in Madrid. In Rome he painted several portraits of members of the Papal Court, culminating in *Pope Innocent X* (1650; Galleria Doria Pamphili, Rome). The realistic characterization of the seated Pope, the tonal rendering of his vestments, and the superbly expressive brushwork make this a masterpiece of formal portraiture. As a preparation for his exacting task, Velázquez had painted an informal half-length portrait of *Juan de Pareja* (1649–50; Metropolitan Museum, New York). Here the handling is vigorous and free, yet so assured that when it was exhibited it achieved immediate fame.

Returning to Madrid in 1651, Velázquez portrayed Philip IV's newly married second wife, *Queen Mariana of Austria* (1652; Prado, Madrid). He also painted a bust of Philip IV (c1652; Prado, Madrid) in which the monarch looks weary and disillusioned. Velázquez' appointment as

Chief Steward of the Palace in 1652 imposed on him responsibilities so onerous that he had little time for painting. His output in the 1650s was considerably reduced, at the time when his artistic powers were at their greatest. They were, however, displayed to the full in the portrait of Mariana's daughter, the *Infanta Margarita* (1653; Kunsthistorisches Museum, Vienna). This is one of the most alluring pictures of childhood ever created, with entrancing color harmonies of silver, pink, and black in the dress, and red, ocher, and blue in the carpet and tablecloth. A freely brushed glass vase of colorful flowers on the table notably extends these harmonies.

All the brilliant qualities of Velázquez' maturity reached their climax in the large interior group portrait of *The Royal Family*, popularly known as *Las Meninas*, "The Maids of Honor" (1656; Prado, Madrid). The Infanta Margarita is in the foreground with two of her maids of honor

Diego Velázquez: The Toilet of Venus (The Rokeby Venus); oil on canvas; 122×177cm (48×70in); c1648–51. National Gallery, London

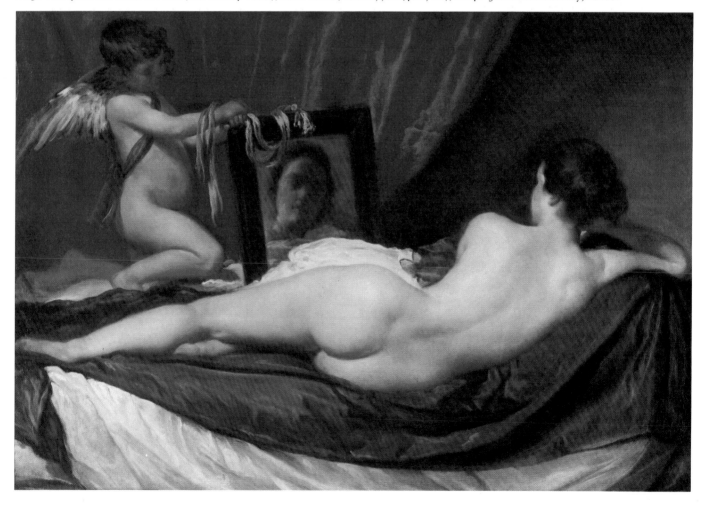

and two dwarfs; Philip IV and Queen Mariana are seen reflected in the mirror in the back wall. Velázquez himself, with his brush in hand, stands in front of his large canvas on the left. With astonishing success, the painter has resolved unusual problems of space, perspective, and light. He has unified a complicated composition by his complete command of color and tones, together with skillfully varied brushwork.

Negotiations for the admission of Velázquez as a Knight of the Order of Santiago began in 1658. The prolonged investigation of the painter's antecedents lasted into the following year; his claim was supported by over 100 witnesses, including the painters Zurbarán and Alonso Cano, who had known him in his youth in Seville. But the honor finally accorded to Velázquez at the end of 1659 was not to give him satisfaction for long. His official duties in connection with the Treaty of the Pyrenees, signed by Philip IV and Louis XIV in June 1660, were so exacting that Velázquez eventually returned to Madrid exhausted and died in August of that year.

Though he never approached the inventiveness of Rubens, or the psychological penetration of Rembrandt, and in composition was often more classical than Baroque, Velázquez is one of the great masters of the Baroque age. He is the greatest of all Spanish painters, through his ability to make a satisfying pattern out of every composition, his characterization, and the technical skill with which he realized his intentions. He was, however, a slow worker, in spite of his apparently free brushwork, and he was a perfectionist—as many *pentimenti* in his paintings demonstrate. The number of his works is thus regrettably small.

The steady output of replicas of royal portraits from Velázquez' studio shows that the master employed many assistants, but few of them are identifiable as individual artistic personalities. Even of Martínez del Mazo and Pareja only a few certain works are known. Velázquez' influence was, however, widespread in Spain, affecting first his contemporaries Zurbarán and Cano, then Carreño, Murillo, and Claudio Coello, and later Goya. The works of Terborch, Manet, and J.S. Sargent bear witness to the appeal his paintings have had in other countries.

Further reading. Ferrari, E.L. *Velázquez*, London and New York (1945). Gudiol, J.

Esaias van de Velde: A Winter Landscape; oil on panel; 26×30cm (10×12in); 1623. National Gallery, London

Velázquez, London (1974). Justi, C. *Velázquez und sein Jahrhundert*, Bonn (1888). López-Rey, J. *Velázquez*, Lausanne (1978). López-Rey, J. *Velázquez: a Catalogue Raisonné of his Oeuvre*, London (1963). Pantorba, B. de *La Vida y la Obra de Velázquez*, Madrid (1955). Trapier, E. du Gué *Velázquez*, New York (1948).

Velde Esaias van de c1591–1630

The Dutch artist Esaias van de Velde was born in Amsterdam. He painted a few semididactic genre pieces of gallant companies feasting, and he also produced pictures of cavalry skirmishes and scenes of plunder. His most typical works, however, are landscapes. These are of his native countryside at different seasons, and are among the first realist landscape paintings of the 17th century. They are characterized by a combination of accuracy of detail and a sense of atmosphere and spaciousness. The color schemes in his mature work tend increasingly towards monochrome. His pictures are often filled with figures, but he abandoned other traditional practices, such as the use of "stage wings" and the bird's eye viewpoint. He had a profound influence on his famous pupil, Jan van Goyen.

Velde Henry van de 1863–1957

Born in Antwerp, the Belgian architect Henry van de Velde studied painting there and in Paris (1884–5). During the early 1890s he was attracted to the work of the English Arts and Crafts movement, and to the ideas of William Morris. In 1892 he turned to graphic design and typography, inventing a style that reflected his interest in Post-Impressionist painting, particularly the work of Gauguin. His first major piece of applied art was the interior of his own house (which he had also built) at Uccle, near Brussels (1895). In 1896 he designed four rooms for Samuel Bing's shop in Paris, "L'Art Nouveau", and in the following year much of this work was exhibited at Dresden.

Unlike that of Victor Horta, van de Velde's brand of Art Nouveau has little direct relationship with nature. Space in his buildings is molded by dynamic but controlled lines of force, further emphasized by the shapes of furniture and furnishings.

Between 1900 and 1914 Van de Velde's career was spent in Germany. In 1901 he was called to Weimar, where he became artistic adviser to the Duke of Saxe-Weimar. His work anticipated the ideals of the Deutscher Werkbund, founded in 1907

Willem van de Velde the Younger: The Battle of Texel; oil on canvas; 150×300cm (59×118in); 1687. National Maritime Museum, Greenwich, London

to improve standards of design in industry. Van de Velde believed in an intuitive approach to design, and could not agree with the Werkbund's new theories of standardization and type. At the Werkbund Exhibition in Cologne in 1914 (to which he contributed the theater), his architecture had already begun to look old-fashioned. In 1914 he resigned his post as Director of the Weimar School of Arts and Crafts, and Walter Gropius took over.

The best-known work of van de Velde's later years is the Kröller-Müller Museum at Otterlo in Holland (1937–54).

Velde family 17th century

Willem van de Velde the Younger (1633–1707), the greatest and most productive of all Dutch marine painters, was the pupil of the marine and landscape artist Simon de Vlieger (c1600–53). His early works are primarily straightforward seascapes, but ships and naval battles become increasingly prominent in his paintings, especially after he arrived in London in 1672 with his father, Willem van de Velde the Elder (1611–93). He was subsequently employed there as an official marine artist. His precise knowledge of ship construction

was mainly learned from his father, who was a nautical draftsman. The two artists collaborated on many paintings, the son coloring his father's outline drawings. Willem the Younger's marine paintings depict every weather condition, from gale to calm. Their accurately observed effects of light and atmosphere—a great advance on the achievements of earlier painters—were imitated by many English followers, and were particularly admired by J.M.W. Turner and John Constable in the 19th century.

Adriaen van de Velde (1636–72), the brother of Willem the Younger, trained under his father and also with the Dutch landscapist Jan Wijnants (c1630/5–84). He painted almost every kind of subject, but is chiefly known for peaceful, sunny landscapes in which figures and grazing animals are prominent. He also produced some winter landscapes, and a few very beautiful beach scenes which have a high-keyed sparkle and lucidity. These paintings, and some etchings of landscapes with cattle, are complemented by a number of idyllic southern landscapes composed of Italianate motifs gleaned from the work of other artists. Adriaen sometimes provided the figures in pictures by other landscape painters.

Verhulst Rombout 1624–98

The Flemish sculptor Rombout Verhulst was active in the northern Netherlands. Born in Malines, Verhulst trained there and in Antwerp. It is uncertain whether he ever visited Italy, but he was living in Amsterdam by 1646. He enlisted as a stonemason in the guild in 1652, and signed several of the most beautiful reliefs, among them *Silence* and *Fidelity*, in the new Amsterdam Town Hall. He obviously enjoyed a higher standing than the other assistants in the workshop of the master sculptor of the project, Artus Quellinus.

Verhulst subsequently turned to carving funeral monuments, including those of Admiral Tromp (c1654; The Old Church, Delft), and Admiral de Ruyter (c1676; The New Church, Amsterdam). He adapted the local tradition of using variously colored marbles for the architecture and figurative carvings, but infused them with a new monumentality. His effigies are extremely realistic, with a sensuous appreciation of surface textures in the flesh of the faces and hands, and in the freely flowing hair. His sculpture has a robust, Rubensian feeling, conveyed with a brilliant technique of handling marble. He modeled in clay as a preliminary to such schemes, and the sketches that survive have an astounding immediacy (there are examples in the Rijksmuseum, Amsterdam).

The monuments have complex, Baroque cartouches framing the inscriptions, and coats of arms, populated by plump *putti* and other allegorical figures. He naturally applied his talent for portraiture to the carved portrait bust, with results that surpass the paintings of his Dutch contemporaries. Verhulst was also expert in carving narrative scenes in low relief; such scenes traditionally appeared on tombs and on the exteriors of certain public buildings in the Netherlands, for example on the Buttery in Leiden. His style of sculpture prevailed throughout the north Netherlands all during the second half of the 17th century, and forms a crucial component in any estimate of Dutch art in that period.

Vermeer Jan 1632–75

Jan Vermeer van Delft was a Dutch painter who came from Delft. His response to the transient beauty of light and colored surfaces, and his impeccable sense of design, place him among the greatest of all European artists. Very little is known of his life. He was the son of a silk-weaver who also dealt in paintings. His teacher is not known, but certain works suggest that he may have been a pupil of Carel Fabritius, three of whose paintings Vermeer owned at his death. He appears to have inherited his father's art-dealing business, and although he joined the Delft Guild of Painters in 1653, dealing seems to have been his primary source of income. His pictures were used as deposits for unpaid bills, but there are no records of any sales during his lifetime. This has been put forward as a reason why there are so few works by him: fewer than 40 certainly attributable works survive, and these are mostly quite small. There may be some truth in the suggestion that he worked only in his spare time, mainly for his own pleasure, producing perhaps only two or three pictures a year. This may also explain why he was so little known as an artist in his lifetime.

Vermeer's earliest works have religious and mythological themes. They include *Christ in the House of Mary and Martha* (National Gallery, Edinburgh), a painting that relates in its forms and colors to those of Utrecht School artists like Hendrick Terbrugghen, and *Diana and her Companions* (Royal Museum of Art, Mauritshuis, The Hague). The earliest dated painting is

The Procuress (1656; Gemäldegalerie Alte Meister, Dresden), in which warm yellows and reds echo the colors of Rembrandt school paintings of the 1650s. The later works are generally domestic interiors; in these we see one or two figures, arrested in a moment of time as they occupy themselves with such recreational activities as reading or writing letters, playing musical instruments, drinking, or talking. Occasionally the theme is that of domestic work (as in *The Lacemaker*; Louvre, Paris). In all these later pictures, Vermeer invests essentially mundane activities with a significance out of all proportion to their apparent importance.

His interiors convey an impression of stillness and serenity; an effect that is largely due to his purity of color (in which, after the early period, cool blues and yellows predominate), and his limpid, radiant light. There is an exhilarating, sensuous quality in Vermeer's light, and also in the pearly, translucent highlights that bathe the objects in his paintings— particularly smooth or semitransparent objects, such as jewels. In later pictures Vermeer emphasized the shimmering effect created by the fall of light by using a meticulous *pointillé* technique in which highlights were broken up into very small touches of paint. The soft translucency of Vermeer's light and color has been compared to the glazes on earthenware; this

Jan Vermeer: The Lacemaker; oil on canvas; 24×21cm (9×8in); c1665. Louvre, Paris

has led some writers to speculate that the artist might once have been engaged in the painting of the tiles and dishes for which Delft was celebrated in the 17th century.

The compositions of Vermeer usually contain very carefully placed horizontals and verticals which are extremely important components of the design. The linear framework formed by rectangular mirrors and maps creates essentially static compositions that enhance the paintings' sense of tranquillity. Spatial organization is generally also complex. There is sometimes little recession, with the image confined to a single figure against a plain background: a figure which, however, has a monumental impact, bearing no relation to the small scale of the painting (for example, *Maidservant Pouring Milk*; Rijksmuseum, Amsterdam). Every object in Vermeer's designs has importance as an abstract volume or shape to the extent that nothing could be altered without destroying the overall harmony. But it is misleading to overemphasize the purely formal aspect of his work: although Vermeer ignores the love of anecdote and incident typical of Dutch genre scenes, his paintings sometimes have a meaning that is not immediately apparent. The musical scenes, for instance, may be representations of profane love; the *Woman Weighing Gold* (National Gallery of Art, Washington, D.C.) represents Vanity.

Symbolism is more obtrusive in a few other paintings, notably in the *Allegory of the New Testament* (Metropolitan Museum, New York) and also in an allegory on the art of painting known as *The Painter in his Studio* (Kunsthistorisches Museum, Vienna). This last work is unusual in Vermeer's oeuvre for its larger scale, as is one of the artist's rare townscapes, the luminous *A View in Delft* (Royal Museum of Art, Mauritshuis, The Hague). In *A View in Delft* (a painting much admired by Van Gogh) and other pictures, the precision of line and detail probably derives from the use of the camera obscura.

Vermeer's work had little influence on other painters. The artist was largely forgotten after his death, and it was not until the 1860s, at the time of the developing interest in naturalism, that he was rescued from relative obscurity. Despite criticisms

that his work lacks invention or emotional content, Vermeer's reputation has increased spectacularly in the 20th century. This is due both to his historical importance and to the intrinsic qualities of his work. His fame has led to many attempts at forgeries.

Further reading. Blankert, A. *Vermeer of Delft*, Oxford (1978). Goldscheider, L. *Jan Vermeer: the Paintings*, London (1967). Gowing, L. *Vermeer*, London (1970).

Vernet Claude-Joseph 1714–89

Claude-Joseph Vernet was a French painter of marine subjects and landscapes. He was trained at Avignon and Aix-en-Provence, and then spent the years 1734 to 1753 working in Italy. There, mainly in Rome, he was the leading painter of marines, evoking the Italian coastline in a manner derived from the early works of Claude Lorrain, or depicting storms and shipwrecks that appealed to pre-Romantic sensibility. He also made landscapes based on Rome and the surrounding Campagna, derived from paintings by Gaspard Dughet, Luigi Vanvitelli, and Andrea Locatelli. He worked for the great Roman families, for French visitors to Rome, and especially for English clients who were making the Grand Tour. His works were admired for their vivid impression of nature, and for their subtle control of tone and light.

In 1753 Vernet began a series of 16 views of the major French seaports (now in the Musée de la Marine, Paris, and the Louvre, Paris); they occupied him until 1765. This was one of the largest official commissions of paintings during the reign of Louis XV. The views are remarkable records of French port life in the 18th century, and important examples of precisely observed realism in a predominantly Rococo age. Vernet continued to paint Italianate landscapes, seascapes, and shipwrecks for an international clientèle, but these eventually became repetitive, and rather dry in style.

Veronese 1528–88

The Venetian painter Paolo Caliari was known as Veronese, because he was born in Verona. By 1541 he was the pupil of the Veronese painter Antonio Badile (1517–60), whose daughter he married in 1566. He is not recorded in Venice until 1555, but he was probably working there a year

or two earlier. Even after he settled in Venice he maintained close contacts with Verona. His use of color differs from that of his older contemporaries educated in Venice: Titian and Tintoretto. Veronese achieves a harmony of clear, sharply defined tones that reflects his training in the Veronese school. His work also shows the influence of Brescian artists such as Alessandro Moretto and Girolamo Savoldo.

Veronese was a supreme decorator. Many of his finest pictures, like *The Marriage at Cana* (1562–3; Louvre, Paris), painted for the refectory of S. Giorgio Maggiore in Venice, suffer from their removal from their original setting. But much of his work remains in position, in such buildings as the Doges' Palace and the church of S. Sebastiano in Venice, and the Villa Barbaro at Maser. To describe Veronese as a decorator is not to diminish his status as a painter. He devised a type of painting that was the necessary compliment to the definitive achievement of his contemporaries Il Sansovino and Andrea Palladio in architecture.

In 1551 Veronese worked on the fresco decoration of the Villa Soranzo near Castelfranco, and fragments of these frescoes survive in the cathedral sacristy there. The qualities of clear color, mastery of perspective, and organized design that we find here are carried further in such canvases as the oval *Age and Youth* (c1553–4; Sale del Consiglio dei Dieci, Doges' Palace, Venice). In 1555 he received the commission for the ceiling of the sacristy of S. Sebastiano, Venice; this commission was followed by one for the ceiling of the nave, where he painted three masterly canvases of *The Story of Esther and Ahasuerus* (1556; S. Sebastiano, Venice). He continued working for this church until 1565. His painting for the high altar (1558–9) represents St Sebastian and other saints below, and the Virgin with the angels in the clouds above. In 1560 he painted the shutters and gallery of the superb organ, the case of which had been made to his design; this was followed by further paintings. The ensemble at S. Sebastiano forms the finest surviving example of Venetian church decoration from the second half of the 16th century.

In the field of private secular decoration, the same position is held by his frescoes in the Villa Barbaro (now Volpi) at Maser, near Asolo. The villa was built by Palladio c1560, and decorated soon afterwards.

Jan Vermeer: The Painter in his Studio; oil on canvas; 130×110cm (51×43in); 1662–5. Kunsthistorisches Museum, Vienna

Veronese: The Feast in the House of Levi; oil on canvas; 555×1280cm (219×504in); 1573. Gallerie dell'Accademia, Venice

Here we find a number of allegorical and mythological compositions, very much in the manner of those from the Villa Soranzo, and the ceilings of the Sale del Consiglio dei Dieci in the Doges' Palace. In a painted setting of feigned architecture, these compositions are linked with *trompe-l'oeil* effects of people in contemporary dress standing on balconies, or entering through doorways, with a background of delightful landscape prospects. In spite of damage and excessive restoration, these frescoes remain a delight, and represent a major achievement. The canvas of *The Family of Darius at the Feet of Alexander* (date disputed; National Gallery, London) is another splendid example of Veronese's work in the field of private secular painting.

Veronese continued to work in the public sphere. The canvases for the ceilings of the Sale del Consiglio dei Dieci in the Doges' Palace were followed by the decorations in the Sala del Collegio (1575–80). He was commissioned to paint a *Paradise* on the vast end wall of the Sala del Maggiore Consiglio, but death prevented him from carrying it out. He devised a splendid style of decoration for conventual refectories, presenting feast scenes from the gospels in a somewhat secular manner, for instance *The Marriage at Cana* (Louvre, Paris) from S. Giorgio Maggiore, and *The Feast in the House of Levi* (1573; Gallerie dell'Accademia, Venice) from the refectory of the

Dominican house of SS. Giovanni e Paolo. In the latter case, the prominence of the secular elements led to his being examined by the Inquisition on a charge of heresy. These paintings combined feigned architecture with figure composition in a manner reminiscent of the decorations at Maser. The backgrounds recall the architecture of the built-in set in the Teatro Olimpico at Vicenza.

In altarpiece design, Veronese favored a type of asymmetrical composition, with a setting of pillars, derived from Titian's altar of Ca' Pesaro in S. Maria dei Frari, Venice. Examples include the *Virgin and Saints* (c1551; S. Francesco della Vigna, Venice), and the *Virgin and Saints* from S. Zaccaria (c1562; Gallerie dell'Accademia, Venice). He also painted smaller religious pictures such as the *Resurrection* (c1570; Gemäldegalerie Alte Meister, Dresden), the *Crucifixion* (c1580; Louvre, Paris), and the wonderfully romantic *St Anthony Preaching to the Fishes* (c1575–80; Museo e Galleria, Borghese, Rome).

Veronese's portraiture is notable for some very fine full-lengths, both of single sitters and family groups, such as the *Family Portrait* (1558; Palace of the Legion of Honor, San Francisco). He excelled in portraying the relationships of children to their elders. He was assisted in his work by his brother Benedetto, and his sons Carlo and Gabriele who carried on his studio after his death.

Further reading. Osmond, P. *Paolo Veronese: his Career and Work*, London (1927). Pignatti, T. *Veronese* (2 vols.), Venice (1976). Piovene, G. and Marini, R. *L'Opera Completa del Veronese*, Milan (1968).

Verrio Antonio c1639–1707

The Italian born artist Antonio Verrio brought the Baroque concept of decorative painting to English art, by collaborating with architects and sculptors at Windsor Castle and Hampton Court. Before coming to England c1672, Verrio worked in Naples, where he was influenced by Luca Giordano. The subject of his decorations at Windsor, painted for King Charles II, was the glorification of the English crown. His speciality was the illusionistic ceiling, and in the Royal Chapel, Windsor, he worked with Grinling Gibbons. Verrio succeeded Sir Peter Lely as Court Painter in 1684, and also worked at Chatsworth, Derbyshire, and at Burghley, Northamptonshire.

Verrocchio Andrea del 1435–88

The Italian sculptor and painter Andrea di Michele di Francesco Cioni was born in Florence, the son of a brickmaker. He probably got his first training in the workshop of a goldsmith, Giuliano da Verrocchi, from whom he took his surname. He passed on the artistic heritage of Donatello, especially as a sculptor in bronze. His chief patrons were members of the Medici family. Lorenzo di Credi and Leonardo da Vinci, whose fame for a long time obscured Verrocchio's genius, excelled among the pupils of his large workshop.

One of his earliest works is a bronze candelabrum (1468; Rijksmuseum, Amsterdam), which was originally destined for the Palazzo Vecchio in Florence. Its floral ornaments and architectural motifs are derived from antique prototypes. Between c1468 and 1470 he painted the seated *Madonna with Child* (Staatliche Museen, Berlin), the style of which was influenced by the Madonnas of Fra Filippo Lippi. The spatial quality of the two

figures, set against a mountainous landscape, shows that he always perceived nature and human figures with a sculptor's eye. Shortly afterwards he painted a small private altar, depicting *Tobias and the Archangel Raphael* (National Gallery, London), which is closely related to an earlier picture of Tobias by Antonio Pollaiuolo.

The monument for Piero and Giovanni de' Medici in the old sacristy of S. Lorenzo, Florence, bears the date of 1472. It excels by its simple construction and abundant decoration. Acanthus leaves grow out of rams' horns, and lions' paws support the sarcophagus, which is set against a diaphanous net of ropes.

Verrocchio's first freestanding statue is

Below: Antonio Verrio: The Heaven Room; oil on plaster; c1693. Burghley House, Northamptonshire

Right: Andrea del Verrocchio: the monument for Piero and Giovanni de' Medici; marble, porphry, and bronze; 1472. Old Sacristy, S. Lorenzo, Florence

the bronze *David* (*c*1473–5; Museo Nazionale, Florence), made for the Medici family. The figure is strongly influenced by its famous forerunner, Donatello's bronze *David* (*c*1433; Museo Nazionale, Florence). However, Donatello's heroic conception here gives place to a calmer and more delicate idealism. The charming bronze *Putto with a Dolphin* (*c*1475–80; Palazzo Vecchio, Florence) originally formed a fountain in a Medici country house. Verrocchio's painting of *The Baptism of Christ* (*c*1474–5; Uffizi, Florence) owes its fame to Leonardo's participation in finishing the picture *c*1480.

At intervals, between 1476 and 1483, Verrocchio worked on the life-sized bronze group of *Christ and St Thomas* (Orsanmichele, Florence), casting Christ *c*1477/8 and St Thomas *c*1482/3. The solemnity of their gestures, and the massive folds of their garments, indicate the master's expressive late style. The famous marble bust of a *Lady with a Bunch of Flowers* (Museo Nazionale, Florence) was carved *c*1478 and was probably influenced by Leonardo's painting of Ginevra dei Benci (*Portrait of a Woman*, *c*1474–6; National Gallery of Art, Washington, D.C.).

Verrocchio's last and undoubtedly greatest work is the bronze equestrian monument of *Bartolommeo Colleoni* (Campo SS. Giovanni e Paolo, Venice), begun *c*1483 and finished, after Verrocchio's death, by Alessandro Leopardi. This gigantic monument combines the lasting influence of Donatello's statuary, as represented by the monument to *Gattamelata* (1446–53; Piazza del Santo, Padua) and the new conception of man as conqueror of his world, which links the late 15th century with the art of the High Renaissance.

Further reading. Passavant, G. (trans. Watson, K.) *Verrocchio: Sculpture, Paintings, and Drawings*, London (1969). Pope-Hennessy, J. *Italian Renaissance Sculpture*, London (1958). Valentiner, R. *Studies of Italian Renaissance Sculpture*, London (1950).

Vieira da Silva Marie 1908–92

The Portuguese painter Marie-Hélène Vieira da Silva studied sculpture under Antoine Bourdelle and Charles Despiau in 1928. She turned to painting in 1929, and became a pupil of François Dufresne, Othon Friesz, and Fernand Léger. William Hayter, with whom she studied engraving in Paris before the Second World War, had a great influence on her work. This is characterized by abstract linear forms, usually derived from architecture; they are painted in neutral tones, and spiral back to form an interior space (for example, *The City*, oil on canvas; 1950–1; Museum of Modern Art, New York). She should be seen in the general context of the lyrical abstraction movement that flourished in Paris after the Second World War and is sometimes referred to as the School of Paris.

Vien Joseph-Marie 1716–1809

The French painter Joseph-Marie Vien was born in Montpellier. From 1743 to 1750 he worked in Rome, where he must have met A.R. Mengs, the teacher of J.-L. David. Vien's work demonstrates the stylistic possibilities available in the mid 18th century: his *Sleeping Hermit* (Louvre, Paris), a great success at the 1753 Salon, is in the line that leads from the work of Guercino to that of Pier Francesco Mola. His *St Denis Preaching* (1767; St Roch, Paris) has genuine grandeur, its pseudo-Classical manner vaguely derived from Raphael. It met with some praise from Diderot. Vien's best-selling works, in that age of nascent Neoclassicism, were his seminude "Greek" virgins in an antique Pompeian setting, such as his *Greek Girl at the Bath* (1767; Museum of Art, Ponce, Puerto Rico). These works are delicate and whimsical, and Neoclassical only in their trappings.

Vigée-Lebrun Marie 1755–1842

The French portrait painter Marie-Louise-Elisabeth Vigée-Lebrun was the daughter of the pastellist Louis Vigée (1715–67). She married the famous art dealer J.-B.-P. Lebrun. She was much influenced by the works of Rubens (1577–1640) and Anthony van Dyck (1599–1641) and by the softer works of her contemporary, Jean-Baptiste Greuze. Her official career began with a commission to paint a portrait, *Marie Antoinette*, 1779 (now in the Kunsthistorisches Museum, Vienna). She became a member of the Académie in 1783. Her most successful works were portraits of women, painted with a lush, neo-Baroque colorism: they are unashamedly and sentimentally decorative. With the Revolution of 1789 she fled

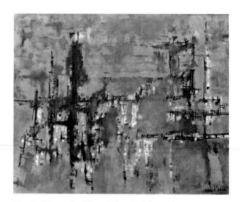

Maria Viera da Silva: The Golden City. Private collection

France because of her connections with the court; she traveled and worked in many parts of Europe until the Restoration. By then her works had become unfashionable, and she retired to write her *Souvenirs* (published 1835–7).

Vignola Jacopo da 1507–73

The Italian architect Jacopo Barozzi da Vignola came from near Bologna; this northern heritage, and with it the patronage of the Farnese family, were all-important in his architectural life. He started his career as a painter, which influenced much of his early architecture in Rome. He arrived in the city *c*1530, probably through the patronage of the younger Cardinal Alessandro Farnese. He worked for the Farnese family at Caprarola, in the Vatican for Pope Paul III (Farnese), and at the new Farnese ducal palace at Piacenza, begun in 1558. The same patronage made him Michelangelo's successor at St Peters, Rome, in 1564, and on the Roman palaces on the Capitoline Hill.

The influence of Michelangelo was strong in Vignola's work at the Villa Giulio, begun in 1551. Here, with Bartolomeo Ammanati and Giorgio Vasari, he produced a series of interlocking courtyards, opening from the rear of the main casino. The axial and visual arrangement was close to Michelangelo's plan for the Palazzo Farnese. In Vignola's castle-villa at Caprarola (1559), however, the intended fortress plan was made to turn in upon itself, in the form of a circular courtyard. It made an impressive effect through its size and novelty, as did his unfinished Palazzo Farnese at Piacenza.

Vignola is particularly associated with the Gesù in Rome, planned for the Society of Jesus *c*1568. Its broad nave, with side chapels set between the coupled pilasters, and its dome over the crossing, established a type associated with the Jesuit order and Tridentine architecture. Once again, the Farnese family were the driving force both in its construction and in the use of Vignola's design. In contrast with the scale and splendor of the Gesù were his two relatively small exercises in the revised central plan of the Renaissance. At S. Andrea in Via Flaminia (c1553), and at S. Anna dei Palafrenieri (1565), he skillfully juggled with two shapes of oval and rectangle. Both these buildings were important during the Roman Baroque period. They strongly influenced the centralized plans of Borromini and Bernini, particu-

larly the latter's S. Andrea al Quirinale, Rome.

In 1562, Vignola published his *Regola delli Cinque Ordini di Architettura* which explained the Classical orders in great detail and established the simple but immensely useful device of the module in correct proportioning. The work was of enormous importance throughout the 16th and 17th centuries and was ultimately published in all the European languages.

Vignon Claude 1593–1670

The French artist Claude Vignon was born at Tours. He trained as a painter in Paris, acquiring there some of the preciosity of

Georges Lallemand. During a stay in Rome, probably in 1617, he was influenced in different ways by followers of Caravaggio and of Adam Elsheimer; his work also showed affinities with that of Domenico Feti and Peter Lastman. He was in Paris again in 1622, but later returned to Italy as a picture-dealer. He was made an Academician in 1651. Representative works are in the Louvre, Paris.

Vignon was principally a painter of religious subjects, though his work showed little religious feeling. His early pictures were striking for their richness of color and sweep of execution, producing a rakish, romantic swagger unusual in France at the time. His later work, modified through the influence of Rubens by 1624, is inclined to slovenliness. He had at least 24 children, of whom three were painters: Claude (1633–1703; a follower of his father), Philippe (1638–1701; a portraitist), and Charlotte (b. 1639; a painter of still lifes).

Villard de Honnecourt *fl.* 1225–45

The French architect, artist, and writer Villard de Honnecourt was probably born around the end of the 12th century in Honnecourt, a small town near Cambrai. The sole source of information on Villard is his autograph illustrated Lodge Book in Paris (Bibliothèque Nationale; MS. Fr. 19093). He may have trained at the nearby Cistercian monastery of Vaucelles. His drawings indicate a knowledge of buildings at Vaucelles and Cambrai, Meaux, Laon, Reims, Chartres, and Lausanne. Villard states that he spent a long time in Hungary, which he probably visited between 1235 and 1242. It may be that his book was begun in connection with his visit, and completed after his return. The manuscript was used as an instruction manual in his Lodge; it bears several annotations and additions in two other hands, which were probably made by his successors. Little is known of buildings Villard actually constructed, although he claimed to have designed the choir of an unidentified church, illustrated in his book, with the assistance of a certain Pierre de Corbie. In addition, it has been suggested that Villard designed the collegiate church of St Quentin (built 1225–57).

The Lodge Book consists of 66 folios, most of which are covered with a wide variety of drawings, often accompanied by explanatory captions. Architectural plans and elevations, furnishings, decorative de-

Marie Vigée-Lebrun: Madame Grand; oil on canvas; 92×72cm (36×28in); 1783. Metropolitan Museum, New York

tails, applied geometry, examples of masonry, carpentry, and machines are all treated, along with over 200 human and animal figures. These sketches reveal Villard's widespread interest not only in the art of his own day and the recent past, but also in Classical art, which may have been transmitted via Romanesque or Byzantine models. His book provides a rare insight into the working method of a 13th-century architect, indicating that sketchbooks were already an important medium for the exchange of ideas. Its broad scope suggests that Gothic architects were highly versatile, with a profound knowledge of the whole range of the arts and crafts.

Villon Jacques 1875–1963

The French painter known as Jacques Villon was born at Dauville. His real name was Gaston Duchamp, and he was the brother of the painter Marcel Duchamp. From 1894 he lived in Paris, where he published humorous drawings and, influenced by Henri de Toulouse-Lautrec, made posters and engravings. He painted in a Fauvist manner from 1906 until 1911, when Cubism became more important in his work. His intellectual approach led him to form the *Section d'Or* group in 1912. After camouflage work during the First World War his paintings became muted and Abstract (for example, *Race Horse*, 1922; Galerie Louis Carré, Paris). He was forced to live by selling engravings until 1930, when he returned to painting and the use of pure colors.

Vischer family
15th and 16th centuries

The Vischer Family were German sculptors and bronze-founders from Nuremberg. For a century, from 1453, theirs was the most important foundry for bronze sculpture in Germany. Also working in Nuremberg, at this time of the city's artistic heyday, were the sculptors Adam Kraft and Veit Stoss, and the painter Albrecht Dürer, who was an important if elusive influence on the later members of the family. The Vischer workshop produced a wide range of bronze sculpture for places all over Germany and eastern Europe. Many works are signed. Whether this indicates responsibility for both casting and design is uncertain, but evidence suggests that such was usually the case.

Hermann the Elder (*ob.* 1488) acquired

Jacques Villon: Portrait of Mlle. Y.D.; oil on canvas; 120×89cm (47×35in); 1913. Los Angeles County Museum of Art, Los Angeles

Nuremberg citizenship in 1453. His many works included the Wittenberg Font (Stadtkirche, Wittenberg) of 1457. It was his son, Peter the Elder (*c*1460–1529) who inherited the business in 1488 and established its great reputation. In that year he supplied a design (Akademie, Vienna) for an architectural framework to surround the shrine of St Sebald (St Sebald, Nuremberg). In the 1490s his work included a powerful bronze figure, the so-called *Branch-breaker* (Bayerisches Nationalmuseum, Munich) and several tomb monuments, for example, the one to Archbishop Ernst von Sachsen (1494–5; Magdeburg Cathedral). He contributed

superb life-size figures of King Arthur and Theodoric for Emperor Maximilian's monument (1512–13; Hofkirche, Innsbruck). Construction of the St Sebald shrine was resumed in 1507, was interrupted from 1512 to 1514, and was completed with the assistance of Peter's sons in 1519. Peter the Elder's work is hard and sharp in finish: it displays a monumental dignity and a Gothic style that may have been influenced by his collection of 14th-century wooden sculptures.

It was probably his eldest son, Hermann the Younger (*c*1486–1517), who transformed the original design of the St Sebald Shrine, replacing with truncated canopies the intended elaborate, late Gothic pinnacles. Some of his architectural drawings, made during a visit to Italy in 1515, have survived (Louvre, Paris). That same year he began work on a screen for the burial chapel in St Anna at Augsburg for the great banking family, the Fuggers. The screen was unfinished at Hermann's death in 1517, but was completed by his brother Hans (c1489–1550) between 1536 and 1540.

Peter the Younger (1487–1528), a third brother, may also have visited Italy. Much of the sculpture of the St Sebald Shrine is attributed to him. It abounds with mythological and allegorical figures such as sea-gods and *putti*—the influence of the Italian Renaissance in both subject and style. The Paduan sculptor Riccio may have been the inspiration for these, and for the independent bronze statuettes that Peter helped to introduce into Germany, such as his inkwell of 1525 (Ashmolean Museum, Oxford). As well as the usual tomb monuments, such as that to Frederick the Wise (1527; Schlosskirche, Wittenberg), Peter made bronze plaquettes and medals.

Georg Vischer (c1520–92), son of Hans, took over the foundry in 1550. Like his uncle he made statuettes, for example an inkwell dated 1547 (Staatliche Museen, Berlin).

Vitale da Bologna 1289/1309–59/69

The Italian painter Vitale d'Aimo de' Cavelli was called Vitale da Bologna, after the city in which he was the most important painter of his period. There are two signed Madonnas by him, one in the Vatican Museums and the other in the Galleria Davia-Bargellini in Bologna, but his work is not easily disentangled from a mass of rather optimistic attributions. Bolognese artists of the 14th century were best known as miniaturists, so that Vitale, a painter of panels and frescoes, is unusual; he seems also to have been a sculptor. To his two signed Madonnas may be added a polyptych in S. Salvatore, Bologna (1353). The style of its narrative panels enables us to attribute to him frescoes in the abbey at Pomposa (1351), frescoes from the church of the Mezzarata (now in the Pinacoteca Nazionale, Bologna) and also the lovely little panels of the *Ador-*

Peter Vischer the Younger: the monument to Peter Frederick the Wise; bronze; height 425cm (167in); 1527. Schlosskirche, Wittenberg

Vitale da Bologna: The Miracles of St Anthony Abbot; panel; 77×37cm (30×15in). Pinacoteca Nazionale, Bologna

ation of the Magi (National Gallery of Scotland, Edinburgh), and *St Anthony Abbot* (Pinacoteca Nazionale, Bologna).

In all these works Vitale displays a feeling for dramatic shapes, blocks of exciting color, and dramatic silhouettes; his works produce an emotional impact almost without regard for subject matter. The *Christ in Majesty* in the apse at S. Maria, Pomposa, is surrounded by a brilliant striped mandorla that dominates the nave; the frescoes at Mezzarata are similarly striking. The Edinburgh *Adoration* is comparatively restful, though highly decorative; the elements of the scene are fitted together with little concern for realistic space, but they tell a complicated story with great economy. This work is probably later than the Davia-Bargellini Madonna and Child (the *Madonna dei Denti*) of 1345, and the Pomposa frescoes of 1351. In his strongly individual art, Vitale was apparently in-

fluenced by the International Gothic style.

Vitruvius 1st Century BC

The Roman architect, military engineer, and author Vitruvius worked for both Julius Caesar and for the Emperor Augustus. His books, *De Architectura*, were intended to explain to his presumed patron, the Emperor, the criteria by which excellence in architecture can be judged and attained. He drew freely on the many earlier treatises by Greek artists, and as a result his work is an important source of information and observations about Greek, rather than Roman, architectural practice. It deals with town planning, materials, the use of the orders of architecture, different building types, water supplies, mensuration, and machines for construction and military purposes. His books served the Renaissance as a guide to Greek architecture, although his examples derive more from the Hellenistic than from the Classical period.

Vittone Bernardo 1702–70

Bernardo Vittone was an Italian architect of the late Baroque period. Except for a brief period of study in Rome (1730–2), he practiced exclusively in his native Piedmont, combining the divergent styles of Guarino Guarini and Filippo Juvarra into a highly original synthesis. All his main works are ecclesiastical, and most of them are centrally planned. Vittone was particularly inventive in the various solutions he devised for effecting the transition from the main centralized space into the area of the dome. An example of his skill can be seen in S. Croce at Villanova di Mondovi (1755); despite the complexity of the geometry, the overall effect is one of gaiety, lightness, and serenity.

Vittoria Alessandro 1525–1608

The Italian sculptor Alessandro Vittoria was born in Trento, and received his early training there in the workshop of the Grandi, who were sculptors and bronzecasters. In 1543 he was sent by Bishop Cristoforo Madruzzo of Trento to the studio of Jacopo Sansovino in Venice. Although Sansovino was a major formative influence on Vittoria, the two men had quite different artistic temperaments. In 1547 after a quarrel, Vittoria left, to work as a *stuccatore* in Vicenza.

Alessandro Vittoria: Neptune; bronze; height 50cm (20in); c1580–5. Victoria and Albert Museum, London

The breach was not healed until 1553, when Vittoria returned to Venice. He based himself there for the rest of his career, becoming the most important and influential sculptor working in Venice in the later 16th century, comparable in importance with his exact contemporary, Giambologna, in Florence. The friend of Titian, Tintoretto, Veronese, and Pietro Aretino, Vittoria was a powerful and inventive artist, and exceptionally versatile. He produced brilliant stucco decorations

(Scala d'Oro of the Doges' Palace, Venice) and architectural sculpture (caryatids for the Biblioteca Marciana, Venice); he was an original medallist, and excelled in his age as a portrait sculptor (seen in his bust of *Tommaso Rangone* in the Ateneo Veneto, Venice).

His major work consists of the altarpieces with marble statues that he made for many Venetian churches, for example S. Salvatore, S. Francesco della Vigna, S. Maria dei Frari, and SS. Giovanni e Paolo. It can be argued that he was an even more powerful artist when he worked on a small scale, in bronze (for example, *St John the Baptist, St Francis*, S. Francesco della Vigna, Venice). Like Tintoretto, Vittoria was deeply interested in the work of Michelangelo, and he introduced elements of Michelangelo's style into Venetian sculpture.

Vivarini family
15th and 16th centuries

The Vivarini were a family of Italian painters of Venetian origin. No certain dates of birth or death are known. The oldest member of the family was Antonio (*fl.* 1440–76/84), but his brother-in-law Giovanni d'Alemagna (*fl.* 1441–*c*50) was certainly his senior, and is usually included within the group, together with Antonio's brother Bartolommeo (*fl.* 1450–99), and his son Alvise (*c*1445–1503/5).

Giovanni and Antonio, and possibly Bartolommeo, worked on the frescoes of the Ovetari Chapel (church of the Eremitani, Padua) from 1448, alongside Mantegna and Niccolo Pizzolo. At Giovanni's death the family left Padua, having completed only part of the vault. A certain eclecticism is noticeable throughout the works of the Vivarini workshop. Their early works, such as the *Coronation of the Virgin* signed and dated by Giovanni and Antonio in 1444 (S. Pantaleone, Venice), show two influences: a highly decorated late Gothic style, characteristic of Pisanello and Gentile da Fabriano, combined with a style probably derived from Donatello, who was in Padua from 1443 to 1453.

Later, their works came to reflect the influence of Mantegna in the depiction of hard, dry folds, as for instance in Bartolommeo's S. Maria Formosa triptych of 1473. Alvise's S. Ambrogio altar (S. Maria dei Frari, Venice; completed posthumously by Marco Basaiti) shows the saint seated in an open loggia. The architecture of the

Antonio Vivarini (attrib.): The Abduction of Helen; panel; 151×294cm (59×116in); 1445–50. Walters Art Gallery, Baltimore

loggia continues that of the picture's frame, in a manner first used in Venice by Antonello and Giovanni Bellini. The quality of lighting, the musical angels, and the poses of some of the figures in this picture are also reminiscent of Bellini's works.

From 1451 the Vivarini family rarely moved from Venice, but received many commissions for altarpieces from provincial towns on the Italian mainland. Antonio and Bartolommeo signed works both independently and in collaboration throughout their working lives, whereas Alvise worked away from the family

Alvise Vivarini: Virgin and Child with Six Saints; tempera on panel; 146×175cm (57×69in); 1480. Gallerie dell'Accademia, Venice

studio. Their only State commission was achieved as the result of his petition to the Doge in 1488, but at Alvise's death the three paintings contracted for remained unfinished. The Vivarini workshop was second only to Bellini's in the production of religious paintings in Venice in the second half of the 15th and early 16th centuries.

Vlaminck Maurice de 1876–1958

The French painter Maurice de Vlaminck was born in Paris. As an artist he was mostly self-taught, in between activities as a racing cyclist and musician. His meeting with André Derain in 1900 was crucial: the two artists shared a studio at Chatou on the outskirts of Paris. In 1901, the Vincent van Gogh exhibition at the Bernheim-Jeune gallery in Paris convinced him of his métier as an artist: "Van Gogh is my father", he wrote. In portraits, landscapes, and still lifes he painted directly from the tube; his brushwork was turbulent, his color violent. He dismissed all forms of Classical and Renaissance art and wanted to burn the École des Beaux-Arts "with my vermilions".

He and Derain formed the *École de Chatou*, in the group that became known as the Fauves, at the Salon d'Automne of 1905. Vlaminck had probably met Matisse by 1902; his fiercely combative nature led him to repeated denials of Matisse's enormous contribution to Fauvism. His love of Van Gogh meant that the color in his paintings was extremely intense; his impasto was more prominent, and his brush strokes were less organized than those of Derain and Matisse.

In such paintings as *Still Life* (c1907; Musée de l'Annonciade, St Tropez) and *Sailing Boat* (1906; private collection) he made forceful contributions to Fauvism. By 1908, however, like many other artists, he became increasingly interested in the work of Cézanne. The bright, strident color was replaced by darker tones (although metallic blues and sharp reds do appear), the spatial organization became more traditional (he developed a liking for wide and deep perspectives), and the mood grew contemplative. His style changed little in his later years. He worked as a printmaker and book illustrator and also wrote works of poetry and prose.

Bartolomeo Vivarini (attrib.): The Adoration of the Magi; panel; 52×28cm (21×11in); c1475. Frick Collection, New York

Above: Maurice Vlaminck: The Circus; oil on canvas; 60×73cm (24×29in); 1906. Galerie Beyeler, Basel

Further reading. Cabanne, P. *Vlaminck*, Paris (1966). Sauvage, M. *Vlaminck: sa Vie et son Message*, Geneva (1956). Selz, J. *Vlaminck*, New York (1963).

Vos Cornelis de *c*1584/5–1651

The Flemish portrait painter Cornelis de Vos also produced large historical, mythological, and allegorical pictures. His portraits (mainly of Antwerp burghers) are characterized by a prosaic attention to detail, but his portrayals of children are more sympathetic (for example, *Daughters of the Artist*; Staatliche Museen, Berlin). The portraits are sometimes mistaken for those of both Rubens and his friend Anthony van Dyck. In 1637 de Vos, his brother Paul (*c*1596–1678), and his brother-in-law Frans Snyders helped Rubens to provide pictures for Philip IV's hunting lodge near Madrid, the Torre de la Parada. In the subject pictures of de Vos there is a stylistic similarity to the largeness of forms and the rhythmic compositional movements of Rubens.

Vos Marten de 1532–1603

Marten de Vos was an Antwerp painter who studied under Frans Floris. He attained his mastership in 1558, and then

Cornelis de Vos: Portrait of the Artist with his Family; oil on canvas; 188×162cm (74×64in); 1621. Musées Royaux des Beaux-Arts de Belgique, Brussels

spent four years in Rome and Venice. He was especially influenced by the work of Tintoretto, whose brushwork style and figure-types are evident in the St Thomas Altar of 1574 (Royal Museum of Fine Arts, Antwerp). De Vos gained many commissions for altarpieces during the reestablishment of Catholicism in the southern Netherlands, after the iconoclasm of the 1570s. His coloring and brushwork become more inhibited in his later years, but there remains an exuberance of style that anticipates Rubens—for example the angels of the St Luke Altar (1602; Royal Museum of Fine Arts, Antwerp).

Vouet Simon 1590–1649

The French painter Simon Vouet was born in Paris. He was in Rome by 1614, after spending some time in Venice. He also

visited Naples and Genoa. In 1624 he was elected president of the Academy of St Luke, the respected Roman art academy. On his return to Paris in 1627 he set up a thriving workshop, taking pupils who included the Mignards, Hubert Le Sueur, François Perrier, and Charles Lebrun.

Vouet's early career in Rome indicates the relative popularity there of the Carracci and of Caravaggio. Vouet unhesitatingly followed the latter: his early work, *Birth of the Virgin* (1615/20; S. Francesco a Ripa, Rome) demonstrated the influence of Caravaggio in its dramatic lighting and use of minor figures pointing in towards brightly lit main figures, against a tenebrous stage. Vouet's other works done in Rome show his interest in the works of Giovanni Lanfranco and Guercino, as in *The Virgin Appearing to St Bruno* (1620; Certosa di S. Martino, Naples).

His return to France in 1627 marks the beginning of the modern French school: Vouet became the most influential French artist working in France (Poussin and Claude lived in Rome). Previously the French had relied on foreign artists, or had continued a Mannerist approach derived from the Italian artistic invasion of the previous century. Here, at last, was the modern Italian manner newly arrived from Rome. Vouet introduced a modified Baroque manner, in which a certain emotionalism, color, and atmosphere are linked with a classical balance and restraint. This appealed to French taste far more than the illusionism and wholehearted emotion of the full Baroque, which, for reasons of temperament and religion, would have been spurned.

Vouet's *Presentation in the Temple* (1641; Louvre, Paris), painted for the high altar of the Jesuit Novitiate, takes a monumental view of form, which is simplified by the rather strong lighting. The architecture enlivens the composition, but, in the presentation of steps and main figure groups, both parallel to the picture plane, the work resembles a Veronese more than a Pietro da Cortona. Vouet made important innovations in decorative painting, particularly at the Hotel Séguier, Paris; he worked there in the chapel (1638), library (until 1640) and lower gallery (until 1649; unfinished at his death). His designs survive only as engravings by M. Dorigny. He revived a type of illusionistic decoration that had not been seen in France since the time of Primaticcio (*ob.* 1570), with painted architecture continuing the actual wall architecture. In the chapel at the Hotel Séguier, he disposes the figures in *Adoration of the Magi* behind a painted balustrade.

No single source is sufficient to describe Vouet's decorative manner, which combines elements from Veronese, Guercino, Correggio, and Giulio Romano, as well as the first School of Fontainebleau. Its silvery lightness can be judged from the much damaged fresco of *Parnassus* in the grotto of the Château de Wideville. This is an early work, the illusionism of which (relatively restrained though it is) must have been considered spectacular in French milieu at that date. Vouet's type of illusionism was an alternative to the Caracci system of ceiling decoration then popular in France. It was not copied until Lebrun and Houasse decorated the *Salon de la Guerre*, the *Salon de la Paix*, and the *Salle de l'Abondance* at Versailles in the 1680s. Vouet's accomplishment as a decorative artist also extended to tapestry design, anticipating the talents of his versatile pupil, Lebrun.

When Poussin visited France in 1640, Louis XIII made the famous comment, "Let's see Vouet get out of this one!" The judgment proved premature. Poussin's art was too severe and small-scale for the decorative demands the King made of it: Vouet's was not.

Voysey Charles 1857–1941

The English architect and designer Charles Francis Annesley Voysey was born at Hessle, Yorkshire. He worked with several London architects before establishing his own practice at Westminster in 1881. He was a member of an Arts and Crafts guild and a successful designer of wallpapers, textiles, and simple but slightly mannered furniture. During an architectural career that lasted from 1889 to 1914, he designed numerous country houses (for example, Perrycroft, Colwall, 1893; Broadleys, Windermere, 1898; The Orchard, Chorleywood, 1900). These were puritan restatements of the small country house of late medieval England, with white roughcast walls, sloping buttresses, and emphatic rooflines.

Vrelant William *fl.* 1456–81

William Vrelant was an illuminator from Utrecht whose name is associated with a distinctive style of manuscript painting prevalent in Bruges during the second half of the 15th century. It is characterized by simple, almost crude, miniatures of great energy and verve, painted in bright colors. The text is in notably large characters that complement the straightforward style of the paintings. Vrelant is documented in Bruges from 1456 until his death; an illuminated *Vita Christi* painted by him is recorded, but this manuscript is no longer identifiable. A copy of the *Chroniques de Hainaut* (probably that in the Bibliothèque Royale Albert I, Brussels) is ascribed to one "Guillaume Wyelant", and is the basis for the attribution to Vrelant of many books illustrated in a similar style. This theory has recently been questioned; if it is correct, Vrelant was the head of the most productive workshop in Bruges.

Vries Adriaen de c1560–1626

Born in Holland, the sculptor Adrien de Vries worked in Rome, and later in Prague for the Emperor Rudolf II. He also maintained a workshop in Augsburg, where many of his bronze works were cast. The large Hercules Fountain (Maximilienstrasse, Augsburg), finished in 1602, takes its theme and figure-style from the work of Giovanni da Bologna, under whom de Vries trained in Italy. Later, the elegant sinuous forms of his Italian master are rendered by de Vries in a more loosely modeled technique, emphasizing light and shade on the surface of flesh. His work was known as far afield as the court at Copenhagen, for which he designed the Neptune Fountain for Fredericksburg Palace (1617–23).

Vries Hans de 1527–?1604

The Flemish artist Hans Vredeman de Vries was one of the most influential figures in the history of design in the later 16th century. His talents spanned the fields of architecture, painting, furniture, and garden design. His engravings carried throughout Europe an exaggerated form of the style of the School of Fontainebleau. His designs for architectural motifs were used on some of the more ambitious country houses of Elizabethan England, such as Wollaton Hall, Nottingham. Work for State occasions, such as triumphal arches for the entry of Charles V into Antwerp in 1549, prompted his few but important pictures of fantastic architectural settings, for example *Christ in the House of Mary and Martha* (Hampton Court Palace, London).

Vrubel Mikhail 1856–1910

The Russian painter Mikhail Aleksandrovich Vrubel trained at the St Petersburg Academy (1880–4). Afterwards he worked mainly in Kiev until 1889, restoring and painting icons and frescoes in the church of St Kirill and the cathedral of St Vladimir. He visited Venice in 1884, and was influenced by Byzantine mosaics and Renaissance painting. After that he painted in a mystical, flat Byzantine style. From 1889 he lived in Moscow, where he associated with the neo-nationalist circle around Marmontov, experimenting with ceramics, and painting myths (for example the mythical knight *Bogatyr*, 1898; State Russian Museum, St Petersburg). He also became obsessed with the spiritual loneliness of the Demon in Mikhail Lermontov's poem *Demon* (1841), which he illustrated and painted constantly from 1890.

Vuillard Jean-Édouard 1868–1940

The French painter, printmaker, and occasional photographer Jean-Édouard Vuillard was born in Paris. He studied at the École des Beaux-Arts and at the Académie Julian, where he met Pierre Bonnard, Paul Sérusier, Maurice Denis, and others who formed the group of the Nabis. Around 1890, Vuillard had a phase during which he used simplified design, strong color, and energetic brushwork. But this, like the time of the Fauves who were to follow, was short-lived, and he is best remembered for his *intimiste* interiors. In these, a predominantly bourgeois setting (often his mother sewing, or reading, or relaxing) is conveyed in flat color areas, sometimes patterned and textured, and always spatially tense.

Like the rest of the Nabis, Vuillard wanted to go beyond painting: he produced many decorative panels and screens, theatrical designs and lithographs. The Nabis contributed to an avant-garde literary magazine, the *Revue Blanche*. In 1894 its editor, Alexandre Natanson, commissioned Vuillard to paint nine canvas panels in tempera showing Paris park scenes. Each of these was some 7 ft (2.2 m) in **height**.

In 1899, his series of colored lithographs, *Paysages et Intérieurs*, was published by Ambrose Vollard. He also made etchings

Jean-Édouard Vuillard: Portrait of Henri Toulouse-Lautrec; oil on card; 25×23cm (10×9in); c1898. Musée Toulouse-Lautrec, Albi

and black-and-white lithographs. He became an enthusiastic photographer—photographs sometimes provided the starting-point for his paintings. He was a founder member of the Salon d'Automne in 1903, but unlike his friend Bonnard, he did not continue to develop artistically after 1900. Instead he tended to retreat into a conventional and easily acceptable form of *intimism*.

Further reading. Preston, S. *Edouard Vuillard*, New York (1972).

Wagner Otto 1841–1918

Otto Wagner was unquestionably the father and leader of the Viennese school of architecture that produced Adolf Loos, Josef Hoffmann, Josef Olbrich, and others. After training in Vienna and Berlin, he began his career with buildings noted for their classicist approach—an approach he never forsook.

It is as an architect who reacted against Viennese historicism that Wagner is chiefly remembered, as well as for his important contributions to town planning. The Vienna *Stadtbahn* (metropolitan railway) project of the mid 1890s was an enterprise of vast scope; it remains today a monument to his imagination, technical ingenuity, and concern for the minutiae of detail. Aesthetically it is predominantly a *Jugendstil* work. Wagner adopted the style at this time, possibly under the influence of pupils like Olbrich; he also used it in two blocks of flats in Vienna, numbers 38 to 40 Linke Wienzeile (1898–9).

Wagner's most influential book of architectural theory was *Moderne Architektur* (1894). Its crucial point was that architecture must create new forms by taking into account both contemporary social needs and advances in technology such as engineering. He also recommended the rejection of unnecessary ornament.

Two of Wagner's post-1900 commissions were of particular importance: the monumental church Am Steinhof (1905), and the Post Office Savings Bank in Vienna (1904–6). The latter work—with its use of aluminum, steel, glass, and marble cladding, its masterly handling of space, and its

Wang Hui: Landscape; ink and colors on hanging scroll; 46×30cm (18×12in). Victoria and Albert Museum, London

logical, practical design—is justly considered a major building in the development of 20th-century architecture.

Walden Herwarth 1878–?1941

The composer, critic, and journalist Herwarth Walden is best known as an energetic propagandist in Germany for Expressionism and the European avant-garde. In 1910, after editing a theater magazine, he founded *Der Sturm*, a Berlin-based publishing house and journal. He was the first to promote the work of Oskar Kokoschka and the *Brücke* group; in 1912 he held the first exhibition of the *Blaue Reiter* school; and later he published the writings of Kandinsky and others. He exhibited Cubism and Futurism in Berlin in 1913 and followed this with a series of important one-man exhibitions, including those of Robert Delaunay (1913) and Lyonel Feininger (1917). Walden had held over 100 exhibitions by the time his gallery closed in 1932.

Wang Chien 1598–1677

The Chinese painter Wang Chien came from T'ai-ts'ang, Kiangsu. He was a contemporary and colleague of Wang Shih-min, although he was not related to him, and was, like him, a member of the Nine Friends group. He rose to be Governor of Lien-Chou Kwangtung, South China. His painting is close in style to that of his contemporary. He is known for his large landscapes in the eclectic, orthodox style of his generation.

Wang Hui 1632–1717

Wang Hui came from Ch'ang-shu, Kiangsu. A gifted Chinese artist who followed the orthodox style, he was discovered by Wang Chien, who introduced him to Wang Shih-min. Both of the older men admired Wang Hui's work, and he was taken as a pupil to work in the studio of the elder Wang at T'ai-ts'ang. This gave him access to works of the old masters in Wang Shih-min's collection, and enlarged his experience and his mastery of the styles of his school. Wang Hui was a graceful painter in the eclectic, orthodox style; he was a man of great personal charm, with a wide circle of friends. He was successful at the court of K'ang Hsi, where he held the post of keeper of the Imperial collections of painting and calligraphy (1691–8).

Wang Meng c1309–85

The Chinese artist Wang Meng was a nephew of Chao Meng-fu, and was a member of a highly educated family. His paintings are among the most original experiments within the closely knit traditions of Chinese Scholar painting. He was interested in composition and in the expression of texture. He painted rich mountain rock formations, occasionally clothing them with colored trees painted in traditional style, but setting up a writhing movement that was quite new. The absence of sky in many of his compositions adds to this rich effect. The scroll *Forest Dwellings at Ch'u-ch'u* (National Palace Museum, Formosa) is an admirable example of the work of this imaginative genius, whose influence on such painters as Wen Chen-ming and Shih T'ao is clear and acknowledged.

Wang Shih-min 1592–1680

The Chinese painter Wang Shih-min came from a prominent scholarly family in T'ai-ts'ang, Kiangsu. He was a contemporary of Tung Ch'i-ch'ang, and was much influenced by him. He was a member of the group called the Nine Friends. He held official posts under the Ming, but retired at the fall of the dynasty and lived in retirement, writing and painting at T'ai-ts'ang for the remainder of his life. He was a great admirer of the Yuan masters, and of Huang Kung-wang in particular. Wang Shih-min, however, used color in the style of Wen Cheng-ming, of whom he must be regarded as a close follower. Although his art was limited in scope, Wang Shih-min worked in a rich, painterly style, but he appears not to have been a great innovator.

Wang Wei 699–759

The Chinese landscape painter Wang Wei was a classically trained scholar poet and official, whose country home was in Wang Ch'uan, Shensi. He was a poet of considerable reputation. He was also a devout Buddhist who, on the death of his mother, created a monastery at his home. Wang Wei admired the poetry of Li Po; his own verse was lyrical and evocative. Su Tung-p'o (Su Shih, the 11th-century artist, poet,

Wang Meng: Fishermen on the Flower Stream; ink on paper hanging scroll; 124×57cm (49×22in). National Palace Museum, Taipei

and critic) remarked, "when enjoying myself with Mo Ch'i's [Wang Wei's] poems I find pictures in them; when looking at Mo Ch'i's pictures, I find in them poems." A poem attributed to Wang Wei reads:

> From the Blue River white stones project,
> On the waters of jade a few red leaves.
> On the mountain paths no rain as yet,
> But the air is moist and wets the clothes.

Wang Wei painted many landscapes, none of which have been preserved. He is credited with the introduction of the art of landscape painting in ink alone, which was regarded, over the centuries, as the greatest school of painting in China. The one work that may bear some echo of his style is the so-called *Wang Ch'uan* scroll, named after his country home. Many copies of the original are recorded; versions in the Seattle Art Museum and the Freer Gallery of Art, Washington, D.C., may be Ming copies of earlier engravings. The gently meandering stream of the title is shown in landscape that is acutely observed, but any hint of the special charm of the painter eludes us. The whole has become formalized and archaized, and a little light color has been added.

Difficult as it is to be certain of the true character of Wang Wei's painting, he stands at the head of the *literati* landscape school. He was revered by all later painters, although his actual paintings quickly became remote in style. He is a striking contrast with his older contemporary, Wu Tao-tzu; although they must have known each other's work, there is no record of their having met.

Wang Yuan-ch'i 1642–1715

Wang Yuan-ch'i was a native of T'ai-ts'ang and a relative of Wang Shih-min. He was thus born into a great family of scholars and achieved considerable distinction, receiving his *chin-shih* degree at the age of 29. He was also recognized by the K'ang Hsi Emperor, and was a member of the board for the compilation of the *Pei-wen chai Shu hua p'u*, a comprehensive catalog of painting and calligraphy.

Wang Yuan-ch'i's paintings are among the most inventive of the eclectic orthodox school. He was interested in volume and the construction of landscape in a way that was never taken up by artists who followed him, but which seems to point the way to an almost Cubist approach to painting.

Warhol Andy 1928–87

The American painter, graphic artist, and filmmaker Andy Warhol was born in Pittsburgh but settled in New York in 1949. During the 1950s he worked as an advertising illustrator. His early creations as an independent artist reveal, in their clarity and visual impact, many of the assumptions underlying advertising (for example his pictures of dollar bills and Campbell's soup cans, as in *Campbell's Soup Cans 200*, 1962; private collection). Warhol was always interested in techniques that enabled multiplication of an image, such as silk-screen printing.

He often used as his starting point a photograph of someone so famous (Marilyn Monroe, Elizabeth Taylor, Jacqueline Kennedy) that the effect, in his pictures, is almost impersonal (for example, *Marilyn Monroe*, 1962, Modern Museum, National Museum, Stockholm; *Elvis I and II*, 1964, Art Gallery of Ontario, Toronto). He also employed prints of horrifying subjects (a bloody car crash, a view of an electric chair), and reduced their impact in the same kind of cool, cunningly packaged way.

The lack of overt emotion, combined with a very strong decorative sense, made Warhol's work particularly appealing to young people in the 1960s. His reputation was increased by a series of films that he began to organize from 1963 (for example, *Chelsea Girls*, 1966; *Lonesome Cowboys*, 1967–8). But to nothing else has he brought so much creative advertising skill as to the promotion of himself. Andy Warhol made himself a household word, even among those who might not care for his artistic style.

Further reading. Gidal, P. *Andy Warhol: Films and Paintings*, New York (1971). Koch, S. *Stargazer: Andy Warhol's World and his Films*, London (1974). Morphet, R. *Warhol*, London (1971). Warhol, A. *Film A to B and Back Again*, London and New York (1975). Wilcock, J. *The Autobiography and Sex Life of Andy Warhol*, New York (1971).

Watteau Antoine 1684–1721

Jean-Antoine Watteau was the outstanding painter of the French Rococo, an artist beside whom the talents of his contemporaries and successors are measured. He was born at Valenciennes; the town had only recently been ceded to France, and during his lifetime he was considered a Flemish artist.

His family was poor and his early years are obscure. He was trained under local artists, and arrived in Paris in 1702 as an assistant to one of them, a painter of scenery for the Paris Opera. This was probably Watteau's first contact with the theater. He later became infatuated with it.

His master left Watteau in Paris, and he was forced to produce copies of popular old masters on a quasi production-line basis. It may have been at this time that he began to paint in his own right, scenes he would have known during his childhood at Valenciennes, executed in the style of **Adriaen Brouwer** and **David Teniers**. Throughout his life his paintings were always based on drawings, and even during these early years in Paris when he was living in poverty, he made many delicate drawings after nature.

Fairly soon after his arrival in Paris he had the good fortune to come into contact with Claude Gillot. By as early as 1703 Watteau may have been his apprentice. Under Gillot he renewed his association with the theater and in particular with the *Commedia dell'Arte*. This troupe of Italian comedians had taken Paris by storm with their fast and irreverent pantomimes; their performances had been considered so scandalous that the company had been expelled from the city in 1697. The memory of the *Commedia dell'Arte* lived on in the productions of French comedians who also based their plays round the traditional characters of Harlequin, Pierrot, and Pantalone. Scenes from the *Commedia* formed most of the subject matter of Gillot's paintings, handled in a rather matter-of-fact way. Not surprisingly, the paintings

Andy Warhol: Marilyn Monroe; silkscreen print on paper; 91×91cm (36×36in); 1967. Tate Gallery, London

Right: Antoine Watteau: Les Fêtes Venitiennes; oil on canvas; 56×46cm (22×18in); c1718–19. National Gallery of Scotland, Edinburgh

that Watteau made during his apprenticeship with Gillot are *Commedia* scenes that seem, like his master's, to have been painted from actual performances.

It was Gillot who ended Watteau's apprenticeship *c*1707 or 1708, possibly for reasons of professional jealousy. He transferred his apprenticeship to Claude Audran III, a decorator who employed a number of artists to carry out his designs. Under Audran, Watteau absorbed a complete Rococo vocabulary of trellises, birds and monkeys, and chinoiserie.

Watteau was fortunate to have studied under Gillot and Audran, both of whom were modern artists outside the main stream of French academic painting, for by inclination as well as by birth Watteau was an outsider in the Parisian art world.

Audran was the curator of the Luxembourg Palace, and through him Watteau had regular access to *The Life of Marie de Medici* cycle of paintings by Rubens. He was able to study and to copy unhindered a series of paintings by his great compatriot. Rubens' technical ability, his draftsmanship, and his handling of paint were far superior to any painting being produced in Paris at that time, and the *Marie de Medici* cycle became the most important influence in the formation of Watteau's style.

In 1709 Watteau submitted a painting to the competition for the coveted Prix de Rome. He came second, and his fortunes began to improve. Sirois, a dealer with whom he later stayed, commissioned him to paint a contemporary battle scene. Watteau returned to Valenciennes, close to the battle lines of the Duke of Marlborough's campaigns, to make his work as natural as possible. Few of his paintings of military scenes survive, but engravings show that what interested Watteau was not the fight or the glamor of battle but the underlying reality: the camps, the soldiers waiting for orders, and the general inactivity of war. His military paintings are like reports from a modern war correspondent, for he had an acute eye which could select the important in everyday life. This perceptiveness was Watteau's greatest gift, and he used it fully in the type of painting with which his name is most closely linked, the *fête galante*.

It was as a painter of *fêtes galantes* that Watteau was enrolled at the Academy; a new category was specially created for him. The painting he chose to submit for membership was entitled *The Pilgrimage*

to *the Island of Cythera* (1717; Louvre, Paris). The painting has it origins in a scene from a contemporary play, *Les Trois Cousines*. It shows the return of a group of people from Cythera, the island of love, at the moment they realize that the pleasures of love are transitory, and that it is time for them to leave their enchanted island for the boat to the mainland.

Here Rubens was once again an inspiration for Watteau: not so much the Rubens of the *Marie de Medici* cycle, but the Rubens who painted *The Garden of Love* (*c*1634; Prado, Madrid). Seriousness of subject is not generally thought to be an attribute of Rococo painting, and Watteau's exquisitely dressed and perfectly mannered courtiers may seem at first sight as unlikely as his Harlequins and Pierrots to be the vehicles of human passions. But Watteau was above all an artist who understood the theater, with its contrasting layers of artifice and reality.

Restlessness, ill health, and financial motives may have encouraged Watteau's visit to London in 1719. It was probably during his year in England that he created *La Toilette* (1719; Wallace Collection, London). Realistic and freely painted, it shows a Venetian sensuousness quite new to French Painting. At Watteau's death, only a year after his return to Paris from London, his priest persuaded him to destroy a number of "offensive" paintings that were probably similar to *La Toilette*.

It was just before his death that Watteau painted the large *Giles* (*c*1719; Louvre, Paris) as a theater placard for a theatrical troupe. "Giles" was the French adaptation of Pierrot, the scapegoat and outcast derided by his companions. In Watteau's painting he stands isolated and vulnerable, with his stupid face and ill fitting clothes. Watteau may have felt an affinity with Giles for he, too, was an outsider, set apart from his contemporaries by temperament as well as by talent.

Further reading. Adhemar, H. and Huyghe, R. *Watteau*, Paris (1950). Brookner, A. *Antoine Watteau*, London (1967). Goncourt, E. and J. de *French Eighteenth-Century Painters*, Oxford (1981).

Watts G.F. 1817–1904

The English painter George Frederick Watts was born in London, the son of an impecunious pianomaker. At 20, he exhi-

bited *The Wounded Heron* (1837; Watts Gallery, Compton, near Guildford), in which the swirling lines characteristic of his later work already appear. In 1843, some prize money won in the competition for the decoration of the new Houses of Parliament enabled him to travel to Florence, where he spent four years. Italian art, and in particular the rich Venetian coloring, made a powerful impression on him; the results can be seen in the vast *Story from Boccaccio* (1844–7; Keble College, Oxford), and in the works he did throughout his career.

Back in England, his aspirations towards monumental painting were frustrated. His pessimistic mood at this time is reflected in the symbolic *Life's Illusions* (1848–9; Tate Gallery, London), and in the realist *Irish Famine* (1848–9; Watts Gallery, Compton, near Guildford). In 1851 he was adopted as "resident" artist at Little Holland House; members of the artistic set centered there sat for many of his portraits, for example *Countess Somers* (begun 1860; Watts Gallery, Compton, near Guildford). These were of a consistently high standard, and his reputation rested upon them until his old age.

After the breakup of the Little Holland House set in 1875, Watts became a near recluse. But the idealized portraits he had always considered to be his most important achievement won increasing public acclaim through exhibitions, such as the one-man show at the Grosvenor Gallery in 1882. He married in 1886, and spent his last years at Compton, near Guildford, where the Watts Gallery is now located.

Webb Philip 1831–1915

The English architect Philip Webb was born in Oxford. Until 1859 he worked as George Street's assistant, becoming involved in the fledgling Arts and Crafts movement. He later designed furniture for William Morris's firm, but otherwise devoted his career to domestic architecture. For Morris he designed the Red House, Bexleyheath (1859); here he made an unashamed use of red brick, and included simple furniture and fittings to complement the rustic atmosphere. His later houses (for instance No. 1 Palace Green, London, 1868; Smeaton Manor, Yorkshire, 1878) were also generally of brick. He drew on various vernacular building types, to illustrate his belief in architecture as "the art of common building".

Weber Max 1881–1961

The American painter Max Weber, one of the leading figures in the development of American Modernism, was born in Russia, his family emigrating to the United States when he was 10. He studied at the Pratt Institute, New York, and later (1905–9) in Paris, where he absorbed the influences of Cézanne, Matisse and Henri Rousseau. Back in New York, he exhibited at Stieglitz' 291 Gallery, and began to respond to diverse influences such as Cubism and Futurism on the one hand, and Pre-Columbian and Pacific art on the other.

Right: Jan Weenix: A Merry Company amid Ancient Ruins; oil on canvas; 80×107cm (31×42in); 1667. Musée du Petit Palais, Paris

Below: G.F. Watts: Paolo and Francesca; oil on canvas; 152×130cm (60×51in); 1872–5. Watts Gallery, Compton, near Guildford

His *Rush Hour, New York* (1915; National Gallery of Art, Washington, D.C.) shows Futurist inspiration, while *Chinese Restaurant* (1915; Whitney Museum of American Art, New York) illustrates his complete assimilation of Cubism. *Spiral Rhythm* (also 1915; Hirsshorn Museum and Sculpture Garden, Washington, D.C.) was one of the first Abstract sculptures in American art. He later turned to more traditional forms, often painting affectionate evocations of his Jewish childhood.

Further reading. Werner, A. *Max Weber*, New York (1975).

Weenix Jan 1640–1719

The Dutch painter Jan Weenix painted portraits and Italianate landscapes in the manner of his father and teacher, Jan Baptist (1621–60?), but his popularity derived mainly from his slight but charming hunting trophy pictures: still lifes in which dead hares, peacocks, and other game or fowl are surrounded by fruit, flowers, and sometimes also weapons of the chase. These objects were frequently arranged around ornamental urns or other examples of garden sculpture, and placed in the twilight setting of a park.

Wen Cheng-ming 1470–1559

Wen Cheng-ming came from a large family of painters. His home was in Ts'ang Chou. A fine calligrapher and painter, he started life as an official, but retired early in order

Wen Cheng-ming: Cypress and Rock; ink on paper; 26×49cm (10×19in); 1550. William Rockhill Nelson Gallery, Kansas City, Mo.

to devote himself to painting. He was a pupil of Shen Chou, and was the leader of the Wu School of the 16th century. His son, nephews, grandsons, and great-nephews all followed in his path; probably the most notable among these was his great-nephew Wen Po-jen (1502–75).

It was the Wu School of Wen Cheng-ming that flourished when Tung Ch'i-ch'ang was writing his treatises on painting. Although Wen Cheng-ming thought himself close to the Yuan painters, and was a most versatile and spirited artist, his skill and grace worried Tung Ch'i-ch'ang, ever suspicious of the clever painter.

Wen Cheng-ming painted bamboo with great feeling, in the *literati* School of Li K'an and Wu Chen. When he painted landscape he took up the use of color, already introduced by Wang Meng in the 14th century, and employed with great distinction by Shen Chou in the 15th century. Wen was working within a tradition that had its roots in the *literati* traditions of the Yuan dynasty, but he was indeed along the path of change that became so clear in the 17th century.

In a sense, Wen Cheng-ming is the last of the intuitive *literati* painters. His art does not reveal the critical, analytical concerns of the period from Tung Ch'i-ch'ang to Mo Shih-lung.

Wesselmann Tom 1931–

The American artist Tom Wesselmann came to prominence as one of the leading exponents of Pop art. In the early 1960s he rejected the influence of Abstract Expressionists such as de Kooning, and began using both the techniques and the imagery of magazine and billboard advertising. His works focused on the themes of consumerism (his *Still Life* series featured familiar products such as cigarettes, food stuffs, automobiles) and, increasingly, eroticism. In his best-known work, the series *The Great American Nude*, he treads a fine line between undermining the eroticism of advertising, and exploiting it. Painted in flat, artificial colors and with sinuous outlines derived from Matisse, Wesselmann's nudes are large and two dimensional (some are in fact cut-outs standing in three-dimensional settings). Languorously seductive and totally depersonalized, they are featureless except for exaggerated lips, nipples and genitals: *Great American Nude # 57* (1964; Whitney Museum of American Art, New York) for example. This fetishism was made all the more explicit with works such as *Smoker, I (Mouth 12)* (1967; Museum of Modern Art, New York), a huge picture in the shape of lips and a cigarette.

Further reading. Hunter, S. *Tom Wesselmann*, New York (1994).

West Benjamin 1738–1820

The American portrait and history painter Benjamin West was born near Springfield, Pennsylvania. In the mid 1750s he taught himself to paint, and in 1760 he traveled to Rome, where he came under the influence of A.R. Mengs and Gavin Hamilton. He settled in London in 1763 and for the next decade he had no serious rival in his preferred field of history painting. His *Landing of Agrippina at Brundisium with the Ashes of Germanicus* (1766; Yale University Art Gallery, New Haven, Conn.), commissioned by the Archbishop of York, typifies the style of his first London period, with its scrupulous attention to correct antique details. West's conviction that such realism enhanced dramatic content was probably due to his appreciation of Poussin. His most important and influential picture was *Death of General Wolfe* (1770; National Gallery of Canada, Ottawa). Here he succeeded in portraying an incident from contemporary history with all the pathos and heroism of a Classical tragedy, without recourse to allegory or the associative value of antique dress and settings. His rapid climb to success as a narrative painter culminated in his appointment in 1772 as History Painter to George III, who remained his patron for 40 years.

West was eclectic in his choice of styles and subjects, which over his long career ranged from the strict Neoclassical to the extravagantly sublime after 1780. He was capable of great innovation, but in the main his inspiration came from the current ideas of other artists. Nevertheless, he was the most successful history painter of his generation in England. A founder member of the Royal Academy, he succeeded Reynolds as President in 1792.

Weyden Rogier van der
1399/1400–64

The Flemish painter Rogier van der Weyden was the son of a master cutler of Tournai. He is first documented in 1427, when he began his apprenticeship with the Master of Flémalle (Robert Campin). He did not discover his vocation until comparatively late in life. Unfortunately we have no record of his earlier activities—a Tournai document of 1426, mentioning a civic gift of wine to a man of the same name, seems to be a coincidental reference to another person. In 1432 he was admitted to the Tournai guild, but by 1435 he had already moved to Brussels. The following year he was made a civic painter of his adopted city. But he retained his business interests in Tournai and was commemorated by the artist's guild there after his death. Although he received commissions

Benjamin West: Penn's Treaty with the Indians; oil on canvas; 193×274cm (76×108in); 1771. Pennsylvania Academy of the Fine Arts, Philadelphia

from a very wide circle of patrons, both within the Netherlands and abroad, there is no record of his having taveled, with the exception of a visit to Rome c1450. None of his paintings is dated, so the chronology of his considerable oeuvre remains uncertain. As he maintained a large workshop, this difficulty is compounded by numerous problems of attribution.

Van der Weyden's earliest surviving works are probably a pair of small diptychs of *The Virgin and Child* and *St Catherine in a Landscape* (Kunsthistorisches Museum, Vienna) and *The Virgin and Child* (Thyssen-Bornemisza Collection, Lugano) and *St George and the Dragon* (National Gallery of Art, Washington). The presence of a number of formal motifs, the handling of light, and the tiny scale of both works betray a knowledge of the work of Jan van Eyck; the facial types of the women and the handling of their drapery indicate a closer association with Robert Campin. A similar

combination of influence appears in another early work, the Louvre *Annunciation*. In a number of respects, this picture seems like a critique of the central panel of Campin's Mérode Altarpiece, with the more glaring perspective errors of its predecessor eliminated. By the time of van der Weyden's *St Luke Drawing a Portrait of the Virgin* (Museum of Fine Arts, Boston) the influence of Campin has become vestigial, while that of Jan van Eyck is paramount. The basic composition is a paraphrase of the latter's *The Madonna of Chancellor Rolin* (c1435; Louvre, Paris). Despite this obvious borrowing, *St Luke Drawing the Virgin* exhibits a linear expressiveness absent in its more composed model. It imparts an emotional tension characteristic of van der Weyden's personal style.

This tendency reaches its ultimate expression in the artist's greatest surviving work, the *Descent from the Cross* in the Prado, Madrid. Probably painted in the second

half of the 1430s, this altarpiece was commissioned by the Louvain Archers' Guild. Rejecting a naturalistic landscape setting, van der Weyden compressed the ten nearly life-size figures in his composition within a gilded niche simulating the appearance of a sculptured altarpiece of polychromed wood. The tightly interlocked figures seem to seethe in a single convulsion of pain which brutally drives home the anguish of the Passion. Although the *Descent from the Cross* is a work of immense formal and coloristic richness, these characteristics are subordinate to the fundamentally emotional purpose of the design.

Van der Weyden was an extremely prosperous master by c1441, but records of this period indicate that he did not disdain to polychrome sculpture and paint banners. During the years 1439 to 1441 he worked on the four panels of *The Justice of the Emperor Trajan and Count Herkinbald* which, until their destruction in 1695,

decorated Brussels Town Hall. A tapestry in Bern records parts of this series, though in a much distorted form. The loss of these pictures is doubly unfortunate, both on account of their evident quality—which is described by several chroniclers—and because they constituted the only major secular narrative cycle that the artist is known to have painted. In 1445 King Juan II gave an altarpiece by master "Rogel" to the charterhouse at Miraflores near Burgos, which indicates that van der Weyden's fame had spread as far as Castile. This work is identical with one of two versions of a triptych dedicated to the Virgin (the smaller in the Staatliche Museen, Berlin, and the larger divided between the Royal Chapel, Granada, and the Metropolitan Museum of Art, New York). During the late 1440s he painted the enormous *Last Judgment* altarpiece, which stands in the hospital founded by the Burgundian Chancellor Nicolas Rolin at Beaune, near Dijon. With its gold background, its sculptural associations (the main composition derives from Gothic tympanum reliefs), and its great emotional intensity, this work is comparable with the earlier *Descent from the Cross*.

Documents reveal that at least one altarpiece by van der Weyden had been exported to Ferrara by 1449. They also show that in 1450 and 1451 he received payments from the Este Court, which were perhaps connected with this lost work. In 1450 he was in Rome, where he is supposed to have admired frescoes by Gentile da Fabriano. It is unlikely that this visit lasted long; he probably visited Florence on the same journey. Two of his surviving works were painted for the Medici: the *Madonna and Child with Four Saints* (Städelsches Kunstinstitut, Frankfurt am Main) and the *Entombment* (Uffizi, Florence). Both were probably painted shortly after his return home, and then shipped to Florence. Although they include certain iconographic motifs derived from Italian art, neither suggests that the artist was particularly interested in Florentine style.

A picture such as the Seven Sacraments Altarpiece (Royal Museum of Fine Arts, Antwerp) probably painted for the Bishop of Tournai in the early 1450s, reveals the continued influence of Jan van Eyck. In the

Rogier van der Weyden: Madonna and Child with Four Saints; oak panel; 53×38cm (21×15in); c1450–1. Städelsches Kunstinstitut, Frankfurt am Main

central panel, the placing of the large-scale figures against a vista down a church nave is based upon Jan van Eyck's *Madonna in Church* (c1425–30; Staatliche Museen, Berlin). By extending this basic idea to embrace all three panels, van der Weyden recast the traditional narrative divisions of the triptych format in a way that suggests a section through the nave and aisles of a Gothic church. His Braque Triptych (Louvre, Paris) is probably of similar date. In this small altarpiece, half-length figures of Christ and the saints are set against a distant landscape background in a remarkably original way. It seems probable that later Northern half-length portraits in a landscape setting, which became common at the turn of the 15th and 16th century, derive ultimately from this painting or a related one by the same artist.

With the St John Altarpiece in the Staatliche Museen, Berlin, van der Weyden returned to the format of a simulated triple portal containing three scenes, similar to the one he had employed a decade earlier in the altarpiece of the Virgin for Miraflores. However, the scenes depicted are visually more complex than those in the Miraflores altarpiece. Increased formal and iconographic complexity is also characteristic of the Berlin Bladelin Triptych (Staatliche Museen). By comparison, the diptych of *Christ on the Cross* and *St John and the Virgin* (John G. Johnson Collection, Philadelphia) is a very austere composition, with every nonessential detail eliminated. Rogier's last major work is the St Columba Altarpiece. Probably painted in c1460 for a church in Cologne, it is now in the Alte Pinakothek, Munich. Reminiscences of the whole span of the artist's work, from the Louvre *Annunciation* to the Bladelin Triptych, are combined in this altarpiece. It is a magisterial work, distinguished by exquisite formal and coloristic harmonies.

In addition to a number of other religious works, van der Weyden painted many portraits, both as independent works and combined with bust-length pictures of the Virgin and Child as devotional diptychs. Few of these are documented and it is difficult to establish their chronology. It is clear, however, that the artist developed a new and refined type of aristocratic portrait, by subjectively manipulating the likenesses of his sitters.

Van der Weyden was the third of the great trio of painters who founded the Early Netherlandish school. Although he

Rogier van der Weyden: Portrait of a Lady; oil on panel; 36×28cm (14×11in); c1450–60. National Gallery, London

drew upon Campin and Jan van Eyck, his elegant and emotive style is quite distinct. His many exported works, and his large atelier, which drew artists even from Italy, broadcast his style throughout Europe. It would be no exaggeration to state that he was the most influential Northern painter of the 15th century.

Further reading. Davies, M. *Rogier van der Weyden*, London (1972). Friedländer, M.J. *Early Netherlandish Painting* vol. 2, *Rogier van der Weyden and the Master of Flémalle*, Brussels and Leiden (1967). Panofsky, E. *Early Netherlandish Painting* (2 vols.), Cambridge, Mass. (1953). *Rogier van der Weyden*, Brussels (1979).

Whistler J.A.M. 1834–1903

The American painter, graphic artist, and designer James Abbott McNeill Whistler was born in Massachusetts. He spent his boyhood in St Petersburg, where his father supervised the construction of the railway to Moscow. He was sent to West Point military academy but was dismissed for failure in his chemistry studies. After a brief spell with the U.S. Coastal Survey, where he learned to etch maps and plans, he left to study in Paris in 1855. He entered the studio of Charles Gleyre, a painter of the Tugier School, and published his first set of etchings, *The French Set*, in 1858.

These were quickly appreciated by fellow artists such as Henri Fantin-Latour and Alphonse Legros. Whistler adopted the pose of a Bohemian, and remained throughout his career true to the figure of a "dandy" as invented by Baudelaire. The image of a butterfly that he adopted for his signature is an apt expression of his character, and one that fitted in well with the young Parisian art world. In 1858 his

first painting, *At the Piano*, was rejected at the Salon (retouched 1859; now in the Taft Museum, Cincinnati). When in the following year it won applause at the Royal Academy, Whistler turned his attention towards London. He was also at this time strongly influenced by Velazquez (1599–1660). He gradually pulled away from the blatant realism of Gustave Courbet towards the restrained light and way of life of England and the English.

In 1859 Whistler bought a house in

London. He began depicting the Thames both in a group of etchings and in a long series of oil paintings: *The Thames in Ice* (1862; Freer Gallery of Art, Washington, D.C.), *The Last of Old Westminster* (1863; Museum of Fine Arts, Boston), *Wapping* (1864; John Hay Whitney Collection, New York), and *Old Battersea Bridge* (c1872; Tate Gallery, London). During this period he also produced *The White Girl* (1862; National Gallery of Art, Washington, D.C.). The painting was rejected by the Paris Salon, and was exhibited instead at the Salon des Refusés in 1863, where it caused a sensation. In it we can see Whistler at his closest to the English Pre-Raphaelites, particularly Dante Rossetti, but still distinctly individual in style. Whistler's paintings, even when they reflect the current fashion, were never derivative. He had learned from the French artists, particularly from Courbet, to enjoy the medium itself, and was thus insured against the sentimental, small-minded qualities of English genre painting.

Through his interest in Japanese art, from c1863, Whistler was able to expand his aesthetic approach. *Japonisme* eventually offered him a path of development along the lines of self-control and concentration of effort. Some of the early "Japanese" pictures, such as *Purple and Rose, the Lange Lijzen of the Six Marks* (1864; John G. Johnson Collection, Philadelphia), are not much more than costume pieces. He was influenced, like his contemporaries, by Japanese works he saw in London and Paris.

After a brief period of impasse, when Whistler attempted a combination of *Japonisme* and classicism, reminiscent of George Moore, he broke through to a deeper style of self-expression. This began after he traveled to Valparaiso, Chile, and saw the Pacific Ocean for the first time. He worked Japanese balance and harmony into his own simplified decorative schemes in a much more organic way (for example, *Three Figures*, c1868; Tate Gallery, London). In his absorption of the ideas of the Orient, he achieved a breakthrough for Western painting. He influenced the art public towards an awareness of Eastern style, not simply bending mannerisms to fit Western ways of seeing, but contributing to a general appreciation of the pure and abstract qualities of Eastern thought and design. It is through his taste for Japanese art and culture that we see Whistler's affinity with Art Nouveau.

J.A.M. Whistler: Finette; drypoint on paper; 29×20cm (11×8in); 1859. British Museum, London

J.A.M. Whistler: Nocturne in Black and Gold: the Falling Rocket; panel; 60×47cm (24×19in); c1874. Detroit Institute of Arts

Whistler's answer was that it contained the experience of a lifetime. In this exchange, two codes, the work ethic and the new aestheticism, met head on. Whistler won the case, was awarded a farthing's damages, and retired abroad, bankrupt.

With the set of etchings he produced in Venice in 1879 and 1880, Whistler brilliantly recouped his losses. On his return he began lecturing on art, publishing his ideas in 1885 in *The Ten o'Clock Lectures*. Here he printed in full the dialogue of the trial, and continued the argument, by declaring his then-radical belief that form and color could exist on their own without material support from subject matter. Whistler made himself known as the chief proponent of the doctrine of "art for art's sake", relating this back to analogies between art and music, and his early use of musical terms in picture titles.

Whistler was elected to the Royal Society of British Artists in 1884. He was married in 1888 and published *The Gentle Art of Making Enemies* in 1890. His final etchings included *The Dutch Series* of the 1890s. He taught at the Académie Carmen from 1898 to 1901, and died in London two years later.

Further reading. Gaunt, W. *The Aesthetic Adventure*, London (1945). Kennedy, E. *The Etched Work of Whistler* (4 vols.), New York (1971). Pennell, R. and J. *The Life of James McNeill Whistler* (2 vols.), London and Philadelphia (1921). Spalding, F. *Whistler*, Oxford (1979). Sutton, D. *James McNeill Whistler: Paintings, Etchings, Pastels, and Watercolours*, London (1966). Weintraub, S. *Whistler: a Biography*, London (1974). Young, A.M., Macdonald, M., and Spencer, R. *The Paintings of James McNeill Whistler* (2 vols.), London and New Haven (1980).

The *Nocturnes* of the 1870s mark the summit of his achievement. His later portraits and his design work, such as the well known *Peacock Room* (1876–7; Freer Gallery of Art, Washington, D.C.), are important steps along the same path. Seen in retrospect, they have won their just place in the development of both American and European painting. But during the artist's lifetime, they seemed as peculiar and outrageous as the public figure that Whistler deliberately cut for himself. It is not surprising that his works and his lifestyle were misunderstood by a critic like John Ruskin: they were a deliberate challenge to the ethics of the previous age.

The notorious Ruskin/Whistler slander trial was caused by the critic's accusation that the painter had slung a pot of paint in the public's face when he produced *Nocturne in Black and Gold: the Falling Rocket* (c1874; Detroit Institute of Arts). One crucial question was, how long had it taken the artist to complete the picture?

Wiligelmo of Modena *fl. c*1100–25

Wiligelmo of Modena was a Romanesque sculptor of great individuality and powers of expression, who had a profound influence on the history of sculpture. Nothing is known about him except that he was the principal sculptor of Modena Cathedral in Emilia, rebuilt from 1099. A boastful inscription praises him, but gives no clues as to his origin or previous career. It seems likely that he was familiar with a newly emerging school of sculpture in Apulia, and that he admired Ottonian ivories.

The principal source for his art, however, was Roman sculpture, of which many more examples existed at that time in Italy than today. During the building of Modena Cathedral, many Roman reliefs were excavated, and some were incorporated into the facade, alongside Wiligelmo's frieze, carved panels, doorways, and capitals. His frieze, showing scenes from Genesis (from the Creation to the Flood), clearly imitates friezes on Roman monuments, although the iconography is Christian. Some of his other reliefs are unmistakable copies of Roman models.

Wiligelmo's style is expressive and monumental. On the jambs of the west doorway, he employed figures of prophets under arcades, placed one above the other; the method was later taken up in St-Denis Abbey, Paris, and in several Gothic cathedrals of the 13th century. His collaborators, pupils, and followers, although lacking his genius, carried the influence of his style throughout northern Italy and beyond—to Aragon and Catalonia, and to Hungary. The frieze on the facade of Lincoln Cathedral was a faint English imitation of Wiligelmo's Modena frieze.

It has recently been arged that Wiligelmo's frieze was intended for a screen inside Modena Cathedral, and was moved on to the facade in the second half of the 12th century. This theory has, however, been conclusively refuted.

Wilkie David 1785–1841

The Scottish painter Sir David Wilkie was born at Cults, Grampian, where his father was a minister. From 1799 to 1804 he trained at the Trustees Academy, Edinburgh. Before moving to London in 1805, he had already produced rustic scenes influenced by both 17th-century Dutch and recent Scottish genre painting. His reputation was established with *The Village Politicians* (1806; private collection). The painting shows an animated discussion in a shabby alehouse, full of anecdotal incident, and reminiscent of work by Adriaen Ostade and David Teniers. The purchasers of such low-life subjects were largely aristocratic, although they reached a wider middle-class audience through engravings. Official recognition soon capped Wilkie's popularity: he was made Associate of the Royal Academy in 1809, and a full member two years later.

In 1812 he mounted an exhibition of his own work, featuring *Blind Man's Buff*

(1812; Collection of H.M. Queen Elizabeth II). The sweetened appearance of the cavorting figures contrasts with that of their boorish predecessors in the first peasant works. *The Letter of Introduction* (1813–14; National Gallery of Scotland, Edinburgh) also represents a branching-out of his art, its subject matter being pitched at a higher social level. In a well-furnished study, a young visitor presents himself to an aged writer, whose suspicious, sidelong look is amusingly echoed in the sniffing of his dog at the stranger's knee. Wilkie's narrative technique was a seminal influence on Victorian genre painting. The tragic tenor of *Distraining for Rent* (1815; private collection) aroused critical displeasure, so the artist, always

seeking to attune his style to the taste of his market, did not pursue this vein.

His best-known picture, *Chelsea Pensioners Reading the Waterloo Despatch* (1821–2; Wellington Museum, London), was shown at the Royal Academy. It was accompanied by a lengthy passage describing each of the veterans who are receiving the news of victory outside a tavern on London's King's Road. Its patriotism and sentimental warmth proved enormously appealing; it had to be roped off from the crowds at the exhibition. The subject brought Wilkie's familiar anecdotal genre towards the "higher" category of modern history painting.

The continental tours he undertook for health reasons between 1825 and 1828,

David Wilkie: The First Earring; oil on panel; 74×61cm (29×24in); 1835. Tate Gallery, London

and especially the Spanish Old Masters he saw, led Wilkie to transform his style. This is evident in, for instance, *Empress Josephine and the Fortune-Teller* (1837; National Gallery of Scotland, Edinburgh), with its loose, rapid brushwork and its imposing scale: it is 7 ft (2.5 m) in height. The adoption of this grander manner may result in part from Wilkie taking over from Sir Thomas Lawrence the distinguished post of Painter-in-Ordinary to the King in 1830. He was knighted in 1836. His principal output was now to be portraiture. His *William IV* (1833; Wellington Museum, London), perhaps the finest example, contains passages of bold impasto, notably the plumes of the military helmet.

In 1840 Wilkie visited the Holy Land. His intention, anticipating that of Holman Hunt, was to collect material for historically accurate paintings of biblical subjects. He died on the return voyage.

William of Sens *fl.* 1174–9

William of Sens was a French master mason. He is named in Gervase's account of the burning and repair of Canterbury Cathedral as the man who directed the rebuilding of the choir after the fire of 1174. Presumably from Sens in France, he was at one time also supposed to have been the architect of Sens Cathedral, but this is no longer accepted. He may have known Sens, however, as well as other more recent French buildings, to judge from the evidence of Canterbury choir, which was the first thoroughgoing Gothic design to be executed in England. In 1178, before work was finished, William fell from a scaffold. He retired to France the following year.

William the Englishman
fl. 1179–84

The master mason known as William the Englishman succeeded William of Sens in 1179, as mason in charge of the new choir of Canterbury Cathedral. He first completed the eastern transepts and then built the Trinity Chapel with Becket's Corona by 1184. The architectural character of these two operations is entirely different: the first is the least French in character, while the other is the most French part of the entire work. For the Trinity Chapel, William of Sens had probably prepared designs which his successor followed faithfully; the transepts, however, called for fresh invention. The transepts were prob-

Richard Wilson: The Valley of Mawddach and Cader Idris; oil on canvas; 102×107cm (40×42in); c1774? Walker Art Gallery, Liverpool

ably the most influential part of the new work at Canterbury.

Willumsen Jens 1863–1958

Jens Ferdinand Willumsen was a Danish artist who was a fringe member of the School of Pont-Aven. His artistic activities extended from painting to architecture, ceramics, sculpture, and art criticism. He trained in Copenhagen. In the summer of 1890, during a visit to the popular artists' resort of Pont-Aven in Brittany, he met Gauguin, who initiated him into Pictorial Symbolism. Willumsen quickly adopted the new style of flat, brightly colored, and simplified painting. His bas-relief *A Work from the Quarry* (1891; State Art Museum, Copenhagen) comes close to Gauguin's work in this medium. But his paintings, such as *Breton Women Walking* (1891; J.F. Willumsen Museum, Fredrikssund, Denmark), owe more to Émile Bernard's crude painted surfaces and Sérusier's simplified but lively silhouettes. He retired to Norway in 1892, in search of the pictorial equivalent of the symbolism of Gauguin's "Bible": *Sartor Resartus*

(published 1836) by Thomas Carlyle.

Wilson Richard 1714–82

The portrait and landscape painter Richard Wilson was the most important British artist before J.M.W. Turner and John Constable to have devoted most of his career to landscape painting in oils.

He was born at Penegoes in Wales, and from 1729 he studied in London with a minor portrait artist. He painted portraits until 1750; *Admiral Thomas Smith* (c1744; National Maritime Museum, Greenwich) is a good example of his work in this field. In 1750 he went to Italy, staying briefly in Venice before establishing himself in Rome. About 1752 he was persuaded, probably by Claude-Joseph Vernet, to become a landscape painter. In the same year he painted *banditti* and history subjects in the styles of Marco Ricci and Poussin. His earliest dated Italian landscape, *View of Rome from the Villa Madama* (1753; Paul Mellon Center for British Art, New Haven, Conn.) was painted for the Earl of Dartmouth, who later commissioned from

Wilson a superb series of finished landscape drawings in chalk. The landscapes of Wilson's Italian sojourn depict standard views in the environs of Rome and Naples. Their principles of composition were derived largely from Claude and Gaspar Dughet. They were specially admired and collected as souvenirs by English aristocrats making the Grand Tour.

About 1757 Wilson, by then master of a fully developed landscape style, returned to London. There he continued to paint Italian views based on the careful studies from nature he had accumulated during his visit. Seeking recognition as a "serious" painter in the Grand Manner, he again essayed historical landscape with *The Destruction of Niobe's Children* (c1760; Paul Mellon Center for British Art, New Haven, Conn.). A version of this painting was shown at the first Society of Artists exhibition in 1760. He was a founder member of the Royal Academy in 1768. In addition to Italian and historical landscapes, Wilson painted country house "portraits" and Welsh views. His five views of Wilton (Collection of the Earl of Pembroke, Wilton, Wiltshire), and his *Snowdon* (1766; Walker Art Gallery, Liverpool), are perhaps his most original contributions to these categories. In his later pictures, the influence of Dutch 17th-century artists, in particular the clear, luminous style of Aelbert Cuyp, becomes increasingly evident. Although he was neglected by patrons toward the end of his life, Wilson had demonstrated the serious purpose of landscape painting. His example inspired English painters well into the next century, and his work foreshadows that of Corot.

Wilton Joseph 1722–1803

The English sculptor Joseph Wilton was born in London, the son of a wealthy plasterer. He had a better training than any English sculptor of his time, being apprenticed to Paul Delvaux at Nivelles, and later joining the workshop of Jean-Baptiste Pigalle in Paris. In 1747 he went to Italy, where he worked successfully for seven years, first in Rome and later in Florence. On his return to London, he established a busy practice in all branches of sculpture. He was a founder member of the Royal Academy in 1769. After inheriting a considerable fortune, he became lazy and extravagant, and too dependent on his large workshop. Although he was the most talented native English sculptor of the 18th

century, Wilton was uneven and indecisive in performance; only occasionally did he show in his work the great brilliance of which he was capable.

Witte Emanuel de c1617–92

The Dutch painter Emanuel de Witte tackled many subjects but is best known for his church interiors, in which he specialized after moving from Delft to Amsterdam in the early 1650s. His interiors are different from the more objective works of Pieter Saenredam (1597–1665), in that the de-

tails and proportions of his buildings are frequently altered, as in *The Choir of the New Church in Amsterdam* (Rijksmuseum, Amsterdam), where the elevation is heightened to stress the church's majestic loftiness. Elsewhere, motifs from different churches are combined in one building, without, however, any loss of architectural homogeneity and authenticity. In some paintings the views are wholly imaginary.

De Witte's massive, silent interiors are generally pierced with dramatic shafts of light, themselves often arbitrary. These,

Emanuel de Witte: The Interior of the Oude Kerk, Amsterdam, during a Sermon; oil on canvas; 79×63cm (31×25in); c1658–9. National Gallery, London

with contrasting pools of shade, heighten the spatial effects and the sense of awesomeness. In this, and in his relatively rich color, de Witte's work is more pictorial than the geometrically organized pictures of Saenredam. De Witte, who achieved little financial success and finally committed suicide, also painted a number of fish-market scenes, some of which contain portraits.

Witz Konrad 1400–45

The Swiss painter Konrad Witz was born at Rottweil in southern Germany. He moved to Basel, becoming a citizen in 1435. The previous year he had been accepted into the artists' guild. About 1435 he was commissioned to paint the so-called "Speculum" Altarpiece. His only signed and dated work, the St Peter Altarpiece, was completed and installed in Geneva Cathedral in 1444.

Witz's altarpieces have long since been dismantled, and many parts are lost. From the Speculum Altarpiece, 12 of the original 16 panels of the wings have survived (Öffentliche Kunstsammlung, Kunstmuseum Basel; Staatliche Museen, Berlin; Musée des Beaux-Arts, Dijon). Their subjects indicate a typological program, wherein scenes from the Old Testament and ancient history prefigure scenes from the New Testament. The latter were probably contained in the missing central section. Only the wings remain of the St Peter Altarpiece (Musée d'Art et d'Histoire, Geneva). They consist of four panels, including the famous *Miraculous Draft of Fishes*—sometimes called *Christ Walking on the Water*. With its view over Lake Geneva, this is one of the first landscape portraits. The painting may be an involved allusion to the deliberations of the Council of Basel (1431–43). Witz's paintings include panels from other dismantled altarpieces, for example, *The Meeting of Joachim and Anna* (Öffentliche Kunstsammlung, Kunstmuseum, Basel).

Witz rejected the Soft style of painting current in southern Germany *c*1430. Through the influence of Robert Campin and Jan van Eyck he forged his own style, whose hallmark is the heavy, firmly molded forms of his figures. With their dignified air, large heads, and narrow shoulders, they dominate the compositions, displaying only restrained emotions. Witz's brand of realism omits the minute detail of Flemish painting, except in the

Konrad Witz: Miraculous Draft of Fishes (Christ Walking on the Water); tempera on panel; 130×155cm (51×61in); 1444. Musée d'Art et d'Histoire, Geneva

depiction of the surface textures of materials such as wood, stone, flaking plaster, and metal.

Wolgemut Michael 1434–1519

The German painter Michael Wolgemut was born in Nuremberg where he was the master of Albrecht Dürer from 1486 to 1490. Earlier Wolgemut had taken over the workshop of Hans Pleydenwurff, after the latter's death in 1472; he also married his widow. Wolgemut's personal style as a painter is difficult to reconstruct. His *Mass of St Gregory* at Andechs (1470–1; Schatzkammer und Reliquienkapelle) was painted while he was active in the workshop of Gabriel Mälesskircher in Nuremberg. Although Wolgemut was the leading painter in the city until Dürer returned in 1495, after his first visit to Italy, his many studio assistants collaborated on the large number of altarpieces executed during the years in which he was master of the

Michael Wolgemut: the frontispiece to Hartmann Schedel's "Weltchronik"; woodcut; 1493

workshop, so the exact contribution of Wolgemut himself is often difficult to define. These altarpieces range from the altar of the church of the Virgin at Zwickau (1479), and the Peringsdörff Altar of 1486–8, painted for the church of the Holy Cross, Nuremberg, to late commissions such as the high altar of the town church of Schwabach (1507–8), where the carved elements were executed by a pupil of Veit Stoss.

In the Peringsdörff panels, the influence of Martin Schongauer (*c*1430–91) is added to the precise Netherlandish treatment Wolgemut inherited from Hans Pleydenwurff; the rich, sober coloring creates an immensely decorative effect. Wolgemut collaborated with Wilhelm Pleydenwurff in the design of the woodcuts for the *Schatzbehalter* published in Nuremberg (1491), and for Hartmann Schedel's *Weltchronik* (1493). Albrecht Dürer paid tribute to Wolgemut in his portrait of the aging master, dated 1516 (Germanisches Nationalmuseum, Nuremberg).

Wols 1913–51

The German painter, printmaker, photographer, and writer, Wolfgang Schülze, known as Wols, was born in Berlin in

Below: Wols: Gouache; gouache on canvas; 22×15cm (9×6in); 1949. Collection of John Craven, Paris

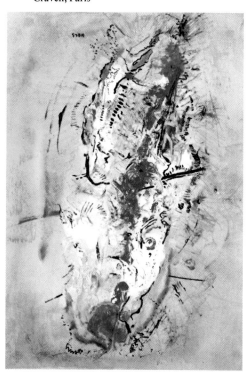

Above: Grant Wood: American Gothic; oil on beaverboard; 76×64cm (30×25in); 1930. Art Institute of Chicago

1913. Although he drew and painted all his life, he had not intended to become an artist. He was a talented musician, but briefly studied ethnography, and then attended the Berlin Bauhaus. In the same year, 1932, he moved to Paris, where he met Amédée Ozenfant, Fernand Léger, Jean Arp, and others.

From 1933 to 1936 Wols lived in Spain with his wife Grety. He then returned to Paris, where he gave his first exhibition of photographs. He continued to paint in his spare time, signing himself "Wols". At the outbreak of the Second World War he was interned for 18 months. It was then that he began his extraordinary improvisations which were first shown in 1946 at the Drouin Gallery, Paris. Done on notepaper, and extremely small in scale, they show a gradual development over a six year period. Their personal imagery derives from variations of figures, creatures, build-

ings, and boats. Some of them are reminiscent of works by Paul Klee, for instance *Dockland* (1941–2; private collection). Later the open, angular line gives way to the characteristic, spidery network of lines which makes the images impossible to identify. He creates a fantasy world of vegetation, micro-organisms, and tangled nerves, as in *Crane de Poète* (1943; private collection).

On his return to Paris Wols began to paint on a larger scale in a semiautomatic style related to *tachisme* and *art informel*. His use of thick paint was partly influenced by Jean Fautrier. The paintings are Abstract and gestural, like *Taches Rouges* (1949–50; private collection), and only occasionally reveal glimpses of his earlier imagery. Wols remained in Paris to the end of his life. His growing reputation led to commissions for illustrations to works by Sartre, Kafka, and others.

Wood Grant 1891–1942

The American painter Grant Wood was born in Iowa and lived there all his life. For family reasons, he began his artistic training late. In the 1920s he paid several visits to Europe, where he was decisively influenced by the meticulous style of the early Flemish and German masters. His subject matter was the Iowa world that he knew, and he brought both to people and to places an unwaveringly precise vision, evident in his best-known work, *American Gothic* (1930; Art Institute of Chicago).

Further reading. Dennis, J. *Grant Wood: A Study in American Art and Culture*, New York (1975).

Wotruba Fritz 1907–75

The Austrian sculptor Fritz Wotruba trained as an engraver, but turned to sculpture, studying under Anton Hanak in 1926. He produced his first stone sculpture in 1928. He took part in the intellectual activity of Vienna during the 1930s; he was particularly associated with Josef Hoffmann. During the Second World War he and his wife lived in Switzerland. In 1945 they returned to Vienna, where he was appointed professor at the Vienna Akademie der Bildenden Kunst. He exhibited widely, and met Henry Moore in 1951. Wotruba worked in stone as well as bronze. His concept of sculpture was architectural and monumental—he portrayed the structure of the human body in a compact mass of geometric forms (for example, *Feminine Rock;* limestone; 1947–8; Middelheim Open-Air Museum of Sculpture, Antwerp).

Wouwermans Philips 1619–68

The Dutch painter Philips Pandsz. Wouwermans was born in Haarlem, the eldest son of a painter; he may have been taught by Frans Hals. He was early influenced by the works of Pieter Verbeecq (c1612–c54) and by the dune landscapes of Jan Wijnants (1630/5–84). Even more influential were the small genre scenes of outdoor life painted by Pieter van Laer, who in 1638 returned to Haarlem from Rome. Yet Wouwermans was a more productive artist whose subjects were more varied and who, especially in his late years, developed an attractive freedom of handling and light palette. He specialized in landscapes, often with horses; and he also painted encampments, hunts, battles, and dune or seashore views.

Further reading. Rosenberg, J. et al. *Dutch Art and Architecture, 1600–1800*, New York (1966).

Wren Christopher 1632–1723

Sir Christopher Wren was England's greatest Baroque architect. His early years were devoted almost exclusively to scientific pursuits. In 1657, when only 25, he was appointed Professor of Astronomy to Gresham College, London; in 1661 he became Savilian Professor of Astronomy at Oxford University. His career as an architect began in 1663, when he was made a commissioner for the restoration of Old St Paul's, London. His first building, Pembroke College Chapel, Cambridge, dates from this year. When he visited France from 1665 to 1666, it was as an architect rather than as a scientist, and the transition was completed in 1667 when, as a commissioner appointed under the Rebuilding Act, he was made responsible for rebuilding St Paul's Cathedral and the 51 City churches destroyed by the Fire of London. Two years later he was appointed Surveyor General of the King's Works. He held this post until 1714, exercising a virtual monopoly over official architecture.

Wren's earliest buildings are competent and academic, but contain little hint of his future development. The Sheldonian Theatre, Oxford (1664–9), was thus more remarkable for its ingeniously constructed roof (replaced in the late 19th century) than for the originality of its design, which carefully reconstructed Serlio's description of the Theater of Marcellus.

The City churches, begun after his return from France, combined a compositional freedom and a spatial ingenuity that had been entirely lacking in his early buildings. His style developed to sudden maturity with the grandiose interior of St Paul's Cathedral (1675–1710). The exterior is equally impressive. It drew heavily upon the example of 17th-century French ecclesiastical architecture, but the composition of dome and flanking towers was probably suggested by engravings of Borromini's church of S. Agnese, Piazza Navona, Rome (1653–7).

His later work falls into two distinct styles: an austere and monumental classicism, well exemplified by the Royal Hospital, Chelsea (1682–91), and a freer, more

Philips Wouwermans: A View on a Seashore with Fishwives Offering Fish to a Horseman; oil on panel; 35×41cm (14×16in). National Gallery, London

Christopher Wren: St Andrew-by-the-Wardrobe, London; 1685–95

ostensibly Baroque style, anticipated by his second project for St Paul's (1773). This found its fullest expression at the end of his career, in his plans for The Royal Hospital, Greenwich (1696–1707), clearly influenced by Louis Levau's masterpiece, the Collège des Quatre Nations, Paris.

As Surveyor General, Wren worked almost exclusively for the Office of Works. Of his few independent commissions, Trinity College Library, Cambridge (1676–84), reveals the Wren style at its most classical. Tom Tower, Christ Church, Oxford (1681–2), is his most ambitious essay in the Gothic style.

As an architect of European stature, Wren exerted an enormous influence over late-17th- and early-18th-century British architecture. His most talented assistant in the Office of Works was Nicholas Hawksmoor. He was also by far the most important formative influence in the careers of Sir John Vanbrugh, William Talman, Thomas Archer, and James Gibbs.

Further reading. Beard, G. *The Work of Christopher Wren*, Edinburgh (1982). Downes, K. *Christopher Wren*, Harmondsworth (1971). Little, B. *Sir Christopher Wren: a Historical Biography*, London (1975). Sebler, E.F. (trans. Murray, P. and L.) *Wren and his Place in European Architecture*, London and New York (1956). Summerson, J. *Wren*, London (1971). Whinney, M. *Wren*, London (1971).

Wright Frank Lloyd 1869–1959

The American architect Frank Lloyd Wright was not only one of the four or five masters of modern architecture, he was also one of its pioneers, of the generation of Peter Behrens, Auguste Perret, and Adolf Loos. His long career spanned some 70 years, and his influence upon European architecture during the crucial second decade of the 20th century was decisive.

Wright was born in Wisconsin; his parents were of English and Welsh origin. In the 1870s he benefited from the Fröbel Kindergarten system of visual and constructive education, which fostered his strong love of natural forms and his craftsman's respect for natural materials.

In 1888 he began work in the Chicago office of the great American architect Louis Sullivan. This apprenticeship, to a man he never ceased to admire, led to his setting up on his own in 1893. After designing a handful of buildings in the 1890s, Wright evolved his first mature domestic style. This can be seen in his Prairie houses, so called because of their similarity to open-planned American frontier farmhouses: low and spreading, with wide projecting eaves and unbroken horizontal window-strips. The interior spaces flow into one another, and interior and exterior interpenetrate.

This was Wright's "organic" architecture, somewhat Japanese in character, which merged harmoniously with the landscape. Its abstract, spatial features, rather than its 19th-century qualities of craftsmanship, were later admired by the younger generation in Europe. Two fine examples of the Prairie house are the Barton house, Buffalo, New York (1903–4), and the Robie house, Chicago (1908).

At the same time that he was designing these largely traditional constructions, Wright was experimenting with concrete and other new materials in his nondomestic building. From this early, influential period two works stand out for their fusion of the monumental with a new conception of space: the Larkin Office Building, Buffalo, New York (1904), and Unity Temple, Oak Park, Chicago (1906).

Between 1910 and 1930 Wright's output declined. He went through a "baroque", ornamental phase, built a series of houses out of precast concrete blocks, and worked on a number of designs. It was not until the mid 1930s, with two outstanding buildings, that he became as well known in the United States as he was abroad. The first was the Kaufmann house (Falling Water) in Pennsylvannia (1936). This proved that its architect had lost neither his remarkable flair for dramatic siting, nor his sensitivity to both natural materials and the techniques of construction favored by the International style.

In the Johnson Wax Factory, Racine, Wisconsin (1936–9), Wright made use of reinforced concrete mushroom columns and glasstube diffused lighting. He later added a Laboratory Tower (1949). The whole effect was slick and streamlined—a far cry from the aesthetic of rock, wood, earth, and water that influenced Wright's two Taliesin communities. Taliesin West, in the Arizona Desert (1938), was built of what Wright called "desert concrete"—

volcanic rocks joined by a minimum of cement.

In the last two decades of his life, Wright became increasingly interested in plans of a nonrectangular format. The Guggenheim Museum, New York (1943–59), is a dazzling triumph of the circle and spiral, and a modern masterpiece of interior space and movement. Despite some wayward projects, Wright was, to the end, an architect of colossal stature.

Further reading. Brooks Pfeiffor, B. (ed.) *The Collected Writings of Frank Lloyd Wright* (3 vols.) New York (1992). Scully, V. Jr. *Frank Lloyd Wright*, London and New York (1960).

Wright of Derby Joseph 1734–97

The English painter Joseph Wright was born at Derby. He was a student of the portrait painter Thomas Hudson, and by 1760 had an established portrait practice in the Midlands. During the next decade he painted his best known pictures, depicting nocturnal industrial scenes and scientific experiments. He emulated in these works the dramatic, artificial lighting effects he had admired in 17th-century Dutch and Flemish pictures, in particular the candle-light scenes of the Utrecht followers of Caravaggio. Wright studied in Italy from 1773 to 1775, and settled permanently at Derby in 1777. At the Royal Academy he exhibited Italian landscapes, portraits, and paintings of literary subjects. In 1784 he

Joseph Wright of Derby: The Earthstopper on the Banks of the Derwent; oil on canvas; 97×121cm (38×48in); 1773. Derby Museums and Art Gallery

Andrew Wyeth: Christina's World; tempera on gesso panel; 81×121cm (32×48in); 1948. Museum of Modern Art, New York

declined an offer of full membership in the Royal Academy because of a quarrel concerning the display of his pictures. Versatile in his painting technique, and innovative in his selection and presentation of subject matter, Wright occupies a secure position in the forefront of the English Romantic movement.

Wu Ch'ang-shih 1844–1927

The Chinese painter Wu Ch'ang-shih came from Huchow in Chekiang. He trained and worked at first as a seal carver, and took up painting later in life. He was a pupil of Jen Po-nien (1839–95) and painted a wide variety of subjects: Buddhist figures, landscape, flowers, bamboo, and trees. His flower painting has survived to epitomize his style, which is bold and yet sensitive. He followed Chu Ta and Li Shan, working in a heavy liquid ink style but adding subtle and beautiful color to produce handsome and often rich painting. His calligraphy is strong and distinctive, and plays an important part in the creation of vitality on the picture surface.

Wu Chen 1280–1354

The Chinese painter Wu Chen was of humble origin, and had a retiring nature. He never undertook official employment,

Wu Chen: Bamboo; ink on paper; 34×44cm (13×17in). National Palace Museum, Taipei

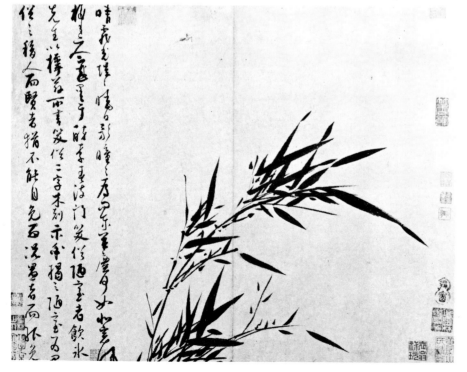

but earned his living as a diviner until his reputation as a painter grew, and he was able to retire from the world to live very quietly in the Chiang Nan area. He was one of the group of painters working in this area, although he was not the most successful of them. His most famous painting is the *Fishermen* handscroll (1342; Freer Gallery of Art, Washington, D.C.), a quiet ink painting on paper depicting the misty landscape of the Hangchow area and the people who live in boats. His ink technique is fluent and gentle, with elements of Kao K'o-kung and Chao Meng-

fu, but also of the Hsia-Ma school, from whom he adopted the use of washes and recession expressed in tone. Wu Chen was not highly estimated in his lifetime, but his free and yet controlled use of ink made him an influential artist, admired for his ability to open up the sophisticated Southern Sung style.

Wu Tao-tzu c680–c740

The Chinese painter Wu Tao-tzu came of humble parentage, and was left an orphan at Yangti, near Loyang in Honan. However, he was educated, studied calligraphy and poetry, and held minor official positions. He was a man of strong character, recorded as having a quick temper and love of wine, and he was capable of flamboyant energy. His reputation as a painter now rests entirely on contemporary stories, for nothing remains of his work except a few pale copies and engravings. Few painters have excited such admiration and respect in their lifetime. Wu's vitality and speed of work gave rise to wonder. He was able to transmit this energy in his painting, and stories of the life-like quality of his paintings of dragons and horses abound. It was said that in his painting of dragons on one of the palace walls "the scales seemed to be moving and, whenever it was going to rain, they emanated vapors and mist".

Wu Tao-tzu was a Buddhist and painted many murals for both Buddhist and Taoist temples in the two capitals of T'ang. Unfortunately these were all destroyed in the anti-Buddhist rioting of the 9th century. However, the copies and contemporary scraps preserved in such treasuries as the Shosoin, Nara, give an impression of a search for vitality of line and movement, and it is probable that Wu was a master of this modulated line. He was also a master of color and the grand composition. In many ways the antithesis of Wang Wei, he was held by his contemporaries to have been the greatest artist of the dynasty in all aspects of painting. He was perhaps the last of the great exponents of many different styles; he became known as the father of the figure-painters of later periods.

Wyatt James 1746–1813

James Wyatt was the most popular English architect of the late 18th century. He was born in Staffordshire and trained in Italy from 1762 to 1768. His early buildings, such as Heveningham Hall, Suffolk (1780–4), were nearly all in an Adam-inspired classical style. Although this developed into an austere and more personal Neoclassicism, his late reputation rested almost entirely on his talents as a Gothicist. His mature works, beginning with Fonthill Abbey, Wiltshire (1796–1813; destroyed), and including Ashridge, Hertfordshire (1808–13), were frequently vast in scale and displayed a mastery of Gothic detail far in advance of that of any other contemporary architect.

Wyeth Andrew 1917–

The American painter Andrew Newell Wyeth was born in Pennsylvania and was trained by his father, the artist and illustrator Newell Convers Wyeth (1882–1944). His talent showed early and he became well known during his teens. He works in a very exact and realistic style that owes something to Surrealism and a good deal more to photography. His great success, and very wide popularity, can be explained by his style and subject matter, usually the scenery and people of rural America. His best work, for example, *Christina's World* (1948; Museum of Modern Art, New York), is also characterized by a certain melancholy.

Further reading. *Andrew Wyeth: Tempera, Watercolors, Dry-Brush, Drawings 1938–1966*, Philadelphia (1966). Corn, W. (ed.) *The Art of Andrew Wyeth*, New York (1974). Merryman, R. *Andrew Wyeth*, Boston (1968). Morgan, A. *Andrew Wyeth: Dry Brush and Pencil Drawings*, New York (1974).

Y

Yeats Jack 1871–1957

The Irish painter Jack Butler Yeats was born in London, the son of the painter John B. Yeats and brother of the poet William Butler Yeats. He spent most of his formative years in Sligo, Ireland, and memories of his boyhood colored his whole artistic career. He attended South Kensington, Chiswick, and Westminster art schools in London, and went on to be a poster artist in Manchester (1892–3). This, and his experiences as a book illustrator, helped give his early oil paintings their strong linearity and bold flat colors (for example, *The Circus Dwarf*, c1911; private collection). Gradually Yeats made his paint surface more expressive and freed his colors from naturalistic description. By the mid 1920s his canvases resembled those of Oskar Kokoschka and late German Impressionism in the bravura handling of their brushstrokes. His subject matter was imbued with his love of Ireland, whose myths, country fairs, and gypsies continually emerged from and disappeared into the windswept landscapes he painted.

Yevele Henry fl. 1356–1400

Henry Yevele was an English master mason; his life is unusually well-documented; its details reveal his enormous versatility, and the achievements that earned him considerable wealth.

Probably born in Derbyshire, Yevele is first recorded in 1356 as a "stonehewer" in London. In 1357 he became mason to the Black Prince and then in 1360 to King Edward III, being granted the office for life in 1369. His most important royal work is the nave of Westminster Abbey, which had been left unfinished in 1269. Building began again in the 1370s. Instead of a Perpendicular design, Yevele completed the remaining six bays in the style of the 13th century. Only the west facade was given the full Perpendicular treatment. At Canterbury Cathedral, it was probably Yevele who rebuilt the Norman nave at the end of the 14th century, but there the design was Perpendicular throughout. It is notable for the illusion of height gained by increasing the size of the arcade at the expense of the clerestory. As at Westminster the aisles, too, are high.

While he was at Canterbury, Yevele was also responsible for the town's fortifications. The massive two-towered west gate is the most prominent of all his surviving military works. These were numerous, and included some building at the Tower of London. It seems likely that Yevele designed the unusual, circular, concentrically planned castle surrounded by a moat at Queenborough, Kent (since demolished).

His domestic buildings probably included the destroyed college at Cobham, Kent, designed as a very early example of the

Jack Yeats: The End of the Season. Private collection

Henry Yevele: the nave of Westminster Abbey; 1370s

Z

Zadkine Ossip 1890–1967

The French sculptor Ossip Zadkine was born in Smolensk, Russia. His mother was of Scottish origin: her family were shipbuilders. He studied and worked in London (1906–8), and settled in 1909 in Paris, to study for a short time at the École des Beaux-Arts under Jean-Antoine Injalbert. From 1914 to 1918 he served in the French Army. He lived in Paris from 1918 to 1941, traveling and exhibiting widely. As an artist in exile, Zadkine lived in New York from 1941 to 1945. On his return to Paris in 1945 he became a Professor of Sculpture at the Académie de la Grande Chaumière. His most famous work is the monument commemorating the 1940 bombing of Rotterdam, *The Destroyed City* (bronze; 1951–3; Quai de Leuvehaven, Rotterdam).

The work done by Zadkine in his late teens and twenties reflects both his involvement with Cubism, and the Parisian circles in which he moved; they included Picasso, Brancusi, Modigliani, and Cocteau. By the time he reached his middle thirties, the geometrical surfaces of his work had opened out, becoming pierced and often elongated.

Further reading. Casson, S. *20th Century Sculptors*, New York (1967). Cogmat, R. *Zadkine*, Paris (1958). Geist, S. "A Memoir of Zadkine", *Artforum*, New York (June 1970). Hammacher, A.M. *Zadkine*, New York (1959). Jianou, I. *Zadkine*, London (1964) and New York (1965).

Zaichu Hara 1750–1837

The individualistic Japanese painter Hara Zaichu was the founder of the *Hara* School. Like many artists of his age, he studied Chinese painters of the Sung and Ming periods, but he formed his true style after adopting some of the naturalistic methods of Okyo, though it is not known whether he met him. The result is sometimes a mixture of *Nanga* and *Shijo* styles, as in *Gathering of Scholars* (British Museum, London). Later in life he added traditional *Yamatoe* techniques and subjects, and the resulting style was favored by royal patrons. His successors, Zaimyo, Zaisho, and Zaisen, all painted for court buildings in Kyoto. The styles used by

quadrangle college plan. More firmly attributed to him are a number of bridges, including work on London Bridge, and the reconstruction of the 11th-century walls of Westminster Hall after 1394.

Finally, Yevele was a designer of monumental works. Tombs, sedilia, and screens all came within his scope, and he may have been responsible for the superbly intricate Neville screen at Durham Cathedral.

Yusho Kaiho 1533–1615

The Japanese painter Kaiho Yusho was (with Eitoku and Tohaku) one of the three great masters of the Momoyama period.

He came from an Omi Province Samurai family that had been almost eliminated in the civil wars. The young Yusho entered the Zen Tofukuji Temple at Kyoto for safety, and was taught by Motonobu. His ink brushwork always retained the forthright vigor found in the work of many Samurai artists, especially in his stabbing tree-boughs. His series of landscape screens in the Kenninji (Kyoto) are among the last great monuments of atmospheric and intellectually powerful ink-painting in the Chinese tradition. In his screens for the Myoshinji (Kyoto), he combined gold and other washes with ink in a masterly manner.

Zaichu were very varied, and included Buddhist works.

Zeuxis *fl. c400 BC*

The Greek painter Zeuxis was born in Heraclea in southern Italy but also worked in Greece. To the science of shading developed by Apollodorus he added the use of highlights, which was the next important step in the progress towards the realism of an artist like Apelles. He was said to have painted a boy with grapes in which the fruit looked so natural that birds flew to them. Another famous work was his *Centaur Family*, described in detail by Lucian for its originality of theme and its coloristic technique. Zeuxis became very rich through his art. No original works by him have survived.

Zimmermann brothers
17th and 18th centuries

The German Zimmermann brothers were originally *stuccatori* of the Wessobrunn School. Johann Baptist Zimmermann (1680–1758) became a leading south German fresco painter, and Dominikus Zimmermann (1685–1766) was active as an architect; they worked in partnership on a number of important projects. Their earliest known joint commission, almost at the outset of their careers as independent masters, was the decoration of the church, sacristy, and library of the monastery of Buxheim (1710–12). Dominikus had already begun the decoration of the monastery's Marienkapelle in the previous year. Meanwhile, working independently, Johann Baptist had decorated the abbey church of Edelstetten with stuccos and

frescoes (1710), and the sacristy of the abbey church of Waldsee (signed and dated 1710).

In early works such as these, the stucco decorations were both designed and executed by the Zimmermanns. Later, in the stair hall and Festsaal of Schloss Schleissheim (1720–5), Johann Baptist was the executant only, working (with Charles-Claude Dubut) to the designs of Effner. Subsequently Johann Baptist painted superb stuccos to the designs of Cuvilliés in the Munich Residenz (1731–3) and the Amalienburg in the park of Schloss Nymphenburg (1734–9). He used Cuvilliés' designs again, at the end of his career, in the Festsaal of Schloss Nymphenburg itself (1755–7).

At Edelstetten the stuccos belong to the early Wessobrunn foliage type, but in the

Johann Zoffany: Cognoscenti in the Uffizi; oil on canvas; 124×155cm (49×61in); 1772–7/8. Collection of H.M. Queen Elizabeth II

ceiling of the abbey library at Ottobeuren (1715–18), the more loosely composed stuccos tend towards the Rococo. The subsidiary frescoes there include short stretches of balustrade, painted illusionistically; in the ceiling of the abbey library at Benediktbeuern (1725), these are instead included in the actual stuccos. The decorative vocabulary employed there by Johann Baptist reveals the impact of Effner's *Régence* style, and leads on directly to the pilgrimage church of Steinhausen which the brothers began in 1728 (work suspended in 1733).

The relative inexperience of Dominikus as an architect is illustrated by his wild underestimate of the cost of the work at Steinhausen. But its longitudinal oval nave, with aisles rising to the full height of the main vault, is the site of some of the finest Bavarian Rococo decoration in existence. The balustrade motif is used to mask the transition between the real world of the stuccos and the visionary world of Johann Baptist's frescoes; naturalistic forms, including birds and insects, are included in the decorations all over the church.

The parish church at Günzburg (1736–41), by Dominikus alone, together with the elegant Annakapelle at Buxheim (1738–40), designed and decorated by both brothers, are intermediate steps in the development leading to the pilgrimage church of Die Wies. The church was built and decorated by the brothers between 1746 and 1754; its oval nave and galleried choir is developed from Günzburg. The richness and vitality of the decoration mark it out as the climax of his phase of the Bavarian Rococo.

Zoffany Johann 1734/5–1810

The painter Johann Zoffany was born in Germany and received his training there, but his reputation rests upon the portraits and conversation pieces he painted in London and in Rome, where he studied under Mengs for several years. He came to England in 1760, and from 1762 painted a series of theatrical portraits. He became a member of the Royal Academy, and after working in Italy returned to London in 1779. Zoffany was a member of a number of Academies in Italy, and in the 1780s worked in India. He vividly represented the social position and the art-collecting activities of the English nobleman who had taken the Grand Tour (for example, *Charles Towneley among his Marbles*,

1790; Towneley Hall Art Gallery and Museum, Burnley).

Zola Émile 1840–1902

The French novelist and art critic Émile Zola was born in Aix-en-Provence. He was a friend of Cézanne, from adolescence until the publication of his novel *L'Oeuvre* in 1886. He took up art criticism in 1866; he defended Manet and the young Impressionists, and attacked the academic hierarchy. He wrote a brochure on Manet in 1867, and Zola's portrait by Manet (*Portrait of Édouard Manet*) was exhibited at the Salon of 1868 (now in the Musée du Jeu de Paume, Paris). Zola's later criticism was intermittent, and in some ways he felt that Cézanne and the Impressionists had not produced the masterpiece he looked for. Nonetheless, his leadership of Naturalism in the novel went hand-in-hand with the Impressionists' desire to depict modern life.

Zuccarelli Francesco 1702–88

Florentine by birth but Venetian by adoption, the Italian painter Francesco Zuccarelli spent some 15 years in England, on two visits between 1752 and 1771, and was a founder member of the Royal Academy. He sweetened the ideal landscape of Claude to conform with Rococo taste, painting in pastel colors and soft, creamy brush strokes. His landscapes, which also show Dutch influence, may be staffed either by peasants or gods, but usually have the same sweetly pastoral mood. Zuccarelli knew and probably influenced Richard Wilson. It is characteristic of the English taste for "fancy pictures", with figures rather than nature landscapes, that during his lifetime his reputation was far higher than Wilson's.

Zuccaro brothers
16th and 17th centuries

The Italian brothers Taddeo (1529–66) and Federico (c1542–1609) Zuccaro were successively the leading exponents of Mannerism in late-16th-century Rome. Both were born near Urbino. It is not known where Taddeo trained, but early in his career he initiated a program designed to reform the art of painting. He deliberately modeled his style on that of the great masters of the earlier 16th-century, such as Raphael and Correggio, and rejected the

Above: Federico Zuccaro: Portrait of Vincenzo Borghini; black and red chalk on paper; 14×9cm (5½×3½in); c1570–4. British Museum, London

excessive complexity of Florentine Mannerism of the mid century.

Federico began his career as an assistant to his brother. After Taddeo's early death in 1566, he was responsible for the completion of two of his large-scale fresco cycles in the Sala Regia of the Vatican, and at the Villa Farnese at Caprarola. Federico was to lend his brother's program of reform a wider currency by traveling extensively, both within Italy and abroad. In 1574 he made a journey to France, Antwerp, and England, where he is supposed to have painted a portrait of Queen Elizabeth. Between 1578 and 1579 he completed Vasari's frescoes in the cupola of Florence Cathedral; during the early 1580s he was active in the Doges' Palace in Venice; and in 1585 he was invited to Spain to work in the Escorial.

The eclectic style of Federico also gained authority from his activities as a teacher and theorist. In 1593 he established an academy in his own palace in Rome, and in 1607 he published a treatise propounding his ideals of beauty and design. This was *L'Idea de' Scultori, Pittori e Architetti*, a major document of Mannerist art theory.

Taddeo Zuccaro: **Study of a Male Nude**; red chalk on paper; 42×29cm (17×11in). Metropolitan Museum, New York

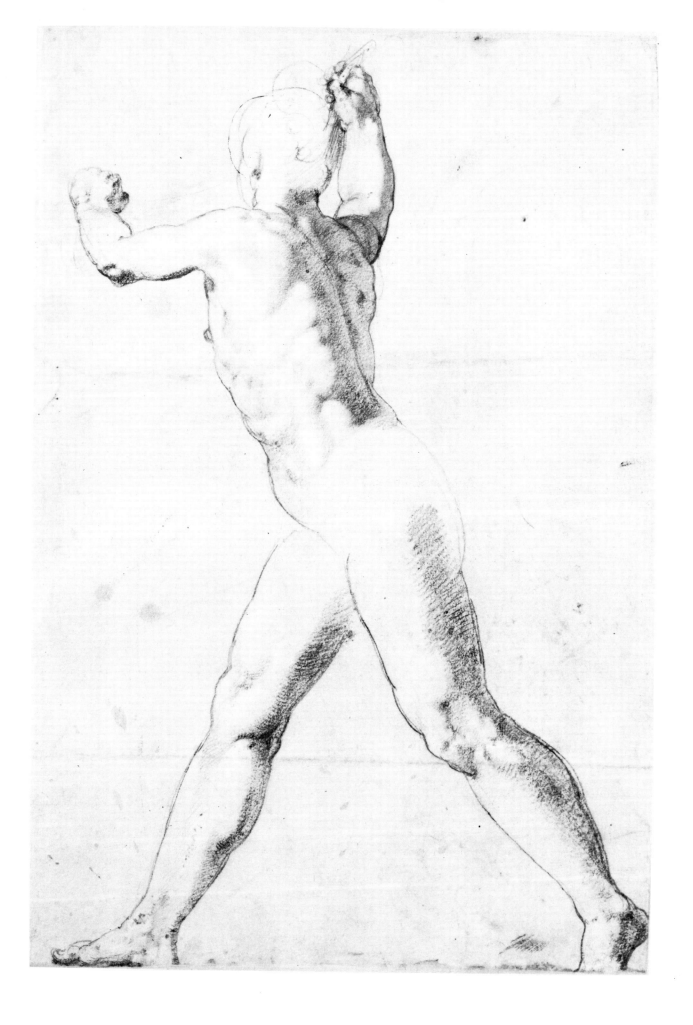

Zurbarán Francisco de 1598–1664

The Spanish painter Francisco de Zurbarán was born in Fuente de Cantos, Badajoz. He was apprenticed in 1614 to Pedro Díaz de Villanueva in Seville. By 1617 he was established in Llerena, Badajoz. There, in 1626, he contracted to paint 21 canvases for the Dominicans of S. Pablo el Real, Seville, and in 1628, 22 canvases for the Merced Calzada in Seville. At the invitation of the municipal authorities he took up residence in Seville in 1629; the move aroused antagonism from the local painters, led by Alonso Cano.

During his apprenticeship in Seville, Zurbarán must have met Velázquez, whose influence is evident in his Llerena period. He early mastered the representation of reality with plastic modeling. His tenebrist style was comparable to that of Caravaggio, as in his *Crucifixion* of 1627 (Art Institute of Chicago). He used the same style in the four works that he contributed in 1629 to the series for the Franciscan College, Seville (surviving panels in the Louvre, Paris, and the Gemäldegalerie Alte Meister, Dresden). These were among many compositions of monastic life that he painted during his career.

In Seville Zurbarán achieved greater luminosity than before in *Birth of the Virgin* (c1629; Norton Simon Museum, Pasadena, Calif.), *The Immaculate Conception* (1630; Diocesan Museum, Sigüenza), and the *House of Nazareth* (c1630; Art Gallery, Cleveland). In the *Still Life* dated 1633 (Norton Simon Museum, Pasadena, Calif.) he reached a perfection in execution and simplicity in composition, together with a deep mystical content, that make this a masterpiece of European painting.

This level of excellence was not maintained in Zurbarán's series of *The Labors of Hercules* and *The Defence of Cadiz* (Prado, Madrid), painted in 1634 in Madrid for the Buen Retiro Palace. But in Seville, from 1638 to 1639, he reached the peak of his achievement in monastic and religious cycles, both in the Hieronymite subjects for the sacristy of the Monastery of Guadalupe (Cáceres), and in the New Testament series for the Charterhouse at Jerez de la Frontera (now in the Musée de Peinture et de Sculpture, Grenoble, and elsewhere).

In the late 1630s Zurbarán had begun to dispatch paintings to the New World, increasingly after 1646, as Murillo's popularity increased, but inevitably their quality

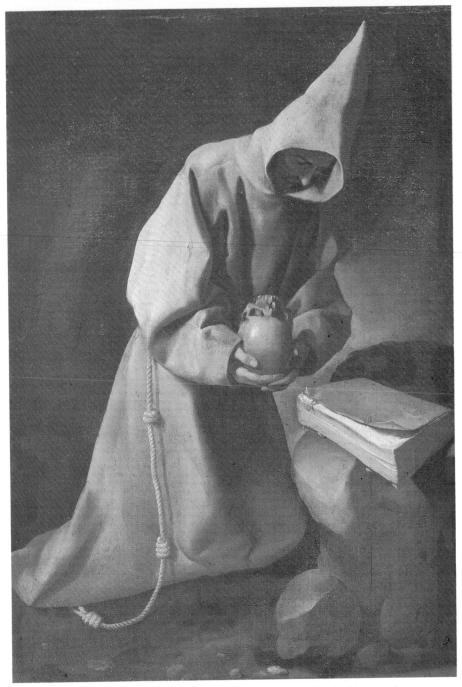

Francisco de Zurbarán: St Francis Meditating; oil on canvas; 114×78cm (45×31in); 1632. Collection of Dr A.E. Shaw, Buenos Aires

declined. In the *Annunciation* (1650; Philadelphia Museum of Art) he lessened the contrast of light and shade, and subsequently he adopted a softer style in parallel with Murillo, as in the *Virgin and Child with St John* (1658; Museum of Art, Diego). After settling in Madrid in 1658, Zurbarán produced a few notable works like the *Immaculate Conception* (1661; Museum of Fine Arts, Budapest) and the *Virgin and Child with St John* (1662; Museum of Fine Arts, Bilbao).

Zurbarán lacked inventiveness. He frequently borrowed compositions from Northern engravings, and his works were sometimes defective in movement, or in cohesion between earthly and celestial figures. Despite this, he has earned increasing fame in modern times through the mystical exaltation or repose reflected in his monastic cycles. He is valued, too, for his skill in naturalistic representation and the subtle use of color and light, both in his monastic pictures and in his rare portraits and still lifes.

During his Seville period, Zurbarán employed many studio assistants, including his son Juan (born 1620), of whom two signed still-life compositions are known (Museum of Art, Kiev, and private collection).

GLOSSARY

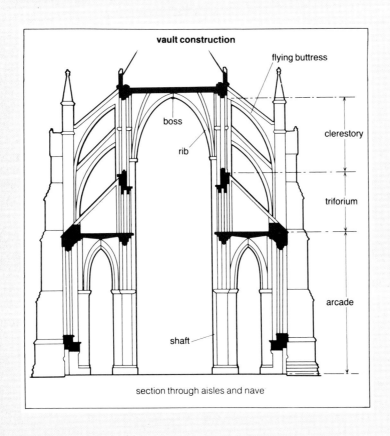

vault construction

flying buttress

boss

rib

clerestory

triforium

arcade

shaft

section through aisles and nave

Abbreviations (arch.) architectural term; (Fr.) French; (Ger.) German; (It.) Italian; (Sp.) Spanish. Words set in SMALL CAPITALS denote glossary headings of related entries. An * indicates that an entry is illustrated in the glossary.

A

abacus (arch.) flat slab on top of CAPITAL supporting ARCHITRAVE; *see* CLASSIC GREEK ARCHITECTURE.

abstract ill-defined and very widely used term which in its most general sense describes any art in which form and color are stressed at the expense, or in the absence of, a representational image.

Abstract Expressionism originally a diverse style of ABSTRACT art developed in the USA during the 1940s and 1950s, and particularly associated with Arshile Gorky and Jackson Pollock; sometimes known as the NEW YORK SCHOOL. After 1952, sometimes known alternatively as ACTION PAINTING.

abstraction the process of making an abstract image; the work created.

Abstraction-Création (Fr.) 1 group of Abstract artists in Paris in 1931 who promoted nonrepresentational art through their exhibitions. 2 the annual magazine published by the group from 1932 to 1936; its full title was *Abstraction-Création: Art non-figuratif.*

abutment (arch.) structure supporting the lateral thrust of an ARCH or VAULT; *see* VAULT CONSTRUCTION.

acacia 1 shrub or tree from which gum arabic is produced. 2 obsolete term for object shaped like a roll or bag, shown in the hands of emperors and consuls on Classical medallions.

academic 1 literally, belonging to an ACADEMY of art. 2 derogatory term meaning conventional, stereotyped, derivative.

academicism the quality of ACADEMIC art.

Academy originally the garden near Athens where Plato taught, and hence the name given to his school of philosophy. During the RENAISSANCE the term was adopted by philosophical and literary groups, and later by schools established for the training of artists. These academies were characterized by their emphasis on the study of Classical art and the human form. In the 19th century the academies were associated with conservatism and rejected by many artists who sought alternative creative outlets.

acanthus decorative motif used in painting and architecture, derived from the scalloped leaf of the acanthus plant.*

acolyte Christian CHURCH officer who assists the priest.

acroterion (arch.) pedestal or figure placed at the three angles of a PEDIMENT.*

acrylic synthetic resin polymer. Used in emulsion form as a modern painting medium, and in sheet form in modern sculpture.

Action Painting Term coined in 1952 by US critic Harold Rosenberg to describe the type of ABSTRACT EXPRESSIONISM practiced by Jackson Pollock and others, in which the emphasis was on the action of applying paint, sometimes splashing or pouring it over a canvas on the floor.

actor print Japanese print showing actor in well-known role; popular from the development of the Kabuki theater in the 17th century as part of the UKIYOE movement of GENRE painting.

adobe brick unbaked, sun-dried clay brick used for building.

adsorption close physical interaction between two substances without chemical reaction.

aedicule (arch.) opening, such as door or window, framed by columns, with a PEDIMENT; *see* CLASSIC GREEK ARCHITECTURE.

Aegean art art from various cultures around the eastern Mediterranean from *c*2800 BC to 1400 BC, including CYCLADIC, Minoan (from Crete), and Mycenaean.

aeolic (arch.) style of Greek architecture found in the 6th century BC; sometimes called Proto-Ionic.

aesthetic concerned with the appreciation of what is beautiful or pleasing.

Aesthetic movement late 19th-century artistic movement in England, promoted by Oscar Wilde and Walter Pater advocating "art for art's sake".

aesthetics philosophy applied to art, which attempts to formulate criteria for the understanding of the AESTHETIC (rather than utilitarian) qualities of art.

agate semiprecious variety of CHALCEDONY, used in jewelry and as a burnishing tool.

airbrush instrument for spraying paint, propelled by compressed air. Invented in 1893, it has been much used by commercial artists, whether for fine lines, large areas, or subtle gradations of color and tone.

aisle (arch.) division of space at the sides of a CHURCH, parallel to the NAVE and separated from it by PIERS or ARCADES.

aiwan (arch.) recess, niche, or reception hall in ancient Parthian building or MOSQUE.*

Ajanta Indian site of series of caves containing wall paintings, based on Buddhist legends, dating from *c*200 BC–AD 700.

ajouré (Fr.) pierced or perforated in elaborate patterns, used especially of METALWORK.

Akbar-nama account of the reign of the Mughal Emperor Akbar (1542–1605; reigned from 1556) written in Persian by Abul Fazl (1551–1602). It was frequently illustrated.

akropolis (or **acropolis**) fortified citadel in Greek cities. "The Acropolis" usually refers to the one in Athens.

alabaster 1 in ANTIQUITY, a carbonate of lime used in Egyptian sculpture, especially for small portable pieces. 2 modern alabaster, a lime sulfate which can be highly polished but is easily scratched, popular in 14th-century Europe for tomb effigies.

alabastron small round-based bottle with broad rim, used by ancient Egyptians and Greeks for ointments. Originally of ALABASTER; later, GLASS or CERAMIC.

albumen proteinaceous substance forming the adhesive element in egg white, which has been used as a painting medium.

all'antica (It.) style of works of art, especially sculpture, that imitate antique models.

alla prima (It.) technique, commonly used in painting since the 19th century, whereby an artist completes a painting in one session without having provided layers of underpainting.

allegory image whose meaning is expressed symbolically.

altar flat-topped block, usually of stone, used for sacrifice to a deity, or, in a Christian CHURCH, as a focal point in services.

altarpiece in Christian CHURCH architecture, the picture or decorated screen behind the ALTAR. It may consist of a single painting or an elaborate group of hinged panels.*

aluminum (Eng. **aluminium**) light, silvery metal, used in modern sculpture, usually in sheet form, sometimes painted.

amber 1 fossilized tree resin, used in its natural form for jewelry and decorative objects. Also dissolved in oil, with other resins, to produce oil varnish. 2 metal alloy consisting of four parts gold to one of silver.

ambo (arch.) reading desk or pulpit in early Christian CHURCH, usually of stone. Normally there were two, facing each other on each side of the CHOIR.

ambulatory continuation of the

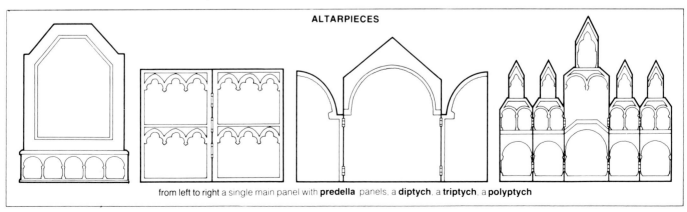

ALTARPIECES

from left to right a single main panel with **predella** panels, a **diptych**, a **triptych**, a **polyptych**

AISLES of the CHOIR around the APSE, sometimes giving access to smaller chapels; *see* CHURCH.

amethyst purple colored precious stone, used in jewelry.

amorino (pl. amorini; It.) small PUTTO; usually winged.

amphitheater arena surrounded by tiered seats. Used from the 1st century BC throughout the Roman world for public spectacles.

amphora large, two-handled jug used in ANTIQUITY to hold oil, wine, etc; *see* GREEK VASES.

amulet charm designed to protect the wearer from evil.

Analytical Cubism early phase of CUBISM, *c*1907–12, in which natural forms were analyzed and reduced to their essential geometric parts.

anatomy structure of the human body. Sometimes refers to the structure of plants or animals.

anchorite hermit, recluse.

Angular style style of painting and sculpture in Northern Europe from *c*1430–1530 characterized by stiff drapery folds.

animalier (Fr.) **1** member of the 19th-century school of French bronze sculptors who specialized in small animal figures. **2** animal-painter.

Animal style 1 ornament representing animal forms. **2** type of nomad art originating in the 7th century BC in southern Russia and the Caucasus; it was characterized by the predominance of animal motifs, frequently distorted, ornamenting all kinds of portable objects including metalwork, textiles, wood and bone.

annular vault (arch.) vaulted roof over a ring-shaped (annular) space, between two concentric walls; *see* VAULT CONSTRUCTION.

antefix (arch.) upright architectural ornament found in Classical buildings, where it decorated or masked the ends of a roof ridge.

antependium covering for the face of an ALTAR, usually textile or precious metal; sometimes called an altar frontal.

antiphonary (sometimes antiphonal) book containing sections of the Mass that were sung as responses by the choir. From *c*AD 1000 antiphonaries were sometimes ILLUMINATED with scenes from the Bible.

Antiquity Greek and Roman civilization until the fall of the Roman Empire in the 5th century AD. Greek and Roman sculpture was admired during the RENAISSANCE as an ideal art, and study of The Antique formed the basis of the curriculum in most art academies.

apex (arch.) uppermost point of a triangular or conical form.

apotheosis (Gr. deification) in Classical art this represented the entry into Olympus of a famous or heroic figure. In the BAROQUE period it was a popular theme for depicting in an allegorical manner the glorification of the artist's patron, usually a prince.

apotropaic having the ability to avert evil influence.

applied art the designing and decorating of functional objects or materials to give them AESTHETIC appeal, e.g. printing type, CERAMICS, GLASS, furniture, METAL-WORK, and TEXTILES. The term is frequently used to differentiate this type of work from the FINE ARTS (painting, drawing, sculpture) whose value is primarily aesthetic.

appliqué (Fr.) TEXTILE decoration in which cut fabric shapes are stitched to a fabric ground as a design.

apse (arch.) semicircular or polygonal end of a CHURCH; usually the end of the CHANCEL, at the east end.

aquatint ETCHING process whereby acid is allowed to bite into a copper plate prepared with resin which is then inked and printed.

arabesque motif based on interlaced plant forms, found in the fine and decorative arts, in architecture, and especially typical of Islamic design.*

arca 1 Indian statue of a deity. **2** (Latin) coffin or carved chest, intended to hold the Eucharist or donations in CHURCH.

arcade (arch.) continuous series of ARCHES supported on COLUMNS or PIERS.*

Arcadia rural area of the Peloponnese idealized in the writings of Virgil, which in the RENAISSANCE became a synonym for a life of rustic idyll, hence arcadian.

arch (arch.) curved architectural structure formed by wedges of brick or stone, held together by pressure and supported only at the sides.

archaic 1 art of the ARCHAIC GREEK period. **2** antiquated, out of date.

Archaic Greek art Greek art of the mid 12th century BC to *c*480 BC; one of four convenient divisions of Greek art, the others being GEOMETRIC, CLASSICAL, and HELLENISTIC.

archaistic tending towards the ARCHAIC, in either sense of the word.

architectonic relating to architecture.

architecture 1 science or art of building. **2** the structure or style of what is built.

architrave (arch.) **1** the lowest main section of an ENTABLATURE. **2** molded frame surrounding a door or window.

archivolt (arch.) curved underside of an ARCH, or sometimes the bands of molding that decorate it.

armature framework or skeleton on which a sculptor molds his clay.

Armory Show international exhibition of modern art held in New York in 1913 in the 69th Regiment Armory building. Exhibits included the work of the more AVANT-GARDE US artists and of the SCHOOL OF PARIS. The exhibition was enormously popular and marked the birth of a real interest in modern art in 20th-century America.

arriccio (It.) coat of lime and sand plaster preparing a wall for painting (especially in FRESCO) on which INTONACO was applied.

Art Deco style of western architecture, APPLIED ARTS, interior and graphic design of the 1920s and 1930s. It was characterized by the combination of decorative ART NOUVEAU with new geometric forms.

arte povera (It., poor/impoverished art) term coined by Italian critic Germano Celani in 1967 to describe the work of artists such as Carl André, Richard Long etc. It stresses the use of ordinary materials such as sand, stones, twigs, etc., and the temporary, noncollectable nature of the work.

articulation manner in which components of architecture or sculpture are put together or jointed.

artifact (or artefact) **1** any object of human workmanship. **2** (archaeology) an object of prehistoric or aboriginal art, as distinguished from a similar but naturally occurring object.

art informel (Fr.) term coined by French critic Michel Tapié, and used from the 1950s to describe the European equivalent to ACTION PAINTING.

Art Nouveau (Fr.) decorative style popular in Europe in the late 19th and early 20th century; it often employed stylized, curvilinear plant forms. It was known in Germany as JUGENDSTIL.

Arts and Crafts Movement mid-19th-century artistic movement in England, inspired by John Ruskin and William Morris; it attempted to raise the standards of design and craftsmanship in the APPLIED ARTS, and to reassert the craftsman's individuality in the face of increasing mechanization.

aryballos 1 tapering oil flask used by ancient Greeks; *see* GREEK VASES. **2** shape of Inca water jar, with conical base.

a secco (It.) technique of MURAL painting on dry plaster.

Ashcan School term used during the 1930s to describe the realist group

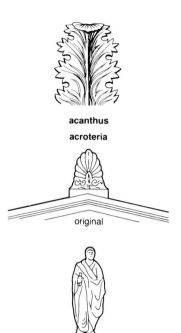

acanthus

acroteria

original

Classical

Baroque

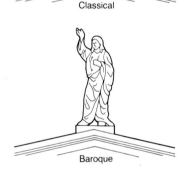

aiwan

the aiwan arch, **above** as used in the early 7th-century palace of Khusrau I at Ctesiphon, **below** as used in a 13th-century *madrasa* in Baghdad

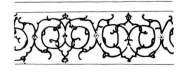

arabesque

of artists which evolved from THE EIGHT in New York *c*1908 and whose subject was usually the urban environment.

ashlar 1 square-cut stone block. **2** masonry of this stone, evenly laid with very fine joints.

assemblage modern art form consisting of objects collected and assembled together; the components are preformed, not made by the artist, and not intended originally as "art material".

atelier (Fr.) studio or workshop.

atlantes (arch.) figures of men used to support an ENTABLATURE. The female equivalent is a CARYATID.

atrium (arch.) **1** forecourt of Roman house leading to various rooms. **2** court in front of Early Christian and ROMANESQUE CHURCHES.

attic 1 in Classical Greece, of Athens or Attica. **2** (arch.) room with sloping ceiling below roof.

attic order (arch.) square COLUMN of Greek architectural order, or PILASTERS applied to upper story of building.

aureole in painting, light shown encircling the head or body of a holy person.

automata animated figures, probably made in Europe since the 5th century BC. Medieval examples are usually linked with clocks, but are also found as table ornaments; in the 19th century they became fashionable as mechanical toys for children.

automatism drawing and painting method associated with SURREALISM in which the artist does not consciously create but doodles, allowing the subconscious mind and virtually uncontrolled movement of the hand to produce an image.

automatist 1 an artist who practices AUTOMATISM; **2** adjective describing the work thus produced.

avant-garde artists whose work is ahead of that of most of their contemporaries; unconventional, experimental, innovative. Also descriptive of the work produced by such artists.

axial related to an AXIS.

axis imaginary line around which the design of a painting, sculpture, or building pivots.

B

bacchanal mythological scene popular in paintings of the RENAISSANCE and 17th century depicting the revels of Bacchus, Roman god of wine.

backcloth painted scenery in theater design; the term is often used figuratively.

background scene in painting which provides setting for main figures or design; sometimes used synonymously with GROUND.

baluster (arch.) small PILLAR or COLUMN supporting rail.

balustrade (arch.) series of BALUSTERS, usually edging terrace or balcony.*

Bamboccianti (It.) group of painters who specialized in *bambocciate* (Fr., *bambochades*): low-life and peasant scenes, popular in the Netherlands and Italy in the 17th century. The name derives from Pieter van Laer (1592–1642), a Dutch painter nicknamed "Il Bamboccio" ("Big Baby").

bamboo tropical giant grasses with woody stems used for furniture in the west in the 19th and 20th centuries. Often incorrectly used to describe 18th- and 19th-century furniture made from other woods, painted and carved to resemble bamboo, in CHINOISERIE style.

banditti (It.) bandits, or similar "picturesque" characters in painting; especially common in 17th-century European paintings.

baptistery place where baptism is performed in CHURCH. In early Christian and medieval times separate buildings were erected and the term applied to them.

Barbizon School group of French landscape painters of the mid 19th century, who painted landscape for its own sake, often directly from nature.

Baroque 1 style of architecture, painting, and sculpture originating principally in Italy, of the late 16th to the early 18th century; it exhibited an increased interest in dynamic movement and dramatic effects. **2** "baroque" is sometimes used in a pejorative sense to mean over-elaborate, florid. **3** The Baroque period refers to the 17th century, when the style was at its height.

Baroque classicism classical style—exemplified in the paintings of Nicolas Poussin and the architecture of Carlo Fontana—which flourished during the BAROQUE period.

basilica (arch.) medieval CHURCH in which the NAVE is taller than the AISLES; early churches had an APSE at one end. It was based on the Roman assembly hall, or the design of colonnaded halls in private houses.*

Basohli Punjab hill state where an individualistic style of painting developed during the later 17th century.

Bauhaus School of architecture and modern art, founded in Weimar, Germany, in 1919 by Walter Gropius, which became the focus of modern design. It moved to Dessau in 1925–6, to Berlin in 1932, and was closed in 1933.

bay (arch.) the space formed, usually within a CHURCH, where the limits are indicated by ORDERS, VAULTS, etc, rather than by walls. On an external wall a bay may be indicated by BUTTRESSES.

beading decorative series of molded beads, found in architecture and furniture.

beam (arch.) horizontal structural member, usually made of wood, bearing a load.

belle peinture (Fr.) expression for the traditionally esteemed, highly accomplished type of painting that employs the full range of painting skills.

Berlin Secession (Ger., *Berliner Sezession*) association led by the German Impressionist painter Max Liebermann which exhibited the work of the BRÜCKE artists in 1908.

bezant 1 gold or silver coin minted at Byzantium. **2** gold ROUNDEL in heraldry.

bezel 1 obliquely cut gem face. **2** rim, groove, or mount holding watchglass or gem in jewelry setting.

Bible moralisée (Fr.) type of Bible originating in the 13th century and designed for the layman, therefore lavishly illustrated.

Biedermeier (Ger.) style of German decorative arts *c*1820–50 emphasizing solid, middle-class comfort; hence style of painting which is banal and sentimental.

biennale biennial art exhibition.

billet (arch.) ornamentation formed by short cylindrical or rectangular blocks placed at regular intervals in hollow moldings.

billon alloy of gold or silver with a larger proportion of base metal.

biomorphic term derived from "biomorphism" which refers to any decorative form that represents a living object.

biscuit unglazed white PORCELAIN, popular in Europe from the mid 17th century.

biting ETCHING term meaning the treatment of a PLATE with acid to etch lines in it.

bitumen (also called asphaltum) a brownish-black pigment formed of a mixture of hydrocarbons with oxygen, sulfur, and nitrogen which occurs naturally. It can be partially dissolved in oil to form a semitransparent red-brown color and was much used in the 18th and 19th centuries.

black-figure technique style of decoration of ancient Greek CERAMICS, chiefly of 6th-century BC Corinth. Designs were painted on the object in black metal oxide paint and then incised through to the reddish clay.

Blaue Reiter group of artists formed in Munich in 1911 by Wassily Kandinsky and Franz Marc. The group was of very varied outlook; other artists who joined it included Paul Klee, Georges Braque, and Picasso.

board various types of stiff paper made from cheap fibers. Boards have been used instead of canvas or paper as a painting support since the 19th century; types include millboard, academy board, and canvas board.

bodegón (Spanish, "tavern"; plural, *bodegones*) painting of a kitchen scene with a predominant interest in STILL LIFE.

Bodhisattva in Buddhist ICONOGRAPHY, one who delays the attainment of nirvana through compassion for human suffering; it may be translated as "Buddha to be".

body color 1 WATERCOLOR made opaque by mixing with white. **2** term used in painting to describe solid, definitive areas of color which are then completed or modified with SCUMBLES and GLAZES.

bole 1 Armenian bole is a red clay (ferruginous aluminum silicate) which can be burnished to a high polish and is used as a preparation for GILDING. **2** white bole is China clay.

Book of Hours book of prayers to be said at canonical hours, used privately by laymen. It was common in the 15th century and sometimes richly illustrated.

border decorative line or design which delineates edges of a drawing, illustration, or manuscript illumination.

boss (arch.) ornamental projection, of wood or stone, placed at the join of vaulting, ribs, etc; *see* VAULT CONSTRUCTION.

bottega (It.) shop, workshop, or artist's studio.

boxwood very hard, fine-grained wood from an evergreen shrub of the genus *Buxus* used for carving and ENGRAVING.

bracelet ornamental wristband, usually of precious metal.

bracket (arch.) projection that functions as a support; may also be decorative.

brass 1 alloy of copper and zinc. **2** an incised or cast sepulchral plate made of the above material.

bravura describes any style that demonstrates technical or artistic flair or brilliance.

brazing process of soldering with an alloy of brass and zinc, much used in modern sculpture.

breviary book containing the prayers, hymns, and lessons to be said by the clergy at the appropriate hours during the day, sometimes illustrated.

bridge-spouted vessel traditional pot shape found in the CERAMIC wares of Central and South America, especially of the central Andes. It has two spouts "bridged" by another piece.

brocade loose term for patterned TEXTILE, especially with woven decoration in gold or silver.

bronze 1 alloy of copper and tin, often used for cast sculpture. 2 a sculpture made from this alloy.

Bronze Age period (mainly 2nd millennium BC) when bronze was the metal chiefly used for weapons and implements.

bronzist maker of BRONZE sculpture, plaques, etc.

Brücke (Ger., *Die Brücke*, "The Bridge") group of German Expressionist painters founded in Dresden in 1905, and including the artists Ernst Ludwig Kirchner and Karl Schmidt-Rottluff.

brush implement for applying paint, usually of hog or sable hair set in a wooden handle.

brush stroke the individual mark made by each application of paint with a BRUSH, usually retaining the mark of the separate brush hairs.

brushwork general term for manner or style in which paint is applied, and often considered by art historians as an identifying characteristic of a particular artist's work.

brutalism architectural style of the 1950s associated with Le Corbusier and Mies van der Rohe, in which no attempt is made to disguise the building materials used.

bucchero 1 red-colored earth used for making jars, or vase made from this material, in the ancient world. 2 black clayey earth used for certain Etruscan vases.

bucranium (Latin; pl. *bucrania*; from Greek *boukranion*, "oxhead") decorative motif in Classical and post-RENAISSANCE art based on an ox-head.*

bugaku type of ancient Japanese dance, sometimes performed at Buddhist ceremonies.

Bunjinga Japanese scholar-painters working from *c*1700; the term also applies to the work they produced.

buon fresco (It.) *see* FRESCO.

burin metal tool used for engraving.

burlap type of coarse canvas, especially jute sacking material.

burnish to polish a surface by rubbing. GOLD LEAF may be burnished by rubbing with a smooth AGATE tool.

bust portrait sculpture showing the sitter's head and shoulders only.

Bustan "The Orchard", a book of ethics in verse written by the Per-

sian poet Sa'di (*c*1213–92). It was often illustrated.

buttress (arch.) reinforced, projecting wall, usually on the exterior of a building, supporting it at a point of stress. A FLYING BUTTRESS transmits the thrust of a vault to an outer support; *see* VAULT CONSTRUCTION.

Byzantine art art of the eastern Roman Empire centered on Constantinople, formerly Byzantium, from the 4th century AD. At various times it embraced both Classical Greek REALISM and stylized, HIERATIC, Oriental art.

C

cabinet picture small or medium-sized painting executed at an easel, and designed for collectors, especially popular from the 17th century; *see* EASEL PICTURE.

cable pattern (arch.) convex rope-like molding found in Norman architecture. Sometimes also refers to similar decoration in goldsmiths' work.

calcite crystalline form of calcium carbonate.

calligraphic style of drawing or painting which is particularly free, flowing, and distinctive, like fine handwriting.

calligraphy the art of fine handwriting.

Camden Town Group group of English POST-IMPRESSIONIST painters formed in 1911 around Walter Sickert, including Spencer Gore, Lucien Pissarro, and Augustus John, who applied some of the principles of Paul Gauguin and Vincent van Gogh to contemporary London subject matter.

cameo gemstone or shell of colored layers with the upper layer carved to form a relief design against the contrasting ground.

camera obscura device that uses a lens to project a reduced image of an object on to a flat surface so that the outline may be traced. Popular with artists from the RENAISSANCE to the 18th century.

camera ottica another name for a CAMERA OBSCURA.

campanile (It.) (arch.) freestanding bell tower of CHURCH.

camposanto (It.) cemetery; churchyard.

candelabrum standing candlestick with holders for more than one candle.

canopy (arch.) suspended or projected miniature roof over an ALTAR, seat, STATUE, or similar.

cantilever (arch.) a beam supported or fixed at one end carrying a load at the other.

capital (arch.) upper part of COLUMN or PILASTER, directly beneath the ENTABLATURE; *see* CLASSIC GREEK ARCHITECTURE.

capomaestro (It.) master builder; chief architect.

caposcuola (It.) founder of artistic or literary movement.

capriccio (It.) literally, a fancy or caprice. In the 18th century it usually referred to a painting in which accurately rendered existing architecture was combined with the imaginary. It also applied to ETCHINGS that represented fantasies rather than actual stories.

Caravaggism tendency to follow the style of Caravaggio, exhibited by the Caravaggisti (17th-century painters working in Rome), who made particularly dramatic use of CHIAROSCURO.

caravansary in the East, an open court surrounded by buildings where caravans rest.

carbon chemical element that occurs in various natural forms including diamond, GRAPHITE, and CHARCOAL, and in all organic compounds. Carbon black, obtained artificially, is one of the oldest black pigments, being derived from the partial burning of wood, bone, and other organic materials.

cardboard board made from pressed paper, used as a support for painting or drawing, and in COLLAGE and SCULPTURE.

caricature painting or drawing, usually a portrait, that exaggerates features for humorous or satirical effect.

carnelian (or cornelian) reddish colored form of CHALCEDONY, used in jewelry and for decorative objects.

Carolingian art European art of the period covered by the reign of Charlemagne (AD 768–814) and his successors until *c* AD 900; usually regarded as the foundation of medieval art.

carpet page in MANUSCRIPT illumination, a page totally filled with decorative design.

cartography map-drawing.

cartoon 1 full-sized drawing for transferring design to painting, MURAL, or TAPESTRY. 2 comic drawing; CARICATURE.

cartouche 1 ornamental frame, whether painted, engraved, printed, or sculpted, often in the form of a SCROLL, and containing an inscription, coat of arms, or similar. 2 in Egyptian HIEROGLYPHICS, an oval or oblong frame enclosing the names of royalty or divinities.

caryatid (Greek; pl. caryatides) (arch.) figure of draped woman that serves as a COLUMN supporting an ENTABLATURE; *see* ATLANTES. Caryatides are also found

arcade

after the Ospedale degli Innocenti, Florence, designed by Brunelleschi and begun in 1419

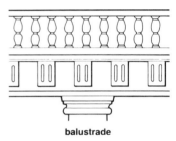

balustrade

basilica

bucranium

as a motif on furniture, for example, as bronze mounts.

casein a phosphoprotein prepared from skimmed milk. When mixed with lime it forms a very strong adhesive that has been extensively used for wood joining, and to a lesser extent as a binding material for paints and GROUNDS.

casino (It.) (arch.) temple or small house, often in a park.

cassone (It.) Italian wooden chest of the 15th and 16th centuries, usually decorated, and often intended to hold a bride's dowry.

castellation (arch.) decoration of a building with battlements and turrets, like a castle; the result may be described as castellated.

casting the duplication of a model in METAL or PLASTER by means of a MOLD; the model thus formed is a cast.

catacomb an underground burial chamber for several tombs; the term applies especially to the Early Christian tombs in Rome.

catafalque decorated structure used to display or carry a coffin during a funeral or lying in state.

cedar tree of the genus *Cedrus* whose hard, reddish wood has been used for making furniture.

ceiling (arch.) lining of roof of room, often painted or decorated.

celadon Chinese PORCELAIN or STONEWARE with a distinctive gray-green GLAZE.

cella (also called *naos*) enclosed chamber in Greek or Roman temple housing a cult-image.

censer portable incense burner for ecclesiastical use, in which incense is sprinkled on burning charcoal.

centaur mythological creature; a horse with a human torso instead of a horse's head and neck.

ceramics the general term used since the 19th century for POTTERY and PORCELAIN, i.e. fired clay.

ceramic sculpture sculpture in ceramic material.

ceramist one who makes ceramics.

Cercle et Carré Group group and periodical of International Constructivists formed in Paris in 1929 by Joaquin Torres-Garciá and others to promote ABSTRACT art.

Chac Mool an important Mayan god, often represented in sculpture.

chaitya term usually reserved for an Indian Buddhist SANCTUARY cut in rock and arranged as a hall with an AISLE on either side separated from it by rows of PILLARS.

chalcedony semiprecious stone; a type of QUARTZ that occurs as different varieties including AGATE and CARNELIAN.

chalice cup, usually of precious metal, used to hold consecrated wine during Mass or Eucharist.

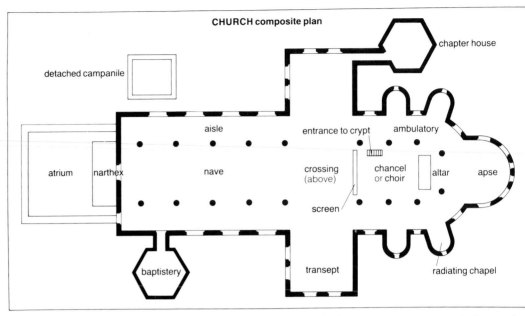

CHURCH composite plan

detached campanile — chapter house — aisle — entrance to crypt — ambulatory — atrium — narthex — nave — crossing (above) — chancel or choir — altar — apse — screen — baptistery — transept — radiating chapel

chalk the common name for calcium carbonate, which is found as a natural deposit all over the world, and is composed of the remains of tiny crustaceans. Traditionally used in painting and drawing.

chamfered capital (arch.) CAPITAL whose square angles are cut obliquely.

champlevé enamel (Fr.) decorated METAL, usually COPPER, especially popular in Europe from the 11th century to the 14th; a hollowed-out pattern in the metal was filled with colored GLASS pastes and the whole object fired, thus fusing glass to metal. (Compare CLOISONNÉ ENAMEL.)

Ch'an Chinese Buddhist sect; equivalent of the Japanese ZEN, which produced a rather mystical type of painting.

chancel (arch.) east end of CHURCH containing the ALTAR.

chapter house (arch.) building attached to a monastic or collegiate CHURCH used for the assembly of clergy.

characterization creation of distinct character.

charcoal form of CARBON used for drawing.

chase 1 to ornament a metal surface by ENGRAVING with steel tools. **2** to apply the final smoothing to a BRONZE cast. Both processes are known as chasing.

chasuble circular ecclesiastical vestment, with a hole in the center for the head.

château (Fr.) **1** a feudal castle. **2** a large country house.

chequer pattern squares of alternate colors.

chert form of QUARTZ.

Che School 15th-century school of Chinese painting, based at

Chekiang, that represented the academic court tradition.

chevron 1 (arch.) zigzag MOLDING in Norman architecture. **2** pattern of V shapes.*

chiaroscuro pictorial representation of light and shade without regard to color.

Chicago School group of architects working in Chicago between 1871 and 1893 including Frank Lloyd Wright and Louis Sullivan.

china term for better quality ceramics such as fine porcelain.

chinoiserie (Fr.) term for a European style of art applied to furniture, ceramics, interior design, based on imaginary pseudo-Chinese motifs.

chin-shih (Chinese, "advanced scholar") the highest grade of the Chinese civil service, from *c*618–1911.

chintz term used in Europe in the 16th and 17th centuries for imported Indian calico, and later for European printed cotton.

chip carving early primitive carved decoration of Northern European oak furniture, executed with a chisel and gouge, until about the 16th century.

Chi-Rho a monogram (the Sacred Monogram) formed by the first two letters—X and P (*chi* and *rho*)—of the Greek word for Christ. In religious art it may refer to the Resurrection of Christ.*

choir (arch.) part of CHURCH where service is sung.

choir stalls seats arranged in rows on either side of CHOIR, often carved.

chromatic of or relating to color.

chromium metallic element often used to plate other METAL, e.g. in sculpture.

chronogram phrase (often an in-

scription) written in Roman letters in which those letters that also represent numerals express a date or an epoch.

chrysocolla 1 classical name for compounds used in soldering gold, especially green copper mineral compounds. **2** natural copper silicate, which has been found as a pigment.

church 1 building designed for Christian worship. The first churches were based on the Roman BASILICA, but soon developed.* **2** the whole body of Christian believers.

ciborium (arch.) **1** vaulted CANOPY over an ALTAR. **2** vessel for holding consecrated host.

cimborio (arch.) (Sp., "drum") a drum-shaped structure, often pierced with windows, and supporting a DOME.*

cinnabar red mercuric sulfide used as pigment. Artificial cinnabar is usually called VERMILION.

cinnabarite mineral ore of CINNABAR.

Cinquecento (It.) the 16th century.

cire perdue (Fr., "lost wax") casting process used in BRONZE sculpture.

cityscape painting or drawing of city scenery.

cladding coating or covering; e.g. material covering the FACADE of a building.

classic 1 the finest art of its kind in any given period. **2** Greek art of the 5th century BC (Classic). **3** art of the Roman and Greek antique world (Classic). **4** art that adheres to high standards of craftsmanship, logic, symmetry, and proportion.

classical synonymous with CLASSIC (2, 3 and 4).

Classic Greek architecture apogee of

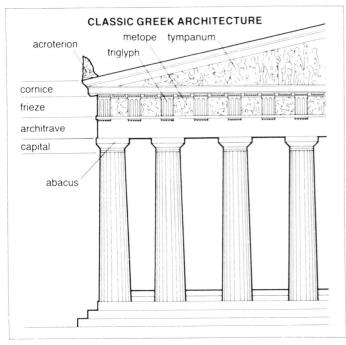

CLASSIC GREEK ARCHITECTURE

acroterion
metope tympanum
triglyph
cornice
frieze
architrave
capital
abacus

Greek architectural design, much imitated in later architecture.*

classicism the quality of classic or classical art. The term is applied in particular to the type of art that was the antithesis of ROMANTICISM during the 18th and 19th centuries, when it was held to represent the virtues of restraint and harmony, in contrast to dramatic individual expression.

classicizing promoting or tending towards the CLASSIC.

clerestory (arch.) upper story of NAVE of CHURCH, pierced with windows; see VAULT CONSTRUCTION.

cloisonné enamel (Fr.) decorated METAL in which a design of metal strips is applied and the compartments (cloisons) formed are filled with colored GLASS pastes. (Compare CHAMPLEVÉ ENAMEL.)

cloisonnisme (Fr.) synonym for SYNTHETISM.

cloister (arch.) covered walk around a space, usually square, with a wall on one side and columns on the other. In Christian monasteries it often links the CHURCH and domestic quarters.

cobalt metallic element from which various colored pigments were produced in the 19th century.

CoBrA an association of Dutch, Danish and Belgian Expressionist artists 1948–51. An acronym of the words Copenhagen, Brussels and Amsterdam.

codex MANUSCRIPT bound as a book.

coffer 1 (arch.) ornamental sunken panel recessed into ceiling or vault, which may then be described as coffered. 2 chest for valuable objects.

collage (Fr., "pasting") technique originating with CUBISM in which paper, photographs, and other everyday materials were pasted on to a support, and sometimes also painted.

collé (Fr.) pasted, glued, stuck.

Cologne School paintings from the Cologne region of Germany, dating, from the late 14th century to the 16th.

Colonial style American painting, art, and architecture of the 17th century to the 19th.

colonnade row of COLUMNS supporting ENTABLATURE.

colonnette small COLUMN.

color field painting painting, usually on a large scale, in which solid areas of color are taken right up to the edge of the canvas, suggesting that they extend to infinity.

coloring the way in which color is used in paintings, or the general impression of color given by a particular painting.

colorism term applied to various periods of painting, e.g. 16th-century Venetian, in which color was emphasized, rather than drawing.

colorist artist who specializes in, or is famed for, his/her use of color.

color modulation composition based on subtle variation of color.

color progression composition based on a clear progression from one color, or group of colors, to another.

colossal order see GIANT ORDER.

colossus gigantic STATUE.

column (arch.) cylindrical pillar, either freestanding or supporting another architectural member. In CLASSICAL architecture it consists of a base, a SHAFT, and a CAPITAL; see CLASSIC GREEK ARCHITECTURE.

column-figure human figure, carved in the round, used to decorate columns at church doorways from the 12th century to the 15th.*

column krater Greek vase for mixing wine and water; see GREEK VASES.

Commedia dell'Arte (It.) professional, improvised Italian comedy of the 16th and 17th centuries.

commission 1 a work of art ordered by a patron. 2 contract to produce work for a patron.

Composite order see ORDERS OF ARCHITECTURE.

composition board BOARD made of cheap pressed or laminated fibers, used as a painting support, in COLLAGE, and in SCULPTURE.

compound pier see PIER.

conceit fanciful device; affectation of style. Used especially of architecture.

Conceptual art art that takes the form of mental images, provoked by various stimuli—visual, tactile, and aural—and in which the concepts and ideas are more important than tangible, concrete works of art.

concha (or conch) (arch.) the domed roof of a semicircular APSE.*

concrete mixture of sand, stone, and cement used as a building material, especially in the 20th century.

Concrete art term coined in 1929 when Theo van Doesburg became editor of the magazine Art Concret; it is sometimes used as a synonym for ABSTRACT art, though the emphasis is not just on geometric or abstract form, but on structure and organization in both design and execution.

condottiere (It.) Italian mercenary; soldier of fortune.

console 1 (arch.) architectural term for scrolled bracket. 2 in furniture, a side table with marble top.

Constructivism international ABSTRACT art movement founded in post-revolutionary Russia by Antoine Pevsner and Naum Gabo, whose aims were expressed in the REALISTIC MANIFESTO.

conté crayon proprietary manufactured CHALK.

contrapposto (It., "opposite", "antithesis", "placed against") posing of human form in painting or sculpture so that head and shoulders are twisted in a different direction from hips and legs.*

contre jour (Fr.) technique used in painting and photography of showing the subject placed against a light source, such as a window, rather than illuminated by a source of light at the side, in the conventional way.

chevron

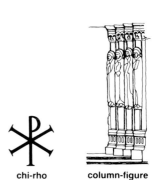

chi-rho   column-figure

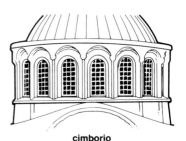

cimborio

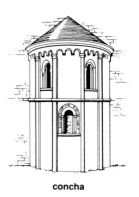

concha

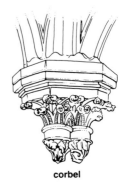

corbel

conversation piece painting of group portrait, especially popular in 18th-century England, showing the sitters talking or involved in some other informal activity.

cool color color tending towards the blue end of the visual SPECTRUM, or which appears to recede in a painting.

cope semicircular ecclesiastical cloak for processions and ceremonies.

copper plate copper plate on which a design is etched or engraved; often used as term for the image produced by this method.

corbel (arch.) projection on a wall, bearing a weight.*

corbeling (arch.) series of CORBELS built one above the other.

corbel table projecting COURSE resting on a series of CORBELS.

cord-impressed pattern pattern applied to early Japanese and other POTTERY by pressing a piece of cord into the CLAY while still soft.

Corinthian order *see* ORDERS OF ARCHITECTURE.

cornelian alternative spelling of CARNELIAN.

cornice (arch.) 1 upper member of an ENTABLATURE. 2 ornamental molding finishing the part to which it is attached, e.g. at the junction of a wall and CEILING.

cornucopia (Latin) goat's horn overflowing with fruit, flowers, and corn, symbolizing plenty.

coroplast a sculptor in Greek ANTIQUITY whose medium was chiefly TERRACOTTA, used particularly for making FIGURINES.

cortile (It., "courtyard") courtyard surrounded by ARCADES.

costume piece painting whose chief subject is a figure or figures in historic or exotic costume.

couching embroidery technique in which thread is sewn on a GROUND using a finer thread, which is visible as a pattern.

coulisse (Fr.) literally, the wings at the side of a stage. In painting, particularly of the BAROQUE period, it refers to a composition in which features at the edge of the picture, e.g. hills and trees, lead the viewer's eye into the painting.

coupled pilaster (arch.) two PILASTERS standing on the same PEDESTAL.

course continuous horizontal layer in the stone of a building.

courtyard (arch.) space enclosed by buildings or walls but often open to the sky.

cove (arch.) concave molding, especially between the CEILING and CORNICE of a room.

cowrie small shell, often used as a design MOTIF.

crenellation (arch.) the formation of battlements, in which the openings are known as *crenelles*.

cresting (arch.) line of ornament finishing a roof or wall.

crewel work textiles made from crewel yarn, a thin, two-threaded strong wool.

crocket (arch.) in Gothic architecture, a carved decoration, usually leaf-shaped, projecting from the sides of pinnacles or gables.

cross-hatching *see* HATCHING.

crossing (arch.) the space in a CHURCH where NAVE, CHANCEL, and TRANSEPTS meet.

cross-in-rectangle (arch.) CHURCH plan, common in Armenia.*

crozier crook-shaped staff carried by bishops.

cruciform cross-shaped; used especially of a CHURCH that has TRANSEPTS.

crypt underground chamber below CHURCH, usually at east end.

crystal (or rock crystal) very hard form of transparent QUARTZ, especially popular in Italy as a carving material.

cube technique MOSAIC technique using cut, cube-shaped stones that can produce more subtle designs than uncut stones.

cubiculum (Latin) 1 term used by the Romans for a bedchamber or reclining room, or a small enclosed space, e.g. a box at the theater. 2 term used by the Roman architectural writer Vitruvius (1st century BC) for a recess in a wall designed to receive the end of a BEAM.

Cubism artistic movement *c*1907 to 1915 initiated by Picasso and Braque as a reaction against IMPRESSIONISM. It aimed to analyze forms in geometric terms (ANALYTICAL CUBISM) or reorganize them in various contexts (SYNTHETIC CUBISM); color remained secondary to form.

Cubo-Futurism specifically Russian art movement associated with Kasimir Malevich, *c*1913, which combined elements of CUBISM and FUTURISM.

cuerda seca (Sp., "dry cord") decorative technique used on tiles; an outline is incised in the soft CLAY and the lines then filled with a greasy medium that acts as a "resist" so that different glazes will not run together.

cult statue statue of non-Christian deity for cult worship.

Cupid synonymous with Amor and Eros; the mythological child of Venus, and Roman god of love, usually depicted as a child holding a bow and arrow. The term is sometimes used to mean simply "cherub" (*see* PUTTO).

cupola (arch.) domed VAULT or roof.*

cup painting Classical Greek decoration of POTTERY vessels that became a highly sophisticated art form.

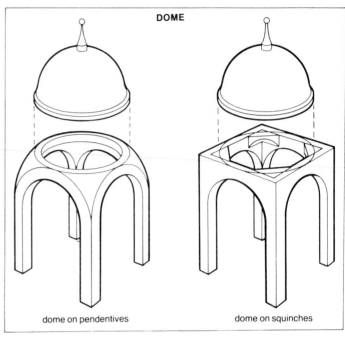

DOME

dome on pendentives   dome on squinches

cursive form/style flowing, like script.

curtain wall (arch.) outer wall of castle joining towers and gatehouse. Also refers to a wall that divides space without bearing weight.

curvilinear based on pattern of curved lines; sinuous.

cushion base base of a CAPITAL associated with early medieval architecture; shaped like a cube but with rounded edges and corners. See CUSHION CAPITAL.

cushion capital (arch.) square capital with rounded corners, found chiefly in ROMANESQUE and early medieval buildings; *see* VAULT CONSTRUCTION.

cusp (arch.) point at which two arcs meet in GOTHIC arch or TRACERY.

Cycladic type of Aegean art from the Cyclades—a group of Greek islands—*c*2800 BC to 1100 BC.

cycle series of paintings linked by a theme, especially used in FRESCO painting.

cylindrical pier *see* PIER.

cypress coniferous tree of the genus *Cupressus*. Often a symbol of mourning. Its rather hard wood may be used for furniture.

D

Dada international "anti-art" movement originating in Zurich *c*1916, involving Marcel Duchamp, Jean Arp, Francis Picabia, among others; a forerunner of SURREALISM; hence Dadaism, Dadaist.

dado (arch.) 1 lower section of a wall, sometimes separated from the upper by a MOLDING. 2 part of a PEDESTAL between the BASE and CORNICE.

Danube School nonexistent as a School, the name loosely refers to several early 16th-century German painters, such as Albrecht Altdorfer and Lucas Cranach, famous for lush landscapes and rich coloristic effects.

dappled of variegated color, or applied in spots and patches.

Dark Ages period of the Middle Ages from *c*5th century AD to 10th century, formerly considered a phase in which philosophy and the arts were ignored or actively hindered.

Decadent Movement *fin-de-siècle* movement associated with Aubrey Beardsley (1872–98).

decalcomania (Fr. *decalcomanie*) American term for LITHOGRAPHY.

decorative aesthetically pleasing, ornamental, nonfunctional.

decorative art near synonymous with APPLIED ART, it involves CERAMICS, GLASS, furniture, TEXTILES, and similar work, excluding FINE ART.

deësis (Greek) in Byzantine iconography, the figure of Christ enthroned between the Virgin and St John the Baptist.

Degenerate art (Ger., *Entartet Kunst*) Nazi propaganda term used from *c*1937 for works of modern art disapproved of by the party.

Delft School 17th-century Dutch genre painting associated with Jan Vermeer and Pieter de Hooch.

depth three-dimensionality or recession, real or suggested.

Der Sturm (Ger., "The Storm") magazine and art gallery in Berlin, founded by Herwarth Walden; from 1910 to 1932 it promoted FUTURISM and EXPRESSIONISM, particularly the BLAUE REITER group.

Dervish Muslim religious man, vowed to a life of poverty.

De Stijl 1 Dutch art magazine founded in 1917 by Theo van Doesburg and Piet Mondrian. **2** artists and architects associated with the journal who were influential in promoting functional BAUHAUS design during the 1920s.

Deutscher Werkbund (Ger., "German Work League") organization founded in Münich in 1907 to promote good design in machine-made objects.

device 1 contrivance or invention. **2** design or heraldic emblem.

devotional associated with, or the object of, religious worship.

diablerie (Fr.) visual representation of the powers of Hell or dealings with the devil.

diadem crown, wreath, or headband.

diaper (arch.) an all-over pattern of small square or lozenge-shaped units, found in ROMANESQUE and GOTHIC buildings. The term is also applied to a similar pattern in STAINED GLASS, and in the gold background of ILLUMINATED MANUSCRIPTS of the 13th, 14th, and 15th centuries.*

diaphane (Fr.) transparent.

diatreton (Greek) chased or engraved drinking cup; *see* GREEK VASES.

die 1 engraved stamp for making a coin or medal. **2** hollow MOLD for shaping extruded METAL.

diluent liquid added to paint to thin it and make it easier to work with, e.g. turpentine, for OIL PAINTING; water, for WATERCOLOR painting.

dinos GREEK VASE, shaped like a KRATER on a tall base.

diorite variety of GREENSTONE or JADE, used for tools, ornaments, and small sculpture.

diptych pair of painted or sculptured panels hinged or joined together; especially popular for devotional pictures in the Middle Ages; *see* ALTARPIECE.

direct carving method of stone sculpture where form is carved immediately out of the block, and not transferred from a model.

direct metal sculpture modern technique of METAL sculpture, shaping metal by beating or with heat, instead of the traditional CASTING technique.

disegno (It.) literally, "drawing" or "design", but which during the RENAISSANCE acquired a broader meaning of overall concept.

di sotto in su (It., "From below upwards") method of illusionistic CEILING painting in which the figures are dramatically FORE-SHORTENED.

distemper paint based on glue or SIZE medium, used for painting walls and theatrical scenery.

Divisionism analytical painting technique developed systematically by Georges Seurat (1859–91); instead of mixing colors on the PALETTE, each color is applied "pure" in individual brush-strokes, so that from a certain distance, the viewer's eye and brain perform the mixing "optically"; *see* POINTILLISM.

dogtooth (arch.) **1** small ornament shaped like a pyramid, with the flat faces cut back. **2** ornament on a MOLDING, in the form of four lobes or leaves radiating from a center, found in 13th-century English architecture.*

dolerite a type of basaltic rock.

dolmen prehistoric monument consisting of a large flat stone on two uprights.

dome (arch.) convex covering set over circular or polygonal base.*

Dong-son prehistoric Indo-Chinese culture; the name derives from the chief site (in Vietnam) in which implements and ornaments have been found.

donor giver of a work of art. From the 6th century AD, often depicted in painting.

Doric *see* ORDERS OF ARCHITECTURE.

draftsman person who draws or sketches plans (particularly of machinery, buildings etc.).

draftsmanship skill in drawing or plan-making.

drapery the arrangement of folds of material, painted or sculpted.

drawing the pictorial representation of objects by a technique that is basically linear, such as pen or pencil. When used of a painting, it refers more specifically to the artist's method of representing form by these means, rather than by the use of color and paint.

drum (arch.) **1** circular or polygonal wall supporting a dome. **2** circular blocks of stone forming a column.

drypoint COPPER ENGRAVING technique.

dynamism the quality or appearance of power, action, movement. The term may be used figuratively of inanimate objects such as sculpture; hence dynamic.

E

earthenware POTTERY made from red or white CLAY, fired in a KILN at less than 1200°C.

easel painting (or picture) small or medium-sized painting executed at an easel. These were usually intended for collectors and connoisseurs, although the term may also be used generally for any portable painting, as opposed to MURAL painting; also called CABINET PICTURE.

eave (arch.) lower edge of a roof, overhanging a wall.

ebony heavy, hard-grained black wood of the species of tree *Diospyros ebenum*, used for furniture and decorative objects.

Ecce homo (Latin, "Behold the man") the pictorial representation of Christ's presentation to the people by Pontius Pilate before the Crucifixion.

École de Paris *see* SCHOOL OF PARIS.

écorché (Fr., "flayed") describes a figure drawn or modeled without skin to show the musculature; used by the artist as an aid to drawing, painting, or sculpture.

Edo 1 former name for Tokyo. **2** name of the period of Japanese history from 1615 to 1868.

effigy portrait or model of a figure, especially when part of a stone tomb.

electrum natural alloy of silver and gold used in the ancient world for METALWORK.

Elementarism modified form of NEO-PLASTICISM propounded by Theo van Doesburg in the 1920s, which caused a rift with Piet Mondrian by introducing diagonals instead of a rigid horizontal and vertical format.

elevation (arch.) **1** the face or side of a structure. **2** drawing or plan of the side of a building.

ellipse an oval shape traced by a point moving in one plane, so that the sum of its distance from two other fixed points remains constant.

emblema elaborate MOSAIC panel set into a plain floor or mosaic. By extension, the term may also be used for any distinct decorative panel set in a larger area, e.g. a carpet.

emboss to MOLD, stamp, or carve a surface to produce a design in RELIEF.

emulsion a combination of two non-miscible liquids in which drops of one are suspended in the other. It is not established how far emulsions have been used as painting media but the technique used by the 15th-century Flemish painters may have employed an egg/oil emulsion.

enamel 1 vitreous substance (usually lead/potash GLASS) fused to METAL at high temperature (about 800°C) and often used for decorative objects; *see* CLOISONNÉ ENAMEL and CHAMPLEVÉ ENAMEL. **2** the object so produced.

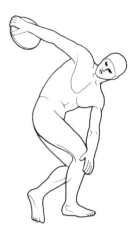

contrapposto

after the Discobolus (Discus-thrower) by Myron; 5th century BC

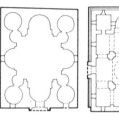

cross-in-rectangle

two examples of Armenian cross-in-rectangle church plan

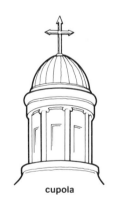

cupola

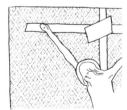

diaper

dogtooth ornament

enamel paint paint based on thickened linseed oil and resin, which dries to a very hard and glossy surface.

enamel painting painting with colored ENAMELS, often used for small objects of METAL or GLASS.

encaustic technique ancient technique of painting with wax and PIGMENTS fused by heat.

engraving 1 the technique of incising lines on wood, METAL, etc. **2** the impression made from the engraved block.

Enlightenment 18th-century philosophical movement that stressed the importance of reason.

enlumineur (Fr.) illuminator (of MANUSCRIPTS).

entablature (arch.) upper section of a Classical ORDER consisting of ARCHITRAVE, FRIEZE, and CORNICE.

entasis (Greek) (arch.) a slight swelling of the contour of a COLUMN, designed to counteract the optical illusion of concavity and generally found in Classical architecture.*

environmental sculpture a development in contemporary sculpture which is conceived as part of the environment shared, rather than just observed, by the viewer.

epistolary (from Latin *epistolarium*) "Book of Epistles" used for the Mass or Eucharist.

equilateral triangle triangle with three equal sides and angles.

erechtheum temple of the Acropolis in Athens, built *c*421–406 BC.

erotic art art devoted to the expression or arousal of sexual feeling.

Erster Deutscher Herbstsalon (Ger., "First German Autumn Salon") art exhibition held in Berlin in 1913, organized by August Macke and Wassily Kandinsky.

etch 1 term used in LITHOGRAPHY for the solution of gum arabic and nitric acid used to render the non-drawn area of a litho stone insensitive to grease. **2** (verb) to eat into, e.g. with acid.

etching 1 process in which the design is drawn on a METAL plate through a wax ground; the design is cut into the plate with acid, and printed. **2** PRINT produced by this method.

ethnographic art art inspired by a particular racial culture, especially of the primitive type.

Euston Road Group group of artists working in a broadly naturalistic style in Euston Rd, London, for a brief period from 1937 to 1939, including William Coldstream, Victor Pasmore, and Lawrence Gowing.

ewer pitcher, jug.

exedra (arch.) semicircular or angular recess in a wall, common in Greek and Roman architecture.

Expressionism artistic movement of the 20th century in which the expression of emotion and feeling is emphasized rather than the representation of nature; hence Expressionist, Expressionistic. *See also* BLAUE REITER and BRÜCKE.

extender inert pigment used to bulk a paint or to lower the tinctorial strength of another pigment.

eye cup BLACK-FIGURE Greek vase with a stylized eye motif.

F

facade (arch.) face of a building, usually the main face.

facet one side of a many sided object e.g. a cut gem.

facture quality or style of execution or handling, especially of a painting.

faience 1 type of tin-glazed EARTHENWARE, often used for architectural purposes. **2** archaeological term for ancient Egyptian wares of glazed powdered QUARTZ.

fantasy (or The Fantastic) dreamlike, visionary, or grotesque image which is the product of the artist's imagination.

Fauves (Fr.) originally a derogatory term (Les Fauves) meaning "wild beasts", used of a group of painters who exhibited at the Salon d'Automne in Paris in 1905, including Matisse; hence Fauvism, Fauvist.

felt 1 watertight fibrous building material used as underlining for roofs etc. **2** in papermaking, the blanket that carries the PAPER and squeezes moisture from it.

fête (Fr.) festival; saint's day; bazaar.

fête champêtre (Fr.) painting of somewhat idealized rural festivities, popular in the 17th and 18th centuries.

fête galante (Fr.) an elegant FÊTE CHAMPÊTRE of the type popularized in the 18th century by Antoine Watteau.

fetish object found in non-Christian cultures (especially African) used as the focus of a magic or religious ceremony.

fiberglass 1 woven glass fiber fabric. **2** molded plastic containing glass fiber, used for sculpture, furniture, etc.

fictive imaginary, creating an illusion. Most frequently used in descriptions of TROMPE L'OEIL painted architecture.

figural figurative, relating to figures or shapes.

figuration 1 form, shape. **2** ornamentation with design. **3** depiction of figures, especially human.

figurative art synonym for REPRESENTATIONAL ART.

figure drawing (and figure painting) drawing or painting in which the human figure predominates, usually full length.

figurine small model or sculpture of the human figure.

filigree fine woven mesh of gold and silver threads, used for mounting precious objects, e.g. GEMS, or in bookbinding.*

Fin de Siècle late 19th-century style of ART NOUVEAU, also associated with the SYMBOLIST and DECADENT movements.

fine art art whose value is considered to be aesthetic rather than functional, i.e. architecture, sculpture, painting and drawing, and the graphic arts. Compare APPLIED ART and DECORATIVE ART.

finial (arch.) the ornamental termination of part of a building such as a SPIRE or PEDIMENT.

fire (verb) to bake in a KILN, especially POTTERY and PORCELAIN. The process converts "raw" CLAY to a hard, usable material.

Flamboyant (arch.) the last phase of French Gothic architecture, from *c*1460, characterized by elaborate, flowing window TRACERY.

flint hard stone, mainly silica, used for making primitive tools and in building.

floral motif design based on flower forms, often used for textiles.

flourish curved ornament used in CALLIGRAPHY or MANUSCRIPT illumination.

flower painting still-life painting of flowers, associated chiefly with Oriental art and the Dutch painters of the 17th century.

fluorescent (adj.) having the property of absorbing radiation in the invisible, ultraviolet range, and emitting it as visible light. Fluorescent paint has been used in modern painting for its vivid color and dramatic optical effect.

flute decoration of shallow vertical grooves in COLUMNS or on furniture; hence fluted, fluting.

flying buttress see BUTTRESS.

fold feature of drapery represented in painting or sculpture, often used to characterize a style; *see* MULDENSTIL.

foliated (arch.) covered with leaf ornamentation.

folio 1 sheet of paper folded to form two leaves. **2** book of the largest common size.

folk art NAIVE art of peasant societies, including their FINE ART and DECORATIVE ART.

font vessel, usually stone, in a CHURCH, used to hold the water for baptism.

foreground in painting, the plane nearest to the viewer.

foreshortening the use of the laws of PERSPECTIVE in art to make an individual form appear three dimensional.

forge 1 to shape metals by heat and hammering. **2** the place where this is done.

form the shape or appearance the artist gives to his subject.

formalism the tendency to adhere to conventional forms at the expense of the subject matter.

format shape, style, or arrangement, which may be repetitive or stereotyped.

formica laminated plastic used for modern furniture and sculpture.

forum Roman public meeting place. "The Forum" refers to the civic center of ancient Rome.

found object an object that is found, not made, by the artist, and is then defined and displayed as a work of art; also known as an *objet trouvé* and associated with SURREALISM and DADA.

free painting painting done for its own sake, and not as decoration of an object.

French chalk finely ground magnesium silicate used with resin in LITHOGRAPHY to protect the image from the acid when ETCHING the stone.

fresco (It.) MURAL painting on fresh plaster; sometimes called *buon fresco* ("true fresco") to distinguish it from painting A SECCO, on dried plaster.

fresco secco (It.) misleading term synonymous with painting A SECCO.

frieze 1 part of an ENTABLATURE between the ARCHITRAVE and CORNICE, sometimes decorated in relief. **2** horizontal band of decoration along the upper part of a wall or on furniture. **3** woolen cloth.

frit 1 mixture of calcified sand used in making GLASS. **2** glass-like composition used in making PORCELAIN. **3** ground glass used in making POTTERY.

frontal 1 facade of, or covering for, the front of an ALTAR. **2** as an adjective, "frontal" describes images of the human figure or of deities in which the face is emphasized; hence frontality.

frontispiece 1 book illustration opposite title page. **2** (arch.) main FACADE, PEDIMENT, or BAY of a building.

frottage (Fr., "rubbing") the technique of placing paper over textured objects or surfaces and rubbing with a wax crayon or graphite, to produce an image.

fu Chinese Bronze Age food vessel of *c*700 BC.

functionalism the artistic theory that form should be determined by function, especially in ARCHITECTURE and the DECORATIVE ARTS, and that this will automatically produce objects that are aesthetically pleasing.

Futurism Italian artistic movement founded in 1909 by Filippo Marinetti, which exalted the modern world of machinery, speed, and violence.

G

gable (arch.) triangular part of a wall at the end of the roof ridge.

gable end (arch.) gable-shaped canopy over a door or window, or a gable-topped wall.

gallery (arch.) 1 an upper story in a CHURCH above the AISLE. 2 in Elizabethan or Jacobean architecture, a long room, usually extending the full length of the house. 3 place where works of art are displayed.

galvanized iron iron coated with zinc to prevent rust.

gargoyle (arch.) waterspout projecting from the gutters of a building (especially in GOTHIC architecture) often in the form of an open-mouthed grotesque human or animal head.

garnet deep red GEM stone.

gem precious or semiprecious stone used in jewelry and decorative objects.

Genji eponymous hero of a Japanese novel, *The Tales of Genji*, written by Lady Murasaki *c* AD 1000.

genre 1 style, type. 2 painting of scenes of daily life, popularized by 17th-century Dutch painters.

Geometric Abstraction loose and somewhat inaccurate term for ABSTRACT art in which the image is composed of nonrepresentational geometric shapes. It has been used of various artists and movements, including the SUPREMATISTS, Piet Mondrian, and Ben Nicholson.

Geometric style Greek style of decoration, flourishing from *c*900 to *c*725 BC, based on linear and angular shapes.

gesso (It.) generally used for any mixture of an inert white PIGMENT with glue, used as a GROUND for painting; strictly, a mixture in which the inert pigment is calcium sulfate. *Gesso grosso* is coarse gesso made from sifted PLASTER of Paris, used for the preliminary ground layer in medieval Italian panel paintings. *Gesso sottile* is fine crystalline gypsum, made by slaking Plaster of Paris in excess water.

Gestural art the type of GEOMETRIC ABSTRACTION that emphasizes brushwork and the artist's movements.

giant order (arch.) COLUMN or PILAS-

TER that extends over more than one story of a building; also known as colossal order.

gilding the coating of a surface with GOLD LEAF; hence gilded.

gilt silver or other METAL, decorated with GOLD LEAF.

giornata (It.) the area of work in MURAL or MOSAIC that could be finished in one day. In FRESCO painting, it refers to the area of INTONACO applied each day. In true fresco, the joins of the *giornate* are usually visible.

glass material produced by fusing silica with an alkaline flux, e.g. potash or soda, by heat.

glass fiber *see* FIBERGLASS.

glass painting technique of decorating GLASS, not very clearly distinguished from glass enameling, although it may be more transparent and smoother. Early glass painting was not fired, and therefore not permanent.

glaze 1 transparent layer of paint applied over another; light passes through and is reflected back, modifying or intensifying the underlayer. 2 vitreous layer made from silica, applied to POTTERY as decoration or to make it watertight.

glazing 1 process of applying glaze. 2 window design or construction.

gloria aureole or NIMBUS around the head of a deity, or a head ornament representing this.

glyptic art term usually used of sculpture in which the design is incised, sometimes to produce an image for CASTING a SEAL.

golden section geometrical proportion, usually expressed as a finite line divided so that the shorter length bears the same relation to the longer as the longer does to the whole. Originally thought to be a naturally harmonious and pleasing relationship.

gold leaf gold, very thinly beaten so that it can be used for GILDING.

gorget piece of armor to protect the throat.

gorgoneion (Greek) representation of the Gorgon's head.

Gospel lectionary volume containing the four Gospels.

Gothic the last period of medieval art and architecture. Early Gothic usually refers to the period 1140–1200; High Gothic *c*1200–50; late Gothic from 1250. "Gothic" was used in the RENAISSANCE as a pejorative adjective for medieval architecture.

gouache 1 opaque WATERCOLOR paint. 2 a work executed in gouache medium.

gradual 1 verses sung or recited immediately after the epistle at Mass. 2 a book of the choral parts of the Mass.

graffiti (It.) drawings or words scribbled in random fashion on a wall.

grande machine (Fr.) phrase meaning literally "great work" or composition, used of paintings of monumental construction.

granite very hard crystalline rock, much used in building.

granulation the decoration of metalwork, particularly gold and jewelry, with a pattern of tiny balls. *

graphic related to drawing or engraving; vividly descriptive.

graphic art broad term for techniques of illustration on paper, particularly in black and white or monochrome, such as drawing, ENGRAVING, LITHOGRAPHY.

graphics design or decoration, including PHOTOGRAPHY, associated with typographic work and illustration.

graphite crystalline form of CARBON, used in PENCILS.

grattage (Fr., "scraping") technique used by 20th-century artists, in which an upper layer of paint is partially scraped away to reveal the contrasting under layer.

Greek cross cross with arms of equal length, often used as an architectural ground plan.

Greek orders of architecture *see* DORIC, IONIC, CORINTHIAN, and ORDERS.

Greek vases range of pots of different sizes, used for different purposes, most of which were often decorated if not painted. *

greenstone nephrite (a variety of JADE) or similar types of stone containing feldspar.

grid-plan term used in town planning to denote a right-angled lattice-like layout, imposed regardless of the terrain. It is thought to have originated in Greece in the 5th century BC.

griffin mythological creature with eagle's head and wings and lion's body.

grisaille technique of monochrome painting in shades of gray, used as underpainting or to imitate the effect of RELIEF.

groin (arch.) ARCH supporting VAULT (*see* VAULT CONSTRUCTION), or the intersection of two barrel vaults.

grotesque fanciful ornament, based on animals, fruit, flowers, and human forms; found in Roman buildings and reused during the RENAISSANCE; also known as *grotesquerie* and *grotteschi*. *

grotto artificially constructed cave, often a feature of landscaped parks and gardens.

ground 1 synonym for BACKGROUND. 2 layer of preparation on a support to receive paint. 3 in ETCHING, the acid-resistant material spread over the metal plate

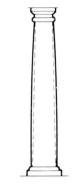

entasis

filigree

granulation

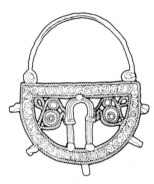

grotesque

GREEK VASES

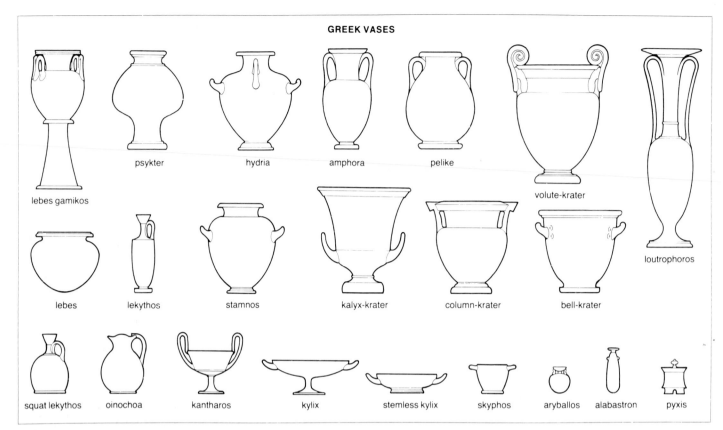

psykter • hydria • amphora • pelike • volute-krater

lebes gamikos

lebes • lekythos • stamnos • kalyx-krater • column-krater • bell-krater • loutrophoros

squat lekythos • oinochoa • kantharos • kylix • stemless kylix • skyphos • aryballos • alabastron • pyxis

before the design is etched. **4** in POTTERY, the CLAY forming the body of a vessel on which a design is executed.

groundline base on which a geometrical design or pattern is constructed, e.g. in Greek vase painting.

ground plan (arch.) plan of building as seen from above.

Groupe Null (or Nul Groep) Dutch art association cofounded in 1960 by Jan Schoonhoven.

guild medieval form of professional association that regulated standards of craftsmanship and commercial activity.

Gulistan (Persian) literally, "The Place of Flowers", the title of one of the two works by the 13th-century poet Sa'di.

gypsum chemically, calcium sulfate dihydrate, an inert white material used in making both PLASTER of Paris and CEMENT. Varieties of gypsum include ALABASTER; *see also* GESSO.

H

haematite red iron oxide, naturally occurring as an ore; the source of red-brown earth PIGMENTS.

Hafiz one of the great Persian lyric poets; he lived from *c*1325 to 1389/90 and worked mainly in Hiraz. His compositions were often illustrated.

haiga Japanese painting illustrating a HAIKU poem.

haiku Japanese poem of three lines and 17 syllables, developed from the 17th century.

half-tone tone in drawing, painting, or in a screen pattern for reproduction; between the darkest and the lightest.

half-tone process printing process using dots to indicate different tones and densities.

hall church (arch.) CHURCH whose NAVE and AISLES are about the same height.*

hallmark official mark for gold, silver, and platinum, to indicate the standard of purity.

halo circle of light surrounding head of saint or divinity; associated with Christian art although it dates back to ancient Greece and Egypt; *see* NIMBUS.

hamam (or *hammam*) in Islamic architecture, the public baths or bath house, usually domed.

happening spontaneous event or display; a feature of American and Western European art since the 1960s.

hard edged 1 of painting, term coined in 1959 to describe ABSTRACT (but not geometric) painting, using large, flat areas of color with precise edges. **2** linear style; the opposite of SFUMATO.

hatching drawing technique that uses closely spaced parallel lines to indicate toned areas. When crossed by other lines in the opposite direction it is known as cross-hatching.

Heian period of Japanese art, from AD 784 to 1185.

Hellenic Greek culture of the 11th century BC to 323 BC.

Hellenistic Greek culture after Alexander the Great (from 323 BC) to the late 1st century BC.

hemicircle semicircular figure.

hemp herbaceous plant producing tough fiber, used in making rope and canvas.

heraldry art or study of armorial devices; hence heraldic.

herm pillar-sculpture that appeared in Greece in the 6th century BC; usually in the form of a bearded male figure.

hexagon plane figure with six sides and angles; hence hexagonal.

hieratic style in which certain fixed types, often sacred, are repeated, e.g. in Egyptian or Byzantine art. It may also be applied to any art that uses severe, rigid figures rather than naturalistic ones.

hieroglyphs 1 picture writing, as used by the Egyptians. **2** during the RENAISSANCE the term was applied to emblems whose message could be deciphered.

Hieronymite belonging to the order of St Jerome.

high art art that strives to attain the highest AESTHETIC and moral qualities in both content and expression.

High Baroque the peak of the Italian BAROQUE style, *c*1625–75.

highlight in painting, a highlight is the lightest, brightest area, indicating light falling on a prominent plane or point; hence highlighting.

hiragana one of the Japanese systems of syllabic writing, used in newpapers etc.

historiated architecture or sculpture decorated with narrative subjects. A historiated initial is an initial in an ILLUMINATED MANUSCRIPT containing a narrative scene.*

history painting painting whose subject is some significant historical event, preferably Classical, actual or literary. From the 16th century to the 19th, history painting was more highly esteemed than other forms of painting, especially by the academies.

horizon the line at which sky and earth appear to meet.

hours in the Christian Church, prayers to be said at set times of day.

hu a Chinese Bronze Age storage vessel.

hydria a Greek pottery water vessel; *see* GREEK VASES.

hydrodynamic concerning the forces acting on or produced by liquid.

hygroscopic having the ability to

readily take up and retain water from the atmosphere.

I

icon (Greek, "image", "portrait") in Byzantine, Greek, and Russian Orthodox church art, the representation of Christ or the Virgin, or saints, in mosaic or painting; tending to be stereotyped or HIERATIC; hence iconic.

iconoclasm (Greek, "image breaking") widespread destruction of religious images, especially in the Byzantine Empire during the 8th and 9th centuries; hence iconoclast, iconoclastic.

iconography the identification of subject matter in works of art; hence iconographic.

iconology the interpretation of subject matter in works of art.

iconostasis in Russian or Byzantine churches, the screen on which ICONS are placed.

ideal art art of various periods that is based on the artist's conception rather than visual perception, e.g. the art of the High RENAISSANCE, or of 17th-century CLASSICISM.

ideated imagined, conceived.

ideogram symbol, e.g. Chinese writing, which expresses an idea without actually expressing the sound of its name.

idiom characteristic, local language or style of art.

ignudi (It.) nude figures.

illuminated manuscript handwritten book on VELLUM or PARCHMENT, usually medieval, decorated with miniature painting, borders, and decorative capital letters; hence illumination.

illusionism the use of optical and perspectival principles to create the illusion of painted objects being three dimensional; hence illusionist, illusionistic.

imagery collection of images or forms giving expression to the artist's idea of objects or people.

impasto thick mass of paint or pastel; hence impasted.

Impressionism 19th-century French art movement, from 1874. Various artists such as Pissarro, Monet, Renoir, and Sisley, were linked by their common interest in capturing immediate visual impressions, and an emphasis on light and color; hence Impressionist; Impressionistic.

incised line line cut into the surface of an object; used in CERAMICS as a decoration, or in painting, when it is made in the GROUND layer, as a guide for painting.

indulgence the remission of a sin by the Roman Catholic Church.

inert pigment white PIGMENTS of low refractive index, therefore poor hiding power e.g. GYPSUM, CHALK, aluminum hydroxide. These may be used in preparing GROUNDS, as EXTENDERS in paint, or as the substrate on which a LAKE PIGMENT is precipitated.

infilling (arch.) area of stone filling a window or ARCH, from which TRACERY is usually cut.

ink fluid for writing or drawing; used also in printing processes.

ink box box containing solid block of ink; used for Oriental drawing and CALLIGRAPHY when mixed with water.

ink painting Japanese and Chinese painting technique, using ink in the same way as WATERCOLOR.

inlay the decoration of furniture, POTTERY, METALWORK, etc by inserting patterns of wood, stone, etc into the body of the object so that the surface is level.

intaglio decoration produced by cutting into a surface, used in ENGRAVING, ETCHING, GEM carving.

intarsia (It.) the decoration of wood with INLAY work, especially in 15th-century Italy.

International Gothic since the 19th century, used to describe the style of art prevalent from *c*1375 to 1425, balanced midway between naturalistic and idealistic values and characterized by delicate and rich coloring.

International style the influential BAUHAUS style of architecture, from the 1920s.

intimisme (Fr.) French genre painting of domestic, intimate interiors, such as the work of Pierre Bonnard and Édouard Vuillard; hence *intimiste*.

intonaco (It.) the smooth layer of LIME plaster that receives the paint in FRESCO painting.

Ionic the second Classic order of Greek architecture; *see* ORDERS OF ARCHITECTURE.

isocephaly characteristic of Greek Classical art whereby figures in a group are all shown at the same height, regardless of distance or recession.

Italianate style 1 in an Italian manner. 2 (arch.) the adaptation of Italian RENAISSANCE palace styles, especially so in America *c*1840–65. ·

Italian Primitives artists and their works in Italy prior to 1400.

J

jade extremely hard stone, which may be blue, green, white, or brown; highly prized in Chinese art for carvings and jewelry. It is composed of calcium and magnesium, with sodium or aluminum.

Jagged style (or *Zackenstil*) sharp, hard-edged style of drapery folds, characteristic of German ROMANESQUE.

jamb vertical side of a doorway or fireplace, or similar.

Japonisme the influence of *Japonaiserie*—Japanese imports e.g. prints and furniture, brought to Europe in the mid 19th century—on European painting.

Jasper ware type of stoneware POTTERY introduced by Josiah Wedgwood in 1774. Originally pure white but sometimes stained with cobalt oxide to produce "Wedgwood blue".

joiner furniture-maker.

journeyman under the medieval GUILD system, a craftsman who had completed his apprenticeship but had not become a MASTER, and therefore worked for a daily wage as a master's assistant.

Jugendstil (Ger.) German term for ART NOUVEAU.

Junk sculpture ASSEMBLAGE sculpture produced since the 1950s, using scrap materials and cast-off everyday objects.

K

kabuki popular Japanese theater of the 17th century, often depicted in prints.

Kalighat Indian temple in Calcutta, built in 1809 and dedicated to the Buddhist deity Kali.

kalyx-krater Greek bowl for mixing wine and water; *see* GREEK VASES.

Kano school of Japanese painting that began with the work of Kano Masánobu (1454–90) and flourished in Kyoto until the 19th century.

kaolin also known as China clay; used in the manufacture of hard-paste PORCELAIN and sometimes in the GROUNDS of paintings. Chemically it is hydrated silicate of ALUMINUM.

karst an underground region where cavities and drainage result from the dissolution of rock. (The term is derived from the name of a region of this kind in Slovenia.)

keros flaring-topped tumbler shape found in PRE-COLUMBIAN pottery and goldwork.

key design geometrical pattern of repeated horizontal and vertical straight lines, found in ancient Greek art.*

keystone (arch.) central wedge-shaped block of an ARCH.

Khamsa "The Quintuplet", the title of the major collection of poems

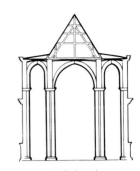

hall church
section through aisles and nave

historiated initial

key design
an example

by the Great Romantic epic Persian poet Nizami (*b. c*1141–1209).

kiln oven in which POTTERY is fired. Sometimes a synonym for a pottery workshop.

kinetic (adj.) sculpture designed to move and thus produce optical effects; first made in the 1920s, but most popular from 1960 onward.

kitsch (Ger.) mass-produced vulgar articles of the kind manufactured for souvenirs; the word has now become a pejorative term for whatever is thought to be in flamboyant bad taste.

knop decorative swelling in the stem of a glass or cup.

kouroi *see* KOUROS.

kouros Archaic Greek statue of standing youth (pl. KOUROI).

krater ancient Greek storage vessel; different shapes were used for water and wine: *see* COLUMN KRATER and KALYX-KRATER.

Kuan yin *see* BODHISATTVA.

Kufic script angular, square type of Arabic script (the more flowing script is NASHKI); sometimes found in decorative ROMANESQUE and GOTHIC art.

Kunstschau (Ger., "Art show") exhibition formed in 1908 by artists who had resigned from the Vienna SECESSION, including Oskar Kokoschka and Gustav Klimt.

kylix shallow, two-handled Greek drinking cup; *see* GREEK VASES.

L

lacquer a waterproof resinous VARNISH that can be highly polished. True lacquer is obtained from the species of tree *Rhus verniciflua* found in China and Japan. Another type is obtained from the lac insect, *Coccus lacca*, and is used in shellac, a commercial polish preparation. Modern commercial "lacquers" are coating materials that dry by the evaporation of solvent.

lake pigment PIGMENT produced by precipitating an organic dye on to an INERT PIGMENT (known as the substrate). Dyes must be treated in this way; otherwise they would dissolve in the medium.

lancet (arch.) tall, narrow, acutely pointed window, a feature of Early English architecture (13th century).

landscape 1 painting, drawing, or ENGRAVING in which the scenery is the principal subject. **2** scenic areas of a painting or drawing.

landscape architecture design or planning of landscape elements; synonymous with landscape gardening.

lantern 1 (arch.) small structure or turret on top of a dome, with windows to allow light to enter.* **2** lamp.

lapis lazuli deep-blue semiprecious stone, used for jewelry, and from which the PIGMENT ultramarine is extracted.

La Tène style style of decorative art that appeared *c*5th century BC in Europe and was fully developed in Celtic art of the pre-Roman period; the name is derived from a site in Switzerland where metal objects and weapons in this style have been found.

lay-in initial stage of traditional oil painting technique, where a drawing is "laid in" with a MONOCHROME to produce a full tonal design.

layout design or plan; particularly used in architecture, garden design, and GRAPHIC ARTS such as book production.

lead heavy, bluish-gray malleable METAL, used as a drawing material, in building, pottery GLAZES, printing, and sculpture.

leather animal skin that is made flexible by dressing and tanning; used for clothing, bags, bottles, footwear, etc.

leitmotif (Ger.) MOTIF that recurs throughout a design and is associated with a particular person or meaning.

lekythos (Greek; pl. *lekythoi*) ancient Greek oil jug; *see* GREEK VASES.

Leonardesque in the style of Leonardo da Vinci (1452–1519).

letter-cutter someone who makes the punches for type founding.

li Chinese Bronze Age food vessel, formed of three cone-shaped containers merged together at the top.

lierne rib (arch.) short RIB connecting the intersections of weight-bearing ribs in GOTHIC vaulting; *see* VAULT CONSTRUCTION.

life drawing drawing from the live human model.

light 1 brightness or illumination, especially in painting. **2** (arch.) division of a window indicated by vertical MULLIONS.

light dynamo type of KINETIC sculpture devised by Heinz Mack in the 1960s; it consists of metal plates and relief surfaces, moved by an electro-motor, behind sheets of curved glass.

lignin the material of which the cell walls of wood are composed.

lime calcium oxide used for making PLASTER.

limestone lime carbonate rock of various types, much used for building.

limner 1 obsolete term for an illuminator of medieval manuscripts. **2** 16th-century term for a miniaturist or portraitist. **3** 18th- and 19th-century term for an untutored, naive portraitist.

linear (adj.) artistic style that emphasizes lines and contours; hence linearity and linearism.

linear perspective method of indicating spatial recession in a picture by placing objects in a series of receding planes; parallel lines receding from the onlooker's viewpoint will appear to meet at a VANISHING POINT.

line engraving 1 the art or process of hand-engraving in INTAGLIO and copper plate, using a BURIN. **2** a PRINT taken from such a plate.

linen cloth woven from flax.

lino cut PRINT produced by carving a design into a block of linoleum.

lintel (arch.) horizontal beam above a door or window.

literati 1 (painting) Chinese scholarly or literary style, developed from the 10th century. **2** literary or scholarly people.

lithography printing method in which a design is drawn on stone with a greasy crayon, and then inked.

local color in painting, the color of an object seen against a white background in daylight, not influenced by cast shadows. Alternatively it may be defined as the color natural to each part, independent of the general color scheme or light and shade.

loggetta (It.) (arch.) small ARCADE or open GALLERY.

loggia (It.) (arch.) covered COLONNADE or ARCADE, open on at least one side.

London Group group of English artists who were influenced by Post-Impressionism, and who exhibited together from 1913.

lost wax *see* CIRE PERDUE.

low life tavern scenes etc depicted in GENRE painting.

low relief *see* RELIEF.

lozenge (arch.) diamond shape with four equal sides.

luminosity appearance of reflecting light, or ability to do so.

lunette semicircular window, or a painting or motif of that shape.

lunula crescent-shaped ornament, particularly from Bronze Age Europe.

lux unit of illuminance expressed as lumen per square meter. (The illuminance of a surface is the luminous flux [quantity of light per second] falling on a unit area.)

Lyrical abstraction term coined by the French painter Georges Mathieu in 1947 to describe the more decorative style of *L'Art Informel* and ABSTRACT EXPRESSIONISM.

lyricism an intensely poetic, decorative quality.

M

macerate (verb) to break up and soften a material in water.

madrasa Muslim school or college.

Maenad mythological female follower of Bacchus.

Maestà (It.) representation of the Madonna and Child enthroned and surrounded by a host of angels and saints.

malachite green copper mineral used for jewelry and in the decorative arts. Chemically, it is natural basic copper carbonate. It is also the source of a green PIGMENT.

mandala circular figure, symbolic of the universe in several religions, particularly Buddhism.

mandorla (It., "almond") in early Christian art, an almond-shaped outline around a divine personage (especially Christ) showing him endowed with divine light.* It was abandoned in the RENAISSANCE.

manganese metallic element or metal oxide; since the 19th century the source of blue and violet PIGMENTS, and used in CERAMICS to produce a purple color.

maniera (It.) according to the writings of Georgio Vasari (1511–74), the "stylishness" associated with the art of 16th-century Italy. *Bella maniera* was considered the highest artistic expression of the age, epitomized in the work of Raphael and Michelangelo.

manikin simple jointed model of the human figure, used by the artist as a model for drapery etc in the absence of a sitter.

maniple ecclesiastical vestment in the form of a strip, hanging from the left arm.

mannered using the exaggerated characteristics of any style. Before the 1930s the term was often synonymous with Italian MANNERISM.

Mannerism artistic style originating in Italy *c*1520–90 that tends to employ distortion of figures, and emphasize an emotional content; hence Mannerist.

man of sorrows the image of Christ, wounded and wearing the crown of thorns. It was a popular theme in the Italian RENAISSANCE and in late medieval German art.

manuscript handwritten or typed (but not printed) book.

maquette model made on a small scale by a sculptor or a stage-designer as a preliminary three-dimensional "sketch" for the final work.

marble type of LIMESTONE used since Antiquity for sculpture and building. It occurs in various colors, from pure white to black, often veined.

marbling decorative effect produced by staining or painting in streaks to resemble MARBLE.

marchigian literally, "of the marches" or border country; often used to refer to the East Italian Marches.

marine painting or drawing of a sea subject.

marl CLAY and LIME soil, applied to the ground as fertilizer.

marouflage (Fr.) the gluing of a canvas to a flat, rigid support; a method employed by artists and in conservation.

mask replica of the face, whether for theatrical purposes or as a portrait made after someone's death.

masonry stonework.

masque theatrical or musical amateur entertainment, with or without dialogue, popular during the 16th and 17th centuries.

mass term generally used figuratively of painting and sculpture that has the appearance of weight, volume, and solidity.

master in the medieval GUILD system, one who was entitled and able to practice his art on his own.

master mason skilled, senior mason.

master mountain landscape style of Chinese landscape painting of the late 10th century, in which small figures and rocks in the foreground are dominated by a massive mountain in the background.

master painter eminent or highly skilled painter who employs assistants and is qualified to teach students.

masterpiece originally a test piece of work done by the medieval apprentice in order to qualify as a MASTER of his GUILD. The term is now used more freely to mean a work of outstanding importance or quality.

mat 1 small carpet. **2** (adj.) non-reflective.

matière (Fr.) material, in the sense of the substance of which something is made.

mat-painted ware pottery decorated mainly with linear patterns in a MAT, manganese paint; chiefly found in mainland Greece c1900–1550 BC.

matrix MOLD, usually of COPPER, for CASTING printing type and other METAL objects.

mausoleum (arch.) **1** the tomb of Mausolus of Caria at Halicarnassus, c350 BC. **2** large, imposing structure erected as a tomb.

meander motif repetitive ornamental pattern of lines, in a SCROLL or KEY DESIGN.

medal small metal commemorative plaque, usually an award.

medallion 1 large MEDAL, usually bearing a portrait. **2** prominent oval or circular MOTIF. **3** the central motif (of any shape) of a Persian carpet.

medium generally, the means or material with which an artist expresses himself. In painting, the medium is the liquid in which PIGMENT is mixed and thinned, e.g. linseed oil.

megalith large monumental stone.

megaron 1 ceremonial hall in Mycenean palace. **2** Mycenaean or Minoan dwelling.

mensuration mathematical rules for determining measurements.

mercedarian from the Spanish *merced*, "market".

Mesolithic period Middle Stone Age, in European history dated c10,000 to 3000 BC, between the Paleolithic and Neolithic periods.

metal 1 solid crystalline substance, usually opaque, ductile, dense, e.g. gold, silver, COPPER, iron. **2** molten GLASS, in glassmaking process.

metalwork objects shaped from METAL.

metamorphic having, or suggesting, the ability to change shape.

Metaphysical painting (It. *Pittura Metafisica*) movement of c1915–18 associated with the painter Giorgio de Chirico; partly a reaction against FUTURISM.

métier (Fr.) subject in which an artist specializes.

metope (arch.) space between TRIGLYPHS in a Doric frieze (*see* ORDERS OF ARCHITECTURE).

mezzanine (arch.) intermediate level between two floors.

mezzotint 1 method of copper ENGRAVING. **2** a PRINT produced by this method.

mica mineral, chiefly composed of aluminum silicate.

Middle Ages in European history, the period between the end of Classical ANTIQUITY and the end of the RENAISSANCE (5th–15th century AD).

mihrab niche in the QIBLA wall of a MOSQUE, indicating the direction of Mecca.

millefiori (It.) pattern formed in glassmaking by fusing rods of colored GLASS in a bundle, and then slicing across the bundle to show a cross section.

mimbar PULPIT in a MOSQUE.

minaret (arch.) slender tower of a MOSQUE from which worshipers are called to prayer.

Ming Chinese dynastic period, 1368–1644; the name is mainly associated with the fine CERAMICS produced at that time.

miniature very small piece of work, such as the illustration in a medieval MANUSCRIPT. During the RE-NAISSANCE and the 18th and 19th centuries, the term was more specifically applied to small portraits painted on ivory.

Minimal art modern art that rejects texture, subject, atmosphere, etc and reduces forms and colors to the simplest; hence Minimalism, Minimalist.

minster a monastic or collegiate CHURCH.

mis-en-page typographical term meaning "making up"; generally, the LAYOUT or composition.

missal book containing all the texts of the Mass, sometimes illustrated.

miter bishop's headdress.

mixed media the combination of different materials in the same work, sometimes including performance.

mobile KINETIC sculpture probably originated by Alexander Calder in 1932; the sculpture is hung from wires so that it is moved by air currents.

möbius strip a mathematical figure: the surface formed by joining the ends of a rectangle after twisting it through 180°, i.e. producing a single continuous surface and continuous curved edge.

model 1 figure to be copied, e.g. in life drawing: PATTERN. **2** (verb) to shape in three dimensions, for example in CLAY. By extension the word also means to paint or draw something that is given the appearance of three-dimensionality, e.g. the human figure.

model book PATTERN BOOK used for reference by artists in the Middle Ages; usually containing copies from existing works.

modeling 1 three-dimensional representation of objects. **2** the artist's depiction or grasp of solid form.

modello (It.) preliminary sketch, drawn or painted. Sometimes quite elaborate and occasionally done in competition for patronage or a COMMISSION.

modernism the theory of modern art that rejects past styles, and promotes contemporary art as the true reflection of the age; hence modernist.

Modern Movement name derived from Nikolaus Pevsner's book *Pioneers of the Modern Movement* for the functionalist architecture and design of the 1920s and 1930s.

modular unit prefabricated building component.

module standardized part used in the construction of architecture, furniture, etc which can therefore be prefabricated.

moiré TEXTILE or METAL textured to produce a rippled effect.

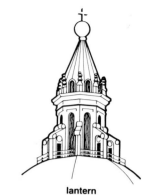

lantern
after the lantern of the duomo, Florence

mandorla

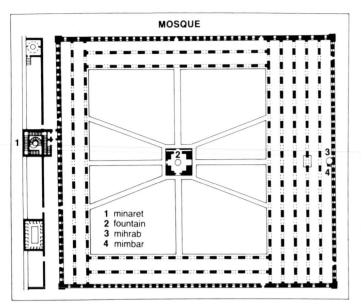

MOSQUE

1 minaret
2 fountain
3 mihrab
4 mimbar

an example of the courtyard mosque,
the groundplan of the mosque of Ibn Tulun, Cairo, built 876–9

mold shape or pattern in which a cast image is reproduced; hence molded, to mold.

molding a strip of stone or wood, plain or decorated, used to ornament a wall or piece of furniture.

Momoyama period of Japanese art from 1573 to 1615.

monel an alloy of 25–30 percent COPPER and 60–70 percent nickel, used as an acid-resist material.

monochrome picture done in various tones of one color only, especially black and white; hence monochromatic.

monogram two or more letters of an artist's name, as a signature.*

monotype printing process that takes an impression from a METAL or GLASS plate, producing only one PRINT of each design, which must then be redrawn.

monstrance in CHURCH, a vessel in which the Host is displayed, on the ALTAR or in procession.

monumental 1 connected with, or serving as, a monument. **2** used figuratively of paintings and other art forms to mean imposing or massive.

Moorish belonging to the culture of the northwest African Muslim peoples of mixed Berber and Arab origin.

morphography the scientific description of form.

morphology study of the form of animals, plants, or language.

mortar building material made from LIME, sand, PLASTER of Paris, and fibrous materials mixed with water, which sets by hydration or carbonation. The term may refer to this mixture in the wet state, or to any similar mixture used as a cement for stone or brick.

mosaic design formed from small pieces of stone, glass, marble, etc.

Mosan art art of the 12th and 13th centuries in the valley of the River Meuse, which flows from northeast France to the Low Countries; it produced the first great school of ENAMEL painters using the CHAMPLEVÉ technique.

mosque Muslim place of worship.*

mother-of-pearl hard, pearly substance forming inner layer of mollusk shells, and used in decorative METALWORK, jewelry, and inlaid furniture.

motif a repeated distinctive feature in a design.*

mouvementé (Fr.) animated, dynamic.

mucilages complex organic compounds of vegetable origin, with glue-like properties, used as an adhesive; hence mucilaginous, pertaining to mucilages.

mud brick brick made from unbaked CLAY.

Mughal art of the courts of the Muslim rulers in India, 1526–1707; also spelt Mogul and Moghal.

Muldenstil (Ger., "troughed style") style of GOTHIC drapery in which the folds form a trough pattern.

mullion (arch.) the vertical member that divides a window into two or more LIGHTS; *see* TRACERY.

multiple art produced since the 1960s, theoretically made in unlimited numbers as consumer articles; the opposite of the traditional "limited edition".

Munich Secession withdrawal in 1892 of German artists in Munich from the traditional institutions; it remained relatively conservative, and was followed by the VIENNA SECESSION (1897) and the BERLIN SECESSION (1908).

mural 1 concerning walls. **2** picture painted on a wall.

muse in Greek and Roman mythology, nine goddesses who inspired poetry, music, etc, and are identified in painting by their various attributes.

mythological painting painting of subjects chosen from Greek and Roman Classical mythology, popular from the 15th century to the 19th.

N

Nabis (Fr., Les Nabis) group of French artists working from *c*1892 to 1899, influenced by Gauguin in their use of color and lightly exotic decorative effects. They included Pierre Bonnard, Jean-Édouard Vuillard, Félix Vallotton and Paul Sérusier.

Nagasaki School 18th-century school of Japanese REALISM in painting, very influential on modern painting.

naive the work, style, or art of untaught artists, usually crudely naturalistic.

Nanga School Japanese school of BUNJINGA or LITERATI painting, active from the late 17th century to the late 19th.

naos synonym for CELLA.

narrative painting painting that relates a story or incident, most popular during the Victorian period.

narthex (arch.) porch across the west end of a CHURCH, used by those not yet taking full communion, e.g. penitents.

nashki the flowing form of Arabic script (compare KUFIC).

natron the natural form of sodium carbonate; also known as soda ash and used chiefly for POTTERY GLAZES.

naturalism accurate, detailed representation of objects or scenes as they appear, whether attractive or otherwise. The term was first used of the 17th-century CARAVAGGISM; (compare REALISM).

nave (arch.) main body or AISLE of CHURCH.

Nazarenes group of German painters working in Rome in the early 19th century; inspired by Northern art of the 15th and early 16th centuries.

neck-amphora Greek POTTERY storage jar; broader-lipped than the ordinary AMPHORA.

necropolis cemetery, especially in the ancient world.

Neoclassicism the late 18th-century European style, lasting from *c*1770 to 1830, which reacted against the worst excesses of the BAROQUE and ROCOCO, reviving the Antique. It implies a return to classical sources which imposed restraint and simplicity on painting and architecture.

Neo-Gothic revival of the Gothic style in 18th-century England, especially in architecture.

Neo-Impressionism the development of IMPRESSIONISM through Georges Seurat's scientific analysis and treatment of color; *see* DIVISIONISM; POINTILLISM.

Neolithic period later Stone Age, *c*8000–1800 BC.

neon inert gas that emits light when an electric current passes through it; neon lights have been used in modern sculpture since the 1950s.

Neo-Palladian *see* PALLADIAN.

Neo-Plasticism synonymous with DE STIJL. The term was coined by Piet Mondrian for his type of GEOMETRIC ABSTRACTION, restricted to nonrepresentational horizontal and vertical forms, primary colors and black and white.

Neoplatonism philosophical and religious system, mixing Platonic ideas and Oriental mysticism, which developed from Alexandria in the 3rd century AD.

Neo-Romanticism broad term for several 20th-century European art movements that draw on mystical, dreamlike subjects; expressive, emotional forms; and SURREALISM.

nephrite variety of JADE; *see* GREENSTONE.

nereid in Greek mythology, a sea nymph.

Netherlands Informal Group Dutch art movement, founded in 1958, that produced the GROUPE NULL association.

net vault (arch.) GOTHIC vault in which the LIERNE RIBS form a netlike pattern; *see* VAULT CONSTRUCTION.

Neue Künstlervereinigung (Ger., "New Artists' Association") founded in Munich in 1909 with Wassily Kandinsky as president, and influenced by the Munich JUGENDSTIL and Fauvism. Kandinsky and Franz Marc later formed the BLAUE REITER group.

New Bauhaus the BAUHAUS founded in Chicago by Laszlo Moholy-Nagy, which later became the Institute of Design.

New English Art Club antiacademic, pro-Impressionist art club founded in 1886. Its founder members included Walter Sickert and Wilson Steer.

New Realism (or *Nouveau Réalisme*) term coined in 1960 by the French critic Pierre Restany for art derived partly from DADA

ORDERS OF ARCHITECTURE

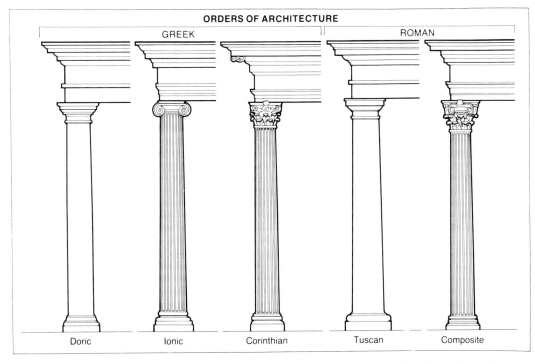

GREEK | ROMAN

Doric   Ionic   Corinthian   Tuscan   Composite

monograms

artists' monograms: **top left** Albrecht Dürer (1471–1528), **top right** Pieter Pourbus(*fl.* (1520–84), **below left** Max Klinger (1857–1920), **below right** John Tenniel (1820–1914)

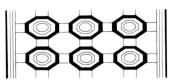

motif

four examples

nimbus

obelisk

---

and SURREALISM, which reacted against more ABSTRACT work, especially by using industrial and everyday objects to make junk art or sculpture.

New Secession a group of artists who broke away from Max Liebermann's BERLIN SECESSION in 1910 under the leadership of Max Pechstein (1881–1955), to promote AVANT-GARDE art.

New York School the core of AB-STRACT EXPRESSIONISM in New York in the 1940s and early 1950s including Jackson Pollock, Willem de Kooning, and Mark Rothko.

niche (arch.) recess in a wall, often containing a statue.

niello 1 black alloy of powdered silver, LEAD, COPPER, and sulfur, fused to METALWORK; especially popular during the RENAISSANCE in Italy. **2** silver plaque decorated with niello.

nimbus halo or light around a sacred image.*

niobid antique statuary of Niobe and her daughters. In Greek mythology, Niobe, the daughter of Tantalus, died weeping for her 12 children who were killed, and was turned to stone.

Nizami Persian poet (1135–1203/17) whose works were frequently illuminated, especially his KHAMSA ("Quintet").

No or **Noh** traditional Japanese dance-drama with heroic theme.

nocturne night scene.

Nomad art name given to decorative art of the 7th century BC, also known as ANIMAL STYLE.

Northern Renaissance non-Italian Western art of the period c1420–c1600.

Nouvelle Tendance (Fr.) short-lived international kinetic art movement of the 1960s.

nymphaeum (arch.) Roman "temple of the nymphs" or house of pleasure, often with statues.

O

obelisk (arch.) tall, four-sided freestanding PILLAR. It originated in Egypt as a solar symbol.*

objet trouvé (Fr.) *see* FOUND OBJECT.

oblate person dedicated to a monastery or religious work.

obsidian type of volcanic rock.

obverse the face of a coin or medal showing the head or main design.

Oceanic art art of the South Pacific.

ocher (or ochre) natural earth of silica and CLAY, colored by iron oxide. It may be yellow, red, or brown and is used as a PIGMENT.

octagon plane figure with eight sides and angles; hence octagonal.

oculus (arch.) originally the circular window at the west end of a CHURCH; it may also mean an illusionistic painting of a window or circular opening.

œil de boeuf (Fr., "bull's eye") a small octagonal vestibule in the Palace of Versailles, lit by a small circular window; the name has been adopted for similar rooms elsewhere.

oeuvre (Fr.) **1** the total output of an artist. **2** a work of art.

offset litho lithographic technique in which ink is transferred from a plate to a rubber roller, and then onto the paper.

oil viscous liquid of vegetable or mineral origin, used in painting and printing. "An oil" or "oils" is often used as shorthand for OIL PAINTING.

oil painting painting in an OIL medium, using linseed, walnut, or poppy oil.

oil sketch *see* SKETCH.

oinochoa ancient Greek vessel for dipping wine from the bowl and filling drinking cups. *See* GREEK VASES.

onyx variety of CHALCEDONY.

opaque impermeable to light; not TRANSPARENT or TRANSLUCENT.

Op art abbreviation of Optical art; 1960s movement in painting in which the illusion of movement was created by the juxtaposition of contrasting geometrical shapes, tones, lines, and colors.

openwork lacy-patterned METAL-WORK of gold and silver threads (*see* FILIGREE). The term is also used for similarly patterned textiles, lace, etc.

order arrangement, sequence.

orders of architecture the five CLAS-SIC orders, each composed of a COLUMN, having a base, SHAFT, CAPITAL, and ENTABLATURE with ARCHITRAVE, FRIEZE, and CORNICE. There are three Greek orders: Doric, Ionic, and Corinthian. These were adapted by the Romans, who added Tuscan and Composite.*

ore naturally occurring mineral, in

aggregate form from which metal is extracted.

organic 1 resembling or related to a living organism **2** (chemically) containing CARBON.

oriel (arch.) bay window on an upper story.

Orientalizing Greek style of art originating in the late 8th century BC in Corinth.

ornament 1 decoration or decorative object. **2** ecclesiastical accessories of worship, e.g. ALTAR, service book.

ornamented decorated, term used especially of three-dimensional objects.

Orphic Cubism term coined *c*1912 by Guillaume Apollinaire for the branch of CUBISM associated with Robert Delaunay, emphasizing color and the analysis of light and its connexion with nature; also known as Orphism.

orthogonal in LINEAR PERSPECTIVE, an orthogonal is a line apparently at right angles to the PICTURE PLANE, which will appear to meet a parallel line at the VANISHING POINT.

Ottoman Turkish dynasty founded in the early 14th century by Othman I. The name is also applied to the later Turkish Empire.

Ottonian art German art of the period 919–early 11th century, under the Ottonian emperors; notable for MANUSCRIPT illumination, BRONZE CASTING, MURAL painting.

outline edge of shape; contour.

oxide chemically, a binary compound with oxygen, i.e. oxygen and one other element, e.g. rust, which is iron oxide. Metal oxides have been used as PIGMENTS and in POTTERY GLAZES.

P

pagoda Chinese or Indian sacred building or tower.

paint PIGMENT dispersed in MEDIUM.

painterly a term coined by the art historian Heinrich Wölfflin to describe one of two contrasting styles in painting: LINEAR, which emphasizes contours; painterly, which emphasizes color and tone; hence painterliness.

painting 1 process of applying paint. **2** object produced by applying paint to a flat support, e.g. a wall or canvas.

palanquin Oriental covered carrying litter.

Paleolithic period the oldest Stone Age culture in Europe, *c*30,000–10,000 BC.

palette 1 slab of wood, METAL, or glass used by the artist for mixing paint. **2** figuratively: the range of colors used by the artist. **3** in ancient Egypt, a carved or plain slab used by scribes or for grinding cosmetics.

palette knife flexible, spatula-shaped knife for mixing or applying thick, bodied paint.

palette knifing use of the palette knife for applying paint.

Palladian style English architectural style, from *c*1715, in imitation of the style of Andrea Palladio; a reaction against the BAROQUE in favor of the CLASSICAL; also called Neo-Palladian.

pallium 1 man's cloak worn by the ancient Greeks. **2** archbishop's vestment. **3** ALTAR cloth.

palmette ornamental palm-leaf motif.

Panathenaic term describing Greek vases made for or acquired at the *Panathenaia*, the national festival of Athens celebrating the union of Attica under Theseus.

pandit Hindu learned in Sanskrit, philosophy and religion; also spelt pundit.

panel 1 flat piece of wood or metal used as a painting support. **2** distinct area or compartment as part of a design.

panel amphora AMPHORA on which the design is set in a PANEL, separated from the body of the vase by a border.

panel painting painting on a wood or METAL PANEL.

panorama painting of a view or landscape; especially large-scale painting around a room, or rolled on a cylinder.

pantheon literally, a temple "of all the gods"; usually the one at Rome, built *c*27–25 BC. Sometimes also used as a collective noun for all the gods.

paper tissue made from vegetable fiber.

papier collé (Fr., "pasted paper") collage of paper and card, first used by Georges Braque, *c*1912.

papier mâché (Fr., "chewed paper") paper pulped with glue, and then molded, baked, and polished.

papyrus reed plant whose stem was used by the Egyptians as writing "paper".

parapet (arch.) low wall around a balcony or similar structure.

parcel gilt silver or furniture gilded in parts.

parchment animal skin from calf, sheep, lamb, goat, or kid, used for writing, painting, bookbinding.

parterre level space in a garden, or ornamental flowerbed.

Parthenon The chief temple of Athena in Athens, on the Acropolis, built *c*447–433 BC.

pastel stick of PIGMENT mixed with gum or work executed in this medium. Because pastel tends to be light and chalky in tone, the word is also used to describe pale, light colors.

pastellist artist working in PASTEL.

pastiche 1 work in the style of another artist. **2** (derogatory) work made from fragments of another work or works.

pastoral idealized landscape painting or country scene.

pastose impasted; thickly painted.

paten shallow dish used for bread of the Mass or Eucharist.

patron someone who patronizes or supports the arts and artists; hence patronage.

pattern model, design, or repeated decorative design.

pattern book book of MOTIFS and designs used as a reference book by artists and industrial designers.

pavilion 1 pleasure house in garden or park. **2** building attached by wings to the main block, or projecting from it.

pearl lustrous GEM produced by mollusks.

pectoral ornamented metal breastplate.

pedestal 1 support for statue etc. **2** part of an ORDER consisting of PLINTH (or base), die (or DADO), and cap (or CORNICE).

pediform foot-shaped.

pediment (arch.) in CLASSIC GREEK ARCHITECTURE, a triangular GABLE under the roof of a building, or similar triangular field.

pelerinage (Fr.) account of a pilgrimage, sometimes illustrated.

pelike (pl. *pelikai*) large Greek storage jar; *see* GREEK VASES.

pen drawing instrument used with ink, sometimes made of quill.

pencil drawing instrument of lead or similar; in the Middle Ages the term also meant a brush.

pendant 1 projecting or suspended BOSS in GOTHIC architecture. **2** decoration at the end of a GABLE roof. **3** one of a pair of works.

pendant vault vault decorated with hanging stone bosses or terminals; found in late GOTHIC architecture; *see* VAULT CONSTRUCTION.

pendentive (arch.) curved triangular section of vaulting in a DOME.

pensieri (It.) small models made as preliminaries to larger models, when making sculpture.

pentimento (It.) area of a painting where the artist has changed his mind. Such changes may become visible in an OIL PAINTING as it ages, because of the increased transparency of the paint, or may be detected by X radiographs or infra-red examination.

peristyle (arch.) COLONNADE around Classical temple or court, or an inner court in a large house surrounded by a colonnade.

Perpendicular (arch.) the English GOTHIC style of *c*1335 to *c*1530 (between Decorated and Tudor); its most characteristic feature is vertical window TRACERY.

personification the image of something embodying ideas or as an example, such as the figure of a deity in human form.

perspective method of representing objects on a two-dimensional surface so that they appear three-dimensional; *see* LINEAR PERSPECTIVE.

perspex *see* PLEXIGLAS.

pewter alloy of tin and lead, used mainly for tableware.

pH the standard measure of acidity, given as a figure on a scale of 14 units. A pH value of less than 7 indicates acidity; a value greater than 7 indicates alkalinity.

phalerae (Latin) metal BOSS or disc, worn as an ornament or decorating a horse's harness.

phiale broad, flat Greek vase.

photography method of producing an image by the chemical action of radiation, such as light, on a sensitive film.

photolithography lithographic process in which the plates are made photographically.

photomontage picture combining juxtaposed photographic images.

physiognomy the study of a person's character from his physical attributes; hence physiognomic.

piano nobile (It.) the first and main floor of an Italian RENAISSANCE palace.

piazza (It.) square, open space surrounded by buildings.

pictogram (or pictograph) pictorial symbol, esp. in PRIMITIVE ART.

pictorial illustrative, or expressed in pictures; hence pictorialism.

picture field the surface area of a painting, also called the picture plane.

picture plane *see* PICTURE FIELD.

picturesque quaint, charming. From the 18th century onwards "The Picturesque" acquired a more specific meaning, particularly in connection with LANDSCAPE painting, landscape gardening, and architecture; it suggested a deliberate roughness or rusticity of design, and was to some extent transitional between CLASSICISM and ROMANTICISM.

pier (arch.) solid support between door or window openings, or supporting a bridge; usually square although it may be cylindrical, hence cylindrical pier. A compound pier in GOTHIC architecture is a group of SHAFTS. *See* VAULT CONSTRUCTION.

Pietà (It.) representation of the Virgin Mary holding the dead body of Christ.

pietra dura (It.) hard or semiprecious

stone, e.g. AGATE, CHALCEDONY, used as inlaid or MOSAIC type work on furniture and other articles; in the plural, *pietre dure*, it implies the use of several different types of stone.

pietra serena (It.) grayish sandstone quarried near Fiesole, Italy, and much used for building.

pigment a colored solid, usually dispersed in a MEDIUM to form paint.

pilaster (arch.) rectangular attached COLUMN that projects from a wall by less than one third of its width.

pillar (arch.) vertical supporting member; unlike a COLUMN, it may be square.

pilotis (Fr., stilts) in modern architecture, the rows of reinforced concrete COLUMNS often used to support a building, while leaving the ground free.*

pinnacle (arch.) conical- or pyramid-shaped ornament on top of a SPIRE, especially in GOTHIC architecture.

plan design or drawing; *see* GROUND PLAN.

plane 1 mathematically a plane is defined as a surface "such that a straight line joining two points lies wholly in it." **2** the term plane may also be used to describe a predominantly flat surface.

plaque decorative or commemorative RELIEF in PLASTER, PORCELAIN, or METAL.

plaquette small metal PLAQUE, usually cast by the CIRE PERDUE method and popular from the 14th century to the 16th.

plaster material for surfacing walls, usually interior. Made by mixing various dry materials, including CLAY, LIME, and GYPSUM, with water, applying it to the wall, and allowing it to set by evaporation, carbonation, or hydration. Plaster of Paris is calcium sulfate hemihydrate. It is often used for making MOLDS.

plastic 1 synthetic polymer that can be molded by heat and pressure. **2** describes anything molded or modeled; the opposite of GLYPTIC. **3** often also used of the three-dimensional values of a painting.

plastic form three-dimensional forms of art such as sculpture, POTTERY, and architecture.

plate 1 shallow dish. **2** piece of METAL or GLASS used in printing, ENGRAVING, and photographic processes. **3** collection of (silver) plated objects. **4** metal tableware, for domestic use.

Plateresque Spanish architectural style from *c*1520, with elaborate relief decoration.

plate tracery (arch.) of windows, early form of GOTHIC TRACERY with simple wide MULLIONS.

plating layer of thin METAL applied to an object, or the application of this layer.

plaza (Sp.) market place, square.

plein air (Fr., "open air") term for a painting executed outdoors, or giving the impression of naturalism by skillful handling of atmosphere.

plexiglas (U.S. trademark) acrylic sheeting used in modern sculpture (also known as perspex). Transparent plexiglas is often used for glazing pictures.

plinth (arch.) **1** the rectangular stone slab or block that forms the lowest member on which a COLUMN or statue stands. **2** projecting base of a wall.

plywood thin board composed of several layers of wood glued together with the grain crossed to give strength.

pochade (Fr.) sketch, especially one made outdoors.

podium (arch.) **1** continuous base of a building or room. **2** raised platform.

poesie (It., "short poems") paintings based on a poetic or literary source, especially from the RENAISSANCE.

pointillism (Fr.) the Neo-Impressionist technique pioneered by Georges Seurat, using dots of pure color instead of mixing paint on the palette; hence *pointillé*, *pointillist*; *see* DIVISIONISM.

polychrome painted in several colors; usually used of sculpture; hence polychromy.

polyester synthetic resin polymer, used to make synthetic fibers and plastic.

polygon many-sided figure; hence polygonal, polygony.

polymorphic painting multiform painting, produced by some modern KINETIC artists. The appearance of the work changes according to the position of the observer.

polyptych painted work (usually an ALTARPIECE) of more than three panels; *see also* DIPTYCH, TRIPTYCH.

polyurethane synthetic resin based on ethyl carbonate, used to make VARNISHES and LACQUERS.

pompe-funèbre (Fr.) funeral ceremony.

Pop art art derived from the popular culture of the 1960s, including commercial illustration, comic strips, and advertising images. British and American equivalent of NEW REALISM.

porcelain hard, refined CERAMIC material, invented by the Chinese in the 7th century.

porch (arch.) covered entrance, usually at the main door of a building.

porphyry hard volcanic stone used since ANTIQUITY for sculpture.

portal (arch.) imposing entrance of a building.

portico (It.) (arch.) covered COLONNADE at the entrance to a building.

porticus (Latin) (arch.) small PORCH built on the north or south side of English pre-Conquest churches. Sometimes a *porticus* was built on both sides, thus forming rudimentary TRANSEPTS.

portrait drawn or painted image of a person, usually naturalistic and identifiable; hence portraiture, portraitist. *See also* BUST.

pose the stance or attitude of the human figure, or group of figures, in painting or sculpture.

poster public placard, developed as an art form from the 19th century onward.

Post-Impressionism term coined by the art theorist Roger Fry for the style of art of Cézanne, van Gogh and Gauguin.

Post-Painterly Abstraction term coined by the American critic Clement Greenberg for a group of Abstract artists working in the 1960s. It includes a number of specific styles and movements, such as COLOR-FIELD PAINTING and MINIMAL ART.

Poussinist adherent of the French late 17th-century theory of *poussinism*: the supremacy of line (draftsmanship) over color.

Pre-Columbian American art and culture before 1492.

predella 1 a platform on which an ALTAR stands. **2** lower part of painted ALTARPIECE.

Prehistoric art art of the Stone Age, which may be divided into PALEOLITHIC, MESOLITHIC, and NEOLITHIC periods.

Pre-Raphaelite Brotherhood English association of artists, *c*1848–54, including Rossetti, Holman Hunt, and Millais. The group had no clear, unifying doctrine but shared an interest in art of the 15th century prior to 1495, start of the High RENAISSANCE.

presbytery (arch.) east end of a CHURCH, between the CHOIR and High ALTAR; sometimes synonymous with SANCTUARY.

primary colors red, blue, and yellow; the colors that can be mixed to produce other colors, but cannot themselves be produced from mixtures.

priming the preparation of a GROUND on which to paint.

primitive art 1 art of a prehistoric culture. **2** early European, non-naturalistic art. **3** untrained, NAIVE art. **4** ETHNOGRAPHIC art (a 19th-century usage). "Primitivism" and "Primitivist" are terms that may refer to any of the above defini-

pilotis

after the Unité d'Habitation, Marseilles, designed by Le Corbusier; built 1947–52

rustication

tions of primitive art, but especially number three.

print 1 any image, pattern, or lettering produced on fabric or PAPER by a variety of GRAPHIC processes. **2** (verb) to make an impression or image by such a process. Usually means letter-printing; printmaking involves producing an image that is aesthetically pleasing, or illustrative.

prismatic prism shaped; related to prisms. Prismatic color is produced by light passing through a TRANSPARENT prism, and synonymous with spectral color.

process works modern works of art in which the process of creation itself becomes the subject of the work.

profile 1 drawing, outline, or silhouette of a figure, especially the human figure viewed from the side. **2** (arch.) section of a MOLDING. **3** cross section of any structure.

proof 1 first impression of a PRINT made for the artist, or as a limited edition. **2** the first example taken from any printing medium.

proportion ratio or relationship of dimensions.

Protogeometric style Greek vase-painting style of the 11th century BC that began to replace the former freehand, LINEAR decoration with more severe, precise shapes; the forerunner of the true GEOMETRIC STYLE.

psalter book containing the text of the psalms, sometimes illustrated.

pueblo (Sp.) communal village built by certain Native American peoples e.g. the Hopi.

pulpit raised platform, from which the sermon is delivered in church.

pumice light volcanic stone consisting of silicates of aluminum, sodium, and potassium; used as an abrasive and for polishing.

Purism movement founded in 1918 by Le Corbusier and Amédée Ozenfant that aimed to purify CUBISM of any decorative elements, emphasizing pure outline and impersonality. It had little influence on painting, more on architecture and design.

putto (It.; pl. *putti*) figure of a child in painting or sculpture; *see also* AMORINO.

pyramid Egyptian stone or brick tomb; rising from a square base to a triangular apex.

pyrolusite natural manganese dioxide; the ore from which manganese is extracted.

pyroxilin (or pyroxylin) cellulose nitrate used as LACQUER or synthetic medium.

pyxis (Greek) (pl. *pyxides*) a small box or casket, usually made of box-wood, used by the ancient Greeks and Romans to hold medicines. It was normally cylindrical; *see* GREEK VASES.

Q

qibla west wall of a MOSQUE, indicating the direction of Mecca.

quadrangle rectangular or square figure, or four-sided courtyard.

quadratura (It.) Italian BAROQUE illusionistic painting of an interior, using PERSPECTIVE to create the impression of an open, limitless space.

quadriga chariot drawn by four horses abreast.

quartz natural, crystalline form of silica; also known as rock crystal.

quatrefoil 1 (arch.) four-arc opening in GOTHIC tracery. **2** four-lobed decorative MOTIF.

Quattrocento (It.) 15th century.

quincunx an arrangement of five objects with four at the corners of a square and one in the center.

R

radiating chapel (arch.) chapel radiating from the APSE or AMBULATORY of a CHURCH.

raku Japanese POTTERY used for the tea ceremony; molded, not thrown on a wheel.

ramie East Asian plant whose strong fiber is used for weaving.

Rayonnant (arch.) style of GOTHIC architecture of the late 13th and 14th centuries, usually referring to the TRACERY of windows, e.g. ROSE WINDOWS. It preceded the FLAMBOYANT style.

Rayonnism development of ABSTRACT art by the Russian artists Michail Larionoff and Natalia Gontcharova, *c*1913, which was an offshoot of CUBISM and in some respects the forerunner of FUTURISM.

ready-made name given by Marcel Duchamp—exponent of DADA principles—to prefabricated objects exhibited as works of art.

realism 1 style of painting dating from the 19th century, typified by Courbet, that makes a deliberate choice of everyday subject matter (Realism). **2** the opposite of ABSTRACT or distorted (similar to NATURALISM). **3** in Greek Classical sculpture, work that is not stylized or idealized.

Realistic Manifesto manifesto produced in 1920 by the brothers Naum Gabo and Antoine Pevsner, which questioned the figurative role of sculpture.

recession in painting, the illusion of depth or distance achieved through the use of color or PERSPECTIVE.

rectilinear based on straight lines; hence rectilinearism.

Rectilinear style of architecture, the last phase of GOTHIC architecture *c*1335–c1530, characterized by vertical TRACERY; also called PERPENDICULAR.

recto the opposite of VERSO, i.e. the front or "right" side of a coin, medal, or painting, or the right-hand page of an open book.

red-figure technique the technique of the finest ancient Greek vase-painting, in which figures were drawn in black and the background blocked in in black so that the figure stood out in the red GROUND-color. Compare BLACK-FIGURE TECHNIQUE.

reductivist Minimalist (*see* MINIMAL ART).

refectory dining hall, especially of a monastery or college.

refractive index a measure of the amount that light is bent on passing from one optical medium to another, e.g. from air to water or from a paint MEDIUM into a PIGMENT particle.

régence style French ROCOCO style of *c*1705–30.

Regency style the style of English art *c*1811–30, i.e. during the regency and reign of King George IV.

Regionalists American painters of the 1930s and 1940s who depicted mid-western life.

register in GRAPHIC art, the alignment of corresponding parts to produce separate colors in the same image.

reinforced concrete concrete reinforced with METAL wire to give increased strength.

relative humidity a measure of atmospheric humidity expressed as a percentage of the maximum amount of moisture that could be contained by a given volume of air at a given temperature (abbreviation, RH).

relief sculpture, carving, etc in which forms project and depth is hollowed out; the type of relief is determined by the degree to which the design stands out; thus *alto rilievo* (high relief) and bas relief (low relief), in which the projection is slight.*

relief line in Greek RED-FIGURE vase painting a "relief line" was used for details of drawing, so-called because it stood out from the surface on which it was drawn.

relief process any GRAPHIC process in which the areas not to be seen are cut away, so that the design stands out in RELIEF on the block; the term is applied to WOODCUTS, LINO CUTS, etc.

reliquary vessel for sacred relics, often in precious METAL.

Renaissance (Fr., "rebirth") the period of Italian art from *c*1400 to 1520 characterized by increased emphasis on REALISM, and the rediscovery of CLASSICAL art. The "Early Renaissance" is sometimes deemed also to include the art of the 14th century. High RENAISSANCE refers to the period of the finest achievements of Leonardo, Raphael, and Michelangelo, *c*1495–1520. *See also* NORTHERN RENAISSANCE.

repoussé (Fr.) METAL decorated by hammering from the side not seen, so that the design stands out in RELIEF.

repoussoir (Fr.) device in painting: objects are placed in the FOREGROUND to direct the eye to the center of the painting.

representational art art that attempts to show objects as they really appear, or at least in some easily recognizable form.

reredos ornamental screen behind an ALTAR.

reserved describes the areas of decoration on CERAMICS, gilded objects, etc, that are left in the color of the base or body of the object.

resin 1 natural organic compound secreted by some plants and insects, used in VARNISHES, LACQUERS, and PAINTS. **2** synthetic substance formulated to resemble the natural resin.

retable 1 raised shelf, ledge, or frame containing ornamental panels, at the back of an ALTAR. **2** painted or carved ALTARPIECE of one or more fixed panels.

retardataire (Fr.) archaic.

reveal (arch.) the inside surface of a door or window, cut at right angles to the face of the wall.

revetment (arch.) wall built to hold back a mass of earth, water, etc; also called a retaining wall.

RH *see* RELATIVE HUMIDITY.

rhyton drinking vessel, usually ceremonial, in the form of an animal head or human figure; found in Greek, Assyrian, and Minoan art; *see* GREEK VASES.

rib (arch.) projecting band or MOLDING on a VAULT or ceiling; *see* VAULT CONSTRUCTION.

rib vault (arch.) a cross VAULT with arched ribs across the sides and diagonals of the BAY that support, or seem to support, the INFILLING; *see* VAULT CONSTRUCTION.

ridgepole (arch.) the horizontal timber at the ridge of a roof where the rafters are fastened.

ridge rib (arch.) a supporting or decorative RIB running along the central axis of a VAULT; *see* VAULT CONSTRUCTION.

Rimpa School School of Japanese painting founded by Tawaraya Sotatsu, *fl. c*1600–30.

rocaille (Fr.) 1 scallop-shell ornament popular from c1730.* 2 shell or stone decoration of rococo gardens and grottoes. 3 among French art historians, sometimes synonymous with ROCOCO.

Rococo elegant, decorative style of c1730–80. During the 19th century the term acquired pejorative connotations, meaning trivial or over-ornate.

Romanesque (arch.) style of architecture that lasted from 1000 to 1150 in France and to the 13th century in the rest of Europe; characterized by massive VAULTS and rounded ARCHES. The term is also applied to the FINE and DECORATIVE ARTS of the period.

Romanist collective name applied particularly to those Northern artists who visited Rome and were influenced by Italian art during the 16th century, e.g. Maerten van Heemskerck.

Romanticism the late 18th- and early 19th-century antithesis to CLASSICISM; the imagination of the artist and the choice of literary themes predominated. Leading Romantic painters included Eugène Delacroix and J.M.W. Turner.

rood screen screen separating the NAVE and CHOIR in a CHURCH.

rosette circular ornament, especially in architecture, shaped like a formalized rose.

rose window (arch.) circular window with radiating TRACERY, found in GOTHIC architecture.

rotunda (arch.) round building or internal room surmounted by a DOME.

roughcast rough preparation of sand and lime applied to a wall prior to the smooth PLASTER.

roundel circular panel, painting, MEDALLION, or ornamental STAINED GLASS window.

rubbing synonymous with FROTTAGE.

rubenisme see RUBENISTE.

Rubeniste adherent of the French late 17th-century theory of *rubenisme*: the supremacy of color over line, in painting. Compare POUSSINIST.

rustication (arch.) masonry in which blocks of stone are emphasized by the deep joints and roughened surfaces; most commonly found in 16th-century Italian palaces.*

S

sacra conversazione (It.) in Christian ICONOGRAPHY, the image of the Virgin and Child with saints, as a group portrait.

sacristy (arch.) room attached to a CHURCH in which the vestments and sacred vessels are kept, and where priests are attired.

Safavid Persian dynastic period, c1502–1736.

salon large room.

Salon French annual exhibition (held from 17th century onwards) of painting and sculpture by members of the ACADEMY; traditionally hostile to innovation.

Salon des Indépendants exhibition of the Société des Artistes Indépendents of 1884, including Seurat and Signac. The society had no selection jury.

Salon des Réfusés exhibition of 1863 promoted by Napoleon III to show works rejected by the Paris SALON.

salon painting the style acceptable to the Paris SALON; by implication dull and stereotyped.

sanctuary (arch.) holiest part of temple or CHURCH, containing the ALTAR.

sand painting applying colored sand to glue on a canvas.

sandstone rock formed of sand or QUARTZ particles bonded together with CLAY, calcium carbonate, and iron oxide; it has a warm color and is easily worked, and has therefore been popular for building and carving.

sarcophagus a stone coffin, often decorated, especially common in ANTIQUITY.

sardonyx onyx in which the white layers alternate with sard (a yellow or orange-red CARNELIAN).

sarsen boulder carried and deposited by ice during the glacial period.

satin silky fabric with a glossy surface.

satyr mythological attendant of the Greek god Dionysos; usually depicted in painting as goat-footed, with horns and tail, or with the feet, ears, and tail of a horse.

scallop shell-shaped ornament.

scalloped capital (arch.) block CAPITAL whose four sides have a series of curves or SCALLOPS.

scapigliatura (It.) Bohemianism.

scarab ancient Egyptian representation of a sacred beetle, associated with the idea of resurrection. Usually made of stone or FAIENCE and inscribed.

scaraboid roughly resembling a SCARAB.

scène galante see FÊTE GALANTE.

scenographic using PERSPECTIVE in painting to create the illusion of depth.

schema (pl. *schemata*) simplified synopsis or representation of a general type.

schematic representing objects by symbols or diagrams.

schematized in SCHEMATIC form.

schist rock composed of bands of different minerals that can be split into thin layers.

scholar-painter the Japanese equivalent of *wen-jen hua* (or "literary men's painting") in Chinese art; a literary-minded amateur who painted for pleasure.

School of Fontainebleau there were two Schools; the First, under Francis I c1528–58 was fundamentally Mannerist, directly influenced by expatriate Italian masters. The Second, under Henry IV (1589–1610) was more mediocre.

School of Paris (École de Paris) 1 broad name for various modern art movements originating in Paris including Nabism (see NABIS), Fauvism (see FAUVES), CUBISM and SURREALISM. 2 school of medieval MANUSCRIPT illuminators in Paris from the mid 13th century to early 15th.

School of Pont-Aven not a true "School" but the group of painters, generally SYMBOLISTS, who worked at Pont-Aven, France, during the late 19th century, including the NABIS and Gauguin.

screen partition, often carved or painted.

scroll 1 architectural ornament similar in form to a scroll of parchment. 2 scroll of paper or silk, popular in Oriental art. A hand scroll is about 30cm (12 in) wide and up to 30m (100 ft) long, and unrolls from right to left to give a continuous picture, viewed section by section. A hanging scroll, as the name implies, is hung like a painting. Both are usually painted in ink or watercolor.

scroll work ornamentation of spiral lines.

sculpture object carved or modeled in wood, stone, etc or cast in metal for an aesthetic, nonfunctional purpose; or the process of producing it; hence sculptor. "Sculptural" is used to describe art (including painting and drawing) that has pronounced three-dimensional qualities.

scumble an OPAQUE or semiopaque layer of paint applied over another so that the first is partially obliterated, producing a slightly broken effect.

scuola (It.) (pl. *scuole*) School of art; a group of artists working under the same influence or master.

seal engraved GEM or METAL stamp used to make an impression in a wax seal on a document; usually identifiable, therefore serves as a signature.

seascape painting or drawing of the sea and shipping.

secco painting (It., "dry") method of wall painting on to dry PLASTER,

high relief

low relief

relief

rocaille

an example of the scallop-shell ornament

using PIGMENTS in lime water, or an egg MEDIUM. Often used for retouching FRESCO.

Secession (Ger. *Sezession*) term used for withdrawal of German and Austrian artists from ACADEMIES in the late 19th century.

section 1 figure or view produced by cutting through an object. **2** in book production, a sheet of PAPER, folded and ready for sewing.

Section d'Or (Fr.) offshoot of CUBISM; members included Fernand Léger, Marcel Duchamp, Frank Kupka, Jacques Villon. The members were linked by an interest in a mathematical system of proportion and the harmonious use of color. There was a *Section d'Or* exhibition in 1912 and a magazine of the same name.

sedilia series of stone seats in a CHURCH on the south side of the CHANCEL, used by the clergy.

segmental arch (arch.) ARCH whose contour is a section of a circle but less than a semicircle.

Seicento (It.) 17th century.

self-portrait portrait of and by the artist.

Semiabstraction the name used by Picasso and his circle for ABSTRACTION.

semidome (arch.) domed ceiling of an APSE, less than the full DOME height.

sennit plaited straw or palm leaf fibers.

sepia blackish brown secretion of ink from cuttlefish and squid, used as a drawing MEDIUM and in WATERCOLOR.

serial painting art form of the 1960s involving the repetition of an image with slight variations.

serpentine sinuous, winding.

Seven and Five Society English art association formed in 1920 by seven painters and five sculptors, including Ben Nicholson and Barbara Hepworth; originally FIGURATIVE, but became ABSTRACT.

sfumato (It., "evaporated") using subtle gradations of tone and softened lines.

shade absence of direct light; tone of a particular color.

shading use of darker tones to indicate shadowed areas.

shaft (arch.) **1** part of a COLUMN between the base and CAPITAL. **2** in medieval architecture, a slender column; *see* VAULT CONSTRUCTION.

Shah-nama "Book of Kings", a verse history of Persian kings written by the Persian poet Firdawsi (*c*935–1020/6). Its text was a popular subject for illustration in the Arab world.

shallow relief low relief or bas relief; *see* RELIEF.

shaped canvas canvas stretched on a frame before painting to form a three-dimensional support.

sheet print single sheet Japanese PRINT.

shell outer case, especially of marine mollusks.

Shijo School of Japanese painting that emphasized NATURALISM and REALISM, founded by Matsumura Goshun (1752–1811). It lasted into the 20th century.

shogun Japanese hereditary commander and ruler, under the Emperor. The institution lasted from 1192 to 1867; the title means "General".

Sibyl Classical prophetess associated with the oracles, e.g. at Delphi.

signet ring ring containing a personal seal.

silhouette 1 MONOCHROME painting, dark on light or light on dark, with a well-defined outline. **2** PROFILE portrait cut from black paper and mounted on white; popular in the 18th and 19th centuries.

silk thread or cloth made from the fiber produced by the silkworm.

silk screen method of color reproduction in which colored inks are squeezed through a stencil prepared on a silk screen.

silver gilt silver gilded with gold.

silver leaf thinly beaten silver, applied like GOLD LEAF.

silverpoint drawing with a silver wire or stylus.

sinopia 1 red-brown earth PIGMENT used in drawings for FRESCO. The name is derived from the place of origin; the town of Sinope on the Black Sea. **2** the name is also generally applied to the drawing on the ARRICCIO, prior to painting the fresco, whether or not it is in this pigment.

Siren 1 mythological creature, half bird, half woman, who lured sailors to their death by sweet singing. **2** mythological serpent.

situationist associated with the "International Situationist" movement formed in 1957 in Italy by Asger Jorn, to cut across national and political divisions.

situla art decorative bronzework that appeared *c*600 BC in the Mediterranean area and later in Celtic art.

size gelatine or animal glue, or other materials such as starch and gums, used to stiffen fabrics, to reduce the porosity of a surface, or as a painting MEDIUM.

sketch 1 rough drawing as the preliminary to a more finished composition. **2** since the 18th century, a complete but slight or quickly executed drawing, painting, or WATERCOLOR.

skyphos ancient Greek drinking cup; *see* GREEK VASES.

slate grayish rock of natural aluminum silicate formed when CLAY is hardened by pressure. It is easily split into plates or sheets and often used in building.

slip CLAY, thinned with water, for decorating or coating pottery.

smalti small pieces of MOSAIC composed of colored vitreous materials or glass fused in a KILN, sometimes on to a TERRACOTTA or PORCELAIN base.

soapstone steatite or hydrated silicate of magnesia; a soft stone, easily carved and polished and often used for small objects; also used as an ingredient in the manufacture of PORCELAIN.

Socialist Realism the official, conservative, post-Revolutionary style of art in Russia.

social realism since the 19th century, the term refers to the convincing portrayal of subjects in a social or political context; in the 20th century it has been applied more specifically to art that deliberately records or comments on the political or social conditions and events in society.

soffit (arch.) underside of an ARCH or some other feature. *

soft ground etching ETCHING technique developed in the late 18th century that renders textures.

Soft style the German equivalent (Ger., *Weicher Stil*) of the INTERNATIONAL GOTHIC, *c*1375–1425, distinguished by soft, curvilinear forms. It was replaced by the sharp, ANGULAR STYLE of drapery.

Sonderbund (full name, *Sonderbund Westdeutscher Kunstfreunde und Künstler*) league of art lovers and artists, founded in Dusseldorf *c*1909. The first president was Karl Ernst Osthaus, a notable patron of modern art.

Sondergotik (Ger.) late Gothic German architectural style equivalent to the French FLAMBOYANT and the English PERPENDICULAR.

spandrel (arch.) **1** triangular area contained by one side of an ARCH. **2** the surface between two adjacent arches and the molding above. **3** surface of vault between two adjacent ribs or any similar triangular surface.

Spazialismo (It.) also known as *Movimento Spaziale*; the movement, founded by Lucio Fontana in 1947, that rejects the idea of EASEL PAINTING in favor of the development of form and color in space.

spectrum the range of colors produced when white light passes through a TRANSPARENT PRISM.

Sphinx the Greek name for a creature with a human head and lion's body; in Egypt, usually male; in Greece, female.

spiral line or form that winds continually along or up a central AXIS; hence spiral COLUMN, spiral staircase, etc.

spire (arch.) tapering, slender cone on top of a tower.

split stitch embroidery stitch used for very fine work; the needle is pushed through an untwisted silk thread as it is sewn, to produce something that looks like a chain stitch.

square up method of transferring or enlarging a preliminary drawing by superimposing a network of squares and transferring each to the intended support.

squinch (arch.) ARCH built diagonally from the corner of a square building supporting a spire or dome.

staffage figure figure in architecture or LANDSCAPE painting, intended to indicate the scale or provide a point of interest.

stained glass GLASS colored with metal oxides; joined with LEAD strips to form designs, mostly for windows in CHURCHES.

stainless steel chrome steel, non-rusting; used in modern sculpture and architecture.

star vault (or stellar vault) medieval VAULT in which the intermediate and LIERNE ribs form a star pattern; *see* VAULT.

stasis stoppage, stagnation.

statuary collection of STATUES, or the making of statues.

statue carved or molded figure in STONE, CLAY, BRONZE, etc.

statuette small statue.

steatite *see* SOAPSTONE.

steel alloy of iron and carbon used in sculpture, building, furniture.

steeple (arch.) tower of a CHURCH, including the SPIRE, LANTERN, etc.

stela (pl. *stele* or *stellae*) Greek stone slab, marking a grave or with an inscription.

stellar vault *see* STAR VAULT.

stellate star shaped.

stemma (It.) escutcheon, coat of arms.

stencil design cut in a card or plate used for brushing color through to the paper beneath.

still life painting of inanimate objects such as fruit, flowers, dead game.

stipple patterning tone built up with small dots and dabs of color.

stirrup jar ancient Greek jar with an arched handle at the top.

stirrup spout pot CERAMIC pot shape, chiefly found in PRE-COLUMBIAN culture and in Mexico and Peru; it has a semicircular hollow handle, leading to a spout shaped rather like a stirrup.

stoa (arch.) roofed PORTICO, usually facing on to a public place, with a wall at the back and a COLONNADE at the front. *

stole ecclesiastical vestment in the

shape of a narrow strip of fabric worn over the shoulders, reaching the knees, or a similar piece in front of the ALTAR.

stone 1 rock used for building and sculpture. 2 gemstone.

stoneware hard POTTERY made from CLAY plus a fusible stone (usually feldspar) and fired at 1200–1400°C so that the stone is vitrified.

stopping out in ETCHING, the protection of certain areas of a PLATE with VARNISH to prevent acid attacking those areas during BITING.

strapwork ornamentation of interlaced bands, like straps of leather, common in the 16th century.*

stretcher frame, usually of wood, on which fabric is stretched prior to painting.

striation 1 pattern of narrow stripes. 2 the representation of drapery by parallel lines, found in BYZANTINE and ROMANESQUE ART.*

strigil ancient Greek or Roman skin scraper, used by athletes.

stringcourse (arch.) MOLDING running horizontally along a wall.

stuccatore (It.) plasterer, someone who works in STUCCO.

stucco slow-setting lime and marble PLASTER that can be modeled and carved for decorating interiors.

stuccoist see STUCCATORE.

studiolo (It.) small office or work room.

study detailed preparatory drawing for a larger work; more detailed and complete than a SKETCH.

stupa ancient Indian burial mound, often housing relics of the Buddha.

style 1 ancient writing implement. 2 manner of artistic expression, particular to an individual, school, or period.

stylized 1 conforming to a recognized style. 2 based on natural forms that are then simplified according to a conventional SCHEMA or stereotype, hence stylization.

stylobate (arch.) continuous base of a COLONNADE.

suite (arch.) a sequence of rooms or a set of matching furniture. It can also mean a series of drawings, paintings, or PRINTS linked by a common theme, often literary.

Sung Chinese dynasty dating from AD 960 to 1278.

support canvas, PAPER, PANEL, wall, etc on which a painting or drawing is executed.

Suprematism Russian ABSTRACT art movement of 1913–15, led by Kasimir Malevich, that used geometric elements.

surimono Japanese color PRINTS commemorating festive occasions, e.g. births, weddings, New Year.

Surrealism movement in art and literature between the two World Wars that tried to fuse actuality with dream and unconscious experience, using AUTOMATISM among other techniques; hence Surreal, Surrealist.

swag carved or painted festoon of garland or drapery.*

swastika ancient symbol, often used in decoration, of a cross with four arms, all bent at right angles to the same direction.

Sweet style sentimental style of marble sculpture associated with the workshop of the della Robbia family in Florence in the mid 15th century.

syllabary a set of SYMBOLS or characters representing syllables, used as an alphabet.

symbol image of something representing something else; hence symbolic, symbolism, symbolize.

Symbolist see SYMBOLIST MOVEMENT.

Symbolist movement (sometimes generally known as Symbolism) art movement that appeared c1885 in France, originating in poetry; a reaction against both REALISM and IMPRESSIONISM, it aimed at the fusion of the real and spiritual worlds, the visual expression of the mystical.

Synchromism an American movement of 1913 promoted by Morgan Russell and Stanton Macdonald-Wright; influenced by Orphism (see ORPHIC CUBISM), using ABSTRACT form and color.

Synthetic Cubism the second phase of CUBISM, after 1912, using COLLAGE.

Synthetism a branch of POST-IMPRESSIONIST painting associated with Gauguin, c1888, chiefly employing flat areas of color, strong contour lines, and simple forms; also called CLOISONNISM.

T

tabernacle (arch.) niche or receptacle containing the Holy Sacrament, usually above the ALTAR.

tableau vivant motionless group of people arranged to represent a scene.

Tachisme term coined in 1952 by the French critic Michel Tapié, for the technique of painting in irregular dabs (taches or spots) and in an apparently haphazard manner.

tactile perceived by touch. The term "tactile values" was introduced to art criticism in 1896 by Bernard Berenson to describe the textural qualities of paintings.

tapestry wall hanging of silk or wool with a nonrepeating pattern or narrative design woven in by hand, during manufacture.

tarashikomi Japanese method of painting "wet on wet".

teak the hard wood of a tropical tree, Tectona grandis, used for furniture and veneers.

technique method of execution.

tectonic related to building and construction.

tempera 1 general term for any MEDIUM used for painting. 2 (egg) tempera, when a whole egg or yolk is used as a medium.

templon COLONNADE in a Middle BYZANTINE CHURCH that closes off the CHANCEL.

tendril ornamental curving line resembling plant stem or curl of hair.* (See overleaf.)

Tenebrism style of 17th-century painting associated with Caravaggio making much use of strong CHIAROSCURO.

Terminal (arch.) PEDESTAL or similar supporting a sculpted head or figure, placed in gardens to define the boundaries; also known as a term or HERM.

terracotta (It., "baked earth") hard, fired but unglazed, brownish-red clay used for POTTERY, SCULPTURE, and building.

terribilità (It.) awesomeness.

tessellation pattern of MOSAIC or pavement floor, composed of blocks of stone, marble, etc.

tesserae (pl. of tessera; Latin from Greek, meaning four-sided) fragments of inorganic material such as stone, GLASS, and MARBLE, cut into cubes for use in MOSAIC.

tetraconch building composed of four CONCHAS.

tetramorph composite figure containing the SYMBOLS of the four Evangelists.

textile woven fabric.

texture the surface of a material, esp. as perceived by touch.

The Antique see ANTIQUITY.

The Eight group of New York artists formed in 1907 and later known by this name. They opposed the restrictive practices of the National Academy of Design, and for their own works turned instead to depicting the contemporary American scene.

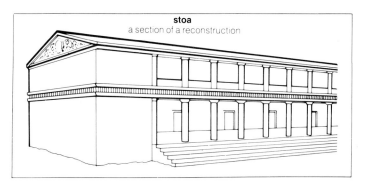

stoa
a section of a reconstruction

decorated soffits

strapwork

striation

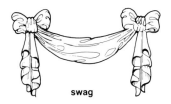

swag

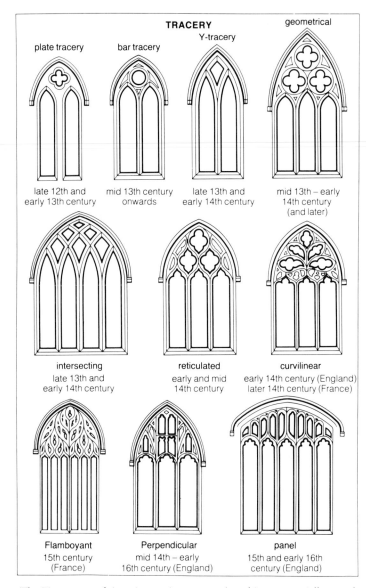

TRACERY

plate tracery
late 12th and
early 13th century

bar tracery
mid 13th century
onwards

Y-tracery
late 13th and
early 14th century

geometrical
mid 13th – early
14th century
(and later)

intersecting
late 13th and
early 14th century

reticulated
early and mid
14th century

curvilinear
early 14th century (England)
later 14th century (France)

Flamboyant
15th century
(France)

Perpendicular
mid 14th – early
16th century (England)

panel
15th and early 16th
century (England)

The Ten group of American painters, *c*1895, influenced by Impressionism.

thiasos company celebrating the festival of the gods, especially Bacchus.

tholos ancient Greek dome-shaped building or underground tomb.

thyrsos spear topped with a pinecone ornament, carried by Dionysos as a symbol of revelry.

tile flat piece of CERAMIC, decorated or used for roofing.

tile hanging wall-covering of overlapping rows of slates or tiles.

tint hue, or shade of a color.

tonality quality of color, light, and shade in painting.

tondo (It.) circular picture or RELIEF.

tone 1 atmosphere, character. **2** intensity of color or hue. **3** degree of lightness or darkness.

topography the art of mapping in detail the features of a geographical region.

toreutics objects, especially metal, that are chased, carved, EMBOSSED, or the study of these.

torsion twisting.

torso human body (or statue) apart from the head and limbs, i.e. the trunk.

Tosa School Japanese School of painting founded in the 15th century that stressed native traditions in art.

totem pole carved wood pillar decorated with mythological figures, made by certain Native American peoples, especially those of the northwest Pacific coast.

tou Chinese bronze vessel; globular, with a cover and a flared base.

tow flax fibers.

town planning science or art of planning the layout of cities.

townscape picture of a town.

trace (verb) draw or copy, especially from a drawing on a superimposed TRANSPARENT sheet.

tracery (arch.) ornamental stone work in window openings, especially in GOTHIC architecture.* Bar tracery dates from *c*1245 and has narrow shafts of stone branching out to form a decorative pattern; it is more delicate and elaborate than plate tracery, which has more solid stone.

transept (arch.) transverse arm of a cross-shaped CHURCH.

transformable synonymous with POLYMORPHIC PAINTING.

transition change of style or, in a painting, of color.

Transitional style (arch.) the style that developed between ROMANESQUE and GOTHIC.

translucency the property of transmitting light without being completely TRANSPARENT.

transparent allowing light to pass through.

trascoro (Sp.) space behind the CHOIR in CHURCH.

travertine very pure LIMESTONE found at the sources of certain Italian rivers; used for building, especially in Rome.

Trecento (It.) 14th century.

trefoil three-lobed ornament, found in GOTHIC TRACERY.

trellis lattice of wood, etc.

tribune (arch.) **1** upper story in a CHURCH, above the AISLE. **2** a bishop's throne. **3** raised floor in a Roman BASILICA.

triclinium ancient Roman dining room or table.

Tridentine derived from the Roman Catholic Council of Trent, Italy (1545–63); orthodox Roman Catholic doctrine.

triforium (arch.) passage in the wall of the NAVE, between the main ARCADE and CLERESTORY; *see* VAULT CONSTRUCTION.

triglyph (arch.) projecting block with three vertical grooves, found alternately with METOPES in a Doric FRIEZE.

Trinità (It.) representation of the Holy Trinity.

triptych picture or carving in three parts; a form of POLYPTYCH common for ALTARPIECES.

triumphal arch Roman monument erected to commemorate a victory; later adopted by 19th-century TOWN PLANNING as an architectural feature.

trompe l'oeil (Fr.) painting that "deceives the eye"; type of illusionistic painting characterized by its very precise NATURALISM.

trumeau (Fr.) (arch.) stone center post in a doorway.

tufa any easily hewn rock such as LIMESTONE, used for building. Also used as a synonym for SANDSTONE.

turquoise blue-green semiprecious stone.

turret (arch.) small tower.

tympan zinc or brass sheet used in a LITHOGRAPHIC transfer press. It lies on top of the PAPER and when pressure is applied to the top of it using the scraper, ink is transferred from the stone to the paper.

tympanum (arch.) triangular surface enclosed by a PEDIMENT, or the semicircle above an arched doorway.*

typography the art of composing type; hence typographer.

U

Ukiyoe (or Ukiyo-e) Japanese, meaning "pictures of the floating world". Genre painting, and later WOODBLOCK prints, whose subjects were actors, domestic scenes, and courtesans.

undercutting term used for CASTING, indicating the area of a MODEL that prevents the removal of the MOLD parts without destroying the impeding parts of the model. Also used to describe the cutting away of the solid matter between an outlying part of a carving and the main part of the block or to describe the area thus cut away.

underpainting the first layer of a painting that establishes forms and tone, and is then modified by GLAZES and SCUMBLES.

Unit One group of avant-garde English artists formed in the 1930s, including Henry Moore, Barbara Hepworth, John Nash, and Ben Nicholson.

urn Roman covered vase used for the ashes of the dead.

ustad the Persian title, "Master".

Utrecht School group of painters in Utrecht including Terbrugghen and Honthorst, 1610–20, who had visited Rome and were influenced by the REALISM and lighting of Caravaggio.

V

Valori Plastici (It.) artists' association and their magazine, produced in Rome in 1918 by the supporters of *Pittura Metafisica*, aiming at a revival of CLASSIC and ACADEMIC art.

value lightness or darkness on a scale of black–white, or from the lightest to the darkest tone of a color.

valve (arch.) leaf of a folding door.

vanishing point point at which the receding parallel lines in a painting appear to meet; *see* LINEAR PERSPECTIVE.

vanitas STILL-LIFE painting, popular from the 17th century, which con-

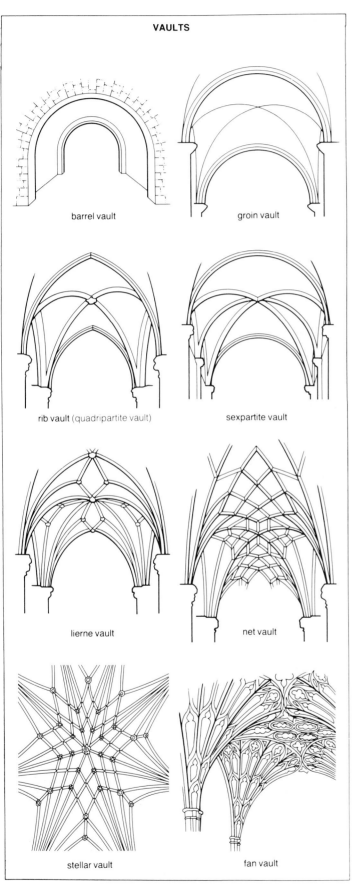

VAULTS

barrel vault

groin vault

rib vault (quadripartite vault)

sexpartite vault

lierne vault

net vault

stellar vault

fan vault

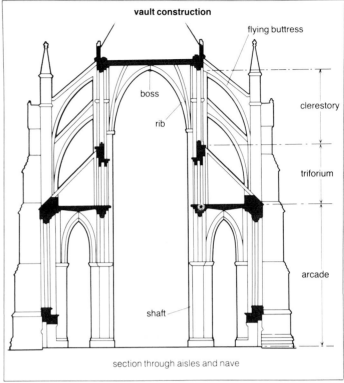

vault construction

flying buttress

boss

rib

clerestory

triforium

arcade

shaft

section through aisles and nave

tains objects as reminders of the impermanence of temporal life and of mortality.

varnish natural or synthetic resinous solution applied to furniture and paintings to saturate color and give a glossy surface, and as a protective layer.

vault (arch.) arched roof or ceiling in stone.*

vault construction in GOTHIC architecture, the architectural structure for directing pressures to maintain VAULTS.*

vaulting series of VAULTS, or style of vault.

vegetal motif plant MOTIF.

vellum fine calf skin, used for writing and painting, and bookbinding.

velvet silk textile, with a soft pile of looped threads. Modern velvets are made from other fibers.

ventail armor protecting the neck, or the lower part of a helmet.

verism extreme REALISM shown by Roman portrait sculpture and some SURREALIST art.

vermilion brilliant red PIGMENT; natural or synthetic mercuric sulfide.

vernacular architectural style; using native, local materials and styles.

verso reverse of coin, MEDAL, or painting or left-hand page of an open book; *see* RECTO.

Vienna Secession radical movement led by Gustav Klimt in an attempt to improve Austrian art, *c*1897. It had strong links with JUGENDSTIL and ART NOUVEAU.

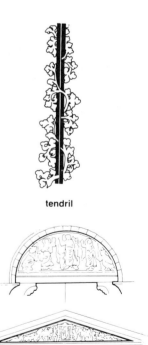

tendril

tympanum
above Romanesque, below Classic Greek

vignette small ornament in a book or on GLASS; or a painting with no obvious edges, or softened edges.

Villanovan belonging to the Iron Age culture of Etruria before 700 BC; after this date it is known as Etruscan.

vine rinceau SCROLL WORK; tendril pattern.

Vingt, Les group of AVANT-GARDE Belgian artists who held annual exhibitions 1883–93.

virtual volume appearance of three dimensionality possessed by an image that is virtual, not real; i.e., from which light rays appear to diverge.

virtues personification of the seven virtues (Faith, Hope, Charity, Prudence, Justice, Temperance, Fortitude) often depicted as CLASSICAL gods and goddesses.

virtuosity special skill of execution.

vista long view, e.g. along an avenue of trees.

vitreous glaze in POTTERY, a glaze that is vitrified (or becomes glass-like) on firing.

Vitruvian derived from the writings of Vitruvius (1st century BC), author of *De Re Architectura*.

volute (arch.) spiral SCROLL ornament, usually on Greek IONIC CAPITALS; also on furniture.*

Vorticism short-lived English AVANT-GARDE movement, the most prominent member of which was Wyndham Lewis. Its name derives from a magazine published by the group in 1914: *Blast! A Review of the Great English Vortex.*

votive offered or consecrated in fulfillment of a vow.

voussoir (Fr.) (arch.) one of a series of wedge-shaped stones forming an ARCH.

W

wall arcade (arch.) series of ARCHES attached to a wall.

wallpaper strong PAPER used to decorate interior walls; it probably came into use by 1480.

warp thread stretched on a loom for weaving, through which the WEFT threads are passed.

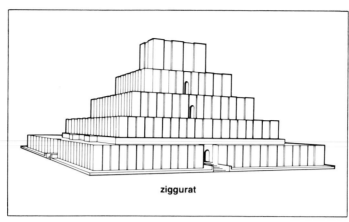

ziggurat

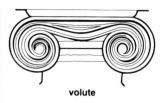

volute

wash the application of diluted WATERCOLOR over a large area to establish a general TONE.

watercolor painting executed in a water-soluble MEDIUM.

wax plastic substance produced by bees, or of vegetable origin, used for modeling.

weft thread that is woven in and out of the WARP threads on a loom.

welding fusing together pieces of metal or plastic with heat.

Westwerk (arch.) west part of CHURCH in CAROLINGIAN and OTTONIAN architecture, having an APSE, towers, sometimes a TRANSEPT, in addition to the usual arrangement at the east end.

whorl spiral or circular pattern.

Wiener Werkstätte an organization of designers formed in Vienna in 1903 to promote JUGENDSTIL arts and crafts.

wing 1 side piece of a composite painting such as an ALTARPIECE. **2** block projecting from main building. **3** sides of stage in the theater.

wood the material obtained from trees; hardwood is dense, close grained, and obtained from deciduous trees; softwood is obtained from coniferous trees.

woodblock PRINT produced from a design on a wooden block.

woodcut PRINT made from a WOODBLOCK, cut so that the design stands out in RELIEF.

workshop place in which art objects or paintings are executed. "Workshop work" is usually not by the MASTER but by his assistants.

wrought iron iron that is forged or rolled (but not cast) into elaborate shapes, e.g. for gates, balconies.

Wu School school of Chinese painting founded by Shen Chou (1427–1509).

Y

Yamato-e the School of Japanese painting from the 10th to the 15th century that preserved the native traditions.

Yellow Book quarterly magazine published from 1894, of which Aubrey Beardsley (1872–98) was art editor.

yew evergreen coniferous tree, the wood of which is used in cabinet making.

Yuan Chinese Mongol dynasty, 1279–1368 (between SUNG and MING).

Z

Zen Japanese form of Buddhism.

Ziggurat (arch.) ancient Babylonian and Assyrian pyramid-shaped construction.*

zigzag pattern formed of lines that make abrupt right and left turns; in Norman architecture, zigzag is synonymous with CHEVRON.

zoomorphic based on animal forms, or the worshiping of gods who have assumed an animal form.

INDEX